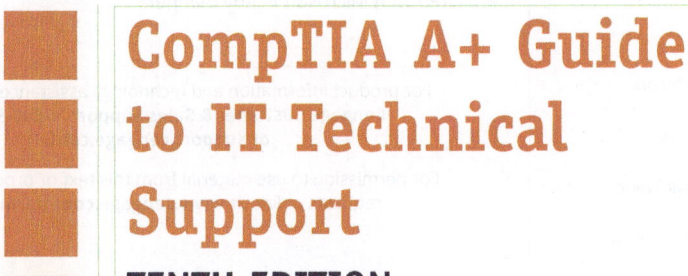

CompTIA A+ Guide to IT Technical Support

TENTH EDITION

Jean Andrews, Joy Dark, Jill West

Australia • Brazil • Mexico • Singapore • United Kingdom • United States

**CompTIA A+ Guide to IT Technical Support,
Tenth Edition, Jean Andrews, Joy Dark,
Jill West**

SVP, Skills Product Management: Jonathan Lau

Product Director: Lauren Murphy

Product Team Manager: Kristin McNary

Product Manager: Amy Savino

Product Assistant: Thomas Benedetto

Executive Director, Content Design:
Marah Bellegarde

Director, Learning Design: Leigh Hefferon

Learning Designer: Natalie Onderdonk

Senior Marketing Director: Michele McTighe

Associate Marketing Manager: Cassie Cloutier

Product Specialist: Mackenzie Paine

Director, Content Delivery: Patty Stephan

Senior Content Manager: Brooke Greenhouse

Digital Delivery Lead: Jim Vaughey

Designer: Erin Griffin

Cover Designer: Joseph Villanova

Cover image: iStockPhoto.com/Tailex

Production Service/Compositor: SPi-Global

For product information and technology assistance, contact us at
**Cengage Customer & Sales Support, 1-800-354-9706
or support.cengage.com.**

For permission to use material from this text or product, submit all requests online at **www.cengage.com/permissions.**

Library of Congress Control Number: 2018953405

ISBN: 978-0-357-10829-1

Cengage
20 Channel Center Street
Boston, MA 02210
USA

Cengage is a leading provider of customized learning solutions with employees residing in nearly 40 different countries and sales in more than 125 countries around the world. Find your local representative at: **www.cengage.com.**

Cengage products are represented in Canada by Nelson Education, Ltd.

To learn more about Cengage platforms and services, register or access your online learning solution, or purchase materials for your course, visit **www.cengage.com.**

Notice to the Reader
Publisher does not warrant or guarantee any of the products described herein or perform any independent analysis in connection with any of the product information contained herein. Publisher does not assume, and expressly disclaims, any obligation to obtain and include information other than that provided to it by the manufacturer. The reader is expressly warned to consider and adopt all safety precautions that might be indicated by the activities described herein and to avoid all potential hazards. By following the instructions contained herein, the reader willingly assumes all risks in connection with such instructions. The publisher makes no representations or warranties of any kind, including but not limited to, the warranties of fitness for particular purpose or merchantability, nor are any such representations implied with respect to the material set forth herein, and the publisher takes no responsibility with respect to such material. The publisher shall not be liable for any special, consequential, or exemplary damages resulting, in whole or part, from the readers' use of, or reliance upon, this material.

Printed at CLDPC, USA, 08-21

Table of Contents

CHAPTER 5

Supporting Hard Drives and Other Storage Devices 213

CHAPTER 6

Supporting I/O Devices. 265

CHAPTER 7

Setting Up a Local Network 321

CHAPTER 8

Network Infrastructure and Troubleshooting. 379

CHAPTER 9

Supporting Mobile Devices 439

CHAPTER 10

Virtualization, Cloud Computing, and Printers 505

CHAPTER 11

Windows Versions and Customer Service 567

CHAPTER 12

Installing Windows. 627

CHAPTER 13

Maintaining Windows. 691

CHAPTER 14

Troubleshooting Windows
After Startup. 757

CHAPTER 15

Troubleshooting Windows Startup. . . . 825

COMPTIA A+ CORE 1 (220-1001) AND A+ CORE 2 (220-1002) EXAM OBJECTIVES MAPPED TO CHAPTERS

CompTIA A+ Guide to IT Technical Support, Tenth Edition fully meets all of the CompTIA's A+ Core 1 (220-1001) and A+ Core 2 (220-1002) Exam Objectives.

COMPTIA A+ CORE 1 (220-1001)

1.0 MOBILE DEVICES

1.1 Given a scenario, install and configure laptop hardware and components.

Objectives	Chapter	Primary Section
• Hardware/device replacement		
- Keyboard	1	First Look at Laptop Components
- Hard drive	5	Hard Drive Technologies and Interface Standards
○ SSD vs. hybrid vs. magnetic disk	5	Hard Drive Technologies and Interface Standards
○ 1.8 in. vs. 2.5 in.	5	Hard Drive Technologies and Interface Standards
- Memory	3	How to Upgrade Memory
- Smart card reader	5	Supporting Other Types of Storage Devices
- Optical drive	5	Supporting Other Types of Storage Devices
- Wireless card/Bluetooth module	6	Identifying and Installing I/O Peripheral Devices
- Cellular card	6	Installing and Configuring Adapter Cards
- Video card	6	Supporting the Video Subsystem
- Mini PCIe	6	Installing and Configuring Adapter Cards
- Screen	6	Supporting the Video Subsystem
- DC jack	4	Troubleshooting the Electrical System
- Battery	1	First Look at Laptop Components
- Touchpad	6	Identifying and Installing I/O Peripheral Devices
- Plastics/frames	1	First Look at Laptop Components
- Speaker	6	Identifying and Installing I/O Peripheral Devices
- System board	2	Motherboard Types and Features
- CPU	3	Selecting and Installing a Processor

1.2 Given a scenario, install components within the display of a laptop.

Objectives	Chapter	Primary Section
• Types	6	Supporting the Video Subsystem
- LCD	6	Supporting the Video Subsystem
- OLED	6	Supporting the Video Subsystem
• Wi-Fi antenna connector/placement	6	Installing and Configuring Adapter Cards
• Webcam	6	Identifying and Installing I/O Peripheral Devices
• Microphone	6	Identifying and Installing I/O Peripheral Devices
• Inverter	6	Supporting the Video Subsystem
• Digitizer/touch screen	6	Identifying and Installing I/O Peripheral Devices

1.3 Given a scenario, use appropriate laptop features.

Objectives	Chapter	Primary Section
• Special function keys	1	First Look at Laptop Components
- Dual displays	1	First Look at Laptop Components
- Wireless (on/off)	1	First Look at Laptop Components

Objectives	Chapter	Primary Section
- Cellular (on/off)	1	First Look at Laptop Components
- Volume settings	1	First Look at Laptop Components
- Screen brightness	1	First Look at Laptop Components
- Bluetooth (on/off)	1	First Look at Laptop Components
- Keyboard backlight	1	First Look at Laptop Components
- Touchpad (on/off)	1	First Look at Laptop Components
- Screen orientation	1	First Look at Laptop Components
- Media options (fast forward/rewind)	1	First Look at Laptop Components
- GPS (on/off)	1	First Look at Laptop Components
- Airplane mode	1	First Look at Laptop Components
• Docking station	1	First Look at Laptop Components
• Port replicator	1	First Look at Laptop Components
• Physical laptop lock and cable lock	1	First Look at Laptop Components
• Rotating/removable screens	1	First Look at Laptop Components

1.4 Compare and contrast characteristics of various types of other mobile devices.

Objectives	Chapter	Primary Section
• Tablets	9	Types of Mobile Devices
• Smartphones	9	Types of Mobile Devices
• Wearable technology devices	9	Types of Mobile Devices
- Smart watches	9	Types of Mobile Devices
- Fitness monitors	9	Types of Mobile Devices
- VR/AR headsets	9	Types of Mobile Devices
• E-readers	9	Types of Mobile Devices
• GPS	9	Types of Mobile Devices

1.5 Given a scenario, connect and configure accessories and ports of other mobile devices.

Objectives	Chapter	Primary Section
• Connection types	9	Configuring and Syncing a Mobile Device
- Wired	9	Configuring and Syncing a Mobile Device
○ Micro-USB/Mini-USB/USB-C	9	Configuring and Syncing a Mobile Device
○ Lightning	9	Configuring and Syncing a Mobile Device
○ Tethering	9	Configuring and Syncing a Mobile Device
○ Proprietary vendor-specific ports (communication/power)	9	Configuring and Syncing a Mobile Device
- Wireless	9	Configuring and Syncing a Mobile Device
○ NFC	9	Configuring and Syncing a Mobile Device
○ Bluetooth	9	Configuring and Syncing a Mobile Device
○ IR	9	Configuring and Syncing a Mobile Device
○ Hotspot	9	Configuring and Syncing a Mobile Device
• Accessories	9	Configuring and Syncing a Mobile Device
- Headsets	9	Configuring and Syncing a Mobile Device
- Speakers	9	Configuring and Syncing a Mobile Device
- Game pads	9	Configuring and Syncing a Mobile Device
- Extra battery packs/battery chargers	9	Configuring and Syncing a Mobile Device
- Protective covers/waterproofing	9	Configuring and Syncing a Mobile Device
- Credit card readers	9	Configuring and Syncing a Mobile Device
- Memory/MicroSD	9	Configuring and Syncing a Mobile Device

1.6   Given a scenario, configure basic mobile device network connectivity and application support.

Objectives	Chapter	Primary Section
• Wireless/cellular data network (enable/disable)	9	Configuring and Syncing a Mobile Device
- Hotspot	9	Configuring and Syncing a Mobile Device
- Tethering	9	Configuring and Syncing a Mobile Device
- Airplane mode	9	Configuring and Syncing a Mobile Device
• Bluetooth	9	Configuring and Syncing a Mobile Device
- Enable Bluetooth	9	Configuring and Syncing a Mobile Device
- Enable pairing	9	Configuring and Syncing a Mobile Device
- Find a device for pairing	9	Configuring and Syncing a Mobile Device
- Enter the appropriate PIN code	9	Configuring and Syncing a Mobile Device
- Test connectivity	9	Configuring and Syncing a Mobile Device
• Corporate and ISP email configuration	9	Configuring and Syncing a Mobile Device
- POP3	9	Configuring and Syncing a Mobile Device
- IMAP	9	Configuring and Syncing a Mobile Device
- Port and SSL settings	9	Configuring and Syncing a Mobile Device
- S/MIME	9	Configuring and Syncing a Mobile Device
• Integrated commercial provider email configuration	9	Configuring and Syncing a Mobile Device
- iCloud	9	Configuring and Syncing a Mobile Device
- Google/Inbox	9	Configuring and Syncing a Mobile Device
- Exchange Online	9	Configuring and Syncing a Mobile Device
- Yahoo	9	Configuring and Syncing a Mobile Device
• PRI updates/PRL updates/baseband updates	9	Configuring and Syncing a Mobile Device
• Radio firmware	9	Configuring and Syncing a Mobile Device
• IMEI vs. IMSI	9	Configuring and Syncing a Mobile Device
• VPN	9	Configuring and Syncing a Mobile Device

1.7   Given a scenario, use methods to perform mobile device synchronization.

Objectives	Chapter	Primary Section
• Synchronization methods	9	Configuring and Syncing a Mobile Device
- Synchronize to the cloud	9	Configuring and Syncing a Mobile Device
- Synchronize to the desktop	9	Configuring and Syncing a Mobile Device
- Synchronize to the automobile	9	Configuring and Syncing a Mobile Device
• Types of data to synchronize	9	Configuring and Syncing a Mobile Device
- Contacts	9	Configuring and Syncing a Mobile Device
- Applications	9	Configuring and Syncing a Mobile Device
- Email	9	Configuring and Syncing a Mobile Device
- Pictures	9	Configuring and Syncing a Mobile Device
- Music	9	Configuring and Syncing a Mobile Device
- Videos	9	Configuring and Syncing a Mobile Device
- Calendar	9	Configuring and Syncing a Mobile Device
- Bookmarks	9	Configuring and Syncing a Mobile Device
- Documents	9	Configuring and Syncing a Mobile Device
- Location data	9	Configuring and Syncing a Mobile Device
- Social media data	9	Configuring and Syncing a Mobile Device
- E-books	9	Configuring and Syncing a Mobile Device
- Passwords	9	Configuring and Syncing a Mobile Device
• Mutual authentication for multiple services (SSO)	9	Configuring and Syncing a Mobile Device
• Software requirements to install the application on the PC	9	Configuring and Syncing a Mobile Device
• Connection types to enable synchronization	9	Configuring and Syncing a Mobile Device

2.0 NETWORKING

2.1 Compare and contrast TCP and UDP ports, protocols, and their purposes.

Objectives	Chapter	Primary Section
• Ports and protocols	8	Understanding TCP/IP and Windows Networking
- 21 – FTP	8	Understanding TCP/IP and Windows Networking
- 22 – SSH	8	Understanding TCP/IP and Windows Networking
- 23 – Telnet	8	Understanding TCP/IP and Windows Networking
- 25 – SMTP	8	Understanding TCP/IP and Windows Networking
- 53 – DNS	8	Understanding TCP/IP and Windows Networking
- 80 – HTTP	8	Understanding TCP/IP and Windows Networking
- 110 – POP3	8	Understanding TCP/IP and Windows Networking
- 143 – IMAP	8	Understanding TCP/IP and Windows Networking
- 443 – HTTPS	8	Understanding TCP/IP and Windows Networking
- 3389 – RDP	8	Understanding TCP/IP and Windows Networking
- 137-139 – NetBIOS/NetBT	8	Understanding TCP/IP and Windows Networking
- 445 – SMB/CIFS	8	Understanding TCP/IP and Windows Networking
- 427 – SLP	8	Understanding TCP/IP and Windows Networking
- 548 – AFP	8	Understanding TCP/IP and Windows Networking
- 67/68 – DHCP	8	Understanding TCP/IP and Windows Networking
- 389 – LDAP	8	Understanding TCP/IP and Windows Networking
- 161/162 – SNMP	8	Understanding TCP/IP and Windows Networking
• TCP vs. UDP	8	Understanding TCP/IP and Windows Networking

2.2 Compare and contrast common networking hardware devices.

Objectives	Chapter	Primary Section
• Routers	7	Setting Up a Multifunction Router for a SOHO Network
• Switches	8	Local Network Infrastructure
- Managed	8	Local Network Infrastructure
- Unmanaged	8	Local Network Infrastructure
• Access points	8	Local Network Infrastructure
• Cloud-based network controller	10	Cloud Computing
• Firewall	8	Local Network Infrastructure
• Network interface card	7	Connecting a Computer to a Local Network
• Repeater	8	Local Network Infrastructure
• Hub	8	Local Network Infrastructure
• Cable/DSL modem	7	Types of Networks and Network Connections
• Bridge	8	Local Network Infrastructure
• Patch panel	8	Setting Up and Troubleshooting Network Wiring
• Power over Ethernet (PoE)	8	Local Network Infrastructure
- Injectors	8	Local Network Infrastructure
- Switch	8	Local Network Infrastructure
• Ethernet over Power	8	Local Network Infrastructure

2.3 Given a scenario, install and configure a basic wired/wireless SOHO network.

Objectives	Chapter	Primary Section
• Router/switch functionality	7	Setting Up a Multifunction Router for a SOHO Network
• Access point settings	7	Setting Up a Multifunction Router for a SOHO Network
• IP addressing	7	Setting Up a Multifunction Router for a SOHO Network
• NIC configuration	7	Connecting a Computer to a Local Network
- Wired	7	Connecting a Computer to a Local Network
- Wireless	7	Connecting a Computer to a Local Network

Objectives	Chapter	Primary Section
• End-user device configuration	7	Connecting a Computer to a Local Network
• IoT device configuration	9	The Internet of Things (IoT)
- Thermostat	9	The Internet of Things (IoT)
- Light switches	9	The Internet of Things (IoT)
- Security cameras	9	The Internet of Things (IoT)
- Door locks	9	The Internet of Things (IoT)
- Voice-enabled, smart speaker/digital assistant	9	The Internet of Things (IoT)
• Cable/DSL modem configuration	7	Types of Networks and Network Connections
• Firewall settings	7	Setting Up a Multifunction Router for a SOHO Network
- DMZ	7	Setting Up a Multifunction Router for a SOHO Network
- Port forwarding	7	Setting Up a Multifunction Router for a SOHO Network
- NAT	7	Setting Up a Multifunction Router for a SOHO Network
- UPnP	7	Setting Up a Multifunction Router for a SOHO Network
- Whitelist/blacklist	7	Setting Up a Multifunction Router for a SOHO Network
- MAC filtering	7	Setting Up a Multifunction Router for a SOHO Network
• QoS	7	Setting Up a Multifunction Router for a SOHO Network
• Wireless settings	7	Setting Up a Multifunction Router for a SOHO Network
- Encryption	7	Setting Up a Multifunction Router for a SOHO Network
- Channels	7	Setting Up a Multifunction Router for a SOHO Network
- QoS	7	Setting Up a Multifunction Router for a SOHO Network

2.4 Compare and contrast wireless networking protocols.

Objectives	Chapter	Primary Section
• 802.11a	7	Setting Up a Multifunction Router for a SOHO Network
• 802.11b	7	Setting Up a Multifunction Router for a SOHO Network
• 802.11g	7	Setting Up a Multifunction Router for a SOHO Network
• 802.11n	7	Setting Up a Multifunction Router for a SOHO Network
• 802.11ac	7	Setting Up a Multifunction Router for a SOHO Network
• Frequencies	7	Setting Up a Multifunction Router for a SOHO Network
- 2.4Ghz	7	Setting Up a Multifunction Router for a SOHO Network
- 5Ghz	7	Setting Up a Multifunction Router for a SOHO Network
• Channels	7	Setting Up a Multifunction Router for a SOHO Network
- 1–11	7	Setting Up a Multifunction Router for a SOHO Network
• Bluetooth	9	Configuring and Syncing a Mobile Device
• NFC	9	Configuring and Syncing a Mobile Device
• RFID	9	The Internet of Things (IoT)
• Zigbee	9	The Internet of Things (IoT)
• Z-Wave	9	The Internet of Things (IoT)
• 3G	7	Types of Networks and Network Connections
• 4G	7	Types of Networks and Network Connections
• 5G	7	Types of Networks and Network Connections
• LTE	7	Types of Networks and Network Connections

2.5 Summarize the properties and purposes of services provided by networked hosts.

Objectives	Chapter	Primary Section
• Server roles	8	Local Network Infrastructure
- Web server	8	Local Network Infrastructure
- File server	8	Local Network Infrastructure
- Print server	8	Local Network Infrastructure

Objectives	Chapter	Primary Section
- DHCP server	8	Local Network Infrastructure
- DNS server	8	Local Network Infrastructure
- Proxy server	8	Local Network Infrastructure
- Mail server	8	Local Network Infrastructure
- Authentication server	8	Local Network Infrastructure
- syslog	8	Local Network Infrastructure
• Internet appliance	8	Local Network Infrastructure
- UTM	8	Local Network Infrastructure
- IDS	8	Local Network Infrastructure
- IPS	8	Local Network Infrastructure
- End-point management server	8	Local Network Infrastructure
• Legacy/embedded systems	8	Local Network Infrastructure

2.6 Explain common network configuration concepts.

Objectives	Chapter	Primary Section
• IP addressing	8	Understanding TCP/IP and Windows Networking
- Static	8	Understanding TCP/IP and Windows Networking
- Dynamic	8	Understanding TCP/IP and Windows Networking
- APIPA	8	Troubleshooting Network Connections
- Link local	8	Understanding TCP/IP and Windows Networking
• DNS	8	Understanding TCP/IP and Windows Networking
• DHCP	8	Understanding TCP/IP and Windows Networking
- Reservations	7	Setting Up a Multifunction Router for a SOHO Network
• IPv4 vs. IPv6	8	Understanding TCP/IP and Windows Networking
• Subnet mask	8	Understanding TCP/IP and Windows Networking
• Gateway	8	Understanding TCP/IP and Windows Networking
• VPN	7	Connecting a Computer to a Local Network
• VLAN	8	Local Network Infrastructure
• NAT	8	Understanding TCP/IP and Windows Networking

2.7 Compare and contrast Internet connection types, network types, and their features.

Objectives	Chapter	Primary Section
• Internet connection types	7	Types of Networks and Network Connections
- Cable	7	Types of Networks and Network Connections
- DSL	7	Types of Networks and Network Connections
- Dial-up	7	Types of Networks and Network Connections
- Fiber	7	Types of Networks and Network Connections
- Satellite	7	Types of Networks and Network Connections
- ISDN	7	Types of Networks and Network Connections
- Cellular	7	Types of Networks and Network Connections
○ Tethering	7	Types of Networks and Network Connections
○ Mobile hotspot	7	Types of Networks and Network Connections
- Line-of-sight wireless Internet service	7	Types of Networks and Network Connections
• Network types	7	Types of Networks and Network Connections
- LAN	7	Types of Networks and Network Connections
- WAN	7	Types of Networks and Network Connections
- PAN	7	Types of Networks and Network Connections
- MAN	7	Types of Networks and Network Connections
- WMN	7	Types of Networks and Network Connections

2.8 Given a scenario, use appropriate networking tools.

3.0 HARDWARE

3.1 Explain basic cable types, features, and their purposes.

3.2   Identify common connector types.

Objectives	Chapter	Primary Section
• RJ-11	7	Types of Networks and Network Connections
• RJ-45	7	Types of Networks and Network Connections
• RS-232	6	Basic Principles for Supporting Devices
• BNC	6	Basic Principles for Supporting Devices
• RG-59	6	Basic Principles for Supporting Devices
• RG-6	6	Basic Principles for Supporting Devices
• USB	6	Basic Principles for Supporting Devices
• Micro-USB	6	Basic Principles for Supporting Devices
• Mini-USB	6	Basic Principles for Supporting Devices
• USB-C	6	Identifying and Installing I/O Peripheral Devices
• DB-9	6	Basic Principles for Supporting Devices
• Lightning	6	Identifying and Installing I/O Peripheral Devices
• SCSI	5	Hard Drive Technologies and Interface Standards
• eSATA	5	Hard Drive Technologies and Interface Standards
• Molex	2	Motherboard Types and Features

3.3   Given a scenario, install RAM types.

Objectives	Chapter	Primary Section
• RAM types	3	Memory Technologies
- SODIMM	3	Memory Technologies
- DDR2	3	Memory Technologies
- DDR3	3	Memory Technologies
- DDR4	3	Memory Technologies
• Single channel	3	Memory Technologies
• Dual channel	3	Memory Technologies
• Triple channel	3	Memory Technologies
• Error correcting	3	Memory Technologies
• Parity vs. non-parity	3	Memory Technologies

3.4   Given a scenario, select, install, and configure storage devices.

Objectives	Chapter	Primary Section
• Optical drives	5	Supporting Other Types of Storage Devices
- CD-ROM/CD-RW	5	Supporting Other Types of Storage Devices
- DVD-ROM/DVD-RW/DVD-RW DL	5	Supporting Other Types of Storage Devices
- Blu-ray	5	Supporting Other Types of Storage Devices
- BD-R	5	Supporting Other Types of Storage Devices
- BD-RE	5	Supporting Other Types of Storage Devices
• Solid-state drives	5	How to Select and Install Hard Drives
- M2 drives	5	How to Select and Install Hard Drives
- NVME	5	How to Select and Install Hard Drives
- SATA 2.5	5	How to Select and Install Hard Drives
• Magnetic hard drives	5	How to Select and Install Hard Drives
- 5,400rpm	5	Hard Drive Technologies and Interface Standards
- 7,200rpm	5	Hard Drive Technologies and Interface Standards
- 10,000rpm	5	Hard Drive Technologies and Interface Standards
- 15,000rpm	5	Hard Drive Technologies and Interface Standards
- Sizes:	5	Hard Drive Technologies and Interface Standards
○ -2.5	5	Hard Drive Technologies and Interface Standards
○ -3.5	5	Hard Drive Technologies and Interface Standards

Objectives	Chapter	Primary Section
• Cooling mechanism	4	Cooling Methods and Devices
- Fans	4	Troubleshooting the Electrical System
- Heat sink	4	Cooling Methods and Devices
- Liquid	4	Cooling Methods and Devices
- Thermal paste	4	Cooling Methods and Devices
• Expansion cards	6	Installing and Configuring Adapter Cards
- Video cards	6	Installing and Configuring Adapter Cards
○ Onboard	6	Basic Principles for Supporting Devices
○ Add-on card	6	Installing and Configuring Adapter Cards
- Sound cards	6	Installing and Configuring Adapter Cards
- Network interface card	6	Installing and Configuring Adapter Cards
- USB expansion card	6	Installing and Configuring Adapter Cards
- eSATA card	5	Hard Drive Technologies and Interface Standards

3.6 Explain the purposes and uses of various peripheral types.

Objectives	Chapter	Primary Section
• Printer	10	Printer Types and Features
• ADF/flatbed scanner	10	Printer Types and Features
• Barcode scanner/QR scanner	6	Basic Principles for Supporting Devices
• Monitors	6	Supporting the Video Subsystem
• VR headset	6	Identifying and Installing I/O Peripheral Devices
• Optical	5	Supporting Other Types of Storage Devices
• DVD drive	5	Supporting Other Types of Storage Devices
• Mouse	6	Identifying and Installing I/O Peripheral Devices
• Keyboard	6	Identifying and Installing I/O Peripheral Devices
• Touchpad	6	Identifying and Installing I/O Peripheral Devices
• Signature pad	6	Identifying and Installing I/O Peripheral Devices
• Game controllers	6	Identifying and Installing I/O Peripheral Devices
• Camera/webcam	6	Identifying and Installing I/O Peripheral Devices
• Microphone	6	Identifying and Installing I/O Peripheral Devices
• Speakers	6	Identifying and Installing I/O Peripheral Devices
• Headset	6	Identifying and Installing I/O Peripheral Devices
• Projector	6	Supporting the Video Subsystem
- Lumens/brightness	6	Supporting the Video Subsystem
• External storage drives	5	How to Select and Install Hard Drives
• KVM	6	Identifying and Installing I/O Peripheral Devices
• Magnetic reader/chip reader	6	Identifying and Installing I/O Peripheral Devices
• NFC/tap pay device	6	Identifying and Installing I/O Peripheral Devices
• Smart card reader	5	Supporting Other Types of Storage Devices

3.7 Summarize power supply types and features.

Objectives	Chapter	Primary Section
• Input 115V vs. 220V	4	Selecting a Power Supply
• Output 5.5V vs. 12V	4	Selecting a Power Supply
• 24-pin motherboard adapter	4	Selecting a Power Supply
• Wattage rating	4	Selecting a Power Supply
• Number of devices/types of devices to be powered	4	Troubleshooting the Electrical System

3.8   Given a scenario, select and configure appropriate components for a custom PC configuration to meet customer specifications or needs.

Objectives	Chapter	Primary Section
• Graphic/CAD/CAM design workstation	6	Customizing Computer Systems
- Multicore processor	6	Customizing Computer Systems
- High-end video	6	Customizing Computer Systems
- Maximum RAM	6	Customizing Computer Systems
• Audio/video editing workstation	6	Customizing Computer Systems
- Specialized audio and video card	6	Customizing Computer Systems
- Large, fast hard drive	6	Customizing Computer Systems
- Dual monitors	6	Customizing Computer Systems
• Virtualization workstation	10	Client-Side Virtualization
- Maximum RAM and CPU cores	10	Client-Side Virtualization
• Gaming PC	6	Customizing Computer Systems
- Multicore processor	6	Customizing Computer Systems
- High-end video/specialized GPU	6	Customizing Computer Systems
- High-definition sound card	6	Customizing Computer Systems
- High-end cooling	6	Customizing Computer Systems
• Standard thick client	10	Client-Side Virtualization
- Desktop applications	10	Client-Side Virtualization
- Meets recommended requirements for selected OS	10	Client-Side Virtualization
• Thin client	10	Client-Side Virtualization
- Basic applications	10	Client-Side Virtualization
- Meets minimum requirements for selected OS	10	Client-Side Virtualization
- Network connectivity	10	Client-Side Virtualization
• Network attached storage device	5	How to Select and Install Hard Drives
- Media streaming	6	Customizing Computer Systems
- File sharing	6	Customizing Computer Systems
- Gigabit NIC	6	Customizing Computer Systems
- RAID array	5	How to Select and Install Hard Drives

3.9   Given a scenario, install and configure common devices.

Objectives	Chapter	Primary Section
• Desktop	10	Client-Side Virtualization
- Thin client	10	Client-Side Virtualization
- Thick client	10	Client-Side Virtualization
- Account setup/settings	7	Connecting a Computer to a Local Network
• Laptop/common mobile devices		
- Touchpad configuration	6	Identifying and Installing I/O Peripheral Devices
- Touch screen configuration	6	Identifying and Installing I/O Peripheral Devices
- Application installations/configurations	9	Configuring and Syncing a Mobile Device
- Synchronization settings	9	Configuring and Syncing a Mobile Device
- Account setup/settings	9	Configuring and Syncing a Mobile Device
- Wireless settings	9	Configuring and Syncing a Mobile Device

3.10 Given a scenario, configure SOHO multifunction devices/printers and settings.

Objectives	Chapter	Primary Section
• Use appropriate drivers for a given operating system	10	Using Windows to Install, Share, and Manage Printers
- Configuration settings	10	Using Windows to Install, Share, and Manage Printers
○ Duplex	10	Printer Types and Features
○ Collate	10	Printer Types and Features
○ Orientation	10	Using Windows to Install, Share, and Manage Printers
○ Quality	10	Using Windows to Install, Share, and Manage Printers
• Device sharing	10	Using Windows to Install, Share, and Manage Printers
- Wired	10	Using Windows to Install, Share, and Manage Printers
○ USB	10	Using Windows to Install, Share, and Manage Printers
○ Serial	10	Using Windows to Install, Share, and Manage Printers
○ Ethernet	10	Using Windows to Install, Share, and Manage Printers
- Wireless	10	Using Windows to Install, Share, and Manage Printers
○ Bluetooth	10	Using Windows to Install, Share, and Manage Printers
○ 802.11(a, b, g, n, ac)	10	Using Windows to Install, Share, and Manage Printers
○ Infrastructure vs. ad hoc	10	Using Windows to Install, Share, and Manage Printers
- Integrated print server (hardware)	10	Using Windows to Install, Share, and Manage Printers
- Cloud printing/remote printing	10	Using Windows to Install, Share, and Manage Printers
• Public/shared devices	10	Using Windows to Install, Share, and Manage Printers
- Sharing local/networked device via operating system settings	10	Using Windows to Install, Share, and Manage Printers
○ TCP/Bonjour/AirPrint	10	Using Windows to Install, Share, and Manage Printers
- Data privacy	10	Using Windows to Install, Share, and Manage Printers
○ User authentication on the device	10	Using Windows to Install, Share, and Manage Printers
○ Hard drive caching	10	Using Windows to Install, Share, and Manage Printers

3.11 Given a scenario, install and maintain various print technologies.

Objectives	Chapter	Primary Section
• Laser	10	Printer Maintenance
- Imaging drum, fuser assembly, transfer belt, transfer roller, pickup rollers, separate pads, duplexing assembly	10	Printer Maintenance
- Imaging process: processing, charging, exposing, developing, transferring, fusing, and cleaning	10	Printer Maintenance
- Maintenance: Replace toner, apply maintenance kit, calibrate, clean	10	Printer Maintenance
• Inkjet	10	Printer Maintenance
- Ink cartridge, print head, roller, feeder, duplexing assembly, carriage, and belt	10	Printer Maintenance
- Calibrate	10	Printer Maintenance
- Maintenance: Clean heads, replace cartridges, calibrate, clear jams	10	Printer Maintenance
• Thermal	10	Printer Maintenance
- Feed assembly, heating element	10	Printer Maintenance
- Special thermal paper	10	Printer Maintenance
- Maintenance: Replace paper, clean heating element, remove debris	10	Printer Maintenance
• Impact	10	Printer Maintenance
- Print head, ribbon, tractor feed	10	Printer Maintenance
- Impact paper	10	Printer Maintenance
- Maintenance: Replace ribbon, replace print head, replace paper	10	Printer Maintenance

Objectives	Chapter	Primary Section
• Virtual	10	Printer Maintenance
- Print to file	10	Printer Maintenance
- Print to PDF	10	Printer Maintenance
- Print to XPS	10	Printer Maintenance
- Print to image	10	Printer Maintenance
• 3D printers	10	Printer Maintenance
- Plastic filament	10	Printer Maintenance

4.0 VIRTUALIZATION AND CLOUD COMPUTING

4.1   Compare and contrast cloud computing concepts.

Objectives	Chapter	Primary Section
• Common cloud models	10	Cloud Computing
- IaaS	10	Cloud Computing
- SaaS	10	Cloud Computing
- PaaS	10	Cloud Computing
- Public vs. private vs. hybrid vs. community	10	Cloud Computing
• Shared resources	10	Cloud Computing
- Internal vs. external	10	Cloud Computing
• Rapid elasticity	10	Cloud Computing
• On-demand	10	Cloud Computing
• Resource pooling	10	Cloud Computing
• Measured service	10	Cloud Computing
• Metered	10	Cloud Computing
• Off-site email applications	10	Cloud Computing
• Cloud file storage services	10	Cloud Computing
- Synchronization apps	9	Configuring and Syncing a Mobile Device
• Virtual application streaming/cloud-based applications	10	Cloud Computing
- Applications for cell phones/tablets	10	Cloud Computing
- Applications for laptops/desktops	10	Cloud Computing
• Virtual desktop	10	Cloud Computing
- Virtual NIC	10	Client-Side Virtualization

4.2   Given a scenario, set up and configure client-side virtualization.

Objectives	Chapter	Primary Section
• Purpose of virtual machines	10	Client-Side Virtualization
• Resource requirements	10	Client-Side Virtualization
• Emulator requirements	10	Client-Side Virtualization
• Security requirements	10	Client-Side Virtualization
• Network requirements	10	Client-Side Virtualization
• Hypervisor	10	Client-Side Virtualization

5.0 HARDWARE AND NETWORK TROUBLESHOOTING

5.1 Given a scenario, use the best practice methodology to resolve problems.

Objectives	Chapter	Primary Section
• Always consider corporate policies, procedures, and impacts before implementing changes	4	Strategies to Troubleshoot Any Computer Problem
1. Identify the problem	4	Strategies to Troubleshoot Any Computer Problem
- Question the user and identify user changes to computer and perform backups before making changes	4	Strategies to Troubleshoot Any Computer Problem
- Inquire regarding environmental or infrastructure changes	4	Strategies to Troubleshoot Any Computer Problem
- Review system and application logs	4	Strategies to Troubleshoot Any Computer Problem
2. Establish a theory of probable cause (question the obvious)	4	Strategies to Troubleshoot Any Computer Problem
- If necessary, conduct external or internal research based on symptoms	4	Strategies to Troubleshoot Any Computer Problem
3. Test the theory to determine cause	4	Strategies to Troubleshoot Any Computer Problem
- Once the theory is confirmed, determine the next steps to resolve problem	4	Strategies to Troubleshoot Any Computer Problem
- If theory is not confirmed, re-establish new theory or escalate	4	Strategies to Troubleshoot Any Computer Problem
4. Establish a plan of action to resolve the problem and implement the solution	4	Strategies to Troubleshoot Any Computer Problem
5. Verify full system functionality and, if applicable, implement preventive measures	4	Strategies to Troubleshoot Any Computer Problem
6. Document findings, actions, and outcomes	4	Strategies to Troubleshoot Any Computer Problem

5.2 Given a scenario, troubleshoot problems related to motherboards, RAM, CPUs, and power.

Objectives	Chapter	Primary Section
• Common symptoms	4	Troubleshooting the Motherboard, Processor, and RAM
- Unexpected shutdowns	4	Troubleshooting the Electrical System
- System lockups	4	Troubleshooting the Motherboard, Processor, and RAM
- POST code beeps	4	Troubleshooting the Motherboard, Processor, and RAM
- Blank screen on bootup	4	Troubleshooting the Motherboard, Processor, and RAM
- BIOS time and setting resets	4	Troubleshooting the Motherboard, Processor, and RAM
- Attempts to boot to incorrect device	4	Troubleshooting the Motherboard, Processor, and RAM
- Continuous reboots	4	Troubleshooting the Motherboard, Processor, and RAM
- No power	4	Troubleshooting the Electrical System
- Overheating	4	Troubleshooting the Motherboard, Processor, and RAM
- Loud noise	4	Troubleshooting the Motherboard, Processor, and RAM
- Intermittent device failure	4	Troubleshooting the Motherboard, Processor, and RAM
- Fans spin – no power to other devices	4	Strategies to Troubleshoot Any Computer Problem
- Indicator lights	4	Troubleshooting the Electrical System
- Smoke	4	Strategies to Troubleshoot Any Computer Problem
- Burning smell	4	Strategies to Troubleshoot Any Computer Problem
- Proprietary crash screens (BSOD/pin wheel)	4	Troubleshooting the Motherboard, Processor, and RAM
- Distended capacitors	4	Troubleshooting the Motherboard, Processor, and RAM
- Log entries and error messages	4	Troubleshooting the Motherboard, Processor, and RAM

5.3   Given a scenario, troubleshoot hard drives and RAID arrays.

Objectives	Chapter	Primary Section
• Common symptoms		
- Read/write failure	5	Troubleshooting Hard Drives
- Slow performance	5	Troubleshooting Hard Drives
- Loud clicking noise	5	Troubleshooting Hard Drives
- Failure to boot	5	Troubleshooting Hard Drives
- Drive not recognized	5	Troubleshooting Hard Drives
- OS not found	5	Troubleshooting Hard Drives
- RAID not found	5	Troubleshooting Hard Drives
- RAID stops working	5	Troubleshooting Hard Drives
- Proprietary crash screens (BSOD/pin wheel)	5	Troubleshooting Hard Drives
- S.M.A.R.T. errors	5	Troubleshooting Hard Drives

5.4   Given a scenario, troubleshoot video, projector, and display issues.

Objectives	Chapter	Primary Section
• Common symptoms	6	Troubleshooting I/O Devices
- VGA mode	6	Troubleshooting I/O Devices
- No image on screen	6	Troubleshooting I/O Devices
- Overheat shutdown	6	Troubleshooting I/O Devices
- Dead pixels	6	Troubleshooting I/O Devices
- Artifacts	6	Troubleshooting I/O Devices
- Incorrect color patterns	6	Troubleshooting I/O Devices
- Dim image	6	Troubleshooting I/O Devices
- Flickering image	6	Troubleshooting I/O Devices
- Distorted image	6	Troubleshooting I/O Devices
- Distorted geometry	6	Troubleshooting I/O Devices
- Burn-in	6	Troubleshooting I/O Devices
- Oversized images and icons	6	Troubleshooting I/O Devices
- Multiple failed jobs in logs	6	Troubleshooting I/O Devices

5.5   Given a scenario, troubleshoot common mobile device issues while adhering to the appropriate procedures.

Objectives	Chapter	Primary Section
• Common symptoms		
- No display	6	Troubleshooting I/O Devices
- Dim display	6	Troubleshooting I/O Devices
- Flickering display	6	Troubleshooting I/O Devices
- Sticking keys	1	First Look at Laptop Components
- Intermittent wireless	9	Troubleshooting Mobile Devices
- Battery not charging	4	Troubleshooting the Electrical System
- Ghost cursor/pointer drift	6	Troubleshooting I/O Devices
- No power	4	Troubleshooting the Electrical System
- Num lock indicator lights	6	Troubleshooting I/O Devices
- No wireless connectivity	9	Troubleshooting Mobile Devices
- No Bluetooth connectivity	9	Troubleshooting Mobile Devices
- Cannot display to external monitor	6	Troubleshooting I/O Devices
- Touch screen non-responsive	9	Troubleshooting Mobile Devices
- Apps not loading	9	Troubleshooting Mobile Devices
- Slow performance	9	Troubleshooting Mobile Devices
- Unable to decrypt email	9	Troubleshooting Mobile Devices

Objectives	Chapter	Primary Section
- Extremely short battery life	9	Troubleshooting Mobile Devices
- Overheating	9	Troubleshooting Mobile Devices
- Frozen system	9	Troubleshooting Mobile Devices
- No sound from speakers	9	Troubleshooting Mobile Devices
- GPS not functioning	9	Troubleshooting Mobile Devices
- Swollen battery	9	Troubleshooting Mobile Devices
• Disassembling processes for proper reassembly	1	First Look at Laptop Components
- Document and label cable and screw locations	1	First Look at Laptop Components
- Organize parts	1	First Look at Laptop Components
- Refer to manufacturer resources	1	First Look at Laptop Components
- Use appropriate hand tools	1	First Look at Laptop Components

5.6 Given a scenario, troubleshoot printers.

Objectives	Chapter	Primary Section
• Common symptoms	10	Troubleshooting Printers
- Streaks	10	Troubleshooting Printers
- Faded prints	10	Troubleshooting Printers
- Ghost images	10	Troubleshooting Printers
- Toner not fused to the paper	10	Troubleshooting Printers
- Creased paper	10	Troubleshooting Printers
- Paper not feeding	10	Troubleshooting Printers
- Paper jam	10	Troubleshooting Printers
- No connectivity	10	Troubleshooting Printers
- Garbled characters on paper	10	Troubleshooting Printers
- Vertical lines on page	10	Troubleshooting Printers
- Backed-up print queue	10	Troubleshooting Printers
- Low memory errors	10	Troubleshooting Printers
- Access denied	10	Troubleshooting Printers
- Printer will not print	10	Troubleshooting Printers
- Color prints in wrong print color	10	Troubleshooting Printers
- Unable to install printer	10	Troubleshooting Printers
- Error codes	10	Troubleshooting Printers
- Printing blank pages	10	Troubleshooting Printers
- No image on printer display	10	Troubleshooting Printers

5.7 Given a scenario, troubleshoot common wired and wireless network problems.

Objectives	Chapter	Primary Section
• Common symptoms	8	Troubleshooting Network Connections
- Limited connectivity	8	Troubleshooting Network Connections
- Unavailable resources	8	Troubleshooting Network Connections
○ Internet	8	Troubleshooting Network Connections
○ Local resources:	8	Troubleshooting Network Connections
○ Shares	8	Troubleshooting Network Connections
○ Printers	8	Troubleshooting Network Connections
○ Email	8	Troubleshooting Network Connections
- No connectivity	8	Troubleshooting Network Connections
- APIPA/link local address	8	Troubleshooting Network Connections
- Intermittent connectivity	8	Troubleshooting Network Connections
- IP conflict	8	Troubleshooting Network Connections
- Slow transfer speeds	8	Troubleshooting Network Connections
- Low RF signal	8	Troubleshooting Network Connections
- SSID not found	8	Troubleshooting Network Connections

COMPTIA A+ CORE 2 (220-1002)

1.0 OPERATING SYSTEMS

1.1 Compare and contrast common operating system types and their purposes.

Objectives	Chapter	Primary Section
• 32-bit vs. 64-bit	12	How to Plan a Windows Installation
- RAM limitations	12	How to Plan a Windows Installation
- Software compatibility	12	How to Plan a Windows Installation
• Workstation operating systems	18	Linux Operating System
- Microsoft Windows	18	Linux Operating System
- Apple Macintosh OS	18	Linux Operating System
- Linux	18	Linux Operating System
• Cell phone/tablet operating systems	9	Mobile Device Operating Systems
- Microsoft Windows	9	Mobile Device Operating Systems
- Android	9	Mobile Device Operating Systems
- iOS	9	Mobile Device Operating Systems
- Chrome OS	9	Mobile Device Operating Systems
• Vendor-specific limitations	18	Linux Operating System
- End-of-life	18	Linux Operating System
- Update limitations	18	Linux Operating System
• Compatibility concerns between operating systems	18	Linux Operating System

1.2 Compare and contrast features of Microsoft Windows versions.

Objectives	Chapter	Primary Section
• Windows 7	11	Windows Interfaces
• Windows 8	11	Windows Interfaces
• Windows 8.1	11	Windows Interfaces
• Windows 10	11	Windows Interfaces
• Corporate vs. personal needs	11	Windows Interfaces
- Domain access	11	Windows Interfaces
- BitLocker	11	Windows Interfaces
- Media center	11	Windows Interfaces
- Branchcache	11	Windows Interfaces
- EFS	11	Windows Interfaces
• Desktop styles/user interface	11	Windows Interfaces

1.3 Summarize general OS installation considerations and upgrade methods.

Objectives	Chapter	Primary Section
• Boot methods	12	How to Plan a Windows Installation
- USB	12	Installing Windows 10, Windows 8.1, and Windows 7
- CD-ROM	12	Installing Windows 10, Windows 8.1, and Windows 7
- DVD	12	Installing Windows 10, Windows 8.1, and Windows 7
- PXE	12	How to Plan a Windows Installation
- Solid state/flash drives	12	Installing Windows 10, Windows 8.1, and Windows 7
- Netboot	18	macOS for Macintosh Computers
- External/hot-swappable drive	12	How to Plan a Windows Installation
- Internal hard drive (partition)	15	Options to Reinstall Windows
• Type of installations	12	How to Plan a Windows Installation
- Unattended installation	12	Special Concerns When Working in a Large Enterprise
- In-place upgrade	12	How to Plan a Windows Installation
- Clean install	12	How to Plan a Windows Installation

Objectives	Chapter	Primary Section
- Repair installation	15	Options to Reinstall Windows
- Multiboot	12	Installing Windows 10, Windows 8.1, and Windows 7
- Remote network installation	12	Special Concerns When Working in a Large Enterprise
- Image deployment	12	Special Concerns When Working in a Large Enterprise
- Recovery partition	15	Options to Reinstall Windows
- Refresh/restore	15	Options to Reinstall Windows
• Partitioning	13	Managing Files, Folders, and Storage Devices
- Dynamic	13	Managing Files, Folders, and Storage Devices
- Basic	13	Managing Files, Folders, and Storage Devices
- Primary	13	Managing Files, Folders, and Storage Devices
- Extended	13	Managing Files, Folders, and Storage Devices
- Logical	13	Managing Files, Folders, and Storage Devices
- GPT	13	Managing Files, Folders, and Storage Devices
• File system types/formatting	13	Managing Files, Folders, and Storage Devices
- ExFAT	13	Managing Files, Folders, and Storage Devices
- FAT32	13	Managing Files, Folders, and Storage Devices
- NTFS	13	Managing Files, Folders, and Storage Devices
- CDFS	13	Managing Files, Folders, and Storage Devices
- NFS	13	Managing Files, Folders, and Storage Devices
- ext3, ext4	18	Linux Operating System
- HFS	18	macOS for Macintosh Computers
- Swap partition	18	Linux Operating System
- Quick format vs. full format	12	Installing Windows 10, Windows 8.1, and Windows 7
• Load alternate third-party drivers when necessary	12	How to Plan a Windows Installation
• Workgroup vs. Domain setup	11	How Windows Controls Access to Network Resources
• Time/date/region/language settings	12	Installing Windows 10, Windows 8.1, and Windows 7
• Driver installation, software, and Windows updates	12	What to Do After a Windows Installation
• Factory recovery partition	15	Options to Reinstall Windows
• Properly formatted boot drive with the correct partitions/format	15	Tools for Least Invasive Solutions
• Prerequisites/hardware compatibility	12	How to Plan a Windows Installation
• Application compatibility	12	How to Plan a Windows Installation
• OS compatibility/upgrade path	12	How to Plan a Windows Installation

1.4 Given a scenario, use appropriate Microsoft command-line tools.

Objectives	Chapter	Primary Section
• Navigation	13	Using a Command-Line Interface (CLI)
- dir	13	Using a Command-Line Interface (CLI)
- cd	13	Using a Command-Line Interface (CLI)
- ..	13	Using a Command-Line Interface (CLI)
• ipconfig	7	Troubleshooting Network Connections
• ping	7	Troubleshooting Network Connections
• tracert	7	Troubleshooting Network Connections
• netstat	7	Troubleshooting Network Connections
• nslookup	7	Troubleshooting Network Connections
• shutdown	13	Using a Command-Line Interface (CLI)
• dism	14	Best Practices to Troubleshoot Windows-Related Problems
• sfc	14	Best Practices to Troubleshoot Windows-Related Problems
• chkdsk	14	Best Practices to Troubleshoot Windows-Related Problems
• diskpart	15	Tools for Least Invasive Solutions

1.5   Given a scenario, use Microsoft operating system features and tools.

Objectives	Chapter	Primary Section
- Assigning/changing drive letters	13	Managing Files, Folders, and Storage Devices
- Adding drives	13	Managing Files, Folders, and Storage Devices
- Adding arrays	13	Managing Files, Folders, and Storage Devices
- Storage spaces	13	Managing Files, Folders, and Storage Devices
• System utilities	14	
- Regedit	14	Slow Startup and Slow Performance
- Command	13	Using a Command-Line Interface (CLI)
- Services.msc	14	Application Errors and Crashes
- MMC	14	Concepts and Windows Tools for Solving Problems with Windows, Applications, and Hardware
- MSTSC	13	Remote Connections
- Notepad	11	Windows Tools for Users and Technicians
- Explorer	11	Windows Tools for Users and Technicians
- Msinfo32	11	Windows Tools for Users and Technicians
- DxDiag	14	Troubleshooting Hardware Problems in Windows
- Disk Defragmenter	13	Managing Files, Folders, and Storage Devices
- System Restore	14	Best Practices to Troubleshoot Windows-Related Problems
- Windows Update	12	What to Do After a Windows Installation

1.6   Given a scenario, use Microsoft Windows Control Panel utilities.

Objectives	Chapter	Primary Section
• Internet Options	16	Securing a Windows Personal Computer
- Connections	16	Securing a Windows Personal Computer
- Security	16	Securing a Windows Personal Computer
- General	16	Securing a Windows Personal Computer
- Privacy	16	Securing a Windows Personal Computer
- Programs	16	Securing a Windows Personal Computer
- Advanced	16	Securing a Windows Personal Computer
• Display/Display Settings	14	Troubleshooting Hardware Problems in Windows
- Resolution	14	Troubleshooting Hardware Problems in Windows
- Color depth	14	Troubleshooting Hardware Problems in Windows
- Refresh rate	14	Troubleshooting Hardware Problems in Windows
• User Accounts	16	Controlling Access to Folders and Files
• Folder Options	11	Windows Tools for Users and Technicians
- View hidden files	11	Windows Tools for Users and Technicians
- Hide extensions	11	Windows Tools for Users and Technicians
- General options	11	Windows Tools for Users and Technicians
- View options	11	Windows Tools for Users and Technicians
• System		
- Performance (virtual memory)	14	Slow Startup and Slow Performance
- Remote settings	13	Remote Connections
- System protection	13	Backup Procedures
• Windows Firewall	16	Securing a Windows Personal Computer
• Power Options	11	Windows Tools for Users and Technicians
- Hibernate	11	Windows Tools for Users and Technicians
- Power plans	11	Windows Tools for Users and Technicians
- Sleep/suspend	11	Windows Tools for Users and Technicians
- Standby	11	Windows Tools for Users and Technicians
• Credential Manager	16	Securing a Windows Personal Computer
• Programs and features	12	What to Do After a Windows Installation
• HomeGroup	11	How Windows Controls Access to Network Resources

Objectives	Chapter	Primary Section
• Devices and Printers	12	What to Do After a Windows Installation
• Sound	11	Windows Tools for Users and Technicians
• Troubleshooting	14	Concepts and Windows Tools for Solving Problems with Windows, Applications, and Hardware
• Network and Sharing Center	11	How Windows Controls Access to Network Resources
• Device Manager	12	What to Do After a Windows Installation
• BitLocker	16	Securing a Windows Personal Computer
• Sync Center	16	Controlling Access to Folders and Files

1.7 Summarize application installation and configuration concepts

Objectives	Chapter	Primary Section
• System requirements	12	What to Do After a Windows Installation
- Drive space	12	What to Do After a Windows Installation
- RAM	12	What to Do After a Windows Installation
• OS requirements	12	What to Do After a Windows Installation
- Compatibility	12	What to Do After a Windows Installation
• Methods of installation and deployment	12	What to Do After a Windows Installation
- Local (CD/USB)	12	What to Do After a Windows Installation
- Network-based	12	What to Do After a Windows Installation
• Local user permissions	12	What to Do After a Windows Installation
- Folder/file access for installation	12	What to Do After a Windows Installation
• Security considerations	12	What to Do After a Windows Installation
- Impact to device	12	What to Do After a Windows Installation
- Impact to network	12	What to Do After a Windows Installation

1.8 Given a scenario, configure Microsoft Windows networking on a client/desktop.

Objectives	Chapter	Primary Section
• HomeGroup vs. Workgroup	11	How Windows Controls Access to Network Resources
• Domain setup	11	How Windows Controls Access to Network Resources
• Network shares/administrative shares/mapping drives	16	Controlling Access to Folders and Files
• Printer sharing vs. network printer mapping	16	Securing a Windows Personal Computer
• Establish networking connections	7	Connecting a Computer to a Local Network
- VPN	7	Connecting a Computer to a Local Network
- Dial-ups	7	Connecting a Computer to a Local Network
- Wireless	7	Connecting a Computer to a Local Network
- Wired	7	Connecting a Computer to a Local Network
- WWAN (Cellular)	7	Connecting a Computer to a Local Network
• Proxy settings	16	Securing a Windows Personal Computer
• Remote Desktop Connection	13	Remote Connections
• Remote Assistance	13	Remote Connections
• Home vs. Work vs. Public network settings	11	How Windows Controls Access to Network Resources
• Firewall settings	16	Securing a Windows Personal Computer
- Exceptions	16	Securing a Windows Personal Computer
- Configuration	16	Securing a Windows Personal Computer
- Enabling/disabling Windows Firewall	16	Securing a Windows Personal Computer
• Configuring an alternative IP address in Windows	7	Connecting a Computer to a Local Network
	7	Connecting a Computer to a Local Network
- IP addressing		
- Subnet mask	7	Connecting a Computer to a Local Network

Objectives	Chapter	Primary Section
- DNS	7	Connecting a Computer to a Local Network
- Gateway	7	Connecting a Computer to a Local Network
• Network card properties	7	Connecting a Computer to a Local Network
- Half duplex/full duplex/auto	7	Connecting a Computer to a Local Network
- Speed	7	Connecting a Computer to a Local Network
- Wake-on-LAN	7	Connecting a Computer to a Local Network
- QoS	7	Connecting a Computer to a Local Network
- BIOS (on-board NIC)	7	Connecting a Computer to a Local Network

1.9 Given a scenario, use features and tools of the Mac OS and Linux client/desktop operating systems.

Objectives	Chapter	Primary Section
• Best practices		
- Scheduled backups	18	macOS for Macintosh Computers
- Scheduled disk maintenance	18	macOS for Macintosh Computers
- System updates/App Store	18	macOS for Macintosh Computers
- Patch management	18	macOS for Macintosh Computers
- Driver/firmware updates	18	macOS for Macintosh Computers
- Antivirus/Anti-malware updates	18	macOS for Macintosh Computers
• Tools		
- Backup/Time Machine	18	macOS for Macintosh Computers
- Restore/Snapshot	18	macOS for Macintosh Computers
- Image recovery	18	macOS for Macintosh Computers
- Disk maintenance utilities	18	macOS for Macintosh Computers
- Shell/Terminal	18	macOS for Macintosh Computers
- Screen sharing	18	macOS for Macintosh Computers
- Force Quit	18	macOS for Macintosh Computers
• Features		
- Multiple desktops/Mission Control	18	macOS for Macintosh Computers
- Key Chain	18	macOS for Macintosh Computers
- Spot Light	18	macOS for Macintosh Computers
- iCloud	18	macOS for Macintosh Computers
- Gestures	18	macOS for Macintosh Computers
- Finder	18	macOS for Macintosh Computers
- Remote Disc	18	macOS for Macintosh Computers
- Dock	18	macOS for Macintosh Computers
- Boot Camp	18	macOS for Macintosh Computers
• Basic Linux commands		
- ls	18	Linux Operating System
- grep	18	Linux Operating System
- cd	18	Linux Operating System
- shutdown	18	Linux Operating System
- pwd vs. passwd	18	Linux Operating System
- mv	18	Linux Operating System
- cp	18	Linux Operating System
- rm	18	Linux Operating System
- chmod	18	Linux Operating System
- chown	18	Linux Operating System
- iwconfig/ifconfig	18	Linux Operating System
- ps	18	Linux Operating System
- su/sudo	18	Linux Operating System
- apt-get	18	Linux Operating System
- vi	18	Linux Operating System
- dd	18	Linux Operating System
- kill	18	Linux Operating System

2.0 SECURITY

2.1 Summarize the importance of physical security measures.

Objectives	Chapter	Primary Section
• Mantrap	17	Protecting Network Resources
• Badge reader	17	Protecting Network Resources
• Smart card	17	Protecting Network Resources
• Security guard	17	Protecting Network Resources
• Door lock	17	Protecting Network Resources
• Biometric locks	17	Protecting Network Resources
• Hardware tokens	17	Protecting Network Resources
• Cable locks	17	Protecting Network Resources
• Server locks	17	Protecting Network Resources
• USB locks	17	Protecting Network Resources
• Privacy screen	17	Protecting Network Resources
• Key fobs	17	Protecting Network Resources
• Entry control roster	17	Protecting Network Resources

2.2 Explain logical security concepts.

Objectives	Chapter	Primary Section
• Active Directory	16	Using Active Directory Domain Services
- Login script	16	Using Active Directory Domain Services
- Domain	16	Using Active Directory Domain Services
- Group Policy/Updates	16	Using Active Directory Domain Services
- Organizational Units	16	Using Active Directory Domain Services
- Home Folder	16	Using Active Directory Domain Services
- Folder redirection	16	Using Active Directory Domain Services
• Software tokens	17	Protecting Network Resources
• MDM policies	17	Protecting Network Resources
• Port security	17	Protecting Network Resources
• MAC address filtering	7	Setting Up a Multifunction Router for a SOHO Network
• Certificates	17	Protecting Network Resources
• Antivirus/Anti-malware	17	Protecting Network Resources
• Firewalls	16	Securing a Windows Personal Computer
• User authentication/strong passwords	16	Securing a Windows Personal Computer
• Multifactor authentication	17	Protecting Network Resources
• Directory permissions	16	Using Active Directory Domain Services
• VPN	17	Protecting Network Resources
• DLP	17	Protecting Network Resources
• Access control lists	17	Protecting Network Resources
• Smart card	17	Protecting Network Resources
• Email filtering	17	Protecting Network Resources
• Trusted/untrusted software sources	17	Protecting Network Resources
• Principle of least privilege	16	Controlling Access to Folders and Files

2.3 Compare and contrast wireless security protocols and authentication methods.

Objectives	Chapter	Primary Section
• Protocols and encryption	7	Setting Up a Multifunction Router for a SOHO Network
- WEP	7	Setting Up a Multifunction Router for a SOHO Network
- WPA	7	Setting Up a Multifunction Router for a SOHO Network
- WPA2	7	Setting Up a Multifunction Router for a SOHO Network
- TKIP	7	Setting Up a Multifunction Router for a SOHO Network
- AES	7	Setting Up a Multifunction Router for a SOHO Network

Objectives	Chapter	Primary Section
• Authentication	17	Protecting Network Resources
- Single-factor	17	Protecting Network Resources
- Multifactor	17	Protecting Network Resources
- RADIUS	17	Protecting Network Resources
- TACACS	17	Protecting Network Resources

2.4 Given a scenario, detect, remove, and prevent malware using appropriate tools and methods.

Objectives	Chapter	Primary Section
• Malware	17	Dealing with Malicious Software on Personal Computers
- Ransomware	17	Dealing with Malicious Software on Personal Computers
- Trojan	17	Dealing with Malicious Software on Personal Computers
- Keylogger	17	Dealing with Malicious Software on Personal Computers
- Rootkit	17	Dealing with Malicious Software on Personal Computers
- Virus	17	Dealing with Malicious Software on Personal Computers
- Botnet	17	Dealing with Malicious Software on Personal Computers
- Worm	17	Dealing with Malicious Software on Personal Computers
- Spyware	17	Dealing with Malicious Software on Personal Computers
• Tools and methods	17	Dealing with Malicious Software on Personal Computers
- Antivirus	17	Dealing with Malicious Software on Personal Computers
- Anti-malware	17	Dealing with Malicious Software on Personal Computers
- Recovery console	17	Dealing with Malicious Software on Personal Computers
- Backup/restore	17	Dealing with Malicious Software on Personal Computers
- End user education	17	Dealing with Malicious Software on Personal Computers
- Software firewalls	17	Dealing with Malicious Software on Personal Computers
- SecureDNS	17	Protecting Network Resources

2.5 Compare and contrast social engineering, threats, and vulnerabilities.

Objectives	Chapter	Primary Section
• Social engineering		
- Phishing	17	Protecting Network Resources
- Spear phishing	17	Protecting Network Resources
- Impersonation	17	Protecting Network Resources
- Shoulder surfing	17	Protecting Network Resources
- Tailgating	17	Protecting Network Resources
- Dumpster diving	17	Protecting Network Resources
• DDoS	17	Dealing with Malicious Software on Personal Computers
• DoS	17	Dealing with Malicious Software on Personal Computers
• Zero-day	17	Dealing with Malicious Software on Personal Computers
• Man-in-the-middle	17	Dealing with Malicious Software on Personal Computers
• Brute force	16	Securing a Windows Personal Computer
• Dictionary	17	Dealing with Malicious Software on Personal Computers
• Rainbow table	17	Dealing with Malicious Software on Personal Computers
• Spoofing	17	Dealing with Malicious Software on Personal Computers
• Non-compliant systems	17	Dealing with Malicious Software on Personal Computers
• Zombie	17	Dealing with Malicious Software on Personal Computers

2.6   Compare and contrast the differences of basic Microsoft Windows OS security settings.

Objectives	Chapter	Primary Section
• User and groups	16	Controlling Access to Folders and Files
- Administrator	16	Controlling Access to Folders and Files
- Power user	16	Controlling Access to Folders and Files
- Guest	16	Controlling Access to Folders and Files
- Standard user	16	Controlling Access to Folders and Files
• NTFS vs. share permissions	16	Controlling Access to Folders and Files
- Allow vs. deny	16	Controlling Access to Folders and Files
- Moving vs. copying folders and files	16	Controlling Access to Folders and Files
- File attributes	16	Controlling Access to Folders and Files
• Shared files and folders	16	Controlling Access to Folders and Files
- Administrative shares vs. local shares	16	Controlling Access to Folders and Files
- Permission propagation	16	Controlling Access to Folders and Files
- Inheritance	16	Controlling Access to Folders and Files
• System files and folders	16	Controlling Access to Folders and Files
• User authentication	16	Securing a Windows Personal Computer
- Single sign-on	16	Securing a Windows Personal Computer
• Run as administrator vs. standard user	14	Concepts and Windows Tools for Solving Problems with Windows, Applications, and Hardware
• BitLocker	16	Securing a Windows Personal Computer
• BitLocker To Go	16	Securing a Windows Personal Computer
• EFS	16	Securing a Windows Personal Computer

2.7   Given a scenario, implement security best practices to secure a workstation.

Objectives	Chapter	Primary Section
• Password best practices	16	Securing a Windows Personal Computer
- Setting strong passwords	16	Securing a Windows Personal Computer
- Password expiration	16	Securing a Windows Personal Computer
- Screensaver required password	16	Securing a Windows Personal Computer
- BIOS/UEFI passwords	16	Securing a Windows Personal Computer
- Requiring passwords	16	Securing a Windows Personal Computer
• Account management	16	Controlling Access to Folders and Files
- Restricting user permissions	16	Controlling Access to Folders and Files
- Logon time restrictions	16	Using Active Directory Domain Services
- Disabling guest account	16	Using Active Directory Domain Services
- Failed attempts lockout	16	Using Active Directory Domain Services
- Timeout/screen lock	16	Using Active Directory Domain Services
- Change default admin user account/password	16	Using Active Directory Domain Services
- Basic Active Directory functions	16	Using Active Directory Domain Services
○ Account creation	16	Using Active Directory Domain Services
○ Account deletion	16	Using Active Directory Domain Services
○ Password reset/unlock account	16	Using Active Directory Domain Services
○ Disable account	16	Using Active Directory Domain Services
• Disable autorun	16	Securing a Windows Personal Computer
• Data encryption	16	Securing a Windows Personal Computer
• Patch/update management	13	Scheduling Preventive Maintenance

2.8   Given a scenario, implement methods for securing mobile devices.

Objectives	Chapter	Primary Section
• Screen locks	9	Securing a Mobile Device
- Fingerprint lock	9	Securing a Mobile Device
- Face lock	9	Securing a Mobile Device
- Swipe lock	9	Securing a Mobile Device
- Passcode lock	9	Securing a Mobile Device
• Remote wipes	9	Securing a Mobile Device
• Locator applications	9	Securing a Mobile Device
• Remote backup applications	9	Securing a Mobile Device
• Failed login attempts restrictions	9	Securing a Mobile Device
• Antivirus/Anti-malware	9	Securing a Mobile Device
• Patching/OS updates	9	Securing a Mobile Device
• Biometric authentication	9	Securing a Mobile Device
• Full device encryption	9	Securing a Mobile Device
• Multifactor authentication	9	Securing a Mobile Device
• Authenticator applications	9	Securing a Mobile Device
• Trusted sources vs. untrusted sources	9	Securing a Mobile Device
• Firewalls	9	Securing a Mobile Device
• Policies and procedures	9	Securing a Mobile Device
- BYOD vs. corporate-owned	9	Securing a Mobile Device
- Profile security requirements	9	Securing a Mobile Device

2.9   Given a scenario, implement appropriate data destruction and disposal methods.

Objectives	Chapter	Primary Section
• Physical destruction	17	Protecting Network Resources
- Shredder	17	Protecting Network Resources
- Drill/hammer	17	Protecting Network Resources
- Electromagnetic (Degaussing)	17	Protecting Network Resources
- Incineration	17	Protecting Network Resources
- Certificate of destruction	17	Protecting Network Resources
• Recycling or repurposing best practices	17	Protecting Network Resources
- Low-level format vs. standard format	17	Protecting Network Resources
- Overwrite	17	Protecting Network Resources
- Drive wipe	17	Protecting Network Resources

2.10   Given a scenario, configure security on SOHO wireless and wired networks.

Objectives	Chapter	Primary Section
• Wireless-specific	7	Setting Up a Multifunction Router for a SOHO Network
- Changing default SSID	7	Setting Up a Multifunction Router for a SOHO Network
- Setting encryption	7	Setting Up a Multifunction Router for a SOHO Network
- Disabling SSID broadcast	7	Setting Up a Multifunction Router for a SOHO Network
- Antenna and access point placement	7	Setting Up a Multifunction Router for a SOHO Network
- Radio power levels	7	Setting Up a Multifunction Router for a SOHO Network
- WPS	7	Setting Up a Multifunction Router for a SOHO Network
• Change default usernames and passwords	7	Setting Up a Multifunction Router for a SOHO Network
• Enable MAC filtering	7	Setting Up a Multifunction Router for a SOHO Network
• Assign static IP addresses	7	Setting Up a Multifunction Router for a SOHO Network
• Firewall settings	7	Setting Up a Multifunction Router for a SOHO Network
• Port forwarding/mapping	7	Setting Up a Multifunction Router for a SOHO Network

3.0 SOFTWARE TROUBLESHOOTING

3.1   Given a scenario, troubleshoot Microsoft Windows OS problems.

3.2   Given a scenario, troubleshoot and resolve PC security issues.

Objectives	Chapter	Primary Section
- Rogue antivirus	17	Dealing with Malicious Software on Personal Computers
- Spam	17	Dealing with Malicious Software on Personal Computers
- Renamed system files	17	Dealing with Malicious Software on Personal Computers
- Disappearing files	17	Dealing with Malicious Software on Personal Computers
- File permission changes	17	Dealing with Malicious Software on Personal Computers
- Hijacked email	17	Dealing with Malicious Software on Personal Computers
○ Responses from users regarding email	17	Dealing with Malicious Software on Personal Computers
○ Automated replies from unknown sent email	17	Dealing with Malicious Software on Personal Computers
- Access denied	17	Dealing with Malicious Software on Personal Computers
- Invalid certificate (trusted root CA)	17	Dealing with Malicious Software on Personal Computers
- System/application log errors	17	Dealing with Malicious Software on Personal Computers

3.3 Given a scenario, use best practice procedures for malware removal.

Objectives	Chapter	Primary Section
1. Identify and research malware symptoms.	17	Dealing with Malicious Software on Personal Computers
2. Quarantine the infected systems.	17	Dealing with Malicious Software on Personal Computers
3. Disable System Restore (in Windows).	17	Dealing with Malicious Software on Personal Computers
4. Remediate the infected systems.	17	Dealing with Malicious Software on Personal Computers
a. Update the anti-malware software.	17	Dealing with Malicious Software on Personal Computers
b. Scan and use removal techniques (safe mode, pre-installation environment).	17	Dealing with Malicious Software on Personal Computers
5. Schedule scans and run updates.	17	Dealing with Malicious Software on Personal Computers
6. Enable System Restore and create a restore point (in Windows).	17	Dealing with Malicious Software on Personal Computers
7. Educate the end user.	17	Dealing with Malicious Software on Personal Computers

3.4 Given a scenario, troubleshoot mobile OS and application issues.

Objectives	Chapter	Primary Section
• Common symptoms	9	Troubleshooting Mobile Devices
- Dim display	9	Troubleshooting Mobile Devices
- Intermittent wireless	9	Troubleshooting Mobile Devices
- No wireless connectivity	9	Troubleshooting Mobile Devices
- No Bluetooth connectivity	9	Troubleshooting Mobile Devices
- Cannot broadcast to external monitor	9	Troubleshooting Mobile Devices
- Touch screen non-responsive	9	Troubleshooting Mobile Devices
- Apps not loading	9	Troubleshooting Mobile Devices
- Slow performance	9	Troubleshooting Mobile Devices
- Unable to decrypt email	9	Troubleshooting Mobile Devices
- Extremely short battery life	9	Troubleshooting Mobile Devices
- Overheating	9	Troubleshooting Mobile Devices
- Frozen system	9	Troubleshooting Mobile Devices
- No sound from speakers	9	Troubleshooting Mobile Devices
- Inaccurate touch screen response	9	Troubleshooting Mobile Devices
- System lockout	9	Troubleshooting Mobile Devices
- App log errors	9	Troubleshooting Mobile Devices

3.5 Given a scenario, troubleshoot mobile OS and application security issues.

Objectives	Chapter	Primary Section
• Common symptoms	9	Troubleshooting Mobile Devices
- Signal drop/weak signal	9	Troubleshooting Mobile Devices
- Power drain	9	Troubleshooting Mobile Devices
- Slow data speeds	9	Troubleshooting Mobile Devices
- Unintended Wi-Fi connection	9	Troubleshooting Mobile Devices
- Unintended Bluetooth pairing	9	Troubleshooting Mobile Devices
- Leaked personal files/data	9	Troubleshooting Mobile Devices
- Data transmission over limit	9	Troubleshooting Mobile Devices
- Unauthorized account access	9	Troubleshooting Mobile Devices
- Unauthorized location tracking	9	Troubleshooting Mobile Devices
- Unauthorized camera/microphone activation	9	Troubleshooting Mobile Devices
- High resource utilization	9	Troubleshooting Mobile Devices

4.0 OPERATIONAL PROCEDURES

4.1 Compare and contrast best practices associated with types of documentation.

Objectives	Chapter	Primary Section
• Network topology diagrams	17	Best Practices for Documentation and Security Policies
• Knowledge base/articles	17	Best Practices for Documentation and Security Policies
• Incident documentation	17	Best Practices for Documentation and Security Policies
• Regulatory and compliance policy	17	Best Practices for Documentation and Security Policies
• Acceptable use policy	17	Best Practices for Documentation and Security Policies
• Password policy	17	Best Practices for Documentation and Security Policies
• Inventory management	17	Best Practices for Documentation and Security Policies
- Asset tags	17	Best Practices for Documentation and Security Policies
- Barcodes	17	Best Practices for Documentation and Security Policies

4.2 Given a scenario, implement basic change management best practices.

Objectives	Chapter	Primary Section
• Documented business processes	17	Best Practices for Documentation and Security Policies
• Purpose of the change	17	Best Practices for Documentation and Security Policies
• Scope the change	17	Best Practices for Documentation and Security Policies
• Risk analysis	17	Best Practices for Documentation and Security Policies
• Plan for change	17	Best Practices for Documentation and Security Policies
• End-user acceptance	17	Best Practices for Documentation and Security Policies
• Change board	17	Best Practices for Documentation and Security Policies
- Approvals	17	Best Practices for Documentation and Security Policies
• Backout plan	17	Best Practices for Documentation and Security Policies
• Document changes	17	Best Practices for Documentation and Security Policies

4.3 Given a scenario, implement basic disaster prevention and recovery methods.

Objectives	Chapter	Primary Section
• Backup and recovery	13	Backup Procedures
- Image level	13	Backup Procedures
- File level	13	Backup Procedures
- Critical applications	13	Backup Procedures
• Backup testing	13	Backup Procedures
• UPS	13	Backup Procedures
• Surge protector	13	Backup Procedures
• Cloud storage vs. local storage backups	13	Backup Procedures
• Account recovery options	15	Troubleshooting Specific Windows Startup Problems

4.4 Explain common safety procedures.

Objectives	Chapter	Primary Section
• Equipment grounding	Apx A	Protecting the Equipment
• Proper component handling and storage	Apx A	Protecting the Equipment
- Antistatic bags	Apx A	Protecting the Equipment
- ESD straps	Apx A	Protecting the Equipment
- ESD mats	Apx A	Protecting the Equipment
- Self-grounding	Apx A	Protecting the Equipment
• Toxic waste handling	Apx A	Protecting the Environment
- Batteries	Apx A	Protecting the Environment
- Toner	Apx A	Protecting the Environment
- CRT	Apx A	Protecting the Environment
- Cell phones	Apx A	Protecting the Environment
- Tablets	Apx A	Protecting the Environment
• Personal safety	Apx A	Protecting Yourself
- Disconnect power before repairing PC	Apx A	Protecting Yourself
- Remove jewelry	Apx A	Protecting Yourself
- Lifting techniques	Apx A	Protecting Yourself
- Weight limitations	Apx A	Protecting Yourself
- Electrical fire safety	Apx A	Protecting Yourself
- Cable management	Apx A	Protecting Yourself
- Safety goggles	Apx A	Protecting Yourself
- Air filter mask	Apx A	Protecting Yourself
• Compliance with government regulations	Apx A	Protecting the Environment

4.5 Explain environmental impacts and appropriate controls.

Objectives	Chapter	Primary Section
• MSDS documentation for handling and disposal	Apx A	Protecting the Environment
• Temperature, humidity level awareness, and proper ventilation	Apx A	Protecting the Equipment
• Power surges, brownouts, and blackouts	Apx A	Protecting the Equipment
- Battery backup	Apx A	Protecting the Equipment
- Surge suppressor	Apx A	Protecting the Equipment
• Protection from airborne particles	Apx A	Protecting the Equipment
- Enclosures	Apx A	Protecting the Equipment
- Air filters/mask	Apx A	Protecting Yourself
• Dust and debris	Apx A	Protecting the Equipment
- Compressed air	Apx A	Protecting the Equipment
- Vacuums	Apx A	Protecting the Equipment
• Compliance to government regulations	Apx A	Protecting the Environment

4.6 Explain the processes for addressing prohibited content/activity, and privacy, licensing, and policy concepts.

Objectives	Chapter	Primary Section
• Incident response	17	Best Practices for Documentation and Security Policies
- First response	17	Best Practices for Documentation and Security Policies
○ Identify	17	Best Practices for Documentation and Security Policies
○ Report through proper channels	17	Best Practices for Documentation and Security Policies
○ Data/device preservation	17	Best Practices for Documentation and Security Policies

4.7 Given a scenario, use proper communication techniques and professionalism.

4.8 Identify the basics of scripting.

Objectives	Chapter	Primary Section
• Script file types	18	Scripting Software and Techniques
- .bat	18	Scripting Software and Techniques
- .ps1	18	Scripting Software and Techniques
- .vbs	18	Scripting Software and Techniques
- .sh	18	Scripting Software and Techniques
- .py	18	Scripting Software and Techniques
- .js	18	Scripting Software and Techniques
• Environment variables	18	Scripting Software and Techniques
• Comment syntax	18	Scripting Software and Techniques
• Basic script constructs	18	Scripting Software and Techniques
- Basic loops	18	Scripting Software and Techniques
- Variables	18	Scripting Software and Techniques
• Basic data types	18	Scripting Software and Techniques
- Integers	18	Scripting Software and Techniques
- Strings	18	Scripting Software and Techniques

4.9 Given a scenario, use remote access technologies.

Objectives	Chapter	Primary Section
• RDP	13	Remote Connections
• Telnet	18	Linux Operating System
• SSH	18	Linux Operating System
• Third-party tools	18	Linux Operating System
- Screen share feature	18	Linux Operating System
- File share	18	Linux Operating System
• Security considerations of each access method	18	Linux Operating System

Introduction: CompTIA A+ Guide to IT Technical Support

CompTIA A+ Guide to IT Technical Support, Tenth Edition was written to be the very best tool on the market today to prepare you to support users and their resources on networks, desktops, laptops, mobile devices, virtual machines, and in the cloud. The text has been updated to include the most current hardware and software technologies; this book takes you from the just-a-user level to the I-can-fix-this level for hardware, software, networks, and virtual computing infrastructures. It achieves its goals with an unusually effective combination of tools that powerfully reinforce both concepts and hands-on, real-world experiences. It also provides thorough preparation for the content on the new CompTIA A+ Core 1 and Core 2 Certification exams. Competency in using a computer is a prerequisite to using this book. No background knowledge of electronics or networking is assumed. An appropriate prerequisite course for this book would be a general course in computer applications.

This book includes:

- ◢ *Several in-depth, hands-on projects* at the end of each chapter that invite you to immediately apply and reinforce critical thinking and troubleshooting skills and are designed to make certain that you not only understand the material, but also execute procedures and make decisions on your own.
- ◢ *Comprehensive review and practice end-of-chapter material*, including a chapter summary, key terms list, critical thinking questions that focus on the type of scenarios you might expect on A+ exam questions, and real-world problems to solve.
- ◢ *Step-by-step instructions* on installation, maintenance, optimization of system performance, and troubleshooting.
- ◢ *A wide array of photos, drawings, and screenshots* support the text, displaying in detail the exact software and hardware features you will need to understand to set up, maintain, and troubleshoot physical and virtual computers and small networks.

In addition, the carefully structured, clearly written text is accompanied by graphics that provide the visual input essential to learning and to help students master difficult subject matter. For instructors using the book in a classroom, instructor resources are available online.

Coverage is balanced—while focusing on new technologies and software, including virtualization, cloud computing, the Internet of Things, and Windows 10, the text also covers the real world of an IT support technician, where some older technologies remain in widespread use and still need support. For example, the text covers M.2 motherboard slots and NVMe, the latest drive interface standard for SSDs, but also addresses how to install SSDs and magnetic hard drives using the older SATA interfaces. The text focuses on Windows 10, the most popular OS for desktops and laptops, but also covers Windows 8/7, macOS, and Linux for desktops, and Android, iOS, Windows Mobile, and Chrome OS for mobile devices. Other covered content that is new with the A+ Core 1 and Core 2 exams includes change management best practices, scripting, SSH, managed switches, VLANs, and Windows Server Active Directory.

This book provides thorough preparation for CompTIA's A+ Core 1 and Core 2 Certification examinations. This certification credential's popularity among employers is growing exponentially, and obtaining certification increases your ability to gain employment and improve your salary. To get more information on CompTIA's A+ certification and its sponsoring organization, the Computing Technology Industry Association, see their website at *www.comptia.org*.

FEATURES

To ensure a successful learning experience, this book includes the following pedagogical features:

- ◢ *Learning Objectives.* Every chapter opens with a list of learning objectives that sets the stage for you to absorb the lessons of the text.
- ◢ *Comprehensive Step-by-Step Troubleshooting Guidance.* Troubleshooting guidelines are included in almost every chapter. In addition, Chapter 4 gives insights into general approaches to troubleshooting that help apply the specifics detailed in each chapter for different hardware and software problems. Chapters 8, 14, and 15 also focus on troubleshooting networks, applications, and Windows.
- ◢ *Step-by-Step Procedures.* The book is chock-full of step-by-step procedures covering subjects from hardware and operating system installations and maintenance to troubleshooting the boot process or a failed network connection and optimizing system performance.
- ◢ *Visual Learning.* Numerous visually detailed photographs, three-dimensional art, and screenshots support the text, displaying hardware and software features exactly as you will see them in your work.
- ◢ *CompTIA A+ Table of Contents.* This table of contents gives the chapter and section that provides the primary content for each certification objective on the A+ exams. This is a valuable tool for quick reference.
- ◢ *Applying Concepts.* These sections offer real-life, practical applications for the material being discussed. Whether outlining a task, developing a scenario, or providing pointers, the Applying Concepts sections give you a chance to apply what you've learned to a typical computer or network problem, so you can understand how you will use the material in your professional life.

 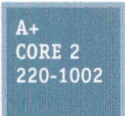 *A+ Icons.* All of the content that relates to CompTIA's A+ Core 1 and A+ Core 2 Certification exams is highlighted with an A+ icon. The icon notes the exam name and the objective number. This unique feature highlights the relevant content at a glance, so that you can pay extra attention to the material.

 Notes. Note icons highlight additional helpful information related to the subject being discussed.

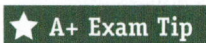 *A+ Exam Tip Boxes.* These boxes highlight additional insights and tips to remember if you are planning to take the CompTIA A+ exams.

 Caution Icons. These icons highlight critical safety information. Follow these instructions carefully to protect the computer and its data and to ensure your own safety.

 OS Differences. These boxes point you to the differences among Windows 10, Windows 8, and Windows 7.

- ◢ *End-of-Chapter Material.* Each chapter closes with the following features, which reinforce the material covered in the chapter and provide real-world, hands-on testing:
  - ◢ *Chapter Summary:* This bulleted list of concise statements summarizes all major points of the chapter.

- ◢ *Key Terms:* The content of each chapter is further reinforced by an end-of-chapter key term list. The definitions of all terms are included with this text in a full-length glossary.

- ◢ *Thinking Critically Questions:* You can test your understanding of each chapter with a comprehensive set of "Thinking Critically" questions to help you synthesize and apply what you've learned in scenarios that test your skills at the same depth as the A+ exams.

- ◢ *Hands-On Projects:* These sections give you practice using the skills you have just studied so that you can learn by doing and know you have mastered a skill.

- ◢ *Real Problems, Real Solutions:* Each comprehensive problem allows you to find out if you can apply what you've learned in the chapter to a real-life situation.

- ◢ *Student Companion Site.* Additional content included on the companion website includes Electricity and Multimeters, and FAT Details. Other helpful online references include Frequently Asked Questions, Sample Reports, a Computer Inventory and Maintenance form, and Troubleshooting Flowcharts.

WHAT'S NEW IN THE TENTH EDITION

Here's a summary of what's new in the *Tenth Edition*:

- ◢ Content maps to all of CompTIA's A+ Core 1 and Core 2 exams.
- ◢ There is now more focus on A+, with non-A+ content moved online to the companion website or eliminated.
- ◢ The chapters focus on Windows 10 with some content about Windows 8/7.
- ◢ New content is added (all new content was also new to the A+ Core 1 and Core 2 exams).

  - ◢ Windows 10 is added. Operating systems covered now include Windows 10, Windows 8, and Windows 7. New content on Linux, macOS, and mobile operating systems (Android, iOS, Windows Phone, and Chrome OS) is added.

  - ◢ New content on Active Directory Domain Services is covered in Chapter 16.

  - ◢ New content on understanding and writing scripts is covered in Chapter 18.

  - ◢ Enhanced content on supporting mobile devices (including the Android OS, iOS, Windows Phone, and Chrome OS) is covered in Chapter 9.

  - ◢ New content on virtualization and cloud computing is covered in Chapter 10.

  - ◢ Hands-On Projects in several chapters use virtual machines so that you get plenty of practice using this essential cloud technology.

  - ◢ New content on change management, network topology diagrams, regulatory and compliance policies, acceptable use policies, inventory management, and regulated data is covered in Chapter 17.

  - ◢ New content on VLANs and managed switches is covered in Chapter 8.

  - ◢ The Internet of Things (IoT) and how to set up a smart home are covered in Chapter 9.

  - ◢ Content on supporting and troubleshooting laptops is integrated throughout the text.

FEATURES OF THE NEW EDITION

Chapter **objectives** appear at the beginning of each chapter, so you know exactly what topics and skills are covered.

A+ Exam Tips include key points pertinent to the A+ exams. The icons identify the sections that cover information you will need to know for the A+ certification exams.

CHAPTER

14

Troubleshooting Windows After Startup

After completing this chapter, you will be able to:

- **Explain the concepts and describe Windows tools used to solve problems with Windows, applications, and hardware**
- **Apply recommended best practices to troubleshoot Windows-related problems**
- **Troubleshoot problems with**

In previous chapters, you learned about the tools and strategies to install and maintain Windows and about the importance of keeping good backups. This chapter takes you one step further as an IT support technician so that you can solve problems with Windows, applications, and hardware using Windows tools and methods. This chapter is about problems that occur after startup. Troubleshooting Windows startup is covered in Chapter 15. We begin the chapter by learning about the Windows concepts and tools you'll need to optimize and troubleshoot Windows. Then we turn our attention to general steps you can follow when solving Windows, applications, and hardware problems, and finally move on to specific problems you might encounter and how to solve them. As you read the chapter, you might consider following along using a Windows 10/8/7 system.

Notes Windows installed in a virtual machine is an excellent environment to use when practicing the skills in this chapter.

Caution When researching a problem, suppose you discover that Microsoft or a manufacturer's website offers a fix or patch you can download and apply. To get the right patch, recall you need to make sure you get a 32-bit patch for a 32-bit installation of Windows, a device driver, or an application. For a 64-bit installation of Windows, make sure you get a 64-bit device driver. An application installed in a 64-bit OS might be a 32-bit application or a 64-bit application.

>> HANDS-ON PROJECTS

Hands-On | Project 2-1 Examining a Motherboard in Detail

1. Look at the back of a desktop computer. Without opening the case, list the ports that you believe come directly from the motherboard.

2. Remove the cover of the case, as you learned to do in Chapter 1. List the different expansion cards in the expansion slots. Was your guess correct about which ports come from the motherboard?

3. To expose the motherboard so you can identify its parts, remove all the expansion cards.

4. Draw a diagram of the motherboard and label these parts:

   - Processor socket
   - Chipset
   - RAM (each DIMM slot)
   - CMOS battery
   - Expansion slots (Identify the slots as PCI, PCIe ×1, PCIe ×4, or PCIe ×16.)
   - Each port coming directly from the motherboard
   - Power supply connections
   - SATA drive connectors

5. What is the brand and model of the motherboard?

6. Locate the manufacturer's website. If you can find the motherboard manual on the site, download it. Find the diagram of the motherboard in the manual and compare it with your diagram. Did you label components correctly?

7. Reassemble the computer, as you learned to do in Chapter 1.

Cautions identify critical safety information.

Hands-On Projects provide practical exercises at the end of each chapter so that you can practice the skills as they are learned.

Notes indicate additional content that might be of student interest or information about how best to study.

APPLYING | CONCEPTS   DISCOLORED CAPACITORS

Jessica complained to Wally, her IT support technician, that Windows was occasionally giving errors, data would get corrupted, or an application would not work as it should. At first, Wally suspected Jessica might need a little more training on how to open and close an application or save a file, but he discovered user error was not the problem. He tried reinstalling the application software Jessica most often used, and even reinstalled Windows, but the problems persisted.

 Notes Catastrophic errors (errors that cause the system not to boot or a device not to work) are much easier to resolve than intermittent errors (errors that come and go).

Wally began to suspect a hardware problem. Carefully examining the motherboard revealed the source of the problem: failing capacitors. Look carefully at Figure 4-37 and you can see five bad discolored capacitors with bulging heads. (Know that sometimes a leaking capacitor can also show crusty corrosion at its base.) When Wally replaced the motherboard, the problems went away.

Bad capacitors

Figure 4-37   These five bad capacitors have bulging and discolored heads

Visual full-color graphics, photos, and screenshots accurately depict computer hardware and software components.

Applying Concepts sections provide practical advice or pointers by illustrating basic principles, identifying common problems, providing steps to practice skills, and encouraging solutions.

Chapter Summary bulleted lists of concise statements summarize
all major points of the chapter, organized by primary headings.

>> CHAPTER SUMMARY

Exploring a Desktop Computer

▲ When hardware support technicians disassemble or reassemble a computer, it is important for them to stay organized, keep careful notes, and follow all the safety procedures to protect the computer equipment and themselves.

▲ Before opening a computer case, shut down the system, unplug it, disconnect all cables, and press the power button to drain residual power.

▲ Common tools for a computer hardware technician include an ESD strap, screwdrivers, tweezers, flashlight, compressed air, and cleaning solutions and pads.

▲ Special tools a hardware technician might need include a POST diagnostic card, power supply tester, multimeter, and loopback plugs.

>> KEY TERMS

For explanations of key terms, see the Glossary for this text.

4-pin 12-V connector	docking port	main board	screen orientation
8-pin 12-V connector	docking station	microATX (mATX)	serial ATA (SATA)
20-pin P1 connector	dual-voltage selector switch	microprocessor	serial port
24-pin P1 connector	DVI (Digital Video Interface) port	modem port	SO-DIMM (small outline DIMM)
airplane mode		Molex connector	
all-in-one computer	electrostatic discharge (ESD)	motherboard	spacers
analog		multimeter	SPDIF (Sony-Philips Digital Interface) sound port
ATX (Advanced Technology Extended)	Ethernet port	netbook	
	expansion card	network port	spudgers
ATX12V power supply	external SATA (eSATA) port	notebook	standoffs
audio ports		optical connector	system board
base station	firmware	PCI Express (PCIe)	Thunderbolt 3 port

>> THINKING CRITICALLY

These questions are designed to prepare you for the critical thinking required for the A+ exams and may use content from other chapters and the web.

1. You purchase a new desktop computer that does not have wireless capability, and then you decide that you want to use a wireless connection to the Internet. What are the two least expensive ways (*choose two*) to upgrade your system to wireless?

   a. Trade in the computer for another computer that has wireless installed.

   b. Purchase a second computer that has wireless capability.

   c. Purchase a wireless expansion card and install it in your system.

   d. Purchase a USB wireless adapter and connect it to the computer by way of a USB port.

Key Terms are defined as they are introduced and listed at the end of each chapter. Definitions can be found in the Glossary.

Thinking Critically sections require you to analyze and apply what you've learned.

>> REAL PROBLEMS, REAL SOLUTIONS

REAL PROBLEM 8-1 Setting Up a Wireless Access Point

As a computer and networking consultant to small businesses, you are frequently asked to find solutions to increasing demands for network and Internet access at a business. One business rents offices in a historical building that has strict rules for wiring. They have come to you asking for a solution for providing Wi-Fi access to their guests in the lobby of the building. Research options for a solution and answer the following questions:

1. Print or save webpages showing two options for a Wi-Fi wireless access point that can mount on the wall or ceiling. For one option, select a device that can receive its power by PoE from the network cable run to the device. For the other option, select a device that requires an electrical cable to the device as well as a network cable.

2. Print or save two webpages for a splitter that can be mounted near the second wireless access point and that splits the power from data on the network cable. Make sure the power connectors for the splitter and the access point can work together.

3. To provide PoE from the electrical closet on the network cable to the wireless access point, print or save the webpage for an injector that injects power into a network cable. Make sure the voltage and wattage output for the injector are compatible with the needs of both wireless access points.

4. You estimate that the distance for network cabling from the switch to the wireless access point is about 200 feet (61 meters). What is the cost of 200 feet of PVC CAT-6a cabling? For 200 feet of plenum CAT-6a cabling?

5. Of the options you researched, which do you recommend? Using this option, what is the total cost of the Wi-Fi hotspot?

REAL PROBLEM 8-2 Exploring Packet Tracer

In Chapter 7 you installed Packet Tracer and created a very basic network. In this project, you work through three chapters of the Packet Tracer Introduction course to take a brief tour of the simulator interface and create a more complex network in Packet Tracer. Notice in the Packet Tracer course that the activities refer to the OSI model instead of the TCP/IP model. Review the section entitled "Compare the TCP/IP Model and OSI Model" in this chapter for a brief refresher. Then complete the following steps to access your course:

1. Return to the Networking Academy website (*netacad.com*), sign in, and click **Launch Course**. You've already downloaded Packet Tracer, so you can skip Chapter 1.

2. Complete Chapters 2, 3, and 4, including the videos and labs, and complete the Packet Tracer Basics Quiz at the end of Chapter 4. The other chapters provide excellent information on Packet Tracer but are not required for this project. Answer the following questions along the way:

   a. What is a simple PDU in Packet Tracer?

   b. What is a .pka file?

   c. Which window shows instructions for a lab activity?

   d. Which Packet Tracer feature do you think will be most helpful for you in learning how to manage a network?

Real Problems, Real Solutions allow you to apply what you've learned in the chapter to a real-life situation.

WHAT'S NEW WITH COMPTIA® A+ CERTIFICATION

The CompTIA A+ certification includes two exams, and you must pass both to become CompTIA A+ certified. The two exams are Core 1 (220-1001) and Core 2 (220-1002).

Here is a breakdown of the domain content covered on the two A+ exams.

CompTIA A+ 220-1001 Exam	
Domain	**Percentage of Examination**
1.0 Mobile Devices	14%
2.0 Networking	20%
3.0 Hardware	27%
4.0 Virtualization and Cloud Computing	12%
5.0 Hardware and Network Troubleshooting	27%
Total	100%

CompTIA A+ 220-1002 Exam	
Domain	**Percentage of Examination**
1.0 Operating Systems	27%
2.0 Security	24%
3.0 Software Troubleshooting	26%
4.0 Operational Procedures	23%
Total	100%

INSTRUCTOR'S MATERIALS

Please visit *cengage.com* and log in to access instructor-specific resources on the Instructor Companion Site, which includes the Instructor's Manual, Solutions Manual, Test creation tools, PowerPoint Presentation, Syllabus, and figure files.

Instructor's Manual: The Instructor's Manual that accompanies this textbook includes additional instructional material to assist in class preparation, including suggestions for classroom activities, discussion topics, and additional projects.

Solutions: Answers to the end-of-chapter material are provided. These include the answers to the Thinking Critically questions and to the Hands-On Projects (when applicable), as well as Lab Manual Solutions.

Cengage Learning Testing Powered by Cognero: This flexible, online system allows you to do the following:
- Author, edit, and manage test bank content from multiple Cengage Learning solutions.
- Create multiple test versions in an instant.
- Deliver tests from your LMS, your classroom, or wherever you want.

PowerPoint Presentations: This book comes with Microsoft PowerPoint slides for each chapter. These are included as a teaching aid for classroom presentation, to make available to students on the network for chapter review, or to be printed for classroom distribution. Instructors, please feel at liberty to add your own slides for additional topics you introduce to the class.

Figure Files: All of the figures in the book are reproduced on the Instructor Companion Site. Similar to the PowerPoint presentations, these are included as a teaching aid for classroom presentation, to make available to students for review, or to be printed for classroom distribution.

TOTAL SOLUTIONS FOR COMPTIA A+

MINDTAP FOR A+ GUIDE TO IT TECHNICAL SUPPORT, TENTH EDITION

MindTap is an online learning solution designed to help students master the skills they need in today's workforce. Research shows employers need critical thinkers, troubleshooters, and creative problem-solvers to stay relevant in our fast-paced, technology-driven world. MindTap helps you achieve this with assignments and activities that provide hands-on practice, real-life relevance, and certification test prep. Students are guided through assignments that help them master basic knowledge and understanding before moving on to more challenging problems.

MindTap activities and assignments are tied to CompTIA A+ certification exam objectives. Live, virtual machine labs allow learners to practice, explore, and try different solutions in a safe, sandbox environment using real Cisco hardware and virtualized Windows, Linux, and UNIX operating systems. The Adaptive Test Prep (ATP) app is designed to help learners quickly review and assess their understanding of key IT concepts. Learners have the ability to test themselves multiple times to track their progress and improvement. The app allows them to filter results by correct answers, by all questions answered, or only by incorrect answers to show where additional study help is needed.

You can test students' knowledge and understanding with graded pre- and post-assessments that emulate the A+ certification exams. Module tests and review quizzes also help you gauge students' mastery of the course topics.

Readings and videos support the lecture, while "In The News" assignments encourage students to stay current with what's happening in the IT field. Reflection activities require students to problem-solve for a real-life issue they would encounter on the job and participate in a class discussion to learn how their peers dealt with the same challenge.

MindTap is designed around learning objectives and provides the analytics and reporting so you can easily see where the class stands in terms of progress, engagement, and completion rates. Use the content and learning path as is or pick and choose how our materials will wrap around yours. You control what the students see and when they see it. Learn more at *http://www.cengage.com/mindtap/*.

- ◢ Instant Access Code: (ISBN: 9780357108314)
- ◢ Printed Access Code: (ISBN: 9780357108321)

LAB MANUAL FOR A+ GUIDE TO IT TECHNICAL SUPPORT, TENTH EDITION

The Lab Manual, now part of your MindTap course, contains over 120 labs to provide students with additional hands-on experience and to help prepare for the A+ exam. The Lab Manual includes lab activities, objectives, materials lists, step-by-step procedures, illustrations, and review questions.

ACKNOWLEDGMENTS

Thank you to the wonderful people at Cengage who continue to give their best and go the extra mile to make the books what they are: Kristin McNary, Amy Savino, and Brooke Greenhouse. I'm grateful for all you've done. Thank you, Dan Seiter, our Developmental Editor extraordinaire, for upholding us with your unwavering, calm demeanor in the face of impossible schedules and inboxes, and to Karen Annett, our excellent copyeditor/proofreader. Thank you, Danielle Shaw, for your careful attention to the technical accuracy of the book.

Thank you to all the people who took the time to voluntarily send encouragement and suggestions for improvements to the previous editions. Your input and help is very much appreciated. The reviewers of this edition provided invaluable insights and showed a genuine interest in the book's success. Thank you to:

     Craig Brigman – Liberty University

     Kimberly Perez – Tidewater Community College

To the instructors and learners who use this book, we invite and encourage you to send suggestions or corrections for future editions. Please write to the author team at *jean.andrews@cengage.com*. We never ignore a good idea! And to instructors, if you have ideas for how to make a class in A+ Preparation a success, please share your ideas with other instructors! You can find us on Facebook at *http://www.facebook.com/JeanKnows*, where you can interact with the authors and other instructors.

This book is dedicated to the covenant of God with man on earth.

            Jean Andrews, Ph.D.
            Joy Dark
            Jill West

ABOUT THE AUTHORS

Jean Andrews has more than 30 years of experience in the computer industry, including more than 13 years in the college classroom. She has worked in a variety of businesses and corporations designing, writing, and supporting application software; managing a help desk for computer support technicians; and troubleshooting wide area networks. She has written numerous books on software, hardware, and the Internet, including the best-selling *CompTIA A+ Core 1 Exam Guide to Computing Infrastructure, Tenth Edition*, and *CompTIA A+ Core 2 Exam Guide to Operating Systems and Security, Tenth Edition*. She lives in northern Georgia.

Joy Dark has worked in the IT field as a help-desk technician providing first-level support for a company with presence in 29 states, a second-tier technician in healthcare IT, and an operations specialist designing support protocols and structures. As a teacher, Joy has taught online courses in IT and has taught English as a Second Language in the United States and South America. She has helped write several technical textbooks with Jean Andrews. She also creates many photographs used in educational content. Joy lives in northwest Georgia with her two daughters and Doberman dog.

Jill West has taught K thru college using a flipped classroom approach, distance learning, hybrid teaching, and educational counseling. She currently teaches computer technology courses at Georgia Northwestern Technical College, both online and in the classroom. She regularly presents on CompTIA certification courses at state and national conferences and international webinars. Jill and her husband Mike live in northwest Georgia, where they homeschool their four children.

READ THIS BEFORE YOU BEGIN

The following hardware, software, and other equipment are needed to do the Hands-On Projects in each chapter:

- ◢ You need a working desktop computer and laptop that can be taken apart and reassembled. You also need a working computer on which you can install an operating system. These computers can be the same or different computers.
- ◢ Troubleshooting skills can better be practiced with an assortment of nonworking expansion cards that can be used to simulate problems.
- ◢ Windows 10 Pro is needed for most chapters. In addition, macOS is used in Chapter 18.
- ◢ Internet access is needed for most chapters.
- ◢ Equipment required to work on hardware includes an ESD strap and flathead and Phillips-head screwdrivers. In addition, a power supply tester, cable tester, and can of compressed air are useful. Network wiring tools needed for Chapter 8 include a wire cutter, wire stripper, and crimper.
- ◢ An iOS or Android smartphone or tablet is needed for Chapter 9.
- ◢ A SOHO router that includes a wireless access point is needed for Chapter 7.

> ⚡ **Caution** Before undertaking any of the lab exercises, starting with Chapter 1, please review the safety guidelines in Appendix A.

Taking a Computer Apart and Putting It Back Together

After completing this chapter, you will be able to:

- Disassemble and reassemble a desktop computer safely while being able to identify various external ports and major components inside a desktop and describe how they connect together and are compatible. You'll be able to identify various tools you will need as a computer hardware technician.

- Disassemble and reassemble a laptop computer safely while being able to identify various external ports and slots and major internal components of a laptop. You will know what special concerns need to be considered when supporting and maintaining laptops.

Like many other computer users, you have probably used your personal computer to play games, update your Facebook profile, write papers, or build Excel worksheets. This text takes you from being an end user of your computer to becoming an information technology (IT) support technician able to support all types of personal computers. The only assumption made here is that you are a computer user—that is, you can turn on your machine, load a software package, and use that software to accomplish a task. No experience in electronics is assumed.

As an IT support technician, you'll want to become A+ certified, which is the industry standard certification for IT support technicians. This text prepares you to pass the A+ 220-1001 Core 1 and 220-1002 Core 2 exams by CompTIA (*comptia.org*). The exams are required by CompTIA for A+ certification.

In this chapter, you take apart and reassemble a desktop computer and laptop while discovering the various hardware components inside the cases. You'll also learn about the tools you'll need to work inside the case.

> ★ **A+ Exam Tip** As you work your way through a chapter, notice the green and blue A+ mapping icons underneath headings. These page elements help you know to which objectives on which exam the content applies. After studying each chapter, take a look at the grid at the beginning of this text and make sure you understand each objective listed in the grid for the chapter just completed.

Taking apart and servicing a computer are tasks that every A+ certified technician needs to know how to do. As part of your preparation to become A+ certified, try to find old desktop and laptop computers you can take apart. If you can locate the service manual for a laptop, you should be able to take it apart, repair it (assuming the parts are still available and don't cost more than the computer is worth), and get it up and running again. Have fun with this chapter and enjoy tinkering with these computers!

EXPLORING A DESKTOP COMPUTER

In this part of the chapter, you learn how to take apart a desktop computer and put it back together. This skill is needed in this chapter and others as you learn to add or replace computer parts inside the case and perhaps even build a system from scratch. As you read the following steps, you might want to refer to the Hands-On Projects at the end of the chapter, which allow you to follow along by taking a computer apart. As you do so, be sure to follow all the safety precautions found in Appendix A. In the steps that follow, each major computer component is identified and described. You learn much more about each component later in the text. Take your time—*don't rush*—as you take apart a computer for the first time. It can be a great learning experience or an expensive disaster! As you work, pay attention to the details and work with care.

STEP 1: PLANNING AND ORGANIZING YOUR WORK AND GATHERING YOUR TOOLS

When you first begin to learn how to work inside a computer case, make it a point to practice good organization skills. If you keep your notes, tools, screws, and computer parts well organized, your work goes more smoothly and is more fun. Here are some tips to keep in mind:

- As you work, make notes using pencil and paper and perhaps take photos with your cell phone so that you can backtrack later if necessary. (When you're first learning to take a computer apart, it's easy to forget where everything fits when it's time to put the computer back together. Also, in troubleshooting, you want to avoid repeating or overlooking things to try.)
- Remove loose jewelry that might get caught in cables and components as you work.
- To stay organized and not lose small parts, keep screws and spacers orderly and in one place, such as a cup or tray.
- Don't stack boards on top of each other: You could accidentally dislodge a chip this way. When you remove a circuit board or drive from a computer, carefully lay it on an antistatic mat or in an antistatic bag in a place where it won't get bumped.
- When handling motherboards, cards, or drives, don't touch the chips on the device. Hold expansion cards by the edges. Don't touch any soldered components on a card, and don't touch the edge connectors unless it's absolutely necessary. All this helps prevent damage from static electricity. Also, your fingerprints on the edge connectors can cause later corrosion.
- To protect a microchip, don't touch it with a magnetized screwdriver.
- Never, ever touch the inside of a computer that is turned on. The one exception to this rule is when you're using a multimeter to measure voltage output.
- Consider the monitor and the power supply to be "black boxes." Never remove the cover or put your hands inside this equipment unless you know about the hazards of charged capacitors and have been trained to deal with them. The power supply and monitor contain enough power to kill you, even when they are unplugged.
- As you work, remember to watch out for sharp edges on computer cases that can cut you.
- In a classroom environment, after you have reassembled everything, have your instructor check your work before you put the cover back on and power up.

TOOLS USED BY A COMPUTER HARDWARE TECHNICIAN

Every IT support technician who plans to repair desktop or laptop computers or mobile devices needs a handy toolbox with a few essential tools. Several hardware and software tools can help you maintain a computer and diagnose and repair computer problems. The tools you choose depend on the amount of money you can spend and the level of hardware support you expect to provide.

Figure 1-1 Tools used by IT support technicians when maintaining, repairing, or upgrading computers

Essential tools for computer hardware troubleshooting are listed here, and several of them are shown in Figure 1-1. You can purchase some of these tools in a computer toolkit, although most toolkits contain items you really can do without.

One of the more important tools is an ESD strap (also called a ground bracelet), which protects against ESD when working inside the computer case. Electrostatic discharge (ESD) is another name for static electricity, which can damage chips and destroy motherboards, even though it might not be felt or seen with the naked eye. Use the strap to connect or ground your hand to the case, as shown in Figure 1-2, and any static electricity between you and the case is dissipated.

Figure 1-2 An ESD strap, which protects computer components from ESD, can clip to the side of the computer case and eliminate ESD between you and the case

Here is a list of essential tools:

▲ An ESD strap (also called a ground bracelet)
▲ Flathead screwdriver
▲ Phillips-head or crosshead screwdriver

◢ Torx screwdriver set, particularly size T15

◢ Tweezers, preferably insulated ones, for picking pieces of paper out of printers or dropped screws out of tight places

◢ Software, including recovery CD or DVD for any operating system (OS) you might work on (you might need several, depending on the OSs you support), antivirus software on bootable CDs or USB flash drives, and diagnostic software

The following tools might not be essential, but they are very convenient:

◢ Cans of compressed air (see Figure 1-3), small portable compressor, or antistatic vacuum cleaner to clean dust from inside a computer case

◢ Cleaning solutions and pads such as contact cleaner, monitor wipes, and cleaning solutions for CDs and DVDs

Figure 1-3 A can of compressed air is handy to blow dust from a
computer case

◢ Multimeter to check cables and the power supply output

◢ Power supply tester

◢ Needle-nose pliers for removing jumpers and for holding objects in place while you screw them in (especially handy for those pesky nuts on cable connectors)

◢ Cable ties to tie cables up and out of the way inside a computer case

◢ Flashlight to see inside the computer case

◢ AC outlet ground tester

◢ Network cable tester

◢ Loopback plugs to test ports

◢ Small cups or bags to help keep screws organized as you work

◢ Antistatic bags (a type of Faraday cage) to store unused parts

◢ Pen and paper for taking notes

◢ POST diagnostic cards

✎ **Notes** It's important to know how to stay safe when working inside computers. Before opening a computer case and using the tools described in this section, be sure to read Appendix A. As you work inside a computer, follow all the safety guidelines discussed in this appendix.

Keep your tools in a toolbox designated for hardware troubleshooting. If you put discs and hardware tools in the same box, be sure to keep the discs inside a hard plastic case to protect them from scratches and dents. In addition, make sure the diagnostic and utility software you use is recommended for the hardware and software you are troubleshooting.

As you turn your attention to the disassembly of a desktop computer, you'll also learn about several IT support technician tools, including loopback plugs, diagnostic cards, power supply testers, and multimeters. Now that you've prepared your work area and tools, put on your ESD strap and let's get started with opening the computer case.

STEP 2: OPENING THE CASE

A+
CORE 1
2.8, 3.2,
3.3, 3.4,
3.5, 3.7,
5.5

Before we discuss the parts inside a desktop case, let's take a quick look at the outside of the case and the ports and switches on it.

WHAT'S ON THE OUTSIDE OF A DESKTOP CASE

A computer case for any type of computer is sometimes called the chassis, and it houses the power supply, motherboard, processor, memory modules, expansion cards, hard drive, optical drive, and other drives. A computer case can be a tower case, a desktop case that lies flat on a desk, an all-in-one case used with an all-in-one computer, or a mobile case used with laptops and tablets. A tower case (see Figure 1-4) sits upright; it can be as high as two feet and has room for several drives. Often used for servers, this type of case is also good for desktop computer users who anticipate upgrading because tower cases provide maximum space for working inside a computer and moving components around. A desktop case lies flat and sometimes serves double-duty as a monitor stand. Later in this chapter, you learn how to work inside a tower case, desktop case, laptop case, and all-in-one case.

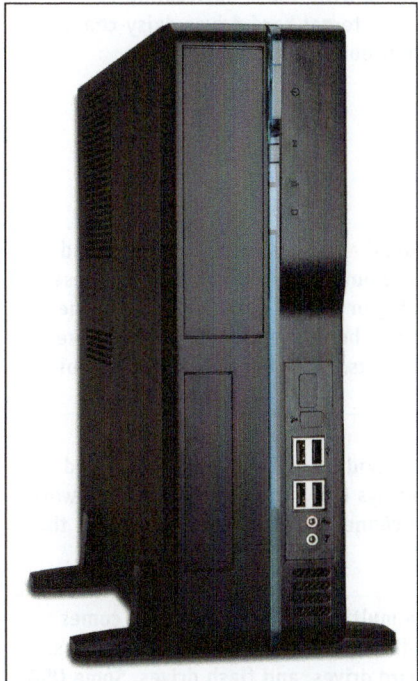

© Courtesy of IN WIN Development, Inc.

Figure 1-4 This slimline tower case supports a microATX motherboard

> ✎ **Notes** Don't lay a tower case on its side when the computer is in use because the CD or DVD drive might not work properly. For the same reason, if a desktop case is designed to lie flat, don't set it on its end when the computer is in use.

Table 1-1 lists ports you might find on a desktop or mobile computer. Consider this table your introduction to these ports so that you can recognize them when you see them. Later in the text, you learn more about the details of each port.

> ★ **A+ Exam Tip** The A+ Core 1 exam expects you to know how to identify the ports shown in Table 1-1.

Port	Description
	A VGA (Video Graphics Array) port, also called a DB-15 port, DB15 port, HD15 port, or DE15 port, is a 15-pin, D-shaped, female port that transmits analog video. (Analog means a continuous signal with infinite variations as compared with digital, which is a series of binary values—1s and 0s.) All older monitors use VGA ports. (By the way, the HD15 [high-definition 15-pin] name for the port is an older name that distinguishes it from the early 9-pin VGA ports.)
	A DVI (Digital Video Interface) port transmits digital or analog video. Three types of DVI ports exist, which you learn about in Chapter 6.
	An HDMI (High-Definition Multimedia Interface) port transmits digital video and audio (not analog transmissions) and is often used to connect to home theater equipment.
	A DisplayPort transmits digital video and audio (not analog transmissions) and is slowly replacing VGA and DVI ports on personal computers.
Source: https://en.wikipedia.org/ wiki/Thunderbolt_(interface)#/media/ File:Thunderbolt_3_interface_USB-C_ ports.jpg	A Thunderbolt 3 port transmits video, data, and power on the same port and cable and is popular with Apple computers. The port is shaped the same as the USB-C port and is compatible with USB-C devices. Up to six peripherals (for example, monitors and external hard drives daisy-chained together) can use the same Thunderbolt port.
	A system usually has three or more round audio ports, also called sound ports, for a microphone, audio in, audio out, and stereo audio out. These types of audio ports can transmit analog or digital data. If you have one audio cable to connect to a speaker or earbuds, plug it into the lime-green sound port in the middle of the three ports. The microphone uses the pink port.
	An SPDIF (Sony-Philips Digital Interface) sound port connects to an external home theater audio system, providing digital audio output and the best signal quality. SPDIF ports always carry digital audio and can work with electrical or optical cable. When connected to a fiber-optic cable, the port is called an optical connector.
	A USB (Universal Serial Bus) port is a multipurpose I/O port that comes in several sizes and is used by many different devices, including printers, mice, keyboards, scanners, external hard drives, and flash drives. Some USB ports are faster than others. Hi-Speed USB 2.0 is faster than regular USB, and Super-Speed USB 3.0 is faster than USB 2.0.

Table 1-1 Ports used with desktop and laptop computers (continues)

Port	Description
	An external SATA (eSATA) port is used by an external hard drive or other device using the eSATA interface.
	A PS/2 port, also called a mini-DIN port, is a round 6-pin port used by a keyboard or mouse. The ports look alike but are not interchangeable. On a desktop, the purple port is for the keyboard and the green port is for the mouse. Many newer computers use USB ports for the keyboard and mouse rather than the older PS/2 ports.
	An older serial port, sometimes called a DB9 port, is a 9-pin male port used on older computers. It has been mostly replaced by USB ports. Occasionally, you see a serial port on a router, where the port is used to connect the router to a device a technician can use to monitor and manage the router.
	A modem port, also called an RJ-11 port, is used to connect dial-up phone lines to computers. A modem port looks like a network port, but is not as wide. In the photo, the right port is a modem port and the left port is a network port shown for comparison.
	A network port, also called an Ethernet port or an RJ-45 port, is used by a network cable to connect to the wired network. Fast Ethernet ports run at 100 Mbps (megabits per second), and Gigabit Ethernet runs at 1000 Mbps or 1 Gbps (gigabits per second). A megabit is one million bits and a gigabit is one billion bits. A bit is a binary value of 1 or 0.

Table 1-1   Ports used with desktop and laptop computers (continued)

LOOPBACK PLUGS

A loopback plug is used to test a network port in a computer or other device to make sure the port is working. It might also test the throughput or speed of the port. Figure 1-5 shows a loopback plug testing a network port on a laptop. You know both the port and the network cable are good because the lights on either side of the port are lit. You can also buy a USB loopback plug to test USB ports.

Figure 1-5   A loopback plug testing a network port and network cable

WHAT'S INSIDE A DESKTOP CASE

Now that you're familiar with the outside of the case, let's open the case to see what is inside. Here are the steps to open a computer case:

1. *Back up important data.* If you are starting with a working computer, make sure important data is backed up first. Copy the data to an external storage device such as a flash drive or external hard drive. If something goes wrong while you're working inside the computer, at least your data will be safe.

2. *Power down the system and unplug it.* Remove discs from the optical drive. Then, power down the system and unplug the power, monitor, mouse, and keyboard cables, and any other peripherals or cables attached. Then, move these cables out of your way.

> ⚡ **Caution** When you power down a computer and even turn off the power switch on the rear of the computer case, know that residual power is still on. Some motherboards even have a small light inside the case to remind you of this fact and to warn you that power is still getting to the system. Therefore, be sure to always unplug the power cord before opening a case.

3. *Press and hold down the power button for a moment.* After you unplug the computer, press the power button for about three seconds to completely drain the power supply (see Figure 1-6). Sometimes when you do so, you'll hear the fans quickly start and go off as residual power is drained. Only then is it safe to work inside the case.

Figure 1-6   Press the power button after the computer is unplugged

4. *Have a plastic bag or cup handy to hold screws.* When you reassemble the computer, you will need to insert the same screws in the same holes. This is especially important with the hard drive because screws that are too long can puncture the hard drive housing, so be careful to label those screws clearly.

5. *Open the case cover.* Sometimes I think figuring out how to open a computer case is the most difficult part of disassembling. If you need help figuring it out, check the user manual or website of the case manufacturer. To remove the computer case cover, do the following:

◢ Some cases require you to start by laying the case on its side and removing the faceplate on the front of the case first. Other cases require you to remove a side panel first, and much older cases require you to first remove all the sides and top as a single unit. Study your case for the correct approach.

◢ Most cases have panels on each side that can be removed. It is usually necessary to remove only one panel to expose the top of the motherboard. To know which panel to remove, look at the port locations on the rear of the case. For example, in Figure 1-7, the ports on the motherboard are on the left side of the case, indicating the bottom of the motherboard is on the left. Therefore, you will want to remove the right panel to expose the top of the motherboard. Lay the case down to its left so that the ports and the motherboard are on the bottom. Later, depending on how drives are installed, it might become necessary to remove the other side panel in order to remove the screws that hold the drives in place.

Motherboard is mounted to this side of the case

Figure 1-7 Decide which side panel to remove

◢ Locate the screws or clips that hold the side panel in place. Be careful not to unscrew any screws besides these. The other screws probably are holding the power supply, fan, and other components in place (see Figure 1-8). Place the screws in the cup or bag used for that purpose. Some cases use clips on a side panel in addition to or instead of screws (see Figure 1-9).

Figure 1-8 Locate the screws that hold the side panel in place

Figure 1-9 On this system, clips hold the side panel in place

▲ After the screws are removed, slide the panel toward the rear and then lift it off the case (see Figure 1-10).

Figure 1-10   Slide the panel to the rear of the case

6. ***Clip your ESD strap to the side of the computer case.*** To dissipate any charge between you and the computer, put on your ESD strap if you have not already done so. Then, clip the alligator clip on the strap cable to the side of the computer case (see Figure 1-11).

Figure 1-11   Attach the alligator clip of your ground bracelet to the side of the computer case

After you open a computer case, as shown in Figure 1-12, the main components you see inside are the power supply, motherboard, expansion card, and drives installed in drive bays. You also see a lot of cables and wires connecting various components. These cables are power cables from the power supply to various components, or cables carrying data and instructions between components. The best way to know the purpose of a cable is to follow it from its source to its destination.

Figure 1-12 Inside the computer case

Here is a quick explanation of the main components installed in the case, which are called internal components:

▲ *The motherboard, processor, and cooler.* The motherboard, also called the main board, the system board, or the techie jargon term, the mobo, is the largest and most important circuit board in the computer. The motherboard contains a socket to hold the processor or CPU. The central processing unit (CPU), also called the processor or microprocessor, does most of the processing of data and instructions for the entire system. Because the CPU generates heat, a fan and heat sink might be installed on top to keep it cool. A heat sink consists of metal fins that draw heat away from a component. The fan and heat sink together are called the processor cooler. Figure 1-13 shows the top view of a motherboard, and Figure 1-14 shows the ports on the side of a motherboard.

Figure 1-13 All hardware components are either located on the motherboard or directly or indirectly connected to it because they must all communicate with the CPU

eSATA 2.0 port
Network port
DVI video port
FireWire port

Six audio ports

SPDIF port
(for coaxial cable)

Two blue USB
3.0 ports

HDMI video port

DisplayPort
video port

Six USB
2.0 ports

Figure 1-14 Ports provided by a motherboard

◢ *Expansion cards.* A motherboard has expansion slots to be used by expansion cards. An expansion card, also called an adapter card, is a circuit board that provides more ports than those provided by the motherboard. Figure 1-15 shows a video card that provides three video ports. Notice the cooling fan and heat sink on the card, which help to keep the card from overheating. The trend today is for most ports in a system to be provided by the motherboard (called onboard ports) and less use of expansion cards.

Cooling fan

Heat sink

Tab used to
stabilize the card

PCI Express
x16 connector

15-pin analog
video port

TV-out connector

DVI port

Figure 1-15 The easiest way to identify this video card is to look at the ports on the end of the card

◢ *Memory modules.* A desktop motherboard has memory slots, called DIMM (dual inline memory module) slots, to hold memory modules. Figure 1-16 shows a memory module installed in one DIMM slot and three empty DIMM slots. Memory, also called RAM (random access memory), is temporary storage for data and instructions as they are being processed by the CPU. The memory module shown in Figure 1-16 contains several RAM chips. Video cards also contain some embedded RAM chips for video memory.

One installed DIMM

Three empty DIMM slots

Figure 1-16   A DIMM holds RAM and is mounted directly on a motherboard

▲ *Hard drives and other drives.* A system might have one or more hard drives and an optical drive. A hard drive, also called a hard disk drive (HDD), is permanent storage used to hold data and programs. For example, the Windows 10 operating system and applications are installed on the hard drive. All drives in a system are installed in a stack of drive bays at the front of the case. The system shown in Figure 1-12 has two hard drives and one optical drive installed. These three drives are also shown in Figure 1-17. The larger hard drive is a magnetic drive, and the smaller hard drive is a solid-state drive (SSD). Each drive has two connections for cables: The power cable connects to the power supply, and another cable, used for data and instructions, connects to the motherboard.

Figure 1-17   Two types of hard drives (larger magnetic drive and smaller solid-state drive) and a DVD drive

▲ *The power supply.* A computer power supply, also known as a power supply unit (PSU), is a box installed in a corner of the computer case (see Figure 1-18) that receives and converts the house current so that components inside the case can use it. Most power supplies have a dual-voltage selector switch on the back of the computer case where you can switch the input voltage to the power supply if necessary—115 V is used in the United States and 220 V is used in other countries. See Figure 1-19. The power cables can connect to and supply power to the motherboard, expansion cards, and drives.

Figure 1-18   A power supply with attached power cables

Power cables

Power supply unit

Figure 1-19   The dual-voltage selector switch sets the input voltage to the power supply

Dual-voltage selector switch

Four screws hold the power supply in the case

> **✎ Notes** If you ever need to change the dual-voltage selector switch, be sure you first turn off the computer and unplug the power supply.

FORM FACTORS USED BY DESKTOP CASES, POWER SUPPLIES, AND MOTHERBOARDS

The desktop computer case, power supply, and motherboard must all be compatible and fit together as an interconnecting system. The standards that describe the size, shape, screw hole positions, and major features of these interconnected components are called form factors. Using a matching form factor for the motherboard, power supply, and case assures you that:

◢ The motherboard fits in the case.
◢ The power supply cords to the motherboard provide the correct voltage, and the connectors match the connections on the board.
◢ The holes in the motherboard align with the holes in the case so you can anchor the board to the case.
◢ The holes in the case align with ports coming off the motherboard.
◢ For some form factors, wires for switches and lights on the front of the case match up with connections on the motherboard.
◢ The holes in the power supply align with holes in the case for anchoring the power supply to the case.

The two form factors used by most desktop and tower computer cases and power supplies are the ATX and microATX form factors. Motherboards use these and other form factors that are compatible with ATX or microATX power supplies and cases. You learn about other motherboard form factors in Chapter 2. Following are important details about ATX and microATX:

◢ ATX (Advanced Technology Extended) is the most commonly used form factor today. It is an open, nonproprietary industry specification originally developed by Intel. An ATX power supply has a variety of power connectors (see Figure 1-20). The power connectors are listed in Table 1-2 and several of them are described next.

Figure 1-20 An ATX power supply with connectors

Connector	Description
	The 20-pin P1 connector is the main motherboard power connector used in the early ATX systems.
	The 24-pin P1 connector, also called the 20+4-pin connector, is the main motherboard power connector used today.
	The 20+4-pin P1 connector has four pins removed so the connector can fit into a 20-pin P1 motherboard connector.
	The 4-pin 12-V connector is an auxiliary motherboard connector, which is used for extra 12-V power to the processor.
	The 8-pin 12-V connector is an auxiliary motherboard connector, which is used for extra 12-V power to the processor, providing more power than the older 4-pin auxiliary connector.
	The 4-pin Molex connector is used for older IDE drives, some newer SATA drives, and to provide extra power to video cards. It can provide +5 V and +12 V to the device.
	The 15-pin SATA power connector is used for SATA (Serial ATA) drives. It can provide +3.3 V, +5 V, and +12 V, although +3.3 V is seldom used.
	The PCIe 6-pin connector provides an extra +12 V for high-end video cards using PCI Express.
	The PCIe 8-pin connector provides an extra +12 V for high-end video cards using PCI Express.
	The PCIe 6/8-pin connector is used by high-end video cards using PCIe ×16 slots to provide extra voltage to the card; it can accommodate a 6-hole or 8-hole port. To get the 8-pin connector, combine both the 6-pin and 2-pin connectors.

Table 1-2   Power supply connectors

Power connectors have evolved because components that use new technologies require more power. As you read about the following types of power connectors and why each came to be, you'll also learn about the evolving expansion slots and expansion cards that drove the need for more power:

◢ **4-pin and 8-pin auxiliary connectors.** When processors began to require more power, the ATX Version 2.1 specifications added a 4-pin auxiliary connector near the processor socket to provide an additional 12 V of power (see Figure 1-21). A power supply that provides this 4-pin 12-volt power cord is called an ATX12V power supply. Later boards replaced the 4-pin 12-volt power connector with an 8-pin motherboard auxiliary connector that provided more amps for the processor. See Figure 1-22.

Figure 1-21   The 4-pin 12-volt auxiliary power connector on a motherboard with a power cord connected

Figure 1-22   An 8-pin, 12-volt auxiliary power connector for extra power to the processor

◢ *24-pin or 20+4-pin P1 connector.* The original P1 connector had 20 pins. Later, when faster PCI Express (PCIe) slots were added to motherboards, more power was required and a new ATX specification (ATX Version 2.2) allowed for a 24-pin P1 connector, also called the 20+4 power connector.

All motherboards today use a 24-pin P1 connector. The extra 4 pins on the 24-pin P1 connector provide +12 volts, +5 volts, and +3.3 volts. Figure 1-23 shows a 24-pin P1 power cord from the power supply and a 24-pin P1 connector on a motherboard. Figure 1-24 shows the pinouts for the 24-pin power cord connector, which is color-coded to wires from the power supply.

Figure 1-23 A 24-pin power cord ready to be plugged into a 24-pin P1 connector on an ATX motherboard

	1 13	
Orange — +3.3V		+3.3V — Orange/Brown
Orange — +3.3V		−12V — Blue
Black — COM		COM — Black
Red — +5V		PS_ON# — Green
Black — COM		COM — Black
Red — +5V		COM — Black
Black — COM		COM — Black
Gray — PWR_ON		NC — White
Purple — +5VSB		+5V — Red
Yellow — +12V1		+5V — Red
Yellow — +12V1		+5V — Red
Orange — +3.3V		COM — Black

Figure 1-24 A P1 24-pin power connector follows ATX Version 2.2 and higher standards

Figure 1-25 shows a PCIe ×16 video card. The edge connector has a break that fits the break in the slot. The tab at the end of the edge connector fits into a retention mechanism at the end of the slot, which helps to stabilize a heavy video card.

PCIe 6-pin power connector on the end of the video card

Edge connector

Figure 1-25 This PCIe ×16 video card has a 6-pin PCIe power connector to receive extra power from the power supply

◢ *6-pin and 8-pin PCIe connectors.* Video cards draw the most power in a system, and ATX Version 2.2 provides for power cables to connect directly to a video card and provide it additional power than what comes through the PCIe slot on the motherboard. The PCIe power connector might have 6 or 8 pins. The video card shown in Figure 1-25 has a 6-pin connector on the end of the card. A PCIe 6-pin power cord from the power supply plugs into the connector. The power supply connector is shown earlier in Table 1-2.

📝 **Notes** For more information about all the form factors discussed in this chapter, check out the form factor website sponsored by Intel at *formfactors.org*.

◢ The microATX (mATX) form factor is a major variation of ATX and addresses some technologies that have emerged since the original development of ATX. MicroATX reduces the total cost of a system by reducing the number of expansion slots on the motherboard, which in turn reduces the power supplied to the board and allows for a smaller case size. A microATX motherboard (see Figure 1-26) will fit into a case that follows the ATX 2.1 or higher standard. A microATX power supply uses a 24-pin P1 connector and is not likely to have as many extra wires and connectors as those on an ATX power supply.

⭐ **A+ Exam Tip** The A+ Core 1 exam expects you to recognize and know the more important features of the ATX and microATX form factors used by power supplies. Given a scenario, you should be able to identify and choose the appropriate form factor.

Figure 1-26 This microATX motherboard by Biostar is designed to support an AMD processor

Now let's learn about the expansion cards you might find installed inside a system.

STEP 3: REMOVING EXPANSION CARDS

A+ CORE 1 3.5, 5.5 If you plan to remove several components, draw a diagram of all cable connections to the motherboard, expansion cards, and drives. You might need this cable connection diagram to help you reassemble. Note where each cable begins and ends and pay particular attention to the small wires and connectors that connect the lights, switches, and ports on the front of the case to the motherboard front panel connectors. It's important to be careful about diagramming these because it is easy to connect them in the wrong position later when you reassemble. If you want, use a felt-tip marker to make a mark across components, which can indicate a cable connection, board placement, motherboard orientation, speaker connection, brackets, and so on. Then, you can simply line up the marks when you reassemble. This method, however, probably won't work for the front case wires because they are so small. For these, consider writing down the colors of the wires and their positions on the pins or taking a photo of the wires in their positions with your cell phone (see Figure 1-27).

Figure 1-27 Diagram the pin locations of the color-coded wires that connect to the front of the case

📝 **Notes** A *header* is a connector on a motherboard that consists of pins that stick up from the board. For example, the group of pins shown in Figure 1-27 is called the **front panel header**.

Computer systems vary in so many ways that it's impossible to list the exact order to disassemble one. Most likely, however, you need to remove the expansion cards first. Do the following to remove the expansion cards:

1. Remove any wire or cable connected to the card.

2. Remove the screw holding the card to the case (see Figure 1-28).

Figure 1-28 Remove the screw holding the expansion card to the case

3. Grasp the card with both hands and remove it by lifting straight up. If you have trouble removing it from the expansion slot, you can *very slightly* rock the card from end to end (*not* side to side). Rocking the card from side to side might spread the slot opening and weaken the connection.

4. As you remove the card, don't put your fingers on the edge connectors or touch a chip, and don't stack the cards on top of one another. Lay each card aside on a flat surface, preferably in an antistatic bag.

> ✎ **Notes** Cards installed in PCI Express × 16 slots use a latch that helps to hold the card securely in the slot. To remove these cards, use one finger to hold the latch back from the slot, as shown in Figure 1-29, as you pull the card up and out of the slot.

Figure 1-29 Hold the retention mechanism back as you remove a video card from its expansion slot

STEP 4: REMOVING THE MOTHERBOARD

**A+
CORE 1
3.5, 5.5**

Depending on the system, you might need to remove the motherboard next or remove the drives next. My choice is to first remove the motherboard. It and the processor are the most expensive and easily damaged parts of the system. I like to get them out of harm's way before working with the drives. However, in some cases, you must remove the drives or the power supply before you can get to the motherboard. Study your situation and decide which to do first. To remove the motherboard, do the following:

1. Unplug the power supply lines to the motherboard.

2. Unplug SATA cables connected to the motherboard.

3. The next step is to disconnect the wires leading from the front or top of the computer case to the motherboard; these wires are called the front panel connectors. If you don't have the motherboard manual handy, be very careful to diagram how these wires connect because they are rarely labeled well on a motherboard. Make a careful diagram and then disconnect the wires. Figure 1-30 shows five leads and the pins on the motherboard front panel header that receive these leads. The pins are color-coded and cryptically labeled on the board.

Figure 1-30 Five leads from the front panel connect to two rows of pins on the motherboard front panel header

4. Disconnect any other cables or wires connected to the motherboard. A case fan might be getting power by a small wire connected to the motherboard. In addition, USB ports on the front of the computer case might be connected by a cable to the motherboard.

5. You're now ready to remove the screws that hold the motherboard to the case. A motherboard is installed so that the bottom of the board does not touch the case. If the fine traces or lines on the bottom of the board were to touch the case, a short would result when the system runs again. To keep the board from touching the case, screw holes are elevated, or you'll see spacers, also called standoffs, which are round plastic or metal pegs that separate the board from the case. Carefully pop off these spacers and/or remove the screws (up to nine) that hold the board to the case (see Figure 1-31) and then remove the board. Set it aside in a safe place. Figure 1-32 shows a motherboard sitting to the side of these spacers. Two spacers are in place and the other is lying beside its case holes. In the figure, also notice the holes in the motherboard where screws are used to connect the board to the spacers.

Figure 1-31   Remove up to nine screws that hold the motherboard to the case

Figure 1-32   This motherboard connects to a case using screws and spacers that keep the board from touching the case

> ✎ **Notes** When you're replacing a motherboard that is not the same size as the original board in a case, you can use needle-nose pliers to unplug a standoff so you can move it to a new hole.

6. The motherboard should now be free and you can carefully remove it from the case, as shown in Figure 1-33. Lift the board by its edges, as shown in the figure.

> ⚡ **Caution** Never lift a motherboard by the cooler because doing so might create an air gap between the cooler and the processor, which can cause the processor to later overheat.

Figure 1-33   Remove the motherboard from the case

> **⚡ Caution**   Some processors have heavy or bulky cooling assemblies installed on top of them. For these systems, it is best to remove the cooler before you take the motherboard out of the case because the motherboard is not designed to support the heavy cooler when the motherboard is not securely seated in the case. Removal of the cooler is covered in Chapter 3.

POST DIAGNOSTIC CARDS

When supporting a motherboard, a POST diagnostic card, also called a POST card or motherboard test card, can be of great help in discovering and reporting computer errors and conflicts that occur after you first turn on a computer but before the operating system (such as Windows 10) is launched. To understand what a POST card does, you need to know about the firmware—the programs and data stored on the motherboard.

Firmware consists of the older BIOS (basic input/output system) firmware and the newer UEFI (Unified Extensible Firmware Interface) firmware, and is usually referred to as BIOS/UEFI. Figure 1-34 shows an embedded firmware chip on a motherboard that contains the BIOS/UEFI programs. BIOS/UEFI is responsible for managing essential devices (for example, keyboard, mouse, hard drive, and monitor) before the OS is launched, starting the computer, and managing motherboard settings. A feature of the newer UEFI is that it can manage a secure boot, assuring that no rogue malware or operating system hijacks the system.

Coin battery

Firmware chip

Figure 1-34   This firmware chip contains BIOS/UEFI, flash ROM, and CMOS RAM; CMOS RAM is powered by the coin battery located near the chip

A POST card is not essential, but it can be quite useful. The POST (power-on self test) is a series of tests performed by the startup BIOS/UEFI when you first turn on a computer. These tests determine if the startup BIOS/UEFI can communicate correctly with essential hardware components required for a successful boot. If you have a problem that prevents the computer from booting and that you suspect is related to hardware, you can install the POST card in an expansion slot on the motherboard. For laptops, some cards install in a USB port. You can then attempt to boot. The card monitors the boot process and reports errors, usually as coded numbers on a small LED panel on the card. You then look up the number online or in the documentation that accompanies the card to get more information about the error and its source. Figure 1-35 shows a POST diagnostic card, the Post Code Master card by Microsystems Developments, Inc. (*postcodemaster.com*).

Figure 1-35   The Post Code Master diagnostic card by Microsystems Developments, Inc., installs in a PCI slot

Before purchasing this or any other diagnostic tools or software, read the documentation about what they can and cannot do, and read some online product reviews. Try using *google.com* and searching on "computer diagnostic card reviews."

> **✎ Notes**   Some Dell computers have lights on the case that blink in patterns to indicate a problem early in the boot before the OS loads. These blinking lights give information similar to that given by POST cards.

STEP 5: REMOVING THE POWER SUPPLY

A+
CORE 1
2.8, 3.7

To remove the power supply from the case, look for screws that attach the power supply to the computer case, as shown in Figure 1-36. Be careful not to remove any screws that hold the power supply housing together. You do not want to take the housing apart. After you have removed the screws, the power supply still might not be free. Sometimes, it is attached to the underside of the case by recessed slots. Turn the case over and look on the bottom for these slots. If they are present, determine in which direction you need to slide the power supply to free it from the case.

Figure 1-36 Remove the power supply mounting screws

POWER SUPPLY TESTER

A power supply tester is used to measure the output of each connector coming from the power supply. You can test the power supply when it is outside or inside the case. As you saw earlier in Figure 1-18, the power supply provides several cables and connectors that power various components inside the computer case. A power supply tester has plugs for each type of cable. Connect a power cable to the tester, plug up the power supply, and turn on the tester. An LCD panel reports the output of each lead (see Figure 1-37).

Figure 1-37 Use a power supply tester to test the output of each power connector on a power supply

MULTIMETER

A multimeter (see Figure 1-38) is a more general-purpose tool that can measure several characteristics of electricity in a variety of devices. Some multimeters can measure voltage, current, resistance, and continuity. (Continuity determines that two ends of a cable or fuse are connected without interruption.) When set to measure voltage, you can use it to measure output of each pin on a power supply connector. When set to measure continuity, a multimeter is useful to test fuses, to determine if a cable is good, or to match pins on one end of a cable to pins on the other end.

Figure 1-38 This digital multimeter can be set to measure voltage, resistance, or continuity

STEP 6: REMOVING THE DRIVES

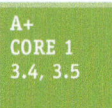

A computer might have one or more hard drives, an optical drive (CD, DVD, or Blu-ray), or some other type of drive. A drive receives power by a power cable from the power supply, and communicates instructions and data through a cable attached to the motherboard. Most hard drives and optical drives today use the serial ATA (SATA) standard.

Figure 1-39 shows a SATA cable connecting a hard drive and motherboard. SATA cables can only connect to a SATA connector on the motherboard in one direction (see Figure 1-40). SATA drives get their power from a power cable that connects to the drive using a SATA power connector (refer back to the photo in Table 1-2).

Figure 1-39 A hard drive subsystem using the SATA data cable

Serial ATA cable

Power cord

Figure 1-40 A SATA cable connects to a SATA connector in only one direction; for this system, use red connectors on the motherboard first

Remove each drive next, handling them with care. Here are some tips:

▲ Some drives have one or two screws on each side of the drive that attach the drive to the drive bay. After you remove the screws, the drive slides to the front or to the rear and then out of the case.

▲ Sometimes, there is a catch underneath the drive that you must lift up as you slide the drive forward.

▲ Some drive bays have a clipping mechanism to hold the drive in the bay. First, release the clip and then pull the drive forward and out of the bay (see Figure 1-41). Handle the drives with care. Some drives have an exposed circuit board on the bottom of the drive. Don't touch this board.

Figure 1-41 To remove this optical drive, first release the clip to release the drive from the bay

▲ Some drives must be removed through the front of the case, especially optical drives. After removing all screws or releasing the clipping mechanism, you might need to remove the front panel of the case to remove the drive. See Figure 1-42.

Figure 1-42 Some cases require you to remove the front panel before removing the optical drive

▲ Some cases have a removable bay for smaller hard drives (see Figure 1-43). The bay is removed first and then the drives are removed from the bay. To remove the bay, first remove the screws or release the clip holding the bay in place, and then slide the bay out of the case. The drives are usually installed in the bay with two screws on each side of each drive. Remove the screws and then the drives (see Figure 1-44).

Figure 1-43 Push down on the clip and then slide the removable bay forward and out of the case

Figure 1-44 Drives in this removable bay are held in place with screws on each side of the bay and drive

STEPS TO PUT A COMPUTER BACK TOGETHER

**A+
CORE 1
3.5, 5.5**

To reassemble a computer, reverse the process of disassembling. Here is where your diagrams will be very useful; having the screws and cables organized will also help. In the directions that follow, we're also considering the possibility that you are installing a replacement part as you reassemble the system. Do the following:

1. Install components in the case in this order: power supply, drives, motherboard, and cards. When installing drives, know that for some systems, it's easier to connect data cables to the drives and then slide the drives into the bay. If the drive is anchored to the bay with screws or latches, be careful to

align the front of the drive flush with the front of the case before installing screws or pushing in the latches (see Figure 1-45).

Push in two latches to secure the drive

Figure 1-45 Align the front of the drive flush with the case front and then anchor with a screw

2. Place the motherboard inside the case. Make sure the ports stick out of the I/O shield at the rear of the case and the screw holes line up with screw holes on the bottom of the case. Figure 1-46 shows how you must align the screw holes on the motherboard with those in the case. There should be at least six screw sets, and there might be as many as nine. Use as many screws as there are holes in the motherboard.

Spacers are installed in the case

Screw holes on the motherboard

Figure 1-46 Align screw holes in the case with those on the motherboard

3. Connect the power cords from the power supply to the motherboard. A system will always need the main P1 power connector and most likely will need the 4-pin auxiliary connector for the processor. Other power connectors might be needed depending on the devices you later install in the system. Here are the details:

▲ Connect the P1 power connector from the power supply to the motherboard (refer back to Figure 1-23).

▲ Connect the 4-pin or 8-pin auxiliary power cord coming from the power supply to the motherboard, as shown in Figure 1-47. This cord supplies the supplemental power required for the processor.

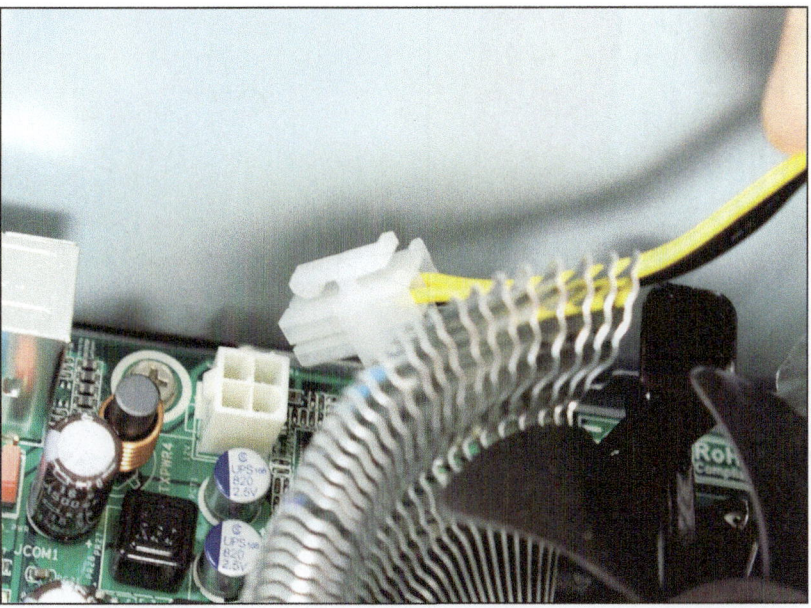

Figure 1-47 The auxiliary 4-pin power cord provides power to the processor

▲ To power the case fan, connect the power cord from the fan to pins on the motherboard labeled Fan Header. Alternately, some case fans use a 4-pin Molex connector that connects to a power cable coming directly from the power supply.

▲ If a CPU and cooler are already installed on the motherboard, connect the power cord from the CPU fan to the pins on the motherboard labeled CPU Fan Header.

4. Connect the wire leads from the front panel of the case to the front panel header on the motherboard. These are the wires for the switches, lights, and ports on the front or top of the computer. Because your case and your motherboard might not have been made by the same manufacturer, you need to pay close attention to the source of the wires to determine where they connect on the motherboard. For example, Figure 1-48 shows a computer case that has seven connectors from the front panel that connect to the motherboard. Figure 1-49 shows the front panel header on the motherboard for these lights and switches. If you look closely at the board in Figure 1-49, you can see labels identifying the pins.

Triangle used to orient connector on pins

Figure 1-48 Seven connectors from the front panel connect to the motherboard

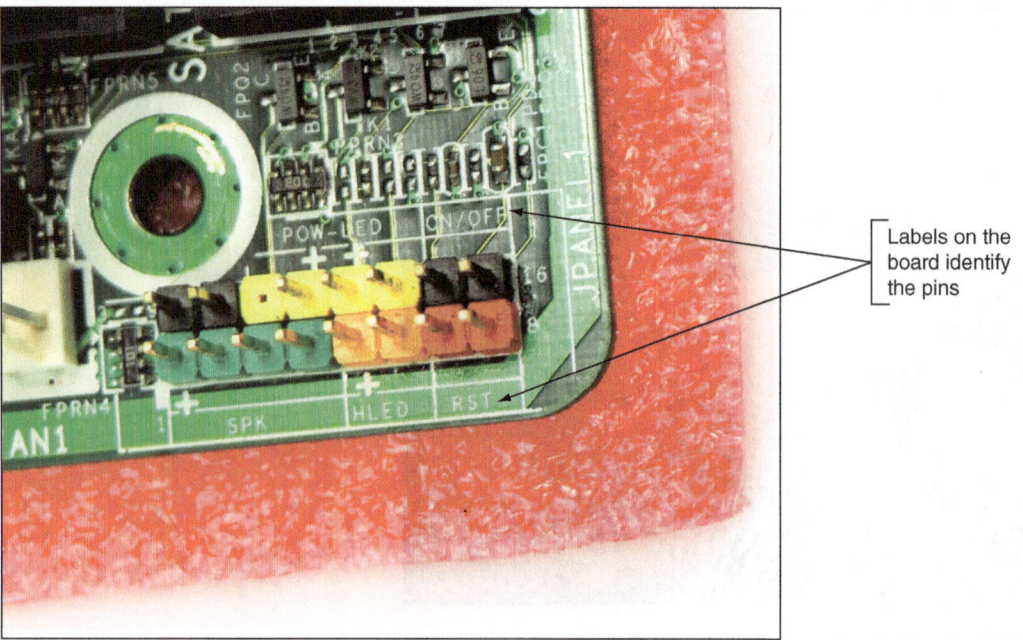

Labels on the board identify the pins

Figure 1-49 The front panel header uses color-coded pins and labels

The five smaller connectors on the right side of Figure 1-48 are labeled from right to left as follows:

▲ *Power SW*. Controls power to the motherboard; must be connected for the PC to power up

▲ *HDD LED*. Controls the drive activity light on the front panel that lights up when any SATA or IDE device is in use (HDD stands for *hard disk drive* and LED stands for *light-emitting diode*; an LED is a light on the front panel.)

▲ *Power LED+*. Positive LED controls the power light and indicates that power is on

▲ *Power LED–*. Negative LED controls the power light; the two positive and negative leads indicate that power is on

▲ *Reset SW*. Switch used to reboot the computer

> 🖉 **Notes** Positive wires connecting the front panel to the motherboard are usually a solid color, and negative wires are usually white or striped.

To help orient the larger connectors on the motherboard pins, look for a small triangle embedded on the connector that marks one of the outside wires as pin 1 (see Figure 1-48). Look for pin 1 to be labeled on the motherboard as a small 1 embedded to either the right or left of the group of pins. If the labels on the board are not clear, turn to the motherboard user guide for help. The diagram in Figure 1-50 shows what you can expect from one motherboard user guide. Notice pin 1 is identified as a square pin in the diagram, rather than round like the other pins.

Pin	Assignment	Function	Pin	Assignment	Function
1	+5 V		9	N/A	N/A
2	N/A	Speaker	10	N/A	
3	N/A	connector	11	N/A	N/A
4	Speaker		12	Power LED (+)	
5	HDD LED (+)	Hard drive	13	Power LED (+)	Power LED
6	HDD LED (−)	LED	14	Power LED (−)	
7	Ground		15	Power button	
8	Reset control	Reset button	16	Ground	Power-on button

Figure 1-50 Documentation for front panel header connections

> ✏ **Notes** If the user guide is not handy, you can download it from the motherboard manufacturer's website. Search on the brand and model number of the board, which is imprinted somewhere on the board.

Sometimes the motherboard documentation is not clear, but guessing is okay when connecting a wire to a front panel header connection. If it doesn't work, no harm is done. Figure 1-51 shows all front panel wires in place and the little speaker also connected to the front panel header pins.

Speaker connected to front panel header

Figure 1-51 A front panel header with all connectors in place

5. Connect wires to ports on the front panel of the case. Depending on your motherboard and case, there might be cables to connect audio ports or USB ports on the front of the case to headers on the motherboard. Audio and USB connectors are the two left connectors shown in Figure 1-48. You can see these ports for audio and USB on the front of the case in Figure 1-52. Look in the motherboard documentation for the location of these connectors. The audio and USB connectors are labeled for one board in Figures 1-53(A) and (B).

Figure 1-52   Ports on the front of the computer case

Figure 1-53   Connectors for front panel ports

6. Install the video card and any other expansion cards. Push the card straight down into the slot, being careful not to rock it side to side, and install the screw to secure the card to the case.

7. Take a few minutes to double-check each connection and make sure it is correct and snug. Verify that all required power cords are connected correctly and the video card is seated solidly in its slot. Also verify that no wires or cables are obstructing fans. You can use cable ties to tie wires up and out of the way.

8. Plug in the keyboard, monitor, and mouse.

9. In a classroom environment, have the instructor check your work before you close the case and power up.

10. Turn on the power and check that the PC is working properly. If the PC does not work, most likely the problem is a loose connection. Just turn off the power and recheck each cable connection and each expansion card. You probably have not solidly seated a card in the slot. After you have double-checked, try again.

Now step back and congratulate yourself on a job well done! By taking a computer apart and putting it back together, you've learned how computer parts interconnect and work.

Now let's turn our attention to how to disassemble and reassemble a laptop.

FIRST LOOK AT LAPTOP COMPONENTS

> **A+
> CORE 1
> 1.1, 1.3,
> 3.3, 3.9,
> 5.5**

A laptop, also called a notebook, is designed for portability (see Figure 1-54A and 1-54B) and can be just as powerful as a desktop computer. More than half of personal computers purchased today are laptops, and almost 30 percent of personal computers currently in use are laptops. Laptops use the same technology as desktops, but with modifications to use less power, take up less space, and operate on the move.

(A)   (B)   (C)

Figure 1-54 A laptop, netbook, and all-in-one computer

Laptops come in several varieties, including some with a touch screen that allows you to handwrite on it with a stylus and some with a rotating or removable screen that allows you to use the laptop as a tablet (see Figure 1-55). Another variation of a laptop is a netbook (Figure 1-54B), which is smaller and less expensive than a laptop and has fewer features. An all-in-one computer (Figure 1-54C) has the monitor and computer case built together and uses components that are common to both a laptop and desktop. Because all-in-one computers use many laptop components and are serviced in similar ways, we include them in this part of the chapter.

Source: iStockphoto.com/Rasslava

Figure 1-55 A laptop with a rotating display can do double-duty as a tablet computer

A laptop provides ports on its sides, back, or front for connecting peripherals (see Figure 1-56). Ports common to laptops as well as desktop systems include USB, network, and audio ports (for a microphone, headset, or external speakers). Video ports might include one or more VGA, DisplayPort, Thunderbolt (on Apple laptops), or HDMI ports to connect to a projector, second monitor, or television. On the side or back of the laptop, you'll see a lock connector that's used to physically secure the laptop with a cable lock (see Figure 1-57) and a DC jack to receive power from the AC adapter. Also, a laptop may have an optical drive, but netbooks usually don't have them.

Figure 1-56 Ports and slots on a laptop computer

Source: Kensington Technology Group

Figure 1-57 Use a cable lock system to secure a notebook computer to a desk to help prevent it from being stolen

Notice the two slots in Figure 1-56 used for flash memory cards: a MagicGate slot and an SD card slot. Each can support several types of flash memory cards that you learn about later in the text.

When a laptop is missing a port or slot you need, you can usually find a USB dongle to provide the port or slot. Here are some possible solutions for a missing or failed port:

▲ *Connect to a local wired network.* Figure 1-58 shows a USB to RJ-45 dongle. Plug the dongle into a USB port and plug a network cable into the RJ-45 port the dongle provides to connect the laptop to a wired network.

1

Figure 1-58 A USB to RJ-45 dongle provides a network port to connect to a wired network

▲ *Connect to a local wireless network.* Figure 1-59 shows a USB to Wi-Fi dongle, which allows you to connect a laptop to a wireless network that doesn't have wireless capability or the laptop's wireless component has failed. Wi-Fi (Wireless Fidelity) is the common name for standards for a local wireless network.

▲ *Connect to a cellular network.* Some laptops have embedded capability to connect to a cellular network. Figure 1-60 shows a USB cellular modem that can be used for a laptop that doesn't have the embedded technology. A cellular network consists of geographic areas of coverage called cells, each controlled by a tower called a base station. Cell phones are so named because they use a cellular network.

Figure 1-59 This USB to Wi-Fi adapter plugs into a USB port to connect to a local wireless network

LED light indicates power

LED light indicates network activity

Figure 1-60   This USB device by Sierra Wireless provides a wireless connection to a cellular network

▲ *Connect to a Bluetooth device*. When a laptop doesn't have Bluetooth capability, you can use a USB to Bluetooth adapter to connect to a Bluetooth wireless device such as a Bluetooth printer or smartphone. Bluetooth is a short-range wireless technology to connect two devices in a small personal network.

▲ *Use an external optical drive*. When a laptop or netbook doesn't have an optical drive, you can use a USB optical drive. Plug the USB optical drive into a USB port so that you can use CDs and DVDs with the laptop or netbook.

> **✎ Notes** When troubleshooting or installing an operating system on a laptop or netbook, you might need to boot from a USB optical drive containing the Windows setup DVD. In this situation, you need to first access BIOS/UEFI setup and change the boot priority order to boot first from an external USB device. This process is covered in Chapter 2.

SPECIAL KEYS, BUTTONS, AND INPUT DEVICES ON A LAPTOP

A+
CORE 1
1.1, 1.3

Buttons or switches might be found above the keyboard, and the top row of keys contains the function keys. To use a function key, hold down the Fn key as you press the function key. Here are the purposes of a few keys and buttons. Some of them change Windows settings. Know that these same settings can also be changed using Windows tools:

▲ *Volume setting*. You can set the volume using the volume icon in the Windows taskbar. In addition, some laptops offer buttons or function keys to control the volume (see Figure 1-61).

Figure 1-61 On this laptop, use the Fn and the F2, F3, or F4 key to control volume; use the Fn key and the F5 or F6 key to control screen brightness; and use the Fn key and the F7 key to manage dual displays

▲ *Keyboard backlight.* Function keys can be used to control the keyboard backlight and light up the keyboard.

▲ *Touch pad on or off.* Other function keys can activate or deactivate the touch pad, which is the most common pointing device on a laptop (see Figure 1-62). Some people prefer to use a USB wired or wireless mouse instead of a touch pad.

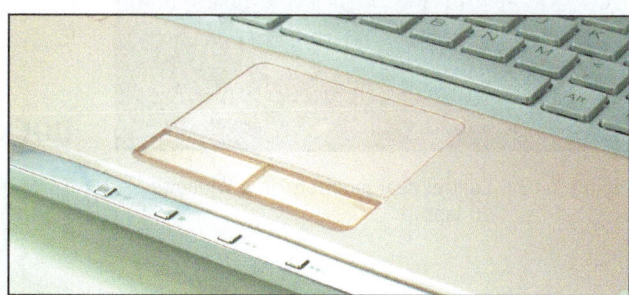

Figure 1-62 The touch pad is the most common pointing device on a notebook

▲ *Screen brightness and screen orientation.* Function keys can control the screen brightness on many laptops. Screen brightness can also be controlled in Windows display settings. Some laptops allow you to use a function key to change the screen orientation to landscape or portrait so you can use the laptop turned on its end.

▲ *Dual displays.* Most laptops use a function key to control dual displays. For example, for one laptop, the combination of the Fn key and the F7 key (refer back to Figure 1-61) displays the box shown in Figure 1-63. Use arrow keys to select only the LCD panel, duplicate or extend output to the external monitor, or use only the external monitor. Dual displays can also be managed using Windows display settings.

Figure 1-63   Control dual monitors on a Windows 10 laptop

▲ *Bluetooth, Wi-Fi, or cellular on or off.* Some laptops use function keys such as Fn with F5 or F6 to toggle Bluetooth, Wi-Fi, or cellular on or off, or a laptop might have a switch for this purpose. You can also control these wireless technologies using Windows settings or software utilities provided by the manufacturer. When you turn off all wireless technologies, the computer is said to be in airplane mode.

▲ *Media options.* Some laptops provide buttons or allow you to use function keys to fast forward, stop, pause, or rewind audio or video media playing in an optical drive.

▲ *GPS on or off.* If a laptop has a GPS (Global Positioning System) receiver to calculate its position on Earth, the laptop might provide a button or function key to turn the GPS on or off. GPS is a system of 24 or more satellites orbiting Earth; a GPS receiver can locate three or more of these satellites at any time and then calculate its own position from these three locations, a process called trilateration.

> 🖉 **Notes** If the keyboard fails and you're not able to immediately exchange it, know that you can plug in an external keyboard to a USB port for use in the meantime.

DOCKING STATIONS AND PORT REPLICATORS

**A+
CORE 1
1.3**

The bottom or sides of some laptops have a proprietary connector, called a docking port, (see Figure 1-64) that connects to a docking station. A docking station provides ports to allow a laptop to easily connect to a full-sized monitor, keyboard, AC power adapter, and other peripheral devices. See Figure 1-65. Laptop manufacturers usually offer a docking station as an additional option on most business laptops and a few consumer laptops as well. A disadvantage of a docking station is that when you upgrade your laptop, you typically must purchase a new compatible docking station.

Figure 1-64   The docking port and sheet battery connector on the bottom of a laptop

Source: Courtesy of Lenovo

Figure 1-65 A docking station for a Lenovo ThinkPad

A *port replicator*, sometimes called a universal docking station, is a device that provides ports to allow a laptop to easily connect to peripheral devices, such as an external monitor, network, printer, keyboard and mouse, or speakers. See Figure 1-66. Some port replicators also supply power to the laptop to charge the battery. The difference between a port replicator and a docking station is that a port replicator isn't proprietary to a single brand or model of laptop because it typically connects to a laptop using a single USB port.

DC power jack
USB to PC
Two USB 3.0
Four USB 2.0   HDMI   DVI   Gigabit Ethernet

Figure 1-66 This port replicator provides USB 3.0, USB 2.0, HDMI, DVI, and network ports

To use a docking station or port replicator, plug all the peripherals into the docking station or port replicator. Then, connect your laptop to the station. No software needs to be installed. When you need to travel with your laptop, you don't have to unplug all the peripherals; all you have to do is disconnect the laptop from the docking station or port replicator.

SPECIAL CONSIDERATIONS WHEN SUPPORTING LAPTOPS

**A+
CORE 1
5.5**

Laptops and their replacement parts cost more than desktop computers with similar features because their components are designed to be more compact and stand up to travel. Laptops use compact hard drives, small memory modules, and CPUs that require less power than regular components. Whereas a desktop computer is often assembled from parts made by a variety of manufacturers, laptop computers are almost always sold by a vendor that either manufactured the laptop or had it manufactured as a consolidated system. Notable factors that generally apply more to laptop than desktop computers are the original equipment manufacturer's warranty, the service manuals and diagnostic software provided by the manufacturer, the customized installation of the OS that is unique to laptops, and the need to order replacement parts directly from the laptop manufacturer or other source authorized by the manufacturer.

In many situations, the tasks of maintaining, upgrading, and troubleshooting a laptop require the same skills, knowledge, and procedures as when servicing a desktop computer. However, you should take some special considerations into account when caring for, supporting, upgrading, and troubleshooting laptops. These same concerns apply to netbooks and all-in-one computers. Let's begin with warranty concerns.

WARRANTY CONCERNS

Most manufacturers or retailers of laptops offer at least a one-year warranty and the option to purchase an extended warranty. Therefore, when problems arise while the laptop is under warranty, you are dealing with a single manufacturer or retailer to get support or parts. After the laptop is out of warranty, this manufacturer or retailer can still be your one-stop shop for support and parts.

> **⚡ Caution** The warranty often applies to all components in the system, but it can be voided if someone other than an authorized service center representative services the laptop. Therefore, you as a service technician must be very careful not to void a warranty that the customer has purchased. Warranties can be voided by opening the case, removing part labels, installing other-vendor parts, upgrading the OS, or disassembling the system unless directly instructed to do so by authorized service center personnel.

Before you begin servicing a laptop, avoid potential problems with a warranty by always asking the customer, "Is the laptop under warranty?" If the laptop is under warranty, look at the documentation to find out how to get technical support. Options are chat sessions on the web, phone numbers, and email. Use the most appropriate option. Before you contact technical support, have the laptop model and serial number ready (see Figure 1-67). You'll also need the name, phone number, and address of the person or company that made the purchase. Consider asking the customer for a copy of the receipt and warranty so you'll have the information you need to talk with support personnel.

Figure 1-67 The model and serial number stamped on the bottom of a laptop are used to identify the laptop to service desk personnel

Based on the type of warranty purchased by the laptop's owner, the manufacturer might send an on-site service technician, ask you to ship or take the laptop to an authorized service center, or help you solve the problem by an online chat session or over the phone. Table 1-3 lists some popular manufacturers of laptops, netbooks, and all-in-ones. Manufacturers of laptops typically also produce all-in-ones because of the features they have in common.

Manufacturer	Website
Acer	*us.acer.com* and *us.acer.com/support*
Apple Computer	*apple.com* and *apple.com/support*
ASUS	*usa.asus.com* and *asus.com/us/support/*
Dell Computer	*dell.com* and *support.dell.com*
Hewlett Packard (HP)	*hp.com* and *support.hp.com*
Lenovo	*lenovo.com* and *support.lenovo.com*
Microsoft	*microsoft.com*
Razer	*razer.com* and *support.razer.com*
Samsung	*samsung.com* and *samsung.com/support*
Sony (VAIO)	*store.sony.com* and *esupport.sony.com*
Toshiba America	*toshiba.com* and *support.toshiba.com*

Table 1-3 Laptop, netbook, and all-in-one manufacturers

SERVICE MANUALS AND OTHER SOURCES OF INFORMATION

Desktop computer cases tend to be similar to one another, and components in desktop systems are usually interchangeable among manufacturers. Not so with laptops. Laptop manufacturers typically take great liberty in creating their own unique computer cases, buses, cables, connectors, drives, circuit boards, fans, and even screws, all of which are likely to be proprietary in design.

Every laptop model has a unique case. Components are installed in unique ways and opening the case for each laptop model is done differently. Because of these differences, servicing laptops can be very complicated, tedious, and time consuming. For example, a hard drive on one laptop is accessed by popping open a side panel and sliding the drive out of its bay. However, to access the hard drive on another model of laptop, you must remove the keyboard. If you are not familiar with a particular laptop model, you can damage the case frame or plastics as you pry and push trying to open it. Trial and error is likely to damage a case. Even though you might successfully replace a broken component, the damaged case will result in an unhappy customer.

Fortunately, a laptop service manual can save you considerable time and effort—if you can locate one (see Figure 1-68). Most laptop manufacturers closely guard these service manuals and release them only to authorized service centers. Two laptop manufacturers, Lenovo and Dell, provide their service manuals online free of charge. HP also does an excellent job of offering online support. For example, Figure 1-69 displays a video that shows the steps to replace the top cover on an HP laptop. I applaud Lenovo, Dell, and HP for the generous documentation about how their laptops are disassembled and the options to purchase proprietary parts without first being an authorized service center.

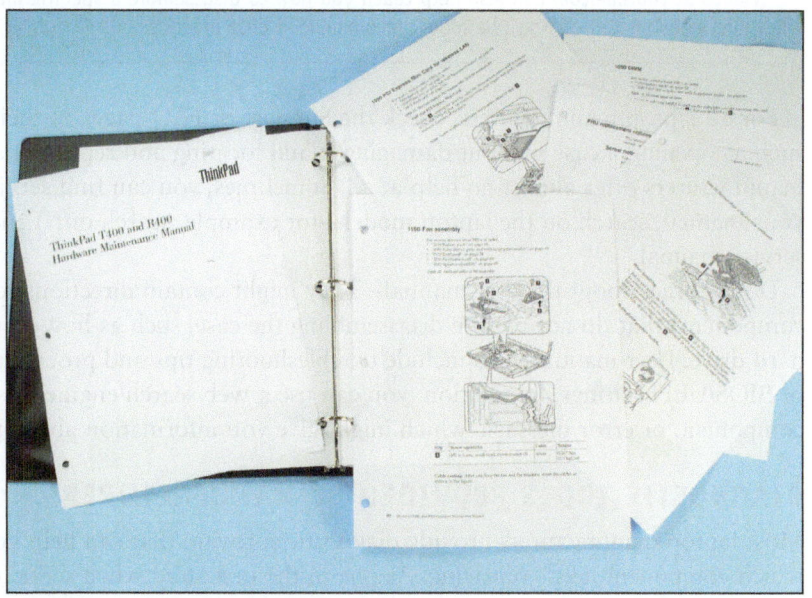

Figure 1-68 A laptop service manual tells you how to use diagnostic tools, troubleshoot a laptop, and replace components

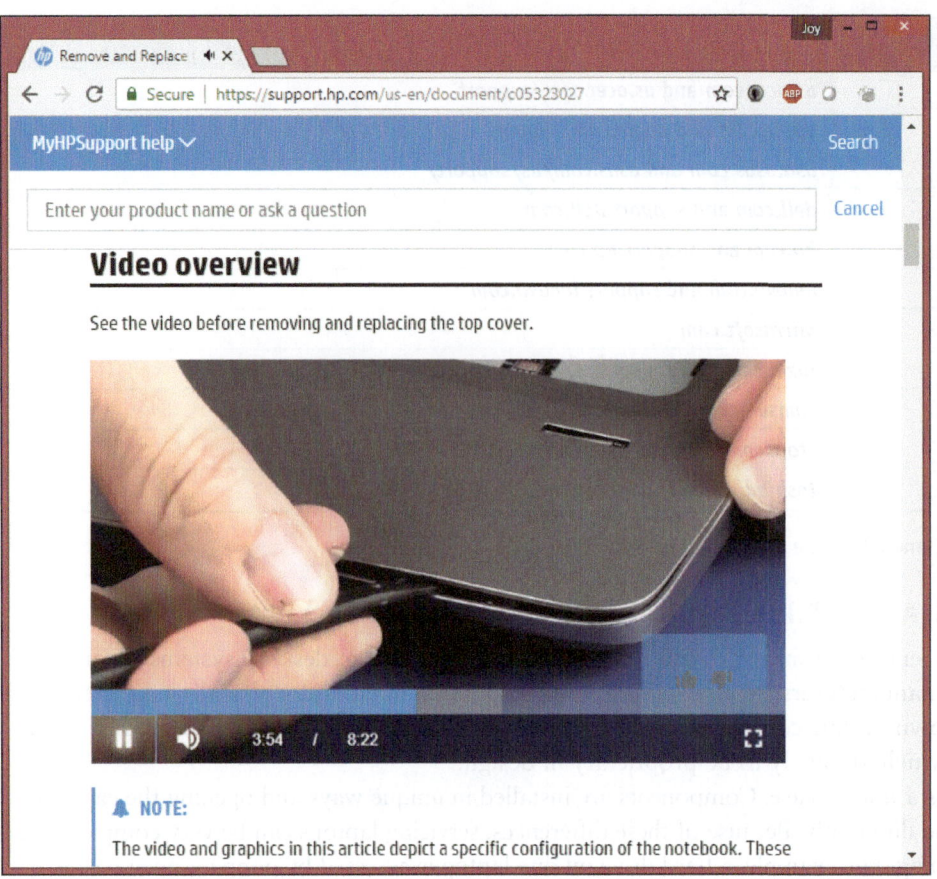

Source: *hp.com*

Figure 1-69   The HP website (*support.hp.com*) provides detailed instructions and videos for troubleshooting and replacing components

> ✎ **Notes** The wiki-type website *ifixit.com* does an excellent job of providing its own teardown and reassembly instructions for many brands and models of laptops. You can also buy parts and tools on the site.
> Videos at *youtube.com* can also help teach you how to disassemble a specific model of laptop. However, beware that not all videos posted on YouTube follow recommended best practices.

For all laptop manufacturers, check the Support or FAQ pages of their websites for help with tasks such as opening a case without damaging it and locating and replacing a component. Be aware that some manufacturers offer almost no help at all. Sometimes, you can find service manuals on the web. To find your manual, search on the laptop model—for example, search on "Lenovo ideapad 310-15ABR laptop service manual."

Don't forget about the user manuals. They might contain directions for upgrading and replacing components that do not require disassembling the case, such as how to upgrade memory or install a new hard drive. User manuals also include troubleshooting tips and procedures and possibly descriptions of BIOS/UEFI settings. In addition, you can use a web search engine to search on the computer model, component, or error message, which might give you information about the problem and solution.

DIAGNOSTIC TOOLS PROVIDED BY MANUFACTURERS

Most laptop manufacturers provide diagnostic software that can help you test components to determine which component needs replacing. As one of the first steps when servicing a laptop, check the user manual, service manual, or manufacturer's website to determine if diagnostic software exists and how to use it. Use the software to pinpoint the problem component, which can then be replaced.

✎ **Notes** When you purchase a replacement part for a laptop from the laptop's manufacturer, most often the manufacturer also sends detailed instructions for exchanging the part and/or phone support to talk you through the process.

Check the manufacturer's website for diagnostics software that can be downloaded for a specific model of laptop or stored on the hard drive or on CDs bundled with the laptop. Figure 1-70 shows a window provided by the diagnostics program installed on the hard drive of one laptop.

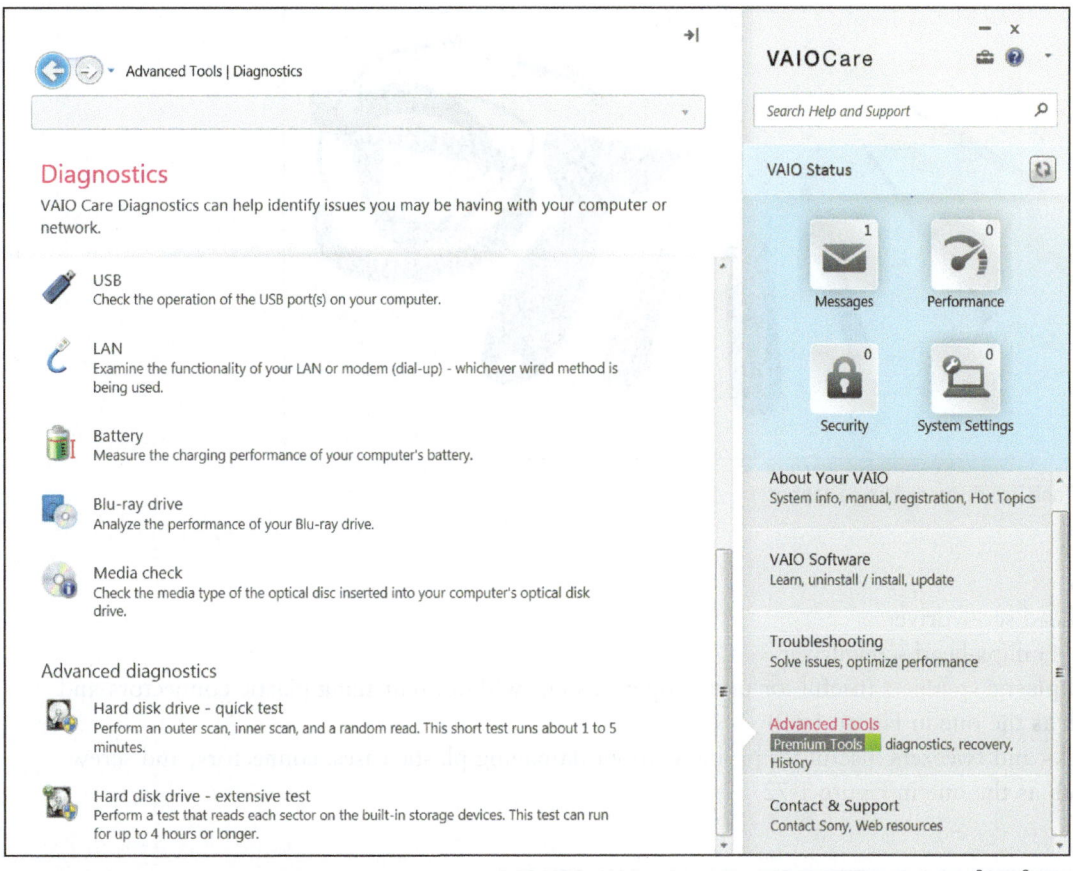

Source: Sony

Figure 1-70 Use diagnostics software provided by a laptop manufacturer to troubleshoot hardware problems

One example of diagnostic software is PC-Doctor (*pc-doctor.com*), which is recommended by several manufacturers, including Lenovo, Fujitsu, and HP. The diagnostic software is stored on the hard drive or on CD. If stored on CD, you can boot from the CD to run the tests. If the software is stored on the hard drive, you can run it from the Windows Start menu or by pressing a function key at startup before Windows loads. Either way, PC-Doctor can run tests on the keyboard, video, speakers, touch pad, optical drive, wireless LAN, motherboard, processor, ports, hard drive, and memory. To learn how to use the software, see the laptop's service manual or user manual. You can find a stand-alone version of PC-Doctor for DOS and PC-Doctor for Windows at *pc-doctor.com*. You can purchase it at this site; it's expensive but might be worth it if you plan to service many laptops.

WORKING INSIDE A LAPTOP COMPUTER

Sometimes it is necessary to open a laptop case so you can upgrade memory, exchange a hard drive, or replace a failed component such as the LCD panel, video inverter, keyboard, touch pad, processor, optical drive, DC jack, fan, motherboard, CMOS battery, Mini PCIe card, wireless card, or speaker. Most laptops sold today are designed so that you can easily purchase and exchange memory modules or hard drives. However, replacing a failing processor or motherboard can be a complex process, taking several hours. Most likely, you will choose to replace the entire laptop rather than doing these labor-intensive and costly repairs.

Screws and nuts on a laptop are smaller than those on a desktop system and therefore require smaller tools. Figure 1-71 shows several tools used to disassemble a laptop, although you can get by without several of them. Here's the list:

Figure 1-71   Tools for disassembling a laptop

◢ ESD strap
◢ Small flathead screwdriver
◢ Number 1 Phillips-head screwdriver
◢ Metal and plastic spudgers (useful for prying open casings without damaging plastic connectors and cases, such as the one in Figure 1-69)
◢ Dental picks and tweezers (useful for prying without damaging plastic cases, connectors, and screw covers, such as the one in Figure 1-72)

Figure 1-72   Use a small screwdriver or dental pick to pry up the plastic cover hiding a screw

◢ Torx screwdriver set, particularly size T5
◢ Something such as a pillbox to keep screws and small parts organized
◢ Notepad for note-taking or digital camera (optional)
◢ Flashlight (optional)

Working on laptops requires extra patience. As with desktop systems, before opening the case of a laptop or touching sensitive components, you should always wear an ESD strap to protect the system against ESD. You can attach the alligator clip end of the strap to an unpainted metallic surface on the laptop. This surface could be, for instance, a port on the back of the laptop (see Figure 1-73). If a ground strap is not available, first dissipate any ESD between you and the laptop by touching a metallic, unpainted part of it, such as a port on the back, before you touch a component inside the case.

Figure 1-73 To protect the system against ESD, attach the alligator clip of a
ground strap to an I/O port on the back of the laptop

Laptops contain many small screws of various sizes and lengths. When reassembling the system, put screws back where they came from so you won't use screws that are too long and that can protrude into a sensitive component and damage it. As you remove a screw, store or label it so you know where it goes when reassembling. One method is to place screws in a pillbox with each compartment labeled. Another way is to place screws on a soft, padded work surface and use white labeling tape to label each set of screws. A third way to organize screws is to put them on notebook paper and write beside them where the screw belongs (see Figure 1-74). My favorite method of keeping up with all these screws is to tape each one beside the manufacturer documentation I'm following to disassemble the laptop (see Figure 1-75). Whatever method you use, work methodically to keep screws and components organized so you know what goes where when reassembling.

Figure 1-74 Using a notepad can help you organize screws so you
know which screw goes where when reassembling

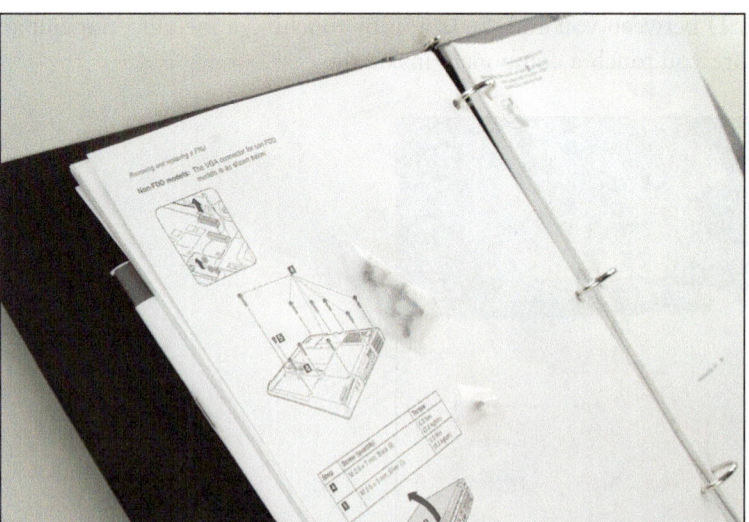

Figure 1-75 Tape screws beside the step in the manufacturer documentation that told you to remove the screw

> ★ **A+ Exam Tip** The A+ Core 1 exam expects you to know the importance of keeping parts organized when disassembling a laptop as well as the importance of having manufacturer documentation to know the steps for disassembly. Given a scenario, you should be able to adhere to appropriate procedures.

If you disassemble a computer and are not following directions from a service manual, keep notes as you work to help you reassemble later. Draw diagrams and label things carefully. Include cable orientations and screw locations in your drawings. You might consider using a digital camera. Photos that you take at each step in the disassembly process will be a great help when it's time to put the laptop back together.

When disassembling a laptop, consider the following tips:

◢ Make your best effort to find the hardware service manual for the particular laptop model you are servicing. The manual should include all the detailed steps to disassemble the laptop and a parts list of components that can be ordered from the laptop manufacturer. If you don't have this manual, your chances of successfully replacing an internal component are greatly reduced! Another helpful resource is searching the Internet for video tutorials for the teardown of the model you are using. If you don't have much experience disassembling a laptop, it is not wise to attempt to do so without the service manual.

◢ Consider the warranty that might still apply to the laptop. Remember that opening the case of a laptop under warranty most likely will void the warranty. Make certain that any component you have purchased to replace an internal component will work in the model of laptop you are servicing.

◢ Take your time. Patience is needed to keep from scratching or marring plastic screw covers, hinges, and the case.

◢ As you work, don't force anything. If you do, you're likely to break it.

◢ Always wear an ESD strap or use other protection against ESD.

◢ When removing cables, know that some ribbon cable connectors are ZIF connectors. To disconnect a cable from a ZIF connector, first pull up on the connector and then remove the cable, as shown in Figure 1-76. Figure 1-77 shows a laptop that uses three ZIF connectors to hold the three keyboard cables in place. For some ribbon cables, you simply pull the cable out of the connector. For these cables, it's best to use two tweezers, one on each side of the connector, to remove the cable.

Figure 1-76 To disconnect a ZIF connector, first lift up on the locking flap to release the latch, and then remove the cable using the pull tab, which is blue on this laptop

Figure 1-77 Three ZIF connectors hold the three keyboard cables in place

◢ Again, use a spudger, dental pick, or very small screwdriver to pry up the plastic cover hiding a screw.

◢ Some laptops use plastic screws that are intended to be used only once. The service manual will tell you to be careful not to overtighten these screws and to always use new screws when reassembling a laptop.

◢ Disassemble the laptop by removing each field replaceable unit (FRU) in the order given by the laptop's service manual. For example, one manufacturer says that to replace the fan assembly and heat sink assembly for a laptop, you must remove components in this order: HDD compartment cover, keyboard bezel, HDD, mini PCIe slot compartment cover and RAM, wireless card, optical drive, and then system board. After all these components are removed, you can then remove the fan assembly and heat sink assembly. Follow the steps to remove each component in the correct order.

◢ At some point in the disassembly process after all appropriate covers and screws have been removed, you must *crack the case*, which means you separate the top and bottom parts of the case. The parts might be tightly sealed together. To separate them, use a plastic or metal spudger to slide along the seal and pry open the case, as shown earlier in Figure 1-69.

When reassembling a laptop, consider these general tips:

◢ Reassemble the laptop in the reverse order you disassembled it. Follow each step carefully.

◢ Be sure to tighten, but not overtighten, all screws. Loose screws or metal fragments in a laptop can be dangerous; they might cause a short as they shift about inside the laptop.

◢ Before you install the battery or AC adapter, verify that there are no loose parts inside the laptop. Pick it up and gently shake it. If you hear anything loose, open the case, find the loose component, screw, spring, or metal flake, and fix the problem.

EXPLORING LAPTOP INTERNAL COMPONENTS

A+
CORE 1
1.1, 3.3,
3.9, 5.5

Here is a list of important components you are likely to be instructed to remove when disassembling a laptop and the typical order you remove them. However, know that the components and the order of disassembly vary from one laptop to another:

1. *Remove or disable the battery pack.* To start the disassembly, disconnect all peripherals, remove discs from the optical drive, and shut down the system. Then, disconnect the AC adapter and remove the battery. Removing the battery (see Figure 1-78) assures you that no power is getting to the system, which keeps the laptop and you safe as you work. Some laptops and netbooks have built-in batteries. For these devices, follow the manufacturer instructions to disable the battery (often called Ship Mode), which prevents it from providing power to any component.

Thumb latch
releases
the battery

Figure 1-78 Remove the battery pack before opening a laptop case

2. *Remove the hard drive.* For some laptops, the hard drive is accessed by removing the hard drive compartment cover from the bottom of the laptop. For example, Figure 1-79 shows the hard drive is secured in its bay with three screws. When you remove the screws and disconnect the ribbon cable, you can lift the drive from its bay. For other hard drives, rather than disconnecting a ribbon cable from the drive, you unplug the drive from its drive socket.

Figure 1-79 Remove all screws that secure the hard drive in its bay

3. *Remove memory.* Laptops use smaller memory modules than the DIMMs used in desktop computers. Figure 1-80 shows a DIMM and a SO-DIMM (small outline DIMM) for size comparison. For one laptop, you first remove the memory/Mini PCI Express Card compartment cover to access the memory modules. Release two latches on both edges of the socket at the same time to remove the memory modules, as shown in Figure 1-81.

Figure 1-80 A DIMM used in desktops compared with a SO-DIMM used in laptop computers

Figure 1-81 Release the latches on both edges of the socket to remove the memory modules

4. *Remove the wireless card.* For the laptop in Figure 1-81, the Mini PCI Express wireless card is installed in the same compartment as the memory modules. Disconnect the two wires leading to the wireless antennas, which are installed in the laptop lid. Next, remove the screw securing the wireless card, then pull the card directly away from the socket, as shown in Figure 1-82.

Figure 1-82 Pull the wireless card directly away from the socket to prevent damage to the card and socket

5. *Remove the optical drive.* The optical drive is secured by a single screw on the bottom of the laptop. Figure 1-83 shows the removal of the single screw holding the drive in place. Next, slide the drive out of the case.

Figure 1-83 Slide the optical drive out of the case after removing the screw securing the optical drive to the laptop

6. *Crack the case.* After removing compartment covers and the components accessible inside these compartments (for example, memory, optical drive, and hard drive), you are ready to remove any other screws as directed in the service manual, and then you can crack the case. Use a spudger to slide along the seal between the case top and bottom, and pry open the plastic casing on the side, as shown in Figure 1-84.

Figure 1-84 Using a spudger helps prevent harming the casing when prying it open

7. ***Remove the keyboard bezel.*** The keyboard bezel is the keyboard casing surrounding the keyboard of a laptop. For some laptops, such as the one shown in Figure 1-85, the keyboard bezel is the top of the case. For other laptops, you remove the case top and then remove the keyboard. Once you remove screws and disconnect the cables from the motherboard, the keyboard bezel should easily lift away from the laptop, as shown in Figure 1-85. You might need a spudger to help.

Figure 1-85 Disconnect both the touch pad board cable and the keyboard cable to remove the keyboard

8. ***Remove the system board.*** Figure 1-86 shows a system board (in laptop documentation, the motherboard is usually called the system board) with heat sink, fan, and processor connected to it. A system board in a laptop also has ports on one side that are easily accessed externally on

the laptop. To remove the system board, you must remove all screws and disconnect all cables for all the components in the laptop, which can be time consuming and difficult. You'll learn how to replace the system board in Chapter 2.

Figure 1-86   The system board, heat sink, and fan are replaceable units in this laptop

9. *Remove the CPU, heat sink, and fan.* The CPU is embedded on the system board in many laptops, which means if the CPU fails, the system board must be replaced to repair the laptop. The heat sink draws heat from the CPU and pipes it to the fan, as labeled in Figure 1-86. The fan blows the heat out of the laptop case. The fan and heat sink assembly is considered a field replaceable component in many laptops.

Other hardware components you are likely to find in a laptop case include the LCD panel and components in the laptop lid. Later in the text, you'll learn how to replace the components in a laptop lid.

EXPLORING INSIDE AN ALL-IN-ONE COMPUTER

An all-in-one computer uses a mix of components sized for a desktop computer and a laptop. Let's get the general idea of what's inside the case of an all-in-one by looking inside the Lenovo ThinkCentre all-in-one, which was shown earlier in Figure 1-54. Figure 1-87 shows the computer with the case cover removed. Notice in the figure that the hard drive is a 3.5-inch drive appropriate for a desktop system, and the memory modules are SO-DIMMs appropriate for a laptop. So goes the hybrid nature of an all-in-one. The fan and heat sink look more like that of a laptop computer, but the processor socket on the motherboard is a desktop processor socket, another hybrid design.

I/O controller board
provides ports on
the side of the
computer

Optical drive

Power supply

Processor is
under this heat sink

SO-DIMMs

Mini PCIe card

CMOS battery

CPU fan

3.5-inch hard drive

Blue bracket holds
hard drive in place

Figure 1-87   Components inside an all-in-one computer

Several components are easy to exchange in this all-in-one without further disassembly. For example, the Mini PCIe card for wireless connectivity is easy to get to, as are the SO-DIMMs you can partly see on the right side of Figure 1-88.

Figure 1-88   A CMOS battery and Mini PCIe wireless card

To work inside an all-in-one, you'll need the service manual to know how to open the case and replace internal components. Replacements for some components, such as the motherboard and power supply, must be purchased from the all-in-one manufacturer because they are likely to be proprietary, as with many laptop components. For specific directions about replacing parts in an all-in-one, see the service manual.

Now that you are familiar with some major components of a laptop, let's learn some special considerations when maintaining laptops.

MAINTAINING LAPTOPS

 A+ CORE 1 1.3, 3.3, 3.9, 5.5
Laptops and mobile devices tend not to last as long as desktop computers because they are portable and therefore subject to more wear and tear. A device's user manual gives specific instructions on how to care for the device. Those instructions follow these general guidelines:

- LCD panels on devices are fragile and can be damaged fairly easily. Take precautions against damaging a laptop or other device's LCD panel. Don't touch it with sharp objects like ballpoint pens.
- Don't pick up or hold a laptop by the lid. Pick it up and hold it by the bottom. Keep the lid closed when the laptop is not in use.
- Only use battery packs and AC adapters recommended by the laptop manufacturer. Keep the battery pack away from moisture or heat, and don't attempt to take the pack apart. When it no longer works, dispose of it correctly. For laptops, you might consider buying an extra battery pack to use when the first one discharges. You can also buy battery chargers so that you can charge one while the other is in use.
- Don't tightly pack a laptop or tablet in a suitcase because the LCD panel might get damaged. Use a good-quality carrying case and make a habit of always transporting the laptop in the carrying case. Don't place heavy objects on top of the laptop case.
- Don't move the laptop while the hard drive is being accessed (when the drive indicator light is on). Wait until the light goes off.
- Don't put the laptop close to an appliance such as a TV, large audio speakers, or refrigerator that generates a strong magnetic field, and don't place your cell phone on a laptop while the phone is in use.
- Always use passwords to protect access to your laptop so you are better protected when connected to a public network or if the device is stolen or used by an unauthorized person.
- Keep your laptop or device at room temperature. For example, never leave it in a car overnight during cold weather, and don't leave it in a car during the day in hot weather. Don't expose your laptop or device to direct sunlight for an extended time.
- Don't leave the laptop or device in a dusty or smoke-filled area. Don't use it in a wet area such as near a swimming pool or in the bathtub. Don't use it at the beach where sand can get in it.
- Don't power it up and down unnecessarily.
- Protect the laptop from overheating by not running it when it's still inside the case, not resting it on a pillow, and not partially covering it with a blanket or anything else that would prevent proper air circulation around it.
- If a laptop has just been brought indoors from the cold, don't turn it on until it reaches room temperature. In some cases, condensation can cause problems. Some manufacturers recommend that when you receive a new laptop shipped to you during the winter, you should leave it in its shipping carton for several hours before you open the carton to prevent subjecting the laptop to a temperature shock.
- Protect a laptop against static electricity. If you have just come in from the cold on a low-humidity day when there is the possibility that you are carrying static electricity, don't touch the laptop until you have grounded yourself.
- Before placing a laptop in a carrying case for travel, remove any CDs, DVDs, or USB flash drives, and put them in protective covers. Verify that the system is powered down and not in sleep mode, which will drain the battery.

◢ If a laptop gets wet, you can partially disassemble it to allow internal components to dry. Give the laptop several days to dry before attempting to turn it on. Don't use heat to speed up the drying time.

◢ Keep current backups of important data on a laptop or device in case it fails or is stolen.

A well-used laptop, especially one that is used in dusty or dirty areas, needs cleaning occasionally. Here are some cleaning tips:

1. Clean the LCD panel with a soft, dry cloth. If the panel is very dirty, you can use monitor wipes to clean it or dampen the cloth with water. Some manufacturers recommend using a mixture of isopropyl alcohol and water to clean an LCD panel. Be sure the LCD panel is dry before you close the lid.

2. Use a can of compressed air meant for use on computer equipment to blow dust and small particles out of the keyboard, trackball, and touch pad. Turn the laptop at an angle and direct the air into the sides of the keyboard. Then, use a soft, damp cloth to clean the key caps and touch pad.

3. Use compressed air to blow out all air vents on the laptop to make sure they are clean and unobstructed.

4. If a laptop is overheating, the CPU fan might be clogged with dust. The overheating problem might be solved by disassembling the laptop and blowing out the fan with compressed air.

5. If keys are sticking, remove the keyboard so you can better spray under the keys with compressed air. If you can remove the key cap, remove it and clean the key contact area with contact cleaner. One example of a contact cleaner you can use for this purpose is Stabilant 22 (*stabilant.com*). Reinstall the keyboard and test it. If the key still sticks, replace the keyboard.

6. Remove the battery and clean the battery connections with a contact cleaner.

★ **A+ Exam Tip** The A+ Core 1 exam expects you to know how to solve the problem of sticking keys on a laptop, given a scenario.

>> CHAPTER SUMMARY

Exploring a Desktop Computer

◢ When hardware support technicians disassemble or reassemble a computer, it is important for them to stay organized, keep careful notes, and follow all the safety procedures to protect the computer equipment and themselves.

◢ Before opening a computer case, shut down the system, unplug it, disconnect all cables, and press the power button to drain residual power.

◢ Common tools for a computer hardware technician include an ESD strap, screwdrivers, tweezers, flashlight, compressed air, and cleaning solutions and pads.

◢ Special tools a hardware technician might need include a POST diagnostic card, power supply tester, multimeter, and loopback plugs.

◢ A computer's video ports might include the VGA, DVI, DisplayPort, and HDMI ports. Other ports include RJ-45, audio, SPDIF, USB, eSATA, PS/2, serial, and RJ-11 ports. A Thunderbolt port can transmit video, data, and power.

◢ Internal computer components include the motherboard, processor, expansion cards, DIMM memory modules, hard drive, optical drive, tape drive, and power supply.

◢ Cases, power supplies, and motherboards use ATX and microATX form factors. The form factor determines how the case, power supply, and motherboard fit together and the cable connectors and other standards used by each.

▲ Power connectors used by the ATX and microATX form factors include the older 20-pin P1, current 24-pin P1, 4-pin and 8-pin CPU auxiliary motherboard, 4-pin Molex, 15-pin SATA, and 6/8-pin PCIe connectors.

▲ An expansion card fits in a slot on the motherboard and is anchored to the case by a single screw or clip.

▲ Firmware consists of the older BIOS (basic input/output system) firmware and the newer UEFI (Unified Extensible Firmware Interface) firmware. This BIOS/UEFI firmware is responsible for managing essential devices (for example, keyboard, mouse, hard drive, and monitor) before the OS is launched, starting the computer, and managing motherboard settings.

▲ Most hard drives and optical drives today use the serial ATA (SATA) standards for the drive to interface with the motherboard and power supply.

First Look at Laptop Components

▲ Laptop computers are designed for travel. They use the same technology as desktop computers, with modifications for space, portability, and power conservation. A laptop generally costs more than a desktop with comparable power and features.

▲ Laptop computers use function keys to control the display, volume, touch pad, media options, GPS, airplane mode, and other features of the laptop. A laptop docking station or port replicator can make it easy to disconnect peripheral devices.

▲ You can use the USB ports for expansion—for example, you can add a USB to RJ-45 dongle, a USB to Wi-Fi dongle, Bluetooth capability, or a USB optical drive.

▲ The laptop manufacturer documentation, including the service manual, diagnostic software, and recovery media, is useful when disassembling, troubleshooting, and repairing a laptop.

▲ Field replaceable units (FRUs) in a laptop can include the memory modules, hard drive, LCD panel, video inverter, keyboard, touch pad, processor, optical drive, DC jack, fan, motherboard, CMOS battery, Mini PCIe card, wireless card, and speakers.

▲ When an internal component needs replacing, consider the possibility of disabling the component and using an external peripheral device in its place. Don't jeopardize the warranty on a laptop by opening the case or using components not authorized by the manufacturer.

▲ Replacing the laptop might be more cost effective than performing labor-intensive repairs, such as replacing the motherboard.

▲ When disassembling a laptop, the manufacturer's service manual is essential.

▲ When upgrading components on a laptop, including memory, use components that are the same brand as the laptop, or use only components recommended by the laptop's manufacturer.

▲ Follow the directions in a service manual to disassemble a laptop. Keep small screws organized as you disassemble a laptop because they come in a variety of sizes and lengths. Some manufacturers use plastic screws and recommend you use new screws rather than reuse the old ones.

▲ Special concerns when supporting a laptop also apply to supporting a netbook or all-in-one computer.

▲ Internal laptop components you might need to remove when replacing a FRU include the keyboard, hard drive, memory, smart card reader, optical drive, wireless card, screen, DC jack, battery pack, touch pad, speaker, system board, CPU, heat sink, and fan.

▲ An all-in-one computer uses a combination of components designed for desktop computers and laptops.

>> KEY TERMS

For explanations of key terms, see the Glossary for this text.

4-pin 12-V connector
8-pin 12-V connector
20-pin P1 connector
24-pin P1 connector
airplane mode
all-in-one computer
analog
ATX (Advanced Technology Extended)
ATX12V power supply
audio ports
base station
BIOS (basic input/output system)
Bluetooth
cellular network
central processing unit (CPU)
chassis
DB9 port
DB15 port
DE15 port
desktop case
digital
DIMM (dual inline memory module)
DisplayPort

docking port
docking station
dual-voltage selector switch
DVI (Digital Video Interface) port
electrostatic discharge (ESD)
Ethernet port
expansion card
external SATA (eSATA) port
firmware
form factors
front panel connectors
front panel header
GPS (Global Positioning System)
hard disk drive (HDD)
hard drive
HD15 port
HDMI (High-Definition Multimedia Interface) port
heat sink
internal components
keyboard backlight
laptop
loopback plug

main board
microATX (mATX)
microprocessor
modem port
Molex connector
motherboard
multimeter
netbook
network port
notebook
optical connector
PCI Express (PCIe)
PCIe 6/8-pin connector
port replicator
POST card
POST diagnostic card
POST (power-on self test)
power supply
power supply tester
power supply unit (PSU)
processor
PS/2 port
RAM (random access memory)
RJ-11 port
RJ-45 port
SATA power connector

screen orientation
serial ATA (SATA)
serial port
SO-DIMM (small outline DIMM)
spacers
SPDIF (Sony-Philips Digital Interface) sound port
spudgers
standoffs
system board
Thunderbolt 3 port
touch pad
tower case
UEFI (Unified Extensible Firmware Interface)
USB (Universal Serial Bus) port
USB optical drive
USB to Bluetooth adapter
USB to RJ-45 dongle
USB to Wi-Fi dongle
VGA (Video Graphics Array) port
video memory
Wi-Fi (Wireless Fidelity)
ZIF connectors

>> THINKING CRITICALLY

These questions are designed to prepare you for the critical thinking required for the A+ exams and may use content from other chapters and the web.

1. You purchase a new desktop computer that does not have wireless capability, and then you decide that you want to use a wireless connection to the Internet. What are the two least expensive ways (*choose two*) to upgrade your system to wireless?

   a. Trade in the computer for another computer that has wireless installed.

   b. Purchase a second computer that has wireless capability.

   c. Purchase a wireless expansion card and install it in your system.

   d. Purchase a USB wireless adapter and connect it to the computer by way of a USB port.

2. What type of computer is likely to use SO-DIMMs, have an internal power supply, and use a desktop processor socket?

3. When troubleshooting a computer hardware problem, which tool might help with each of the following problems?

   a. You suspect the network port on a computer is not functioning.

   b. The system fails at the beginning of the boot and nothing appears on the screen.

   c. A hard drive is not working and you suspect the Molex power connector from the power supply might be the source of the problem.

4. You disassemble and reassemble a desktop computer. When you first turn it on, you see no lights and hear no sounds. Nothing appears on the monitor screen. What is the most likely cause of the problem? Explain your answer.

   a. A memory module is not seated properly in a memory slot.

   b. You forgot to plug in the monitor's external power cord.

   c. A wire in the case is obstructing a fan.

   d. Power cords to the motherboard are not connected.

5. You are looking to buy a laptop on a budget that requires you to service and repair the laptop yourself, and you want to save money by not purchasing an extended service agreement beyond the first year. To limit your search, what should you consider when choosing manufacturers? Which manufacturers would you choose and why?

6. A four-year-old laptop will not boot and presents error messages on screen. You have verified with the laptop technical support that these error messages indicate the motherboard has failed and needs replacing. What is the order of steps you should take to prepare for the repair?

   a. Ask yourself if replacing the motherboard will cost more than purchasing a new laptop.

   b. Find a replacement motherboard.

   c. Find the service manual to show you how to replace the motherboard.

   d. Ask yourself if the laptop is still under warranty.

7. Why are laptops usually more expensive than desktop computers with comparable power and features?

8. When a laptop internal device fails, what three options can you use to deal with the problem?

9. A friend was just promoted to a new job that requires part-time travel, and he has also been promised a new laptop after his first month with the company. He needs an easy way to disconnect and reconnect all his peripheral devices to his old laptop. Devices include two external monitors (one HDMI, one DVI), a USB wireless mouse, USB wireless keyboard, Ethernet network, USB printer, headphones, and microphone. He has a budget of $100. What kind of device would best suit his needs? Why? Research online to find a recommendation for a device that will work best for him. What is your recommendation and why?

10. Your laptop LCD panel is blank when you boot up. You can hear the laptop turn on, and the keyboard backlight is on. You have checked the brightness using the function keys, and that is not the problem. What is an easy next step to determine if the LCD panel has failed? Describe how that next step can also help if the LCD panel has failed, but the replacement components won't arrive for a week and you still need to use your laptop.

11. A foreign exchange student brought his desktop computer from his home in Europe to the United States. He brought a power adapter so that the power cord would plug into the power outlet. He tried turning on his computer, but it wouldn't power on. What is likely the problem? What should you warn him about when he returns home at the end of the year?

12. You're building a new desktop computer from parts you picked out and purchased. You invested a good deal of money in this computer and want to be sure to protect your investment while you assemble it. What precautions should you take to protect your computer from damage and electrostatic discharge?

13. Your friend asks for your help because her laptop screen is too dim to read anything. What is the first step you should take to fix the problem?

14. Your boss asks you to give a presentation and you need to use a projector to show a slideshow. What are the steps to display the slideshow on both your laptop and the projector simultaneously?

15. After troubleshooting a problem, you decide that the wireless card has failed in a laptop. What do you do first before you disassemble the laptop?

>> HANDS-ON PROJECTS

Hands-On | Project 1-1 Opening a Computer Case

Using a desktop or tower computer, identify all the ports on the front or rear of the case. If you need help, see Table 1-1. Look at the rear of the case. On which side is the motherboard? Examine the case and determine how to open it. Shut down the system and unplug the power cable. Disconnect all other cables. Press the power button on the front of the case to discharge residual power. Carefully open the case. Remember not to touch anything inside the case unless you are using an ESD strap or antistatic gloves to protect components against ESD.

Draw a diagram of the inside of the case and label all drives, the motherboard, the cooler, DIMM memory modules, the power supply, and any expansion cards installed, then do the following:

1. Write down how many power cables are coming from the power supply. How many of these cables are connected to the motherboard? To other devices inside the computer? Identify each type of power cable the system is using.

2. For the motherboard, list the number and type of expansion slots on the board. Does the board have a 20-pin or 24-pin P1 connector? What other power connectors are on the board? How many memory slots does the board have? Locate the screws that attach the motherboard to the case. How many screws are used? Do you see screw holes in the motherboard that are not being used? As a general rule of thumb, up to nine screws can be used to attach a motherboard to a case.

3. For expansion cards, examine the ports on the back of the card. Can you determine the purpose of the card by looking at its ports? What type of slot does the card use?

Leave the case open so you'll be ready for Hands-On Project 1-2 next.

Hands-On | Project 1-2 Identifying Connectors Used on an Installed Motherboard

If necessary, remove the case cover to your desktop computer. Next, remove the expansion cards from your system. With the expansion cards out of the way, you can more clearly see the power cables and other cables and cords connected to the motherboard. Diagrams and notes are extremely useful when disassembling and reassembling a system. To practice this skill, draw a large rectangle that represents the motherboard. On the rectangle, label every header or connector that is used on the board. Note on the label the type of cable that is used and where the other end of the cable connects.

Hands-On | Project 1-3 Identifying Drives and Their Connectors

If your instructor has provided a display of drives, identify the purpose of each drive (for example, a hard drive or optical drive) and the type of power connector each drive uses (for example, SATA or Molex). If you have access to a computer with the case cover removed, answer the following questions:

1. List the drives installed, the purpose of each drive, and the type of interface and power connector it uses.
2. How many connectors does the motherboard have for drives? Identify each type of connector (SATA or PATA).

Hands-On | Project 1-4 Closing the Case

The case cover to your desktop computer is off from doing the previous exercises. Before you close your case, it's always a good idea to quickly clean it first. Using a can of compressed air, blow the dust away from fans and other components inside the case. Be careful not to touch components unless you are properly grounded. When you're done, close the case cover.

Hands-On | Project 1-5 Observing Laptop Features

Do the following to find a service manual for a laptop you have available, such as one that belongs to you or a friend:

1. What are the brand, model, and serial number of the laptop?
2. What is the website of the laptop manufacturer? Print or save a webpage on that site that shows the documentation and/or drivers available for this laptop.
3. If the website provides a service manual for disassembling the laptop, download the manual. Print two or three pages from the manual showing the title page and table of contents for the manual.
4. If the website does not provide a service manual, search the Internet for the manual. If you find it, download it and print the title page and table of contents.

After examining a laptop, its documentation, and the manufacturer's website, answer these questions:

1. What ports are on the laptop?
2. What type of memory slots does the laptop have?
3. List the purpose of each function key on the keyboard.
4. List the purpose of each button on the top or bottom of the keyboard.
5. What is the cost of a new battery pack?

>> REAL PROBLEMS, REAL SOLUTIONS

REAL PROBLEM 1-1 Planning Your Computer Repair Toolkit

Do research on the web to find the following tools for sale: ESD strap, set of flathead and Phillips-head screwdrivers, can of compressed air, monitor cleaning wipes, multimeter, power supply tester, cable ties, flashlight, loopback plug to test an Ethernet port, POST diagnostic card, and toolbox.

   Print or save the webpages that show each tool and its price. What is the total cost of this set of tools? If you were building your own computer repair toolkit, which tools would you purchase first if you could not afford the entire set of tools? Which tools not listed would you add to your toolbox?

REAL PROBLEM 1-2 Setting Up a Service Center for Laptops

If you intend to set up your own computer repair shop, you might want to consider becoming a service center for a few brands of the more popular laptops. Reasons to become an authorized service center include having access to service manuals, parts lists, and wholesale parts for laptops. Do the following to research becoming an authorized service center:

1. Select a brand of laptops that you think you would like to service.

2. Research the website of this manufacturer and answer these questions:

   a. Where is the closest authorized service center for this brand of laptops?

   b. What are the requirements to become an authorized service center? Print or save the webpage showing the requirements.

   c. Is A+ certification one of those requirements?

   d. Some laptop manufacturers offer a program that falls short of becoming an authorized service center but does provide support for IT professionals so that repair technicians can order laptop parts. Does the manufacturer offer this service? If so, what must you do to qualify?

   If you try one brand of laptop and can't find the information you need, try another brand. Sometimes this information can only be obtained by contacting the manufacturer directly. And one more hint: To use *google.com* to search a particular site, begin the search string with *site:hostname.com*.

REAL PROBLEM 1-3 Taking Apart a Laptop

If you enjoy putting together thousand-piece jigsaw puzzles, you'll probably enjoy working on laptop computers. With desktop systems, replacing a component is not a time-consuming task, but with laptops, the job could take half a day. If you take the time to carefully examine the laptop's case before attempting to open it, you will probably find markings provided by the manufacturer to assist you in locating components that are commonly upgraded. If you have a service manual, your work will be much easier than without one.

   The best way to learn how to disassemble a laptop is to practice on an old one that you can afford to break. Find an old Dell, Lenovo, or IBM ThinkPad for which you can download the service manual from the appropriate website. Carefully and patiently follow the disassembly instructions and then reassemble the laptop. When done, you can congratulate yourself and move on to newer laptops.

All About Motherboards

After completing this chapter, you will be able to:

- Describe and contrast various types and features of motherboards

- Configure a motherboard using BIOS/UEFI firmware

- Maintain a motherboard by updating drivers and firmware, using jumpers to clear BIOS/UEFI settings, and replacing the CMOS battery

- Select, install, and replace a desktop motherboard or laptop system board

In Chapter 1, you learned how to work inside a desktop or laptop computer and began the process of learning about each major component or subsystem in a computer case. In this chapter, you build on all that knowledge to learn about motherboards, which techies sometimes call the mobo. You'll learn about motherboard sizes (called form factors), connectors, expansion slots, sockets, onboard ports, and chipsets. Then you'll learn how to support a motherboard, which includes configuring, maintaining, installing, and replacing it. A motherboard is considered a field replaceable unit, so it's important to know how to replace one, but the good news is you don't need to know how to repair one that is broken. Troubleshooting a motherboard works hand in hand with troubleshooting the processor and other components that must work to boot up a computer, so we'll leave troubleshooting the motherboard until later chapters.

MOTHERBOARD TYPES AND FEATURES

**A+
CORE 1
1.1, 3.5**

A motherboard is the most complicated component in a computer. When you put together a computer from parts, generally you start by deciding which processor and motherboard you will use. Everything else follows these two decisions. Take a look at the details of Figure 2-1, which shows an ATX motherboard, the Asus Prime Z370-P, that can hold various Intel Core i7, Core i5, Core i3, or Pentium processors in the LGA1151 8th generation processor socket. When selecting a motherboard, generally you need to pay attention to the form factor, processor socket, chipset, expansion slots, and other connectors, slots, and ports. In this part of the chapter, we'll look at the details of each of these features so that you can read a technical motherboard ad with the knowledge of a pro and know how to select the right motherboard when replacing an existing one or building a new system.

Four PCIe ×4 slots

LGA1151 socket
with CPU installed

Intel Z370 chipset

Two PCIe ×16 slots

Three DIMM slots with two
DDR4 DIMMs installed

Figure 2-1 The Asus Prime Z370-P gaming motherboard uses the ATX form factor and LGA1151 8th generation process socket

MOTHERBOARD FORM FACTORS

**A+
CORE 1
3.5**

The motherboard form factor determines the size of the board and its features that make it compatible with power supplies and cases. The most popular motherboard form factors are ATX, microATX (a smaller version of ATX, sometimes called the mATX), and Mini-ITX, also called mITX (a smaller version of microATX). You saw an ATX motherboard in Figure 2-1. Figure 2-2 shows an mATX board, and a Mini-ITX board is shown in Figure 2-3. The Mini-ITX board is also commonly referred to as an ITX board.

Conventional PCI slot
Two PCIe ×1 slots
PCIe ×16 slot

Cooler with
CPU below

Four memory
modules
(DIMMs)

Chipset under
heat sink

Figure 2-2 The Intel desktop motherboard DH676D uses the mATX form factor and has the processor, cooler, and memory modules installed

Source: Courtesy of ASUSTeK Computer, Inc.

Figure 2-3 A Mini-ITX motherboard

Table 2-1 lists form factor sizes and descriptions, and Figure 2-4 shows a comparison of the sizes and hole positions of the boards. Each of these three boards can fit into an ATX computer case and use an ATX power supply.

Form Factor	Motherboard Size	Description
ATX, full size	Up to 12" × 9.6" (305mm × 244mm)	A popular form factor that has had many revisions and variations.
microATX (aka mATX)	Up to 9.6" × 9.6" (244mm × 244mm)	A smaller version of ATX.
Mini-ITX (aka mITX and ITX)	Up to 6.7" × 6.7" (170mm × 170mm)	A small form factor (SFF) board used in low-end computers and home theater systems. The boards are often used with an Intel Celeron or Atom processor and are sometimes purchased as a motherboard-processor combo unit.

Table 2-1   Three motherboard form factors

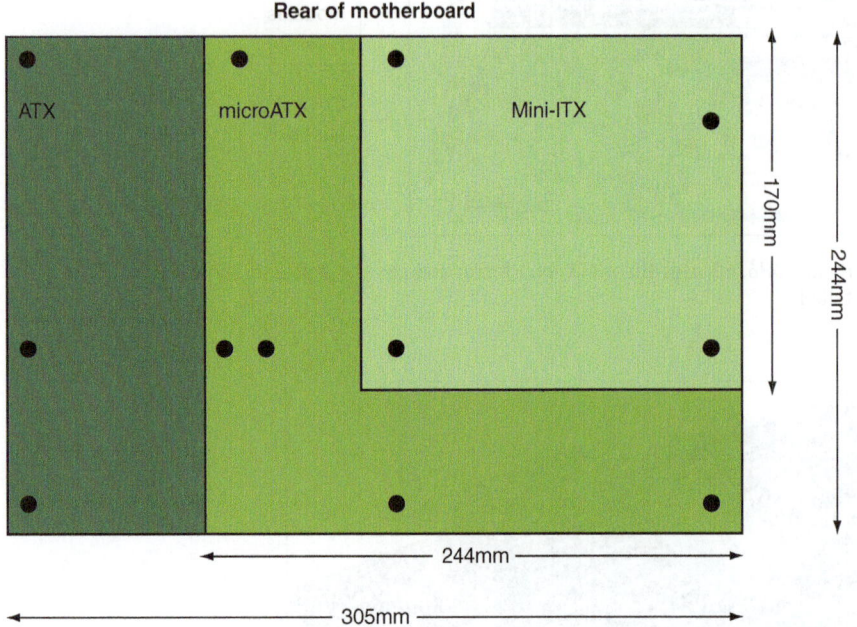

Figure 2-4   Sizes and hole positions for the ATX, microATX, and Mini-ITX motherboards

★ A+ Exam Tip The A+ Core 1 exam expects you to know how to match up an ATX, mATX, ITX, or mITX motherboard with the appropriate case and power supply that support the same form factor.

INTEL AND AMD CHIPSETS AND PROCESSOR SOCKETS

A+ CORE 1 3.5

A chipset is a set of chips on the motherboard that works closely with the processor to collectively control the memory, buses on the motherboard, and some peripherals. The chipset must be compatible with the processor it serves. A socket is rectangular with pins or pads to connect the processor to the motherboard and a mechanism to hold the processor in place. This chipset and socket determine which processors a board can support.

The two major chipset and processor manufacturers are Intel (*intel.com*) and AMD (*amd.com*). Intel dominates the chipset market for several reasons: It knows more about its own Intel processors than other manufacturers do, and it produces the chipsets most compatible with the Intel family of processors.

INTEL CHIPSETS

Intel makes desktop, mobile, and server chipsets and processors. To see a complete comparison chart of all Intel chipsets and processors, start at the Intel link *ark.intel.com*. Intel groups its chipsets and processors in generations, and each generation has a code name. Here is the list of generations from the past five years or so:

▲ *Coffee Lake.* The latest generation of chipsets and processors is the 8th generation, also called Coffee Lake, which began shipping at the end of 2017. The desktop processors use a revised version of the older LGA1151 socket and the new 300 Series chipset—for example, the Z370 chipset. The Coffee Lake LGA1151 socket is not backward compatible with 7th or 6th generation processors that use the first version of LGA1151. (The number of pins is the same, but how the pins are used is different; the newer socket also provides more wattage for processors.) The Coffee Lake 300 Series chipset uses only DDR4 memory, currently the fastest type of memory for personal computers. The 8th generation mobile processors fall into two groups: the Coffee Lake H-series processors and the Kaby Lake Refresh processors. Look back at Figure 2-1 where the Z370 chipset and LGA1151 8th generation socket and processor are labeled. A close-up of this open socket is shown in Figure 2-5.

Figure 2-5   The 8th generation LGA1151 socket with the cover removed and load
plate lifted, ready to receive the processor

▲ *Kaby Lake.* The 7th generation desktop processors and chipsets, also called Kaby Lake, began shipping in 2016 and mobile processors were launched in 2017. Desktop processors use the first version of the LGA1151 socket.

▲ *Skylake.* The 6th generation processors and chipsets, also called Skylake, was launched in 2015. The processors were the first to use the LGA1151 socket. Other improvements over previous generations include faster and more efficient chipsets and use of faster DDR4 memory. Skylake chipsets are able to use the older and slower DDR3 memory only if it is low-voltage DDR3.

▲ *Broadwell and Haswell.* The 5th generation (Broadwell) and the 4th generation (Haswell) processors work with the older LGA1150 and LGA2011 processor sockets.

🖉 **Notes** The 9th generation, or Cannon Lake processors and chipsets, is expected to be released by the time this text is published.

Since the release of the 2nd generation Intel Core family of processors, you can know which generation a processor fits in by the four digits in the model number. The first of the four digits is the generation. For example, the Core i5-6200U processor is a 6th generation processor, and the Core i5-7500 processor is a 7th generation processor.

SOCKETS FOR INTEL PROCESSORS

The Intel name for a socket includes the number of pins the socket has. Intel uses a land grid array (LGA) for all its current sockets. These sockets have blunt pins that project up to connect with lands on the bottom of the processor. You can see these lands when you look closely at Figure 2-5.

Here are the current Intel sockets for desktop computers:

▲ The LGA1151 socket was first released in 2015. The first release of the socket works with Intel's 7th and 6th generation processors and chipsets and is shown in Figure 2-6. The second release works with Intel 8th generation processors and chipsets.

Figure 2-6 The 7th and 6th generation LGA1151 open socket and the bottom of an Intel processor

▲ The LGA1150 socket, shown in Figure 2-7, works with the 5th and 4th generation of chipsets and processors.
▲ The LGA1155 socket is used for 3rd and 2nd generation chipsets and processors.

Figure 2-7 The LGA1150 socket with the protective cover installed

Here are the Intel sockets used in servers and high-performance workstations:

▲ The LGA2066 socket is used with 8th through 6th generation processors and chipsets. It was introduced with Skylake-X high-end 6th generation processors in 2017.

▲ LGA2011 is used with 5th through 2nd generation processors and chipsets and has several variations for different generations, including LGA2011-0, LGA2011-1, and LGA2011-v3.

▲ LGA1366 is used with 4th through 1st generation processors and chipsets; it was discontinued in 2012 and introduced in 2008. The LGA1366 socket is shown in Figure 2-8.

Figure 2-8 The LGA1366 socket with the socket cover removed and the load plate lifted ready to receive a processor

> ⚡ **Caution** When a processor is installed in a socket, extreme care must be taken to protect the socket and the processor against ESD and from damage caused by bending the pins or scratching the processor pads during the installation. Take care not to touch the bottom of the processor or the pins of the socket, which can leave finger oil on the gold plating of the contact surfaces. This oil can later cause tarnishing and lead to a poor contact.

So that even force is applied when inserting the processor in the socket, sockets have one or two levers on the sides. These sockets are called zero insertion force (ZIF) sockets, and the levers are used to lift the processor up and out of the socket. When you push the levers down, the processor moves into its pin connectors with equal force over the entire housing. Because the socket and processor are delicate, processors generally should not be removed or replaced repeatedly.

AMD CHIPSETS AND SOCKETS

Currently, AMD has four chipset and socket categories for personal computers:

▲ The TR4 (Threadripper 4) socket is a land grid array (LGA) socket that supports Threadripper processors and uses the AMD X399 chipset. The Threadripper processors are part of the AMD Ryzen series of high-end processors.

▲ The AM4 chipset family and AM4 socket is used with AMD Ryzen and Athlon processors. AMD chipsets in the AM4 family include A300, B300, and X300. The processors and chipsets support mainstream desktop systems. The socket has 1331 pins in a pin grid array (PGA), which means the socket has 1331 holes and the AMD processor has 1331 pins that fit into the socket holes.

▲ The AM3+ and AM3 are PGA sockets used with AMD Piledriver and Bulldozer processors and the 9-series chipsets, including 970, 980G, and 990X. The processors and chipsets are used in high-end gaming systems. AM3+ and AM3 processors can fit in either socket. Figure 2-9 shows the AM3+ socket and the bottom of the AMD FX processor.

Figure 2-9 The AMD AM3+ open socket; notice the holes in the socket and pins on the bottom of the processor

◢ The FM2+ is an older PGA socket used with AMD Athlon, Steamroller, and Excavator processors and A-series chipsets such as the A58 and A68H.

MATCH A PROCESSOR TO THE SOCKET AND MOTHERBOARD

For both Intel and AMD, the processor families (for example, Intel Core i3, Intel Core i5, AMD Athlon, or AMD Ryzen) are used with various chipset generations and sockets. Therefore, you must pay close attention to the actual model number of the processor to know which socket it requires and which motherboards can support it. If you install a processor on a motherboard that can fit the socket but has the wrong chipset for the processor, you can damage both the motherboard and the processor. Sometimes, you can install a newer processor on an older motherboard by first updating the firmware on the motherboard, which you learn to do later in this chapter. To match a processor to a motherboard and socket:

◢ Look at the motherboard manufacturer's website or user guide for a list of processors the motherboard supports. If a motherboard requires a firmware update to use a newer processor, the motherboard manufacturer's website will alert you and provide the downloaded firmware update. How to update chipset firmware is covered later in this chapter. If an update is required, you must update the firmware before you install the new processor.

◢ You can also search the Intel (*ark.intel.com*) or AMD (*amd.com*) website for the exact processor to make sure the socket it uses is the same as the socket on the motherboard. You can also use the website to find other information about the processor.

> ⭐ **A+ Exam Tip** The A+ Core 1 exam does not expect you to be familiar with the processor sockets used by laptop computers. It is generally more cost effective to replace a laptop that has a damaged processor than to replace the processor. If you are called on to replace a laptop processor, however, always use a processor the laptop manufacturer recommends for the particular laptop model and system board CPU socket.

BUSES AND EXPANSION SLOTS

When you look carefully at a motherboard, you may see many fine lines on both the top and the bottom of the board's surface (see Figure 2-10). These lines, sometimes called traces, are circuits or paths that enable data, instructions, timing signals, and power to move from component to component on the board. This system of pathways used for communication and the protocol and methods used for transmission are collectively called a bus. (A protocol is a set of rules and standards that any two entities use for communication.)

Figure 2-10   On the bottom of the motherboard, you can see bus lines terminating at the processor socket

The specifications of a motherboard always include the expansion slots on the board. Take a look at a motherboard ad that shows detailed specifications and identify the types of expansion slots on the board. Table 2-2 lists the various expansion slots found on today's motherboards.

Expansion Slot or Internal Connector	Performance	Year Introduced
Each revision of PCI Express basically doubles the throughput of the previous revision.		
PCI Express Version 5.0	Up to 63 GB/sec for 16 lanes	Expected in 2019
PCI Express Version 4.0	Up to 32 GB/sec for 16 lanes	2017
PCI Express Version 3.0	Up to 16 GB/sec for 16 lanes	2010
PCI Express Version 2.0	Up to 8 GB/sec for 16 lanes	2007
Conventional **PCI (Peripheral Component Interconnect)** slots transfer data at about 500 MB/sec and have gone through several variations, but only the latest variation is seen on today's motherboards. A notch in the slot prevents the wrong type of PCI card from installing. The standard has been replaced by PCI Express.		
SATA (Serial Advanced Technology Attachment or Serial ATA) connectors on a motherboard are mostly used by storage devices, such as hard drives or optical drives.		
SATA3 (Revisions 3.2 and 3.3) aka SATA 6.0 (for speed)	6 Gb/sec or 600 MB/sec	2008
SATA2 (Revision 2) aka SATA 3.0 (for speed)	3 Gb/sec or 300 MB/sec	2004
USB (Universal Serial Bus) might have internal connectors and external ports, which are used by a variety of USB devices.		
USB 3.2, 3.1, and 3.0	Up to 5 Gb/sec	2011–2017
USB 2.0	480 Mb/sec	2001

Table 2-2   Expansion slots and internal connectors listed by throughput

Now let's look at the details of the PCI and PCIe expansion slots used in desktops.

PCI EXPRESS

PCI Express (PCIe) currently comes in four different slot sizes called PCI Express ×1 (pronounced "by one"), ×4, ×8, and ×16. Figure 2-11 shows three of these slots. Notice in the figure the notch in the slot, which prevents a card from being inserted in the wrong direction or in the wrong slot.

Figure 2-11 Three types of expansion slots: PCIe ×1, PCIe ×16, and conventional PCI

A PCIe ×1 slot contains a single lane for data. PCIe ×4 has 4 lanes, PCIe ×8 has 8 lanes, and PCIe ×16 has 16. The more lanes an add-on card uses, the more data is transmitted in a given time. Data is transferred over 1, 4, 8, or 16 lanes, which means that a 16-lane slot is faster than a shorter slot when the add-on card in the slot is using all 16 lanes. If you install a short card in a long slot, the card uses only the lanes it connects to. PCIe is used by a variety of add-on cards. The PCIe ×16 slot is used by graphics cards that require large throughput.

Less expensive motherboards may not have a full PCIe ×16 bus and yet provide PCIe ×16 slots. The longer cards can fit in the ×16 slot but only use 4 lanes for data transfers. The version of PCIe also matters; the latest currently available is Version 4, which is the fastest. (Version 5 is expected to be released in 2019.) Learn to read motherboard ads carefully. For example, look at the ad snippet shown in Figure 2-12. One of the longer PCIe ×16 slots operates in ×4 mode, only using 4 lanes, and uses the PCIe Version 2 standard. If you were to install a graphics card in one of these two PCIe ×16 slots, you would want to be sure you install it in the faster of the two ×16 slots.

2

Slots	- 1 x PCI Express 3.0 x16 Slot (PCIE2: x16 mode)
	- 1 x PCI Express 2.0 x16 Slot (PCIE4: x4 mode)
	- 2 x PCI Express 2.0 x1 Slots
	- 2 x PCI Slots
	- Supports AMD Quad CrossFireX™ and CrossFireX™
	*If PCIE1 or PCIE3 slot is occupied, PCIE4 slot will run at x2 mode.

Figure 2-12 PCIe documentation for one motherboard

A graphics card that uses a PCIe ×16 slot may require as much as 450 watts. A typical PCIe ×16 slot provides 75 watts to a card installed in it. To provide the extra wattage for the card, a motherboard may have power connectors near the ×16 slot, and the graphics card may have one, two, or even three connectors to connect the card to the extra power (see Figure 2-13). Possibilities for these connectors are a 6-pin PCIe (which provides 75 watts) and/or an 8-pin PCIe connector (which provides 150 watts), a 4-pin Molex connector, or a SATA-style connector. Connect power cords from the power supply to the power connector type you find on the graphics card. Alternately, some motherboards provide Molex or SATA power connectors on the board to power PCIe graphics cards. See Figure 2-14. When installing a graphics card, always follow the manufacturer's directions for connecting auxiliary power for the card. If the card requires extra wattage, the package will include power cords you need for the installation.

Figure 2-13 The graphics card has a PCIe 8-pin power connector on top

Molex-style power connector

SATA-style power connector

Figure 2-14 Auxiliary power connectors to support PCIe

PCI

Conventional PCI slots and buses are slower than those of PCI Express. The slots are slightly taller than PCIe slots (look carefully at the two PCI slots labeled in Figure 2-11); they are positioned slightly closer to the rear of the computer case, and the notch in the slot is near the front of the slot. The PCI bus transports 32 data bits in parallel and operates at about 500 Mbps. The PCI slots are used for all types of add-on cards, such as Ethernet network cards, wireless cards, and sound cards. Although most graphics cards use PCIe, you can buy PCI video cards to use if your PCIe slots are not working.

RISER CARDS USED TO EXTEND THE SLOTS

Suppose you are installing a Mini-ITX or microATX motherboard into a low-profile or slimline case that does not give you enough room to install an expansion card standing up in a slot. In this situation, a riser card can solve the problem. The riser card installs in the slot and provides another slot at a right angle (see Figure 2-15). When you install an expansion card in this riser card slot, the card sits parallel to the motherboard, taking up less space. These riser cards come for all types of PCI and PCIe slots.

Inserts in
motherboard
slot

Right-angle slot
for expansion
card

Figure 2-15   The PCI riser card provides a slot for an expansion card installed
parallel to the motherboard

> **Notes** Be careful that cards installed in slots on a riser card are properly supported. It's not a good idea to install a heavy and expensive graphics card in an improperly supported riser card slot.

ONBOARD PORTS AND CONNECTORS

In addition to expansion slots, a motherboard might also have several ports and internal connectors. Ports coming directly off the motherboard are called onboard ports or integrated components. For external ports, the motherboard provides an I/O panel of ports that stick out the rear of the case. These ports may include multiple USB ports, PS/2 mouse and keyboard ports, video ports (HDMI, DVI-D, DVI-I, or DisplayPort), sound ports, a LAN RJ-45 port (to connect to the network), and an eSATA port (for external SATA drives). Figure 2-16 shows ports on an entry-level desktop motherboard.

PS/2 keyboard/
mouse combo port

Ethernet (RJ-45) port

Three sound ports

Two USB 2.0
ports

DVI-D port

HDMI port

Four blue
USB 3.0 ports

Figure 2-16 A motherboard provides ports for common I/O devices

When you purchase a motherboard, the package includes an I/O shield, which is the plate you install in the computer case that provides holes for the I/O ports. The I/O shield is the size designed for the case's form factor, and the holes in the shield are positioned for the motherboard ports (see Figure 2-17).

Figure 2-17 The I/O shield fits the motherboard ports to the computer case

A motherboard might have several internal connectors, including USB, M.2, SATA, and IDE connectors. When you purchase a motherboard, look in the package for the motherboard manual, which is either printed or on DVD; you can also find the manual online at the manufacturer's website. The manual will show a diagram of the board with a description of each connector. For example, the connectors for the motherboard in Figure 2-18 are labeled as the manual describes them. If a connector is a group of pins sticking up on the board, the connector is called a header. You will learn to use most of these connectors in later chapters.

Next is a rundown of the internal connectors you need to know about.

| Audio connector | Serial connector | Two USB 2.0 connectors | USB 3.1 connector | System panel header |

Figure 2-18   Internal connectors on a motherboard for front panel ports

SATA

SATA (Serial Advanced Technology Attachment or Serial ATA), pronounced "*say*-ta," is an interface standard used mostly by storage devices. To attach a SATA drive to a motherboard, you need a data connection to the motherboard and a power connection to the power supply. Figure 2-19 shows a motherboard with seven SATA connectors. Six use the SATA3 standard and one is a shorter SATA Express connector.

Figure 2-19   Seven SATA connectors on a motherboard

The following are currently used versions of SATA:

◢ SATA Express (SATAe) combines SATA and PCIe to provide a faster bus than SATA3, although the standard is seldom used.
◢ SATA3 (generation 3) is commonly known by its throughput as SATA 6Gb/s.
◢ SATA2 (generation 2) is commonly known by its throughput as SATA 3Gb/s.

M.2

The M.2 connector, formally known as the Next Generation Form Factor (NGFF), uses the PCIe, USB, or SATA interface to connect a mini add-on card. The card fits flat against the motherboard and is secured with a single screw. Figure 2-20 shows the slot and three screws for M.2 cards. The three screws allow for the installation of cards of three different lengths.

Figure 2-20 An M.2 slot and three possible screw positions to secure a card to the motherboard

The M.2 connector or slot was first used on laptops and is now common on desktop motherboards. It is commonly used by wireless cards and solid-state drives (SSDs). When the PCIe interface is used, the slot is faster than all the SATA standards normally used by hard drives; therefore, the M.2 slot is often the choice to support the SSD that will hold the Windows installation. However, before you plan to install Windows on an M.2 drive, make sure the motherboard BIOS/UEFI firmware will boot from an M.2 device. (Look for the option in the boot priority order in BIOS/UEFI setup, which is discussed later in this chapter.)

Be aware there are multiple M.2 standards and M.2 slots. An M.2 slot is keyed for certain M.2 cards by matching keys on the slot with notches on the card. Figure 2-21 shows three popular options, although other options exist. Before purchasing an M.2 card, make sure the card matches the M.2 slot and uses an interface standard the slot supports. For example, for one motherboard, the M.2 slot uses either the PCIe or SATA interface. When a card that uses the SATA interface is installed in the slot, the motherboard uses SATA for the M.2 interface and disables one of the SATA connectors. When a PCIe M.2 card is installed, the motherboard uses the PCIe interface for the slot.

Figure 2-21 An M.2 slot is keyed with a notch to hold an M.2 card with a B key or M key edge connector

IDE

Years ago the IDE (Integrated Drive Electronics) standard was used to interface storage devices with the motherboard. An IDE connector has 40 pins and uses a wide ribbon with a 40-pin connector in the middle of the cable and another connector at the other end of the cable to connect two storage devices (hard drives or optical drives). Figure 2-22 shows an IDE connector on a motherboard and an IDE cable. These older storage devices received their power from the power supply by way of a Molex power cord.

Figure 2-22 An IDE connector and cable

★ **A+ Exam Tip** The A+ Core 1 exam expects you to be able to recognize SATA, IDE, M.2, and USB internal motherboard connectors and decide which connector to use in a given scenario.

USB

A motherboard may have USB headers or USB connectors. (Recall that a header is a connector with pins sticking up.) The USB header is used to connect a cable from the motherboard to USB ports on the front of the computer case (see Figure 2-23).

Two USB 2.0 connectors

Figure 2-23 Two USB headers are used to connect the motherboard to USB ports on the front of the computer case

APPLYING | CONCEPTS   FINDING THE MOTHERBOARD DOCUMENTATION

The motherboard manual or user guide is essential to identifying components on a board and knowing how to support the board. This guide can be a PDF file stored on the CD or DVD that came bundled with the motherboard. If you don't have the CD, you can download the user guide from the motherboard manufacturer's website.

(continues)

To find the correct user guide online, you need to know the board manufacturer and model. If a motherboard is already installed in a computer, you can use BIOS/UEFI setup or the Windows System Information utility (msinfo32.exe) to report the brand and model of the board. To access System Information for Windows 10 or Windows 7, enter **msinfo32.exe** in the search box. (For Windows 8 or 8.1, right-click **Start**, click **Run**, and enter **msinfo32.exe** in the Run box.) In the System Information window, click **System Summary**. In the System Summary information in the right pane, look for the motherboard information labeled as the System Manufacturer and System Model (see Figure 2-24).

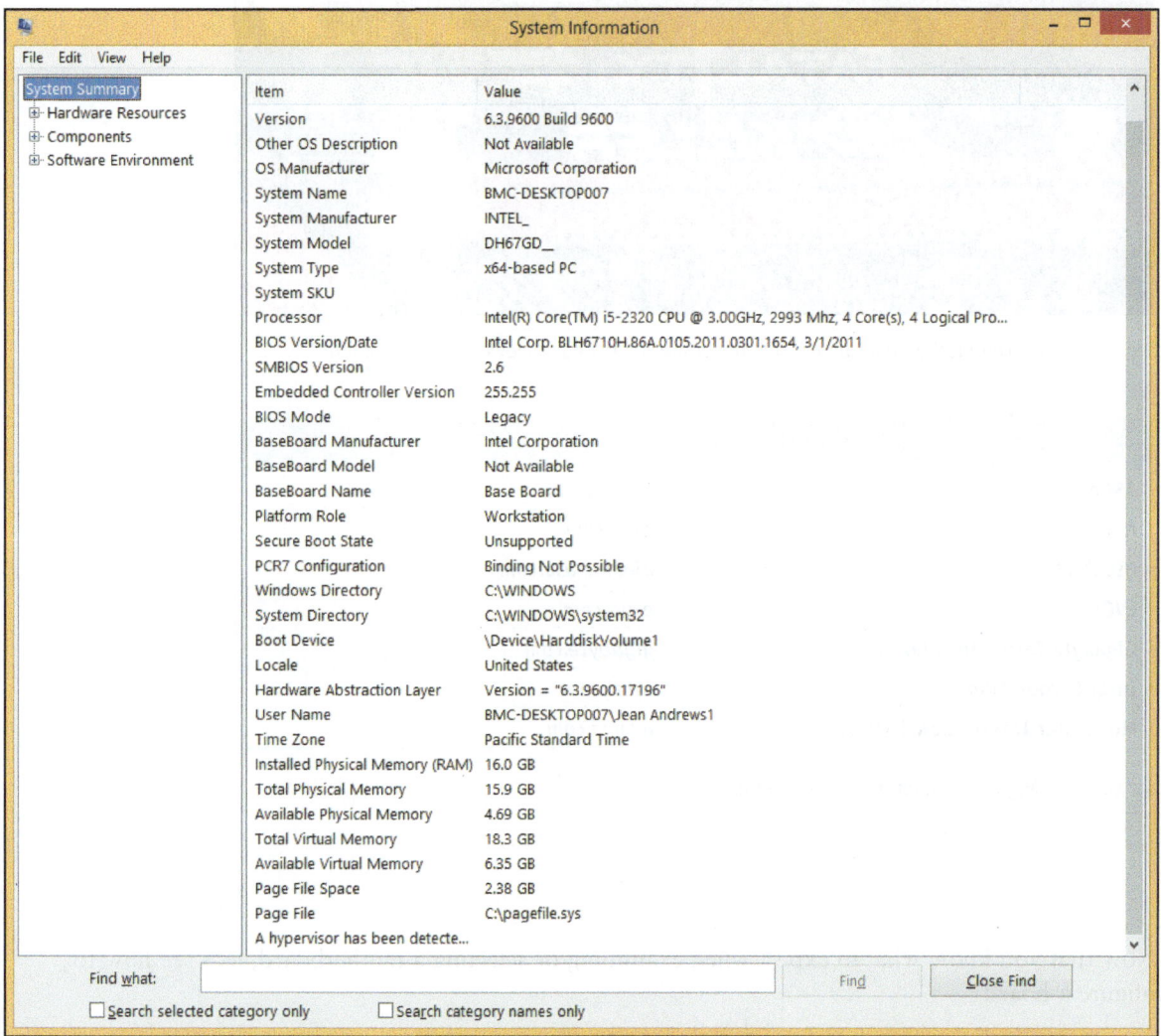

Figure 2-24   Use the system information window to identify the motherboard brand and model

If the motherboard is not installed or the system is not working, look for the brand and model imprinted somewhere on the motherboard (see Figure 2-25). Next, go to the website of the motherboard manufacturer and download the user guide. Websites for several motherboard manufacturers are listed in Table 2-3. The diagrams, pictures, charts, and explanations of settings and components in the user guide will be invaluable to you when supporting this board.

(continues)

Figure 2-25   The motherboard brand and model are imprinted somewhere on the board

Manufacturer	Web Address
ASRock	asrock.com
ASUS	asus.com
BIOSTAR	biostar-usa.com
EVGA	evga.com
Gigabyte Technology Co., Ltd.	gigabyte.com
Intel Corporation	intel.com
Micro-Star International (MSI)	us.msi.com

Table 2-3   Major manufacturers of motherboards

Now that you know what to expect when examining or selecting a motherboard, let's see how to configure a board.

USING BIOS/UEFI SETUP TO CONFIGURE A MOTHERBOARD

**A+
CORE 1
3.5**

Firmware on the motherboard is used to enable or disable a connector, port, or component; control the frequency and other features of the CPU; manage security features; control what happens when the computer first boots; and monitor and log various activities of the board.

Motherboards made after 2012 use BIOS/UEFI firmware; prior to 2012, all motherboards used BIOS firmware. UEFI (Unified Extensible Firmware Interface) improves on BIOS but includes BIOS for backward compatibility with older devices. UEFI is managed by several manufacturers and developers under the UEFI Forum (see *uefi.org*).

Facts you need to know about UEFI include:

⬛ Microsoft requires UEFI in order for a system to be certified for Windows 10/8.
⬛ UEFI is required for hard drives larger than 2 TB. (One terabyte or TB equals 1000 gigabytes or GB.) A hard drive uses one of two methods for partitioning the drive: The Master Boot Record (MBR) method is older, allows for four partitions, and is limited to 2-TB drives. The GUID Partition Table (GPT) method is newer, allows for any size of hard drive, and, for Windows, can have up to 128 partitions on the drive. GPT is required for drives larger than 2 TB or for systems that boot using UEFI firmware.
⬛ UEFI offers Secure boot, which prevents a system from booting up with drivers or an OS that is not digitally signed and trusted by the motherboard or computer manufacturer. For Secure boot to work, the OS must support UEFI.
⬛ For backward compatibility, UEFI can boot from an MBR hard drive and provide a BIOS boot through its Compatibility Support Module (CSM) feature. CSM is backward compatible with devices and drivers that use BIOS.

The motherboard settings don't normally need to be changed except, for example, when you are first setting up the system, when there is a problem with hardware or the OS, or a power-saving feature or security feature (such as a power-on password) needs to be disabled or enabled.

> ⭐ **A+ Exam Tip** The A+ Core 1 exam expects you to know about BIOS/UEFI settings for boot options, firmware updates, security settings, and interface configurations. Security settings include passwords, drive encryption, the TPM chip, LoJack, and Secure boot. All these settings and features are covered in this part of the chapter. In a given scenario, you need to know which BIOS/UEFI setting to use to solve a problem, install a new component or feature, or secure a system.

ACCESSING THE BIOS/UEFI SETUP PROGRAM

You access the BIOS/UEFI setup program by pressing a key or combination of keys during the boot process; for some laptops, you press a button on the side of the laptop. For most motherboards, you press F12, F2, or Del during the boot. Sometimes, a message such as *Press F12 or Del to enter UEFI BIOS Setup* appears near the beginning of the boot, or a boot menu with the option to access BIOS setup appears after you have pressed a special button. See the motherboard documentation to know for sure which key or button to press.

When you press the appropriate key or button, a setup screen appears with menus and Help features that are often very user-friendly. Although the exact menus depend on the BIOS/UEFI maker, the sample screens that follow will help you become familiar with the general contents of BIOS/UEFI setup screens.

> ✏️ **Notes** BIOS firmware uses only the keyboard for input, while UEFI firmware can use the keyboard and mouse. Some manufacturers use BIOS firmware with integrated UEFI functionality, and the setup screens are controlled only by the keyboard.

VIEWING AND MONITORING INFORMATION

The first screen you see in the firmware utility usually gives you information about the system, including the BIOS/UEFI version and information about the CPU, memory, hard drive, optical drive, date, and time. BIOS/UEFI menus and screens differ, so you might need to browse through the screens to find what you're looking for. For example, Figure 2-26 shows information on the Configuration screen about installed hard drives and optical drives. This system has five internal SATA and eSATA ports and one external eSATA port. As you can see, a 120-GB hard drive is installed on SATA port 0, and another 1000-GB hard drive is installed on SATA port 1. Both ports are internal SATA connectors on the motherboard. Notice the optical drive is installed on SATA port 3, which is also an internal connector on the motherboard.

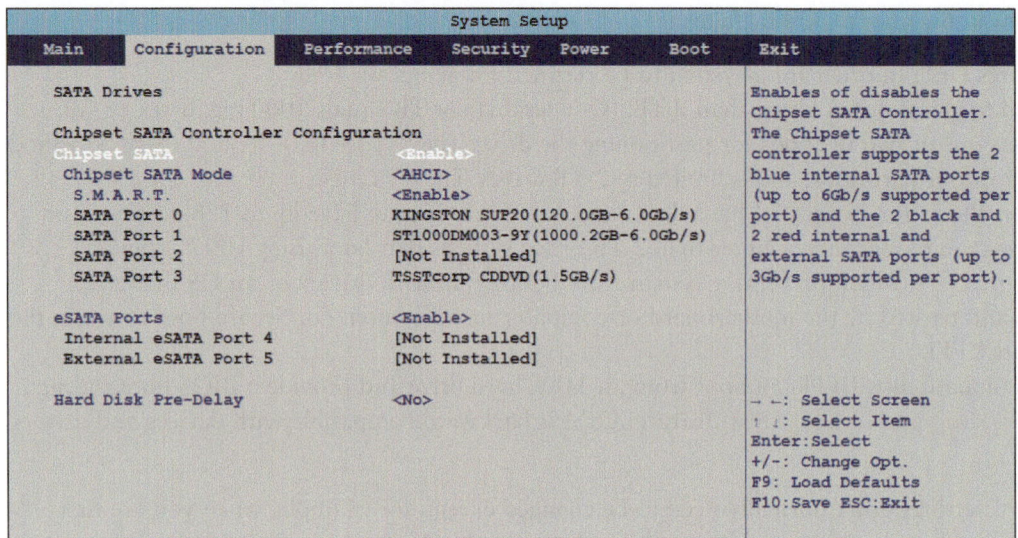

Source: Intel

Figure 2-26   A BIOS/UEFI setup screen showing a list of drives installed on the system

Figure 2-27 shows the BIOS/UEFI screen for another system with a graphical BIOS/UEFI interface. Notice information about the BIOS version, CPU type, total memory installed, current temperature and voltage of the CPU, how the two memory slots on the motherboard are used (one is populated and one is empty), and RPMs of CPU fans.

Source: American Megatrends, Inc.

Figure 2-27   Information about the system is reported when you first access BIOS/UEFI setup

When you click **Advanced Mode**, you see the SATA configuration. For example, Figure 2-28 shows a 1000-GB hard drive using the first SATA6G yellow port and a DVD device using the second SATA3G brown port. The other SATA ports are disabled. Also notice in the figure that S.M.A.R.T is enabled. S.M.A.R.T.

(Self-Monitoring Analysis and Reporting Technology) monitors statistics reported by a hard drive and can predict when the drive is likely to fail. It displays a warning when it suspects a failure is about to happen.

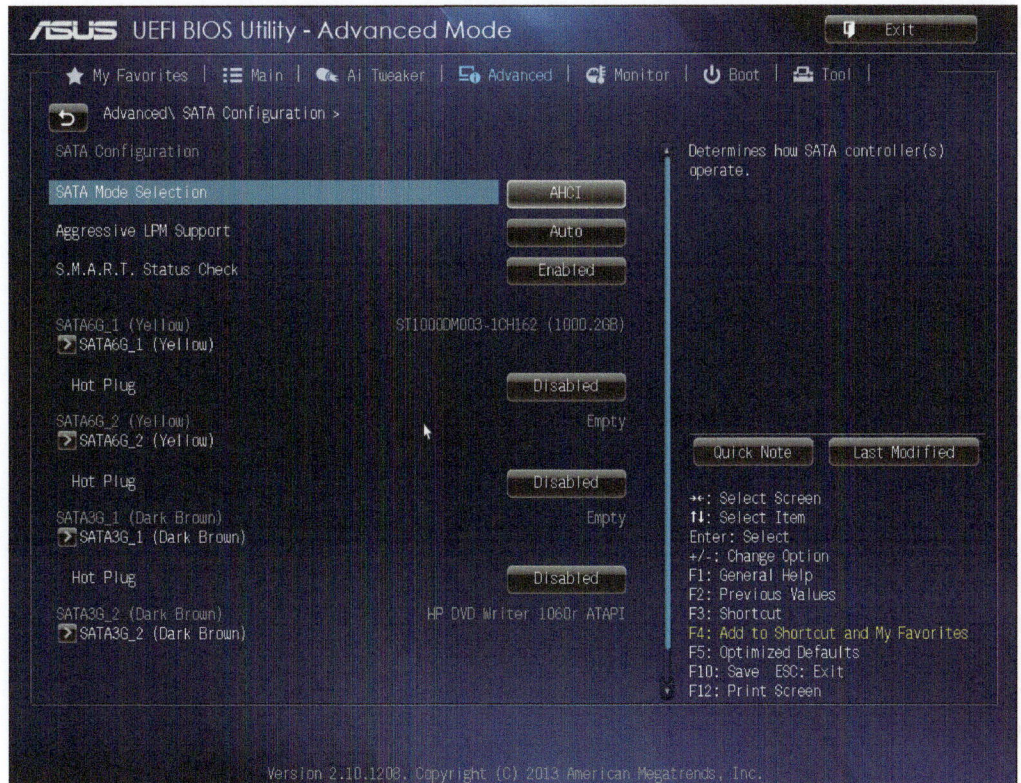

Source: American Megatrends, Inc.

Figure 2-28 SATA configuration displayed by the Asus BIOS/UEFI utility shows the status of four SATA connectors on the motherboard

CHANGING BOOT OPTIONS

Figure 2-29 shows an example of a boot menu in BIOS/UEFI setup. Here, you can set the order in which the system tries to boot from certain devices (called the boot priority order or boot sequence).

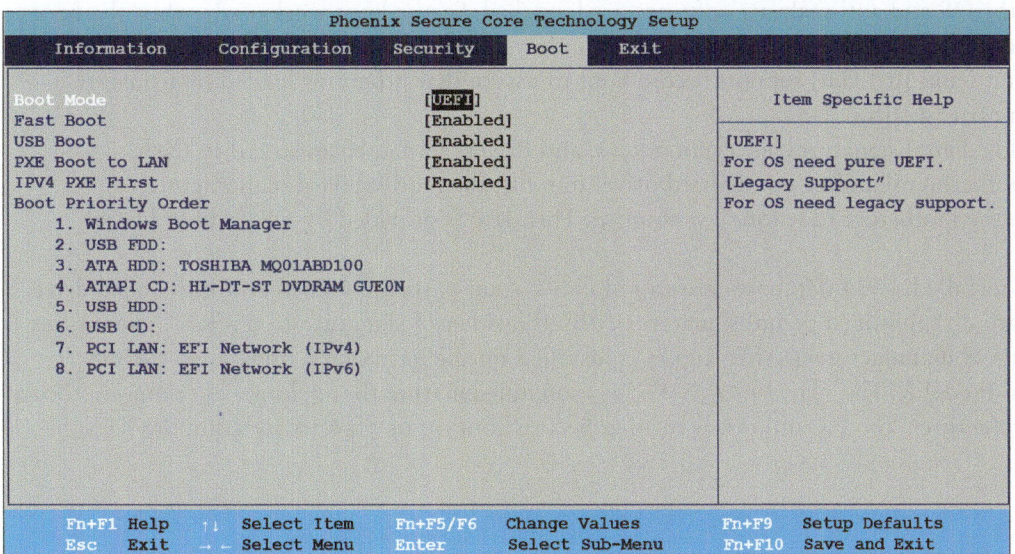

Source: Intel

Figure 2-29 Set the boot priority order in BIOS setup

BOOT PRIORITY ORDER

Here are some examples where you might want to change the boot priority order:

▲ Some distributions of the Linux operating system (OS) can be installed on a USB flash drive; you can boot the OS from this drive when you put the USB device first in the boot priority order.

> **⚡ Caution** Booting the system directly from a USB flash drive causes the system to ignore any OS that might be installed on the hard drive, which can be a security issue because data stored on the hard drive might be vulnerable. To help close this security hole, set the boot priority order to first boot from the hard drive and password-protect access to BIOS/UEFI setup so that others cannot change the boot order. Other ways to protect the OS and data on the hard drive are addressed later in this text.

▲ When you first install an OS on the hard drive, you might want BIOS/UEFI to first boot from a DVD so that you can install Windows from the Windows setup DVD.

▲ If you are installing the OS from a server on the network, put the *PCI LAN: EFI Network* option at the top of the boot priority order and enable *PXE Boot to LAN*. This causes the computer to boot to the firmware program called the Preboot eXecution Environment or Pre-Execution Environment (PXE), which then searches the network for an OS it receives from a deployment server. Notice in Figure 2-29 that when booting to access a deployment server on the network, you must choose whether your network is using IPv4 or IPv6 for IP addressing. You learn more about these concepts later in the text.

▲ When Windows is installed on the hard drive but refuses to start, you can boot from the Windows setup DVD to troubleshoot and repair the installation.

After the OS is installed, you can prevent accidental or malicious boots from a DVD or other removable media by changing the boot priority order to boot first from the hard drive. Also, BIOS/UEFI screens might give you options regarding built-in diagnostics that occur at the boot. You can configure some motherboards to perform a fast boot and bypass the extensive POST. When troubleshooting a boot problem, be sure to set BIOS/UEFI to perform the full POST.

MANAGE SECURE BOOT

You also need to know how to manage Secure boot, which was invented to help prevent malware from launching before the OS and anti-malware software are launched. Secure boot works only when the boot mode is UEFI (and not CSM) and the OS supports it. Windows 10/8 and several distributions of Linux (for example, Ubuntu and Red Hat) support Secure boot to assure that programs loaded by firmware during the boot are trustworthy.

Secure boot holds digital signatures, encryption keys, and drivers in databases stored in flash memory on the motherboard and/or on the hard drive. Initially, the motherboard manufacturer stores the data on the motherboard before it is shipped. This date is provided by OS and hardware manufacturers.

After the OS is installed, UEFI databases are stored in a system partition named efi on the hard drive. Database names are db (approved digital signatures), dbx (blacklist of signatures), and KEK (signatures maintained by the OS manufacturer). After an OS is installed on the hard drive, updates to the OS include updates to the KEK. The Platform Key (PK) is a digital signature that belongs to the motherboard or computer manufacturer. The PK authorizes turning Secure boot on or off and updating the KEK database.

2

When Secure boot is enabled, it checks each driver, the OS, and applications before UEFI launches these programs during the early stages of the boot to verify it is signed and identified in the Secure boot databases. After the OS is launched, it can load additional drivers and applications that UEFI Secure boot does not verify.

For normal operation, you would not be required to change Secure boot settings unless you want to install hardware or an OS (for example, Kali Linux) that is not certified by the computer manufacturer. In this situation, you could disable Secure boot. Before you make any changes to the Secure boot screen, be sure to use the option to save Secure boot keys, if that option is available. Doing so saves all the databases to a USB flash drive so that you can backtrack your changes later if need be.

Take a look at Figure 2-30, which shows the Security screen for one laptop where Secure boot can be enabled or disabled. Also notice the option highlighted to Restore Factory Keys. This option may be helpful if BIOS/UEFI refuses to allow a fresh installation of an OS or hardware device. On this system, before you can enable Secure boot, you must go to the Boot screen and select UEFI as the Boot Mode.

```
                    Phoenix Secure Core Technology Setup
    Information    Configuration    Security    Boot    Exit

    Administrator Password         Cleared                      Item Specific Help
    User Password                  Cleared
    HDD Password                   Cleared              [Enter]
                                                        Restore all secure boot
    Set Administrator Password     [Enter]              database to factory default
    Set Hard Disk Password         [Enter]              include PK, KEK, db and
                                                        dbx.
    AMD Platform Security Processor  [Enabled]
    Clear AMD PSP Key              [Clear AMD PSP Key]

    Secure Boot                    [Enabled]
    Secure Boot Status             Enabled
    Platform Mode                  User Mode
    Secure Boot Mode               Standard
    Reset to Setup Mode            [Enter]
    Restore Factory Keys           [Enter]


    Fn+F1  Help    ↑↓  Select Item    Fn+F5/F6  Change Values    Fn+F9   Setup Defaults
    Esc    Exit    →←  Select Menu    Enter     Select Sub-Menu  Fn+F10  Save and Exit
```

Source: Intel

Figure 2-30   Manage Secure boot on the Security screen of BIOS/UEFI setup

> ✎ **Notes** On laptops and other computers that have the Windows 8 logo imprinted on them, the computer manufacturer is required to configure Secure boot so that it cannot be disabled, which assures that only certified OSs and drivers can be loaded by UEFI.

MANAGE CSM AND UEFI BOOT

The Boot screen allows you to select UEFI mode or CSM (also called Legacy Support) mode. UEFI mode is required for Secure boot to be enabled. For example, in Figure 2-31, you first must disable Fast Boot and then you can select either CSM (Compatibility Support Module) or Secure boot. When you select Secure boot, UEFI mode is enabled. Use CSM for backward compatibility with older BIOS devices and drivers and MBR hard drives.

Source: American Megatrends, Inc.

Figure 2-31 Use CSM to boot a legacy BIOS system or disable it to implement UEFI Secure boot

CONFIGURING ONBOARD DEVICES

You can enable or disable some onboard devices (for example, a wireless LAN, a network port, USB ports, or video ports) using BIOS/UEFI setup. For one system, the Configuration screen shown in Figure 2-32 does the job. On this screen, you can enable or disable a port or group of ports; you can configure the Front Panel Audio ports for Auto, High Definition audio, and Legacy audio; or you can disable these audio ports. What you can configure on your system depends on the onboard devices the motherboard offers.

```
                            System Setup

  Main    Configuration   Performance   Security   Power    Boot    Exit

  Onboard Devices                                  Enables or Disables
                                                   Enhanced Consumer Infrared
  Enhanced Consumer IR        <Disable>            (CIR)
  Audio                       <Enable>
    Front Panel Audio         <Auto>
  HDMI/DisplayPort Audio      <Enable>
  LAN                         <Enable>
  1394                        <Enable>

  USB                         <Enable>
  Num Lock                    <On>
  PCI Latency Timer           <32>




                                                   → ←: Select Screen
                                                   ↑ ↓: Select Item
                                                   Enter:Select
                                                   +/-: Change Opt.
                                                   F9: Load Defaults
                                                   F10:Save ESC:Exit
```

Source: Intel

Figure 2-32 Enable and disable onboard devices

2

> 🖉 **Notes** You don't have to replace an entire motherboard if one port fails. For example, if the network port fails, use BIOS/UEFI setup to disable the port. Then use an expansion card for the port instead.

PROCESSOR AND CLOCK SPEEDS

Overclocking is running a processor, memory, motherboard, or video card at a higher speed than the manufacturer recommends. Some motherboards and processors allow overclocking, but it is not a recommended best practice. If you decide to overclock a system, pay careful attention to the temperature of the processor so it does not overheat; overheating can damage the processor.

CONFIGURING SECURITY FEATURES

Other security features besides Secure boot are power-on passwords, LoJack, drive password protection, the TPM chip, and drive encryption. All are discussed next.

POWER-ON PASSWORDS

Power-on passwords are assigned in BIOS/UEFI setup to prevent unauthorized access to the computer and/or the BIOS/UEFI setup utility. For one motherboard, this security screen looks like the one shown in Figure 2-33, where you can set a supervisor password and a user password. In addition, you can configure how the user password works.

Source: Intel

Figure 2-33 Set supervisor and user passwords in BIOS/UEFI setup to help lock down a computer

The choices under User Access Level are *No Access* (the user cannot access the BIOS/UEFI setup utility), *View Only* (the user can access BIOS/UEFI setup, but cannot make changes), *Limited* (the user can access BIOS/UEFI setup and make a few changes such as date and time), and *Full Access* (the user can access the BIOS/UEFI setup utility and make any changes). When supervisor and user passwords are both set and you boot the system, a box to enter a password is displayed. The access you have depends on which password you enter. Also, if both passwords are set, you must enter a valid password to boot the system. By setting both passwords, you can totally lock down the computer from unauthorized access.

> ⭐ **A+ Exam Tip** The A+ Core 1 exam expects you to know how to use BIOS/UEFI setup to secure a workstation from unauthorized use.

> **⚡ Caution** In the event that passwords are forgotten, know that supervisor and user passwords to the computer can be reset by setting a jumper (group of pins) on the motherboard to clear all BIOS/UEFI customized settings and return BIOS/UEFI setup to its default settings. To keep someone from using this technique to access the computer, you can use a computer case with a lockable side panel and install a lock on the case. Using jumpers is covered later in this chapter.
>
> Also, the BIOS/UEFI utility might have an intrusion detection alert feature that requires a cable to be connected to a switch on the case. When the case is opened, the action is logged in BIOS/UEFI and a message appears at the beginning of the boot that an intrusion has been detected. This security feature is easily bypassed by hackers and is therefore not considered a best practice.

LOJACK FOR LAPTOPS TECHNOLOGY

LoJack and Computrace Agent technology are embedded in the firmware of many laptops to protect a system against theft. When you subscribe to the LoJack for Laptops service by Absolute (*absolute.com*) and later report a theft to Absolute, the company can locate your laptop whenever it connects to the Internet. Absolute reports its location to the police, and even before it is recovered, you can give commands through the Internet to lock the laptop or delete all data on it.

DRIVE PASSWORD PROTECTION

Some laptop BIOS/UEFI utilities offer the option to set a hard drive password. For example, look back at Figure 2-30 and the option Set Hard Disk Password. Using this option, you can set Master and User passwords for all hard drives installed in the system. When you first turn on the computer, you must enter a power-on password to boot the computer and a hard drive password to access the hard drive.

Using a hard drive password does not encrypt all the data on the drive but encrypts only a few organizational sectors. Therefore, a hacker can move the drive to another computer and use software that can read sectors where data is kept without having to read the organizational sectors. Password-protected drives are therefore not as secure as drive encryption, which is discussed next.

THE TPM CHIP AND HARD DRIVE ENCRYPTION

Many motherboards contain a chip called the TPM (Trusted Platform Module) chip. The BitLocker Encryption tool in Windows 10/8/7 is designed to work with this chip; the chip holds the BitLocker encryption key (also called the startup key). The TPM chip can also be used with encryption software other than BitLocker that may be installed on the hard drive. If the hard drive is stolen from the computer and installed in another computer, the data will be safe because BitLocker has encrypted all contents on the drive and will not allow access without the startup key stored on the TPM chip. Therefore, this method assures that the drive cannot be used in another computer. However, if the motherboard fails and is replaced, you'll need a backup copy of the startup key to access data on the hard drive.

> **★ A+ Exam Tip** The A+ Core 1 exam expects you to know about drive encryption, the TPM chip, and how to use both to secure a workstation or laptop.

When you use Windows to install BitLocker Encryption, the initialization process also initializes the TPM chip. Initializing the TPM chip configures it and turns it on. After BitLocker is installed, you can temporarily turn it off, which also turns off the TPM chip. For example, you might want to turn off BitLocker to test the BitLocker recovery process. Normally, BitLocker will manage the TPM chip for you, and there is no need for you to manually change TPM chip settings. However, if you are having problems installing BitLocker, one thing you can do is clear the TPM chip. *Be careful!* If the TPM chip is being used to hold an encryption key to protect data on the hard drive and you clear the chip, the encryption key will be lost. That means all the data will be lost, too. Therefore, don't clear the TPM chip unless you are certain it is not being used to encrypt data.

> **Notes** Drive encryption might be too secure at times. I know of a situation where an encrypted hard drive became corrupted. Normally, you might be able to move the drive to another computer and recover some data. However, this drive asked for the encryption password but then could not confirm it. Therefore, the entire drive, including all the data, was inaccessible.

BIOS SUPPORT FOR VIRTUALIZATION

Virtualization in computing is when one physical computer uses software to create multiple virtual computers and each virtual computer or virtual machine (VM) simulates the hardware of a physical computer. Each VM running on a computer works like a physical computer and is assigned virtual devices such as a virtual motherboard and virtual hard drive. Examples of VM software are Microsoft Hyper-V and Oracle VirtualBox. For most VM software to work, virtualization must be enabled in BIOS/UEFI setup. Looking back at Figure 2-33, you can see the option to enable Intel VT, the name Intel gives to its virtualization technology.

EXITING THE BIOS/UEFI SETUP MENUS

When you finish with BIOS/UEFI setup, an exit screen such as the one shown in Figure 2-34 gives you various options, such as saving your changes and exiting or discarding your changes and exiting. Notice in the figure that you also have the option to Load Optimized Defaults. This option can sometimes solve a problem when a user has made several inappropriate changes to the BIOS/UEFI settings or you are attempting to recover from an error created while updating the firmware.

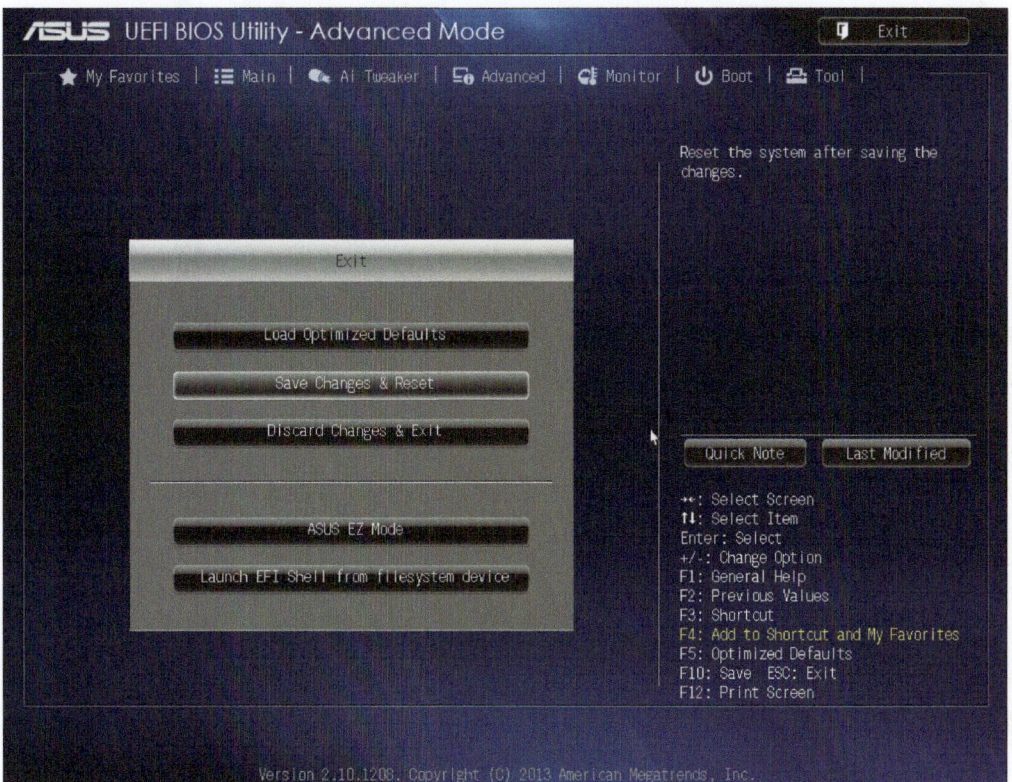

Source: American Megatrends, Inc.

Figure 2-34 The BIOS/UEFI Utility Exit screen

APPLYING | CONCEPTS   MANAGING THE TPM CHIP

To manage the TPM chip, follow these steps:

1. In BIOS/UEFI, verify that the TPM chip is enabled.

2. Sign in to Windows using an administrator account.

3. In the Windows 10/8/7 search box, enter the **tpm.msc** command. If necessary, respond to the UAC box. The TPM Management console opens.

4. If no TPM chip is present or it's not enabled in BIOS/UEFI setup, the console reports that. If your system has a TPM chip that is not yet initialized, the Status pane in the console reports TPM is not ready for use (see Figure 2-35). To initialize the TPM, click **Prepare the TPM** in the Actions pane. After Windows initializes the TPM and you close the dialog box, the console will report that the TPM is ready for use (also shown in Figure 2-35).

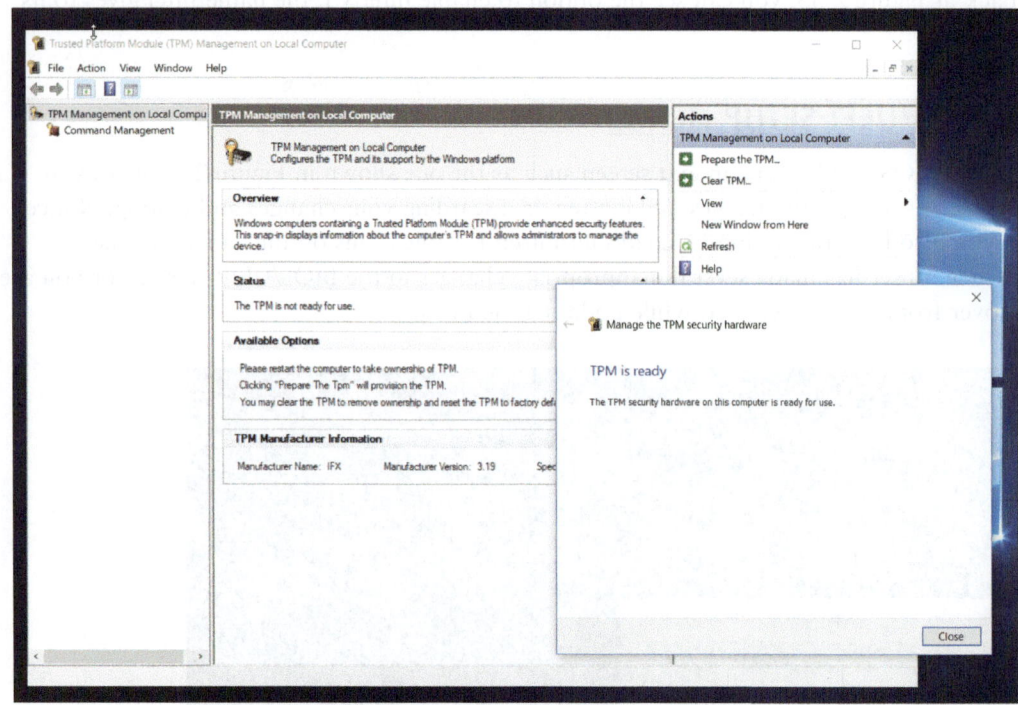

Figure 2-35   Use the TPM Management console to manage the TPM chip in Windows

5. Using the console, you can change the TPM owner password, turn TPM on or off in Windows, reset the TPM when it has locked access to the hard drive, and clear the TPM, which resets it to factory defaults. After you have made changes to the TPM chip, you will most likely be asked to restart the computer for the changes to take effect.

UPDATING MOTHERBOARD DRIVERS AND BIOS/UEFI

When a motherboard is causing problems or you want to use a new OS or hardware device, you might need to update the motherboard drivers or update the BIOS/UEFI firmware. Both skills are covered in this part of the chapter.

INSTALLING OR UPDATING MOTHERBOARD DRIVERS

Device drivers are small programs stored on the hard drive that an operating system such as Windows or Linux uses to communicate with a specific hardware device—for example, a printer, network port on the motherboard, or video card. The CD or DVD that comes bundled with the motherboard contains a user guide and drivers for its onboard components (for example, chipset, graphics, audio, network, and USB drivers), and these drivers need to be installed in the OS. After installing a motherboard, you can install the drivers from CD or DVD and later update them by downloading updates from the motherboard manufacturer's website. Updates to motherboard drivers are sometimes included in updates to Windows.

✎ **Notes** The motherboard CD or DVD or the manufacturer's website might contain useful utilities—for example, a utility to monitor the CPU temperature and alert you if overheating occurs, or a diagnostics utility for troubleshooting. You might also find a utility that works in Windows or Linux to update the BIOS/UEFI firmware.

If you don't have the CD or DVD that came with the motherboard or you want to update the drivers already installed on the system, go to the motherboard manufacturer website to find the downloads you need. Figure 2-36 shows the download page for the Asus Prime Z370-P motherboard shown earlier in Figure 2-1. On this page, you can download manuals, drivers, utility tools, and BIOS/UEFI updates for the board. You can also access a list of CPUs and memory modules the board can use. Be sure to get the correct drivers for the OS edition and type (for example, Windows 10 64-bit) you are using with the board.

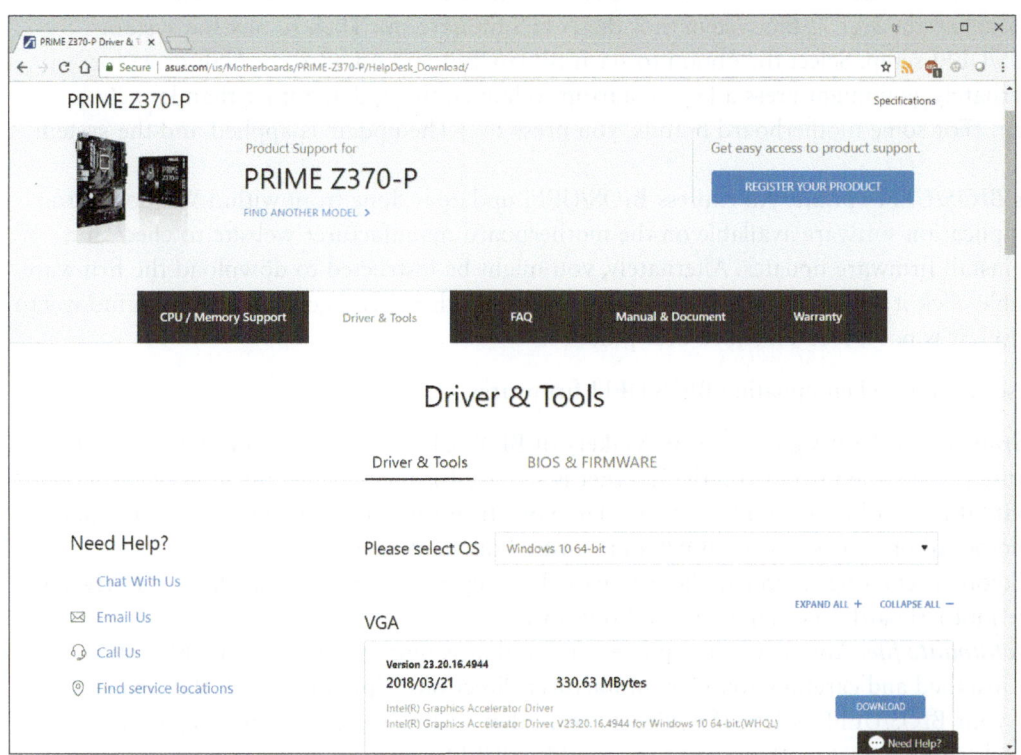

Source: ASUSTeK Computer, Inc.

Figure 2-36 Download drivers, utilities, BIOS/UEFI updates, documentation, and other help software from the motherboard manufacturer's website

✎ **Notes** To know what edition and type of Windows you are using, use the System Information utility (msinfo32.exe).

UPDATING FIRMWARE

The process of upgrading or refreshing the programming and data stored on the firmware chip is called updating firmware, flashing BIOS/UEFI, or flashing BIOS. Here are some good reasons to flash the BIOS/UEFI:

◢ The system hangs at odd times or during the boot.
◢ Some motherboard functions have stopped working or are causing problems. For example, the onboard video port is not working.
◢ You get errors when trying to install a new OS or hardware device.
◢ You want to incorporate some new features or a new component on the board. For example, a BIOS upgrade might be required before you upgrade the processor.

> ⚡ **Caution** It's extremely important that you use the correct motherboard brand and model when selecting the BIOS/UEFI update on the manufacturer's website. Trying to use the wrong update can cause problems. Also, get your updates directly from the manufacturer website rather than other third-party sites.

To flash BIOS/UEFI, always follow the directions that you can find in the user guide for your motherboard. Motherboards can use one or more of these methods:

◢ **Download and update from within BIOS/UEFI setup.** Some motherboards allow you to enter BIOS/UEFI setup and select the option for BIOS/UEFI to connect to the Internet, check for updates, download the update, and apply it.
◢ **Update from a USB flash drive using BIOS/UEFI setup.** Download the latest firmware update file for your BIOS/UEFI version from the manufacturer website and store it on a USB flash drive that is formatted using the FAT32 file system (not the NTFS file system). Then restart the system and launch BIOS/UEFI setup. Select the option to flash BIOS/UEFI and point to the USB drive for the update. Alternately, you might press a key at startup to launch the update rather than launch BIOS/UEFI setup. (For some motherboard brands, you press F7.) The update is applied and the system restarts.
◢ **Run an express BIOS/UEFI update.** An express BIOS/UEFI update is done from within Windows. You use Windows application software available on the motherboard manufacturer website to check for, download, and install firmware updates. Alternately, you might be instructed to download the firmware update and double-click it to start the update. Because too many things can go wrong using Windows to update BIOS/UEFI, it is not a recommended best practice.

Be aware of these cautions when updating BIOS/UEFI firmware:

◢ **Don't update firmware without a good reason.** Makers of BIOS/UEFI are likely to provide updates frequently because putting the upgrade on the Internet is so easy for them. Generally, however, follow the principle that "if it's not broke, don't fix it." Update your firmware only if you're having a problem with your motherboard or there's a new BIOS/UEFI feature you want to use.
◢ **Back up first.** Before attempting to update the firmware, back up the firmware to a USB flash drive, if possible. See the motherboard user manual to find out how.
◢ **Select the correct update file.** Always use an update version that is more recent than the BIOS/UEFI version already installed and carefully follow manufacturer directions. Upgrading with the wrong file could make your BIOS/UEFI useless. If you're not sure that you're using the correct upgrade, *don't guess.* Check with the technical support for your BIOS/UEFI before moving forward. Before you call technical support, have the information available that identifies your BIOS/UEFI and motherboard.
◢ **Don't interrupt the update.** Be sure not to turn off your computer while the update is in progress. For laptops, make sure the AC adapter is plugged in and powering the system.

> **✎ Notes** To identify the BIOS/UEFI version installed, look for the BIOS version number displayed on the main menu of BIOS/UEFI setup. Alternately, you can use the System Information utility (msinfo32.exe) in Windows to display the BIOS version.

If the BIOS update is interrupted or the update creates errors, you are in an unfortunate situation. Search the motherboard manufacturer website for help. Here are some options:

- ▲ **Back flash.** You might be able to revert to the earlier version, which is called a back flash. To do this, generally you download the recovery file from the website and copy the file to a USB flash drive. Then set the jumper on the motherboard to recover from a failed BIOS update. When you reboot the system, the BIOS automatically reads from the device and performs the recovery. Then reset the jumper to the normal setting and boot the system.
- ▲ **Bootable media and restore defaults.** You might be instructed to make a bootable CD or DVD using support tools from the motherboard manufacturer. Boot the system from the CD or DVD and enter commands to attempt the update again from the file stored on the USB flash drive. Then enter BIOS/UEFI setup and restore defaults.

> **✎ Notes** If a BIOS/UEFI update fails to complete, BIOS/UEFI may reboot and try again up to three times. After the third attempt, the update will be discarded and the firmware will roll back a partial update.

USING JUMPERS TO CLEAR BIOS/UEFI SETTINGS

A motherboard may have jumpers that you can use to clear BIOS/UEFI settings, which returns the BIOS/UEFI setup to factory default settings. You might want to clear settings if flashing BIOS/UEFI didn't work or failed to complete correctly, or if a power-on password is forgotten and you cannot boot the system.

A jumper is two small posts or metal pins that stick up on the motherboard; it's used to hold configuration information. An open jumper has no cover, and a closed jumper has a cover on the two pins (see Figure 2-37). Look at the jumper cover in Figure 2-37(B) that is "parked," meaning it is hanging on a single pin for safekeeping, but is not being used to turn on a jumper setting.

A   B   C

Figure 2-37 A 6-pin jumper group on a circuit board: (A) has no jumpers set to on, (B) has a cover parked on one pin, and (C) is configured with one jumper setting turned on

Figure 2-38 shows one example of a group of three jumpers. (The tan jumper cap is positioned on the first two jumper pins on the left side of the group.) Figure 2-39 shows the motherboard documentation for how to use these jumpers. When jumpers 1 and 2 are closed, which they are in the figure, normal booting happens. When jumpers 2 and 3 are closed, passwords to BIOS/UEFI setup can be cleared on the next boot. When no jumpers are closed, the BIOS/UEFI will recover itself on the next boot from a failed update. Once set for normal booting, the jumpers should be changed only if you are trying to recover when a power-up password is lost or flashing BIOS/UEFI has failed. To learn how to set jumpers, see the motherboard documentation.

BIOS jumper group

Figure 2-38   This group of three jumpers controls the BIOS configuration

Jumper Position	Mode	Description
1 ... 3	Normal (default)	The current BIOS configuration is used for booting.
1 ... 3	Configure	After POST, the BIOS displays a menu in BIOS setup that can be used to clear the user and supervisor power-on passwords.
1 ... 3	Recovery	Recovery is used to recover from a failed BIOS update. Details can be found in the motherboard manual.

Figure 2-39   BIOS configuration jumper settings

REPLACING THE CMOS BATTERY

A motherboard stores its data in flash memory in the firmware or in CMOS RAM. CMOS (complementary metal-oxide semiconductor) is a method of manufacturing microchips, and CMOS RAM is a small amount of memory stored on the motherboard that retains data even when the computer is turned off because it is charged by a nearby lithium coin-cell battery (see Figure 2-40). If the CMOS battery is disconnected or fails, setup information is lost. An indication that the battery is getting weak is that the system date and time are incorrect after power has been disconnected to the computer. A message about a low battery can also appear at startup.

Figure 2-40   The coin-cell battery powers CMOS RAM when the system is turned off and unplugged

The CMOS battery on the motherboard is considered a field replaceable unit. The battery is designed to last for years and recharges when the motherboard has power. However, on rare occasions, you might need to replace one if the system loses BIOS/UEFI settings when it is unplugged. Make sure the replacement battery is an exact match to the original or is one the motherboard manufacturer recommends for the board. Power down the system, unplug it, press the power button to drain the power, and remove the case cover. Use your ESD strap to protect the system against ESD. The old battery can be removed with a little prying using a flathead screwdriver. The new battery pops into place. For more specific directions, see the motherboard documentation.

Now let's see what other tasks you might need to do when you are installing or replacing a motherboard.

INSTALLING OR REPLACING A MOTHERBOARD

A motherboard is considered a field replaceable unit, so you need to know how to replace one when it goes bad. In this part of the chapter, you learn how to select a motherboard and then how to install or replace one in a desktop or laptop computer.

HOW TO SELECT A DESKTOP MOTHERBOARD

Because the motherboard determines so many of your computer's features, selecting the motherboard is often your most important decision when you purchase a desktop computer or assemble one from parts. Depending on which applications and peripheral devices you plan to use with the computer, you can take one of three approaches to selecting a motherboard. The first approach is to select the board that provides the most room for expansion, so you can upgrade and exchange components and add devices easily. A second approach is to select the board that best suits the needs of the computer's current configuration, knowing that when you need to upgrade, you will likely switch to new technology and a new motherboard. The third approach is to select a motherboard that meets your present needs with moderate room for expansion.

Ask the following questions when selecting a motherboard:

1. How is the motherboard to be used? (For example, it might be used for light business and personal use, as a gaming system, for a server, or for a high-powered workstation.)
   Knowing how the board will be used helps you decide about the most important features and overall power of the board. For example, a motherboard to be used in a server might need support for RAID (an array of multiple hard drives to improve performance and fault tolerance). In another example, a motherboard used in a gaming system will not need RAID support, but might need a chipset that supports two high-end graphics adapters.

2. What form factor does the motherboard use?

3. Which brand (Intel or AMD) and model processors does the board support? Which chipset does it use? Which processors does it support?
   Most motherboard manufacturers offer a motherboard model in two versions: one version with an Intel chipset and a second version with an AMD chipset. Here are the criteria to decide which brand of chipset to use:

   ◢ If price is a concern, boards with AMD chipsets generally cost less than comparable boards with Intel chipsets.

   ◢ AMD is popular in the hobbyist and gaming market, and many of its chipsets and processors are designed with high-end graphics in mind. AMD puts graphics first and processing power second. For the hobbyist, many AMD processors can be overclocked.

◢ Intel offers the most options in processor models and chipset and processor features. Intel typically targets the consumer, business, and server markets, and generally is strong in power conservation, processing power, and graphics.

◢ Intel dominates the laptop, pre-built desktop, consumer, and server markets.

4. Which type and speed of memory does the board support?

5. What are the embedded expansion slots, internal and external connectors, and devices on the board? (For example, the board might provide multiple PCIe ×16 v4 slots, SATA3 connectors, a network port, a wireless component, multiple USB ports, an M.2 slot, HDMI port, DVI-D port, and so forth.)

6. Does the board fit the case you plan to use?

7. What are the price and the warranty on the board? Does the board get good reviews?

8. How extensive and user friendly is the documentation and how helpful is the manufacturer website?

9. What warranty and how much support does the manufacturer supply for the board?

Sometimes a motherboard contains an onboard component more commonly offered as a separate device. One example is support for video. The video port might be on the motherboard or might require a video card. A motherboard with embedded video is less expensive than a motherboard and a graphics card you plan to install in a PCIe ×16 slot, but the latter plan gives higher-quality video.

> 🖉 **Notes** If you have an embedded component, make sure you can disable it so you can use another external component if needed. Components are disabled in BIOS/UEFI setup.

Table 2-3, shown earlier in the chapter, lists some manufacturers of motherboards and their web addresses. For motherboard reviews, do a general search of the web.

> 🖉 **Notes** Get really familiar with the manufacturer's website of the motherboard you plan to purchase. It tells you which processors and memory modules the board can support. Make sure the processor and memory you plan to use with the board are on these lists.

HOW TO INSTALL OR REPLACE A MOTHERBOARD

When you purchase a motherboard, the package comes with the board, I/O shield, documentation, drivers, and various screws, cables, and connectors. When you replace a motherboard, you pretty much have to disassemble an entire computer, install the new motherboard, and reassemble the system, which you learned to do in Chapter 1. The following steps are meant to be a general overview of the process and are not meant to include the details of all possible installation scenarios, which can vary according to the components and case you are using. The best place to go for detailed installation instructions is the motherboard user guide.

> ⚡ **Caution** As with any installation, remember the importance of using an ESD strap to ground yourself when working inside a computer case to protect components against ESD. Other precautions to protect the hardware and you are covered in Appendix A.

The general process for replacing a motherboard is as follows:

1. *Verify that you have selected the right motherboard to install in the system.* The new motherboard should have the same form factor as the case, support the RAM modules and processor you want to install on it, and have other internal and external connectors you need for your system.

2. *Get familiar with the motherboard documentation, features, and settings.* Especially important are any connectors and jumpers on the motherboard. It's a great idea to read the motherboard user guide from cover to cover. At the least, get familiar with what it has to offer and study the diagrams in it that label all the components on the board. Learn how each connector and jumper is used. You can also check the manufacturer's website for answers to any questions you might have.

3. *Remove components so you can reach the old motherboard.* Use an ESD strap. Turn off the system and disconnect all cables and cords. Press the power button to dissipate the power. Open the case cover and remove all expansion cards. Disconnect all internal cables and cords connected to the old motherboard. To safely remove the old motherboard, you might have to remove drives. If the processor cooler is heavy and bulky, you might remove it from the old motherboard before you remove the motherboard from the case.

4. *Install the I/O shield.* The I/O shield is a metal plate that comes with the motherboard and fits over the ports to create a well-fitting enclosure for them. A case might come with a standard I/O shield already in place. Hold the motherboard up to the shield and make sure the ports on the board will fit the holes in the shield (see Figure 2-41). If the holes in the shield don't match up with the ports on the board, punch out the shield and replace it with the one that came bundled with the motherboard.

I/O shield installed on the back of the case

Figure 2-41 Make sure the holes in the I/O shield match up with the ports on the motherboard

5. *Install the motherboard.* Place the motherboard into the case and, using spacers or screws, securely fasten the board to the case. Because coolers are heavy, most processor instructions say to install the motherboard before installing the processor and cooler to better protect the board or processor from being damaged. On the other hand, some motherboard manufacturers say to install the processor and cooler and then install the motherboard. Follow the order given in the motherboard user guide. The easiest approach is to install the processor, cooler, and memory modules on the board and then place the board in the case (see Figure 2-42).

Figure 2-42 A motherboard with processor, cooler, and memory modules installed is ready to go in the case

6. *Install the processor and processor cooler.* The processor comes already installed on some motherboards, in which case you just need to install the cooler. The steps for installing a processor and cooler are covered in Chapter 3.

7. *Install RAM into the appropriate slots on the motherboard.* You learn how to install RAM in Chapter 3.

8. *Attach the wires and cables.* Attach the wire leads from the front panel to the front panel connector or header on the motherboard, as you learned to do in Chapter 1. You'll also need to attach the P1 power connector, fan connectors, processor auxiliary power connector, and SATA cables to the internal drives. If the case has ports on the front, such as USB or sound ports, connect cables from the ports to the appropriate headers on the motherboard. Position and tie cables neatly together to make sure they don't obstruct the fans and the airflow.

9. *Install the video card on the motherboard.* If the motherboard does not have onboard video, install the video card now. It should go into the primary PCI Express ×16 slot. If the motherboard has onboard video, use the video port and check out how the system functions until you know everything else is working. Then go back and install an optional video card. If you plan to install two video cards, verify that one is working before installing the second one.

10. *Plug the computer into a power source, and attach the monitor, keyboard, and mouse.* Initially install only the devices you absolutely need.

11. *Boot the system and enter BIOS/UEFI setup.* Make sure the settings are set to the defaults. If the motherboard comes new from the manufacturer, it will already be at default settings. If you are salvaging a motherboard from another system, you might need to reset settings to the defaults. You will need to do the following while you are in BIOS/UEFI setup:

   ◢ Check the time and date.

   ◢ Make sure fast boot (also called abbreviated POST) is disabled. While you're installing a motherboard, you generally want it to do as many diagnostic tests as possible. After you know the system is working, you can choose fast boot.

   ◢ Set the boot order to the hard drive, and then the optical drive, if you will be booting the OS from the hard drive.

◢ Leave everything else at their defaults unless you know that particular settings should be otherwise.

◢ Save and exit.

12. *Observe POST and verify that no errors occur.*

13. *Verify that Windows starts with no errors.* If Windows is already installed on the hard drive, boot to the Windows desktop. Use Device Manager to verify that the OS recognizes all devices and that no conflicts are reported.

14. *Install the motherboard drivers.* If your motherboard comes with a CD or DVD that contains some motherboard drivers, install them now. You will probably need Internet access so that the setup process can download the latest drivers from the motherboard manufacturer's website. Reboot the system one more time, checking for errors.

15. *Install any other expansion cards and drivers.* Install each device and its drivers, one device at a time, rebooting and checking for conflicts after each installation.

16. *Verify that everything is operating properly and make any final OS and BIOS/UEFI adjustments, such as setting power-on passwords.*

> 🖊 **Notes** Whenever you install or uninstall software or hardware, keep a notebook with details about the components you are working on, configuration settings, manufacturer specifications, and other relevant information. This helps if you need to backtrack later and can also help you document and troubleshoot your computer system. Keep all hardware documentation for this system together with the notebook in an envelope in a safe place.

REPLACING A LAPTOP SYSTEM BOARD

**A+
CORE 1
1.1**
Replacing the system board (motherboard) on a laptop probably means you'll need to fully disassemble the entire laptop except the LCD assembly in the lid. Therefore, before you tackle the job, consider alternatives. If available, use diagnostic software from the laptop manufacturer to verify that the problem is a failed system board. If a port or component on the system board has failed, consider installing an external device rather than replacing the entire board. Make sure the laptop is not still under a warranty that might be voided if you crack the case. Replacing the system board is a big deal, so consider that the cost of repair, including parts and labor, might be more than the laptop is worth. A new laptop might be your best solution.

> 🖊 **Notes** You will need the teardown instructions to disassemble the laptop. Also, check for videos online about the teardown. For example, go to *youtube.com* and search on "disassemble lenovo ideapad 310."

If you do decide to replace the system board, use a replacement purchased from the laptop manufacturer. Most likely, the board comes with teardown instructions to install it. As our example, we use the Lenovo Ideapad 310, which has a system board with an embedded processor. Here is the general procedure for replacing the board and processor:

1. Update Windows and device drivers and make sure Windows is working properly before you shut down the system.

2. This laptop has a built-in battery. Disconnect the AC adapter. Press **Fn + S + V** to set the battery in Ship Mode so it does not supply power to the system. To verify Ship Mode is set, press the power button; the system should not power up.

3. As you learned to do in Chapter 1, remove the hard drive slot compartment cover and the hard drive. Next, remove the slot compartment cover that gives access to the memory and Mini PCIe card, and

then remove these two components. Remove the optical drive. Figure 2-43 shows the bottom of the laptop with all these components removed.

Figure 2-43   The bottom of a laptop with the hard drive, memory, Mini PCI Express card, and optical drive removed

4. To remove the keyboard bezel, first remove the 13 screws, which are circled in Figure 2-43. Next, detach the touch pad and keyboard ribbon cables from the two FPC (flexible printed circuit) connectors. You can now turn the laptop over, crack the case, and lift off the keyboard bezel. Figure 2-44 shows the system board now exposed.

Figure 2-44   Remove the keyboard bezel to expose the system board

5. To detach the system board, first remove the 5 screws holding it in place and then remove the 6 ribbon cables (circled in red in Figure 2-44) connecting the speakers, hard drive, optical drive, USB ports, battery, camera, and LCD panel. You can then remove the system board by pushing it to the right

to dislodge it from the jacks on the side of the laptop (see Figure 2-45) and then lifting the board up and out of the case. See Figure 2-46. Handle the board carefully, making sure you don't bend it as you work.

Figure 2-45 Detach the system board from jacks on the left side of the case and then lift the system board up and out of the case

Figure 2-46 Disconnect the fan cable and screws holding the fan assembly to the system board

6. Follow directions in reverse order to reassemble the system. Be careful to delicately, yet firmly, push the system board into the jacks on the left side of the case without damaging these jack connections. Also, double-check to make certain each ribbon cable is securely attached to its connector. After the system is assembled, attach the AC adapter, which switches the battery out of Ship Mode. Power up the system. After you have verified that Windows comes up with no errors, be sure to update BIOS/UEFI on the new board.

>> *CHAPTER SUMMARY*

Motherboard Types and Features

▲ The motherboard is the most complicated of all components inside the computer. It contains the processor socket and accompanying chipset, firmware holding the BIOS/UEFI, memory slots, expansion slots, jumpers, ports, and power supply connections. Sometimes, the processor is embedded on the board. The motherboard you select determines both the capabilities and limitations of your system.

▲ The most popular motherboard form factors are ATX, microATX, and Mini-ITX. The form factor determines the size of the board and the case and power supply the board can use.

▲ The chipset embedded on the motherboard determines what kind of processor and memory the board can support.

▲ Typically, a motherboard will have one or more Intel sockets for an Intel processor or one or more AMD sockets for an AMD processor.

▲ Major advancements in past Intel chipsets and processors are labeled as generations and include Coffee Lake (8th gen), Kaby Lake (7th gen), Skylake (6th gen), Broadwell (5th gen), and Haswell (4th gen).

▲ Current Intel desktop processors use the LGA1151, LGA1150, or LGA1155 socket. Server processors use the LGA2066, LGA2011, or LGA1366 socket.

▲ Current AMD processors use the TR4, AM4, AM3+, AM3, or FM2+ socket. These sockets are used to identify the current AMD generations of chipsets and processors.

▲ When matching a motherboard to a processor, use only processors the motherboard manufacturer recommends for the board. Even though a processor might fit the processor socket on a board, using a match not recommended by the manufacturer can damage both the board and the processor.

▲ Current buses and expansion slots used on motherboards include PCI Express ×1, ×4, ×8, and ×16, Versions 2, 3, 4, and 5, conventional PCI, SATAe, SATA3, SATA2, M.2, and USB.

▲ Components that are built into the motherboard are called onboard components. Other components can be attached to the system in some other way, such as on an expansion card, internal connector, or external port.

▲ A 40-pin IDE connector on a motherboard was designed to use older IDE storage devices and is seldom seen on modern motherboards.

Using BIOS/UEFI Setup to Configure a Motherboard

▲ The firmware that controls current motherboards is a combination of the older BIOS and the newer UEFI. Microsoft requires UEFI firmware in order for a system to be certified for Windows 10/8.

▲ UEFI supports the GPT partitioning system for hard drives, which supports hard drives larger than 2 TB. The older MBR partitioning system is limited to drives smaller than 2 TB.

▲ Booting using UEFI mode is required to use Windows Secure boot, which protects a system against malware launching before Windows or anti-malware software is started. For legacy hardware and operating systems, a UEFI system can be booted in CSM or legacy mode, which is a BIOS boot.

▲ Motherboard settings that can be configured using BIOS/UEFI setup include changing the boot priority order, managing Secure boot options, selecting UEFI mode or CSM mode, enabling or disabling onboard devices, overclocking the CPU, and managing power-on passwords, LoJack for Laptops, the TPM chip, and support for virtualization. You can also view information about the installed processor, memory, storage devices, CPU and chassis temperatures, fan speeds, and voltages.

◢ Secure boot uses databases to verify that hardware drivers are digitally signed by their manufacturers. These databases are stored in firmware on the motherboard before the board ships and later on the Windows hard drive. Updating firmware can update databases in firmware, and you can restore these databases to their factory state. In addition, Microsoft can include updates to its Secure boot databases kept on the hard drive in normal Windows updates.

Updating Motherboard Drivers and BIOS/UEFI

◢ Device drivers for motherboard components are installed in the operating system when you first install a motherboard. These drivers might need updating to fix a problem with a board component or to use a new feature provided by the motherboard manufacturer. Drivers come bundled on CD or DVD with the motherboard and can be downloaded from the motherboard manufacturer website.

◢ Update motherboard firmware when a component on the board is causing problems or you want to incorporate a new feature or component on the board.

◢ To update BIOS/UEFI, you can use BIOS/UEFI setup to check online for updates and apply them, or you can apply updates previously downloaded to a USB flash drive. Alternately, you might be able to install an app in Windows that can check for BIOS/UEFI updates and apply them. This last option is not recommended.

◢ When flashing BIOS/UEFI, don't update firmware without a good reason, back up the firmware before you update it, be certain to select the correct update file, and make sure the update process is not interrupted.

◢ Jumpers on the motherboard may be used to clear BIOS/UEFI settings, restoring them to factory defaults. The CMOS battery that powers CMOS RAM might need replacing.

Installing or Replacing a Motherboard

◢ When selecting a motherboard, pay attention to the form factor, chipset, expansion slots and memory slots used, and the processors supported. Also notice the internal and external connectors and ports the board provides.

◢ When installing a motherboard, first study the motherboard and its manual, and set jumpers on the board. Sometimes it is best to install the processor and cooler before installing the motherboard in the case. When the cooling assembly is heavy and bulky, you should install it after the motherboard is securely seated in the case.

◢ For laptops, it's usually more cost effective to replace the laptop than to replace a failed system board.

>> KEY TERMS

For explanations of key terms, see the Glossary for this text.

AM3+	CMOS RAM	IDE (Integrated Drive Electronics)	mATX
AM4	Compatibility Support Module (CSM)	I/O shield	microATX
ATX	device drivers	ITX	Mini-ITX
back flash	flashing BIOS	jumper	mITX
BitLocker Encryption	flashing BIOS/UEFI	land grid array (LGA)	Molex connector
bus	FPC (flexible printed circuit) connectors	LGA1150	onboard ports
chipset	GUID Partition Table (GPT)	LGA1151	overclocking
CMOS (complementary metal-oxide semiconductor)	header	LoJack	PCI (Peripheral Component Interconnect)
CMOS battery		M.2 connector	PCI Express (PCIe)
		Master Boot Record (MBR)	pin grid array (PGA)

Platform Key (PK)	SATA (Serial Advanced Technology Attachment or Serial ATA)	socket	USB (Universal Serial Bus)
Preboot eXecution Environment or Pre-Execution Environment (PXE)		TPM (Trusted Platform Module) chip	virtualization
	Secure boot	TR4 (Threadripper 4)	virtual machine (VM)
	small form factor (SFF)	traces	zero insertion force (ZIF) sockets
protocol	S.M.A.R.T. (Self-Monitoring Analysis and Reporting Technology)	UEFI (Unified Extensible Firmware Interface)	
riser card			

>> *THINKING CRITICALLY*

These questions are designed to prepare you for the critical thinking required for the A+ Core 1 exam and may use information from other chapters or the web.

1. After trying multiple times, a coworker is not able to fit a motherboard in a computer case, and is having difficulty aligning screw holes in the motherboard to standoffs on the bottom of the case. Which is most likely the source of the problem?

   a. The coworker is trying to use too many screws to secure the board; only four screws are required.

   b. The form factors of the case and motherboard don't match.

   c. The form factors of the motherboard and power supply don't match.

   d. The board is not oriented correctly in the case. Rotate the board.

2. Which type of boot authentication is more secure?

   a. Power-on password or supervisor password

   b. Drive password

   c. Full disk encryption

   d. Windows password

3. You are replacing a processor on an older motherboard and see that the board has the LGA1155 socket. You have three processors on hand: Intel Core i3-2100, Intel Core i5-8400, and Intel Core i5-6500. Which of these three processors will most likely fit the board? Why?

4. You are looking at a motherboard that contains *B370* in the motherboard model name, and the socket appears to be an Intel LGA socket. Which socket is this board most likely using?

   a. LGA1150

   b. LGA1151, 7th generation

   c. LGA1151, 8th generation

   d. LGA1151, all generations

5. Windows is displaying an error about incompatible hardware. You enter BIOS/UEFI setup to change the boot priority order so that you can boot from the Windows setup DVD to troubleshoot the system. However, when you get to the Boot screen, you find that the options to change the boot priority order are grayed out and not available. What is most likely the problem?

   a. You signed in to BIOS/UEFI with the user power-on password rather than the supervisor power-on password.

   b. A corrupted Windows installation does not allow you to make changes in BIOS/UEFI setup.

   c. Motherboard components are malfunctioning and will not allow you to change BIOS/UEFI options.

   d. The keyboard and mouse are not working.

6. Your supervisor has asked you to set up a RAID hard drive array in a tower system, which has a motherboard that uses the B360 chipset. You have installed the required three matching hard drives to hold the array. When you enter BIOS/UEFI to configure the RAID, you cannot find the menus for the RAID configuration. What is most likely the problem?

   a. A RAID array requires at least four matching hard drives.

   b. RAID arrays are not configured in BIOS/UEFI.

   c. Your supervisor did not give you the necessary access to BIOS/UEFI to configure RAID.

   d. The B360 chipset does not support RAID.

7. A customer asks you over the phone how much it will cost to upgrade memory on her desktop system to 16 GB. She is a capable Windows user and able to access BIOS/UEFI setup using the user power-on password you set up for her. Which actions can you ask the customer to perform as you direct her over the phone to get the information you need and develop an estimate of the upgrade's cost?

   a. Use BIOS/UEFI to view how much memory is installed and how much memory the system can hold.

   b. Enter info32.exe to determine how much memory is currently installed.

   c. Use BIOS/UEFI to show which memory slots are used and how much memory is installed in each slot.

   d. View the System Information window to determine how much memory is currently installed.

8. The GeForce GTX 1060 graphics card requires 120 W of power. You plan to install it in a PCIe 3.0 ×16 slot. Will you need to also install extra power to the card? If so, how can you do that?

   a. Yes. The PCIe 3.0 ×16 slot provides 75 W, and you need to connect the card using a PCIe 8-pin connector to gain additional power.

   b. No. The PCIe 3.0 ×16 slot provides all the necessary power and no extra power connection is required.

   c. Yes. The PCIe 3.0 ×16 slot provides 75 W, and you need to connect the card using a PCIe 6-pin connector to gain additional power.

   d. Yes. The PCIe 3.0 ×16 slot provides 100 W, and you need to connect the card using a Molex connector to gain an additional 20 W.

9. While building a high-end gaming system, you are attempting to install the EVGA GeForce GTX 1080 graphics card and discover there is not enough clearance above the motherboard for the card. What is your best solution?

   a. Use a different case that allows for the height of the expansion card.

   b. Use a riser card to install the card parallel to the motherboard.

   c. Use an onboard component rather than the graphics card.

   d. Use a conventional PCI graphics card that fits the motherboard and case.

10. Your boss has purchased a new laptop for business use and has asked you to make sure the data he plans to store on the laptop is secure. Which of the following security measures is the most important to implement to keep the data secure? Second in importance?

   a. Use BitLocker Encryption with the TPM chip.

   b. Enable Secure boot.

   c. Set a supervisor password to BIOS/UEFI.

   d. Disable booting from the optical drive.

11. Which of the following might cause you to flash BIOS/UEFI? Select all that apply.

   a. Windows displays error messages on the screen at startup and refuses to start.

   b. You are installing an upgraded processor.

   c. You are installing a new graphics card to replace onboard video.

   d. Windows continually shows the wrong date and time.

12. Which of the following must be done before you can install the Intel Core i7-7700 processor on the Gigabyte GA-H110M-S2 motherboard? Select all that apply.

   a. Flash BIOS/UEFI.

   b. Install motherboard drivers.

   c. Clear CMOS RAM.

   d. Exchange the LGA1151 socket for one that can hold the new processor.

13. Does Windows 7 support Secure boot in UEFI? Windows 8? Linux Ubuntu version 14?

14. Which partitioning method must be used for partitioning a 4-TB hard drive?

15. If a USB port on the motherboard is failing, what can you do that might fix the problem?

16. What is the purpose of installing standoffs or spacers between the motherboard and the case?

17. When installing a motherboard, suppose you forget to connect the wires from the case to the front panel header. Will you be able to power up the system? Why or why not?

18. When you turn off the power to a computer and unplug it at night, it loses the date, and you must reenter it each morning. What is the problem and how do you solve it?

19. When troubleshooting a desktop motherboard, you discover the network port no longer works. What is the best and least expensive solution to this problem? If this solution does not work, which solution should you try next?

   a. Replace the motherboard.

   b. Disable the network port and install a network card in an expansion slot.

   c. Use a wireless network device in a USB port to connect to a wireless network.

   d. Return the motherboard to the factory for repair.

   e. Update the motherboard drivers.

20. A computer freezes at odd times. At first you suspected the power supply or overheating, but you have eliminated overheating and replaced the power supply without solving the problem. What do you do next?

   a. Replace the processor.

   b. Replace the motherboard.

   c. Reinstall Windows.

   d. Replace the memory modules.

   e. Flash BIOS/UEFI.

>> HANDS-ON PROJECTS

Hands-On | Project 2-1 Examining a Motherboard in Detail

1. Look at the back of a desktop computer. Without opening the case, list the ports that you believe come directly from the motherboard.

2. Remove the cover of the case, as you learned to do in Chapter 1. List the different expansion cards in the expansion slots. Was your guess correct about which ports come from the motherboard?

3. To expose the motherboard so you can identify its parts, remove all the expansion cards.

4. Draw a diagram of the motherboard and label these parts:

   ◢ Processor socket
   ◢ Chipset
   ◢ RAM (each DIMM slot)
   ◢ CMOS battery
   ◢ Expansion slots (Identify the slots as PCI, PCIe ×1, PCIe ×4, or PCIe ×16.)
   ◢ Each port coming directly from the motherboard
   ◢ Power supply connections
   ◢ SATA drive connectors

5. What is the brand and model of the motherboard?

6. Locate the manufacturer's website. If you can find the motherboard manual on the site, download it. Find the diagram of the motherboard in the manual and compare it with your diagram. Did you label components correctly?

7. Reassemble the computer, as you learned to do in Chapter 1.

Hands-On | Project 2-2 Examining Motherboard Documentation

Using the motherboard brand and model installed in your computer, or another motherboard brand and model assigned by your instructor, download the user guide from the motherboard manufacturer website and answer these questions:

1. List up to 10 processors the board supports.

2. What type of RAM does the board support?

3. What is the maximum RAM the board can hold?

4. Which versions of PCIe does the board use?

5. What chipset does the board use?

6. On the motherboard diagram, locate the jumper group on the board that returns BIOS/UEFI setup to default settings. It is often found near the CMOS battery. Some boards might have more than one, and some have none. Label the jumper group on your own diagram.

Hands-On | Project 2-3 Matching a Processor to a Motherboard and Socket

You are designing a desktop system and your friend has offered to sell you his unused Core i5-8600T processor at a reduced price. Research the processor and possible motherboards that will support it and answer the following questions:

1. What is the best online price you can find for the processor?
2. What socket does the processor use?
3. What is one Gigabyte motherboard that supports this processor? Which chipset does the board use? Does the board require a firmware (BIOS) update to use this processor?
4. What is one Asus (*asus.com*) motherboard that supports this processor? Which chipset does the board use? Which firmware (BIOS/UEFI) version is necessary to use this processor?

Hands-On | Project 2-4 Identifying the Intel Chipset and Processor on Your Computer

Intel offers two utilities you can download and run to identify an installed Intel processor or chipset. Do the following to use the utilities:

◢ If you are using a computer with an Intel processor, download and run the Processor Identification Utility available at:

downloadcenter.intel.com/download/7838

◢ If you are using a computer with an Intel processor, download and run the Chipset Identification Utility available at:

downloadcenter.intel.com/product/2715/Intel-Chipset-Identification-Utility

Websites change often, so if these links don't work, try searching the Intel website for each utility. What information does each utility provide about your processor and chipset?

Hands-On | Project 2-5 Researching the Intel ARK Database

Intel provides an extensive database of all its processors, chipsets, motherboards, and other products at *ark.intel.com*. Research the database and answer these questions:

1. List three fifth generation Core i7 processors. For each processor, list the processor number (model), the maximum memory it supports, the PCI Express version it supports (version 2.0, 3.0, or 4.0), and the socket it uses.
2. List three Intel motherboards for desktops: an ATX board, a microATX board, and a Mini-ITX board. For each motherboard, list the processor socket it provides, the chipset it uses, the maximum memory it supports, and the number of PCIe slots it has.
3. The Z370 chipset is designed for gaming computers. What is the launch date for the Z370 chipsets? What Intel generation is the chipset? How many displays does the chipset support?

Hands-On | Project 2-6 Examining BIOS/UEFI Settings

Access the BIOS/UEFI setup program on your computer and answer the following questions:

1. What key(s) did you press to access BIOS/UEFI setup?
2. What brand and version of BIOS/UEFI are you using?
3. What is the frequency of your processor?
4. What is the boot sequence order of devices?
5. Do you have an optical drive installed? What are the details of the installed drive?
6. What are the details of the installed hard drive(s)?
7. Does the BIOS/UEFI offer the option to set a supervisor or power-on password? What is the name of the screen where these passwords are set?
8. Does the BIOS/UEFI offer the option to overclock the processor? If so, list the settings that apply to overclocking.
9. Can you disable the onboard ports on the computer? If so, which ports can you disable, and what is the name of the screen(s) where this is done?
10. List up to three BIOS/UEFI settings that control how power is managed on the computer.

Hands-On | Project 2-7 Inserting and Removing Motherboards

Using old or defective expansion cards and motherboards, practice inserting and removing expansion cards and motherboards. In a lab or classroom setting, the instructor can provide extra cards and motherboards for exchange.

>> REAL PROBLEMS, REAL SOLUTIONS

REAL PROBLEM 2-1 Labeling the Motherboard

Figure 2-47 shows a diagram of an ATX motherboard. Label as many of the 19 components as you can. If you would like to print the diagram, look for "Figure 2-47" in the online content that accompanies this text at *cengage.com*. For more information on accessing this content, see the Preface.

Figure 2-47 Label the 19 components on the motherboard

Source: Asus

REAL PROBLEM 2-2 Selecting a Replacement Motherboard

When a motherboard fails, you can select and buy a new board to replace it. Suppose the motherboard in your computer has failed and you want to buy a replacement and keep your repair costs to a minimum. Try to find a replacement motherboard on the web that can use the same case, power supply, processor, memory, and expansion cards as your current system. If you cannot find a good match, what other components might have to be replaced (for example, the processor or memory)? What is the total cost of the replacement parts? Save or print webpages that show what you need to purchase.

REAL PROBLEM 2-3 Researching How to Maintain a Motherboard

Using the motherboard user guide that you downloaded in Hands-On Project 2-2, answer the following questions:

1. How many methods can be used to flash BIOS/UEFI on the motherboard? Describe each method. What can you do to recover the system if flashing BIOS/UEFI fails?

2. Locate the CMOS battery on the diagram of the motherboard. What are the steps to replace this battery?

Using a computer in your school lab, do the following to practice replacing the CMOS battery:

1. Locate the CMOS battery on your motherboard. What is written on top of the battery? Using the web, find a replacement for this battery. Print the webpage that shows the battery. How much does the new battery cost?

2. Enter BIOS/UEFI setup on your computer. Write down any BIOS/UEFI settings that are not default settings. You'll need these settings later when you reinstall the battery. Alternately, you might find a way to save current settings to a USB flash drive.

3. Turn off and unplug the computer, press the power button to drain the system of power, open the case, remove the battery, and boot the computer. What error messages appear? What is the system date and time?

4. Power down the computer, unplug it, press the power button to drain the power, replace the battery, and boot the computer. Close the case and return BIOS/UEFI settings to the way you found them. Make sure the system is working normally.

Supporting Processors and Upgrading Memory

After completing this chapter, you will be able to:

- Compare characteristics and features of Intel and AMD processors used for personal computers

- Select, install, and upgrade a processor

- Compare the different kinds of physical memory and how they work

- Upgrade memory

Previously, you learned about motherboards. In this chapter, you learn about the two most important components on the motherboard, which are the processor and memory. You learn how a processor works, about the many different types and brands of processors, and how to match a processor to the motherboard.

Memory technologies have evolved over the years. When you support an assortment of desktop and laptop computers, you'll be amazed at all the variations of memory modules used not only in newer computers, but also in older computers still in use. A simple problem of replacing a bad memory module can become a complex research project if you don't have a good grasp of current and past memory technologies.

The processor and memory modules are considered field replaceable units (FRUs), so you'll learn how to install and upgrade a processor and memory modules. Upgrading the processor or adding more memory to a system can sometimes greatly improve performance. You will learn how to troubleshoot problems with the processor or memory in Chapter 4.

TYPES AND CHARACTERISTICS OF PROCESSORS

The processor installed on a motherboard is the primary component that determines the computing power of the system (see Figure 3-1). Recall that the two major manufacturers of processors are Intel (*intel.com*) and AMD (*amd.com*).

Figure 3-1 An AMD FX processor installed in an AM3+ socket with the cooler not yet installed

Here are the features of a processor that affect performance and compatibility with motherboards:

◢ *Feature 1: Processor speed*. The processor frequency is the speed at which the processor operates internally and is measured in gigahertz, such as 3.3 GHz. Current Intel and AMD processors run from about 2.0 GHz up to more than 4.4 GHz.

◢ *Feature 2: Lithography*. The lithography is the average space between transistors printed on the surface of the silicon chip. The measurement is in nanometers (nm); 1 nm is 1 billionth of a meter. Current processor lithography ranges from 14 nm to 35 nm. The lower the measurement, the better and faster the processor performs.

◢ *Feature 3: Socket and chipset the processor can use*. Recall that current Intel sockets for desktop and server systems are LGA1151, LGA1150, LGA1155, LGA1156, LGA2066, LGA2011, and LGA1366. AMD's current desktop sockets are TR4, AM4, AM3+, AM3, AM2+, and FM2+.

◢ *Feature 4: Multiprocessing abilities*. The ability of a system to do more than one task at a time is accomplished by several means:

　　◢ *Multiprocessing*. Using two processing units (called arithmetic logic units or ALUs) installed within a single processor is called multiprocessing. With multiprocessing, the processor, also called the core, can execute two instructions at the same time.

　　◢ *Multithreading*. Each processor or core processes two threads at the same time. When Windows hands off a task to the CPU, it is called a thread and might involve several instructions. To handle two threads, the processor requires extra registers, or holding areas, within the processor housing that it uses to switch between threads. In effect, you have two logical processors for each physical processor or core. Intel calls this technology Hyper-Threading and AMD calls it HyperTransport. The feature must be enabled in BIOS/UEFI setup and the operating system (OS) must support the technology.

▲ *Multicore processing*. A single processor in the processor package is called single-core processing and using multiple processors installed in the same processor housing is called multicore processing. Multicore processing might contain up to eight cores (dual-core, triple-core, quad-core, and so forth). In Figure 3-2, the quad-core processor contains four cores or CPUs. Using multithreading, each core can handle two threads. Therefore, the processor appears to have up to eight logical processors, as it can handle eight threads from the operating system.

Figure 3-2 This quad-core processor has four cores and each core can handle two threads

▲ *Dual processors*. A server motherboard might have two processor sockets, called dual processors or a multiprocessor platform (see Figure 3-3). A processor (for example, the Xeon processor for servers) must support this feature.

Source: intel.com/content/www/us/en/motherboards/server-motherboards/server-board-s2600st-brief.html

Figure 3-3 This Intel Server Board S2600ST has two Xeon processor sockets and 16 slots for DDR4 memory

▲ *Feature 5: Memory cache, which is the amount of memory included within the processor package.* Today's processors all have some memory on the processor chip (called a die). Memory on the processor die is called Level 1 cache (L1 cache). Today's processors might have 4 MB to 12 MB of L1 cache. In addition to L1 cache, a processor may have some Level 2 cache (L2 cache), which is memory in the processor package but not on the processor die. Some processors use a third cache farther from the processor's core, but still in the processor package, which is called Level 3 cache (L3 cache).

> **✎ Notes** Memory used in a memory cache is static RAM (SRAM; pronounced "S-Ram"). Memory used on the motherboard loses data rapidly and must be refreshed often. It is therefore called dynamic RAM (DRAM; pronounced "D-Ram"). SRAM is faster than DRAM because it doesn't need refreshing. Both SRAM and DRAM are called volatile memory because they can only hold data as long as power is available.

▲ *Feature 6: The memory features on the motherboard that the processor can support*. DRAM memory modules used on a motherboard that a processor might support include DDR2, DDR3, or DDR4. Besides the type of memory, a processor can support certain amounts of memory, memory speeds, and a number of memory channels (single, dual, triple, or quad channels). All these characteristics of memory are discussed later in the chapter.

▲ *Feature 7: Support for virtualization*. A computer can use software to create and manage multiple virtual machines and their virtual devices. Most processors sold today support virtualization. The feature must be enabled in BIOS/UEFI setup.

▲ *Feature 8: Integrated graphics*. A processor might include an integrated GPU. A graphics processing unit (GPU) is a processor that manipulates graphic data to form the images on a monitor screen. The GPU might be on a video card, on the motherboard, or embedded in the CPU package. When inside the CPU package, it is called integrated graphics. Many AMD processors and all Intel second-generation and higher processors have integrated graphics.

▲ *Feature 9: Overclocking*. Some processors are designed to allow for overclocking, which is to run the processor at a higher frequency than recommended by the processor manufacturer. As you learned in Chapter 2, if a CPU and motherboard support overclocking, it is managed in BIOS/UEFI.

> **★ A+ Exam Tip** The A+ Core 1 exam expects you to be able to select a processor for a given motherboard, considering these processor features: Hyper-Threading, number of cores, virtualization, integrated GPU, overclocking, and the motherboard CPU socket.

Older processors could process 32 bits at a time and were known as x86 processors because Intel used the number 86 in their model number. Today's processor architectures fall into two categories:

▲ *Hybrid processors can process 32 bits or 64 bits*. All of today's processors for desktop systems can process either 32 bits or 64 bits. These hybrid processors are known as x86-64 bit processors. An operating system such as Windows or Linux is installed as a 32-bit OS or a 64-bit OS. For most situations, when the OS installation gives you the option, you should choose to install it as a 64-bit OS to get the best performance. Applications are created as 32-bit apps or 64-bit apps, and both can be installed in a 64-bit OS. However, you cannot install a 64-bit app in a 32-bit installation of an OS.

▲ *64-bit processors*. Intel makes several 64-bit processors for workstations or servers that use fully implemented 64-bit processing, including the Itanium and Xeon processors. Intel calls the technology IA64, but they are also called x64 processors. They require a 64-bit operating system and can handle 32-bit applications only by simulating 32-bit processing.

3

Figure 3-4   The System window displays the type of operating system installed

INTEL PROCESSORS

**A+
CORE 1
3.5**

As you learned in Chapter 2, Intel groups its processors in generations. (Recall that the 8th generation, also called Coffee Lake, was released in 2017, and the 9th generation, Cannon Lake, is expected to be released in 2019.) Intel also groups its processors in families that can span several generations. To find details about any Intel processor, search the Intel ARK database at *ark.intel.com*. Current families of processors for desktops and laptops include the following.

◢ The Intel Core processors, first introduced in the 2nd generation, target the mid- to high-end consumer market and are currently Intel's most popular processor family:

  ◢ Core i9 and Core i7 are made for high-end desktops and laptops. The latest Core i9 processor has 18 cores, 4.2 GHz, and a 24.75-MB cache.

  ◢ Core i5 is well suited for mainstream desktops and laptops (see Figure 3-5).

  ◢ Core i3 is an entry-level processor for desktops and laptops.

◢ Pentium processors are designed for entry-level desktops and laptops.

◢ Atom is made for low-end desktops, netbooks, and laptops, and the Celeron is made for low-end netbooks and laptops.

Figure 3-5 The Intel Core i5-8600K 14-nm, 3.60-GHz, 9-MB cache processor
installs in the 8th generation LGA1151 socket

> ✎ **Notes** Notice the processor in Figure 3-5 is advertised as unlocked, which means it can be overclocked.

Some Intel mobile processors are packaged in the Centrino processor technology. Using the Centrino technology, the Intel processor, chipset, and wireless network adapter are all interconnected as a unit, which improves laptop performance. Several Intel mobile processors have been packaged as a Centrino processor.

Intel dominates the processor and chipset market for servers with highly stable and powerful processors. Models of the Core i9, Core i7, Core i5, and Core i3 processors are designed for server use, and some of the Atom processors target energy-efficient servers. For high-end servers, Intel offers the Xeon, Xeon Phi, and Itanium. Processors designed for servers are more expensive because they are more stable and error-free than comparable desktop processors.

AMD PROCESSORS

**A+
CORE 1
3.5**

Processors by Advanced Micro Devices, Inc., or AMD (*amd.com*), are popular in the game and hobbyist markets, and are generally less expensive than comparable Intel processors. Recall that AMD processors use different sockets than Intel processors, so the motherboard must be designed for one manufacturer's processor or the other, but not both. Many motherboard manufacturers offer two comparable motherboards—one for an Intel processor and one for an AMD processor.

3

The current AMD processor families include:

◢ For desktops, the Ryzen, Ryzen Pro, Ryzen Threadripper, A-Series, A-Series Pro, and FX. The Threadripper can have up to 16 cores. Figure 3-6 shows an FX processor by AMD.
◢ For laptops, the Ryzen, Ryzen Pro, A-Series, and A-Series Pro.
◢ For servers, the EPYC and Opteron. The EPYC can have up to 32 cores.

Figure 3-6 The AMD FX processor installs in the AMD AM3+ socket and has eight cores

In the next part of the chapter, you learn the detailed steps to select and install a processor in several of the popular Intel and AMD sockets used by desktop and laptop computers.

SELECTING AND INSTALLING A PROCESSOR

A+
CORE 1
1.1, 3.5

A hardware technician is sometimes called on to assemble a desktop computer from parts, exchange a processor that is faulty, add a second processor to a dual-processor system, or upgrade an existing processor to improve performance. In each situation, it is necessary to know how to match a processor for the system in which it is installed. Next, you need to know how to install the processor on the motherboard for each of the current Intel and AMD sockets used for desktop and laptop systems.

SELECTING A PROCESSOR TO MATCH SYSTEM NEEDS

A+
CORE 1
3.5

When selecting the motherboard and processor, recall you must choose between the AMD and Intel chipset and processor. How to make this decision between the two brands was covered earlier in the text. When selecting a processor to match a motherboard you already have, the first requirement is to select one that the motherboard is designed to support. Among the processors the board supports, you need to select the one that best meets the general requirements of the system and the user's needs. Here are some processor features to consider:

◢ To get the best performance, use the highest-performing processor the board supports. Performance can be measured by clock speed, the number of tasks a CPU can run per clock cycle, and the size of the processor cache.
◢ Understand the processor's ability to multitask, considering the number of cores and multithreading abilities. Know, however, that applications must be able to take advantage of multiple cores. If not, some cores can sit idly while others do all the work. If the system will only be used for browsing the web, a

single-core processor will do the job. However, Adobe Premier, AutoCAD, Star Wars Battlefront, and Excel are examples of applications that take full advantage of multiple CPU cores.

▲ Balance the performance and power of the CPU with that of the entire system. For example, if the system has a high-performing graphics adapter, don't install a low-performing processor or hard drive to save on cost. One bottleneck can slow down the entire system.

▲ Be sure to read reviews of the processors you are considering and look for reviews that include comparison benchmarks of several processors. Also, you sometimes need to sacrifice performance and power for cost.

APPLYING | CONCEPTS   SELECTING A PROCESSOR

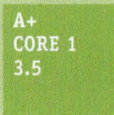

Your friend, Alice, is working toward her A+ certification. She has decided that the best way to get the experience she needs before she sits for the exam is to build a system from scratch. She has purchased an Asus motherboard and asked you for some help selecting the right processor. She tells you that the system will later be used for light business needs and she wants to install a processor that is moderately priced to fit her budget. She says she doesn't want to install the most expensive processor the motherboard can support, but neither does she want to sacrifice too much performance or power.

The documentation on the Asus website (*support.asus.com*) for the ASUS Prime Z370-A motherboard provides this information:

▲ The ATX board contains the Z370 chipset and 8th generation LGA1151 socket and uses up to 64 GB of DDR4 memory.

▲ CPUs supported include a long list of 8th generation, 14-nm CPU Core i3, Core i5, Core i7, and Pentium processors. Here are five processors found in this list:
  ▲ Intel Core i7-8086K, 4.0 GHz, 95 W, 12-MB L3 cache, 6 cores
  ▲ Intel Core i5-8400T, 1.7 GHz, 35 W, 9-MB L3 cache, 6 cores
  ▲ Intel Core i3-8300, 3.7 GHz, 62 W, 8-MB L3 cache, 4 cores
  ▲ Intel Core i3-8100, 3.6 GHz, 65 W, 6-MB L3 cache, 4 cores
  ▲ Intel Pentium G5400T, 3.1 35W, 4-MB L3 cache, 2 cores

Based on what Alice has said, you decide to eliminate the most expensive processors (the Core i7 and i5) and the least-performing processor (the Pentium). That decision narrows your choices down to a Core i3. Before you select one of these processors, you need to check the list on the Asus site to make sure the specific Core i3 processor is included. Look for the exact processor number—for example, the Core i3-8300.

You will also need a cooler assembly. If your processor doesn't come boxed with a cooler, select a cooler that fits the processor socket and gets good reviews. You'll also need some thermal compound if it is not included with the cooler.

The cooler is bracketed to the motherboard using a wire or plastic clip. A creamlike thermal compound is placed between the bottom of the cooler heat sink and the top of the processor. This compound eliminates air pockets, helping to draw heat off the processor. The thermal compound transmits heat better than air and makes an airtight connection between the fan and the processor. When processors and coolers are boxed together, the cooler heat sink might have thermal compound already applied to the bottom (see Figure 3-7).

Figure 3-7 Thermal compound is already applied to the bottom of this cooler that was purchased boxed with the processor

INSTALLING A PROCESSOR AND COOLER ASSEMBLY

**A+
CORE 1
3.5**

Now let's look at the details of installing Intel and AMD processors and the cooler assembly.

⭐ **A+ Exam Tip** The A+ Core 1 exam expects you to know how to install Intel and AMD processors.

INSTALL AN INTEL PROCESSOR

If you are building a new system and the motherboard is not already installed in the case, follow the directions of the motherboard manufacturer to install the motherboard and then the processor, or follow the directions to install the processor and then the motherboard. The order of installation varies among manufacturers. Also, a cooler assembly might have nuts, bolts, screws, and plates that must be installed on the motherboard before you install the motherboard in the case. Here is the general procedure for installations, but always read and follow the specific directions for your motherboard and cooler assembly during your installation:

1. Use an ESD strap or antistatic gloves to protect the processor, motherboard, and other components against ESD.

2. When replacing a processor in an existing system, power down the system, unplug the power cord, press the power button to drain the system of power, and open the case.

3. For a new motherboard, look for a protective cover over the processor socket (see Figure 3-8). Remove this socket cover and keep it in a safe place. If you ever remove the processor, put the cover back on the socket to protect it.

Figure 3-8 The Intel LGA1151 socket with a protective cover in place

4. While the socket is exposed, as in Figure 3-9, be *very careful* not to touch the pins in the socket. Open the socket by pushing down on the socket lever and gently pushing it away from the socket to lift the lever.

Figure 3-9   The exposed socket is extremely delicate

5. As you lift the lever, the socket load plate is raised, as shown in Figure 3-10. Notice the two posts on either side of the socket next to the hinge. These posts help orient the processor in the socket.

Figure 3-10   Lift the socket load plate to expose the processor socket

6. Open the clear plastic protective cover around the processor and locate the two notches and one gold triangle that help you orient the processor in the socket. Figure 3-11 shows the posts on the socket that are used with the notches on the processor to orient the processor in the socket. You can then carefully remove the plastic cover. While the processor contacts are exposed, take extreme care not to touch the bottom of the processor. Hold it only at its edges. (It's best to use antistatic gloves as you work, but the gloves make it difficult to handle the processor.) Put the processor cover in a safe place and use it to protect the processor if you ever remove the processor from the socket.

Two posts match up with two notches on processor package

Figure 3-11 Two posts near the socket hinges help you orient the processor in the socket

7. Hold the processor with your index finger and thumb and orient the processor so that the two notches on its edge line up with the posts embedded on the socket. Gently lower the processor straight down into the socket. See Figure 3-12. Don't allow the processor to tilt, slide, or shift as you put it in the socket. To protect the pads, the processor needs to go straight down into the socket.

Gold triangle on edge of processor package

Right-angle mark on motherboard socket

Figure 3-12 Align the processor in the socket using the gold triangle and the right-angle mark

8. Check carefully to make sure the processor is aligned correctly in the socket. Closing the socket without the processor fully seated can destroy the socket. Figure 3-13 shows the processor fully seated in the socket. Close the socket load plate so that it catches under the screw head at the front of the socket.

Notches on processor align with posts on socket

Figure 3-13 Verify that the processor is seated in the socket with notches aligned to socket posts

9. Push down on the lever and gently return it to its locked position.

INSTALL THE COOLER ASSEMBLY

You are now ready to install the cooler. Some coolers are lightweight with heat sinks and a fan on top. Some are heavier with heat sinks, fins, and a fan on the side, and they require a plate installed on the bottom of the motherboard to strengthen the board for the heavy cooler (see Figure 3-14).

Figure 3-14 A heavy-duty cooler may have a strengthening plate, heat sink, fins, a fan, and several screws, nuts, and bolts

Before installing a cooler, read the directions carefully and make sure you understand them. The cooler may be designed for either an Intel or AMD socket and may have to be installed differently depending on the socket type, so be sure you're following the correct directions.

Notes For complicated cooler assemblies such as the Cooler Master Hyper 212 EVO shown in Figure 3-14, look for helpful YouTube videos that show how to install the assembly.

Here are the general steps for installing a cooler assembly:

1. Motherboards with Intel sockets have four holes to anchor the cooler (for example, see Figure 3-15). Examine the cooler posts that fit over these holes and the clips, nuts, bolts, screws, or plates that will hold the cooler firmly in place. Make sure you understand how this mechanism works because it may be difficult to install.

Four holes in motherboard to attach cooler assembly

Thermal compound applied

Figure 3-15 If the cooler does not have preapplied thermal compound, apply it on top of the processor

2. If the cooler has thermal compound preapplied, remove the plastic from the compound. If the cooler does not have thermal compound applied, put a small dot of compound (about the size of a small pea) in the center of the processor, as shown in Figure 3-15. When the cooler is attached and the processor is running, the compound spreads over the surface. Don't use too much—apply just enough to later create a thin layer. If you use too much compound, it can slide off the housing and damage the processor or circuits on the motherboard. To get just the right amount, you can buy individual packets that each contain a single application of thermal compound.

Notes When removing and reinstalling a processor, use a soft, dry cloth to carefully remove all the old thermal compound from both the processor and the cooler. Don't try to reuse the compound.

3. Some heavy coolers provide a plate that fits underneath the motherboard, with nuts, bolts, and screws to secure it to the board. The plate strengthens the board to help protect it from bending when the heavy cooler is installed. Install the plate, such as the one shown in Figure 3-16. The bolts on top of the board are now ready to receive the cooler.

Figure 3-16 A cooler assembly plate on the bottom of the motherboard prevents a heavy cooler from bending the board

4. After the plate is installed, install the cooler on top of the processor. Be very careful to place the cooler straight down on the processor without shifting it so you don't smear the thermal compound off the top of the processor. Work very slowly and deliberately. To help keep the cooler balanced and in position, partly secure screws in two opposite bolts and then into the other two bolts. Rotate among the screws to partially tighten each one several times and keep the cooler in balance. See Figure 3-17. You can then clip the fan to the side of the cooler fins.

Figure 3-17 To keep the cooler balanced, rotate among the four screws as you partially tighten each screw in turn

5. For lighter coolers with locking pins, verify that the locking pins are turned as far as they will go in a counterclockwise direction. (Make sure the pins don't protrude into the hollow plastic posts that go down into the motherboard holes.) Align the cooler over the processor so that all four posts fit into the

3

four holes on the motherboard and the fan power cord can reach the fan header on the motherboard. Then push down on each locking pin until you hear it pop into the hole. To help keep the cooler balanced and in position, push down two opposite pins and then push the remaining two pins in place. Using a flathead screwdriver, turn each locking pin clockwise to secure it. Figure 3-18 shows a cooler with locking pins secured. (Later, if you need to remove the cooler, turn each locking pin counterclockwise to release it from the hole.)

Fan header

Figure 3-18 The pins are turned clockwise to secure the cooler to the motherboard

Notes If you later notice the CPU fan is running far too often, you might need to tighten the connection between the cooler and the processor.

6. The fan on a cooler receives its power from a 4-pin CPU fan header on the motherboard. Connect the power cord from the cooler fan to this 4-pin header, which you should find on the board near the processor (see Figure 3-19).

Figure 3-19 Connect the cooler fan power cord to the motherboard 4-pin CPU fan header

After the processor and cooler are installed and the motherboard is installed in the case, make sure cables and cords don't obstruct fans or airflow, especially airflow around the processor and video card. Use cable ties to tie cords and cables up and out of the way.

Make one last check to verify that all power connectors are in place and that other cords and cables are connected to the motherboard correctly. You are now ready to plug the system back in, turn it on, and verify all is working. If the power comes on (you hear the fan spinning and see lights) but the system fails to work, most likely the processor is not seated solidly in the socket or some power cord has not yet been connected or is not solidly connected. Turn everything off, unplug the power cord, press the power button to drain power, open the case, and recheck your installation.

If the system comes up and begins the boot process but suddenly turns off before the boot is complete, most likely the processor is overheating because the cooler is not installed correctly. Turn everything off, unplug the power cord, press the power button to drain power, open the case, and verify that the cooler is securely seated and connected.

After the system is up and running, you can check BIOS/UEFI setup to verify that the system recognized the processor correctly. The setup screen for one processor is shown in Figure 3-20. Also, check the CPU and motherboard temperatures in BIOS/UEFI setup to verify that the CPU is not overheating. In the BIOS/UEFI utility shown in Figure 3-20, you can see the temperatures and fan RPMs.

Source: American Megatrends, Inc.

Figure 3-20   Verify that the CPU is recognized correctly by BIOS/UEFI and that CPU and motherboard temperatures are within acceptable range

The maximum processor temperature varies by processor; to know the maximum, download the datasheet specifications for the processor from the Intel website (*ark.intel.com*). For example, the Intel Core i5-8600K 6-core processor shown earlier in this chapter will stop execution if the temperature rises above 100 degrees. If you see the temperature rising this high, open the case cover and verify that the processor fan is running. Perhaps a wire is in the way and preventing the fan from turning or the fan power wire is not connected. Other troubleshooting tips for processors are covered in Chapter 4.

INSTALL AN AMD PROCESSOR AND COOLER ASSEMBLY

When installing an AMD processor, do the following:

1. Open the socket lever. If there's a protective cover over the socket, remove it.

2. Holding the processor very carefully so you don't touch the bottom, orient the four empty pin positions on the bottom with the four filled hole positions in the socket (see Figure 3-21). For some AMD sockets,

a gold triangle on one corner of the processor matches up with a small triangle on a corner of the socket. Carefully lower the processor straight down into the socket. Don't allow it to tilt or slide as it goes into the socket. The pins on the bottom of the processor are very delicate, so take care as you work.

Four alignment positions

Figure 3-21 Orient the four alignment positions on the bottom of the processor with those in the socket

3. Check carefully to make sure the pins in the processor are sitting slightly in the holes. Make sure the pins are not offset from the holes. If you try to use the lever to put pressure on these pins and they are not aligned correctly, you can destroy the processor. You can actually feel the pins settle into place when you're lowering the processor into the socket correctly.

4. Press the lever down and gently into position (see Figure 3-22).

Figure 3-22 Lower the lever into place, which puts pressure on the processor

5. You are now ready to apply the thermal compound and install the cooler assembly. For most AMD sockets, the black retention mechanism for the cooler is already installed on the motherboard (see Figure 3-23). Set the cooler on top of the processor, aligning it inside the retention mechanism.

Figure 3-23 Align the cooler over the retention mechanism

6. Next, clip the clipping mechanism into place on one side of the cooler. Then push down firmly on the clip on the opposite side of the cooler assembly; the clip will snap into place. Figure 3-24 shows the clip on one side in place for a system that has a yellow retention mechanism and a black cooler clip. Later, if you need to remove the cooler, use a Phillips screwdriver to remove the screws holding the retention mechanism in place. Then remove the retention mechanism along with the entire cooler assembly.

Figure 3-24 The clips on the cooler attach the cooler to the retention mechanism on the motherboard

7. Connect the power cord from the fan to the 4-pin CPU fan header on the motherboard next to the processor.

> ✎ **Notes** You will learn how to troubleshoot problems with the processor, motherboard, and RAM in Chapter 4.

REPLACING THE PROCESSOR IN A LAPTOP

**A+
CORE 1
1.1**

Before replacing the processor in a laptop, consider that the laptop might still be under warranty. Also consider that it might be more cost effective to replace the laptop rather than replacing the processor, when you include the cost of parts and labor. If you decide to replace a processor in a laptop, be sure to select a processor supported by the manufacturer of the particular laptop model. The range of processors supported by a laptop does not usually include as many options as those supported by a desktop motherboard.

Follow the directions in the service manual to remove the old processor. For some laptops, removing the cover on the bottom exposes the processor fan and heat sink assembly. When you remove this assembly, you can then open the socket and remove the processor. For example, looking at the laptop shown in Figure 3-25, you can see the processor heat sink and fan assembly exposed. To remove the assembly, remove the seven screws and the fan power connector (see Figure 3-26). Then lift the assembly straight up, being careful not to damage the processor underneath.

Figure 3-25 The cover is removed from the bottom of a laptop, exposing several internal components

Figure 3-26 Seven screws hold the processor heat sink and fan assembly in place

In the laptop shown in Figure 3-27, the heat sink and fan assembly are also exposed when you remove the cover on the bottom of the laptop. Notice that the heat sink on this laptop extends to the processor and chipset. You remove several screws and then lift the entire assembly out as a unit. For the laptop shown in Figures 3-25 and 3-26, the heat sink fits on top of the processor and the fan sits to the side of the processor. This design is typical of many laptops. However, some laptops require you to remove the keyboard and the keyboard bezel to reach the fan assembly and processor under the bezel.

Processor socket is under this portion of the heat sink

Figure 3-27 Remove the cover from the bottom of the laptop to expose the heat sink and fan assembly and to reach the processor

Figure 3-28 shows the heat sink and fan assembly removed in a laptop, exposing the processor. Notice the thermal compound on the processor. To remove the processor, turn the CPU socket screw 90 degrees to open the socket, as shown in the figure. Most Intel and AMD sockets have this socket screw on the side of the socket, as shown in Figure 3-28, although other sockets have the screw on the corner.

Figure 3-28 Open the CPU socket

Lift the CPU from the socket. Be careful to lift straight up without bending the CPU pins. Figure 3-29 shows the processor out of the socket. If you look carefully, you can see the missing pins on one corner of the processor and socket. This corner is used to correctly orient the processor in the socket.

3

Figure 3-29 The processor removed from the socket

Before you place the new processor into the socket, be sure the socket screw is in the open position. Then delicately place the processor into its socket. If it does not drop in completely, consider that the screw might not be in the full open position. Be sure to use new thermal compound on top of the processor. Intel recommends 0.2 grams of compound, which is about the size of a small pea. To make sure you use just the right amount of compound, consider buying it in individual packets that are measured for a single application.

Now let's turn our attention to the various memory technologies used in personal computers and learn how to upgrade memory.

MEMORY TECHNOLOGIES

A+ CORE 1 1.1, 3.3 Recall that random access memory (RAM) temporarily holds data and instructions as the CPU processes them and that the memory modules used on a motherboard are made of dynamic RAM or DRAM. DRAM loses its data rapidly, and the memory controller must refresh it several thousand times a second. RAM is stored on memory modules, which are installed in memory slots on the motherboard (see Figure 3-30).

One populated black slot and one empty black slot

Two empty blue slots

Figure 3-30 RAM on motherboards today is stored in DIMMs

> ★ **A+ Exam Tip** The A+ Core 1 exam expects you to know the purposes and characteristics of DDR2, DDR3, DDR4, and SO-DIMM memory technologies and how to match memory for an upgrade to memory already installed in a system.

Several variations of DRAM have evolved over the years. Here are the two major categories of memory modules:

▲ All current motherboards for desktops use a type of memory module called a DIMM (dual inline memory module).

▲ Laptops use a smaller version of a DIMM called a SO-DIMM (small outline DIMM, pronounced "sew-dim"). MicroDIMMs are used on subnotebook computers and are smaller than SO-DIMMs.

DIMMs have seen several evolutions and you need to know about the last three, which are shown in Table 3-1. Notice the notches on the edge connector of each module, which prevent the wrong type of module from being inserted into a memory slot on the motherboard.

Description of Module	Example
A 288-pin DDR4 DIMM is currently the fastest memory with lower voltage requirements. It can support quad or dual channels or function as single DIMMs. It has one notch near the center of the edge connector.	Source: kingston.com
A 240-pin DDR3 DIMM can support quad, triple, or dual channels or function as single DIMMs. It has an offset notch farther from the center than a DDR2 DIMM.	
A 240-pin DDR2 DIMM can support dual channels or function as single DIMMs. It has one notch near the center of the edge connector.	

Table 3-1   Types of memory modules

Many DIMM technologies exist because they have evolved to improve capacity, speed, and performance without greatly increasing the cost. A quick Google search for buying RAM turns up details such as those shown in Figure 3-31. In this part of the chapter, you learn about these technologies so that you can make the best selections of memory for a particular motherboard and customer needs.

> ✎ **Notes** JEDEC (*jedec.org*) is the organization responsible for standards used by solid-state devices, including RAM technologies.

Figure 3-31 Evolving memory technologies result in many details and options

We'll now look at each of the types of DIMM and SO-DIMM modules and the technologies they use.

DIMM AND SO-DIMM TECHNOLOGIES

To understand the details of a memory ad, let's start with a few important acronyms:

- The "D" in DIMM stands for "dual," named for the independent pins on both sides of the module's edge connector. All DIMMs have a 64-bit data path.
  - A SIMM (single inline memory module) is an older technology that has pins on only one side of the module edge connector. You hardly ever see them used today.
- A DDR (Double Data Rate) DIMM gets its name from the fact that it ran twice as fast as earlier DIMMs when it was invented. It was able to double the effective data rate because a DDR DIMM processes data at the rise and fall of the motherboard clock beat, rather than at each clock beat.
- DDR2 is faster and uses less power than DDR.
- DDR3 is faster and uses less power than DDR2. Both DDR2 and DDR3 DIMMs use 240 pins. They are not compatible because their notches are not in the same position.
- DDR4 is faster and uses less power than DDR3. A DDR4 module uses 288 pins and has a single notch in the edge connector.

Factors that affect the capacity, features, and performance of DIMMs include the number of channels they use, how much RAM is on one DIMM, the speed, error-checking abilities, and buffering. All these factors are discussed next.

SINGLE, DUAL, TRIPLE, AND QUAD CHANNELS

Early DIMMs only used a single channel, which means the memory controller can access only one DIMM at a time. To improve overall memory performance, dual channels allow the memory controller to communicate with two DIMMs at the same time, effectively doubling the speed of memory access. A motherboard that supports triple channels can access three DIMMs at the same time, and a quad channel motherboard can access four DIMMs at the same time. DDR2, DDR3, and DDR4 DIMMs can use dual channels. DDR3 DIMMs can also use triple channels. DDR3 and DDR4 DIMMs can use quad channels. For dual, triple, or quad channels to work, the motherboard and the DIMM must support the technology.

Motherboard manufacturers typically color-code DIMM slots to show you how to configure dual, triple, or quad channeling. For example, Figure 3-32 shows how dual channeling works on a board with two black DIMM slots and two gray slots. The board has two memory channels, channel 1 and channel 2. With dual channeling, two DIMMs installed in the two gray slots are each using a different channel, and therefore can be addressed at the same time. If two more DIMMs are installed in the two black slots, they can be accessed at the same time.

Figure 3-32 Using dual channels, the memory controller can read from two DIMMs at the same time

When setting up dual channeling, know that the pair of DIMMs to be addressed at the same time must be equally matched in size, speed, and features, and it is recommended they come from the same manufacturer. (Two matching DIMMs are often sold as a DIMM kit.) A motherboard that supports dual channels was shown in Figure 3-30. To use dual channeling, this motherboard requires matching DIMMs to be installed in the black slots and another matching pair in the blue slots, as shown in Figure 3-33.

Know that the second pair of DIMMs does not have to match the first pair of DIMMs because the blue slots run independently of the black slots. If the two DIMM slots of the same color are not populated with matching pairs of DIMMs, the motherboard will revert to single channeling.

DIMMs in channel A slots

DIMMs in channel B slots

Figure 3-33 Matching pairs of DIMMs installed in four DIMM slots that support dual channeling

⭐ **A+ Exam Tip**   The A+ Core 1 exam expects you to be able to distinguish among single-channel, dual-channel, and triple-channel memory installations and to configure these installations for best performance.

For a triple-channel installation, three DIMM slots must be populated with three matching DDR3 DIMMs (see Figure 3-34). The three DIMMs are installed in the three blue slots on the board. The motherboard in the figure has a fourth black DIMM slot. You can barely see this black slot behind the three populated slots in the photo. If the fourth slot is used, then triple channeling is disabled, which can slow down performance. If a matching pair of DIMMs is installed in the first two slots and another matching pair of DIMMs is installed in the third and fourth slots, then the memory controller will use dual channels. Dual channels are not as fast as triple channels, but they are certainly better than single channels.

Fourth slot is empty

Figure 3-34 Three identical DDR3 DIMMs installed in a triple-channel configuration

Expect a motherboard that uses quad channeling to have eight memory slots. For example, the Gigabyte AMD X399 Gaming motherboard has four DIMM slots on each side of the AMD TR4 processor socket (see Figure 3-35). The eight DIMM slots support four channels; each channel has two slots. The processor can address four slots or four channels at the same time. To know which of the eight slots to populate for optimum performance, see the motherboard user manual; in the figure, the manufacturer did not color-code the slots.

Figure 3-35   The Gigabyte AMD X399 Gaming motherboard has eight DIMM DDR4 slots and supports quad channeling

DIMM SPEEDS

DIMM speeds are measured either in MHz (such as 3,000 MHz or 1,600 MHz) or PC rating (such as PC4 24000 or PC3 12800). A PC rating is a measure of the total bandwidth (in MB/second) of data moving between the module and the CPU. To calculate the PC rating for a DDR4 DIMM, multiply the speed by 8 bytes because a DIMM has an 8-byte or 64-bit data path. For example, a DDR4 DIMM that runs at 3,000 MHz has a bandwidth or transfer rate of $3,000 \times 8$ or 24,000 MB/second, which is expressed as a PC rating of PC4 24000. (A DDR4 PC rating is labeled PC4.)

A second example calculates the PC rating for a DDR3 DIMM running at 1,600 MHz:

PC rating = $1,600 \times 8 = 12,800$, which is written as PC3 12800.

★ **A+ Exam Tip**   The A+ Core 1 exam expects you to be able to calculate PC ratings, given the transfers per second. To get the PC rating, multiply the transfers per second by eight. To get the speed, divide the PC rating by eight.

ERROR CHECKING AND PARITY

Because DIMMs intended to be used in servers must be extremely reliable, error-checking technology called ECC (error-correcting code) is sometimes used. Figure 3-36 shows two modules with ECC designed for server use.

M393A2G40EB2-CTD Samsung 16GB 1X16GB 2666MHZ PC4-21300 CI17 Ecc Registered Dual Rank X4 DD

$186.00 from 5+ stores

Brand New . . Product # M393A2G40Eb2-Ctd . . The Samsung 16Gb Ddr4 Rdimm **Server** Memory is a memory module with 16 GB storage ...

Samsung · DDR4 · 16 GB · 2,666 MHz · ECC · Registered

Samsung M393A4K40BB0-CPB4Q 32GB 2133Mhz Pc4-17000 Registered DDR4 New

$390.00 from 5+ stores

Brand New. In Stock.

Samsung · DDR4 · 32 GB · 2,133 MHz · ECC · Registered

Figure 3-36   Server memory uses ECC for fault tolerance

Some DDR2, DDR3, and DDR4 memory modules support ECC. A DIMM that supports ECC will have an extra chip, the ECC chip. ECC compares bits written to the module to what is later read from the module, and it can detect and correct an error in a single bit of the byte. If there are errors in 2 bits of a byte, ECC can detect the error but cannot correct it. The data path width for DIMMs is normally 64 bits, but with ECC, the data path is 72 bits. The extra 8 bits are used for error checking. ECC memory costs more than non-ECC memory, but it is more reliable. For ECC to work, the motherboard and all installed modules must support it. Also, it's important to know that you cannot install a mix of ECC and non-ECC memory on the motherboard—the resulting system will not work.

As with most other memory technologies discussed in this chapter, when adding memory to a motherboard, match the type of memory to the type the board supports. To see if your motherboard supports ECC memory, look for the ability to enable or disable the feature in BIOS/UEFI setup, or check the motherboard documentation.

Older SIMMs and DIMMs used an error-checking technology called parity. Using parity checking, a ninth bit is stored with every 8 bits in a byte. If memory is using odd parity, it makes the ninth or parity bit either a 1 or a 0 so that the number of 1s in the 9 bits is odd. If memory uses even parity, it makes the parity bit a 1 or a 0 to make the number of 1s in the 9 bits even.

> ★ **A+ Exam Tip**   The A+ Core 1 exam expects you to know that parity memory uses 9 bits (8 bits for data and 1 bit for parity). You also need to be familiar with ECC and non-ECC memory technologies and to know when each technology is recommended or required in a given scenario.

Later, when the byte is read back, the memory controller checks the odd or even state. If the number of bits is not an odd number for odd parity or an even number for even parity, a parity error occurs. A parity error always causes the system to halt. On the screen, you see the error message "Parity Error 1" or "Parity Error 2" or a similar error message about parity. Parity Error 1 is a parity error on the motherboard; Parity Error 2 is a parity error on an expansion card.

Figure 3-37 shows a DIMM and SO-DIMM for sale. The DIMM is advertised as parity memory and the SO-DIMM is non-parity. Expect parity memory to be more expensive and more reliable than non-parity memory.

MT18HTF25672PY-667E1 Micron 2GB Pc2-5300p DDR2-667
Parity Ecc 1rx4 Cl5 240 Pin Memory. New

$79.00 from 10+ stores

★★★★★ 1 product review

Micron · DDR2 · 2 GB · 667 MHz · ECC · 240-pin

92G7315 - 8MB EDO SO Dimm NON-PARITY Memory Board

$4.95 from Impact Computers & Electronics

8MB EDO SO Dimm NON-**PARITY Memory** Board

IBM · 8 MB

Figure 3-37 Parity and ECC memory is more reliable than non-parity and non-ECC memory

Notes RAM chips on DIMMs can cause errors if they become undependable and cannot hold data reliably. Sometimes this happens when chips overheat or power falters.

BUFFERED AND REGISTERED DIMMS

Buffers and registers hold data and amplify a signal just before the data is written to the module, and they can increase memory performance in servers. (Buffers are an older technology than registers.) Some DIMMs use buffers, some use registers, and some use neither. If a DIMM doesn't support registers or buffers, it's referred to as an unbuffered DIMM or UDIMM. Looking back at the ad in Figure 3-31, you can see two modules listed as Unbuffered, one listed as Registered, and another that's not identified, so we can assume it is unbuffered. You might see registered memory written as RDIMM.

CAS LATENCY

Another memory feature is CAS Latency (CAS stands for "column access strobe"), which is a way of measuring access timing. The feature refers to the number of clock cycles it takes to write or read a column of data off a memory module. Lower values are better than higher ones. For example, CL8 is a little faster than CL9.

Notes In memory ads, CAS Latency is sometimes written as CL.

Ads for memory modules might give the CAS Latency value within a series of timing numbers, such as 5-5-5-15. The first value is CAS Latency, which means the module is CL5. Looking back at Figure 3-37, you can see the CL rating for the first module is CL5.

Notes When selecting memory, use the memory type that the motherboard manufacturer recommends.

TYPES OF MEMORY USED IN LAPTOPS

Today's laptops use DDR4, DDR3L, DDR3, or DDR2 SO-DIMM memory. Table 3-2 lists current SO-DIMMs. All these memory modules are smaller than regular DIMMs and use the same technologies as DIMMs.

3

★ **A+ Exam Tip** The A+ Core 1 exam expects you to know that DDR3, DDR2, and DDR memory can be found on SO-DIMMs and to know when to use each type of memory in a given scenario.

Memory Module Description	Sample Memory Module
A 2.74" 260-pin SO-DIMM contains DDR4 memory. The one notch on the module is offset from the center of the module.	![crucial memory module] Source: crucial.com
A 2.66" 204-pin SO-DIMM contains DDR3 memory. The one notch on the module is offset from the center of the module. A DDR3L SO-DIMM uses less power than a regular DDR3 SO-DIMM.	![Kingston HyperX module] Courtesy of Kingston Technology Corporation
A 2.66" 200-pin SO-DIMM contains DDR2 SDRAM. One notch is near the side of the module.	![Kingston memory module] Courtesy of Kingston Technology Corporation

Table 3-2 Memory modules used in laptop computers

As with memory modules used in desktop computers, you can only use the type of memory the laptop is designed to support. The number of pins and the position of the notches on a SO-DIMM keep you from inserting the wrong module in a memory slot.

HOW TO UPGRADE MEMORY

To upgrade memory means to add more RAM to a computer. Adding more RAM might solve a problem with slow performance, applications refusing to load, or an unstable system. When Windows does not have adequate memory to perform an operation, it displays an "Insufficient memory" error or it slows down to a painful crawl.

When first purchased, many computers have empty slots on the motherboard, allowing you to add DIMMs or SO-DIMMs to increase the amount of RAM. Sometimes a memory module goes bad and must be replaced.

When you add more memory to your computer, you need answers to these questions:

▲ How much RAM do I need and how much is currently installed?
▲ What type of memory is currently installed?
▲ How many and what kind of modules can I fit on my motherboard?
▲ How do I select and purchase the right modules for my upgrade?
▲ How do I physically install the new modules?

All these questions are answered in the following sections.

HOW MUCH MEMORY DO I NEED AND HOW MUCH IS CURRENTLY INSTALLED?

With the demands today's software places on memory, the answer is probably, "All you can get." When deciding how much memory the system can support, consider the limitations of the motherboard, processor, and operating system. For the motherboard, research the motherboard user manual or manufacturer website. For the processor, see the Intel or AMD website. Here are the limitations when considering the operating system:

◢ Windows 10/8/7 requires a minimum of 1 GB for a 32-bit installation and 2 GB for a 64-bit installation, but more is better.

◢ For 64-bit installations, Windows 10 Pro can support up to 2 TB of memory, Windows 8 Pro can support up to 512 GB, and Windows 7 Pro can support up to 192 GB, although no motherboard can support that much memory.

◢ A 32-bit Windows 10/8/7 installation can support no more than 4 GB of memory.

APPLYING | CONCEPTS

HOW MUCH AND WHAT KIND OF MEMORY IS CURRENTLY INSTALLED?

When you execute **msinfo32.exe** in Windows, the System Information window shown in Figure 3-38 reports the amount of installed physical memory. Notice in the window that 16 GB is installed.

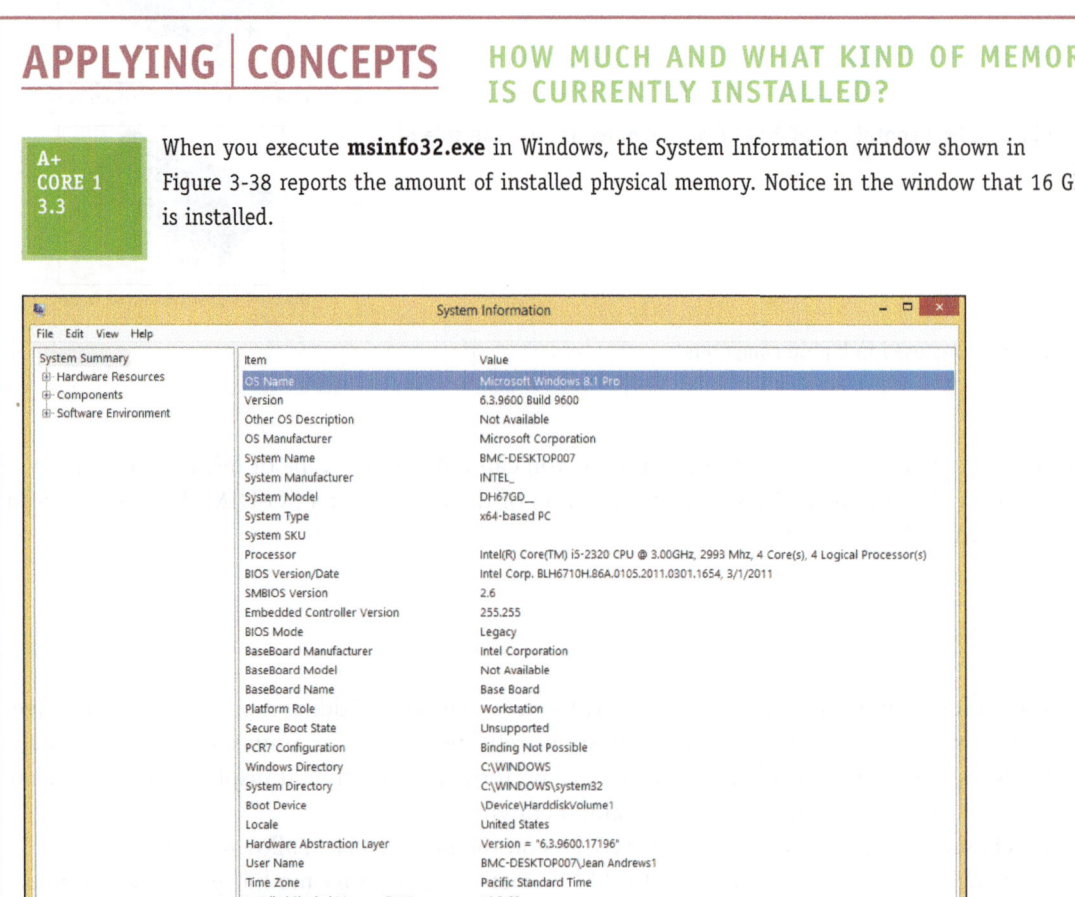

Figure 3-38 The System Information window reports installed physical memory

(continues)

The BIOS/UEFI setup screen shows more information about installed memory than Windows does. Reboot the computer and access BIOS/UEFI setup, as you learned in Chapter 2. The BIOS/UEFI setup main menu for one system is shown in Figure 3-39. This screen shows that there are four memory slots and that each contains a 4-GB DIMM. You can also see that the memory speed is 1,333 MHz and the board supports dual channeling.

```
                              System Setup
 Main     Configuration   Performance   Security   Power   Boot   Exit

   BIOS Version              BLH6710H.86A.0105.2011.0301.1654      Number of cores to
                                                                   enabled in each
   Processor Type            Intel(R) Core(TM) i5-2320 CPU @       processor package
                             3.00GHz

   Active Processor Cores    <ALL>
   Host Clock Frequency      100MHz
   Processor Turbo Speed     3.30 GHz
   Memory Speed              1333 MHz

   L2 Cache RAM              4 x 256 KB
   L3 Cache RAM              6 MB
   Total Memory              16 GB
   DIMM3 (Memory Channel A Slot 0)   4 GB
   DIMM1 (Memory Channel A Slot 1)   4 GB
   DIMM4 (Memory Channel B Slot 0)   4 GB
   DIMM2 (Memory Channel B Slot 1)   4 GB

   System Identification Information

   System Date              [Thu 05/01/2012]            → ←: Select Screen
   System Time              [09:35:49]                  ↑ ↓: Select Item
                                                        Enter:Select
                                                        +/-: Change Opt.
                                                        F9: Load Defaults
                                                        F10:Save ESC:Exit
```

Source: Intel

Figure 3-39 BIOS/UEFI setup reports the memory configuration and amount

Because all the slots are populated, you know you must replace existing 4-GB DIMMs with larger-capacity DIMMs, which will increase the price of the upgrade.

On other BIOS/UEFI screens, you should be able to identify the motherboard brand and model. For the BIOS/UEFI in Figure 3-39, select **System Identification Information**; you see that the motherboard is the Intel DH67GD.

WHAT TYPE OF MEMORY IS ALREADY INSTALLED?

A+ CORE 1 3.3

If the board already has memory installed, you want to do your best to match the new modules with the existing modules. To learn what type of memory modules are already installed, do the following:

1. Open the case and look at the memory slots. How many slots do you have? How many are filled? Remove each module from its slot and examine it for the imprinted type, size, and speed. In Figure 3-40, the module is 4 GB PC4-17000 CL 15-15-15-36 and the brand of RAM is GEIL.

Figure 3-40 Use the label on this DIMM to identify its features

2. If you have not already identified the motherboard, examine it for the imprinted manufacturer and model (see Figure 3-41).

Model

Manufacturer

Figure 3-41   Look for the manufacturer and model of a motherboard imprinted somewhere on the board

3. Find the motherboard documentation online and read it to find the type of memory the board supports. Look in the documentation to see if the board supports dual channels, triple channels, or quad channels. If the board supports multiple channels and modules are already installed, verify that matching DIMMs are installed in each channel, as recommended in the documentation.

4. If you still have not identified the module type, you can take the motherboard and the old memory modules to a good computer store and they should be able to match it for you.

HOW MANY AND WHAT KIND OF MODULES CAN FIT ON MY MOTHERBOARD?

> **A+**
> **CORE 1**
> **3.3**

Now that you know what memory modules are already installed, you're ready to decide how much memory and what kind of modules you can add to the board. Keep in mind that if all memory slots are full, you can sometimes take out small-capacity modules and replace them with larger-capacity modules, but you can only use the type, size, and speed of modules that the board can support. Also, if you must discard existing modules, the price of the upgrade increases.

To know how much memory your motherboard can physically hold, read the documentation that comes with the board. You can always install DIMMs as single modules, but you might not get the best performance by doing so. For best performance, install matching DIMMs in each channel (two, three, or four slots). Now let's look at two examples, one using dual channels and another using triple channels.

MOTHERBOARD USING DDR4 DUAL-CHANNEL DIMMs

The Asus Prime Z370-P motherboard has four 288-pin DDR4 DIMM slots and is shown earlier in Figure 3-41. It supports 2-GB, 4-GB, 8-GB, and 16-GB unbuffered, non-ECC DDR4 DIMMs with dual channeling. DIMM voltage cannot exceed 1.35 V and DIMMs with the same CAS Latency must be installed. The user manual recommends installing memory from the same manufacturer and same product line. It also says the maximum speed of the DIMMs supported varies by the processor. The processor shown in Figure 3-41 is the Intel Core i5-8600K; a quick check at *ark.intel.com* tells us that the maximum memory speed supported by this processor is 2,666 MHz. The information imprinted on the two DIMMs currently installed (see Figure 3-42) is DDR4 3,000 MHz 15-17-17-35 1.35 V Vengeance by Corsair.

Figure 3-42   Look for imprinted information about a DIMM

You want to upgrade memory from the current 16 GB to 32 GB. To get the full benefit of dual channeling, based on your research, you need to purchase two matching DIMMs using these specifications:

◢ Corsair Vengeance DDR4 DIMM
◢ CAS Latency 15, unbuffered, non-ECC
◢ Minimum speed of 2,666 MHz

To support dual channeling, the two existing DIMMs are installed in the two gray slots on the board; you plan to install the two new DIMMs in the two black slots.

MOTHERBOARD USING DDR3 TRIPLE-CHANNEL DIMMs

The Intel motherboard shown earlier in Figure 3-34 has four DDR3 memory slots that can be configured for single, dual, or triple channeling. The four empty slots are shown in Figure 3-43. If triple channeling is used, three matching DIMMs are used in the three blue slots. If the fourth slot is populated, the board reverts to single channeling. For dual channeling, install two matching DIMMs in the two blue slots farthest from the processor and leave the other two slots empty. If only one DIMM is installed, it goes in the blue slot in the farthest position from the processor.

Figure 3-43   Four DDR3 slots on a motherboard

The motherboard documentation says that these types of DIMMs can be used:

◢ DIMM voltage rating no higher than 1.6 V
◢ Non-ECC DDR3 memory

◢ Serial Presence Detect (SPD) memory only
◢ Gold-plated contacts (some modules use tin-plated contacts)
◢ 1333 MHz, 1066 MHz, or 800 MHz (best to match the system bus speed)
◢ Unbuffered, nonregistered single- or double-sided DIMMs
◢ Up to 16 GB total installed RAM

The third item in the list needs an explanation. SPD is a DIMM technology that declares the module's size, speed, voltage, and data path width to system BIOS/UEFI at startup. If the DIMM does not support SPD, the system might not boot or boot with errors. Today's memory always supports SPD.

HOW DO I SELECT AND PURCHASE THE RIGHT MEMORY MODULES?

You're now ready to make a purchase. As you select your memory, it might be difficult to find an exact match to DIMMs already installed on the board. Compromises might be necessary, but understand that there are some you can make and some you cannot:

◢ Mixing unbuffered memory with buffered or registered memory won't work.
◢ When matching memory, you should also match the module manufacturer for best results. But, in a pinch, you can try using memory from two different manufacturers.
◢ If you mix memory speeds, know that all modules will perform at the slowest speed.

Now let's look at how to use a website or computer ad to search for the right memory.

USE A WEBSITE TO RESEARCH YOUR PURCHASE

When purchasing memory from a website such as Crucial Technology's site (*crucial.com*) or Kingston Technology's site (*kingston.com*), look for a search utility that will match memory modules to your motherboard. These utilities are easy to use and help you confirm you have made the right decisions about type, size, and speed to buy. They can also help if motherboard documentation is inadequate and you're not exactly sure what memory to buy.

Let's look at one example on the Crucial site, where we are looking to install memory in the Asus Prime Z370-P motherboard discussed earlier in the chapter. After selecting the manufacturer, product, and model (see Figure 3-44), click **find upgrade**.

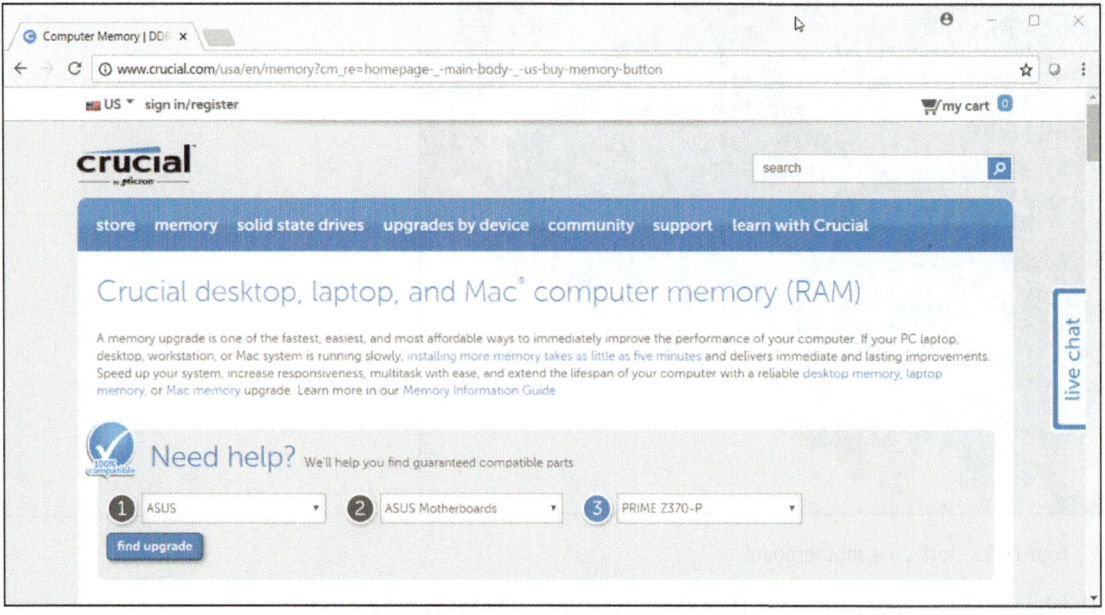

Source: crucial.com

Figure 3-44 Use the Crucial upgrade utility to find the correct memory for an upgrade

The search results include the DIMMs shown in Figure 3-45. You can see all our criteria are met (unbuffered, CAS Latency 15, Non-ECC, 3,000 MHz, and 1.35 V) except the brand. These criteria validate what we have already determined based on our research, and we can now search for the matching brand on other memory sites. If we can't find the matching brand, this hit will certainly work for our upgrade.

Source: crucial.com

Figure 3-45   Selecting memory off the Crucial website

> ✎ **Notes** RAM modules may have heat spreaders, which are fins or heat sinks on the side of the module to keep it from overheating. Some modules have cool lights for visual appeal in see-through cases.

HOW DO I INSTALL THE NEW MODULES?

A+ CORE 1 3.3

When installing RAM modules, be careful to protect the chips against static electricity, as you learned in Chapters 1 and 2. Follow these precautions:

- Always use an ESD strap as you work.
- Turn off the power, unplug the power cord, press the power button, and remove the case cover.
- Handle memory modules with care.
- Don't touch the edge connectors on the memory module or on the memory slot.
- Don't stack cards or modules because you can loosen a chip.
- Usually modules pop into place easily and are secured by spring catches on both ends. Make sure that you look for the notches on one side or in the middle of the module; these notches orient the module in the slot.

Let's now look at the details of installing a DIMM.

INSTALL DIMMs

For DIMM modules, small clips latch into place on each side of the slot to hold the module in the slot, as shown in Figure 3-46. Some motherboards have only one latch on the slot. To install a DIMM, first pull the supporting arms on the sides of the slot outward. Look on the DIMM edge connector for the notches, which help you orient the DIMM correctly over the slot, and insert the DIMM straight down into the slot. When the DIMM is fully inserted, the supporting clips should pop back into place. Figure 3-47 shows a DIMM being inserted into a slot on a motherboard. Apply pressure on both ends of the DIMM at the same time, being careful not to rock the module from side to side or backward and forward.

Clip holds module in place

Open clip on empty slot

Figure 3-46   Clips on each side of a slot hold a DIMM in place

Figure 3-47   Insert the DIMM into the slot by pressing down until the support clips lock into position

When the computer powers up, it counts the memory present without any further instruction and senses the features that the modules support, such as ECC or buffering. During the boot you can enter BIOS/UEFI to verify that the memory is recognized or allow Windows to start and use the System Information window to verify the expected amount of installed memory. If the new memory is not recognized, power down the system and reseat the module. Most likely it's not installed solidly in the slot.

HOW TO UPGRADE MEMORY ON A LAPTOP

Before upgrading memory, make sure you are not voiding the laptop's warranty. Search for the best buy, but make sure you use memory modules made by or authorized by your laptop's manufacturer and designed for the exact model of your laptop. Installing generic memory might save money but might also void the laptop's warranty.

Upgrading memory on a laptop works about the same way as upgrading memory on a desktop: Decide how much memory you can upgrade and what type of memory you need, purchase the memory, and install it. As with a desktop computer, be sure to match the type of memory to the type the laptop supports.

APPLYING | CONCEPTS   UPGRADING MEMORY ON A LAPTOP

Most laptops are designed to allow easy access to memory. Follow these steps to exchange or upgrade memory for a typical laptop:

1. Back up data and shut down the system. Remove peripherals, including the AC adapter. Remove the battery. Be sure to use an ESD strap as you work.

2. Many laptops have a RAM door on the bottom. For some laptops, this door is in the battery cavity. Turn the laptop over and loosen the screws on the RAM door. (It is not necessary to remove the screws.)

3. Raise the door (see Figure 3-48) and remove it from its hinges. The two memory slots are exposed.

Figure 3-48   Raise the DIMM door on the bottom of the notebook

> ✏ **Notes** Some laptops have SO-DIMM slots stacked on top of each other. When you remove one SO-DIMM from these laptops, you can see the slot under it that holds a second SO-DIMM.

4. Notice in Figure 3-49 that one slot is filled and one is available for a memory upgrade. Also notice in the figure that when you remove the RAM door, the CMOS battery is exposed. This easy access to the battery makes exchanging it very easy. To remove a SO-DIMM, pull the clips on the side of the memory slot apart slightly (see Figure 3-49). The SO-DIMM will pop up and out of the slot and can then be removed. If it does not pop up, you can hold the clips apart as you pull the module up and out of the slot.

(continues)

Figure 3-49 Pull apart the clips on the memory slot to release the SO-DIMM

5. To install a new SO-DIMM, insert the module at an angle into the slot (see Figure 3-50) and gently push it down until it snaps into the clips (see Figure 3-51). Replace the RAM door.

Figure 3-50 Insert a new SO-DIMM into a memory slot

Figure 3-51 Push down on the SO-DIMM until it pops into the clips

6. Replace the battery, plug in the power adapter, and power up the laptop.

>> CHAPTER SUMMARY

Types and Characteristics of Processors

◢ The most important component on the motherboard is the processor, or central processing unit. The two major manufacturers of processors are Intel and AMD.

◢ Processors are rated by their processor speed, lithography, the socket and chipset they can use, multiprocessing features (multithreading, multicore rating, and dual processors), memory cache, memory features supported, virtualization, integrated graphics, overclocking, and processor architecture (32-bit or 64-bit).

◢ A processor's memory cache inside the processor housing can be an L1 cache (contained on the processor die), L2 cache (off the die), and L3 cache (farther from the core than L2 cache).

- The core of a processor has two arithmetic logic units (ALUs). Multicore processors have two, three, or more cores (called dual core, triple core, quad core, and so forth). Each core can process two threads at once if the feature is enabled in BIOS/UEFI setup.

- The current families of Intel processors for desktops include Core, Pentium, Atom, and Celeron. Several different processors and generations are within each family.

- The current AMD desktop and laptop processor families are Ryzen, Ryzen Pro, Ryzen Threadripper, A-Series, A-Series Pro, and FX. In addition, the Ryzen Threadripper is the latest processor for desktops. Several processors exist within each family.

Selecting and Installing a Processor

- Select a processor that the motherboard supports. A board is likely to support several processors that vary in performance and price.

- When installing a processor, always follow the directions in the motherboard user guide and be careful to protect the board and processor against ESD. Current Intel sockets use a socket lever and socket load plate. When opening these sockets, lift the socket lever and then the socket load plate, install the processor, and then close the socket. Many AMD sockets have a socket lever but not a socket load plate.

- Always apply thermal compound between the processor and cooler assembly to help draw heat from the processor.

Memory Technologies

- DRAM is stored on DIMMs for desktop computers and SO-DIMMs for laptops.

- Types of current DIMMs are DDR4, which have 288 pins, and DDR3 and DDR2 DIMMs, which have 240 pins.

- Matching DIMMs can work together in dual channels, triple channels, and quad channels so that the memory controller can access more than one DIMM at a time to improve performance. In a channel, all DIMMs must match in size, speed, and features. DDR3 DIMMs can use dual, triple, or quad channeling, but DDR2 DIMMs can only use dual channels. DDR4 DIMMs can use dual or quad channels.

- DIMM speeds are measured in MHz (for example, 3,000 MHz) or PC rating (for example, PC4 24000).

- The memory controller can check memory for errors and possibly correct them using ECC (error-correcting code). Using parity, an older technology, the controller could recognize that an error had occurred, but could not correct it.

- Buffers and registers are used to hold data and amplify a data signal. A DIMM is rated as a buffered, registered (RDIMM), or unbuffered DIMM (UDIMM).

- CAS Latency (CL) measures access time to memory. The lower values are faster than the higher values.

- Today's laptops use DDR4, DDR3L, DDR3, or DDR2 SO-DIMMs.

How to Upgrade Memory

- When upgrading memory, use the type, size, and speed the motherboard supports and match new modules to those already installed. Features to match include DDR4, DDR3, DDR2, size in MB or GB, speed (MHz or PC rating), buffered, registered, unbuffered, CL rating, tin or gold connectors, support for dual, triple, or quad channeling, ECC, and non-ECC. Using memory made by the same manufacturer is recommended.

- When upgrading components on a laptop, including memory, use components that are the same brand as the laptop, or use only components recommended by the laptop's manufacturer.

>> KEY TERMS

For explanations of key terms, see the Glossary for this text.

CAS Latency	dual processors	multicore processing	single-core processing
Centrino	dynamic RAM (DRAM)	multiprocessing	SO-DIMM (small outline
DDR (Double Data Rate)	ECC (error-correcting code)	multiprocessor platform	DIMM)
DDR2	graphics processing unit	parity	static RAM (SRAM)
DDR3	(GPU)	parity error	thermal compound
DDR3L	Hyper-Threading	processor frequency	thread
DDR4	HyperTransport	quad channel	triple channels
DIMM (dual inline	Level 1 cache (L1 cache)	SIMM (single inline	x86 processors
memory module)	Level 2 cache (L2 cache)	memory module)	x86-64 bit processors
dual channels	Level 3 cache (L3 cache)	single channel	

>> THINKING CRITICALLY

These questions are designed to prepare you for the critical thinking required for the A+ Core 1 exam and may use information from other chapters or the web. As always, remember Google is your friend!

1. An experienced user has installed Oracle VM VirtualBox on her workstation and is attempting to use it to create a virtual machine (VM). The software is causing error messages while attempting to create the VM. What is the most likely problem?

   a. The user does not know how to use the software.

   b. Virtualization is not enabled in BIOS/UEFI.

   c. The version of Windows she is using is not rated for installations of Oracle software.

   d. The processor is not rated to support VirtualBox and VMs.

2. A friend has asked you to help him find out if his computer is capable of overclocking. How can you direct him? Select all that apply.

   a. Show him how to find System Summary data in the System Information utility in Windows and then do online research.

   b. Show him how to access BIOS/UEFI setup and browse through the screens.

   c. Explain to your friend that overclocking is not a recommended best practice.

   d. Show him how to open the computer case, read the brand and model of his motherboard, and then do online research.

3. A customer has a system with a Gigabyte B450 Aorus Pro motherboard. He wants to upgrade the processor from the AMD Athlon X4 950 to the AMD Ryzen 7 2700X. Which of the following accurately describes this upgrade?

   a. The upgrade is possible and will yield a significant increase in performance.

   b. The upgrade is not possible because the new processor is not supported by this motherboard.

   c. The upgrade is possible, but will not yield a significant increase in performance.

   d. The upgrade is not possible because this motherboard has an embedded processor that cannot be exchanged.

4. What new parts will you need to replace a failing processor? Select all that apply.

   a. Power cable

   b. Processor

3

   c. Cooling assembly

   d. Thermal compound

5. How many threads can a quad-core processor handle at once?

6. A motherboard has four DIMM slots; three slots are gray and the fourth is black. What type of memory is this board designed to use?

   a. DDR4

   b. DDR3

   c. DDR2

   d. All of the above

7. What prevents a DDR3 DIMM from being installed in a DDR2 DIMM slot on a motherboard?

8. In memory ads for DIMMs, you notice DDR 2400 CL15 in one ad and PC4 21300 CL9 in another. Which ad is advertising the faster memory?

9. When planning a memory upgrade, you discover that Windows 8 reports 4 GB of memory installed. In BIOS/UEFI, you see that two of four slots are populated. You install two 2-GB DIMMs in the two empty DIMM slots. When you boot the system, Windows 8 still reports 4 GB of memory. Order the four steps you should take to troubleshoot the problem of missing memory.

   a. Open the case and verify that the DIMM modules are securely seated.

   b. Go into BIOS/UEFI and verify that it recognized 8 GB of installed memory.

   c. Open the System Information window to verify the edition or version of Windows 8 installed.

   d. Inspect the DIMMs you installed to verify that they match the existing DIMMs and those the motherboard can support.

10. If 2 bits of a byte are in error when the byte is read from ECC memory, can ECC detect the error? Can it fix the error?

11. A DIMM memory ad displays 5-5-5-15. What is the CAS Latency value of this DIMM?

12. What is the speed in MHz of a DIMM rated at PC4 24000?

13. A motherboard uses dual channeling, but you have four DIMMs available that differ in size. The motherboard supports all four sizes. Can you install these DIMMs on the board? Will dual channeling be enabled?

14. Which is faster, CL3 memory or CL5 memory?

15. If your motherboard supports ECC DDR3 memory, can you substitute non-ECC DDR3 memory?

16. You have just upgraded memory on a computer from 4 GB to 8 GB by adding one DIMM. When you first turn on the PC, the memory count shows only 4 GB. Which of the following is most likely the source of the problem? What can you do to fix it?

   a. Windows is displaying an error because it likely became corrupted while the computer was disassembled.

   b. The new DIMM you installed is faulty.

   c. The new DIMM is not properly seated.

   d. The DIMM is installed in the wrong slot.

17. Your motherboard supports dual channeling and you currently have two slots populated with DIMMs; each module holds 2 GB. You want to install an additional 4 GB of RAM. Will your system run faster if you install two 2-GB DIMMs or one 4-GB DIMM? Explain your answer.

Hands-On | Project 3-1   Researching a Processor Upgrade or Replacement

To identify your motherboard and find out what processor and processor socket a motherboard is currently using, you can use BIOS/UEFI setup, Windows utilities, or third-party software such as Speccy at *ccleaner.com/speccy/ download/standard*. To research which processors a board can support, you can use the motherboard user guide, the website of the motherboard manufacturer, and for Intel processors, the Intel site at *ark.intel.com*. Research the current processor and processor socket of your computer's motherboard, research which processors your board can support, and answer the following questions:

1. What is the brand and model of your motherboard? What processor socket does it use? How did you find your information?
2. Identify the currently installed processor, including its brand, model, speed, and other important characteristics. How did you find your information?
3. List three or more processors the board supports, according to the motherboard documentation or website.
4. Search the web for three or more processors that would match this board. Save or print three webpages that show the details and prices of a high-performing, moderately performing, and low-performing processor the board supports.
5. If your current processor fails, which processor would you recommend for this system? Explain your recommendation.

Now assume the Core i5-8600K processor that you saw installed in Figure 3-12 has gone bad. The motherboard in which it is installed is the Asus Prime Z370-P desktop board. The owner of the motherboard has requested that you keep the replacement cost as low as possible without sacrificing too much performance. What processor would you recommend for the replacement? Save or print a webpage that shows the processor and its cost.

Hands-On | Project 3-2   Removing and Inserting a Processor

In this project, you remove and install a processor. As you work, be very careful not to bend pins on the processor or socket, and protect the processor and motherboard against ESD. Do the following:

1. Verify that the computer is working. Turn off the system, unplug it, press the power button, and open the computer case. Put on your ESD strap. Remove the cooler assembly, remove all the thermal compound from the cooler and processor, and then remove the processor.
2. Reinstall the processor and thermal compound. Have your instructor check the thermal compound. Install the cooler.
3. Replace the case cover, power up the system, and verify that everything is working.

Hands-On | Project 3-3 Examining BIOS/UEFI Settings

On your home or lab computer, use BIOS/UEFI setup to answer these questions:

1. Which processor is installed? What is the processor frequency?
2. What are the BIOS/UEFI settings that apply to the processor and how is the processor configured?
3. What information does BIOS/UEFI report about total memory installed and how each memory slot is populated? Does the board support dual, triple, or quad channeling? How do you know?

Hands-On | Project 3-4 Planning and Pricing a Memory Upgrade

Research your own computer or a lab computer to determine how much and what type of memory is currently installed and how much the system can support. Then research the web to determine the total cost of a memory upgrade so you can max out the total memory on your system. Take into account the maximum memory your motherboard, processor, and operating system can support. You can keep the cost down by using the modules you already have, but don't forget to match important features of the modules already installed. Save or print webpages from two retail sites that show modules you would purchase. Answer the following questions:

1. How much memory is currently installed? After the upgrade, how much memory would be installed?
2. Which component—the motherboard, processor, or OS—dictated the maximum memory that could be installed in your system?
3. Describe the details of the currently installed memory. Describe the details of the new memory you would purchase for the upgrade.
4. How much will the upgrade cost?

Hands-On | Project 3-5 Explaining Triple and Quad Channeling

You have volunteered to help tutor some learners who are preparing to take the A+ Core 1 exam, and they have asked you to explain triple channeling and quad channeling. Draw a diagram similar to the dual-channeling diagram in Figure 3-32 to explain triple channeling, and then draw another diagram to explain quad channeling. Compare your diagrams with others in your class and make any necessary changes.

Hands-On | Project 3-6 Upgrading Memory

To practice installing additional memory in a computer in a classroom environment, remove the DIMMs from one computer and place them in another computer. Boot the second computer and check that it counts the additional memory. When finished, return the borrowed modules to the original computer.

Hands-On | Project 3-7   Upgrading Laptop Memory

A friend, Tangela, is looking for ways to improve the performance of her Windows 10 Lenovo laptop and has turned to you for advice. She has cleaned up the hard drive and is now considering the possibility of upgrading memory. In a phone conversation, Tangela reported the following:

1. When she opened the System Information window, she saw 8.0 GB as Installed Physical Memory.
2. When she looked on the bottom of the laptop, she saw the model "IdeaPad 310-15ABR."
3. When she opened a cavity cover on the bottom of the case, she discovered one SO-DIMM slot filled with a SO-DIMM that has "4GB PC4-2400T" imprinted on it.

Tangela is now puzzled why Windows reports 8 GB of memory, but the one SO-DIMM contains only 4 GB. With this information in hand, research the possible upgrade and answer the following:

1. Explain why Windows reports 8 GB of memory and the one SO-DIMM contains 4 GB of memory.
2. Can the laptop receive a memory upgrade? Save or print a webpage showing a SO-DIMM that can fit the system. How much will the upgrade cost?

>> REAL PROBLEMS, REAL SOLUTIONS

REAL PROBLEM 3-1 Using Memory Scanning Software

A great shortcut to research a memory upgrade is an online memory scanner. Follow these directions to use three free products to scan your system and report information about it. (As you work, be careful not to download extra software advertised on these sites.)

1. Go to *crucial.com/systemscanner* by Crucial and then download and run the Crucial System Scanner.
2. Go to *cpuid.com/softwares/cpu-z.html* and then download and run the CPU-Z scanner.
3. Go to *ccleaner.com/speccy/download/standard* and then download and run the Speccy scanner.
4. Using any of these scanners, answer these questions:
   a. Which motherboard do you have installed?
   b. How much memory is installed?
   c. How many memory slots does the board have?
   d. How many are populated?
   e. What is the CAS Latency of memory?
   f. How many cores does your processor have?
   g. What is the maximum memory the board supports?
   h. What type of memory does the board support?
   i. What would be the total cost of the memory upgrade if you were to max out the total memory on the board?
   j. Which scanner did you use to answer these questions? Why did you select this particular scanner?

REAL PROBLEM 3-2 Troubleshooting Memory

Follow the rules outlined earlier in the text to protect the computer against ESD as you work. Remove the memory module in the first memory slot on a motherboard, and boot the PC. Did you get an error? Why or why not?

REAL PROBLEM 3-3 Playing the Memory Research Game

Play the Memory Research game. You will need a group with three other players, Internet access, and a fifth person who is the scorekeeper. The scorekeeper asks a question and then gives players one minute to find the best answer. Five points are awarded to the player who has the best answer at the end of each one-minute play. The scorekeeper can use the following questions or make up his or her own. If you use these questions, mix up the order:

1. What is the fastest DDR4 DIMM sold today?

2. What is the largest DDR3 DIMM sold today?

3. What is the largest fully buffered ECC 240-pin DDR2 DIMM sold today?

4. What is the lowest price for an 8-GB 240-pin ECC DDR3 DIMM?

Supporting the Power System and Troubleshooting Computers

I n the first chapters of this text, you learned about the motherboard, processor, and RAM. This chapter focuses on how to keep these heat-producing components cool by using fans, heat sinks, and other cooling devices and methods. You also learn about one more essential component of a computer system, the power supply, including how to select a power supply to meet the wattage needs of a system.

Then we focus on troubleshooting these various hardware subsystems and components. You study the troubleshooting techniques and procedures to get the full picture of what it's like to have the tools and knowledge in hand to solve any computer-related problem. Then you learn to practically apply these skills to troubleshooting the electrical system, motherboard, processor, and memory. By the end of this chapter, you should feel confident that you can face a problem with hardware and understand how to zero in on the source of the problem and its solution.

COOLING METHODS AND DEVICES

The processor, motherboard, memory modules, expansion cards, and other components in the case produce heat. If they get overheated, the system can become unstable and components can fail or be damaged. As a hardware technician, you need to know how to keep a system cool. Devices that are used to keep a system cool include CPU fans, case fans, coolers, heat sinks, and liquid cooling systems.

In this part of the chapter, you learn about several methods to keep the system cool, beginning with these general rules to cool the inside of a computer case:

- ◢ *Keeping the case closed*. This may seem counterintuitive as you might think an open case allows for better airflow, but consider the dust that will clog your fans and how fans are designed to draw hot air out of a closed case. If airflow is disrupted, an open case is a temporary fix to an overheating computer and should not be used long term.
- ◢ *Cleaning the inside of the computer*. Dust and debris clog your computer. Dirt and dust cake on the equipment and essentially insulate the heat-sensitive components. Use a can of compressed air to blow clean the inside of the case and its components.
- ◢ *Moving the computer*. If the computer is in a fairly dusty or warm space, the computer might overheat. If overheating is a problem, try moving the computer to a new area that is cleaner and cooler.

PROCESSOR COOLERS, FANS, AND HEAT SINKS

Because a processor generates so much heat, computer systems use a cooling assembly designed for a specific processor to keep temperatures below the processor maximum temperature. If a processor reaches its maximum temperature, it automatically shuts down. Good processor coolers maintain a temperature of 90–110 degrees F (32–43 degrees C). The cooler (see Figure 4-1) sits on top of the processor and consists of a fan and a heat sink. A heat sink is made of metal that draws the heat away from the processor into the fins. The fan can then blow the heat away. You learned to install a cooler in Chapter 3.

Figure 4-1   A cooler sits on top of a processor to help keep it cool

A cooler is made of aluminum, copper, or a combination of both. Copper is more expensive, but does a better job of conducting heat. For example, the Thermaltake (*thermaltake.com*) multisocket cooler shown in Figure 4-2 is made of copper and has an adjustable fan control.

Figure 4-2   The Thermaltake V1 copper cooler is a multisocket cooler that fits several Intel and AMD sockets

Recall that the cooler is bracketed to the motherboard using a wire or plastic clip and thermal compound is placed between the bottom of the cooler heat sink and the top of the processor. To get its power, the cooler fan power cord connects to a 4-pin fan header on the motherboard (see Figure 4-3). The fan connector will have three or four holes. A three-hole connector can fit onto a 4-pin header; just ignore the last pin. A 4-pin header on the motherboard supports pulse width modulation (PWM) that controls fan speed in order to reduce the overall noise in a system. If you use a cooler fan power cord with three pins, know that the fan will always operate at the same speed.

3-pin CPU fan power cord

4-pin CPU fan header

Figure 4-3   A cooler fan gets its power from a 4-pin PWM header on the motherboard

CASE FANS, OTHER FANS, AND HEAT SINKS

**A+
CORE 1
3.5**

To prevent overheating, you can also install additional case fans. Most cases have one or more positions to hold a case fan to help draw air out of the case. Figure 4-4 shows holes on the rear of a case designed to hold a case fan.

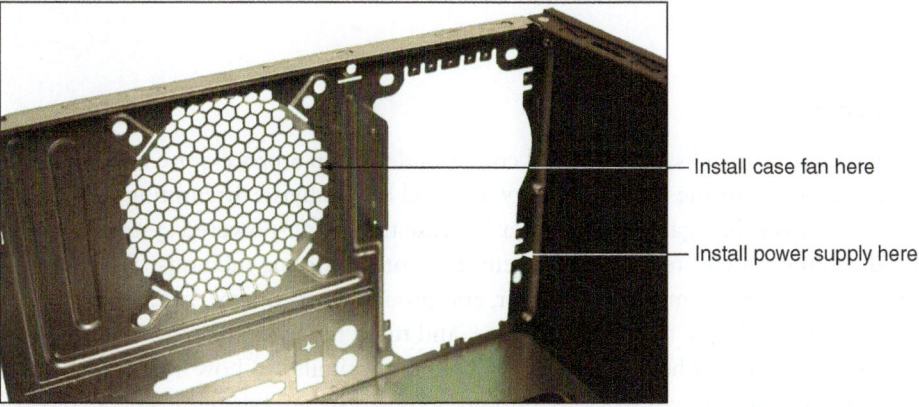

Install case fan here

Install power supply here

Figure 4-4   Install a case fan on the rear of this case to help keep the system cool

A computer case might need as many as seven or eight fans mounted inside the case; however, the trend is to use fewer and larger fans. Generally, large fans tend to perform better and run quieter than small fans.

Processors and video cards, also called graphics cards, are the two greatest heat producers in a system. Some graphics cards come with a fan on the side of the card. You can also purchase heat sinks and fans to mount on an expansion card to keep it cool. Another solution is to use a fan card mounted next to the graphics card. Figure 4-5 shows a PCI fan card. Be sure you select the fan card that fits the expansion slot you plan to use, and make sure there's enough clearance beside the graphics card for the fan card to fit and for airflow.

For additional cooling, consider a RAM cooler such as the one shown in Figure 4-6. It clips over a DIMM. A fan might be powered by a SATA power connector

Source: Courtesy of Vantec Thermal Technologies

Figure 4-5 A PCI fan card by Vantec can be used next to a high-end graphics card to help keep it cool

or 4-pin Molex power connector. The fan shown in Figure 4-6 uses a Molex connector. If you need a different or extra power connector that isn't available on a power supply, you can use an adapter to change an unused SATA or Molex connector into the connector you need.

4-pin power connector

DIMM cover

Figure 4-6 A RAM cooler keeps memory modules cool

When selecting any fan or cooler, take into consideration the added noise level and the ease of installation. Some coolers and fans can use a temperature sensor that controls the fan. Also consider the guarantee made by the cooler or fan manufacturer.

LIQUID COOLING SYSTEMS

**A+
CORE 1
3.5**

In addition to using fans, heat sinks, and thermal compound to keep a processor cool, a liquid cooling system can be used. For the most part, they are used by hobbyists attempting to overclock to the max a processor in a gaming computer because these high-powered systems tend to run hot. Liquid cooling systems tend to run quieter than other cooling methods. They might include a PCIe card that has a power supply, temperature sensor, and processor to control the cooler.

Using liquid cooling, a small pump sits inside the computer case, and tubes move liquid around components and then away from them to a place where fans can cool the liquid, similar to how a car radiator works. Figure 4-7 shows one liquid cooling system where the liquid is cooled by fans sitting inside a large case. Sometimes, however, the liquid is pumped outside the case, where it is cooled.

4

Figure 4-7 A liquid cooling system pumps liquid outside and away from components where fans can then cool the liquid

Now let's turn our attention to the power supply.

SELECTING A POWER SUPPLY

A+ CORE 1 3.7

In Chapter 1, you learned how to uninstall and install a power supply unit (PSU). You might need to replace a power supply when it fails or if the power supply in an existing system is not adequate. When building a new system, you can purchase a computer case with the power supply already installed (see Figure 4-8), or you can purchase a power supply separate from the case.

Figure 4-8 This case comes with a power supply, power cord, and bag of screws

TYPES AND CHARACTERISTICS OF POWER SUPPLIES

A+ CORE 1 3.7

As you select the right power supply for a system, you need to be aware of the following power supply features:

▲ *ATX or microATX form factor.* The form factor of a power supply determines the dimensions of the power supply and the placement of screw holes and slots used to anchor the power supply to the case.

▲ *Wattage ratings.* A power supply has a wattage rating for total output maximum load (for example, 500 W, 850 W, or 1000 W) and individual wattage ratings for each of the voltage output circuits. These wattage capacities are listed in the documentation and on the side of a power supply, as shown in Figure 4-9.

+12 V rail capacity

Figure 4-9 Consider the number and type of power connectors and the wattage ratings of a power supply

When selecting a power supply, pay particular attention to the capacity for the +12 V rail. (A *rail* is the term used to describe each circuit provided by the power supply.) The +12 V rail is the one most used, especially in high-end gaming systems. Notice in Figure 4-9 that the +12 V rail gets 360 W of the maximum 525-W load. Sometimes you need to use a power supply with a higher-than-needed overall wattage to get enough wattage on this one rail.

> **Notes** To calculate wattage, know that the power in watts (W) is equal to the current in amps (A) times the voltage in volts (V): $W = A \times V$

▲ *Number and type of connectors.* Consider the number and type of power cables and connectors the unit provides. Connector types are shown in Table 1-2 in Chapter 1. Table 4-1 lists some common connectors and the voltages they supply. Some power supplies include detached power cables, sometimes called modular cable systems, that you can plug into connectors on the side of the unit. By using only the power cables you need, extra power cables don't get in the way of airflow inside the computer case.

Connector	Voltages	Description
SATA	+3.3 V, +5 V, +12 V	Power to SATA drives, 5 pin
Molex	+5 V, +12 V	Power to older IDE drives and used with some older SATA drives, 4 pin
24-pin P1	+3.3 V, ±5 V, ±12 V	Newer main power connector to motherboard

Table 4-1 Power supply connectors and voltages

> ⭐ **A+ Exam Tip** The A+ Core 1 exam expects you to know the voltage output of the power connectors listed in Table 4-1. Consider memorizing the table.

> ✏️ **Notes** If a power supply doesn't have the connector you need, it is likely you can buy an adapter to convert one connector to another. For example, Figure 4-10 shows an adapter that converts two Molex cables to one 12-V 6-pin PCIe connector.

Figure 4-10 This adapter converts two Molex cables to a single 12-V 6-pin PCIe connector

◢ *Fans inside the PSU*. Every power supply has a fan inside its case; some have two fans. The fan may be mounted on the back or top of the PSU. Fans range in size from 80 mm to 150 mm wide. The larger the fan, the better job it does and the quieter it runs. Some PSUs can automatically adjust the fan speed based on the internal temperature of the system.

> ✏️ **Notes** Some power supplies are designed without fans so that they can be used in home theater systems or other areas where quiet operation is a requirement.

◢ *Dual voltage options*. Expect a power supply to have a dual-voltage selector switch on the back where you can switch input voltage to 115 V for the United States or 220 V for other countries.

◢ *Extra features*. Consider the warranty of the power supply and the overall quality. Some power supplies are designed to support two video cards used in a gaming computer. Two technologies used for multiple video cards are SLI by NVIDIA and Crossfire by AMD. If you plan to use multiple video cards, use a PSU that supports SLI or Crossfire. Know that more expensive power supplies are quieter, last longer, and don't put off as much heat as less expensive ones. Also, expect a good power supply to protect the system against overvoltage. A power supply rated with Active PFC (power factor correction) runs more efficiently and uses less electricity than other power supplies.

HOW TO CALCULATE WATTAGE CAPACITY

> **A+ CORE 1 3.7** When deciding what wattage capacity you need for the power supply, consider the total wattage requirements of all components inside the case as well as USB devices that get their power from ports connected to the motherboard.

> ⭐ **A+ Exam Tip** The A+ Core 1 exam expects you to know how to select and install a power supply. You need to know how to decide on the wattage, connectors, and form factor of the power supply.

Keep these two points in mind when selecting the correct wattage capacity for a power supply:

◢ *Video cards draw the most power*. Video cards draw the most power in a system, and they draw from the +12 V output. If your system has a video card, pay particular attention to the +12 V rating. The current trend is for the motherboard to provide the video components and video port, thus reducing the overall wattage needs for a system. Video cards are primarily used in gaming computers or other systems that require high-quality graphics.

▲ *The power supply should be rated about 30 percent higher than expected needs*. Power supplies that run at less than peak performance last longer and don't overheat. In addition, a power supply loses some of its capacity over time. Also, don't worry about a higher-rated power supply using too much electricity. Components only draw what they need. For example, a power supply rated at 1000 W and running at a 500-W draw will last longer and give off less heat than a power supply rated at 750 W and running at a 500-W draw.

To know what size of power supply you need, add up the wattage requirements of all components and then add 30 percent. Technical documentation for these components should give you the information you need. Table 4-2 lists appropriate wattage ratings for common devices. Alternately, you can use a wattage calculator provided on the website of many manufacturers and vendors. Using the calculator, you enter the components in your system and then the calculator will recommend the wattage you need for your power supply.

Devices	Approximate Wattage
Motherboard, processor, memory, keyboard, and mouse	200–300 W
Fan	5 W
SATA hard drive	15–30 W
BD/DVD/CD drive	20–30 W
PCI video card	50 W
PCI card (network card or other PCI card)	20 W
PCIe ×16 video card	150–300 W
PCIe ×16 card other than a video card	100 W

Table 4-2   To calculate the power supply rating you need, add up total wattage

⚡ **Caution**   Some older Dell motherboards and power supplies do not use the standard P1 pinouts for ATX, although the power connectors look the same. For this reason, never use a Dell power supply with a non-Dell motherboard, or a Dell motherboard with a non-Dell power supply, without first verifying that the power connector pinouts match; otherwise, you might destroy the power supply, the motherboard, or both.

Table 4-3 lists a few case and power supply manufacturers.

Manufacturer	Website
Antec	*antec.com*
Cooler Master	*coolermaster.com*
Corsair	*corsair.com*
EVGA	*evga.com*
FirePower Technology	*firepower-technology.com*
Rosewill	*rosewill.com*
Seasonic	*seasonic.com*
Sentey	*sentey.com*
Silverstone	*silverstonetek.com*
Thermaltake	*thermaltakeusa.com*
Zalman	*zalman.com*

Table 4-3   Manufacturers of cases and power supplies for personal computers

So far in the text, you have learned about motherboards, processors, RAM, and the electrical system, which are the principal hardware components of a computer. With this hardware foundation in place, you're ready to learn about computer troubleshooting. Let's start with an overview of how to approach any hardware problem, and then we'll turn our attention to the details of troubleshooting the electrical system, motherboard, RAM, and CPU.

STRATEGIES TO TROUBLESHOOT ANY COMPUTER PROBLEM

4

A+ CORE 1 5.1 When a computer doesn't work and you're responsible for fixing it, you should generally approach the problem first as an investigator and discoverer, always being careful not to compound the problem through your actions. If the problem seems difficult, see it as an opportunity to learn something new. Ask questions until you understand the source of the problem. Once you understand it, you're almost done because most likely the solution will be evident. If you take the attitude that you can understand the problem and solve it, no matter how deeply you have to dig, you probably *will* solve it.

One systematic method used by most expert troubleshooters to solve a problem is the six steps diagrammed in Figure 4-11, which can apply to both software and hardware problems. As an IT technician, expect that you will build your own style and steps for troubleshooting based on your own experiences over time.

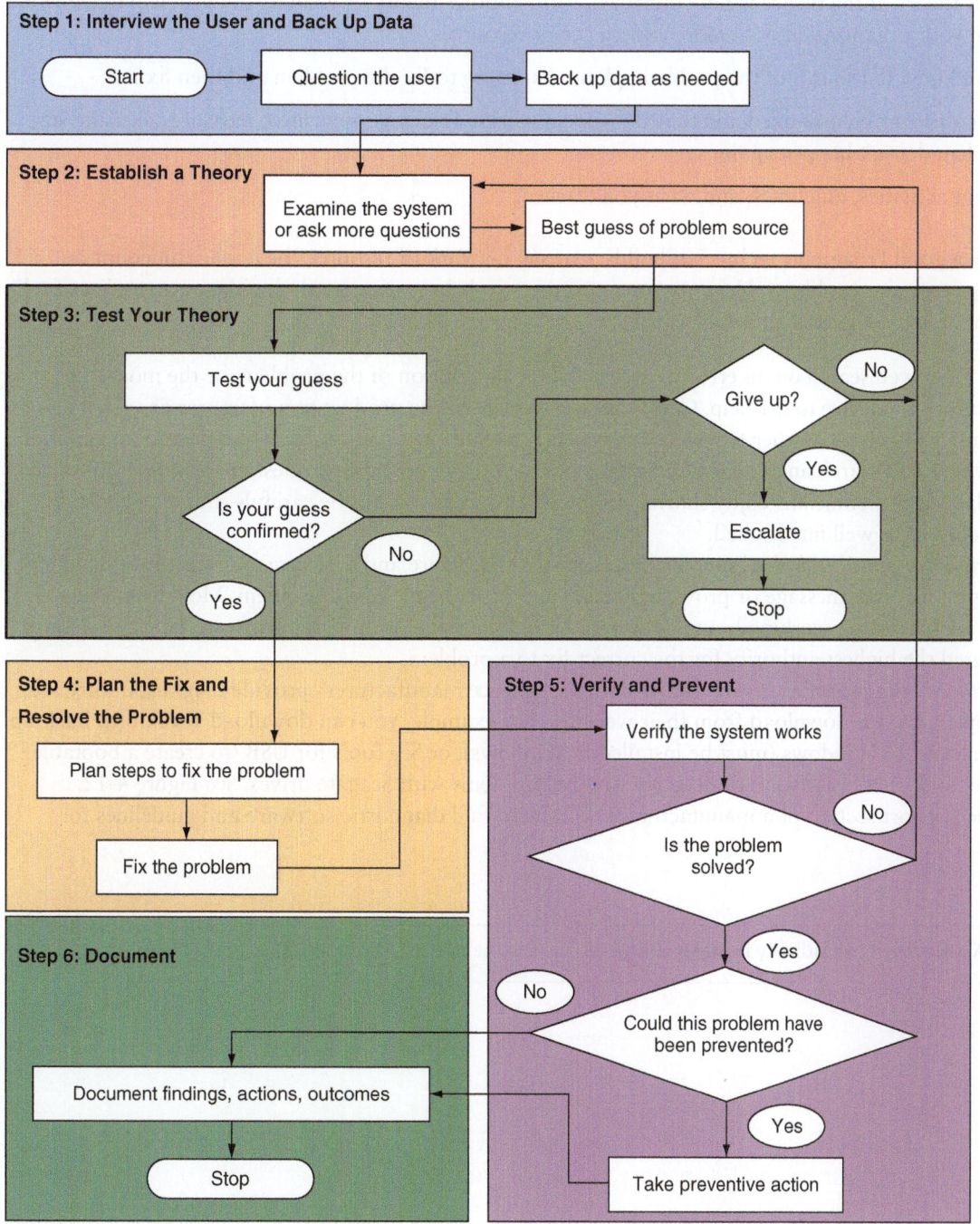

Figure 4-11 A general approach to problem solving

> ⭐ **A+ Exam Tip** The A+ Core 1 exam expects you to know about all the aspects of troubleshooting theory and strategy and how to apply the troubleshooting procedures and techniques described in this section. Read A+ Core 1 Objective 5.1 and compare it with Figure 4-11. You'll find the objectives with this text.

Here are the steps:

1. Interview the user and back up data before you make any changes to the system.

2. Examine the system, analyze the problem, and make an initial determination of the source of the problem.

3. Test your theory. If the theory is not confirmed, form another theory or escalate the problem to someone higher in your organization with more experience or resources.

4. After you know the source of the problem, plan what to do to fix the problem and then fix it.

5. Verify that the problem is fixed and that the system works. Take any preventive measures to make sure the problem doesn't happen again.

6. Document activities, outcomes, and what you learned.

Over time, a good IT support technician builds a strong network of resources he or she can count on when solving computer problems. Here are some resources to help you get started with your own list of reliable and time-tested sources of help:

▲ *The web*. Do a web search on an error message, a short description of the problem, or the model and manufacturer of a device to get help. Check out the website of the product manufacturer or search a support forum. It's likely that other technicians have encountered the same problem and posted the question and answer. If you search and cannot find your answer, you can post a new question. *Youtube.com* videos might help. Many technicians enjoy sharing online what they know, but be careful—not all technical advice is correct or well intentioned.

▲ *Chat, forums, or email technical support*. Support from hardware and software manufacturers can help you interpret an error message or provide general support in diagnosing a problem. Most technical support is available during working hours by way of an online chat session. Support from the manufacturer is considered the highest authority for the correct fix to a problem.

▲ *Manufacturer's diagnostic software*. Many hardware device manufacturers provide diagnostic software, which is available for download from their websites. For example, you can download Toolkit (to back up data), SeaTools for Windows (must be installed in Windows), or SeaTools for USB (to create a bootable USB drive) and use the software to diagnose and fix problems with Seagate drives. See Figure 4-12. Search the support section of a manufacturer's website to find diagnostic software and guidelines for using it.

> ✎ **Notes** Always check compatibility between utility software and the operating system (OS) you plan to use.

4

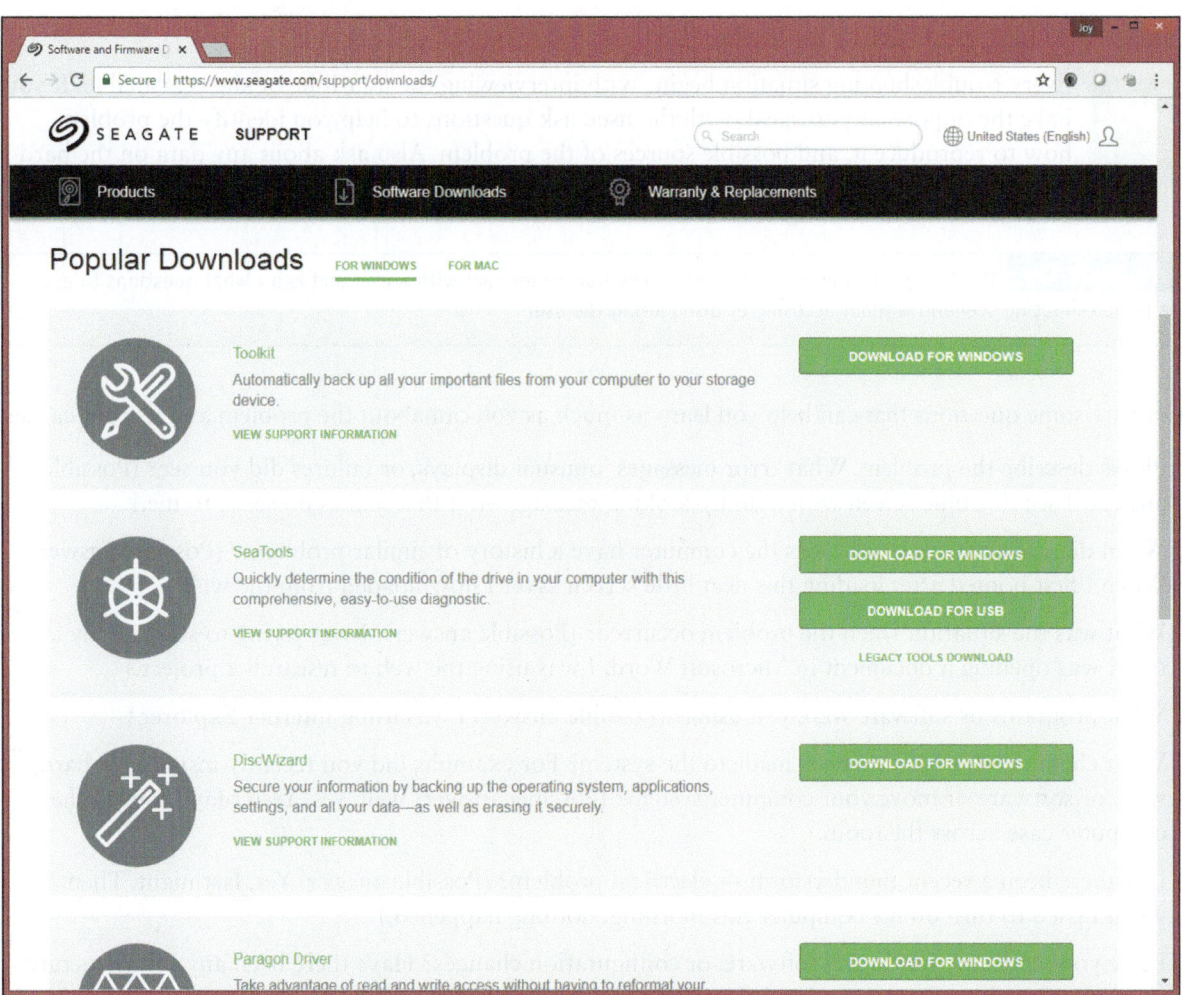

Figure 4-12 Download diagnostic software tools from a manufacturer's website

▲ *User manuals*. Refer to your user manuals, which often list error messages and their meanings. They also might contain a troubleshooting section and list any diagnostic tools available.

▲ *Technical associates in your organization*. Be sure to ask for advice when you're stuck. Also, after making a reasonable and diligent effort to resolve a problem, getting the problem fixed could become more important than resolving it yourself. There comes a time when you might need to turn the problem over to a technician who is more experienced or has access to more resources. (In an organization, this process is called escalating the problem.)

Now let's examine the process step by step. As you learn about these six steps, you'll also learn about 13 rules useful when troubleshooting. Here's the first rule.

Rule 1: Approach the Problem Systematically
When trying to solve the problem, start at the beginning and walk through the situation in a thorough, careful way. This rule is invaluable. Remember it and apply it every time. If you don't find the explanation to the problem after one systematic walk-through, then repeat the entire process. Check and double-check to find the step you overlooked the first time. Most problems with computers are simple, such as a loose cable or incorrect Windows setting. Computers are logical through and through. Whatever the problem is, it's also very logical. Also, if you are faced with more than one problem on the same computer, work on only one problem at a time. Trying to solve multiple problems at the same time can get too confusing.

STEP 1: INTERVIEWING THE USER AND BACKING UP DATA

 Every troubleshooting situation begins with interviewing the user if he or she is available. If you have the opportunity to speak with the user, ask questions to help you identify the problem, how to reproduce it, and possible sources of the problem. Also ask about any data on the hard drive that is not backed up.

> ★ **A+ Exam Tip** The A+ Core 1 exam expects you to know how to interact with a user and know what questions to ask in a troubleshooting scenario without accusing or dishonoring the user.

Here are some questions that can help you learn as much as you can about the problem and its root cause:

1. Please describe the problem. What error messages, unusual displays, or failures did you see? (Possible answer: I see this blue screen with a funny-looking message on it that makes no sense to me.)

2. When did the problem start? Does the computer have a history of similar problems? (Possible answer: When I first booted after loading this neat little screen saver I downloaded from the web.)

3. What was the situation when the problem occurred? (Possible answers: I was trying to start up my laptop. I was opening a document in Microsoft Word. I was using the web to research a project.)

4. What programs or software were you using? (Possible answer: I was using Internet Explorer.)

5. What changes have recently been made to the system? For example, did you recently install new hardware or software or move your computer system? (Possible answer: Well, yes. Yesterday I moved the computer case across the room.)

6. Has there been a recent thunderstorm or electrical problem? (Possible answer: Yes, last night. Then when I tried to turn on my computer this morning, nothing happened.)

7. Have you made any hardware, software, or configuration changes? Have there been any infrastructure changes? (Possible answer: No, but I think my sister might have.)

8. Has someone else used your computer recently? (Possible answer: Sure, my son uses it all the time.)

9. Is there some valuable data on your system that is not backed up that I should know about before I start working on the problem? (Possible answer: Yes! Yes! My term paper! It's not backed up! You gotta save that!)

10. Can you show me how to reproduce the problem? (Possible answer: Yes, let me show you what to do.)

Based on the answers you receive, ask more penetrating questions until you feel the user has given you all the information he or she knows that can help you solve the problem. As you talk with the user, keep in mind rules 2, 3, and 4.

> **Rule 2: Establish Your Priorities**
> This rule can help make for a satisfied customer. Decide what your first priority is. For example, it might be to recover lost data or to get the computer back up and running as soon as possible. When practical, ask the user or customer for help deciding on priorities. For most users, data is the first priority unless they have a recent backup.

> **Rule 3: Beware of User Error**
> Remember that many problems stem from user error. If you suspect this is the case, ask the user to show you the problem and carefully watch what the user is doing. Be careful to handle a user error delicately because some people don't like to hear that they made a mistake.

4

Rule 4: Keep Your Cool and Don't Rush
In some situations, you might be tempted to act too quickly and to be drawn into the user's sense of emergency. But keep your cool and don't rush. For example, if a computer stops working and unsaved data is still in memory or if data on the hard drive has not been backed up, look and think carefully before you leap! A wrong move can be costly. The best advice is not to hurry. Carefully plan your moves. Research the problem using documentation or the web if you're not sure what to do, and don't hesitate to ask for help. Don't simply try something, hoping it will work, unless you've run out of more intelligent alternatives!

After you have talked with the user, be sure to back up any important data that is not currently backed up before you begin work on the computer. Here are three options:

▲ *Use File Explorer to copy the data to another system.* If the computer is working well enough to boot to the Windows desktop, you can use Windows 10/8 File Explorer or Windows 7 Windows Explorer to copy data to a flash drive, another computer on the network, or other storage media.

▲ *Move the hard drive to another system.* If the computer is not healthy enough to use Explorer, don't do anything to jeopardize the data. If you must take a risk with the data, let it be the user's decision to do so, not yours. When a system won't boot from the hard drive, consider removing the drive and installing it as a second drive in a working system. If the file system on the problem drive is intact, you might be able to copy data from the drive to the primary drive in the working system.

To move the hard drive to a working computer, you don't need to physically install the drive in the drive bay. Open the computer case. Carefully lay the drive on the case and connect a power cord and data cable (see Figure 4-13). Then turn on the computer. While you have the computer turned on, be *very careful* not to touch the drive or touch inside the case. Also, while a tower case is lying on its side like the one in Figure 4-13, don't use the optical drive.

Start the computer and sign in to Windows using an Administrator account. (If you don't sign in with an Administrator account, you must provide the password to an Administrator account before you can access the files on the newly connected hard drive.) When Windows finds the new drive, it assigns a drive letter. Use Explorer in Windows 10/8/7 or third-party software to copy files from this drive to the primary hard drive in this system or to other storage media. Then return the drive to the original system and turn your attention to solving the original problem.

Figure 4-13   Move a hard drive to a working computer to recover data on the drive

🖊 **Notes**   An easier way to temporarily install a hard drive in a system is to use a USB port. Figure 4-14 shows a USB-to-SATA converter kit. The SATA connector can be used for desktop or laptop hard drives because a SATA connector is the same for both. A USB-to-SATA converter is really handy when recovering data and troubleshooting problems with hard drives that refuse to boot.

Figure 4-14   Use a USB-to-SATA converter to recover data from a drive that has a SATA connector

▲ *Hire a professional file recovery service.* If your data is extremely valuable and other methods have failed, you might want to consider a professional data recovery service. They're expensive, but getting the data back might be worth it. To find a service, do a web search on "data recovery." Before selecting a service, be sure to read reviews, understand the warranty and guarantees, and perhaps get a recommendation from a satisfied customer.

> ★ **A+ Exam Tip**   The A+ Core 1 exam expects you to know the importance of making backups before you make changes to a system.

If possible, have the user verify that all important data is safely backed up before you continue to the next troubleshooting step.

> ⚡ **Caution**   Don't take chances with a user's important data. If the user tells you the data has already been backed up, ask him to verify that he can recover the data from the backup website or media before you assume the data is really backed up.

If you're new to troubleshooting and don't want the user looking over your shoulder while you work, you might want to let him or her know you'd prefer to work alone. You can say something like, "Okay, I think I have everything I need to get started. I'll let you know if I have another question."

STEP 2: EXAMINING THE SYSTEM AND MAKING YOUR BEST GUESS

You're now ready to start solving the problem. Rules 5 and 6 can help.

Rule 5: Make No Assumptions
This rule is the hardest to follow because there is a tendency to trust anything in writing and assume that people are telling you exactly what happened. But documentation is sometimes wrong, and people don't always describe events as they occurred, so do your own investigating. For example, if the user tells you that the system boots up with no error messages but that the software still doesn't work, boot for yourself. You never know what the user might have overlooked.

Rule 6: Try the Simple Things First
The solutions to most problems are so simple and obvious that we overlook them because we expect the problem to be difficult. Don't let the complexity of computers fool you. Most problems are easy to fix. Really, they are! To save time, check the simple things first, such as whether a power switch is not turned on or a cable is loose. Generally, it's easy to check for a hardware problem before you check for a software problem. For example, if a USB drive is not working, verify that the drive works on another port or another computer before verifying the drivers are installed correctly.

Follow this process to form your best guess (best theory) and test it:

1. *Reproduce the problem and observe for yourself what the user has described.* For example, if the user tells you the system is totally dead, find out for yourself. Plug in the power and turn on the system. Listen for fans and look for lights and error messages. Suppose the user tells you that Internet Explorer will not open. Try opening it yourself to see what error messages might appear. As you investigate the system, refrain from making changes until you've come up with your theory for the source of the problem. Can you duplicate the problem? Intermittent problems are generally more difficult to solve than problems that occur consistently.

2. *Decide if the problem is hardware- or software-related.* Sometimes you might not be sure, but make your best guess. For example, if the system fails before Windows starts to load, chances are the problem is a hardware problem. If the user tells you the system has not worked since the lightning storm the night before, chances are the problem is electrical. If the problem is that Explorer will not open even though the Windows desktop loads, you can assume the problem is software-related. In another example, suppose a user complains that his Word documents are getting corrupted. Possible sources of the problem might be that the user does not know how to save documents properly, the application or the OS might be corrupted, the computer might have a virus, or the hard drive might be intermittently failing. Investigate for yourself, and then decide if the problem is caused by software, hardware, or the user.

3. *Make your best guess as to the source of the problem, and don't forget to question the obvious.* Here are some practical examples of questioning the obvious and checking the simple things first:

   ◢ The video doesn't work. Your best guess is the monitor cables are loose or the monitor is not turned on.

   ◢ Excel worksheets are getting corrupted. Your best guess is the user is not saving the workbook files correctly.

   ◢ The DVD drive is not reading a DVD. Your best guess is the DVD is scratched.

   ◢ The system refuses to boot and displays the error that the hard drive is not found. Your best guess is internal cables to the drive are loose.

Rule 7: Become a Researcher
Following this rule is the most fun. When a computer problem arises that you can't easily solve, be as tenacious as a bulldog. Search the web, ask questions, read more, make some phone calls, and ask more questions. Take advantage of every available resource, including online help, documentation, technical support, and books such as this one. Learn to perform advanced searches using a good search engine on the web, such as *google.com*. What you learn will be yours to take to the next problem. This is the real joy of computer troubleshooting. If you're good at it, you're always learning something new.

If you're having trouble deciding what might be the source of the problem, keep rule 7 in mind and try searching these resources for ideas and tips:

◢ The specific application, operating system, or hardware you support must be available to you to test, observe, and study and to use to re-create a customer's problem whenever possible.

◢ Verify any system or application changes by referring to the system or application event logs. Windows keeps comprehensive logs about the system, hardware, applications, and user activities; these logs can be viewed using Windows Event Viewer. Many applications keep logs of events or changes to the system or application. Some applications might pop up error messages, such as a low disk space error. Open the application log to evaluate the error more closely and to see if any more details are provided in the log.

▲ In a corporate setting, hardware and software products generally have technical documentation available. If you don't find it on hand, know that you are likely to find user manuals and technical support manuals as .pdf files that can be downloaded from the product manufacturers' websites. These sites might offer troubleshooting and support pages, help forums, chat sessions, email support, and links to submit a troubleshooting ticket to the manufacturer (see Figure 4-15). For Windows problems, the best websites to search are *technet.microsoft.com* and *support.microsoft.com*.

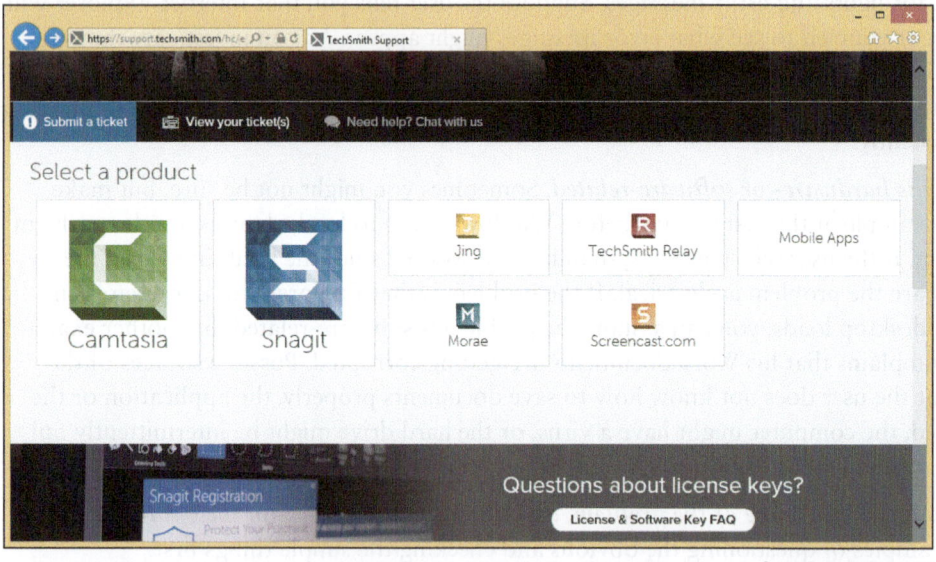

Source: Techsmith Corporation

Figure 4-15 Search manufacturer websites for help with a hardware or software product

▲ Use a search engine to search the web for help. In your search string, include an error message, symptom, hardware device, or description of the problem. The chances are always good that someone has had exactly the same problem, presented the problem online, and someone else has presented a step-by-step solution. All you have to do is find it! As you practice this type of web research, you'll get better and better at knowing how to form a search string and knowing which websites are trustworthy and present the best information. If your first five minutes of searching doesn't turn up a solution, please don't give up! It might take patience and searching for 20 minutes or more to find the solution you need. As you search, most likely you'll learn more and more about the problem, and you'll slowly zero in on a solution.

▲ Some companies offer an expert system for troubleshooting. An expert system is software that is designed and written to help solve problems. It uses databases of known facts and rules to simulate human experts' reasoning and decision making. Expert systems for IT technicians work by posing questions about a problem to be answered by the technician or the customer. The response to each question triggers another question from the software until the expert system arrives at a possible solution or solutions. Many expert systems are "intelligent," meaning the system will record your input and use it in subsequent sessions to select more questions to ask and approaches to try. Therefore, future troubleshooting sessions on the same type of problem tend to zero in more quickly toward a solution.

> ✎ **Notes** To limit your search to a particular site when using *google.com*, use the *site:* parameter in the search box. For example, to search only the Microsoft site for information about the defrag command, enter this search string: `defrag site:microsoft.com`

STEP 3: TESTING YOUR THEORY

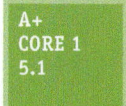

A+
CORE 1
5.1

As you test your theories, keep in mind rules 8 through 11.

Rule 8: Divide and Conquer

This rule is the most powerful. Isolate the problem. In the overall system, remove one hardware or software component after another until the problem is isolated to a small part of the whole system. As you divide a large problem into smaller components, you can analyze each component separately. You can use one or more of the following to help you divide and conquer:

- ◢ In Windows, perform a clean boot to eliminate all nonessential startup programs and services as a possible source of the problem.
- ◢ Boot from a bootable DVD or flash drive to eliminate the Windows installation and the hard drive as the problem.
- ◢ Remove any unnecessary hardware devices, such as a second video card, optical drive, or even the hard drive. You don't need to physically remove the optical drive or hard drive from the bays inside the case. Simply disconnect the data cable and the power cable.

Rule 9: Write Things Down

Keep good notes as you're working. They'll help you think more clearly. Draw diagrams. Make lists. Clearly and precisely write down what you're learning. If you need to leave the problem and return to it later, it's difficult to remember what you have observed and already tried. When the problem gets cold like this, your notes will be invaluable.

Rule 10: Don't Assume the Worst

When it's an emergency and your only copy of data is on a hard drive that is not working, don't assume that the data is lost. Much can be done to recover data. If you want to recover lost data on a hard drive, don't write anything to the drive; you might write on top of lost data, eliminating chances of recovery.

Rule 11: Reboot and Start Over

This is an important rule. Fresh starts are good, and they uncover events or steps that might have been overlooked. Take a break! Get away from the problem. Begin again.

Most computer problems are simple and can be simply solved, but you do need a game plan. That's how Figure 4-16 can help. The flowchart focuses on problems that affect the boot. As you work your way through it, you're eliminating one major computer subsystem after another until you zero in on the problem. After you've discovered the problem, many times the solution is obvious.

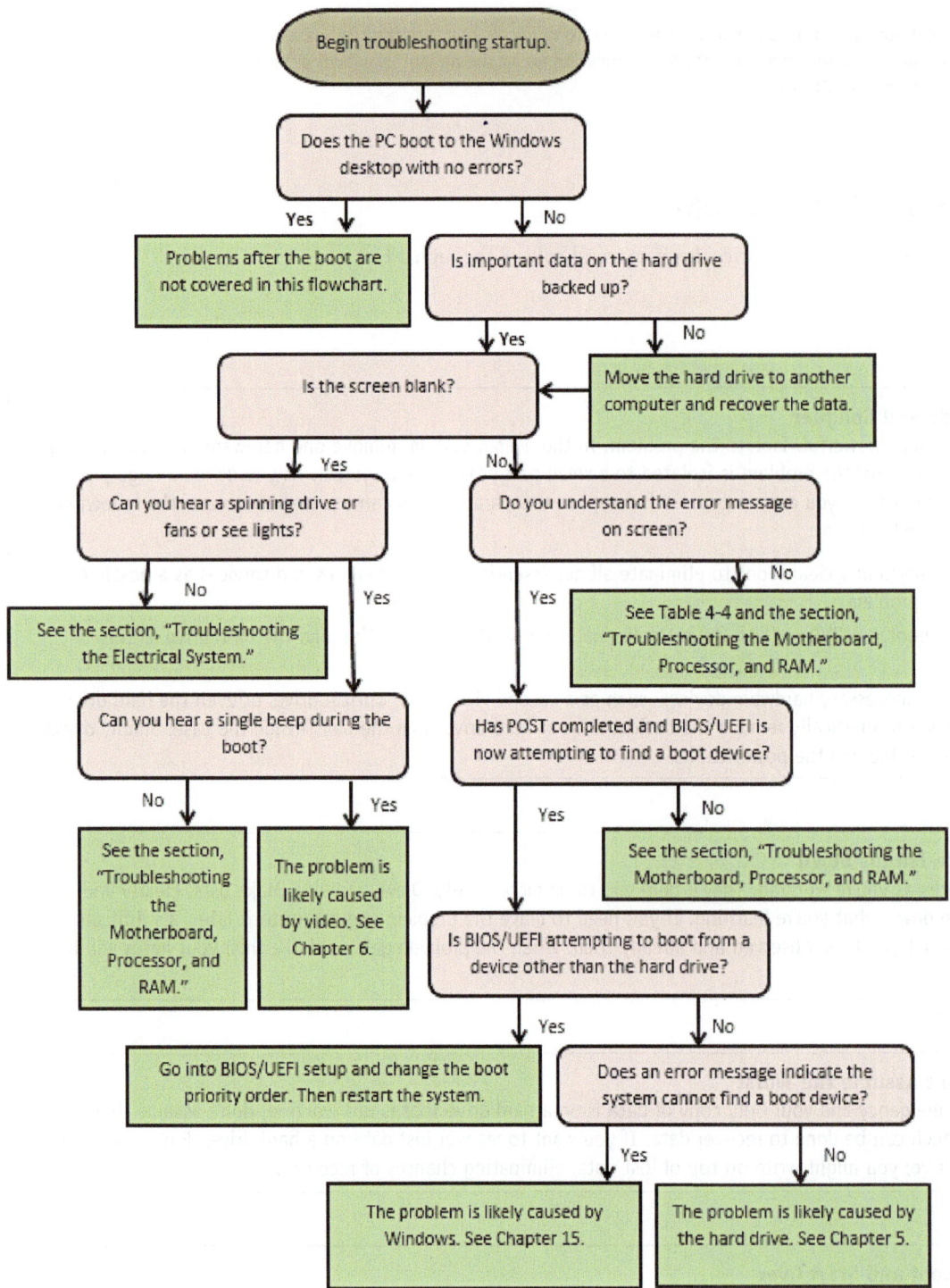

Figure 4-16 Use this flowchart when first facing a computer problem

As Figure 4-16 indicates, troubleshooting a computer problem is divided into problems that occur during the boot and those that occur after the Windows Start screen or desktop has successfully loaded. Problems that occur during the boot might happen before Windows starts to load or during Windows startup. Read the flowchart in Figure 4-16 very carefully to get an idea of the symptoms that would cause you to suspect each subsystem.

Also, Table 4-4 can help as a general guideline for the primary symptoms and what are likely to be the sources of a problem.

4

The A+ Core 1 exam might give you a symptom and expect you to select a probable source of a problem from a list of sources. These examples of what can go wrong can help you connect problem sources to symptoms.

Symptom or Error Message	What to Do About the Problem
System shuts down unexpectedly	Try to find out what was happening at the time of the shutdowns to pinpoint an application or device causing the problem. Possible sources of the problem are overheating, faulty RAM, the motherboard, or the processor.
System shuts down unexpectedly and starts back up	Begin by checking the system for overheating. Is the processor cooler fan working? Go to BIOS/UEFI setup and check the temperature of the processor. When the processor overheats and the system restarts, the problem is called a processor thermal trip error.
System locks up with an error message on a blue screen, called a blue screen of death (BSOD)	Figure 4-17 shows an example of a BSOD error. These Windows errors are caused by problems with devices, device drivers, or a corrupted Windows installation. Begin troubleshooting by searching the Microsoft website for the error message and a description of the problem.
System locks up with an error message on a black screen	These error messages on a black background, such as the one shown in Figure 4-18, are most likely caused by an error at POST. Begin troubleshooting the device mentioned in the error message.
System freezes or locks up without an error message	If the system locks up without an error screen and while still displaying the Windows Start screen or desktop, the problem is most likely caused by an application not responding. Sometimes you'll see the Windows pinwheel indicating the system is waiting for a response from a program or device. Open the Windows Task Manager utility and end any application that is not responding. If that doesn't work, restart Windows.
POST code beeps	One or no beep indicates that all is well after POST. However, startup BIOS/UEFI communicates POST errors as a series of beeps before it tests video. Search the website of the motherboard or BIOS/UEFI manufacturer to know how to interpret a series of beep codes. You might need to restart the system more than once so you can carefully count the beeps. Table 4-5 lists some common beep codes.
No power	If you see no lights on the computer case and hear no spinning fans, make sure the surge protector or wall outlet has power. Is the switch on the rear of the case on? Is the dual-voltage selector switch set correctly? Are power supply connectors securely connected? Is the power supply bad?
Blank screen when you first power up the computer, and no noise or indicator lights	Is power getting to the system? If power is getting to the computer, address the problem as electrical. Make sure the power supply is good and power supply connectors are securely connected.
Blank screen when you first power up the computer, and you can hear the fans spinning and see indicator lights	Troubleshoot the video subsystem. Is the monitor turned on? Is the monitor data cable securely connected at both ends? Is the indicator light on the front of the monitor on?
BIOS/UEFI loses its time and date settings "CMOS battery low" error message appears during the boot	The CMOS battery is failing. Replace the battery.
System reports less memory than you know is installed	A memory module is not seated correctly or has failed. Begin troubleshooting memory.
System attempts to boot to the wrong boot device	Go into BIOS/UEFI setup and change the boot device priority order.
Fans spin, but no power to other devices	Begin by checking the power supply. Are connectors securely connected? Use a power supply tester to check for correct voltage outputs.
Smoke or burning smell	Consider this a serious electrical problem. Immediately unplug the computer.

Table 4-4 Symptoms or error messages caused by hardware problems and what to do about them (continues)

Symptom or Error Message	What to Do About the Problem
Loud whining noise	Most likely the noise is made by the power supply or a failing hard drive. There might be a short. The power supply might be going bad or is under-rated for the system.
Clicking noise	A clicking noise likely indicates the magnetic hard drive is failing. Replace the drive as soon as possible.
Intermittent device failures	Failures that come and go might be caused by overheating or failing RAM, the motherboard, the processor, or the hard drive. Begin by checking the processor temperature for overheating. Then check RAM for errors and run diagnostics on the hard drive.
Distended capacitors	Failed capacitors on the motherboard or other circuit board are sometimes distended and discolored on the top of the capacitor. Replace the motherboard.
Error appears during boot: *Intruder detection error*	An intrusion detection device installed on the motherboard has detected that the computer case was opened. Suspect a security breach.
Error appears during boot: *Overclocking failed. Please enter setup to reconfigure your system*	Overclocking should be discontinued. However, this error might not be related to overclocking; it can occur when the power supply is failing.
Possible error messages: *No boot device available* *Hard drive not found* *Fixed disk error* *Invalid boot disk* *Inaccessible boot device or drive* *Invalid drive specification*	Startup BIOS/UEFI did not find a device to use to load the operating system. Make sure the boot device priority order is correct in BIOS/UEFI setup. Try booting from a bootable USB flash drive or DVD. If this works, begin troubleshooting the hard drive, which is covered in Chapter 5.
Possible error messages: *Missing operating system* *Error loading operating system*	Windows startup programs are missing or corrupted. How to troubleshoot Windows startup is covered in Chapter 15.
Continuous reboots	See the explanation later in this chapter.

Table 4-4 Symptoms or error messages caused by hardware problems and what to do about them (continued)

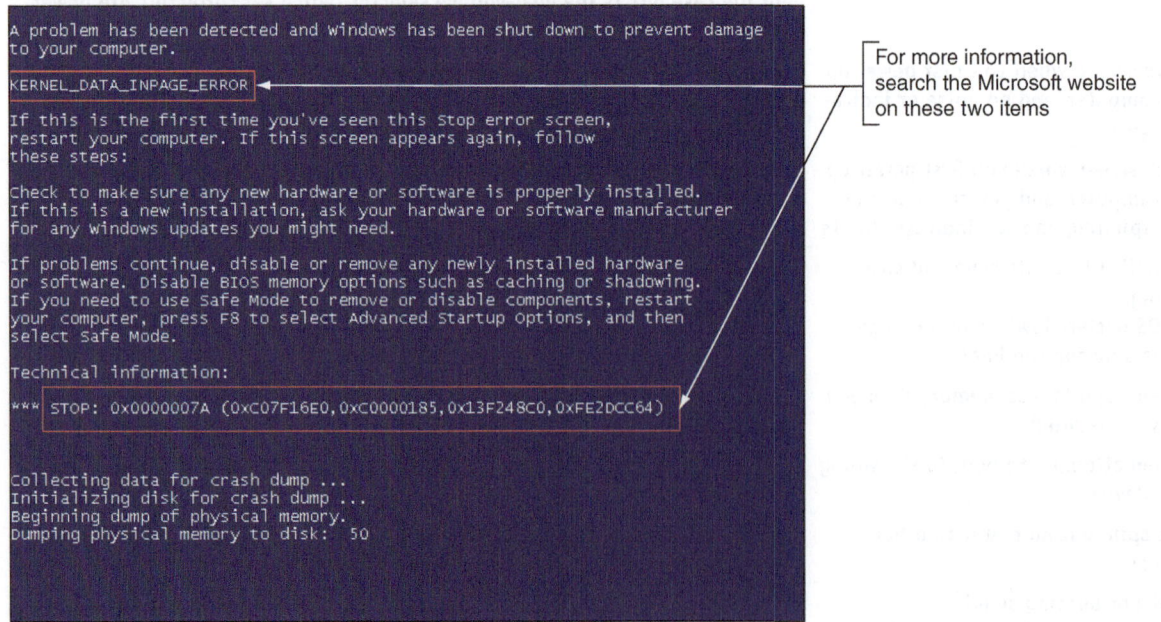

For more information, search the Microsoft website on these two items

Figure 4-17 Search the Microsoft website for information about a BSOD error

```
HardWare Monitor
_____

CPU Vcore       :       1.32V          NB/SB Voltage   :       1.24V
+ 3.3 V         :       3.37V          + 5.0 V         :       5.13V
+12.0 V         :       12.22V         VDIMM           :       2.01V
HT Voltage      :       1.26V          5V(SB)          :       5.05V
Voltage Bat     :       3.08V          CPU Temp        :       32°C
CPU FAN         :       2755 RPM       System FAN      :       0 RPM


Verifying  DMI Pool Data . . . . . . . . . .  Update Success

A disk read error occurred

Press Ctrl+Alt+Del to restart
```

Source: Intel

Figure 4-18 A POST error message on a black screen shown early in the boot

Beeps During POST	Description
1 short beep or no beep	The computer passed all POST tests
1 long and 2 short beeps	Award BIOS: A video problem, no video card, bad video memory Intel BIOS: A video problem
Continuous short beeps	Award BIOS: A memory error Intel BIOS: A loose card or short
1 long and 1 short beep	Intel BIOS: Motherboard problem
1 long and 3 short beeps	Intel BIOS: A video problem
3 long beeps	Intel BIOS: A keyboard controller problem
Continuous 2 short beeps and then a pause	Intel BIOS: A video card problem
Continuous 3 short beeps and then a pause	Intel BIOS: A memory error
8 beeps followed by a system shutdown	Intel BIOS: The system has overheated
Continuous high and low beeps	Intel BIOS: CPU problem

Table 4-5 Common beep codes and their meanings for Intel and Award BIOS

By the time you have finished Step 3, the problem might already be solved or you will know the source of the problem and will be ready to plan a solution.

STEP 4: PLANNING YOUR SOLUTION AND THEN FIXING THE PROBLEM

Some solutions, such as replacing a hard drive or a motherboard, are expensive and time consuming. You need to carefully consider what you will do and the order in which you will do it. When planning and implementing your solution, keep rules 12 and 13 in mind.

Rule 12: Use the Least Invasive Solution First

As you solve computer problems, always keep in mind that you don't want to make things worse, so you should use the least invasive solution. You want to fix the problem in such a way that the system is returned to normal working condition with the least amount of effort and fewest changes. For example, don't format the hard drive until you've first tried to fix the problem without having to erase everything on the drive. As another example, don't reinstall Microsoft Office until you have tried applying patches to the existing installation.

> **Rule 13: Know Your Starting Point**
> Find out what works and doesn't work before you take anything apart or try a possible fix. Suppose you decide to install a new anti-malware program. After the installation, you discover Microsoft Office gives errors and you cannot print to the network printer. You don't know if the anti-malware program is causing problems or the problems existed before you began work. As much as possible, find out what works or what doesn't work before you attempt a fix.

Do the following to plan your solution and fix the problem:

1. Consider different solutions and select the least invasive one. When appropriate, talk with the user or owner about the best solution.

2. Before applying your solution, do your best to determine what works and doesn't work in the system so you know your starting point.

3. Fix the problem. This might be as simple as plugging up a new monitor, or it might be as difficult as reinstalling Windows and applications software and restoring data from backups.

STEP 5: VERIFYING THE FIX AND TAKING PREVENTIVE ACTION

After you have fixed the problem, reboot the system and verify that all is well. Can you reach the Internet, use the printer, or use Microsoft Office? If possible, have the user check everything and verify that the job is done satisfactorily. If either of you finds a problem, return to Step 2 in the troubleshooting process to examine the system and form a new theory as to the cause of the problem.

After you and the user have verified all is working, ask yourself the question, "Could this problem have been prevented?" If so, go the extra mile to instruct the user, set Windows to automatically install updates, or do whatever else is appropriate to prevent future problems.

STEP 6: DOCUMENTING WHAT HAPPENED

Good documentation helps you take what you learned into the next troubleshooting situation, train others, develop effective preventive maintenance plans, and satisfy any audits or customer or employer queries about your work. Most companies use call-tracking software for this purpose. Be sure to include initial symptoms, the source of the problem, your troubleshooting steps, and what you did to ultimately fix it. Make the notes detailed enough so that you can use them later when solving similar problems.

For on-site support, a customer expects documentation about your services. Include in the documentation sufficient details broken down by cost of individual parts, hours worked, and cost per hour. Give the documentation to the customer at the end of the service and keep a copy for yourself. For phone support, the documentation stays in-house.

APPLYING | CONCEPTS   TAKING GOOD NOTES

Daniel had not been a good note taker in school, and this lack of skill was affecting his work. His manager, Jonathan, had been watching Daniel's notes in the ticketing system at the help desk and was not happy with what he saw. Jonathan had pointed out to Daniel more than once that his cryptic, incomplete notes with sketchy information would one day cause major problems. On Monday morning, calls were hammering the help desk because a server had gone down over the weekend and many internal customers were not able to get to their data. Daniel escalated one call from a customer named Matt to a tier-two help desk. Later that day, Sandra, a tier-two technician, received the escalated ticket, and to her dismay the phone number of the customer was missing. She called Daniel. "How am I to call this customer? You only have his first name, and these notes about the problem don't even make sense!" Daniel apologized to Sandra, but the damage was done.

Two days later, an angry Matt calls the manager of the help desk to complain that his problem is still not solved. Jonathan listens to Matt vent and apologizes for the problem his help desk has caused. It's a little embarrassing to Jonathan to have to ask Matt for his call-back information and to repeat the details of the problem. He gives the information to Sandra and the problem gets a quick resolution.

Discuss this situation in a small group and answer the following questions:

1. If you were Daniel, what could you do to improve note taking in the ticketing system?

2. After Sandra called, do you think Daniel should have told Jonathan about the problem? Why or why not?

3. If you were Jonathan, how would you handle the situation with Daniel?

Two students play the roles of Daniel and Jonathan when Jonathan calls Daniel into his office to discuss the call he just received from Matt. The other students in the group can watch and make suggestions as to how to improve the conversation.

Now you're ready to look at how to troubleshoot each subsystem that is critical to booting up the computer. We begin with the electrical system.

TROUBLESHOOTING THE ELECTRICAL SYSTEM

APPLYING | CONCEPTS   EXPLORING A COMPUTER PROBLEM

Your friend Sharon calls to ask for your help with a computer problem. Her system has been working fine for over a year, but now strange things are happening. Sometimes the system powers down for no apparent reason while she is working, and sometimes Windows locks up. As you read this section, look for clues as to what the problem might be. Also, think of questions to ask your friend that will help you diagnose the problem.

A+
CORE 1
5.2, 5.5

Electrical problems can occur before or after the boot and can be consistent or intermittent. Repair technicians often don't recognize the cause of a problem to be electrical because of the intermittent nature of some electrical problems. In these situations, the hard drive, memory, the OS, or even user error might be suspected as the source of the problem and then systematically eliminated before the electrical system is suspected. This section will help you to be aware of symptoms of electrical problems so that you can zero in on the source of an electrical problem as quickly as possible.

Possible symptoms of a problem with the electrical system are:

- The computer appears "dead"—no indicator lights and no spinning drive or fan.
- The computer sometimes locks up during booting. After several tries, it boots successfully.
- Error codes or beeps occur during booting, but they come and go.
- You smell burnt parts or odors. (Definitely not a good sign!)
- The computer powers down at unexpected times.
- The computer appears dead, but you hear a whine coming from the power supply.

Without opening the computer case, the following list contains some questions you can ask and things you can do to solve a problem with the electrical system. The rule of thumb is "Try the simple things first." Most computer problems have simple solutions.

◢ If you smell any burnt parts or odors, don't try to turn the system on. Identify the component that is fried and replace it.

◢ When you first plug up power to a system and hear a whine coming from the power supply, the power supply might be inadequate for the system or there might be a short. Don't press the power button to start up the system. Unplug the power cord so that the power supply will not be damaged. The next step is to open the case and search for a short. If you don't find a short, consider upgrading the power supply.

◢ Is the power cord plugged in? If it is plugged into a power strip or surge suppressor, is the device turned on and plugged in?

◢ Is the power outlet controlled by a wall switch? If so, is the switch turned on?

◢ Are any cable connections loose?

◢ Is the circuit breaker blown? Is the house circuit overloaded?

◢ Are all switches on the system turned on? Computer? Monitor? Surge suppressor or UPS (uninterruptible power supply)?

◢ Is there a possibility the system has overheated? If so, wait a while and try turning on the computer again. If the system comes on but later turns itself off, you might need additional cooling fans inside the unit. How to solve problems with overheating is covered later in this chapter.

◢ Older computers might be affected by electromagnetic interference (EMI). Check for sources of electrical or magnetic interference such as fluorescent lighting or an electric fan or copier sitting near the computer case.

> ⚡ **Caution**   Before opening the case of a brand-name computer, such as an HP or Dell, consider the warranty. If the system is still under warranty, sometimes the warranty is voided if the case is opened. If the warranty prevents you from opening the case, you might need to return the system to a manufacturer's service center for repairs.

If the problem is still not solved, it's time to look inside the case. First, turn off the computer, unplug it, press the power button to drain residual power, and then open the case. Next, do the following:

◢ Check all power connections from the power supply to the motherboard and drives. Also, some cases require the front panel to be in place before the power-on button will work. Are all cards securely seated?

◢ If you smell burnt parts, carefully search for shorts and for frayed and burnt wires. Disassemble the parts until you find the one that is damaged.

◢ If you suspect the power supply is bad, test it with a power supply tester.

PROBLEMS THAT COME AND GO

If a system boots successfully to the Windows Start screen or desktop, you still might have a power system problem. Some problems are intermittent; that is, they come and go. Generally, intermittent problems are more difficult to solve than a dead system. There can be many causes of intermittent problems, such as an inadequate power supply, overheating, and devices and components damaged by ESD. Here are some symptoms that might indicate an intermittent problem with the electrical system after the boot:

◢ The computer stops or hangs for no reason. Sometimes it might even reboot itself.

◢ Memory errors appear intermittently.

◢ Data is written incorrectly to the hard drive or files are corrupted.

4

▲ The keyboard stops working at odd times.
▲ The motherboard fails or is damaged.
▲ The power supply overheats and becomes hot to the touch.
▲ The power supply fan whines and becomes very noisy or stops.

Here is what to do to eliminate the electrical system as the source of an intermittent problem:

1. *Consider the power supply is inadequate.* If the power supply is grossly inadequate, it will whine when you first plug up the power. If you have just installed new devices that are drawing additional power, verify that the wattage rating of the power supply is adequate for the system.
   You can also test the system to make sure you don't have power problems by making all the devices in your system work at the same time. For instance, you can make two hard drives and the DVD drive work at the same time by copying files from one hard drive to the other while playing a movie on the DVD. If the drives and the other devices each work independently, but data errors occur when all work at the same time, suspect a shortage of electrical power.

2. *Suspect the power supply is faulty.* You can test it using either a power supply tester (the easier method) or a multimeter (the more tedious method). However, know that a power supply that gives correct voltages when you measure it might still be the source of problems because power problems can be intermittent. Also be aware that an ATX power supply monitors the range of voltages provided to the motherboard and halts the motherboard if voltages are inadequate. Therefore, if the power supply appears "dead," your best action is to replace it.

3. *The power supply fan might not work.* Don't operate the computer if the fan does not work because computers without cooling fans can quickly overheat. Usually just before a fan stops working, it hums or whines, especially when the computer is first turned on. If this has just happened, replace the power supply. If the new fan does not work after you replace the power supply, you have to dig deeper to find the source of the problem. You can now assume the problem wasn't the original fan. A short drawing too much power somewhere else in the system might cause the problem. To troubleshoot a nonfunctional fan, which might be a symptom of another problem and not of the fan itself, follow these steps:

   a. Turn off the power and remove all power cord connections to all components except the motherboard. Turn the power back on. If the fan works, the problem is with one of the systems you disconnected, not with the power supply, the fan, or the motherboard.
   b. Turn off the power and reconnect one card or drive at a time until you identify the device with the short.
   c. If the fan does not work when all devices except the motherboard are disconnected, the problem is the motherboard or the power supply. Because you have already replaced the power supply, you can assume that the motherboard needs to be replaced.

POWER PROBLEMS WITH THE MOTHERBOARD

A+
CORE 1
5.2

A short might occur if some component on the motherboard makes improper contact with the chassis. This short can seriously damage the motherboard. For some cases, check for missing standoffs (small plastic or metal spacers that hold the motherboard a short distance away from the bottom of the case). A missing standoff most often causes these improper connections. Also check for loose standoffs or screws under the board that might be touching a wire on the bottom of the board and causing a short. Shake the case gently and listen for loose screws.

Shorts in the circuits on the motherboard might also cause problems. Look for damage on the bottom of the motherboard. These circuits are coated with plastic, and quite often damage is difficult to spot. Also look for burned-out capacitors that are spotted brown or corroded. You'll see examples of burned-out capacitors later in the chapter.

> ⚡ **Caution**   Never replace a damaged motherboard with a good one without first testing or replacing the power supply. You don't want to subject another good board to possible damage.

APPLYING CONCEPTS   INVESTIGATING A COMPUTER PROBLEM

Back to Sharon's computer problem. Here are some questions that will help you identify the source of the problem:

- ◢ Have you added new devices to your system? (These new devices might be drawing too much power from an overworked power supply.)
- ◢ Have you moved your computer recently? (It might be sitting beside a heat vent or electrical equipment.)
- ◢ Does the system power down or hang after you have been working for some time? (This symptom might have more than one cause, such as overheating or a power supply, processor, memory, or motherboard about to fail.)
- ◢ Has the computer case been opened recently? (Someone working inside the case might not have used a ground bracelet, and components are now failing because of ESD damage.)
- ◢ Are case vents free so that air can flow? (The case might be close to a curtain covering the vents.)

Intermittent problems like the one Sharon described are often heat-related. If the system only hangs but does not power off, the problem might be caused by faulty memory or bad software, but because it actually powers down, you can assume the problem is related to power or heat.

If Sharon tells you that the system powers down after she's been working for several hours, you can probably assume overheating. Check that first. If that's not the problem, the next thing to do is replace the power supply.

PROBLEMS WITH OVERHEATING

As a repair technician, you're sure to eventually face problems with computers overheating. Overheating can happen as soon as you turn on the computer or after it has been working a while. Overheating can cause intermittent errors, the system to hang, or components to fail or not last as long as they normally would. (Overheating can significantly shorten the life span of the CPU and memory.) Overheating happens for many reasons, including improper installation of the CPU cooler or fans, overclocking, poor airflow inside the case, an underrated power supply, a component going bad, or the computer's environment (for example, heat or dust).

Here are some symptoms that a system is overheating:

- ◢ The system hangs or freezes at odd times or freezes just a few moments after the boot starts.
- ◢ A Windows BSOD error occurs during the boot.
- ◢ You cannot hear a fan running or the fan makes a whining sound.
- ◢ You cannot feel air being pulled into or out of the case.

If you suspect overheating, go into BIOS/UEFI setup and view the temperature monitors for the system. To protect the expensive processor and other components, you can also purchase a temperature sensor. The sensor plugs into a power connection coming from the power supply and mounts on the side of the case or in a drive bay. The sensor sounds an alarm when the inside of the case becomes too hot. To decide which temperature sensor to buy, use one recommended by the case manufacturer. You can also install utility software that can monitor system temperatures. For example, SpeedFan by Alfredo Comparetti is freeware that can monitor fan speeds and temperatures (see Figure 4-19). A good website to download the freeware is *filehippo.com/download_speedfan*. Be careful not to download other freeware available on the site.

4

Source: SpeedFan by Alfredo Milani Comparetti

Figure 4-19 SpeedFan monitors fan speeds and system temperatures

Here are some simple things you can do to solve an overheating problem:

1. If the system refuses to boot or hangs after a period of activity, suspect overheating. Immediately after the system hangs, go into BIOS/UEFI setup and find the screen that reports the CPU temperature. The temperature should not exceed that recommended by the CPU manufacturer.

2. Excessive dust insulates components and causes them to overheat. Use compressed air, a blower, or an antistatic vacuum to remove dust from the power supply, the vents over the entire computer, and the processor cooler fan (see Figure 4-20). To protect the fan, don't allow it to spin as you blow air into it. Overspinning might damage a fan.

Figure 4-20 Dust in this cooler fan can cause the fan to fail and the processor to overheat

Notes When working in a customer's office or home, be sure you clean up any mess you create from blowing dust out of a computer case.

3. Check airflow inside the case. Are all fans running? You might need to replace a fan. Is there an empty fan slot on the rear of the case? If so, install a case fan in the slot (see Figure 4-21). Orient the fan so that it blows air out of the case. The power cord to the fan can connect to a fan header on the motherboard or to a power connector coming directly from the power supply.

Figure 4-21 Install one exhaust fan on the rear of the case to help pull air through the case

4. If there are other fan slots on the side or front of the case, you can also install fans in these slots. However, don't install more fans than the case is designed to use.

5. Can the side of the case hold a chassis air guide that guides outside air to the processor? If it has a slot for the guide and the guide is missing, install one. However, don't install a guide that obstructs the CPU cooler. How to install an air guide is covered later in this section.

6. A case is generally designed for optimal airflow when slot openings on the front and rear of the case are covered and when the case cover is securely in place. To improve airflow, replace missing faceplates over empty drive bays and replace missing slot covers over empty expansion slots. See Figure 4-22.

7. Are cables in the way of airflow? Use tie wraps to secure cables and cords so that they don't block airflow across the processor or get in the way of fans turning. Figure 4-23 shows the inside of a case where cables are tied up and neatly out of the way of airflow from the front to the rear of the case.

Figure 4-22 For optimum airflow, don't leave empty expansion slots and bays uncovered

Figure 4-23 Use cable ties to hold cables out of the way of fans and airflow

4

8. A case needs some room to breathe. Place it so there are at least a few inches of space on both sides and the top of the case. If the case is sitting on carpet, put it on a computer stand so that air can circulate under the case and to reduce carpet dust inside the case. Many cases have a vent on the bottom front, and carpet can obstruct airflow into this vent (see Figure 4-24). Make sure drapes are not hanging too close to fan openings.

Figure 4-24   Keep a tower case off carpet to allow air to flow into the bottom air vent

9. Verify that the cooler is connected properly to the processor. If it doesn't fit well, the system might not boot and the processor will overheat. If the cooler is not tightly connected to the motherboard and processor or the cooler fan is not working, the processor will quickly overheat as soon as the computer is turned on. Has thermal compound been installed between the cooler and processor?

10. After you close the case, leave your system off for at least 30 minutes. When you power up the computer again, let it run for 10 minutes, go into BIOS/UEFI setup, check the temperature readings, and reboot. Next, let your system run until it shuts down. Power it up again and check the temperature in BIOS/UEFI setup again. A significant difference in this reading and the first one you took after running the computer for 10 minutes indicates an overheating problem.

11. Check BIOS/UEFI setup to see if the processor is being overclocked. Overclocking can cause a system to overheat. Try restoring the processor and system bus frequencies to default values.

12. Have too many peripherals been installed inside the case? Is the case too small for all these peripherals? Larger tower cases are better designed for good airflow than smaller slimline cases. Also, when installing expansion cards, try to leave an empty slot between each card for better airflow. The same goes for drives. Try not to install a group of drives in adjacent drive bays. For better airflow, leave empty bays between drives. Take a close look at Figure 4-23, where you can see space between each drive installed in the system.

13. Flash BIOS/UEFI to update the firmware on the motherboard. How to flash BIOS/UEFI is covered in Chapter 2.

14. Thermal compound should last for years, but eventually it will harden and need replacing. If the system is several years old, replace the thermal compound.

★ **A+ Exam Tip**   The A+ Core 1 exam expects you to recognize that a given symptom is possibly power- or heat-related.

If you try the preceding list of things to do and still have an overheating problem, it's time to move on to more drastic solutions. Consider whether the case design allows for good airflow; the problem might be caused by poor air circulation inside the case. The power supply fan in ATX cases blows air out of the case, pulling outside air from the vents in the front of the case across the processor to help keep it cool. Another exhaust fan is usually installed on the back of the case to help the power supply fan pull air through the case. In addition, most processors require a cooler with a fan installed on top of the processor. Figure 4-25 shows a good arrangement of vents and fans for proper airflow and a poor arrangement.

Good arrangement for proper airflow   Poor arrangement for proper airflow

Figure 4-25   Vents and fans need to be arranged for best airflow

For better ventilation, use a power supply that has vents on the bottom and front, as shown in Figure 4-26. Compare that with the power supply in Figure 4-21, which has vents only on the front and not on the bottom.

Figure 4-26   This power supply has vents on the bottom to provide better airflow inside the case

An intake fan on the front of the case might help pull air into the case. Intel recommends you use a front intake fan for high-end systems, but AMD says a front fan for ATX systems is not necessary. Check with the processor and case manufacturers for specific instructions as to the placement of fans and what type of fan and heat sink to use.

4

Intel and AMD both recommend a chassis air guide (CAG) as part of the case design. This air guide is a round air duct that helps to pull and direct fresh air from outside the case to the cooler and processor (see Figure 4-27). The guide should reach inside the case very close to the cooler, but not touch it. Intel recommends the clearance be no greater than 20 mm and no less than 12 mm. If the guide obstructs the cooler, you can remove the guide, but optimum airflow will not be achieved.

Chassis air guide

Figure 4-27 Use a chassis air guide to direct outside air over the cooler

Be careful when trying to solve an overheating problem. Excessive heat can damage the CPU and the motherboard. Never operate a system if the case fan, power-supply fan, or cooler fan is not working.

PROBLEMS WITH LAPTOP POWER SYSTEMS

A+
CORE 1
5.2, 5.5

A laptop can be powered by an AC adapter (which uses regular house current to power the laptop) or an installed battery pack. Battery packs today use lithium ion technology. Most AC adapters today are capable of auto-switching from 110 V to 220 V AC power. Figure 4-28 shows an AC adapter that has a green light indicating the adapter is receiving power.

Figure 4-28 This AC adapter for a laptop uses a green light to indicate power

Some mobile users like to keep an extra battery on hand in case the first one uses up its charge. When the laptop signals that power is low, shut down the system, remove the old battery, and replace it with a charged one. To remove a battery, you usually must release a latch first.

📝 **Notes** If you're using the AC adapter to power your laptop when the power goes out, the installed battery serves as a built-in UPS. The battery immediately takes over as your uninterruptible power supply (UPS). Also, a laptop has an internal surge protector. However, for extra protection, you might want to use a power strip that provides surge protection.

Here are some problems you might encounter with laptop power systems and their solutions:

◢ If power is not getting to the system or the battery indicator light is lit when the AC adapter should be supplying power, verify that the AC adapter is plugged into a live electrical outlet. Is the light on the AC adapter lit? Check if the AC adapter's plug is secure in the electrical outlet. Check the connections on both sides of the AC adapter transformer. Check the connection at the DC jack on the laptop. Try exchanging the AC adapter for one you know is good. The DC jack might need replacing. Most laptops allow you to replace the DC jack without replacing the entire system board. Check the service manual for the laptop to see how labor-intensive the repair is before you decide to proceed.

◢ If the battery is not charging when the AC adapter is plugged in, the problem might be with the battery or the motherboard. A hot battery might not charge until it cools down. If the battery is hot, remove it from the computer and allow it to cool to room temperature. Check the battery for physical damage. If the battery is swollen or warped, replace it. If it shows no physical signs of damage, try to recharge it. If it does not recharge, replace the battery pack. If a known good battery does not recharge, you have three options: (1) Replace the system board, (2) replace the laptop, or (3) use the laptop only when it's connected to power using the AC adapter.

APPLYING CONCEPTS TESTING AN AC ADAPTER

If the system fails only when the AC adapter is connected, it might be defective. Try a new AC adapter, or, if you have a multimeter, use it to verify the voltage output of the adapter. Do the following for an adapter with a single center-pin connector:

1. Unplug the AC adapter from the computer, but leave it plugged into the electrical outlet.

2. Most laptops run on 19 V DC, but a few run on 45 V DC. To be on the safe side, set the multimeter to measure voltage in the range of 1-200 V DC. Place the red probe of the multimeter in the center of the DC connector that would normally plug into the DC outlet on the laptop. Place the black probe on the outside cylinder of the DC connector (see Figure 4-29).

3. The voltage range should be plus or minus 5 percent of the accepted voltage. For example, if a laptop is designed to use 16 V, the voltage should measure somewhere between 15.2 and 16.8 V DC.

Figure 4-29 To use a multimeter to test this AC adapter, place the red probe in the center of the connector and the black probe on the outside

TROUBLESHOOTING THE MOTHERBOARD, PROCESSOR, AND RAM

The field replaceable units (FRUs) on a motherboard are the processor, the processor cooler assembly, RAM, and the CMOS battery. Also, the motherboard itself is an FRU. As you troubleshoot the motherboard and discover that some component is not working, such as a network port, you might be able to disable that component in BIOS/UEFI setup and install a card to take its place.

> ⭐ **A+ Exam Tip** The A+ Core 1 exam expects you to know how to troubleshoot problems with motherboards, processors, and RAM.

When you suspect a bad component, a good troubleshooting technique is to substitute a known good component for the one you suspect is bad. Be cautious here. A friend once had a computer that wouldn't boot. He replaced the hard drive, with no change. He replaced the motherboard next. The computer booted up with no problem; he was delighted, until it failed again. Later he discovered that a faulty power supply had damaged his original motherboard. When he traded the bad one for a good one, the new motherboard also got zapped! If you suspect problems with the power supply, check the voltage coming from the power supply before putting in a new motherboard.

The following symptoms can indicate that a motherboard, processor, or memory module is failing:

◢ The system begins to boot but then powers down.
◢ An error message is displayed during the boot. Investigate this message.
◢ The system reports less memory than you know is installed.
◢ The system becomes unstable, hangs, or freezes at odd times. (This symptom can have multiple causes, including a failing power supply, RAM, hard drive, motherboard, or processor, Windows errors, and overheating.)
◢ Intermittent Windows or hard drive errors occur.
◢ Components on the motherboard or devices connected to it don't work.

Remember the troubleshooting principle to check the simple things first. The motherboard and processor are expensive and time consuming to replace. Unless you're certain the problem is one of these two components, don't replace either until you first eliminate other components as the source of the problem.

If you can boot the system, follow these steps to eliminate Windows, software, RAM, BIOS/UEFI settings, and other software and hardware components as the source of the problem:

1. If an error message appears, Google the error message. Pay particular attention to hits on the motherboard or processor manufacturer or Microsoft websites. Search forums for information about the error.

2. The problem might be a virus. If you can boot the system, run a current version of antivirus software to check for viruses.

3. A memory module might be failing. In Windows 10/8/7, use the Memory Diagnostics tool to test memory. Even if Windows is not installed, you can still run the tool by booting the system from the Windows setup DVD. How to use the Memory Diagnostics tool is coming up later in this chapter.

> ✎ **Notes** Besides the Windows Memory Diagnostics tool, you can use the Memtest86 utility to test installed memory modules. Check the site *memtest86.com* to download this program.

4. Suspect the problem is caused by an application or by Windows. In Windows, Device Manager is the best tool to check for potential hardware problems.

5. In Windows, check Event Viewer logs for a record about a hardware or application problem. You learn to use Event Viewer in a project at the end of this chapter.

6. In Windows, download and install any Windows updates or patches. These updates might solve a hardware or application problem.

7. Ask yourself what has changed since the problem began. If the problem began immediately after installing a new device or application, uninstall it.

8. A system that does not have enough RAM can sometimes appear to be unstable. Using the System window, find out how much RAM is installed, and compare that with the recommended amounts. Consider upgrading RAM.

9. The BIOS/UEFI might be corrupted or have wrong settings. Check BIOS/UEFI setup. Have settings been tampered with? Is the CPU speed set incorrectly or is it overclocked? Reset BIOS/UEFI setup to restore default settings.

10. Disable any quick booting features in BIOS/UEFI so that you get a thorough report of POST. Then look for errors reported on the screen during the boot.

11. Flash BIOS/UEFI to update the firmware on the board.

12. Check the motherboard manufacturer's website for diagnostic software that might identify a problem with the motherboard.

13. Update all drivers of motherboard components that are not working. For example, if the USB ports are not working, try updating the USB drivers with those downloaded from the motherboard manufacturer's website. This process can also update the chipset drivers.

14. If an onboard port or device isn't working, but the motherboard is stable, follow these steps:

   a. Verify that the problem is not with the device using the port. Try moving the device to another port on the same computer or move the device to another computer. If it works there, return it to this port. The problem might have been a bad connection.

   b. Go into BIOS/UEFI setup and verify that the port is enabled.

   c. Check Device Manager and verify that Windows recognizes the device or port with no errors. For example, Device Manager shown in Figure 4-30 reports the onboard Bluetooth device is disabled. Try to enable the device.

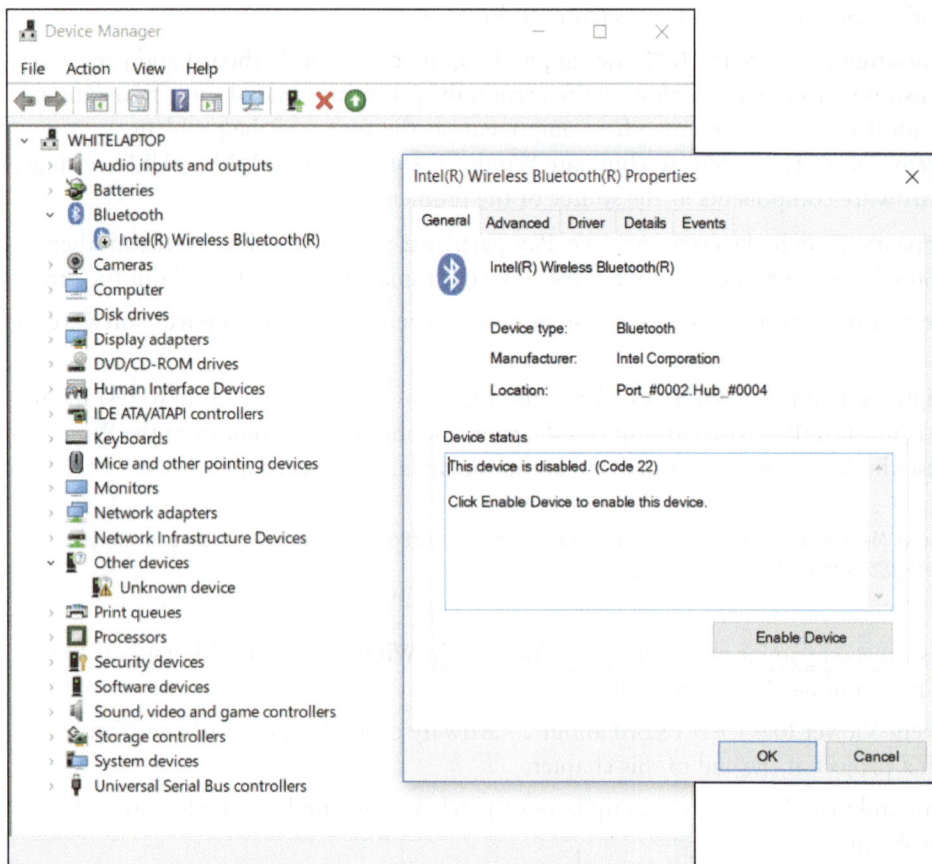

Figure 4-30 Device Manager reports a problem with an onboard device

d. Next try updating the motherboard drivers for this device from the motherboard manufacturer's website.

e. If you have a loopback plug, use it to test the port.

f. If the problem is still not solved, disable the port in BIOS/UEFI setup and install an expansion card to provide the same type of port or connector.

15. Suspect the problem is caused by a failing hard drive. How to troubleshoot a failing drive is covered in Chapter 5.

16. Suspect the problem is caused by overheating. How to check for overheating is covered earlier in this chapter.

17. Verify that the installed processor is supported by the motherboard. Perhaps someone has installed the wrong processor.

APPLYING | CONCEPTS   USING WINDOWS MEMORY DIAGNOSTICS

Errors with memory are often difficult to diagnose because they can appear intermittently and might be mistaken as application errors, user errors, or other hardware component errors. Sometimes these errors cause the system to hang, a blue screen error might occur, or the system continues to function with applications giving errors or data getting corrupted. You can quickly identify a problem with memory or eliminate memory as the source of a problem by using the Windows 10/8/7 Memory Diagnostics tool. Use one of these two methods to start the utility:

▲ **Use the mdsched.exe command in Windows**. To open a command prompt window from the Windows 10/8/7 desktop, enter the **cmd** command in the Windows start or run box. In the command prompt window, enter **mdsched.exe** and press **Enter**. A dialog box appears (see Figure 4-31) and asks if you want to run the test now or on the next restart.

Figure 4-31   Use the mdsched.exe command to test memory

▲ **Boot from the Windows setup DVD**. If Windows is not the installed operating system or you cannot boot from the hard drive, boot the computer from the Windows setup USB drive or DVD to test memory for errors. Follow these steps:

1. If necessary, change the boot priority order in BIOS/UEFI setup to boot first from the optical drive or USB drive. Boot from the Windows setup DVD or USB drive.

2. On the opening screen for Windows 10/8, select your language and click **Next**. On the next screen (see Figure 4-32), click **Repair your computer**. Next choose **Troubleshoot**. For Windows 10, the Advanced options screen appears; for Windows 8, you must click **Advanced options** to see this screen.

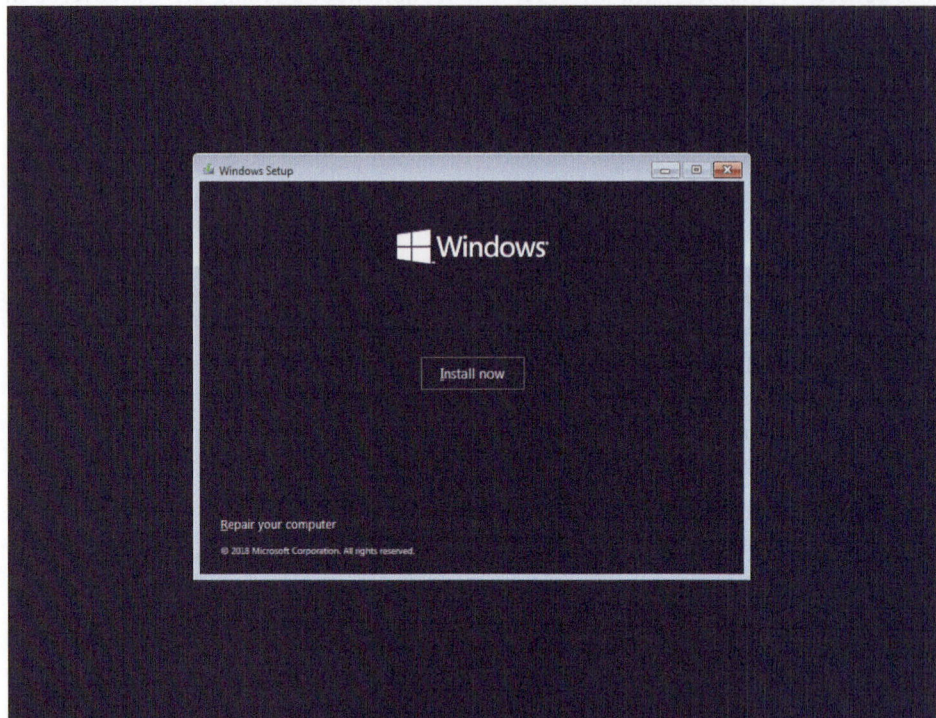

Figure 4-32   The opening menu when you boot from Windows 10 setup media

3. On the Advanced options screen (see Figure 4-33), choose **Command Prompt**. In the command prompt window, enter the **mdsched.exe** command.

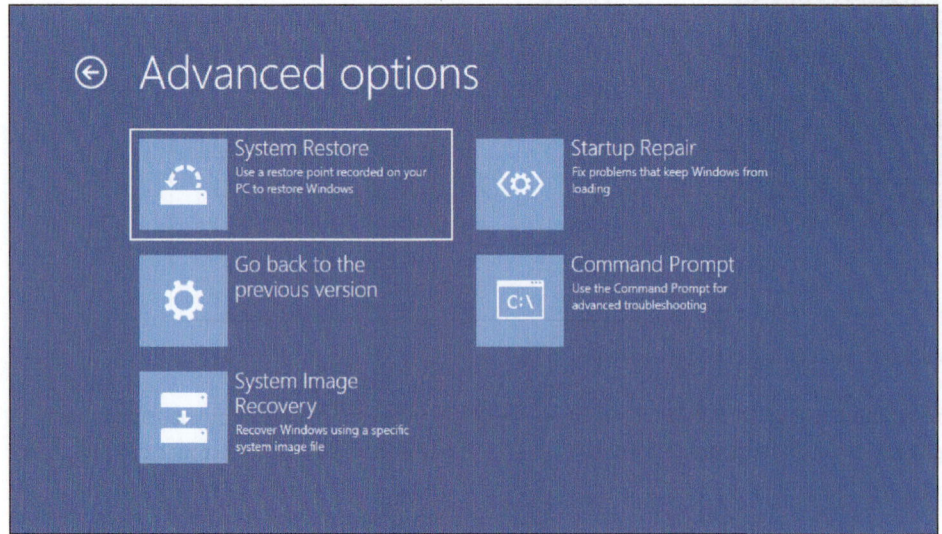

Figure 4-33   The Windows 10 Advanced options screen launched from Windows 10 setup media

> **◇ OS Differences** For Windows 7, after booting from the Windows 7 setup DVD, select the Windows installation to repair. On the System Recovery Options screen (see Figure 4-34), click **Windows Memory Diagnostic**. For Windows 7, it is not necessary to open a command prompt window to test memory.

Figure 4-34 Test memory using the Windows 7 System Recovery Options menu

If the tool reports memory errors, replace all memory modules installed on the motherboard.

APPLYING | CONCEPTS   USING DEVICE MANAGER TO DELETE THE DRIVER STORE

One thing you can do to solve a problem with a device is to uninstall and reinstall the device. When you first install a device, Windows stores a copy of the driver package in a driver store. When you uninstall the device, you can also tell Windows to delete the driver store. If you don't delete the driver store, Windows uses it when you install the device again. That's why the second time you install the same device, Windows does not ask you for the location of the drivers. Windows might also use the driver store to automatically install the device on the next reboot without your involvement.

All this is convenient unless there is a problem with the driver store. To get a true fresh start with an installation, you need to delete the driver store. First sign in to Windows using an account with administrative privileges and then follow these steps:

1. To open Device Manager from the Windows 10/8 desktop, right-click **Start** and click **Device Manager**. (In Windows 7, click **Start** and click **Control Panel**. In Control Panel Classic icon view, click **Device Manager**.) Device Manager opens.

(continues)

> ⭐ **A+ Exam Tip**   The A+ Core 1 exam expects you to be familiar with Control Panel in Classic icon view. If Control Panel is showing Category view, click **Category**, and then click **Large icons** or **Small icons**. Also, you are expected to know commands for various Windows tools. For example, to start Device Manager, you can enter the devmgmt.msc command in a command line window.

2. Right-click the device and click **Properties** in the shortcut menu. Click the **Driver** tab and click **Uninstall Device**. In the Uninstall Device box, check **Delete the driver software for this device**, and click **Uninstall**. See Figure 4-35. The installed drivers and the driver store are both deleted. When you reinstall the device, you'll need the drivers on CD or downloaded from the web.

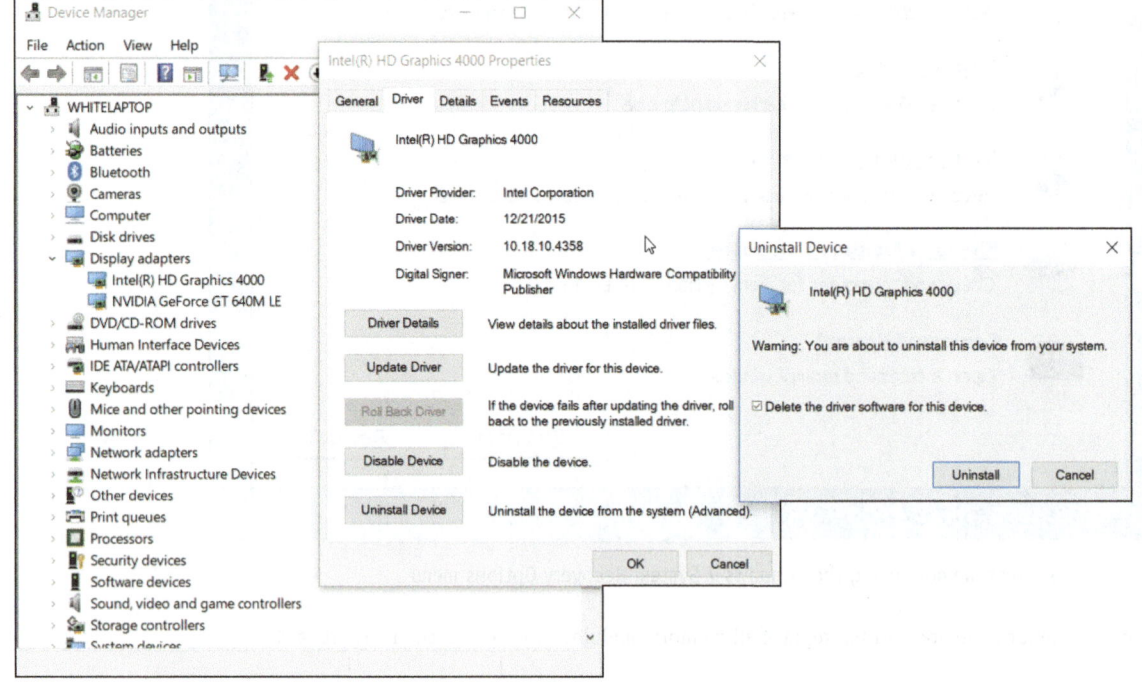

Figure 4-35   Use Device Manager to uninstall the drivers and delete the driver store for a device

Also know that if the check box is missing on the Confirm Device Uninstall box, the drivers are embedded in Windows and you cannot delete the driver store for these devices. Examples of these devices are the optical drive, hard drive, and generic keyboard, which all have embedded Windows drivers.

We're working our way through what to do when the system locks up, gives errors, or generally appears unstable. Another problem that can occur at the boot is continuous reboots, which can be caused by overheating, a failing processor, motherboard, or RAM, or a corrupted Windows installation.

WINDOWS STARTUP REPAIR

A+ CORE 1 5.2   For Windows 10/8/7, many continuous restart errors can be solved by performing a Startup Repair process. The Startup Repair utility restores many of the Windows files needed for a successful boot. After several restarts, Windows 10 will try to automatically run the Startup Repair process. If Startup Repair does not automatically start or does not fix the problem, try running it from Windows setup media.

Follow these steps to run Startup Repair from the Windows 10/8 setup DVD or USB drive:

1. If necessary, change the boot priority order in BIOS/UEFI setup to boot first from the optical drive or USB drive. Boot from the Windows setup DVD or USB drive.

2. On the opening screen, select your language and click **Next**. On the next screen, click **Repair your computer**. Next, choose **Troubleshoot**. For Windows 10, the Advanced options screen appears (refer back to Figure 4-33); for Windows 8, you must click **Advanced options** to see this screen. On the Advanced options screen, choose **Startup Repair**, and select your operating system. Windows will attempt to repair the system and restart to the Windows desktop.

◇ OS Differences For Windows 7, error messages disappear before they can be read as the system reboots. To disable these automatic restarts, press F8 as Windows starts up. The Advanced Boot Options menu appears (see Figure 4-36). Select **Disable automatic restart on system failure**. When you restart Windows, the error message stays on screen long enough for you to read it. Search the Microsoft websites (*support.microsoft.com* and *technet.microsoft.com*) for information about the hardware component causing the problem and what to do about it. BSOD errors might apply to the motherboard, video card, RAM, processor, hard drive, or some other device for which Windows is trying to load device drivers. From the Advanced Boot Options menu, you can click **Repair Your Computer**, which launches the Windows 7 version of Startup Repair.

Figure 4-36 Press F8 during the boot to see the Windows 7 Advanced Boot Options menu

If you have tried to repair Windows, checked BIOS/UEFI settings, searched the web for help, and still have not identified the source of the problem, it's time to open the case and check inside. Be sure to use an ESD strap and follow other procedures to protect the system against ESD. With the case open, follow these steps:

1. Check that all the system power and data cables are securely connected. Try reseating all expansion cards and DIMM modules.

2. Look for physical damage on the motherboard. Look for frayed traces on the bottom of the board or discolored, distended, or bulging capacitors on the board.

3. Reduce the system to essentials. Remove any unnecessary hardware, such as expansion cards, and then watch to see if the problem goes away. If it does, replace one component at a time until the problem returns and you have identified the component causing the trouble.

4. Try using a POST diagnostic card. It might offer you a clue as to which component is giving a problem.

5. Suspect the problem is caused by a failing power supply. It's less expensive and easier to replace than the motherboard or processor, so eliminate it as a cause before you move on to the motherboard or processor.

6. Exchange the processor.

7. Exchange the motherboard, but before you do, measure the voltage output of the power supply or simply replace it, in case it is producing too much power and has damaged the board.

APPLYING | CONCEPTS   DISCOLORED CAPACITORS

Jessica complained to Wally, her IT support technician, that Windows was occasionally giving errors, data would get corrupted, or an application would not work as it should. At first, Wally suspected Jessica might need a little more training on how to open and close an application or save a file, but he discovered user error was not the problem. He tried reinstalling the application software Jessica most often used, and even reinstalled Windows, but the problems persisted.

> ✎ **Notes** Catastrophic errors (errors that cause the system not to boot or a device not to work) are much easier to resolve than intermittent errors (errors that come and go).

Wally began to suspect a hardware problem. Carefully examining the motherboard revealed the source of the problem: failing capacitors. Look carefully at Figure 4-37 and you can see five bad **discolored capacitors** with bulging heads. (Know that sometimes a leaking capacitor can also show crusty corrosion at its base.) When Wally replaced the motherboard, the problems went away.

Bad capacitors

Figure 4-37   These five bad capacitors have bulging and discolored heads

APPLYING | CONCEPTS   LESSONS LEARNED

Sophia is putting together a computer from parts for the first time. She has decided to keep costs low and is installing an AMD processor on a microATX motherboard, using all low-cost parts. She installed the hard drive, optical drive, and power supply in the computer case. Then she installed the motherboard in the case, followed by the processor, cooler, and memory. Before powering up the system, she checked all connections to make sure they were solid and read through the motherboard documentation to make sure she did not forget anything important. Next, she plugs in the monitor to the onboard video port and then plugs in the keyboard and power cord. She takes a deep breath and turns on the power switch on the back of the computer. Immediately, she hears a faint whine, but she's not sure what is making the noise. When she presses the power button on the front of the case, nothing happens. No fans, no lights. Here are the steps Sophia takes to troubleshoot the problem:

1. She turns off the power switch and unplugs the power cord. She remembers to put on her ground bracelet and carefully checks all power connections. Everything looks okay.

2. She plugs in the system and presses the power button again. Still all she hears is the faint whine.

3. She presses the power button a second and third time. Suddenly a loud pop followed by smoke comes from the power supply, and the strong smell of electronics fills the room! Sophia jumps back in dismay.

4. She removes a known good power supply from another computer, disconnects the blown power supply, and connects the good one to the computer. When she turns on the power switch, she hears that same faint whine. Quickly she turns off the switch and unplugs the power cord. She does not want to lose another power supply!

5. Next, Sophia calls technical support of the company that sold her the computer parts. A very helpful technician listens carefully to the details and tells Sophia that the problem sounds like a short in the system. He explains that a power supply might whine if too much power is being drawn. As Sophia hangs up the phone, she begins to think that the problem might be with the motherboard installation.

6. She removes the motherboard from the case, and the source of the problem is evident: She forgot to install spacers between the board and the case. The board was sitting directly on the bottom of the case, which had caused the short.

7. Sophia installs the spacers and reinstalls the motherboard. Using the good power supply, she turns on the system. The whine is gone, but the system is dead.

8. Sophia purchases a new power supply and motherboard, and this time carefully uses spacers in every hole used by the motherboard screws. Figure 4-38 shows one installed spacer and one ready to be installed. The system comes up without a problem.

Figure 4-38   Spacers installed in case holes keep the motherboard from causing a short

(continues)

In evaluating her experience with her first computer build, Sophia declares the project a success. She was grateful she had decided to use low-cost parts for her first build. She learned much from the experience and will never, ever forget to use spacers. She told a friend, "I made a serious mistake, but I learned from it. I feel confident I know how to put a system together now, and I'm ready to tackle another build. When you make mistakes and get past them, your confidence level actually grows because you learn you can face a serious problem and solve it."

>> CHAPTER SUMMARY

Cooling Methods and Devices

⏃ Devices that are used to keep a processor and system cool include CPU coolers and fans, thermal compound, case fans, heat sinks, and liquid cooling.

⏃ Liquid cooling systems use liquids pumped through the system to keep it cool and are sometimes used by hobbyists when overclocking a system.

Selecting a Power Supply

⏃ Important features of a power supply to consider before purchase are its form factor, wattage capacity, number and type of connectors it provides, and warranty.

⏃ To decide on the wattage capacity of a power supply, add up the wattage requirements for all components in a system and then increase that total by about 30 percent. The wattage provided by the +12 V rail is also important.

Strategies to Troubleshoot Any Computer Problem

⏃ The six steps in the troubleshooting process are (1) interview the user and back up data, (2) examine the system and form a theory of probable cause (your best guess), (3) test your theory, (4) plan a solution and implement it, (5) verify that everything works and take appropriate preventive measures, and (6) document what you did and the final outcome.

⏃ If possible, always begin troubleshooting a computer problem by interviewing the user. Find out when the problem started and what happened about the time it started. You also need to know if important data on the computer is not backed up. When troubleshooting, set your priorities based on user needs.

⏃ Sources that can help with hardware troubleshooting are the web, online technical support and forums, diagnostic software, user manuals, and your network of technical associates.

⏃ When troubleshooting, check the simple things first. For example, you can scan for viruses, test RAM, and run diagnostic software before you begin the process of replacing expensive components.

⏃ Decide if a computer problem occurs before or after a successful boot and if it is caused by hardware or software. After you have fixed the problem, verify the fix and document the outcome.

⏃ When troubleshooting laptops, consider the warranty and that replacing a component might cost more than replacing the device. If possible, substitute an external component for an internal one.

Troubleshooting the Electrical System

⏃ To determine if a system is getting power, listen for spinning fans or drives and look for indicator lights.

⏃ Use a power supply tester to test the power supply.

▲ Intermittent problems that come and go are the most difficult to solve and can be caused by hardware or software. The power supply, motherboard, RAM, processor, hard drive, and overheating can cause intermittent problems.

▲ Removing dust from a system, providing for proper ventilation, and installing extra fans can help to keep a system from overheating.

▲ The battery and the DC jack in a laptop are considered field replaceable units that pertain to the power system.

▲ Use a multimeter to check the voltage output of an AC adapter.

Troubleshooting the Motherboard, Processor, and RAM

▲ BIOS/UEFI gives beep codes when a POST error occurs during the boot before it tests video.

▲ Error messages on a black screen during the boot are usually put there by startup BIOS/UEFI during POST.

▲ Error messages on a blue screen during or after the boot are put there by Windows and are called the blue screen of death (BSOD).

▲ The motherboard, processor, RAM, processor cooler assembly, and CMOS battery are field replaceable units.

▲ An unstable system that freezes or hangs at odd times can be caused by a faulty power supply, RAM, hard drive, motherboard, or processor, a Windows error, or overheating.

▲ A POST diagnostic card can troubleshoot problems with the motherboard.

>> KEY TERMS

For explanations of key terms, see the Glossary for this text.

AC adapter	chassis air guide (CAG)	Event Viewer	Memory Diagnostics
auto-switching	cooler	expert system	processor thermal trip error
blue screen of death	discolored capacitors	heat sink	Startup Repair
(BSOD)	driver store	lithium ion	technical documentation
case fan			

>> THINKING CRITICALLY

These questions are designed to prepare you for the critical thinking required for the A+ Core 1 exam and may use information from other chapters or the web.

1. How much power is consumed by a load drawing 5 A with 120 V across it?

2. What is a reasonable wattage capacity for a power supply to be used with a system that contains a DVD drive, three hard drives, and a high-end video card?

   a. 250 W

   b. 1000 W

   c. 700 W

   d. 150 W

3. You upgrade a faulty PCIe video card to a recently released higher-performing card. Now the user complains that Windows 10 hangs a lot and gives errors. Which is the most likely source of the problem? Which is the least likely source?

   a. A component of the computer is overheating.

   b. Windows does not support the new card.

   c. The drivers for the card need updating.

   d. Memory is faulty.

4. What should you immediately do if you turn on a computer and smell smoke or a burning odor?

   a. Unplug the computer.

   b. Dial 911.

   c. Find a fire extinguisher.

   d. Press a key on the keyboard to enter BIOS setup.

5. When you boot up a computer and hear a single beep, but the screen is blank, what can you assume is the source of the problem?

   a. The video card or onboard video

   b. The monitor or monitor cable

   c. Windows startup

   d. The processor

6. You suspect that a power supply is faulty, but you use a power supply tester to measure its voltage output and find it to be acceptable. Why is it still possible that the power supply may be faulty?

7. Someone asks you for help with a computer that hangs at odd times. You turn it on and work for about 15 minutes, and then the computer freezes and powers down. What do you do first?

   a. Replace the surge protector.

   b. Replace the power supply.

   c. Wait about 30 minutes for the system to cool down and try again.

   d. Install an additional fan.

8. You own a small computer repair company and a customer comes to you with a laptop that will not boot. After investigating, you discover the hard drive has crashed. What should you do first?

   a. Install a hard drive that's the same size and speed as the original.

   b. Ask the customer's advice about the size of the drive to install, but select a drive that's the same speed as the original drive.

   c. Ask the customer's advice about the size and speed of the new drive to install.

   d. If the customer looks like he can afford it, install the largest and fastest drive the system can support.

9. You have repaired a broken LCD panel in a laptop computer. However, when you disassembled the laptop, you bent the hinge on the lid so that it now does not latch solidly. When the customer receives the laptop, he notices the bent hinge and begins shouting at you. What do you do first? Second?

   a. Explain to the customer you are sorry but you did the best you could.

   b. Listen carefully to the customer and don't get defensive.

   c. Apologize and offer to replace the bent hinge.

   d. Tell the customer he is not allowed to speak to you like that.

10. As a help-desk technician, list four good detective questions to ask if a user calls to say, "My computer won't boot."

11. If the power connector from the CPU fan has only three pins, it can still connect to the 4-pin header, but what functionality is lost?

12. How do you determine the wattage capacity needed by a power supply?

13. You've decided to build a new gaming computer and are researching which power supply to buy. Which component in a high-end gaming computer is likely to draw the most power? What factor in a power supply do you need to consider to make sure this component has enough wattage?

14. Your friend Suzy calls to ask for help with her computer. She says when she first turns on the computer, she doesn't hear a spinning drive or fan or see indicator lights, and the monitor is blank. Is the problem hardware- or software-related?

15. Which two components in a system might make a loud whining noise when there is a problem? Why?

16. Your boss assigns you a trouble ticket that says a computer is randomly shutting off after about 15 minutes of use. You have a theory that the computer is overheating. What utility program can you use to read system temperatures?

17. What are two reasons to tie cables up and out of the way inside a computer case?

18. You suspect a component in a computer is fried. You remove any unnecessary hardware devices one by one to narrow down where the problem exists. Which step in the troubleshooting process is this?

>> HANDS-ON PROJECTS

Hands-On | Project 4-1   Calculating Wattage Capacity for Your System

Do the following to compare the wattage capacity of the power supply installed in your computer with the recommended value:

   1. Search the web for a power supply wattage calculator. Be sure the one you use is provided by a reliable website. For example, the ones at *newegg.com* and *outervision.com* are reliable. (At *newegg.com*, click **Computer Hardware** and then click **Power Supply Wattage Calculator**. At *outervision.com*, click **Outervision Power Supply Calculator**.)

   2. Enter the information about your computer system. Print or save the webpage showing the resulting calculations.

   3. What is the recommended wattage capacity for a power supply for your system?

   4. Look on the printed label on the power supply currently installed in your computer. What is its wattage capacity?

   5. If you had to replace the power supply in your system, what wattage capacity would you select?

Hands-On | Project 4-2   Researching Beep Codes

Identify the motherboard and BIOS/UEFI version installed in your computer. Locate the motherboard user guide on the web and find the list of beep codes that the BIOS/UEFI might give at POST. If the manual doesn't give this information, search the support section on the website of the motherboard manufacturer or search the website of the BIOS/UEFI manufacturer. List the beep codes and their meanings for your motherboard.

Hands-On | Project 4-3   Identifying Airflow Through a Case

Turn on a computer and feel the front and side vents to decide where air is flowing into and out of the case. Identify where you believe fans are working to produce the airflow. Power down the computer, unplug it, and press the power button to completely drain the power. Then open the computer case. Are fans located where you expected? Which fans were producing the strongest airflow through the case when the system was running? In which direction is each case fan drawing air: into the case or out of the case?

Hands-On | Project 4-4   Blowing Dust Out of a Case

If necessary, open the case cover to your desktop computer. Using a can of compressed air, blow the dust away from all fans and other components inside the case. Be careful not to touch components unless you are properly grounded. When you're done, close the case cover.

Hands-On | Project 4-5   Troubleshooting Memory

Do the following to troubleshoot memory:

1. Open the Windows System Information window and record the amount of memory in your system.
2. Follow the rules to protect a computer against ESD as you work. Remove the memory module in the first memory slot on the motherboard and boot the computer. Did you get an error? Why or why not? Replace the module, verify that the system starts with no errors, and verify that the full amount of memory is recognized by Windows.
3. Use the Windows 10/8/7 Memory Diagnostics tool to test memory. About how long did the test take? Were any errors reported?

Hands-On | Project 4-6   Sabotaging and Repairing a Computer

Open the computer case and create a hardware problem with your computer that prevents it from booting without damaging a component. For example, you can disconnect a data cable or power cable or loosen a DIMM in a memory slot. Close the computer case and restart the system. Describe the problem as if you were a user who does not know much about computer hardware. Power down the system and fix the problem. Boot up the system and verify that all is well.

## 4

Hands-On | Project 4-7 Documenting an Intermittent Problem

Intermittent problems can make troubleshooting challenging. The trick in diagnosing problems that come and go is to look for patterns or clues as to when the problems occur. If you or the user can't reproduce the problem at will, ask the user to keep a log of when the problems occur and exactly what messages appear. Tell the user that intermittent problems are the hardest to solve and might take some time, but you won't give up. Show the user how to take a screenshot of the error messages when they appear. It might also be appropriate to ask him to email the screenshot to you. Do the following:

1. Use the Windows 10/8/7 Snipping Tool to take a snip of your Windows desktop showing the File Explorer or Windows Explorer window open. If you need help using the Snipping Tool, see Windows Help and Support or search the web.

2. Save the snip and email it to your instructor.

Hands-On | Project 4-8 Researching IT Support Sites

The web is an excellent resource to use when problem solving, and it's helpful to know which websites are trustworthy and useful. Access each of the websites listed in Table 4-6, and print one webpage from each site that shows information that might be useful for a support technician. If the site offers a free email newsletter, consider subscribing to it. Answer the following questions about these sites:

1. Which site can help you find out what type of RAM you can use on your computer?

2. Which site explains Moore's Law? What is Moore's Law?

3. Which site offers a free download for data recovery software?

4. Which site gives a review about registry cleaning software?

5. Which two sites allow you to post a question about computer repair to a forum?

6. Which site offers a tutorial to learn C programming?

7. Which site offers free antivirus software published by the site owners?

Organization	Website
CNET, Inc.	cnet.com
Experts Exchange (subscription site)	experts-exchange.com
F-Secure Corp.	f-secure.com
How Stuff Works	howstuffworks.com
How-To Geek	howtogeek.com
IFixit	ifixit.com
Kingston Technology (information about memory)	kingston.com
Microsoft Technical Resources	support.microsoft.com technet.microsoft.com
PC World	pcworld.com
TechRepublic	techrepublic.com

Table 4-6 Technical information websites

List some other websites you found when answering these questions. Would you consider these websites authoritative and why?

>> REAL PROBLEMS, REAL SOLUTIONS

REAL PROBLEM 4-1 Replacing a Power Supply

Suppose you turn on a system and everything is dead—no lights, nothing on the monitor screen, and no spinning fan or hard drive. You verify that the power to the system works, all power connections and power cords are securely connected, and all pertinent switches are turned on. You can assume the power supply has gone bad. It's time to replace it. To prepare for this situation in a real work environment, exchange power supplies with another student in your lab who is using a computer that has a power supply rated at about the same wattage as yours. Then verify that your system starts up and works.

REAL PROBLEM 4-2 Using Event Viewer to Troubleshoot a Hardware Problem

Just about anything that happens in Windows is recorded in Event Viewer (Eventvwr.msc). You can find events such as a hardware or network failure, OS error messages, or a device that has failed to start. When you first encounter a Windows, hardware, application, or security problem, get in the habit of checking Event Viewer as one of your first steps toward investigating the problem. To save time, first check the Administrative Events log because it filters out all events except Warning and Error events, which are the most useful for troubleshooting. Do the following to practice using Event Viewer:

1. For Windows 10/8/7, enter **eventvwr.msc** in the Windows 10/7 search box, in the Windows 8 run box, or in a command prompt window. Event Viewer opens. Drill down into the **Custom Views** list in the left pane and click **Administrative Events**. Scroll through the list of Error or Warning events and list any that indicate a possible hardware problem. Make note of the first event in the list.

2. Disconnect the network cable.

3. In the Event Viewer menu bar, click **Action** and **Refresh** to refresh the list of events. How many new events do you see? Click each new event to see its details below the list of events until you find the event that tells you the network cable was unplugged. Figure 4-39 shows Event Viewer for Windows 10. Describe the details of the event about the network cable.

Figure 4-39 Use Event Viewer to find logs that can help you troubleshoot hardware problems

4. Tinker around with other hardware on your computer. What actions did you take that triggered a Warning or Error event in Event Viewer?

REAL PROBLEM 4-3 Troubleshooting a Hung System

A user complains to you that her system hangs for no known reason. After asking her a few questions, you identify these symptoms:

◢ The system hangs after about 15–20 minutes of operation.

◢ When the system hangs, it doesn't matter what application is open or how many applications are open.

◢ When the system hangs, it appears as though power is turned off: There are no lights, spinning drives, or other evidence of power.

You suspect overheating might be the problem. To test your theory, you decide to do the following:

1. You want to verify that the user has not overclocked the system. How do you do that?

2. You decide to check for overheating by examining the temperature of the system immediately after the system is powered up and then again immediately after the system hangs. Describe the steps you take to do this.

3. After doing the first two steps, you decide overheating is the cause of the problem. What are four things you can do to fix the problem?

Supporting Hard Drives and Other Storage Devices

After completing this chapter, you will be able to:

- Describe and contrast technologies used inside a hard drive and how a computer communicates with a hard drive

- Select, install, and support a hard drive

- Support optical drives, solid-state storage, and flash memory devices

- Troubleshoot hard drives

The hard drive is the most important permanent storage device in a computer, and supporting hard drives is one of the more important tasks of a computer support technician. This chapter introduces the different kinds of hard drive technologies and the ways a computer interfaces with a hard drive. You learn how to select and install the different types of hard drives and how to troubleshoot hard drive problems. You also learn how to select and install optical drives in desktops and laptops. This chapter also covers solid-state storage, including flash memory cards and which type of card to buy for a particular need.

HARD DRIVE TECHNOLOGIES AND INTERFACE STANDARDS

A+
CORE 1
1.1, 3.1,
3.2, 3.4,
3.5

A hard disk drive (HDD), most often called a hard drive, is rated by its physical size, capacity, speed, technologies used inside the drive, and interface standards. First, we look at the features of a hard drive and then turn to how the drive interfaces with the computer.

> 🖊 **Notes** In technical documentation, you might see a hard drive abbreviated as HDD (hard disk drive). However, this chapter uses the term *hard drive*.

TECHNOLOGIES AND FORM FACTORS OF HARD DRIVES

A+
CORE 1
1.1, 3.1,
3.4

The two types of hardware technologies used inside the drive are magnetic and solid-state. In addition, some hybrid drives use a combination of both technologies. Each hard drive technology uses several form factors, all discussed in this part of the chapter.

MAGNETIC HARD DRIVES

A magnetic hard drive has one, two, or more platters, or disks, that stack together and spin in unison inside a sealed metal housing that contains firmware to control reading and writing data to the drive and to communicate with the motherboard. The top and bottom of each disk have a read/write head that moves across the disk surface as all the disks rotate on a spindle (see Figure 5-1). All the read/write heads are controlled by an actuator, which moves the read/write heads across the disk surfaces in unison. The disk surfaces are covered with a magnetic medium that can hold data as magnetized spots. The spindle rotates at 5400, 7200, 10,000, or 15,000 RPM (revolutions per minute). The faster the spindle, the better the drive performs. Most consumer hard drives are rated at 5400 or 7200 RPM.

Figure 5-1 Inside a magnetic hard drive

Data is organized on a magnetic hard drive in concentric circles called tracks (see Figure 5-2). Each track is divided into segments called sectors (also called records). Older hard drives used sectors that contained 512 bytes. Most current hard drives use 4096-byte sectors.

Figure 5-2 A hard drive is divided into tracks and sectors

Form factors for internal magnetic hard drives are 3.5" for desktops and 2.5" for laptop computers. See Figure 5-3. In addition, a smaller 1.8" hard drive (about the size of a credit card) is used in some low-end laptops and other equipment such as MP3 players.

Figure 5-3 A magnetic hard drive for a desktop is larger than that used in laptops

SOLID-STATE DRIVES

A solid-state drive (SSD), also called a solid-state device, is so named because it has no moving parts. The drives are built using nonvolatile memory, which is similar to that used for USB flash drives and smart cards. Recall that this type of memory does not lose its data even after the power is turned off.

Source: istock.com/AlexLMX

Figure 5-4 A circuit board with NAND memory inside an SSD

In an SSD, flash memory is stored on chips on a circuit board inside the drive housing (see Figure 5-4). The chips contain grids of rows and columns with two transistors at each intersection that hold a 0 or 1 bit. One of these transistors is called a floating gate and accepts the 0 or 1 state according to a logic test called NAND (stands for "Not AND"). Therefore, the memory in an SSD is called NAND flash memory.

Transistors are limited to the number of times they can be reprogrammed. Therefore, the life span of an SSD is based on the number of write operations to the drive, and can be expressed as TBW (TeraBytes Written) or DWPD (Drive Writes Per Day) over its expected life. (The number of read operations does not affect the life span.) For example, one SSD manufacturer guarantees its SSDs for 70 TBW, which means 70 TB or 70,000 GB write operations for the duration of the drive. Another manufacturer might rate the drive as DWPD—for example, 70 GB write operations per day for five years. For normal use, a drive would not be used that much and would last much longer. However, the drive warranty is only for five years.

Because flash memory is expensive, solid-state drives are much more expensive than magnetic hard drives of the same capacity, but they are faster, more reliable, last longer, and use less power than magnetic drives.

You need to be aware of three popular form factors used by SSDs:

▲ **2.5" SSD.** The 2.5" SSD (see the left side of Figure 5-5) is used in desktops and laptops and can mount in the same bays and use the same cable connectors as those used by 2.5" magnetic drives. (Occasionally, you might see a 1.8" SSD for netbooks and other mobile devices, but they are rare.)

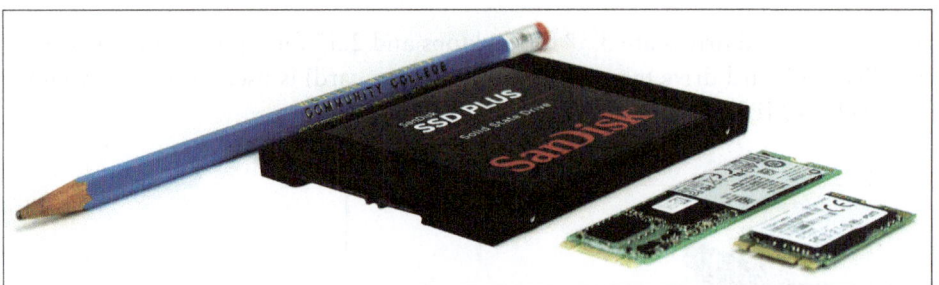

Figure 5-5 Solid-state drives in two form factors: 2.5" SSD and two lengths of M.2 SSD cards

▲ **M.2 SSD card.** The M.2 SSD form factor (see the right side of Figure 5-5) is a small M.2 card that uses the motherboard M.2 slot you learned about in Chapter 2.
▲ **PCI Express SSD expansion card.** An SSD can be embedded on a PCIe expansion card (see Figure 5-6). These drives generally have a faster interface with the CPU than 2.5" SSDs and may also be faster than an M.2 SSD, depending on how the M.2 slot interfaces with the CPU. A PCIe SSD uses the NVMe interface discussed later in the chapter.

Source: www.goplextor.com/Product/Detail/M9Pe(Y)#/Features

Figure 5-6 This SSD by Plextor is embedded on a PCIe ×4 version 3.0 expansion card and uses the NVMe interface standard

HYBRID HARD DRIVES

A hybrid hard drive (H-HDD), sometimes called a solid-state hybrid drive (SSHD), contains both magnetic and SSD technologies. The magnetic drive in the drive housing permanently holds data while the flash component serves as a buffer to improve drive performance. Some hybrid drives perform just as well as an SSD. For a hybrid drive to function, the operating system must support it.

LOGICAL BLOCK ADDRESSING AND CAPACITY

Before a magnetic drive leaves the factory, sector markings are written to it in a process called low-level formatting. (This formatting is different from the high-level formatting that Windows does after a drive is installed in a computer.) The hard drive firmware, BIOS/UEFI on the motherboard, and the OS use a simple sequential numbering system called logical block addressing (LBA) to address all the sectors on the drive. SSDs are marked into blocks, which are communicated to the motherboard and OS; they read/write to the drive in blocks, just as with magnetic drives. SSDs are also low-level formatted before they leave the factory.

The size of each block and the total number of blocks on the drive determine the drive capacity. Today's drive capacities are usually measured in GB (gigabytes) or TB (terabytes, each of which is 1024 gigabytes). Magnetic drives are generally much larger in capacity than SSDs.

5

> **✎ Notes** Many solid-state drive manufacturers reserve blocks on the drive that are used when other blocks begin to prove they are no longer reliable. Also, a technique called **wear leveling** assures that the logical block addressing does not always address the same physical blocks in order to distribute write operations more evenly across the device.

S.M.A.R.T.

You need to be aware of one more technology supported by both SSD and magnetic hard drives: **S.M.A.R.T. (Self-Monitoring Analysis and Reporting Technology)**, which is used to predict when a drive is likely to fail. System BIOS/UEFI uses S.M.A.R.T. to monitor drive performance, temperature, and other factors. For magnetic drives, it monitors disk spin-up time, distance between the head and the disk, and other mechanical activities of the drive. Many SSDs report to the BIOS/UEFI the number of write operations, which is the best measurement of when the drive might fail. If S.M.A.R.T. suspects a drive failure is about to happen, it displays a warning message. S.M.A.R.T. can be enabled and disabled in BIOS/UEFI setup.

> **✎ Notes** Malware has been known to give false S.M.A.R.T. alerts.

Now let's look at how the drive's firmware or controller communicates with the motherboard and processor.

INTERFACE STANDARDS USED BY HARD DRIVES

| A+ CORE 1 3.1, 3.2, 3.4, 3.5 | Four interface standards used by hard drives include IDE (outdated), SCSI (also outdated), SATA (the most popular current standard), and NVMe (the latest and fastest standard.) |

> **★ A+ Exam Tip** The A+ Core 1 exam expects you to recognize the cables and connectors for the IDE, SCSI, SATA, and NVMe interfaces. Given a scenario, you may be expected to decide which interface to use (SATA or NVMe) and be able to install and configure devices that use these interfaces.

IDE

Years ago, hard drives used the Parallel ATA (PATA) standards, also called the IDE (Integrated Drive Electronics) standards, to connect to a motherboard. PATA allowed for one or two IDE connectors on a motherboard, each using a 40-pin data cable. Two drives could connect to one cable (see Figure 5-7).

Figure 5-7 A computer's hard drive subsystem using an IDE interface to the motherboard

Two types of IDE cables are the older cable with a 40-pin connector and 40 wires and a newer cable with the same 40-pin connector and 80 thinner wires (see Figure 5-8). The additional 40 wires reduce crosstalk (interference that can lead to corrupted communication) on the cable. The later IDE standards required the 80-wire cable. The maximum recommended length of an IDE cable is 18". The IDE standard is seldom used today.

Figure 5-8 In comparing the 80-conductor cable with the 40-conductor cable, note they are about the same width, but the 80-conductor cable has twice as many fine wires

SCSI

In the distant past, a few personal computer hard drives designed for high-end workstations used the SCSI (Small Computer System Interface) interface standard. SCSI (pronounced "scuzzy") can support up to 7 or 15 SCSI-compliant devices in a system. Most often, a SCSI expansion card (see Figure 5-9), called the SCSI host adapter, used a PCIe slot and provided one external connector for an external SCSI device, such as a SCSI printer, and one internal connector for internal SCSI devices, such as hard drives and optical drives.

Figure 5-10 shows a long SCSI cable. One end of the cable connects to the host adapter and the other connectors are used for internal SCSI devices. SCSI evolved over the years with various connector types and cables but is no longer used in personal computers.

Figure 5-9 This Adaptec SCSI card uses a PCIe ×1 slot and supports up to 15 devices in a SCSI chain

SATA

Most hard drives in today's personal computers use the SATA interface standards to connect to the motherboard. The serial ATA or SATA (pronounced "*say*-ta") standard uses a serial data path, and a SATA data cable can accommodate a single SATA drive (see Figure 5-11). The three SATA standards are:

- ▲ SATA3 or SATA III, rated at 6 Gb/sec, is sometimes called SATA 6 Gb/s.
- ▲ SATA2 or SATA II, rated at 3 Gb/sec, is sometimes called SATA 3 Gb/s.
- ▲ SATA1 or SATA I, rated at 1.5 Gb/sec, is seldom seen today.

Figure 5-10 This 68-pin internal SCSI ribbon cable can connect several SCSI devices

✎ **Notes** Interface standards for drives define data speeds and transfer methods between the drive controller, the BIOS/UEFI, the chipset on the motherboard, and the OS. The standards also define the type of cables and connectors used by the drive and the motherboard or expansion cards. SATA cables work for all three SATA standards.

Figure 5-11   A SATA cable connects a single SATA drive to a motherboard SATA connector

SATA interfaces are used by all types of drives, including hard drives, CD, DVD, and Blu-ray. SATA supports hot-swapping, also called hot-plugging. With hot-swapping, you can connect and disconnect a drive while the system is running. Hard drives that can be hot-swapped cost significantly more than regular hard drives and are generally used in servers or other network storage devices.

A SATA drive connects to one internal SATA connector on the motherboard by way of a 7-pin SATA data cable and uses a 15-pin SATA power connector (see Figure 5-12). An internal SATA data cable can be up to 1 meter in length. A motherboard might have two or more SATA connectors; use the connectors in the order recommended in the motherboard user guide. For example, for the four connectors shown in Figure 5-13, you are told to use the red ones before the black ones.

SATA power connectors

SATA data connectors

Figure 5-12   A SATA data cable and SATA power cable

Figure 5-13 This motherboard has two black and two red SATA II ports

SATA Express connector

Two SATA connectors grouped with the SATA Express connector

Figure 5-14 One SATA Express port is grouped with two normal SATA ports

The SATA 3.2 revision allows for PCIe and SATA to work together in a technology called **SATA Express**, which uses a new SATA connector. The speed of SATA Express is about three times that of SATA 3.0. However, because SATA Express is not as fast as NVMe, hard drive manufacturers have been slow to invest in SATA Express drives, and only a few motherboards have SATA Express slots. Figure 5-14 shows a board with seven SATA ports. When the one SATA Express port is used, the two normal SATA ports grouped with it are disabled.

In addition to internal SATA connectors, the motherboard or an expansion card can provide **external SATA (eSATA)** ports for external drives (see Figure 5-15). External SATA drives use a special external shielded SATA cable up to 2 meters long. Seven-pin eSATA ports run at the same speed as the internal ports using SATA I, II, or III standards. The eSATA port is shaped differently from an internal SATA connector so as to prevent people from using the unshielded internal SATA data cables with the eSATA port.

Figure 5-15 Two eSATA ports on a motherboard

> **Notes** External hard drives can connect to a computer by way of external SATA (eSATA) or USB. Be sure the port provided by the computer uses the same standard that the external drive uses—for example, SuperSpeed USB 3.0 or eSATA III. If the port is not fast enough, you can install an expansion card to provide faster ports.

When purchasing a SATA hard drive, keep in mind that the SATA standards for the drive and the motherboard need to match. If either the drive or the motherboard uses a slower SATA standard than the other device, the system will run at the slower speed.

NVMe

Whereas the SATA interface is used by both magnetic and solid-state drives, the newer NVMe (Non-Volatile Memory Express or NVM Express) interface standard is used only by SSDs. Magnetic hard drives are slow enough that a SATA interface is adequate, but SSDs are so fast that the SATA interface becomes a performance bottleneck. NVMe uses the faster PCI Express ×4 interface to communicate with the processor. Here are the comparisons:

▲ The most common SATA standard, SATA3, transfers data at 6 Gb/sec.

▲ NVMe uses the most common PCIe standard, PCIe 3.0, which transfers data at 1 GB/sec per lane. Converted from Gigabyte to Gigabit, PCIe 3.0 transfers data at 8 Gb/sec per lane. NVMe uses four lanes (PCIe ×4), yielding a transfer rate of 8 Gb/sec x 4 = 32 Gb/sec. Therefore, the NVMe transfer rate of 32 Gb/sec is more than five times faster than SATA3's transfer rate of 6 Gb/sec.

The PCIe NVMe interface might be used in three ways:

▲ *PCIe expansion card*. The NVMe interface is used by SSDs embedded on PCIe expansion cards. Refer back to Figure 5-6.

▲ *U.2 slot*. A 2.5" SSD can support the NVMe interface using a U.2 connector on the drive and a U.2 port on the motherboard. See Figure 5-16. These drives might be advertised as a PCIe drive, U.2 drive, or NVMe solid-state drive.

Figure 5-16 A U.2 2.5" SSD uses the NVMe and PCIe interface standards and connects to a U.2 port on the motherboard

▲ *M.2 port*. An M.2 SSD card might use the NVMe or SATA standard. Recall that an M.2 slot on a motherboard might interface with the processor using the USB, SATA, or PCIe bus. If the slot uses the PCIe bus and the M.2 SSD card uses the NVMe interface, the 32-Gb/sec transfer rate can be attained. If your motherboard does not have an M.2 port, you can use a PCIe adapter card (also called a carrier card) to provide M.2 ports for M.2 SSDs (see Figure 5-17).

Figure 5-17 A PCIe ×4 adapter card provides one M.2 slot for an M.2 SSD

Most motherboards today have PCIe expansion slots, and M.2 slots are more common on motherboards than U.2 ports. For M.2 slots, check the motherboard documentation to find out which bus the M.2 slot uses and whether you can boot the system from the SSD card installed in the slot. Some motherboards, such as the Asus Prime Z370P, provide two M.2 slots, which can be configured in a RAID array. For this board, you can purchase the Asus Hyper M.2 ×16 card (see Figure 5-18) to install in the first PCIe ×16 slot and install up to four M.2 SSDs on the card. These four drives can be configured in a RAID array and you can use BIOS/UEFI to enable the card so that you can boot the system from this RAID array of SSDs. You learn more about RAID later in this chapter.

Source: https://www.asus.com/us/Motherboard-Accessory/HYPER-M-2-X16-CARD/overview/

Figure 5-18 Install up to four M.2 SSDs in a bootable RAID array on this adapter card by Asus

Now that you know about the various hard drive technologies and interfaces, let's see how to select and install a hard drive.

HOW TO SELECT AND INSTALL HARD DRIVES

**A+
CORE 1
1.1, 3.4.
3.8**

In this part of the chapter, you learn how to select a hard drive for your system. Then, you learn the details of installing a SATA drive. Next, you learn how to deal with using removable bays, the problem of installing a hard drive in a bay that is too wide for it, and special considerations to install a hard drive in a laptop. You also learn how to set up a RAID system.

SELECTING A HARD DRIVE

When selecting a hard drive, keep in mind that to get the best performance from the system, the motherboard and drive must support the same interface standard. If they don't support the same standard, they revert to the slower standard that both can use, or the drive will not work at all. There's no point in buying an expensive hard drive with features that your system cannot support.

Therefore, when making purchasing decisions, you need to know the standards for the motherboard slot or port and perhaps for the expansion card that might provide the drive interface. Find out by reading the motherboard manual. Here are some options for compatibility:

◢ SATA ports on a motherboard are usually color-coded to indicate which SATA standard the port supports. A motherboard typically has a mix of SATA3 and SATA2 ports. A SATA drive is rated for one SATA standard but can run at the slower speed of the SATA port.

◢ M.2 slots might support PCIe 3.0, PCIe 2.0, SATA2, SATA3, or USB 3.0. M.2 ports might be keyed to one notch or two and can accommodate up to three sizes of cards. Match the card to the slot and its fastest standard.

◢ When an M.2 port with a card installed is using the SATA bus, one of the SATA ports might be disabled. Be sure to know which one so you don't attempt to use it for another device.

◢ NVMe expansion cards most likely use a PCIe ×4 version 3.0 slot. A motherboard might have multiple PCIe ×4 slots; use one that supports PCIe version 3.0.

Besides compatibility, consider the features already discussed in this chapter when purchasing a hard drive:

◢ Technology (SSD is faster and lasts longer than a hybrid drive, which is faster than a magnetic drive)
◢ Form factor (3.5" or 2.5" for magnetic drives or 2.5", M.2, U.2, or PCIe card for SSDs)
◢ Capacity (in GB or TB)
◢ Data transfer rate as determined by the drive interface (SATA 6.0 Gb/s, SATA 3.0 Gb/s, PCIe ×4 32 Gb/s, and so forth)
◢ For magnetic drives, the spindle speed (5400, 7200, 10,000, or 15,000 RPM), which affects performance
◢ For hybrid drives, the cache or buffer size, which affects performance (A magnetic drive with a cache is a hybrid drive.)

Some hard drive manufacturers are listed in Table 5-1. Most manufacturers of memory also make solid-state drives.

Manufacturer	Website
Kingston Technology (SSD only)	kingston.com
Samsung (SSD only)	samsung.com
Seagate Technology (magnetic and SSD)	seagate.com
Western Digital (magnetic and SSD)	wdc.com
Toshiba (magnetic and SSD)	toshiba.com

Table 5-1 Hard drive manufacturers

Now let's turn our attention to the step-by-step process of installing a SATA drive.

STEPS TO INSTALL A SATA DRIVE

 In Figure 5-19, you can see the back of a SATA hard drive. A SATA drive might have jumpers used to set features such as the ability to power up from standby mode. Most likely, if jumpers are present on a SATA drive, the factory has set them as they should be and advises you not to change them.

Figure 5-19 The rear of a SATA drive

> ★ **A+ Exam Tip** The A+ Core 1 exam expects you to know how to configure SATA devices in a system. What you learn in this chapter about installing a SATA hard drive in a system also applies to installing a SATA optical drive. Hard drives and optical drives use a SATA data connector and a power connector.

Some SATA drives have two power connectors, as does the one in Figure 5-20. Choose between the SATA power connector (which is preferred) or the legacy 4-pin Molex connector, but never install two power cords to the drive at the same time because it could damage the drive.

Figure 5-20 The rear of a SATA drive with two power connectors

STEP 1: AS BEST YOU CAN, PROTECT THE USER'S DATA

Recall from Chapter 4 that before you work on solving any computer problem, you need to establish your priorities. Your first priority might be the user's data. If the user tells you there is important data on the current hard drive and you can boot from it, back up the data to other media and verify that you can access the data on that media. If the current hard drive will not boot, recall you can move it to another computer and transfer data to other media. Make every effort possible to protect the user's data before you move on to the next step.

STEP 2: KNOW YOUR STARTING POINT

As with replacing or installing any other devices, make sure you know your starting point before you begin installing a hard drive. Answer these questions: How is your system configured? Is everything working properly? Verify which of your system's devices are working before installing a new one. Later, if a device does not work, the information will help you isolate the problem. Keeping notes is a good idea whenever you install new hardware or software or make any other changes to your computer system. Write down what you know about the system that might be important later.

> ✎ **Notes** When installing hardware and software, don't install too many things at once. If something goes wrong, you won't know what's causing the problem. Install one device, start the system, and confirm that the new device is working before installing another.

STEP 3: READ THE DOCUMENTATION AND PREPARE YOUR WORK AREA

Before you take anything apart, carefully read all the documentation for the drive and controller card, as well as the part of your motherboard documentation that covers hard drive installation. Make sure that you can visualize all the steps in the installation. If you have any questions, keep researching until you locate the answer. You can do a Google search, have a chat session with technical support, or ask a knowledgeable friend for help. As you get your questions answered, you might discover that what you are installing will not work on your computer, but that is better than coping with hours of frustration and a disabled computer. You cannot always anticipate every problem, but at least you can know that you made your best effort to understand everything in advance. What you learn with thorough preparation pays off every time!

You're now ready to set out your tools, documentation, new hardware, and notebook. Remember the basic rules concerning static electricity. Be sure to protect against electrostatic discharge (ESD) by wearing an ESD strap during the installation. You also need to avoid working on carpet in the winter when there's a lot of static electricity.

Some added precautions for working with a hard drive are as follows:

◢ Handle the drive carefully.
◢ Do not touch any exposed circuitry or chips.
◢ Prevent other people from touching exposed microchips on the drive.
◢ When you first take the drive out of the static-protective package, touch the package containing the drive to a screw holding an expansion card or cover, or to a metal part of the computer case, for at least two seconds. This drains the static electricity from the package and from your body.
◢ If you must set down the drive outside the static-protective package, place it component-side-up on a flat surface.
◢ Do not place the drive on the computer case cover or on a metal table.

If you're assembling a new system, it's usually best to install drives before you install the motherboard so that you will not accidentally bump sensitive motherboard components with the drives.

STEP 4: INSTALL THE DRIVE

Now you're ready to get started. Follow these steps to install the drive in the case:

1. Shut down the computer, unplug it, and press the power button to drain residual power. Remove the computer case cover. Check that you have an available power cord from the power supply for the drive.

> ✎ **Notes** If there are not enough power cords from a power supply, you can purchase a Y connector that can add another power cord.

2. For 2.5" or 3.5" drives, decide which bay will hold the drive by examining the locations of the drive bays and the length of the data cables and power cords. Bays designed for hard drives do not have access to the outside of the case, unlike bays for optical drives and other drives in which discs are inserted. Also, some bays are wider than others to accommodate wide drives such as a DVD drive. Will

the data cable reach the drives and the motherboard connector? If not, rearrange your plan for locating the drive in a bay, or purchase a custom-length data cable. Some bays are stationary, meaning the drive is installed inside the bay because it stays in the case. Other bays are removable; you remove the bay, install the drive in it, and then return the bay to the case.

3. For a stationary bay, slide the drive in the bay and then use a screwdriver to secure one side of the drive with one or two short screws (see Figure 5-21). It's best to use two screws so the drive will not move in the bay, but sometimes a bay only provides a place for a single screw on each side. Some drive bays provide one or two tabs that you pull out before you slide the drive in the bay and then push in to secure the drive. Another option is a sliding tab (see Figure 5-22) that is used to secure the drive. Pull the tab back, slide in the drive, and push the tab forward to secure the drive.

Figure 5-21 Secure one side of the drive with one or two screws

> ⚡ **Caution** Be sure the screws are not too long. If they are, you can screw too far into the drive housing, which will damage the drive itself.

Figure 5-22 This drive bay uses tabs to secure the drive

4. When using screws to secure the drive, carefully turn the case over without disturbing the drive and put one or two screws on the other side of the drive (see Figure 5-23). To best secure the drive in the case, use two screws on each side of the drive.

Hard drive

Figure 5-23 Secure the other side of the drive with one or two screws

📝 **Notes** Do not allow torque to stress the drive. In other words, don't force a drive into a space that is too small for it. Also, placing two screws in diagonal positions across the drive can place pressure diagonally on the drive.

5. Check the motherboard documentation to find out which SATA connectors on the board to use first. For example, five SATA connectors are shown in Figure 5-24. The documentation says the two blue SATA connectors support 6.0 Gb/s and slower speeds, and the two black and one red SATA connectors support 3.0 Gb/s and slower speeds. On this board, be sure to connect your fastest hard drive to a blue connector. For some boards, the hard drive that has the bootable OS installed must be connected to the first SATA connector, which is usually labeled SATA 0. For both the drive and the motherboard, you can only plug the cable into the connector in one direction. A SATA cable might provide a clip on the connector to secure it (see Figure 5-25).

Figure 5-24 Five SATA connectors support different SATA standards

Figure 5-25 A clip on a SATA connector secures the connection

6. Connect a 15-pin SATA power connector or 4-pin Molex power connector from the power supply to the drive (see Figure 5-26).

Figure 5-26 Connect the SATA power cord to the drive

7. Check all your connections and power up the system.

8. To verify that the drive was recognized correctly, enter BIOS/UEFI setup and look for the drive. Figure 5-27 shows a BIOS/UEFI setup screen on one system that has four SATA connectors. A hard drive is installed on one of the faster yellow SATA connectors and a DVD drive is installed on one of the slower brown SATA connectors.

Notes If the drive light on the front panel of the computer case does not work after you install a new drive, try reversing the LED wire on the front panel header on the motherboard.

Source: American Megatrends, Inc.

Figure 5-27   A BIOS/UEFI setup screen showing a SATA hard drive and DVD drive installed

You are now ready to prepare the hard drive for first use. If you are installing a new hard drive in a system that will be used for a new Windows installation, boot from the Windows setup DVD or USB drive and follow the directions on the screen to install Windows on the new drive. If you are installing a second hard drive in a system that already has Windows installed on the first hard drive, use the Disk Management utility in Windows to prepare the drive for first use (called partitioning and formatting the drive).

INSTALLING A DRIVE IN A REMOVABLE BAY

Now let's see how a drive installation goes when you are dealing with a removable bay. Figure 5-28 shows a computer case with a removable bay that has a fan at the front of the bay to help keep the drives cool. (The case manufacturer calls the bay a fan cage.) The bay is anchored to the case with three black locking pins. The third locking pin from the bottom of the case is disconnected in the photo.

Three locking pins used to hold the bay in the case

Figure 5-28   The removable bay has a fan in front and is anchored to the case with locking pins

Unplug the cage fan from its power source. Turn the handle on each locking pin counterclockwise to remove it. Then slide the bay to the front and out of the case. Insert the hard drive in the bay and use two screws on each side to anchor the drive in the bay (see Figure 5-29). Slide the bay back into the case and reinstall the locking pins. Plug in the cage fan power cord.

Figure 5-29 Install the hard drive in the bay using two screws on each side of the drive

INSTALLING A SMALL DRIVE IN A WIDE BAY

A+
CORE 1
3.4

Because 2.5" drives are smaller than the bays designed for 3.5" drives, you'll need a universal bay kit to fit these drives into most desktop computer cases. These inexpensive kits should create a tailor-made fit. In Figure 5-30, you can see how the universal bay kit adapter works. The adapter spans the distance between the sides of the drive and the bay. Figure 5-31 shows a SATA SSD with the brackets connected.

Side brackets connect to hard drive

Figure 5-30 Use the universal bay kit to make the drive fit the bay

Figure 5-31 An SSD with a bay kit connected

INSTALLING AN M.2 SSD CARD

As always, read the motherboard manual to find out the types of M.2 cards the board supports. For SSD cards, the manual or motherboard website is likely to list specific SSD brands and models the board can use. Also be aware that if the M.2 slot is used and the SSD card uses the SATA interface standard, it might disable a SATA Express or SATA connector on the board. Do the following to install the card:

1. Measure the length of the card and decide which screw hole for the M.2 slot the card requires. Install a standoff in the hole.

2. Slide the card straight into the slot, but not from an upward angle because you might bend open the slot and prevent a good connection. Make sure the card is installed securely in the slot. In Figure 5-32, you can see the card has two notches and can be used in either a B-key M.2 slot (the key on the left of the slot) or an M-key M.2 slot (the key on the right of the slot). This motherboard has an M-key slot. Also notice in the figure that the standoff is installed, ready to secure the card to the board.

Figure 5-32 Slide an SSD card straight into an M.2 slot

3. Install the one screw in the standoff to secure the card to the motherboard. Don't overtighten the screw because you might damage the card.

4. Start the system, go into BIOS/UEFI setup, and make sure the M.2 card is recognized by the system. If it will be the boot device, make the appropriate changes in BIOS/UEFI.

INSTALLING A HARD DRIVE IN A LAPTOP

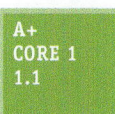

A+ CORE 1 1.1

When purchasing and installing an internal hard drive or optical drive in a laptop, see the laptop manufacturer's documentation about specific capacities, form factors, and connectors that will fit the laptop. Before deciding to replace a hard drive, consider these issues:

◢ Be aware of voiding a warranty if you don't follow the laptop manufacturer's directions.
◢ If the old drive has crashed, you'll need the recovery media to reinstall Windows and the drivers. Make sure you have the recovery media before you start.
◢ If you are upgrading from a low-capacity drive to a higher-capacity drive, you need to consider how you will transfer data from the old drive to the new one. One way is to use a USB-to-SATA converter. Using this converter, both drives can be up and working on the laptop at the same time, so you can copy files.

Here is what you need to know when shopping for a laptop hard drive:

◢ Purchase a hard drive recommended by the laptop manufacturer. The drive might be magnetic or SSD, and you'll need a 2.5" or 1.8" drive. Some high-end laptops use an M.2 SSD.
◢ For a 2.5" drive, expect it to use the SATA interface. SATA data and power connectors on a laptop hard drive look the same as those in a desktop installation.

To replace a hard drive, older laptop computers required that you disassemble the laptop. With newer laptops, you should be able to easily replace a drive. For the laptop shown in Figure 5-33, first power down the system, remove peripherals, including the AC adapter, and remove the battery pack. Then remove a screw that holds the drive in place (see Figure 5-33).

> ⚡ **Caution** To protect sensitive components, never open a laptop case without first unplugging the AC adapter and removing the battery pack.

Figure 5-33 This one screw holds the hard drive in position

Open the lid of the laptop slightly so that the lid doesn't obstruct your removing the drive. Turn the laptop on its side and push the drive out of its bay (see Figure 5-34). Then remove the plastic cover from the drive. Move the cover to the new drive, and insert the new drive in the bay. Next, replace the screw and power up the system.

Figure 5-34 Push the drive out of its bay

When the system boots up, BIOS/UEFI should recognize the new drive and search for an operating system. If the drive is new, boot from the Windows setup or recovery DVD or USB flash drive and install the OS.

> ✎ **Notes** It is possible to give general directions on desktop computer repair that apply to all kinds of brands, models, and systems. Not so with laptops. Learning to repair laptops involves learning unique ways to assemble, disassemble, and repair components for specific brands and models of laptops.

For some laptops, such as the one shown in Figure 5-35, you remove a cover on the bottom of the computer to expose the hard drive. You then remove one screw that anchors the drive. You can then remove the drive.

Figure 5-35 Remove a cover on the bottom of the laptop to exchange the hard drive, which is attached to a proprietary bracket

SETTING UP HARDWARE RAID

For most personal computers, a single hard drive works independently of any other installed drives. A technology that configures two or more hard drives to work together as an array of drives is called RAID (redundant array of inexpensive disks or redundant array of independent disks). Two reasons you might consider using RAID are:

◢ To improve performance by writing data to two or more hard drives so that a single drive is not excessively used.

▲ To improve fault tolerance, which is a computer's ability to respond to a fault or catastrophe, such as a hardware failure or power outage, so that data is not lost. If data is important enough to justify the cost, you can protect the data by continuously writing two copies of it, each to a different hard drive. This method is most often used on high-end, expensive file servers, but it is occasionally appropriate for a single-user workstation.

TYPES OF RAID

Several types of RAID exist; the four most commonly used are RAID 0, RAID 1, RAID 5, and RAID 10. Following is a brief description of each, including another method of two disks working together called spanning. The first four methods are diagrammed in Figure 5-36:

Figure 5-36 Ways that hard drives can work together

▲ Spanning, sometimes called JBOD (just a bunch of disks), uses two hard drives to hold a single Windows volume, such as drive E:. Data is written to the first drive, and when it is full, the data continues to be written to the second. The purpose of spanning is to increase the disk space available for a single volume.

▲ RAID 0 also uses two or more physical disks to increase the disk space available for a single volume. RAID 0 writes to the physical disks evenly across both disks so that neither receives all the activity; this improves performance. Windows calls RAID 0 a striped volume. To understand that term, think of data striped—or written across—several hard drives. RAID 0 is preferred to spanning.

> 🖉 **Notes** A Windows volume is a logical hard drive that is assigned a drive letter like C: or E:. The volume can be part or all of a physical hard drive or can span multiple physical hard drives. Earlier in the chapter you learned about the Asus Prime Z370-P motherboard, which has two M.2 slots. When you install matching M.2 SSD cards in these slots, you can use BIOS/UEFI setup to configure these two cards in a RAID-0 array, which creates a superfast single logical hard drive or Windows volume.

▲ RAID 1 is a type of mirroring that duplicates data on one drive to another drive and is used for fault tolerance. Each drive has its own volume, and the two volumes are called mirrors. If one drive fails, the other continues to operate and data is not lost. Hot-swapping is allowed in RAID 1. Windows calls RAID 1 a mirrored volume.

▲ RAID 5 stripes data and parity information across three or more drives and uses parity checking, so that if one drive fails, the other drives can re-create the data stored on the failed drive by using the parity information. Data is not duplicated, and therefore RAID 5 makes better use of volume capacity. RAID-5 drives increase performance and provide fault tolerance. Hot-swapping is allowed in RAID 5. Windows calls these drives **RAID-5 volumes**.

▲ **RAID 10**, also called **RAID 1+0** and pronounced "RAID one zero" (*not* "RAID ten"), is a combination of RAID 1 and RAID 0. It takes at least four disks for RAID 10. Data is mirrored across pairs of disks, as shown at the top of Figure 5-37. In addition, the two pairs of disks are striped, as shown at the bottom of Figure 5-37. To help you better understand RAID 10, notice the data labeled as A, A, B, B across the first stripe. RAID 10 is the most expensive solution that provides the best redundancy and performance and allows for hot-swapping.

RAID 1: Two pairs of mirrored disks

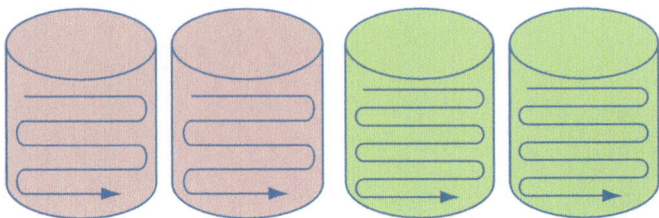

RAID 10: Mirrored and striped

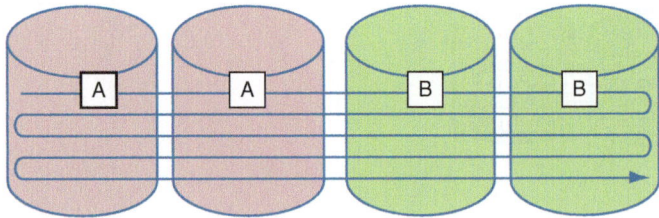

Figure 5-37 RAID 1 and RAID 10

> ★ **A+ Exam Tip** The A+ Core 1 exam may give you a scenario and expect you to select the appropriate RAID-0, RAID-1, RAID-5, or RAID-10 configuration. You are also expected to be able to install and configure a RAID system.

All RAID configurations can be accomplished at the hardware level (called hardware RAID) or at the operating system level (called software RAID). In Windows 10/8/7, you can use the Disk Management utility to group hard drives in a RAID array. Windows 10/8 also offers the Storage Spaces utility to implement software RAID. However, software RAID is considered an unstable solution and is not recommended by Microsoft. Configuring RAID at the hardware level is considered best practice because if Windows gets corrupted, the hardware might still be able to protect the data. Also, hardware RAID is generally faster than software RAID.

HOW TO IMPLEMENT HARDWARE RAID

Hardware RAID can be set up by using a RAID-enabled motherboard that is managed in BIOS/UEFI setup or by using a RAID controller card. When using a RAID controller card, run the software that comes with the card to set up your RAID array.

For best performance in any RAID system, all hard drives in an array should be identical in brand, size, speed, and other features. Also, if Windows will be installed on a hard drive that is part of a RAID array, RAID must be implemented before Windows is installed because all data on the drives will be lost when you configure RAID. As with installing any hardware, first read the documentation that comes with the motherboard or RAID controller and follow those specific directions rather than the general guidelines given here. Make sure you understand which RAID configurations the board or card supports.

> ★ **A+ Exam Tip** The A+ Core 1 exam expects you to be able to set up hardware RAID and, given a scenario, know when it is appropriate to require hot-swappable drives for the array.

For one motherboard that has six SATA connectors that support RAID 0, 1, 5, and 10, here are the general directions to install three matching hard drives in a RAID-5 array:

1. Install the three SATA drives in the computer case and connect each drive to a SATA connector on the motherboard (see Figure 5-38). To help keep the drives cool, install them with an empty bay between each drive.

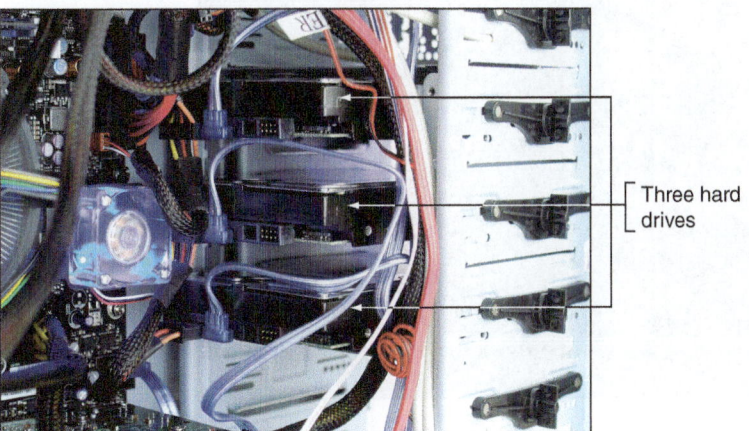

Figure 5-38   Install three matching hard drives in a system

2. Boot the system and enter BIOS/UEFI setup. On the Advanced setup screen, verify that the three drives are recognized. Select the option to configure SATA and then select RAID from the menu (see Figure 5-39).

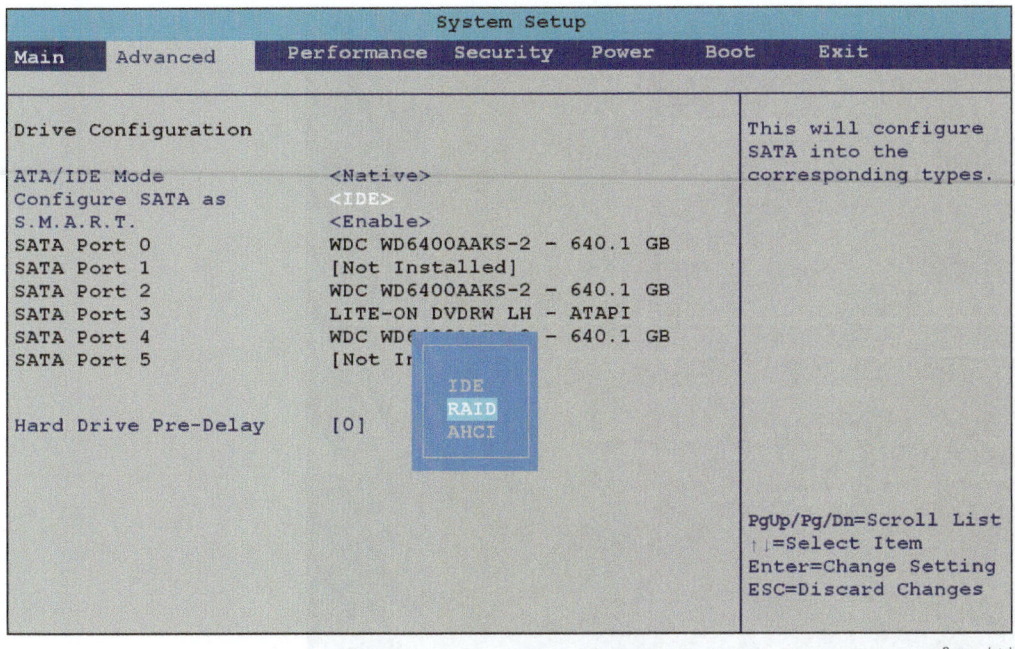

Source: Intel

Figure 5-39   Configure SATA ports on the motherboard to enable RAID

3. Reboot the system. A message is displayed on screen: "Press <Ctrl+I> to enter the RAID Configuration Utility." Press **Ctrl** and **I** to enter the utility (see Figure 5-40). Notice in the information area that the three drives are recognized and their current status is Non-RAID Disk.

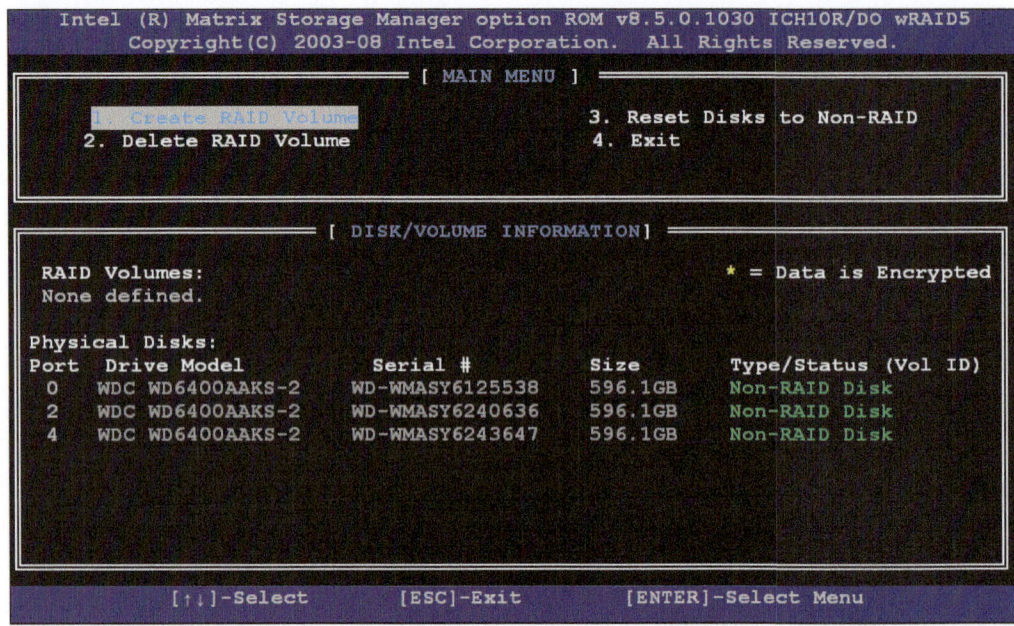

Source: Intel

Figure 5-40 Use a BIOS/UEFI utility to configure a RAID array

4. Select option 1 to **Create RAID Volume**. On the next screen shown in Figure 5-41, enter a volume name (FileServer in our example).

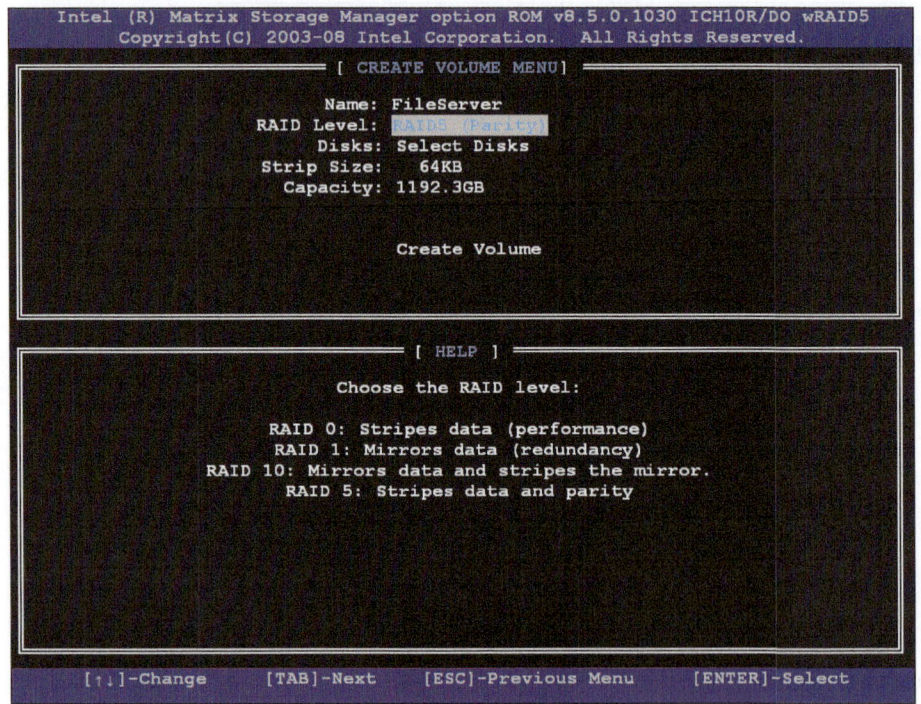

Source: Intel

Figure 5-41 Make your choices for the RAID array

5. Under RAID Level, select **RAID5 (Parity)**. Because we are using RAID 5, which requires three hard drives, the option to select the disks for the array is not available. All three disks will be used in the array.

6. Select the value for the Strip Size. (This is the amount of space devoted to one strip across the striped array. Choices are 32 KB, 64 KB, or 128 KB.)

7. Enter the size of the volume. The available size is shown in Figure 5-41 as 1192 GB, but you don't have to use all the available space. The space you don't use can later be configured as another array. (In this example, I entered 500 GB.)

8. Select **Create Volume** to complete the RAID configuration. A message warns that if you proceed, all data on all three hard drives will be lost. Type **Y** to continue. The array is created and the system reboots.

You are now ready to install Windows. Windows 10/8/7 has built-in hardware RAID drivers and therefore automatically "sees" the RAID array as a single 500-GB hard drive. After Windows is installed on this one logical drive, Windows will call it volume C:.

APPLYING | CONCEPTS   TROUBLESHOOTING HARD DRIVE INSTALLATIONS

A+ CORE 1 5.3

Sometimes, trouble crops up during an installation. Keeping a cool head, thinking things through carefully several times, and using all available resources will most likely get you out of any mess.

Installing a hard drive is not difficult unless you have an unusually complex situation. For example, your first hard drive installation should not involve the extra complexity of installing a RAID array. If a complicated installation is necessary and you have never installed a hard drive, ask for expert help.

The following list describes errors that cropped up during a few hard drive installations; the list also includes the causes of the errors and what was done about them. Everyone learns something new when making mistakes, and you probably will, too. You can then add your own experiences to this list:

- When first turning on a previously working computer, Susan received the following error message: "Hard drive not found." She turned off the machine, checked all cables, and discovered that the data cable from the motherboard to the drive was loose. She reseated the cable and rebooted. POST found the drive.
- Lucia physically installed a new hard drive, replaced the cover on the computer case, and booted the computer with a Windows setup DVD in the drive. POST beeped three times and stopped. Recall that diagnostics during POST are often communicated by beeps if the tests take place before POST has checked video and made it available to display the messages. Three beeps on some computers signal a memory error. Lucia turned off the computer and checked the memory modules on the motherboard. A module positioned at the edge of the motherboard next to the cover had been bumped as she replaced the cover. She reseated the module and booted again, this time with the cover still off. The error disappeared.
- Jason physically installed a new hard drive and turned on the computer. He received the following error: "No boot device available." He had forgotten to insert a Windows setup DVD. He put the disc in the drive and rebooted the machine successfully.
- The hard drive did not physically fit into the bay. The screw holes did not line up. Juan got a bay kit, but it just didn't seem to work. He took a break, went to lunch, and came back to make a fresh start. Juan asked others to help him view the brackets, holes, and screws from a fresh perspective. It didn't take long to discover that he had overlooked the correct position for the brackets in the bay.

⚡ Caution When things are not going well, you can tense up and make mistakes more easily. Be certain to turn off the machine before doing anything inside! Not doing so can be a costly error. For example, a friend had been trying and retrying to boot for some time and got frustrated and careless. She plugged the power cord into the drive without turning the computer off. The machine began to smoke and everything went dead. The next thing she learned was how to replace a power supply!

NAS DEVICES AND EXTERNAL STORAGE

**A+
CORE 1
3.8**

Hard drives are sometimes installed in external enclosures, such as the one shown in Figure 5-42. These enclosures make it easy to expand the storage capacity of a single computer or to make hard drive storage available to an entire network. For network attached storage (NAS), the enclosure connects to the network using an Ethernet port. When the storage is used by a single computer, the connection is made using a USB or eSATA port. Regardless of how the enclosure connects to a computer or network, the hard drives inside the enclosure might use a SATA connection.

Here is what you need to know about supporting these external enclosures:

◢ An enclosure might contain firmware that supports RAID. For example, a switch on the rear of one enclosure for two hard drives can be set for RAID 0, RAID 1, or stand-alone drives. Read the documentation for the enclosure to find out how to manage the RAID volumes.

◢ To replace a hard drive in an enclosure, see the documentation for the enclosure to find out how to open it and replace the drive.

◢ If a computer case is overheating, one way to solve the problem is to remove the hard drives from the case and install them in an external enclosure. However, it's better to leave the hard drive that contains the Windows installation in the case.

◢ You can purchase a SATA controller card that provides external eSATA connectors to be used when (1) the motherboard eSATA port is not functioning, or (2) the motherboard does not support a fast SATA standard that your hard drives use. Figure 5-43 shows a PCIe storage controller card that offers two internal SATA III connections and two eSATA III ports.

Courtesy of D-Link Corporation

Figure 5-42 The NAS ShareCenter Pro 1100 by D-Link can hold four hot-swappable SATA hard drives totaling 12 TB of storage, has a dual-core processor and 512 MB of RAM, and supports RAID

Source: Ableconn at ableconn.com

Figure 5-43 This PCIe x2 eSATA card by Ableconn has two eSATA ports and supports the SATA3 6-Gb/sec standard

Now let's move on to other types of storage devices, including optical drives and flash cards.

SUPPORTING OTHER TYPES OF STORAGE DEVICES

**A+
CORE 1
1.1, 3.4,
3.6**

Before we explore the details of several other types of storage devices, including optical discs, USB flash drives, and memory cards, let's start with the file systems they might use.

FILE SYSTEMS USED BY STORAGE DEVICES

**A+
CORE 1
3.4**

A storage device, such as a hard drive, CD, DVD, USB flash drive, or memory card, uses a file system to manage the data stored on the device. A file system is the overall structure the operating system uses to name, store, and organize files on a drive. In Windows, each storage device or group of devices, such as a RAID array, is treated as a single logical drive. When Windows first recognizes a new logical drive in the system, it determines which file system the drive is using, assigns it a drive letter (for example, C: or D:), and calls it a volume. Use File Explorer in Windows 10/8 or Windows Explorer in Windows 7 to see volumes and devices in Windows (see Figure 5-44). To see information about the volume or device, right-click it and select **Properties** from the shortcut menu. The device or volume Properties box appears, which shows its file system and storage capacity (see the right side of Figure 5-44).

5

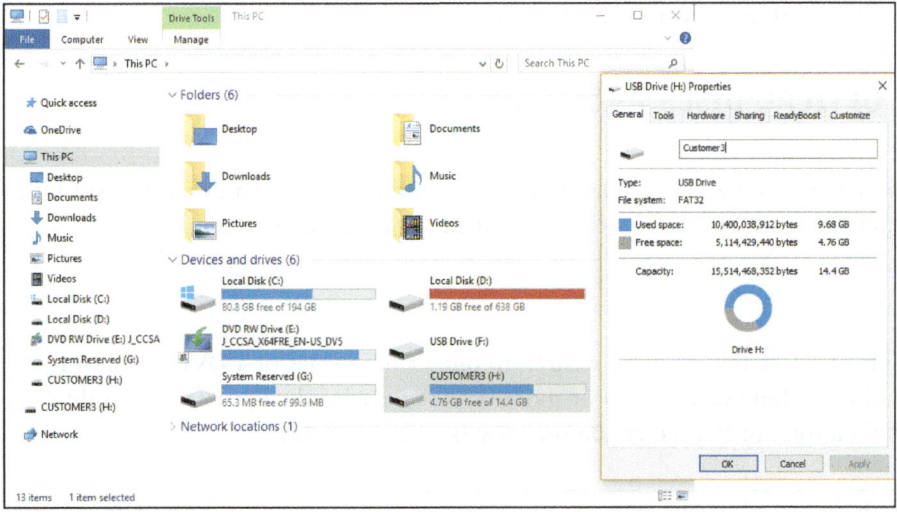

Figure 5-44 This 16-GB USB flash drive is using the FAT32 file system

Using Windows to install a new file system on a device or logical drive is called formatting, a process that erases all data on the device or drive. One way to format a device is to right-click it and select **Format** from the shortcut menu. In the box that appears, you can select the file system that works for this device (see Figure 5-45). If you have problems with a device, make sure it's using a file system appropriate for your situation:

- ◢ NTFS (New Technology file system) is primarily used by hard drives.
- ◢ The exFAT file system is used by large-capacity removable storage devices, including some USB flash drives, memory cards, and external hard drives.
- ◢ FAT32 and FAT file systems are used by smaller-capacity devices.
- ◢ CDFS (Compact Disc File System) or the UDF (Universal Disk Format) file system is used by CDs.
- ◢ A newer version of the UDF file system is used by DVDs and BDs (Blu-ray discs).

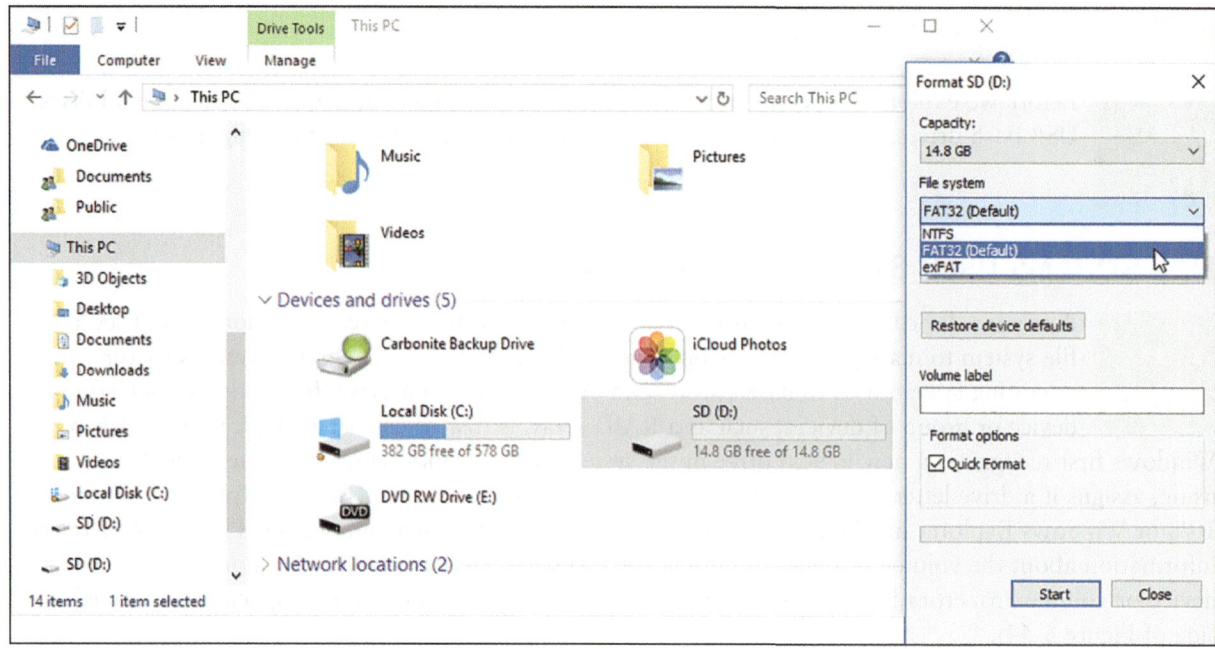

Figure 5-45 A storage device can be formatted using File Explorer

Now let's look at the types of optical drives you might be called on to support.

STANDARDS USED BY OPTICAL DISCS AND DRIVES

<table><tr><td>A+
CORE 1
3.6</td><td>CDs (compact discs), DVDs (digital versatile discs or digital video discs), and BDs (Blu-ray discs) use similar laser technologies. Tiny lands and pits on the surface of a disc represent bits, which a laser beam can read. This is why they are called optical storage technologies.</td></tr></table>

OPTICAL DISCS

Data is written to only one side of a CD, but it can be written to one or both sides of a DVD or Blu-ray disc. Also, a DVD or Blu-ray disc can hold data in two or more layers on each side. For example, a dual-layer, double-side DVD can hold a total of four layers on one disc (see Figure 5-46).

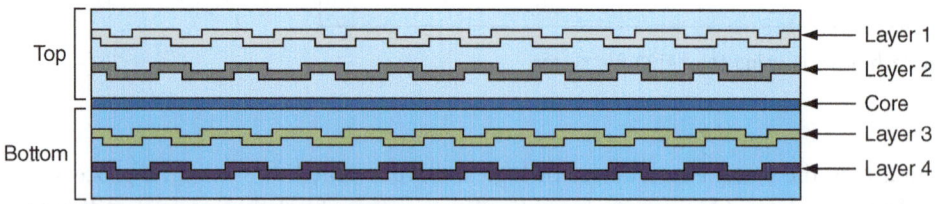

Figure 5-46 A DVD can hold data in double layers on both the top and bottom of the disc, yielding a maximum capacity of 17 GB

The breakdown of how much data can be held on CDs, DVDs, and BDs is shown in Figure 5-47. The capacities for DVDs and BDs depend on the number of sides and layers used to hold the data.

> ✎ **Notes** The discrepancy in the computer industry between 1 billion bytes (1,000,000,000 bytes) and 1 GB (1,073,741,824 bytes) exists because 1 KB equals 1024 bytes. Even though documentation might say that a DVD holds 17 GB, it actually holds 17 billion bytes, which is only 15.90 GB.

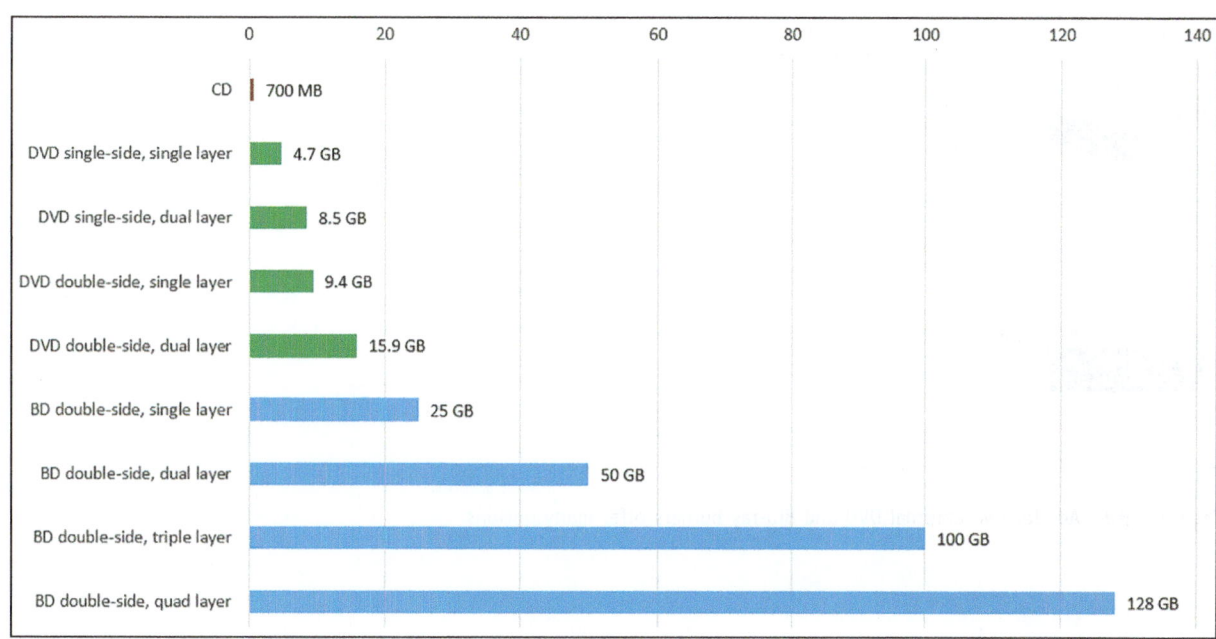

Figure 5-47 Storage capacities for CDs, DVDs, and BDs

OPTICAL DRIVES AND BURNERS

Blu-ray drives are backward compatible with DVD and CD technologies, and DVD drives are backward compatible with CD technologies. Depending on the drive features, an optical drive might be able to read and write to BDs, DVDs, and CDs. A drive that can write to discs is commonly called a burner. Today's internal optical drives interface with the motherboard by way of a SATA connection. An external drive might use an eSATA or USB port. Figure 5-48 shows an internal DVD drive, and Figure 5-49 shows an external DVD drive.

Rear of drive

Figure 5-48 This internal DVD drive uses a SATA connection

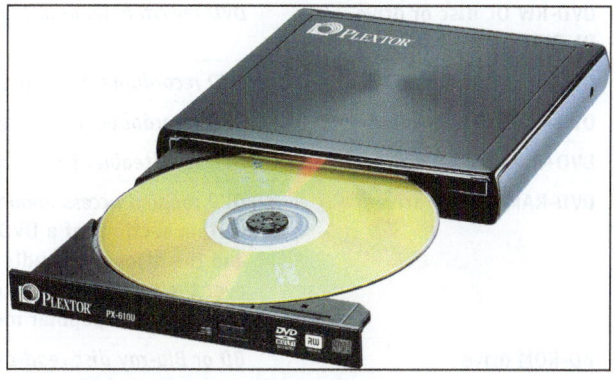

Courtesy of Plextor

Figure 5-49 The PX-610U external DVD±RW drive by Plextor uses a USB 2.0 port

When shopping for an optical drive or burner, suppose you see a couple of ads like those shown in Figure 5-50. To sort out the mix of disc standards, Table 5-2 can help. The table lists the popular CD, DVD, and Blu-ray disc and drive standards.

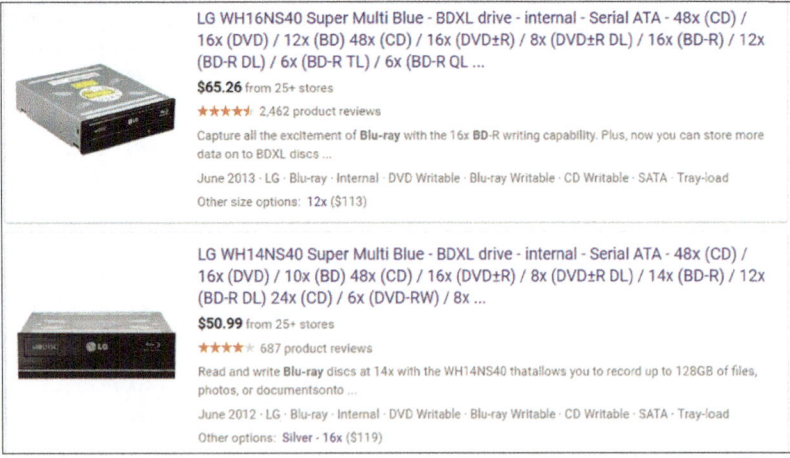

Figure 5-50 Ads for two external DVD and Blu-ray burners offer many options

Standard	Description
CD-ROM disc or drive	*CD read-only memory.* A CD-ROM disc burned at the factory can hold music, software, or other data. The bottom of a CD-ROM disc is silver. A CD-ROM drive can read CDs.
CD-R disc	*CD recordable.* A CD-R disc is a write-once CD.
CD-RW disc or drive	*CD rewriteable.* A CD-RW disc can be written to many times. A CD-RW drive can write to a CD-RW or CD-R disc and overwrite a CD-RW disc.
DVD-ROM drive	*DVD read-only memory.* A DVD-ROM drive can also read CDs or DVDs.
DVD-R disc	*DVD recordable, single layer.* A DVD-R disc can hold up to 4.7 GB of data and is a write-once disc.
DVD-R DL disc	*DVD recordable in dual layers.* Doubles storage to 8.5 GB of data on two layers.
DVD-RW disc or drive	*DVD rewriteable.* A DVD-RW disc is also known as an erasable, recordable disc or a write-many disc. The speeds in an ad for an optical drive indicate the maximum speed supported when burning this type of disc—for example, DVD-RW 6X.
DVD-RW DL disc or drive, aka. DL DVD drive	*DVD rewriteable, dual layers.* A DVD-RW DL disc has a storage capacity of 8.5 GB.
DVD+R disc or drive	*DVD recordable.* Similar to DVD-R but faster. Discs hold about 4.7 GB of data.
DVD+R DL disc or drive	*DVD recordable, dual layers.* A DVD+R DL disc has 8.5 GB of storage.
DVD+RW disc or drive	*DVD rewriteable.* Faster than DVD-RW.
DVD-RAM disc or drive	*DVD random access memory.* Rewriteable and erasable. You can erase or rewrite certain sections of a DVD-RAM disc without disturbing other sections of the disc, and the discs can handle many times the number of rewrites (around 100,000) over the thousand rewrites expected for most DVD-RW and DVD+RW discs. DVD-RAM discs are popular media used in camcorders and set-top boxes.
BD-ROM drive	*BD or Blu-ray disc read-only memory.* A BD-ROM drive can also read DVDs, and some can read CDs.
BD-R disc or drive	*BD recordable.* The drive reads/writes only one layer of data, for a capacity of 25 GB. A BD-R disc handles one-time recording and is designed for large HD video and audio files.

Table 5-2 Optical disc and drive standards (continues)

Standard	Description
BD-R DL disc or drive	*BD recordable dual-layer*. A BD-R DL drive or disc handles dual layers, yielding a 50-GB capacity. The discs support one-time recording.
BD-RE disc or drive	*BD rewriteable*. A BD-RE drive may read/write single layers, yielding a 25-GB capacity. A BD-RE disc can handle rewriting to the disc up to 1,000 times.
BD-RE DL disc or drive	*BD rewriteable dual-layer*. A BD-RE DL disc with a capacity of 50 GB can handle rewriting up to 1,000 times and is designed to hold backups of video and music libraries.
BD-R TL disc or drive BD-R XL TL disc or drive	*BD recordable triple-layer*. A BD-R TL disc uses three layers, yielding 100-GB capacity, and supports one-time recording.
BD-R QL disc or drive BD-R XL QL disc or drive	*BD recordable quad-layer*. BD-R QL discs have four layers, yielding 128-GB capacity. These discs are primarily used in data centers and cloud computing.

Table 5-2 Optical disc and drive standards (continued)

> ⭐ **A+ Exam Tip** The A+ Core 1 exam expects you to know about combo optical drives and burners, including CD-ROM, CD-RW, DVD-ROM, DVD-RW, DVD-RW DL, Blu-ray, BD-R, and BD-RE combo drives. To prepare for the exam, study the details of Table 5-2. You need to know how to select the appropriate type of disc, given a scenario.

> ✏️ **Notes** CDs, DVDs, and BDs are expected to hold their data for many years; however, you can prolong the life of a disc by protecting it from exposure to light.

INSTALLING AN OPTICAL DRIVE

A+ CORE 1 3.4

Internal optical drives on today's computers use a SATA interface. Figure 5-51 shows the rear of a SATA optical drive. An optical drive is usually installed in the drive bay at the top of a desktop case (see Figure 5-52). After the drive is installed in the bay, connect the data and power cables.

SATA power connector

SATA data connector

Figure 5-51 The rear of a SATA optical drive

Figure 5-52 Slide the drive into the bay flush with the front panel

★ **A+ Exam Tip** The A+ Core 1 exam expects you to know how to select and install a CD, DVD, or Blu-ray drive.

Windows 10/8/7 supports optical drives using its own embedded drivers without add-on drivers. Therefore, when Windows first starts up after the drive is installed, it recognizes the drive and installs drivers. Use Device Manager to verify that the drive installed with no errors and is ready to use.

REPLACING AN OPTICAL DRIVE ON A LAPTOP

**A+
CORE 1
1.1**

Because the need to have an optical drive on a computer is decreasing, some newer laptops don't include it, which saves on size and weight of the laptop. If you find you need an optical drive with a laptop, use an external model that connects by way of a USB port. If an internal optical drive goes bad on a laptop, it is likely cheaper to replace the optical drive than the laptop. For some systems, you'll need to first remove the keyboard to expose an optical drive. Follow along as we remove the DVD drive from one laptop system:

1. *Very important*: Shut down the system, unplug the AC adapter, and remove the battery pack.

2. To remove the keyboard from this laptop, you first remove one screw on the bottom of the case and then turn the case over and pry up the keyboard. You can then move the keyboard to one side. You can leave the ribbon cable from the motherboard to the keyboard connected. When you move the keyboard out of the way, the DVD drive is exposed, as shown in Figure 5-53.

Figure 5-53 Remove the keyboard to expose the optical drive

3. Remove the screw that holds the DVD drive to the laptop (see Figure 5-54).

Figure 5-54   Remove the screw that holds the DVD drive

4. Slide the drive out of the bay (see Figure 5-55).

5. When you slide the new drive into the bay, make sure you push it far enough into the bay so that it solidly connects with the drive connector at the back of the bay. Replace the screw.

For other systems, the optical drive can be removed by first removing a cover from the bottom of the laptop. Then you remove one screw that secures the drive. Next, push the optical drive out of the case (see Figure 5-56).

Figure 5-55   Slide the drive out of the bay

Figure 5-56   Push the optical drive out the side of the case

SOLID-STATE STORAGE

A+
CORE 1
3.4, 3.6

Types of solid-state storage include SSDs, USB flash drives, and memory cards. Current USB flash drives range in size from 256 MB to 2 TB and go by many names, including a flash pen drive, jump drive, thumb drive, and key drive. Several USB flash drives are shown in Figure 5-57. Flash drives might work at USB 2.0 or USB 3.0 speed and use the FAT (for small-capacity drives) or exFAT file system (for large-capacity drives). Windows 10/8/7 has embedded drivers to support flash drives. To use one, simply insert the device in a USB port. It then appears in Windows 10/8 File Explorer or Windows 7 Windows Explorer as a drive with an assigned letter.

Figure 5-57 USB flash drives come in a variety of styles and sizes

> 🖊 **Notes** To make sure that data written to a flash drive is properly saved, right-click the drive in File Explorer or Windows Explorer and select **Eject** from the shortcut menu. It is then safe to remove the drive.

Memory cards might be used in digital cameras, tablets, smartphones, MP3 players, digital camcorders, and other portable devices, and most laptops have memory card slots provided by a built-in smart card reader. If there is not a memory card slot in the device, you can add an external smart card reader/writer that uses a USB connection. For a desktop, you can install a universal smart card reader/writer in a drive bay. For example, the device shown in Figure 5-58 reads and writes to several types of smart cards. It installs in a desktop drive bay and connects to the motherboard by way of a 9-pin USB cable. Plug the cable into an empty 9-pin USB 2.0 header on the motherboard.

Source: https://www.sabrent.com/product/CRW-UINB/7-slot-usb-2-0-internal-memory-card-reader-writer/

Figure 5-58 This 7-slot USB 2.0 Internal Memory Card Reader and Writer by Sabrent supports multiple types of smart cards

The most popular memory cards are Secure Digital (SD) cards, which follow the standards of the SD Association (*sdcard.org*) and are listed in Table 5-3. The three standards for capacity used by SD cards are 1.x (regular SD), 2.x (SD High Capacity or SDHC), and 3.x (SD eXtended Capacity or SDXC). Besides capacity, SD cards come in three physical sizes (full-size, MiniSD, and MicroSD) and are rated for speed in classes.

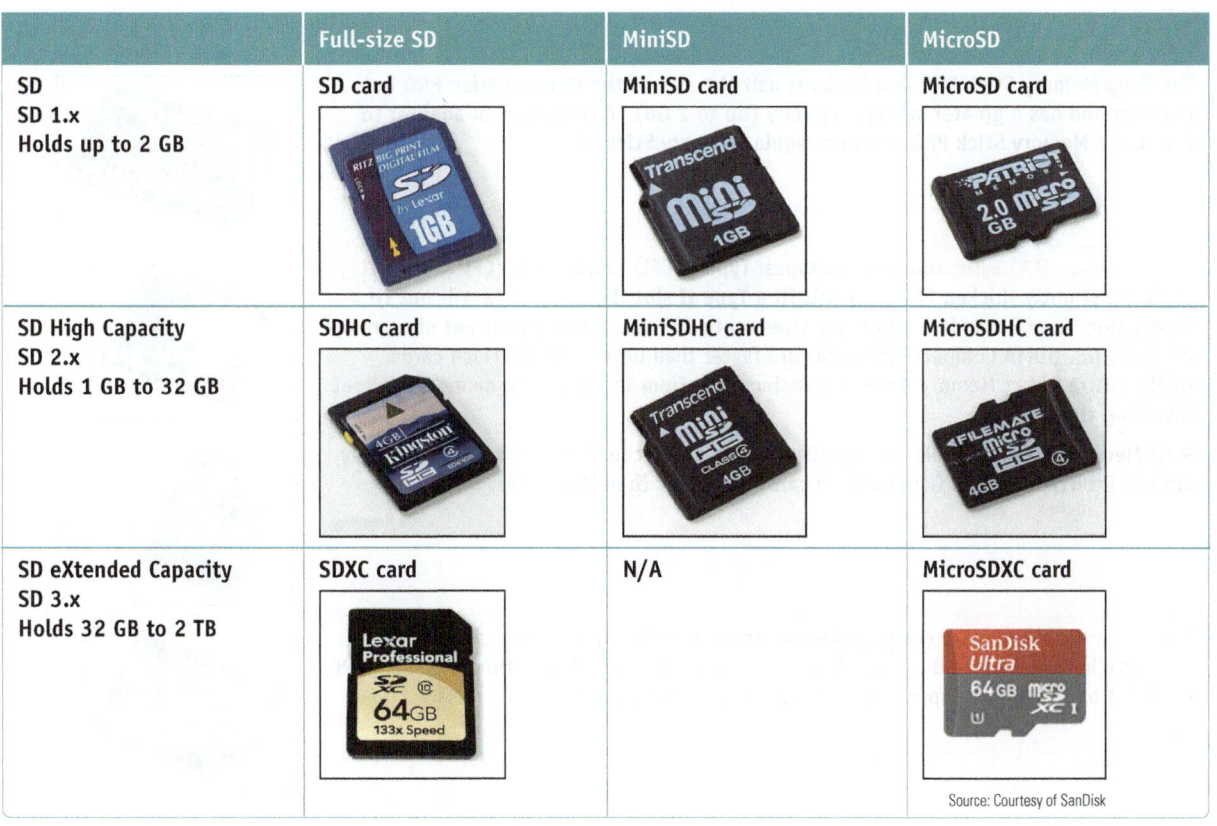

	Full-size SD	MiniSD	MicroSD
SD **SD 1.x** **Holds up to 2 GB**	SD card	MiniSD card	MicroSD card
SD High Capacity **SD 2.x** **Holds 1 GB to 32 GB**	SDHC card	MiniSDHC card	MicroSDHC card
SD eXtended Capacity **SD 3.x** **Holds 32 GB to 2 TB**	SDXC card	N/A	MicroSDXC card Source: Courtesy of SanDisk

Table 5-3   Flash memory cards that follow the SD Association standards

Source: https://www.howtogeek.com/189897/how-to-buy-an-sd-card-speed-classes-sizes-and-capacities-explained/

Figure 5-59   Look for one of these symbols on an SD card to indicate class rating speed

Popular classes for rating speeds, from slowest to fastest, are class 2, 4, 6, 10, Ultra High Speed class 1 (UHS class 1), and UHS class 3. For digital cameras, class 4 or 6 should be fast enough. For high-resolution video recording, use class 10 or higher. To know the class rating, look for a symbol (see Figure 5-59) on the card. Generally, the higher the speed, the more expensive the card becomes. For SD cards rated in UHS classes, the device must also be rated for UHS to get the higher speeds.

SDHC and SDXC slots are backward compatible with earlier standards for SD cards. However, you cannot use an SDHC card in an SD slot, and you cannot use an SDXC card in an SDHC slot or SD slot. Only use SDXC cards in SDXC slots.

SD and SDHC cards use the FAT file system, and SDXC cards use the exFAT file system. Windows 10/8/7 supports both file systems, so you should be able to install an SD, SDHC, or SDXC card in an SD slot on a Windows laptop with no problems (assuming the slot supports the SDHC or SDXC card you are using).

Memory cards other than SD cards are shown in Table 5-4. Some of the cards in the table are seldom used today.

★ **A+ Exam Tip**   The A+ Core 1 exam expects you to know about SD, MicroSD, MiniSD, CompactFlash, and xD memory cards. Given a scenario, you need to know which type of flash storage device is appropriate for the situation.

Flash Memory Device	Example
The Sony Memory Stick PRO Duo is about half the size of the Memory Stick PRO but is faster and has a greater storage capacity (up to 2 GB). You can use an adapter to insert the Memory Stick PRO Duo in a regular Memory Stick slot.	
CompactFlash (CF) cards come in two types, Type I (CFI) and Type II (CFII). Type II cards are slightly thicker. CFI cards will fit a Type II slot, but CFII cards will not fit a Type I slot. The CF standard allows for sizes up to 137 GB, although current sizes range up to 64 GB. UDMA CompactFlash cards are faster than other CompactFlash cards. UDMA (Ultra Direct Memory Access) transfers data from the device to memory without involving the CPU.	
MultiMediaCard (MMC) looks like an SD card, but the technology is different and they are not interchangeable. Generally, SD cards are faster than MMC cards.	
The **xD-Picture Card** has a compact design (about the size of a postage stamp), and currently holds up to 2 GB of data. You can use an adapter to insert this card into a PC Card slot on a laptop computer or a CF slot on a digital camera.	

Table 5-4   Flash memory cards

Figure 5-60 shows several flash memory cards together so you can get an idea of their relative sizes. Sometimes a memory card is bundled with one or more adapters so that a smaller card will fit a larger card slot.

Figure 5-60   Flash memory cards

TROUBLESHOOTING HARD DRIVES

In this part of the chapter, you learn how to troubleshoot problems with hard drives. Hard drive problems during the boot can be caused by the hard drive subsystem, the file system on the drive, or files required by Windows when it begins to load. When trying to solve a problem with the boot, you need to decide if the problem is caused by hardware or software. All the problems discussed in this section are caused by hardware.

SLOW PERFORMANCE

**A+
CORE 1
5.3**

One of the most common complaints about a computer is that it is running slowly. In general, the overall performance of a system depends on the individual performances of the processor, motherboard, memory, and hard drive; often, the hard drive (for example, a 5400-RPM magnetic drive) or the hard drive interface (SATA2, for example) is the bottleneck.

If not managed well, hard drives can run slower over time, and full hard drives run slower than others. For best performance, don't allow an SSD to exceed 70% capacity and a magnetic drive to exceed 80% capacity.

You can use Windows tools or tools provided by the hard drive manufacturer to optimize a drive.

5

WINDOWS AUTOMATICALLY OPTIMIZES A DRIVE

First, let's understand why performance might slow down for magnetic drives and SSDs:

- ▲ *Magnetic drives*. When a magnetic drive is new, files are physically written in contiguous sectors (one following another without a break). Over time, as more files are written and deleted, files are stored in disconnected fragments on the drive and slow performance can result. To improve performance, every week Windows automatically defragments a magnetic drive, rearranging fragments or parts of files in contiguous clusters.
- ▲ *SSDs*. For SSDs, data is organized in blocks and each block contains many pages. A file can spread over several pages in various blocks. Each time a new page is written to the drive, the entire block to which it belongs must be read into a buffer, erased, and then rewritten with the new page included. When a file is deleted, information about the file is deleted, but the actual data in the file is not erased. This can slow down SSD performance because the unused data must still be read and rewritten in its block. To improve performance, Windows sends the trim command to an SSD to erase a block that no longer contains useful data so that a write operation does not have to manage the data. Once a week, Windows 10/8 also sends a retrim command to the SSD to erase all blocks that are filled with unused data. (Windows 7 does not retrim to optimize SSDs.)

You can use the Windows Defrag and Optimization tool (dfrgui.exe) to verify that Windows is defragmenting a magnetic drive and trimming an SSD. When you run the **dfrgui** command in Windows, the Optimize Drives window appears and reports the status of each drive installed in the system (see Figure 5-61 for Windows 8). To verify the settings, click **Change settings**. If a drive has not been recently optimized, click **Optimize**.

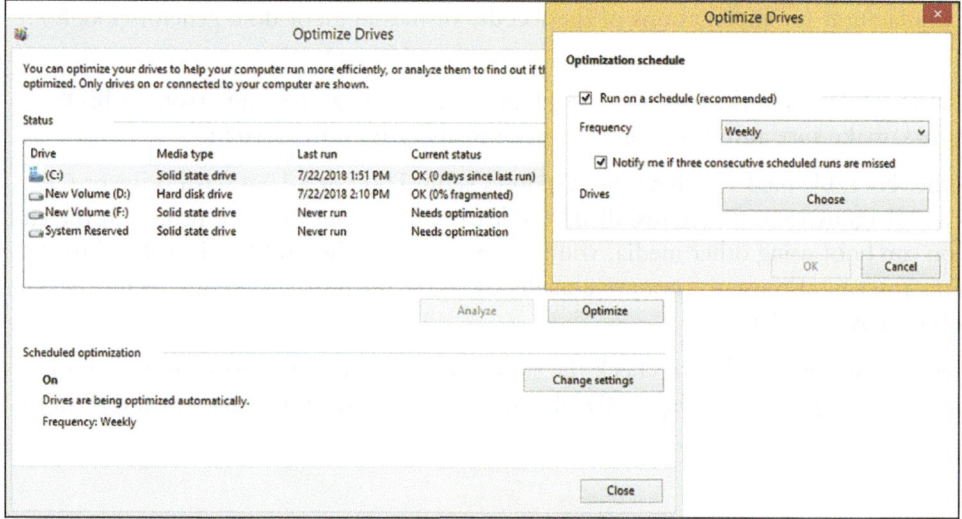

Figure 5-61 Windows reports volume C: is trimmed and volume D: is not fragmented

> ✎ **Notes** To run a command in Windows, enter the command (for example, dfrgui) in the Windows 10 or Windows 7 search box or in the Windows 8 run box.

DRIVE MANUFACTURER UTILITIES

Most magnetic drive and SSD manufacturers offer free utilities you can download and use to update drive firmware and optimize and troubleshoot a drive. For example, Intel offers Solid State Drive Toolbox for its SSDs, Seagate has SeaTools for its magnetic drives and SSDs, and Kingston offers SSD Toolbox for its drives. Search the manufacturer website to find and download the tools and get other hard drive support.

HARD DRIVE PROBLEMS DURING THE BOOT

Hardware problems usually show up at POST, unless there is physical damage to an area of the hard drive that is not accessed during POST. Hardware problems often make the hard drive totally inaccessible. If BIOS/UEFI cannot find a hard drive at POST, it displays an error message similar to one of the following. Most likely, the error message is in white text on a black background.

```
No boot device available
Hard drive not found
OS not found
Read/write failure
Fixed disk error
Invalid boot disk
Inaccessible boot device
Drive not recognized
RAID not found
RAID stops working
Numeric error codes in the 1700s or 10400s
S.M.A.R.T. errors during the boot
```

If BIOS/UEFI cannot access the drive, the cause might be the drive, the data cable, the electrical system, the motherboard, or a loose connection. Here is a list of things to do and check before you open the case:

1. If BIOS/UEFI displays numeric error codes or cryptic messages during POST, check the website of the motherboard manufacturer for explanations of these codes or messages, or do a general Google search.

2. Check BIOS/UEFI setup for errors in the hard drive configuration. If you suspect an error, set BIOS/UEFI to default settings, make sure autodetection is turned on, and reboot the system.

3. Try booting from other bootable media such as the Windows setup DVD or a USB flash drive or CD with the Linux OS and diagnostics software installed. You learn more about this in a project at the end of this chapter. If you can boot using other media, you have proven that the problem is isolated to the hard drive subsystem. You can also use the bootable media to access the hard drive, run diagnostics on the drive, and possibly recover its data.

4. For a RAID array, use the firmware utility to check the status of each disk in the array and to check for errors. Press a key at startup to access the RAID BIOS/UEFI utility. This utility lists each disk in the

array and its status. You can search the website of the motherboard or RAID controller manufacturer for an interpretation of the messages on this screen and what to do about them. If one of the disks in the array has gone bad, it might take some time (as long as two days for large-capacity drives) for the array to rebuild using data on the other disks. In this situation, the status for the array is likely to show as Caution.

5

After the array has rebuilt, your data should be available. However, if one of the hard drives in the array has gone bad, you need to replace the hard drive. After you have replaced the failed drive, you must add it back to the RAID array. This process is called rebuilding a RAID volume. How to do this depends on the RAID hardware you are using. For some motherboards or RAID controller cards, you use the RAID firmware. For others, you use the RAID management software that came bundled with the motherboard or controller. You install this software in Windows and use the software to rebuild the RAID volume using the new hard drive.

If the problem is still not solved, open the case and check the following things. Be sure to protect the system against ESD as you work:

1. Remove and reattach all drive cables.

2. If you're using a RAID or SATA controller card, remove and reseat it or place it in a different slot. Check the documentation for the card, looking for directions for troubleshooting.

3. Inspect the drive for damage, such as bent pins on the cable or drive connection.

4. Determine if a magnetic hard drive is spinning by listening to it or lightly touching the metal drive (with the power on).

5. Check the cable for frayed edges or other damage.

6. Check the installation manual for things you might have overlooked. Look for a section about system setup and carefully follow all directions that apply.

7. S.M.A.R.T. errors that display during the boot result from BIOS/UEFI reporting that the drive has met a threshold point of failure. Back up the data and replace the drive as soon as possible.

8. When Windows is installed on a hard drive but cannot launch, it might present a blue screen with error messages, called a BSOD (blue screen of death), or it might hang and display a never-ending, spinning Windows pinwheel or wait icon. Windows includes several tools for checking a hard drive for errors and repairing a corrupted Windows installation, as you will learn in Chapter 15. Without getting into the details of supporting Windows, here are a few simple things you can try:

   a. *Use Windows 10/8/7 Startup Repair*. In Chapter 4, you learned that the Startup Repair utility restores many of the Windows files needed for a successful boot. Following directions given in that chapter, boot from the Windows 10/8/7 setup DVD or flash drive, select the option to **Repair your computer**, and perform a **Startup Repair**.

   b. *Use the chkdsk command*. To make sure the hard drive does not have bad sectors that can corrupt the file system, you can use the chkdsk command. The command works from Windows, but if you cannot start Windows from the hard drive, you can use the command after booting the system from Windows setup media and selecting the option to **Repair your computer**. Then, for Windows 10/8, go to the **Advanced options** screen (see Figure 5-62); for Windows 7, go to the **System Recovery Options** screen. Next select **Command Prompt**. At the command prompt that appears, use this chkdsk command to search for bad sectors on drive C: and recover data:

```
chkdsk C: /r
```

Figure 5-62 Select Command Prompt, where you can execute the chkdsk command

---

✎ Notes Early in the boot, BIOS/UEFI error messages usually display in white text on a black screen. Windows BSOD boot error messages display on a blue screen. As an IT help-desk technician, you might find yourself talking on the phone with a customer about his boot problem. To help you decide if the problem is happening during POST or as Windows is loading, ask the customer to tell you the color of the screen that shows the error message.

---

9. Before Windows can format and install a file system on a drive, it first separates the drive into one or more partitions using the older MBR (Master Boot Record) or newer GPT (Global Partition Table) partitioning system. Here are steps you can take to repair an MBR hard drive:

   a. *Repair the BCD*. The BCD (Boot Configuration Data) is a small database that holds parameters Windows needs for a successful boot. At a command prompt, use this bootrec command to rebuild the BCD:

   ```
   bootrec /RebuildBCD
   ```

   b. *Repair the boot sector*. The first sector of a hard drive is called the boot sector and holds the MBR partition table, which maps the locations of partitions on the drive. To repair a corrupted boot sector, use this command:

   ```
   bootrec /FixBoot
   ```

   c. *Repair the MBR*. The bootrec command can be used to fix problems with the MBR program in the boot sector that is needed to start Windows. Use this command:

   ```
   bootrec /FixMBR
   ```

10. Check the drive manufacturer's website for diagnostic software such as SeaTools, which is used to diagnose problems with Seagate drives. Sometimes these types of software, including SeaTools, can be run from a bootable USB flash drive or CD. Run the software to test the drive for errors.

11. If it is not convenient to create a bootable USB flash drive or CD with hard drive diagnostic software installed, you can move the drive to a working computer and install it as a second drive in the system. Then you can use the diagnostic software installed on the primary hard drive to test the problem drive. While you have the drive installed in a working computer, be sure to find out if you can copy data from it to the good drive, so that you can recover any data not backed up. Remember that you set the drive on the open computer case (see Figure 5-63) or use a SATA-to-USB converter to connect the drive to a USB port. If you have the case open with the computer turned on, be *very careful* not to touch the drive or touch inside the case.

Figure 5-63 Temporarily connect a faulty hard drive to another system to diagnose the problem and try to recover data

12. After you have tried to recover the file system and data on the drive and before you decide to replace the hard drive, try these things to clean the drive and get a fresh start:

   a. *Format a hard drive volume*. If you decide the hard drive volume is corrupted and you want to start over, boot the system from Windows setup media and open a Windows command prompt. Then use the format command to erase everything on the volume. In this example, D: is the drive letter for the volume:

   ```
   format D:
   ```

   b. *Use diskpart to start over with a fresh file system*. If formatting the volume doesn't work, you can erase the hard drive partitions using the diskpart command. When you enter diskpart at a command prompt, the DISKPART> prompt appears. Then use the following commands to wipe everything off the hard drive. In the example, you are erasing partition 1 on disk 0.

   ```
   list disk
   select disk 0
   list partition
   select partition 1
   clean
   ```

   Use the **exit** command to exit the diskpart utility. You can then reinstall Windows, which partitions the hard drive again. If Windows cannot recognize the drive, it's probably time to replace hardware in the hard drive subsystem.

13. If the drive still does not boot, exchange the three field replaceable units—the data cable, the storage card (if the drive is connected to one), and the hard drive itself—for a hard drive subsystem. Do the following, in order, and test the hard drive after each step:

   a. Try connecting the drive data cable to a different SATA connector on the motherboard. A SATA connector might be disabled when the system is using an M.2 slot.

   b. Reconnect or swap the drive data cable.

   c. Reseat or exchange the drive controller card, if one is present.

   d. Exchange the hard drive for a known good drive.

14. Sometimes older drives refuse to spin at POST or a failing drive can make a loud clicking noise. Drives that have trouble spinning often whine at startup for several months before they finally refuse to spin altogether. If your drive whines loudly when you first turn on the computer, *do not* turn off the computer, and replace the drive as soon as possible. One of the worst things you can do for a drive that has difficulty starting is to leave the computer turned off for an extended period of time. Some drives, like old cars, refuse to start if they are unused for a long time. A drive making a loud clicking noise most likely is not accessible and must be replaced.

15. A bad power supply or a bad motherboard also might cause a disk boot failure.

If the problem is solved by exchanging the hard drive, take the extra time to reinstall the old hard drive and verify that the problem was not caused by a bad connection.

>> CHAPTER SUMMARY

Hard Drive Technologies and Interface Standards

◢ A hard disk drive (HDD) can be a magnetic drive, a solid-state drive, or a hybrid drive. A magnetic drive comes in three sizes: 3.5" for desktop computers and 2.5" and 1.8" for laptops.

◢ A solid-state drive contains NAND flash memory and is more expensive, faster, more reliable, and uses less power than a magnetic drive. Form factors used by SSDs include 2.5", M.2, and PCIe cards.

◢ A hybrid hard drive (H-HDD) is a magnetic drive with an SSD buffer that improves performance.

◢ S.M.A.R.T. is a self-monitoring technology whereby the BIOS/UEFI monitors the health of the hard drive and warns of an impending failure.

◢ Interface standards used by hard drives and optical drives include the outdated IDE and SCSI standards, SATA (the most popular standard), and NVMe (applies only to SSDs and the fastest standard).

◢ Three SATA standards provide data transfer rates of 1.5 Gb/sec (using SATA I), 3 Gb/sec (using SATA II), and 16 Gb/sec (using SATA III).

◢ The NVMe standard can be used by SSDs embedded on PCIe expansion cards, SSDs using a U.2 connector, and SSD M.2 cards using an M.2 slot.

How to Select and Install Hard Drives

◢ When selecting a hard drive, consider the interface standards, storage capacity, technology (solid-state or magnetic), spindle speed (for magnetic drives), interface standard, and buffer size (for hybrid drives).

◢ SATA drives require no configuration and are installed using a power cord and a single SATA data cable.

◢ Laptop hard drives plug directly into a SATA connection on the system board.

◢ RAID technology uses an array of hard drives to provide fault tolerance and/or improved performance. Choices for RAID are RAID 0 (striping using two drives and improves performance), RAID 1 (mirroring using two drives and provides fault tolerance), RAID 5 (parity checking using three drives, provides fault tolerance, and improves performance), and RAID 10 (striping and mirroring combined using four drives, and provides optimum fault tolerance and performance).

◢ Hardware RAID is implemented using the motherboard BIOS/UEFI or a RAID controller card. Software RAID is implemented in Windows. The best practice is to use hardware RAID rather than software RAID.

◢ Multiple hard drives can be installed in a single external enclosure to expand the storage capacity of a single computer or to make hard drive storage available on a network as network attached storage (NAS).

Supporting Other Types of Storage Devices

◢ File systems a storage device might use in Windows include NTFS, exFAT, FAT32, FAT, CDFS (used by CDs), and UDF (used by CDs, DVDs, and BDs).

◢ CDs, DVDs, and BDs are optical discs with data physically embedded into the surface of the disc. Laser beams are used to read data off the disc by measuring light reflection.

◢ Optical discs can be recordable (such as a CD-R disc) or rewriteable (such as a DVD-RW disc). A BD QL (Blu-ray disc quad-layer) can hold 128 GB.

◢ Flash memory cards are a type of solid-state storage. Types of flash memory card standards by the SD Association include SD, MiniSD, MicroSD, SDHC, MiniSDHC, MicroSDHC, SDXC, and MicroSDXC. Other memory cards include Memory Stick PRO Duo, CompactFlash I and II, MMC, and xD-Picture Card.

Troubleshooting Hard Drives

◢ Defragmenting a magnetic hard drive can sometimes improve slow performance of the drive. Trimming an SSD improves performance.

◢ Hard drive problems during the boot can be caused by the hard drive subsystem, the file system on the drive, or files required by Windows when it begins to load. After the boot, bad sectors on a drive can cause problems with corrupted files.

◢ To determine if the hard drive is the problem when booting, try to boot from other media, such as the Windows setup DVD or a bootable USB flash drive.

◢ For problems with a RAID volume, use the RAID controller firmware (on the motherboard or on the RAID controller card) or RAID management software installed in Windows to report the status of the array and to rebuild the RAID volume.

◢ To determine if a drive has bad sectors, use the chkdsk command. You can run the command after booting the system using Windows setup media.

◢ Use the format command to erase everything on a Windows volume.

◢ Use commands within the diskpart utility to completely erase a partition on a hard drive.

◢ Field replaceable units in the hard drive subsystem are the data cable, optional storage card, and hard drive.

>> KEY TERMS

For explanations of key terms, see the Glossary for this text.

BCD (Boot Configuration Data)
BD (Blu-ray disc)
bootrec
BSOD (blue screen of death)
CD (compact disc)
CDFS (Compact Disc File System)
chkdsk
CompactFlash (CF) card
Defrag and Optimization tool (dfrgui.exe)

diskpart
DVD (digital versatile disc or digital video disc)
eSATA (external SATA)
external enclosures
fault tolerance
file system
formatting
hard disk drive (HDD)
hard drive
hot-swapping
hybrid hard drive (H-HDD)

IDE (Integrated Drive Electronics)
low-level formatting
magnetic hard drive
MBR (Master Boot Record)
mirrored volume
NAND flash memory
NAS (network attached storage)
NVMe (Non-Volatile Memory Express or NVM Express)

RAID (redundant array of inexpensive disks or redundant array of independent disks)
RAID 0
RAID 1
RAID 5
RAID-5 volume
RAID 10 or RAID 1+0
read/write head
SATA Express
SCSI (Small Computer System Interface)

SD (Secure Digital) card
serial ATA or SATA
S.M.A.R.T. (Self-Monitoring
  Analysis and Reporting
  Technology)

smart card reader
solid-state hybrid drive
  (SSHD)
spanning

SSD (solid-state drive or
  solid-state device)
striped volume
UDF (Universal Disk Format)

volume
wear leveling
xD-Picture card

>> THINKING CRITICALLY

These questions are designed to prepare you for the critical thinking required for the A+ exams and may use content from other chapters and the web.

1. Your friend has a Lenovo IdeaPad N580 laptop, and the hard drive has failed. Her uncle has offered to give her a working hard drive he no longer needs, the Toshiba MK8009GAH 80-GB 4200-RPM drive. Will this drive fit this laptop? Why or why not?

   a. Yes, the drive form factor and interface connectors match.

   b. No, the drive form factor matches but the interface does not match.

   c. Yes, the drive form factor, spindle speed, and interface all match.

   d. No, the drive form factor and interface do not match.

2. You have four 2.5" hard drives on hand and need a replacement drive for a desktop system. The documentation for the motherboard installed in the system says the board has six SATA 3 Gb/s connectors and one IDE connector. Which of the four hard drives will work in the system and yield the best performance?

   a. Ultralock IDE ATA 4500-RPM 3.5" HDD

   b. WD 3.5" 7200-RPM SATA 3.0 HDD

   c. Seagate IDE ATA 4500-RPM 3.5" HDD

   d. WD 2.5" 4500-RPM SATA 6 Gb/s HDD

3. You are setting up a RAID system in a server designed for optimum fault tolerance, accuracy, and minimal downtime. Which HDD is best for this system, assuming the motherboard supports it?

   a. Hot-swap 2.5" SATA 2.0 SSD

   b. Hot-swap 3.5" SATA 3.0 10,000-RPM drive

   c. 3.5" SATA 3.0 15,000-RPM drive

   d. 2.5" SATA 6 Gb/s SSD

4. You have two matching HDDs in a system, which you plan to configure as a RAID array to improve performance. Which RAID configuration should you use?

   a. RAID 0

   b. RAID 1

   c. RAID 5

   d. RAID 10

5. Which RAID level stripes data across multiple drives to improve performance and provides fault tolerance?

6. Which of the following situations allows for data not to be lost in a RAID array?

   a. RAID 0 and one hard drive fails

   b. RAID 1 and one hard drive fails

    c. RAID 5 and two hard drives fail

    d. RAID 10 and three hard drives fail

7. A laptop has an SD card slot that no longer reads cards inserted in the slot. Which is the first and best solution to try? The second?

    a. Download and install the latest drivers from the laptop manufacturer for the card slot.

    b. Purchase a USB memory card adapter to replace the SD card slot.

    c. Replace the card reader on the system board, being careful to only use parts sold or recommended by the laptop manufacturer.

    d. Update Windows on the laptop.

    e. Reinstall Windows on the laptop.

8. Explain how a DVD manufacturer can advertise that a DVD can hold 4.7 GB, but Explorer reports the DVD capacity as 4,706,074,624 bytes or 4.38 GB.

    a. Manufacturers are allowed to overadvertise their products.

    b. The manufacturer measures capacity in decimal and the OS measures capacity in binary.

    c. The actual capacity is 4.7 GB, but the OS requires overhead to manage the DVD and the overhead is not included in the reported DVD capacity.

    d. The DVD was formatted to have a capacity of 4.38 GB, but it could have been formatted to have a capacity of 4.7 GB.

9. You discover Event Viewer has been reporting hard drive errors for about one month. What is the first solution you should try to fix the problem?

    a. Use the chkdsk command to repair the drive.

    b. Use Explorer to reformat the drive.

    c. Replace the drive with a known good one.

    d. Download and install firmware updates to the drive from the hard drive manufacturer.

10. You install a SATA hard drive and then turn on the computer for the first time. You access BIOS/UEFI setup and see that the drive is not recognized. Which of the following do you do next?

    a. Turn off the computer, open the case, and verify that memory modules on the motherboard have not become loose.

    b. Turn off the computer, open the case, and verify that the data cable and power cable are connected correctly.

    c. Update BIOS/UEFI firmware to make sure it can recognize the new drive.

    d. Reboot the computer and enter BIOS/UEFI setup again to see if it now recognizes the drive.

11. You want to install an SSD in your desktop computer, but the drive is far too narrow to fit snugly into the bays of your computer case. Which of the following do you do?

    a. Install the SSD in a laptop computer.

    b. Buy a bay adapter that will allow you to install the narrow drive in a desktop case bay.

    c. This SSD is designed for a laptop. Flash BIOS/UEFI so that your system will support a laptop hard drive.

    d. Use a special SATA controller card that will support the narrow hard drive.

12. Mark each statement as true or false:

    a. PATA hard drives are older and slower than SATA hard drives.

    b. SATA1 is about 10 times faster than SATA3.

    c. RAID 0 can be implemented using only a single hard drive.

    d. RAID 5 requires five hard drives working together at the same speed and capacity.

    e. You can use an internal SATA data cable with an eSATA port.

    f. A SATA internal data cable has seven pins.

13. Why do hard drives tend to slow down over time?

    a. Drives can reach full capacity, which hinders where data can be written to the drive.

    b. SSDs must erase a block before a block can be written.

    c. Magnetic drives take longer when having to read data from noncontiguous locations on the drive.

    d. All of the above

14. Of the following hard drives, which one is fastest?

    a. SATA 6 Gb/s SSD

    b. SATA 6 Gb/s 10,000-RPM drive

    c. M.2 SSD using a SATA3 interface

    d. PCIe NVMe SSD card

15. You install an M.2 SSD card in an M.2 slot on a motherboard. When you boot up the system, you discover the DVD drive no longer works. What are likely causes of this problem? Select two.

    a. The DVD drive SATA connector is disabled.

    b. The DVD drive cable is loose or disconnected.

    c. The installation corrupted the DVD drivers.

    d. The DVD drive has failed and must be replaced.

>> HANDS-ON PROJECTS

Hands-On | Project 5-1 Examining BIOS/UEFI Settings for a Hard Drive

Following the directions given in Chapter 2, view the BIOS/UEFI setup information on your computer and write down all the BIOS/UEFI settings that apply to your hard drive. Explain each setting that you can. The web and motherboard documentation can help. What is the size of the installed drive? Does your system support S.M.A.R.T.? If so, is it enabled?

Hands-On | Project 5-2 Selecting a Replacement Hard Drive

Suppose one of the 640-GB Western Digital hard drives installed in the RAID array shown in Figure 5-38 has failed. Search the Internet and find a replacement drive as close to this drive as possible. Save or print three webpages showing the sizes, features, and prices of three possible replacements. Which drive would you recommend as the replacement drive and why?

Hands-On | Project 5-3 Preparing for Hard Drive Hardware Problems

1. Boot your computer and make certain that it works properly. Turn off your computer, remove the computer case, and disconnect the data cable to your hard drive. Turn on the computer again. Write down the message that appears.

2. Turn off the computer and reconnect the data cable. Reboot and make sure the system is working again.

3. Turn off the computer and disconnect the power supply cord to the hard drive. Turn on the computer. Write down the error message that appears.

4. Turn off the computer, reconnect the power supply, and reboot the system. Verify that the system is working again.

5

Hands-On | Project 5-4 Installing a Hard Drive

In a lab that has one hard drive per computer, you can practice installing a hard drive by removing it from one computer and installing it as a second drive in another computer. When you boot up the computer with two drives, verify that both drives are accessible in File Explorer (or Windows Explorer in Windows 7). Then remove the second hard drive and return it to its original computer. Verify that both computers and drives are working.

Hands-On | Project 5-5 Shopping for Storage Media

Shop online and print or save webpages showing the following devices. One way to shop online is to do a general Google search and then click **Shopping**. Select ads to answer these questions.

1. DVD+R DL discs are usually sold in packs. What is the storage capacity of each disc? How many discs are in the pack? What is the price per disc?

2. DVD+RW discs are usually sold as singles or in packs. What is the price per disc? How many more times expensive is a DVD+RW disc than a DVD+R disc?

3. BD-R 100-GB discs are sold as singles or in packs. What is the price per disc?

4. What is the largest-capacity USB flash drive you can find? What is its capacity and price?

5. The eight types of SD memory cards are listed in Table 5-3. What is the storage capacity and price of each card? Which type of SD card gives you the most storage per dollar?

Hands-On | Project 5-6 Using Speccy to Inspect Your System

In a project at the end of Chapter 3, you downloaded and installed Speccy at *ccleaner.com/speccy/download/standard*. If Speccy is not still installed, install it now. Run it to inspect your system and answer the following questions:

1. What is the manufacturer and product family of your primary hard drive? What is the capacity of the drive? Is the drive magnetic or SSD?

2. Looking at the S.M.A.R.T. data reported by Speccy, how many read errors has S.M.A.R.T. reported? Of the many drive attributes that S.M.A.R.T. monitors, has it reported a status other than good? If so, which attributes have led to problems?

(continues)

3. Which SATA type is your hard drive using?

4. For your optical drive, which read capabilities does the drive support? Which write capabilities does the drive support?

5. List three ways Speccy might be able to help you when troubleshooting hard drive problems.

>> REAL PROBLEMS, REAL SOLUTIONS

REAL PROBLEM 5-1 Recovering Data

Your friend has a Windows 10 desktop system that contains important data. He frantically calls you to say that when he turns on the computer, the lights on the front panel light up, he can hear the fan spin for a moment, and then all goes dead. His most urgent problem is the data on his hard drive, which is not backed up. The data is located in several folders on the drive. What is the quickest and easiest way to solve the most urgent problem, recovering the data? List the major steps in that process.

REAL PROBLEM 5-2 Using Hardware RAID

You work as an IT support technician for a boss who believes you are really bright and can solve just about any problem he throws at you. Folks in the company have complained one time too many that the file server downtime is just killing them, so he asks you to solve this problem. He wants you to figure out what hardware is needed to implement hardware RAID for fault tolerance.

You check the file server's configuration and discover it has a single hard drive using a SATA connection with Windows Server 2016 installed. There are four empty bays in the computer case and four extra SATA power cords. You also discover an empty PCIe ×4 slot on the motherboard. BIOS/UEFI setup does not offer the option to configure RAID, but you think the slot might accommodate a RAID controller.

Complete the investigation and do the following:

1. Decide what hardware you must purchase and save or print webpages showing the products and their cost.

2. What levels of RAID does the RAID controller card support? Which RAID level is best to use? Cite any important information in the RAID controller documentation that supports your decisions.

3. What is the total hardware cost of implementing RAID? Estimate how much time you think it will take for you to install the devices and test the setup.

REAL PROBLEM 5-3 Creating a Live Ubuntu Bootable USB Drive with Persistent Storage

Every IT technician who works on personal computers needs a bootable USB flash drive, CD, or DVD in his toolkit to use when he cannot boot from the hard drive. If you can boot from other media, you have proven the problem is not the motherboard, processor, or memory and can turn your attention to the hard drive subsystem and Windows. In this project, you create an Ubuntu bootable USB flash drive, called a Live USB, with persistent storage. (A live Ubuntu flash drive or disc is one that can boot and launch Ubuntu from the drive without changing anything on the hard drive. The term "persistent storage" means that you can write files to the Ubuntu flash drive and the files will still be there next time you launch Ubuntu from the drive.) You'll need at least 2 GB of free space (4 GB of free space is recommended) on a

USB flash drive that has been formatted with the FAT32 file system. Follow these steps to create and test the drive:

1. Go to *ubuntu.com/download/desktop* and download the latest Ubuntu desktop OS to your computer.

2. Go to *linuxliveusb.com/en/home* and download the LinuxLive USB Creator app.

3. Install and launch the Creator app. In the app window, make these five selections:

    a. For Step 1, *Choose a USB key*, select your USB drive.

    b. For Step 2, *Choose a source*, click **ISO/IMG/ZIP** and point to the ISO file you downloaded.

    c. For Step 3, *Persistence*, move the slider all the way to the right to select the maximum amount for persistent storage.

    d. For Step 4, *Options*, no changes are needed.

    e. For Step 5, *Create*, click to start the process to create the Live USB drive. The process can take 5 to 15 minutes.

4. You can use the flash drive on this or another computer to launch Ubuntu from the drive. First make sure the BIOS/UEFI boot priority is set to boot first from the USB drive. Then shut down the system and restart it. Ubuntu Desktop loads. Save your Live USB drive for another project you'll do in Chapter 18.

5. Some systems don't give the option to boot to a USB drive. For these systems, you'll need a bootable CD or DVD. Search the web for directions to create a live Ubuntu bootable CD. Ubuntu calls this CD a Live CD. Which site gives the best directions?

5

Supporting I/O Devices

This chapter is packed full of details about the many I/O (input/output) devices an IT support technician must be familiar with and must know how to install and support. Most of us learn about new technologies when we need to use a device or when a client or customer requests our help with purchasing decisions or solving a problem with a device. Good technicians soon develop the skills of searching the web for explanations, reviews, and ads about a device and can quickly turn to support websites for how to install, configure, or troubleshoot a device. This chapter can serve as your jump start for learning about many computer parts and devices used to enhance a system. It contains enough information to get you started toward becoming an expert with computer devices.

We begin with the basic skills common to supporting any device, including how to use Device Manager and how to select the right port for a new peripheral device. Then you learn to install I/O devices and adapter cards and to support the video subsystem. Next, you learn how to troubleshoot problems with I/O devices. Finally, we wrap up the chapter with a discussion of how to select appropriate parts for a customized computer system to satisfy your customer's specifications.

BASIC PRINCIPLES FOR SUPPORTING DEVICES

An I/O or storage device can be either internal (installed inside the computer case) or external (installed outside the case and called a peripheral device). These basic principles apply to supporting both internal and external devices:

▲ *Every device is controlled by software.* When you install a new device, such as a barcode reader or scanner, you must install both the device and the device drivers to control it. These device drivers must be written for the OS (operating system) you are using. Recall from earlier chapters that the exceptions to this principle are some simple devices, such as the keyboard, which are controlled by the system BIOS/UEFI. Also, Windows has embedded device drivers for many devices. For example, when you install a video card, Windows can use its embedded drivers to communicate with the card, but to use all the features of the card, you can install the drivers that came bundled with it.

▲ *When it comes to installing or supporting a device, the manufacturer knows best.* In this chapter, you learn a lot of principles and procedures for installing and supporting a device, but when you're on the job installing a device or fixing a broken one, read the manufacturer's documentation and follow those guidelines first. For example, for most installations, you install the device before you install the device driver. However, for some devices, such as a wireless keyboard, you might need to install the device driver first. Check the device documentation to know which to do first.

▲ *Some devices need application software to use the device.* For example, after you install a scanner and its device drivers, you might also need to install Adobe Photoshop to use the scanner.

▲ *A device is no faster than the port or slot it is designed to use.* When buying a new external device, pay attention to the type of port for which it is rated. For example, an external hard drive designed to use a USB 2.0 port will work using a USB 3.0 port, but it will work at the USB 2.0 speed even when it's connected to the faster USB 3.0 port. For another example, a video card in a PCI slot will not work as fast as a video card in a PCI Express slot because of the different speeds of the slots.

▲ *Use an administrator account in Windows.* When installing hardware devices under Windows, you need to be signed in to the system with a user account that has the highest level of privileges to change the system. This type of account is called an administrator account.

▲ *Problems with a device can sometimes be solved by updating the device drivers.* Device manufacturers often release updates to device drivers. Update the drivers to solve problems with the device or to add new features. You can use Device Manager in Windows to manage devices and their drivers.

▲ *Install only one device at a time.* If you have several devices to install, install one and restart the system. Make sure that device is working and all is well with the system before you move on to install another device.

Recall that Device Manager (its program file is named devmgmt.msc) is your primary Windows tool for managing hardware. It lists almost all installed hardware devices and the drivers they use. (Printers and many USB devices are not listed in Device Manager.) Using Device Manager, you can disable or enable a device, update its drivers, uninstall a device, and undo a driver update (called a driver rollback).

Before we move on to installing devices, you need to be familiar with the ports on a computer. When selecting a new device, you can get the best performance by selecting one that uses the fastest wired or wireless connection standard available on your computer.

WIRED AND WIRELESS CONNECTION STANDARDS USED BY PERIPHERAL DEVICES

When deciding which connection standard to use for a new device, the speed of the transmission standard is often a tiebreaker. Table 6-1 shows the speeds of various wired and wireless standards, from fastest to slowest. This table can help you decide whether speed should affect your purchasing decisions—for example, when you are deciding between a USB 2.0 printer connection and a Bluetooth wireless connection. Standards for video transmissions are not included in this table.

6

Port or Wireless Type	Maximum Speed	Maximum Cable Length or Wireless Range
Thunderbolt 3	40 Gbps	Copper cables up to 2 meters; requires USB-C connector
Thunderbolt 2	20 Gbps	Copper cables up to 100 meters
SuperSpeed+ USB (USB 3.2)	20 Gbps	For maximum speed, cable length up to 1 meter; requires USB-C connector
SuperSpeed+ USB (USB 3.1)	10 Gbps	Cable lengths up to 3 meters
eSATA Version 3 (eSATA-600)	6.0 Gbps	Cable lengths up to 2 meters
SuperSpeed USB (USB 3.0)	5.0 Gbps	Cable lengths up to 3 meters
eSATA Version 2 (eSATA-300)	3.0 Gbps	Cable lengths up to 2 meters
eSATA Version 1 (eSATA-150)	1.5 Gbps or 1500 Mbps (megabits per second)	Cable lengths up to 2 meters
Wi-Fi 802.11ac RF (radio frequency) of 5.0 GHz	1.3 Gbps or 1300 Mbps	Range up to 70 meters
Wi-Fi 802.11n RF of 2.4 GHz or 5.0 GHz	Up to 600 Mbps	Range up to 70 meters
Lightning	480 Mbps	Cable lengths up to 2 meters
Hi-Speed USB (USB 2.0)	480 Mbps	Cable lengths up to 5 meters
Original USB (USB 1.1)	12 Mbps or 1.2 Mbps	Cable lengths up to 3 meters
Wi-Fi 802.11g RF of 2.4 GHz	Up to 54 Mbps	Range up to 100 meters
Wi-Fi 802.11a RF of 5.0 GHz	Up to 54 Mbps	Range up to 50 meters
Wi-Fi 802.11b RF of 2.4 GHz	Up to 11 Mbps	Range up to 100 meters
Bluetooth wireless RF of 2.45 GHz	Up to 3 Mbps	Range up to 10 meters
Near Field Communication (NFC) RF of 13.56 MHz	Up to 424 kbps	Range up to 4 centimeters

Table 6-1 Data transmission speeds for various wired and wireless connections

CONNECTORS AND PORTS USED BY PERIPHERAL DEVICES

Take a look at the back of a computer and you're likely to see a group of ports, several of which you saw in Table 1-1 in Chapter 1. In this part of the chapter, we survey ports used by a variety of I/O devices and ports used for video, TV, and other specific uses. We begin our survey with USB.

USB CONNECTIONS AND PORTS

Here is a summary of important facts you need to know about USB connections:

▲ The USB Implementers Forum, Inc. (*usb.org*), the organization responsible for developing USB, uses the symbols shown in Figure 6-1 to indicate SuperSpeed+ USB (USB 3.2 and USB 3.1), SuperSpeed USB (USB 3.0), Hi-Speed USB (USB 2.0), or Original USB (USB 1.1).

Source: USB Forum

Figure 6-1 SuperSpeed+, SuperSpeed, Hi-Speed, and Original USB logos appear on products certified by the USB Forum

◢ As many as 127 USB devices can be daisy-chained together using USB cables. In a daisy chain, one device provides a USB port for the next device.

◢ USB uses serial transmissions, and USB devices are hot-swappable, meaning that you can plug in or unplug one without first powering down the system.

◢ A USB cable has four wires, two for power and two for communication. The two power wires (one is hot and the other is ground) allow the host controller to provide power to a device. Three general categories of USB ports and connectors are regular USB, micro USB, and mini USB. Mini USB connectors are smaller and more durable than micro USB, which are smaller than regular USB connectors. Table 6-2 shows the different USB connectors on USB cables.

> ✎ **Notes** Sometimes a mouse that uses USB 2.0 gives problems when plugged into a USB 3.0 port. If a mouse refuses to work or is unstable, try moving it to a USB 2.0 port.

Cable and Connectors	Description
A-Male to B-Male cable	The A-Male connector on the left is flat and wide and connects to an A-Male USB port on a computer or USB hub. The B-Male connector on the right is square and connects to a USB 1.x or 2.0 device such as a printer.
Mini-B to A-Male cable	The Mini-B connector has five pins and is often used to connect small electronic devices to a computer.
A-Male to Micro-B cable	The Micro-B connector has five pins and has a smaller height than the Mini-B connector. It's used on tablets, cell phones, and other small electronic devices.
A-Male to Micro-A cable	The Micro-A connector has five pins and is smaller than the Mini-B connector. It's used on cell phones and other small electronic devices.

Table 6-2 USB connectors (continues)

Cable and Connectors	Description
USB 3.0 A-Male to USB 3.0 B-Male cable	This USB 3.0 B-Male connector is used by SuperSpeed USB 3.0 devices such as printers or scanners. Devices that have this connection can also use regular B-Male connectors, but this USB 3.0 B-Male connector will not fit the connection on a USB 1.1 or 2.0 device. USB 3.0 A-Male and B-Male connectors and ports are blue.
USB 3.0 A-Male to USB 3.0 Micro-B cable	The USB 3.0 Micro-B connector is used by SuperSpeed USB 3.0 devices. The connectors are not compatible with regular Micro-B connectors.
USB 3.1 A-Male to USB-C 3.1 cable	The USB-C connector (also called the USB Type-C connector) on the right is flat with rounded sides and connects to a USB-C port on a computer or device, such as the latest smartphones or a graphics tablet. USB-C connectors do not have a specific orientation and are backward compatible with USB 2.0 and USB 3.0. The connector is required to attain maximum speeds with USB 3.2 devices.

Table 6-2   USB connectors (continued)

Notes A USB 3.0 A-Male connector or port has additional pins compared with USB 1.1 or 2.0 ports and connectors but still is backward compatible with USB 1.1 and 2.0 devices. A USB 3.0 A-Male or B-Male connector or port is usually blue. Take a close look at the blue and black USB ports shown in Figure 1-14 in Chapter 1.

VIDEO CONNECTORS AND PORTS

Video ports are provided by a video card or the motherboard. Video cards (see Figure 6-2) are sometimes called graphics adapters, graphics cards, or display cards. Most motherboards sold today have one or more video ports integrated into the motherboard and are called onboard ports. If you are buying a motherboard with a video port, make sure that you can disable the video port on the motherboard if it gives you trouble. You can then install a video card and use its video port rather than the port on the motherboard. Recall that a video card can use a PCI or PCI Express slot on the motherboard. The fastest slot to use is a PCIe ×16 slot.

Figure 6-2   The PCX 5750 graphics card by MSI Computer Corporation uses the PCI Express ×16 local bus

Recall that types of video ports include VGA, DVI, DisplayPort, and HDMI connectors. In addition to these ports, you also need to know about mini-HDMI, DVI-I, and DVI-D ports. These ports are described here:

▲ *VGA.* The 15-pin VGA port is the standard analog video port and transmits three signals of red, green, and blue (RGB). A VGA port is sometimes called a DB-15 port.

▲ *DVI ports.* DVI ports were designed to replace VGA, and variations of DVI can transmit analog and/or digital data. The DVI standards specify the maximum length for DVI cables as 5 meters, although some video cards produce a strong enough signal to allow for longer DVI cables.

Here are the variations of DVI:

▲ *DVI-D.* The DVI-D port only transmits digital data. Using an adapter to convert a VGA cable to the port won't work. You can see a DVI-D port in Figure 6-3A.

(A) (B)

Figure 6-3   Two types of DVI ports: (A) DVI-D, (B) DVI-I

▲ *DVI-I.* The DVI-I port (see Figure 6-3B) supports both analog and digital signals. Analog data is transmitted using the extra four holes on the right side of the connector. If a computer has this type of port, you can use a digital-to-analog adapter to connect an older analog monitor to the port using a VGA cable (see Figure 6-4). If a video card has a DVI port, most likely it will be the DVI-I port (the one with the four extra holes) so that you can use an adapter to convert the port to a VGA port.

Figure 6-4   A digital-to-analog video port converter using a DVI-I connector with four extra pins

◢ *DisplayPort*. DisplayPort was designed to replace DVI and can transmit digital video and audio data. It uses data packet transmissions similar to those of Ethernet, USB, and PCI Express, and is expected to ultimately replace VGA, DVI, and HDMI on desktop and laptop computers. Besides the regular Display-Port used on video cards and desktop computers, laptops might use the smaller Mini DisplayPort. Figure 6-5 shows a DisplayPort to Mini DisplayPort cable. The maximum length for DisplayPort cables is 15 meters.

BIOS/UEFI setup can be used to manage onboard DisplayPort and HDMI ports. For example, Figure 6-6 shows the BIOS screen where you can enable or disable the audio transmissions of DisplayPort and HDMI ports and still use these ports for video.

Figure 6-5 A DisplayPort to Mini DisplayPort cable

```
                          System Setup
  Main    Configuration    Performance    Security    Power    Boot    Exit

  Onboard Devices                                          If enabled,
                                                           HDMI/DisplayPort output
  Enhanced Consumer IR        <Disable>                    includes both audio and
  Audio                       <Enable>                     video. If disabled,
      Front Panel Audio       <Auto>                       HDMI/DisplayPort output is
  HDMI/DisplayPort Audio      <Enable>                     video only.
  LAN                         <Enable>
  1394                        <Enable>

  USB

  Num Lock                    <On>
  PCI Latency Timer           <32>




                                                           → ←: Select Screen
                                                           ↑ ↓: Select Item
                                                           Enter:Select
                                                           +/-: Change Opt.
                                                           F9: Load Defaults
                                                           F10:Save ESC:Exit
```

Source: Intel

Figure 6-6 Use BIOS/UEFI setup to enable or disable onboard ports

◢ *HDMI and HDMI mini connectors*. HDMI transmits both digital video and audio, and was designed to be used by home theater equipment. The HDMI standards allow for several types of HDMI connectors. The best known, which is used on most computers and televisions, is the Type A 19-pin HDMI connector. Small mobile devices can use the smaller Type C 19-pin HDMI mini connector, also called the mini-HDMI connector. Figure 6-7 shows a cable with both connectors that is useful when connecting devices like a smartphone to a computer. Figure 6-8 shows an HDMI to DVI-D cable. An HDMI connector works only on DVI-D and DVI-I ports. The maximum length of an HDMI cable depends on the quality of the cable; no maximum length has been specified.

Figure 6-7   An HDMI to mini-HDMI cable

Source: Courtesy of Belkin Corporation

Figure 6-8   An HDMI to DVI cable can be used to connect a computer that has a DVI port to home theater equipment that uses an HDMI port

★ **A+ Exam Tip**   The A+ Core 1 exam expects you to know about these video connector types: VGA (DB-15), HDMI, mini-HDMI, DisplayPort, DVI-D, and DVI-I. You must also be able to choose which connector type is the right solution given a scenario.

ADDITIONAL CONNECTORS AND PORTS

Besides USB and video, here are a few other ports and connectors you need to know about:

▲ *Thunderbolt*. Thunderbolt is a multipurpose connector used for high-end displays, external storage devices, and to charge power for smartphones and laptops (see Figure 6-9). Earlier versions of Thunderbolt were limited to Apple products and used the DisplayPort base connection. The latest Thunderbolt 3 uses the USB-C connection (marked with a lightning bolt symbol), which opens the compatibility of Thunderbolt connections to non-Apple products. The USB-C Thunderbolt 3 port can support data transfer rates up to 40 Gbps.

▲ *eSATA*. The eSATA port is used for connecting external storage devices to a computer (see Figure 6-10).

Source: https://www.apple.com/shop/product/MQ4H2AM/A/thunderbolt-3-usb%E2%80%91c-cable-08-m

Figure 6-9   The Thunderbolt 3 cable uses the USB-C connector

6

Source: https://www.amazon.com/StarTech-3-Feet-Shielded-External-ESATA3/dp/B000ENUCR4/ref=sr_1_
5?ie=UTF8&qid=1534146766&sr=8-5&keywords=esata+cable

Figure 6-10   An eSATA connection is used to connect external
storage devices to a computer

▲ *Lightning*. The Lightning connector is an Apple-specific connector for its mobile devices (see Figure 6-11). It is used to charge mobile devices, for data transfer, and to connect peripheral devices, such as a credit card payment device or headphone jack, to the Apple mobile device. The connector is reversible.

Source: https://www.apple.com/shop/product/MQGJ2AM/A/usb-c-to-lightning-cable-1-m?fnode=91

Figure 6-11   This Lightning-to-USB-C cable connects an Apple
mobile device to a USB-C port

These connectors and ports are mostly outdated, although you might still see them in use:

▲ *BNC, RG-6, and RG-59*. Coaxial cable has a *single* copper wire down the middle and a braided shield around it (see Figure 6-12). The cable is stiff and difficult to manage, and is no longer used for networking. RG-6 coaxial cable is used for cable TV, having replaced the older and thinner RG-59 coaxial cable once used for cable TV. Coaxial cable uses a twist-on connector called a BNC connector. One type of BNC connector, called the F connector, is shown in Figure 6-13.

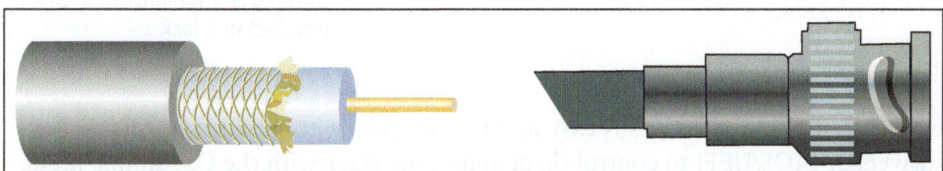

Figure 6-12   A coaxial cable uses a twist-on BNC connector

Figure 6-13   An RG-6 coaxial cable with an F connector used for connections to TV has a single copper wire

▲ *RS-232*. USB or other connectors have replaced the serial RS-232 connectors once used with mice, keyboards, dial-up modems, and peripheral connections. However, you might see a serial RS-232 connector on a rack server to set up a terminal to access the server. An earlier version of RS-232 had a 25-pin connector, but all RS-232 connectors today use 9 pins and are often called DB-9 connectors (see Figure 6-14).

Now that you know about the connection standards, ports, and connectors for external devices, let's see how to install them.

Source: https://www.cablestogo.com/product/52035/6ft-db9-f-f-serial-rs232-cable-black

Figure 6-14   The DB-9 connector may be used to connect a terminal to a server installed in a rack

IDENTIFYING AND INSTALLING I/O PERIPHERAL DEVICES

**A+
CORE 1
1.1, 1.2,
3.6, 3.9**

Installing peripheral or external devices is easy and usually goes without a hitch. All devices need device drivers or BIOS/UEFI to control them and to interface with the OS. Simple input devices, such as the mouse and keyboard, can be controlled by the BIOS/UEFI or have embedded device drivers built into the OS. For these devices, you usually don't have to install additional device drivers.

Peripheral devices you might be called on to install include a keyboard, mouse, touch pad, barcode reader, biometric device (for example, a fingerprint reader), touch screen, motion controller, scanner, microphone, game pad, joystick, digitizer, smart card reader, webcam, MIDI-enabled devices, speakers, and display devices. These installations are similar, so learning to do one will help you do another. Here are the general procedures to install any peripheral device:

1. *Read the manufacturer's directions.* I know you don't want to hear that again, but when you follow these directions, the installation goes smoother. If you later have a problem with the installation and you ask the manufacturer for help, being able to say you followed the directions exactly as stated goes a long way toward getting more enthusiastic help and cooperation.

2. *Make sure the drivers provided with the device are written for the OS you are using.* Recall that 64-bit drivers are required for a 64-bit OS, and 32-bit drivers are required for a 32-bit OS. You can sometimes use drivers written for older Windows versions in newer Windows versions, but for best results, use drivers written for the OS installed. You can download the drivers you need from the manufacturer's website.

3. *Make sure the motherboard port you are using is enabled.* Most likely it is enabled, but if the device is not recognized when you plug it in, go into BIOS/UEFI setup and make sure the port is enabled. In addition, BIOS/UEFI setup might offer the option to configure a USB port to use SuperSpeed+ (USB 3.2 or 3.1), SuperSpeed (USB 3.0), Hi-Speed USB (USB 2.0), or original USB (USB 1.1). Refer back to Figure 6-6, which shows the BIOS setup screen for one system where you can enable or disable onboard devices. In addition, if you are having problems with a motherboard port, don't forget to update the motherboard drivers that control the port.

4. *Install drivers or plug in the device.* Some devices, such as a USB printer, require that you plug in the device before installing the drivers, and some devices require you to install the drivers before plugging in the device. For some devices, it doesn't matter which is installed first. Carefully read and follow the device documentation. For example, the documentation for one scanner says that if you install the camera before installing the driver, the drivers will not install properly.
   If you plug in the device first, Device Setup launches and steps you through the installation of drivers (see Figure 6-15). As Device Setup works, an icon appears in the taskbar. To see the Device Setup box, as shown in the figure, click the icon.

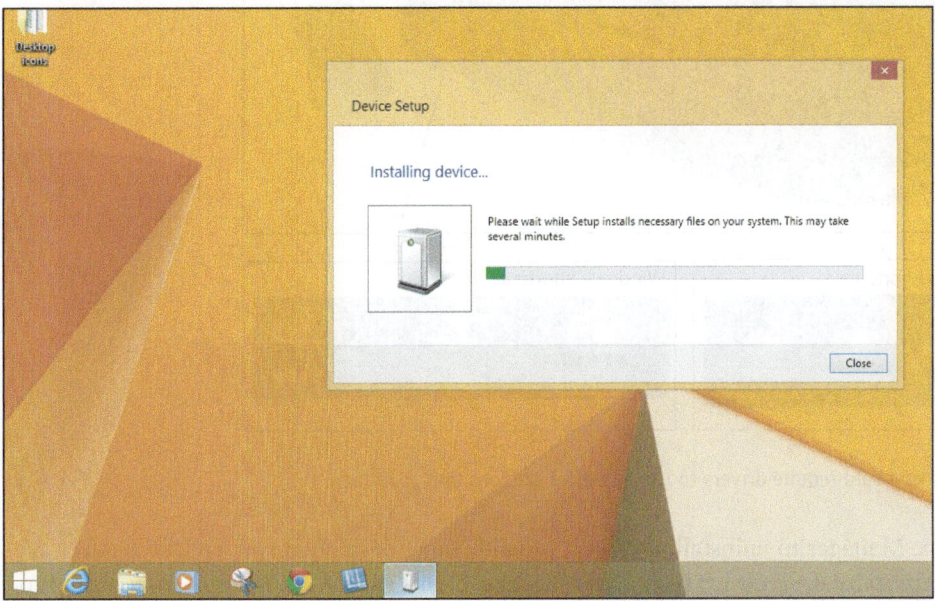

Figure 6-15 Device Setup begins installing a new device

If you need to install the drivers first, run the setup program on CD or DVD. If you downloaded drivers from the web, double-click the driver file and follow the directions on screen. It might be necessary to restart the system after the installation. After the drivers are installed, plug the device into the port. The device should immediately be recognized by Windows. If you have problems using the device, turn to Device Manager for help.

5. *Install the application software to use the device*. For example, a USB camcorder is likely to come bundled with video-editing software. Run the software to use the device.

Now let's look at some key features and any specific installation concerns for several peripheral devices.

MOUSE OR KEYBOARD

**A+
CORE 1
1.1, 3.6**

When you plug a mouse or keyboard into a USB port, Windows should immediately recognize it and install generic drivers. (Older computers used PS/2 ports for the mouse and keyboard. Because these ports were not hot-pluggable, you had to restart Windows after plugging in a mouse or keyboard.) For keyboards with special features such as the one shown in Figure 6-16, you need to install the drivers that came with the keyboard before you can use these features.

Figure 6-16 The mouse and keyboard require drivers to use the extra buttons and zoom bar

You can later use Device Manager to uninstall, disable, or enable most devices. However, USB devices are managed differently. To uninstall a USB device such as the USB keyboard shown in Figure 6-16, use the Programs and Features window. To open the window in Windows 10, press **Win+X**, click **Apps and Features**, and then click **Programs and Features**. In the Programs and Features window, select the device and click **Uninstall**. Follow the directions on screen to uninstall the device.

OS Differences To open the Programs and Features window in Windows 8, press **Win+X** and click **Programs and Features**. See Figure 6-17. For Windows 7, click **Start**, click **Control Panel**, and click **Programs and Features**.

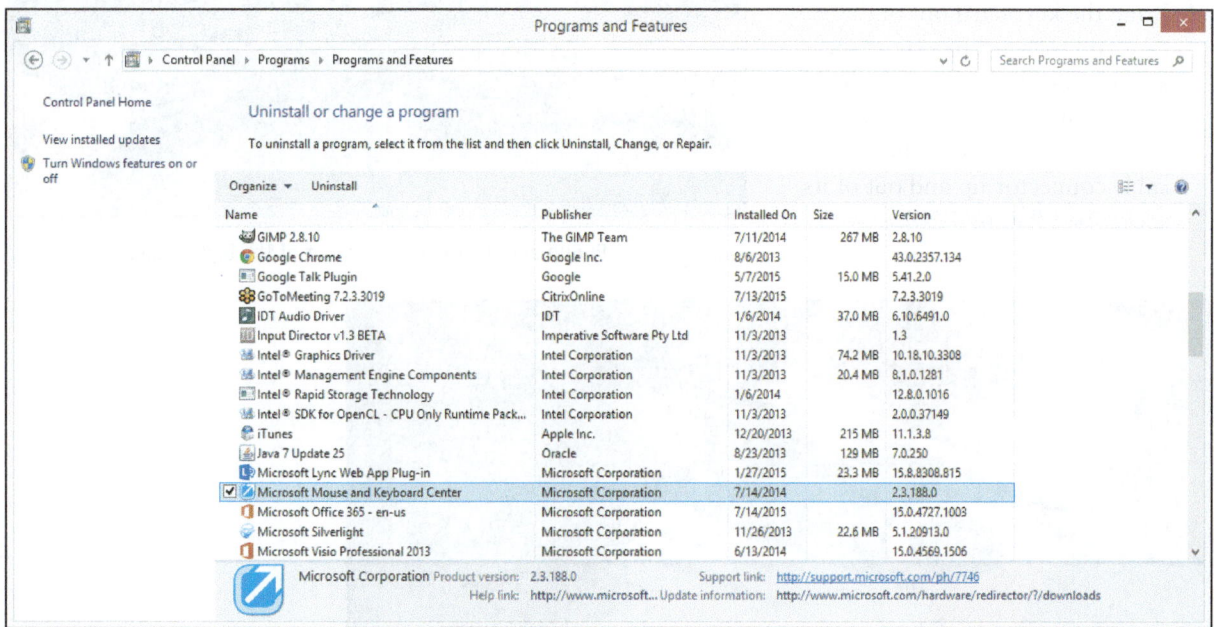

Figure 6-17 USB devices are listed as installed programs

Notes The A+ Core 1 exam expects you to use Control Panel in Classic view, which presents a list of individual items. If Control Panel is in Category view, which presents items in groups, you can get Classic view by clicking **Category** and then clicking **Small icons** or **Large icons**.

REPLACE THE KEYBOARD AND TOUCH PAD IN A LAPTOP

Replacing the keyboard is pretty easy. Before you begin any disassembly of a laptop, refer to the manufacturer documentation. Here are typical steps that are similar for many models of laptops:

1. Power down the laptop and remove the AC adapter and the battery pack.

2. Remove two or more screws on the bottom of the laptop, as shown in Figure 6-18. (Only the manufacturer documentation can tell you which ones because there are probably several used to hold various components in place.)

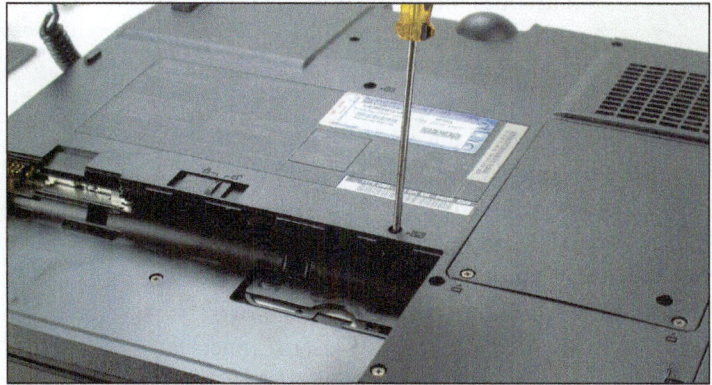

Figure 6-18 Remove screws on the bottom of the laptop

3. Turn the laptop over and open the lid. Gently push the keyboard toward the lid hinges while pulling it up to release it from the case (see Figure 6-19).

4. Bring the keyboard out of the case and forward to expose the keyboard ribbon cable attached underneath the board. Use a spudger or tweezers to lift the cable connector up and out of its socket (see Figure 6-20).

Figure 6-19 Pry up and lift the keyboard out of the laptop case

Figure 6-20 Disconnect the keyboard cable from the motherboard

5. Replace the keyboard following the steps in reverse order.

Sometimes the touch pad and keyboard are one complete field replaceable unit (FRU). If the touch pad is a separate component, it might be part of the keyboard bezel, also called the palm rest. This bezel is the flat cover that surrounds the keyboard. Most likely you have to remove the keyboard before you can remove the keyboard bezel.

BARCODE READERS

A barcode reader is used to scan barcodes on products at the point of sale (POS) or when taking inventory. The reader might use a wireless connection, a serial port, a USB port, or a keyboard port. If the reader uses a keyboard port, most likely it contains a splitter (called a keyboard wedge) for the keyboard to use, and data read by the barcode reader is input into the system as though it were typed using the keyboard. Figure 6-21 shows a barcode reader by Intermec that is a laser scanner and uses Bluetooth to connect wirelessly to the computer.

Source: Courtesy of Intermec Technologies

Figure 6-21 A handheld or hands-free barcode scanner by Intermec Technologies

PAY DEVICES

A+
CORE 1
3.6

A **magnetic stripe reader** and **chip reader** can read from the stripe or chip to pull information from a card or license (see Figure 6-22). A card reader sends information to the computer through a serial connection, USB connection, Lightning connection, 3.5-mm headphone jack, or a stripe reader wedge mounted on a keyboard. A wireless card reader uses Bluetooth.

Source: https://www.staples.com/ID-TECH-Omni-WCR32-Magnetic-Stripe-Reader/product_IM1VS3392
Figure 6-22 A card reader makes financial transactions faster

A **tap pay device** connects wirelessly or by cable to a computer or mobile device to turn it into a point-of-sale system. For example, the PayPal tap pay device shown in Figure 6-23 is a magnetic chip and card reader and a tap pay device all in one; it can connect via a USB cable or Bluetooth wireless connection to a vendor's smartphone or tablet. When a customer taps the device with her smartphone, as shown in the figure, an encrypted NFC connection sends the payment to the PayPal tap pay device. The payment is then sent by encrypted Bluetooth to the vendor's PayPal Here mobile app installed on the vendor's device, which passes it on to the vendor's PayPal account.

6

Source: https://www.staples.com/paypal-chip-and-tap-credit-card-reader/product_2774174
Figure 6-23 A tap pay device receives a transaction from a customer smartphone via NFC communication

SIGNATURE PADS

> A+
> CORE 1
> 3.6

A signature pad uses a sensitive touch screen to capture a handwritten signature made using a stylus or finger for a receipt, contract, or ID card (see Figure 6-24). The signature pad LCD panel displays electronic ink. Signature pads typically use a serial or USB connection to a computer and include software installed on the computer to process the signature. In addition to a signature pad peripheral device, an app can be installed on a smartphone or tablet to allow the mobile device touch screen to receive signatures.

Source: https://www.staples.com/Topaz-SigLite-1x5-T-S460-BSB-R-Virtual-Serial-via-USB-Electronic-Signature-Pad/product_IM1VL7673

Figure 6-24 The LCD panel on a signature pad captures a signature

BIOMETRIC DEVICES

> A+
> CORE 1
> 3.6

A biometric device inputs biological data about a person to identify the person's fingerprint, handprint, face, voice, eye, or handwritten signature. For example, you can use a fingerprint reader to sign in to Windows or to access a smartphone using Touch ID technology. These fingerprint readers should not be considered the only authentication to control access to sensitive data: for that, use a strong password—one that is as long as you can remember or can be stored securely.

Fingerprint readers can look like a mouse and use a wireless or USB connection, such as the one shown in Figure 6-25, or they can be embedded on a keyboard, flash drive, or laptop case. For mobile devices, the fingerprint reader can be activated by pressing a button or touch screen. Most fingerprint readers that are not embedded in other devices use a USB connection. As with other USB devices, read the documentation to know if you should install the drivers first or the device first.

(A) (B)

Figure 6-25 Fingerprint readers can (A) look like a mouse, but smaller, or (B) be embedded on a keyboard

WEBCAMS

> A+
> CORE 1
> 3.6

A webcam (web camera) is embedded in most laptops and can also be installed as a peripheral device using a USB port or some other port. For example, the webcam shown in Figure 6-26 works well for personal chat sessions and videoconferencing and has a built-in microphone. First, use the setup CD to install the software and then plug in the webcam to a USB port.

Source: iStock.com/blyjak

Figure 6-26 This personal web camera clips to the top of your laptop and has a built-in microphone

A webcam comes with a built-in microphone. You can use this microphone or use the microphone port on the computer. Most software allows you to select these input devices. For example, Figure 6-27 shows the Tools Options box for Camtasia Recorder by TechSmith (*techsmith.com*).

Source: Camtasia Recorder by TechSmith

Figure 6-27 The Camtasia Recorder application allows you to change the input devices used for video and sound

GRAPHICS TABLETS

A+
CORE 1
3.6

Another input device is a graphics tablet, also called a digitizing tablet or digitizer, that is used to hand draw and is likely to connect using a USB port (see Figure 6-28). It comes with a stylus that works like a pencil on the tablet and controls the pointer on the screen. The graphics tablet and stylus can be a replacement for a mouse or touch pad on a laptop, and some graphics tablets come with a mouse. Graphics tablets are popular with graphic artists and others who use desktop publishing applications.

Figure 6-28 A graphics tablet and stylus are used to digitize a hand drawing

Install the graphics tablet the same way you do other USB devices. Additional software might be bundled with the device to enhance its functions, such as inputting handwritten signatures into Microsoft Word documents.

TOUCH SCREENS

A touch screen is an input device that uses a monitor or LCD panel as the backdrop for input options. In other words, the touch screen is a grid that senses taps, finger pinches, and slides and sends these events to the computer by way of a USB port or other type of connection. Some laptops have built-in touch screens, and you can also install a touch screen on top of a monitor screen as an add-on device. As an add-on device, the touch screen has its own AC adapter to power it. Some monitors for desktop systems have built-in touch screen capability.

For add-on desktop monitors, clamp the touch screen over the monitor. For most installations, you install the drivers before you connect the touch screen to the computer by way of a USB port. After you install the drivers and the touch screen, you must use management software that came bundled with the device to decide how much of the monitor screen is taken up by the touch screen and to calibrate the touch screen. Later, if the monitor resolution is changed, the touch screen must be recalibrated.

VIRTUAL REALITY HEADSETS

A VR (virtual reality) headset is a device worn on the head that creates a visual and audible virtual experience for the user using a lens display, speakers, microphone, and head-tracking sensors for interaction (see Figure 6-29). VR headsets are often used for extreme gaming experiences but are also used in medical and military training. VR headsets can be programmed independently of a computer or the headset can be connected to a computer using USB for more programming input or recording the experience. Some VR headsets include a dock for a smartphone to create the visual and audible experience and use motion sensors for interaction.

Source: https://www.newegg.com/Product/Product.aspx?Item=9SIAG797579575

Figure 6-29 A VR headset creates a visual and audible virtual experience

KVM SWITCHES

A KVM (Keyboard, Video, and Mouse) switch allows you to use one keyboard, monitor, and mouse for multiple computers. A KVM switch can be useful in a server room or testing lab where you use more than one computer and want to keep desk space clear of multiple keyboards, mice, and monitors; or, you may simply want to lower the cost of peripherals. Figure 6-30 shows a KVM switch that can connect a keyboard, monitor, mouse, microphone, and speakers to two computers. The device uses USB ports for the keyboard and mouse.

Connectors for computer 1   Connectors for computer 2

Press button on wired remote   Connectors for monitor,
to toggle between computers   keyboard, and mouse

Figure 6-30 This KVM switch connects two computers to a keyboard, mouse, monitor, microphone, and speakers and uses USB for the keyboard and mouse

6

A KVM switch does not require that you install device drivers to use it. Just plug in the cables from each computer to the device. Also plug in one set of a monitor, mouse, keyboard, and possibly a microphone and speakers to the device. Switch between computers by using a hot key on the keyboard, buttons on the top of the KVM switch, or a wired remote such as the one shown in Figure 6-30.

INSTALLING AND CONFIGURING ADAPTER CARDS

A+
CORE 1
1.1, 3.5

In this part of the chapter, you learn to install and configure adapter cards. These cards include a video card, sound card, network interface card (NIC), and USB expansion card. The purpose of adding an adapter card to a system is to add external ports or internal connectors the card provides.

Regardless of the type of card you are installing, be sure to verify and do the following when preparing to install one:

▲ *Verify that the card fits an empty expansion slot*. Recall that there are several PCI and PCI Express standards; therefore, make sure the card will fit the slot. To help with airflow, try to leave an empty slot between cards. Especially try to leave an empty slot beside the video card, which puts off a lot of heat. PCIe slots on a motherboard might support different PCIe standards. The motherboard manual tells you which slot is rated for which PCIe standard.

▲ *Verify that the device drivers for your OS are available*. Check the card documentation and make sure you have the drivers for your OS. For example, you need to install 64-bit Windows 10 device drivers in a 64-bit installation of Windows 10. It might be possible to download drivers for your OS from the website of the card manufacturer.

▲ *Back up important data that is not already backed up*. Before you open the computer case, be sure to back up important data on the hard drive.

▲ *Know your starting point*. Know what works and doesn't work on the system. Can you connect to the network and the Internet, print, and use other installed adapter cards without errors? After installing a new card, verify your starting point again before installing another card.

Here are the general directions to install an adapter card. They apply to any type of card.

1. Read the documentation that came with the card. For most cards, you install the card first and then the drivers, but some installations might not work this way.

2. If you are installing a card to replace an onboard port, access BIOS/UEFI setup and disable the port.

3. Wear an ESD strap as you work to protect the card and the system against ESD. Shut down the system, unplug power cords and cables, and press the power button to drain the power. Remove the computer case cover.

4. Locate the slot you plan to use and remove the faceplate cover from the slot if one is installed. Sometimes a faceplate punches or snaps out, and sometimes you have to remove a faceplate screw to remove the faceplate. Remove the screw in the top of the expansion slot or raise the clip on the top of the slot. Save the screw; you'll need it later.

5. Remove the card from its antistatic bag and insert it into the expansion slot. Be careful to push the card straight down into the slot without rocking the card from side to side. Rocking the card can widen the expansion slot, making it difficult to keep a good contact. If you have a problem getting the card into the slot, resist the temptation to push the front or rear of the card into the slot first. You should feel a slight snap as the card drops into the slot.

   Recall that PCIe ×16 slots use a retention mechanism in the slot to help stabilize a heavy card (see Figure 6-31). For these slots, you might have to use one finger to push the stabilizer to the side as you push the card into the slot. Alternately, the card might snap into the slot and then the retention mechanism snaps into position. Figure 6-32 shows a PCIe video card installed in a PCIe ×16 slot.

Figure 6-31 A white retention mechanism on a PCIe ×16 slot pops into place to help stabilize a heavy video card

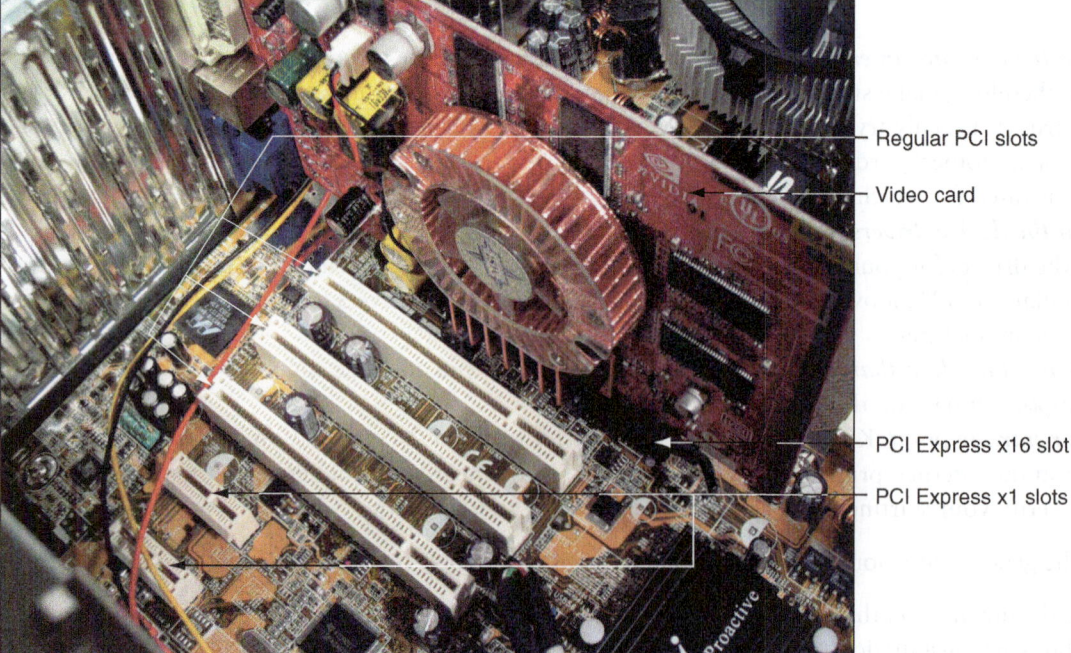

Regular PCI slots

Video card

PCI Express x16 slot

PCI Express x1 slots

Figure 6-32 A PCIe video card installed in a PCIe ×16 slot

6. Insert the screw that anchors the card to the top of the slot (see Figure 6-33). Be sure to use this screw. If it's not present, the card can creep out of the slot over time, causing a loose connection.

Figure 6-33 Secure the card to the case with a single screw

7. Connect any power cords or data cables the card might use. For example, a video card might have a 6-pin or 8-pin PCIe power connector for a power cord from the power supply to the card, as shown in Figure 6-34. (If the power supply does not have the right connector, you can buy an inexpensive adapter to convert a 4-pin Molex connector to a PCIe connector.)

Figure 6-34 Connect a power cord to the PCIe power connector on the card

8. Make a quick check of all connections and cables, and then replace the case cover. (If you want, you can leave the case cover off until you've tested the card, in case it doesn't work and you need to reseat it.) Plug up the external power cable and essential peripherals.

9. Start the system. When Windows starts, it should detect that a new hardware device is present and attempt to automatically install the drivers. As the drivers are installed, a message might appear above the taskbar. When you click the message, the Device Setup box appears (refer back to Figure 6-15). You can cancel the wizard and manually install the drivers.

10. Insert the CD that came bundled with the card and launch the setup program on the CD. The card documentation will tell you the name of the program (examples are Setup.exe and Autorun.exe). Figure 6-35 shows the opening menu for one setup program for a video card. Click **Install Video Drivers** and follow the on-screen instructions to install the drivers. If you are using downloaded driver files, double-click the file to begin the installation and follow the directions on screen.

> **✎ Notes** All 64-bit drivers must be certified by Microsoft to work in Windows. However, some 32-bit drivers might not be. During the driver installation, if you see a message that 32-bit drivers have not been certified, go ahead and give permission to install the drivers if you obtained them from the manufacturer or another reliable source.

Source: EVGA

Figure 6-35   An opening menu to install video drivers

11. After the drivers are installed, you might be asked to restart the system. Then you can configure the card or use it with application software. If you have problems with the installation, turn to Device Manager and look for errors reported about the device. The card might not be properly seated in the slot.

   Now let's turn our attention to sound cards you might be called on to install. As with any adapter card you install, be sure to become familiar with the user guide before you start the installation so that you know the card's hardware and software requirements and what peripheral devices it supports.

SOUND CARDS AND ONBOARD SOUND

A+ CORE 1 3.5

A sound card (an expansion card with sound ports) or onboard sound (sound ports embedded on a motherboard) can play and record sound and save it in a file. Figure 6-36 shows a sound card by Creative (*creative.com*). This Sound Blaster card uses a PCIe ×1 slot and supports up to eight surround sound version 7.1 speakers. The color-coded speaker ports are for these speakers: front left and right, front center, rear left and right, subwoofer, and two additional rear speakers. The two SPDIF (Sony-Philips Digital InterFace) ports are used to connect to external sound equipment such as a CD or DVD player.

Source: Courtesy of Creative Technology Ltd.

Figure 6-36 The Sound Blaster X-Fi Titanium sound card by Creative uses a PCIe ×1 slot

✎ Notes If you are using a single speaker or two speakers with a single sound cable, connect the cable to the lime-green sound port on the motherboard, which is usually the middle port.

REPLACING EXPANSION CARDS IN A LAPTOP

A+ CORE 1 1.1

A laptop does not contain the normal PCI Express or PCI slots found in desktop systems. Newer laptops are likely to use the Mini PCI Express slots (also called Mini PCIe slots) that use the PCI Express standards applied to laptops. Mini PCI Express slots use 52 pins on the edge connector. These slots can be used by many kinds of Mini PCIe cards. These cards are often used to enhance communications options for a laptop, including Wi-Fi wireless, cellular WAN, video, and Bluetooth Mini PCIe cards. Figure 6-37 shows a Mini PCI Express card by Sierra Wireless that provides mobile broadband Internet.

For many laptops, you can remove a cover on the bottom to expose expansion cards so that you can exchange them without an extensive disassembly. For example, to remove the cover on the bottom of one Lenovo laptop, first remove several screws and then lift the laptop cover up and out. Several internal components are exposed, as shown in Figure 6-38.

Source: Sierra Wireless

Figure 6-37 The MC8775 Mini PCI Express card by Sierra Wireless used for voice and data transmissions on cellular networks

Processor fan

Processor
heat sink

SO-DIMMs

Hard drive

Mini PCIe
wireless card

Figure 6-38   Removing the cover from the bottom of a laptop exposes several internal components

The half-size Mini PCIe wireless Wi-Fi card shown in Figure 6-39 has two antennas. To remove the card, first remove the one screw shown in the photo and disconnect the two black and white antenna wires. Note the black and white triangles labeled with a 1 and a 2 on the label of the card so you know which wire goes on which connector when replacing the card. Then slide the card forward and out of the slot. You can then install a new card.

Figure 6-39   This half-size Mini PCIe wireless card is anchored in the expansion slot with one screw

Figure 6-40 shows a full-size Mini PCIe card installed in a laptop. First remove the one screw at the top of the card and disconnect the two antenna wires, and then pull the card forward and out of the slot.

(A)

1. Remove screw

2. Disconnect antenna

3. Pull and lift card from slot

(B)

Figure 6-40 How to remove a Mini PCI Express card

> ★ **A+ Exam Tip** The A+ Core 1 exam expects you to be able to determine when you would need to replace a Mini PCIe card in a laptop given a scenario.

After you have installed a Mini PCIe card that is a Bluetooth, cellular WAN, or other wireless adapter, try to connect the laptop to the wireless network. If you have problems making a connection, verify that Device Manager reports the device is working properly and that Event Viewer has not reported error events about the device.

SUPPORTING THE VIDEO SUBSYSTEM

**A+
CORE 1
1.1, 1.2,
3.1, 3.5,
3.6**

The primary output device of a computer is the monitor. The two necessary components for video output are the monitor and the video card (also called the video adapter and graphics adapter) or a video port on the motherboard. In this part of the chapter, you learn about monitors and how to support the video subsystem.

MONITOR TECHNOLOGIES AND FEATURES

The most popular type of monitor for laptop and desktop systems is an LCD flat-screen monitor (see Figure 6-41), but you have other choices as well. Here is a list and description of each type of monitor:

Figure 6-41   An LCD monitor

▲ *LCD monitor*. The LCD (liquid crystal display) monitor, also called a flat-panel monitor, was first used in laptops. The monitor produces an image using a liquid crystal material made of large, easily polarized molecules. Figure 6-42 shows the layers of the LCD panel that together create the image. At the center of the layers is the liquid crystal material. Next to it is the layer responsible for providing color to the image. These two layers are sandwiched between two grids of electrodes forming columns and rows. Each intersection of a row electrode and a column electrode forms one pixel on the LCD panel. Software can address each pixel to create an image.

Figure 6-42   Layers of an LCD panel

▲ *OLED monitor*. An OLED (organic light-emitting diode) monitor uses a thin LED (light-emitting diode) layer or film between two grids of electrodes and does not use backlighting. It does not emit as much light as an LCD monitor, and therefore can produce deeper blacks, provide better contrast, work in darker rooms, and use less power than an LCD monitor. On the other hand, LCD monitors give less glare than OLED monitors. OLED screens are used by mobile devices and other portable electronic devices. OLED monitors are just now appearing for desktop systems.

◢ *Projector.* A digital projector (see Figure 6-43) shines a light that projects a transparent image onto a large screen and is often used in classrooms or with other large groups. Several types of technologies are used by projectors, including LCD. A projector is often installed as a dual monitor on a computer, which you learn how to do later in the chapter.

Source: Courtesy of Panasonic Corporation of North America

Figure 6-43   A portable XGA projector by Panasonic

⭐ **A+ Exam Tip**   The A+ Core 1 exam expects you to compare LCD and OLED monitor types so that you can choose which one is the best fit for a given scenario.

A laptop display almost always uses LCD technology, although laptops that use an OLED display are available. Some laptop LCD panels use LED backlighting to improve display quality and conserve power. For desktops, LCD is by far the most popular monitor type. Figure 6-44 shows an ad for one best-selling LCD monitor. Table 6-3 explains the features mentioned in the ad.

⭐ **A+ Exam Tip**   The A+ Core 1 exam expects you to know about the components within the display of a laptop, including the components used in LCD, LED, and OLED displays. You also need to know about backlighting, the function of an inverter, and how to replace one.

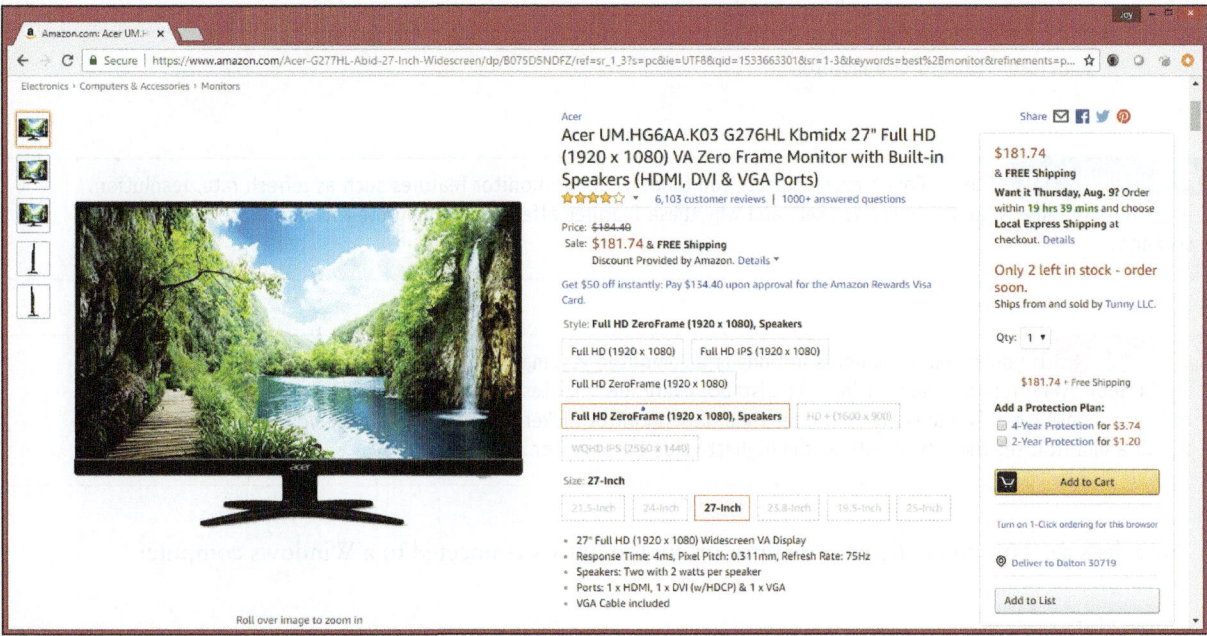

Source: amazon.com

Figure 6-44   An ad for a monitor lists monitor features

6

Monitor Characteristic	Description
Screen size	The screen size is the diagonal length of the screen surface in inches.
Refresh rate	The refresh rate is the number of times a monitor screen is built or refreshed in 1 second, measured in Hz (cycles per second). The ad in Figure 6-44 shows the monitor refresh rate as 75 Hz (75 frames per second)—the higher, the better. Related to refresh rate, the response time is the time it takes to build one frame, measured in ms (milliseconds)—the lower, the better. The ad in Figure 6-44 shows a response time of 4 ms.
Pixel pitch	A pixel is a spot or dot on the screen that can be addressed by software. The pixel pitch is the distance between adjacent pixels on the screen—the smaller the number, the better. For example, Figure 6-44 shows a pixel pitch of 0.311 mm.
Resolution	The resolution is the number of spots or pixels on a screen that can be addressed by software. Values can range from 640 × 480 up to 4096 × 2160 for high-end monitors. Popular resolutions are 1920 × 1080 and 1366 × 768.
Contrast ratio	Contrast ratio is the contrast between true black and true white on the screen—the higher the contrast ratio, the better. 1000:1 is better than 700:1. An advertised dynamic contrast ratio is much higher than the contrast ratio, but is not a true measurement of contrast. Dynamic contrast adjusts the backlighting to give the effect of an overall brighter or darker image. For example, if the contrast ratio is 1000:1, the dynamic ratio is 20,000,000:1. When comparing quality of monitors, pay more attention to the contrast ratio than the dynamic ratio.
Viewing angle	The viewing angle is the angle at which a monitor becomes difficult to see from the side. A viewing angle of 170 degrees is better than 140 degrees.
Backlighting or brightness	Brightness is measured in cd/m^2 (candela per square meter), which is the same as lumens/m^2 (lumens per square meter). In addition, the best LED backlighting for viewing photography is class IPS (in-plane switching), which provides the most accurate color.
Connectors	Popular options for connectors are VGA, DVI-I, DVI-D, HDMI, DisplayPort, and Apple's Thunderbolt. Some monitors offer more than one connector (see Figure 6-45).
Other features	LCD monitors can also provide a privacy or antiglare surface, tilt screens, microphone input, speakers, USB ports, adjustable stands, and perhaps even an input for your smartphone. Some monitors are also touch screens, so they can be used with a stylus or finger touch.

Table 6-3 Important features of a monitor

★ **A+ Exam Tip** The A+ Core 1 exam expects you to know about monitor features such as refresh rate, resolution, brightness in lumens, and connectors used, and why these features affect which monitor you would choose given a scenario.

⚡ **Caution** If you spend many hours in front of a computer, you may strain your eyes. To protect your eyes from strain, look away from the monitor into the distance every few minutes. Use a good monitor with a high refresh rate or low response time. The lower refresh rates that cause monitor flicker can tire and damage your eyes. When you first install a monitor, set the refresh rate at the highest value the monitor can support.

Now let's see how to configure a monitor or dual monitors connected to a Windows computer.

Power port

Sound ports

Analog VGA
connector

DVI-D connector

Figure 6-45 The rear of this LCD monitor shows digital and analog video ports to accommodate a video
cable with either a 15-pin analog VGA connector or a digital DVI connector

CHANGING MONITOR SETTINGS

A+
CORE 1
3.6, 5.4

Settings that apply to the monitor can be managed by using the monitor buttons, function keys
on a keyboard, and Windows utilities. Using the monitor buttons, you can adjust the horizontal
and vertical position of the screen on the monitor surface and change the brightness and contrast settings. Adjust these settings to correct a distorted image. For laptops, the brightness and
contrast settings can be changed using function keys on the laptop.

APPLYING | CONCEPTS INSTALLING DUAL MONITORS

To increase the size of your Windows desktop, you can install more than one monitor for a single computer. To install
dual monitors, you need two video ports on your system, which can come from motherboard video ports, a video card
that provides two video ports, or two video cards.

To install a second monitor in a dual-monitor setup using two video cards, follow these steps:

1. Verify that the original video card works properly and decide whether it will be the primary monitor.

2. Boot the computer and enter BIOS/UEFI setup. If BIOS/UEFI setup has the option to select the order in which
video cards are initialized, verify that the currently installed card is configured to initialize first. For example,
for the BIOS/UEFI system in Figure 6-46, the video adapter in the PCIe slot initializes first before other video
adapters. If it does not initialize first and you install the second card, video might not work at all when you
first boot with two cards.

(continues)

Figure 6-46   In BIOS/UEFI setup, verify that the currently installed video adapter is set to initialize first

3. Install a second video card in an empty slot. A computer might have a second PCIe slot or an unused PCI slot you can use. Attach the second monitor.

4. Boot the system. Windows recognizes the new hardware and launches Device Setup. You can use the utility to install the video card drivers or cancel the utility and install them manually, as you learned to do earlier in the chapter.

Here are the steps to configure dual monitors:

1. Connect two monitors to your system. In Windows 10, open the **Settings** app and click the **System** group. The display settings appear, as shown in Figure 6-47.

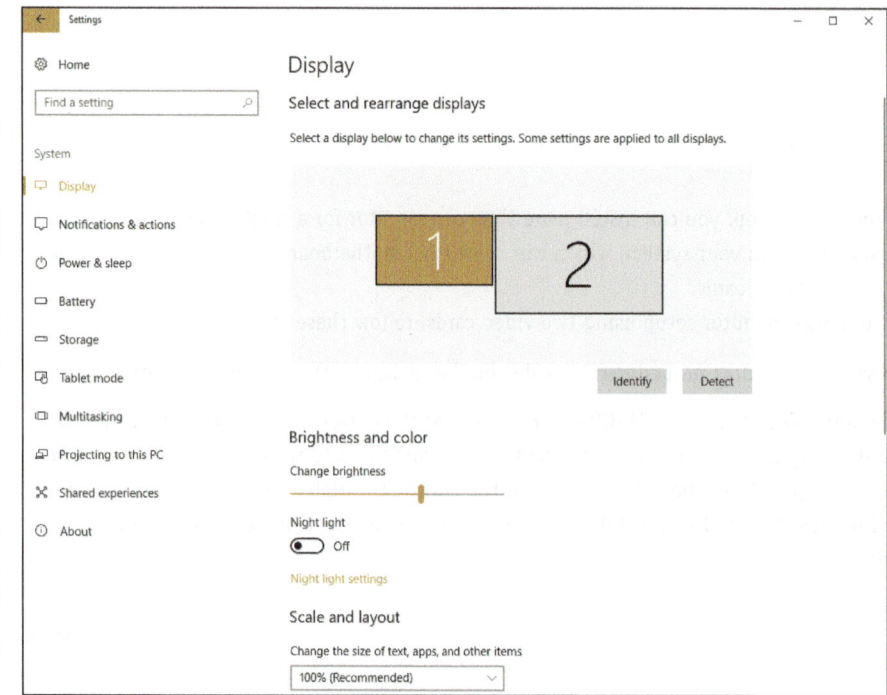

Figure 6-47   Configure each monitor in a dual-monitor configuration

(continues)

> **OS Differences** In Windows 8/7, open **Control Panel** in Classic view, click **Display**, and then click **Adjust resolution**. The Screen Resolution window appears.

2. Notice the two numbered boxes that represent your two monitors. When you click one of these boxes, the settings then apply to the selected monitor, and the screen resolution and orientation (Landscape, Portrait, Landscape flipped, or Portrait flipped) follow the selected monitor. This lets you customize the settings for each monitor separately. If necessary, use drag-and-drop to arrange the boxes so that they represent the physical arrangement of your monitors.

> **Notes** If you see both numbered displays in the same box, the Multiple displays setting is set to Duplicate these displays. To separate the displays, change the Multiple displays setting to **Extend these displays**. Then click **Keep changes**.

> **Notes** In Figure 6-47, if you arrange the two boxes side by side, your extended desktop will extend left or right. If you arrange the two boxes one on top of the other, your extended desktop will extend up and down.

3. Adjust the screen resolution according to your preferences. Most often the highest resolution is the best resolution for the monitor.

4. The Multiple displays setting allows you to select how to handle multiple displays. You can extend your desktop onto the second monitor, duplicate displays, or disable the display on either monitor. To save the settings, click **Keep changes**. The second monitor should initialize and show the extended or duplicated desktop.

5. Close the **Settings** app. For an extended desktop, open an application and verify that you can use the second monitor by dragging the application window over to the second monitor's desktop.

After you add a second monitor to your system, you can move from one monitor to another simply by moving your mouse over the extended desktop. Switching from one monitor to the other does not require any special keystroke or menu option.

Most laptop computers are designed to be used with projectors and provide a VGA, DisplayPort, or HDMI port for this purpose. To use a projector, plug it in to the extra port and then turn it on. For a laptop computer, use a function key to activate the video port and toggle between extending the desktop to the projector, using only the projector, duplicating the screen on the projector, or not using the projector. When giving a presentation, most people prefer to see it duplicated on the LCD screen and the projector.

> **Notes** For group presentations that require a projector, the most common software used is Microsoft PowerPoint. If you configure your projector as a dual monitor, you can use PowerPoint to display a presentation to your audience on the projector at the same time you are using your LCD display to manage your PowerPoint slides. To do so, select the **Slide Show** tab in PowerPoint. In the Set Up group, click **Set Up Slide Show**. In the Set Up Show box under Multiple monitors, check **Show Presenter View** or **Use Presenter View** and click **OK**.

TROUBLESHOOTING I/O DEVICES

> **A+ CORE 1 5.4, 5.5**

A computer usually has so many types of peripheral devices that you'll probably troubleshoot at least one of each at some point in your technical career. When this happens, always try the least invasive and least expensive solutions first. For example, try updating drivers of a graphics tablet before replacing it. Now let's learn how to handle some of the errors or problems you might encounter.

NUMLOCK INDICATOR LIGHT

 A+ CORE 1 5.5
If a user complains she cannot sign in to Windows even when she's certain she is entering the correct password, ask her to make sure the NumLock key is set correctly. Laptops use this key to toggle between the keys interpreted as letters and numbers. Most laptops have a NumLock indicator light near the keyboard.

DEVICE MANAGER

A+ CORE 1 5.4, 5.5
Device Manager is usually a good place to start troubleshooting. A Device Manager window is shown on the left side of Figure 6-48. Click a white arrow to expand the view of an item and click a black arrow to collapse the view. Notice the yellow triangle beside the SM Bus Controller, which indicates a problem with this motherboard component. To see a device's properties box, right-click the device and click **Properties**.

Figure 6-48   Use Device Manager to solve problems with hardware devices

First try updating the drivers. Click **Update Driver** on the General tab or the Driver tab. If a driver update creates a problem, you can roll back (undo) the update if the previous drivers were working. (Windows does not save drivers that were not working before the driver update.) If you are still having a problem with a device, try uninstalling it and installing it again. To uninstall the device, click **Uninstall** on the Driver tab. Then reboot and reinstall the device, looking for problems during the installation that point to the source of the problem. Sometimes reinstalling a device is all that's needed to solve the problem.

If Windows is not able to locate new drivers for a device, locate and download the latest driver files from the manufacturer's website to your hard drive. Be sure to use 64-bit drivers for a 64-bit OS and 32-bit drivers for a 32-bit OS. If possible, use Windows 10 drivers for Windows 10, Windows 8 drivers for Windows 8, and Windows 7 drivers for Windows 7. You can double-click the downloaded driver files to launch the installation.

UPDATE PORT OR SLOT DRIVERS ON A LAPTOP

If you ever have a problem with a port or slot on a laptop, first turn to Device Manager to see if errors are reported and to update the drivers for the port or slot. The laptop manufacturer has probably stored backups of the drivers on the hard drive under support tools and on the recovery media if available. You can also download the latest drivers from the manufacturer's website. If the problem is still not solved after updating the drivers, try using Device Manager to uninstall the port or slot drivers and then use the support tools to reinstall the drivers.

> ✏ **Notes** If a port or slot on a desktop or laptop fails even after updating the drivers, you can install an external device to replace the port or slot. For example, if the network port fails, you can purchase a USB to Ethernet adapter dongle to connect an Ethernet cable to the system using a USB port.

TROUBLESHOOTING VIDEO, MONITORS, AND PROJECTORS

For monitor and video problems, as with other devices, try doing the easy things first. For instance, try to make simple hardware and software adjustments. Many monitor problems are caused by poor cable connections or bad contrast/brightness adjustments. Typical monitor and video problems and how to troubleshoot them are described next, and then you learn how to troubleshoot video problems on laptop computers.

> ✏ **Notes** A user very much appreciates a support technician who takes a little extra time to clean a system being serviced. When servicing a monitor, take the time to clean the screen with a soft, dry cloth or monitor wipe.

PROBLEMS WITH VIDEO CARD INSTALLATIONS

When you install a video card, here is a list of things that can go wrong and what to do about them:

- *When you first power up the system, you hear a whining sound.* This is caused by the card not getting enough power. Make sure a 6-pin or 8-pin power cord is connected to the card if it has this connector. The power supply might be inadequate.
- *When you first start up the system, you see nothing but a black screen.* Most likely this is caused by the onboard video port not being disabled in BIOS/UEFI setup. Disable the port.
- *When you first start up the system, you hear a series of beeps.* BIOS/UEFI cannot detect a video card. Make sure the card is securely seated. The video slot or video card might be bad.
- *Error messages about video appear when Windows starts.* This can be caused by a conflict between onboard video and the video card. Try disabling onboard video in Device Manager.
- *Games crash or lock up.* Try updating drivers for the motherboard, the video card, and the sound card. Also install the latest version of DirectX. Then try uninstalling the game and installing it again. Then download all patches for the game.

MONITOR INDICATOR LIGHT IS NOT ON; NO IMAGE ON SCREEN

If you hear one or no beep during the boot and you see a blank screen, then BIOS/UEFI has successfully completed POST, which includes a test of the video card or onboard video. You can then assume the problem must be with the monitor or the monitor cable. Ask these questions and try these things:

1. Is the monitor power cable plugged in?

2. Is the monitor turned on? Try pushing the power button on the front of the monitor. An indicator light on the front of the monitor should turn on, indicating it has power.

3. Is the monitor cable plugged into the video port at the back of the computer and the connector on the rear of the monitor?

4. Try a different monitor and a different monitor cable that you know are working.

> **Notes** When you turn on your computer, the first thing you see on the screen is the firmware on the video card identifying itself. You can use this information to search the web, especially the manufacturer's website, for troubleshooting information about the card.

MONITOR INDICATOR LIGHT IS ON; NO IMAGE ON SCREEN

For this problem, try the following:

1. Make sure the video cable is securely connected at the computer and the monitor. Most likely the problem is a bad cable connection.

2. If the monitor displays POST but goes blank when Windows starts to load, the problem is Windows and not the monitor or video. Boot from the Windows setup DVD and perform a Startup Repair, which you learned to do in Chapter 4. If this works, change the driver and resolution. Other tools for troubleshooting Windows are covered later in the text.

3. The monitor might have a switch on the back for choosing between 110 volts and 220 volts. Check that the switch is in the correct position.

4. The problem might be with the video card. If you have just installed the card and the motherboard has onboard video, go into BIOS/UEFI setup and disable the video port on the motherboard.

5. Verify that the video cable is connected to the video port on the video card and not to a disabled onboard video port.

6. Using buttons on the front of the monitor, check the contrast adjustment. If there's no change, leave it at a middle setting.

7. Check the brightness or backlight adjustment. If there's no change, leave it at a middle setting.

8. If the monitor-to-computer cable detaches from the monitor, exchange it for a cable you know is good or check the cable for continuity. If this solves the problem, reattach the old cable to verify that the problem was not simply a bad connection.

9. As a test, use a monitor you know is good on the computer you suspect to be bad. If you think the monitor is bad, make sure that it also fails to work on a good computer.

10. Open the computer case and reseat the video card. If possible, move the card to a different expansion slot. Clean the card's edge connectors using a contact cleaner purchased from a computer supply store.

11. If there are socketed chips on the video card, remove the card from the expansion slot and then use a screwdriver to press down firmly on each corner of each socketed chip on the card. Chips sometimes loosen because of temperature changes; this condition is called chip creep.

12. Trade a good video card for the video card you suspect is bad. Test the video card you think is bad on a computer that works. Test a video card you know is good on the computer that you suspect is bad. Whenever possible, do both.

13. Test the RAM on the motherboard with memory diagnostic software.

14. For a motherboard that is using a PCI Express video card, try using a PCI video card in a PCI slot or a PCIe ×1 video card in a PCIe ×1 slot. A good repair technician keeps an extra PCI video card around for this purpose.

15. Trade the motherboard for one you know is good. Sometimes, though rarely, a peripheral chip on the motherboard can cause the problem.

SCREEN GOES BLANK 30 SECONDS OR ONE MINUTE AFTER THE KEYBOARD IS LEFT UNTOUCHED

A Green motherboard (one that follows energy-saving standards) used with an Energy Saver monitor can be configured to go into standby or sleep mode after a period of inactivity. Using this feature can also help prevent burn-in. Burn-in is when a static image stays on a monitor for many hours, leaving a permanent impression of that image on the monitor. An alternate method to avoid burn-in is to use a screen saver that has a moving image or a rotation of varying images. To wake up the computer, press any key on the keyboard or press the power button. Use the Power Options applet in Control Panel to configure the sleep settings on a computer.

> **Notes** Problems might occur if the motherboard power-saving features or the Windows screen saver is turning off the monitor. If the system hangs when you try to get the monitor going again, try disabling one or the other. If this doesn't work, disable both.

POOR DISPLAY

In general, you can solve problems with poor display by using controls on the monitor and using Windows settings. Do the following:

▲ *LCD monitor controls*. Use buttons on the front of an LCD monitor to adjust color, brightness, contrast, focus, and horizontal and vertical positions.

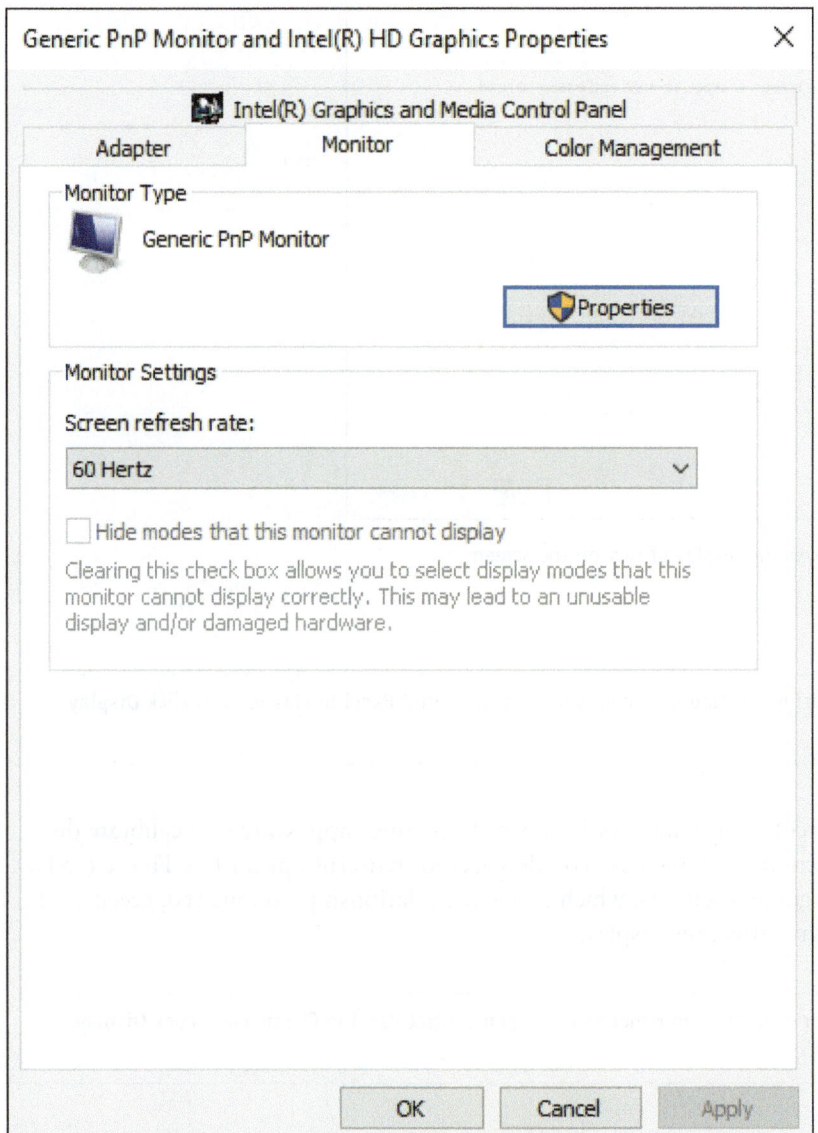

▲ *Windows display settings*. Use Windows settings to adjust font size, refresh rate, screen resolution, brightness, color, and ClearType text. To adjust display settings in Windows 10, right-click the desktop and click **Display settings**. Here are a few settings:

  ▲ *Resolution*. The resolution is the number of horizontal and vertical pixels used to build one screen. In the Resolution drop-down menu, select the highest resolution. If the monitor shows distorted geometry where images are stretched inappropriately, make sure the resolution is set to its highest value. Also, a low resolution can cause oversized images or icons.

  ▲ *Refresh rate*. The refresh rate is the number of times the monitor refreshes the screen in 1 second. To adjust the refresh rate, click **Display adapter properties**. On the Monitor tab, select the highest refresh rate available (see Figure 6-49).

Figure 6-49 Use the highest refresh rate the system supports

> ○ **OS Differences** To open the video properties box in Windows 8/7, use Control Panel to open the **Screen Resolution** window. Click **Advanced settings**. The video properties box appears.

◢ *ClearType*. In Windows 10, open the **Settings** app and open the **System** group to find display settings. To open the ClearType Text Tuner, search on **ClearType** in the search box of the Settings app, select **Adjust ClearType text**, and check **Turn on ClearType** (see Figure 6-50). Then follow the steps in the wizard to improve the quality of text displayed on the screen.

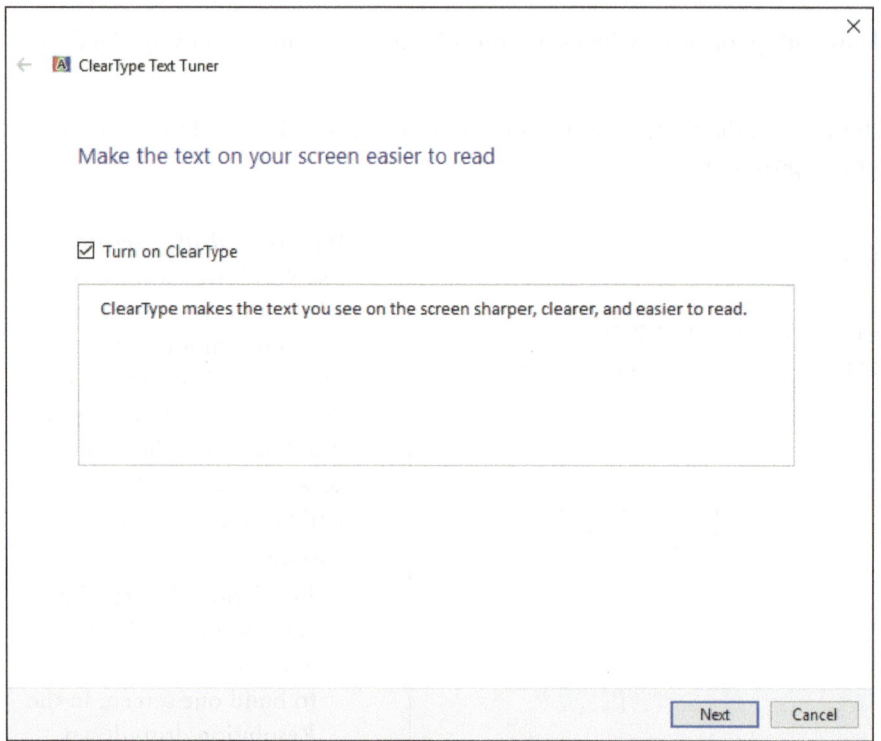

Figure 6-50 ClearType in Windows improves the display of text on the screen

> ○ **OS Differences** To change the ClearType setting in Windows 8/7, open Control Panel in Classic view, click **Display**, and click **Adjust ClearType text**.

◢ *Color calibration*. To calibrate colors in Windows 10, open the Settings app, search on **calibrate display color**, and follow the directions on screen. As you do so, color patterns appear (see Figure 6-51). Use these screens to adjust the gamma settings, which define the relationships among red, green, and blue, as well as other settings that affect the display.

> ○ **OS Differences** To change the color calibration in Windows 8/7, open Control Panel in Classic view, click **Display**, and then click **Calibrate color**.

(A)

(B)

Figure 6-51 Two screens in the Windows 10 color calibration wizard

▲ *Update the video drivers.* The latest video drivers can solve various problems with the video subsystem, including poor display.

🖊 **Notes** If adjusting the resolution doesn't correct distorted geometry or oversized images or icons, try updating the video drivers.

Here are a few other display problems and their solutions:

◢ *Dead pixels*. An LCD monitor might have pixels that are not working. These dead pixels can appear as small white, black, or colored spots on your screen. A black or white pixel is likely to be a broken transistor, which cannot be fixed. Having a few dead pixels on an LCD monitor screen is considered acceptable and usually is not covered under the manufacturer's warranty.

> ✎ **Notes** A pixel might not be a dead pixel (a hardware problem), but only a stuck pixel (a software problem). You might be able to use software to fix stuck pixels. For example, run the online software at *flexcode.org/lcd2.html* to fix stuck pixels. The software works by rapidly changing all the pixels on the screen. (Be aware the screen flashes rapidly during the fix.)

◢ *Dim image*. A laptop computer dims the LCD screen when the computer is running on battery power to conserve the charge. You can brighten the screen using the Windows display settings. In Windows 10, open the **Settings** app, click **System,** and then adjust the brightness slide bar (see Figure 6-47). To check whether settings to conserve power are affecting screen brightness, open **Control Panel** in Classic view and click **Power Options**. Note the power plan that is selected. Click **Change plan settings** for this power plan. On the next screen, you can adjust when or if the screen will dim (see Figure 6-52). If the problem is still not resolved, it might be a hardware problem. How to troubleshoot hardware in laptops is covered later in this chapter.

> ↻ **OS Differences** To adjust the brightness in Windows 8/7, open Control Panel in Classic view, click **Display,** and then click **Adjust brightness**.

Figure 6-52 Change power plan options to affect how or if the screen dims

A dim image in a desktop monitor might be caused by a faulty video card or a faulty monitor. To find out which is the problem, connect a different monitor. If the LCD monitor is the problem, most likely the backlighting is faulty and the monitor needs replacing.

◢ *Artifacts*. Horizontally torn images on screen are called artifacts (see Figure 6-53), and happen when the video feed from the video controller gets out of sync with the refresh of the monitor screen. The problem can be caused by hardware or software. A common cause is when the GPU on the video card overheats.

Figure 6-53 A simulation of horizontal tears on an image, called artifacts

You can test that possibility by downloading and running freeware to monitor the temperature of the CPU and the GPU while you're playing a video game. If you notice the problem occurs when the GPU temperature is high, install extra fans around the video card to keep it cool. Two freeware programs to monitor temperatures are CPU-Z by CPUID (*cpuid.com/softwares/cpu-z.html*) and GPU-Z by TechPowerUp (*techpowerup.com/gpuz*). See Figure 6-54.

> ✎ **Notes** In this text, we've given several options for various freeware utilities. It's a good idea to know about your options for several reasons: Each freeware utility has different options, owners of freeware might not update their utilities in a timely manner, and websites might decide to include adware with their downloads.

TechPowerUp GPU-Z 0.8.4	— □ ✕

Graphics Card	Sensors	Validation	PowerColor Giveaway	📷

GPU Core Clock	▼	600.0 MHz	
GPU Memory Clock	▼	666.7 MHz	
GPU Temperature	▼	34.0 °C	
GPU Power	▼	0.1 W	
GPU Load	▼	2 %	
Memory Usage (Dedicated)	▼	16 MB	
Memory Usage (Dynamic)	▼	52 MB	

☐ Log to file   Sensor refresh rate: 1.0 sec ▼
☑ Continue refreshing this screen while GPU-Z is in the background

Intel(R) HD Graphics 4600 ▼   Close

Source: GPU-Z by TechPowerUp

Figure 6-54 GPU-Z monitors the GPU temperature

Try updating the video drivers. However, if you see artifacts on the screen before Windows loads, then you know the problem is not caused by the drivers. The problem might be caused by the monitor. Try using a different monitor to see if the problem goes away. If it doesn't, replace the monitor.

Overclocking can cause artifacts. Other causes of artifacts are the motherboard or video card going bad, which can happen if the system has been overheating or video RAM on the card is faulty. Try replacing the video card. The power supply also might be the problem.

In general, you can improve video quality by upgrading the video card and/or monitor. Poor display might be caused by inadequate video RAM. Your video card might allow you to install additional video RAM. See the card's documentation.

CANNOT CONNECT TO EXTERNAL MONITOR OR PROJECTOR

If the connection to the external monitor or projector fails when you're setting up dual monitors for a desktop, using a projector for a presentation, or connecting a monitor to a laptop to troubleshoot video problems with the laptop, try the following solutions:

1. Make sure the monitor or projector is getting power. Is the power cord securely connected? Is the electrical outlet working?

2. Check the connection at both ends of the video cable.

3. Is the monitor or projector turned on? For some projectors, a remote control is used to turn on the projector or wake it from sleep mode. The remote control batteries might be dead and need replacing.

4. Use the Function keys on a laptop to toggle between the laptop display and the external monitor or projector. (Alternately, you can press Win+P to toggle between displays.)

5. Try using a different video cable.

6. Try using a different video connection if the laptop and monitor have another option available.

7. If the projector shuts off unexpectedly, it might have entered sleep mode because of inactivity. Press the power button to wake the projector. If you can't wake it, the problem might be overheat shutdown. Allow the projector lamp to cool down. Make sure the air vents are not obstructed and the room temperature is not too hot. The air filters inside the projector might be clogged with dust and need replacing.

APPLYING | CONCEPTS CORRECTING WINDOWS DISPLAY SETTINGS WHEN THE SCREEN IS UNREADABLE

When the display settings don't work, you can easily return to standard VGA settings called VGA mode, which includes a resolution of 640 × 480 or 800 × 600 for some systems.

To use VGA mode when Windows 10/8 is able to boot and you can use at least one monitor, do the following:

1. Press **Win+X** and click **Run**. In the Run box, type **msconfig.exe** and press **Enter**. The System Configuration box appears. Click the **Boot** tab (see Figure 6-55).

2. On the Boot tab, check **Base video** and click **OK**. In the box that appears, click **Restart**. The system will restart in VGA mode. You can now adjust display settings or reinstall video drivers.

3. After you fix any problems with video, open the System Configuration box and click **Normal startup** on the General tab. Then restart Windows.

Figure 6-55 Control how Windows boots

○ **OS Differences** To use VGA mode in Windows 7, reboot the system and press the **F8** key after the first beep. The Advanced Boot Options menu appears. Select **Safe Mode** to boot up with minimal configurations of Windows, which includes standard VGA mode. Alternately, to boot Windows normally and use VGA mode, select **Enable low-resolution video (640 × 480)**. Change the display settings and then restart Windows.

VIDEO SYSTEM IN A LAPTOP

If the LCD panel in a laptop shows a black screen but the power light indicates that power is getting to the system, the video subsystem might be the source of the problem. Do the following:

1. Look for an LCD cutoff switch or button on the laptop (see Figure 6-56). The switch must be on for the LCD panel to work.

LCD cutoff button

Figure 6-56 The LCD cutoff button on a laptop

2. Try to use an onboard video port to connect an external monitor. After you connect the monitor, use a function key to toggle between the LCD panel, the external monitor, and both the panel and monitor. If the external monitor works but the LCD panel does not, try these things using the external monitor:

   ◢ Check Device Manager for warnings about the video controller and to update the video drivers.

   ◢ Check Event Viewer for reported problems or multiple failed jobs in the logs with the video subsystem. You learned about Event Viewer in Chapter 4.

3. If you still can't get the LCD panel to work but the external monitor does work, you have proven the problem is with the LCD panel assembly. In a laptop, a dim screen or no display can be caused by a bad inverter. If replacing the inverter does not help, the next task is to replace the LCD panel. Be aware that the replacement components might cost more than the laptop is worth. Steps to replace the LCD panel in a laptop are covered later in the chapter.

FLICKERING, DIM, OR OTHERWISE POOR VIDEO

Use these tips to solve problems with bad video:

◢ Verify Windows display settings. Try using the highest resolution for the LCD panel. This resolution will be the best available unless the wrong video drivers are installed.

◢ Try adjusting the brightness, which is a function of the backlight component of the LCD panel.

◢ Try updating the video drivers. Download the latest drivers from the laptop manufacturer's website. Bad drivers can cause an occasional ghost cursor on screen. A ghost cursor is a trail left behind when you move the mouse.

◢ If the cursor drifts on the screen when the mouse or touch pad isn't being used, try using a different port on the computer or replacing the batteries in the mouse.

◢ A flickering screen can be caused by bad video drivers, a low refresh rate, a bad inverter, or loose connections inside the laptop. After setting the refresh rate to its highest setting, updating the video drivers, and checking for loose connections, try replacing the inverter.

REPLACE THE LCD PANEL IN A LAPTOP

Because the LCD panel is so fragile, it is one component that is likely to be broken when a laptop is not handled properly. If the LCD display is entirely black, most likely you'll have to replace the entire LCD assembly. However, for a laptop that uses fluorescent backlighting, the problem might be the inverter if the screen is dim but you can make out that some display is present. The inverter board converts DC to the AC used to power the backlighting of the LCD panel (see Figure 6-57). Check with the laptop manufacturer to confirm that it makes sense to first try replacing the relatively inexpensive inverter board before you replace the entire LCD panel assembly. If the entire assembly needs replacing, the cost of the assembly might exceed the value of the laptop.

Figure 6-57   A ThinkPad inverter board

A laptop LCD panel, including the entire cover and hinges, is sometimes considered a single field replaceable unit, and sometimes components within the LCD assembly are considered FRUs. For example, the field replaceable units for the display panel in Figure 6-58 are the LCD front bezel, the hinges, the LCD panel, the

Figure 6-58   Components in an LCD assembly

inverter board, the LCD interface cables, the LCD USB cover, and the rear cover. Also know that an LCD assembly might include a microphone, webcam, and speakers that are embedded in the laptop lid. For other laptops, the microphone and speakers are inside the case. The speakers are considered a field replaceable unit. In addition, a Wi-Fi antenna might be in the lid of the laptop, which is why you should raise the lid if you need a better Wi-Fi signal. When you disassemble the lid, you must disconnect the antenna from the bottom part of the laptop.

Some high-end laptops contain a video card that has embedded video memory. This video card might also need replacing. In most cases, you would replace only the LCD panel and perhaps the inverter board.

Before you begin any disassembly of a laptop, refer to the manufacturer documentation. The following are some general directions to replace an LCD panel:

1. Remove the AC adapter and the battery pack.

2. Remove the upper keyboard bezel, which is the band around the keyboard that holds it in place. You might also need to remove the keyboard.

3. Remove the screws holding the hinge in place and remove the hinge cover. Figure 6-59 shows a laptop with a metal hinge cover, but some laptops use plastic covers that easily break as you remove them. Be careful with the plastic ones.

Figure 6-59 Remove the hinge cover from the laptop hinge

4. Remove the screws holding the LCD panel to the laptop.

5. You're now ready to remove the LCD panel from the laptop. Be aware there might be wires running through the hinge assembly, cables, or a pin connector. Cables might be connected to the motherboard using ZIF connectors. As you remove the LCD top cover, be careful to notice how the panel is connected. Don't pull on wires or cables as you remove the cover, but first carefully disconnect them.

6. Next, remove screws that hold the top cover and LCD panel together. Sometimes, these screws are covered with plastic or rubber circles or pads that match the color of the case. First use a dental pick or small screwdriver to pick off these covers. You should then be able to remove the front bezel and separate the rear cover from the LCD panel. For one LCD panel, you can see the inverter board when you separate the LCD assembly from the lid cover. Figure 6-60 shows the inverter being compared with the new one to make sure they match. The match is not identical but should work.

Figure 6-60 The inverter is exposed and is compared with the new one

7. Disconnect the old inverter and install the new one. When disconnecting the ribbon cable from the old inverter, notice you must first lift up on the lock holding the ZIF connector in place, as shown in Figure 6-61.

8. Install the new inverter. Reassemble the LCD panel assembly. Make sure the assembly is put together with a tight fit so that all screws line up well.

9. Reattach the LCD panel assembly to the laptop.

Figure 6-61 Lift up on the ZIF connector locking mechanism before removing the ribbon cable

CUSTOMIZING COMPUTER SYSTEMS

> **A+**
> **CORE 1**
> **3.8**

Many computer vendors and manufacturers offer to build customized systems to meet specific needs of their customers. As a technical retail associate, you need to know how to recommend computer components that meet your customers' needs. You also might be called on to select and purchase components for a customized system, and perhaps even build this system from parts. In this part of the chapter, we focus on several types of customized systems you might be expected to know how to configure and what parts to consider when configuring these systems.

Here are important principles to keep in mind when customizing a system to meet customer needs:

▲ *Meet applications requirements*. Consider the applications the customer will use and make sure the hardware meets or exceeds the recommended requirements for these applications. Consider any special hardware the applications might require, such as a game controller for gaming or a digital tablet for graphics applications.

▲ *Balance functionality and budget.* When working with a customer's budget, put the most money on the hardware components that are most needed for the primary intended purposes of the system. For example, if you are building a customized gaming PC, a RAID hard drive configuration is not nearly as important as the quality of the video subsystem.

▲ *Consider hardware compatibility.* When selecting hardware, start with the motherboard and processor. Then select other components that are compatible with this motherboard.

Now let's look at the components you need to consider when building the following four types of customized systems: a graphics or CAD/CAM design workstation, an audio and video editing workstation, a gaming PC, and a network attached storage device.

> ★ **A+ Exam Tip** The A+ Core 1 exam might give you a scenario that requires you to customize any of seven types of computers: a graphics or CAD/CAM design workstation, an audio and video editing workstation, a virtualization workstation, a gaming PC, a network attached storage device, a thick client, and a thin client. Four of these types are covered in this chapter, and the other three types are covered in Chapter 10.

GRAPHICS OR CAD/CAM DESIGN WORKSTATION

**A+
CORE 1
3.8**

You might be called on to configure a workstation used for graphics or CAD/CAM (computer-aided design/computer-aided manufacturing). People who use these systems might be an engineer working with CAD software to design bridges, an architect who designs skyscrapers, a graphics designer who creates artistic pages for children's books, or a landscape designer who creates lawn and garden plans. Examples of the applications these professionals might use include AutoCAD by Autodesk (*autodesk.com*) and Adobe Illustrator by Adobe Systems (*adobe.com*).

Graphics-intensive, advanced applications perform complex calculations, use large and complex files, and can benefit from the most powerful of workstations. Because rendering 3D graphics is a requirement, a high-end or ultra-high-end video card is needed. Figure 6-62 shows a high-end, customized CAD workstation from Orbital Computers (*orbitalcomputers.com*).

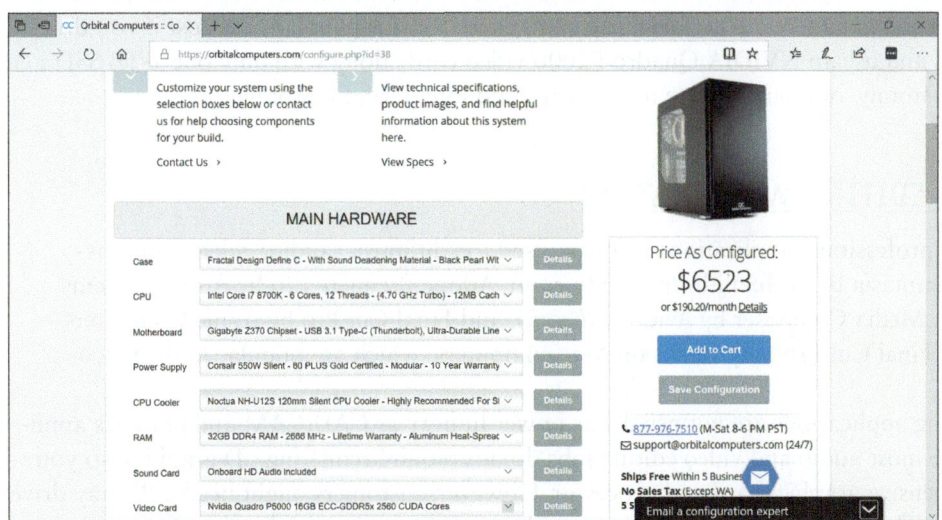

Source: orbitalcomputers.com

Figure 6-62 A high-end CAD workstation customized for maximum performance

Here is a breakdown of the requirements for these high-end workstations:

▲ *Motherboard that provides at least dual channels for memory and plenty of memory slots, and a generous amount of RAM.* In the ad shown in Figure 6-62, the system has 32 GB of installed DDR4 RAM. For best performance, you can install the maximum amount of RAM the board supports.

◢ *Powerful multicore processor with a large CPU cache.* In the ad shown in Figure 6-62, the Intel 8th generation Core i7 processor, which is rated for high-end workstations and low-end servers, has six cores and a 12-MB cache. This processor can handle the high demands of complex calculations performed by advanced software.

◢ *Fast hard drives with plenty of capacity.* Although you can't see them listed in Figure 6-62, the system has two solid-state drives (SSDs) with a total capacity of 2 TB to accommodate large amounts of data. Also consider the speed of the drive interface—recall from Chapter 5 that the fastest current SSD interface for desktop systems is NVMe using PCIe 3.0. (For magnetic hard drives, the fastest standard is SATA3.)

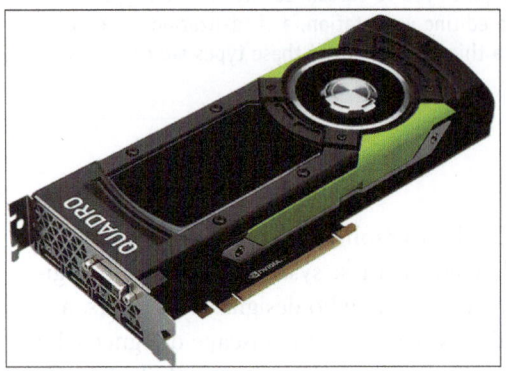

Source: NVIDIA Corporation

Figure 6-63   This high-end precision video card by NVIDIA costs about $1,800

◢ *High-end video card.* To provide the best 3D graphics experience, use a high-end video card that is built more for precision than fast loading. Whereas gaming systems emphasize speed and smooth transitions, CAD/CAM workstations require high-precision graphics for complex 3D images. Two high-end manufacturers for CAD/CAM video cards are NVIDIA (*nvidia.com*) and AMD (*amd. com*). The ad in Figure 6-62 mentions the NVIDIA Quadro P5000 (see Figure 6-63). It uses a PCIe ×16 slot and has 16 GB of GDDR5x video memory using a 256-bit video bus. The card has four HDMI ports and one DVI port. The card alone costs about $1,800 and accounts for a major portion of the total system cost, which is over $6,500.

Wouldn't it be fun to build this system? However, not all graphics workstations need to be this powerful or this expensive. You can still get adequate performance in a system for less than half the cost if you drop the RAM down to 16 GB and use an NVIDIA Quadro P2000 video card, along with only one 1-TB SSD while relying on network storage or cloud storage for backups and long-term file storage.

AUDIO AND VIDEO EDITING WORKSTATION

Examples of professional applications software used to edit music, audio, video, and movies include Camtasia by TechSmith (*techsmith.com*), Adobe Premiere Pro by Adobe Systems (*adobe.com*), Media Composer by Avid (*avid.com*), and Final Cut Pro by Apple Computers (*apple.com*). Final Cut Pro only works on Mac computers, which are popular in the video-editing industry.

Audio- and video-editing applications are not usually as power-hungry as CAD/CAM and graphics applications, primarily because most audio and video editing jobs do not require rendering 3D graphics, so you can get by with a less expensive graphics card and processor. However, customers might need a Blu-ray drive and at least two monitors. The best LCD monitors that provide the most accurate color are LED monitors with a class IPS (in-plane switching) rating. Figure 6-64 shows the specs for one customized video-editing workstation designed by Logical Increments (*logicalincrements.com*).

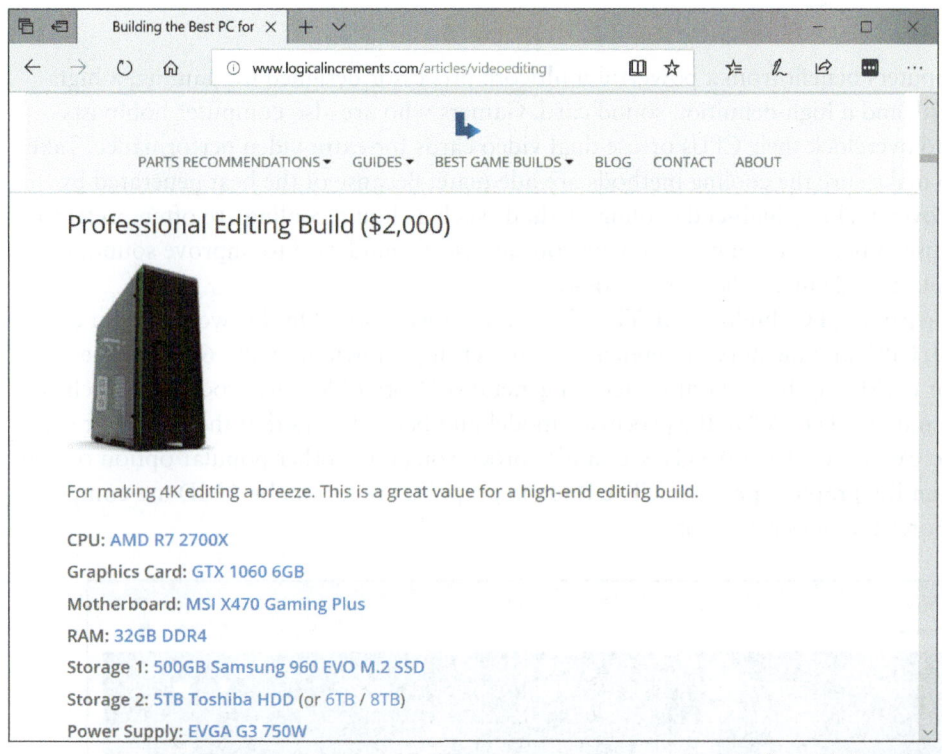

Source: LogicalIncrements.com

Figure 6-64 This mid-range video-editing workstation uses a Core i7 processor and GTX graphics processor

Here is what you need for a mid-range to high-end audio/video editing workstation:

- ◢ *Core i7-equivalent or higher processor.* Both Intel and AMD make high-quality CPUs.
- ◢ *High-end motherboard.* Choose a motherboard that supports at least dual-channel memory running at 1600-MHz RAM speed or higher.
- ◢ *At least 16 GB of RAM.* More is better, and make sure the RAM cards are well-matched and slotted correctly on the motherboard.
- ◢ *Video card with a GeForce GTX graphics processor or better.* GeForce is a family of graphics processors designed by NVIDIA that is not as high-end as the Quadro graphics processors but still yields good video performance. Note that AMD also offers impressive graphics card options. Most users will require dual or triple monitors, so you might need to consider dual video cards for optimum video performance or for more than two simultaneous-use video ports.
- ◢ *Audio card for higher-quality sound output.* One example is the Creative Sound Blaster Zx (*us.creative.com*), which requires a PCIe slot. Before you purchase, research reviews online for highly rated options.
- ◢ *Maximum storage space.* Use one or more large and fast hard drives running at least 7200 RPM with the SATA3 interface, or even better, use SSDs using M.2 slots and the NVMe interface.
- ◢ *Double-sided, dual-layer DVD burner and possibly a Blu-ray burner.* Recall from Chapter 5 that Blu-ray discs come in various standards and can have capacities of 25, 50, 100, or 128 GB. Make sure the Blu-ray burner is rated for the capacity the customer requires.

GAMING PC

Gaming computers benefit from a powerful multicore processor designed for gaming, a high-end video card, and a high-definition sound card. Gamers who are also computer hobbyists might want to overclock their CPUs or use dual video cards for extra video performance. Take extra care to make sure the cooling methods are adequate. Because of the heat generated by multiple video cards and overclocking, high-end cooling methods such as liquid cooling are often preferred. Most gaming computers use onboard surround sound, or you can use a sound card to improve sound. A lighted case with a clear plastic side makes for a great look.

Figure 6-65 shows some gaming PCs built by iBUYPOWER (*ibuypower.com*). On this website, you can adjust the sliders for CPU, GPU, and memory preferences. At the settings shown in Figure 6-65, all the systems use at least 16 GB of RAM and the powerful Intel 8th generation Core i7-8700K processor, which is designed with the gamer in mind. The "K" in the processor model number indicates that the processor can be overclocked. The video cards use a GeForce GTX graphics processor, and another popular option on the website is an AMD Radeon RX graphics processor. The Radeon graphics processors by AMD are comparable to the NVIDIA GeForce graphics processors.

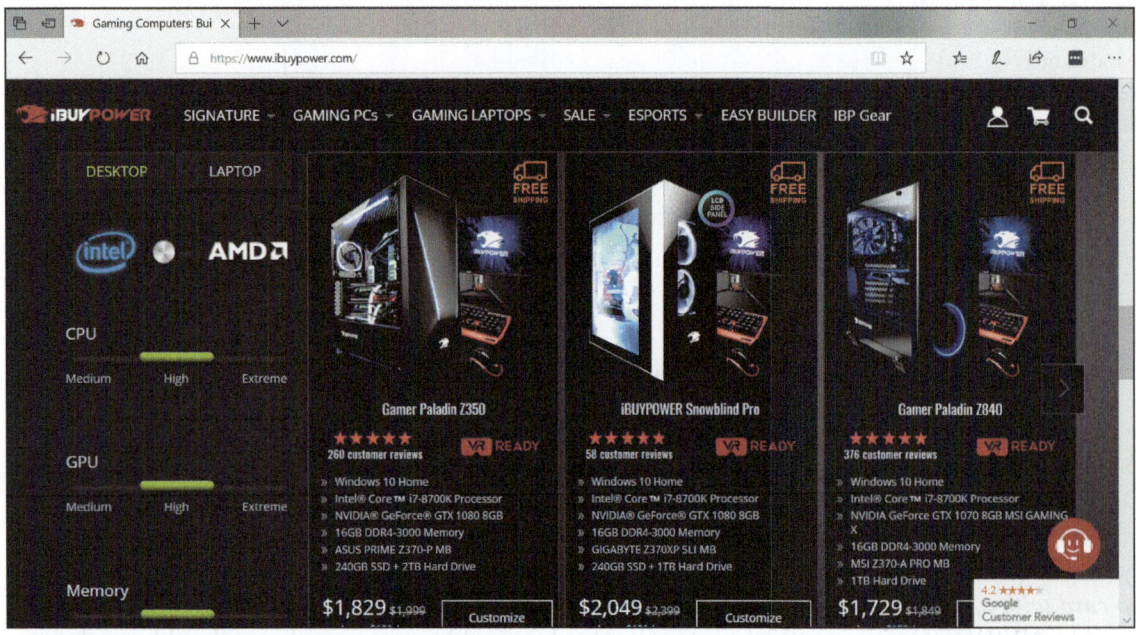

Source: ibuypower.com

Figure 6-65 A group of Intel Core i7 gaming PCs

NAS (NETWORK ATTACHED STORAGE) DEVICE

Recall from Chapter 5 that an NAS (network attached storage) device contains a collection of hard drives providing storage services to a network. This is useful when you have several computers on a small business or home network and want to share files among them or access these files from the Internet. You can use the NAS device to serve up these files and to stream media files and movies to client computers, or you can stream media files to the NAS device for storage, such as a video feed from a security camera. On the small end, My Cloud by WD (*wdc.com*) sells for just over $150 and includes a single 2-, 3-, or 4-TB disk that can be backed up to an external hard drive. A much more capable—and expensive—option is the DiskStation DS1817 by Synology (*synology.com*) shown in Figure 6-66. This NAS device includes eight bays that can each hold a maximum 12-TB drive with many backup and load-balancing configuration options. It also has 8 GB of RAM with the option to add another 8 GB on the dual-channeled motherboard, and the option to add a 10-Gigabit Ethernet network card or dual M.2 SSD adapter cards.

Figure 6-66 An eight-bay NAS device

Source: Synology.com

Here are the features and hardware you need to consider when customizing an NAS device:

▲ ***Processor with moderate power.*** A moderate amount of RAM is sufficient—for example, 6 to 8 GB.

▲ ***RAID array.*** Make sure the motherboard supports hardware RAID and implement RAID on the motherboard to provide fault tolerance and high performance. Use fast hard drives (at least 7200 RPM) or, better yet, SSDs with plenty of storage capacity, accounting for the extra space needed for the RAID implementation you intend to use. Know that some storage drives are designed for energy efficiency by shutting down when not in use; this feature does not work well in RAID systems. Check the NAS device manufacturer's website for a list of compatible storage drives.

▲ ***Appropriately sized chassis.*** Make sure the case has plenty of room for all the storage drives a customer might require.

▲ ***Gigabit NIC.*** Network transfers need to be fast, especially for streaming videos and movies. Make sure the network port is rated for Gigabit Ethernet (1000 Mbps) or, if the network will support it, 10 Gigabit Ethernet. All devices and computers on the LAN should use the same speed.

▲ ***Media streaming capability.*** If you plan to stream media from the NAS device, make sure it supports UPnP/DLNA standards. UPnP is a feature included in many residential and small business routers that helps computers on the network discover and communicate with services provided by other computers. DLNA is a derivative of UPnP that is specific to media streaming services.

>> CHAPTER SUMMARY

Basic Principles for Supporting Devices

▲ Adding new devices to a computer requires installing hardware and software. Even if you generally know how to install an I/O device, always follow the specific instructions of the product manufacturer.

▲ Use Device Manager in Windows to manage hardware devices and to solve problems with them.

▲ Wired data transmission types include USB, eSATA, Thunderbolt, and Lightning. Wireless data transmission types include Wi-Fi, Bluetooth, and NFC.

▲ USB connectors include the A-Male, Micro-A, B-Male, Mini-B, Micro-B, and USB-C.

▲ Popular I/O ports on a desktop or laptop motherboard include eSATA and USB. Older computers sometimes used serial RS-232 ports.

▲ Video ports that a video card or motherboard might provide are VGA, DVI-I, DVI-D, DisplayPort, HDMI, HDMI mini, and multipurpose Thunderbolt ports.

▲ Other peripheral connectors and ports include eSATA, Lightning, BNC, RG-6, RG-59, and RS-232.

Identifying and Installing I/O Peripheral Devices

▲ When installing devices, use 32-bit drivers for a 32-bit OS and 64-bit drivers for a 64-bit OS.

▲ A touch screen is likely to use a USB port. Software is installed to calibrate the touch screen to the monitor screen and receive data input.

◢ Biometric input devices, such as a fingerprint reader, collect biological data and compare it with that recorded about a person to authenticate the person's access to a system.

◢ A KVM switch lets you use one keyboard, monitor, and mouse with multiple computers.

Installing and Configuring Adapter Cards

◢ Generally, when an adapter card is physically installed in a system and Windows starts up, it detects the card and then you install the drivers using the Windows wizard. However, always follow specific instructions from the device manufacturer when installing an adapter card because the order of installing the card and drivers might be different.

◢ A sound card allows you to input audio and use multispeaker systems.

Supporting the Video Subsystem

◢ Types of monitors include LCD and OLED.

◢ Technologies and features of LCD monitors include screen size, refresh rate, pixel pitch, resolution, contrast ratio, viewing angle, backlighting, and connectors that a monitor uses.

◢ Use the Windows 10 Settings app or the Windows 8/7 Screen Resolution window to configure monitor resolution and configure dual monitors.

Troubleshooting I/O Devices

◢ Use Device Manager to update drivers on I/O devices giving trouble.

◢ Video problems can be caused by the monitor, video cable, video card, onboard video, video drivers, or Windows display settings.

◢ To bypass Windows display settings, boot the system to the Advanced Boot Options menu and select Safe Mode or Enable low-resolution video (640 × 480) to enable VGA mode.

◢ A few dead pixels on an LCD monitor screen are considered acceptable by the manufacturer.

◢ Artifacts on the monitor screen can be caused by hardware, software, overheating, or overclocking. Try updating video drivers and checking for high temperatures.

Customizing Computer Systems

◢ As a technician, you might be called on to customize a system for a customer, including a graphics or CAD/CAM workstation, an audio- and video-editing workstation, a gaming PC, and an NAS device.

◢ A high-end video card is a requirement in a graphics, CAD/CAM, or video-editing workstation, or for a gaming PC. These systems also need powerful processors and ample RAM.

>> KEY TERMS

For explanations of key terms, see the Glossary for this text.

artifact			
barcode reader	coaxial cable	digitizer	DVI-I
biometric device	DB-9	digitizing tablet	flat-panel monitor
BNC connector	DB-15	DisplayPort	ghost cursor
burn-in	dead pixel	distorted geometry	graphics tablet
chip reader	Device Manager	DVI-D	HDMI connector

HDMI mini connector
hot-swappable
KVM (Keyboard, Video, and Mouse) switch
LCD (liquid crystal display) monitor
Lightning
magnetic stripe reader
micro USB

Mini DisplayPort
mini-HDMI connector
Mini PCIe
Mini PCI Express
mini USB
OLED (organic light-emitting diode)
overheat shutdown

pixel
projector
RG-6 coaxial cable
RG-59 coaxial cable
RS-232
signature pad
sound card
stylus

tap pay device
Thunderbolt
touch screen
USB 2.0
USB 3.0
USB-C
VGA mode
VR (virtual reality) headset

>> THINKING CRITICALLY

These questions are designed to prepare you for the critical thinking required for the A+ exams and may use content from other chapters and the web.

1. You want to connect an external hard drive for backups. Which is the fastest connection used by current external hard drives? What is the speed?

2. You're working on a server in a server room and need to connect a keyboard. The port available is a 9-pin serial port. What type of port is this?

3. You have a contactless magnetic stripe and chip reader by Square. What type of wireless transmission does the device use to receive encrypted data?

4. Your boss bought a new printer with a USB 3.0 port, and it came with a USB 3.0 cable. Your boss asks you: Will the printer work when I connect the printer's USB cable into a USB 2.0 port on my computer?

   a. No, the printer can only use a USB 3.0 port.

   b. Yes, but at the USB 2.0 speed.

   c. Yes, it will work at the USB 3.0 speed.

   d. Yes, but at the UBS 1.1 speed.

5. What is the easiest way to tell if a USB port on a laptop computer is using the USB 3.0 standard?

6. Your friend Amy calls you asking for help with her new LCD monitor. She says the monitor isn't showing the whole picture. What is the resolution you should recommend for her to use?

7. Your boss has asked you what type of monitor he should use in his new office, which has a wall of windows. He is concerned there will be considerable glare. Which gives less glare, an LED monitor or an OLED monitor?

8. Which Windows utility is most likely the best one to use when uninstalling an expansion card?

9. Would you expect all the devices listed in BIOS/UEFI setup to also be listed in Device Manager? Would you expect all devices listed in Device Manager to also be listed in BIOS/UEFI setup?

10. Why is it best to leave a slot empty between two expansion cards?

11. You're connecting a single speaker to your computer. Which speaker port should you use?

12. What can you do if a port on the motherboard is faulty and a device requires this type of port?

13. What are two screen resolutions that might be used by VGA mode?

14. Which type of drivers must always be certified in order to be installed in Windows?

15. Your desktop computer has DVI and HDMI video ports. If a DVI monitor does not work on your system and yet you know the monitor is good, what is the best solution?

    a. Use a DVI to HDMI adapter to use the current DVI monitor and cable.

    b. Buy a new HDMI monitor to use with the HDMI port.

    c. Install a video card in your computer with a DVI port.

    d. Replace the motherboard with another motherboard that has a DVI port.

16. You plug a new scanner into a USB port on your Windows system. When you first turn on the scanner, what should you expect to see?

    a. A message displayed by the scanner software telling you to reboot your system.

    b. Windows Device Setup launches to install drivers.

    c. Your system automatically reboots.

    d. An error message from the USB controller.

17. You turn on your Windows computer and see the system display POST messages. Then the screen goes blank with no text. Which of the following items could be the source of the problem?

    a. The video card

    b. The monitor

    c. Windows

    d. Microsoft Word software installed on the system

18. You have just installed a new sound card in your system, and Windows says the card installed with no errors. When you plug up the speakers and try to play a music CD, you hear no sound. What is the first thing you should do? The second thing?

    a. Check Device Manager to see if the sound card is recognized and has no errors.

    b. Reinstall Windows.

    c. Use Device Manager to uninstall the sound card.

    d. Identify your sound card by opening the case and looking on the card for the manufacturer and model.

    e. Check the volume controls on the speaker amplifier and in Windows.

    f. Use Device Manager to update the sound card drivers.

19. You have just installed a new DVD drive and its drivers in Windows 10. The drive will read a CD but not a DVD. You decide to reinstall the device drivers. What is the first thing you do?

    a. Open the Settings app and click the System group.

    b. Open Device Manager and choose Update Driver.

    c. Remove the data cable from the DVD drive so Windows will no longer recognize the drive and allow you to reinstall the drivers.

    d. Open Device Manager and uninstall the drive.

20. Match the following ports to the diagrams in Figure 6-67: Dual Link DVI-I, USB Type A, USB Type B, VGA, DisplayPort, Mini DisplayPort, HDMI, and serial RS-232. (Note that some port diagrams are not used.)

Figure 6-67 Identify ports

21. Three hardware priorities for a CAD workstation are a multicore processor, maximum RAM, and a high-end video card. How do each of these components meet the specific demands of this type of computer system?

22. You just received a shipment of two customized computer systems and need to figure out which workstation is the CAD computer and which is the video-editing workstation. While examining the specifications for each, what telltale differences will help you to identify them correctly?

23. Your customer, Mykel, is ordering a custom-built computer for his home office and isn't sure which components should be the highest priority to meet his needs. He's a software developer and runs multiple VMs to test his applications. He also designs some of his own graphics, and he plays online games when he's not working. Which of the following priorities would be most important for Mykel's computer?

    a. High-end graphics card, RAID array, and lots of RAM

    b. High-end CPU, lots of RAM, and high-end graphics card

    c. Multiple hard drives, lots of RAM, and high-end CPU

    d. High-end graphics card, expansion audio card, and lots of RAM

24. Your customer, Maggie, wants to buy a gaming PC, and she specifically mentions that she wants an Intel CPU and intends to overclock the CPU. How can you identify which Intel CPUs are capable of overclocking? What are two other components that must be selected with overclocking in mind?

>> HANDS-ON PROJECTS

Hands-On | Project 6-1 Installing a Device

Install a device on a computer. If you are working in a classroom environment, you can simulate an installation by moving a device from one computer to another. Devices that you might consider installing are a video card, webcam, or fingerprint reader.

Hands-On | Project 6-2   Researching Connection Adapters

Research the web and find devices that can be used as solutions to the following problems. Print or save the webpage showing the device and price:

1. Find an adapter that allows you to connect a DVI port on a computer to an HDMI monitor using a DVI cable.
2. Find an adapter that allows you to connect an Ethernet cable to a USB port on your laptop.
3. Find an adapter that allows you to use a VGA cable to connect a DVI-I port on your desktop to a VGA monitor.

Hands-On | Project 6-3   Updating Device Drivers

Using your home or lab computer connected to the Internet, go to Device Manager and attempt to update the drivers on all your installed devices. Which devices did Windows find newer drivers for?

Hands-On | Project 6-4   Adjusting Windows Display Settings

To practice changing display settings, do the following:

1. Using the Windows 10 Settings app, open the Color Calibration window and calibrate the color displayed on your monitor screen. Using the Windows 10 Settings app, verify that ClearType text is enabled.
2. Try different screen resolutions supported by your monitor. Then verify that the monitor is set to use the highest refresh rate it supports.
3. To view your Windows desktop in VGA mode, use the instructions given earlier to boot to Windows 10/8 Base video or the "Enable low-resolution video (640 × 480)" setting in Windows 7. Then restart Windows and return your system to normal Windows display settings.

Hands-On | Project 6-5   Designing a Customized System

Working with a partner, design a gaming computer, a CAD computer, or a video-editing computer by doing the following:

1. Search the web for a prebuilt system that you like. Print or save the webpage showing the detailed specifications for the system and its price. Which parts in the system do you plan to use for your system? Which parts would you not use or upgrade for your own system?
2. Search the web for the individual parts for your system. Save or print webpages showing all the parts you need to build this computer. Don't forget the case, power supply, motherboard, processor, RAM, hard drive, and other specialized components.
3. Make a list of each part with links to the webpage that shows the part for sale. What is the total cost of all parts?
4. Exchange your list and webpages with your partner and have the partner check your work to make sure that each part is compatible with the entire system and nothing is missing. Do the same for your partner's list of parts.
5. After you are both convinced your lists of parts are compatible and nothing is missing, submit your work to your instructor.

>> REAL PROBLEMS, REAL SOLUTIONS

REAL PROBLEM 6-1 Helping with Upgrade Decisions

Upgrading an existing system can sometimes be a wise thing to do, but sometimes the upgrade costs more than the system is worth. Also, if existing components are old, they might not be compatible with components you want to use for the upgrade. A friend, Renata, asks your advice about several upgrades she is considering. Answer these questions:

1. Renata has a four-year-old desktop computer that has a Core2 Duo processor and 2 GB of memory. It does not have an eSATA port. She wants to use an external hard drive that has an eSATA interface to her computer to back up and store her entertainment media. How would she perform the upgrade, and what is the cost? Save or print webpages to support your answers.

2. Her computer has one USB port, but she wants to use her USB printer at the same time she uses her USB scanner. How can she do this, and how much will it cost? Save or print webpages to support your answers.

3. Renata also uses her Windows 8 computer for gaming and wants to get a better gaming experience. The computer is using onboard video and has an empty PCI Express video slot. What is the fastest and best graphics card she can buy? How much does it cost? Save or print webpages to support your answer.

4. What is the total cost of all the upgrades Renata wants? Do you think it is wise for her to make these upgrades or would it be wiser to purchase a new system? How would you explain your recommendation to her?

REAL PROBLEM 6-2 Using Input Director

Input Director is software that lets you use one keyboard and mouse to control two or more computers that are networked together. You can download the free software from *inputdirector.com*. To use the software, you need to know the host name of each computer that will share the keyboard and mouse. To find out the host name in Windows 10/8, right-click **Start** and select **System**. In Windows 7, right-click **Computer** and select **Properties**. The host name is listed as the PC or Computer name.

Working with a partner, download and install Input Director and configure it so that you and your partner are using the same keyboard and mouse for your computers.

REAL PROBLEM 6-3 Researching a Computer Ad

Pick a current website or magazine ad for a complete, working desktop computer system, including computer, monitor, keyboard, and software, together with extra devices such as a mouse or printer. Research the details of the ad and write a two- to four-page report describing and explaining these details. This project provides a good opportunity to learn about the latest offerings on the market as well as current pricing.

REAL PROBLEM 6-4 Working with a Monitor

Do the following to practice changing monitor settings and troubleshooting monitor problems:

1. Practice changing the display settings, including the wallpaper, screen saver, and appearance. If you are not using your own computer, be sure to restore each setting after making changes.

2. Change the monitor resolution. Try several resolutions. Make a change and then make the change permanent. You can go back and adjust it later if you want.

3. Work with a partner who is using a different computer. Unplug the monitor in the computer lab or classroom, loosen or disconnect the computer monitor cable, or turn the contrast and brightness all

the way down while your partner does something similar to the other computer. Trade computers and troubleshoot the problems.

4. Wear an ESD strap. Turn off the computer, press the power button, remove the case cover, and loosen the video card. Turn on the computer and write down the problem as a user would describe it. Turn off the computer, reseat the card, and verify that everything works.

5. Turn off your system. Insert into the system a defective video card provided by your instructor. Turn on the system. Describe the resulting problem in writing, as a user would.

REAL PROBLEM 6-5 Starting Windows 10 in VGA Mode

Suppose the user has selected a combination of foreground and background colors that makes it impossible to read the screen and correct the display settings. Practice correcting the problem by booting Windows 10 into Safe Mode, which loads VGA mode with basic display settings:

1. Shut down your Windows 10 computer and reboot. When you get to the Windows sign-in screen, hold down the **Shift key** and press the power icon and **Restart**.

2. On the Choose an Option screen, click **Troubleshoot**. Then click **Advanced options** and click **Startup Settings**. On the Startup Settings screen, click **Restart**.

3. A list of options appears. Type **3** to select *Enable low-resolution video*.

4. When the system restarts, you can correct display settings and restart Windows normally.

Setting Up a Local Network

After completing this chapter, you will be able to:

• Describe network types and the Internet connections they use

• Connect a computer to a wired or wireless network

• Configure and secure a multifunction router on a local network

• Troubleshoot network connections using the command line

In this chapter, you learn about the types of networks and the technologies used to build networks. You also learn to connect a computer to a network and how to set up and secure a small wired or wireless network.

This chapter prepares you to assume total responsibility for supporting both wired and wireless networks in a small office/home office (SOHO) environment. Later, you'll learn more about the hardware used in networking, including network devices, connectors, cabling, networking tools, and the types of networks used for Internet connections. Let's get started by looking at the types of networks you might encounter as an IT support technician and the types of connections they might use to connect to the Internet.

★ **A+ Exam Tip** Much of the content in this chapter applies to both the A+ Core 1 220-1001 exam and the A+ Core 2 220-1002 exam.

TYPES OF NETWORKS AND NETWORK CONNECTIONS

A+
CORE 1
2.2, 2.3,
2.4, 2.7

A computer network is created when two or more computers can communicate with each other. Networks can be categorized by several methods, including the technology used and the size of the network. When networks are categorized by their size or physical area they cover, these are the categories used, listed from smallest to largest:

A+
CORE 2
1.8

▲ *PAN.* A PAN (personal area network) consists of personal devices such as cell phones and laptop computers communicating at close range. PANs can use wired connections (such as USB or Lightning) or wireless connections (such as Bluetooth or Wi-Fi, also called 802.11).

▲ *LAN.* A LAN (local area network) covers a small local area, such as a home, office, or a small group of buildings. LANs can use wired (most likely Ethernet) or wireless technologies (most likely Wi-Fi). A LAN allows workstations, servers, printers, and other devices to communicate and share resources.

▲ *WMN.* A WMN (wireless mesh network) consists of many wireless devices communicating directly with each other rather than through a single, central device. Some or all of the devices on the WMN can serve as connection points for other devices to communicate across longer distances. This technology is commonly used in IoT (Internet of Things) wireless networks, where many types of devices, such as thermostats, light switches, door locks, and security cameras, are connected to the network and on to the Internet.

▲ *MAN.* A MAN (metropolitan area network) covers multiple buildings in a large campus or a portion of a city, such as a downtown area. It's usually the result of a cooperative effort to improve service to its users. Network technologies used can be wireless (most likely LTE) and/or wired (for example, Ethernet with fiber-optic cabling).

▲ *WAN.* A WAN (wide area network) covers a large geographical area and is made up of many smaller networks. The best-known WAN is the Internet. Some technologies that connect a single computer or LAN to the Internet include DSL, cable Internet, satellite, cellular WAN, and fiber optic.

★ **A+ Exam Tip** The A+ Core 1 exam expects you to be able to compare LAN, WAN, PAN, MAN, and WMN networks.

Now let's look at network technologies used for Internet connections.

INTERNET CONNECTION TECHNOLOGIES

A+
CORE 1
2.2, 2.3,
2.4, 2.7

A+
CORE 2
1.8

To connect to the Internet, a device or a network first connects to an Internet service provider (ISP), such as Xfinity or Spectrum. The most common types of connections for SOHO networks are DSL and cable Internet (commonly called cable or cable modem). See Figure 7-1. When connecting to an ISP, know that upload speeds are generally slower than download speeds. These rates differ because users typically download more data than they upload. Therefore, an ISP devotes more of the available bandwidth to downloading and less of it to uploading.

Figure 7-1 An ISP stands between a LAN and the Internet

Networks are built using one or more technologies that provide varying degrees of bandwidth. Bandwidth is the theoretical number of bits that can be transmitted over a network connection at one time, similar to the number of lanes on a highway. The networking industry refers to bandwidth as a measure of the maximum rate of data transmission in bits per second (bps), thousands of bits per second (Kbps), millions of bits per second (Mbps), or billions of bits per second (Gbps). Bandwidth is the theoretical or potential speed of a network, whereas data throughput is the average of the actual speed. In practice, network transmissions experience delays, called latency, that result in slower network performance. For example, wired signals traveling across long cables or wireless signals crossing long distances through the air can cause signal strength degradation, resulting in latency. Latency is measured by the round-trip time it takes for a message to travel from source to destination and back to source.

Table 7-1 lists network technologies used by local networks to connect to the Internet. The table is more or less ordered from slowest to fastest maximum bandwidth within each category, although latency can affect the actual bandwidth of any particular network. We'll explore each of these technologies in more depth throughout this chapter.

Technology (Wireless or Wired)	Maximum Speed	Description
Wireless Internet connection: Satellite and WiMAX		
Satellite	Up to 15 Mbps	Requires a dish to send to and receive from a satellite, which is in a relative fixed position with the Earth.
WiMAX	Up to 30 Mbps	Requires a transmitter to send to and receive from a WiMAX tower up to 30 miles away. WiMAX was once popular in rural areas for wireless Internet connections, but it is losing this market space to cellular solutions such as LTE.
Wireless Internet connection: Cellular		
3G cellular (third-generation cellular)	At least 200 Kbps, but can be up to 4 Mbps	Improved over earlier technologies and allows for transmitting data and video. Uses either CDMA or GSM mobile phone services. Speeds vary widely according to the revision standards used.
4G cellular (fourth-generation cellular)	100 Mbps to 1 Gbps	Higher speeds are achieved when the mobile device stays in a fixed position. A 4G network typically uses LTE (Long Term Evolution) technology.
5G cellular (fifth-generation cellular)	10–50 Gbps and beyond	At the time of this writing, 5G devices are expected on the market as soon as 2019 with more widespread use beginning in 2020, and additional improvements to the technology in later years.
Wired Internet connection: Telephone		
Dial-up or regular telephone (POTS, for plain old telephone service)	Up to 56 Kbps	Slow access to an ISP using a modem and dial-up connection over phone lines.
ISDN	64 Kbps or 128 Kbps	ISDN (Integrated Services Digital Network) is an outdated business-use connection to an ISP over dial-up phone lines.
SDSL (Symmetric Digital Subscriber Line)	Up to 22 Mbps	Equal bandwidth in both directions. SDSL is a type of broadband technology. (Broadband refers to a networking technology that carries more than one type of signal on the same cabling infrastructure, such as DSL and telephone or cable Internet and TV.) DSL uses regular phone lines and is an always-up or always-on connection that does not require a dial-up.
ADSL (Asymmetric DSL)	640 Kbps upstream and up to 24 Mbps downstream	Most bandwidth is allocated for data coming from the ISP to the user. Slower versions of ADSL are called ADSL Lite or DSL Lite. ISP customers pay according to a bandwidth scale.
VDSL (very-high-bit-rate DSL)	Up to 70 Mbps	A type of asymmetric DSL that works only over a short distance.

Table 7-1 Networking technologies (continues)

Technology (Wireless or Wired)	Maximum Speed	Description
Other wired Internet connections		
Cable Internet	Up to 160 Mbps, depending on the type of cable	Connects a home or small business to an ISP, usually comes with a cable television subscription, and shares cable TV lines. If available, fiber-optic cable gives highest speeds.
Dedicated line using fiber optic	Up to 43 Tbps	Dedicated fiber-optic line from ISP to business or home. Speeds vary widely with price.
Wired local network: Ethernet		
Fast Ethernet (100BaseT)	100 Mbps	Used for local networks.
Gigabit Ethernet (1000BaseT)	1000 Mbps or 1 Gbps	Fastest Ethernet standard for small, local networks.
10-Gigabit Ethernet (10GBaseT)	10 Gbps	Typically requires fiber media, is mostly used on the backbone of larger enterprise networks, and can also be used on WAN connections.
Wireless local network: Wi-Fi		
802.11a	Up to 54 Mbps	No longer used.
802.11b	Up to 11 Mbps	Experiences interference from cordless phones and microwaves.
802.11g	Up to 54 Mbps	Compatible with and has replaced 802.11b.
802.11n	Up to 600 Mbps	Uses multiple input/multiple output (MIMO), which means an access point can have up to four antennas to improve performance.
802.11ac	Theoretically up to 7 Gbps, but currently at 1.3 Gbps	Supports up to eight antennas and supports beamforming, which detects the locations of connected devices and increases signal strength in those directions.
802.11ad	Up to 7 Gbps	This throughput can only be achieved when the device is within 3.3 m of the access point.

Table 7-1   Networking technologies (continued)

> ✎ **Notes**   Pending Wi-Fi standards include 802.11 ax, which is designed to improve performance in highly populated areas, and 802.11 ay, which is expected to achieve maximum throughput of 20 Gbps and extend the range of 802.11 ad. Approval of both standards is expected in 2019.

Currently, cable Internet and DSL are the two most popular ways to make an Internet connection for a home network. Let's first compare these two technologies and then we'll look at fiber-optic dedicated lines, satellite, dial-up, and cellular WAN connections.

> ★ **A+ Exam Tip**   The A+ Core 1 exam expects you to be able to compare these network types used for Internet connections: cable, DSL, dial-up, fiber, satellite, ISDN, and cellular (tethering and mobile hotspot).

COMPARE CABLE INTERNET AND DSL

Here are the important facts about cable Internet and DSL:

▲ **Cable Internet** is a broadband technology that uses cable TV lines and is always connected (always up). With cable Internet, the TV signal to your television and the data signals to your computer or LAN share the same **coaxial (coax) cable**, an older cable form that is rarely used today in a local area network. The **cable modem** converts a computer's digital signals to analog when sending them and converts incoming analog data to digital.

▲ **DSL (Digital Subscriber Line)** is a group of broadband technologies that covers a wide range of speeds. DSL uses ordinary copper phone lines and a range of frequencies on the copper wire that are not used by voice, making it possible for you to use the same phone line for voice and DSL at the same time. When you make a regular phone call, you dial in as usual. However, the DSL part of the line is always connected (always up) for most DSL services.

When deciding between cable Internet and DSL, consider these points:

▲ Both cable Internet and DSL can sometimes be purchased on a sliding scale, depending on the bandwidth you want to buy. Subscriptions offer residential and more expensive business plans. Business plans are likely to have increased bandwidth and better support when problems arise.

▲ With cable Internet, you share the TV cable infrastructure with your neighbors, which can result in service becoming degraded if many people in your neighborhood are using cable Internet at the same time. With DSL, you're using a dedicated phone line, so your neighbors' surfing habits are not important.

▲ With DSL, static over phone lines in your house can be a problem. The DSL company provides filters to install at each phone jack (see Figure 7-2), but still the problem might not be fully solved. Also, your phone line must qualify for DSL; some lines are too dirty (too much static or noise) to support DSL. Figure 7-3 shows a **DSL modem** that can connect directly to a computer or to a router on your network.

Figure 7-2 When DSL is used in your home, filters are needed on every phone jack except the one used by the DSL modem

Figure 7-3 This DSL modem connects to a phone jack and a computer or router to provide a broadband connection to an ISP

▲ Both cable and DSL connections typically require a modem device at the entry to your SOHO network. Although you might be able to find the modem's default login instructions online, you'll likely never have to change any settings on the modem itself. Configuring a DSL or cable modem consists of plugging the correct cables into the correct ports. For example, Figure 7-4 shows a cable modem with the ISP cable connected on the right. The yellow Ethernet cable connects to the local network, and a phone line is plugged into the Voice-over-IP (VoIP) phone service provided by the ISP over the Internet. Also notice the Reset button in the figure, which you can use to reset a modem to its factory default settings. When troubleshooting a modem, try rebooting it first, and only use the reset as a last resort.

Figure 7-4 Use a cable modem to connect the ISP's coaxial cable to the LAN's Ethernet cable

DEDICATED LINE USING FIBER OPTIC

Another broadband technology used for Internet access is fiber optic. The technology connects a dedicated line from your ISP to your place of business or residence. This dedicated line is called a point-to-point (PTP) connection because no other business or residence shares the line with you. Television, Internet data, and voice communication all share the broadband fiber-optic cable, which reaches all the way from the ISP to your home. Alternatively, the provider might install fiber-optic cabling up to your neighborhood and then run coaxial cable (similar to that used in cable Internet connections) for the last leg of the connection to your business or residence. Upstream and downstream speeds and prices vary.

SATELLITE

People who live in remote areas and want high-speed Internet connections often have limited choices. DSL and cable options might not be available where they live, but satellite access is available from pretty much anywhere. Internet access by satellite is available even on airplanes. Passengers can connect to the Internet using a wireless hotspot and satellite dish on the plane. A satellite dish mounted on top of your house or office building communicates with a satellite used by an ISP offering the satellite service (see Figure 7-5). One disadvantage of satellite is that it requires line-of-sight wireless connectivity without obstruction from mountains, trees, and tall buildings. Another disadvantage is that it experiences higher delays in transmission (called latency), especially when uploading, and is therefore not a good solution for an Internet connection that will be used for videoconferencing or voice over Internet.

Figure 7-5 Communication by satellite can include television and Internet access

DIAL-UP

Of all the types of networking connections, dial-up or POTS (plain old telephone service) is the least expensive and slowest connection to the Internet. Dial-up connections are painfully slow, but you might still need them when traveling, and they're good at home when your broadband connection is down.

CELLULAR WAN

A **wireless wide area network (WWAN)**, also called a **cellular network** or cellular WAN because it consists of cells, is provided by companies such as Verizon and AT&T. Each cell is controlled by a base station (see Figure 7-6), which might include more than one transceiver and antenna on the same tower to support various technologies for both voice and data transmission. Two established cellular technologies are GSM (Global System for Mobile Communications) and CDMA (Code Division Multiple Access). In the United States, Sprint and Verizon use CDMA, while AT&T and T-Mobile—along with most of the rest of the world—use GSM. **Long Term Evolution (LTE)** and Voice over LTE (VoLTE) provide both data and voice transmissions and are expected to ultimately replace both GSM and CDMA.

Figure 7-6 A cellular WAN is made up of many cells that provide coverage over a wide area

Cellular devices that use GSM or LTE require a **SIM (Subscriber Identification Module) card** to be installed in the device; the card contains the information that identifies your device to the carrier (see Figure 7-7). CDMA networks don't require SIM cards unless they also use LTE. Most carriers today use a combination of GSM and LTE or CDMA and LTE.

Installed SIM card

Figure 7-7 A SIM card contains proof that your device can use a cellular network

Most smartphones are linked by the manufacturer to a specific cellular provider and will need to be validated on that provider's network to connect to it. To connect a computer using mobile broadband to a cellular network, you need the hardware and software to connect and, for most networks, a SIM card. Here are your options for software and hardware devices that can connect to a cellular network, and general steps for how to create each connection. Keep in mind that when you purchase any of these devices from a carrier or manufacturer, detailed instructions are most likely included for connecting to the cellular network.

▲ *Embedded mobile broadband modem.* A laptop or other mobile device might have an embedded broadband modem. In this situation, you still need to subscribe to a carrier. If a SIM card is required, insert the card in the device. For some laptops, the card slot might be in the battery bay, and you must remove the battery to find the slot. Then use a setting or application installed on the device to connect to the cellular network.

Figure 7-8 Tether your laptop to your cell phone using a USB cable

▲ *Cell phone tethering.* You can tether your computer or another device to your cell phone. The cell phone connects to the cellular network and provides communication to the tethered device. To use your phone for tethering, your carrier contract must allow it. The phone and other device can connect by way of a USB cable (see Figure 7-8), a proprietary cable provided by your cell phone manufacturer, or a Bluetooth or Wi-Fi wireless connection. Your carrier is likely to provide you software to make the connection, or the setting might be embedded in the phone's OS. If software is provided, install the software first and then use the software to make the connection. Otherwise, enable the tether in your phone's OS.

▲ *USB broadband modem.* For any computer, you can use a USB broadband modem (sometimes called an air card), such as the one shown in Figure 7-9. The device requires a contract with a cellular carrier. If needed when using a USB broadband modem, insert the SIM card in the modem (see Figure 7-10). When you insert the modem into a USB port, Windows finds the device, and the software stored on the device automatically installs and runs. A window provided by the software then appears and allows you to connect to the cellular network.

LED light indicates power

LED light indicates network activity

Figure 7-9 A USB broadband modem by Sierra Wireless

Slot for SIM card

Remove the back cover to reveal the SIM card

Figure 7-10 A SIM card with subscription information on it might be required to use a cellular network

▲ *LTE installed Internet.* Some cellular companies offer home Internet service through their cellular WAN infrastructure. Verizon calls its service LTE Internet Installed, and AT&T calls its service FWI (Fixed Wireless Internet). The ISP installs an LTE router at the home, possibly with an external antenna, which then connects wirelessly to the ISP's cellular network. The router provides a Wi-Fi hotspot as well as a few Ethernet ports for wired devices. Typically, the router can't be moved to other locations like a smartphone can—it's designed to be used only at the location where the subscription is established. Data usage caps also may apply.

▲ *Mobile hotspot.* Some mobile devices can create a mobile hotspot that computers and other mobile devices can connect by Wi-Fi to your device and on to the Internet. Some cellular ISPs, such as AT&T, also offer devices dedicated to this purpose.

Now that you understand some basics about the different types of networks and methods of connecting those networks to the Internet, you're ready to learn about different ways to connect computers to local networks.

CONNECTING A COMPUTER TO A LOCAL NETWORK

A+
CORE 1
2.2, 2.3,
2.6, 3.2

Connecting a laptop or desktop computer to a network is quick and easy in most situations. Here, we begin with a summary of how to connect to a wired or wireless network, and then you learn how to connect to a VPN. (In Chapter 9, you learn how to connect smartphones and tablets to networks.)

A+
CORE 2
1.8

★ **A+ Exam Tip** The A+ Core 2 exam expects you to know which type of network connection (VPN, wired, wireless, cellular, or dial-up) is appropriate for a given scenario and to know how to make the connection.

CONNECTING TO AN ETHERNET WIRED OR WI-FI WIRELESS LOCAL NETWORK

A+
CORE 1
2.3, 3.2

To connect a computer to a network using an Ethernet wired or Wi-Fi wireless connection, follow these steps:

A+
CORE 2
1.8

1. In general, before you connect to any network, the network adapter and its drivers must be installed and Device Manager should report no errors.

2. Do one of the following to connect to the network:

   ▲ For a wired network, plug in the network cable to the Ethernet port. The port is also called an RJ-45 port and looks like a large phone jack. An RJ-45 connector looks similar to an RJ-11 connector, only larger (see Figure 7-11). Indicator lights near the network port should light up to indicate connectivity and activity. For Ethernet, Windows should automatically configure the connection.

   ▲ For a wireless network, click the **Network** icon in the taskbar on the desktop and select a wireless network. Click **Connect**. If the network is secured, you must enter the security key to the wireless network to connect.

3. If this is the first time you've connected to a local network, you'll be asked if you want to make the PC discoverable. For private networks (such as your home or business), click **Yes**, and for public networks (such as a coffee shop hotspot), click **No**.

Figure 7-11 RJ-45 and RJ-11 connectors

> ✏ **Notes** For a private corporate or enterprise network, Windows Server or Microsoft Azure is likely to manage access to the network using a Windows domain. You must sign in to the Windows domain with a user name and password. Press **Ctrl+Alt+Del** to access the sign-on screen. The user name might be text such as Jane Smith or an email address such as *JSmith@mycompany.com*. You learn more about private networks, public networks, and Windows domains in Chapter 11.

4. Open your browser and make sure you can access the web. For wireless connections, some hotspots provide an initial page called a captive portal, where you must enter a code or agree to the terms of use before you can use the network. On a private network, open File Explorer or Windows Explorer and drill down into the Network group to verify that network resources are available (see Figure 7-12).

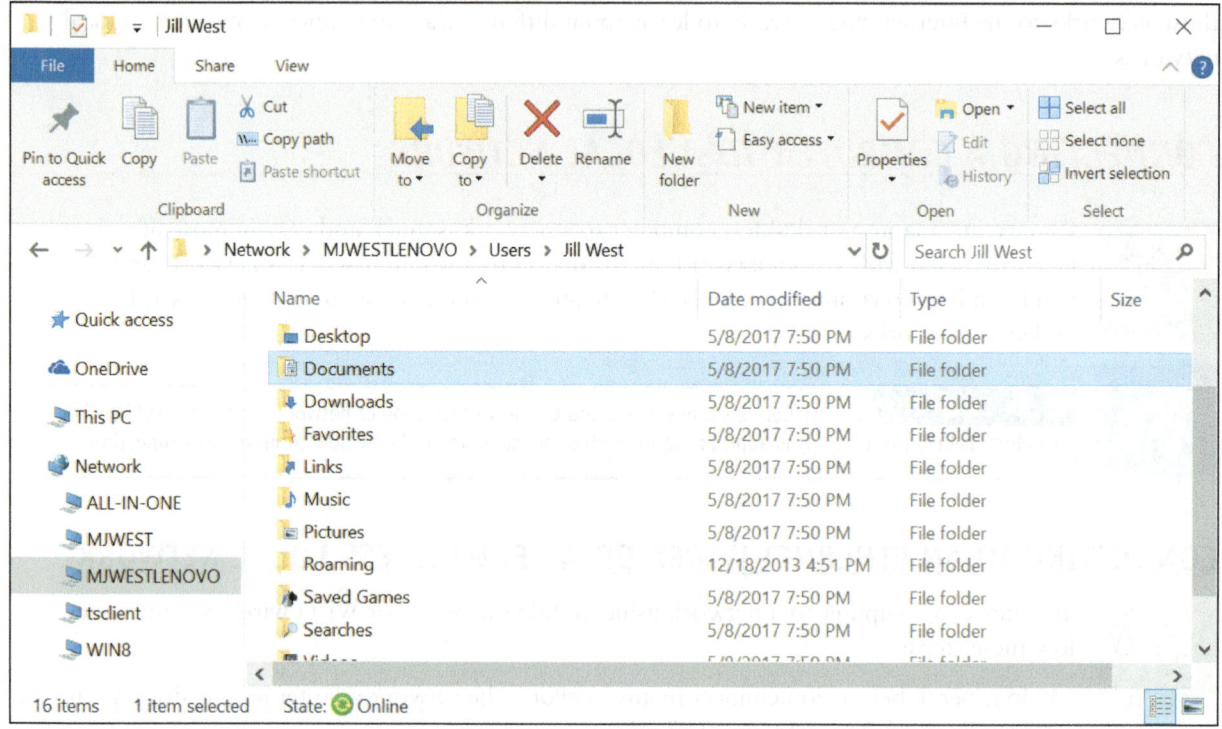

Figure 7-12 File Explorer shows resources on the network

To view and change network security settings in Windows 10, open the Settings app and click **Network & Internet**. Click **Change connection properties**, and then select either **Public** or **Private**.

> ↻ **OS Differences** To verify or change security settings in Windows 8, click the **Settings** charm and click **Change PC settings**. On the PC settings screen, click **Network**. On the Network screen, if necessary, click **Connections**. To set the network security to Private, turn on **Find devices and content**. To set the network security to Public, turn this setting off.
>
> In Windows 7, open the **Network and Sharing Center** window. If the network location is **Home network** or **Work network**, click it. The Set Network Location box appears. Select a network type and click **Close**.

For wireless connections, you can view the status of the connection, including the security key used to make the connection. Do the following:

1. Open **Control Panel** and open the **Network and Sharing Center**. Alternately, you can right-click the **Network** icon in the desktop taskbar in Windows 10 and click **Open Network & Internet settings**, which opens the Network & Internet group in the Settings app. In Windows 8/7, click **Open Network**

and Sharing Center. In the Network and Sharing Center (see Figure 7-13), click Change adapter settings, or in the Network & Internet window, click Change adapter options. The Network Connections window appears (see Figure 7-14).

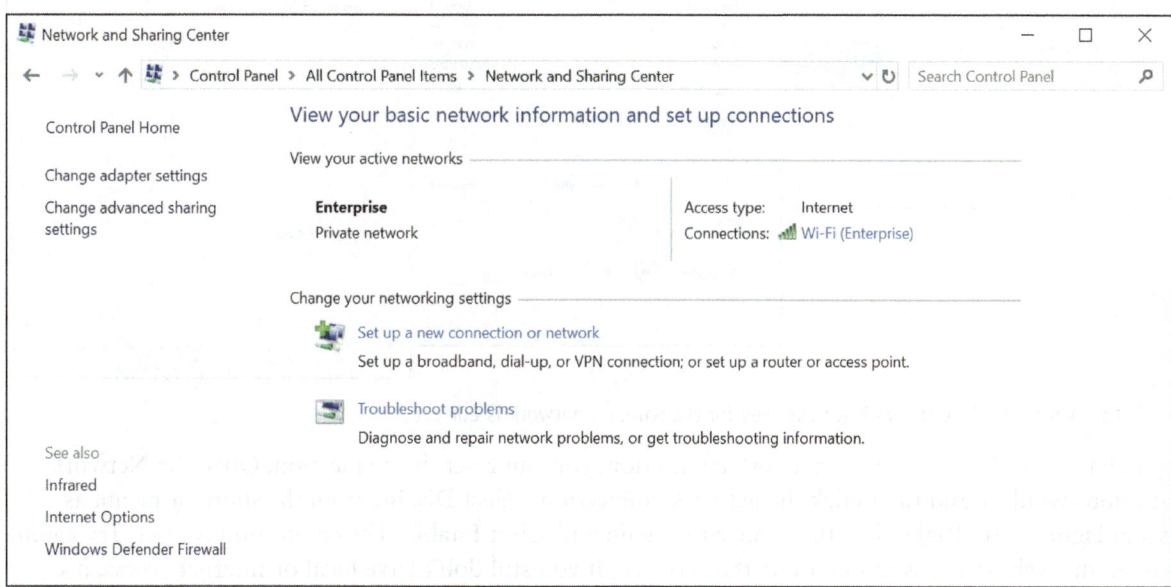

Figure 7-13 The Network and Sharing Center reports a healthy wireless network connection

Figure 7-14 The Network Connections window can be used to repair broken connections

> **Notes** For Windows 10, a shortcut to open the Network & Internet window in the Settings app is to press **Win+X** and click **Network Connections**. For Windows 8, the same shortcut will open the Network Connections window.

2. In the Network Connections window, right-click the **Wi-Fi** connection and click **Status**. In the Wi-Fi Status box (see Figure 7-15), click **Wireless Properties**. In the Wireless Network Properties box, select the **Security** tab. To view the security key, check **Show characters**. You can also see the security and encryption types that Windows automatically detected and applied when it made the connection.

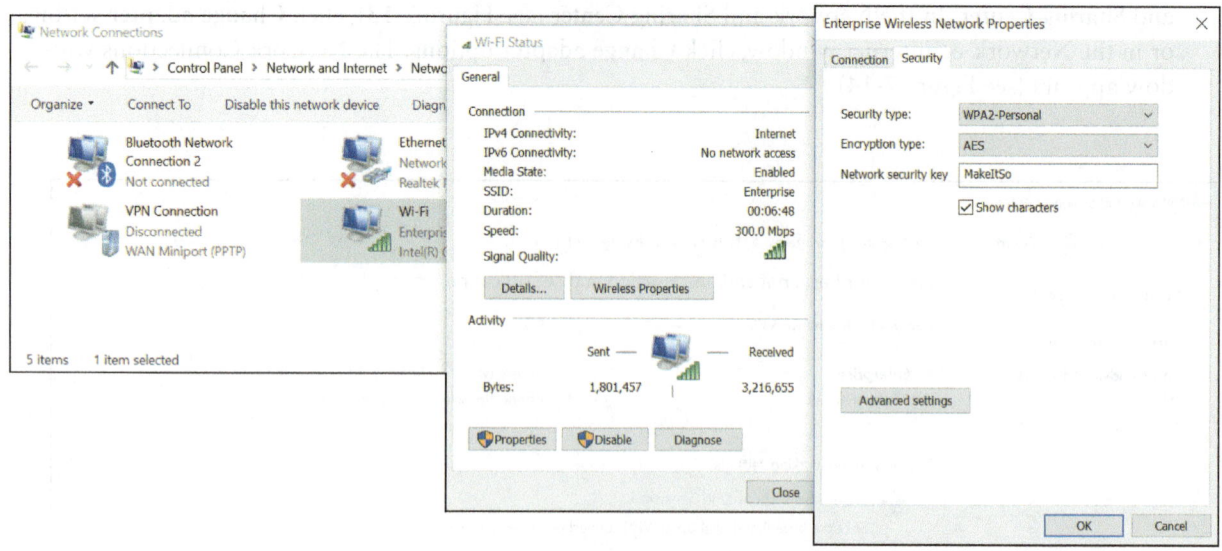

Figure 7-15 Verify that the Network security key for the wireless network is correct

If you have a problem making a network connection, you can reset the connection. Open the Network Connections window and right-click the network connection. Select **Disable** from the shortcut menu, as shown in Figure 7-16. Right-click the connection again and select **Enable**. The connection is reset. Try again to browse the web or access resources on the network. If you still don't have local or Internet access, it's time to dig a little deeper into the source of the problem. More network troubleshooting tools and solutions are covered later in this chapter.

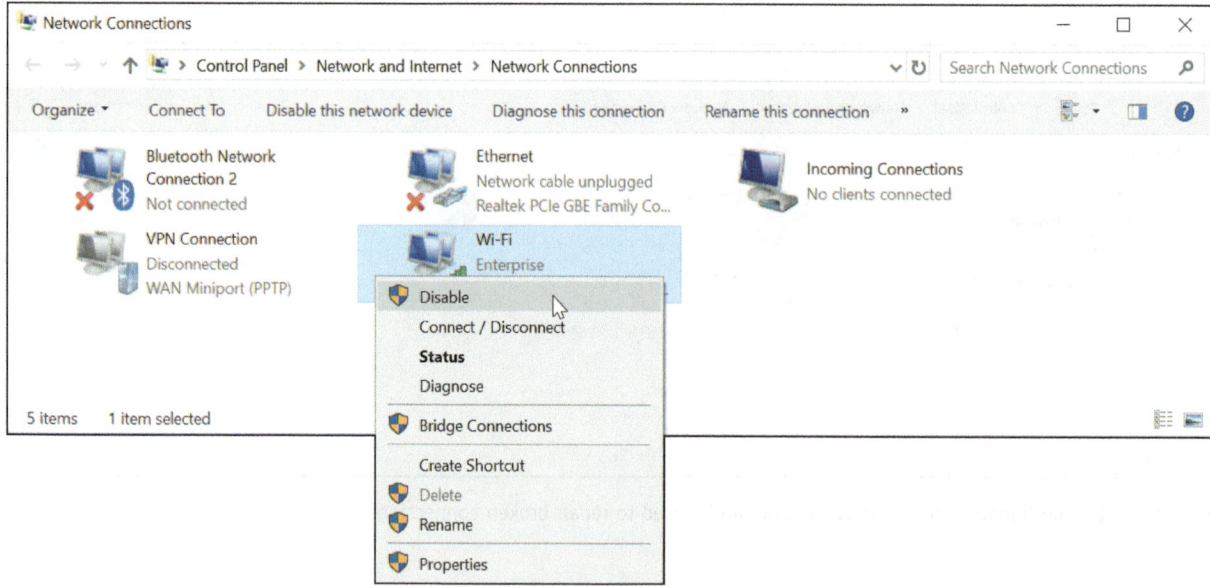

Figure 7-16 To repair a connection, disable and then enable the connection

CREATING A VPN CONNECTION

A **virtual private network (VPN)** is often used by telecommuting employees to connect to the corporate network by way of the Internet. A VPN protects data by encrypting it from the time it leaves the remote computer until it reaches a server on the corporate network, and vice versa. The encryption technique is called a tunnel or tunneling (see Figure 7-17).

Figure 7-17 With a VPN, tunneling is used to send encrypted data over wired and wireless networks and the Internet

A VPN can be managed by operating systems, routers, or third-party software such as OpenVPN (*openvpn.net*). A VPN connection is a virtual connection, which means you are setting up the tunnel over an existing connection to the Internet. When creating a VPN connection on a personal computer, always follow directions given by the network administrator who hosts the VPN. The company website might provide VPN client software to download and install on your computer. Then you might be expected to double-click a configuration file to complete the VPN connection. OpenVPN uses an .ovpn file for this purpose.

Here are the general steps using Windows to connect to a VPN:

1. In the Network and Sharing Center (refer back to Figure 7-13), click **Set up a new connection or network**. Then select **Connect to a workplace - Set up a dial-up or VPN connection to your workplace** (see Figure 7-18) and click **Next**.

Figure 7-18 Create a dial-up connection to an ISP

2. In the Connect to a Workplace dialog box, click **Use my Internet connection (VPN)**. In the next dialog box, enter the IP address or domain name of the network (see Figure 7-19). Your network administrator can provide this information. Name the VPN connection and click **Create**.

Figure 7-19 Enter connection information to the VPN

Whenever you want to use the VPN connection, click the **Network** icon in the taskbar. In the list of available networks, click the **VPN connection** and click **Connect**. Enter your user name and password (see Figure 7-20) and click **OK**. Your user name and password are likely to be the same network ID and password to your user account on the Windows domain on the corporate network.

After the connection is made, you can use your browser to access the corporate secured intranet websites or other resources. The resources you can access depend on the permissions assigned to your user account.

Figure 7-20 Enter your user name and password to connect to your VPN

Problems connecting to a VPN can be caused by the wrong authentication protocols used when passing the user name and password to the VPN. To configure these settings, return to the Network and Sharing Center and click **Change adapter settings**. In the Network Connections window, right-click **VPN Connection** and click **Properties**. In the Properties box, select the **Security** tab (see Figure 7-21). Here you can select security settings for the type of VPN, encryption requirements, and authentication protocols given to you by the network administrator.

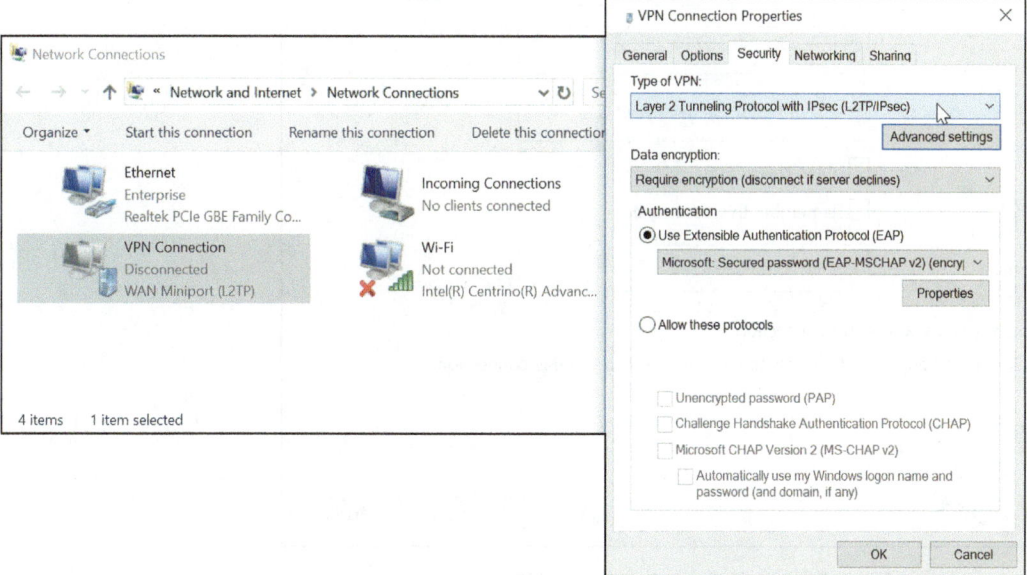

Figure 7-21   Configure the VPN's security settings

CREATING A DIAL-UP CONNECTION

Here are the bare-bones steps you need to set up and support a dial-up connection:

1. Install an internal or external dial-up modem in your computer. Make sure Device Manager recognizes the card without errors.

2. Plug the phone line into the dial-up modem port on your computer and into the wall jack. Phone lines use RJ-11 connectors (RJ stands for registered jack), which are the same connectors used for wired telephones.

3. Open the **Network and Sharing Center** window. In Windows 10/8/7, open the Control Panel and click **Network and Sharing Center**.

> ★ **A+ Exam Tip**   Windows 10 includes many options for accessing the Network and Sharing Center, and the A+ Core 2 exam expects you to be familiar with multiple methods for accessing any of the common utilities. One of the quickest ways to get to the Network and Sharing Center is to right-click **Start**, click **Network Connections**, then click **Network and Sharing Center**.

4. In the Network and Sharing Center window, click **Set up a new connection or network**. In the dialog box that appears (refer back to Figure 7-18), select **Connect to the Internet - Set up a broadband or dial-up connection to the Internet** and click **Next**.

5. In the next dialog box, click **Dial-up**. In the next box (see Figure 7-22), enter the phone number to your ISP, your ISP user name and password, and the name you decide to give the dial-up connection. Then click **Create**.

Figure 7-22 Enter a phone number and account information to your ISP

To use the connection, click your **Network** icon in the taskbar. In the list of available connections, select your dial-up connection (see Figure 7-23A). In Windows 10, this opens the Dial-up page in the Settings app, where you click the dial-up connection again and click **Connect**. In Windows 8/7, click **Connect**. The Connect dialog box appears, where you can enter your password (see Figure 7-23B). Click **Dial**. You will hear the modem dial the ISP and make the connection.

Figure 7-23 (A) Select your dial-up connection, and (B) enter the password to your ISP

If the dial-up connection won't work, here are some things you can try:

- Is the phone line working? Plug in a regular phone and check for a dial tone. Is the phone cord securely connected to the computer and the wall jack?
- Does the modem work? Check Device Manager for reported errors about the modem. Does the modem work when making a call to another phone number (not your ISP)?
- Check the Dial-up Connection Properties box for errors. To do so, click **Change adapter settings** in the Network and Sharing Center, and then right-click the dial-up connection and select **Properties** from the shortcut menu. Is the phone number correct? Has a 1 been added in front of the number by mistake? Does the number need to start with a 9 to get an outside line? If you need to add a 9, you can put a comma in the field (for example, "9,4045661200"), which causes a slight pause after the 9 is dialed.
- Try dialing the number manually from a phone. Do you hear beeps on the other end? Try another phone number.
- When you try to connect, do you hear the number being dialed? If so, the problem is most likely with the phone number, the phone line, or the user name and password.
- Try removing and reinstalling the dial-up connection.

Now let's turn our attention to how to configure settings for a network connection, including dynamic, static, and alternate address configurations.

DYNAMIC AND STATIC IP CONFIGURATIONS

**A+
CORE 1
2.3**

Computers use IP addresses to find each other on a network. An IP address is assigned to a network connection when the connection is first made and can be:

**A+
CORE 2
1.8**

- A 32-bit string, written as four decimal numbers called octets and separated by periods, such as 192.168.100.4
- A 128-bit string, written as eight hexadecimal numbers separated by colons, such as 2001:0000:B80:0000:0000:D3:9C5A:CC

Most networks use 32-bit IP addresses, which are defined by IPv4 (Internet Protocol version 4). Some networks use both 32-bit addresses and 128-bit addresses, which are defined by IPv6 (Internet Protocol version 6).

> 📝 **Notes** The suite of rules that define network communication is called **TCP/IP (Transmission Control Protocol/Internet Protocol)**. IP (Internet Protocol) is a set of rules for IP addressing. IPv4 is an earlier version of IP, and IPv6 is the latest version. A **protocol** is a set of rules computers must follow in order to communicate.

A host is any device, such as a desktop computer, laptop, or printer, on a network that requests or serves up data or services to other devices. To communicate on a network or the Internet, a host needs this TCP/IP information:

- Its own IP address—for example, 192.168.100.4.
- A subnet mask, which is four decimal numbers separated by periods—for example, 255.255.255.0. When a computer wants to send a message to a destination computer, it uses its subnet mask to decide whether the destination computer is on its own network or another network.
- The IP address of a default gateway. Computers can communicate directly with each other on the same network. However, when a computer sends a message to a computer on a different network, it sends the message to its default gateway, which is connected to the local network and at least one other network. The gateway sends the message on its way to other networks. For small businesses and homes, the default gateway is a router.

▲ The IP addresses of one or more DNS (Domain Name System or Domain Name Service) servers. Computers use IP addresses to communicate, but people use computer names, such as *www.cengage.com*, to address a computer. When you enter *www.cengage.com* in your browser address box, your computer must find the IP address of the *www.cengage.com* web server and does so by querying a DNS server. DNS servers can access databases spread all over the Internet that maintain lists of computer names (such as *www.cengage.com*) and their IP address assignments. This group of databases is called the Internet namespace and finding the IP address for a computer name is called name resolution. In the Internet namespace, *cengage.com* is the name of the Cengage domain and *www.cengage.com* is the name of a web server in that domain. You'll learn more about these concepts in Chapter 8.

The IP address, subnet mask, default gateway, and DNS server addresses can be manually assigned to a computer's network connection; the computer's IP address is called a static IP address. Alternately, all of this information can be requested from a server on the network when a computer first connects to the network. The IP address it receives is called a dynamic IP address, and the server that assigns the address from a pool of addresses it maintains is called a DHCP (Dynamic Host Configuration Protocol) server. A computer or other device (such as a network printer) that requests address information from a DHCP server is called a DHCP client. It is said that the client is leasing an IP address. A DHCP server that serves up IPv6 addresses is often called a DHCPv6 server. You'll learn more about DHCP in Chapter 8.

> ⭐ **A+ Exam Tip** The A+ Core 1 exam expects you to know what a DHCP server is and may give you a scenario that requires you to use static and dynamic IP addressing.

Most networks use dynamic IP addressing. By default, Windows requests dynamic IP configuration from the DHCP server and there is nothing for you to configure. In some situations, however, a computer must have a static IP address, so as an IT support technician, you need to know how to configure static IP addressing.

Follow these steps to configure static IP addressing:

1. Open the **Network Connections** window. Right-click the network connection and click **Properties**. In the Properties box on the **Networking** tab (as shown in the middle box of Figure 7-24), select **Internet Protocol Version 4 (TCP/IPv4)** and click **Properties**. The TCP/IPv4 Properties box appears (see the right side of Figure 7-24).

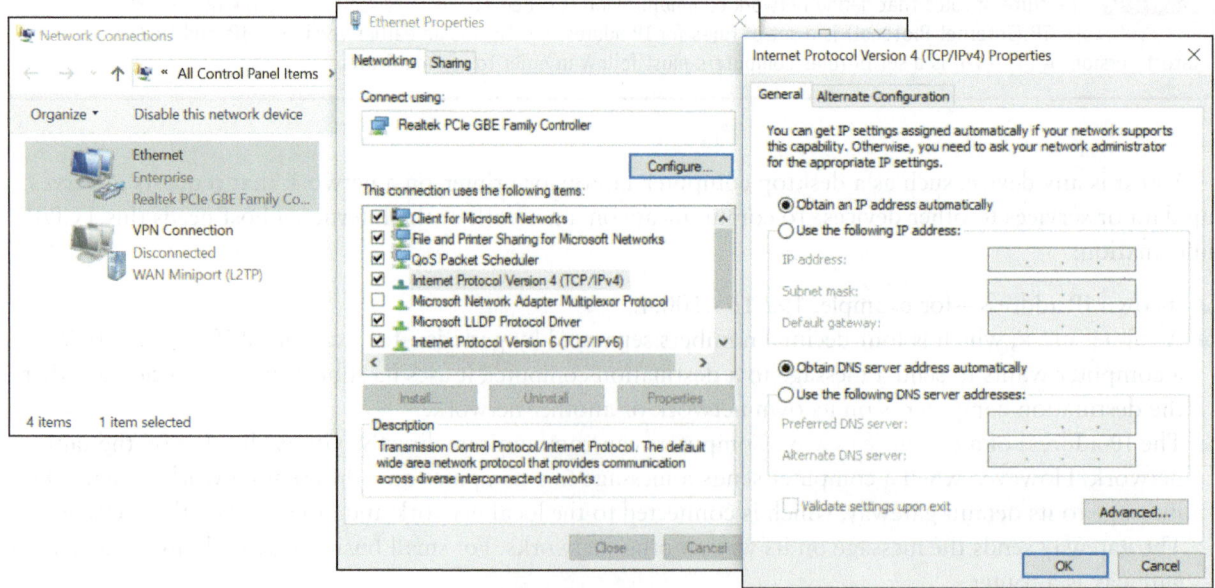

Figure 7-24 Configure TCP/IPv4 for static or dynamic addressing

2. By default, dynamic IP addressing is used, which selects *Obtain an IP address automatically* and *Obtain DNS server address automatically*. To change the settings to static IP addressing, select **Use the following IP address**. Then enter the IP address, subnet mask, and default gateway.

3. If your network administrator has given you the IP addresses of DNS servers, select **Use the following DNS server addresses** and enter up to two IP addresses. If you have additional DNS IP addresses, click **Advanced** and enter them on the **DNS** tab of the Advanced TCP/IP Settings box.

> 📝 **Notes** As an IT support technician, it's unlikely you'll ever be called on to configure static IPv6 addressing. However, to do so, use the Ethernet Properties box in the middle of Figure 7-24. Select **Internet Protocol Version 6 (TCP/IPv6)** and click **Properties**.
> You can also uncheck **Internet Protocol Version 6 (TCP/IPv6)** to disable it. For most situations, you need to leave it enabled. A bug in Windows 7 might prevent you from joining a homegroup if IPv6 is disabled. You'll learn more about IPv6 in Chapter 8.

> 📝 **Notes** In Windows 10, you can use the Settings app to configure static IP addressing. On the Status page in the Network & Internet group, click **Change connection properties**. Scroll down and click **Edit** under *IP settings*. Automatic (DHCP) is the default setting (see Figure 7-25A). To enter static IP address information, click **Manual**. In the Edit IP settings box (see Figure 7-25B), turn on IPv4 and enter the information.

7

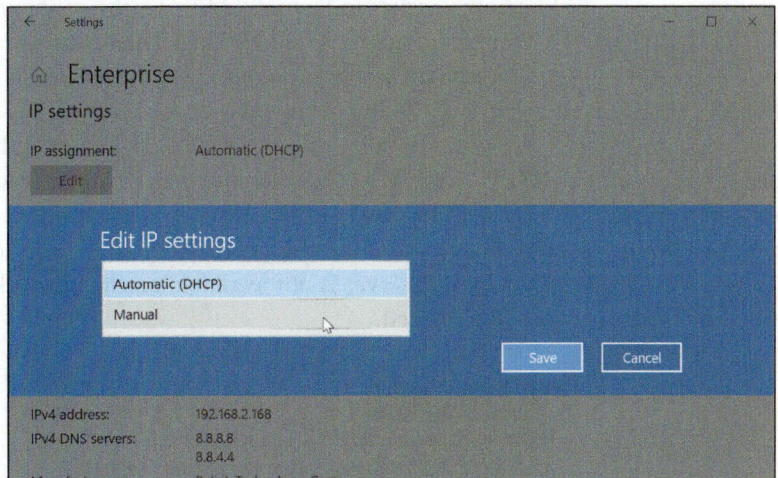

Figure 7-25 Set static IP addressing information in the Settings app

Internet Protocol Version 4 (TCP/IPv4) Properties   ×

General   Alternate Configuration

If this computer is used on more than one network, enter the alternate IP settings below.

○ Automatic private IP address
○ User configured

IP address: [. . . .]

Subnet mask: [. . . .]

Default gateway: [. . . .]

Preferred DNS server: [. . .]

Alternate DNS server: [. . .]

Preferred WINS server: [. . .]

Alternate WINS server: [. . .]

☐ Validate settings, if changed, upon exit

                          [OK]   [Cancel]

Figure 7-26   Create an alternate static IP address configuration

ALTERNATE IP ADDRESS CONFIGURATION

A+ CORE 1 2.3

A+ CORE 2 1.8

Suppose an employee with a laptop often travels, and her work network uses static IP addressing, even though most public networks use dynamic IP addressing. How do you configure her computer's network connection settings? For travel, you would configure the computer to use dynamic IP addressing in order to connect to public networks. However, when the computer attempts to connect to the corporate network, it needs a static IP address. The solution is to create an alternate configuration that the computer will use only if needed.

To create an alternate configuration, first use the General tab of the TCP/IPv4 Properties box shown earlier in Figure 7-24 to set the configuration for dynamic IP addressing. Then click the **Alternate Configuration** tab. As you can see in Figure 7-26, by default Windows sets an **Automatic private IP address (APIPA)**, which is an IP address beginning with 169.254, when it cannot find a DHCP server. Select **User configured**. Then enter a static IP address, subnet mask, default gateway, and DNS server addresses for the alternate configuration to be used on the company network. Click **OK** and close all boxes. Now the computer will first attempt to gather network connection settings from a DHCP server. If a DHCP server is not available on the network, the computer will instead use the new static IP settings you just entered.

Figure 7-27   USB devices provide wired and wireless network connections

★ **A+ Exam Tip**   The A+ Core 2 exam expects you to know in a scenario when it is appropriate to configure an alternate IP address, including setting the static IP address, subnet mask, DNS addresses, and gateway address.

MANAGING NETWORK ADAPTERS

A+ CORE 1 2.2, 2.3

A+ CORE 2 1.8

A computer makes a wired or wireless connection to a local network by way of a network adapter, which might be a network port embedded on the motherboard or a **network interface card (NIC)** installed in an expansion slot on the motherboard. In addition, the adapter might be an external device plugged into a USB port (see Figure 7-27). A network adapter is often called a network interface card or NIC even when it's not really a card but a USB device or a device embedded on the motherboard. It might also be called a network controller or network adapter.

Here are a network adapter's features you need to be aware of:

▲ *The drivers a NIC uses.* A NIC usually comes bundled with drivers on CD or the drivers can be downloaded from the web. Windows has several embedded NIC drivers. After you install a NIC, you install its drivers. Problems with the network adapter can sometimes be solved by using Device Manager to update the drivers or uninstall the drivers and then reinstall them.

▲ *Ethernet speeds.* For wired networks, the four speeds for Ethernet are 10 Mbps, 100 Mbps (Fast Ethernet), 1 Gbps (Gigabit Ethernet), and 10 Gbps (10-gigabit Ethernet). Most network adapters sold today for local networks use Gigabit Ethernet and support the two slower speeds. To see the speeds a NIC supports, open its Properties box in **Device Manager**. Select the **Advanced** tab. In the list of properties, select **Speed & Duplex**. You can then see available speeds in the Value drop-down list (see the right side of Figure 7-28). If the adapter connects with slower network devices on the network, the adapter works at the slower speed. Notice that the drop-down list has options for half duplex or full duplex. Full duplex sends and receives transmissions at the same time. Half duplex works in only one direction at a time. Select **Auto Negotiation** for Windows to use the best possible speed and duplex for a particular connection.

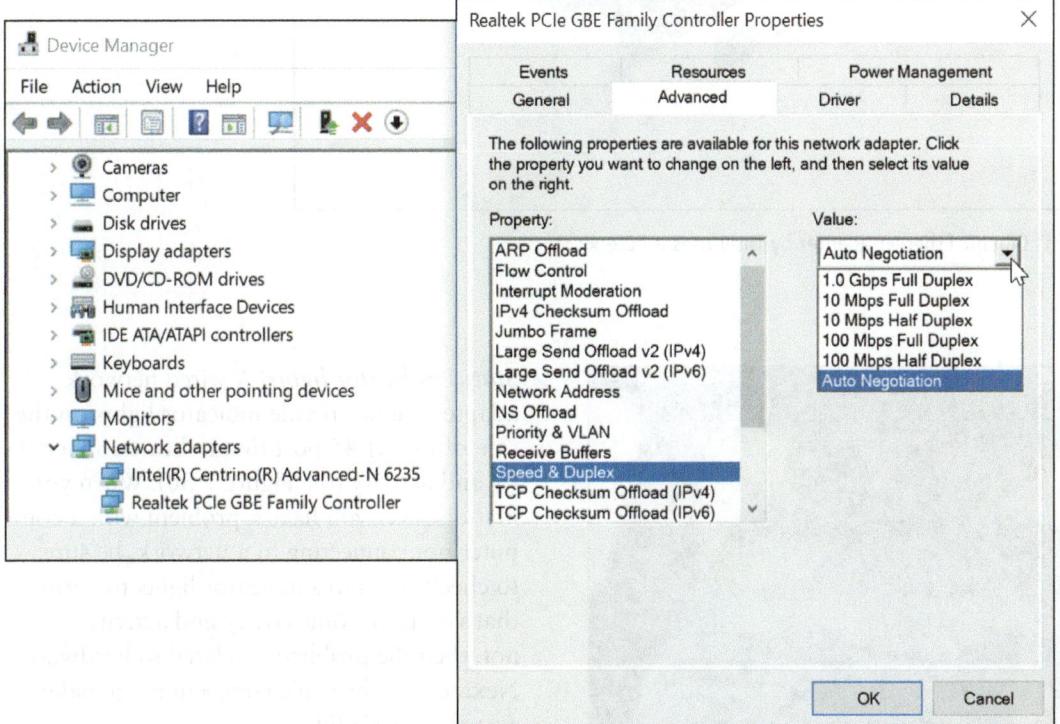

Figure 7-28 Set the speed and duplex for the network adapter

✎ **Notes** The speed of a network depends on the speed of each device on the network and how well a router or switch manages that traffic. SOHO network devices typically offer three speeds: Gigabit Ethernet (1000 Mbps or 1 Gbps), Fast Ethernet (100 Mbps), or Ethernet (10 Mbps). If you want your entire network to run at the fastest speed, make sure all your devices are rated for Gigabit Ethernet.

▲ *MAC address.* Every NIC (wired or wireless) has a 48-bit (6-byte) identification number, called the MAC address or physical address, hard-coded on the card by its manufacturer. The MAC address is unique for that adapter and is used to identify the adapter on the local network. An example of a MAC address is 00-0C-6E-4E-AB-A5. Most likely, the MAC address is printed on the device (see Figure 7-29).

Figure 7-29   This Gigabit Ethernet adapter by Intel uses a PCIe ×1 slot

Figure 7-30   Status indicator lights for the onboard network port

▲ *Status indicator lights.* A wired network adapter might provide indicator lights on the side of the RJ-45 port that indicate connectivity and activity (see Figure 7-30). When you first discover you have a problem with a computer not connecting to a network, be sure to check the status indicator lights to verify that you have connectivity and activity. If not, then the problem is related to hardware. Next, check the cable connections to make sure they are solid.

▲ *Wake-on-LAN.* A NIC might support Wake-on-LAN, which allows it to wake up the computer when it receives certain communication on the network. To use the feature, it must be enabled on the NIC. Open the NIC's Properties box in Device Manager and click the **Advanced** tab. Make sure **Wake on Magic Packet** and **Wake on pattern match** are both enabled (see Figure 7-31A).

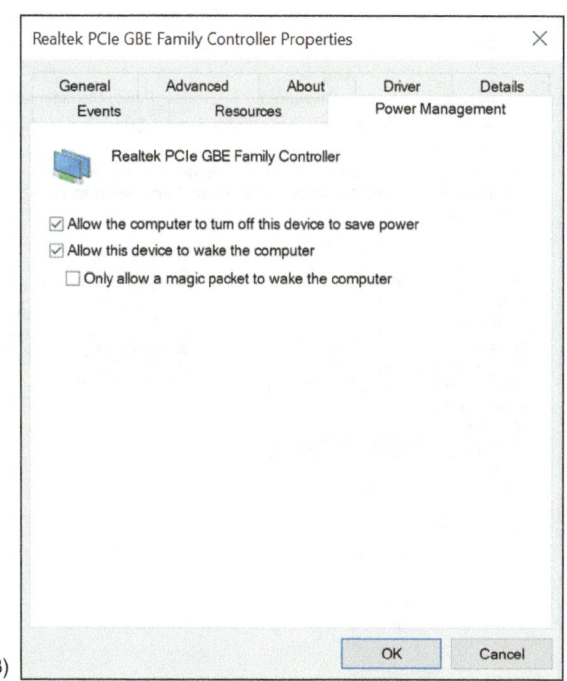

(A)   (B)

Figure 7-31 Enable Wake-on-LAN (A) using the Advanced tab, or (B) using the Power Management tab of the network adapter's Properties box

> **Notes** Some NICs provide a Power Management tab in the Properties box. To use the Power Management tab to enable Wake-on-LAN, check **Allow this device to wake the computer** (see Figure 7-31B).

For an onboard NIC, you must also enable Wake-on-LAN in BIOS/UEFI setup. Reboot the computer, enter BIOS/UEFI setup, and look for the option on a power-management screen. Figure 7-32 shows the BIOS/UEFI screen for one onboard NIC. It is not recommended that you enable Wake-on-LAN for a wireless network adapter.

Source: Intel

Figure 7-32 Use the Power screen in the BIOS/UEFI setup to enable Wake-on-LAN

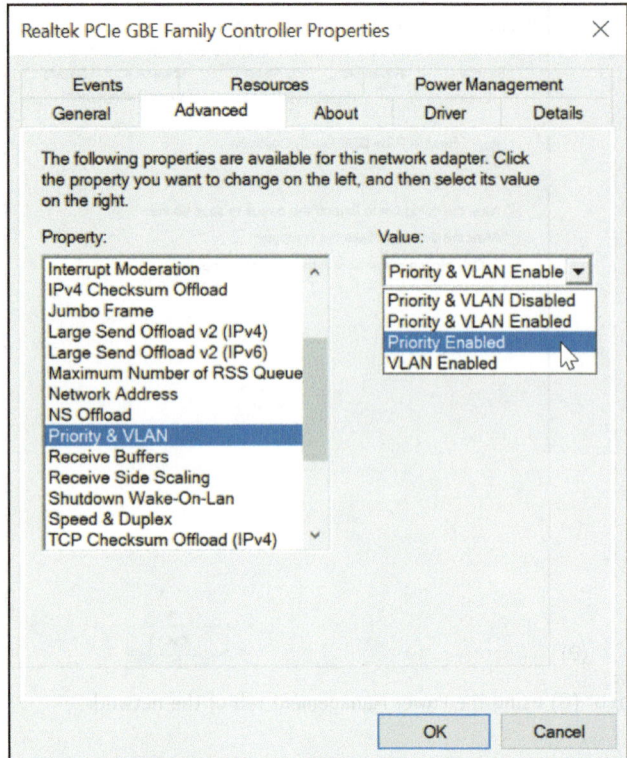

Figure 7-33 Select Priority Enabled to allow the network adapter to support QoS on the network

◢ *Quality of Service (QoS).* Another feature on a network adapter is Quality of Service (QoS), the ability to control which applications' traffic have priority on the network. The feature must be enabled and configured on the router, enabled on the network adapters, and configured in Windows for every computer on the network that uses the high-priority applications. Later in this chapter, you learn how to configure a router to use QoS. To enable QoS on a Windows computer's NIC, open the network adapter Properties box in Device Manager. On the Advanced tab, make sure **Priority Enabled** or **Priority & VLAN Enabled** is selected, as shown in Figure 7-33. If the option is not listed, the adapter does not support QoS.

> 📝 **Notes** A VLAN is a virtual LAN, and QoS is sometimes implemented using VLAN technology. You'll learn more about VLANs when you study virtualization.

Now that you know how to connect a computer to a network, let's look at how to set up the network itself. The process of building and maintaining a large, corporate network is outside the scope of this text. However, working with smaller networks, such as those used in homes and small businesses, helps prepare you to work in larger network environments.

SETTING UP A MULTIFUNCTION ROUTER FOR A SOHO NETWORK

> **A+
> CORE 1
> 2.2, 2.3,
> 2.4, 2.6**

An IT support technician is likely to be called on to set up a small office or home office (SOHO) network. As part of setting up a small network, you need to know how to configure a multipurpose router to stand between the network and the Internet. A router (see Figure 7-34) is a device that manages traffic between two or more networks and can help find the best path for traffic to get from one network to another.

> **A+
> CORE 2
> 2.2, 2.3,
> 2.6, 2.10**

> ⭐ **A+ Exam Tip** The A+ Core 1 and A+ Core 2 exams may require you to evaluate the needs of a business or residence in a given scenario and to install, configure, and secure a SOHO wired and wireless router based on these needs.

Figure 7-34 A router connects the local network to the Internet

FUNCTIONS OF A SOHO ROUTER

A+
CORE 1
2.2, 2.3

Routers can range from small ones designed to manage a SOHO network that connects to an ISP (costing around $50 to $300) to those that manage multiple networks and extensive traffic (costing several thousand dollars). On a small office or home network, a router stands between the ISP network and the local network (see Figure 7-35), and the router is the local network's gateway to the Internet.

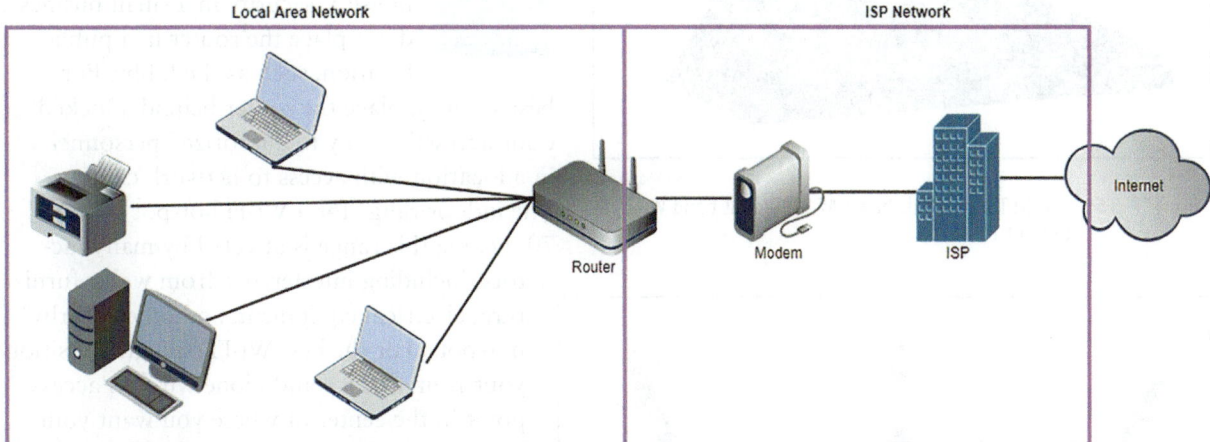

Figure 7-35 A router stands between a local network and the ISP network and manages traffic between them

Note in the figure that computers can connect to this router using wired or wireless connections. This is because a SOHO router often serves different functions in a single device. A typical SOHO router usually combines these functions:

- As a router, it stands between two networks—the ISP network and the local network—and routes traffic between the two networks.
- As a switch, it manages several network ports that can be connected to wired computers on the local network or to a dedicated switch that provides even more ports for locally networked computers.
- As a DHCP server, it can provide IP addresses to computers and other devices on the local network.
- As a wireless access point (WAP), it enables wireless devices to connect to the network. These wireless connections can be secured using wireless security features.
- As a firewall, it blocks unwanted traffic from the Internet and can restrict Internet access for local devices behind the firewall. Restrictions on local devices can apply to days of the week, time of day, keywords used, certain websites, and specific applications. It can also limit network and Internet access to specified computers, based on their MAC addresses.
- If the router is used as an FTP (File Transfer Protocol) server, you can connect an external hard drive to the router, and the FTP firmware on the router can be used to share files with network users.

An example of a multifunction router is the Nighthawk AC1900 by NETGEAR, shown in Figures 7-36 and 7-37. It has one Internet port for the broadband modem (cable modem or DSL modem) and four ports for devices on the network. The USB port can be used to plug in a USB external hard drive for file sharing on the network. The router is also a wireless access point with multiple antennas to increase speed and range.

Source: Amazon.com

Figure 7-36   The NETGEAR Nighthawk AC1900 dual band Wi-Fi Gigabit router

Reset button	Ethernet LAN ports 1–4	Internet port	USB 2.0 port	Power On/Off	Power connector

Source: NETGEAR

Figure 7-37   Connections and ports on the back of the NETGEAR router

INSTALLING AND CONFIGURING A ROUTER ON THE LOCAL NETWORK

A+ CORE 1 2.3, 2.6

A+ CORE 2 2.2, 2.6, 2.10

When deciding where to physically place a router, consider its physical security. If the router will be used as a wireless access point, make sure it is centrally located to create the best Wi-Fi hotspot for users. For physical security in a small business, don't place the router in a public location, such as the lobby. For best security, place the router behind a locked door accessible only to authorized personnel in a location with access to network cabling. The indoor range for a Wi-Fi hotspot is up to 70 meters; this range is affected by many factors, including interference from walls, furniture, electrical equipment, and other nearby hotspots. For the best Wi-Fi strength, position your router or a stand-alone wireless access point in the center of where you want your hotspot, and know that a higher position (near the ceiling) works better than a lower position (on the floor).

For routers that have external antennas, raise the antennas to vertical positions. Plug in the router and connect network cables to devices on the local network. Connect the network cable from the ISP modem or other device to the uplink port on the router.

To configure a router for the first time or change its configuration, always follow the directions of the manufacturer. You can use any computer on the network that uses a wired connection (it doesn't matter which computer) to configure the firmware on the router. You'll need the IP address of the router and the default user name and password to the router setup. To find this information, look in the router documentation or search online for your model and brand of router.

Here are the general steps for one router, the Nighthawk AC1900 by NETGEAR, although the setup screens for your router may be different:

1. Open your browser and enter the IP address of the router in the address box. In our example, the address is 192.168.1.1. The Windows Security box appears (see Figure 7-38). For our router, the default user name and password are both **admin**, although yours might be different.

Figure 7-38 Enter the user name and password to the router firmware utility

2. The main setup page of the router firmware appears in your browser window. Figure 7-39 shows the main page for a router that has already been configured. Notice the BASIC tab is selected. Most of the settings you'll need are on the ADVANCED tab. Begin by poking around to see what's available and to find the settings you need. If you make changes, be sure to save them. When finished, click **Logout** and close the browser window.

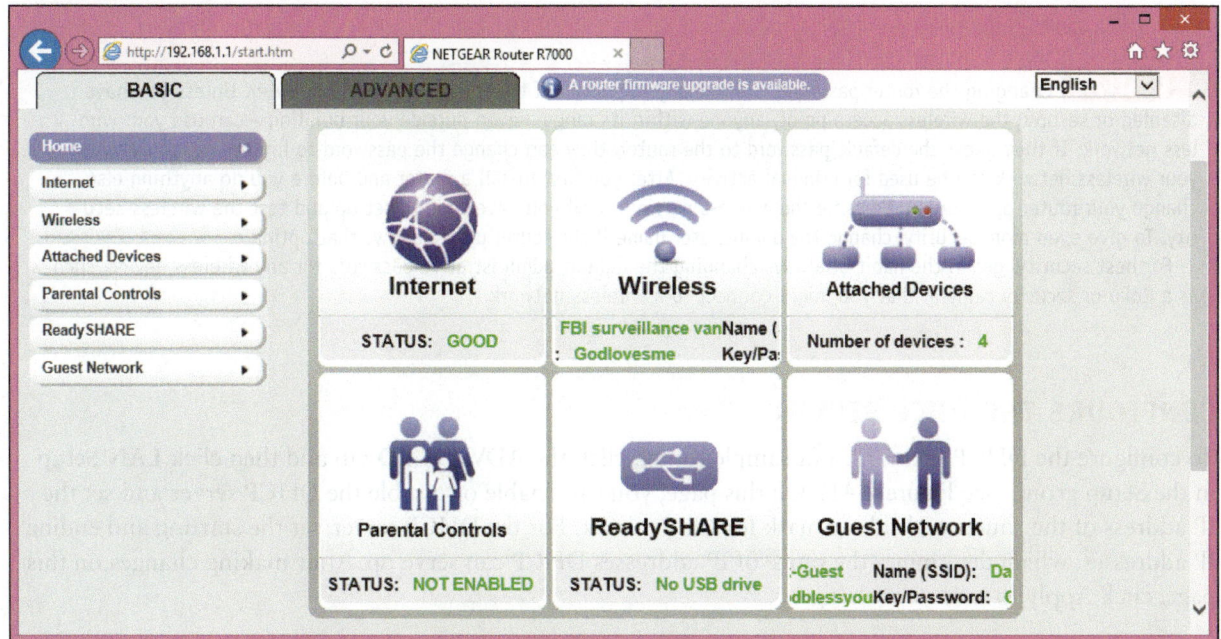

Source: NETGEAR

Figure 7-39 The main screen for router firmware setup

Following are some changes you might need to make to the router's configuration. To secure your router, always change the router password, which is described next.

CHANGE THE ROUTER PASSWORD

It's extremely important to protect access to your network and prevent others from hijacking your router. If you have not already done so, change the router's default administrative password. For our router, click the **ADVANCED** tab, click **Administration**, and click **Set Password** (see Figure 7-40). Change the password and click **Apply**. If the firmware offers the option, disable the ability to configure the router over the wireless network. Know that this password to configure the router firmware is different from the password needed to access the router's wireless network.

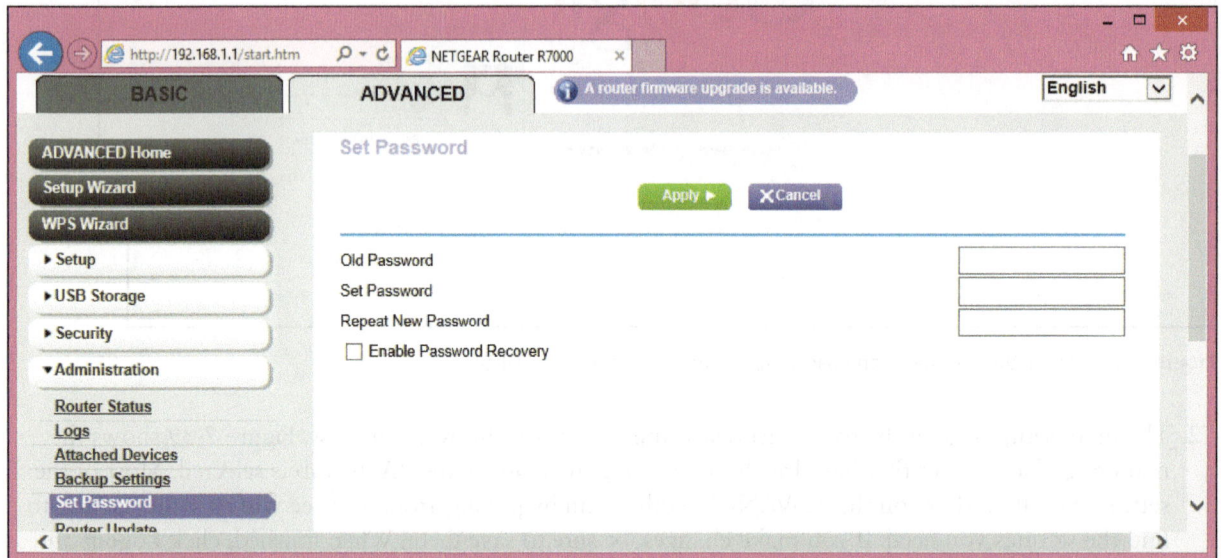

Figure 7-40   Change the router firmware password

Source: NETGEAR

> **⚡ Caution**   Changing the router password is especially important if the router is a wireless router. Unless you have disabled or secured the wireless access point, anyone within its range—even outside your building—can use your wireless network. If they guess the default password to the router, they can change the password to hijack your router. Also, your wireless network can be used for criminal activity. After you first install a router and before you do anything else, change your router password and disable the wireless network until you have time to set up and test the wireless security. To give even more security, change the default user name if the router utility allows that option.
>
>   For best security, get in the habit of always changing the default administrative password for any wireless device, such as a Roku or security camera, that you might connect to a wireless network.

CONFIGURE THE DHCP SERVER

To configure the DHCP server for our sample router, click the **ADVANCED** tab and then click **LAN Setup** in the Setup group (see Figure 7-41). On this page, you can enable or disable the DHCP server and set the IP address of the router and subnet mask for the network. For the DHCP server, set the starting and ending IP addresses, which determines the range of IP addresses DHCP can serve up. After making changes on this page, click **Apply** to save your changes.

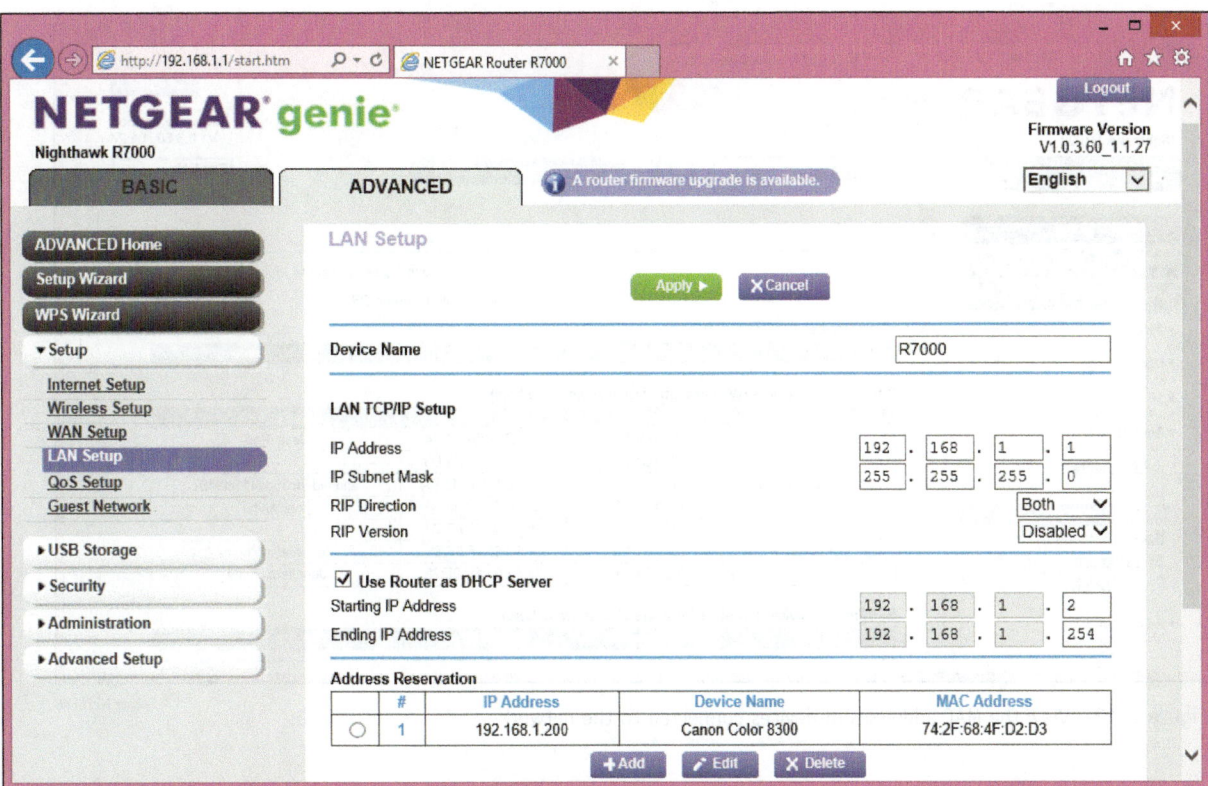

Figure 7-41 Configure the DHCP server in the router firmware

Source: NETGEAR

> ✎ **Notes** As you advance in your networking skills, you'll learn how to choose subnet masks and ranges of IP addresses to divide a large network into more manageable subnets. For now, know that if your range of IP addresses varies only in the last octet, the subnet mask is 255.255.255.0. If the range of IP addresses varies in the last two octets, the subnet mask is 255.255.0.0. You'll learn more about subnets in Chapter 8.

RESERVE IP ADDRESSES

A network device such as a printer needs a consistent IP address at all times so computers that access the printer don't need to be told its new IP address each time it reconnects to the network. In addition, a computer that is running a service, such as a web server for other computers on the network, needs a consistent IP address so that other computers can consistently find the web server. You could assign the printer and web server IP addresses by configuring the device or computer for static IP addressing. Alternately, you can assign static IP addresses to a device or computer by creating an address reservation on the DHCP server so that the DHCP client receives the same IP address from the server every time it connects to the network. Do the following to reserve an IP address:

1. To identify the computer or printer, you'll need its MAC address. When the client is connected to the network, click the **ADVANCED** tab and click **Attached Devices** in the Administration group (see Figure 7-42). Copy the MAC address (select it and press **CTRL+C**) or write it down.

Figure 7-42   View the MAC addresses of devices connected to the network

Source: NETGEAR

2. To assign a reserved IP address to the client, go to the LAN Setup page shown in Figure 7-41 and click **Add** under **Address Reservation**. In the IP address field, enter the IP address to assign to the computer or printer. Be sure to use an IP address in the range of IP addresses assigned by the DHCP server. Select the MAC address from the list of attached devices or copy or type the MAC address in the field. Click **Apply** to save your changes. In Figure 7-43, a Canon network printer is set to receive the IP address 192.168.1.200 each time it connects to the network. It's helpful to network users to write this IP address on a label taped in plain sight on the printer or web server.

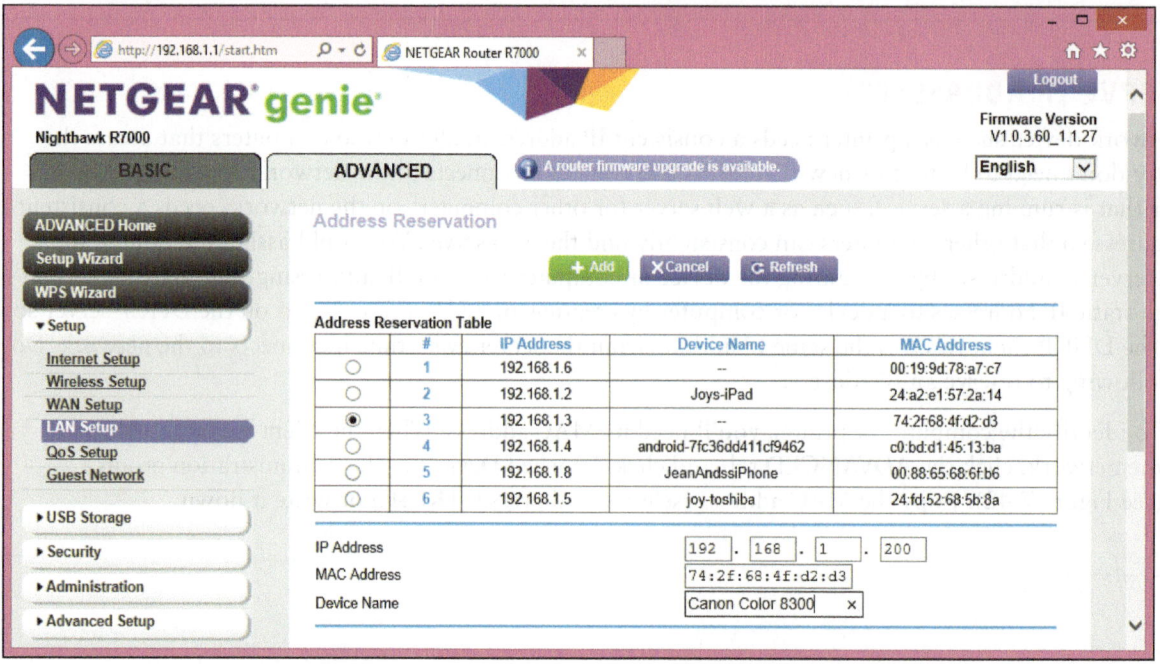

Figure 7-43   Use address reservation to assign a reserved IP address to a computer or other device

Source: NETGEAR

MAC ADDRESS FILTERING

MAC address filtering allows you to restrict access to your network to certain computers or devices. If a MAC address is not entered in the table of MAC addresses, the device is not allowed to connect to the network. For our sample router, the MAC address table can be viewed and edited on the ADVANCED tab of the Access Control page in the Security group (see Figure 7-44). To turn on Access Control, check the **Turn on Access Control** check box and then allow or block each MAC address in the table.

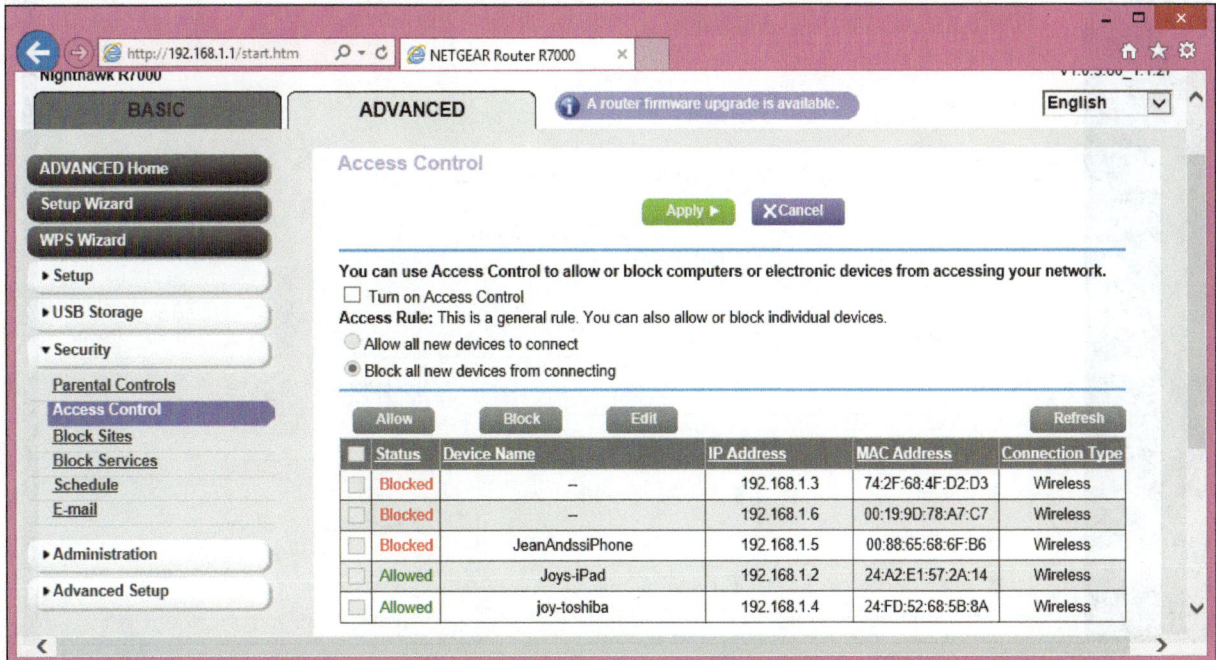

Figure 7-44 Use MAC address filtering to allow and block devices on the network

Source: NETGEAR

> **Notes** It's fairly easy to fake a MAC address when attacking a network. Therefore, MAC address filtering is not considered an effective security measure.

QOS FOR AN APPLICATION OR DEVICE

As you use your network and notice that one application or device is not getting the best service, you can improve its network performance using the Quality of Service (QoS) feature discussed earlier in this chapter. Wireless devices used for streaming multimedia (for example, a Roku) and applications used for video conferencing (for example, Skype) might need a high priority. For one sample router, do the following:

1. Sign in to the router firmware and go to the **Media Prioritization** page (see Figure 7-45). Turn on **Prioritization**. Then you can drag a device into the High Priority list. You can also select an application or online game from one of the two drop-down lists on the right and drag it to the High Priority list.

2. Notice in the figure that a Roku device is listed for the highest priority, followed by the Skype application. Click **OK** to save your changes.

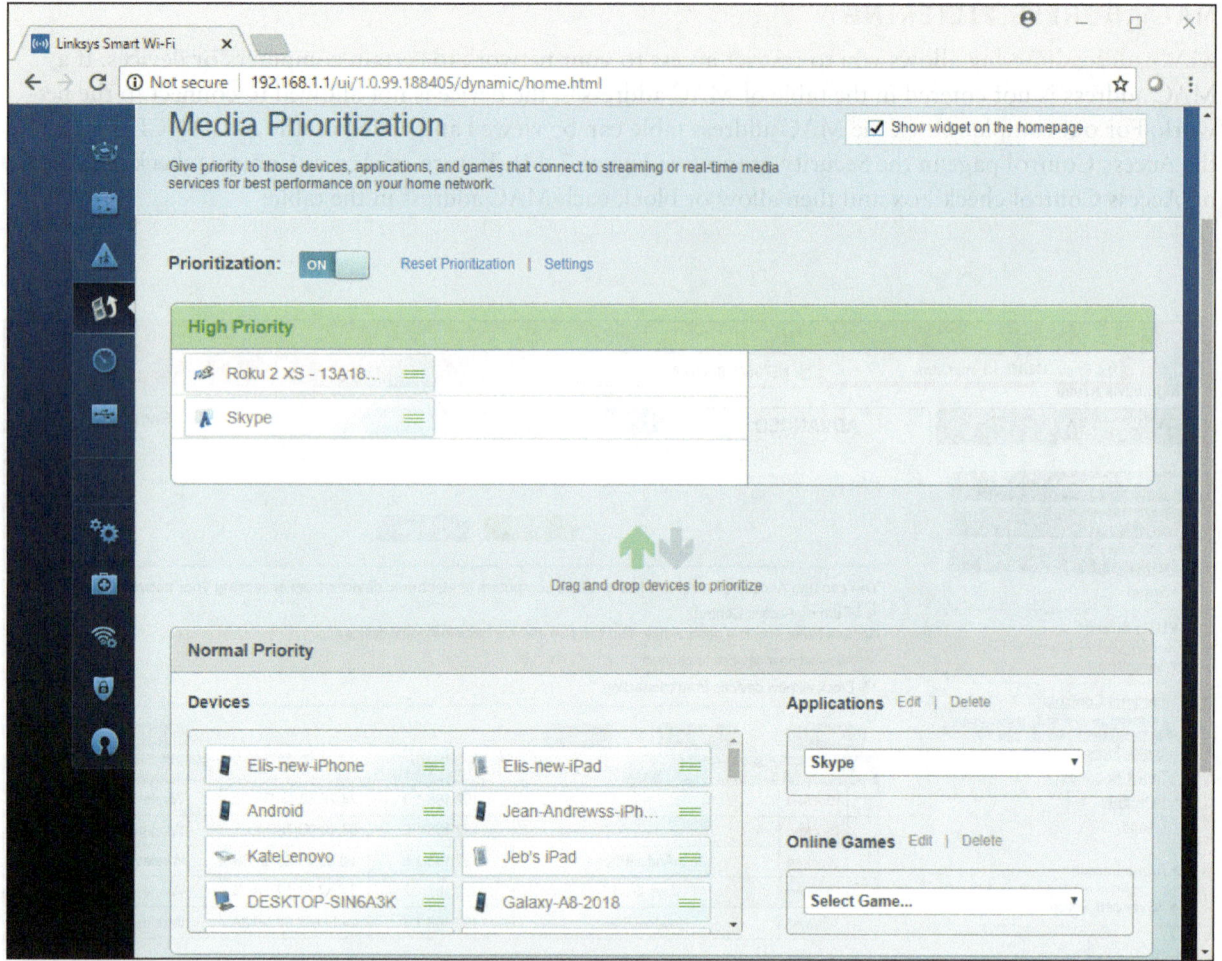

Figure 7-45   High priority is given to a device or app for best QoS

UNIVERSAL PLUG AND PLAY

Universal Plug and Play (UPnP) helps computers on the local network automatically discover and communicate with services provided by other computers on the local network. Enable UPnP if computers on the network use applications, such as messaging, gaming, or Windows Remote Assistance, which run on other local computers and there is a problem establishing communication. Basically, a computer can use the router to advertise its service and automatically communicate with other computers on the network. UPnP is considered a security risk because shields between computers are dropped, which hackers might exploit. Therefore, use UPnP with caution.

For our sample router, UPnP is enabled on the UPnP page in the Advanced Setup group on the ADVANCED tab (see Figure 7-46). Any computers and their ports that are currently using UPnP are listed.

UPDATE ROUTER FIRMWARE

As part of maintaining a router, know that router manufacturers occasionally release updates to the router firmware. The router setup utility can be used to download and apply these updates. For our sample router, you can click **A router firmware upgrade is available** on any of the setup screens (for example, see Figure 7-46) to see the Firmware Upgrade Assistant page (see Figure 7-47). Use this page to perform the upgrade.

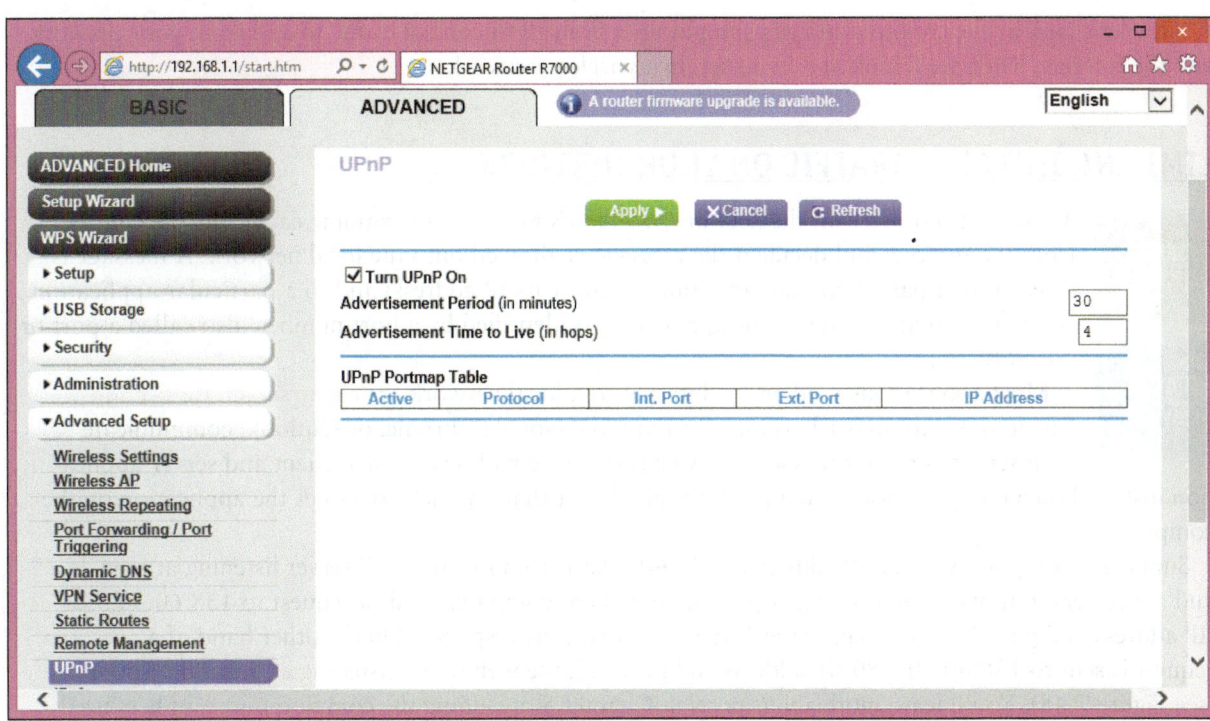

Figure 7-46 Turn on UPnP

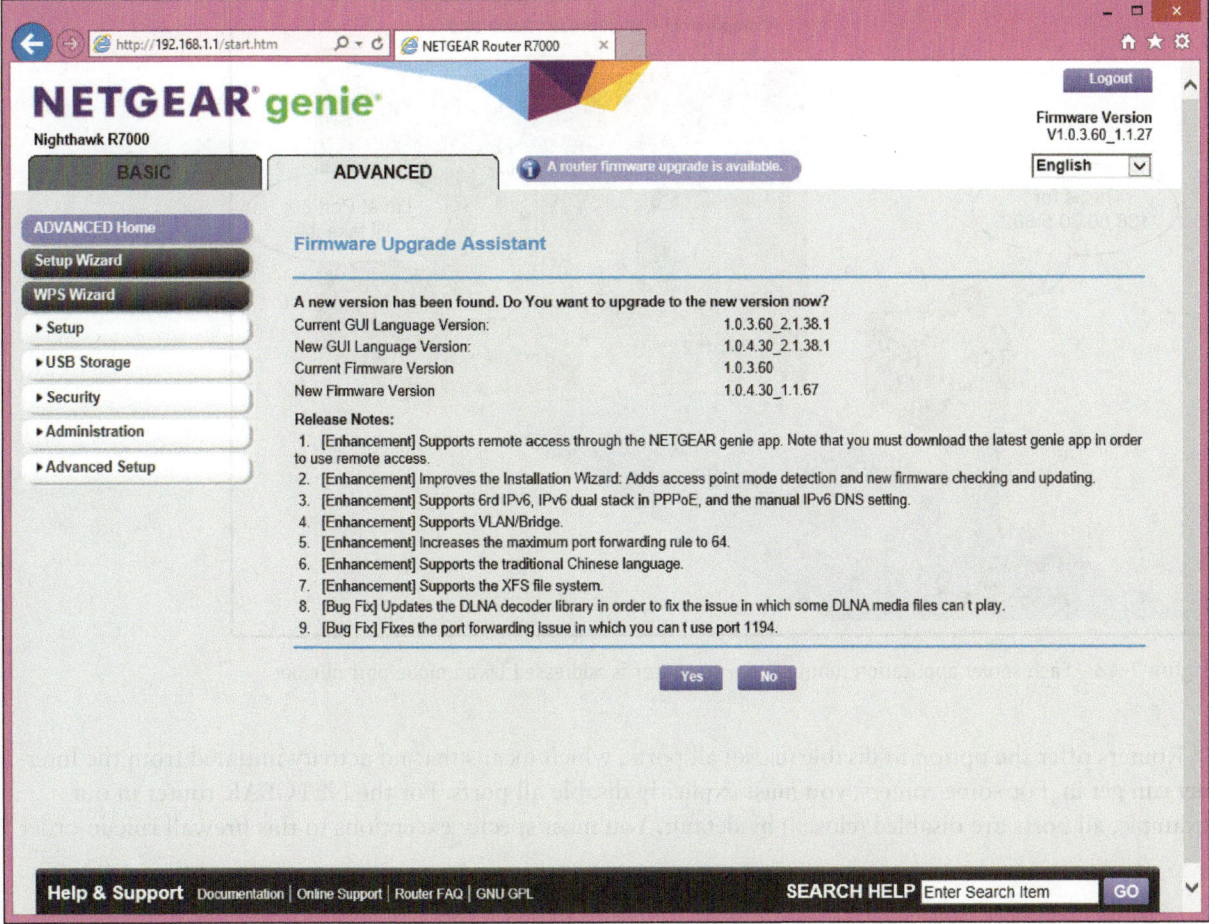

Figure 7-47 Update router firmware

Now let's look at the concepts and steps to put up a firewall to control traffic to and from your network and the Internet. Then we'll look at how to set up a wireless network.

LIMITING INTERNET TRAFFIC ON YOUR NETWORK

A+
CORE 1
2.2, 2.3

To protect resources on the network, a router's firewall can examine each message coming from the Internet and decide if the message is allowed onto the local network. A message is directed to a particular computer (identified by its IP address) and to a particular application running on that computer. The application is identified by a port number, also called a port or port address.

A+
CORE 2
2.10

Most applications used on the Internet or a local network are client/server applications. Client applications, such as Internet Explorer, Google Chrome, or Outlook, communicate with server applications such as a web server or email server. Each client and server application installed on a computer listens at a predetermined port that uniquely identifies the application on the computer.

Suppose a computer with an IP address of 138.60.30.5 is running an email server listening at port 25 and a web server application listening at port 80. If a client computer sends a request to 138.60.30.5:25 (IP address and port 25), the email server listening at that port responds. On the other hand, if a request is sent to 138.60.30.5:80 (IP address and port 80), the web server listening at port 80 responds (see Figure 7-48). You'll learn more about ports in Chapter 8, including the common port numbers used by several popular applications.

Figure 7-48   Each server application running on a computer is addressed by a unique port number

Routers offer the option to disable (close) all ports, which means that no activity initiated from the Internet can get in. For some routers, you must explicitly disable all ports. For the NETGEAR router in our example, all ports are disabled (closed) by default. You must specify exceptions to this firewall rule in order to allow unsolicited traffic from the Internet. Exceptions are allowed using port forwarding or a DMZ. In addition to managing ports, you can also limit Internet traffic by filtering content. All these techniques are discussed next.

> ★ **A+ Exam Tip** The A+ Core 1 and A+ Core 2 exams may give a scenario that expects you to resolve a problem by implementing port forwarding/mapping, whitelists, blacklists, content filtering, parental controls, and a DMZ.

PORT FORWARDING

Suppose you're hosting an Internet game or website or want to use Remote Desktop to access your home computer from the Internet. In these situations, you need to enable (open) certain ports to certain computers so that activity initiated from the Internet can get past your firewall. This technique, called port forwarding or port mapping, means that when the firewall receives a request for communication from the Internet to the specific computer and port, the request will be allowed and forwarded to that computer on the network. The computer is defined to the router by its static IP address. For example, in Figure 7-49, port 80 is open and requests to port 80 are forwarded to the web server listening at that port. This one computer on the network is the only one allowed to receive requests at port 80.

Figure 7-49 Port forwarding on a network

To configure port forwarding for our sample router, click the **ADVANCED** tab, click **Port Forwarding/ Port Triggering** in the Advanced Setup group (see Figure 7-50), and verify that **Port Forwarding** is selected. Select the **Service Name**, enter the static IP address of the computer providing the service in the Server IP Address field, and click **Add**. Notice in the figure that the Remote Desktop application on a device outside the network can use port forwarding to communicate with the computer whose IP address is 192.168.1.90 using port 3389. The situation is illustrated in Figure 7-51. This computer is set to support the Remote Desktop server application.

> ✏ **Notes** If you want to use a domain name rather than an IP address to access a computer on your network from the Internet, you'll need to purchase the domain name and register it in the Internet namespace to associate it with your static IP address assigned by your ISP. Several websites on the Internet let you do both; one site is by Network Solutions at *networksolutions.com*.

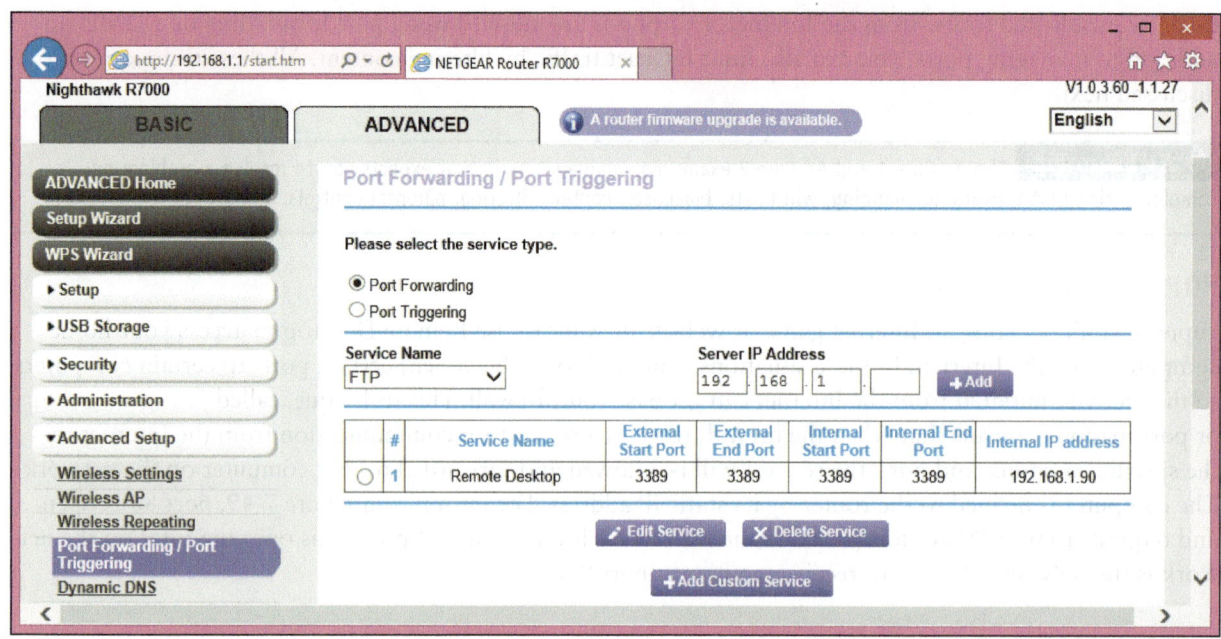

Source: NETGEAR

Figure 7-50 Using port forwarding, activity initiated from the Internet is allowed access to a computer on the network

Figure 7-51 With port forwarding, a router allows messages past the firewall that are initiated outside the network

Also notice the IP address for the message in Figure 7-51 is directed to the router's IP address. With port forwarding, the router forwards all traffic to port 3389 to the one computer with this open port, even through traffic is directed to the router's IP address. Here are some tips to keep in mind when using port forwarding:

▲ You must lease a static IP address for your router from your ISP so that people on the Internet can find you. Most ISPs will provide you a static IP address for an additional monthly fee.

▲ For port forwarding to work, the computer on your network must have a static IP address so that the router knows where to send the communication.

▲ Using port forwarding, your computer and network are more vulnerable because you are allowing external users directly into your private network. For better security, turn on port forwarding only when you know it's being used.

DMZ

A DMZ (demilitarized zone) in networking is a computer or network that is not protected by a firewall or has limited protection. You can drop all your shields protecting a computer by putting it in a DMZ, and the firewall no longer protects it. If you are having problems getting port forwarding to work, putting a computer in a DMZ can free it to receive any communication from the Internet. All unsolicited traffic from the Internet that the router would normally drop is forwarded to the computer designated as the DMZ server.

> **⚡ Caution** If a DMZ computer is compromised, it can be used to attack other computers on the network. Use it only as a last resort when you cannot get port forwarding to work. It goes without saying you should not leave the DMZ enabled unless you are using it.

7

To set up a DMZ server for our sample router, click the **ADVANCED** tab and select **WAN Setup** in the Setup group (see Figure 7-52). Check **Default DMZ Server** and enter the static IP address of the computer.

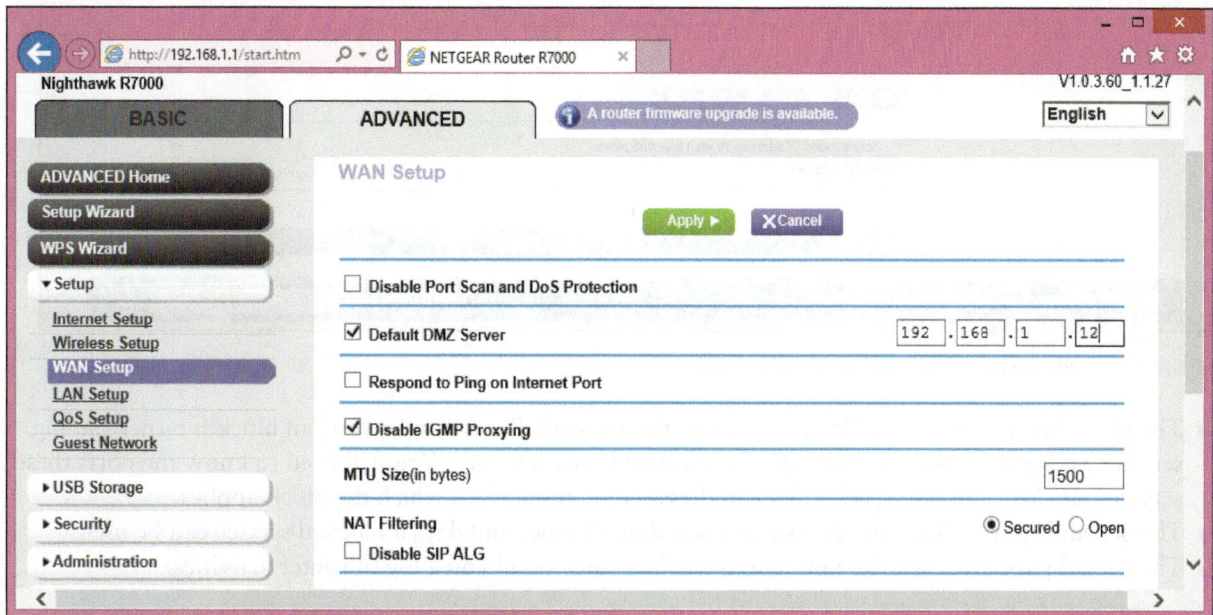

Source: NETGEAR

Figure 7-52 Set up an unprotected DMZ server for the network

CONTENT FILTERING AND PARENTAL CONTROLS

Routers normally provide a way for employers or parents to limit the content that computers on the local network can access on the Internet. Filtering can apply to specific computers, users, websites, categories of websites, keywords, services, time of day, and day of the week. Criteria for filtering can draw from blacklists (lists of what cannot be accessed) or whitelists (lists of what can be accessed).

For our sample router, content filtering and parental controls are managed in the Security group on the ADVANCED tab. Here are the options:

▲ The Parental Controls page provides access to the Live Parental Controls application and website at *netgear.com/lpc,* where parents can manage content allowed from the Internet and monitor websites and content accessed.

▲ The Block Sites page (see Figure 7-53) allows you to create a blacklist of keywords or websites to block. Notice you can also specify a trusted IP address of a computer on the network that is allowed access to this content.

Figure 7-53 Block sites by keyword or domain names

Source: NETGEAR

▲ The Block Services page can block services on the Internet. For example, you can block Internet gaming services or email services, or allow the service based on a schedule. You will need to know the ports these services use. You can also specify the IP addresses of computers to which the block applies.

▲ The Schedule page allows you to specify a schedule of times and days a blocked service can be used.

▲ The E-mail page gives you the option to have the router email you a log of router activities.

Now let's turn our attention to configuring a wireless access point provided by a router.

SETTING UP A WIRELESS NETWORK

**A+
CORE 1
2.3, 2.4**

A wireless network is created by a wireless access point. The standards for a local wireless network are called **Wi-Fi (Wireless Fidelity)**, and their technical name is IEEE 802.11. The IEEE 802.11 standards, collectively known as the 802.11 a/b/g/n/ac standards, have evolved over the years. This list details the progression of ranges and frequencies for each standard:

**A+
CORE 2
2.3, 2.10**

▲ *802.11a.* Short range up to 50 meters with radio frequency of 5.0 GHz

▲ *802.11b.* Longer range of 100 meters (indoor ranges are less than outdoor ranges) and radio frequency of 2.4 GHz

▲ *802.11g.* Same range and frequency as 802.11b but with faster speeds up to 54 Mbps

▲ *802.11n.* Can use either 5.0-GHz or 2.4-GHz radio frequency with an indoor range up to 70 meters and an outdoor range up to 250 meters

▲ *802.11ac.* Uses the 5.0-GHz radio frequency and has the same ranges as 802.11n, except performance stays stronger at the edges of its reach

7

Figure 7-54 A wireless network adapter with two antennas supports 802.11a/b/g/n/ac Wi-Fi standards

Wireless computers and other devices on the wireless LAN (WLAN) must support the latest wireless standard for it to be used. If not, the connection uses the latest standard both the WAP and client support. Figure 7-54 shows a wireless adapter that has two antennas and supports the 802.11ac standard. Most new adapters, wireless computers, and mobile devices support 802.11ac and are backward compatible with older standards.

Now let's look at the various features and settings of a wireless access point and how to configure them.

Notes When configuring your wireless access point, it's important you are connected to the router using a wired connection. If you change a wireless setting and you are connected wirelessly, your wireless connection will be dropped immediately and you cannot continue configuring the router until you connect again.

SECURITY KEY

The most common and effective method of securing a wireless network is to require a security key before a client can connect to the network. By default, a network that uses a security key encrypts data traversing the network. Use the router firmware to set the security key. For best security, enter a security key that is different from the password for the router's configuration utility.

Notes When it comes to making secure passwords and passphrases, longer is better and randomness is crucial. To make the strongest passphrase or security key, use a random group of numbers, uppercase and lowercase letters, and, if allowed, at least one symbol. At the bare minimum, use at least eight characters in the passphrase.

For our sample router, the security key can be set on the ADVANCED tab of the Wireless Setup page in the Setup group (see Figure 7-55). Here, the security key is called the Password or Network Key. Click **Apply** to save your changes.

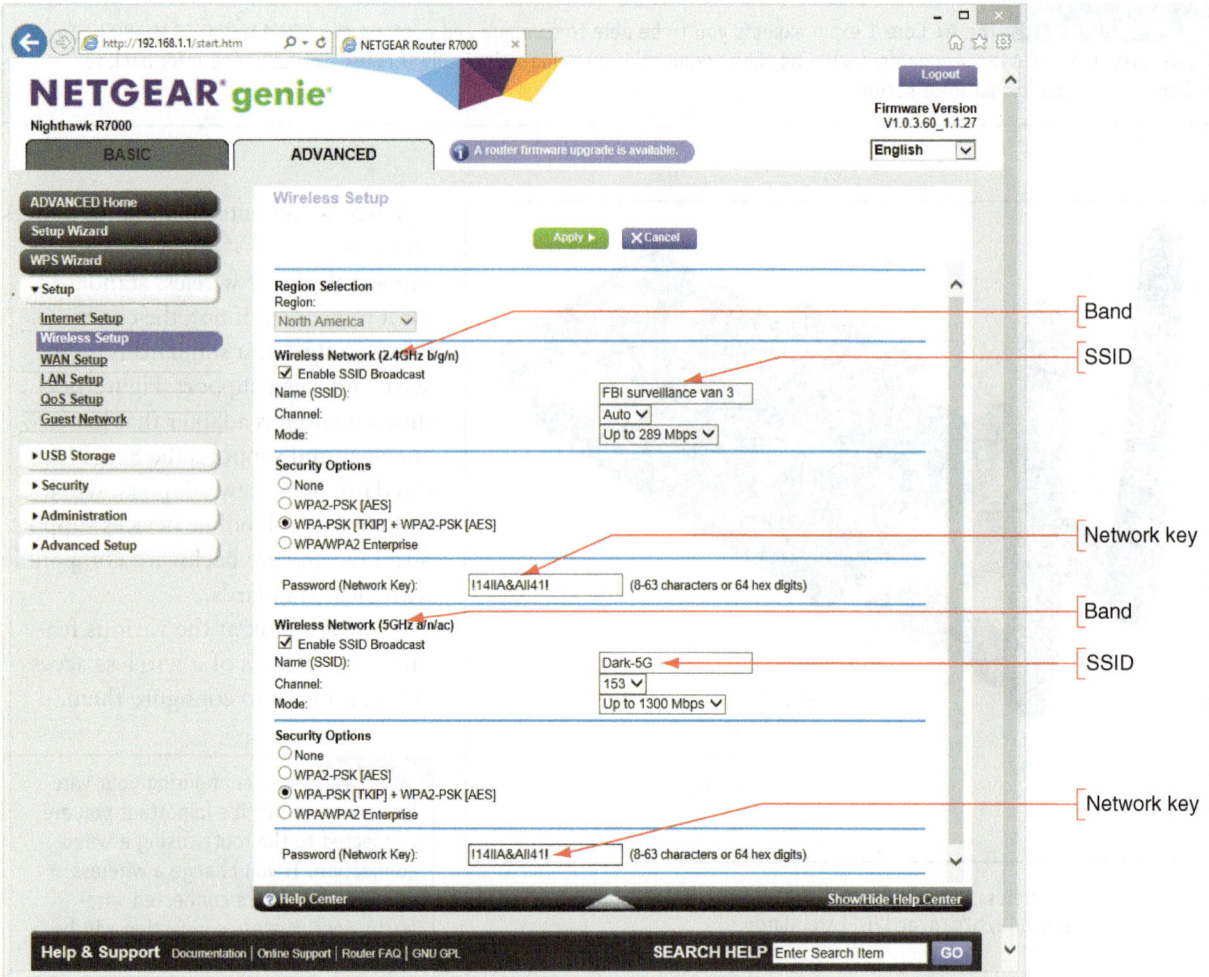

Figure 7-55   Configure the router's wireless access point

Source: NETGEAR

SET ENCRYPTION

When you set a security key, routers by default encrypt wireless transmissions. You can change the encryption protocols used or disable encryption. (Encrypting transmissions increases security but slows down the network; disabling encryption can improve performance and might be appropriate when you are not concerned about transmissions being hacked.) The three main security standards for 802.11 wireless networks are:

▲ **WEP.** WEP (Wired Equivalent Privacy) is no longer considered secure because the key used for encryption is static (it doesn't change).

▲ **WPA.** WPA (Wi-Fi Protected Access) is stronger than WEP and was designed to replace it. WPA typically uses TKIP (Temporal Key Integrity Protocol, pronounced *tee-kip*) for encryption. TKIP generates a different key for every transmission; however, the encryption algorithm used for its calculations is no longer considered secure.

▲ **WPA2.** WPA2 (Wi-Fi Protected Access 2), also called the 802.11i standard, is the current wireless security standard. WPA2 typically uses AES (Advanced Encryption Standard) for encryption, which provides faster and more secure encryption than TKIP. All wireless devices sold today support the WPA2 standard.

▲ **WPA3.** WPA3 (Wi-Fi Protected Access 3) offers better encryption and additional features over WPA2. For example, you can securely configure a nearby wireless device, such as a wireless webcam or motion sensor, over the wireless network, eliminating the need to connect the device with a wired connection to configure it. Another feature is Individual Data Encryption, which allows a secure connection for your laptop or other wireless device over a public, unsecured Wi-Fi network.

To configure Wi-Fi encryption for our sample router, first notice in Figure 7-55 that this router supports two wireless frequencies or bands: 2.4 GHz used by 802.11 b/g/n standards and 5 GHz used by 802.11 a/n/ac. Each band can have its own encryption type and security key. For the most flexibility, set both bands to allow any encryption standard the router supports. For our router, that's **WPA-PSK [TKIP] + WPA2-PSK [AES]** encryption. This setting means a wireless connection will use WPA2 encryption unless an older device does not support it, in which case the connection reverts to WPA encryption. Alternately, for best security, set both bands to require the highest standard the router supports. For our router, that's **WPA2-PSK [AES]**. Using this setting, the router will reject any older devices not capable of supporting this encryption standard. Click **Apply** to save your changes.

> ✎ **Notes** WPA/WPA2 Enterprise is more secure than WPA/WPA2 PSK, also known as WPA/WPA2 Personal. PSK (pre-shared key) relies on a passphrase shared with all network users, which could be compromised. Enterprise relies on a secure authentication server to manage all users on the network. However, very few SOHO networks have the resources to set up and host an authentication service. In most cases, when setting up a SOHO network, your most secure option is WPA2-PSK or, better yet, WPA2 Personal with AES encryption.

CHANGE THE DEFAULT SSID AND DISABLE SSID BROADCASTING

The Service Set Identifier (SSID) is the name of a wireless network. When you look at Figure 7-55, you can see that each frequency band has its own SSID and you can change that name. Each band is its own wireless network, which the access point (router) connects to the local wired network. When you give each band its own SSID and connect a wireless computer to your network, you can select the band by selecting the appropriate SSID. If your computer supports 802.11ac, you would want to select the SSID for the 5-GHz band in order to get the faster speeds of the 802.11ac standard. If you selected the SSID for the 2.4-GHz band, the connection would revert to the slower 802.11n standard.

Also notice in Figure 7-55 the option to Enable SSID Broadcast. When you disable SSID broadcasting, the wireless network will appear as Unnamed or Unknown Network on an end user's device. When a client selects this network, she is given the opportunity to enter the SSID. If she doesn't enter the name correctly, she will not be able to connect. This security method is not considered strong because software can be used to discover an SSID that is not being broadcast.

SELECT CHANNELS FOR THE WLAN

A channel is a specific radio frequency within a broader frequency. For example, two channels in the 2.4-GHz band are 2.412 GHz and 2.437 GHz. In the United States, eleven channels are available for wireless communication in the 2.4-GHz band. In order to avoid channel overlap, however, devices in the 2.4-GHz band select channels 1, 6, or 11, resulting in three nonoverlapping channels available for use. The 5-GHz band offers up to 24 nonoverlapping channels in the United States, although some of those channels are restricted in certain areas, such as near an airport. For most networks, you can allow auto channel selection so the device scans for the least busy channel. However, if you are trying to solve a problem with interference from a nearby wireless network, you can manually set each network to a different channel and make the channels far apart to reduce interference. For example, in the 2.4-GHz band, set the network on one WAP to channel 1 and set a nearby WAP's network to channel 11. For one router, the Wi-Fi Settings page provides a drop-down menu to select a specific channel or allow the router to automatically select the least busy channel (see Figure 7-56).

7

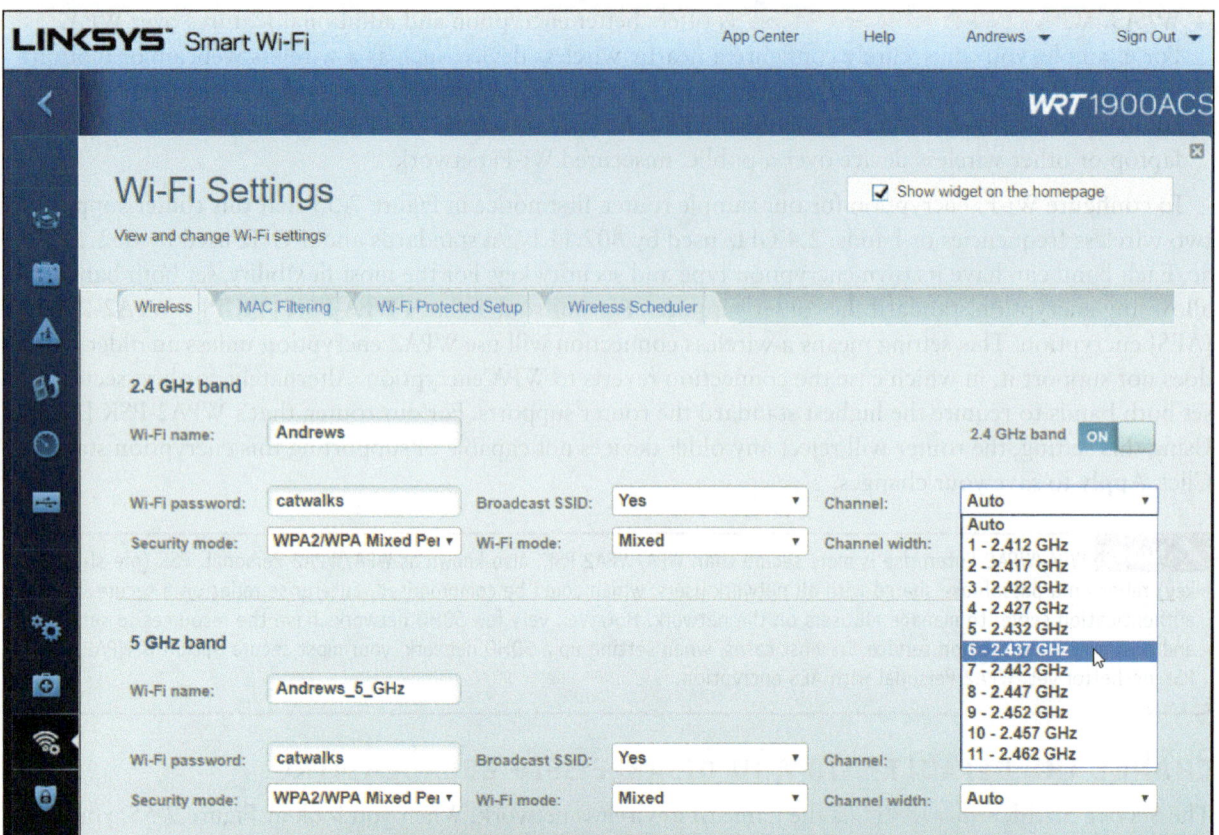

Figure 7-56 Select a channel in the 2.4-GHz band

Source: Linksys

RADIO POWER LEVELS AND WAP PLACEMENT

You've already learned that an access point should be placed in a central location to maximize its range in the target area. This also minimizes the signal's reach outside of the target area, which increases security. A wireless signal that reaches to public areas, such as a parking lot or the street, invites unauthorized users to park nearby and take their time attempting to crack your wireless security measures. Some high-end access points allow you to adjust the radio power levels the wireless network can use. To reduce interference, save on electricity, or limit the range of the network to your own property, reduce the power level.

WIRELESS QOS

Earlier, you learned you can improve QoS for a device, online game, or other application by assigning it to a high-priority list. In addition, for wireless devices, you can further improve QoS by enabling WMM (Wi-Fi Multimedia). When WMM is enabled, the wireless access point will prioritize wireless traffic for audio, video, and voice over other types of wireless network traffic. For one sample router, look back at Figure 7-45. When you click **Settings** on this router firmware page, the Settings box shown in Figure 7-57 appears. Turn on **WMM Support** and click **OK**. The Roku shown in Figure 7-45 is already prioritized as a device. Now multimedia traffic on the Wi-Fi network has priority.

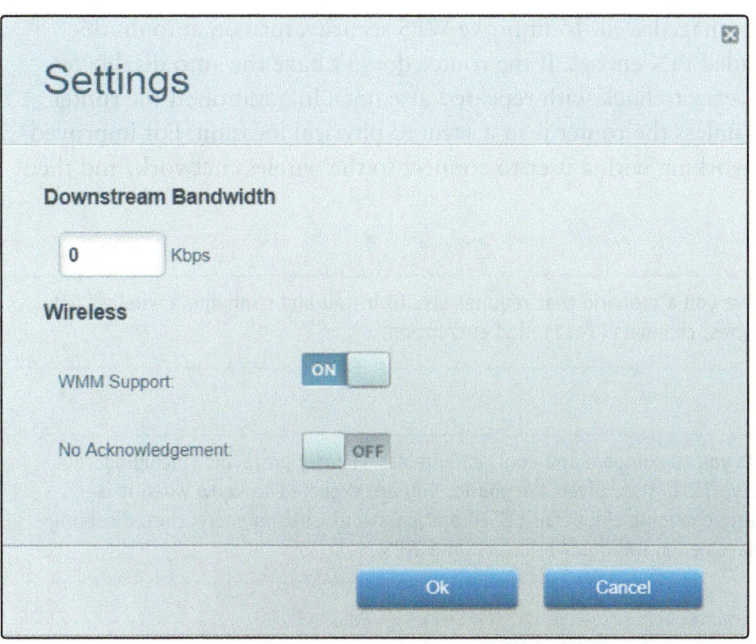

Source: Linksys

Figure 7-57 Prioritize multimedia traffic over the wireless portion of the network

WI-FI PROTECTED SETUP (WPS)

You also need to know about Wi-Fi Protected Setup (WPS), which is designed to make it easier for users to connect their computers to a wireless network when a hard-to-remember SSID and security key are used. WPS generates the SSID and security key using a random string of hard-to-guess letters and numbers. The SSID is not broadcast, so both the SSID and security key must be entered correctly to connect. Rather than having to enter these difficult strings, a user presses a button on a wireless computer or on the router, or enters an eight-digit PIN assigned to the router (see Figure 7-58). All computers on the wireless network must support WPS for it to be used, and you must enable WPS on the router, as shown in the figure.

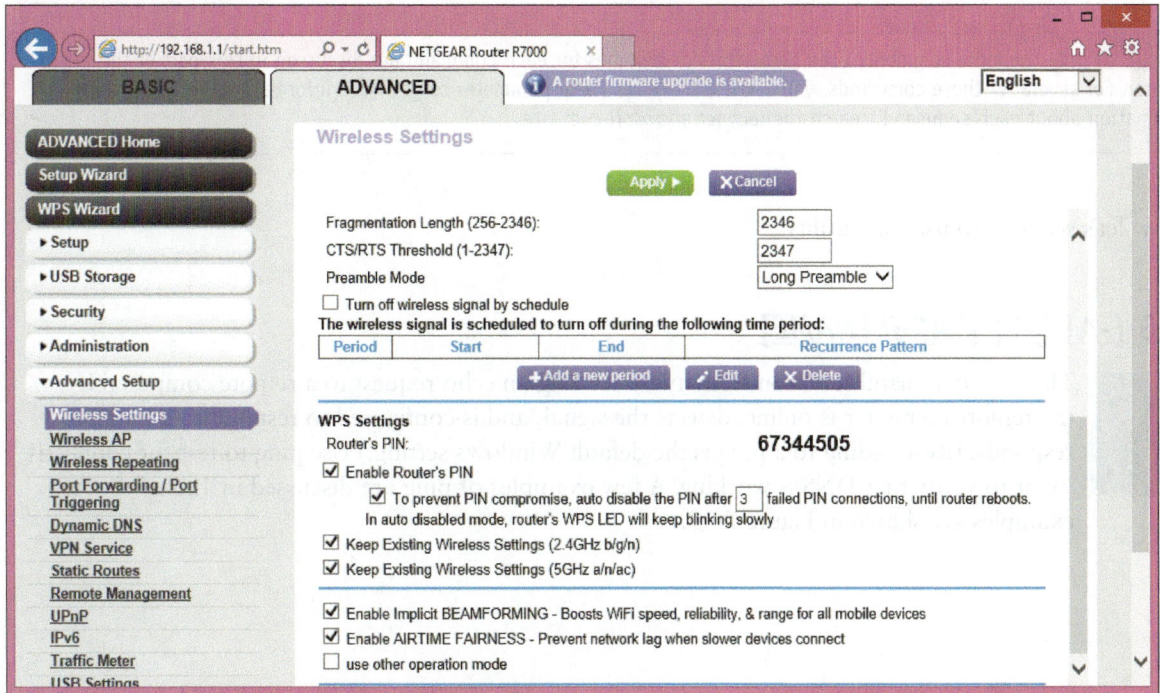

Source: NETGEAR

Figure 7-58 Enable WPS and decide how the router's PIN is used

WPS might be a security risk if it's not managed well. To improve WPS security, turn on auto disable so that WPS will be disabled after a few failed PIN entries. If the router doesn't have the auto disable feature, don't use WPS—an eight-digit PIN is easy to hack with repeated attempts. In addition, if the router has a WPS button to push, don't use WPS unless the router is in a secured physical location. For improved security, turn on WPS only when you are working with a user to connect to the wireless network, and then turn it off.

> ⭐ **A+ Exam Tip** The A+ Core 1 exam may give you a scenario that requires you to install and configure a wireless network, including Wi-Fi 802.11 standards, frequencies, channels (1–11), and encryption.

> ⭐ **A+ Exam Tip** The A+ Core 2 exam expects you to compare and contrast wireless security protocols (including WEP, WPA, WPA2, TKIP encryption, and AES encryption). Also, given a scenario, you are expected to know when it is appropriate to use SOHO router features, including changing the default SSID and password, setting encryption, disabling SSID broadcasting, antenna and access point placements, radio power levels, and WPS.

TROUBLESHOOTING NETWORK CONNECTIONS

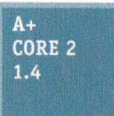

Windows includes several utilities you can use to troubleshoot networking problems. In this part of the chapter, you learn to use ping, ipconfig, nslookup, tracert, two net commands, and netstat. Most of these program files are found in the \Windows\System32 folder.

> ⭐ **A+ Exam Tip** The A+ Core 2 exam expects you, when given a scenario, to know when and how to use these network utilities: ping, ipconfig, ifconfig, tracert, netstat, net use, net user, and nslookup. You should know when and how to use each utility and how to interpret results.

> ✏️ **Notes** Only the more commonly used parameters or switches for each command are discussed in this part of the chapter. For several of these commands, you can use the /? or /help parameter to get more information. For even more information about each command, search the *technet.microsoft.com* site.

Now let's see how to use each utility.

PING [-A] [-T] [*TARGETNAME*]

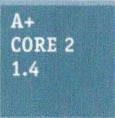

The ping command tests connectivity by sending an echo request to a remote computer. If the remote computer is online, detects the signal, and is configured to respond to a ping, it responds. (Responding to a ping is the default Windows setting.) Use ping to test for connectivity or to verify that DNS is working. A few examples of ping are discussed in Table 7-2. Two examples are shown in Figure 7-59.

Ping Command	Description
ping 69.32.208.75	Ping tests for connectivity using an IP address. If the remote computer responds, the round-trip times are displayed.
ping -a 69.32.208.75	The –a parameter tests for name resolution. Use it to display the host name and verify that DNS is working.
ping -t 69.32.208.75	The –t parameter causes pinging to continue until interrupted. To display statistics, press Ctrl+Break. To stop pinging, press Ctrl+C.
ping 127.0.0.1	This is called a loopback address test. The IP address 127.0.0.1 always refers to the local computer. If the local computer does not respond, you can assume there is a problem with the network connection's configuration.
ping cengage.com	Use a host name to find out the IP address of a remote computer. If the computer does not respond, suspect there is a problem with DNS. On the other hand, some computers are not configured to respond to pings.

Table 7-2 Examples of the ping command

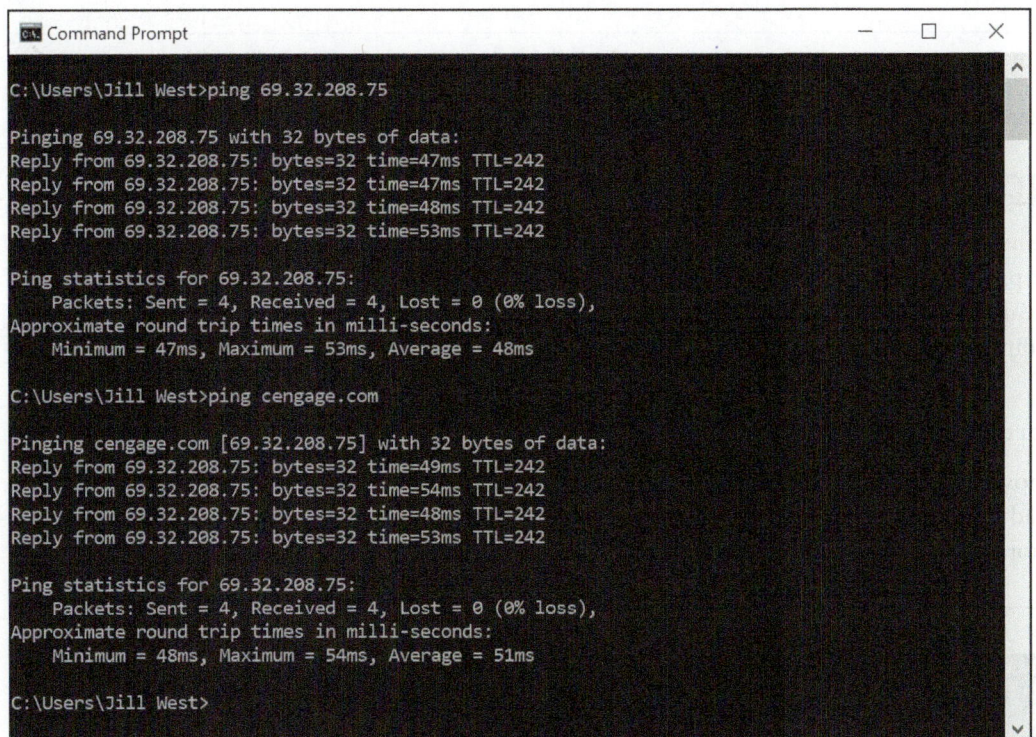

```
Command Prompt                                          —    □    ×

C:\Users\Jill West>ping 69.32.208.75

Pinging 69.32.208.75 with 32 bytes of data:
Reply from 69.32.208.75: bytes=32 time=47ms TTL=242
Reply from 69.32.208.75: bytes=32 time=47ms TTL=242
Reply from 69.32.208.75: bytes=32 time=48ms TTL=242
Reply from 69.32.208.75: bytes=32 time=53ms TTL=242

Ping statistics for 69.32.208.75:
    Packets: Sent = 4, Received = 4, Lost = 0 (0% loss),
Approximate round trip times in milli-seconds:
    Minimum = 47ms, Maximum = 53ms, Average = 48ms

C:\Users\Jill West>ping cengage.com

Pinging cengage.com [69.32.208.75] with 32 bytes of data:
Reply from 69.32.208.75: bytes=32 time=49ms TTL=242
Reply from 69.32.208.75: bytes=32 time=54ms TTL=242
Reply from 69.32.208.75: bytes=32 time=48ms TTL=242
Reply from 69.32.208.75: bytes=32 time=53ms TTL=242

Ping statistics for 69.32.208.75:
    Packets: Sent = 4, Received = 4, Lost = 0 (0% loss),
Approximate round trip times in milli-seconds:
    Minimum = 48ms, Maximum = 54ms, Average = 51ms

C:\Users\Jill West>
```

Figure 7-59 Use ping to test for connectivity and name resolution

IPCONFIG [/ALL] [/RELEASE] [/RENEW] [/DISPLAYDNS] [/FLUSHDNS]

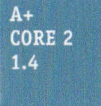

A+
CORE 2
1.4

The ipconfig (IP configuration) command can display network configuration information and refresh the TCP/IP assignments for a connection, including its IP address. Some examples of the command are listed in Table 7-3.

Ipconfig Command	Description
`ipconfig /all`	Displays a network connection's configuration information, including the MAC address.
`ipconfig /release`	Releases the IP address and other TCP/IP assignments when dynamic IP addressing is being used.
`ipconfig /release6`	Releases an IPv6 address and other TCP/IP assignments.
`ipconfig /renew`	Leases a new IP address from a DHCP server. Make sure you release the IP address before you renew it.
`ipconfig /renew6`	Leases a new IPv6 address from a DHCP IPv6 server. Make sure you release the IPv6 address before you renew it.
`ipconfig /displaydns`	Displays information about name resolutions that Windows currently holds in the DNS resolver cache.
`ipconfig /flushdns`	Flushes the name resolver cache, which might solve a problem when the browser cannot find a host on the Internet.

Table 7-3 Examples of the ipconfig command

📝 **Notes** The **ifconfig (interface configuration)** command is similar to ipconfig, and is used on UNIX, Linux, and macOS operating systems. You'll learn more about how to use Linux and macOS in Chapter 18.

NSLOOKUP [*COMPUTERNAME*]

A+ CORE 2 1.4

The **nslookup (namespace lookup** or **name server lookup)** command is used to test name resolution problems with DNS servers by allowing you to request information from a DNS server's zone data. Zone data is the portion of the DNS namespace that the server knows about. For example, to find out what your DNS server knows about the domain name *microsoft.com*, use this command:

```
nslookup microsoft.com
```

Figure 7-60 shows the results. Notice in the figure that the DNS server reports five different IPv4 addresses assigned to *microsoft.com*. It also reports that this information is nonauthoritative, meaning that it is not the authoritative, or final, name server for the *microsoft.com* domain name.

```
C:\Users\Jill West>nslookup microsoft.com
Server:  google-public-dns-a.google.com
Address:  8.8.8.8

Non-authoritative answer:
Name:    microsoft.com
Addresses:  104.43.195.251
          23.96.52.53
          23.100.122.175
          191.239.213.197
          104.40.211.35

C:\Users\Jill West>
```

Figure 7-60 The nslookup command reports information about the Internet namespace

A reverse lookup is when you use the nslookup command to find the host name when you know a computer's IP address, such as:

```
nslookup 69.32.208.75
```

To find out the default DNS server for a network, enter the nslookup command with no parameters.

TRACERT [*TARGETNAME*]

> **A+**
> **CORE 2**
> **1.4**

The tracert (trace route) command can be useful when you're trying to resolve a problem reaching a destination host such as an FTP site or website. The command sends a series of requests to the destination computer and displays each hop to the destination. (A hop happens when a message moves from one router to another.) For example, to trace the route to the *cengage.com* web server, enter this command in a command prompt window:

```
tracert cengage.com
```

The results of this command for one location are shown in Figure 7-61; your results will be different. A message is assigned a Time to Live (TTL), which is the number of hops it can make before a router drops the message and sends an error message back to the host that sent the original message (see Figure 7-62). The tracert command creates its report from these messages. If a router doesn't respond, the *Request timed out* message appears.

```
C:\Users\Jill West>tracert cengage.com

Tracing route to cengage.com [69.32.208.75]
over a maximum of 30 hops:

  1     2 ms     2 ms     2 ms  192.168.2.1
  2      *        *        *     Request timed out.
  3    11 ms    11 ms    12 ms  96-34-119-245.static.unas.tx.charter.com [96.34.119.245]
  4    14 ms    15 ms    53 ms  96-34-119-135.static.unas.tx.charter.com [96.34.119.135]
  5    17 ms    19 ms    16 ms  96-34-119-144.static.unas.tx.charter.com [96.34.119.144]
  6    21 ms    21 ms    21 ms  crr02spbgsc-bue-401.spbg.sc.charter.com [96.34.69.254]
  7    22 ms    29 ms    36 ms  bbr01spbgsc-bue-4.spbg.sc.charter.com [96.34.2.50]
  8    38 ms    50 ms    38 ms  bbr01gnvlsc-bue-800.gnvl.sc.charter.com [96.34.0.134]
  9      *        *        *     Request timed out.
 10    52 ms    54 ms    49 ms  4.69.216.229
 11    50 ms    48 ms    47 ms  CINCINNATI.bar1.Cincinnati1.Level3.net [4.59.40.178]
 12    53 ms    50 ms    58 ms  69.32.128.159
 13      *        *        *     Request timed out.
 14    51 ms    49 ms    49 ms  us-store.cengage.com [69.32.208.75]

Trace complete.

C:\Users\Jill West>
```

Figure 7-61 The tracert command traces a path to a destination computer

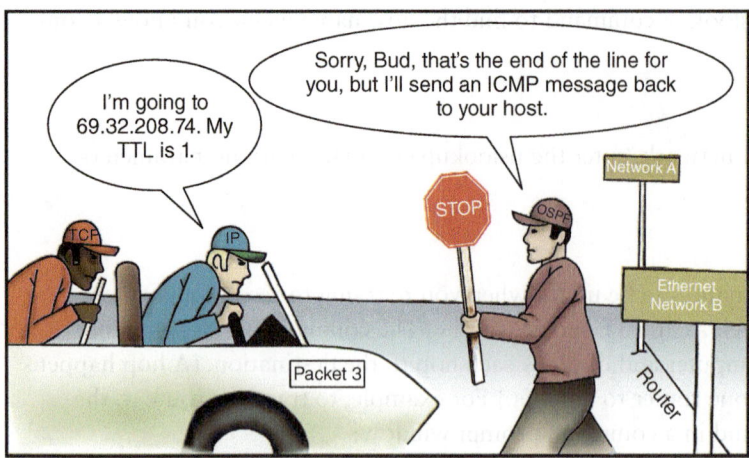

Figure 7-62   A router eliminates a message that has exceeded its TTL

THE NET COMMANDS

**A+
CORE 2
1.4**

The net command is several commands in one, and most of the net commands require an elevated command prompt window, which allows commands that require administrator privileges in Windows. In this section, you learn about the net use and net user commands. The net use command connects or disconnects a computer from a shared resource or can display information about connections.

> **✎ Notes**   One way to get an elevated command prompt window is to open **Task Manager**, click **File**, click **Run new task**, type **cmd**, check **Create this task with administrative privileges**, and click **OK**. See Figure 7-63. The command prompt window that appears has Administrator in the title bar.

Figure 7-63   Open an elevated command prompt window

Use the following commands to pass a user name and password to the \\bluelight remote computer, and then map a network drive to the \Medical folder on that computer:

```
net use \\bluelight\Medical /user:"Jean Andrews" mypassword
net use z: \\bluelight\Medical
```

The double quotation marks are needed in the first command above because the user name has a space in it.

A persistent network connection is one that happens at each logon. To make the two commands persistent, add the /persistent parameter like this:

```
net use \\bluelight\Medical /user:"Jean Andrews" mypassword /persistent:yes
net use z: \\bluelight\Medical /persistent:yes
```

The net user command manages user accounts. For example, the built-in administrator account is disabled by default. To activate the account, use this net user command:

```
net user administrator /active:yes
```

> **📝 Notes** Other important net commands are net localgroup, net accounts, net config, net print, net share, and net view. Consider doing a Google search on these commands to find out how they work.

NETSTAT [-A] [-B] [-O]

A+ CORE 2 1.4

The netstat (network statistics) command gives statistics about network activity and includes several parameters. Table 7-4 lists a few netstat commands.

Netstat Command	Description
netstat	Lists statistics about the network connection, including the IP addresses of active connections.
netstat >>netlog.txt	Directs output to a text file.
netstat -b	Lists programs that are using the connection (see Figure 7-64) and is useful for finding malware that might be using the network. The –b switch requires an elevated command prompt.
netstat -b -o	Includes the process ID of each program listed. When you know the process ID, you can use the taskkill command to kill the process.
netstat -a	Lists statistics about all active connections and the ports the computer is listening on.

Table 7-4   Netstat commands

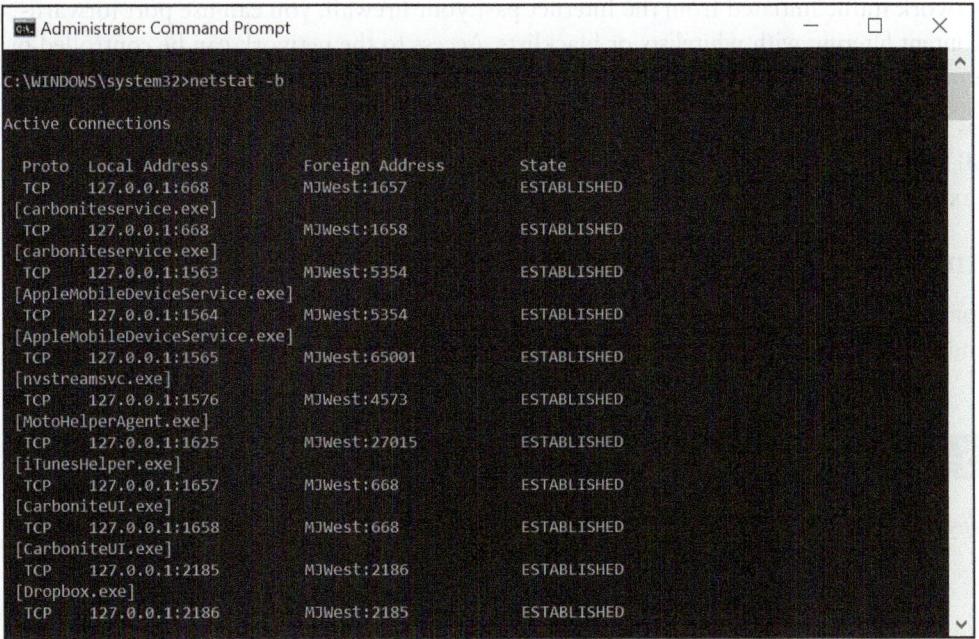

Figure 7-64   Netstat -b lists programs that are using a network connection

> ✏️ **Notes** Many commands other than netstat can use the >> parameter to redirect output to a text file. For example, try the ping or tracert command with this parameter:
>
> ```
> tracert cengage.com >>C:\Users\"Jill West"\Documents\testfile.txt
> ```

>> CHAPTER SUMMARY

Types of Networks and Network Connections

◢ Networks are categorized by size as a PAN, LAN, WMN, MAN, or WAN.

◢ Performance of a network technology is measured in bandwidth and latency.

◢ The two most popular ways to connect to the Internet are cable Internet and DSL. Other methods used include dedicated fiber optic, satellite, dial-up, and cellular wireless technologies (3G, 4G, 5G, and/or LTE).

Connecting a Computer to a Local Network

◢ A VPN protects data by encrypting it from the time it leaves the remote computer until it reaches a server on the corporate network, and vice versa.

◢ A host needs an IP address, subnet mask, default gateway, and IP addresses for DNS servers to communicate with other hosts on the local or remote networks.

◢ Network adapters, commonly called NICs, are rated by speed and each has a MAC address. Some NICs have status indicator lights and wake-on-LAN and QoS features.

Setting Up a Multifunction Router for a SOHO Network

◢ A multifunction router for a small office/home office network might serve several functions, including router, switch, DHCP server, wireless access point, firewall, and FTP server.

◢ It's extremely important to change the administrative password on a router as soon as you install it, especially if the router also serves as a wireless access point.

◢ To allow certain network traffic initiated from the Internet past your firewall, you can use port forwarding, a DMZ, and content filtering with whitelists or blacklists. Access to the network can be controlled by MAC address filtering.

◢ To secure a wireless access point, you can require a security key, enable encryption (WEP, WPA, WPA2, or WPA3), disable SSID broadcasting, and adjust radio power levels. You can also set wireless channels and wireless QoS to maximize the efficiency of a wireless network.

Troubleshooting Network Connections

◢ Useful Windows command-line utilities for network troubleshooting are ping, ipconfig, nslookup, tracert, net use, net user, and netstat. The Linux ifconfig command is similar to the Windows ipconfig command.

>> KEY TERMS

For explanations of key terms, see the Glossary for this text.

3G	802.11a	802.11g	AES (Advanced Encryption
4G	802.11ac	802.11n	Standard)
5G	802.11b	address reservation	

APIPA (Automatic private IP address)
bandwidth
beamforming
blacklist
broadband
cable Internet
cable modem
cellular network
channel
client/server application
coaxial (coax) cable
data throughput
default gateway
DHCP (Dynamic Host Configuration Protocol)
DHCP client
DHCP server
DHCPv6 server
DMZ (demilitarized zone)
DNS (Domain Name System or Domain Name Service)
DNS server
DSL (Digital Subscriber Line)
DSL modem
dynamic IP address
elevated command prompt window

fiber optic
fiber-optic cable
firewall
FTP (File Transfer Protocol)
FTP server
full duplex
half duplex
host
ifconfig (interface configuration)
IP address
ipconfig (IP configuration)
IPv4 (Internet Protocol version 4)
IPv6 (Internet Protocol version 6)
ISDN (Integrated Services Digital Network)
ISP (Internet service provider)
LAN (local area network)
latency
line-of-sight wireless connectivity
LTE (Long Term Evolution)
MAC address
MAC address filtering
MAN (metropolitan area network)

MIMO (multiple input/ multiple output)
mobile hotspot
name resolution
net use
net user
netstat (network statistics)
NIC (network interface card)
nslookup (namespace lookup or name server lookup)
PAN (personal area network)
physical address
ping
port address
port forwarding
protocol
QoS (Quality of Service)
reverse lookup
RJ-11
RJ-45
router
SIM (Subscriber Identification Module) card
SSID (Service Set Identifier)
static IP address
subnet mask
switch

TCP/IP (Transmission Control Protocol/Internet Protocol)
tether
TKIP (Temporal Key Integrity Protocol)
tracert (trace route)
UPnP (Universal Plug and Play)
VPN (virtual private network)
Wake-on-LAN
WAN (wide area network)
WAP (wireless access point)
WEP (Wired Equivalent Privacy)
whitelist
Wi-Fi (Wireless Fidelity)
WLAN (wireless LAN)
WMN (wireless mesh network)
WPA (Wi-Fi Protected Access)
WPA2 (Wi-Fi Protected Access 2)
WPA3 (Wi-Fi Protected Access 3)
WPS (Wi-Fi Protected Setup)
WWAN (wireless wide area network)

>> THINKING CRITICALLY

These questions are designed to prepare you for the critical thinking required for the A+ exams and may use content from other chapters and the web.

1. You have just finished installing a network adapter and booted up the system, installing the drivers. You open File Explorer on a remote computer and don't see the computer on which you installed the new NIC. What is the first thing you check? The second thing?

   a. Has IPv6 addressing been enabled?

   b. Is the computer using dynamic or static IP addressing?

   c. Do the lights on the adapter indicate it's functioning correctly?

   d. Has the computer been assigned a computer name?

2. As an IT technician, you arrive at a customer's home office to troubleshoot problems he's experiencing with his printer. While questioning the customer to get an understanding of his network, you find that he has a new Wi-Fi router that connects wirelessly to a new desktop and two new laptops, in addition to multiple smartphones, tablets, and the network printer. He also has several smart home devices, including security cameras, light switches, door locks, and a thermostat supported by an IoT controller hub. To work on the printer, which type of network will you be interacting with?

    a. PAN

    b. WAN

    c. WMN

    d. LAN

3. While you work on the customer's printer, he continues chatting about his network and problems he's been experiencing. One complaint is that his Internet service slows down considerably in the evening. You suspect you know the cause of this problem: His neighbors arrive home in the evening and bog down the ISP's local infrastructure. To be sure, you take a quick look at the back of his modem. What type of cable connected to the WAN port would confirm your suspicions and why?

4. Your customer then asks you if it would be worth the investment for him to have Ethernet cabling installed to reach each of his workstations, instead of connecting them by Wi-Fi to his network. Specifically, he wants to know if that would speed up communications for the workstations. You examine his router and find that it's using 802.11ac Wi-Fi. Would you advise him to upgrade to Ethernet? Why or why not?

    a. Yes, because Ethernet is faster than 802.11ac.

    b. Yes, because wired connections are always faster than wireless connections.

    c. No, because installing Ethernet cabling is more expensive than the increased speed is worth.

    d. No, because 802.11ac speeds are faster than Ethernet.

5. You run the ipconfig command on your computer, and it reports an IP address of 169.254.75.10 on the Ethernet interface. Which device assigned this IP address to the interface?

    a. The ISP's DNS server

    b. The local network's DHCP server on the SOHO router

    c. The cable modem

    d. The local computer

6. A friend of yours is having trouble getting good Internet service. He says his house is too remote for cable TV—he doesn't even have a telephone line to his house. He's also really frustrated with satellite service because cloudy skies or storms often disrupt the signal. You ask him what provider he uses for his cell phone. He says he has Verizon for his cell, which gets a good signal at his house. What Internet service will you recommend he look into getting for his home network?

    a. Dial-up

    b. LTE installed Internet

    c. DSL

    d. Cable Internet

7. You've just received a call from Human Resources asking for assistance with a problem. One of your company's employees, Renee, has recently undergone extensive surgery and will be homebound for 3–5 months. She plans on working from home and needs a solution to enable frequent and extended access to the company network's resources. Which WAN technology will you need to configure for Renee and which tool will you use to configure it?

    a. WWAN using the Network Connections window

    b. Dial-up using the Network and Sharing Center

    c. Ethernet using the Network Connections window

    d. VPN using the Network and Sharing Center

8. Describe two different methods of opening the Network and Sharing Center in Windows 10.

9. In this chapter, you learned how to set a static IP address in Windows. Most Linux OSs allow these settings to be changed from the command line. Search online to see how to do this. What Linux command is used to set the interface to a static IP address?

10. Your boss has asked you to configure a DHCP reservation on the network for a Windows computer that is used to configure other devices on a network. To do this, you need the computer's MAC address. What command can you enter at the command line to access this information?

11. You're setting up a Minecraft gaming server so that you and several of your friends can share a realm during your gameplay. To do this, your friends will need to access your server over the Internet, which means you must configure your router to send this traffic to your game server. Which router feature will you use and which port must you open?

12. While troubleshooting an Internet connection problem for your network, you restarted the modem and then the router. The router is now communicating with the Internet, which you can confirm by observing the blinking light on the router's WAN indicator. However, now your laptop is not communicating with the router. Order the commands below to fix the problem and confirm connectivity.

   a. ping

   b. ipconfig /renew

   c. nslookup microsoft.com

   d. ipconfig /release

13. You have just installed a SOHO router in a customer's home and the owner has called to say his son is complaining that Internet gaming is too slow. His son is using a wireless laptop. Which possibilities should you consider to speed up the son's gaming experience? Select all that apply.

   a. Verify that the wireless connection is using the fastest wireless standard the router supports.

   b. Disable encryption on the wireless network to speed up transmissions.

   c. Suggest the son use a wired Gigabit Ethernet connection to the network.

   d. Enable QoS for the gaming applications on the router and on the son's computer.

14. You need a VPN to connect to a private, remote network in order to access some files. You click the network icon in your taskbar to establish the connection, and realize there is no VPN option available on the menu. What tool do you need to use to fix this problem?

   a. net command

   b. netstat command

   c. Network and Sharing Center

   d. Network Connections window

15. You're troubleshooting a network connection for a client at her home office. After pinging the network's default gateway, you discovered that the cable connecting the desktop to the router had been damaged by foot traffic and was no longer providing a reliable signal. You replaced the cable, this time running the cable along the wall so it won't be stepped on. What do you do next?

>> HANDS-ON PROJECTS

Hands-On | Project 7-1   Investigating Verizon FiOS

Verizon (*verizon.com*) offers FiOS, an alternative to DSL and cable for wired broadband Internet access to a residence or small business. FiOS is a fiber-optic Internet service that uses fiber-optic cable all the way to your house or business to provide both telephone service and Internet access. Search the web for answers to these questions about FiOS:

1. Give a brief description of FiOS and how it is used for Internet access.

2. What downstream and upstream speeds can FiOS support?

3. When using FiOS, does your telephone voice communication share the fiber-optic cable with Internet data?

4. Is FiOS available in your area?

Hands-On | Project 7-2   Investigating Network Connection Settings

Using a computer connected to a network, answer these questions:

1. What is the hardware device used to make this connection (network card, onboard port, wireless)? List the device's name as Windows sees it in the Device Manager window.

2. What is the MAC address of the wired or wireless network adapter? What command or window did you use to get your answer?

3. For a wireless connection, is the network secured? If so, what is the security type?

4. What is the IPv4 address of the network connection?

5. Are your TCP/IP version 4 settings using static or dynamic IP addressing?

6. What is the IPv6 address of your network connection?

7. Disable and enable your network connection. Now what is your IPv4 address?

Hands-On | Project 7-3   Researching a Wireless LAN

Suppose you have a DSL connection to the Internet in your home and you want to connect two laptops and a desktop computer in a wireless network to the Internet. You need to purchase a multifunction wireless router like the ones you learned to configure in this chapter. You also need a wireless adapter for the desktop computer. (The two laptops have built-in wireless networking.) Use the web to research the equipment needed to create the wireless LAN and answer the following:

1. Save or print two webpages showing two different multifunctional wireless routers. What is the brand, model, and price of each router?

2. Save or print two webpages showing two different wireless adapters a desktop computer can use to connect to the wireless network. Include one external device that uses a USB port and one internal device. What is the brand, model, and price of each device?

3. Which router and wireless adapter would you select for your home network? What is the total cost of both devices?

Hands-On | Project 7-4   Viewing and Clearing the DNS Cache

Open a command prompt window and use the ipconfig /displaydns command to view the DNS cache on your computer. Then use the ipconfig /flushdns command to clear the DNS cache.

>> REAL PROBLEMS, REAL SOLUTIONS

REAL PROBLEM 7-1 Setting Up a Small Network

The simplest possible wired network is two computers connected together using a crossover cable. In a crossover cable, the send and receive wires are crossed so that one computer can send and the other computer receives on the same wire. At first glance, a crossover cable looks just like a regular network cable (also called a patch cable) except for the labeling, as shown in Figure 7-65. (In Chapter 8, you learn how to distinguish between the cables by examining their connectors.)

Figure 7-65   A patch cable and crossover cable look the same but are labeled differently

Do the following to set up and test a small network:

1. Connect two computers using a crossover cable. Using the Network and Sharing Center, verify that your network is up. Using ipconfig, determine each computer's IP address. What is the IPv4 address of Computer A? Of Computer B?

2. On each computer, try to ping the other computer. Does it work? Why or why not? What specific output do you get?

3. Convert the TCP/IP configuration to static IP addressing. Assign 192.168.10.4 to one computer and 192.168.10.5 to the other computer. The subnet mask for both computers is 255.255.255.0.

4. Ping each computer from the other computer. Does it work? Why or why not?

5. Without changing the subnet masks, change the IP address of one computer to 192.168.90.1. Can you still ping each computer? What specific output do you get?

6. Return the computers to the same subnet and IP addresses you used in step 3. Verify that each computer can ping the other.

REAL PROBLEM 7-2 Using the Hosts File

The hosts file in the C:\Windows\System32\drivers\etc folder has no file extension and contains computer names and their associated IP addresses on the local network. An IT support technician can manually edit the hosts file when the association is needed for address resolution on the local network and a DNS server is not available on the local network.

> ✎ **Notes** For an entry in the hosts file to work, the remote computer must always have the same IP address.

Using your small network you set up in Real Problem 7-1, do the following to use the hosts file:

1. Verify that each computer can ping the other.

2. What is the name of each computer? For Windows 10/8, press **Win+X** and click **System** to find out.

3. Try to ping each computer using its computer name rather than its IP address. Did the ping work?

4. On Computer A, copy the hosts file to a new location and edit it using Notepad. Add the entry that associates the IP address of Computer B with its computer name. As you save the file, be sure not to assign it a file extension. Rename the original hosts file and then copy the edited hosts file to the C:\ Windows\System32\drivers\etc folder.

5. Repeat step 4 for the hosts file on Computer B to associate the name and IP address of Computer A.

6. Try to ping each computer, this time using its computer name rather than IP address. Did the ping work?

REAL PROBLEM 7-3 Installing and Using Packet Tracer

If you plan to pursue networking or security as your area of specialty in IT, you might consider earning a few Cisco networking certifications after you complete your CompTIA A+, Network+, and Security+ certifications. The Cisco Networking Academy website provides many useful tools for advancing your networking education. One of those tools is a network simulator called Packet Tracer. In this project, you download and install Packet Tracer, and create a very basic network using simulated devices in Packet Tracer. This version of Packet Tracer is free to the public, and your school does not have to be a member of Cisco's Networking Academy for you to download and use it.

To get the Packet Tracer download, you must first sign up for the free Introduction to Packet Tracer online course on the Cisco Networking Academy website. Complete the following steps to create your account:

1. In your browser, navigate to **netacad.com/courses/packet-tracer**. Enroll in the course.

2. Open the confirmation email and confirm your email address. Configure your account and save this information in a safe place. You will need this information again.

3. Click Courses and select the Introduction to Packet Tracer course.

   Now you are ready to download and install Packet Tracer. If you need help with the download and installation process, launch the course and navigate to Chapter 1, Section 1.1, Topic 1.1.2 for additional guidance. Complete the following steps:

4. Inside the course, click **Student Resources**, and then click **Download and install the latest version of Packet Tracer**. Download the latest version for your computer, and then install Packet Tracer. Note that the download might not complete in the MS Edge browser; if you encounter a problem, try Google Chrome instead. When the installation is complete, run **Cisco Packet Tracer**.

5. When Packet Tracer opens, sign in with your Networking Academy account that you created earlier. If you see a Windows Security Alert, allow access through your firewall. Cisco Packet Tracer opens. The interface window is shown in Figure 7-66.

Figure 7-66 Explore the Packet Tracer window

Source: Cisco Systems, Inc.

The Introduction to Packet Tracer course presents an excellent introduction to Packet Tracer and provides lab activities. We'll revisit the Packet Tracer course in Chapter 8. In the meantime, let's build a very simple network in Packet Tracer so you can begin to get familiar with the user interface.

6. First you need a router. In Packet Tracer (and in most network diagrams), routers look like a hockey puck with four arrows on top. In the Devices pane, make sure the **Network Devices** group is selected and the **Routers** subgroup, is selected. Drag a **2901** router from the selection pane into the workspace.

7. Next, add a switch. In network diagrams, switches look like rectangular boxes with four arrows on top. Click to select the **Switches** subgroup, then drag a **2960-24TT** switch to the workspace.

8. Now you're ready to add a couple of computers. Select the **End Devices** group. Drag a **Generic PC** and a **Generic Laptop** to the workspace. Arrange all the devices as shown in Figure 7-67.

Figure 7-67 Arrange the devices on your network diagram

Source: Cisco Systems, Inc.

9. Now you're ready to connect the devices with Ethernet cables. Click the orange lightning icon to select the **Connections** group. Use the lightning icon from the selection pane to automatically select the correct connection type for each connection you make. In Chapter 8, you'll learn more about different types of cables so you can make those decisions yourself. After you click the **Automatically Choose Connection Type** lightning icon, click **PC0** to start the connection, then click **Switch0** to complete the connection. The link starts as orange, and as the connection is negotiated between the PC and the switch, the link turns to green on both ends.

10. Create an automatic connection from **Laptop0** to **Switch0**, and another automatic connection from **Switch0** to **Router0**. The laptop-to-switch connection will come up automatically. The switch-to-router connection will remain red because it requires additional configuration before it will work.

11. Click **Router0** to see its configuration window. On the Physical tab, you can see a picture of the device itself, both front and back. Explore this window to see what information is available to you, but don't change anything. When you're ready, click the **Config** tab.

    In Packet Tracer, you can perform all the configurations at the CLI (command line interface) or through a GUI (graphic user interface). In this project, you'll use the GUI options, and watch the *Equivalent IOS Commands* pane at the bottom of the window to see what commands you're executing.

12. To activate the router's interface, click the **GigabitEthernet0/0** interface in the left pane. Position the configuration window off to the side of the workspace so you can see Router0 and monitor any changes to the connection. Change the Port Status to **On**. What happens to the connection in the workspace?

13. Let's add IP configuration information. Give the connection the IP Address of **192.168.43.1** and a Subnet Mask of **255.255.255.0**. Then close Router0's configuration window.

14. Next, add IP address configuration information to the endpoint devices. Click **PC0** to open its configuration window. Here, you could use the Config tab or tools from the Desktop tab. Click **Desktop**, then click **IP Configuration**. You have two options: DHCP or Static. For now, you'll have to use Static. Why?

15. Make sure **Static** is selected, then give the PC the following IP configuration:
    - IP Address: **192.168.43.100**
    - Subnet Mask: **255.255.255.0**
    - Default Gateway: **192.168.43.1**

    With this configuration, what device will the PC use as its default gateway?

16. Close PC0's configuration window, then use the same steps to give Laptop0 the following IP configuration:
    - IP Address: **192.168.43.200**
    - Subnet Mask: **255.255.255.0**
    - Default Gateway: **192.168.43.1**

17. On Laptop0, close the IP Configuration pane. On the Desktop tab, click **Command Prompt**. Ping PC0 from Laptop0. What command did you use? Did it work?

18. You can use Simulation mode to watch the ping messages travel over the network. Close Laptop0's configuration window, then click the **Simulation mode** tab in the bottom right of the Packet Tracer window (refer back to Figure 7-66). Open Laptop0's **Command Prompt** window again, and position this window off to the side of the workspace so you can see the devices. Ping the router. What command did you use? Did it work?

19. This network is not connected to a simulated WAN connection, although it could be. Which device in this network would you connect to the modem for the ISP's network?

20. Packet Tracer gives you a safe and fun environment to explore networking concepts. Take a few minutes to look around the Packet Tracer menus and options, and perhaps add more devices to your network. When you're ready, close all open windows. You do not need to save your Packet Tracer file unless you want to.

Network Infrastructure and Troubleshooting

After completing this chapter, you will be able to:

- Explain the TCP/IP protocols and standards Windows uses for networking

- Identify, compare, and contrast hardware used to build local networks

- Set up and troubleshoot the wiring in a small network

- Troubleshoot network connectivity problems caused by firmware, operating systems, and applications

You've already learned how to connect a computer to a network and how to set up and secure a wired and wireless router for a small network. This chapter takes you a step further in supporting networks. You learn how Windows uses TCP/IP protocols and standards to create and manage network connections, including how computers are identified and addressed on a network. You also learn about the hardware devices, cables, and connectors used to construct a network. Next, you learn about networking tools, how to terminate network cables, and how to troubleshoot problems with network hardware and software.

UNDERSTANDING TCP/IP AND WINDOWS NETWORKING

A+
CORE 1
2.1, 2.2,
2.3, 2.6

The more you understand how networks work, the more likely you will be able to solve problems with network connections. This part of the chapter focuses on how a network works. When two computers communicate using a local network or the Internet, communication happens essentially at four levels: the hardware, the operating system, the application for each computer on the network, and the network itself. Communication begins when one computer tries to find the other computer on the local or remote network. For example, in Figure 8-1, someone uses a web browser on a client to request a webpage from a web server. To handle this request, the client computer looks for the web server, the protocols for communication are established, and then the request is made and answered. Hardware, network devices, the OS, and the applications on both computers are all involved in this process.

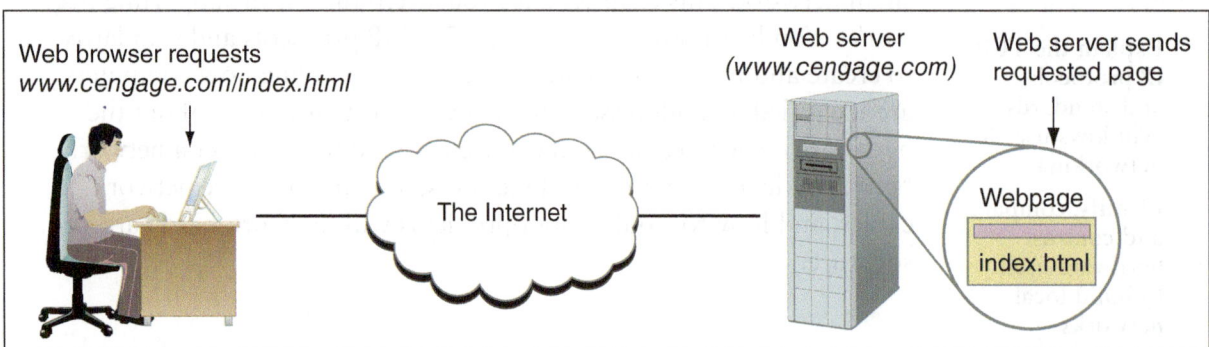

Figure 8-1   A web browser (client software) requests a webpage from a web server (server software); the web server returns the requested data to the client

Let's first look at the layers of communication that involve hardware, network devices, the OS, and applications, and then see how computers are addressed and found on a network or the Internet. Then we'll see how a client/server request is made by the client and answered by the server.

LAYERS OF NETWORK COMMUNICATION

A+
CORE 1
2.2

When your computer at home is connected to your Internet service provider (ISP) off somewhere in the distance, your computer and a computer on the Internet must be able to communicate. When two devices communicate, they must use the same protocols so that the communication makes sense. Recall that, for almost all networks today, including the Internet, the group or suite of protocols used is called TCP/IP (Transmission Control Protocol/Internet Protocol).

TCP/IP MODEL FOR NETWORK COMMUNICATION

Let's consider network communication that starts when a browser (an application) requests a webpage from a web server (another application). The layers of communication are shown in Figure 8-2 with the blue arrows. The request is passed to the OS, which passes the request to the network card, which passes the request on to the network. When the request reaches the network card on the server, the network card passes the request on to the OS and then the OS passes it on to the application (the web server).

Figure 8-2 Network communication happens in layers

When studying networking theory, a simple model used to divide network communication into four layers is the TCP/IP model. In this model, protocols used by hardware function at the Link layer, and protocols used by the OS are divided into three layers (Internet, Transport, and Application layers). These four layers are shown on the left and right sides of Figure 8-2 and listed in Table 8-1.

Layer	Addressing	Description
Layer 4: Application layer		Application-to-application communication is managed by the OS, using protocols specific to the application (HTTP, Telnet, FTP, and so forth). This layer of communication happens after the OSs have made a connection at the Transport layer.
Layer 3: Transport layer	Port numbers	Host-to-host communication, managed by the OS, primarily using TCP and UDP protocols.
Layer 2: Internet layer	IP addresses	Host-to-host on the local network or network-to-network communication, managed by the OS and network devices.
Layer 1: Link layer	MAC addresses	Device-to-device on local network, managed by firmware on NICs. Layer 1 is also called the Network interface layer or Network access layer.

Table 8-1 TCP/IP model has four layers of communication

Let's follow a message from browser to web server, paying attention to each layer of communication:

▲ *Source Step 1: Application layer*. Recall from Chapter 7 that most applications that use a network are client/server applications. When a browser client makes a request to a web server, the browser passes the request to the OS. The OS formats the message using the appropriate application protocol (for example,

HTTP, FTP, Telnet, DNS, and SSH). In our example, an HTTP message is created and passed down in the TCP/IP stack of protocols to the Transport layer.

▲ *Source Step 2: Transport layer.* The Transport layer adds information to the message to address the correct server application. Depending on the type of application, the protocol TCP (Transmission Control Protocol) or UDP (User Datagram Protocol) adds the port assigned to the server application (TCP uses port 80 for HTTP communication in our example). The message with Transport data added is then passed down to the Internet layer.

▲ *Source Step 3: Internet layer.* The Internet layer is responsible for getting the message to the destination computer or host on the local network, an intranet, or the Internet. An intranet is any private network that uses TCP/IP protocols. A large enterprise might support an intranet that is made up of several local networks. The primary protocol used at the Internet layer is IP (Internet Protocol), which uses a 32-bit and/or 128-bit IP address to identify each host. (Other Internet layer protocols include EIGRP, OSPF, BGP, and ICMP.) IP adds address information to the message and then passes it down to the Link layer.

▲ *Source Step 4: Link layer.* The Link layer is the physical network, including the hardware and its firmware for every device connected to the network. A computer's network interface card (NIC) is part of this physical network. As you know, each NIC is able to communicate with other NICs on the local network using each NIC's MAC address. The MAC address is a 48-bit (6-byte) unique number hard-coded on the card by its manufacturer. Part of the MAC address identifies the manufacturer, who is responsible for making sure that no two network adapters have the same MAC address. Every device on a network (for example, computers, printers, smart thermostats, refrigerators, and smartphones) connects to the network by way of its NIC and MAC address. For a local network, recall the hardware or physical connection might be wireless (most likely using Wi-Fi) or wired (most likely using Ethernet). The NIC receives the message from IP, adds information for Ethernet or Wi-Fi transmission, and places the message on the network.

📝 **Notes**   You can have Windows tell you the MAC address of an installed NIC by entering the ipconfig /all command in a command prompt window (see Figure 8-3).

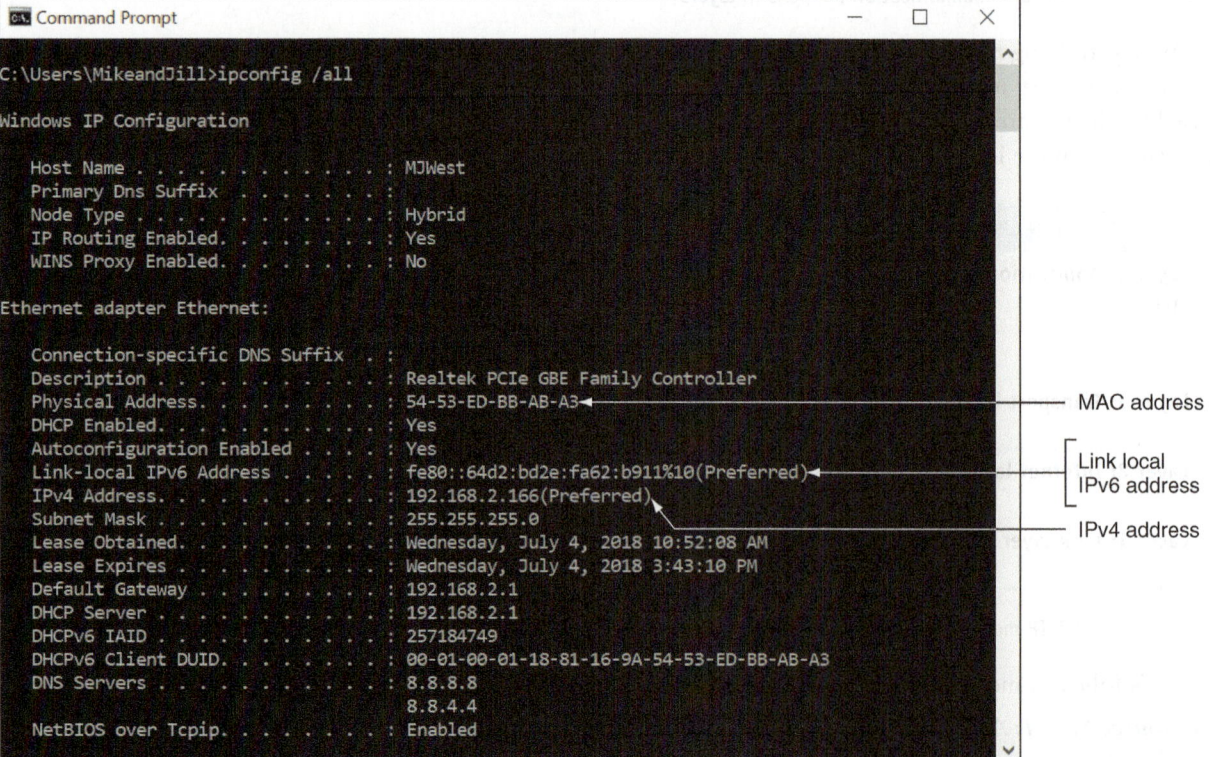

Figure 8-3   Use the ipconfig /all command to show the MAC address, also called the physical address, of a network adapter

▲ *Step 5: Network transmission*. IP at the Internet layer is responsible to make sure the message gets from one network to the next until it reaches its destination network (see Figure 8-4) and destination computer on that network. Whereas a MAC address at the hardware Link layer is only used to find a computer or other host on a local network, an IP address can be used to find a computer on a local network, anywhere on the Internet (see Figure 8-5), or on an intranet.

Figure 8-4 A host (router, in this case) can always determine if an IP address is on its network

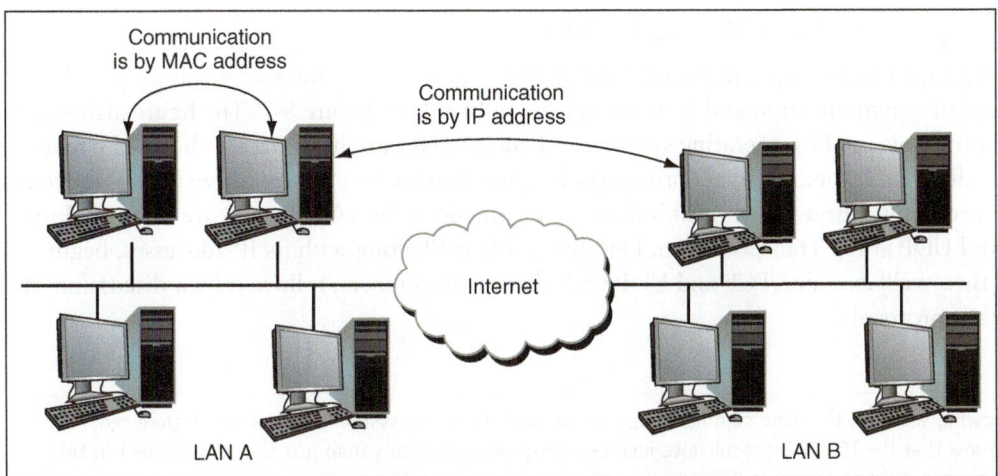

Figure 8-5 Computers on the same LAN can use MAC addresses to communicate, but computers on different LANs use IP addresses to communicate over the Internet

◢ *Step 6: Destination.* On the destination computer, its NIC receives the message, strips off Ethernet or Wi-Fi information at the Link layer, and passes the message up to the Internet layer. The Internet layer strips off IP address information and passes the message up to the Transport layer. The Transport layer strips off TCP or UDP information and passes the message to the correct port (see Figure 8-6) and on to the Application layer. The Application layer passes the message to the web server application.

Figure 8-6   Each server running on a computer is addressed by a unique port number

> ✎ **Notes**   Messages on a TCP/IP network might have different names depending on which layer's protocols have added information to the message, either at the beginning of the message (called a header) or at the end (called a trailer). For example, messages with IP address header information added are called packets. Messages with source and destination MAC addresses are called frames. In general, all of these messages can be referred to with the more technical term **protocol data unit (PDU)**.

COMPARE THE TCP/IP MODEL AND OSI MODEL

Besides the TCP/IP model, a more complicated model is the OSI (Open Systems Interconnection) model, which has seven layers of communication and is shown on the right side of Figure 8-7. The figure also shows many of the TCP/IP protocols used by operating systems and client/server applications and how they relate to one another at the different layers. As you continue reading the chapter, this figure can serve as your road map to the different protocols. Three of the most important protocols in the TCP/IP suite are IP at the Internet layer, and TCP and UDP at the Transport layer. Let's first look at IP along with its IP addresses, beginning with IPv4, and then we'll examine TCP and UDP with their port numbers, followed by a discussion of several other important protocols.

> ✎ **Notes**   In the following sections, the more significant application and operating system protocols are introduced. However, you should know that the TCP/IP protocol suite includes many more protocols than just those mentioned in this chapter; only some of them are shown in Figure 8-7.

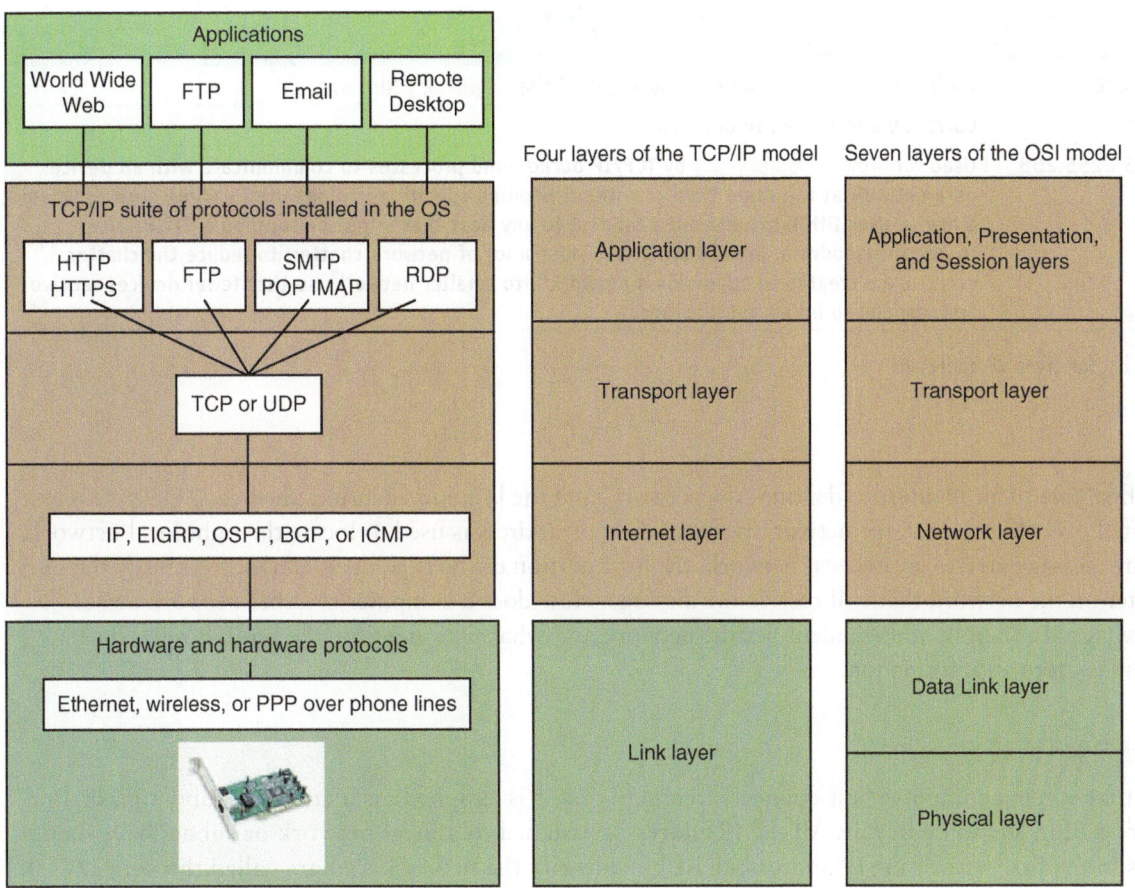

Figure 8-7 How software, protocols, and technology on a TCP/IP network relate to each other

HOW IPV4 ADDRESSES ARE USED

A+
CORE 1
2.3, 2.6

A MAC address is embedded on every NIC at the factory, but each time a computer connects to a network, the interface with the network is assigned an IP address. Recall from Chapter 7 that an IP address can be a dynamic IP address assigned by a DHCP server or a static IP address manually assigned by the user or a technician. An IP address has 32 bits or 128 bits. When the Internet and TCP/IP were first invented, it seemed that 32 bits were more than enough to satisfy any needs we might have for IP addresses because IPv4 created about four billion potential IP addresses. Today we need many more than four billion IP addresses over the world. Partly because of a shortage of 32-bit IP addresses, IPv6 was designed to use an IP address with 128 bits. Currently, the Internet uses a mix of 32-bit and 128-bit IP addresses. The Internet Assigned Numbers Authority (IANA at *iana.org*) is responsible for keeping track of assigned IP addresses and has already released all of its available 32-bit IPv4 addresses. IPv6 addresses leased from IANA today are all 128-bit addresses.

A 32-bit IPv4 address is organized into four groups of 8 bits each, which are presented as four decimal numbers separated by periods, such as 72.56.105.12. The largest possible 8-bit number is 11111111, which is equal to 255 in decimal, so the largest possible IPv4 address in decimal is 255.255.255.255, which in binary is 11111111.11111111.11111111.11111111. Each of the four numbers separated by periods is called an octet (for 8 bits) and can be any decimal value from 0 to 255, making a total of about 4.3 billion IPv4 addresses (256 × 256 × 256 × 256). Some IP addresses are reserved, so these numbers are approximations. IP addresses that are reserved for special use by TCP/IP and should not be assigned to a device on a network are listed in Table 8-2.

IP Address	How It Is Used
127.0.0.1	Indicates your own computer and is called the loopback address.
0.0.0.0	Currently unassigned IP address.
255.255.255.255	Used for broadcast messages by TCP/IP background processes to communicate with all devices on a network at the same time or without needing specific recipient information, such as when a device uses DHCP to send out a request to any host that might be running a DHCP server to get an IP address. Broadcasting can cause a lot of network chatter; to reduce the chatter, subnets are created to subdivide a network into smaller networks so that fewer devices receive and respond to broadcast messages.

Table 8-2   Reserved IP addresses

The first part of an IP address identifies the network, and the last part identifies the host. When messages are routed over the Internet, the network portion of the IP address is used to locate the right local network. After the message arrives at the local network, the host portion of the IP address is used to identify the one computer on the network that will receive the message. How does a computer or other network device know what part of an IP address identifies the network and what part identifies the host? It relies on a subnet mask for this information.

SUBNET MASKS

Recall that when a computer first connects to a network, it is assigned an IP address, subnet mask, and IP address of its default gateway. All the IP addresses assigned to a local network or subnet have matching bits in the first part of the IP address; these bits identify the network and are called the network ID. For example, the range of IP addresses assigned to a local network might be 192.168.80.1-100. The first three octets (192.168.80) identify the network and the last octet (1 through 100) identifies each host. The last bits in each IP address that identify the host must be unique for each IP address on the network.

Before a computer can send a message to another computer, it must decide whether it can communicate directly with the computer on its local network or must go through the default gateway to a remote network. To decide, the computer compares the network ID portion of its IP address to the network ID portion of the remote computer's IP address. How does it know how many bits in its IP address identify its network? That's the job of the subnet mask.

A subnet mask has 32 bits and is a string of 1s followed by a string of 0s—for example, 11111111.11111 111.11110000.00000000. The 1s in a subnet mask say, "On our network, this part of an IP address identifies our network," and the group of 0s says, "On our network, this part of an IP address identifies the host." Usually a subnet mask is displayed in decimal—for example, the subnet mask of 11111111.11111111.0000 0000.00000000 is 255.255.0.0 in decimal.

Figure 8-8 shows how a subnet mask serves as a type of filter to decide whether a destination IP address is on the local network or a remote network. In the figure, you can see that the subnet mask has 24 ones. Therefore, the computer compares the first 24 bits of the destination IP address to its own first 24 bits. If they match, it directs the message to the computer on its local network. If they don't match, it sends the message to its default gateway.

In another example, suppose the IP address of a computer is 201.18.20.160 and the subnet mask is 255.255.0.0, which is 11111111.11111111.00000000.00000000 in binary. The subnet mask tells Windows that the first 16 bits, or two octets (201.18), of the IP address is the network ID. Therefore, when Windows

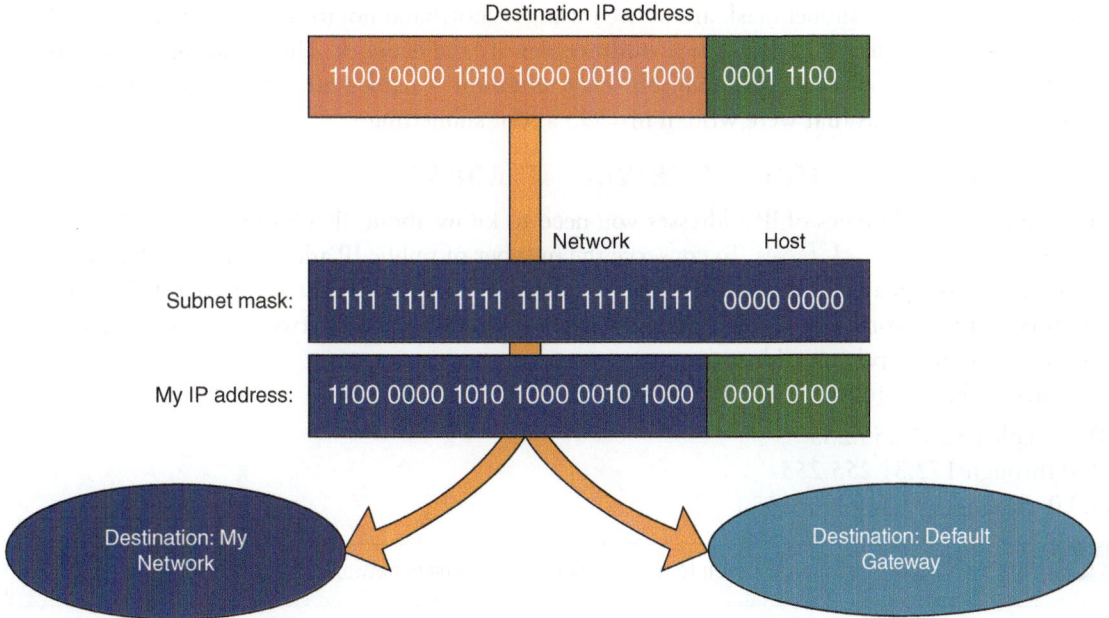

Destination IP address

1100 0000 1010 1000 0010 1000   0001 1100

Network   Host

Subnet mask: 1111 1111 1111 1111 1111 1111   0000 0000

My IP address: 1100 0000 1010 1000 0010 1000   0001 0100

Destination: My
Network

Destination: Default
Gateway

8

Figure 8-8   The subnet mask serves as a filter to decide whether a destination IP address is on its own or
another network

is deciding how to communicate with a computer that has an IP address of 201.18.20.208, it knows the computer is on its own network, but a computer with an IP address of 201.19.23.160 is on a different network.

Let's look at one more example. Suppose the IP address of a computer is 19.200.60.6 and its subnet mask is 255.255.240.0. Is a computer with the IP address 19.200.51.100 on its network? Table 8-3 shows the logic to find out:

Question	Answer
1. What is my IP address in binary?	19.200.60.6 in binary is: 00010011.11001000.00111100.00000110.
2. What is my subnet mask in binary?	255.255.240.0 in binary is: 11111111.11111111.11110000.00000000.
3. How many bits in my IP address identify my network?	There are 20 ones in the subnet mask. Therefore, 20 bits identify the network.
4. What is the other IP address in binary?	19.200.51.100 in binary is: 00010011.11001000.00110011.01100100.
5. Do the first 20 bits in my IP address match the first 20 bits in the other IP address?	Compare the 20 red bits in the two IP addresses: 00010011.11001000.00111100.00000110 00010011.11001000.00110011.01100100 Yes, they match.
6. Is the other IP address on my network?	Yes.

Table 8-3   Logic of a subnet mask

Sometimes an IP address and subnet mask are written using a shorthand notation like 15.50.212.59/20, where the /20 means that the first 20 bits in the IP address identify the network. This notation is sometimes called slash notation or CIDR notation (pronounced "*cider notation*"), named after the CIDR (Classless Interdomain Routing) standards that were written in 1993 about subnetting.

PUBLIC, PRIVATE, AND AUTOMATIC PRIVATE IP ADDRESSES

There are a few more special ranges of IP addresses you need to know about. IP addresses available to the Internet are called public IP addresses. To conserve the number of public IP addresses, some blocks of IP addresses have been designated as private IP addresses that are not allowed on the Internet. Private IP addresses are used within a company's private network, and computers on this network can communicate with one another using these private addresses.

IEEE recommends that the following IP addresses be used for private networks:

◢ 10.0.0.0 through 10.255.255.255
◢ 172.16.0.0 through 172.31.255.255
◢ 192.168.0.0 through 192.168.255.255

> ★ **A+ Exam Tip** The A+ Core 1 exam expects you to have memorized the private network IP address ranges.

There's also a special type of private IP address range. If a computer first connects to a network that is using dynamic IP addressing and is unable to lease an IP address from the DHCP server, it generates its own Automatic Private IP Address (APIPA) in the address range 169.254.*x*.*y*.

> 🖉 **Notes** If you are running a web server on the Internet, you will need a public IP address for your router and either a static or reserved private IP address for the web server. For this situation, you can lease a public IP address from your ISP at an additional cost. You will also need to enable port forwarding to the server, which is discussed in Chapter 7.

NAT (Network Address Translation) is a technique designed to conserve the number of public IP addresses needed by a network. A router stands between a private network and the Internet. It substitutes the private IP addresses used by computers on the private network with its own public IP address when these computers need access to the Internet. See Figure 8-9. Besides conserving public IP addresses, another advantage of NAT is security; the router hides the entire private network behind this one address. For a SOHO router, expect that NAT is enabled by default.

Figure 8-9 NAT allows computers with private IP addresses to access the Internet

> 🖉 **Notes** IEEE, a nonprofit organization, is responsible for many Internet standards. Standards are proposed to the networking community in the form of an RFC (Request for Comment). RFC 1918 outlines recommendations for private IP addresses. To view an RFC, visit the website *rfc-editor.org*.

HOW IPV6 ADDRESSES ARE USED

 A+ CORE 1 2.6 Moving on to the IPv6 standards, more has changed than just the number of bits in an IP address. To improve routing capabilities and speed of communication, IPv6 changed the way IP addresses are used to find computers on the Internet. Let's begin our discussion of IPv6 by looking at how IPv6 addresses are written and displayed:

▲ An IPv6 address has 128 bits that are written as eight blocks of hexadecimal numbers separated by colons, like this: 2001:0000:0B80:0000:0000:00D3:9C5A:00CC.

▲ Each block is 16 bits. For example, the first block in the address above is 2001 in hex, which can be written as 0010 0000 0000 0001 in binary.

▲ Leading zeroes in a four-character hex block can be eliminated. For example, the IP address above can be written as 2001:0000:B80:0000:0000:D3:9C5A:CC, where leading zeroes have been removed from three of the hex blocks.

▲ If blocks contain all zeroes, they can be written as double colons (::). The IP address above can be written two ways:

  ▲ 2001::B80:0000:0000:D3:9C5A:CC

  ▲ 2001:0000:B80::D3:9C5A:CC

To avoid confusion, only one set of double colons is used in an IPv6 address. In this example, the preferred method is the second one: 2001:0000:B80::D3:9C5A:CC because the address is written with the fewest zeroes.

The way computers communicate using IPv6 has changed the terminology used to describe TCP/IP communication. Here are a few terms used in the IPv6 standards:

▲ A link is a local area network (LAN) or wide area network (WAN).

▲ A node is any device that connects to the network, such as a computer, printer, or router. The connection can be a logical attachment, such as when a virtual machine connects to the network, or a physical attachment, such as when a network adapter connects to the wired network.

▲ The last 64 bits or 4 blocks of an IPv6 address identify the interface and are called the interface ID or interface identifier. These 64 bits uniquely identify an interface on the local network.

▲ Neighbors are nodes on the same local network.

Recall that with IPv4 broadcasting, messages are sent to every node on a local network. However, IPv6 doesn't use broadcasting, thereby reducing network traffic. Instead, IPv6 uses multicasting, anycasting, and unicasting, as illustrated in Figure 8-10 and described next:

▲ A multicast address is used to deliver messages to all nodes in a targeted, multicast group, such as when video is streaming from a server to multiple nodes on a network.

▲ An anycast address is used by routers and can identify multiple destinations; a message is delivered only to the closest destination.

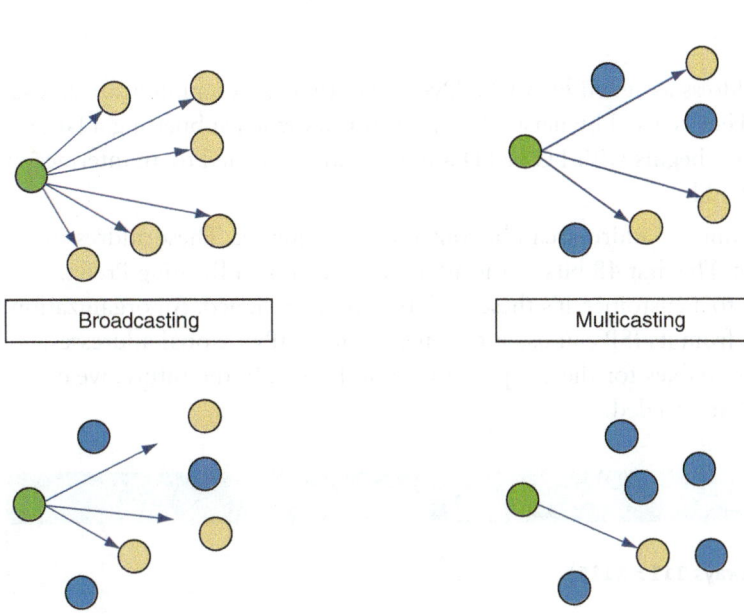

Figure 8-10 Concepts of broadcasting, multicasting, anycasting, and unicasting

▲ A unicast address is used to send messages to a single node on a network. Three types of unicast addresses are link local addresses, unique local addresses, and global addresses. A single interface might have more than one unicast address assigned to it at any given time:

  ▲ A link local address, also called a link local unicast address or local address, can be used for limited communication with neighboring nodes in the same link (the local network). These local addresses are similar to IPv4 APIPA addresses in that they are assigned to the computer by itself as opposed to coming from a DHCPv6 server, and are not guaranteed to be unique on the network. Most link local addresses begin with FE80::/64. This prefix notation means the address begins with FE80 followed by enough zeroes to make 64 bits, as shown in Figure 8-11. Link local addresses are not allowed on the Internet or allowed to travel outside private networks. Look back at Figure 8-3 to see an example of a link local address where the wired interface has the IPv6 address of fe80::64d2:bd2e:fa62:b911%10. The first 64 bits are fe80::, and the interface ID is 64d2:bd2e:fa62:b911. IPv6 addresses are followed by a % sign and a number; for example, %10 follows this IP address. This number is called the zone ID or scope ID and is used to identify the interface in a list of interfaces for this computer.

Link Local Address

64 bits	64 bits
Prefix 1111 1110 1000 0000 0000 0000 ... 0000 FE80::/64	Interface ID

Unique Local Address

48 bits	16 bits	64 bits
Network ID	Subnet ID	Interface ID

Global Address

48 bits	16 bits	64 bits
Global Routing Prefix	Subnet ID	Interface ID

Figure 8-11   Three types of IPv6 addresses: A link local address has a 64-bit prefix followed by 64 bits to identify the host

  ▲ A unique local address is a private address assigned by a DHCPv6 server that can communicate across subnets within the private network. They're used by network administrators when subnetting a large network. A unique local address always begins with FC or FD and is usually assigned to an interface in addition to its self-assigned link local address.

  ▲ A global address, also called a global unicast address, can be routed on the Internet. These addresses are similar to IPv4 public IP addresses. The first 48 bits of the address is the Global Routing Prefix. When an ISP assigns a global address to a customer, it's these 48 bits that are assigned. An organization that leases one Global Routing Prefix from its ISP can use it to generate many IPv6 global addresses.

Table 8-4 lists the currently used address prefixes for these types of IPv6 addresses. In the future, we can expect more prefixes to be assigned as they are needed.

IP Address Type	Address Prefix
Multicast	FF00::/8 (The first 8 bits are always 1111 1111)
Link local address	FE80::/64 (The first 64 bits are always 1111 1110 1000 0000...)

Table 8-4   Address prefixes for types of IPv6 addresses (continues)

IP Address Type	Address Prefix
Unique local address	FC00::/7 (The first 7 bits are always 1111 110; today's local networks assign 1 for the 8th bit, so the prefix typically shows as FD00::/8)
Global address	2000::/3 (The first 3 bits are always 001)
Unassigned address	0::0 (All zeroes)
Loopback address	0::1, also written as ::1 (127 zeroes followed by 1)

Table 8-4   Address prefixes for types of IPv6 addresses (continued)

> ★ **A+ Exam Tip**   The A+ Core 1 exam expects you to understand what a link local address is and how it's used.

> ✎ **Notes**   IPv6 uses subnetting but doesn't need a subnet mask because the subnet ID is part of the IPv6 address. The **subnet ID** is the 16 bits following the first 48 bits of the address. When a large IPv6 network is subnetted, a DHCPv6 server assigns a node in a subnet a global address or unique local address that contains the correct subnet ID for the node's subnet.
> An excellent resource for learning more about IPv6 and how it works is the e-book, *TCP/IP Fundamentals for Microsoft Windows*. To download the free PDF, search for it at *microsoft.com/download*.

VIEWING IP ADDRESS SETTINGS

A+ CORE 1 2.6   In summary, let's use the ipconfig command to take a look at the IPv4 and IPv6 addresses assigned to all network connections on a computer (see Figure 8-12).

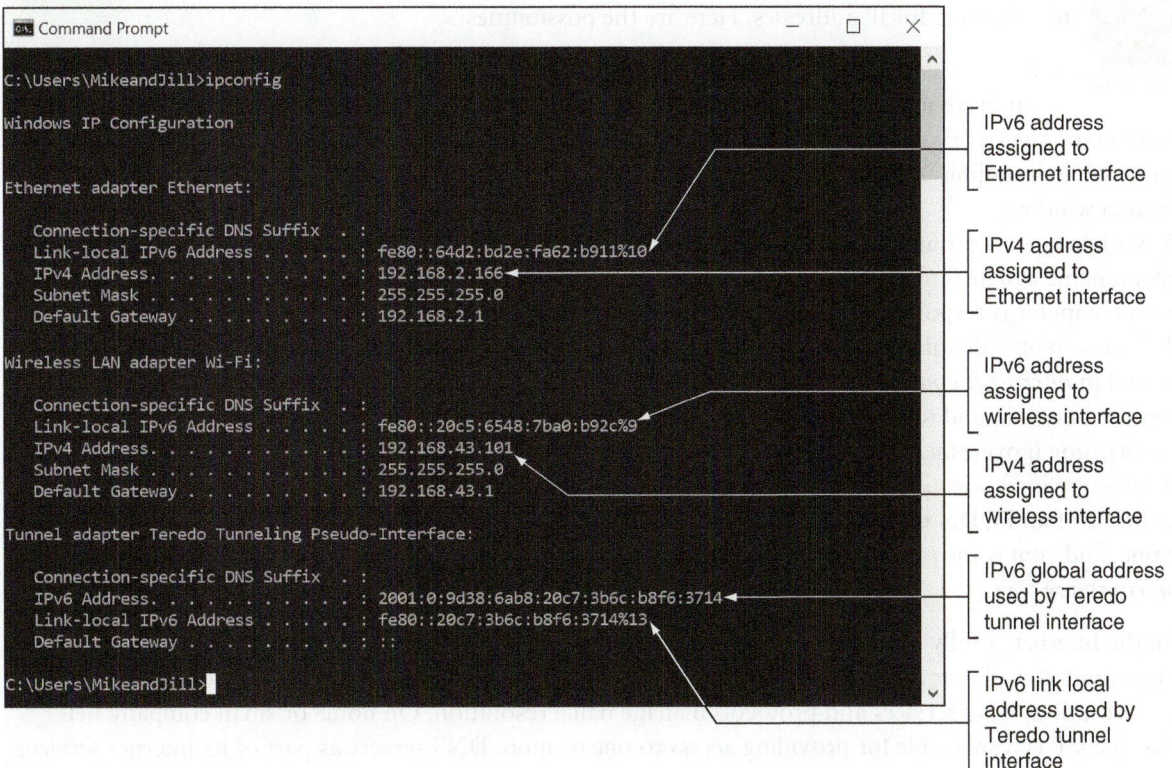

Figure 8-12   The ipconfig command showing IPv4 and IPv6 addresses assigned to this computer

Notice in the figure the four IP addresses that have been assigned to the physical connections:

◢ TCP/IP has assigned the Ethernet connection two IP addresses: one IPv4 address and one IPv6 address.

◢ The wireless LAN connection on a different subnet has also been assigned an IPv4 address and an IPv6 address.

> ✎ **Notes** Very few networks solely use IPv6. Tunneling is used to allow IPv6 messages to traverse IPv4 networks. A tunnel works by encapsulating an IPv6 message inside an IPv4 message. Figure 8-12 shows a Teredo (pronounced "ter-EE-do") tunnel that is assigned IPv6 global and link local addresses. Teredo is named after the Teredo worm that bores holes in wood.

IPv6 addressing is designed so that a computer can self-configure its own link local IP address, which is similar to how IPv4 uses an Automatic Private IP Address (APIPA). Here's what happens when a computer using IPv6 first makes a network connection:

1. The computer creates its IPv6 address by using the FE80::/64 prefix and uses its MAC address to generate an interface ID for the last 64 bits.

2. It then performs a duplicate address detection process to make sure its IP address is unique on the network.

3. Next, it asks if a DHCPv6 server is present on the network to provide configuration information. If a server responds with DHCP information, such as the IP addresses of DNS servers or the default gateway's IP address, the computer uses it. It also keeps its original link local address. Because a computer can generate its own link local IP address, a DHCPv6 server usually serves up only global or unique local addresses.

CHARACTER-BASED NAMES IDENTIFY COMPUTERS AND NETWORKS

**A+
CORE 1
2.6**

Remembering an IP address is not always easy for humans, so character-based names are used to substitute for IP addresses. Here are the possibilities:

◢ A *host name* is the name of a computer and can be used in place of its IP address. The name can have up to 63 characters, including letters, numbers, and special characters. Examples of computer names are www, ftp, Jean's Computer, TestBox3, and PinkLaptop. You can assign a computer name while installing Windows. In addition, you can change the computer name at any time using the System window.

◢ A workgroup is a group of computers on a peer-to-peer network that are sharing resources. The workgroup name assigned to this group is only recognized within the local network. In a peer-to-peer network, each computer is responsible for sharing and securing its own resources.

◢ A *domain name* identifies a network. Examples of domain names are the names that appear before the period in *microsoft.com*, *cengage.com*, and *mycompany.com*. The letters after the period are called the top-level domain and tell you something about the domain. Examples are .com (commercial), .org (nonprofit), .gov (government), and .info (general use).

◢ A *fully qualified domain name (FQDN)* identifies a computer and the network to which it belongs. An example of an FQDN is *www.cengage.com*. The host name is *www* (a web server), *cengage* is the domain name, and *com* is the top-level domain name of the Cengage network. Another FQDN is *joesmith. mycompany.com*.

On the Internet, a fully qualified domain name must be associated with an IP address before the computer can be found. Recall that this process of associating a character-based name with an IP address is called name resolution; DNS services and protocols manage name resolution. On home or small company networks, the ISP is responsible for providing access to one or more DNS servers as part of its Internet service. (Recall from Chapter 7 that a DNS server looks up and returns an IP address for a computer name when a DNS client requests this namespace lookup.) Larger corporations have their own DNS servers to perform name resolution for the enterprise network. When an individual or organization, which has its own DNS servers, leases a public IP address and domain name and sets up a website, it is responsible for entering the name resolution information into its primary DNS server. This server can present the information to other DNS servers on the web and is called the authoritative name server for the website.

> ★ **A+ Exam Tip** The A+ Core 1 exam expects you to understand the purpose of DNS servers and be familiar with client-side DNS.

When Windows is trying to resolve a computer name to an IP address, it first looks in the DNS cache it holds in memory. If the computer name is not found in the cache, Windows then turns to a DNS server if it has the IP address of the server. When Windows queries the DNS server for a name resolution, it is called the DNS client.

APPLYING | CONCEPTS VIEWING AND CLEARING THE DNS CACHE

Suppose a user is unable to reach a website on her computer but you can access it from your help-desk computer. One good step to use when troubleshooting name resolution problems is to clear the DNS cache. Open a command prompt window and use the **ipconfig /displaydns** command to view the DNS cache on your computer. Then use the **ipconfig /flushdns** command to clear the DNS cache. Windows will rebuild its cache by collecting up-to-date DNS information from the DNS servers you've configured Windows to use.

TCP AND UDP DELIVERY METHODS

A+ CORE 1 2.1 Looking back at Figure 8-7, you can see three layers of protocols working at the Application, Transport, and Internet layers. These three layers make up the heart of TCP/IP communication. In the figure, TCP or UDP manages communication with the applications protocols above them as well as the protocols in the lower layers, which control communication on the network. There are a few key differences between TCP and UDP that determine which of these two protocols is most appropriate for each situation.

> ★ **A+ Exam Tip** The A+ Core 1 exam expects you to be able to contrast the TCP and UDP protocols.

TCP GUARANTEES DELIVERY

Remember that all communication on a network happens by way of messages delivered from one location on a network to another. TCP (Transmission Control Protocol) guarantees message delivery. TCP makes a connection, sends the data, checks whether the data is received, and resends it if it is not. TCP is therefore called a connection-oriented protocol. TCP is used by applications such as web browsers and email. Guaranteed delivery takes longer and is used when it is important to know that the data reached its destination.

For TCP to guarantee delivery, it uses protocols at the Internet layer to establish a session between client and server to verify that communication has taken place. When a TCP message reaches its destination, an acknowledgment is sent back to the source (see Figure 8-13). If the source TCP does not receive

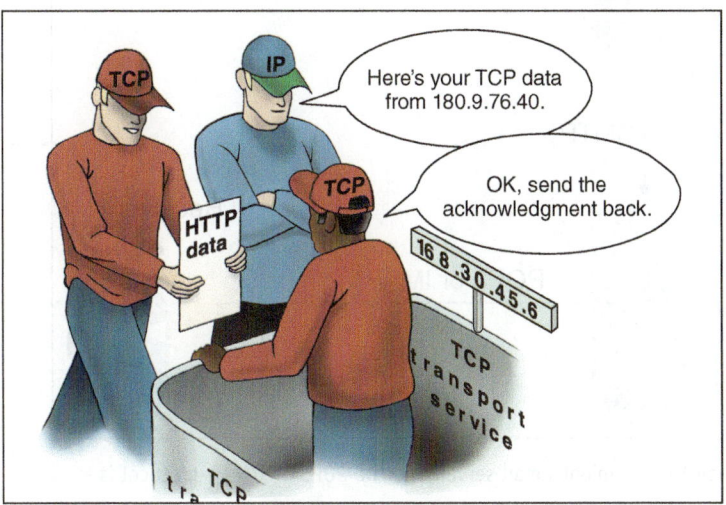

Figure 8-13 TCP guarantees delivery by requesting an acknowledgment

the acknowledgment, it resends the data or passes an error message back to the higher-level application protocol.

UDP PROVIDES FAST TRANSMISSIONS

On the other hand, UDP (User Datagram Protocol) does not guarantee delivery by first establishing a connection or by checking whether data is received; thus, UDP is called a connectionless protocol or best-effort protocol. UDP is used for broadcasting, such as streaming live video or sound over the web, where guaranteed delivery is not as important as fast transmission; however, TCP is preferred for video on demand. UDP is also used to monitor network traffic.

TCP/IP PROTOCOLS USED BY APPLICATIONS

 Some common applications that use the Internet are web browsers, email, chat, FTP, Telnet, Remote Desktop, and Remote Assistance. Here is a bit of information about several of the Application-layer protocols used by these applications and others:

- ◢ *HTTP.* HTTP (Hypertext Transfer Protocol) is the protocol used for the World Wide Web and by web browsers and web servers to communicate. You can see when a browser is using this protocol by looking for "http" at the beginning of a URL in the address bar, such as *http://www.microsoft.com*.
- ◢ *HTTPS.* HTTPS (HTTP secure) refers to the HTTP protocol working with a security protocol such as Secure Sockets Layer (SSL) or Transport Layer Security (TLS) to create a secured socket. (TLS is better than SSL.) A socket is a connection between a browser and web server. HTTPS is used by web browsers and servers to secure the socket by encrypting the data before it is sent and then decrypting it on the receiving end before the data is processed. To know a secured protocol is being used, look for "https" in the URL, as in *https://www.wellsfargo.com*.
- ◢ *SMTP.* SMTP (Simple Mail Transfer Protocol) is used to send an email message to its destination (see Figure 8-14). The email server that takes care of sending email messages (using the SMTP protocol) is often referred to as the SMTP server.

Figure 8-14 The SMTP protocol is used to send email to a recipient's mail server, and the POP3 or IMAP4 protocol is used by the client to receive email

▲ *POP and IMAP*. After an email message arrives at the destination email server, it remains there until the recipient requests delivery. The recipient's email server uses one of two protocols to deliver the message: POP3 (Post Office Protocol, version 3) or IMAP4 (Internet Message Access Protocol, version 4). Using POP3, email is downloaded to the client computer and, unless the default setting is changed, the email is then deleted from the email server. Using IMAP4, the client application manages the email while it is still stored on the server.

▲ *RDP*. Remote Desktop Protocol (RDP) is used by the Windows Remote Desktop and Remote Assistance utilities to connect to and control a remote computer.

▲ *Telnet*. The Telnet protocol is used by Telnet client/server applications to allow an administrator or other user to control a computer remotely. Telnet is not considered secure because transmissions in Telnet are not encrypted.

▲ *SSH*. The Secure Shell (SSH) protocol encrypts communications so hackers can't read the data if they intercept a transmission. SSH is used in various situations for encryption, such as when remotely controlling a computer or when communicating with a web server. SSH is commonly used in Linux to pass sign-in information to a remote computer and control that computer over a network. Because it's secure, SSH is preferred over Telnet.

▲ *FTP*. FTP (File Transfer Protocol) is used to transfer files between two computers over a WAN or LAN connection. Web browsers can use the protocol, as can File Explorer in Windows. Also, third-party FTP client software, such as CuteFTP by GlobalSCAPE (*cuteftp.com*) or open source FileZilla (*filezilla-project.org*), offer additional features. By default, FTP transmissions are not secure. Two protocols that encrypt FTP transmissions are FTPS (FTP Secure), which uses SSL encryption, and SFTP (SSH FTP), which uses SSH encryption.

▲ *SMB*. Server Message Block (SMB) is a file access protocol originally developed by IBM and used by Windows to share files and printers on a network. The current release of the SMB protocol is SMB 3; older versions include SMB 2 and a spinoff protocol called CIFS (Common Internet File System).

▲ *AFP*. AFP (Apple Filing Protocol) is a file access protocol used by early editions of the Mac operating system by Apple and is one protocol in the old suite of Apple networking protocols called AppleTalk. (TCP/IP has replaced AppleTalk for most networking protocols in the macOS.) Current macOS releases use SMB 3 for file access, and support both AFP and CIFS for backward compatibility.

▲ *LDAP*. Lightweight Directory Access Protocol (LDAP, often pronounced "l-dap") is used by various client applications when the application needs to query a database. For example, an email client on a corporate network might query a database that contains the email addresses for all employees, or an application might query a database of printers looking for a printer on the corporate network or the Internet. Data sent and received using the LDAP protocol is not encrypted; therefore, an encryption layer using SSL is sometimes added to LDAP transmissions.

▲ *SNMP*. Simple Network Management Protocol (SNMP) is a versatile protocol used to monitor network traffic and manage network devices. It can help create logs for monitoring device and network performance, it can make some automatic changes to devices being monitored, and it can be used to alert network technicians when a bottleneck or other performance issues are causing problems on the network. The SNMP server is called the manager, and a small application called an agent is installed on devices being managed by SNMP.

APPLYING | CONCEPTS   FILE EXPLORER AND FTP

To use FTP in File Explorer, enter the address of an FTP site in the address bar—for example, *ftp.cengage.com*. A logon dialog box appears where you can enter a user name and password (see Figure 8-15). When you click **Log On**, you can see folders on the FTP site and the FTP protocol displays in the address bar, as in *The Internet > ftp.cengage.com*. You can copy and paste files and folders between your computer and the FTP server.

(continues)

Figure 8-15   Log on to an FTP site

Recall that client/server applications use ports to address each other. Table 8-5 lists the port assignments for common applications.

Port	Protocol and Role	Description
20	FTP client	The FTP client receives data on port 20 from the FTP server.
21	FTP server	The FTP server listens on port 21 for commands from an FTP client.
22	SSH server	A server using the SSH protocol listens at port 22.
23	Telnet server	A Telnet server listens at port 23.
53	DNS server	A DNS server listens at port 53.
67	DHCP server	A DHCP server listens on port 67.
68	DHCP client	A DHCP client receives messages on port 68.
80	Web server using HTTP	A web server listens at port 80 when receiving HTTP requests.
443	Web server using HTTPS	A web server listens at port 443 when receiving HTTPS transmissions.
25	SMTP email server	An email server listens at port 25 to receive email from an email client.
465	SMTP secure	An email client sends secured email to an SMTP server listening at port 465. SMTP secure is also known as SMTPS and uses SSL/TLS to secure transmissions.
110	POP3 email server	An email client requests email from a POP3 server listening at port 110.
995	POP3 secure	An email client requests secured email from a POP3 server listening at port 995. POP3 secured is also known as POP3S and uses SSL/TLS to secure transmissions.
143	IMAP email server	An email client requests email from an IMAP server listening at port 143.
993	IMAP secure	An email client requests secured email from an IMAP server listening at port 993. IMAP secure is also known as IMAPS and uses SSL/TLS to secure transmissions.

Table 8-5   Common TCP/IP port assignments for client/server applications (continues)

Port	Protocol and Role	Description
137, 138, and 139	SMB over NetBIOS	**NetBIOS** is a legacy suite of protocols used by Windows before TCP/IP. To support legacy NetBIOS applications on a TCP/IP network, Windows offers **NetBT (NetBIOS over TCP/IP)**. Earlier versions of SMB required NetBT to be enabled. Ports used on these networks are: ▲ SMB over UDP uses ports 137 and 138. ▲ SMB over TCP uses ports 137 and 139. Current versions of SMB don't require NetBT.
445	SMB direct over TCP/IP	SMB 3, SMB 2, and closely related CIFS use port 445 for both TCP and UDP traffic.
161	SNMP agent	An SNMP-managed device receives requests from the manager on port 161.
162	SNMP manager	An SNMP manager listens on port 162.
389	LDAP	A database or directory service listens at port 389 for LDAP communication from a client. LDAP (or its secure version, LDAPS, at port 636) is often used for network authentication services.
427	SLP and AFP	**Service Location Protocol (SLP)** uses port 427 to find printers and file sharing devices on a network. AFP relies on SLP and port 427 to find resources on a local network.
548	AFP	AFP over TCP/IP is used for file sharing and file services.
3389	RDP apps, including Remote Desktop and Remote Assistance	Remote Desktop and Remote Assistance services listen at port 3389.

Table 8-5 Common TCP/IP port assignments for client/server applications (continued)

> ★ **A+ Exam Tip** The A+ Core 1 exam expects you to know the common port assignments of the FTP, SSH, Telnet, SMTP, DNS, HTTP, POP3, IMAP, HTTPS, RDP, NetBIOS, SMB, CIFS, SLP, AFP, DHCP, LDAP, and SNMP protocols, and to understand the purposes of these protocols. Before sitting for this exam, be sure to memorize the ports listed in Table 8-5. You also might be given a scenario that requires you to put this information to use.

As you work with network connections, keep in mind that the connections must work at all layers. When things don't work right, it helps to understand that you must solve the problem at one or more layers. In other words, the problem might be with the NIC, with the OS or application on the host, or with a router or other device on the local or remote network.

Now that you have an understanding of TCP/IP and Windows networking, let's apply that knowledge to manage, set up, and troubleshoot networks.

LOCAL NETWORK INFRASTRUCTURE

In this part of the chapter, you learn about the hardware devices that create and connect to networks. We discuss desktop and laptop devices, hubs, switches, bridges, and other network devices, and the cables and connectors these devices use.

SWITCHES AND HUBS

Today's Ethernet networks use a design called a star bus topology, which means that nodes are connected to one or more centralized devices, which are connected to each other (see Figure 8-16). A centralized device can be a switch or a hub. Each of these devices handles a network message differently.

Figure 8-16 A star bus network formed by nodes connected to multiple switches

Here are the differences between a hub and a switch:

▴ An Ethernet **hub** transmits the message to every device except the device that sent the message, as shown in Figure 8-17A. A hub is just a pass-through and distribution point for every device connected to it, without regard for what kind of data is passing through and where the data might be going. Hubs are outdated technology, having been replaced by switches. Figure 8-18 shows a hub that supports 10-Mbps and 100-Mbps Ethernet speeds. (You can't find hubs these days to support faster networks.)

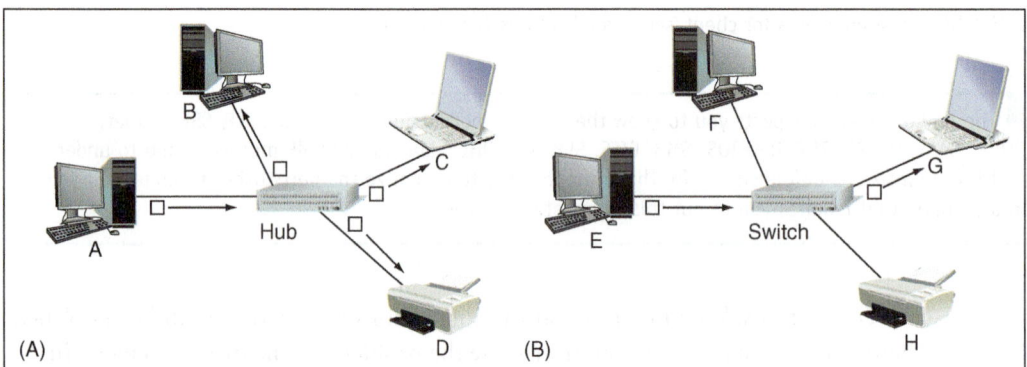

Figure 8-17 (A) A hub is a simple pass-through device to connect nodes on a network, and (B) a switch sends a message to the destination node based on its MAC address

Figure 8-18 This hub supports 10-Mbps and 100-Mbps Ethernet speeds

Figure 8-19 This Gigabit Ethernet switch by NETGEAR has eight Ethernet ports

◢ A switch (see Figure 8-19) is smarter and more efficient than a hub because it keeps a table of all the MAC addresses for devices connected to it. When the switch receives a message, it searches its MAC address table for the destination MAC address of the message and sends the message only to the interface for the device using this MAC address (see Figure 8-17B). At first, a switch does not know the MAC addresses of every device connected to it. It learns this information as it receives messages and records each source MAC address in its MAC address table. When it receives a message destined to a MAC address not in its table, the switch acts like a hub and broadcasts the message to all devices except the one that sent it.

Two types of switches are managed and unmanaged switches. An unmanaged switch requires no setup or configuration other than connecting network cables to its ports. It does not require an IP address and is appropriate for SOHO networks. A managed switch has firmware that can be configured to monitor and manage network traffic. It's appropriate for larger networks and can be used to manage QoS for prioritizing network traffic and to control speeds for specific ports.

You can also use a managed switch to subnet a large LAN into smaller subnets called virtual LANs (VLANs), which can reduce network traffic. Subnetting is done by assigning a group of ports on the switch to a different VLAN and directing the router as a DHCP server to assign a unique range of IP addresses to each VLAN to create a subnet. In Figure 8-20, the one physical LAN is subnetted into two virtual LANs. With subnetting, broadcast traffic is reduced because it is limited to each VLAN. The firmware on a managed switch is accessed through a browser using the switch's IP address, which is similar to how you access the firmware on a router. A switch requires an IP address only for the purpose of accessing its firmware.

Figure 8-20 Ports on a managed switch can be assigned to a VLAN to subnet a network

Here are reasons you might add switches to your network:

◢ *To add network connections.* A SOHO router usually has four to eight ports in a built-in switch. When you need more connections, add a switch in a location where you have multiple workstations or printers that need to connect to the network. In practice, a small network might begin as one switch and three or four computers. As the need for more computers grows, new switches are added to provide these extra connections.

◢ *To regenerate the network signal.* An Ethernet cable should not exceed 100 meters (about 328 feet) in length. If you need to reach distances greater than that, you can add a switch in the line, which regenerates the signal.

◢ *To manage network traffic.* Managed switches can be installed in strategic places on the network to subnet the network and manage network traffic to improve performance.

Figure 8-16, shown earlier in the chapter, uses three switches in sequence. Physically, the network cables that run between two switches or between a switch and a computer might be inside a building's walls, with a network jack on the wall providing an RJ-45 connector. You plug a network cable into the jack to make the connection.

WIRELESS ACCESS POINTS AND BRIDGES

A+
CORE 1
2.2

You've already learned that a router can also be a wireless access point. In addition, a wireless access point can be a dedicated device. The wireless access point can also serve as a bridge, as shown in Figure 8-21. A bridge is a device that stands between two segments of a network and manages network traffic between them. For example, one network segment might be a wireless network and the other segment might be a wired network; the wireless access point (AP) connects these two segments. Functioning as a bridge, the AP helps to reduce the overall volume of network traffic by not allowing messages across the bridge if it knows that the messages are addressed to a destination on its own segment. Figure 8-22 demonstrates the concept of a network bridge. (Logically, you can think of a switch as a multiport bridge.)

Figure 8-21 A ceiling-mount wireless access point by TP-Link

Figure 8-22 A bridge is an intelligent device that makes decisions concerning network traffic

Similar to a switch, a bridge at first doesn't know which nodes are on each network segment. It learns that information by maintaining a table of MAC addresses from information it collects from each message that arrives at the bridge. Eventually, it learns which nodes are on which network segment and becomes more efficient at preventing messages from getting on the wrong segment, which can bog down network traffic.

> **✎ Notes** If your wireless access point does not reach the entire area you need to cover, you can add a **repeater** or an extender, which amplifies and retransmits the signal to a wider coverage area. Repeaters and extenders capture the Wi-Fi signal, boost it, and retransmit it to the new area. The difference between a repeater and an extender is that a repeater rebroadcasts the signal using a new network name, whereas an extender keeps the original network name.

> **★ A+ Exam Tip** The A+ Core 1 exam expects you to know the functions and features of a hub, switch, router, access point, bridge, repeater, firewall, and modem.

NETWORK SERVERS

A+ CORE 1 2.5 Recall that a client computer contacts a server in order to request information or perform a task, such as when a web browser connects with a web server and requests a webpage. Many other types of server resources exist on a typical network. Some of these servers are stand-alone devices, but often multiple network services are provided by a single server computer, or servers might be embedded in other devices. For example, servers are sometimes embedded in router firmware (such as a SOHO router providing DHCP services) or in an operating system (such as web server capabilities embedded in Windows Server). On large networks, network services are often provided by multiple servers so that if one goes down, others can fill in the gap. This is called redundancy. It adds reliability but also adds complexity. Each time any of these components is updated, any legacy technology present on the network must be taken into consideration, which can result in a complex web of network server resources. Here's a brief list of several popular client/server resources used on networks and the Internet:

◢ *Web server*. A web server serves up webpages to clients. Many corporations have their own web servers, which are available privately on the corporate network. Other web servers are public, accessible from anywhere on the Internet. The most popular web server application is Apache (see *apache.org*), which primarily runs on UNIX or Linux systems and can also run on Windows. The second most popular web server is Internet Information Services (IIS), which is embedded in the Windows Server operating system.

▲ *Mail server.* Email is a client/server application that involves two mail servers. Recall that SMTP is used to send email messages, and either POP3 or IMAP4 is used to deliver an email message to a client. An example of a popular email server application is Microsoft Exchange Server. Outlook, an application in the Microsoft Office suite of applications, is a popular email client application.

▲ *File server.* A file server stores files and makes them available to other computers. A network administrator can make sure this data is backed up regularly and kept secure.

▲ *Print server.* A print server manages network printers and makes them available to computers throughout the network. Expensive network printers can handle high-capacity print jobs from many sources, eliminating the need for a desktop printer at each workstation. If a network printer fails, a technician can sometimes diagnose and solve the problem from her workstation. Windows business and professional versions include the Print Management console for this purpose.

▲ *DHCP server.* Recall from Chapter 7 that a DHCP server leases an IP address to a computer when it first attempts to initiate a connection to the network and requests an IP address. The DHCP server is configured to pull from a range of IP addresses, which is called the DHCP scope.

▲ *DNS server.* DNS servers, as you've learned, store domain names and their associated IP addresses for computers on the Internet or a large enterprise network. DNS servers are responsible for name resolution, which happens when a client computer sends an FQDN (fully qualified domain name) to a DNS server and requests the IP address associated with this character-based name.

> ✎ **Notes** A telltale sign that the network's DNS server is malfunctioning is when you can reach a website by its IP address, but not by its FQDN.

▲ *Proxy server.* A proxy server is a computer that intercepts requests that a client, such as a browser, makes of another server, such as a web server. The proxy server substitutes its own IP address for the request using NAT protocols. It might also store data that is used frequently by its clients. An example of using a proxy server is when an ISP caches webpages to speed up requests for the same pages. After it caches a page and another browser requests the same content, the proxy server can provide the content that it has cached. In addition, a proxy server sometimes acts as a router to the Internet, a firewall to protect the network, a filter for email, and to restrict Internet access by employees to prevent them from violating company policies.

▲ *Authentication server.* An authentication server authenticates users or computers to the network so that they can access network resources. Active Directory, which is a directory service included in Windows Server, is often used for this purpose on a Windows domain. The authentication server stores user or device credentials such as user names and passwords, validates an authentication request, and determines the permissions assigned to each user, device, or group.

▲ *Syslog server.* Syslog is a protocol that gathers event information about various network devices, such as errors, failures, maintenance tasks, and users logging in or out. The messages about these events are sent to a central location called a Syslog server, which collects the events into a database. Some Syslog servers can generate alerts or notifications to inform network administrators of problems that might need attention.

UNIFIED THREAT MANAGEMENT (UTM) APPLIANCE

> **A+**
> **CORE 1**
> **2.5**

Recall that a router stands between the Internet and a private network to route traffic between the two networks. It can also serve as a firewall to protect the network. A next-generation firewall (NGFW) combines firewall functions with antivirus/anti-malware functions and perhaps other functions as well. NGFW components might be installed on a dedicated appliance, a router, servers, or even in the cloud. In addition, an NGFW device can offer comprehensive Unified Threat

Management (UTM) services. A UTM appliance, also called a security appliance, network appliance, or Internet appliance, stands between the Internet and a private network, as does a router, and protects the network (see Figure 8-23).

Figure 8-23 A UTM appliance is considered a next-generation firewall that can protect a private network

A UTM appliance might offer these types of protections and services:

▲ *Firewall.* The firewall software filters incoming and outgoing network traffic according to IP addresses, ports, the type of messages the traffic contains, and how the message was initiated.

▲ *Antivirus and anti-malware software.* This software is usually much more advanced than what might be installed on a server or workstation.

▲ *Identity-based access control lists.* These lists control access of users or user groups and can log and report activity of these users and groups to reveal misuse, data leaks, or unauthorized access to resources. The company can use this feature to satisfy legal auditing requirements for detecting and controlling data leaks.

▲ *Intrusion detection system.* An intrusion detection system (IDS) monitors all network traffic and creates alerts when suspicious activity happens. IDS software can run on a UTM appliance, router, server, or workstation.

▲ *Intrusion prevention system.* An intrusion prevention system (IPS) not only monitors and logs suspicious activity, it can prevent the threatening traffic from burrowing into the system.

▲ *Endpoint management server.* Also called an endpoint security management system, an endpoint management server provides monitoring of various endpoint devices on the network, from computers and laptops to mobile devices like smartphones, tablets, or even barcode readers. The service can ensure that endpoints are kept up to date with current anti-malware requirements, operating system patches, and application updates. The system will restrict the device's access to the network until that device meets the security requirements, which gives an additional layer of protection to other network resources.

▲ *VPN.* The appliance can provide a VPN (virtual private network) to remote users of the network. You learned how to create a VPN connection in Chapter 7.

Figure 8-24 shows a UTM appliance by NETGEAR.

Source: Fortinet.com

Figure 8-24 The ProSECURE UTM appliance by NETGEAR

★ **A+ Exam Tip** The A+ Core 1 exam expects you to be able to summarize the purposes of services provided by a UTM Internet appliance, including an IDS, IPS, and endpoint management server.

ETHERNET CABLES AND CONNECTORS

Several variations of Ethernet cables and connectors have evolved over the years. They are primarily identified by their speeds and the types of connectors used to wire the networks. Table 8-6 compares cable types and Ethernet versions.

> ★ **A+ Exam Tip** The A+ Core 1 exam expects you to know the details listed in Table 8-6. Given a scenario, you need to recognize that when a cable exceeds its recommended maximum length, limited connectivity problems can result.

Cable System	Speed	Cables and Connectors	Example of Connectors	Maximum Cable Length
10Base2 (ThinNet)	10 Mbps	Coaxial cable, an older cable typically used for cable TV, uses a BNC connector.	Source: Courtesy of *Cables4Computer.com*	185 meters or 607 feet
10BaseT, 100BaseT (Fast Ethernet), 1000BaseT (Gigabit Ethernet), and 10GBaseT (10-Gigabit Ethernet)	10 Mbps, 100 Mbps, 1 Gbps, or 10 Gbps	Twisted-pair (UTP or STP) uses an RJ-45 connector.	Source: Courtesy of Tyco Electronics	100 meters or 328 feet
100BaseFL, 100BaseFX, 1000BaseFX, or 1000BaseX (fiber optic)	100 Mbps, 1 Gbps, or 10 Gbps	Fiber-optic cable uses ST or SC connectors (shown to the right) or LC and MT-RJ connectors (not shown).	Source: Courtesy of Black Box Corporation	Up to 2 kilometers (6562 feet)

Table 8-6 Variations of Ethernet and Ethernet cabling

ETHERNET STANDARDS AND CABLES

Ethernet can run at four speeds. Each version of Ethernet can use more than one cabling method. Here is a brief description of the transmission speeds and the cabling methods they use:

▲ *10-Mbps Ethernet.* This first Ethernet specification was invented by Xerox Corporation in the 1970s, and later became known as Ethernet.

▲ *100-Mbps Ethernet or Fast Ethernet.* This improved version of Ethernet, called Fast Ethernet, operates at 100 Mbps and typically uses copper cabling rated CAT-5 or higher. Fast Ethernet networks can support slower speeds of 10 Mbps so devices that run at either 10 Mbps or 100 Mbps can coexist on the same LAN.

▲ *1000-Mbps Ethernet or Gigabit Ethernet.* This version of Ethernet operates at 1000 Mbps (1 Gbps) and uses twisted-pair cable and fiber-optic cable. Gigabit Ethernet is becoming the most popular choice for LAN technology. Because it can use the same cabling and connectors as Fast Ethernet, a company can upgrade from Fast Ethernet to Gigabit without rewiring the network.

▲ *10-Gigabit Ethernet.* This version of Ethernet operates at 10 billion bits per second (10 Gbps) and typically uses fiber-optic cable. It can be used on LANs, MANs, and WANs, and is also a good choice for network backbones. (A network backbone is a channel whereby local networks can connect to wide area networks or to each other.)

TWISTED-PAIR CABLE

As you can see from Table 8-6, the three main types of cabling used by Ethernet are twisted-pair, coaxial, and fiber optic. Twisted-pair cabling uses pairs of wires twisted together to reduce crosstalk, which is interference that degrades a signal on the wire. It's the most popular cabling method for local networks and uses an RJ-45 connector. The cable comes in two varieties: unshielded twisted-pair (UTP) cable and shielded twisted-pair (STP) cable. UTP cable is less expensive than STP and is commonly used on LANs. STP cable uses a covering or shield around each pair of wires inside the cable that protects it from electromagnetic interference caused by electrical motors, transmitters, or high-tension lines. It costs more than unshielded cable, so it's used only when the situation demands it. Twisted-pair cable is rated by category (cat), as listed in Table 8-7.

Twisted-Pair Category	Cable System	Frequency	Shielded or Unshielded	Comment
CAT-5	10/100BaseT	Up to 100 MHz	Either	Has two wire pairs and is seldom used today
CAT-5e (Enhanced)	10/100BaseT, Gigabit Ethernet	Up to 350 MHz	Either	Has four twisted pairs and a heavy-duty sheath to help reduce crosstalk
CAT-6	10/100BaseT, Gigabit Ethernet, 10Gig Ethernet at shorter distances	Up to 250 MHz	Either	Less crosstalk because it has a plastic core that keeps the twisted pairs separated

Table 8-7 Twisted-pair categories

Figure 8-25 shows unshielded twisted-pair cables and the RJ-45 connector. Twisted-pair cable has four pairs of twisted wires for a total of eight wires. You learn more about how the eight wires are arranged later in this chapter.

Figure 8-25 Unshielded twisted-pair cables and an RJ-45 connector used for local wired networks

> ✏️ **Notes** Normally, the plastic covering of a cable is made of **PVC (polyvinyl chloride)**, which is not safe when used inside **plenums** (areas between the floors of buildings). In these situations, plenum cable covered with Teflon is used because it does not give off toxic fumes when burned. Plenum cable is two or three times more expensive than PVC cable. Figure 8-25 shows plenum cable and PVC cable. Because they can look essentially the same, check for labels printed on the cable to determine whether it's PVC or plenum-rated.

Loose configuration

Tight configuration

Plastic encasement

Liquid gel

Glass or plastic fiber

Strength wires

Plastic sheath

Figure 8-26 Fiber-optic cables contain a glass or plastic core for transmitting light

FIBER OPTIC

Fiber-optic cables transmit signals as pulses of light over glass or plastic strands inside protective tubing, as illustrated in Figure 8-26. Fiber-optic cable comes in two types: single-mode (thin, difficult to connect, expensive, and best performing) and multimode (most popular). A single-mode cable uses a single path for light to travel through it and multimode cable uses multiple paths for light. Both single-mode and multimode fiber-optic cables can be constructed as loose-tube cables for outdoor use or tight-buffered cables for indoor or outdoor use. Loose-tube cables are filled with gel to prevent water from soaking into the cable, and tight-buffered cables are filled with synthetic or glass yarn, called strength wires, to protect the fiber-optic strands, as shown in Figure 8-26.

> ★ **A+ Exam Tip** The A+ Core 1 exam expects you to know about these cables and connectors: BNC, RJ-45, RJ-11, coaxial, Ethernet, STP, UTP, CAT-5, CAT-5e, CAT-6, plenum, and fiber.

POWERLINE NETWORKING OR ETHERNET OVER POWER (EOP)

A+ CORE 1 2.2 If you need network access to a remote location in a building where network cabling and Wi-Fi cannot reach, you have another option. The HomePlug standard introduced in 2001, called powerline networking or Ethernet over Power (EoP), uses power lines in a building to transmit data. Powerline networking is simple to set up, inexpensive, and can run at Gigabit speeds. Like Wi-Fi, the data is sent out on a network that you cannot necessarily contain because power lines are not confined to a single building. If a building or apartment is sharing a phase (electrical signal) with another building or apartment, the data might leak and be intercepted by a neighbor. For this reason, powerline adapters offer 128-bit AES encryption that is activated by pairing the adapters to each other. Alternately, you can install the manufacturer's utility on your computer to create a network key.

To use powerline networking, you need at least two powerline adapters (see Figure 8-27), which can be bought in pairs called a kit.

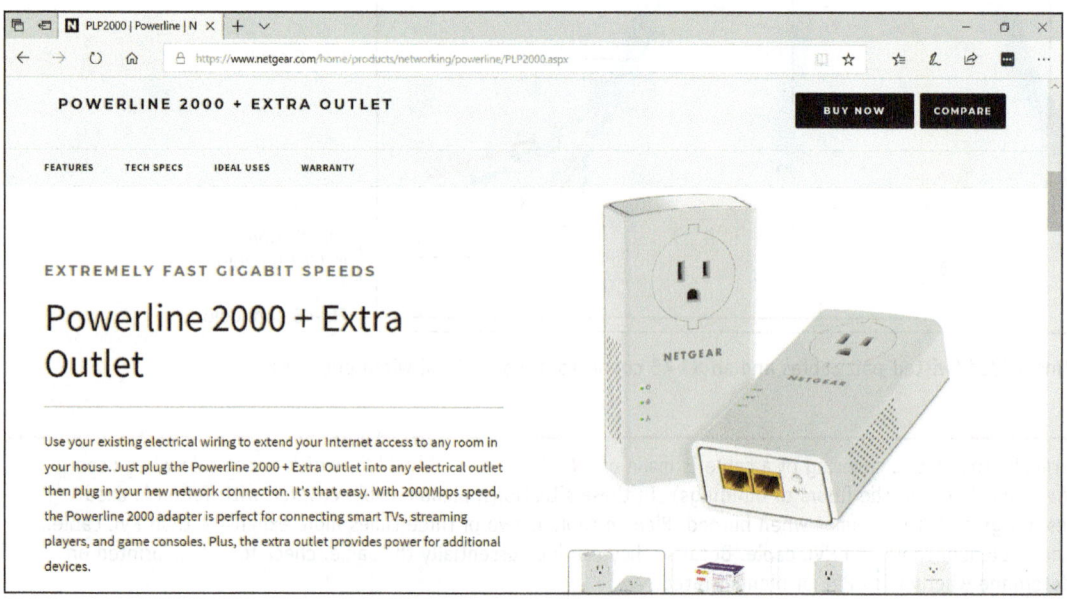

Source: *NETGEAR.com*

Figure 8-27 A starter kit for powerline networking includes two adapters

Powerline networks are not without problems. Consider the following issues powerline networking presents:

- ◢ Powerline adapters must be plugged directly into a wall outlet. Plugging a powerline adapter into a power strip or surge protector or sharing an outlet with an energy hog like a space heater hinders the function of the device.
- ◢ Powerline adapters might be large and cover both outlets on a single wall plate. A few powerline adapters offer a pass-through outlet, but most do not.
- ◢ Sometimes people forget to use the encryption options and end up with an unsecured network.
- ◢ Distance degrades quality. If you have a map of the building's circuits, try to keep the two adapters as close on the same circuit as possible. Jumping circuits decreases signal strength.

When shopping for powerline adapters, consider these things:

- ◢ Most powerline manufacturers belong to the HomePlug Alliance group (*homeplug.org*). Make sure the adapter you are considering is HomePlug certified.
- ◢ Make sure the adapter is rated for the latest HomePlug AV2 speed standard for Gigabit-class data transfers.
- ◢ If you have limited wall outlets, you might need a powerline adapter that offers a pass-through outlet.

POWER OVER ETHERNET (POE)

A+
CORE 1
2.2

If you have the opposite problem of needing to get power where your network cabling has gone, you can use Power over Ethernet (PoE), a feature that might be available on high-end wired network adapters to allow power to be transmitted over Ethernet cable. Using this feature, you can place a wireless access point, webcam, IP phone, or other device that needs power in a position in a building where you don't have an electrical outlet. The Ethernet cable to the device provides both power and data transmissions. PoE can provide up to 25.5 W from a single Ethernet port, although the amount of power that reaches a device degrades with the length of the cable. Most high-quality switches provide PoE. If your switch doesn't offer PoE, you can attach a PoE injector (see Figure 8-28), which adds power to an Ethernet cable.

Figure 8-28 A PoE injector introduces power to an Ethernet cable

Some devices, such as a webcam, are designed to receive both power and data from the Ethernet cable. For other devices, you must use a splitter that splits the data and power transmissions before connecting to the non-PoE device. Figure 8-29 shows a PoE switch and a splitter used to provide power to a non-PoE access point. When setting up a device to receive power by PoE, make sure the device sending the power, the splitter, and the device receiving the power are all compatible. Pay special attention to the voltage and wattage requirements and the type of power connector of the receiving device.

Figure 8-29   Use a PoE splitter if the receiving device is not PoE compatible

SETTING UP AND TROUBLESHOOTING NETWORK WIRING

In Chapter 7 you learned to configure a workstation and SOHO router to create a small network and connect it to a device (for example, a DSL or cable modem) that provides Internet access. If your network is not strictly a wireless network, you also need cabling and perhaps one or more switches to create a wired network. This section covers what you need to know to set up and troubleshoot a wired network.

DESIGNING A WIRED NETWORK

Begin your network design by deciding where to place your router. If the router is also your wireless access point, take care in where you place it. Recall from Chapter 7 that a wireless access point should be placed near the center of the area where you want your wireless hotspot to maximize its range for users and minimize your Wi-Fi network's exposure to unauthorized users outside your building. The router also needs to have access to your cable modem or DSL modem. The modem needs access to the cable TV or phone jack where it receives service. For a business, the router, modem, and servers are often placed in an electrical closet that can be locked for security and additional wireless access points are placed where hotspots are needed. Next, consider where the wired workstations will be placed. Position switches in strategic locations to provide extra network drops to multiple workstations.

Some network cables might be wired inside walls of your building with wall jacks that use RJ-45 ports. These cables might converge in an electrical closet or server room to connect to switches. If network cables are lying on the floor, be sure to install them against the wall so they won't be a trip hazard. To get the best performance from your network, follow these tips:

▲ Make sure cables don't exceed the recommended length (100 meters for twisted pair).
▲ Use twisted-pair cables rated at CAT-5e or higher. (CAT-6 gives better performance than CAT-5e for Gigabit Ethernet, but it's harder to wire and more expensive.)

▲ Use switches rated at the same speed as your router and network adapters.

▲ For Gigabit speed on the entire network, use all Gigabit switches, network adapters, and router. However, if some devices run at slower speeds, most likely a switch or router can still support the higher speeds for other devices on the network.

Figure 8-30 shows a possible inexpensive wiring job where two switches and a router are used to wire two rooms for five workstations and a network printer. The only inside-wall wiring that is required is two back-to-back RJ-45 wall jacks on either side of the wall between the two rooms. The plan allows for all five desktop computers and a network printer to be wired with cabling neatly attached to the baseboards of the office without being a trip hazard.

Figure 8-30 Plan the physical configuration of a small network

Now let's look at the tools you need to solve problems with network cabling, the details of how a network cable is wired, and how you can create your own network cables by installing RJ-45 connectors on twisted-pair cables.

TOOLS USED BY NETWORK TECHNICIANS

A+
CORE 1
2.8

Here's a list of tools a network technician might want in his or her toolbox:

▲ *Loopback plug.* A loopback plug can be used to test a network cable or port. To test a port, insert the loopback plug into the port; to test a cable, connect one end of the cable to a network port on a computer or other device, and connect the loopback plug to the other end of the cable (see Figure 8-31). If the LED lights on the network port light up, the cable and port are good. Another way to use a loopback plug is to find out which port on a switch in an electrical closet matches up with a wall jack. Plug the loopback plug into the wall jack. The connecting port on the switch in the closet lights up. When buying a loopback plug, pay attention to the Ethernet speeds it supports. Some only support 100 Mbps; others support 100 Mbps and 1000 Mbps.

Network activity and connection LED lights indicate cable and port are good

Loopback plug is testing cable and Ethernet port

Figure 8-31 A loopback plug verifies that the cable and network port are good

▲ *Cable tester.* A cable tester is used to determine if a cable is good or to find out what type it is if the cable is not labeled. You can also use a cable tester to locate the ends of a network cable in a building. A cable tester has two components, the remote and the base (see Figure 8-32).

Figure 8-32 Use a cable tester pair to determine the type of cable and/or if the cable is good

To test a cable, connect each component to the ends of the cable and turn on the tester. Lights on the tester will show you if the cable is good and what type of cable you have. You'll need to read the user manual that comes with the cable tester to know how to interpret the lights.

You can also use the cable tester to find the two ends of a network cable installed in a building. Suppose you see several network jacks on walls in a building, but you don't know which jacks connect back to the switch. Install a short cable in each of the two jacks or a jack and a port in a patch panel. A patch panel (see Figure 8-33) provides multiple network ports for cables that converge in one location such as an electrical closet or server room. Each port is numbered on the front of the panel. Use the cable tester base and remote to test the continuity between remote wall jacks and ports in the patch panel, as shown in Figure 8-34. Whereas a loopback plug works with live cables and ports, a cable tester works on cables that are not live. You might damage a cable tester if you connect it to a live circuit, so before you start connecting the cable tester to wall jacks, be sure that you turn off all devices on the network.

Source: Courtesy of Tripp Lite

Figure 8-33   A patch panel provides Ethernet ports for cables converging in an electrical closet

Figure 8-34   Use cable testers to find the two ends of a network cable in a building

▲ *Network multimeter.* You've already learned about multimeters. A network multimeter (see Figure 8-35) is a multifunctional tool that can test cables, ports, and network adapters. When you connect it to your network, it can also detect the Ethernet speed, duplex status, default router on the network, lengths of cables, voltage levels of PoE, and other network statistics and details. Many network multimeters can document test results and upload results to a computer. Good network multimeters can cost several hundred dollars.

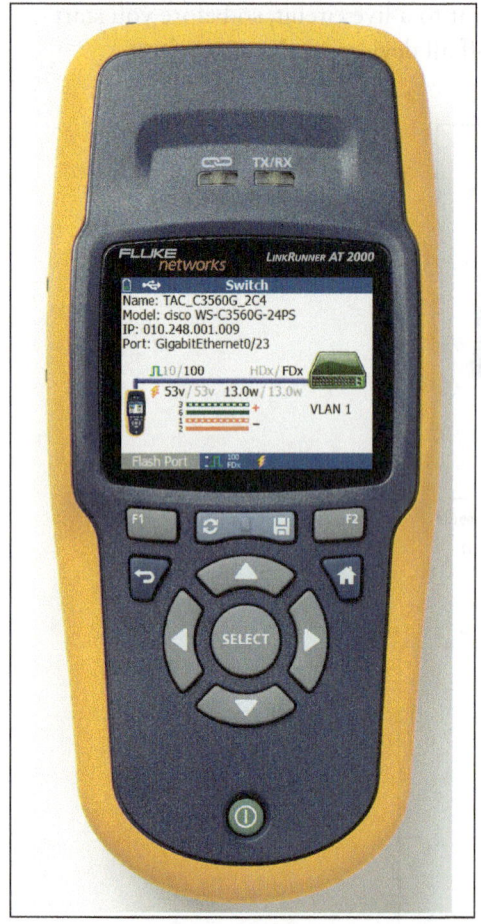

Source: Courtesy of Fluke Corporation

Figure 8-35 The LinkRunner Pro network multi-meter by Fluke Corporation works on Gigabit Ethernet networks using twisted-pair copper cabling

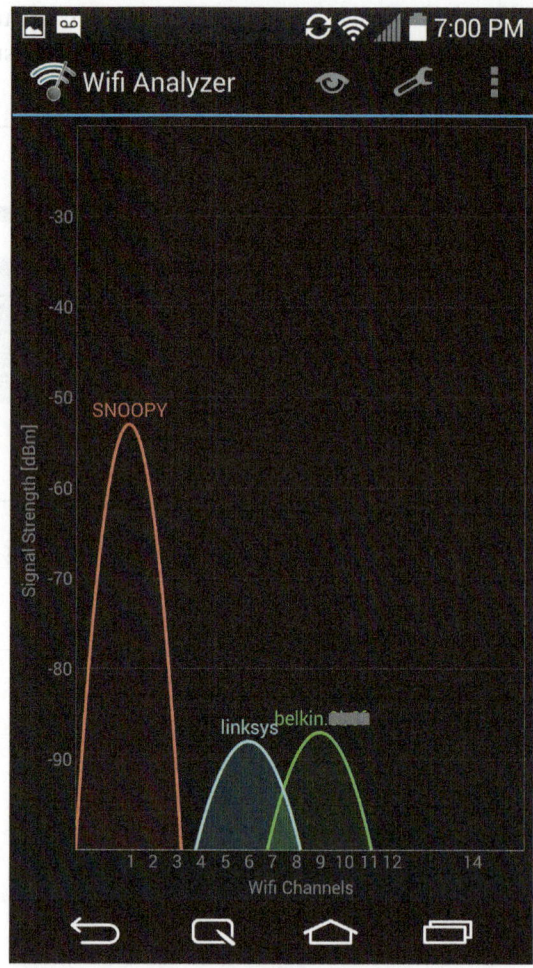

Source: Wi-Fi Analyzer app for Android

Figure 8-36 This Wi-Fi Analyzer app detected three wireless networks

▲ *Wi-Fi analyzer.* A **Wi-Fi analyzer** is software that can find Wi-Fi networks, determine signal strengths, help optimize Wi-Fi signal settings, and help identify Wi-Fi security threats. For example, you can use a Wi-Fi analyzer to find out which Wi-Fi channels are being used before you pick your channels. You can turn your smartphone into a Wi-Fi analyzer by installing a free or inexpensive app through your phone's app store (see Figure 8-36).

▲ *Toner probe.* A **tone generator and probe**, sometimes called a **toner probe**, is a two-part kit that is used to find cables in the walls of a building. See Figure 8-37. The toner connects to one end of the cable and puts out a continuous or pulsating tone on the cable. While the toner is putting out the tone, you use the probe to search the walls for the tone. The probe amplifies the tone so you hear it as a continuous or pulsating beep. The beeps get louder when you are close to the cable and weaker when you move the probe away from the cable. With a little patience, you can trace the cable through the walls. Some toners can put out tones up to 10 miles on a cable and offer a variety of ways to connect to the cable, such as clips and RJ-45 and RJ-11 connectors.

Connectors to connect to cable or wire

Toner

Probe

Figure 8-37 A toner probe kit by Fluke Corporation

▲ *Cable stripper.* A cable stripper is used to build your own network cable or repair a cable. Use the cable stripper to cut away the plastic jacket or coating around the wires inside a twisted-pair cable so that you can install a connector on the end of the cable. How to use cable strippers is covered later in the chapter.

▲ *Crimper.* A crimper is used to attach a terminator or connector to the end of a cable. It applies force to pinch the connector to the wires in the cable to securely make a solid connection. Figure 8-38 shows a multifunctional crimper that can crimp an RJ-45 or RJ-11 connector. It also serves double duty as a wire cutter and wire stripper.

Crimp cavity for RJ-45 connector

Crimp cavity for RJ-11 connector

Wire cutter

Wire stripper

Figure 8-38 This crimper can crimp RJ-45 and RJ-11 connectors

◢ *Punchdown tool.* A punchdown tool (see Figure 8-39) is used to punch individual wires in a network cable into their slots in a keystone RJ-45 jack that is used in an RJ-45 wall jack. In a project at the end of this chapter, you practice using the tool with a keystone jack.

Blade that cuts
the wire

Figure 8-39   A punchdown tool forces a wire into a slot and cuts off the wire

Now that you know about the tools you'll need to wire networks, let's see how the cables and connectors are wired.

HOW TWISTED-PAIR CABLES AND CONNECTORS ARE WIRED

A+
CORE 1
2.8, 3.1

Two types of network cables can be used when building a network: a straight-through cable and a crossover cable. A straight-through cable (also called a patch cable) is used to connect a computer to a switch or other network device. A crossover cable is used to connect two like devices such as a switch to a switch or a computer to a computer (to make the simplest network of all).

The difference between a straight-through cable and a crossover cable is the way the transmit and receive lines are wired in the connectors at each end of the cables. A crossover cable has the transmit and receive lines reversed so that one device receives off the line on which the other device transmits. Before the introduction of Gigabit Ethernet, 10BaseT and 100BaseT required that a crossover cable be used to connect two like devices such as a switch to a switch. Today's devices that support Gigabit Ethernet use auto-uplinking, which means you can connect a switch to a switch using a straight-through cable and the devices will negotiate the transmit and receive links so data crosses the connection successfully. Crossover cables are seldom used today except to connect a computer to a computer to create a simple two-node network.

Twisted-pair copper wire cabling uses an RJ-45 connector that has eight pins, as shown in Figure 8-40. 10BaseT and 100BaseT Ethernet use only four of these pins: pins 1 and 2 for transmitting data and pins 3 and 6 for receiving data. The other pins can be used for phone lines or for power (using PoE). Gigabit Ethernet uses all eight pins to transmit and receive data and can also transmit power on these same lines.

Figure 8-40 Pinouts for an RJ-45 connector

Twisted-pair cabling used with RJ-45 connectors is color-coded in four pairs: blue, orange, green, and brown, as shown in Figure 8-40. Each pair has one solid wire and one striped wire. Two standards have been established in the industry for wiring twisted-pair cabling and RJ-45 connectors: T568A and T568B. Both are diagrammed in Figure 8-40 and listed in Table 8-8. The T568A standard has the green pair connected to pins 1 and 2 and the orange pair connected to pins 3 and 6. The T568B standard has the orange pair using pins 1 and 2 and the green pair using pins 3 and 6, as shown in the diagram and the table. For both standards, the blue pair uses pins 4 and 5, and the brown pair uses pins 7 and 8.

Pin	100BaseT Purpose	T568A Wiring	T568B Wiring
1	Transmit+	White/green	White/orange
2	Transmit-	Green	Orange
3	Receive+	White/orange	White/green
4	(Used only on Gigabit Ethernet)	Blue	Blue
5	(Used only on Gigabit Ethernet)	White/blue	White/blue
6	Receive-	Orange	Green
7	(Used only on Gigabit Ethernet)	White/brown	White/brown
8	(Used only on Gigabit Ethernet)	Brown	Brown

Table 8-8 The T568A and T568B Ethernet standards for wiring RJ-45 connectors

Notes The T568A and T568B standards as well as other network wiring standards and recommendations are overseen by the Telecommunications Industry Association (TIA), Electronics Industries Alliance (EIA), and American National Standards Institute (ANSI).

If the wiring on one end of the cable matches the wiring on the other end, be it the T568A or T568B standard, you have a straight-through cable. If you're working on a 10BaseT or 100BaseT network and you use T568A wiring on one end of the cable and T568B on the other end, you have a crossover cable (see the diagram on the left side of Figure 8-41). For Gigabit Ethernet (1000BaseT) that transmits data on all four pairs, you must cross the green and orange pairs as well as the blue and brown pairs to make a crossover cable (see the diagram on the right side of Figure 8-41). Recall, however, that crossover cables are seldom used on Gigabit Ethernet. When you buy a crossover cable, most likely it is wired only for 10BaseT or 100BaseT networks. If you ever find yourself needing to make a crossover cable, be sure to cross all four pairs so the cable will work on 10BaseT, 100BaseT, and 1000BaseT networks. You can also buy an adapter to convert a straight-through cable to a crossover cable, but most likely the adapter only crosses two pairs and works only for 10BaseT or 100BaseT networks, such as the adapter shown in Figure 8-42.

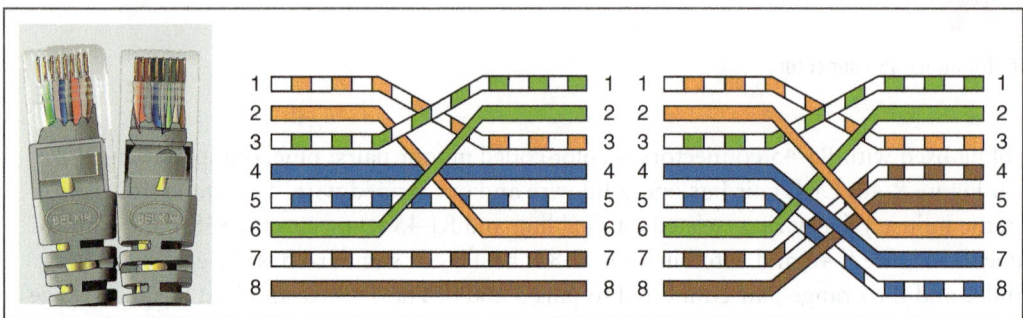

Figure 8-41 Two crossed pairs in a crossover cable is compatible with 10BaseT or 100BaseT Ethernet; four crossed pairs in a crossover cable is compatible with Gigabit Ethernet

Figure 8-42 A crossover adapter converts a patch cable to a crossover cable for a 10BaseT or 100BaseT network

Although it's possible to mix standards on the same network, you should always be *consistent with which standard you use*. When you are wiring a network in a building that already has network wiring, be sure to find out if the wiring is using T568A or T568B, and then be sure you always use that standard. If you don't know which to use, use T568B because it's the most common. However, if you are working for the U.S. government, know that it requires T568A for all its networking needs.

APPLYING | **CONCEPTS**   MAKING A STRAIGHT-THROUGH CABLE USING T568B WIRING

It takes a little practice to make a good network straight-through cable, but you'll get the hang of it after doing only a couple of cables. Figure 8-43 shows the materials and tools you'll need to make a network cable.

Figure 8-43 Tools and materials to make a network cable

Here are the steps to make a straight-through cable using the T568B standard:

1. Use wire cutters to cut the twisted-pair cable the correct length plus a few extra inches.

2. If your RJ-45 connectors include boots, slide two boots onto the cable. Be sure they're each facing the correct direction.

3. Use wire strippers to strip off about two inches of the plastic jacket from the end of the wire. To do that, put the wire in the stripper and rotate the stripper around the wire to score the jacket (see Figure 8-44). You can then pull off the jacket.

Figure 8-44 Rotate a wire stripper around the jacket to score it so you can slide it off the wire

4. Use wire cutters to start a cut into the jacket, and then use the rip cord to pull the jacket back a couple of inches (see Figure 8-45). Next, cut off the rip cord and the jacket. You take the extra precaution of removing the jacket because you might have nicked the wires with the wire strippers.

(continues)

Figure 8-45   Rip back the jacket, and then cut off the extra jacket and rip cord

5. Untwist each pair of wires so you have eight separate wires. Smooth each wire to straighten out the kinks. Line up the wires in the T568B configuration (refer to Table 8-8).

6. Holding the tightly lined-up wires between your fingers, use wire cutters to cut the wires off evenly, leaving a little over an inch of wire. See Figure 8-46. To know how short to cut the wires, hold the RJ-45 connector up to the wires. The wires must go all the way to the front of the connector. The jacket must go far enough into the connector so that the crimp at the back of the connector will be able to solidly pinch the jacket.

Figure 8-46   Evenly cut off wires measured to fit in the RJ-45 connector with the jacket protruding into the connector

✎ Notes You'll find several YouTube videos on network wiring. An excellent video by Ferrules Direct for making a straight-through cable is posted at *youtube.com/watch?v=WvPODOjiyLg*.

7. Be sure you have pin 1 of the connector lined up with the orange-and-white wire. Then insert the eight wires in the RJ-45 connector. Guide the wires into the connector, making sure they reach all the way to the front. (It helps to push up a bit as you push the wires into the connector.) You can jam the jacket firmly into the connector. Look through the clear plastic connector to make sure the wires are lined up correctly, that they all reach the front, and that the jacket goes past the crimp.

8. Insert the connector into the crimper tool. Use one hand to push the connector firmly into the crimper as you use the other hand to crimp the connector. See Figure 8-47. Use plenty of force to crimp. The eight blades at the front of the connector must pierce through to each copper wire to complete each of the eight connections, and the crimp at the back of the connector must solidly crimp the cable jacket to secure the cable to the connector (see Figure 8-48). Remove the connector from the crimper and make sure you can't pull the connector off the wire.

Figure 8-47   Use the crimper to crimp the connector to the cable

Figure 8-48   The crimper crimps the cable and cable jacket, and eight blades pierce the jacket of each individual copper wire

(continues)

9. Slide the boot into place over the connector. Now you're ready to terminate the other end of the cable. Configure it to also use the T568B wiring arrangement. Figure 8-49 shows the straight-through cable with only one boot in place.

Figure 8-49   A finished patch cable with one boot in place

10. Use a cable tester to make sure the cable is good.

 Notes According to networking standards for wiring a keystone RJ-45 jack and a straight-through cable, you can avoid crosstalk by removing the cable jacket to expose no more than three inches of twisted-pair wires, and you should untwist exposed twisted-pair wires no more than a half inch.

TROUBLESHOOTING NETWORK CONNECTIONS

A+
CORE 1
2.8, 5.7

With tools in hand, including hardware tools described in this chapter and software tools you learned about in Chapter 7, you're now ready to tackle network troubleshooting, including problem solving when there is no connectivity or it is limited or intermittent. Some guidelines to follow when troubleshooting a network problem are outlined in Figure 8-50 and listed here:

1. To check for local connectivity, ping the local router, then try pinging other devices on the network. No connectivity to any network devices might be caused by the network cable or its connection, a wireless switch not turned on, a bad network adapter, or network settings in Windows.

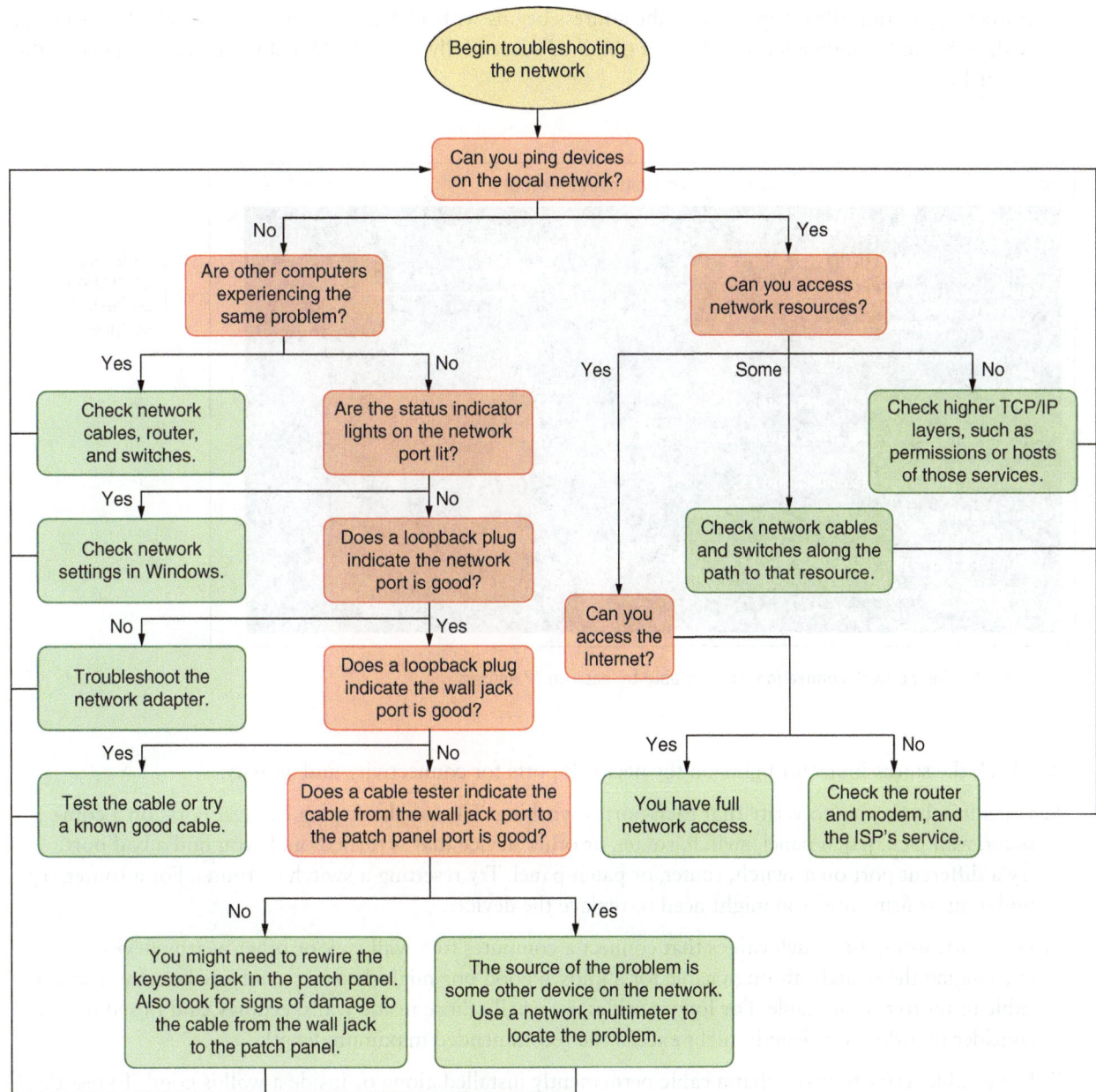

Figure 8-50 A flowchart to troubleshoot networking problems related to hardware

2. Determine whether other computers on the network are experiencing the same problem you've noticed on the first computer. If the entire network is down, the problem is not isolated to the computer you are working on.

3. To find out if a computer with limited or no connectivity was able to initially connect to a DHCP server on the network, check for an Automatic Private IP Address (APIPA) on an IPv4 network. On an IPv6 network, check for a link local address for the interface with no unique local address. Recall that on an IPv4 network, a computer assigns itself an APIPA if it is unable to find a DHCP server when it first connects to the network. On an IPv6 network, the computer always assigns itself a link local address, but it will only have a unique local address if it can get one from a DHCPv6 server. Use the ipconfig command to find out the IP addresses (see Figure 8-51). In the results, an APIPA presents itself as the

Autoconfiguration IPv4 Address, and the address begins with 169.254. An IPv6 link local address begins with FE80 and a unique local address, if obtained successfully from the DHCPv6 server, will begin with FC or FD.

Figure 8-51 The network connection was not able to lease an IP address

4. Check the status indicator lights on the network ports for connectivity and activity.

5. Use a loopback plug to verify that each port is working. The loopback plug can test ports on a computer, wall jack, patch panel, switch, router, or other device that is turned on. If you find a bad port, try a different port on a switch, router, or patch panel. Try resetting a switch or router. For a router, try updating its firmware. You might need to replace the device.

6. For short, straight-through cables that connect a computer to a wall jack or other nearby device, exchanging the straight-through cable for a known good one might be easier and quicker than using a cable tester to test the cable. For longer cables, especially those inside walls, ceilings, and raised floors, consider that the cable length might exceed the recommended maximum length.

7. Use a cable tester to verify that a cable permanently installed along or inside a wall is good. To test the cable, you have to first disconnect it from a computer, patch panel, switch, or other device at both ends of the cable. Common problems with networks are poorly wired termination in patch panels and wall jacks. If the cable proves bad, first try reinstalling the two jacks before you replace the cable.

8. Test for access to other network resources, such as file shares, network printers, or email services. If you can successfully ping the devices hosting those resources, but you can't access the resources themselves, this indicates a problem at a higher TCP/IP layer, such as permission configurations, or problems at the host for that network service.

9. If you can access some but not all devices on the network, the limited connectivity might be caused by cables or a switch on the network or a problem at the other computers you're trying to reach.

10. To test for Internet access, use a browser to surf the web. Problems with no Internet access can be caused by cables, a SOHO router, a broadband modem, or problems at the ISP.

Now let's see how to handle problems with no connectivity or intermittent connectivity and then we'll look at problems with Internet access.

PROBLEMS WITH NO CONNECTIVITY OR INTERMITTENT CONNECTIVITY

A+
CORE 1
2.8, 5.7

When a computer has no network connectivity or intermittent connectivity, begin by checking hardware and then move on to checking Windows network settings.

Follow these steps to solve problems with hardware:

1. Check the status indicator lights on the NIC or the motherboard Ethernet port. A steady light indicates connectivity and a blinking light indicates activity (see Figure 8-52). Check the indicator lights on the router or switch at the other end. Try a different port on the device. If the router or switch is in a server closet and the ports are not well labeled, you can use a loopback plug to find out which port the computer is using. If you don't see either light, this problem must be resolved before you consider OS or application problems.

Figure 8-52 Status indicator lights verify connectivity for a network port

2. Check the network cable connection at both ends. Is the cable connected to a port on the motherboard that is disabled? It might need to be connected to the network port provided by a network card. A cable tester can verify that the cable is good or if it is the correct cable (patch cable or crossover cable). Try a different network cable.

3. For wireless networking, make sure the wireless radio on the computer is turned on. If you have no connectivity, limited connectivity, or intermittent connectivity, consider moving the computer to a new position in the hotspot or shift the wireless access point's location. Use a wireless locator to find the best position. Try turning the wireless connection off, wait a few seconds, then turn it back on. Rebooting a computer might solve the problem of not receiving a signal. Problems with a low RF (radio frequency) signal can sometimes be solved by moving the laptop or connecting to a different wireless access point that has a stronger RF signal.

4. If the problem still persists after you've checked cable connections and the wireless radio, turn to Windows to repair the network connection. Use one of these methods:

   ◢ In a command prompt window, use these two commands: **ipconfig /release** followed by **ipconfig /renew**.

   ◢ In the Network and Sharing Center, click **Troubleshoot problems** to access a diagnostic tool for Windows network connectivity (see Figure 8-53).

> ✎ **Notes** In Windows 10, you can also access the troubleshooter tools by right-clicking the network connection icon in the taskbar, clicking **Open Network & Internet settings**, and then clicking **Network troubleshooter**.

▲ If that doesn't work, return to the Network and Sharing Center, click **Change adapter settings**, right-click the connection, and click **Disable**. Then right-click the connection again and click **Enable**.

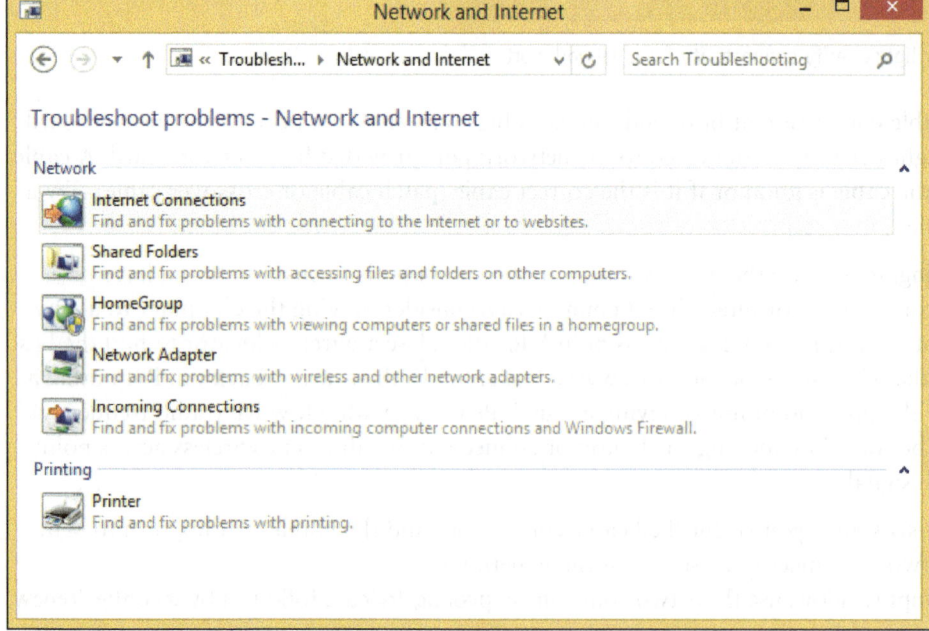

Figure 8-53 Windows 10 and Windows 8/7 troubleshooter tools

If the problem is still not resolved, you need to dig deeper. Perhaps the problem is with the network adapter drivers. To solve problems with device drivers, which might also be related to a problem with the NIC, follow these steps:

1. Make sure the network adapter and its drivers are installed by checking for the adapter in Device Manager. Device Manager should report the device is working with no problems.

2. If errors are reported, try updating the device drivers. (Use another computer to download new drivers to a USB flash drive and then move the flash drive to this computer.) If the drivers still install with errors, look on the manufacturer's website or the installation CD that came bundled with the adapter for diagnostic software that might help diagnose the problem.

3. Try uninstalling and reinstalling the network adapter.

4. If Device Manager still reports errors, try running anti-malware software and updating Windows. Then try replacing your network adapter. If that doesn't work, the problem might be a corrupted Windows installation.

PROBLEMS WITH INTERNET CONNECTIVITY

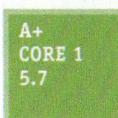

If you have local connectivity, but not Internet access, do the following:

1. Try recycling the connection to the ISP. Follow these steps:

   ◢ Go to the power source of the cable modem, DSL modem, or other device that you use to connect to your ISP, and unplug the power. Unplug the router. Wait about five minutes for the connection to break at the ISP.

   ◢ Plug in the cable modem, DSL modem, or other ISP device. Wait until the lights settle. Then plug in your router.

   ◢ On any computer on your network, use the Network and Sharing Center to repair the network connection. Open your browser and try to browse to some websites.

2. For a cable modem, check to make sure your television works. The service might be down. For a DSL connection, check to make sure your landline phone gives a dial tone. The phone lines might be down.

3. To eliminate the router as the source of the problem, connect one computer directly to the broadband modem. If you can access the Internet, you have proven the problem is with the router or cables going to it. Connect the router back into the network and check all the router settings. The problem might be with DHCP, the firewall settings, or port forwarding. Try updating the firmware on the router. If you are convinced all settings on the router are correct, but the connection to your ISP works without the router and does not work with the router, it's time to replace the router.

4. To eliminate DNS as the problem, follow these steps:

   ◢ Try substituting a domain name for the IP address in a ping command. First ping an IP address, such as Google's DNS server:

   ```
   ping 8.8.8.8
   ```

   Then ping a domain name:

   ```
   ping google.com
   ```

   If both pings work, then you can conclude that DNS works. If an IP address works but the domain name does not work, the problem lies with DNS.

   ◢ Try pinging your DNS server. To find out the IP address of your DNS server, use the nslookup command with no parameters or open the firmware utility of your router and look on a status screen.

◢ Try changing your DNS servers to public DNS servers, such as Google's (see Figure 8-54). In the Network Connections window, right-click the active connection and click **Properties**. Click **Internet Protocol Version 4 (TCP/IPv4)** and click **Properties**. Select **Use the following DNS server addresses**. Google's DNS servers are 8.8.8.8 and 8.8.4.4, and there are several other public DNS servers available. You can use a different computer to search for other DNS services as well.

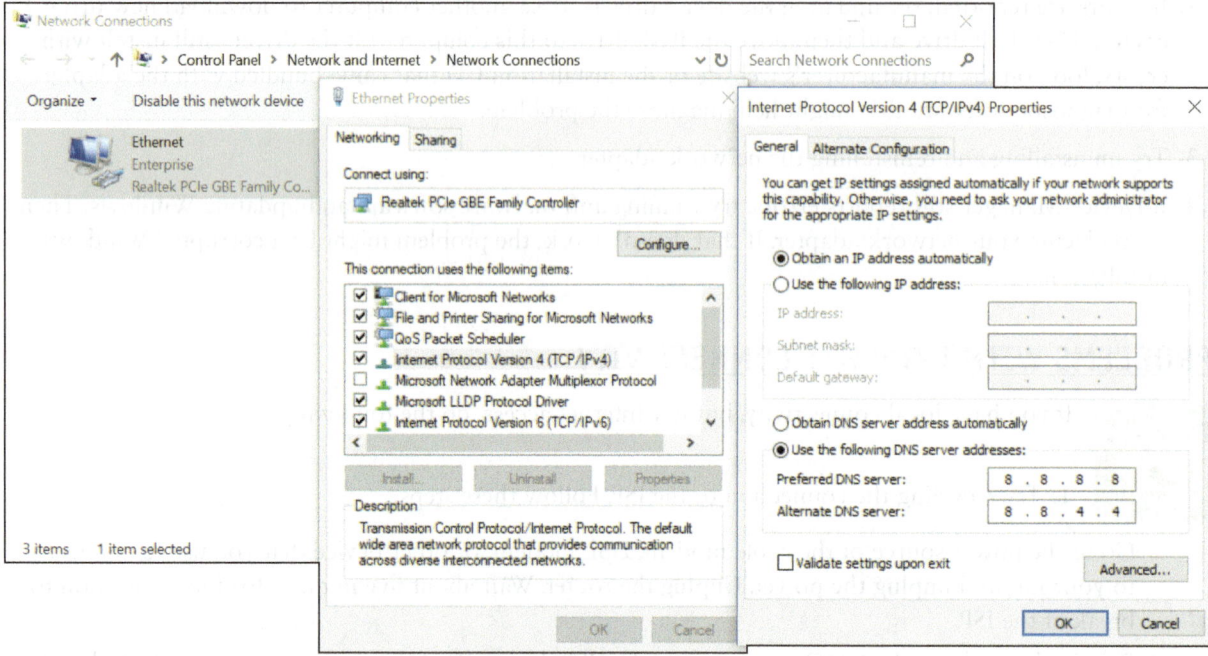

Figure 8-54 Several organizations offer public DNS services if your ISP's DNS servers are down

5. If you're having a problem accessing a particular computer on the Internet, try using the tracert command. For example:

```
tracert cengage.com
```

The results show computers along the route that might be giving delays.

6. If one computer on the network cannot access the Internet but other computers can, make sure MAC address filtering on the router is disabled or the computer is allowed access.

7. Perhaps the problem is with your router firewall or Windows Firewall. How to verify router firewall settings is covered in Chapter 7. Windows Firewall is covered in Chapter 16.

8. If you still cannot access the Internet, contact your ISP.

If some computers on the network have both local and Internet connectivity, but one computer does not, move on to checking problems on that computer, which can include TCP/IP settings and problems with applications.

USING TCP/IP UTILITIES TO SOLVE CONNECTIVITY PROBLEMS

The problem of no connectivity or no Internet access can be caused by Windows TCP/IP configuration and can be solved using Windows TCP/IP utilities. Follow these steps to verify that the local computer is communicating over the network:

1. Using the Network and Sharing Center or the ipconfig command, try to release the current IP address and lease a new address. This process solves the problem of an IP conflict with other computers on the network when using DHCP and dynamic IP addresses or your computer's failure to connect to the network.

2. For static IP addressing, consider that duplicate static IP addresses may have been assigned to hosts on the network. You need to go to each computer or device that is using static IP addresses and verify that no two addresses are the same.

3. To find out if you have local connectivity, try to ping another computer on the network. To find out if you have Internet connectivity and DNS is working, try to ping a computer on the Internet using its host address. Enter **ping cengage.com**. If this last command doesn't work, try the tracert command to find out if the problem is outside or inside your local network. Enter **tracert cengage.com**.

4. In a command prompt window, enter **ipconfig /all**. Verify the IP address, subnet mask, and default gateway. For dynamic IP addressing, if the computer cannot reach the DHCP server, it assigns itself an APIPA, which is listed as an Autoconfiguration IPv4 Address that begins with 169.254 (refer back to Figure 8-51). In this case, suspect that the computer is not able to reach the network or the DHCP server is down.

5. Next, try the loopback address test. Use the **ping 127.0.0.1** command. Your computer should respond. If you get an error, assume the problem is TCP/IP settings on your computer. Compare the configuration with that of a working computer on the same network.

6. If you're having a problem with slow transfer speeds, suspect a process is hogging network resources. Use the **netstat –b** command to find out if the program you want to use to access the network is actually running. In Chapter 14, you learn to use Resource Monitor to look for processes hogging network resources. Recall from Chapter 7 that you can use QoS features in Windows and on the router to give priority to an application or device that needs to perform better on the network.

7. Firewall settings might be wrong. Are port forwarding settings on the router and in Windows Firewall set correctly? You learn to configure Windows Firewall in Chapter 16.

8. If you're having problems getting a network drive map to work, try making the connection with the net use command, like this:

```
net use z: \\computername\folder
```

To disconnect a mapped network drive, use this command:

```
net use z: /delete
```

SLOW TRANSFER SPEEDS

 Perhaps you have network connectivity, but the network seems sluggish with slow file transfer speeds, lagging websites or network-based applications, and possibly a variety of error messages. It's best to look first for simple problems causing these delays. Using your critical thinking skills, start at the hardware level of the TCP/IP model and work your way up the layers:

▲ There's an unofficial layer affectionately called the User layer. If the user is present, interview the user and have the user reproduce the problem while you watch. Ask questions such as, "When did the problem start?" and "What has changed since the problem started?" Determine if you might have some tips for how to access network resources more efficiently and effectively.

▲ *Link layer*. Check cables for secure connections, status lights for consistent connectivity, and network devices for indications of errors being reported. Also use Device Manager to check the NIC's speed and duplex settings on Ethernet connections, ensuring that Auto Negotiation is selected.

▲ *Internet layer*. Ping the computer's loopback address, default gateway, another device on the network, and a server on the Internet. Watch for indications of delayed responses, and use tracert if needed to help identify the exact location of the slowdown.

▲ *Transport layer*. Check firewall settings for blocked ports. Also confirm that QoS settings are configured as expected, and consider experimenting with different settings to see if that improves network performance.

▲ *Application layer*. If everything below the Application layer is working, you'll know to focus your troubleshooting efforts on application installation, configuration, and compatibility concerns. Try the same operations using different but similar applications. For example, try using a different browser, or use a different FTP client application. Keep in mind that both the server and the client might need some troubleshooting to identify and solve an Application-layer problem.

Now we move on to problems with wireless connectivity.

WI-FI NETWORK NOT FOUND

Recall that a wireless access point broadcasts an SSID. Your computer should easily find the SSID of a Wi-Fi network and connect after entering the security key, if one is needed. If your computer does not detect an SSID that you know should be available, it might be because the SSID is hidden. If you know the SSID name and the security key, you can still connect to the network by following these steps:

1. Open the Network and Sharing Center.

2. Click **Set up a new connection or network**.

3. Select **Manually connect to a wireless network** (see Figure 8-55), and click **Next**.

Figure 8-55 Set up a manual connection to a hidden SSID

4. Enter the network name, choose the security type, and enter the security key. Click **Next**.

5. Your wireless network is set up and you should be connected. Click **Close**.

>> CHAPTER SUMMARY

Understanding TCP/IP and Windows Networking

▲ According to the TCP/IP model, networking communication must happen at four layers: Link, Internet, Transport, and Application.

▲ At the Link layer, a network adapter has a MAC address that uniquely identifies it on the network.

▲ At the Internet layer, the OS identifies a network connection by an IP address. At the Transport layer, a port address identifies an application.

▲ IP addresses can be dynamic or static. A dynamic IP address is assigned by a DHCP server when the computer first connects to a network. A static IP address is manually assigned.

▲ An IPv4 address has 32 bits, and an IPv6 address has 128 bits. Some IP addresses are private and can only be used on a local network.

▲ Using IPv4, the string of 1s in a subnet mask determines the number of left-most bits in an IP address that identify the local network. The string of 0s determines the number of right-most bits in the IP address that identify the host.

▲ Using IPv6, three types of IP addresses are a multicast address (used for one-to-many transmissions), anycast address (used by routers), and unicast address (used by a single node on a network).

▲ Types of unicast addresses are a link local address (used on a private network), unique local address (used on subnets in a large enterprise), and global address (used on the Internet).

▲ A computer can be assigned a computer name, and a network can be assigned a domain name. A fully qualified domain name (FQDN) includes the computer name and the domain name. An FQDN can be used to find a computer on the Internet if this name is associated with an IP address kept by DNS servers.

▲ TCP/IP uses several protocols at the Application layer (such as FTP, HTTP, and Telnet) and at the Transport layer (such as TCP and UDP). The Internet layer primarily relies on IP, and the Link layer mostly uses Ethernet and Wi-Fi protocols.

Local Network Infrastructure

▲ Networking hardware used on local networks can include hubs, switches, routers, wireless access points, bridges, cables, and connectors.

▲ Switches and older hubs are used as centralized connection points for devices on a wired network. A bridge stands between two network segments and controls traffic between them.

▲ A client computer contacts a server to request information or to perform a task. Examples of network servers are a web server, mail server, file server, print server, DHCP server, DNS server, proxy server, authentication server, and Syslog server.

▲ Most wired local networks use twisted-pair cabling that can be unshielded twisted-pair (UTP) cable or shielded twisted-pair (STP) cable. Twisted-pair cable is rated by category, with the most common being CAT-5, CAT-5e, and CAT-6.

▲ Fiber-optic cables can use one of four connectors: ST, SC, LC, or MT-RJ. Any one of the four connectors can be used with single-mode or multimode fiber-optic cable.

▲ Powerline networking, also called Ethernet over Power (EoP), sends Ethernet transmissions over the power lines of a building or house. Power over Ethernet (PoE) sends power over Ethernet cables.

Setting Up and Troubleshooting Network Wiring

▲ Tools used to manage and troubleshoot network wiring and connectors are a loopback plug, cable tester, network multimeter, Wi-Fi analyzer, toner probe, cable stripper, crimper, and punchdown tool.

▲ The RJ-45 connector has eight pins. Four pins (pins 1, 2, 3, and 6) are used to transmit and receive data using the 10BaseT and 100BaseT speeds. Using 1000BaseT speed, all eight pins are used for transmitting and receiving data.

▲ Two standards used to wire network cables are T568A and T568B. The difference between the two standards is that the orange twisted-pair wires are reversed in the RJ-45 connector from the green twisted-pair wires.

▲ Either T568A or T568B can be used to wire a network. To avoid confusion, don't mix the two standards in a building.

▲ Use wire strippers, wire cutters, and a crimper to make network cables. A punchdown tool is used to terminate cables in a patch panel or keystone RJ-45 jack. Be sure to use a cable tester to test or certify a cable you have just made.

Troubleshooting Network Connections

▲ When troubleshooting network problems, check hardware, device drivers, Windows, and the client or server application, in that order.

▲ Use the ping command to verify connectivity and the tracert command to solve problems with connecting to a particular host on the Internet. The nslookup command can verify that DNS is working. Use ipconfig to verify that the computer leased an IP address from the DHCP server. The netstat command can verify a process that uses the network is running. The net use command can be used to map a network drive.

▲ Use the Network and Sharing Center to connect to a Wi-Fi network when the SSID is hidden.

>> KEY TERMS

For explanations of key terms, see the Glossary for this text.

AFP (Apple Filing Protocol)
anycast address
authentication server
best-effort protocol
BNC connector
bridge
broadcast message
cable stripper
cable tester
CAT-5
CAT-5e
CAT-6
CIDR (Classless Interdomain Routing) notation
CIFS (Common Internet File System)

connectionless protocol
connection-oriented protocol
crimper
crossover cable
DNS client
domain name
endpoint device
endpoint management server
EoP (Ethernet over Power)
Fast Ethernet
file server
FQDN (fully qualified domain name)
FTP (File Transfer Protocol)

Gigabit Ethernet
global address
host name
HTTP (Hypertext Transfer Protocol)
HTTPS (HTTP secure)
hub
IDS (intrusion detection system)
IMAP4 (Internet Message Access Protocol, version 4)
interface ID
intranet
IP (Internet Protocol)
IPS (intrusion prevention system)

LDAP (Lightweight Directory Access Protocol)
link
link local address
loopback address
managed switch
multicast address
NAT (Network Address Translation)
neighbor
NetBIOS
NetBT (NetBIOS over TCP/IP)
network ID
network multimeter
NGFW (next-generation firewall)

node
octet
OSI (Open Systems Inter-
    connection) model
patch cable
patch panel
PDU (protocol data unit)
plenum
PoE (Power over Ethernet)
PoE injector
POP3 (Post Office Protocol,
    version 3)
powerline networking
print server
private IP address
proxy server

public IP address
punchdown tool
PVC (polyvinyl chloride)
RDP (Remote Desktop
    Protocol)
repeater
SLP (Service Location
    Protocol)
SMB (Server Message
    Block)
SMTP (Simple Mail
    Transfer Protocol)
SNMP (Simple Network
    Management Protocol)
socket
SSH (Secure Shell)

STP (shielded twisted-pair)
    cable
straight-through cable
subnet
subnet ID
subnet mask
switch
Syslog
Syslog server
T568A
T568B
TCP (Transmission Control
    Protocol)
TCP/IP (Transmission
    Control Protocol/Internet
    Protocol)

TCP/IP model
Telnet
tone generator and probe
toner probe
twisted-pair cabling
UDP (User Datagram
    Protocol)
unicast address
unique local address
unmanaged switch
UTM (Unified Threat
    Management)
UTP (unshielded
    twisted-pair) cable
virtual LAN (VLAN)
Wi-Fi analyzer

8

>> THINKING CRITICALLY

These questions are designed to prepare you for the critical thinking required for the A+ exams and may use content from other chapters and the web.

1. While investigating the settings on your SOHO router, you find two IP addresses reported on the device's routing table, which is used to determine where to send incoming data. The two IP addresses are 192.168.2.1 and 71.9.200.235. Which of these IP addresses would you see listed as the default gateway on the devices in your local network? How do you know?

2. Different network devices function at different network communication layers, depending on their purpose. Using the TCP/IP model, identify the highest layer accessed by each of the following devices:

   a. Router

   b. Unmanaged switch

   c. Wireless access point

   d. Firewall

3. Your boss asks you to transmit a small file that includes sensitive personnel data to a server on the network. The server is running a Telnet server and an FTPS server. Why is it not a good idea to use Telnet to reach the remote computer?

   a. Telnet transmissions are not encrypted.

   b. Telnet is not reliable and the file might arrive corrupted.

   c. FTP is faster than Telnet.

   d. FTP running on the same computer as Telnet causes Telnet not to work.

4. While troubleshooting an IPv4 network connection problem, you start to wonder if the local computer's NIC is working correctly. What command should you enter at the command prompt to test your theory?

5. Which of the following are valid IPv6 addresses? Select all that apply.

   a. fe80::64d2:bd2e:fa62:b911

   b. fe80::g90p:bd2e:fa62:b911

   c. fe80::64d2:bd2e::b911

   d. ::1

6. You're setting up a secure email server on your local network that you want clients to be able to access from the Internet using IMAP4 and SMTP. Which ports should you open in your firewall?

   a. 25 and 143

   b. 587 and 993

   c. 80 and 443

   d. 25 and 110

7. Lately your IPv6 network has experienced problems connecting new clients to the network. As part of your troubleshooting, you run an ipconfig command on one of the client computers and find two IPv6 addresses reported on the Ethernet interface: fe80::894d:c173:fef2 and fdb9::75f8:e30c:7cf4. Which one indicates the DHCPv6 server is probably working correctly? How do you know?

8. FTP requires confirmation that a file was successfully transmitted to a client, but it has no built-in mechanism to track this information for itself. What protocol does FTP rely on at the Transport layer of the TCP/IP model to ensure delivery is complete?

   a. UDP

   b. HTTP

   c. SSH

   d. TCP

9. A hub transmits all incoming messages to all of its ports except the port where the messages came in. A switch usually sends messages only to the destination computer. What information does a switch collect from messages crossing its interfaces so it knows where to send data in future transmissions?

   a. IP address

   b. MAC address

   c. Port number

   d. FQDN

10. Your customer recently installed a new router in her dance studio, as shown in the diagram in Figure 8-56. She then ran Ethernet cables through the drop ceiling to computers in various offices. Without any further testing, which computers do you suspect are experiencing connection problems? Choose all that apply.

    a. Computer A

    b. Computer B

    c. Computer C

    d. None of them

Figure 8-56 A diagram of a dance studio

11. Your SOHO router has failed and you have installed a new router. The old router's static IP address on the network is 192.168.0.1. The new router has a static IP address of 10.0.0.1. You go to a computer to configure the new router and enter 10.0.0.1 in the browser address box. The router does not respond. You open a command prompt window and try to ping the router, which does not work. Next, you verify that the router has connectivity and you see that its local connection light is blinking, indicating connectivity. What is the most likely problem and its best solution?

    a. The computer you are using to configure the router has a corrupted TCP/IP configuration. Restart the computer.

    b. The router is defective. Return it for a full refund.

    c. The computer and the router are not in the same subnet. Release and renew the IP address of the computer.

    d. The computer and the router are not in the same subnet. Change the subnet mask assigned to the computer.

12. While troubleshooting a network connection problem, you run the command ipconfig /all in a command prompt window and get the following output:

```
Ethernet adapter Ethernet:

   Connection-specific DNS Suffix.:
   Description...................: Realtek PCIe GBE Family Controller
   Physical Address..............: 54-53-ED-BB-AB-A3
   DHCP Enabled..................: Yes
   Autoconfiguration Enabled......: Yes
   Link local IPv6 Address.......: fe80::64d2:bd2e:fa62:b911%10 (Preferred)
   IPv4 Address..................: 192.168.2.166(Preferred)
   Subnet Mask...................: 255.255.255.0
   Lease Obtained................: Sunday, August 19, 2018 10:56:41 AM
   Lease Expires.................: Sunday, August 19, 2018 1:56:41 PM
```

```
Default Gateway.................: 192.168.2.1
DHCP Server....................: 192.168.2.1
DHCPv6 IAID...................: 257184749
DHCPv6 Client DUID............: 00-01-00-01-18-81-16-9A-54-53-ED-BB-AB-A3
DNS Servers...................: 8.8.8.8      8.8.4.4
NetBIOS over Tcpip............: Enabled
```

Is the computer using a wired or wireless network connection? What is the local computer's MAC address? What is the IP address of the router on the local network?

13. Which two of the following hosts on a corporate intranet are on the same subnet?

   a. 192.168.2.143 255.255.255.0

   b. 172.54.98.3 255.255.0.0

   c. 192.168.5.57 255.255.255.0

   d. 172.54.72.89 255.255.0.0

14. You are configuring email on a customer's computer. Which port should you configure for *pop.companymail.com*? For *smtp.companymail.com*?

   a. 143, 25

   b. 110, 143

   c. 110, 25

   d. 25, 110

15. Which of the following tools can be used to determine if a network cable is good? Choose all that apply.

   a. Cable tester

   b. Crimper

   c. Loopback plug

   d. Network multimeter

16. You've been hired to help with installing cable at a new office building for the local branch of the Social Security Administration. You're wiring a connection into the first room on your list. List the colors of the wires in the order you should place them into the connector, starting with pin 1.

>> HANDS-ON PROJECTS

Hands-On | Project 8-1 Using Subnet Masks

To practice your skills using subnet masks, fill in Table 8-9. First, convert decimal values to binary and then record your decisions in the last column.

Local IP Address	Subnet Mask	Other IP Address	On the Same Network? (Yes or No)
15.50.212.59 Binary: _____	255.255.240.0 Binary: _____	15.50.235.80 Binary: _____	
192.168.24.1 Binary: _____	255.255.248.0 Binary: _____	192.168.31.198 Binary: _____	

Table 8-9   Practice using subnet masks (continues)

Local IP Address	Subnet Mask	Other IP Address	On the Same Network? (Yes or No)
192.168.0.1 Binary: _____	255.255.255.192 Binary: _____	192.168.0.63 Binary: _____	
192.168.0.10 Binary: _____	255.255.255.128 Binary: _____	192.168.0.120 Binary: _____	

Table 8-9 Practice using subnet masks (continued)

Hands-On | Project 8-2 Researching a Network Upgrade

An IT support technician is often called on to research equipment to maintain or improve a computer or network and make recommendations for purchase. Suppose you are asked to upgrade a small network that consists of one switch and four computers from 100BaseT to Gigabit Ethernet. The switch connects to a router that already supports Gigabit Ethernet. Do the following to price the hardware needed for this upgrade:

1. Find three switches by different manufacturers that support Gigabit Ethernet and have at least five ports. Save or print the webpages describing each switch.

2. Compare the features and prices of the three switches. What additional information might you want to know before you make your recommendation for a small business network?

3. Find three network adapters by different manufacturers to install in the desktop computers to support Gigabit Ethernet. Save or print webpages for each NIC.

4. Compare features of the three network adapters. What additional information do you need to know before you make your recommendation?

5. Make your recommendations based on the moderate (middle-of-the-road) choices. What is the total price of the upgrade, including one switch and four network adapters?

6. What is one more question you need to have answered about other equipment before you can complete the price of the upgrade? Explain how you would find the answer to your question.

Hands-On | Project 8-3 Wiring a Keystone Jack

A keystone RJ-45 jack is used in a network wall jack. To practice wiring a keystone jack, you'll need a wire stripper, wire cutter, twisted-pair cabling, keystone jack, and punchdown tool. Here are the instructions to wire one:

1. Using a wire stripper and wire cutter, strip and trim back the jacket from the twisted-pair wire, leaving about two inches of wire exposed. Untwist the wires only so far as necessary so each wire can be inserted in the color-coded slot in the jack. The untwisted wire should be no longer than a half inch. Why are twists so important when wiring connectors and jacks?

2. Insert each wire into the appropriate slots for either the T568A or T568B standard, depending on the network where you might use this keystone jack. Figure 8-57 shows the wires in position for T568B wiring. Notice how the cable jacket goes into the keystone jack. Which wiring standard did you use? How did you choose that standard?

(continues)

Figure 8-57 Eight wires are in position in a keystone jack for T568B wiring

3. Using the punchdown tool, make sure the blade side of the tool is on the outside of the jack. (The punchdown tool has "Cut" embedded on the blade side of the tool.) Push down with force to punch each wire into its slot and cut off the wire on the outside edge of the slot. It might take a couple of punches to do the job. See the left side of Figure 8-58. Place the jack cover over the jack, as shown on the right side of Figure 8-58.

Figure 8-58 Use a punchdown tool to punch the wires into the keystone jack, and then place the cover in position

4. The jack can now be inserted into the back side of a wall faceplate (see Figure 8-59). Make sure the wires in the jack are at the top of the jack. If you look closely at the faceplate, you can see the arrow pointing up. It's important that the wires in the jack be at the top so dust doesn't settle on these wires over time. Use screws to secure the faceplate to the wall receptacle. Be sure to use a cable tester to check the network cable from its jack to the other end to make sure the wiring is good. When wiring a building, testing the cable and its two connections is called certifying the cable.

(continues)

Figure 8-59 Insert the jack in the faceplate, making sure the wire connectors are at the top of the jack

📝 **Notes** To see a video by DIY Telecom of using a punchdown tool to make an RJ-45 keystone jack, see *youtube.com/watch?v=Xkbz-uywLJs.*

Hands-On | Project 8-4 Researching Network Tools

Use the web to research the features and prices for the network tools you learned about in this chapter that you can include among your computer and network repair tools. Suppose you have a budget of $200 to buy a wire stripper, wire cutter, crimper, cable tester, loopback plug, punchdown tool, toner probe, and/or network multimeter. Save or print webpages showing the features and price of each tool you select for your toolkit. Which tools, if any, did you decide not to purchase? Why?

Hands-On | Project 8-5 Making Network Cables

Using the tools and skills you learned about in this chapter, practice making a straight-through cable and a crossover cable. Use a cable tester to test both cables.

Answer the following questions:

1. Which wiring standard did you use for the straight-through cable? List the pinouts (pin number and wire color) for each of the eight pins on each connector.

2. Will your crossover cable work on a Gigabit Ethernet network? List the pinouts (pin number and wire color) for each of the eight pins on each connector.

Hands-On | Project 8-6 Networking Two Computers with a Crossover Cable

In Real Problem 7-1 at the end of Chapter 7, you used a crossover cable to connect two computers in a simple network. Again connect two computers in a simple network, but this time use the crossover cable you just made. What are the Ethernet speeds that each computer supports? Which speed is the network using? Verify the network connectivity by copying a file from one computer to the other.

>> REAL PROBLEMS, REAL SOLUTIONS

REAL PROBLEM 8-1 Setting Up a Wireless Access Point

As a computer and networking consultant to small businesses, you are frequently asked to find solutions to increasing demands for network and Internet access at a business. One business rents offices in a historical building that has strict rules for wiring. They have come to you asking for a solution for providing Wi-Fi access to their guests in the lobby of the building. Research options for a solution and answer the following questions:

1. Print or save webpages showing two options for a Wi-Fi wireless access point that can mount on the wall or ceiling. For one option, select a device that can receive its power by PoE from the network cable run to the device. For the other option, select a device that requires an electrical cable to the device as well as a network cable.

2. Print or save two webpages for a splitter that can be mounted near the second wireless access point and that splits the power from data on the network cable. Make sure the power connectors for the splitter and the access point can work together.

3. To provide PoE from the electrical closet on the network cable to the wireless access point, print or save the webpage for an injector that injects power into a network cable. Make sure the voltage and wattage output for the injector are compatible with the needs of both wireless access points.

4. You estimate that the distance for network cabling from the switch to the wireless access point is about 200 feet (61 meters). What is the cost of 200 feet of PVC CAT-6a cabling? For 200 feet of plenum CAT-6a cabling?

5. Of the options you researched, which do you recommend? Using this option, what is the total cost of the Wi-Fi hotspot?

REAL PROBLEM 8-2 Exploring Packet Tracer

In Chapter 7 you installed Packet Tracer and created a very basic network. In this project, you work through three chapters of the Packet Tracer Introduction course to take a brief tour of the simulator interface and create a more complex network in Packet Tracer. Notice in the Packet Tracer course that the activities refer to the OSI model instead of the TCP/IP model. Review the section entitled "Compare the TCP/IP Model and OSI Model" in this chapter for a brief refresher. Then complete the following steps to access your course:

1. Return to the Networking Academy website (*netacad.com*), sign in, and click **Launch Course**. You've already downloaded Packet Tracer, so you can skip Chapter 1.

2. Complete Chapters 2, 3, and 4, including the videos and labs, and complete the Packet Tracer Basics Quiz at the end of Chapter 4. The other chapters provide excellent information on Packet Tracer but are not required for this project. Answer the following questions along the way:

   a. What is a simple PDU in Packet Tracer?

   b. What is a .pka file?

   c. Which window shows instructions for a lab activity?

   d. Which Packet Tracer feature do you think will be most helpful for you in learning how to manage a network?

Supporting Mobile Devices

Previous chapters have focused on supporting personal computers. This chapter moves on to discuss operating systems on mobile devices such as smartphones and tablets. As mobile devices become more common, many people use them to surf the web, access email, and manage apps and data. This chapter is intended to show you how to support a device that you might not own or normally use. Technicians are often expected to do such things! As an IT support technician, you need to know about the operating systems and hardware used with mobile devices and how to help a user configure and troubleshoot these devices.

Many employees expect to be able to use their mobile devices to access, synchronize, and edit data on the corporate network. Therefore, to protect this data, corporations require that employee mobile devices be secured and that data, settings, and apps be synchronized to other storage locations. In this chapter, you learn how you can synchronize content on mobile devices to a personal computer or to storage in the cloud (on the Internet). You learn how to secure mobile devices. You also learn about some connection technologies specific to the Internet of Things, which includes many non-computing devices such as door locks and security cameras. Finally, in this chapter, you learn about tools and resources available for troubleshooting mobile operating systems.

> ★ **A+ Exam Tip** Much of the content in this chapter applies to both the A+ Core 1 220-1001 exam and the A+ Core 2 220-1002 exam.

TYPES OF MOBILE DEVICES

A+
CORE 1
1.4

Mobile devices vary considerably by size, functionality, available connection types, and primary purpose(s), not to mention cost. Here's a list of the mobile devices that you might be called on to support as an IT support technician:

▲ *Smartphone.* A smartphone is primarily a cell phone that also includes abilities to send text messages with photos, videos, or other multimedia content attached; surf the web; manage email; play games; take photos and videos; and download and use small apps. Most smartphones use touch screens for input (see Figure 9-1) and a few have a physical keyboard plus a touch screen. Many smartphones allow for voice input.

Source: iStockphoto.com/Hocus-focus

Figure 9-1 Most smartphones don't have a physical keyboard and use a touch screen with an on-screen keyboard for input

▲ *Tablets and lightweight laptops.* A tablet is a computing device with a touch screen that is larger than a smartphone and has functions similar to a smartphone. As you can see in Figure 9-2, it might come with a detachable keyboard or a stylus. Most tablets can connect to Wi-Fi networks and use Bluetooth or NFC (Near Field Communication), which you'll learn about later in this chapter, to wirelessly connect to nearby devices. Some tablets have the ability to use a cellular network for data transmissions and phone calls. Installed apps, such as Skype, can make voice phone calls, send text, and make video calls. When a tablet can be used to make a phone call, the distinction between a smartphone and a tablet is almost nonexistent, except for size.

Source: Samsung

Figure 9-2 Tablets are larger than smartphones and smaller than laptops

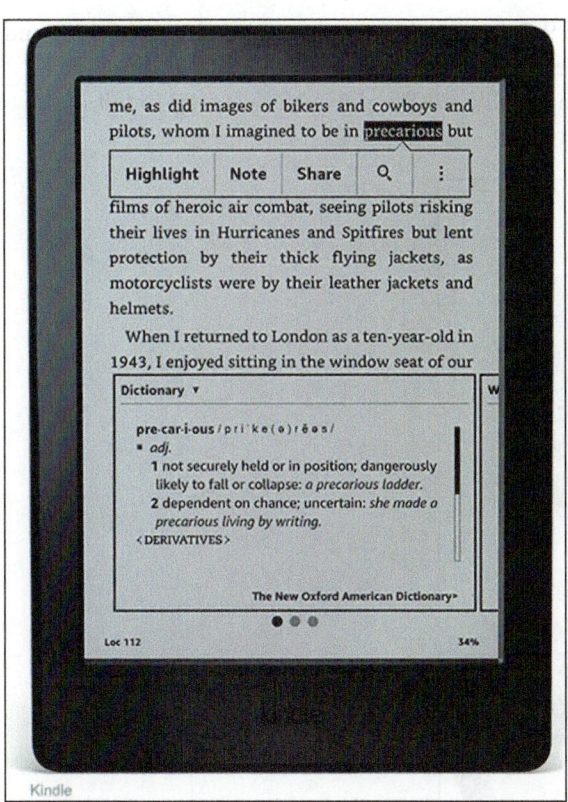

Kindle

Source: amazon.com

Figure 9-3 An e-reader includes tools optimized for reading, making notes, and looking up definitions of words

- *E-readers.* An e-reader, as shown in Figure 9-3, is a mobile device that holds digital versions of books, newspapers, magazines, and other printed documents, which are usually downloaded to the device from the web. An e-reader can connect to the Internet using a Wi-Fi wireless connection or a wired connection to a computer that is connected to the Internet. In addition, content can be stored on a flash memory card, which is inserted in the e-reader. Some e-readers, such as Amazon's Kindle Fire, have other apps that allow for surfing the web, playing games, handling email, and more. Devices such as these blur the line between e-readers and tablets.
- *GPS.* A GPS (Global Positioning System) feature is often embedded in many mobile devices, including smartphones, smart watches, tablets, and even automobiles, making it possible to identify the device's location in relation to multiple satellites in orbit around the Earth. Dedicated GPS devices are also available from Garmin (*garmin.com*), TomTom (*tomtom.com*), and a few others. A mobile device determines its location by using Bluetooth and GPS information as well as crowd-sourced Wi-Fi and cellular databases built from anonymous, encrypted, geo-tagged locations of Wi-Fi hotspots and cell towers.

- *Wearable technology devices.* Wearable technology devices, including smart watches (see Figure 9-4), wristbands, arm bands, eyeglasses, headsets, clothing, tracking tags, and even action cameras can be used as computing devices to make phone calls, send text messages, transmit data, and/or check email. Wearable technology often includes fitness monitoring capability where the device can measure heart rate, calculate calories burned, count pool laps or miles jogged or biked, and a host of other activities. These devices can sync up with a computer for power and communication, similar to how other mobile devices work. Many people believe smart watches will eventually replace smartphones as the personal communication device of choice.

Source: iStockphoto.com/Mutlu Kurtbas

Figure 9-4 The app screen on a smart watch by Apple, Inc.

- *VR/AR headsets.* A special type of wearable technology, virtual reality (VR) headsets, can help a user feel immersed in a virtual experience even to the point of moving physically through 3D space. Devices are used primarily for extreme gaming experiences, and are also used in military and medical training. The two main categories of VR headsets are mobile, which is basically a headset shell to hold a smartphone behind the lenses, or tethered, which requires a wired connection to a robust computer. Mobile VR headsets are inexpensive (as low as $30) and, accordingly, the experience leaves much to be desired.

Tethered VR headsets, such as the Oculus Rift in Figure 9-5, are much more expensive (around $400) and often come with a variety of accessories to maximize the VR experience. Microsoft has also developed a line of augmented reality (AR) headsets with native compatibility to Windows 10 that tend to fall in the middle ground between mobile and tethered VR headsets.

Source: amazon.com

Figure 9-5 The Oculus Rift communicates with a computer through a wired connection

MOBILE DEVICE OPERATING SYSTEMS

A+
CORE 1
3.9

A+
CORE 2
1.1, 4.6

The operating system for a mobile device is installed at the factory. Here are the four most popular ones:

▲ Android OS by Google (*android.com*) is based on Linux and is used on various smartphones and tablets. At the time of this writing, Android is the most popular OS for smartphones in the world. Nearly 80 percent of smartphones sold today use Android. Combining both smartphones and tablets, Android holds over 70 percent of the worldwide market.

▲ iOS by Apple (*apple.com*) is based on macOS and is currently used on the iPhone and iPad. Almost 20 percent of smartphones sold today are made by Apple and use iOS, and over 20 percent of smartphones and tablets combined use iOS.

▲ Windows 10 Mobile by Microsoft (*microsoft.com*) is based on Windows 10 and is used on various smartphones. (Tablets use the 32-bit version of the same Windows 10 operating system used on desktop and laptop systems.) About half a percent of smartphones sold today use Windows 10 Mobile or one of its predecessors, such as Windows Phone 8.1.

▲ Chrome OS by Google is built on the open source Chromium OS (*chromium.org*). Open source means the source code for the operating system is available for free and anyone can modify and redistribute the source code. Chrome OS is designed solely for use on Google's Chromebook (*google.com/chromebook*), which is available from many different manufacturers as a lightweight laptop, a tablet, or a convertible laptop-tablet. Chrome OS looks and works like the familiar Chrome browser and relies heavily on web-based apps and storage. While technically a desktop OS, Chrome OS on Chromebooks bridges both the desktop and mobile markets, and it's rising in popularity due to increased availability of compatible apps, decreasing prices, quick response times in the OS, and reliable security features.

⭐ **A+ Exam Tip** The A+ Core 2 exam expects you to understand the similarities and differences among the Android, iOS, Windows Mobile, and Chrome OS operating systems used with mobile devices.

ANDROID MANAGED BY GOOGLE

A+ CORE 1 3.9

A+ CORE 2 1.1

The Android operating system is based on the Linux OS and uses a Linux kernel. Linux and Android are both open source. Google (*google.com* and *android.com*) manages but does not own Android, and assumes a leadership role in development, quality control, and distributions of the Android OS and Android apps. Ongoing development of the Android OS code by Google and other contributors is released to the public as open source code.

GET TO KNOW AN ANDROID DEVICE

Releases of Android are named after desserts and include Honeycomb (version 3.x), Ice Cream Sandwich (version 4.0.x), Jelly Bean (version 4.1-4.3.x), KitKat (version 4.4+), Lollipop (version 5.0-5.1.1), Marshmallow (version 6.0), Nougat (versions 7.0 and 7.1), Oreo (versions 8.0 and 8.1), and the recently released Pie (version 9.0). Future releases of Android will follow in alphabetic order. At the time of this writing, most new phones and tablets ship with Oreo installed, although Android Pie is released on some phone models.

Android's graphical user interface (GUI) starts with multiple home screens and supports windows, panes, and 3D graphics. The Android OS can use an embedded browser, manage a database using SQLite, and connect to Wi-Fi, Bluetooth, and cellular networks. Most current Android mobile devices have a power button and volume control buttons on the side, and no physical buttons on the front of the device. However, three soft buttons on the navigation bar at the bottom of the screen include back (goes back to the previous screen), home (goes directly to the home screen), and overview (shows all running apps—swipe an app to the side to close it). See Figure 9-6.

Source: Android

Figure 9-6 This Nexus smartphone has the Android Oreo OS installed

On Android phones, up to five apps or groups of apps can be pinned to the favorites tray just above the navigation bar. Apps in the favorites tray stay put as you move from home screen to home screen by swiping left or right. Tap the small arrow above the favorites tray or swipe up anywhere on the screen to access the app drawer, which lists and manages all apps installed on the phone. Press and hold an app in the app drawer to add it to an existing home screen or to add more home screens.

Notifications provide alerts and related information about apps and social media. Notifications are accessed by swiping down from the top of the screen, as shown in Figure 9-7A. The notifications shade provides access to the quick settings panel, such as Wi-Fi, Bluetooth, and Brightness. Tap the **Settings** gear icon near the upper-right corner to open the Settings app (see Figure 9-7B), or tap the **back** button in the navigation bar to return to the home screen.

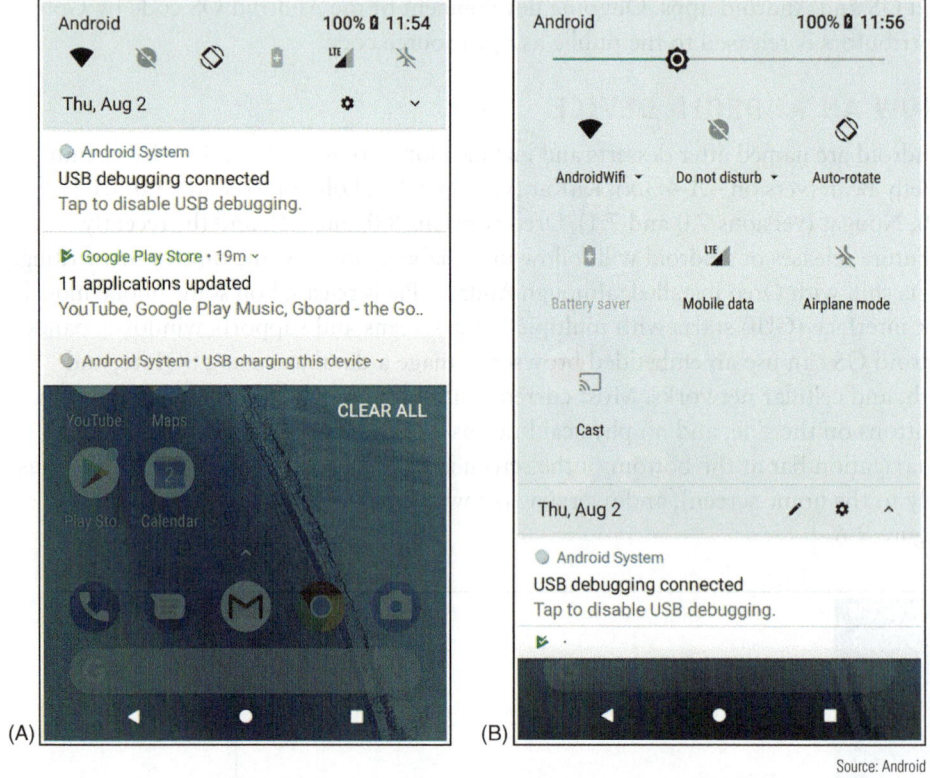

Source: Android

Figure 9-7   (A) The notifications shade includes quick access to the Settings app; (B) swipe down again to access quick settings on the notifications shade

A digital assistant service or app, also called a personal assistant, responds to a user's voice commands with a personable, conversational interaction to perform tasks and retrieve information. Popular examples are Apple's Siri (*apple.com*), Amazon's Alexa (*amazon.com*), Microsoft's Cortana (*microsoft.com*), and the Google Assistant (*assistant.google.com*). Google Assistant can be accessed on most Android devices with the voice command "Ok Google" or "Hey Google," or by touching and holding the Home button. See Figure 9-8. Give Google Assistant voice commands to send a message, start a phone call, look up information, and do many other tasks.

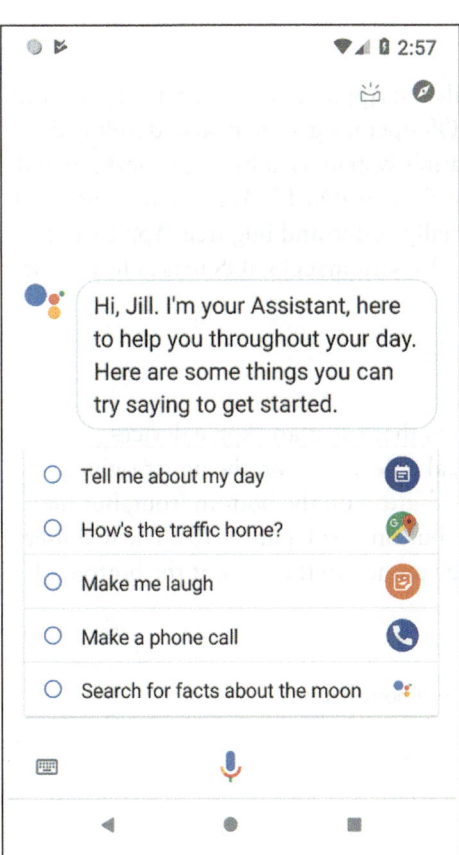

Source: Android

Figure 9-8 Google Assistant responds to voice commands

ANDROID APPS

Android apps are sold or freely distributed from any source or vendor. For example, you can open the Chrome browser and download an app from a website, such as the Amazon Appstore for Android at *amazon.com* or directly from the website of a developer. However, the official source for apps is Google Play at *play.google.com*. A Google account is required to download content from Google Play and can be associated with any valid email address.

To download an app using the Play Store app, tap the **Play Store** app on the home screen. (If you don't see the app icon on the home screen, tap the **app drawer** and then tap **Play Store**.) The app takes you to Google Play, where you can search for apps, games, movies, music, e-books, and magazines (see Figure 9-9A). You can also use the Play Store app to manage updates to installed apps, as shown in Figure 9-9B.

To develop Android apps, an app developer can download Android Studio to his computer from *developer.android.com*. Included in the download are Android SDK tools and an Android emulator. An SDK (Software Development Kit) is a group of tools that developers use to write apps, and an Android emulator is software that creates a virtual Android device complete with virtual hardware (buttons, camera, and even device orientation), a working installation of Android, and native apps. Android Studio is free and is released as open source. In a project at the end of this chapter, you'll download and install Android Studio and then use it to create virtual Android devices.

9

(A)

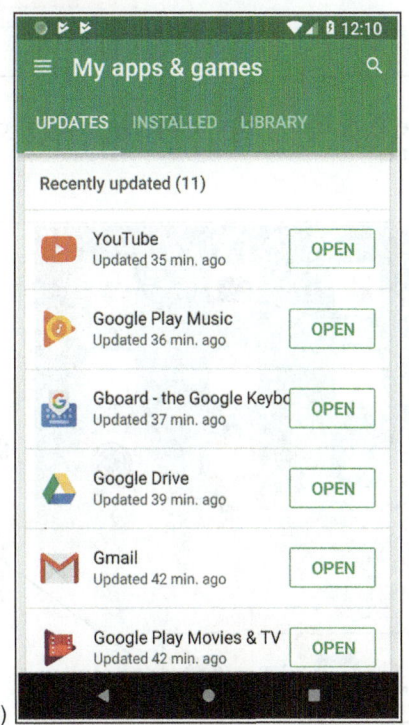

(B)

Source: Android

Figure 9-9 Use the Play Store app to (A) search Google Play for apps, music, e-books, movies, and more that you can download, as well as (B) updates to installed apps

IOS BY APPLE

A+ CORE 1 3.9

A+ CORE 2 1.1

Apple, Inc. (*apple.com*) develops, manufactures, and sells the Apple iPhone (a smartphone) and iPad (a handheld tablet). Both of these devices use the iOS operating system, also developed and owned by Apple. iOS is based on macOS, the operating system used by Apple desktop and laptop computers. The latest release at the time of this writing is iOS 12. Apple maintains strict standards on its products, which means iOS is exceptionally stable and bug free. Apple's iOS is also a very easy and intuitive operating system to use. As with macOS, iOS makes heavy use of icons.

GET TO KNOW AN IOS DEVICE

Because Apple is the sole owner and distributor of iOS, the only devices that use it are Apple devices (currently the iPhone and iPad). iPhones and iPads each have a physical Side button on the upper-right side of the device. All iPads and older models of iPhones have a Home button on the bottom front, but the newer iPhone X (pronounced *iPhone ten*) models don't have a Home button (see Figure 9-10). The iOS user interface as it appears on an iPad is shown in Figure 9-11. Apps can be pinned to the dock at the bottom of the screen.

Source: https://www.apple.com/iphone/compare/

Figure 9-10   The iPhone X series does not have the Home button that comes on all previous models of iPhones

Source: iOS

Figure 9-11   Access the dock on an iPad by swiping up from the bottom of the screen

Knowing a few simple navigation tips on an iOS device can help you get around a little more easily:

▲ *Open and close apps.* Tap an app icon to open it. Use the app switcher to switch to a different open app or to close apps. On an iPad, swipe up on the screen or double-click the Home button to show the app switcher and control center on the same screen (see Figure 9-12). On an older iPhone, double-click the Home button to see the app switcher. On an iPhone X, swipe up from the bottom and briefly hold to see the app switcher, or you can swipe side to side to move among open apps. In the app switcher, swipe up to close an app. Closing apps you're not using can save battery life.

Source: iOS

Figure 9-12 Access the app switcher and control center from any screen

▲ *Control center.* Use the control center to change basic settings such as brightness, volume, Wi-Fi, and Bluetooth. For the iPad and older iPhones, swipe up to show the control center (see the right side of Figure 9-12 for an iPad). On an iPhone X, swipe down from the upper-right corner to show the control center. Use the Settings app to adjust which settings are available in the control center.

▲ *Notification screen.* Swipe down from the top of the screen to see the notifications screen. The types of notifications shown and other notification settings can be customized in the Settings app, which you can open from the Home screen by tapping the Settings icon.

▲ *Delete and move apps.* To delete or move an app icon on the screen, press and hold the icon until all icons start to jiggle. As the icons jiggle, press the **X** beside the icon to delete it. To move an icon, press and drag it to a new location. You can add new home screens by dragging an app icon off the screen to the right. To stop the jiggling, press the Home button on the iPad and older iPhones. For iPhone X, press the **Done** button that appears in the upper-right corner of the screen.

▲ *Siri.* For iPhone X, press and hold the Side button to open Siri, iOS's digital assistant service, as shown in Figure 9-13. For all other iPhones and iPads, press and hold the **Home** button to open Siri. Siri was the first of the digital assistant services and has been around long enough to have become quite sophisticated. Siri uses information within the user's account to provide a customized experience.

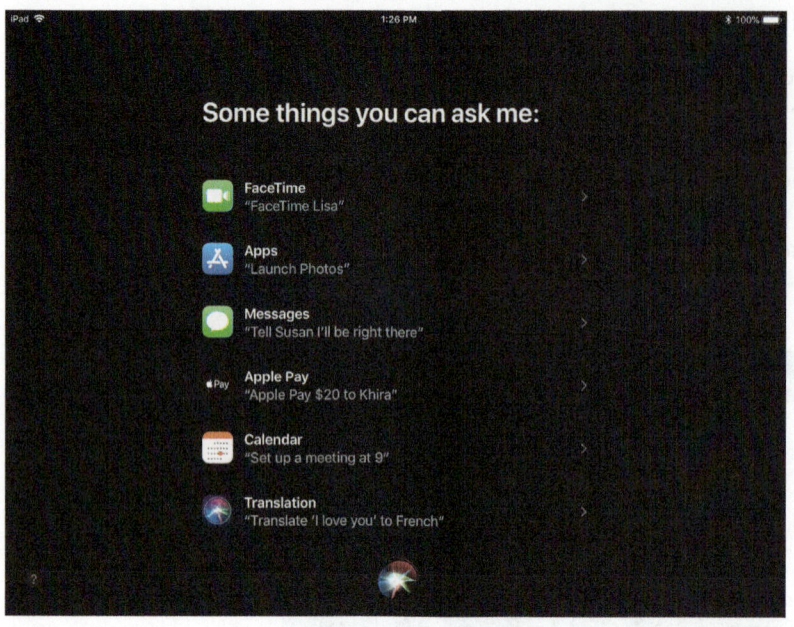

Source: iOS

Figure 9-13   Siri follows voice commands

IOS APPS

You can get Android apps from many sources, but the only place to go for an iOS app is Apple. Apple is the sole distributor of iOS apps at its App Store. Other developers can write apps for the iPhone or iPad, but these apps must be sent to Apple for close scrutiny. If they pass muster, they are distributed by Apple on its website. Apple offers app development tools, including the iOS SDK (Software Development Kit) at *developer. apple.com*.

When you first purchase an iPad or iPhone, you activate it by signing into the device with an Apple ID, or user account, using a valid email address and password, and associating the account with a credit card number. Here are options for obtaining apps and other content:

▲ *App Store.* Use the App Store app on your mobile device (see Figure 9-14 for an iPad example) to search, purchase, and download apps, games, e-books, and periodical content such as newspapers and magazines. Some downloads are free.

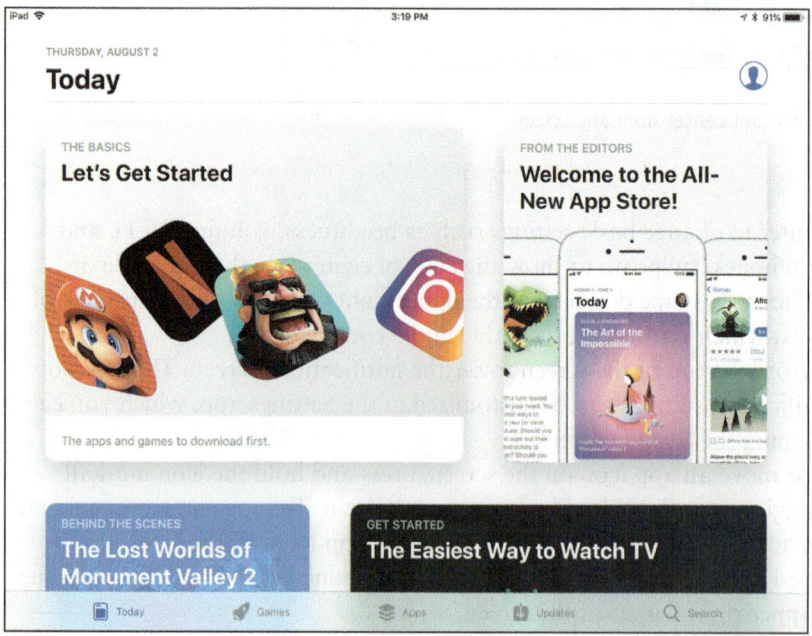

Source: iOS

Figure 9-14   Use Apple's App Store app to download new apps

▲ *iTunes*. Use the iTunes Store app to search, purchase, and download media content, including music, movies, TV shows, and podcasts. (Again, some downloads are free.) You also have the option to download and install the iTunes software on a Mac or Windows personal computer. When you connect your mobile device to the computer by way of a USB port, you can use the iTunes software to sync the device to iOS updates downloaded from *iTunes.com* and to content on your computer, which can be a helpful troubleshooting option, as you'll see later.

WINDOWS MOBILE BY MICROSOFT

**A+
CORE 1
3.9**

**A+
CORE 2
1.1**

The Windows Mobile operating system by Microsoft is more or less a simplified version of the Windows operating system designed for desktop computers, laptops, and tablets. Windows Mobile and Windows version numbers correspond: Windows Mobile 10 corresponds to Windows 10. One of the biggest differences between Windows and Windows Mobile is that Windows Mobile does not have a desktop screen. Everything is accessed from the Start screen.

GET TO KNOW A WINDOWS MOBILE DEVICE

Most Windows phones have three buttons below the screen (see Figure 9-15). These buttons might be physical buttons or software buttons. The start button accesses the Start screen, the back button goes back one screen, and the search button opens a Cortana search box. (Recall that Cortana is the Windows digital assistant app.) Also, if you press and hold the **back** button, it displays recent apps. For most phones, these buttons aren't true software buttons, but they're also not true physical buttons because they might not work when the OS is malfunctioning.

Windows phones rely primarily on the Start screen for accessing apps. Just as with Windows 10, the Start screen is full of live tiles; each represents an app and many show live data on the tile from that app. Here are some tips for getting around Windows Mobile:

▲ Tap a tile on the Start screen to open its app. Scroll up or down to see more tiles. Press and hold to resize or reposition tiles. On many smartphones, pressing and holding a link functions like right-clicking with a mouse on a Windows desktop computer.

▲ Swipe down from the very top of the screen to see notifications in the Action Center (Figure 9-16A), similar to both Android and iOS. Like Android, there is also a Settings icon here to open the Settings app, shown in Figure 9-16B. Settings can also be accessed via the Settings tile on the Start screen.

Figure 9-15 Press and hold the search button to activate Cortana, the Windows digital assistant

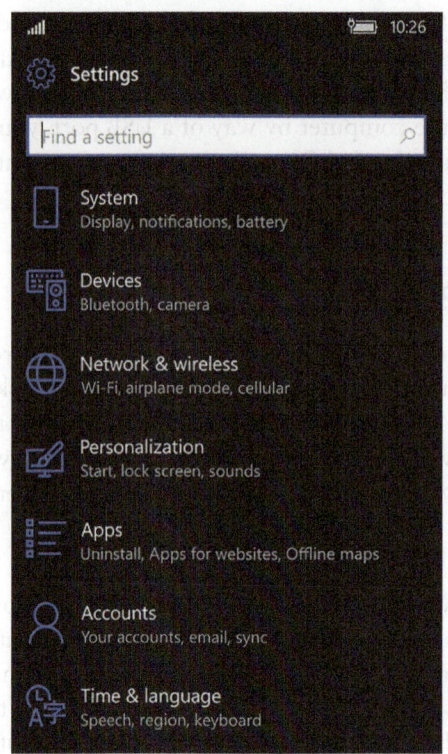

Figure 9-16   (A) Notifications appear in the Action Center; (B) the Settings app provides an extensive toolkit for customizing a Windows smartphone

⊿ Swipe from the right to see the apps list. Press and hold an app on the list to pin the app to the Start screen (see Figure 9-17). On the Start screen, you can press and hold the app tile and then change its size and other characteristics. Tap the **Store** tile on the Start screen to find more apps.

⊿ While a menu is displayed in the Settings app, you can sometimes swipe from the right to see a submenu. Windows Mobile is rich with settings options, making it easier to integrate Windows phones in an enterprise environment.

⊿ Windows Mobile 10 has a digital assistant called Cortana that also customizes the user's experience.

WINDOWS MOBILE APPS

The availability of apps for Windows mobile devices is much more limited than that for Android or iOS. Windows apps are obtained through the Microsoft Store app. Additionally, like Android apps, Windows Mobile apps can be obtained from third-party websites via the browser on the mobile device.

CHROME OS BY GOOGLE

Chrome OS is deeply integrated with Google's Chrome browser: Most of Chrome OS's native apps open directly in the Chrome browser and rely heavily on having an active Internet connection. While there are some apps that will function offline, such as Gmail, Docs, and Calendar, functionality is limited to data that is temporarily stored on the Chromebook until it can again be synced with the user's online account. Chrome OS functions exclusively on Chromebooks, although

Figure 9-17   To pin an app to the Start screen, press and hold the app's icon and then tap *Pin to Start*

Figure 9-18 A Chromebook can be a lightweight laptop, a tablet, or a hybrid laptop-tablet

many manufacturers build and sell Chromebooks. See Figure 9-18.

GET TO KNOW A CHROMEBOOK

Chromebooks come with a variety of external ports, depending on the manufacturer and model. Many feature USB and USB-C ports as well as HDMI. Some include SD card slots for adding extra storage space. The keyboard on a Chromebook (see Figure 9-19) looks similar to the typical laptop keyboard, with a few notable differences. The unique keys mostly run along the top of the keyboard and include these keys: search, previous and next pages, refresh, immersive mode (hides tabs and launcher), and overview mode (shows all open apps). Keyboard shortcuts, a popular feature with Chromebooks, use combinations of key presses to accomplish tasks such as opening a new Chrome window (**ctrl+n**) or tab (**ctrl+t**), taking a screenshot (**ctrl+overview**), locking the screen (**search+L**), and showing all keyboard shortcuts (**ctrl+alt+/**).

Figure 9-19 A Chromebook keyboard

Figure 9-20 shows the Chrome OS desktop with the Settings app and Chrome browser open. Also notice the shelf on the bottom left and the open status tray on the bottom right. The app launcher is in the shelf. To open the Settings app, click anywhere in the status tray, which opens the tray, and then click the **Settings app** gear icon in the open status tray.

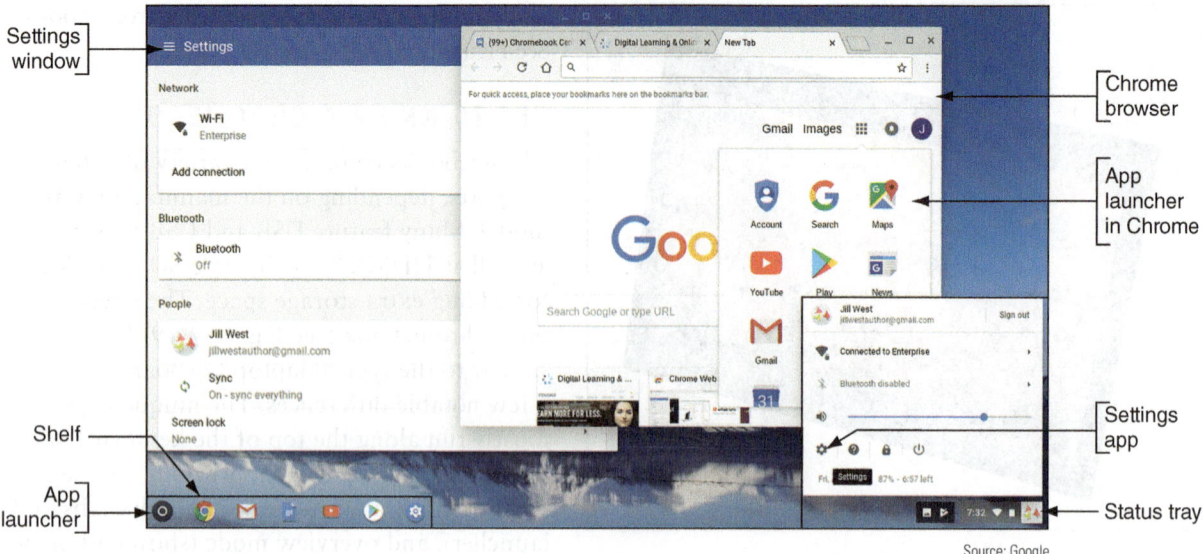

Figure 9-20   The Chrome OS desktop

Source: Google

Chrome OS is automatically updated about every six weeks and includes some significant security measures to protect the computer from malware, including built-in virus protection. Google took a four-pronged approach to security with Chrome OS:

- *Sandboxing.* Each tab in the Chrome browser is isolated from the underlying OS and from processes in other tabs.
- *Verified boot.* Similar to the Windows Secure boot, it protects the OS from changes being made to its underlying system files, automatically entering recovery mode if modifications are detected.
- *Power washing.* The user can perform a simple and quick reset to factory settings in the event a malware infection does manage to take hold.
- *Quick updates.* The OS updates itself in the background without user intervention about every six weeks. If an update is needed for a security patch, it can happen within 48 hours.

The end effect is a very stable and secure OS that even security professionals rely on when traveling to techie, hacker, or security conferences, where the persistent threat of hacking attacks is an integral part of the overall experience.

CHROME OS APPS

The Chrome shelf contains icons for important apps; tap an icon to open the app. To view and open any installed app, tap the app launcher icon in the shelf (refer back to Figure 9-20) and tap an app in the launcher (see Figure 9-21). Most apps open in the Chrome browser, and several apps offer Chrome extensions that add functionality to the Chrome browser even when the app is not open. Users can get more apps through the Chrome Web Store app, and some newer Chromebooks also support Android apps downloaded through the Google Play Store app.

> ⚡ **Caution**   Know that if you download Android apps to the Chromebook and then turn off the Play Store app, you'll lose all the Android apps' data and settings from the Chromebook.

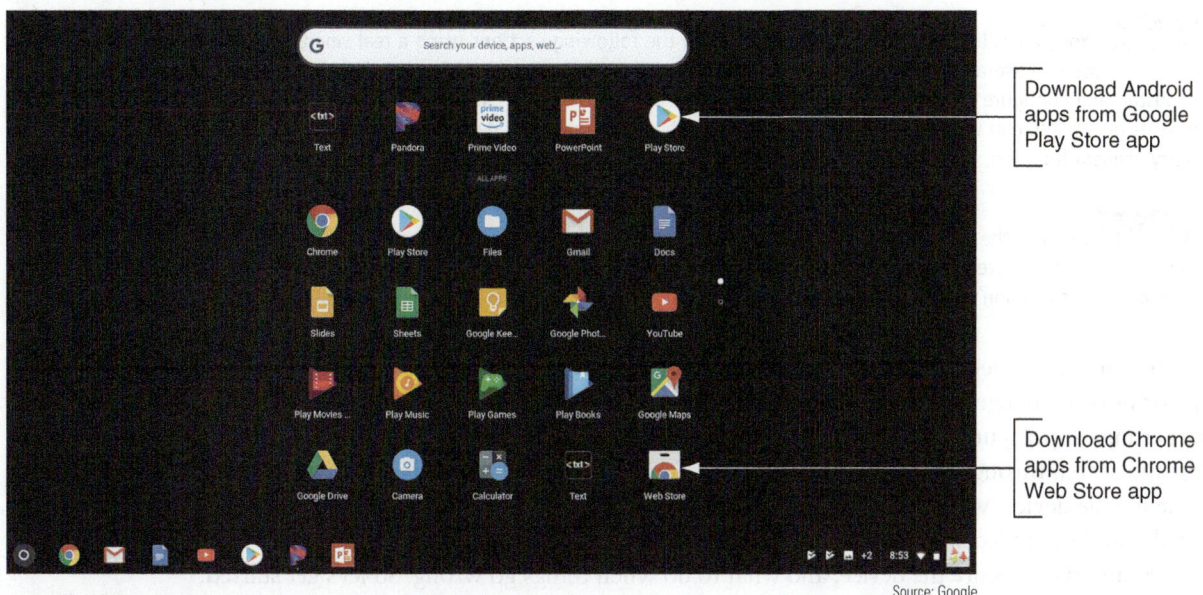

Source: Google

Figure 9-21 Open apps from the Chrome OS app launcher

COMPARING OPEN SOURCE AND CLOSED SOURCE OPERATING SYSTEMS

A+
CORE 1
3.9

A+
CORE 2
1.1, 4.6

Open source operating systems (such as Android and Chrome OS) and closed source operating systems (such as iOS and Windows Mobile) have their advantages and disadvantages. Closed source systems are also called vendor-specific or commercial license operating systems. Here are some key points to consider about releasing or not releasing source code:

▲ Apple carefully guards its iOS source code and internal functions of the OS. Third-party developers of apps have access only to APIs, which are requests to the OS to perform a function, such as to access data provided by the embedded GPS. An app must be tested and approved by Apple before it can be sold in Apple's online App Store. These policies assure users that apps are high quality. It also assures developers they have a central point of contact for users to buy their apps, and their copyrights are better protected.

▲ In the interest of openness and innovation, the Android and Chrome OS source code and the development and sale of apps are not as closely guarded. Apps can be purchased or downloaded from Google Play or Chrome Web Store, but they can also be obtained from other sources such as *amazon.com* or directly from a developer. This freedom comes with a cost because users are not always assured of high-quality, bug-free apps, and developers are not always assured of a convenient market for their apps.

▲ For Android, because any smartphone or tablet manufacturer can modify the source code, many variations of Android exist. These variations can make it difficult for developers to write apps that are compatible with any given Android platform. These inconsistencies can also make it difficult for users to learn to use new Android devices.

CONFIGURING AND SYNCING A MOBILE DEVICE

A+
CORE 1
1.5, 1.6,
1.7, 2.4,
3.1, 3.9

A+
CORE 2
1.1

In this part of the chapter, you learn to configure network connections and to update and back up data, content, and settings on mobile devices. You don't need to memorize these steps—it's sufficient to be familiar with the general idea of where these features are located in the OS and how to use them, especially because the specific steps change with almost every new version of any mobile OS. We'll use examples of both Android and iOS because they're by far the most popular mobile OSs.

9

> ✏️ **Notes** You can follow along with the steps given in the following sections using a real smartphone or tablet (Android or iOS) or you can use an Android emulator. Real Problem 9-1 at the end of this chapter gives you step-by-step instructions to install and configure the free Android Studio, which includes an Android emulator. You can then create emulated Android devices on your screen with real features that work like those on a physical device, including a power button, rotate capability, camera function, and much more.

> ✏️ **Notes** Because the Android operating system is open source, manufacturers can customize the OS and how it works. Therefore, specific step-by-step directions will vary from device to device, even when the devices all use the same Android release. Remember that you don't need to memorize the steps—just learn general procedures for supporting a variety of mobile devices.

When you are called on to support a device that you don't own or normally use, it's helpful to begin by looking for how to change settings. Most of the settings you need to use to support a mobile device are contained in the Settings app. Figure 9-22 shows the Settings apps for Android and iOS. Basically, you can open the Settings app and search through its menus and submenus until you find what you need. If you get stuck, check the user guide for the device, which you can download from the device manufacturer's website. The user guide is likely to tell you the detailed steps of how to connect to a network, configure email, update the OS, sync and back up settings and data, secure the device, and what to do when things go wrong. So let's get started.

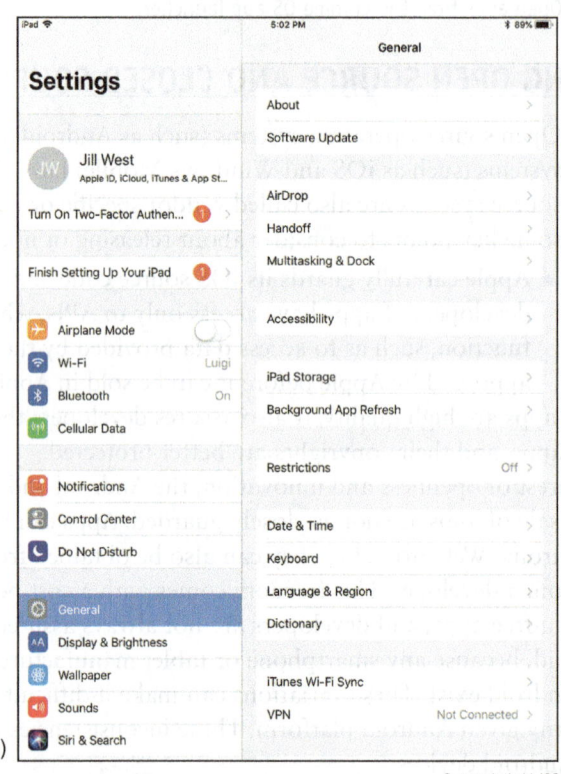

(A) (B)

Source: Android, iOS

Figure 9-22 (A) The Android Settings app, and (B) the iOS Settings app

> ✏️ **Notes** Most of us rarely follow step-by-step directions when learning to use a new device until when "all else fails, read the directions." This part of the chapter can give you an idea of what to look for, and you can likely figure out the specific steps for yourself.

MOBILE DEVICE LAN/WAN CONNECTIONS

A+
CORE 1
1.5, 1.6,
3.9

A mobile device might have several antennas—primarily Wi-Fi, GPS, Bluetooth, NFC, and cellular. The device uses a Wi-Fi or cellular antenna to connect to a LAN (local area network) or WAN (wide area network) and uses Bluetooth or NFC to connect to a PAN (personal area network). Settings on the device allow you to enable or disable each antenna. Network connections are configured using the Settings app. Let's look at LAN and WAN network connections first, then we'll look at technologies used for connecting mobile device accessories in PANs.

> **✎ Notes** You can automatically disable the antennas in a mobile device that can transmit signals by enabling **airplane mode** so that the device can neither transmit nor receive the signals. Many newer devices do not disable the GPS or NFC antennas; GPS only receives and never transmits, and NFC signals don't reach very far. While airplane mode is on, you can manually enable some wireless connections, such as Bluetooth or Wi-Fi.

> **★ A+ Exam Tip** The A+ Core 1 exam might give you a scenario that expects you to decide how to configure a Wi-Fi, cellular data, Bluetooth, or VPN connection on a mobile device.

WI-FI CONNECTION

Most mobile devices have Wi-Fi capability and can connect to a Wi-Fi local wireless network. On the Wi-Fi settings screen, you can add a Wi-Fi connection, manage existing networks, view available Wi-Fi hotspots, see which Wi-Fi network you are connected to, turn Wi-Fi off and on, and decide whether the device should ask the user before joining a Wi-Fi network. When the device is within range of Wi-Fi networks, it displays the list of networks. Select one to connect. If the Wi-Fi network is secured, enter the security key to complete the connection. To change a network's settings, tap the name of the network (see Figure 9-23). Searching for a Wi-Fi network can drain battery power. To make a battery charge last longer, disable Wi-Fi when you're not using it.

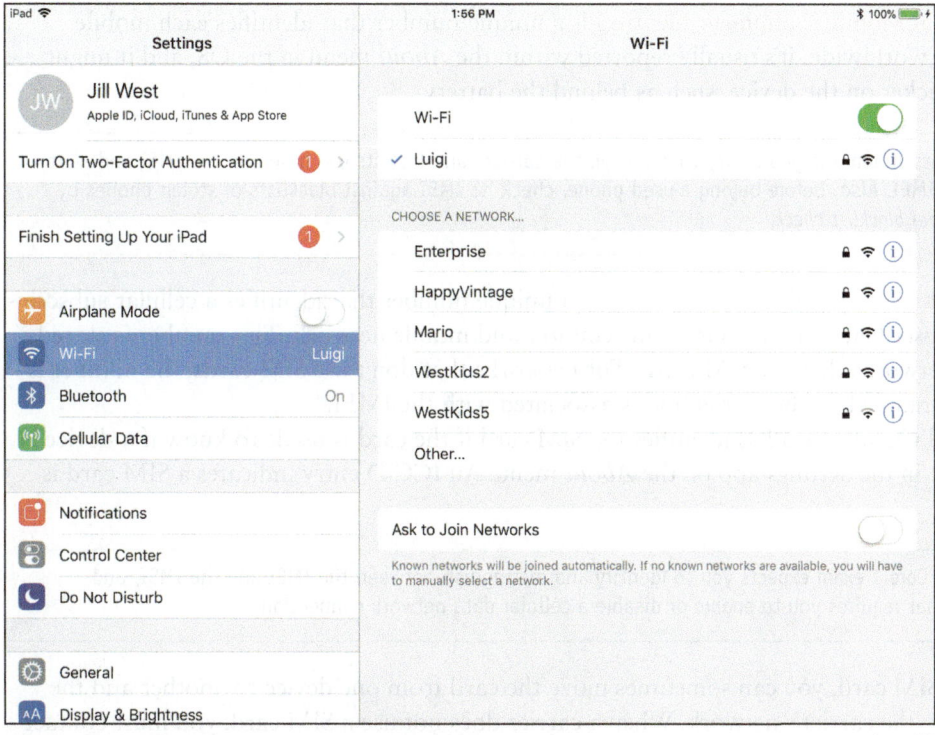

Source: iOS

Figure 9-23 Configure Wi-Fi connection settings

TETHERING AND MOBILE HOTSPOTS

When a mobile device is connected to the Internet by way of its cellular network, recall from Chapter 7 that you can allow other computers and devices to use this same connection. For example, in Figure 9-24, the smartphone is tethered by USB to a laptop so that the laptop can use the cellular network to connect to the Internet. If the smartphone has Wi-Fi capabilities, it can create its own Wi-Fi hotspot for other computers

Figure 9-24 Tether your smartphone to your laptop using a USB cable

and devices to connect to wirelessly. An app on the smartphone controls these connections. To use your phone for tethering and for providing mobile hotspots, your carrier subscription must allow it.

CELLULAR DATA CONNECTION

Smartphones and some laptops, tablets, and wearable mobile devices can connect to a cellular network if they have cellular capability and a subscription to the cellular network carrier. Recall from Chapter 7 that a cellular network provided by a carrier (for example, AT&T or Verizon) is used for voice, text, and data communication. A cellular network uses GSM or CDMA for voice and another layer of technology for data transmissions, such as 3G, 4G, 5G, and LTE. GSM and LTE require a SIM card installed in the device, and CDMA does not use a SIM card unless the network is also using LTE, which does require a SIM card. To make a cellular data connection, you must have a subscription with your carrier that includes a cellular data plan.

Here is information that might be used when a connection is first made to the network:

◢ The **IMEI (International Mobile Equipment Identity)** is a unique number that identifies each mobile phone or tablet device worldwide. It's usually reported within the *About* menu in the OS, and it might also be printed on a sticker on the device, such as behind the battery.

> 🖉 **Notes** If your phone gets stolen and you notify your carrier, the carrier can block its use based on the IMEI and alert other carriers to the stolen IMEI. Also, before buying a used phone, check its IMEI against blacklists of stolen phones by doing a Google search on *imei blacklist check*.

◢ The **IMSI (International Mobile Subscriber Identity)** is a unique number that identifies a cellular subscription for a device or subscriber, along with its home country and mobile network. This number is stored on the SIM card for networks that use SIM cards. For networks that don't use SIM cards, the number is kept in a database maintained by the carrier and is associated with the IMEI.
◢ The ICCID (Integrated Circuit Card ID) identifies the SIM card if the card is used. To know if a device is using a SIM card, look in the Settings app on the *About* menu. An ICCID entry indicates a SIM card is present.

> ★ **A+ Exam Tip** The A+ Core 1 exam expects you to identify and distinguish between the IMEI and the IMSI, and might give you a scenario that requires you to enable or disable a cellular data network connection.

When a carrier uses a SIM card, you can sometimes move the card from one device to another and the new device can connect to the carrier's network. When a carrier does not use a SIM card, you must contact the carrier and request permission to switch devices. If the carrier accepts the new device, the new IMEI will be entered in the carrier's database.

The carrier typically configures the phone to make calls on its network; however, you might find that you want to disable cellular data at times, or disable cellular roaming. The advantage of disabling cellular data and using Wi-Fi for data transmissions is that these transmissions are not charged against your cellular data subscription plan. Also, Wi-Fi is generally faster than most cellular connections. Disabling roaming can prevent roaming charges on your bill incurred from using other carriers' cellular networks when you travel outside your home territory.

To disable roaming on an Android device, go to the Network & Internet menu in the Settings app, tap **Mobile network**, then turn off **Mobile data** or **Roaming**. On an iOS device, open the Settings app, tap **Cellular Data**, then turn off **Cellular Data**. Next, tap **Cellular Data Options**, then turn off roaming.

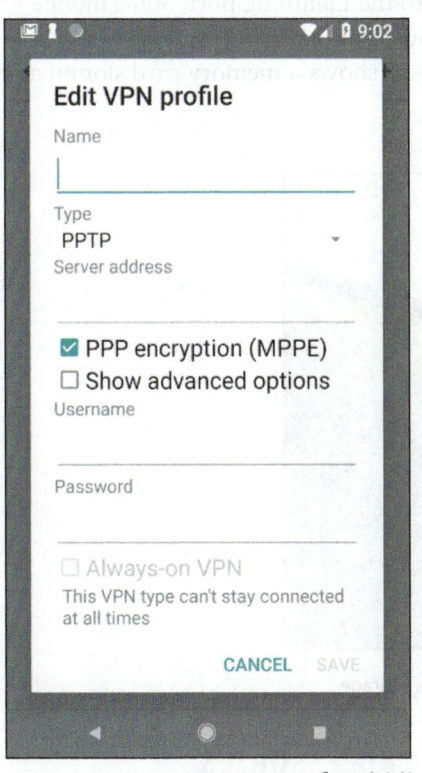

Edit VPN profile

Name

Type
PPTP
Server address

☑ PPP encryption (MPPE)
☐ Show advanced options
Username

Password

☐ Always-on VPN
This VPN type can't stay connected at all times

CANCEL   SAVE

Source: Android

Figure 9-25   Configure a VPN connection

If you have roaming enabled, especially for a CDMA device, you'll want to keep the PRL (Preferred Roaming List) updated. The PRL is a database file that lists the preferred service providers or radio frequencies your carrier wants the device to use when outside your home network. You can reset or update the list in the Settings app. For Android devices, go to the **System updates** menu and tap **Update PRL**. For an iOS device, open the Settings app, tap **General**, then scroll down and tap **Reset, Subscriber Services**, and **Reprovision Account**.

VPN CONNECTION

Like desktop computers, a mobile device can be configured to communicate information securely over a virtual private network (VPN) connection. To create a VPN connection in the Settings app, tap **VPN** and then add a new VPN connection. Follow directions to complete the connection, which will require you to know the type of encryption protocol used (PPTP, L2TP, or IPsec), the IP address or domain name of the VPN server, and the user name and password to the corporate network. Figure 9-25 shows the configuration options on an Android smartphone. In addition to the built-in Android VPN client shown in the figure, some Android devices also provide proprietary VPN configuration options. To access VPN settings in iOS, open the **Settings** app, tap **General**, and then tap **VPN**.

MOBILE DEVICE ACCESSORIES AND THEIR PAN CONNECTIONS

A+
CORE 1
1.5, 1.6,
2.4, 3.1,
3.9

You can buy all kinds of accessories for mobile devices, such as wireless keyboards, speakers, earbuds, headsets, game pads, docking stations, printers, extra battery packs and chargers, USB adapters, memory cards (usually the microSD form factor) to expand storage space, credit card readers for accepting payments by credit card, and protective covers for waterproofing. For example, Figure 9-26 shows a car docking station for a smartphone. Using this car dock, the smartphone serves as a GPS device giving driving directions.

Figure 9-26   A smartphone and a car docking station

When buying accessories for a mobile device, be sure to check what ports and slots are available on the device. For example, many mobile devices no longer include replaceable batteries. Current iPhones no longer have audio ports—to use a wired headset, you have to plug a dongle into the Lightning port. Some mobile devices have a slot for a memory card, which might be located on the side of the case or inside it; however, Apple mobile devices and many others don't offer this feature. Figure 9-27 shows a memory card slot on an Android tablet, and Figure 9-28 shows a MicroSD card.

Figure 9-27   An Android device might provide a memory card slot to allow for extra storage

Figure 9-28   A mobile device might use a MicroSD card to add extra flash memory storage to the device

WIRED CONNECTIONS FOR ACCESSORIES

Smartphones, tablets, and wearable devices can make a wired connection to a computer. This connection can be used to charge the device, download software updates, upload data to the computer, back up data, and restore software or data. The device's port used for power and communication may be a type of USB port or a proprietary, vendor-specific port. Some USB connectors used for this purpose include microUSB (see Figure 9-29A), the smaller miniUSB (see Figure 9-29B), and the newer USB-C (see Figure 9-29C). Newer Apple iPhones, iPods, and iPads use the proprietary Lightning port and connector for power and communication (see Figure 9-30).

(A)   (B)   (C)

Figure 9-29   Some mobile devices may connect to a computer's USB port by way of a (A) microUSB, (B) miniUSB, or (C) USB-C cable

Figure 9-30 A Lightning cable by Apple, Inc., has a USB connector for the computer end and a Lightning connector for an iPhone or iPad

WIRELESS CONNECTIONS FOR ACCESSORIES

Mobile devices typically have the capability to connect to other nearby wireless devices and accessories using a Bluetooth, IR, or NFC wireless connection:

Figure 9-31 An iPad and a wireless keyboard can connect using Bluetooth

▲ *Bluetooth*. Bluetooth is a short-range wireless technology to connect two devices in a small PAN. To create a Bluetooth connection, the two devices must be paired, a process you'll learn more about later in this chapter. Figure 9-31 shows an iPad connected to a keyboard using Bluetooth.

▲ *Infrared*. Infrared (IR) is a wireless connection that requires an unobstructed "line of sight" between transmitter and receiver, which must be within about 30 m of each other. IR relies on light waves just below the visible red-light portion of the spectrum. This means you can't see infrared light, but you can feel it as heat. TV or other multimedia devices and a remote control often use an IR wireless interface. Apps on smartphones and tablets that support IR can be used in place of an IR remote control.

▲ *NFC*. Near Field Communication (NFC) is a wireless technology that establishes a communication link between two NFC devices that are within 10 cm (about 4 inches) of each other. For example, when two smartphones get within close range, they can use NFC to exchange contact information. NFC connections are also used for contactless credit card payments at a store. An NFC tag (see Figure 9-32) contains a small microchip that can be embedded in just about anything, including a key chain tag, printed flyer, or billboard (see Figure 9-32). The NFC tag dispenses information to any NFC-enabled smartphone or other device that comes within 4 inches of the tag. Learn more about NFC at *nearfieldcommunication.org*.

Figure 9-32 These programmable NFC tags have sticky backs for attaching to a flat surface like a wall, desk, or car dashboard

APPLYING | CONCEPTS   PAIRING BLUETOOTH DEVICES

To configure a Bluetooth connection, complete the following steps:

1. Turn on the Bluetooth device, such as a speaker, headset, or keyboard, to which you want to connect your mobile device.

2. Enable Bluetooth on that device and enable pairing mode. Sometimes just turning on Bluetooth enables pairing automatically for a limited period of time. The device might have a pairing button or combination of buttons to enable pairing. When you press this button, a pairing light blinks, indicating the device is ready to receive a Bluetooth connection. This makes the device discoverable, which means it's transmitting a signal to identify itself to nearby Bluetooth devices.

3. On your mobile device, turn on Bluetooth. The mobile device searches for Bluetooth devices. If it discovers the Bluetooth device, tap it to connect. The two Bluetooth devices now begin the pairing process.

4. The devices might require a code to complete the Bluetooth connection. For example, in Figure 9-33, an iPad and Bluetooth keyboard are pairing. To complete the connection, enter the four-digit code on the keyboard.

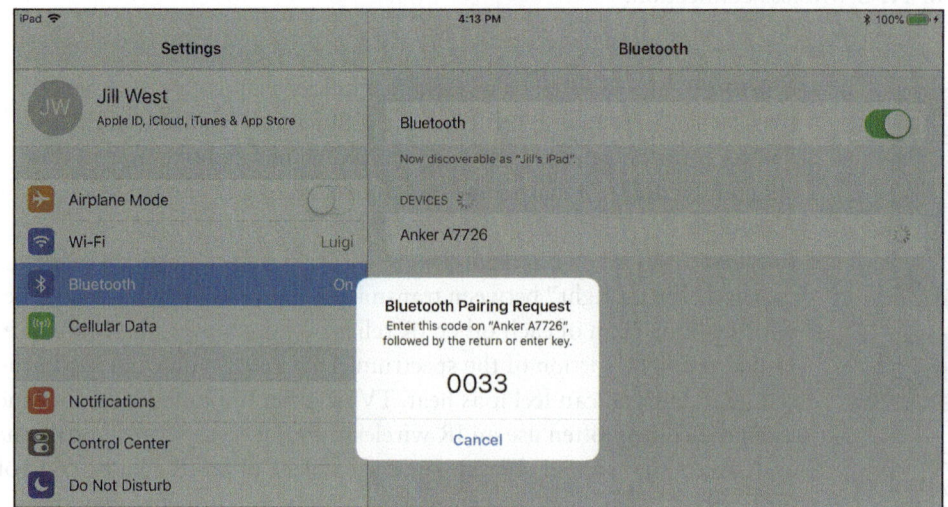

Source: iOS

Figure 9-33   A code is required to pair these two Bluetooth devices

5. Test the connection. For an audio device, play a video or audio recording on the mobile device, and for a keyboard, type into a notes application or text box.

> ★ **A+ Exam Tip**   The A+ Core 1 exam might give you a scenario that requires you to pair Bluetooth devices and then test connectivity after the connection is established.

CONFIGURING MOBILE DEVICE EMAIL

A+
CORE 1
1.6, 3.9

Using a personal computer or mobile device, email can be managed in one of two ways:

◢ *Using a browser.* In a browser, go to the website of your email provider and manage your email on the website. In this situation, your email is never downloaded to your computer or mobile device, and your messages remain on the email server until you delete them.

◢ *Using an email client.* An email client application, such as Microsoft Outlook, can be installed on your personal computer or on your mobile device. The app can either download email messages to your device (using the POP3 protocol) or can manage messages on the server (using the IMAP protocol). When the app downloads messages, you can configure the server to continue to store these messages for later use or delete the messages from the server.

Email providers include Gmail (by Google), iCloud (by Apple), Yahoo! (owned by Verizon), or Outlook/ Hotmail/Live (Microsoft's public email services for individuals). Microsoft also offers Exchange, its private enterprise email service that is hosted on corporation or ISP servers, or Exchange Online, which is hosted on Microsoft servers. As for apps on your mobile device, Android includes the Gmail app, which can be used with any email provider, and iOS includes its Mail app. In either OS, a different email app can be installed, such as Microsoft Outlook, Google Inbox, Yahoo Mail, or K-9 Mail.

To configure email on a mobile device, open the email app and add an email account directly in the app. Here is the information you'll need to configure an email app on a mobile device:

▲ *Your email address and password.* If your email account is with Google, Microsoft, Apple, or Yahoo!, your email address and password are all you need because the OS can automatically set up these accounts.

If your email account is with any other provider, you'll also need the following information:

▲ *Names of your incoming and outgoing email servers.* To find this information, check the support page of your email provider's website. For example, the server you use for incoming mail might be *imap.mycompany.com*, and the server you use for outgoing mail might be *smtp.mycompany.com*. The two servers might have the same name.

▲ *Type of protocol your incoming server uses.* The incoming server will use POP3 or IMAP4. Using IMAP4, you are managing your email on the server. For example, you can move a message from one folder to another and that change happens on the remote server. Using POP3, the messages are downloaded to your device where you manage them locally. Most POP3 mail servers give you the option to leave the messages on the server or delete them after they are downloaded.

▲ *Security used.* Most likely, if email is encrypted during transmission, the configuration will happen automatically without your involvement. However, if you have problems, you need to be aware of these possible settings:

   ▲ An IMAP server uses port 143 unless it is secured and using SSL. IMAP over SSL (IMAPS) uses port 993.

   ▲ A POP3 server uses port 110 unless it is secured and using SSL. POP3 over SSL uses port 995.

   ▲ Outgoing email is normally sent using the protocol SMTP. A more secure alternative is S/MIME (Secure/ Multipurpose Internet Mail Extensions), which encrypts the email message and includes a digital signature to validate the identity of the sender. This feature is enabled after the email account is set up on the device. The activation process is automated for accounts through Microsoft Exchange and can be set up manually for other types of accounts. Look for this security option on the Advanced settings screen.

> ★ **A+ Exam Tip** The A+ Core 1 exam expects you to know about POP3 and IMAP4, and the SSL and port settings they use, and might require you to use this information in configuring email on a mobile device. Before you sit for the exam, memorize the ports (including secure ports) and protocols discussed in this section and understand how this information is used to configure email on a mobile device. A project at the end of this chapter will give you practice with this process.

SYNCING AND BACKING UP MOBILE DEVICES

> A+
> CORE 1
> 1.6, 1.7,
> 3.9
>
> A+
> CORE 2
> 1.1

Synchronization, backup, and restore functions are much simpler now than they were in the past and require almost no attention from the user. Also, compatibility concerns between operating systems are less of an issue now as manufacturers continue to standardize file types and communication protocols. In this part of the chapter, you learn to sync with online accounts or third-party apps, sync with your desktop, update the OS, and back up settings. First, here's the difference between syncing and backups:

▲ Syncing mirrors app data and other content among your devices and/or the cloud that use the same Apple or Google account. A photo taken or a calendar event created on one device is available in the cloud and all other devices. As another example, when you sync email, the Gmail app on your phone will show the same email messages and configuration settings as the Gmail interface in your browser on your computer.

◢ Backups are copies of app data, configuration settings, and other content stored in case you need it to recover from a failed, lost, or corrupted device.

SYNC TO THE CLOUD

Syncing data to the cloud means that you can access your data from any device or any computer with a web browser connected to the Internet. (Google products work best in Google Chrome, of course.) You can sync contacts, application purchases and installations, email, pictures, music, videos, calendars, bookmarks, documents, location data on map apps, social media data, e-books, and even passwords.

> ⚡ **Caution** It's not safe to store passwords in your browser. It's much more secure to use a password manager app, such as KeePass or LastPass. KeePass stores passwords only on the local computer, which is more secure but less convenient. LastPass can store passwords in the cloud and sync passwords across devices, which is more convenient but less secure.

When you're signed in to your Google or Apple account, both Google's cloud and Apple's iCloud can automatically sync nearly all content created in their OS-native apps across your devices. (You can choose whether to sync only over Wi-Fi so syncing doesn't use up your cellular data allotment.) Here's how it works:

◢ *Google storage in the cloud.* Android syncs Google apps or third-party apps on your device to your Google storage at *google.com*; the first 15 GB of cloud storage is free. Use the Settings app on your device to manage what is synced. To access your content in the cloud, use any browser to go to *google.com* and sign in to your Google account. A single sign-on (SSO), also called mutual authentication for multiple services, gives access to Gmail, Google Drive, Calendar, Contacts, and all other Google apps. Click the **Google apps** icon to select different apps, as shown in Figure 9-34. Many third-party apps can also sync their data through the Google account the mobile device is registered to, although the sync settings might be managed within the app rather than through the device's Settings app.

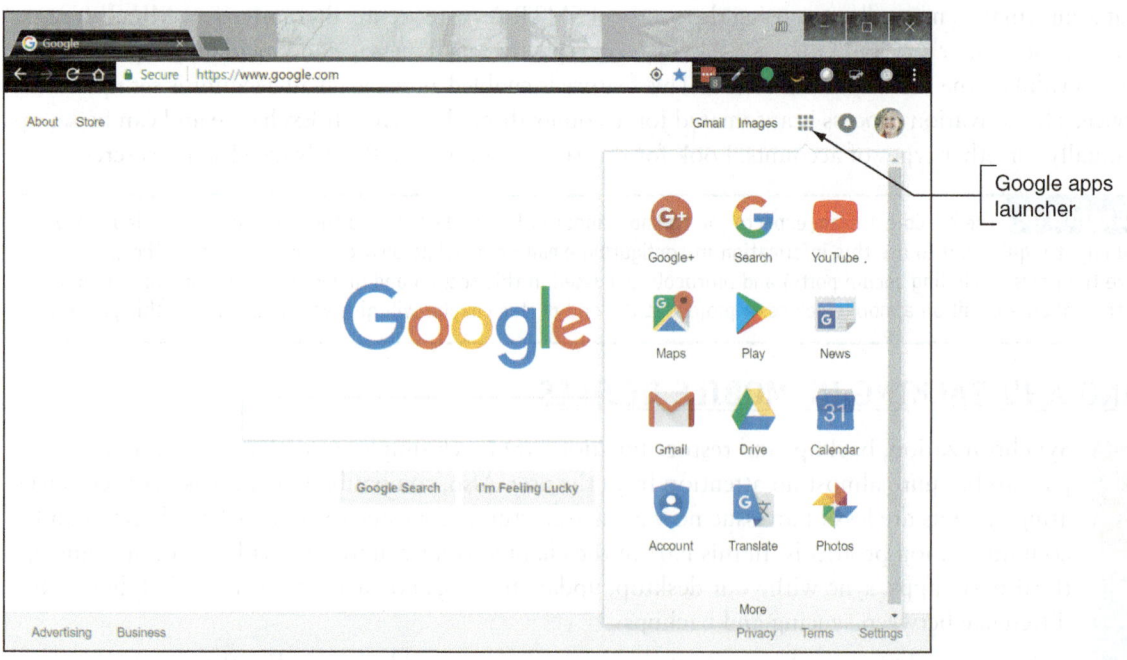

Source: Google

Figure 9-34 Access Android content at *google.com*

▲ *iCloud storage in the cloud.* iOS syncs content to the Apple website at *icloud.com*; the first 5 GB of cloud storage is free. To set up iCloud syncing, go to the **Settings** app on your iPad or iPhone, tap the user name, and tap **iCloud** to go to the screen (see Figure 9-35) where you can decide which apps and data get synced and manage your iCloud storage.

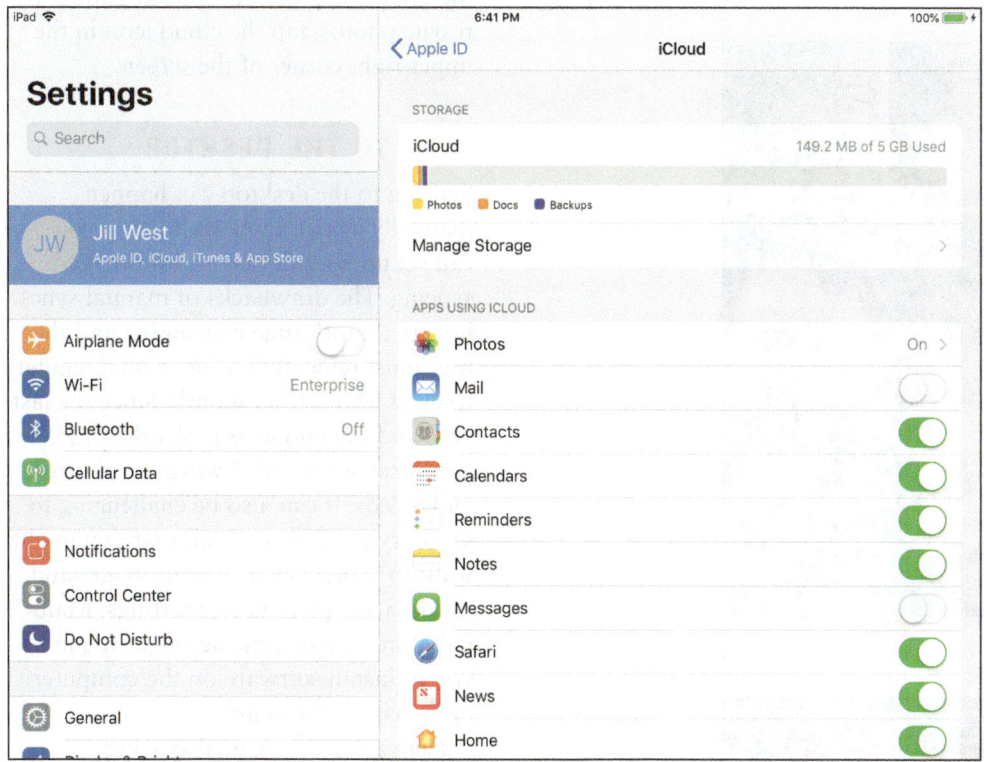

Source: iOS

Figure 9-35   Manage iCloud synchronization on a mobile device

You can access synced data in the cloud from your computer by signing in to your Apple account at *icloud.com*. For example, the Launchpad or home page for your iCloud content (see Figure 9-36) shows synced apps, including Mail, Contacts, Calendar, iCloud Drive, and Photos.

Source: iCloud.com

Figure 9-36   Access iOS content at *icloud.com*

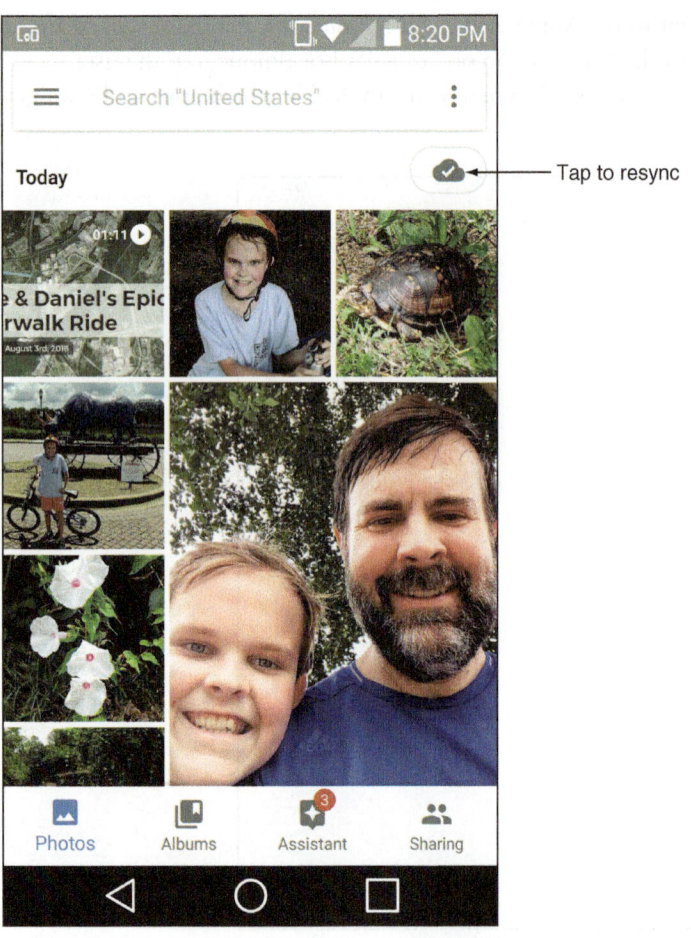

Tap to resync

Source: Android

Figure 9-37   If content fails to sync automatically, resync manually

If you notice an account is not syncing correctly, resync information for the account through the app that holds the data. For example, Figure 9-37 shows the Photos app on an Android phone. To resync photos, tap the cloud icon in the upper-right corner of the screen.

SYNC TO THE DESKTOP

Syncing to the desktop can happen manually as you think to do it or you can set up your device for automatic syncing. The drawbacks of manual syncing are that it's time consuming and the user must remember to do it on a regular basis. If it's been six months since the last sync and the phone or tablet dies, the user loses six months' worth of photos and videos. It can also be challenging to set up syncing to cover all that you might want to sync, such as text messages and third-party app data and settings. Manual or automatic syncing might require you to install software on the computer to manage the syncing.

Here are some manual syncing options:

▲ *USB connection and File Explorer.* The tried-and-true method for syncing photos and videos from a phone or tablet directly to the desktop is to plug the device into a USB connection with the computer (or a Lightning to USB connection on a Mac) and copy files from the device to the computer. For a Windows computer, you can use File Explorer to copy files from the device to your computer, which preserves the original quality of the media files, unlike some cloud-based sync services, which reduce resolution before storing in the cloud. An advantage of this type of syncing to a computer is that no extra software needs to be installed on your computer.

▲ *iTunes with iOS.* For iOS devices, you can install iTunes on a computer and use it to sync and back up the mobile device. After you install and start iTunes, connect your mobile device through a USB connection and iTunes will then recognize the device. For example, Figure 9-38 shows the iTunes window on a Mac with backup options at the top right and sync options at the lower right. After selecting the sync or backup settings you want, click **Sync** to sync the device and computer or **Back Up Now** to back up the device to your computer.

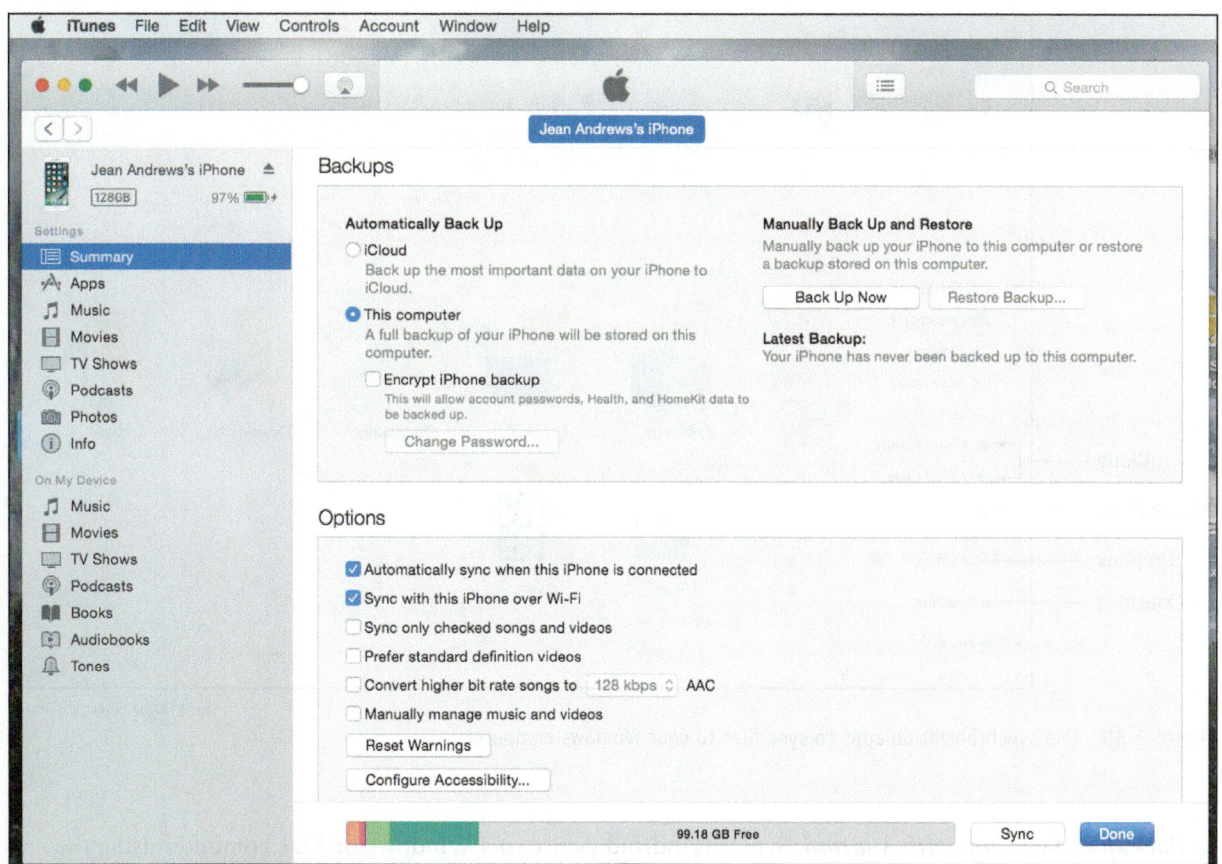

Source: iTunes

Figure 9-38 iTunes can sync or back up a mobile device with a Mac or Windows computer

The following three options provide automatic syncing to the desktop. Each option requires you to install an application on the computer and configure the sync settings. Before you install the app, make sure the computer meets the minimum hardware and OS requirements needed to support the app:

▲ *Third-party syncing apps*. OneDrive, Dropbox, and other apps provide cloud-based file storage services and will sync entire folders in the background with no user intervention required to any computer or device that has the app installed and signed in. Make a change on one device and you immediately see it on another or in the cloud. OneDrive, Dropbox, and other syncing apps can install in Android and iOS mobile devices and in Windows and Linux on the desktop. Figure 9-39 shows File Explorer on a Windows 10 computer with synced folders for iCloud Photos, iCloud Drive, Google Drive, Dropbox, and OneDrive, all of which are also installed on one or more of the user's mobile devices.

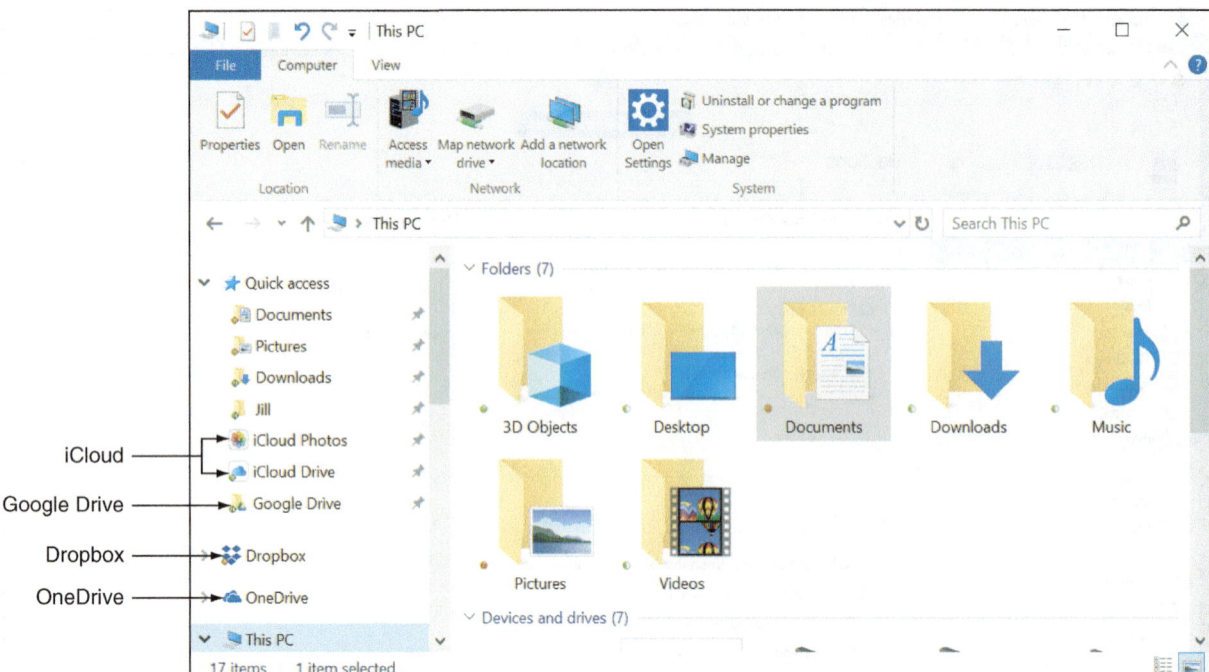

Figure 9-39   Use synchronization apps to sync files to your Windows computer

▲ *Backup & Sync app with Android*. Sync an Android device to a Windows or Mac computer using the Backup & Sync app. When you install the app on your computer, it installs a Google Drive folder and can automatically sync files to the mobile device, the computer, and the cloud.

▲ *iCloud Drive with iOS*. As you know, you can sync app settings and other data on your iOS device to the Apple cloud at *icloud.com*. In addition, when you turn on iCloud Drive, the Files app on an iPad or iPhone syncs files across devices and you can share these files with people in your contacts list. You can also install the iCloud Drive app on a computer so that files can sync to your desktop (refer back to Figure 9-39), which is similar to the way Dropbox works. To turn on iCloud Drive on a device, open the **Settings** app, tap the user name, then tap **iCloud**. Verify that **iCloud Drive** is turned on and syncing the apps you want to sync. If iCloud Drive is installed on your Windows computer, content will also sync there.

SYNC AN ACTIVITY WITH HANDOFF AND CONTINUE ON PC

In addition to syncing files and other content, you can sync activity in progress. For example, suppose you're visiting a webpage on your smartphone, and you want to open that webpage in your desktop's browser without searching for it again. Or suppose you're working on a document on one device, and you want to continue your work on the other device. You can transfer the activity from the mobile device to the desktop and back, picking up on one device where you left off on the other.

▲ *Apple Handoff*. In macOS and iOS, the feature is called Handoff. Enable Handoff in the Settings menu on the iPhone or iPad and in the System Preferences menu on the Mac. When the device and computer are on the same Wi-Fi or Bluetooth network and signed in to the same Apple account, the Handoff icon appears on each device for activities transferrable from the other. Tap or click the icon to pick up an activity from the other device.

▲ *Microsoft Launcher or Continue on PC*. Windows 10 offers an Android app called Microsoft Launcher or an iOS app called Continue on PC. Both of these apps add a share option, called Continue on PC, into certain activities you perform on your phone and send to a Windows computer (see Figure 9-40A).

Android launchers are apps that can replace Android's default home screen (called the Pixel Launcher) to add different features and functionality. In the case of Microsoft Launcher, as shown in Figure 9-40B and Figure 9-40C, the app makes the Android's home screen look and function more like a Windows Mobile phone, including synchronization with your Windows desktop. Compare the home screen in Figure 9-40B with the home screen in Figure 9-6 to identify subtle differences. To get started with Windows 10, open the **Settings** app and click **Phone**.

(A)

(B)

(C)

Source: Android

Figure 9-40   (A) Tap Continue on PC to pick up an Android activity on your Windows desktop; (B) the Microsoft launcher has made subtle changes to the Android home screen; (C) the launcher's All apps screen is similar to the Windows Start screen

> ✎ **Notes**   Many apps also include the ability to sync activities between devices, either within one user's account or between accounts. Google Chrome, for example, syncs browsing history, settings, and bookmarks with all devices signed into Chrome using the same account. Microsoft's OneNote syncs notes across devices and can sync notes to devices that belong to other people when you share a notebook.

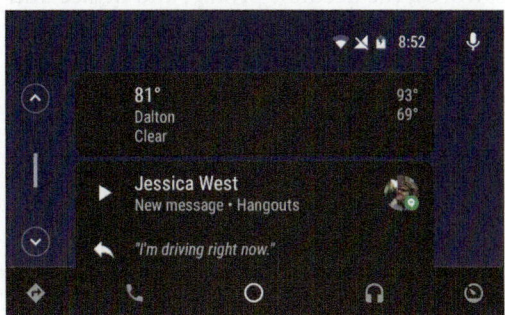

Source: Android Auto

Figure 9-41   Android Auto lets users check the weather, send a Hangouts message, or make a phone call using their vehicle's touch screen

SYNC TO AN AUTOMOBILE

Many newer automobiles offer the option to use Bluetooth to pair a smartphone with the car's computer for easy access to the phone's music, navigation, and call features through the car's media screen. While this is not true synchronization because most of the phone's content stays on the phone and is not stored on the car's computer, it does allow the user to control the phone through the car's control panel or touch screen. Figure 9-41 shows information from an Android phone on a Kia Sedona's touch screen using the Android Auto app. Apple devices use the Apple CarPlay app instead. Both apps include navigation, music, phone, and text message activities to interact with the user directly on the car's screen.

> ✏️ **Notes** You can emulate a car's touch screen in Android Studio for testing apps in the Android Auto interface. You'll need to download and install the testing tool Desktop Head Unit (DHU) in the SDK Manager, and you'll need a real smartphone to connect with the DHU (not an emulated one). Learn more at *developer.android.com/training/auto/testing/*.

UPDATE THE OS

Updates to the Android OS are automatically pushed to the device from the manufacturer. Because each manufacturer maintains its own versions of Android, these updates might not come at the same time Google announces a major update, which limits availability of updates for some devices. Also, vendors don't continue to make these modifications indefinitely—eventually a device ages out of the vendor's updates in what's called an end-of-life limitation. When the device does receive notice of an update, it might display a message asking permission to install the update. With some devices, you can also manually check for updates at any time, although not all devices provide this option.

To see if manual updates can be performed on your device, go to the **Settings** app and tap **About**. On the About screen, tap **System updates**, **Software update**, or a similar item. The device turns to the manufacturer's website for information and reports any available updates.

Before installing an OS update, you might want to go to the website and read the release instructions about the update, called Product Release Instructions (PRI), which typically describe new features or patches the update provides and how long the update will take. Later, if a device is giving problems after an OS update, check the PRI for information that might help you understand the nature of the problem.

To check for and install updates on an iOS device, you must first be signed in to your device with an Apple ID, which requires an associated credit card number. Then open the **Settings** app and tap **General** in the left pane. On the right side, tap **Software Update**. Any available updates will be reported here and can be installed.

It's a good idea to back up your mobile device's files, settings, configurations, and profiles before performing an update. How to back up a device is discussed next.

BACK UP AND RECOVERY

Suppose your mobile device is lost, stolen, or damaged beyond repair. Backups and recovery options need to be in place to prepare for these events. Here are some options:

▲ *File-level backup.* Syncing emails, contacts, calendars, photos, and other data through online accounts or to your computer is called a file-level backup, because each file is backed up individually. File-level backups, however, don't include your app data or OS settings, such as your Wi-Fi passwords, account profile, or device and app configuration.

▲ *Partial image-level backup.* A true image-level backup includes everything on the device and can completely restore the device to its previous state. However, a mobile device OS offers only a partial image-level backup that includes settings, native app data, Wi-Fi passwords, the account profile, and device and app configuration. Third-party app configurations and their data are not included in the OS backup.

▲ *Combination of file-level and partial image-level backups.* To prepare for catastrophic failure or loss, you need to use both backup methods: Sync data files to your computer or the cloud and use the OS backup for other types of data and settings. Make sure that syncing and backups include critical apps, their configuration, and data. In reality, though, backups for mobile devices will miss a few configurations, such as app installations or third-party app configurations. For this reason, you might need to use an additional method of backing up data and settings for any critical third-party applications.

Generally, you can back up to the cloud or to your computer. Android provides a way to back up to Google Drive:

▲ *Google Drive backup.* To enable Android's backup feature, open the **Settings** app, go to **System**, and then tap **Backup**. Make sure that **Back up to Google Drive** is turned on and change the backup account if needed. You can also fine-tune what content is included in the backup. Your backup data is stored on Google's servers and is associated with your Google account.

▲ *Back up to computer*. You need a third-party app or a manufacturer's app to create a detailed backup of the device configuration and content to your computer.

iOS can back up to a computer using iTunes or to the cloud using iCloud. The best practice is to use both methods:

▲ *iCloud Backup*. Go to **Settings** and tap the user name, then tap **iCloud**. Scroll down and tap **iCloud Backup**. When you turn on iCloud Backup, it backs up whenever the device is plugged into a power source and connected to Wi-Fi, the screen is locked, and there's enough unused iCloud storage to hold the backup. However, you can also create a new backup at any time by clicking **Back Up Now**. iCloud backs up app data, call history, device settings, text, photos, and videos unless these items are already included in iCloud syncing.

▲ *iTunes backup*. Open iTunes on your computer and connect your mobile device to the computer. You might have to enter your device passcode. In iTunes, select your device and click **Back Up Now**.

When deciding whether to back up to the cloud or a computer, consider that cloud backups using Google Drive or iCloud are readily accessible from any computer and happen automatically when you're connected to Wi-Fi. The disadvantages are that you have less control over security of your data and you have to pay for cloud storage.

Here are two situations when you might want to recover from a backup:

▲ *To the original mobile device*. If you have reset the device while troubleshooting a problem and have a backup in the cloud, sign in to the device using your Google or Apple account. You will then be given the option to recover from backup or to set up the device as a new device. You'll learn more about resetting a device later in this chapter. For iOS, if you have a backup on your computer and connect the device to your computer, iTunes gives you the option to recover from backup.

▲ *To a new device*. The same recovery options are offered when you first sign in to a new mobile device using your Google or Apple account—or, for iOS, when you connect a new device to your computer and the iTunes app.

🖉 **Notes** If you're about to buy a new phone or tablet, be sure to back up your old device before you switch your carrier service or your Google or Apple account to the new device. If possible, also back up your phone or tablet before taking it in for repair at a service center.

Whatever backup method you use, it's important to occasionally test the backup recovery process to verify that you know how to use it, the recovery works, and you know exactly what's being recovered. After you test the recovery process, you might realize you need additional backup methods in place to make sure everything is covered.

SECURING A MOBILE DEVICE

Because smartphones and tablets are so mobile, they get stolen more often than other types of computers. Therefore, protecting data on a mobile device is especially important. Consider what might be revealed about your life if someone stole your smartphone or tablet and the data on it.

▲ Your apps and personal data could expose email, calendars, call logs, voice mail, text messages, Dropbox, iCloud Drive, Google Maps, Hangouts, Gmail, QuickMemo, YouTube, Amazon, Facebook, videos, photos, notes, contacts, and bookmarks and browsing history in web browsers.

▲ Videos and photos might reveal private information and be tagged with date and time stamps and GPS locations.

▲ Network connection settings include Wi-Fi security keys, email configuration settings, user names, and email addresses.

⬛ Purchasing patterns and history as well as credit card information might be stored—or at least accessible for use—in mobile payment apps, in apps developed by retailers, through membership card databases, or through email records.

To keep your data safe, consider controlling access to your devices and consider what apps you can use to protect the data. These methods are discussed in this part of the chapter along with BYOD (Bring Your Own Device) policies that might be used in an enterprise environment to secure corporate data stored on a device.

DEVICE ACCESS CONTROLS

Consider the following lock methods to control access to the device.

⬛ **Screen lock.** A screen lock requires the correct input to unlock the device. Mobile devices provide a variety of options for unlocking the screen. As the complexity of a lock code increases, so does the security of the device:

⬛ **Swipe lock.** Swipe your finger across the screen to unlock the device. (This is not very secure but it prevents a pocket dial.)

⬛ **PIN lock.** Enter a numeric code with numbers.

⬛ **Passcode lock.** Enter an alphanumeric code with letters and/or numbers.

⬛ **Pattern lock.** Draw a pattern across a display of dots on the screen.

⬛ **Fingerprint lock.** Use a specialized scanner that collects an optical, electrical, or ultrasonic reading of a person's fingerprint and then compares this information to stored data.

⬛ **Face lock.** Use the device's camera to perform facial recognition.

Figure 9-42A shows screen lock options on an Android smartphone, including a swipe lock, pattern lock, PIN lock, and passcode lock. Android also allows the user to set exceptions to the screen lock, as shown in Figure 9-42B. Using these options, the smartphone might stay unlocked when it detects it's being carried or when it detects its location, such as the user's home or office.

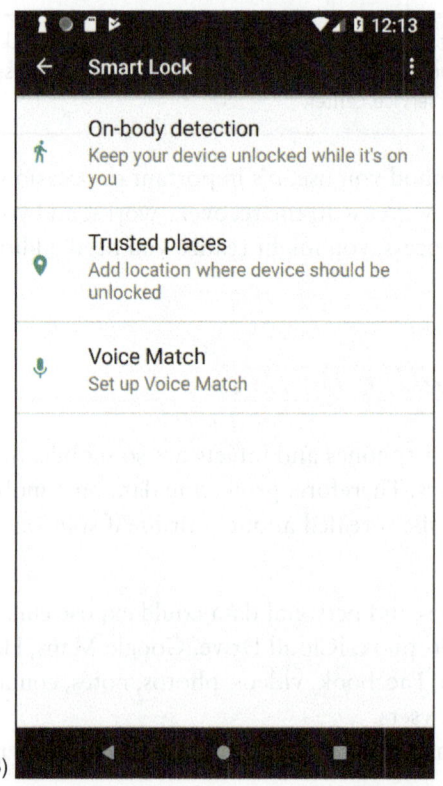

Source: Android

Figure 9-42   (A) Screen lock options on an Android smartphone; (B) Smart Lock exceptions to keep the screen unlocked

> **✎ Notes** Fingerprint and facial recognition are both forms of biometric authentication. **Biometric authentication** collects biological data about a person's fingerprints, handprints, face, voice, retina, iris, and handwritten signatures to confirm the person's identity. In some states, you cannot legally be forced to give your phone's password to investigators, but you can be required to give your fingerprint.

▲ *Restrict failed login attempts.* When you set a screen lock, you can specify that data be erased after a certain number of failed login attempts, or you can simply block further attempts. With iOS, the device locks after six failed attempts and you must wait before you can try again. If the device permanently locks and you've created a backup in iTunes, you can sync to the backup to access the phone. Otherwise, you'll have to use recovery mode, which erases the device. With Android devices, login attempt restriction options vary by manufacturer. You can change the lock code online using the device's associated Google account on the Find My Device website (*google.com/android/find*), which also locates the device.

> **⚡ Caution** If you set your device to erase data after failed login attempts, be sure to keep backups of your data and other content. A small child can pick up your smartphone and accidentally erase all your data with a few finger taps.

▲ *Full device encryption.* Both Android and iOS devices offer full device encryption, which encrypts all the stored data on a device. Encrypting a device's stored data makes it essentially useless to a thief. However, encryption might slow down device performance and data is only as safe as the strength of the password keeping the data encrypted. Also, data might be vulnerable again when it's being viewed or transmitted because device encryption only encrypts data while it's stored on the device, not when it's in motion or in use. When enabling encryption for the first time, it might take an hour or more to complete the encryption. Also, if the encryption process is interrupted during that time, some or all of the data will be lost.

▲ *Multifactor authentication.* Smartphones can be used to authenticate to services and networks (for example, email, cloud services, corporate network accounts, VPNs, or even Facebook) as one of the two or more techniques required for multifactor authentication. For example, you might first enter a password on a computer as the first authentication and then a code is sent as a text message to your smartphone; you must then enter the code in the computer as the second authentication. Another example might be that you enter a code in a computer that is at a certain location and the system you're signing in to checks the GPS location of your smartphone to make sure it is near the computer. In addition, authenticator applications can be installed on your smartphone and configured to provide multifactor authentication support for a huge variety of account types. Popular examples are Google Authenticator or Microsoft Authenticator, both of which work on either Android or iOS devices, or an independent competitor like Authy (*authy.com*), which also works in Chrome OS.

SOFTWARE SECURITY

In addition to controlling access to a device, software can help secure data. Most of the methods discussed here require the user to understand the importance of a security measure and how to use it:

▲ *OS updates and patches.* Apply OS updates and patches to plug up security holes. Android automatically pushes updates to many of its devices, but iOS devices and many other mobile devices require manual updates.

▲ *Antivirus/anti-malware.* Because Apple closely protects iOS and its apps, it's unlikely an Apple device will need anti-malware software. The Android OS and apps are not as closely guarded, so Android anti-malware apps are recommended. Before installing one, be sure to read reviews about it. Most of the major anti-malware software companies provide Android anti-malware apps.

▲ *Trusted sources.* iOS devices are limited to installing apps only from Apple's App Store. Android and Windows devices can download and install apps from other sources, only some of which are trustworthy. Trusted sources generally include well-known app stores, such as Amazon Appstore for Android (*amazon.com/appstore*) or SlideME (*slideme.org*). Other trusted sources might include your bank's website, your employer, or your school, although often their apps are posted in Google Play (*play.google.com*) as well. Before downloading an app, look for lots of reviewer feedback as one measure of safety.

Android versions before Oreo allow you to limit app sources to only the Google Play Store, which can help reduce the threat of untrusted sources for apps. In the **Settings** app, tap **Security** and make sure that **Unknown sources** is unchecked. Beginning with Oreo, you can decide which apps are allowed to install other apps. To choose, go to **Settings > Apps & notifications > Advanced > Special app access > Install unknown apps** (see Figure 9-43A). If you decide to use third-party app sources, be sure you already have a good anti-malware program and a firewall running on your device.

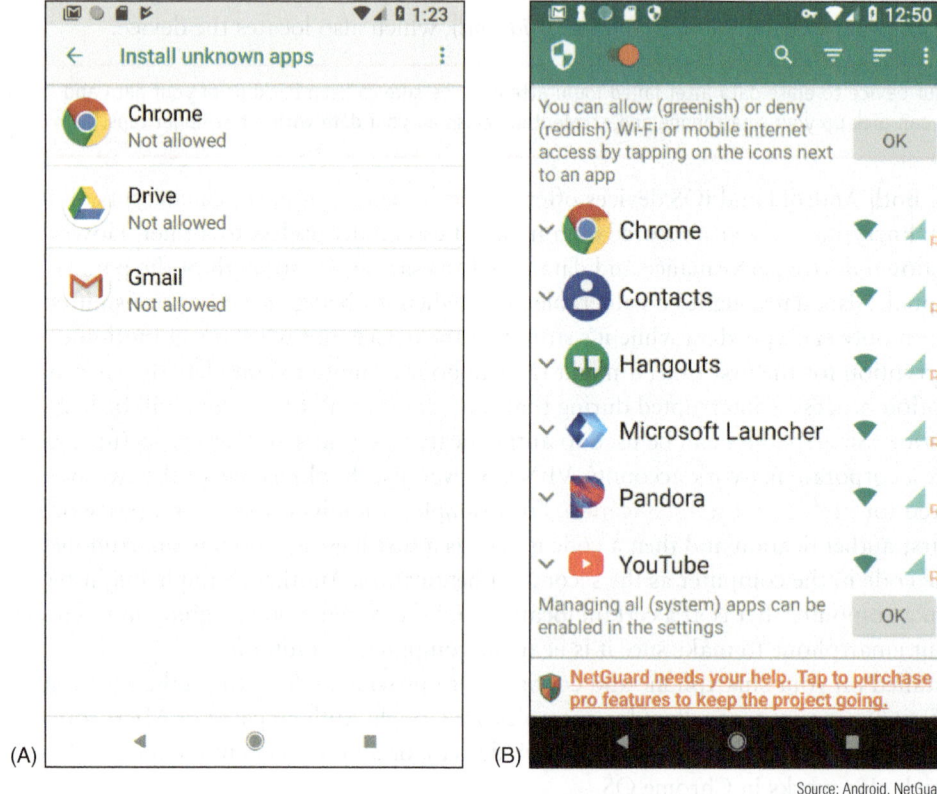

Source: Android, NetGuard

Figure 9-43 (A) Choose which apps can install apps from sources other than the Play Store;
(B) choose which apps can access the Internet

▲ *Firewalls.* As with Windows computers, a firewall on a mobile device helps control which apps or services can use network connections. When you install an app, you're required to agree to the permissions it requests in order to get the app. A firewall gives you more control over an app's network access. For example, a firewall can prevent the Facebook app from sending SMS messages.

Most firewall apps for mobile devices mimic a VPN connection, which forces all network communication to be routed through the firewall. Figure 9-43B shows an example of one firewall app, NetGuard (*netguard.me*), on an Android smartphone; the app allows you to decide which other apps can use the networks.

▲ *Android locator application and remote wipe.* You can use Find My Device (*google.com/android/find*), Android's built-in locator application, to locate your phone on a map, force it to ring at its highest volume, change the device password, or remotely erase all data from the device to protect your privacy, which is called a remote wipe. See Figure 9-44. To use the locator app to locate your device or perform a remote wipe, Find My Device must already be turned on in the **Security & location** menu in the Settings app. Third-party locator applications are also available in the Play Store.

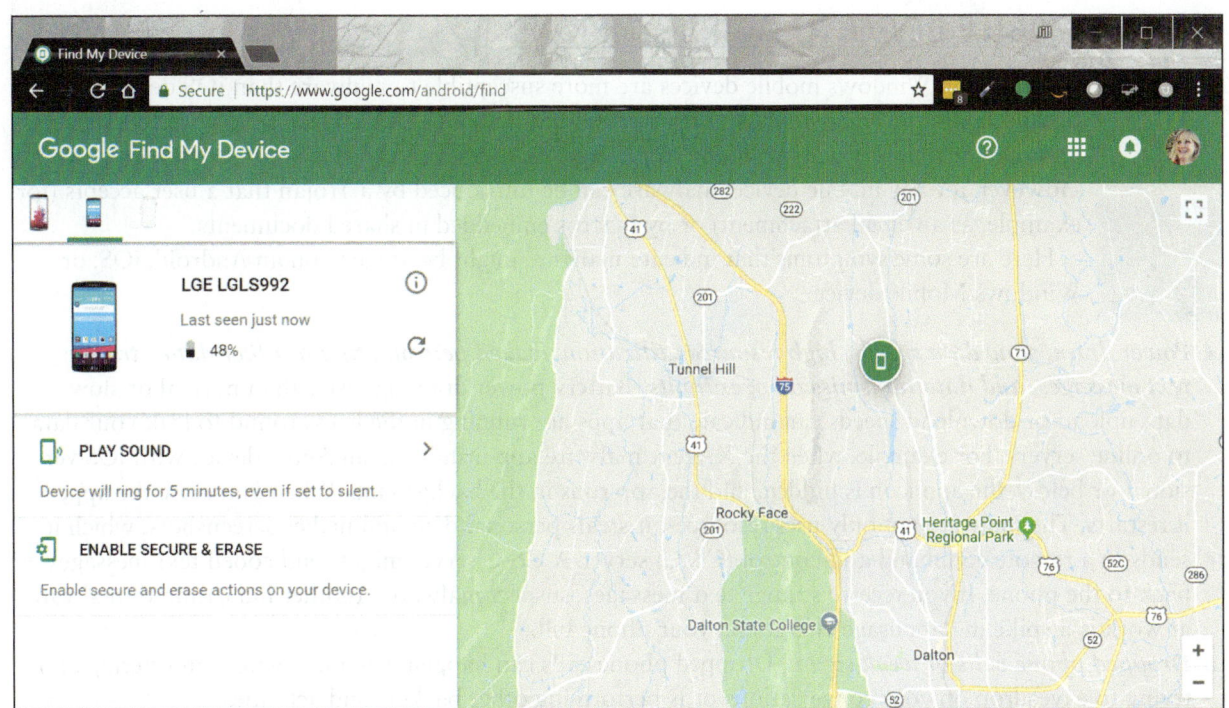

Source: Google

Figure 9-44 Locate a lost Android device using any web-enabled computer or mobile device and your Google account

▲ *iOS locator application and remote wipe.* Similar to Android's Find My Device, iCloud offers the ability to locate a lost iOS device if the feature is already enabled on the device before it's lost. On an iPad or iPhone, open the Settings app, tap the *user name*, tap **iCloud**, and then turn **Find my iPad** or **Find my iPhone** on or off. Besides using a browser on a computer to find your device, you can also download Find My iPhone or Find My iPad to another Apple device and use it to locate your lost device. Both apps are free. If your device was stolen or you have given up on finding your device, you can use iCloud to perform a remote wipe.

MOBILE SECURITY IN CORPORATE ENVIRONMENTS

A+ CORE 2 2.8

Corporations and schools might provide corporate-owned devices, which are secured and managed by corporate policies and procedures, or the organization might have BYOD (Bring Your Own Device) policies and procedures. With BYOD, an employee or student is allowed to connect his own device to the corporate network. For security purposes, an organization configures the person's device before allowing it to connect to the network.

Employees or employee groups in an organization are assigned security profiles, which are a set of policies and procedures to restrict how a user can access, create, and edit the organization's resources. Profile security requirements can be partially implemented by configuration requirements placed on BYOD and corporate-owned devices an employee uses. These device requirements, such as full device encryption, remote wipes, location apps, access control, authenticator apps, multifactor authentication, firewalls, anti-malware measures, or use of VPN connections, must be clearly outlined. Users must be educated on how to use them, and they must include assurance that devices continue to meet the baseline requirements.

Part of these requirements will likely include installation of a remote backup application, which remotely backs up the device's data to a company file server. For example, Canopy Remote Backup by Atos (*canopy-cloud.com*) provides cloud-based backups for laptops, tablets, and smartphones.

COMMON MOBILE DEVICE MALWARE SYMPTOMS

A+
CORE 1
5.5

A+
CORE 2
3.4, 3.5

Android and Windows mobile devices are more susceptible to malware than iOS devices because apps can be downloaded from sites other than Google or Microsoft. With iOS devices, apps can be obtained only from the Apple App Store and are therefore more strictly vetted. However, for any mobile device, malware can be introduced by a Trojan that a user accepts (for example, as an email attachment) or by macros embedded in shared documents.

Here are some symptoms that indicate malware might be at work on an Android, iOS, or Windows Mobile device:

▲ *Power drain, slow data speeds, high resource utilization, leaked personal files or other data, strange text messages, and data transmission over limits.* Battery power draining faster than normal or slow data upload or download speeds can indicate that apps are running in the background to leak your data to online servers. For example, when the XAgent malware app installs on an Apple device with iOS version 7 or below, the app icon is hidden, and the app runs in the background. When you close the app, it restarts. The malware not only uses resources, it steals personal data and makes screenshots, which it sends to a remote command-and-control (C&C) server. A C&C server might send coded text messages back to the phone. If you receive strange text messages, suspect malware. Another indication of malware at work is a spike in data usage charges on your phone bill.

▲ *Dropped phone calls or weak signal.* Dropped phone calls can happen when malware is interfering and trying to eavesdrop on your conversations or is performing other background activities.

▲ *Unintended Wi-Fi and Bluetooth connections.* Malicious Wi-Fi hotspots and Bluetooth devices can hijack a device or inject it with malware. When a mobile device connects to a malicious Wi-Fi hotspot, the device can receive a malicious script that repeatedly reboots the device, which makes it unusable. To prevent this type of attack, avoid free Wi-Fi hotspots or use a VPN connection. To prevent a device from pairing with a malicious Bluetooth device, turn off Bluetooth when it's not in use.

▲ *Unauthorized account access.* A malicious app can steal passwords and data from other apps and can pretend to be a different app to get access to online accounts. If you suspect an online account has been hacked, consider malware might be on the mobile device that uses this account.

▲ *Unauthorized location tracking.* Spyware apps installed on a mobile device can report its location to a C&C server.

▲ *Unauthorized use of camera or microphone.* Unauthorized surveillance is a sure sign of malware. Stalker spyware apps have been known to take photos and send them to a C&C server; send a text alert to a hacker and then add the hacker to a live call; use the microphone to record live conversations and then send the recording to a C&C server; report Facebook, Skype, Viber, and iMessage activity, including passwords and location data; and upload all photos, videos, and text messages to a C&C server.

Notes When is spyware legal? Parents can legally install spyware (politely called monitoring software) on a minor child's phone, tablet, or computer, and employers can monitor employee devices when they are company owned. One example is FlexiSPY (*flexispy.com*), an app that runs in the background to monitor text, email, Facebook and other visited websites, apps, photos, videos, contacts, bookmarks, location tracking, and phone calls. It can also record calls and surrounding sounds. It comes with a mobile viewer app installed on the parent's or employer's smartphone.

MOBILE DEVICE MALWARE REMOVAL

A+
CORE 2
2.8

Here are general steps for removing malware from a mobile device, listed from least to most invasive:

▲ *Uninstall the offending app.* If you can identify the malware app, close the app and uninstall it. If the app won't uninstall, you can force stop the app or any background processes that belong to the app. For Android apps running in the background, open the Settings app, tap **Apps**, and tap a running app to force it to stop. Then try again to uninstall the app.

▲ *Update the OS*. Check to see if any updates are available for the device. For an iOS device, consider using iTunes on your computer to perform the update rather than updating iOS directly from the device.

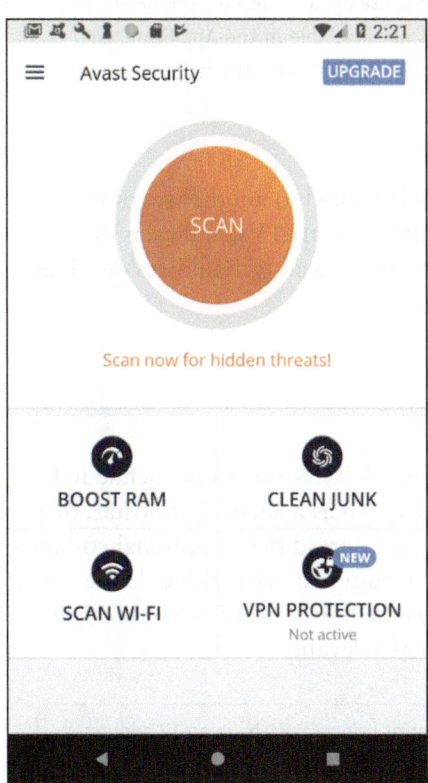

Figure 9-45 Avast performs regular scans on an Android device

Source: Avast

▲ *Perform a factory reset*. The most surefire way to remove malware is to back up data and other content, reset the device to its factory default state, and then restore the content from backup. Reset options for Android and iOS are discussed later in this chapter.

After you have removed malware on a mobile device, you will want to keep it clean. Here are a few tips:

▲ Keep OS updates current.
▲ Educate users about the importance of privacy settings (for example, disable cookies and turn off Bluetooth when it's not in use). Also, users should not open email attachments or download shared files from untrusted sources.
▲ Consider installing an anti-malware app. Apple claims that an iOS device cannot be infected with malware and does not make anti-malware apps available in the App Store. However, you can get an app from the App Store that monitors your device and scans for malware that might be in stored files, but is not installed. For Android and Windows Mobile devices, search online reviews and consider the features offered before deciding on an anti-malware app. An anti-malware app, such as Avast shown in Figure 9-45, can scan apps and files for malware, scan for unauthorized surveillance, monitor security and privacy settings, find the device when it's lost, lock and remote wipe it, and maintain automatic updates. It might even include a firewall or a VPN feature.

APPLYING | CONCEPTS   ROOTING AND JAILBREAKING

To get more control over what can be done with an Android or iOS device, some people have discovered they can get root or administrative privileges to the OS and the entire file system (all files and folders), and complete access to all commands and features. For Android, the process is called **rooting**, and for iOS, the process is called **jailbreaking**. After jailbreaking, an iOS phone can get apps from any source, but Apple has the right to void the warranty or refuse to provide support. Rooting and jailbreaking might also violate BYOD policies in an enterprise environment. In addition, rooting or jailbreaking makes a device more susceptible to malware. Here is how you can tell if a device is rooted or jailbroken:

▲ *Rooted Android device*. Use one of these methods to find out if an Android device has been rooted:
  ▲ Download and run a root checker app from Google Play, which will tell you if the device is rooted.
  ▲ Download and run a terminal window app from Google Play. (A terminal window in Linux is similar to a command prompt window in Windows.) When you open the app, look at the command prompt. If the prompt is a #, the device is rooted. If the prompt is a $, the device is likely not rooted. With the $ prompt showing, try the **sudo su root** command, which in Linux allows you root access. If the prompt changes to #, the device is rooted.

> 🖉 **Notes** In Linux, the # command prompt displays when a user has root access and the $ command prompt displays when a user does not.

(continues)

◢ **Jailbroken iOS device.** To find out if an iOS device has been jailbroken, look for an unusual app on the home screen—for example, the Electra, Meridian, Cydia, or Icy app. If any of these apps is present, the device has been jailbroken. If you have any app icon on your home screen that is not available in the App Store, the app is most likely a jailbreak app or other malware. When you update iOS using iTunes, the jailbreak will be removed.

Mobile devices and their reliance on wireless communication are closely related to another set of technologies, the Internet of Things or IoT. You might have heard of smart lights, smart TVs, and even smart houses. Let's take a look at what the IoT is all about and begin exploring the special technologies developed for these purposes.

THE INTERNET OF THINGS (IOT)

There's some debate on what makes up the Internet of Things (IoT). Most people define IoT to be devices connected to the Internet for a specific purpose, such as a smart thermostat, that normally would not be connected to the Internet. Generally, it's agreed that traditional computing devices, such as desktops, laptops, and smartphones, or traditional networking devices, such as routers, firewalls, and cable modems, are not IoT devices. However, as the line between "computer" and "Internet-connected non-computer" blurs, this distinction will become less relevant.

🖊 **Notes** For a device to be considered part of the IoT, the device or its controller or bridge must have an IP address. After all, a node can't connect to the Internet without an IP address.

In this part of the chapter, you learn about the wireless technologies used by IoT devices and how to set up a smart home network of IoT devices.

IOT WIRELESS TECHNOLOGIES

In most cases, IoT devices are monitored and controlled by wireless connections. Besides Wi-Fi and Bluetooth, Z-Wave and Zigbee are two other wireless technologies commonly used by smart locks, smart light bulbs, and other IoT smart home devices. Here are the primary facts about Z-Wave and Zigbee:

◢ Z-Wave transmits around the 900-MHz band and requires less power than Wi-Fi. It has a larger range than Bluetooth, reaching a range of up to 100 m in open air (though significantly less inside buildings).

◢ Zigbee operates in either the 2.4-GHz band or the 900-MHz band, requires less power than Wi-Fi, and generally reaches a range of about 20 m inside but can reach much farther.

◢ Z-Wave and Zigbee are not compatible. Zigbee is faster than Z-Wave. Z-Wave and Zigbee use encryption and are considered safe from hackers.

◢ Both Z-Wave and Zigbee devices can connect in a mesh network, which means that devices can "hop" through other devices to reach the destination device. Z-Wave and Zigbee devices don't inherently use TCP/IP without another protocol at work, such as Z/IP or Zigbee IP, that manages TCP/IP networking.

◢ Typically, Zigbee and Z-Wave compete about equally for the smart home device wireless standard of choice. Zigbee is the choice for large-scale commercial or industrial use because it is more robust.

🖊 **Notes** When worker honeybees return to their nest, they do a dance that looks like a zig-zag pattern. Zigbee was named after this phenomenon: *zig bee.*

Another wireless standard used in the IoT industry is RFID (radio-frequency identification), which is traditionally used in small tags that attach to and identify clothing inventory, car keys, bags, luggage, pets, cattle, hospital patients, and much more. An RFID tag contains a microchip and antenna and can be a passive or active tag. Active RFID tags have built-in batteries and transmitters to respond to commands or requests for information. Passive RFID tags, which cost much less, are essentially electronic barcodes that can be read from a few feet away without requiring line-of-sight access. Recently, RFID has been used for real-time IoT inventory management. RFID readers placed in manufacturing plants, warehouses, transportation systems, and stores can track inventory in real time to get products to customers faster and with less overhead.

SETTING UP A SMART HOME

As an IT support technician, you might be called on to set up and support a smart home that uses IoT devices. For the most basic of smart homes, you'll need:

▲ *Smartphone or tablet and Wi-Fi home network with Internet access.* Use a smartphone or tablet to set up and control smart devices by way of the device manufacturer's app you install on the phone or tablet. Internet access is often required to use the app.
▲ *Smart home devices.* Examples are smart light bulbs, thermostats, security cameras, door locks, doorbells, refrigerators, televisions, and sound systems. Smart devices can be controlled by the manufacturer's app installed on a phone or tablet. Some smart devices, such as a smart thermostat by Nest (*nest.com*), can connect directly to a Wi-Fi network via an embedded Wi-Fi radio (see Figure 9-46). Alternately, devices such as a door lock or thermostat might use Bluetooth to communicate with a phone or tablet within Bluetooth range or might use a bridge to connect to the Wi-Fi network. Other devices, such as smart light bulbs or a door lock, might use Zigbee, Z-Wave, or another wireless technology that the phone or tablet does not use. Such devices require a bridge device to connect them to the Wi-Fi network, as shown in Figure 9-46.

Figure 9-46 IoT devices connected to a smart home network may use a variety of wireless technologies

For smart devices to truly be IoT devices, you must be able to control them over the Internet. For that to happen, they must connect directly or through a bridge to a home Wi-Fi network that has Internet access. Notice in Figure 9-46 that the manufacturer's website is involved when managing many IoT devices. For example, Figure 9-47 shows the webpage where two exterior webcams and two thermostats by Nest (*nest.com*) can be monitored and managed from anywhere on the web.

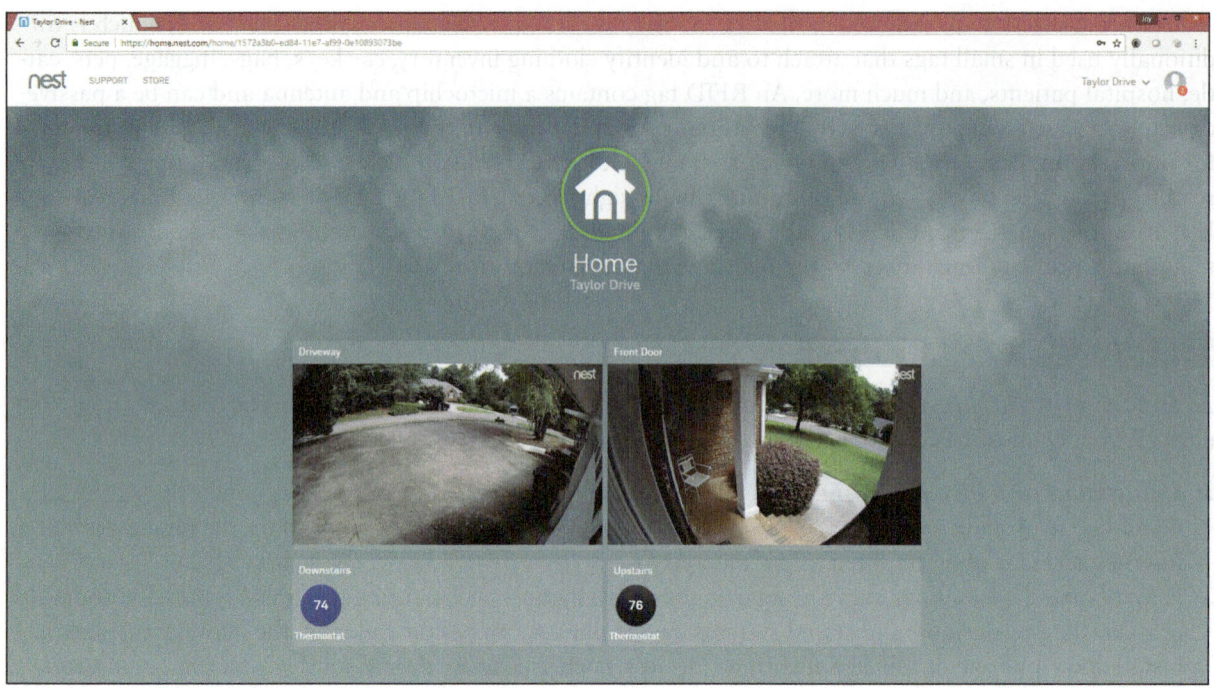

Figure 9-47   IoT device manufacturers provide websites to manage their devices

You can enhance a smart home network with smart speakers and controller hubs:

▲ *Smart speaker*. A smart speaker includes digital assistant software that is voice activated. Amazon, Google, and Apple offer competing smart speakers, which connect by Wi-Fi to the Internet and include a search engine. For example, you can command a smart speaker to play music available over Pandora radio on the web. You can also ask it to tell you the capital of Myanmar. When you sign in to your Amazon, Google, or Apple account on the web, you can set up smart devices so that a smart speaker can turn them on or off and tell you information the devices provide. For example, you can ask a smart speaker with a screen, such as an Echo Show, to show you the live feed from a security camera at your front door. Here are three options for smart speakers:

Figure 9-48   The orange light indicates the Echo Dot is on but not connected to a Wi-Fi network

▲ *Alexa and Echo devices by Amazon*. An Echo smart speaker is voice activated and may include a screen. The embedded digital assistant is called Alexa. You can say, "Alexa, turn on the lights," and the app does it. One low-end Echo product is the Echo Dot shown in Figure 9-48. You'll need the Alexa app on an Android or iOS device to set up an Echo device.

▲ *Google Assistant and Google Home*. Google Assistant is an app on an Android phone and is also embedded in a Google Home smart speaker. You control Google Assistant by starting with the spoken command "OK Google." You set up the Google Home smart speaker using an app on your phone (see Figure 9-49). You can also install the Google Assistant app on an iPhone or iPad so it can control smart devices set up to use the app.

Source: google.com

Figure 9-49 Use a smartphone to set up a Google Home smart speaker

◢ *Siri and HomePod by Apple.* Siri is the digital assistant included with an iPhone or iPad and is also embedded in a HomePod smart speaker. A HomePod is set up using an iPhone or iPad.

◢ *Controller hub.* A smart speaker can access the web and turn Wi-Fi-connected smart devices on or off, but for a completely automated smart home experience, you need a controller hub. A controller hub, also called a smart home hub, can control smart devices that use different manufacturer apps and different wireless technologies, such as Wi-Fi, Bluetooth, Zigbee, or Z-Wave, to create an integrated smart home experience. For example, you can use a controller hub to coordinate dinner:

When you approach your home, the garage door opens, the range turns on to warm up the soup, the room temperature is raised, and the kitchen lights are turned on. Two examples of hubs are Wink Hub (*wink.com*) and Samsung SmartThings (*smartthings.com*). In addition, software hubs such as Yonomi (*yonomi.co*) install as apps on smartphones and tablets.

Some people start a smart home by installing one or two smart devices controlled from a smartphone. Later they add a smart speaker and other smart devices to manage lighting, climate, convenience features, security, and entertainment. They also add controller hubs to make all the devices work together.

APPLYING | CONCEPTS   SETTING UP A DIGITAL ASSISTANT AND SMART SPEAKER

One significant goal of manufacturers of IoT smart home devices is to make them easy to set up and connect to the home's Wi-Fi network. However, the steps for setting up these devices vary somewhat among manufacturers, their products, and product models. Here, we'll look at the general steps for configuring an Echo Dot from Amazon; you should use the more specific steps from your product's manufacturer.

1. The Echo Dot and Alexa are set up and controlled from the Alexa app on a smartphone. Download and install the Alexa app first and sign in to your Amazon account. After Alexa is set up, you can also control Alexa from your Amazon account at *amazon.com*.

2. Plug the Echo Dot into a wall outlet. After it powers up and the light turns orange, it's ready to be paired with a smartphone. Refer back to Figure 9-48.

3. On the smartphone in the Alexa app, choose the Echo Dot from the device setup menu (see Figure 9-50A).

(continues)

(A)   (B)

Source: amazon.com

Figure 9-50   (A) Choose the Echo Dot in the setup options; (B) connect the phone to the Dot's Wi-Fi hotspot

4. Echo Dot provides its own Wi-Fi hotspot to do the initial setup for another Wi-Fi network. First, connect the phone to the Dot's Wi-Fi hotspot (see Figure 9-50B). You can then configure the Dot to connect to your home's Wi-Fi network.

5. Once the Dot is communicating with your local network, it's ready to respond to voice commands. Use the wake word "Alexa" to activate the Dot, then say your command or request. You can change the wake word in the Alexa app. If you're setting up a smart home network, you're ready to add smart home devices to your Alexa account.

✎ **Notes** Some people like to use Alexa when traveling. In late 2018, Amazon introduced Echo Auto, which connects to your smartphone and vehicle for the Alexa experience on the road. Be aware, however, that Echo Auto uses data on your smartphone's cellular data plan.

APPLYING | CONCEPTS   SETTING UP AN IOT SMART HOME DEVICE

The following general steps apply to setting up many types of IoT devices:

1. Download the manufacturer's app.

2. Open the app to follow the instructions for installation and configuration and to control the device from your smartphone. You might also need to install a bridge for devices that don't use Wi-Fi.

3. To control the device with voice communication, enable the smart home device in your digital assistant account.

Using these general steps, we're adding a smart door lock, the August Smart Lock Pro (see Figure 9-51), to a smart home network. This smart lock by default is controlled via Bluetooth by your smartphone within Bluetooth range. In addition, we're installing the August Connect, which is a bridge to connect the smart lock to your home Wi-Fi network so that you can control the smart lock from anywhere on the Internet or through a smart speaker such as Alexa.

Smart lock

Wi-Fi connect bridge

Figure 9-51   The August Smart Lock Pro automatically unlocks or locks as the user's Bluetooth-enabled smartphone moves closer or farther away

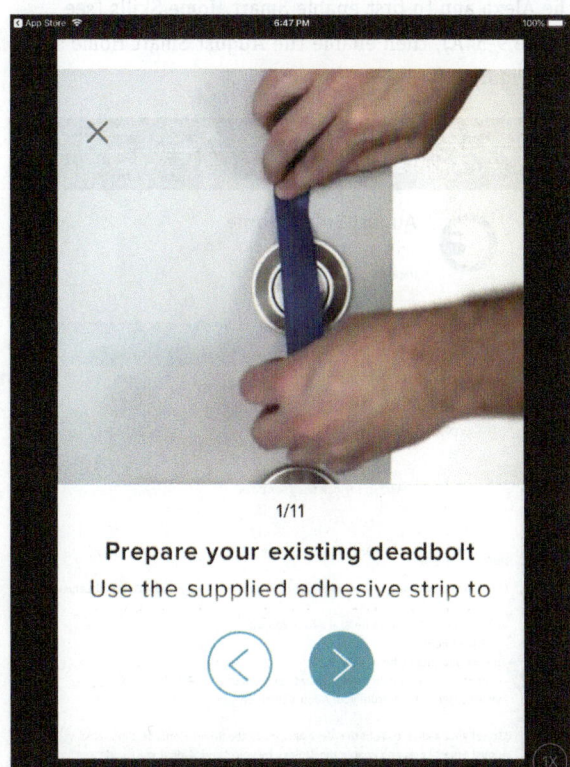

Source: August Home Inc.

Figure 9-52   Install the smart lock on existing deadbolt hardware

The steps above are general steps; you should follow the more specific directions provided by your device's manufacturer:

1. Smart home device manufacturers usually provide their own app to control the device. Download and install the August Home app on your smartphone and create an account. This process might include security measures such as providing a photo of yourself, verifying your phone number with a texted security code, and verifying your email with an emailed security code.

2. Set up your smart lock in the app. The August Home app gives step-by-step video instruction for the lock installation (see Figure 9-52). You can also search YouTube for demonstrations of this process for your device. A good video for the August Smart Lock is posted by Silver Eagle Locksmith at *youtube.com/watch?v=omrbvCVOcI8*.

3. With your smartphone within Bluetooth range of the door lock, the app will connect to the lock via Bluetooth and continue setup. You can name your house and the specific location of the lock, such as "Front Door." The app might also install a firmware update at this time.

4. Calibrate the lock if instructed to do so. This involves setting the lock to "locked" and "unlocked" multiple times so the detectors inside the lock know how far to turn the latch.

(continues)

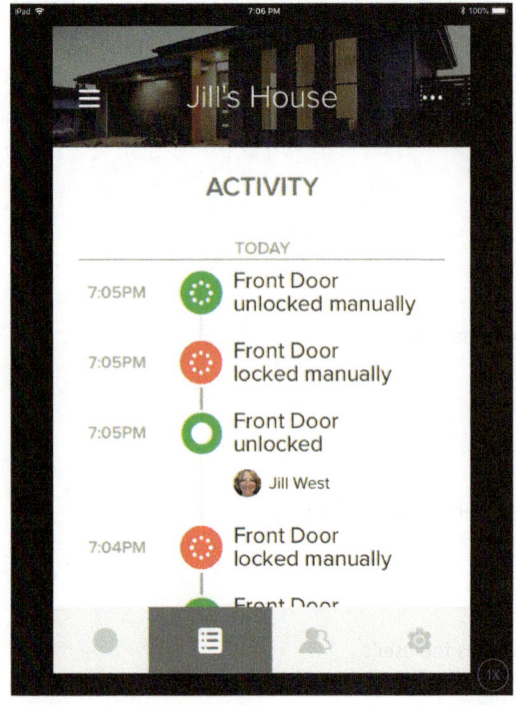

Figure 9-53 See the lock's recent activity, including which users have locked or unlocked the door

5. Next, if you're using an iPhone or iPad, you have the option to link the lock to HomeKit, which is the software used by HomePod, Apple's smart speaker that works with Siri. We're going to use Alexa, so we skip this step.

6. August Connect is a small box, called a bridge, that is mounted near the door lock and connects to the lock via Bluetooth and to your Wi-Fi home network so that you can control the lock from your smartphone anywhere on the Internet. To install the Connect, make sure your smartphone is connected to the home Wi-Fi network, then plug the Connect into a wall outlet near the lock's location. The app detects the Connect and configures it for your home Wi-Fi network.

   You can now control the lock from anywhere using the August Home app, and you can view a log of the lock's activity, as shown in Figure 9-53. However, we want to also link it to the Alexa app.

7. Alexa relies on "skills" to add functionality to an Alexa account. Think about skills as apps within the Alexa app. To add smart home devices to Alexa, use the Alexa app to first enable Smart Home Skills (see Figure 9-54A), then enable the August Smart Home skill (see Figure 9-54B).

(A)

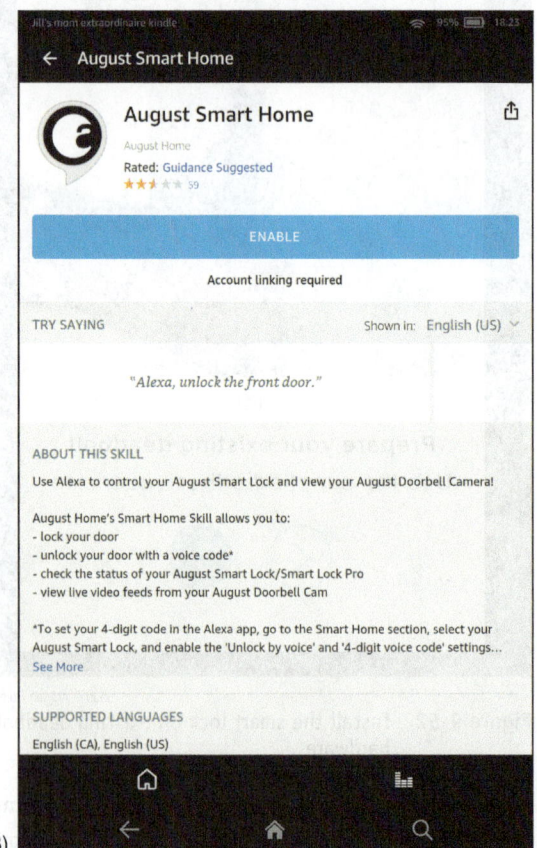

(B)

Figure 9-54 Using the Alexa app, (A) enable Smart Home Skills; (B) enable the August Smart Home skill

Figure 9-55 Install this smart light switch to remotely control a room's light, fan, or electric outlets

8. After you link your August account and give Alexa permission to manage the lock, Alexa will discover the lock. Alexa will now respond to voice commands such as, "Alexa, tell August to lock the front door" and "Alexa, tell August to unlock the front door," in which case you'll also need to tell Alexa your PIN.

Let's look at a couple more examples of IoT smart devices. The smart light switch by Meross (*meross.com*), shown in Figure 9-55, uses Wi-Fi and the Meross app and can be controlled by Amazon Alexa or Google Assistant. The Honeywell wireless thermostat in Figure 9-56 uses Honeywell proprietary RedLINK wireless transmissions and can communicate with a Wi-Fi network via the RedLINK-to-Wi-Fi bridge, also shown in the figure, so that it can interact with Honeywell's Total Comfort Care app. Both devices can also link to Amazon Alexa or Google Assistant.

RedLINK wireless to Wi-Fi bridge

Figure 9-56 Use your phone, an Echo Dot, or a Google Home smart speaker to control this wireless thermostat

The setup for both the Wi-Fi smart light switch and the thermostat using RedLINK wireless is similar to how the Bluetooth thermostat was set up:

1. Install the app.

2. Install the device in the app. If the device does not use Wi-Fi, install an optional bridge device.

3. Connect the device to a smart speaker.

TROUBLESHOOTING MOBILE DEVICES

A+
CORE 1
1.6, 5.5

As an IT support technician for mobile devices, know that they contain few field replaceable units (FRU), or hardware that can be replaced by field technicians. The cost of replacement, including parts and labor, generally exceeds the value of fixing the device. Although it is possible to replace the screens in some mobile devices, a support technician is generally not expected to take the time to do so.

A+
CORE 2
3.4, 3.5
There are, however, many problems with a device that you can troubleshoot using tools within the OS. When learning to troubleshoot any OS or device, remember the web is a great source of information. Depend on the *support.google.com/googleplay* and *support.apple.com* websites to give you troubleshooting tips and procedures for their respective mobile devices. In this section, we'll first explore troubleshooting tools for mobile device OSs, and then we'll consider many common symptoms and problems and what to do about them.

TROUBLESHOOTING TECHNIQUES

A+
CORE 1
5.5

A+
CORE 2
3.4, 3.5
The following steps are ordered to solve a problem while making the least changes to the system (i.e., try the least invasive solution first). Try the first step; if it does not solve the problem, move on to the next step. With each step, first make sure the device is plugged in or already has sufficient charge to complete the step. After you try one step, check to see if the problem is solved before you move on to the next step. Here are the general steps we're following, although some might not be possible, depending on the situation:

1. Close, uninstall, and reinstall an app. Too many open apps can shorten battery life and slow down device performance. If you suspect an app is causing a problem, uninstall it and use the app store to reinstall it.

2. Restart the device (also called a soft boot) and reboot the device (also called a hard boot).

3. Update, repair, or reinstall the OS, or recover the system from the last backup.

4. Start over by resetting the device to its factory state (all data and settings are lost).

Earlier in the chapter, you learned how to close, uninstall, and reinstall an app. Let's look at the last three steps in a little more detail. For more specific instructions, search the website of the device manufacturer.

RESTART OR REBOOT THE DEVICE

A restart powers down the device and restarts it, which is similar to a Windows restart. A reboot, also called a hard boot, is similar to a Windows shutdown and performs a full clean boot. First try a restart, and if that doesn't fix the problem, try a hard boot:

1. *Restart the device, also called a soft boot.* To restart an Android device, press and hold the power button, and select **restart**. To restart an iOS device, press and hold the Side button and slide the power-off message to the right. To turn the device back on, press and hold the Android power button or iOS Side button. Power cycling a smartphone every few days is a good idea to keep the phone functioning at peak efficiency.

2. *Reboot the device using a hard boot.* When the menus in a device don't work or the device freezes entirely, a full clean boot might help. For most Android devices, hold down the power button and volume-down button at the same time. (Check Android device manufacturers for details.) To reboot an iPhone X, hold down either volume button and the Side button until the Apple logo appears; for an iPad or older iPhone, press and hold the Side button and the Home button.

If the device has a removable battery and it refuses to hard boot, you can open the back of the device and then remove and reinstall the battery as a last resort (unless the device is under warranty).

UPDATE, REPAIR, OR RESTORE THE SYSTEM

As you progress through troubleshooting steps, try these options to update, repair, or restore a device:

1. *Back up content and settings.* Before you try any of the techniques in this section, first try to back up data and settings using one or more of the methods discussed earlier in the chapter.

2. *Update the OS.* Try installing any updates, if available.

For Android devices, you can try these options to repair and restore your system:

1. *Boot into Android Safe Mode.* Similar to Windows computers, Android offers a Safe Mode for trouble-shooting. In Safe Mode, only the original software installed on the phone will run so that you can elimi-nate third-party software as the source of the problem. Be aware, however, that booting to Safe Mode might result in the loss of some settings, such as synchronization accounts. The combination of buttons to access Safe Mode varies by device, so see the manufacturer's website for specific instructions. For Google's Pixel smartphone, you access Safe Mode by holding down the power button until the power menu appears. Tap and hold the **Power Off** option until the pop-up shown in Figure 9-57A appears. Tap **OK** to restart the phone in Safe Mode, as shown in Figure 9-57B. Notice the *Safe mode* flag at the bot-tom of the screen. In Safe Mode, only apps native to the Android installation can run, and troubleshoot-ing tools can be accessed through the Settings app to back up data, test configuration issues, or reset the device. To exit Safe Mode, restart the phone normally.

(A)

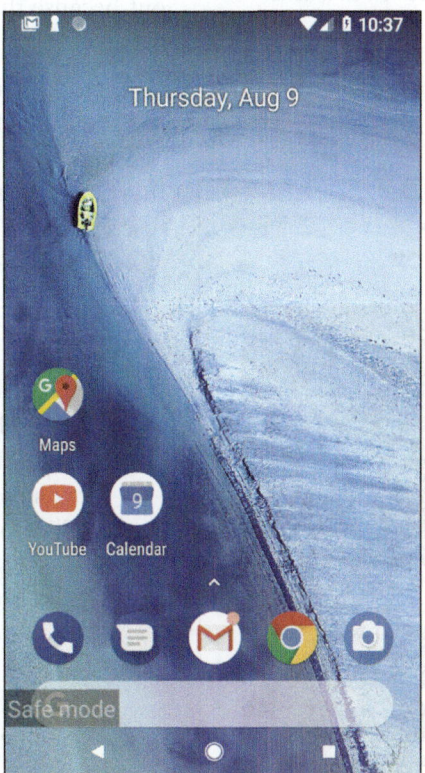
(B)

Source: Android

Figure 9-57 (A) Restart in Safe Mode; (B) in Safe Mode, third-party apps don't load

2. *Restore from backup.* If you have used Google Drive or a third-party app to back up the Android OS, its data or settings, now is the time to restore the system from this backup.

Several troubleshooting apps have been developed to help resolve Android problems. Most of these apps work only if they have already been installed before the problem occurs. If you have not already installed a troubleshooting app, your best resource at this point is to do a Google search on the problem and depend as much as possible on the device manufacturer's website.

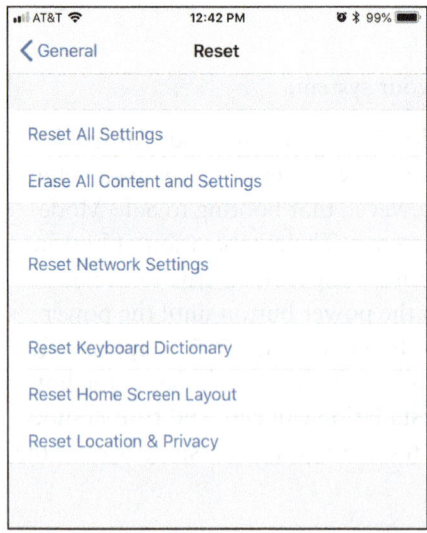

Source: iOS

Figure 9-58 The Reset screen on an iPhone

For iOS devices, you have several options for repairing and restoring your system, which are listed beginning with the least invasive:

1. *Reset all iOS settings*. To erase settings, open the **Settings** app and tap **General** and **Reset**. On the Reset screen (see Figure 9-58), tap **Reset All Settings**.

2. *Restore from backup*. Use one of these methods to restore from backup:

   ▲ *Restore the device from iCloud*. If you have an iCloud backup, open the **Settings** app and tap **General, Reset,** and **Erase All Content and Settings** (see Figure 9-58). Then tap **Restore** and **iCloud backup**. You'll need to sign in to iCloud.

   ▲ *Restore the device from iTunes*. If you have used iTunes to back up the device, connect the device to your computer, start **iTunes**, and click **Restore Backup**. Refer back to Figure 9-38. In the figure, notice the option is grayed out because there is no iTunes backup for this connected iPhone.

3. *Reinstall iOS*. If an iOS device won't turn on or start up, first consider that the battery might be dead. Try to charge it for at least an hour. If you still can't turn it on, you can use iTunes to try to reinstall iOS without losing your data. (You can use iTunes on any computer, even if you have not previously used it to back up your device.)

   a. If necessary, download and install iTunes. Make sure iTunes is updated and then close it.

   b. Connect the iPhone or iPad to the computer and start iTunes. For an iPhone X or iPhone 8, press and release the volume-up button followed by the volume-down button, and then press and hold the Slide button until you see the recovery mode screen (see Figure 9-59A). For older iPhones or iPads, press and hold the Home button and Side button. Follow the directions until you see the screen shown in Figure 9-59B, and then click **Update**. The latest version of iOS that works on your device should install and keep your data.

Source: https://support.apple.com/en-us/HT201412

Figure 9-59 Use recovery mode with iTunes to reinstall iOS on an iOS device that will not start

START OVER WITH A FACTORY RESET

As a last resort, you can perform a factory reset. The reset erases all data and settings and resets the device to its original factory default state. You can then apply a backup if you have one, so try to back up all data and settings before performing the reset, if possible.

1. *Factory reset from the Settings app.* In Android, open the **Settings** app, tap **System**, tap **Reset options**, and then tap **Erase all data (factory reset)**. In iOS, open the **Settings** app, and then tap **General** and **Reset**. On the Reset screen, tap **Erase All Content and Settings**.

2. *Factory reset from a hard boot (Android only).* If you cannot start Android or cannot get to the Settings app after a reboot, you can perform a factory reset from a hard boot. For most Android devices, hold down the power button and volume-down button at the same time until you see the Android bootloader menu. Select **Recovery Mode** and then check the device manufacturer's website for other options on the Recovery Mode screen that you can try before a full factory reset. If you decide that you have no other options, select **Factory reset** on the Recovery Mode screen.

3. *Factory reset and restore from iTunes backup (iOS only).* If an iOS device won't turn on and you've already tried to reinstall iOS using iTunes, as discussed above, you can perform a factory reset using iTunes. Connect the device to a computer that has iTunes installed and go to recovery mode in iTunes, as you learned to do earlier. Then click **Restore** (see Figure 9-59B). All data and settings on the device are erased and iOS is reinstalled. If you have previously used iTunes on this computer to back up your device, the device is restored from the backup. If you have an iCloud backup, you will be given the opportunity to restore from iCloud the first time you sign on to the device with your Apple ID.

> ✎ **Notes** If you have forgotten your iOS passcode, you are given six attempts to enter it before the device is disabled. You will need to use iTunes to reinstall iOS and you will lose all your data and settings unless you have an iTunes backup to restore the device from backup. If you have backed up to iCloud and you sign into iOS for the first time with your Apple ID, you are given the chance to restore the device from the iCloud backup.

If you've tried the previous steps and your device is still not working properly, search for more troubleshooting tips online, review the list of common problems below, or take the device to the place of purchase for repair.

COMMON PROBLEMS AND SOLUTIONS

A+
CORE 1
1.6, 5.5

A+
CORE 2
3.4, 3.5

Several common problems with mobile devices can be addressed with a little understanding of what has gone wrong behind the scenes. Here's a description of how to handle some common problems:

- ◢ *Short battery life or power drain.* Too many apps or malware running in the background will drain the battery quickly, as will Wi-Fi, Bluetooth, or other wireless technologies. Disable wireless connections and close apps when you're not using them to save battery juice. Consider that malware might be at work; how to address malware is covered earlier in the chapter. If the battery charge still lasts an extremely short time, try exchanging the AC adapter (charger). If that doesn't work, exchange the battery unless the device is under warranty. Many Android devices have replaceable batteries, so if a battery is performing poorly, consider replacing it.

- ◢ *Inaccurate touch screen response.* A cover on the screen can result in inaccurate touch screen responses. Also, accessibility settings can alter a touch screen's performance. Check accessibility settings in the Settings app. Hold duration is a particular suspect, as are touch location assistance and screen auto-rotate.

- ◢ *Touch screen nonresponsive.* Here are some tips to try when a touch screen is giving you problems:

  - ◢ Clean the screen with a soft, lint-free cloth.

  - ◢ Don't use the touch screen when your hands are wet or you are wearing gloves.

▲ Restart the device.

▲ Remove any plastic sheet or film protecting the touch screen. Some screen protectors are too thick and interfere with the touch screen interface, or bubbles and debris under the screen protector can cause problems. Use a screen protector that is approved for your device and carefully follow instructions for installing it. Turn on the screen protector's touch sensitivity setting if available.

▲ If you recently installed a third-party app when the touch screen became unresponsive, try uninstalling that app. Sometimes third-party apps can cause a touch screen to freeze.

▲ *No sound or distorted sound from speakers*. This might seem obvious, but first make sure the volume is turned up by pressing the device's physical **Up** volume button. Also, the problem could be that the sound output for the device is being misdirected. Check to see if Bluetooth is on; if it is, turn it off to make sure the device is not inadvertently connected to a Bluetooth headset or car stereo system. Also check Accessibility settings. Some of the Accessibility audio settings can interfere with normal operation of the device's built-in speaker system.

▲ *Dim display*. Try increasing the brightness. This is especially helpful when trying to view the screen in bright daylight, but increasing the brightness level will also drain the battery more quickly. For Android, open the notifications shade, then slide the brightness slider to the right to brighten the screen. Make sure the Auto option is not selected so that you have more control over the screen's brightness level.

For the iPad and older iPhones, swipe up to show the control center; on an iPhone X, swipe down from the upper-right corner to show the control center. In the control center, you can adjust the screen brightness.

Sometimes individual apps will control the screen brightness separately from the OS, so also check brightness settings within an app. Also check color and contrast settings on the accessibility menu in the Settings app (for Android, see Figure 9-60).

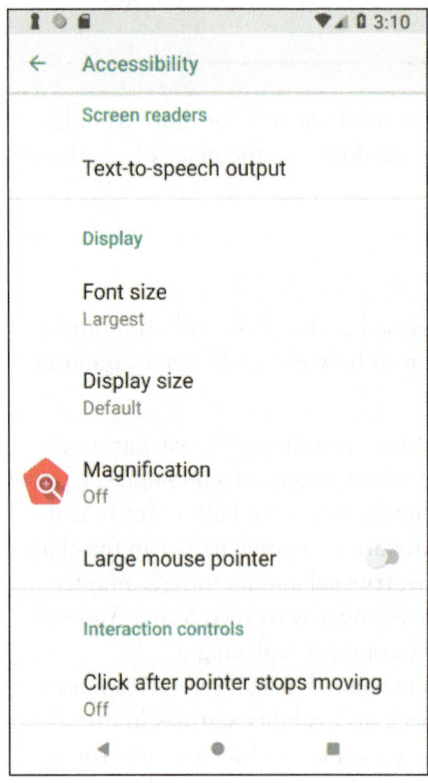

Source: Android

Figure 9-60 Accessibility settings can make a mobile device act in unexpected ways

▲ *Cannot broadcast to external monitor*. Many mobile devices can wirelessly mirror, or cast, their displays to a TV, monitor, projector, or to a dongle attached to one of these display devices. Android devices rely on Miracast technology, while iOS devices use AirPlay. When troubleshooting, first confirm that both devices are turned on (and not in sleep mode), placed closely enough to each other, casting is enabled where needed, and devices are connected to the same Wi-Fi network. You can also check for available updates on each device. Next, consider sources of interference, such as crowded Wi-Fi bands, and check that the Wi-Fi router is set to prioritize Wi-Fi multimedia (WMM) traffic. A VPN app on the device sometimes disables the casting feature because of the way cast technology seems to pose a threat to VPN security. It might be necessary to uninstall third-party VPN apps for casting to work properly.

▲ *Bluetooth connectivity issues*. Turn the Bluetooth radio off and then back on again. Devices typically limit the time they're available for pairing, so reactivating Bluetooth restarts the pairing process. In Bluetooth settings, you might be able to adjust the visibility timeout so devices have more time to discover each other. You can also delete all known Bluetooth devices in the Settings app to try the pairing process from the beginning. Sometimes an OS update will cause issues with Wi-Fi network connectivity or Bluetooth pairings. In this case, reset network settings in the Settings app. This restores network settings to factory defaults, and then you can attempt pairing again.

▲ *Wi-Fi connectivity problems*. Intermittent connectivity problems or no wireless connectivity might be caused by problems with the signal that is being broadcast from the router or access point. First make sure the access point and router are working correctly, that they're positioned closely enough to each other, that the Wi-Fi network you want to connect to is visible to the device (not hidden), and that you're using the correct security key. For Wi-Fi issues on the device side, first start with Wi-Fi settings in the Settings app for the network to which you're trying to connect. Try renewing the IP address, and if that doesn't work, tell the device to forget the network and then retry connecting to the network. Finally, try resetting the network settings. By default, many mobile devices stop attempting to reconnect to a weak Wi-Fi signal to conserve battery power, but you can sometimes change this setting so the device will attempt to maintain a connection even with a weak signal.

▲ *Signal drop/weak signal*. Sometimes updating the device's firmware can solve problems with dropped calls or network connections due to a weak signal because the update might apply to the radio firmware, which manages the cellular, Wi-Fi, and Bluetooth radios. This is sometimes referred to as a baseband update. For most of today's mobile devices, firmware updates are pushed out by the manufacturer at the same time as OS updates. If your device allows for managing firmware updates separately, usually that option will be available in the Settings app (see Figure 9-61) in the same place as the OS update option. You might also be able to download software from the device's manufacturer that can apply updates to the device through a USB connection with your computer. Examples are iTunes (*apple.com/itunes*) for Apple devices, LG PC Suite (*lg.com/us/support/software-firmware-drivers*) for LG devices, and HTC Sync Manager (*htc.com/us/software/htc-sync-manager*) for HTC devices. These apps can also be used for synchronization and backup functions. Be careful when applying a firmware update, as a failed update can "brick" the device, which means to make it useless.

▲ *GPS not functioning*. Geotracking, which is the identification of a device's location to track the device's movements, relies heavily on GPS location information. For example, Siri checks the device's current location before recommending Italian restaurants in the area. Many apps can only access this information if Location services are enabled on the device (however, emergency calls can use location information even if Location services are not enabled). If an app is having trouble accessing location-specific information, check the Location services settings in the Settings app, as shown in Figure 9-62.

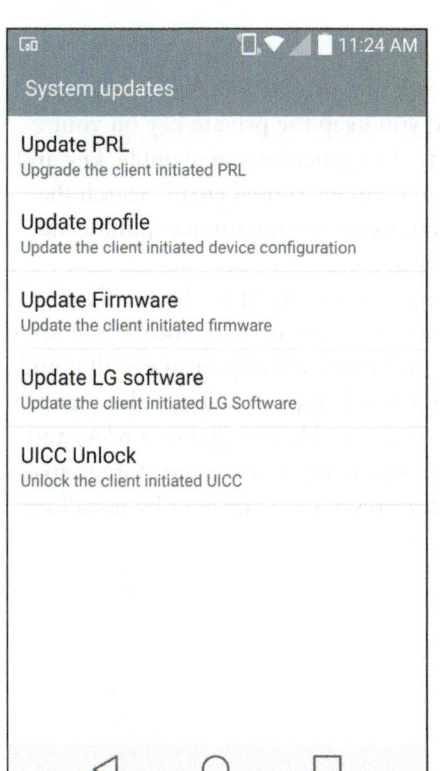

Source: Android

Figure 9-61 This LG phone lists several options for applying updates

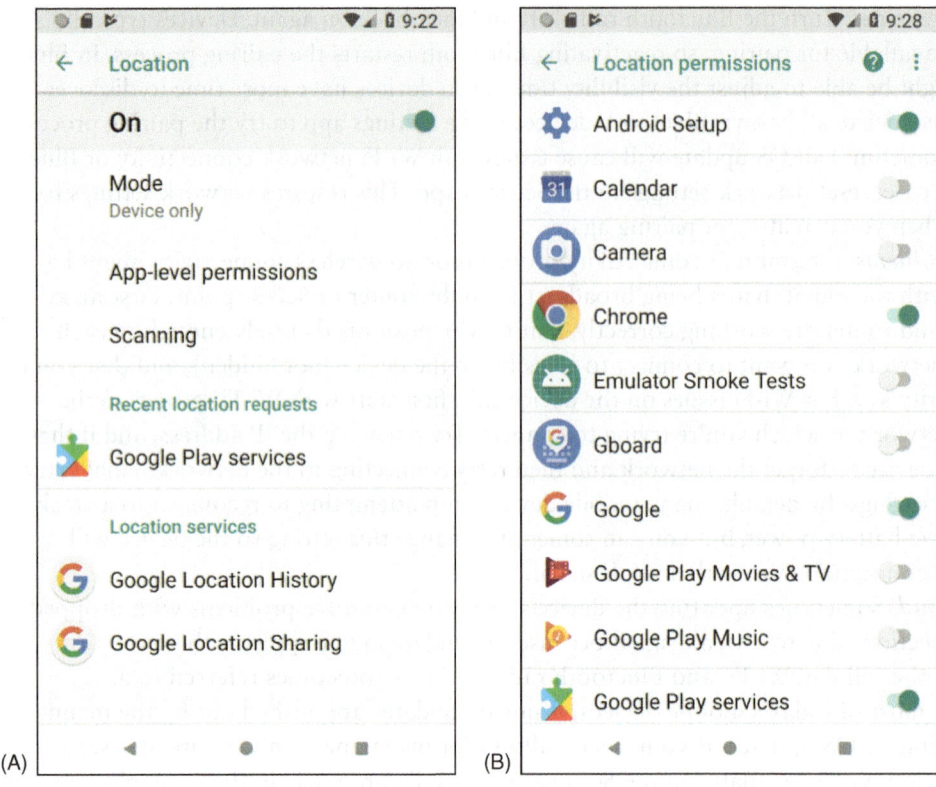

Source: Android

Figure 9-62   (A) Manage Location services in the Settings app, and (B) fine-tune which apps can use Location services

▲ *Unable to decrypt email.* Email encryption is done using a public key and a private key. You distribute your public key to those who want to send you encrypted email and you keep the private key on your device. If your device is unable to decrypt email, most likely you'll need to generate a new public key and private key and then distribute your new public key to those who send you encrypted email. Search the website of the email app you are using for encryption to find instructions for setting up new public and private keys and for other tips on troubleshooting decrypting problems.

▲ *Apps not loading.* When apps load slowly or not at all, a hot or failing battery might be the problem. Having too many apps open at once will use up memory and slow down overall performance. Close apps you're not using, clean cached data, and disable live wallpapers. Try to update the app or uninstall it and install it again. The device might be short on storage space; uninstall unused apps and delete files that are no longer needed. The Settings app displays how much storage space is available (see Figure 9-63A) and what content can be removed (see Figure 9-63B). Consider downloading an app to clean up storage space or monitor how apps are using memory. Consider performing a factory reset and start over by installing only the apps you actually use.

Source: Android

Figure 9-63   (A) Android reports how storage is used and (B) makes suggestions to free some storage space

- ◢ *App log errors*. Some apps maintain logs of errors that can be useful to technical support staff for the app. When helping you troubleshoot a problem, an app support technician might give you specific steps for accessing those logs.
- ◢ *Frozen system*. Consider that the battery may be low. Try recharging the battery for at least an hour. Then follow directions given earlier to reboot the device using a hard boot. If that doesn't work, move on to reinstall the OS, recover the system from backup, and finally reset the device to its factory state.
- ◢ *System lockout*. If a device is locked because of too many failed attempts to sign in (such as when a child has attempted to unlock your device or you have forgotten the passcode), wait until the timer on the device counts down and try to sign in again. With Android devices, you might also be able to sign in using your Google account and the password associated with the device. After you have entered the account and password, you must reset your passcode or screen swipe pattern. If you still can't unlock the device, know that Google offers many solutions to this problem. Go to *accounts.google.com* and search for additional methods and tools to unlock your device.

  If you have forgotten the passcode for an iOS device, Apple advises that your only solution is to reset the device, which erases all data and settings, and then restore the device from a backup. You can restore from a backup stored in iTunes on your computer or from iCloud.
- ◢ *Overheating*. For a true overheating problem where the device is too hot to touch safely, power off and replace the device. However, all devices can get fairly warm if the display is left on for too long, if the surrounding environment is particularly hot, if the device is sitting on a blanket or other soft surface, if the case is not properly vented, if the battery is going bad, or if the device remains plugged in to a power source for a long period of time. Don't use a mobile device for too long in direct sunlight, turn off the display when you're not using it, and close apps that you're not using. This will also help conserve battery power.

If you know where the battery is located inside a mobile device, check for heat originating from that area of the device. If the area is hot, replacing the battery might be your solution. First check if the phone is under warranty. If the phone is not under warranty, open the case and examine the battery for damage. Is it swollen or warped? If so, replace the battery. For most mobile devices, you can find teardown instructions, videos, tools, and replacement parts for purchase online at various websites, such as *ifixit.com* (see Figure 9-64). If the phone is under warranty, you might be able to tell if the battery is swollen or warped by laying the phone on a flat surface. If the phone itself appears warped, take it in for repair.

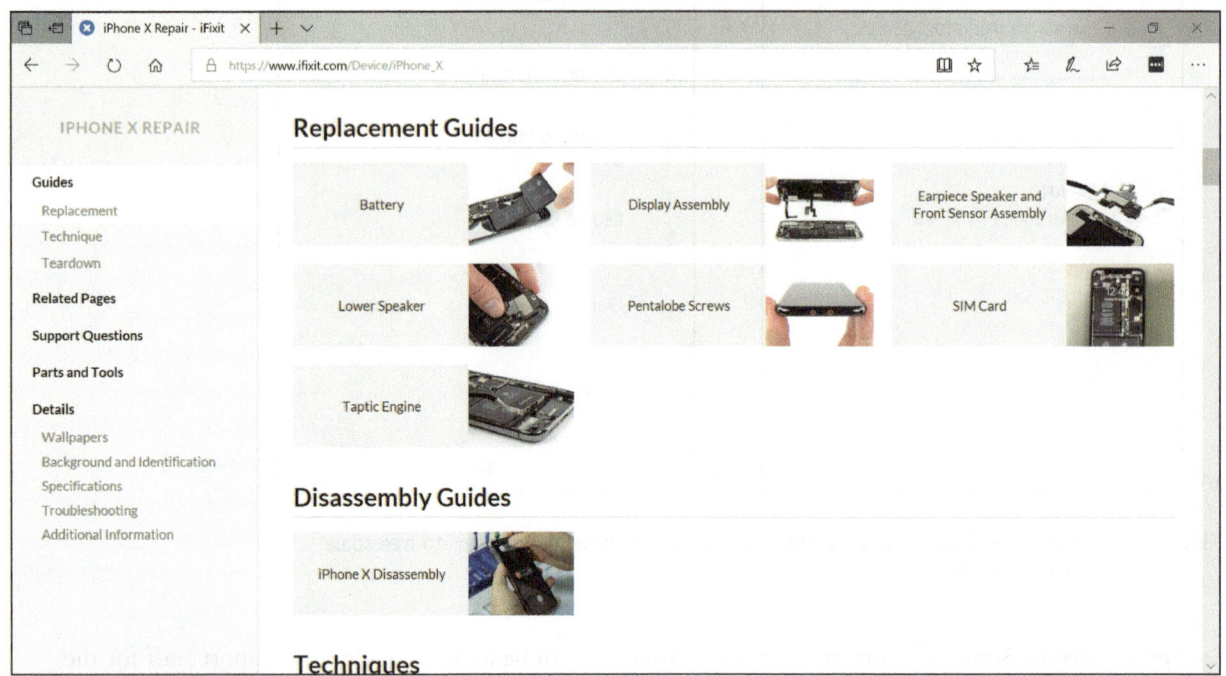

Source: ifixit.com

Figure 9-64 At *ifixit.com*, you can find instructions and purchase tools or parts to replace an iPhone battery

> ✎ **Notes** Some Android smartphones provide information about the device when you enter `*#*#4636#*#*` in the phone's dialer keypad. In the screen that appears, select **Battery Information**. If the Battery Health screen reports "unknown," suspect a bad battery. The screen also reports the temperature of the battery, which should be less than 40° C.

>> CHAPTER SUMMARY

Types of Mobile Devices

◢ Mobile devices an IT support technician might be called on to service include smartphones, tablets, lightweight laptops, e-readers, GPS devices, and wearable technology devices such as smart watches, fitness monitors, and VR or AR headsets.

Mobile Device Operating Systems

◢ The most popular operating systems used on mobile devices include Android by Google, iOS by Apple, Windows and Windows Mobile by Microsoft, and Chrome OS by Google.

◢ Android is an open source OS, and anyone can develop and sell Android apps or variations in the Android OS. Google is the major distributor of Android and Android apps are available on its Google Play website.

- iOS by Apple is used only on Apple devices, including the iPhone and iPad. Apps for iOS are distributed solely by Apple.

- Windows Mobile by Microsoft installs on smartphones and uses the same version numbers as Windows for desktops, laptops, and tablets.

- Chrome OS is designed solely for use on Google's Chromebook, which is a tablet, lightweight laptop, or convertible laptop-tablet available from many different manufacturers. Chrome OS relies heavily on the Chrome browser and an active Internet connection. Chrome OS apps are distributed through the Chrome Web Store, and apps for the newer Chromebooks are distributed from the Google Play Store.

Configuring and Syncing a Mobile Device

- A mobile device might have several antennas for wireless connections—primarily Wi-Fi, GPS, Bluetooth, NFC, and cellular. The device uses a Wi-Fi or cellular antenna to connect to a LAN (local area network), a WAN (wide area network), or to create its own hotspot, and it uses Bluetooth or NFC to connect to a PAN (personal area network). A wired connection might use a microUSB, miniUSB, USB-C, or proprietary port, such as the Lightning port by Apple, for syncing with a computer or tethering to provide the computer with cellular WAN access.

- Email can be accessed on a mobile device through a browser or an email client. Email providers include Gmail (by Google), iCloud (by Apple), Yahoo! (owned by Verizon), or Outlook/Hotmail/Live (Microsoft's public email services for individuals). Microsoft also offers Exchange, its private enterprise email service that is hosted on corporation or ISP servers, or Exchange Online, which is hosted on Microsoft servers.

- Syncing mirrors app data and other content among your devices and/or the cloud that use the same Apple or Google account. Backups are copies of app data, configuration settings, and other content in case you need it to recover from a failed, lost, or corrupted device.

Securing a Mobile Device

- Control access to a mobile device by restricting failed login attempts, encrypting the device, and configuring a screen lock such as a swipe lock, PIN lock, passcode lock, pattern lock, fingerprint lock, or face lock. You can also use the mobile device as an authentication factor to increase security for access to other services and networks.

- Secure mobile device data and resources by regularly updating and patching the OS, using an antimalware app, getting apps only from trusted sources, implementing a firewall, and configuring a locator app and the ability to remote wipe the device.

- In corporate environments, profile security might require the use of full device encryption, remote backups, remote wipes, access control to the device, firewalls, anti-malware measures, and VPN connections to protect company resources on the mobile device.

- Symptoms of malware on mobile devices include slow performance, short battery life, power drain, slow data speeds, leaked personal files or data, data transmission over limits, signal drops, weak signal, unintended Wi-Fi connections, unintended Bluetooth pairing, unauthorized account access, unauthorized location tracking, unauthorized camera or microphone activation, and high resource utilization.

- To remediate an infected device, uninstall the offending app, update the OS, and/or do a factory reset on the device.

The Internet of Things (IoT)

- The IoT is made up of any device connected to a network or to the Internet, including a plethora of devices from thermostats and light switches to security cameras and door locks, but not including traditional computing devices, such as desktops, laptops, and smartphones, or traditional networking devices, such as routers, firewalls, and cable modems.

◢ Wireless technologies used by IoT devices include Wi-Fi, Bluetooth, Z-Wave, and Zigbee. RFID is used to passively or actively track items and inventory, such as shipped packages, clothing inventory, hospital patients, and your car keys, and can be used in an automated IoT inventory system.

◢ Zigbee is faster and more robust than Z-Wave and is better suited for industrial and large-scale commercial use.

◢ A smart home requires a Wi-Fi network with Internet access, a smartphone or tablet, smart home devices, and optional smart speakers, controller hubs, and bridges.

Troubleshooting Mobile Devices

◢ To troubleshoot a mobile device using tools in the OS, you can close running apps, uninstall and reinstall an app, reboot the device, update the OS, reset all settings (iOS only), use Safe Mode (Android only), use Recovery mode, or perform a factory reset.

◢ To address specific, common symptoms on a mobile device, you might need to check accessibility settings, replace the battery if it's not under warranty, change the way a device is used, remove protective coverings that are causing interference, check wired or wireless connection configurations, adjust device settings, or consult with tech support for the device manufacturer or app.

>> KEY TERMS

For explanations of key terms, see the Glossary for this text.

airplane mode	favorites tray	IR (infrared)	remote wipe
Android	file-level backup	iTunes	RFID (radio-frequency
app drawer	fitness monitoring	jailbreaking	identification)
App Store	FRU (field replaceable unit)	launcher	rooting
Apple ID	full device encryption	Lightning port	SDK (Software Development Kit)
AR (augmented reality) headset	geotracking	locator application	security profile
authenticator application	Gmail	macOS	Side button
baseband update	Google account	Microsoft Store	smartphone
biometric authentication	Google Play	microUSB	smart speaker
Bluetooth	GPS (Global Positioning System)	miniUSB	S/MIME (Secure/Multi-purpose Internet Mail Extensions)
BYOD (Bring Your Own Device)	Home button	multifactor authentication	SSO (single sign-on)
cast	iCloud	NFC (Near Field Communication)	tablet
Chrome OS	iCloud Drive	notification	trusted source
commercial license	image-level backup	open source	USB-C
controller hub	IMEI (International Mobile Equipment Identity)	paired	VR (virtual reality) headset
digital assistant	IMSI (International Mobile Subscriber Identity)	PRI (Product Release Instructions)	wearable technology device
dock	iOS	PRL (Preferred Roaming List)	Windows 10 Mobile
emulator	IoT (Internet of Things)	profile security requirements	Yahoo!
end-of-life limitation	iPad	radio firmware	Zigbee
e-reader	iPhone	remote backup application	Z-Wave
Exchange Online			

>> THINKING CRITICALLY

These questions are designed to prepare you for the critical thinking required for the A+ exams and may use content from other chapters and the web.

1. Which of these network connections would allow your smartphone to sync your photos to your online account? Choose all that apply.

    a. Wi-Fi

    b. Bluetooth

    c. GPS

    d. Cellular

2. While visiting a coffee shop, you see a poster advertising a concert for a music group you'd love to see. You notice there's an NFC tag at the bottom with additional information about the concert. Which of the following devices would likely be able to read the NFC tag?

    a. GPS

    b. Smartphone

    c. E-reader

    d. VR headset

3. Which of the following mobile device OSs are open source? Choose all that apply.

    a. iOS

    b. Windows 10 Mobile

    c. Chrome OS

    d. Android

4. A smart speaker has no screen or keypad for changing its settings. Order three steps to configure the speaker.

    a. Connect the smartphone to the speaker's Wi-Fi hotspot.

    b. Download the speaker's app to a smartphone.

    c. Enter the password to the home Wi-Fi network.

    d. Enter the password to the speaker's Wi-Fi hotspot.

5. Which Chromebook security feature ensures that malware can't change the OS's system files?

    a. Quick updates

    b. Power washing

    c. Sandboxing

    d. Verified boot

6. You work for a company that provides dozens of the same smartphone model for its employees. While troubleshooting one smartphone that won't connect to the cellular network, you call the provider's tech support number for some assistance. The technician asks for the device's IMEI. What is she trying to determine?

    a. The OS version on the phone

    b. The specific device you're calling about

    c. The SIM card installed in the device

    d. The IP address of the phone on the cellular provider's data network

7. Which encryption protocols might be used to secure a VPN connection? Choose all that apply.

    a. L2TP

    b. SSH

    c. PPTP

    d. IPsec

8. You're at the store to buy a car charger for your dad's iPhone. There are several options with many different types of connectors. Which of these connectors should you choose?

   a. USB-C

   b. microUSB

   c. Lightning

   d. VGA

9. Place the following information in the correct fields in Figure 9-65 to add an email account to a smartphone using port 143 for the incoming mail server and port 25 for the outgoing mail server (not all information will be used):

   imap-mail.sample.com

   p@ssw0rd

   pop-mail.sample.com

   mjones@sample.com

   smtp-mail.sample.com

   Mary Jones

Figure 9-65   Configure email for a smartphone

10. Congratulations! You just bought a new-to-you car, and it comes with a media system that can sync with your iPhone. You're concerned about data usage on your cell phone, so before you go pick up your car, you decide to download the necessary app at home while you're connected to Wi-Fi. What app do you need to download?

11. You're traveling across the country for a much-anticipated vacation. When you get there, your smartphone seems to be having trouble connecting to the local cellular network. You call the provider, and the technician suggests you update the PRL. Why might this help? Where would you find this option on your Android smartphone to perform the update?

12. Your company has recently been hired to install a smart security system for a large office building. The system will include security cameras, voice-controlled lights, smart locks, and smart thermostats. Some of the security cameras will be installed outdoors throughout the parking lot. Which wireless IoT protocol should your company use for the installation?

a. Wi-Fi because it is always encrypted

b. Zigbee because it is always encrypted

c. Z-Wave because it is the fastest wireless standard

d. Bluetooth because it is easiest to configure

13. You're trying to cast a video presentation from your tablet to a projector for a training session with some new hires. Although you tested it successfully yesterday, today the connection is not cooperating. You've closed apps you're not using, and you've checked that the projector and the tablet are working otherwise. Of the following troubleshooting steps, which should you try first? Second?

a. Restart the projector.

b. Restart the tablet.

c. Reinstall the presentation app.

d. Verify that you have Internet access on the tablet.

14. An app that cost you $4.99 is missing from your Android. What is the best way to restore the missing app?

a. Go to backup storage and perform a restore to recover the lost app.

b. Purchase the app again.

c. Go to the Play Store where you bought the app and install it again.

d. Go to the Settings app and perform an application restore.

15. Suppose you and your friend want to exchange lecture notes taken during class. She has an iPhone and you have an iPad. What is the easiest way to do the exchange?

a. Copy the files to an SD card and move the SD card to each device.

b. Drop the files in OneDrive and share notebooks with each other.

c. Send a text to each other with the files attached.

d. Transfer the files through an AirDrop connection.

16. You have set up your Android phone using one Google account and your Android tablet using a second Google account. Now you would like to download the apps you purchased on your phone to your tablet. What is the best way to do this?

a. Set up the Google account on your tablet that you used to buy apps on your phone and then download the apps.

b. Buy the apps a second time from your tablet.

c. Back up the apps on your phone to your SD card and then move the SD card to your tablet and transfer the apps.

d. Call Google support and ask them to merge the two Google accounts into one.

17. Of the 10 devices shown earlier in Figure 9-46, how many of them are assigned IP addresses?

a. Four: two phones, a web server, and a router

b. Three: two phones and a web server

c. Seven: a thermostat, a router, two phones, two bridges, and a web server

d. All 10 are assigned IP addresses.

>> HANDS-ON PROJECTS

Hands-On | Project 9-1   Selecting a Mobile Device

Shop for a new smartphone or tablet that uses iOS or Android. Be sure to read some reviews about a device you are considering. Select two devices that you might consider buying and answer the following questions:

1. What is the device brand, model, and price?

2. What is the OS and version? Amount of storage space? Screen size? Types of network connections? Battery life? Camera pixels?

3. What do you like about each device? Which would you choose and why?

Hands-On | Project 9-2   Exploring *ifixit.com*

Replacing the battery in a smartphone or tablet is a handy skill for an IT support technician to have. If you have a smartphone or tablet or know a friend who has one, find out the brand and model of the device, or use one of the devices you researched for Hands-On Project 9-1. Search the *ifixit.com* website, which is a wiki-based site with tons of guides for tearing down, repairing, and reassembling all kinds of products, including smartphones, tablets, and laptops.

Does the site offer a guide for replacing the battery in your device or your friend's device? If so, list the high-level steps for the repair. If not, choose another device and list the high-level steps for that device. What tools would you need to actually make the repair?

Hands-On | Project 9-3   Researching Apps for Mobile Payment Services

iPhone and Android phones both offer some kind of mobile payment service, which allows you to use your smartphone to pay for merchandise or services at a retail checkout counter. iPhone has Apple Pay, and Android uses Google Pay. Mobile payment services rely on NFC (Near Field Communication) technology to exchange financial information between your phone and the reader at the checkout counter. You might want to pay with a credit card stored on your phone or get discounts with a store rewards account reported by your phone as you check out. But how secure is your sensitive financial information?

Research the following topics and answer the following questions:

1. Research how mobile payment systems use NFC technology. How does NFC work? How can you activate NFC on an Android phone for making a payment with Google Pay? On an iPhone for making a payment with Apple Pay?

2. Find and read some articles online or watch videos that describe the details of storing financial information for mobile payment systems, accessing the information when needed, and transmitting the information securely. What security measures are in place? Where is the data actually stored? What information is actually transmitted at the point of transaction?

3. List three third-party mobile payment apps available either in Apple's App Store or in Google's Play Store. On which mobile OS versions will the apps work? What are advantages and disadvantages of each app? How much do the apps cost? What security measures do the apps use?

4. If you were to purchase one of these apps, which one would it be? Why?

Hands-On | Project 9-4 Practicing Locating Your iOS or Android Device

Whether you have an Android device or an iOS device, knowing how to locate it when it gets lost or stolen or how to perform a remote wipe can be crucial skills in an emergency. Using your own device or a friend's, complete the following steps to find out how these tasks work:

1. If you have an iOS device, go to *iCloud.com/#find*. If you have an Android device, go to *google.com/android/find*.

2. Sign in and make sure the correct device is selected. Was the website able to locate your device? If not, check your device settings and make any adjustments necessary until the website successfully locates the device.

3. Explore the site to see how to make the device ring, how to lock the device by changing the passcode, and how to erase the device. What did you learn about your device?

One potential snag in finding or remotely wiping your device would be relying on passwords stored in your device to access your Google or iCloud account. Be sure to store your sign-in information for these accounts in password vault software or memorize the information.

9

>> REAL PROBLEMS, REAL SOLUTIONS

REAL PROBLEM 9-1 Using Android Studio to Run an Android Emulator

For this project, you might want to work with a partner so that you will have someone with whom to discuss the project in case the installation requires some troubleshooting. Make sure you're using a computer that meets the minimum requirements. While Android Studio works on macOS and Linux platforms, these instructions apply specifically to Windows 10. Here are the Windows system requirements:

▲ Microsoft Windows 10/8/7 (32- or 64-bit)

▲ 3 GB RAM minimum, 8 GB RAM recommended; plus 1 GB for the Android Emulator

▲ 2 GB of available storage space minimum, 4 GB recommended

▲ 1280 × 800 minimum screen resolution

Complete the following steps:

1. Make sure that your computer does not have Hyper-V enabled. To check this, open **Control Panel**, click **Programs and Features**, and click **Turn Windows features on or off**. Make sure that **Hyper-V** is not checked. If it is, uncheck it. Click **OK**. If you had to disable Hyper-V, restart your computer.

2. Make sure that hardware virtualization is enabled in your motherboard's BIOS/UEFI. The name and steps to access this feature vary by motherboard. Check your motherboard's documentation to determine how to enable this feature. What steps did you take to check or enable virtualization on your motherboard?

3. Download the current stable version of Android Studio at *developer.android.com/studio*. You might need to use Chrome to download the file, as the Edge browser is more likely to cause an error. Run the .exe file that you downloaded. At the time of this writing, the file name is android-studio-ide-173.4907809-windows.exe. What is the name of the file you downloaded?

4. Follow the setup wizard and accept all default settings, installing any SDK packages that it recommends. When you reach the SDK Components Setup window shown in Figure 9-66, click to select

Android SDK Platform with **API 28** (or a more current version, if available) and **Android Virtual Device**. If your computer has an Intel CPU, be sure that **Performance (Intel ® HAXM)** is also selected. Click **Next** and continue the setup with all default selections.

Source: Google

Figure 9-66 Select all available components here to install

5. When installation is complete, run **Android Studio**. The user interface is shown in Figure 9-67.

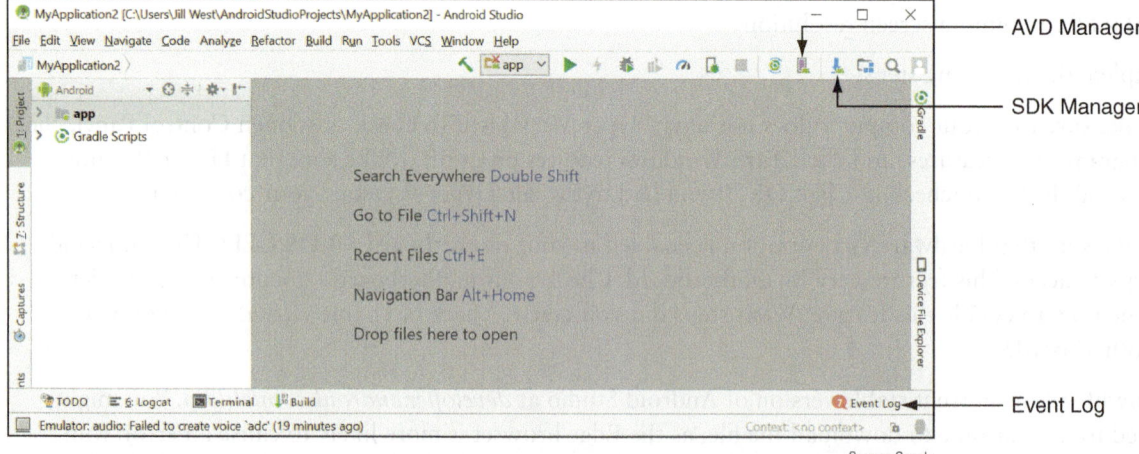

Source: Google

Figure 9-67 Android Studio is designed for app developers to build and test their products

6. Click to launch the AVD Manager, which is shown in Figure 9-68.

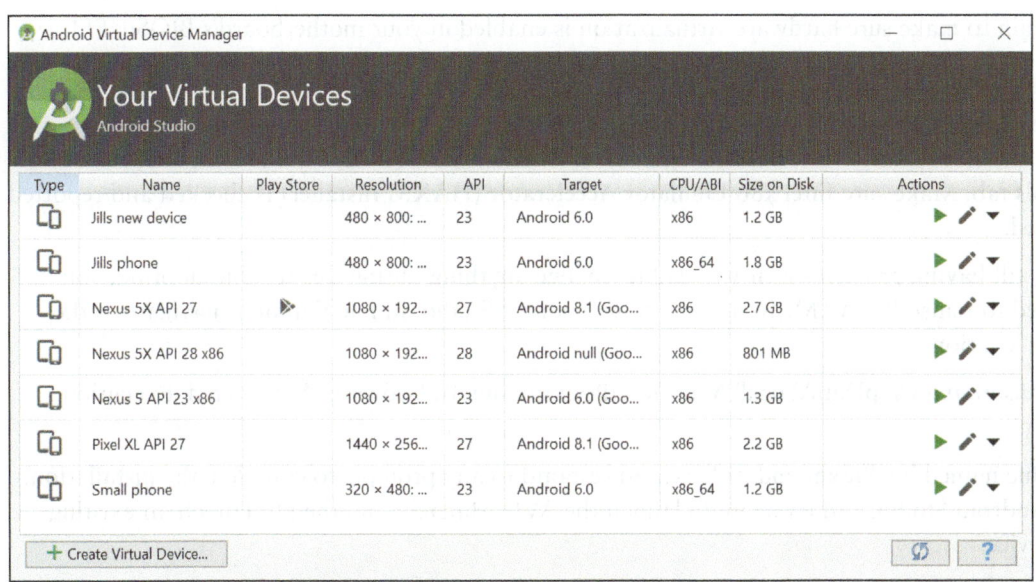

Source: Google

Figure 9-68 Use an existing virtual device or create a new one

9

7. To make sure everything is working so far, click a green **Launch** arrow next to an existing virtual device. If it works, you should see an emulated Android phone (see Figure 9-69A), although it might take a minute or two to fully launch. If you get an error message at this point, use the troubleshooting tips below or search online for possible solutions to your specific error message, which you can see in the Event Log.

(A)   (B)

Source: Google

Figure 9-69 (A) An emulated Nexus 5 with Android Marshmallow, and (B) an emulated Pixel XL with Android Oreo

a. Check again to make sure hardware virtualization is enabled in your motherboard's BIOS/UEFI.

b. Check again to make sure Hyper-V is disabled in Windows.

c. If your computer is using an Intel CPU, make sure HAXM is updated and installed properly. To check this, click to launch the **SDK Manager**. With **Android SDK** selected in the left pane, click the **SDK Tools** tab. Make sure **Intel x86 Emulator Accelerator (HAXM Installer)** is checked and reported as **Installed**.

d. If you're still having problems or if you had to change anything during this troubleshooting, you might need to reinstall HAXM. To do this, close Android Studio. In **File Explorer**, navigate to the following location:

C:\Users*username*\AppData\Local\Android\sdk\extras\intel\Hardware_Accelerated_Execution_Manager\

Run the file named **intelhaxm-android.exe** and respond to any prompts to complete the installation. Restart Android Studio, and try again to launch the AVD Manager and then to launch an existing virtual device.

8. What troubleshooting did you have to perform? What did you learn from this process?

9. Close the virtual device so you can create a new one with an updated OS. In the AVD Manager, click **Create Virtual Device**. Choose the **Pixel XL** phone and click **Next**. Choose the **Oreo Android 8.1** release. You might have to download the system image from the Play Store. If so, click **Download**, then select the release and click **Next**. If desired, give the device a name and then click **Finish**. Your new device should appear in your list of devices. Click its green **Launch** arrow to launch the device, as shown in Figure 9-69B.

10. Play around with the UI to see how well it emulates a real smartphone. Try some of the features discussed in this chapter. Which features did you test?

REAL PROBLEM 9-2 Configuring Email on a Mobile Device

For this project, use your own Android device or an emulated Android device. If you've not already set up Android Studio's phone emulator, complete Real Problem 9-1 before completing this project. You'll need a legitimate email account for this project. If you don't already have one you can use, you can create a free email account using *mail.google.com*, *outlook.live.com*, or *mail.yahoo.com*.

Follow these steps to manually configure the email client on a mobile device:

1. Open the **Gmail** app and then tap **Add another email address**. Gmail can automatically configure email from many providers. Because it's essential that you know how to manually configure email on a mobile device, tap **Other**.

2. Add your email address and tap **MANUAL SETUP**. Check with your email provider to determine whether to use POP3 or IMAP. What's the main difference between these two protocols? What are the ports for these two protocols? What are the secure ports for these protocols?

3. Enter the password, check **Keep me signed in**, and tap **Sign in**. On the next screen, tap **Yes** to agree to the needed permissions.

4. Add the incoming server settings for your email provider, or check the server suggested by the Gmail app. Which incoming email server are you required to use? When you're ready, tap **NEXT**.

5. Add the outgoing server settings for your email provider, or check the server suggested by the Gmail app. Which outgoing email server are you required to use? When you're ready, tap **NEXT**.

6. Set your account options as desired, then tap **NEXT**.

7. If you were successful, you'll get a notice confirming your account is set up. Set the account name and your name as desired, then tap **NEXT**. If you weren't successful, backtrack and troubleshoot to solve the problem.

8. When you're finished, send an email to a classmate, and check an email sent from someone else to confirm your email account is working on your smartphone.

9. You need to know how to change the settings on an account. What steps are required to change the server settings for the account you just added?

10. You should also know how to remove an email account from a mobile device. What steps are required to remove the email account you just added?

Virtualization, Cloud Computing, and Printers

After completing this chapter, you will be able to:

- Implement and configure virtual machines and hypervisors
- Support cloud computing services on a network
- Discuss printer types and features
- Install and share printers and manage printer features, add-on devices, and the printer queue
- Perform routine maintenance tasks necessary to support printers
- Troubleshoot printer problems

Continuing our exploration of network infrastructure and its resources, this chapter begins with coverage of virtualization and cloud computing. Infrastructure and resources on a network can be virtualized on a single machine, reducing hardware costs. Other resources can be outsourced to third-party providers over the Internet, reducing costs even further. The chapter then explores in depth the most popular types of network printers and how to support them. As you work through the chapter, you learn about printer types and features, how to install a local or network printer, and how to share a printer with others on a network. You learn how to manage printer features, add-on devices, shared printers, and print jobs. Finally, you learn about maintaining and troubleshooting printers.

CLIENT-SIDE VIRTUALIZATION

A+
CORE 1
3.8, 4.1,
4.2

Virtualization in computing is when one physical machine hosts multiple activities that are normally done on multiple machines. Two types of virtualization are:

▲ *Application virtualization*. One computer can serve up multiple applications such as web servers, email servers, file servers, and desktop applications such as Microsoft Office and Adobe Acrobat. Later in the chapter you learn more about application virtualization.

▲ *Desktop virtualization*. Desktop virtualization, also called client-side virtualization, client virtualization, and client-side desktop virtualization, is when one computer provides multiple desktops for users. Each virtual desktop is contained in its own virtual machine.

With desktop virtualization, software called a hypervisor creates and manages virtual machines (VMs). Each VM managed by a hypervisor has its own virtual hardware (virtual motherboard, processor, RAM, hard drive, NIC, and so forth) and acts like a physical computer. After an OS is installed in a VM, applications can be installed.

Figure 10-1 shows a Windows 10 Professional desktop with two virtual machines running that were created by Oracle VirtualBox, which is hypervisor software. One VM is running Windows 10 and the other VM is running Ubuntu Desktop, which is a Linux OS. You'll learn about Linux in Chapter 18.

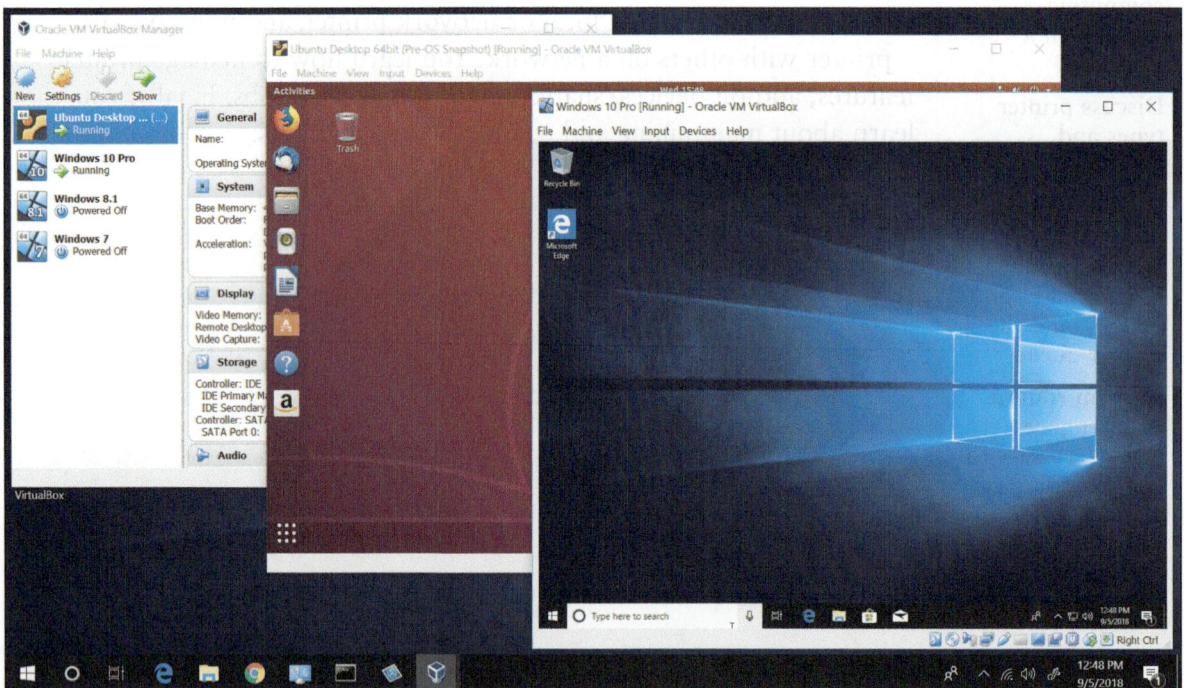

Source: Oracle Corporation and Canonical Group Limited

Figure 10-1 Two virtual machines running on a Windows 10 host, each with its own virtual hardware and OS (Windows 10 and Ubuntu Linux)

TYPE 1 AND TYPE 2 HYPERVISORS

A+
CORE 1
4.2

Hypervisor software can be a Type 1 or Type 2 hypervisor, the main difference being whether the host computer has its own OS. The differences are diagrammed in Figure 10-2.

Figure 10-2 Type 1 and Type 2 hypervisors

Here is an explanation of the two types of hypervisors:

◢ A Type 1 hypervisor installs on a computer before any operating system, and is therefore called a bare-metal hypervisor. After it installs, it partitions the hardware computing power into multiple VMs. A different OS can be installed in each VM. Examples of Type 1 hypervisors are the open-source XenServer by Citrix (*xenserver.org*), KVM by Red Hat (*redhat.com*), the free ESXi by VMware (*vmware.com*), and Microsoft's Hyper-V (*microsoft.com*), which is embedded in Windows Server. When a server provides virtual desktops or VMs to multiple users over the local network or the cloud, this is called remote or server-hosted desktop virtualization. For server-hosted desktops, most likely the hypervisor used is a Type 1 hypervisor.

◢ A Type 2 hypervisor installs in a host operating system as an application and is sometimes called a hosted hypervisor. Examples of Type 2 hypervisors include VMware Workstation or Player (*vmware.com*), Windows Client Hyper-V by Microsoft (*microsoft.com*), and Oracle VirtualBox (*virtualbox.org*). A Type 2 hypervisor is not as powerful as a Type 1 hypervisor because it is dependent on the host OS to allot its computing power. A VM in a Type 2 hypervisor is not as secure or as fast as a VM in a Type 1 hypervisor. When a workstation is used to host a hypervisor with its VMs, this is called local or client-hosted desktop virtualization. For the most part, client-hosted desktops are provided by a Type 2 hypervisor.

Here are some ways that client-hosted VMs created by Type 2 hypervisors might be used:

◢ Developers often use VMs to test applications. If you save a copy of a virtual hard drive (VHD) that has a fresh installation of Windows, you can easily build a new VM to test an application.

◢ Help-desk technicians use VMs so they can easily switch from one OS to another when a user asks for help with a particular OS.

◢ Honeypots are single computers or a network of computers that lure hackers to protect the real network. Virtual machines can give the impression to a hacker that he has found a computer or an entire network of computers. Administrators can monitor the honeypot for unauthorized activity.

◢ Students use VMs to install and practice using and supporting different operating systems.

SETTING UP CLIENT-SIDE VIRTUALIZATION

As an IT support technician, you might be called on to set up client-side virtualization on a workstation to host multiple VMs. The first step is to make sure the workstation can support the hypervisor and VMs.

CUSTOMIZE A VIRTUALIZATION WORKSTATION

Here are the requirements for a workstation that will host multiple virtual machines:

◢ *Maximum CPU cores*. Each VM has its own virtual processor, so it's important that the host's processor is a multicore processor. All dual-core or higher processors sold today support hardware-assisted virtualization (HAV), which is a technology that enhances the processor support for virtual machines.

For Intel processors, this feature is called Intel VT. For AMD processors, the technology is called AMD-V.

▲ *The motherboard BIOS/UEFI*. Most of today's motherboards support HAV, and it must be enabled in BIOS/UEFI setup. Figure 10-3 shows the UEFI setup screen for one motherboard where the HAV feature is called Intel Virtualization Technology. When you enable the feature, also verify that all subcategories are enabled under the main category for hardware virtualization.

Source: American Megatrends, Inc.

Figure 10-3 A UEFI setup screen to enable hardware virtualization

▲ *Maximum RAM*. Some hypervisors are designed so that each VM that is running ties up all the RAM assigned to it. Therefore, you need extra amounts of RAM when a computer is running several VMs. Other hypervisors allow a VM to tie up only the RAM it is using, which is called dynamic allocation of memory.

▲ *Lots of storage space*. Each VM has its own virtual hard drive (VHD), which is a file stored on the physical hard drive that acts like an independent hard drive, complete with its own boot sectors and file systems. You can configure this VHD to be a fixed size or dynamically expanding. The fixed size takes up hard drive space whether the VM uses the space or not. A dynamically allocated VHD increases in capacity as the VM uses the space. Each VM must have an operating system installed, which takes about 20 GB for a Windows 10/8/7 installation. In addition, each application installed in a VM requires storage space. Make sure you have adequate storage space for all the VMs the customer plans to create. See the requirements provided by the hypervisor manufacturer for additional recommendations.

▲ *Network requirements*. If multiple VMs on the workstation will be running at the same time, you'll need a fast network connection; make sure the NIC supports Gigabit Ethernet. Later, when you set up the workstation, it might require a static IP address so that others on the network can reach the VMs. Also consider using two NICs in the workstation: The hypervisor can run all the VMs through one NIC that has the static IP address assignment and the other NIC is used for other network activity on the workstation. Some network administrators may also choose to set up the VMs in their own VLAN.

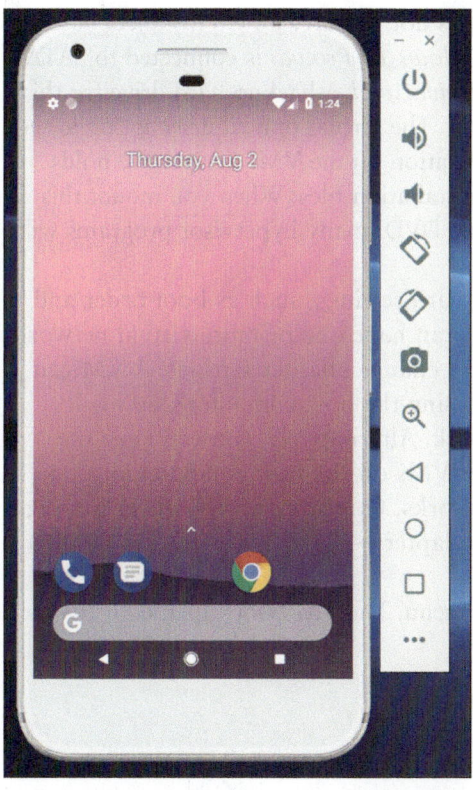

Figure 10-4 Android Studio emulates a Google Pixel XL phone running Android Oreo

Source: Android

▲ *Emulator requirements.* Some hypervisors can emulate hardware devices and present this virtual hardware to each VM. For example, in Chapter 9, you learned how to use the hypervisor included in Android Studio to run an Android device emulator (see Figure 10-4). The emulator not only includes the Android OS and applications, it also emulates the hardware of a smartphone, tablet, or other mobile devices. Emulators might include a virtual processor, memory, motherboard, hard drive, optical drive, keyboard, mouse, monitor, network adapter, SD card, USB device, smartphone, printer, hardware buttons, and other components and peripherals. Research the hypervisor software to find out the system requirements for emulators the hypervisor can create and make sure the workstation can support the emulator system requirements.

When deciding how to use the overall budget for a virtualization workstation, prioritize the number of CPU cores and the amount of installed RAM.

INSTALL AND CONFIGURE A TYPE 2 HYPERVISOR

A hypervisor offers a way to configure each VM, including which virtual hardware is installed. For example, when you launch **Oracle VirtualBox**, the VirtualBox Manager window shown on the left side of Figure 10-5 appears. To create a new VM, click **New** in the upper-left corner and follow the directions on screen. To change the configuration of a VM, select the VM in the left pane and click **Settings**. The Settings box appears. Click the **Storage** menu, shown on the right side of Figure 10-5, to install and uninstall virtual hard drives and optical drives in the VM.

Two hard drives and an optical drive

Mounted .iso file

Figure 10-5 Emulated (virtual) hard drives and an optical drive are installed in a VM on VirtualBox

Source: Oracle VirtualBox

Notice in the Settings box in Figure 10-5 that this VM, which does not yet have an OS installed, has two hard drives and an optical drive. The virtual hard drive named *Windows 10 Pro.vdi* is connected to SATA port 0 and will contain the Windows 10 installation. *VirtualHardDrive1.vhd*, a backup hard drive for this VM, is the same size (50 GB) and is connected through SATA port 1. The virtual optical drive is connected to SATA port 2 and holds the Windows 10 ISO file, ready for installation on the VM. An ISO file holds the image of a CD or DVD and can be used to provide Windows installation files. When you mount this file to the VM, you can install Windows in the VM from this virtual DVD; many hypervisor programs will perform this step for you during setup of a new VM.

Click the **System** menu (see Figure 10-6) to configure motherboard settings, such as boot order and memory. Also consider network requirements for the VM. A VM can have one or more virtual network adapters, called a virtual NIC. Click **Network** (see Figure 10-7) to change adapter settings. A VM can connect to a local network in the same way as other computers using the host computer's network interface, and it can share and use shared resources on the network. Alternatively, you can keep the VM isolated from the physical network while connected to other VMs on the host computer, or you can keep it completely isolated from all physical and virtual networks. On the right side of the Settings box, you can control the number and type of installed network adapters—up to four adapters for this hypervisor.

To boot up a VM, select it in the left pane and click **Start** in the menu. The VM boots up and works the same way as a physical computer.

Source: Oracle VirtualBox

Figure 10-6 Configure motherboard settings in the VM to change the boot order

Figure 10-7 Configure up to four network adapters for a VM in Oracle VirtualBox

Source: Oracle VirtualBox

SECURING A VIRTUAL MACHINE

A virtual machine is susceptible to hackers and malware just like a physical machine. When supporting a VM that holds sensitive data and has network and Internet connectivity or is located in a public area, keep these points in mind for securing VM resources:

▲ *Secure the VM within the VM*. Using the OS installed in the VM, follow all the security measures you are learning throughout this text. For example, be sure to configure the OS firewall in the VM, keep updates current, install and run anti-malware software, require passwords for all user accounts in the VM, and encrypt data folders.

▲ *VMs should be isolated for best security*. One major advantage of using VMs on a workstation is that a VM on one workstation is better isolated from a VM on another because the workstations provide an extra layer of protection. Also, the host workstation for VMs should not be used for web surfing or other activities that might compromise its VMs. If a workstation has more than one NIC, a VM that should be kept especially secure can be isolated by dedicating a NIC solely to this VM and putting this NIC on its own subnet.

▲ *Secure the files that hold a VM*. You can move a VM from one computer to another by moving the files that contain the VM. Be sure these files that hold the VM are secured with permissions that allow access only to specific local or network users and apply file encryption to the files.

▲ *Secure the host computer*. Protect your VMs by applying security measures to protect the host computer that holds the VMs. For example, run anti-malware, keep Windows updated, require password authentication to sign in to the host computer, harden the host computer's firewall, and isolate it on the network in a protected subnet.

> ★ **A+ Exam Tip** The A+ Core 1 exam might give you a scenario that requires you to secure a virtual machine installed on a host computer.

CLOUD COMPUTING

In Chapter 8, you learned about server resources available on a network, and in this chapter, you've learned some ways to virtualize network resources. Not all of a network's resources reside on the local network. Cloud computing is when a vendor or corporation makes computing resources available over the Internet. In Chapter 9 you learned about Google Drive, iCloud Drive, Dropbox, and OneDrive, which are examples of cloud file storage services where you can store your files in the cloud. These services work with synchronization apps on mobile devices and computers to sync data and settings to cloud storage accounts such as Google Cloud and iCloud and between devices. Cloud computing can also provide many other types of services and resources, including applications, network services, websites, database servers, specialized developer applications, and virtual desktops in VMs.

The current trend for both small and large businesses is to use cloud computing rather than local computing resources to expand current and future computing needs. As an IT technician, you need to understand how cloud computing works and how to support it.

DEPLOYMENT MODELS FOR CLOUD COMPUTING

Cloud computing services are delivered by a variety of deployment models, depending on who manages the cloud and who has access to it. The main deployment models you are likely to encounter are:

▲ *Public cloud*. In a public cloud, services are provided over the Internet to the general public. Google or Yahoo! email services are examples of public cloud deployment.

▲ *Private cloud*. In a private cloud, services are established on an organization's own servers or established virtually for a single organization's private use. For example, an insurance company might have a centralized data center that provides private cloud services to its branch offices throughout the United States. A corporation might provide access to its email servers for employees working remotely using a browser or an off-site email application such as Outlook.

▲ *Community cloud*. In a community cloud, services are shared between multiple organizations with a common interest, but the services are not available publicly. For example, a medical database might be shared among all hospitals in a geographic area or government agencies might share regulatory requirements. In these cases, the community cloud could be hosted internally by one or more of the organizations involved, or hosted externally by a third-party provider.

▲ *Hybrid cloud*. A hybrid cloud is a combination of public, private, and community clouds used by the same organization. For example, a company might store inventory databases in a private cloud but use a public cloud email service.

ELEMENTS OF CLOUD COMPUTING

Regardless of the service provided, all cloud computing service models incorporate the following elements:

▲ *Service at any time*. On-demand service is available to users at any time. Cloud computing vendors often advertise uptime of their services, which is the percentage of time in any given year when their services are available online without disruption. Downtimes are minimized to a number of hours or even minutes per year.

▲ *Elastic services and storage*. Rapid elasticity refers to the service's ability to be scaled up or down as the need level changes for a particular customer without requiring hardware changes that could be costly for the customer. Layers of services, such as applications, storage space, or number of users, can be added or removed when requested. Services can also be adjusted automatically, depending on the options made available by the service vendor.

▲ *Support for multiple client platforms*. Platform refers to the operating system, the runtime libraries or modules the OS provides to applications, and the hardware on which the OS runs. Cloud resources are made available to clients through standardized access methods that can be used with a variety of platforms, such as Windows, Linux, or macOS, on any number of devices, such as desktops, laptops, tablets, and smartphones from various manufacturers.

▲ *Resource pooling and consolidation*. With resource pooling, services to multiple customers are hosted on shared physical resources, which are dynamically allocated to meet customer demand. Customers generally don't know the geographical location of the physical devices providing cloud services, which is called location independence.

▲ *Measured service*. Resources offered by a cloud computing vendor, such as storage, applications, bandwidth, and other services, are measured, or metered, for billing purposes and/or for the purpose of limiting any particular customer's use of that resource according to the service agreement. These measured services have reporting policies in place to ensure transparency between vendors and customers.

CLOUD COMPUTING SERVICE MODELS

**A+
CORE 1
2.2, 4.1**

Cloud computing service models are categorized by the types of services they provide. The National Institute of Standards and Technology (NIST) has developed a standard definition for each category, which varies by the division of labor implemented. For example, as shown on the left side of Figure 10-8, an organization is traditionally responsible for its entire network, top to bottom. In this arrangement, the organization has its own network infrastructure devices, manages its own network services and data storage, and purchases licenses for its own operating systems and applications. The three cloud computing service models illustrated on the right side of Figure 10-8 incrementally increase the amount of management responsibilities outsourced to cloud computing vendors.

Figure 10-8 At each progressive level, the vendor takes over more computing responsibility for the customer

The following list describes these service models:

▲ *IaaS*. With IaaS (Infrastructure as a Service), the customer rents hardware, including servers, storage, and networking, and can use these hardware services virtually. Customers are responsible for their own application installations, data management, and backup. In most situations, customers are also responsible for their own operating systems. For example, customers might rent several VMs and use them for servers by installing an OS in each VM and hosting applications such as web servers, email servers, DNS servers, or DHCP services, or by hosting productivity software such as Microsoft Office for employees. IaaS is ideal for fast-changing applications, to test software, or for startup businesses looking to save money by not having to invest in hardware. Examples of IaaS providers are Amazon Web Services (*aws.amazon.com*), Windows Azure (*azure.microsoft.com*), and Google Compute Engine (*cloud.google.com*).

> **Notes** A good example of an IaaS product is a **cloud-based network controller**, which provides remote management of network resources over a WAN connection. These network resources might include Wi-Fi access points, network servers, network routers, switches, and firewalls, and these resources might be located on-site or in the cloud at a third-party service provider's data center. All of these resources can be controlled through a browser interface from anywhere with an Internet connection. For example, while traveling for a conference, a network admin using a product such as CloudTrax (*cloudtrax.com*) can manage wireless mesh network configuration issues back at the office simply by signing into his network controller dashboard through a browser.

▲ *PaaS*. With PaaS (Platform as a Service), a customer rents hardware, operating systems, and some applications that might support other applications the customer may install. PaaS is popular with software developers who require access to multiple platforms during the development process. A developer can build and test an application on a PaaS virtual machine made available over the web, and then throw out the machine and start over with a new one with a few clicks in his browser window. Applications that a PaaS vendor might provide to a developer are tailored to the specific needs of the project, such as an application to manage a database of test data. Examples of PaaS services include Google Cloud Platform and Microsoft Azure.

▲ *SaaS*. With SaaS (Software as a Service), customers use applications hosted on the service provider's hardware and operating systems, and typically access the applications through a web browser. Applications are provided through an online user interface and are compatible with a multitude of devices and operating systems. Online email services, such as Gmail and Yahoo!, are good examples of SaaS. Google offers an entire suite of virtual software applications through Google Cloud and their other embedded products. Except for the interface itself (the device and whatever browser software is required to access the website), the vendor provides every level of support from network infrastructure through data storage and application implementation.

▲ *XaaS (Anything as a Service or Everything as a Service)*. In the XaaS model, the "X" represents an unknown, just as it does in algebra. Here, the cloud can provide any combination of functions depending on a customer's exact needs. The XaaS model is not shown in Figure 10-8.

APPLICATION VIRTUALIZATION

A+
CORE 1
4.1

Using application virtualization, an application is made available to users by a virtualization server and does not need to be installed on the user's computer. For laptops and desktops, especially in an enterprise environment, this means ready access to many more applications than can reasonably be installed on a computer, freeing up more of its storage space, and personalizing apps to the needs of many users without having to manage tedious customizations.

Here are two options for application virtualization:

▲ *Cloud-based applications*. With cloud-based applications, which is a form of SaaS, the software resides on a server in the cloud and the user accesses the software through a browser. For example, many companies are moving toward rentable software or software by subscription, such as with Adobe and Microsoft. When you buy an annual subscription to Office 365, you might access the software through a browser, and you might install the software on your own computer. This particular service also includes built-in data storage, if desired by the user, by connecting the licensed account with OneDrive, a virtual data storage service.

▲ *Application streaming*. Application streaming is a cross between cloud-based applications, where the application is never installed on the local computer and runs only in the cloud, and installed applications, which is the traditional method of installing an app for use on the local device. With application streaming, parts of the application are downloaded, at least temporarily, on the local device only when needed; other parts of the application might continue to run in the cloud from a distant server. The application is never fully installed on the local device—only the pieces of the application that the user currently needs, and those pieces stay on the device only while they're being used.

A good example of application streaming is Android's Instant Apps, which allows a user to tap an app in Google Play and try the app without first having to install it (see Figure 10-9). If you turn on the Instant Apps feature in Android and then open your browser, you can search for and run an instant app right in your browser. This works great for an app you want to use temporarily but don't want to install.

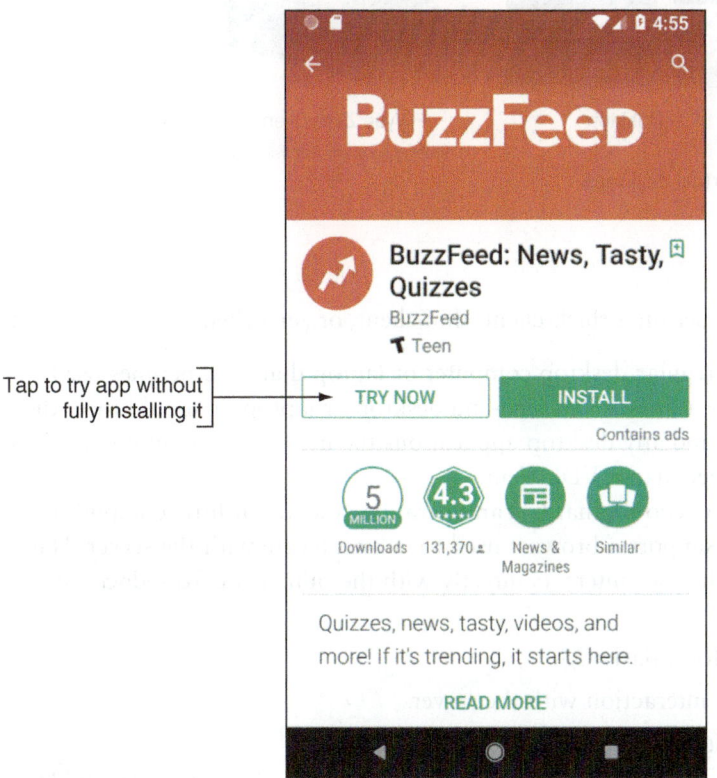

Tap to try app without fully installing it

Source: Android and BuzzFeed, Inc.

Figure 10-9 Give an app a test drive without having to install it

SETTING UP CLIENT COMPUTERS TO USE CLOUD RESOURCES

A+
CORE 1
3.8, 3.9

With the trend of providing more virtual desktops and applications in the cloud, fewer resources need to be devoted to high-end workstations required to support installed applications. When a hypervisor on a server in the cloud presents a virtual desktop to a client computer, the technology is called Virtual Desktop Infrastructure (VDI). See Figure 10-10. In this part of the chapter, you learn how to configure a client computer to use a virtual desktop.

Figure 10-10   Using VDI, a hypervisor serves up virtual desktops

THICK CLIENT AND THIN CLIENT

The VDI virtual desktop is presented to the user on a thick client, thin client, or zero client:

▲ A *thick client*, also called a fat client, is a regular desktop computer or laptop that is sometimes used as a client by a hypervisor server. It can be a low-end to high-end desktop or laptop. It should meet the recommended requirements to run its OS and any desktop applications the user might require when it is being used as a stand-alone computer rather than a VDI client.

▲ A *thin client* is a computer, such as a Chromebook, that has an operating system but little computing power of its own and might only need to support a browser used to communicate with the server. The server does most of the processing while the user interacts directly with the thin client. To reduce the cost of the computer, configure it to:

  ◢ Meet only the minimum requirements for a basic OS.

  ◢ Support basic applications required for interaction with the server.

  ◢ Support high-speed network connectivity.

▲ A *zero client*, also called a dumb terminal, such as the Wyse Zero Client by Dell, does not have an OS and is little more than an interface to the network with a keyboard, monitor, and mouse.

VDI VIRTUAL DESKTOP ACCOUNTS

Setting up a zero client requires special software provided by the VDI vendor. Setting up a thick client or thin client to receive a VDI virtual desktop is simple. First, know there are two approaches to VDI: The virtual desktop presented to the user is persistent or nonpersistent. The user's account determines which type of desktop the user receives:

▲ *Persistent VDI*. With persistent VDI, the user owns the virtual desktop, which can be customized for the user and saved for future use. Each time the user signs on, he picks up the desktop where it left off the last time he signed off.

▲ *Nonpersistent VDI*. With nonpersistent VDI, a user receives a desktop from a pool of desktops; each time the user signs on, she gets a desktop that reverts to its original state.

To access the virtual desktop, open a browser, go to the virtual desktop provider's website, and sign in with a user account and password.

PRINTER TYPES AND FEATURES

So far in this chapter, you've explored the basics of virtualization and cloud computing. These skills and concepts give you ways to customize and expand your network. When supporting a network, you'll also likely be expected to support printers on the network. So let's take a look at what that entails.

As an output device, a printer converts digital data to hard copy on paper. Some printers are also a multifunction input device that can work as a scanner to scan printed paper and print additional hard copies of that information or create a digital file from it. The file can then be saved on a computer or sent out over a phone or network connection. A scanner can also be a dedicated device with no printing, copying, or faxing capability. Scanners, whether dedicated devices or integrated in a printer, come in two primary types:

▲ **Flatbed scanners** must be fed one page at a time, with each page being lined up on a glass surface.
▲ **ADF (automatic document feeder) scanners** can automatically process a stack of papers, cards, or envelopes, pulling each page individually into a roller system for scanning and then spitting it out into a separate tray.

> 🖉 **Notes** For heavy business use, sometimes it's best to purchase a dedicated machine for each purpose instead of bundling many functions into a single machine. For example, if you need a scanner and a printer, purchase a good printer and a good scanner rather than a combo machine. Routine maintenance and troubleshooting are easier and less expensive on single-purpose machines, although the initial cost is higher. On the other hand, for home or small office use, a combo device can save money and counter space.

As for the output side of this process, the major categories of printer types include laser, inkjet (ink dispersion), impact, thermal, and 3D printers. In the following sections, we look at the different types of printers for desktop computing. Table 10-1 lists some popular printer manufacturers.

Printer Manufacturer	Website
Brother	*brother-usa.com*
Canon	*usa.canon.com*
Epson	*epson.com*
Hewlett-Packard	*hp.com*
Konica Minolta	*kmbs.konicaminolta.us*
Lexmark	*lexmark.com*
Oki Data	*okidata.com*
Xerox	*xerox.com*
Zebra Technologies	*zebra.com*

Table 10-1 Printer manufacturers

> ⭐ **A+ Exam Tip** The A+ Core 1 exam might give you a scenario that requires you to perform installation or maintenance steps on these types of printers: laser, inkjet, thermal, impact, and 3D printers. You also need to know about virtual printers.

LASER PRINTERS

A+
CORE 1
3.11

A **laser printer** is a type of electro-photographic printer that can range from a small, personal desktop model to a large network printer capable of handling and printing large volumes continuously. Figure 10-11 shows an example of a typical laser printer for a small office.

Laser printers require the interaction of mechanical, electrical, and optical technologies. They work by placing toner on an electrically charged rotating drum called the **imaging drum**, transferring the toner onto paper as the paper moves through the system, and then fusing the toner to the paper. Figure 10-12 shows the seven steps of laser printing.

Note that Figure 10-12 shows only a cross-section of the drum, mechanisms, and paper. Remember that the drum is as wide as a sheet of paper. The mirror, blades, and rollers in the drawing are also as wide as paper. Also know that toner responds to a charge and moves from one surface to another if the second surface has a more positive charge than the first.

Figure 10-11 A Samsung Xpress color multifunction laser printer

> ★ **A+ Exam Tip** The A+ Core 1 exam might give you a scenario that requires you to solve a problem using your knowledge of the seven steps of laser printing. Be sure you know the order of steps.

LASER PRINTING STEPS

The seven steps of laser printing are described next:

1. *Processing the image.* A laser printer processes and prints an entire page at one time. The page comes to the printer encoded in a language the printer understands, and the firmware inside the printer processes the incoming data to produce a bitmap (a bunch of bits in rows and columns) of the final page, which is stored in the printer's memory. One bitmap image is produced for monochrome images. For color images, one bitmap is produced for each of four colors. (The colors are blue, red, yellow, and black, better known as cyan, magenta, yellow, and black, and sometimes written as CMYK.)

Figure 10-12 The seven progressive steps of laser printing

2. *Charging or conditioning.* During charging, the drum is conditioned by a roller that places a high uniform electrical charge of -600 V to -1000 V on the surface of the drum. The roller is called the primary charging roller or primary corona, which is charged by a high-voltage power supply assembly. For some printers, a corona wire is used instead of the charging roller to charge the drum.

3. *Exposing or writing.* A laser beam controlled by motors and a mirror scans across the drum until it completes the correct number of passes. The laser beam is turned on and off continually as it makes a single pass down the length of the drum, once for each raster line, so that dots are exposed only where toner should go to print the image. For example, for a 1200 dots per inch (dpi) printer, the beam makes 1200 passes for every inch of the drum circumference. This means that 1200 dots are exposed or not exposed along the drum for every inch of linear pass. The 1200 dots per inch down this single pass, combined with 1200 passes per inch of drum circumference, accomplish the resolution of 1200 × 1200 dots per square inch of many laser printers. For each exposed dot, the laser beam applies a charge of -100 V, which is significantly more positive than for the unexposed dots on the drum. The charge on this image area will be used in the developing stage to transmit toner to the drum surface.

4. *Developing.* The developing cylinder applies toner to the surface of the drum. The toner is charged between -200 V and -500 V, and sticks to the developing cylinder because of a magnet inside it. A control blade prevents too much toner from sticking to the cylinder surface. As the cylinder rotates very close to the drum, the toner is attracted to the parts of the drum surface that have a -100 V charge and is repelled from the more negatively charged parts of the drum surface. The result is that toner sticks to the drum where the laser beam has hit and is repelled from the areas where the laser beam has not hit.

5. *Transferring.* During transfer, a strong electrical charge draws the toner off the drum onto the paper. This is the first step that takes place outside the cartridge and the first step that involves the paper. The soft, black transfer roller puts a positive charge on the paper to pull the toner from the drum onto the paper. Then the static charge eliminator weakens the charges on both the paper and the drum so that the paper does not stick to the drum. The stiffness of the paper and the small radius of the drum also help the paper move away from the drum and toward the fusing assembly. Very thin paper can wrap around the drum, which is why printer manuals usually instruct you to use only paper designated for laser printers.

6. *Fusing.* The fuser assembly uses heat and pressure to fuse the toner to the paper. Up to this point, the toner is merely sitting on the paper. The fusing rollers apply heat to the paper, which causes the toner to melt, and the rollers apply pressure to bond the melted toner into the paper. The temperature of the rollers is monitored by the printer. If the temperature exceeds an allowed maximum value (for example, 410 degrees F), the printer shuts down.

7. *Cleaning.* A sweeping blade cleans the drum of any residual toner. The charge left on the drum is then neutralized. Some printers use erase lamps in the top cover of the printer for this purpose. The lamps use red light so they won't damage the photosensitive drum.

For color laser printers, the writing process repeats four times, one for each toner color of cyan, magenta, yellow, and black. Each color might require a separate image drum, although many color printers can use the same drum for all four colors. Then, the paper passes to the fusing stage, where the fuser bonds all toner to the paper and aids in blending the four tones to form specific colors.

⭐ **A+ Exam Tip** The A+ Core 1 exam expects you to know these laser printer terms: imaging drum, fuser assembly, transfer belt, transfer roller, pickup roller, separate pads, and duplexing assembly.

CARTRIDGES AND OTHER REPLACEABLE PARTS

The charging, exposing, developing, and cleaning steps use the printer components that undergo the most wear. To make the printer last longer, some or all of these steps are done inside a removable cartridge that can be replaced as a single unit. For older printers, all four steps are done inside one cartridge. For newer printers, the cleaning, charging, and exposing steps are done inside the image drum cartridge. The developing cylinder is located inside the toner cartridge. The transferring is done using a transfer belt that can be replaced on some printers, and the fusing is done inside a fuser cartridge, which also might be replaceable.

By using these multiple cartridges inside laser printers, the cost of maintaining a printer is reduced. You can replace one cartridge without having to replace them all. The toner cartridge needs replacing the most often, followed by the image drum, the fuser cartridge, and the transfer assembly, in that order.

Other printer parts that might need replacing include the pickup roller that pushes a sheet of paper forward from the paper tray and the separation pad (also called a separate pad) that keeps more than one sheet of paper from moving forward. If the pickup roller is worn, paper misfeeds into the printer. If the separation pad is worn, multiple sheets of paper will be drawn into the printer. Sometimes you can clean a pickup roller or separation pad to prolong its life before it needs replacing.

> 📝 **Notes** Before replacing expensive parts in a printer, consider whether a new printer might be more cost effective than repairing the old one.

DUPLEXING ASSEMBLY

A printer that is able to print on both sides of the paper is called a duplex printer or a double-sided printer. Many laser printers and a few inkjet printers offer this feature. After the front of the paper is printed, a duplexing assembly, which contains several rollers, turns the paper around and draws it back through the print process to print on the back of the paper. Alternately, some high-end printers have two print engines so that both sides of the paper are printed at the same time.

Figure 10-13 An example of an inkjet printer with feeder trays open

INKJET PRINTERS

A+
CORE 1
3.11

An inkjet printer (see Figure 10-13) uses a type of ink-dispersion printing and doesn't normally provide the high-quality resolution of laser printers. Inkjet printers are popular because they are small and can print color inexpensively. Most inkjet printers today can print high-quality photos, especially when used with photo-quality paper.

An inkjet printer uses a print head that moves across the paper, creating one line of the image with each pass. The printer puts ink on the paper using a matrix of small dots. Different types of inkjet printers form their droplets of ink in different ways. Printer manufacturers use several technologies, one of which is the bubble-jet. Bubble-jet printers use tubes of ink that have tiny resistors near the end of each tube. These resistors heat up and cause the ink to boil. Then a tiny air bubble of ionized ink (ink with an electrical charge) is ejected onto the paper. A typical bubble-jet print head has 64 or 128 tiny nozzles, all of which can fire a droplet simultaneously. (High-end printers can have as many as 3000 nozzles.) Plates carrying a magnetic charge direct the path of ink onto the paper to form shapes.

Inkjet printers include one or more ink cartridges to hold the different colors of ink for the printer. Figure 10-14 shows four ink cartridges. A black cartridge is on the left and the three color cartridges are cyan, yellow, and magenta. For this printer, a print head is built into each ink cartridge.

Figure 10-14 The ink cartridges of an inkjet printer

A stepper motor moves the print head and ink cartridges across the paper using a carriage and belt to move the assembly and stabilizing bars to control the movement (see Figure 10-15). A paper tray can hold a stack of paper, or a paper feeder on the back of the printer can hold a few sheets of paper. The sheets stand up in the feeder and are dispensed one at a time. Rollers pull a single sheet into the printer from the paper tray or paper feeder. A motor powers these rollers and times the sheet going through the printer in the increments needed to print the image. When the printer is not in use, the assemblage sits in the far-right position, which is called the home position or parked position. This position helps protect the ink in the cartridges from drying out. Figure 10-15 shows the assemblage positioned so that the ink cartridges are accessible for replacement.

Figure 10-15 The belt and stabilizing bars used to move the print head across the page

Some inkjet printers offer duplex printing. These printers are larger than normal inkjet printers because of the added space required for the duplexing assembly. For duplex printing, be sure to use heavy paper (rated at 24-pound paper or higher) so the ink doesn't bleed through.

Even with single-sided printing, inkjet printers tend to smudge on inexpensive paper, and they are slower than laser printers. If a printed page later becomes damp, the ink can run and get quite messy. The quality of the paper used with inkjet printers significantly affects the quality of printed output. You should use only paper that is designed for an inkjet printer, and you should use a high-grade paper to get the best results.

> **✎ Notes** Weight and brightness are the two primary ways of measuring paper quality. The rated weight of paper (for example, 20 pounds to 32 pounds) determines the thickness of the paper. Brightness is measured on a scale of 92 to 100.

> **✎ Notes** Photos printed on an inkjet printer tend to fade over time, more so than photos produced professionally. To make your photos last longer, use high-quality photo paper (rated at high gloss or studio gloss) and use fade-resistant ink (such as Vivera ink by HP). Then protect these photos from exposure to light, heat, humidity, and polluted air. To best protect photos made by an inkjet printer, keep them in a photo album rather than displayed and exposed to light.

When purchasing an inkjet printer, look for the kind that uses two or four separate cartridges. One cartridge is used for black ink. Three cartridges, one for each color, give better-quality color than one cartridge that holds all three colors. Some low-end inkjet printers use a single three-color cartridge and don't have a black ink cartridge. These printers must combine all colors of ink to produce a dull black. Having a separate cartridge for black ink means that it prints true black and, more important, does not use the more expensive colored ink for black print. To save money, you should be able to replace an empty cartridge without having to replace all cartridges.

> **✎ Notes** It's possible to refill an ink cartridge, and many companies will sell you the tools and ink you need as well as show you how to do it. You can also purchase refilled cartridges at reduced prices. When you purchase ink cartridges, make sure you know if they are new or refilled. Also, for best results, don't refill a cartridge more than three times. Many manufacturers and retail shops will accept empty cartridges for recycling.

IMPACT PRINTERS

An impact printer creates a printed page by using some mechanism that touches or hits the paper. The best-known impact printer is a dot matrix printer, which prints only text that it receives as raw data. It has a print head that moves across the width of the paper, using pins to print a matrix of dots on the page. The pins shoot against a cloth ribbon, which hits the paper, depositing the ink. The ribbon provides both the ink for printing and the lubrication for the pinheads. The quality of the print is poor compared with other printer types. However, you still see impact printers in use for three reasons:

▲ They use continuous tractor feeds and fanfold paper (also called computer paper) rather than individual sheets of paper, making them useful for logging ongoing events or data.
▲ They can use carbon paper to print multiple copies at the same time.
▲ They are extremely durable, give little trouble, and seem to last forever.

> **★ A+ Exam Tip** The A+ Core 1 exam might give you a scenario that requires you to install or maintain an impact printer's print head, ribbon, and tractor feed, or to work with the impact paper used in the printer.

Maintaining a dot matrix impact printer is easy. The impact paper used by these printers comes as a box of fanfold paper or in rolls (used with receipt printers). When the paper is nearing the end of the stack or roll, a color on the edge alerts you to replace the paper. Occasionally, you should replace the ribbon of a dot matrix printer. If the print head fails, check on the cost of replacing the head versus the cost of buying a new printer. Sometimes, the cost of the head is so high that it's best to just buy a new printer. Overheating can damage a print head (see Figure 10-16), so keep it as cool as possible to make it last longer. Keep the printer in a cool, well-ventilated area, and don't use it to print more than 50 to 75 pages without allowing the head to cool down.

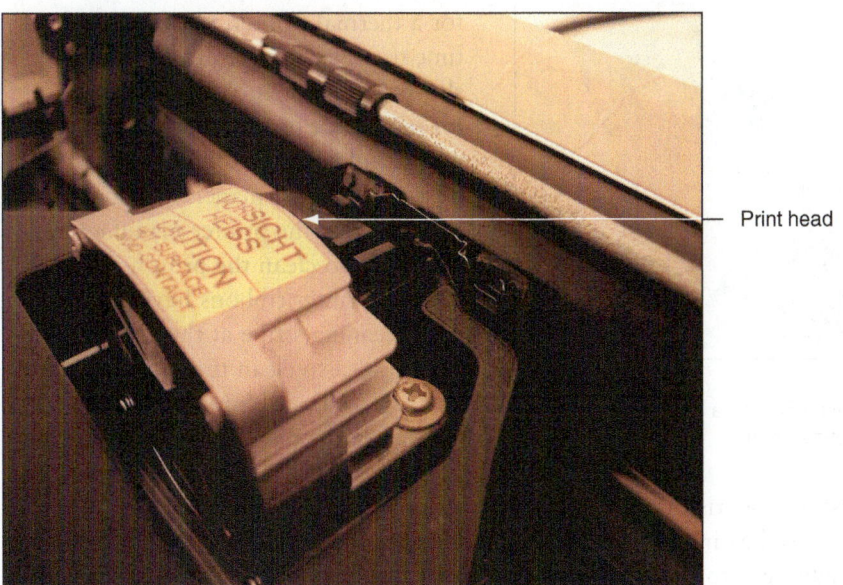

Print head

10

Figure 10-16 Keep the print head of a dot matrix printer as cool as possible so that it will last longer

Courtesy of EPSON America, Inc.

Figure 10-17 The TM-T88V direct thermal printer by EPSON

A+
CORE 1
3.11

THERMAL PRINTERS

Thermal printers use heat to create an image. Two types of thermal printers are a direct thermal printer and a thermal transfer printer. The older direct thermal printer burns dots onto specially coated paper called thermal paper; this process was used by older fax machines. The process requires no ink and does not use a ribbon. Direct thermal printers are often used as receipt printers that use rolls of thermal paper (see Figure 10-17). The printed image can fade over time or if it interacts with another heat source or ultraviolet light.

A thermal transfer printer uses a ribbon that contains wax-based ink. The heating element melts the ribbon (also called foil) onto special thermal paper so that it stays glued to the paper as the feed assembly moves it through the printer. Thermal

Courtesy of Zebra Technologies

Figure 10-18 The GC420 printer by Zebra is both a thermal transfer printer and a direct thermal printer

transfer printers are used to print receipts, barcode labels, clothing labels, or container labels. Figure 10-18 shows a thermal transfer printer used to make barcodes and other labels.

Thermal printers are reliable and easy to maintain. When you are responsible for a thermal printer, you know it's time to replace the paper roll when it shows a color strip down one edge. It's important to regularly clean the print head because buildup can harden over time and permanently damage the head. Follow the printer manufacturer's directions to clean the print head. Some thermal printer ribbons have a print head cleaning stripe at the end, and it's a good idea to clean the head each time you replace the ribbon. Additionally, some manufacturers suggest cleaning the head with isopropyl alcohol wipes.

When cleaning, remove any dust and debris that get down in the print head assembly. As you work, ground yourself to protect the sensitive heating element against static electricity. Don't touch the heating element with your fingers. You might need to clean it with a lint-free cotton swab dabbed in isopropyl alcohol. Also, to prolong the life of the print head, use the lowest heat setting for the heating element that still gives good printing results.

> ⭐ **A+ Exam Tip** The A+ Core 1 exam might give you a scenario that requires you to install or maintain the feed assembly or heating element used in thermal printers, or you might need to work with the special thermal paper used in the older direct thermal printers.

3D PRINTERS

 While impact printers and thermal printers have been around for a very long time, a new type of printer is the 3D printer. 3D printers use a plastic filament to build a 3D model of a digital image. In Figure 10-19, notice the coil of plastic filament on the left that is fed into the 3D printer, which heats the plastic and deposits thin layer upon layer to build three-dimensional objects.

When setting up a 3D printer, make sure the printer is level. When you're ready to print, you can buy

Source: iStock.com/izusek

Figure 10-19 A 3D printer heats a plastic filament and layers the plastic to build three-dimensional objects premade images online. If you want to design your own images, you'll need a 3D modeling program. Some of these are free and simple to learn, such as Sketchup (*sketchup.com*) and Tinkercad (*tinkercad.com*). Others require a much steeper learning curve and a higher price in exchange for more features. As discussed in Chapter 6, any computer used for 3D imaging and design will perform more quickly and gracefully with more RAM and CPU power. Before you start printing, do some research online for tips on getting a cleaner finished product. YouTube has several informative videos by 3D Printing Nerd (*the3dprintingnerd.com*), Matter Hackers (*matterhackers.com*), and others.

Now let's turn our attention to using Windows to install, share, and manage printers.

USING WINDOWS TO INSTALL, SHARE, AND MANAGE PRINTERS

**A+
CORE 1
3.10, 3.11**

In this part of the chapter, you learn to install local and network printers, share an installed printer, and remotely use a shared printer. You also learn about virtual printing and cloud printing, and how to configure printer add-ons and features. We begin with local and network printers.

LOCAL OR NETWORK PRINTER

**A+
CORE 1
3.10**

A printer connects to a single computer or to the network:

- A local printer connects directly to a computer by way of a USB port, serial port, or wireless connection (Bluetooth or Wi-Fi). Most printers these days support more than one method.
- A network printer has an Ethernet port to connect directly to the network or uses Wi-Fi to connect to a wireless access point.

Some printers have both an Ethernet port and a USB-B port (see Figure 10-20), as well as multiple wireless connection options. These printers can be installed as either a network printer (connecting directly to the network) or a local printer (connecting directly to a computer).

Figure 10-20   This printer has an Ethernet port and USB-B port

Status indicator lights for the Ethernet port

Ethernet port

USB-B port

10

The two ways to install a printer and make it available on a network are:

▲ *Shared local printer.* Connect a local printer to a computer on the network, and then share the printer through the computer's network connection. See Computer A in Figure 10-21. Two requirements to keep in mind include:

   ▲ For a shared local printer to be available to other computers on the network, the host computer must be turned on and not in sleep or standby mode.

   ▲ For another computer on the network to use the shared printer, the appropriate printer drivers for the computer's OS must be installed on the remote computer.

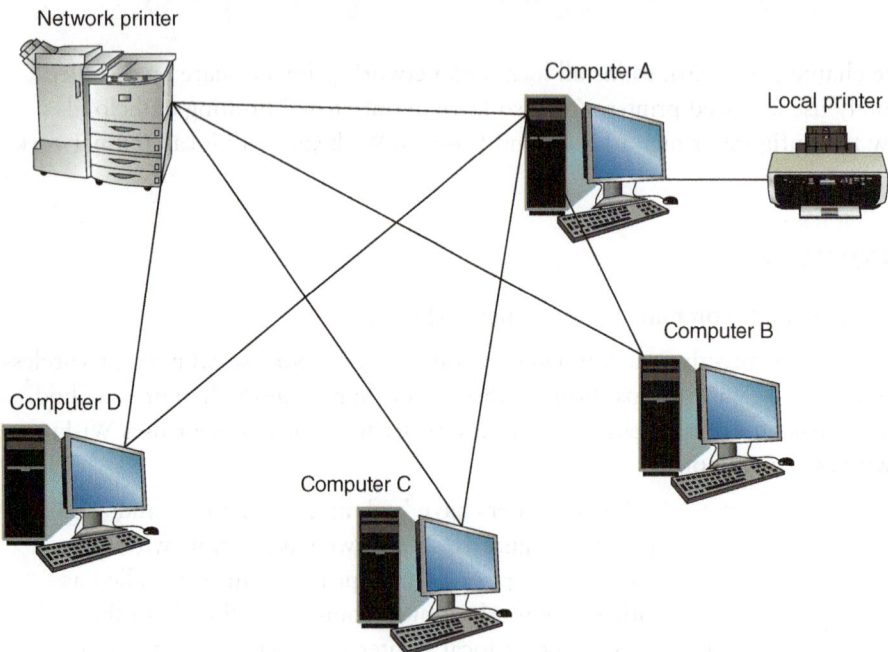

Figure 10-21 A shared local printer and a network printer

▲ *Network printer.* A network printer can connect directly to a network with its own NIC (see the network printer in Figure 10-21), and is identified on the network by its IP address or host name. To use the printer, any computer on the network can install this printer and print to it, which is called remote printing.

> ✎ **Notes** A computer can have several printers installed. Of these, Windows designates one printer to be the default printer, which is the one Windows prints to unless another is selected.

WIRED OR WIRELESS PRINTER CONNECTIONS

A+
CORE 1
3.10

Connecting a wired printer (USB or Ethernet) is easy:

   ▲ *USB.* Plug the USB cable into the printer and computer, and Windows installs the printer automatically.

   ▲ *Serial.* For a printer with a serial port, plug the serial cable into the printer and computer and install the printer as a local printer.

▲ *Ethernet.* Plug the Ethernet cable into the printer and network wall jack, switch, or router and install the printer as a network printer on any computer on the network.

Connecting a wireless printer is a little more complex:

▲ *Bluetooth.* For a Bluetooth printer installed as a local printer, turn on Bluetooth in Windows, move the printer within range of the computer, and watch as the two Bluetooth devices pair up. While you might need to navigate some of the Bluetooth settings on the printer's display to enable pairing, the process works like most other Bluetooth connections.

▲ *Wi-Fi infrastructure mode.* In infrastructure mode, Wi-Fi devices connect to a Wi-Fi access point, such as a SOHO router. Put the Wi-Fi printer within range of the access point and use controls on the printer to select the Wi-Fi network using the highest IEEE standard (802.11 a, b, g, n, or ac) supported by both the access point and the printer. Enter the security key to the network if one is required. All Wi-Fi printers support infrastructure connections and some Wi-Fi printers can handle ad hoc connections, which are discussed next.

▲ *Wi-Fi ad hoc mode.* Some Wi-Fi printers can connect directly to a nearby computer in a Wi-Fi ad hoc mode network to be installed as a local printer. This is accomplished in different ways depending on the technology available in the printer and the computer:

    ▲ Many modern Wi-Fi printers include the ability to host a Wi-Fi hotspot to which nearby computers can connect. The main disadvantage here is that most computers can connect to only one Wi-Fi network at a time, so if a computer is connected to the printer's Wi-Fi network, it can't communicate with the Internet or other network resources.

    ▲ The reverse arrangement might work better: Set up a mobile hotspot on the computer and connect the printer to the computer's hotspot. In Windows 10, you click the computer's network icon in the taskbar and click the **Mobile hotspot** tile to turn it on. Right-click the tile and click **Go to Settings**, where you'll find the hotspot's network name and network password. On the printer, use that information to connect to the computer's hotspot. (Windows 8 supports mobile hotspots, but it requires using several netsh commands not covered in this text.)

    ▲ Windows 7 computers can create a device-to-device Wi-Fi connection called an ad hoc network. Open the **Network and Sharing Center**, click **Set up a new connection or network**, click **Set up a wireless ad hoc (computer-to-computer) network**, and follow the directions on screen.

> ✎ **Notes** Apple computers and mobile devices can use an AirPrint printer without you having to install it. For a Mac or iOS device to use an AirPrint printer, simply open the Print menu in any app. If an AirPrint printer is on the network, it will appear in the list of printers. All AirPrint-enabled printers are capable of Wi-Fi connections to a wireless network and some have a USB or Ethernet port for wired connections. AirPrint printers are also capable of cloud printing, as discussed later in this chapter.

INSTALLING A LOCAL OR NETWORK PRINTER

A+ CORE 1 3.10 When you install a printer, printer drivers are required that are compatible with the installed operating system. Be sure to use 32-bit drivers for a 32-bit OS and 64-bit drivers for a 64-bit OS. Windows has many printer drivers built in. The drivers might also come on a CD bundled with the printer or you can download them from the printer manufacturer's website.

With some printers, you launch the installation program that came bundled on the setup CD or was downloaded from the printer manufacturer's website. With others, use the Windows 10 Settings app or the Windows 10/8/7 Devices and Printers window in Control Panel to install a printer. These windows are also used to manage and uninstall printers, as you'll see throughout the rest of this chapter.

APPLYING | CONCEPTS   INSTALLING A PRINTER

**A+
CORE 1
3.10**
Installing a network printer is sometimes called mapping a printer. Windows 10 has many preinstalled printer drivers that make printer installation particularly easy and straightforward. However, some manufacturers recommend that you install their drivers before connecting the printer to your computer or the network. This provides additional printer configuration and management tools that are not included in the Windows drivers. Follow these steps to install a wired or Wi-Fi network printer, serial-port printer, or Bluetooth printer using the Windows drivers, or follow more specific instructions from the printer's manufacturer:

1. Make sure the printer is connected to the network or the computer. In Windows 10, open the Settings app and click **Devices**, then click **Printers & scanners**. Click **Add a printer or scanner**. Windows searches for available printers and lists them (see Figure 10-22).

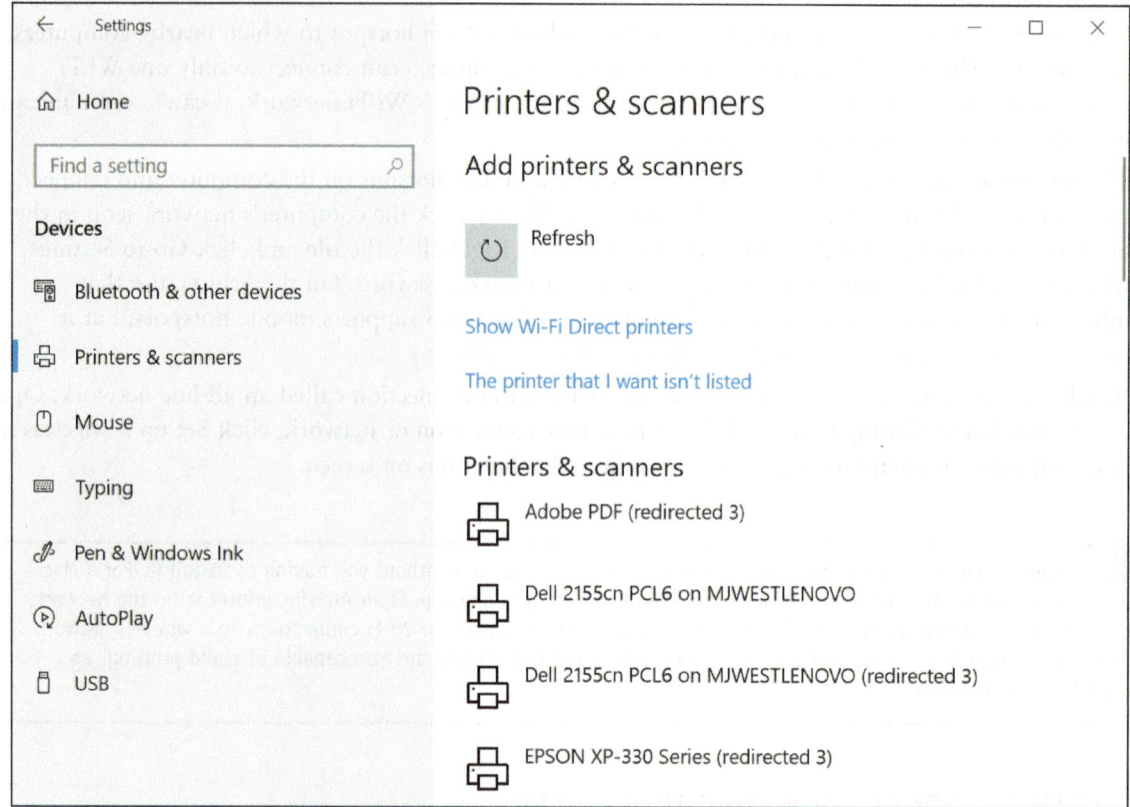

Figure 10-22   Use the Printers & scanners window to install a printer

2. Select the printer and click **Manage** to change printer settings.

3. If your printer isn't listed, click **The printer that I want isn't listed**. Choose one of the following options:
   a. **My printer is a little older** searches for older printer drivers.
   b. **Select a shared printer by name** allows you to enter a network location for the printer.
   c. **Add a printer using a TCP/IP address or hostname** allows you to address the printer by IP address or host name.
   d. **Add a Bluetooth, wireless or network discoverable printer** searches again for printers connected through Bluetooth or the network.

e. **Add a local printer or network printer with manual settings** gives you the option to make more granular changes to the printer's installation, use a setup CD provided by the manufacturer, or select an appropriate driver from a list of available Windows printer drivers. In the next box, choose the port where the printer is connected and click **Next**. Then you can select the brand and printer model to use drivers provided by Windows (see the left side of Figure 10-23), or you can use drivers stored on CD or previously downloaded from the web by clicking **Have Disk**. The Install From Disk box appears (see the right side of Figure 10-23). Click **Browse** to locate the drivers; Windows is looking for an .inf file. Be sure to select 32-bit or 64-bit drivers, depending on which type of OS you are using, then click **OK**.

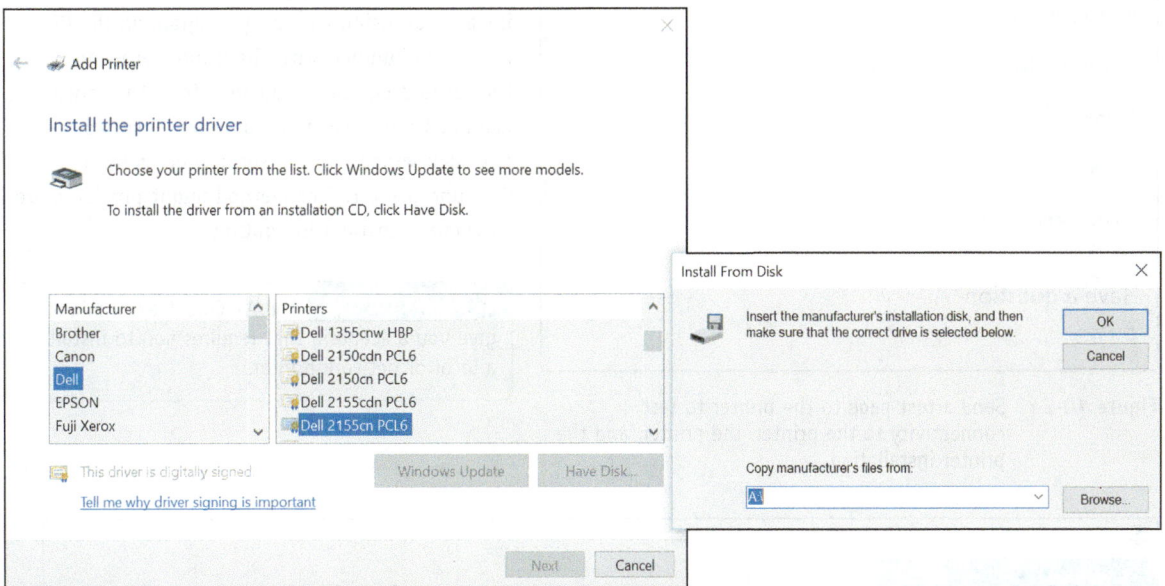

Figure 10-23   Locate printer drivers on CD or downloaded from the web

---

📝 **Notes** Use the System window to find out if a 32-bit or 64-bit OS is installed. To open the System window in Windows 10/8, press **Win+X** and click **System**. In Windows 7, click **Start**, right-click **Computer**, and select **Properties**.

🔄 **OS Differences** To use Control Panel to add a printer in Windows 10/8/7, open Control Panel in Classic view and click **Devices and Printers**. In the Devices and Printers window, click **Add a printer**. Select the printer and click **Next**. If your printer isn't listed, click **The printer that I want isn't listed** and select one from a list of printers for which Windows has drivers. In the next box, select the brand and printer model to use the drivers provided by Windows. To use drivers stored on CD or previously downloaded from the web, click **Have Disk**. The Install From Disk box appears. Click **Browse** to locate the drivers; Windows is looking for an .inf file. Be sure to select 32-bit or 64-bit drivers, depending on which type of OS you are using.

---

4. Continue to follow the wizard to install the printer. Dialog boxes give you the opportunity to change the name of the printer and designate it as the default printer. You can also test the printer. It's always a good idea to print a test page when you install a printer to verify that the installation works.

You can send a test page to the printer at any time. Click the printer in the Printers & scanners window, click **Manage**, and then click **Print a test page** (see Figure 10-24).

(continues)

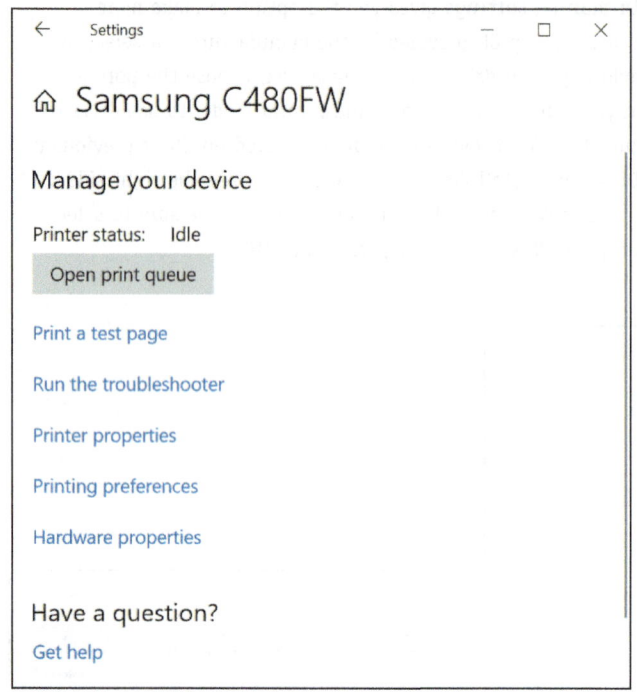

Figure 10-24 Send a test page to the printer to test connectivity to the printer, the printer, and the printer installation

OS Differences To use Control Panel to print a test page in Windows 10/8/7, right-click the printer in the Devices and Printers window and select **Printer properties**. On the General tab of the Properties box, click **Print Test Page**.

Rather than using Windows tools to start a printer installation, you can also start the installation using the setup program on the CD that came bundled with the printer or using the setup program downloaded from the printer manufacturer's website. Figure 10-25 shows one such window in the setup process for a Samsung printer. This method might provide more customized installation options.

★ A+ Exam Tip The A+ Core 1 exam might give you a scenario that requires you to install a local or network printer.

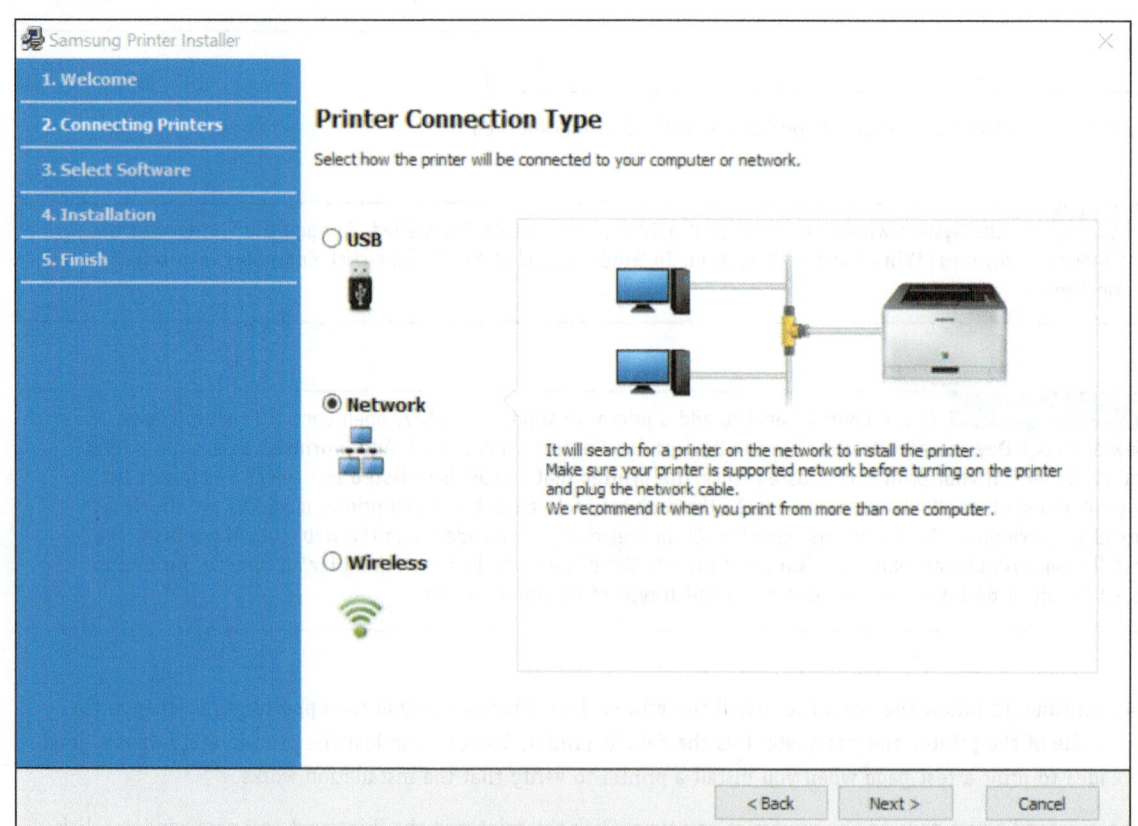

Source: Samsung

Figure 10-25 A menu provided by a setup program that came bundled with a printer

SHARING A PRINTER ON A NETWORK

**A+
CORE 1
3.10**

Recall from Chapter 8 that a print server manages network printers and makes them available to computers and other devices on the network. Any time a computer sends a print job to a printer through the network, whether that printer is a shared local printer or a network printer, print server functions play a role. However, the device that provides the print server can vary depending on how the printer is set up. Let's look at the available options:

◢ *Integrated print server.* Most printers today include network capability—you can connect them directly to a router or switch, and devices on the network can find and access the printer. In this case, the printer is providing its own integrated print server embedded in the firmware on the printer's hardware. Some integrated printers allow you to manage print protocols, start or stop jobs in the print queue, reorder jobs in the queue, cancel specific jobs coming from a particular computer on the network, monitor printer maintenance tasks, and set up your email address so the printer alerts you by email when it has a problem.

◢ *Computer as a print server.* When a computer shares its local printer with other computers on the network, the computer is considered to be a print server. If a network has several print servers, you might find it convenient as an IT support technician to use the Print Management console on your workstation to manage these print servers. Using Print Management, you can stop, start, and clear print jobs on any print server on the network and troubleshoot other printer problems from your workstation. You learn to use Print Management in Chapter 14.

◢ *Other network hardware.* Print server software might be embedded in other network devices, such as a router or firewall. Connect the printer to the network device and use its configuration interface to manage the printer.

10

APPLYING | CONCEPTS   CONFIGURING AND USING A SHARED PRINTER

**A+
CORE 1
3.10**

To share an installed local or network printer with others on the network, follow these steps:

1. In the printer Properties dialog box, which you access through the Settings app or Control Panel, click the **Sharing** tab. Check **Share this printer** (see the middle box in Figure 10-26).

Figure 10-26 Share the printer and decide how printer sharing is handled

(continues)

2. You can then change the share name of the printer. Notice in Figure 10-26 the option to control where print jobs are rendered. A print job can be prepared (rendered) on the remote computer (client computer) or this computer (print server). Your choice depends on which computer you think can best handle the computing burden. You can test several print jobs on remote computers with rendering at either location and see which method best uses computing resources on the network.

3. If you want to make drivers for the printer available to remote users who are using an operating system other than the OS on this computer, click **Additional Drivers**.

4. The Additional Drivers box opens (see the right side of Figure 10-26). For 32-bit operating systems, select **x86**. For 64-bit operating systems, select **x64**. Click **OK** to close the box. You might be asked for the Windows setup DVD or other access to the installation files.

5. Click **OK** to close the Properties box. A shared printer shows a two-friends icon under it or in the status bar in the Devices and Printers window. The printer is listed in the Network group in File Explorer or Windows Explorer on other network computers.

For the printer share to be successful, the following requirements must be met:

▲ The computer sharing the printer and the computer using the shared printer must both be connected to the same network.

▲ The shared printer and the computer sharing it must be turned on.

▲ Both computers must allow file and printer sharing.

SECURE A SHARED PRINTER

Consider the security of your shared printer and the privacy of data embedded in documents to be printed:

▲ *Secure the printer.* On the printer's Properties box (refer back to Figure 10-26), click the **Security** tab to manage who has access to the printer and permissions allowed. Notice in Figure 10-27 that the Everyone group can print but is not allowed to manage the printer or documents sent to it. Just as with shared files and folders, you can share the printer with specific users and/or set up a customized user group that is allowed to use a printer. In this way, user authentication is required before giving a user access to the printer.

▲ *Secure the data.* By default, documents sent to the printer are cached (spooled) to the hard drive of the print server and cached on a hard drive that might be installed in a high-end printer. To prevent these print jobs from being hacked,

Figure 10-27   Security settings for a printer

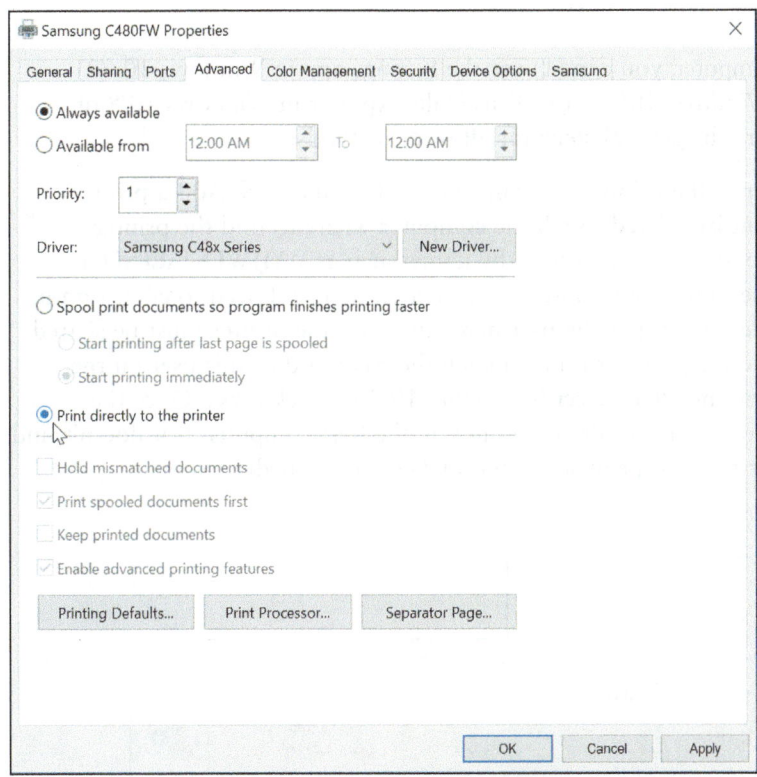

Figure 10-28   For best security, bypass caching print jobs to the hard drive

don't allow caching to either hard drive. To change the Windows default setting for spooling, click the **Advanced** tab of the printer's Properties box (see Figure 10-28). Select **Print directly to the printer**. Not spooling to the hard drive slows down the printing process in exchange for better security.

Notes When print jobs are spooled and the printer is not working or is turned off, the documents can back up in the print queue. To manage the print queue from the Settings app in Windows 10, click **Devices**, click the printer in the list, and click **Open queue** (see Figure 10-29). Use the menu bar in the queue window to manage the printer's queue. In Windows 10/8/7, double-click the printer in the Devices and Printers window from Control Panel. Click the queue link to open the queue window.

10

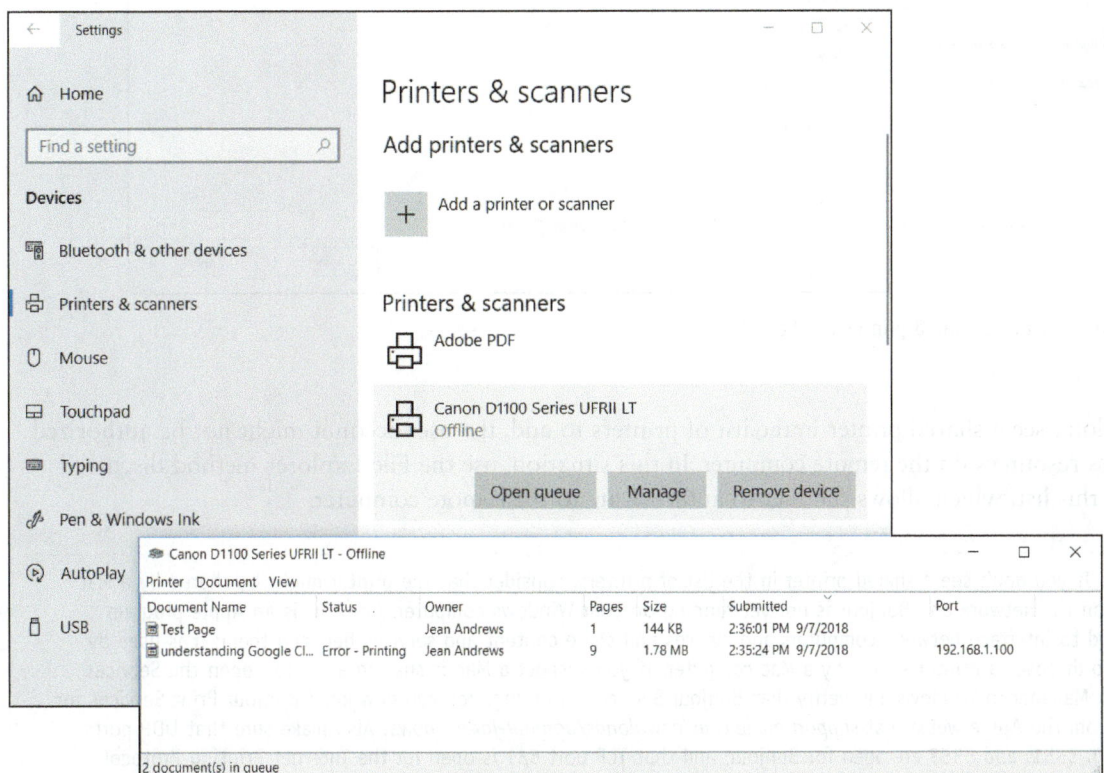

Figure 10-29   Use the print queue to pause printing or cancel a print job

USE A SHARED PRINTER

To install a shared printer on a remote computer, you can (1) use the Settings app in Windows 10, (2) use the Devices and Printers window in Windows 10/8/7, or (3) use File Explorer in Windows 10/8 or Windows Explorer in Windows 7. Here are the general steps for all three methods:

▲ *Settings app.* On a remote computer, open the Printers & scanners window and click **Add a printer or scanner**. Click **The printer that I want isn't listed** to tell the computer where to find the printer. Choose **Select a shared printer by name** to locate the printer by name, such as **\\MJWEST\EPSON XP-330 Series (jillwest)**, or click **Browse** to find the printer on the network. You'll need to enter sign-in credentials for the computer sharing the printer. For the user name to work, the printer must be shared with this specific user or user group and the password must match the password of this user on the remote computer. Then select the printer and click **Select** (see Figure 10-30). Click **Next**. Once the printer is selected, Windows attempts to use printer drivers found on the host computer. If it doesn't find the drivers, you will be given the opportunity to provide them on CD or other media.

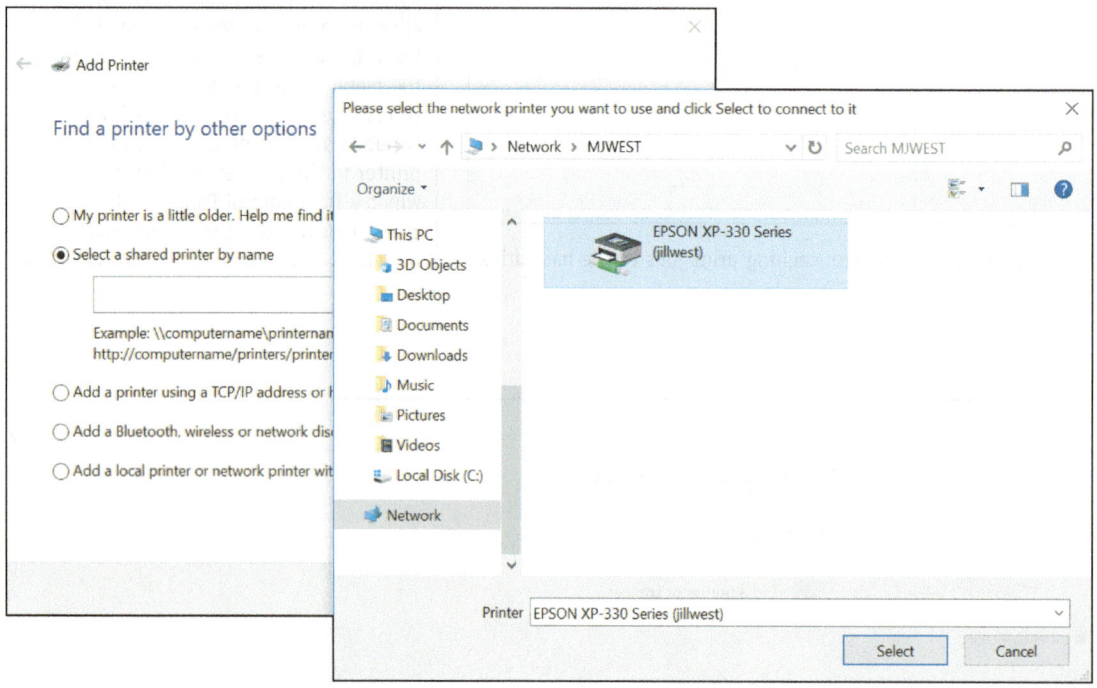

Figure 10-30   Locate a shared printer on the network

If you don't see a shared printer in the list of printers to add, the user account might not be authorized to access resources on the remote computer. In this situation, use the File Explorer method discussed later in this list, which allows the user to authenticate to the remote computer.

> 🖊 **Notes** If you don't see a shared printer in the list of printers, consider that the printer might be shared by a Mac computer on the network and Bonjour is not yet running on your Windows computer. **Bonjour** is an Apple program that is used to interface between computers and devices and share content and services between them; it is used by Windows to discover a printer shared by a Mac computer. If you suspect a Mac is sharing a printer, open the Services tab of Task Manager in Windows and verify that Bonjour Service is running. You can download Bonjour Print Services for Windows from the Apple website at *support.apple.com/downloads/bonjour-for-windows*. Also make sure that UDP ports 1900, 5350, 5351, and 5353 are open for Bonjour, and that TCP port 631 is open for the Internet Printing Protocol (IPP), which is used by macOS printer sharing services.

▲ *Devices and Printers window.* On a remote computer, open the Devices and Printers window, click **Add a printer**, and follow the directions on screen to add a network printer. Select the shared printer, which shows the sharing computer's host name and the printer name in the printer address column, or click **The printer I want isn't listed** and browse the network to find the printer. Windows attempts to use printer drivers found on the host computer. If it doesn't find the drivers, you will be given the opportunity to provide them on CD or other media.

▲ *File Explorer or Windows Explorer.* In the Explorer window, drill down into the computer that is sharing the printer. If required, authenticate to the remote computer with a valid user account and password on the remote computer. For the user name to work, the printer must be shared with this specific user or user group and the password must match the password of this user on the remote computer. After authentication, you can see the shared printer. Right-click the printer and select **Connect** (see Figure 10-31). In the warning box that appears, click **Install driver** and follow the directions on screen.

Figure 10-31 Use File Explorer to connect to a shared printer

After the printer is installed, be sure to send a test page to the printer to verify that the installation is successful.

VIRTUAL PRINTING

A+
CORE 1
3.11

Printing to a file instead of producing a hard copy at a printer is called virtual printing. The types of files you can virtually print depend on the software installed on your system. To see your options for virtual printing, open the Print menu or dialog box for an application. For example, Figure 10-32 shows the results on one system using Word 2016.

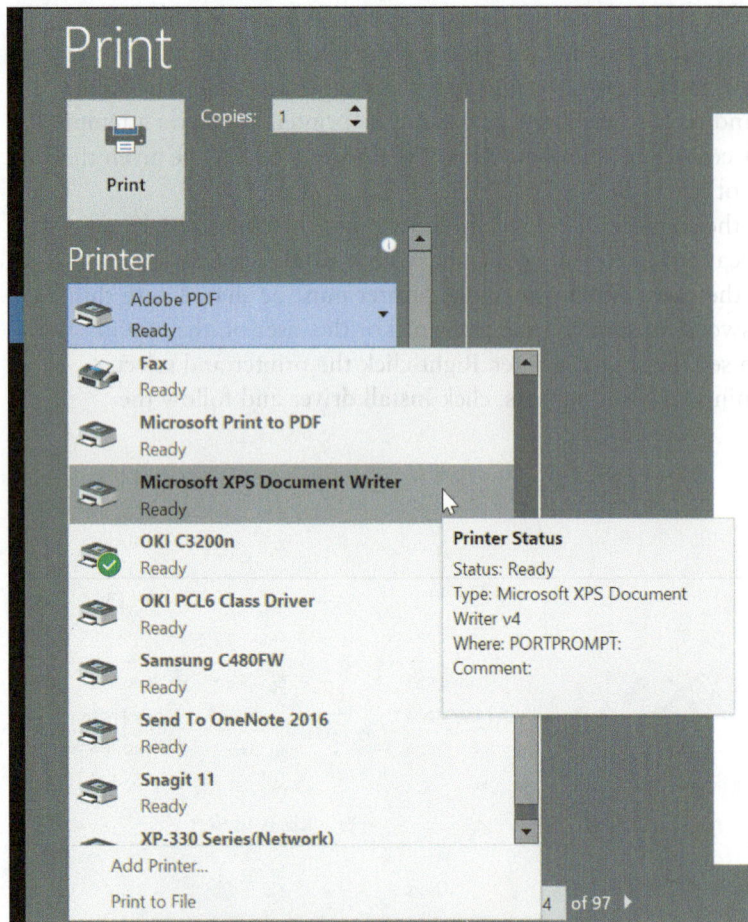

Figure 10-32 The file types available for virtual printing depend on software installed in the system

The items of interest listed in the figure are the following types of files:

▲ *PDF (Portable Document Format) file.* Windows 10 includes the Microsoft Print to PDF tool, which sends a print job to a PDF file. Notice in Figure 10-32 that Adobe Acrobat is installed on this system, which provides the option to use the Acrobat application to virtually print to a PDF file.

▲ *Image file, also called a bitmap file.* Snagit is imaging software normally used to take screenshots. When you print to Snagit, you create an image that appears in the Snagit window. Then, you can use Snagit to save the image as a PNG, GIF, JPG, BMP, TIF, or other image file format.

▲ *XPS (XML Paper Specification) file.* Windows includes the Microsoft XPS Document Writer, which creates an XPS file. The file is similar to a PDF and can be viewed, edited, printed, faxed, emailed, or posted on websites. In Windows, the file is viewed in a browser window.

▲ *Print to file.* When you check **Print to file** on a Print menu, the print job is created for the currently selected printer and saved to a PRN file. The file contains the information a printer needs to print the document. Saving a print job to a PRN file and later printing it worked with older printers, but doesn't work with modern printers. Today, it's better to create a PDF or XPS document.

> ★ **A+ Exam Tip** The A+ Core 1 exam might give you a scenario that requires you to perform virtual printing to PDF, XPS, or image files, or to use the option to Print to file.

CLOUD PRINTING

**A+
CORE 1
3.10**

With cloud printing, you can print to a printer anywhere on the Internet from a personal computer or mobile device connected to the Internet. Cloud printing is a type of client/server application. Client software on a computer or mobile device sends a document (which might be encrypted) or a print job to server software on a network that funnels the print jobs to a printer on its network. The printer might be a privately owned printer, a shared network printer, or a public printer run by a business. The computer or mobile device with the client software installed can be anywhere on the Internet. Examples of cloud printing services include Google Cloud Print (*google.com/cloudprint*), which you can set up on any cloud-ready printer, and enterprise-grade UniPrint Infinity (*uniprint.net*). For best security, make sure your software can encrypt a document or print job sent over the Internet. You learn to print using Google Cloud Print in a project at the end of this chapter.

CONFIGURING PRINTER FEATURES AND ADD-ON DEVICES

A+
CORE 1
3.10

After the printer is installed, use the printer Properties box to manage printer features and hardware devices installed on the printer. To access settings for the EPSON printer shown in Figure 10-33, click the **General** tab and then click **Preferences**, which shows the available options on the right side of the figure. Other printers might show a **Device Settings** tab. The options depend on the installed printer. As you can see in the figure, the **Main** tab lets you control the size of the paper, page orientation (landscape or portrait), quality of printing (for example, draft, standard, or high quality), color options (color or black/grayscale), 1-sided or 2-sided (called duplex printing), collated or uncollated, and various add-on devices depending on the printer, such as a printer hard drive, stapler, or stacker unit.

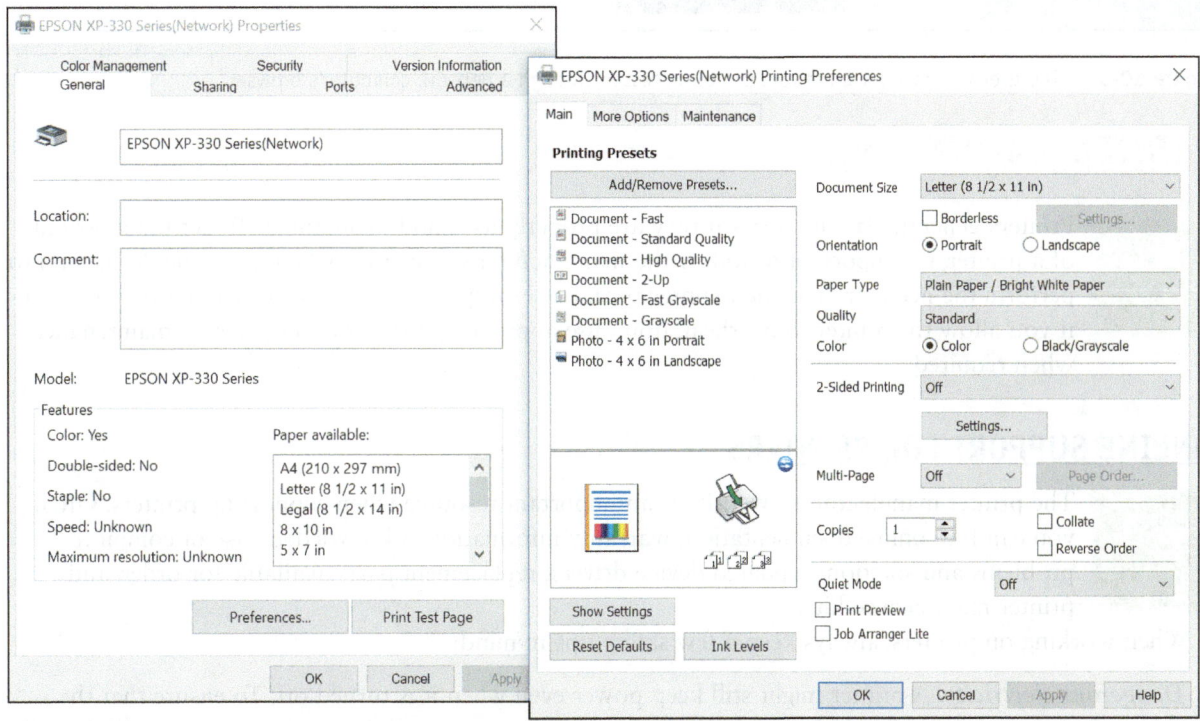

Figure 10-33   The Printing Preferences dialog box for an EPSON printer

You can also manage many printer settings and features through the printer's own utility, which might be installed as an application on your computer or might be a firmware utility in the printer that is accessed through your browser. For example, for one Oki Data printer, enter the IP address of the printer in a browser and then enter the administrative password to the printer firmware. The firmware utility (see Figure 10-34) allows you to manage printer settings and features.

Now let's turn our attention to tasks you might be called on to do when maintaining and upgrading a printer.

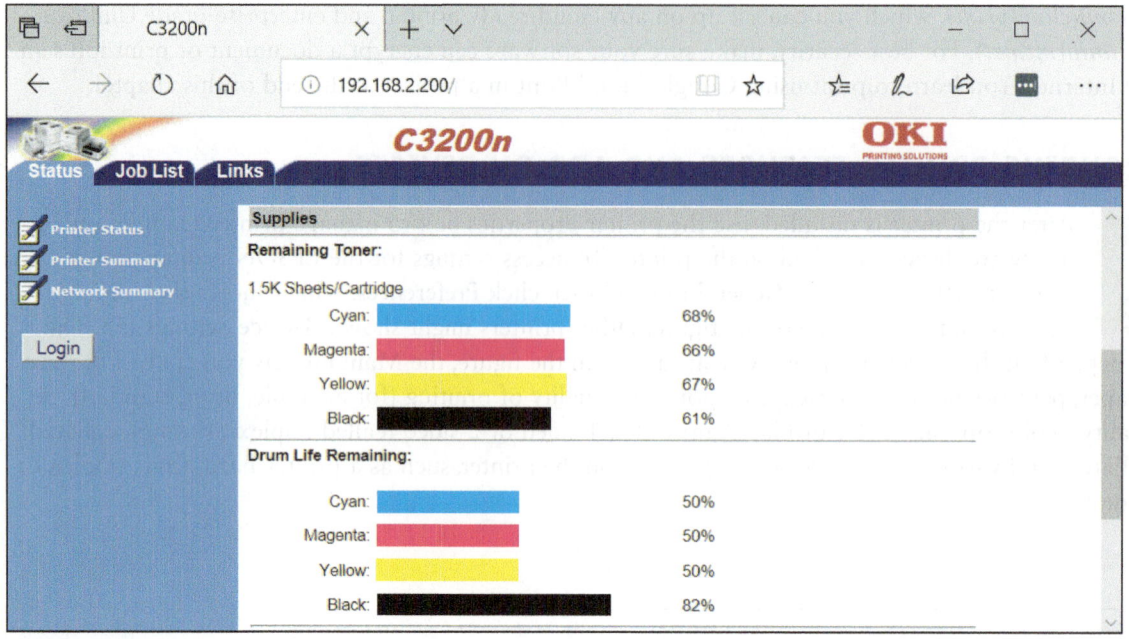

Source: Oki Data

Figure 10-34 The user interface for a network printer accessed through a network computer's browser

PRINTER MAINTENANCE

Printers generally last for years if they are properly used and maintained. To get the most out of a printer, it's important to follow the manufacturer's directions when using the device and to perform the necessary routine maintenance. For example, the life of a printer can be shortened if you allow the printer to overheat, don't use approved paper, or don't perform maintenance when required.

ONLINE SUPPORT FOR PRINTERS

The printer manufacturer's website is an important resource when supporting printers. Often, you can find online documentation, warranty information, a knowledge base of common problems and solutions, updated device drivers, replacement parts available for order, and printer maintenance kits.

When working on printers, always keep a few safety tips in mind:

▲ *Dangerous electricity.* A printer might still keep power even when it is turned off. To ensure that the printer has no power, unplug it. Even when a laser printer is unplugged, internal components might still hold a dangerous electrical charge for some time.

▲ *Hot to touch.* Some laser printer parts can get hot enough to burn you while in operation. Before you work inside a laser printer, turn it off, unplug it, and wait about 30 minutes for it to cool down.

▲ *Laser beam.* For your protection, the laser beam in a laser printer is always enclosed inside a protective case. Therefore, when servicing a laser printer, you should never have to look at the laser beam, which can damage your eyes.

▲ *Static electricity.* To protect sensitive memory modules and hard drives inside printers, be sure to use an ESD strap when installing them. You don't need to wear an ESD strap when exchanging consumables such as toner cartridges, fuser assembles, or image drums.

▲ *When no one is around.* Here's one more tip to stay safe, but I don't want it to frighten you: When you work inside high-voltage equipment such as a laser printer, don't do it when no one else is around. If you have an emergency, someone needs to be close by to help you.

Figure 10-35 shows an ink cartridge being installed in an inkjet printer. To replace an inkjet cartridge, turn on the printer and open the front cover. The printer releases the cartridges from their parked positions. You can then open the latch on top of the cartridge and remove it. Install the new cartridge as shown in the figure.

Figure 10-35   Installing an ink cartridge in an inkjet printer

CLEANING A PRINTER

A printer gets dirty inside and outside as stray toner, ink, dust, and bits of paper accumulate. As part of routine printer maintenance, you need to regularly clean the printer. How often depends on how much the printer is used and the work environment. Some manufacturers suggest that a heavily used printer be cleaned weekly, and others suggest you clean it whenever you exchange the toner, ink cartridges, or ribbon.

Clean the outside of the printer with a damp cloth. Don't use ammonia-based cleaners. Clean the inside of the printer with a dry cloth and remove dust, bits of paper, and stray toner. Picking up stray toner can be a problem. Don't try to blow it out with compressed air because you don't want the toner in the air. Also, don't use an antistatic vacuum cleaner. You can, however, use a vacuum cleaner designed to pick up toner, called a toner vacuum. This type of vacuum does not allow the toner that it picks up to touch any conductive surface.

Some printer manufacturers also suggest you use an extension magnet brush. The long-handled brush is made of nylon fibers that are charged with static electricity and easily attract the toner like a magnet. For a laser printer, wipe the rollers from side to side with a dry cloth to remove loose dirt and toner. Don't touch the soft, black roller (the transfer roller), or you might affect the print quality. You can find specific instructions for cleaning a printer on the printer manufacturer's website.

CALIBRATING A PRINTER

An inkjet printer might require calibration to align and/or clean the inkjet nozzles, which can solve a problem when colors appear streaked or out of alignment. To calibrate the printer, you might use the menu on the printer's control panel or use software that came bundled with the printer. How to access these tools differs from one printer to another. See the printer manual to learn how to perform the calibration. For some printers, a Services tab is added to the printer Properties window. Other printer installations might put utility programs in the Start menu. The first time you turn on a printer after installing ink cartridges, it's a good idea to calibrate the printer.

If an inkjet printer still does not print after calibrating it, you can try to manually clean the cartridge nozzles. Check the printer manufacturer's website for directions. For most inkjet printers, you are directed to use clean, distilled water and cotton swabs to clean the face of the ink cartridge, being careful not to touch the nozzle plate. To prevent the inkjet nozzles from drying out, don't leave the ink cartridges out of their cradle for longer than 30 minutes. Here are some general directions:

1. Following the manufacturer's directions, remove the inkjet cartridges from the printer and lay them on their sides on a paper towel.

2. Dip a cotton swab in distilled water (not tap water) and squeeze out any excess water.

3. Hold an ink cartridge so that the nozzle plate faces up and use the swab to clean the area around the nozzle plate, as shown in Figure 10-36. Do not clean the plate itself.

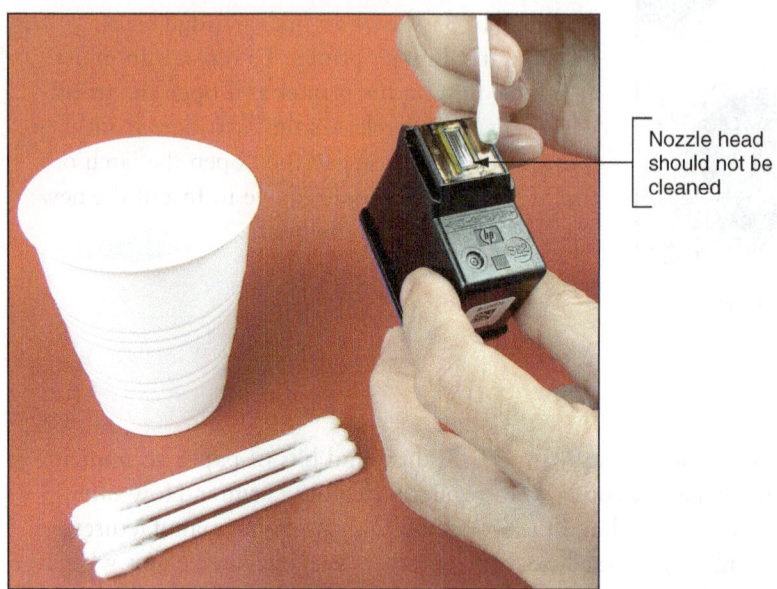

Nozzle head should not be cleaned

Figure 10-36   Clean the area around the nozzle plate with a damp cotton swab

4. Hold the cartridge up to the light and make sure that no dust, dirt, ink, or cotton fibers are left around the face of the nozzle plate. Make sure the area is clean.

5. Clean all the ink cartridges the same way and replace the cartridges in the printer.

6. Print a test page. If print quality is still poor, try calibrating the printer again.

7. If you still have problems, you need to replace the ink cartridges.

Laser printers automatically calibrate themselves periodically. You can instruct a laser printer to calibrate at any time by using the controls on the front of the printer or the browser-based utility program that is included in the firmware of a network printer. To access the utility, enter the IP address of the printer in the browser address box and sign in.

PRINTER MAINTENANCE KITS

Manufacturers of high-end printers provide printer maintenance kits, which include specific printer components, step-by-step instructions for performing maintenance, tips for how often maintenance should be done, and information on any special tools or equipment you need to do maintenance. For example, the maintenance plan for the HP Color LaserJet 4600 printer says to replace the transfer roller assembly after printing 120,000 pages and to replace the fusing assembly after 150,000 pages. The plan also says the black ink cartridge should last for about 9,000 pages and the color ink cartridge should last about 8,000 pages. HP sells the image transfer kit, the image fuser kit, and the ink cartridges designed for this printer.

To find out how many pages a printer has printed so you'll know if you need to do the maintenance, have the printer give you the page count since the last maintenance. You can tell the printer to display the information or print a status report by using buttons on the front of the printer (see Figure 10-37),

or you can use utility software using a computer connected to the printer. See the printer documentation to know how to get this report. For network printers that offer a browser-based utility, enter the IP address of the printer in your browser and use the utility to find the counters. (Figure 10-38 shows such a utility for an Oki Data network printer.)

Figure 10-37 Use buttons on the front of the printer to display information, including the page count

Source: Oki Data

Figure 10-38 Use the web-based printer utility to read the printer counters

After you have performed the maintenance, be sure to reset the page count so it will be accurate when you need to do the next routine maintenance. Keep a written record of the maintenance and other service done.

As examples of replacing printer consumables, let's look at how to replace a toner cartridge, image drum, and fuser for an Oki Data color laser printer.

> ★ **A+ Exam Tip** The A+ Core 1 exam might give you a scenario that requires you to replace a toner cartridge or apply a maintenance kit for a laser printer.

A toner cartridge for this printer generally lasts for about 1,500 pages. Here are the steps to replace a color toner cartridge:

1. Turn off and unplug the printer. Press the cover release button on the upper-left corner of the printer and open the printer cover (see Figure 10-39).

Figure 10-39 Open the printer cover

2. Figure 10-40 shows the cover up. Notice the four erase lamps on the inside of the cover. Look inside the printer for the four toner cartridges and the fuser assembly labeled in Figure 10-41. Push or pull the blue toner cartridge release button forward to disconnect and release the cartridge from the image drum below it (see Figure 10-42).

Four erase lamps

Figure 10-40 The cover is lifted

Four toner cartridges

Fuser assembly

Figure 10-41 Inside the Oki Data printer

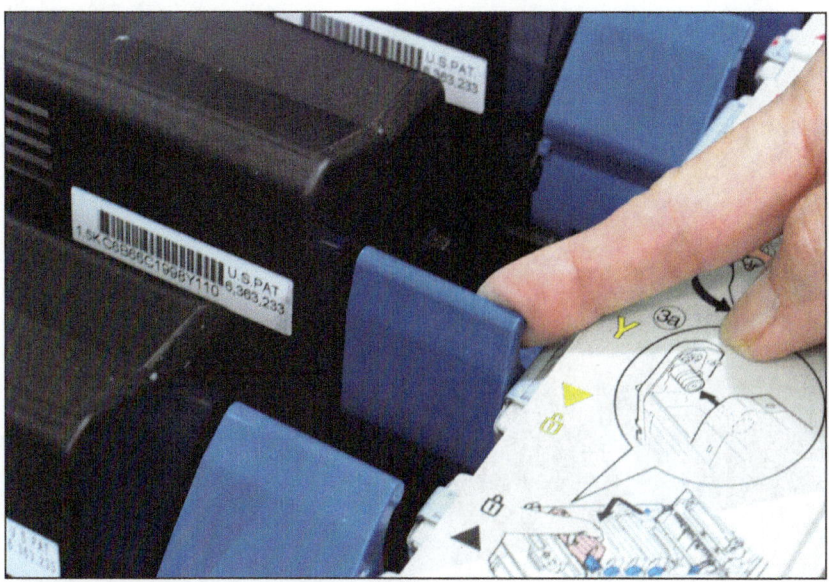

Figure 10-42   Push the blue lever forward to release the toner cartridge

3. Lift the cartridge out of the printer, lifting up on the right side first and then removing the left side (see Figure 10-43). Be careful not to spill loose toner.

4. Unpack the new cartridge. Gently shake it from side to side to loosen the toner. Remove the tape from underneath the cartridge, and place the cartridge in the printer by inserting the left side first and then the right side. Push the cartridge lever back into position to lock the cartridge in place. Close the printer cover.

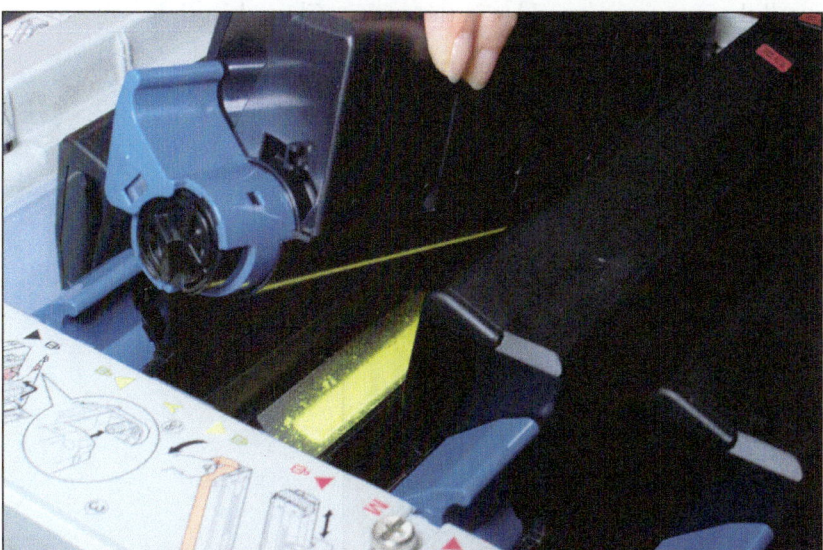

Figure 10-43   Remove the toner cartridge

This printer has four image drums, one for each color. The drums are expected to last for about 15,000 pages. When you purchase a new drum, the kit comes with a new color toner cartridge. Follow these steps to replace the cartridge and image drum. In these steps, we are using the yellow drum and cartridge:

1. Turn off and unplug the printer. Wait about 30 minutes for it to cool down, then open the printer cover. The toner cartridge is connected to the image drum. Lift the drum together with the toner cartridge out of the printer (see Figure 10-44). Be sure to dispose of the drum and cartridge according to local regulations.

Figure 10-44   Remove the image drum and toner cartridge as one unit

2. Unpack the new image drum. Peel the tape off the drum and remove the plastic film around it. As you work, be careful to keep the drum upright so as not to spill the toner. Because the drum is sensitive to light, don't allow it to be exposed to bright light or direct sunlight. Don't expose it to normal room lighting for longer than five minutes.

3. Place the drum in the printer. Install the new toner cartridge in the printer. Close the printer cover.

The fuser should last for about 45,000 pages. To replace the fuser, follow these steps:

1. Turn off and unplug the printer. Allow the printer to cool and open the cover.

2. Pull the two blue fuser levers forward to unlock the fuser (see Figure 10-45).

Figure 10-45   Pull the two fuser levers forward to release the fuser

3. Lift the fuser out of the printer using the handle on the fuser, as shown in Figure 10-46.

Figure 10-46 Remove the fuser

4. Unpack the new fuser and place it in the printer. Push the two blue levers toward the back of the printer to lock the fuser in place.

As a last step whenever you service the inside of this printer, always carefully clean the LED erase lamps on the inside of the top cover (see Figure 10-47). The printer maintenance kits you've just learned to use all include a wipe to clean these strips.

Figure 10-47 Clean the LED strips on the inside top cover

TROUBLESHOOTING PRINTERS

| A+ CORE 1 3.11, 5.6 | In this part of the chapter, you learn some general and specific printer troubleshooting tips. As with all computer problems, begin troubleshooting by interviewing the user, finding out what works and doesn't work, and making an initial determination of the problem. When you think the problem is solved, ask the user to check things out to make sure he is satisfied with your |

work. After the problem is solved, be sure to document the symptoms of the problem and what you did to solve it.

PRINTER DOES NOT PRINT

| A+ CORE 1 3.11, 5.6 | When a printer does not print, the problem can be caused by any number of things. As you can see in Figure 10-48, the problem can be isolated to one of the following areas: |

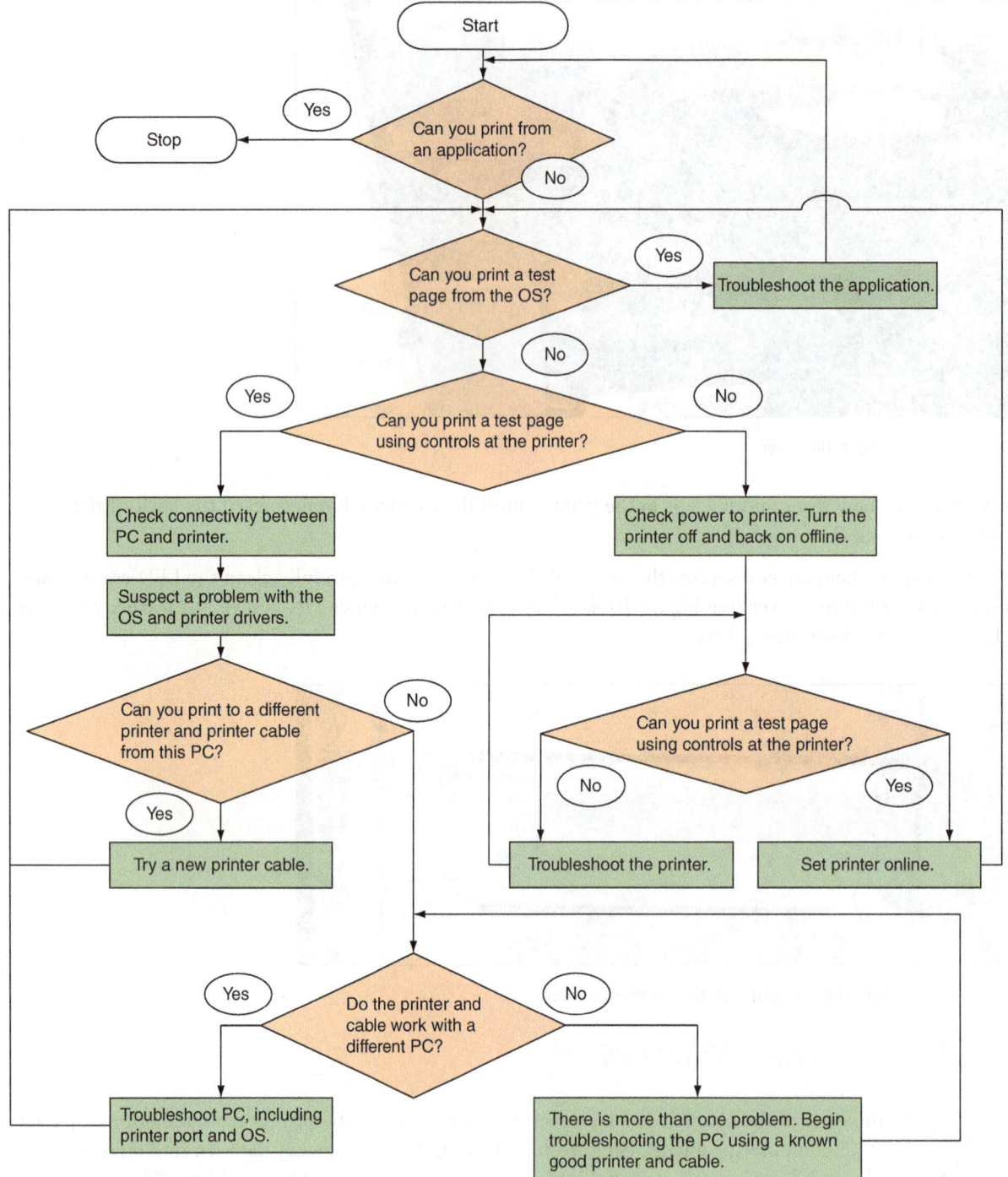

Figure 10-48   How to isolate a printer problem

◢ The application attempting to use the printer
◢ Windows, Windows settings, or printer drivers
◢ The printer itself
◢ Connectivity between the computer and its local printer or a network printer

In addition, if this is the first time you have tried to use the printer after installing it, the printer drivers or the printer installation might be the problem. The following sections address printer problems caused by all of these categories, starting with the application trying to use the printer.

PROBLEMS PRINTING FROM AN APPLICATION

If you have trouble printing from an application on a client computer, try these steps:

1. On the client computer, try to print a Windows test page. If the Windows test page prints, you have proven the problem is with the application or the file it is attempting to print.

2. Make sure the correct printer is selected in the application print menu.

3. Try using the application to print a different file.

4. Try to print to a different file type, then print that file from a different application. For example, you can print to an XPS document by selecting Microsoft XPS Document Writer in the list of installed printers. Then you can double-click the .xps file, which opens in the XPS Viewer window, and you can print from this window.

5. Verify that enough hard drive space is available for the OS to create temporary print files.

6. Try repairing or reinstalling the application.

> ★ **A+ Exam Tip** The A+ Core 1 exam might give you a scenario that expects you to determine if connectivity between the printer and the computer is the problem when troubleshooting printer issues.

PROBLEMS PRINTING FROM WINDOWS

If the Windows test page does not print from the client computer, do the following:

1. The print spool might be stalled. Open the printer's queue and try deleting all print jobs in the queue. To cancel one document, right-click it and click **Cancel** in the shortcut menu (see Figure 10-49). To cancel all documents, click **Printer** and click **Cancel All Documents**. Try printing a Windows test page again.

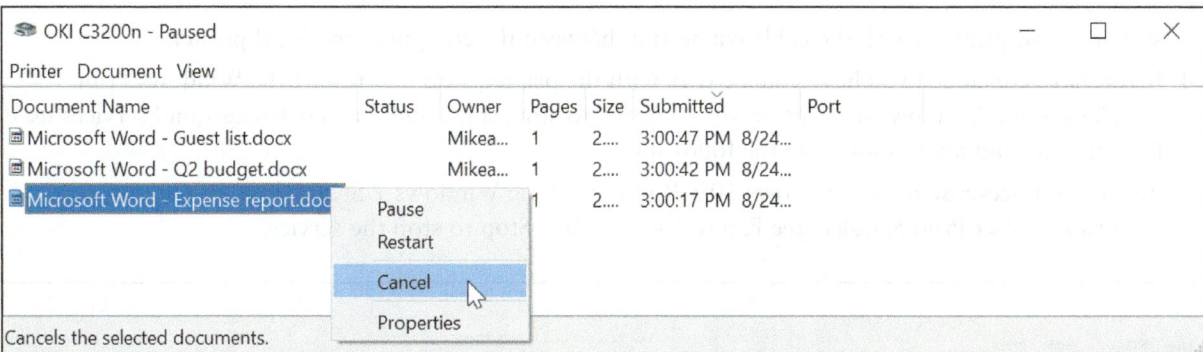

Figure 10-49 Cancel a print job in the printer queue

> ★ **A+ Exam Tip** The A+ Core 1 exam might give you a scenario that requires you to solve problems with the print queue.

2. If the Windows test page also stalls in the queue, go to the printer and check the simple things at the printer:

   a. Is the printer on? Is it getting power?

   b. Is there paper in the printer?

   c. Does the control panel on the printer show an error code?

d. Can you print a printer self-test page by using controls at the printer? For directions to print a self-test page, see the printer's user guide. For example, you might need to hold down a button or combination of buttons on the printer's front panel. If this test page prints correctly, then the printer is working. If the test page does not print, solve the problem with the printer itself.

3. If the printer is working, do a quick check to be sure you have communication with the printer before you continue troubleshooting. Do the following:

a. Try pinging the printer. Open a command prompt window, enter **ping**, and then enter the IP address of your printer. In Figure 10-50, the address is **192.168.2.200**. If the printer replies (see Figure 10-50), the problem is not network connectivity.

Figure 10-50 Use the ping command to determine if you have network connectivity with the printer

b. If the ping does not work, move on to the section, "Problems with Connectivity for a Network Printer or Shared Printer."

c. For a USB printer, check the cable connection between the computer and local printer.

4. If you have concluded you have connectivity with the printer, stop and restart the Windows Print Spooler service. Windows uses the Services console to stop, start, and manage background services used by Windows and applications. Do the following:

a. Enter **services.msc** in the Windows 10/8 Run box or the Windows 7 Search box. In the Services console, select **Print Spooler** (see Figure 10-51). Click **Stop** to stop the service.

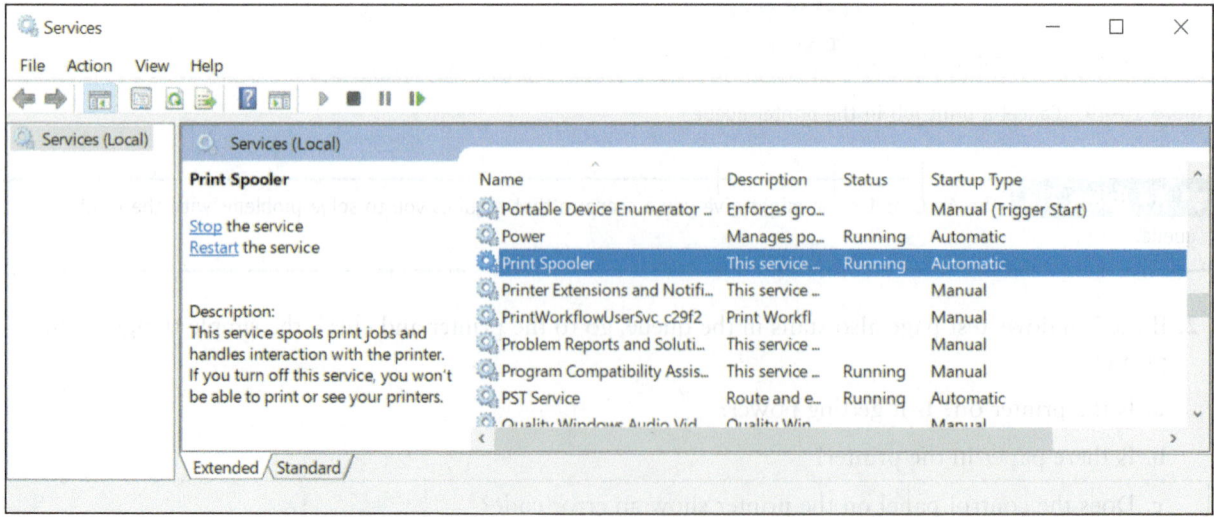

Figure 10-51 Use the Services console to stop and start the print spooler

b. To delete any print jobs left in the queue, open File Explorer or Windows Explorer and delete all files in the C:\Windows\System32\spool\PRINTERS folder.

c. Restart the print spooler. Return to the Services console, make sure Print Spooler is selected, and click **Start**. Close the Services console window.

5. If you still cannot print, reboot the computer. Try deleting the printer and then reinstalling it.

6. Check the printer manufacturer's website for an updated printer driver. Download and install the correct driver.

7. Try disabling printer caching, which you learned to do earlier in the chapter, so that print jobs are not cached but are sent directly to the printer.

PROBLEMS WITH THE PRINTER ITSELF

To eliminate the printer as the problem, check these things:

1. Is the printer on? Is it getting power? If there's no image on the printer's control panel display, the printer is not getting power or it is turned off.

2. Does the printer have paper?

3. Look for an error message or error code in the control panel on the front of the printer. If the control panel reports "Ready" or "Online," then you can assume a network printer is communicating with the network.

> 🖉 **Notes** If you see an error code you don't understand, search the printer documentation or website to find out its meaning. Follow the directions on the printer manufacturer's website to address the error code.

4. Can you print a printer self-test page, as described earlier? If this test page prints correctly, then the printer is working.

> 🖉 **Notes** A printer self-test page might tell you the printer resolution and how much memory is installed. If this information is not correct, try upgrading firmware on the printer.

5. Try resetting the printer. (For some printers, press the Reset button on the printer.) Try powering down or unplugging the printer and starting it again. As it starts up, look for any new error messages that appear.

6. Is the paper installed correctly? Are the printer cover and rear access doors properly closed and locked? Is there a paper jam?

7. If paper is jammed inside the printer, follow the directions in the printer documentation to remove the paper. Don't jerk the paper from the printer mechanism, but pull evenly on the paper, with care. You don't want to leave pieces of paper behind. Check for jammed paper from both the input tray and the output bin. Check both sides. Laser and inkjet printers likely have a door in the back that you can open to gently clear the jammed paper, as shown in Figure 10-52.

Figure 10-52 Open the door on the back of an inkjet printer to remove jammed paper

10

8. Is the paper not feeding? Remove the paper tray and check the metal plate at the bottom of the tray. Can it move up and down freely? If not, replace the tray. When you insert the tray in the printer, does the printer lift the plate as the tray is inserted? If not, the lift mechanism might need repair.

9. Damp paper can cause paper jams, creases, and wrinkles. Is the paper in the printer dry? Paper that is too thin can also crease or wrinkle in the printer.

10. For an inkjet printer, check if nozzles are clogged. Sometimes, leaving the printer on for a while will heat up the ink nozzles and unclog them.

11. If the print head of an impact printer moves back and forth but nothing prints, check the ribbon. Is it installed correctly between the plate and print head? Is it jammed? If the ribbon is dried out, it needs to be replaced.

12. Check the service documentation and printer page count to find out if routine maintenance is due or if the printer has a history of similar problems. Check the user guide for the printer and the printer manufacturer's website for other troubleshooting suggestions.

If you still cannot get a printer to work, you might need to take the printer to a certified repair shop. Before you do, though, try contacting the manufacturer. You might also be able to open a chat session on the printer manufacturer's website.

PROBLEMS WITH CONNECTIVITY FOR A NETWORK PRINTER OR SHARED PRINTER

If the printer's self-test page prints correctly (the printer is working) but you cannot ping the printer from the computer where the print job was issued, the next step is to suspect no connectivity between the printer and computer. We call this computer the client computer in the following steps for a network printer:

1. Consider that the entire network might be down or the client computer is offline. Can the client computer communicate with other devices or computers on the network? Can another computer on the network communicate with the printer?

2. Consider that the IP address of the printer might have changed, which can happen if the printer is receiving a dynamic IP address. Using Windows, delete the printer, and then install the printer again. If this solves the problem, assign a static IP address to the printer to keep the problem from reoccurring.

3. Can you print to another network printer? If so, there might be a problem with the first printer's configuration. Try uninstalling and installing the printer at the client computer.

4. Check the network port on the printer and the switch or router to which the printer connects. Do the network status indicator lights indicate connectivity and network activity? If not, try replacing the network cable to the printer.

5. Use the printer's browser-based utility and check for status reports and error messages. Run diagnostic software that might be available on the utility menu. Try flashing the printer's firmware if updates are recommended by the manufacturer.

6. Is the printer installed directly on the client computer or on another host computer that is acting as a print server?

Even though you are using a network printer, it might have been installed as a printer that is shared on the network by the host computer. Let's look at an example of this situation. Figure 10-53 shows a Devices and Printers window with several installed printers. Notice the two installations of the EPSON XP-330 Series printer. The first installation was done by using a printer that was shared by another computer on the network. The second installation was done by installing the Epson printer as a network printer addressed by its IP address. When you print using the second installation of the Epson printer, you print directly over the network to the printer. When you print to the first installation of the Epson printer, you print by way of the other computer on the network. If this computer is offline, the print jobs back up in the print queue until the computer is available.

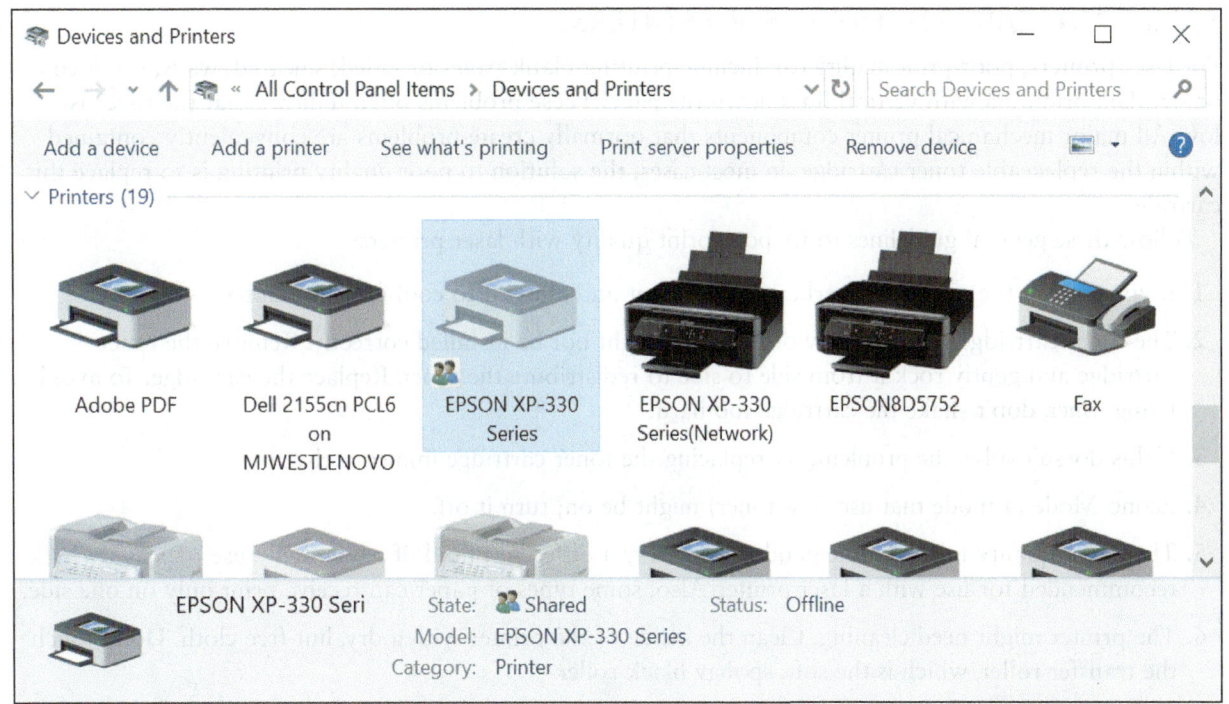

Figure 10-53 A network printer installed using two methods

When a computer has shared a local or network printer with others on the network, follow these steps to solve problems with these shared printers:

1. Is enough hard drive space available on the client or host computer?

2. Did you get an "Access denied" message when you tried to print from the client computer? If so, you might not have access to the host computer. On the client computer, go to File Explorer or Windows Explorer and attempt to drill down into resources on the printer's computer. Perhaps you have not entered a correct user account and password to access this computer; if so, you will be unable to use the computer's resources. Make sure you have a matching Windows user account and password on each computer.

3. On the host computer, open the printer's Properties box and click the **Security** tab. Select **Everyone** and make sure Permissions for Everyone includes permission to print (refer back to Figure 10-27).

4. Using Windows on the client computer, delete the printer, and then install the printer again. For best results, install the printer directly over the network and not through another computer. Watch for and address any error messages that might appear.

POOR PRINT QUALITY

**A+
CORE 1
3.11, 5.6**

Poor print quality can be caused by the printer drivers, the application, Windows, or the printer. Let's start by looking at what can cause poor print quality with laser printers and then move on to other problems that affect printouts.

> ★ **A+ Exam Tip** The A+ Core 1 exam might give you a scenario that requires you to resolve problems with streaks, faded prints, ghost images, garbled characters on a page, vertical lines, low memory errors, wrong print colors, and printing blank pages. All these problems are covered in this part of the chapter.

POOR PRINT QUALITY FOR LASER PRINTERS

For laser printers, poor print quality can include printing blank pages or faded, smeared, wavy, speckled, or streaked printouts with vertical lines down the page. These problems often indicate that the toner is low. All major mechanical printer components that normally create problems are conveniently contained within the replaceable toner cartridge. In most cases, the solution to poor-quality printing is to replace this cartridge.

Follow these general guidelines to fix poor print quality with laser printers:

1. If you suspect the printer is overheated, unplug it and allow it to cool for 30 minutes.

2. The toner cartridge might be low on toner or might not be installed correctly. Remove the toner cartridge and gently rock it from side to side to redistribute the toner. Replace the cartridge. To avoid flying toner, don't shake the cartridge too hard.

3. If this doesn't solve the problem, try replacing the toner cartridge immediately.

4. Econo Mode (a mode that uses less toner) might be on; turn it off.

5. The paper quality might not be good enough. Try a different brand of paper. Only use paper recommended for use with a laser printer. Also, some types of paper can receive print only on one side.

6. The printer might need cleaning. Clean the inside of the printer with a dry, lint-free cloth. Don't touch the transfer roller, which is the soft, spongy black roller.

7. If the transfer roller is dirty, the problem will probably correct itself after several sheets print. If not, take the printer to an authorized service center.

8. Does the printer require routine maintenance? Check the website of the printer's manufacturer to see how often to perform maintenance and to purchase the required printer maintenance kit.

> **Notes** Extreme humidity can cause the toner to clump in the cartridge and give a Toner Low message. If this is a consistent problem in your location, you might want to invest in a dehumidifier for the room where your printer is located.

9. Streaking is usually caused by a dirty developer unit or corona wire. The developer unit is contained in the toner cartridge. Replace the cartridge or check the printer documentation for directions on how to remove and clean the developer unit. Allow the corona wire to cool and clean it with a lint-free swab.

10. Speckled printouts can be caused by the laser drum. If cleaning the printer and replacing the toner cartridge don't solve the problem, replace the laser drum.

> **Notes** If loose toner comes out with your printout, the fuser is not reaching the proper temperature and toner is not being fused to the paper. Professional service is required.

11. Distorted images can be caused by foreign material inside the printer that might be interfering with the mechanical components. Check for debris that might be interfering with the printer operation.

12. If the page has a gray background or gray print, the image drum is worn out and needs to be replaced.

13. If a ghost image appears a few inches below the actual darker image on the page, the problem is usually with the image drum or toner cartridge. The drum is not fully cleaned in the cleaning stage, and toner left on it causes the ghost image. If the printer utility installed with the printer offers the option to clean the drum, try that first. The next solution is to replace the toner cartridge. If the problem is still not solved, replace the image drum.

POOR PRINT QUALITY FOR INKJET PRINTERS

To troubleshoot blank pages or poor print quality for an inkjet printer, check the following:

1. Is the correct paper for inkjet printers being used? The quality of paper determines the final print quality, especially with inkjet printers. In general, the better the quality of the paper you use with an inkjet printer, the better the print quality. Don't use less than 20-pound paper in any type of printer unless the printer documentation specifically states that a lower weight is satisfactory.

2. Is the ink supply low, or is there a partially clogged nozzle?

3. Remove and reinstall the cartridge(s).

4. Follow the printer's documentation to clean each nozzle. Is the print head too close to or too far from the paper?

5. There is a little sponge in some printers near the carriage rest that can become clogged with ink. It should be removed and cleaned.

6. If you are printing transparencies, try changing the fill pattern in your application.

7. Missing lines or dots on the printed page can be caused by the ink nozzles drying out, especially when the printer sits unused for a long time. Follow the directions given earlier in the chapter for cleaning inkjet nozzles.

8. Streaks or lines down the page can be caused by dust or dirt in the print head assemblage. Follow the manufacturer's directions to clean the inkjet nozzles.

10

GARBLED CHARACTERS ON PAPER

If scrambled or garbled characters print on all or part of a page, the problem can be caused by the document being printed, the application, connectivity between the computer and the printer, or the printer. Follow these steps to zero in on the problem:

1. First, cancel all print jobs in the print queue. Then try printing a different document from the same application. If the second document prints correctly, the problem is with the original document.

2. Try printing using a different application. If the problem is resolved, try repairing or reinstalling the application.

3. For a USB printer, the problem might be with a USB hub, port, or cable. Is the USB cable securely connected at both ends? If you are using a USB hub, remove the hub, connecting the printer directly to the computer. Try a different USB cable or USB port.

4. Recycle the printer by powering it down and back up or by pressing a Reset button.

5. Update the printer drivers. Go to the website of the printer manufacturer to find the latest drivers and follow the directions to install them.

6. If the problem is still not solved, the printer might need servicing. Does the printer need maintenance? Search the website of the printer manufacturer for other solutions.

LOW MEMORY ERRORS

For some printers, an error occurs if the printer does not have enough memory to hold the entire page. For other printers, only a part of the page prints. Some might signal this problem by flashing a light or displaying an error message on their display panels, such as "20 Mem Overflow," "Out of memory," or "Low Memory." The solution is to install more memory or to print only simple pages with few graphics. Print a self-test page to verify how much memory is installed. Some printers give you the option to install a hard drive in the printer to provide additional printer storage space.

WRONG PRINT COLORS

For a printer that is printing the wrong colors, do the following:

1. Some paper is designed to print on only one side. You might need to flip the paper in the printer.

2. Try adjusting the print quality. These adjustments vary by printer. For one color laser printer, open the **Printing Preferences** box and click the **Quality** tab (see the left side of Figure 10-54). You can try different selections in this box. To manually adjust the color, check **Manual Color Settings** and then click **Color Settings**. The box on the right side of Figure 10-54 appears.

Source: Canon

Figure 10-54 Adjust printing quality and color

3. For an inkjet printer, try cleaning the ink cartridges and calibrating the printer. One step in this process prints a self-test page. If the self-test page shows missing or wrong colors, the problem is with the ink cartridges. Try cleaning the ink nozzles. If that doesn't work, replace the ink cartridges.

4. For a laser printer, try calibrating the printer.

APPLYING | CONCEPTS   SOLVING PROBLEMS WITH PRINTER INSTALLATIONS

A+
CORE 1
3.11, 5.6

Here are some steps you can take if the printer installation fails or installs with errors:

1. If you have problems, consider that Windows might be using the wrong or corrupted printer drivers. Try removing the printer and then installing it again. To remove a printer in the Windows 10 Settings app, click a printer and click **Remove device**. To use Control Panel, right-click the printer in the Devices and Printers window and click **Remove device**. Try to install the printer again.

2. If the problem is still not solved, completely remove the printer drivers by using the printui command. The Printer User Interface command, printui, is used by administrators to manage printers and printer drivers on remote computers. You can also use it to delete drivers on the local computer. Follow these steps:

   a. If the printer is listed in the Settings app or the Devices and Printers window, remove it. (Sometimes Windows automatically puts a printer there when it finds printer drivers are installed.)

b. Before you can delete printer drivers, you must stop the print spooler service. Open the Services console and use it to stop the Print Spooler (refer to Figure 10-51). To delete any print jobs left in the queue, open Explorer and delete all files in the C:\Windows\System32\spool\PRINTERS folder.

c. You can now start the print spooler back up. Because the printer is no longer listed in the Settings app or the Devices and Printers window, starting the spooler will not tie up these drivers.

d. Open an **elevated command prompt window**, which is a window used to enter commands that have administrator privileges. To open this window in Windows 10, click **Start**, click the **Windows System** folder, right-click **Command Prompt**, point to **More**, and click **Run as administrator**. Respond to the UAC box.

> **⟳ OS Differences** To open the elevated command prompt in Windows 8, press **Win+X** and click **Command Prompt (Admin)**. In Windows 7, click **Start**, **All Programs**, and **Accessories**. Right-click **Command Prompt** and click **Run as administrator**. Respond to the UAC box.

e. At the command prompt (see the left side of Figure 10-55), enter the command **printui /s /t2**. In the command line, the /s causes the Print Server Properties box to open and the /t2 causes the Drivers tab to be the selected tab.

Figure 10-55 Use the printui command to delete printer drivers and possibly delete the driver package (driver store)

f. The Print Server Properties box opens, as shown in the middle of Figure 10-55. Select the printer and click **Remove**. In the Remove Driver And Package dialog box (see the right side of Figure 10-55), select **Remove driver only** and click **OK**. It is not necessary to remove the driver package. (This driver package, also called the driver store, can be installed on this computer or a remote computer; it holds a backup of the printer drivers.)

g. When a warning box appears, click **Yes**. Close all windows.

3. Try to install the printer again. Start the installation from the CD that came bundled with the printer or by using the printer setup program downloaded from the printer manufacturer's website.

>> CHAPTER SUMMARY

Client-Side Virtualization

◢ Client-side virtualization is done by creating multiple virtual machines, each with its own virtual desktop, on a physical machine using a hypervisor.

◢ A Type 1 hypervisor installs before an OS is installed and is called a bare-metal hypervisor. A Type 2 hypervisor is an application that installs in an OS. A Type 1 hypervisor is faster and more secure than a Type 2 hypervisor.

◢ When customizing a virtualization workstation, maximize the available budget for CPU cores and the amount of installed RAM. Make sure the NIC supports Gigabit Ethernet, consider adding a second NIC to the workstation, and account for system requirements needed to support the hypervisor software and its hardware emulator.

Cloud Computing

◢ Cloud computing is providing computing resources over the Internet to customers.

◢ A public cloud service is available to the public, and a private cloud service is kept on an organization's own servers or made available by a vendor only for a single organization's private use. A community cloud is shared between multiple organizations, and a hybrid cloud is any combination of these deployment models.

◢ All cloud computing service models incorporate on-demand service, rapid elasticity, multiplatform compatibility, resource pooling, and measured service.

◢ Cloud computing service models, including IaaS, PaaS, SaaS, and XaaS, are categorized by the types of services they provide and the degree that a third-party service or vendor is responsible for the resources.

◢ Application virtualization makes an application available to remote users from a virtualization server and does not install the application on the user's system.

◢ A thick client needs to meet recommended requirements for its OS and applications, and a thin client is a low-end computer that only needs to meet the minimum requirements for a lightweight OS.

Printer Types and Features

◢ The two most popular types of printers are laser and inkjet. Other types of printers are thermal printers, impact printers (dot matrix), and 3D printers. Laser printers produce the highest quality, followed by inkjet printers. Dot matrix printers have the advantage of being able to print multicopy documents. 3D printers use a plastic filament to build a 3D model of a digital image.

◢ The seven steps that a laser printer performs to print are processing, charging, exposing, developing, transferring, fusing, and cleaning. The charging, exposing, developing, and cleaning steps take place inside removable cartridges, which makes the printer easier to maintain.

◢ Inkjet printers print by shooting ionized ink at a sheet of paper. The quality of the printout largely depends on the quality of paper used with the printer.

◢ Dot matrix printers are a type of impact printer. They print by projecting pins from the print head against an inked ribbon that deposits ink on the paper.

◢ Direct thermal printers use heat to burn dots into special paper, and thermal transfer printers melt the ribbon or foil during printing.

◢ If you want to design your own images for three-dimensional printing, you'll need a 3D modeling program.

Using Windows to Install, Share, and Manage Printers

◢ A printer is installed as a local printer connected directly to a computer or as a network printer that works as a device on the network. Local printers can connect to a computer via a USB, serial, Bluetooth, or Wi-Fi connection. Network printers can connect to the network via an Ethernet or Wi-Fi connection. USB printers are installed automatically in Windows.

◢ Windows 10 installs, manages, and removes a printer using the Printers & scanners window in the Settings app. Windows 10/8/7 uses the Devices and Printers window in Control Panel. You can also install a printer using a setup program provided by the printer manufacturer. Always print a test page after installing a printer.

◢ A print server can be a computer on the network, firmware embedded in a network printer, or other network hardware such as a router or firewall.

◢ A printer can be shared in Windows so that others on the network can use it. To use a shared printer, the printer drivers must be installed on the remote computer.

◢ Network printers are identified on the network by their IP address.

◢ The Windows print queue is managed from the Printers & scanners window or from the Devices and Printers window.

◢ Virtual printing prints to a file, and cloud printing prints to a printer via the Internet.

◢ Printer features, such as duplexing, collating, and page orientation, are managed in a printer Properties box.

Printer Maintenance

◢ An inkjet or laser printer can be calibrated to align the color on the page. The nozzles of an inkjet printer tend to clog or dry out, especially when the printer remains unused. The nozzles can be cleaned automatically by means of printer software or buttons on the front panel of the printer.

◢ Check the page count of the printer to know when service is due and you need to order a printer maintenance kit. The page count can be reported on the printer panel or through a web-based utility in the printer firmware.

◢ Memory and a hard drive can be added to a printer to improve performance and prevent errors.

Troubleshooting Printers

◢ When troubleshooting printers, first isolate the problem. Narrow the source to the printer, connectivity between the computer and its local printer, the network, Windows, printer drivers, the application using the printer, or the printer installation. Test pages printed directly to the printer or within Windows can help narrow the source of the problem.

◢ Poor print quality can be caused by the printer drivers, the application, Windows, or the printer. For a laser printer, consider that low toner can be the problem. For an inkjet printer, consider that the ink cartridges need cleaning or replacing. The quality of paper can also be a problem.

>> KEY TERMS

For explanations of key terms, see the Glossary for this text.

3D printer	ad hoc mode	application virtualization	charging
ADF (automatic document feeder) scanner	AirPrint	Bonjour	client-hosted desktop virtualization
	application streaming	calibration	

client-side virtualization
cloud-based application
cloud-based network
   controller
cloud computing
cloud file storage service
cloud printing
community cloud
default printer
direct thermal printer
duplex printer
duplexing assembly
elevated command prompt
   window
extension magnet brush
flatbed scanner
fuser assembly
HAV (hardware-assisted
   virtualization)

hybrid cloud
hypervisor
IaaS (Infrastructure as a
   Service)
imaging drum
impact paper
impact printer
infrastructure mode
ink cartridge
inkjet printer
integrated print server
laser printer
local printer
measured service
network printer
on-demand
PaaS (Platform as a
   Service)
pickup roller

platform
print head
printer maintenance kit
printer self-test page
printui
private cloud
public cloud
rapid elasticity
remote printing
resource pooling
SaaS (Software as a
   Service)
separate pad
separation pad
Services console
synchronization app
thermal paper
thermal printer
thermal transfer printer

thick client
thin client
toner vacuum
tractor feed
transfer belt
transfer roller
Type 1 hypervisor
Type 2 hypervisor
VDI (Virtual Desktop
   Infrastructure)
virtual desktop
virtualization
virtualization server
virtual NIC
virtual printing
VM (virtual machine)
zero client

>> THINKING CRITICALLY

These questions are designed to prepare you for the critical thinking required for the A+ exams and may use content from other chapters and the web.

1. You're setting up some VMs to test an application you're considering making available to employees of the small company you work for. You need to test the app in a variety of OSs, and you don't expect to need these VMs after testing is complete. You'd like setup to be as simple and straightforward as possible without needing to make any changes to the servers on your network. Which of these hypervisors will best serve your needs?

   a. XenServer

   b. Client Hyper-V

   c. Hyper-V

   d. ESXi

2. You have three VMs running on a Windows 10 computer. Two of the VMs, machines A and B, are able to communicate with the Internet and other network resources, as is the host Windows 10 machine. However, one VM, machine C, cannot access websites on the Internet. What is the first component you check? The second component?

   a. The host machine's network adapter

   b. The switch connected to the host machine

   c. VM C's virtual NIC

   d. The host machine's hypervisor

3. You're installing VirtualBox on a Windows 10 Home computer and you get the following error message:

   `VT-x is disabled in the BIOS for all CPU modes`

   What is the problem? How do you fix it?

4. Which component in a thin client might need a higher rating than other components?

   a. The CPU because most of the processing is done on the thin client

   b. RAM because the system must have enough to hold a virtual desktop

   c. The hard drive because a VM takes up a large amount of hard drive space

   d. The NIC because most of the processing is done on the server

5. Your boss has instructed you to set up a virtualization workstation that will provide help-desk users with access to Windows 10 Pro and Home, Windows 7 Pro and Home Basic, Ubuntu Desktop, Linux Mint, and Android Oreo and Pie. She also wants you to use Client Hyper-V as the hypervisor. In what order should you install the operating systems and hypervisor?

   a. Ubuntu Desktop, Client Hyper-V, remaining OSs in VMs

   b. Client Hyper-V, Windows 10 Pro, remaining OSs in VMs

   c. Client Hyper-V, OSs in VMs

   d. Windows 10 Pro, Client Hyper-V, remaining OSs in VMs

6. You work for a small startup company that just hired five new employees, doubling its number of team members. In preparation for the new employees' first day in the office, you add five new user accounts to your CRM (customer relationship management) software subscription, a service that is hosted in the cloud. What aspect of cloud computing has worked to your advantage?

   a. On-demand

   b. Rapid elasticity

   c. Measured service

   d. Resource pooling

7. Doctors at a regional hospital access an online database of patient records that is being developed and tested by a conglomerate of health insurance agencies. The database contains records of hundreds of thousands of patients and is regulated by HIPAA restrictions on protected health information (PHI). What kind of cloud deployment is this database?

8. You're responding to a troubleshooting ticket about a laser printer in HR that isn't working. According to reports, the printer runs the print job and successfully sends the paper through. The paper shows the text prints correctly. However, the toner smudges easily and sticks to other papers, equipment, and clothes. Which part in the printer probably needs replacing?

   a. Fuser assembly

   b. Imaging drum

   c. Transfer roller

   d. Toner cartridge

9. You are not able to print a Word document on a Windows computer to a printer on the network. The network printer is connected directly to the network, but when you look at the Devices and Printers window, you see the name of the printer as \\BRYANT\HP LaserJet Pro MFP. In the following list, select the possible sources of the problem. Select all that apply.

   a. The BRYANT computer is not turned on.

   b. The HP LaserJet printer is not online.

   c. The BRYANT computer does not have file and printer sharing enabled.

   d. The Windows computer has a stalled print spool.

10

10. Gmail is an example of what type of cloud computing service model?

    a. IaaS

    b. Application streaming

    c. PaaS

    d. SaaS

11. You are not able to print a test page from your Windows 10 computer to your local, USB-connected Canon Pixma printer. Which of the following are possible causes of the problem? Select all that apply.

    a. The network is down.

    b. The printer cable is not connected properly.

    c. The Windows print spool is stalled.

    d. File and printer sharing is not enabled.

12. Which of the following resources are shared between the host computer and a VM? Select all that apply.

    a. NIC

    b. Operating system

    c. Hard drive

    d. Applications

13. What should you do if an inkjet printer prints with missing dots or lines on the page?

    a. Change the ink cartridge.

    b. Clean the heating element.

    c. Replace the image drum.

    d. Clean the inkjet nozzles.

14. Your boss, an avid user of Apple devices, has asked you to print some contracts to her shared printer. You send the documents from your Windows 10 workstation, but the print job doesn't go through. What is the first thing you need to do? Second?

    a. Verify that the Bonjour service is running on your computer.

    b. Verify that your boss can print a test page from her printer.

    c. Verify that you can view the boss's computer in File Explorer.

    d. Restart your computer.

15. Why might you assign a static IP address to a printer?

>> HANDS-ON PROJECTS

Hands-On | Project 10-1   Using Google Cloud

Google Cloud Platform is an example of a PaaS. To use the service, do the following:

1. Go to *cloud.google.com* and click **Try free**. You will need to sign in using a Google account. If you don't have an account, you can create one with any valid email address. When you first set up an account, you

(continues)

must enter payment information, which Google promises not to use during your free trial period. Create an individual account type, enter your information, and click **START MY FREE TRIAL**.

2. You begin on the Getting started page for your first project, aptly named My First Project. Click **Compute Engine**. When the system is ready, click **Create** in the VM instances box to create a VM. Use the default settings, except change the Boot disk to **Windows Server 2016 Datacenter**. Click **Create** and then wait for Google to create the instance.

3. In the VM instances list, click the instance, which takes you to the VM instance details page. Click **Set Windows password** and assign a user name to your VM instance. Google Cloud assigns a password, which displays on screen. Copy the password, save it somewhere safe, then click **Close**. Note the External IP assigned to the VM instance under the Network Interfaces section, shown near the center of Figure 10-56.

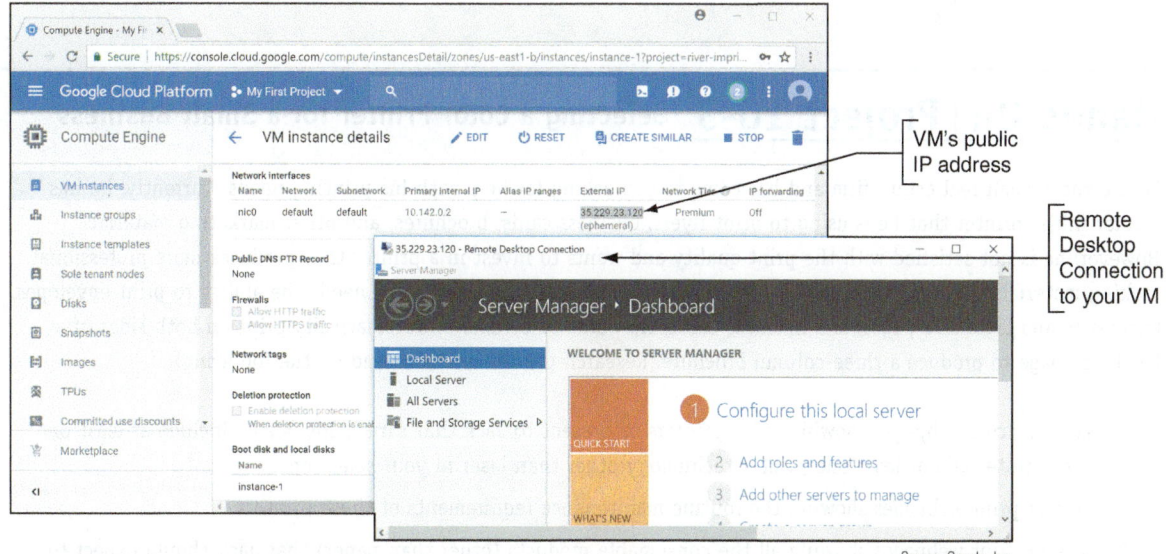

Source: Google, Inc.

Figure 10-56   Google Cloud Platform serves up a VM that has Windows Server 2016 installed

4. On your computer, you can use Remote Desktop with screen and file sharing to access your VM. Follow these steps:

   a. Enter the **mstsc** command in the Windows 10/7 Search box or the Windows 8 Run box. In the Remote Desktop Connection box, enter the External IP address of your VM, which is its public IP address available on the Internet. Click **Connect**.

   b. In the *Enter your credentials* box, your Windows user name appears. If your VM's user name is not the same as your Windows user name, click **More choices** and then click **Use a different account**. You can then enter the VM's user name and password. Click **OK** to connect.

   The lower window in Figure 10-56 shows the VM in a Remote Desktop Connection window. This Windows Server setup screen is the first screen that appears immediately after the first restart when you've installed Windows Server 2016. Take a few minutes to explore your Windows Server VM.

5. To avoid accumulating any charges against your free quota, shut down the server VM in the Remote Desktop Connection window. You learn more about Remote Desktop in Chapter 13.

> ✎ **Notes**   You will use the Google Cloud Platform service for other projects in Chapters 16 and 18. Do not disable your Google Cloud Platform account until after you have completed these projects.

Hands-On | Project 10-2 Researching Printer Support

Your company plans to purchase a new printer, and you want to evaluate the printer manufacturers' websites to determine which site offers the best support. Research three websites listed in Table 10-1 and answer these questions, supporting your answers with pages that you have saved or printed from the websites:

1. Which website made it easiest for you to select a new printer, based on your criteria for its use?
2. Which website made it easiest for you to find help for troubleshooting printer problems?
3. Which website gave you the best information about routine maintenance for its printers?
4. Which website gave you the best information about how to clean its printers?

Hands-On | Project 10-3 Selecting a Color Printer for a Small Business

Jack owns a small real estate firm and has come to you asking for help with his printing needs. Currently, he has a color inkjet printer that he is using to print flyers, business cards, brochures, and other marketing materials. However, he is not satisfied with the print quality and wants to invest in a printer that produces more professional-looking materials. He expects to print no more than 8,000 sheets per month and needs the ability to print envelopes, letter-size and legal-size pages, and business cards. He wants to be able to automatically print on both sides of a legal-size page to produce a three-column brochure. Research printer solutions and do the following:

1. Save or print webpages showing three printers to present to Jack that satisfy his needs. Include at least one laser printer and at least one printer technology other than laser in your selections.
2. Save or print webpages showing the routine maintenance requirements of these printers.
3. Save or print webpages showing all the consumable products (other than paper) that Jack should expect to have to purchase in the first year of use.
4. Calculate the initial cost of the equipment and the total cost of consumables for one year (other than paper) for each printer solution.
5. Prepare a list of advantages and disadvantages for each solution.
6. Based on your research, which of the three solutions do you recommend? Why?

Hands-On | Project 10-4 Printing in the Cloud

To practice cloud printing using Google Cloud Print, you'll need a computer with an installed printer and another computer somewhere on the Internet. For the easiest solution to using Google Cloud Print, both computers need Google Chrome installed. You'll also need a Google account.

On the computer with an installed printer, do the following to register your printer as a cloud printer:

1. If you don't already have Google Chrome, go to *google.com/chrome/*, download it, and install it.
2. Open Google Chrome and enter **chrome://devices** in the address box. Click **Add printers**. Sign in to Google with your Google account. If you don't already have an account, you can click **Create account** to create one.

(continues)

3. The list of installed printers appears. Uncheck all printers except the one you want to use for cloud printing. Click **Add Printer(s)**.

4. To confirm which printers are registered, click **Manage your printers**.

On a computer anywhere on the Internet, do the following:

5. If necessary, install Google Chrome.

6. Open Google Chrome and sign in with your Google account. Navigate to a webpage you want to print. Click the menu icon in the upper-right corner of the Chrome window and click **Print**.

7. On the Print page, click **Change** and select the printer; if you don't see your printer listed, click **Show All**. Click **Print**. The page prints over the web to your printer.

> **Notes** You can share your cloud printer with others who have a Google account. To do so, sign in to your Google account and go to *google.com/cloudprint*. There you'll see a list of print jobs sent to your printer. Click **Printers**. Select the printer you want to share and click **Share**. Enter the email address of your friend and click **Share**. Click **Close**. When your friend is signed in to Google, he can print to your printer from anywhere on the web.

>> REAL PROBLEMS, REAL SOLUTIONS

REAL PROBLEM 10-1 Creating a VM

Installing a hypervisor on a computer opens a whole new world of possibilities for exploring various operating systems and networking options. In this project, you download and install VirtualBox, a free hypervisor that is compatible with Windows, Linux, and macOS host operating systems, and then you create a VM. In the next project, you'll install Linux on the VM.

> **Notes** If you don't want to use VirtualBox as your hypervisor, you can substitute another client hypervisor, such as VMware Player or Client Hyper-V, which is available in professional and business editions of Windows. Note that Client Hyper-V does not work well on the same computer with other hypervisors, and can cause problems such as failed network connectivity. For that reason, don't enable Hyper-V on a Windows computer that has another hypervisor installed.

Complete the following steps on a Windows 10/8/7 computer:

1. If you're using VirtualBox as your hypervisor, confirm that Hyper-V is not enabled. Right-click **Start** and click **Apps and Features**. Scroll to the bottom of this window and click **Programs and Features**. In the left pane, click **Turn Windows features on or off**. Make sure **Hyper-V** is unchecked and click **OK**. Not all Windows computers list Hyper-V as an option.

2. Go to the Oracle VirtualBox website (*virtualbox.org*) and download and install VirtualBox on your computer.

3. To set up a new virtual machine, open VirtualBox and click **New** at the top of the VirtualBox window. The *Create Virtual Machine* window shown in Figure 10-57 appears.

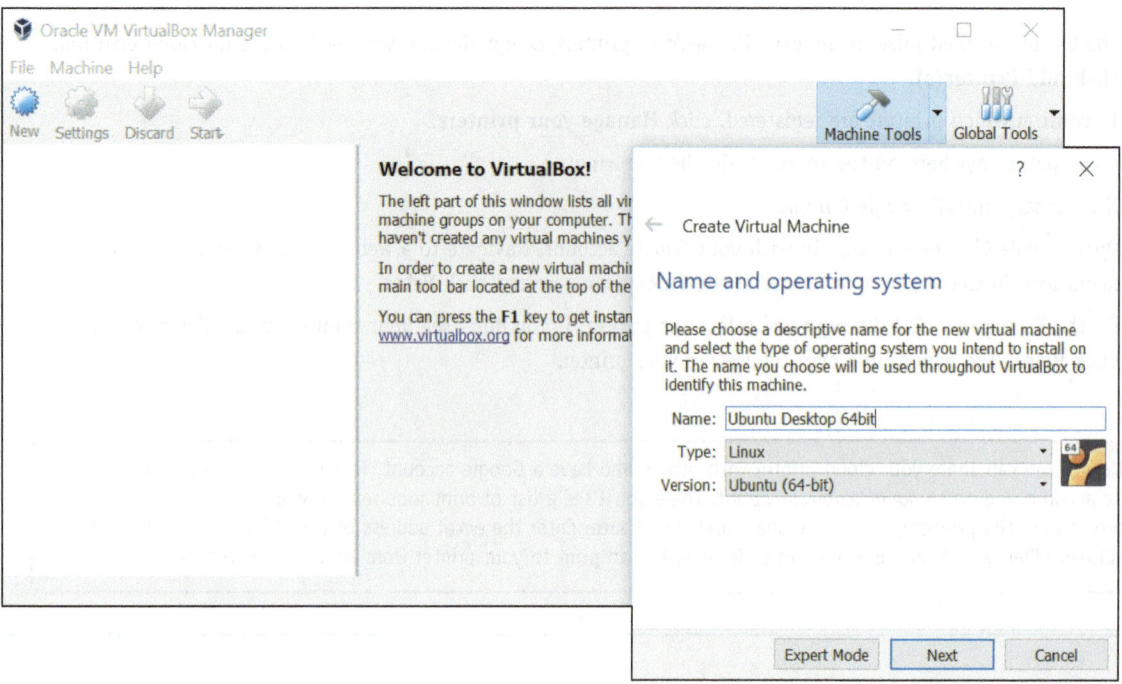

Figure 10-57 Using VirtualBox to set up a new virtual machine

Source: Oracle Corporation

4. Assign the VM a name, select **Linux** from the Type drop-down menu, and select **Ubuntu (64-bit)** from the Version drop-down menu. Click **Next**.

5. Set the memory size selection to **4096 MB** and click **Next**.

Figure 10-58 While a 64-bit Linux installation requires at least 10 GB of hard drive space, 16 GB is better

Source: Oracle Corporation

6. Be sure that **Create a virtual hard disk now** is checked and click **Create**. For the hard drive file type, make sure the default selection **VDI (VirtualBox Disk Image)** is checked, unless directed otherwise by your instructor, and click **Next**.

7. Be sure the default selection **Dynamically allocated** is checked so that space on the physical computer's hard drive is used only when it's needed by the VM. Click **Next**. Change the size of the virtual hard drive to **16 GB**, as shown in Figure 10-58, and click **Create**. When you complete the wizard, the new virtual machine is listed in the left pane of the VirtualBox window.

8. Don't start the VM yet—you'll install Ubuntu Desktop on this VM in the next Real Problem. For now, explore the VirtualBox window's menus, tools, and options. A snapshot of a VM saves a copy of the VM's disk file and can be used to restore the VM to an earlier state or clone (copy) of the VM. How can you make a snapshot of your VM? Take a snapshot and name it **Pre-OS snapshot**.

9. To change the boot order of a physical computer, you would enter the motherboard's BIOS/UEFI setup screen and change the boot order settings. How can you change the boot order for your VM?

REAL PROBLEM 10-2 Installing Linux in a VM

In Real Problem 10-1, you installed VirtualBox and created a VM. In this project, you install Ubuntu Desktop, a popular Linux distro (short for *distribution*). Complete the following steps:

1. Go to *ubuntu.com* and download the Ubuntu Desktop OS to your hard drive, or get this file from your instructor. This is a free download, so you can decline to make any donations. The file that downloads is an ISO file. Ubuntu is a well-known version of Linux and offers both desktop and server editions.

2. Open **VirtualBox**. Select the VM and click **Settings**. In the VM's Settings box, click **Storage** in the left pane. In the Storage Devices area, to the right of *Controller: SATA*, click the **Adds optical drive** icon, which looks like a disc with a green plus (+) symbol on it, as shown in Figure 10-59.

Source: Oracle Corporation

Figure 10-59 Mount an ISO image as a virtual CD in the VM

3. A dialog box appears. Click **Choose disk**. Browse to the location of the ISO file that contains the Ubuntu Desktop operating system setup files. Select the ISO file, click **Open**, and then click **OK**. You will return to the Oracle VM VirtualBox Manager window.

4. With the VM selected, click **Start** on the toolbar. Your VM starts up and begins the process of installing the operating system. Click **Install Ubuntu**. Follow the prompts and make any adjustments to default settings as directed by your instructor, or accept all default settings. If given the option, don't install any extra software bundled with the OS. You'll need to restart the VM when the installation is finished. When prompted to remove the installation media, press **Enter** because the ISO file was automatically removed already.

5. In the welcome windows, read about Ubuntu and skip the Livepatch setup. Install any OS updates offered. Monitor the update by clicking the **Software Updater** app in the dock, as shown in Figure 10-60, and restart when it's ready. To verify that you have an Internet connection, open the **Mozilla Firefox** browser and surf the web.

Software Updater app listed in dock

Source: Canonical Group Limited

Figure 10-60   The Software Updater app manages updates in Ubuntu

6. Good IT technicians must know how to use many operating systems. Poke around in the Ubuntu Desktop interface and get familiar with it. You can also search the web for tutorials and YouTube videos on how to use Ubuntu Desktop. How do you open the Settings app to change settings in the OS, such as background image, notifications, privacy, and network connections?

7. When you're ready to shut down your VM, click the power icon in the upper-right corner of the Ubuntu Desktop screen, click the next power icon, and click **Power Off** in the menu that appears. As with physical computers, it's important to properly shut down a VM to prevent corruption of its OS and other files.

REAL PROBLEM 10-3 Preparing for the A+ Core 1 Exam

Chapters 1 through 10 prepare you for the A+ Core 1 exam. Now that you have studied these chapters, you are ready to make your final review of the A+ Core 1 objectives and sit for the exam. Read through the objectives listed at the beginning of this text and make sure you understand each objective. Your instructor might suggest other exam-prep tasks. You can go to the CompTIA website at *comptia.org* to sign up for the exam or use another method suggested by your instructor. A+ Certification requires you to pass the A+ Core 1 and A+ Core 2 exams.

Windows Versions and Customer Service

After completing this chapter, you will be able to:

- Use Windows to interface with users, files and folders, applications, and hardware

- Use Windows tools to explore, examine, and support the system

- Explain the various ways Windows secures resources on the network and secures a network connection

- Support customers with professionalism and respect, in addition to your technical skills

In this chapter, you learn about the versions of Microsoft Windows and how this operating system provides an interface between users and applications and between applications and hardware devices. You learn to use several Windows tools and utilities that are useful to view and manage storage devices, examine a system, and troubleshoot simple problems with hardware and applications. Finally, you learn about interpersonal skills (people skills, sometimes called soft skills) needed by an IT support technician.

> ★ **A+ Exam Tip** In this text, you learn about Windows 10, Windows 8.1, Windows 8.0, and Windows 7. All these operating systems are covered on the A+ Core 2 exam. In the text, we use Windows 8 to refer to Windows 8.0 and Windows 8.1.

WINDOWS INTERFACES

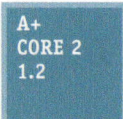

An operating system (OS) is software that controls a computer. In general, you can think of an operating system as the middleman between applications and hardware, between the user and hardware, and between the user and applications (see Figure 11-1).

Figure 11-1 Users and applications depend on the OS to relate to all applications and hardware components

Several applications might be installed on a computer to meet various user needs, but a computer really needs only one operating system. Although there are important differences among them, all operating systems share the following four main functions:

◢ *Function 1:* Provide a user interface

  ◢ Performing storage and housekeeping procedures requested by the user, such as reorganizing a hard drive, deleting files, copying files, and changing the system date

  ◢ Providing a way for the user to manage the desktop, hardware, applications, and data

◢ *Function 2:* Manage files

  ◢ Managing files on hard drives, DVD drives, CD drives, USB flash drives, and other drives

  ◢ Creating, storing, retrieving, deleting, and moving files

◢ *Function 3:* Manage hardware

  ◢ Managing the BIOS/UEFI (programs permanently stored on hardware devices)

  ◢ Managing memory, which is a temporary place to store data and instructions as they are being processed

  ◢ Diagnosing problems with software and hardware

  ◢ Interfacing between hardware and software (that is, interpreting application software needs to the hardware and vice versa)

◢ *Function 4:* Manage applications

  ◢ Installing and uninstalling applications

  ◢ Running applications and managing the interface to the hardware on behalf of an application

Windows 10 is the latest Microsoft operating system and is an upgrade to Windows 8, which was preceded by Windows 7. Windows 8.1 is a free update or release of the original Windows 8. Every IT support technician needs to be a power user of Windows 10 and familiar with Windows 8/7.

✎ **Notes** This chapter assumes Windows 10 is already installed on your computer, and it would be helpful if you have access to the Windows 8 and Windows 7 operating systems as you work your way through this chapter. If Windows is not yet installed, read Chapter 12 and install Windows 10, 8, or 7. Then you can return to this chapter to learn how to use the OS.

Every Windows OS offers a graphical user interface (GUI; pronounced "GOO-ee") that uses graphics instead of a command-driven interface. Windows 10 offers two graphical user interfaces—the desktop and Tablet mode via a feature called Continuum. Windows 8 has two graphical user interfaces—the modern interface and the desktop. Windows 7 offers one graphical user interface, the desktop. We next examine these interfaces.

> ✎ **Notes** The figures and steps in this text use Windows 10 Professional, Windows 8.1 Professional, and Windows 7 Professional. If you are using a different edition of Windows 10, 8, or 7, your screens and steps may differ slightly from those presented here.

WINDOWS 10 INTERFACE

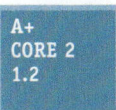
A+
CORE 2
1.2

Let's take a quick look at the Windows 10 desktop and Start menu, as well as other features you'll find useful when supporting Windows 10.

WINDOWS 10 DESKTOP

The application and utility hub in Windows 10 is the Start menu on the desktop (see Figure 11-2). Tools used by technicians to support, secure, and troubleshoot Windows, as well as productivity software such as Microsoft Office, QuickBooks, and Dreamweaver, can be accessed from the Start menu, desktop, and taskbar. The taskbar is normally located at the bottom of the Windows desktop, displaying information about open programs and providing quick access to others. By default, Windows 10 pins the Task View, Microsoft Edge, File Explorer, and Store icons in the Quick Launch toolbar on the left side of the taskbar. Click an icon to open the program. An open application displays a program icon in the taskbar to the right of the toolbar; if a pinned application is open, it is underlined.

11

Figure 11-2   Windows 10 uses a Start menu with live tiles

The Windows 10 Start menu has live tiles on the right side of the menu that offer continuous real-time updates. Click a tile or program name to open its app. The left side of the Start menu includes lists of: (1) recently added apps, if there are any, (2) apps used most often, (3) suggested apps for downloading from the Windows Store, and (4) an alphabetical list of all apps available on the computer. To expand the view of the links on the left side of the Start menu, click the three horizontal bars (sometimes called a hamburger button) at the top-left corner of the menu, as shown in Figure 11-2.

The bottom-left corner of the Start menu has a few icons that you can use to access important functions. Click the **Account** icon to change account settings, lock Windows, or sign out of Windows. Other icons allow you to access File Explorer, the Settings app, and the Power menu. Click the **Power** icon to put the computer in sleep mode, shut it down, or restart.

> **✎ Notes** To customize the Start menu, open the Start menu and click the **Settings app** icon. In the Settings app, open the **Personalization** group and select **Start**. If you prefer to use the Windows 8 Start screen in Windows 10, apply the full-screen Start menu option in the Personalization group of the Settings app.

The notification area, also called the system tray or systray, is located on the right side of the taskbar by default and displays open services. A service is a program that runs in the background to support or serve Windows or an application. The services in the notification area include the volume or sound control and network connectivity.

To launch a program from the desktop, use one of these methods:

◢ *Start menu*. Click the **Start** button and find the program in the list of all programs on the left, or find the pinned app or a live tile on the right. To pin an app to the Start menu, find the app in the alphabetical apps list, right-click the app tile, and click **Pin to Start**. To unpin an app from the Start menu, right-click the pinned app tile and click **Unpin from Start**.

◢ *Windows 10 search box with Cortana.* Cortana is the new voice-enabled search feature of Windows 10 and is accessed using the search box on the taskbar (shown earlier in Figure 11-2). If you know the name of the program file, you can type that name in the search box and press **Enter**, or click the microphone button to the right of the search box and then say the command to Cortana. For example, the program name of the Notepad text editor is notepad.exe. When you type **notepad** in the search box and press **Enter**, the Notepad window opens. (Windows assumes the file extension for a program is .exe, so it's not necessary to type the extension.) Alternatively, you can click the microphone button and then say, "**Open Notepad.**" The Notepad window opens.

◢ *Quick Launch menu*. To launch most Windows support tools, right-click the **Start** button to display the Quick Launch menu (see Figure 11-3) and then click an item to open it. You can also press **Win+X** to launch the menu from anywhere in Windows 10.

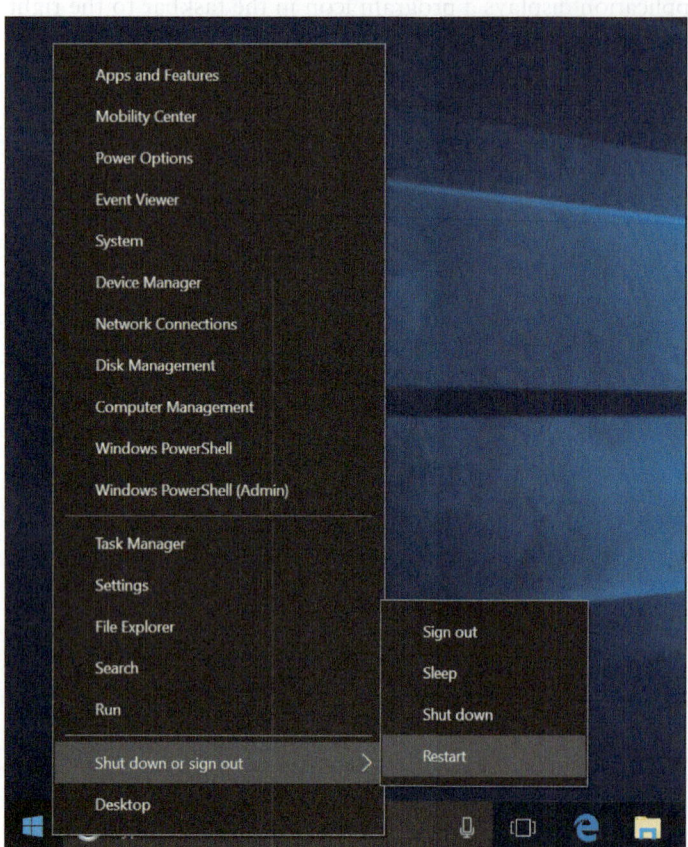

Figure 11-3 Use the Quick Launch menu from anywhere in Windows to access useful Windows utilities and screens

Here are some important items on the Quick Launch menu. You'll learn to use these and other items on the menu in this chapter and later chapters:

▲ Use the Settings app to change Windows settings. To change more advanced settings, you'll need to use the Control Panel. You'll have a chance to explore the Settings app and Control Panel later in this chapter.

▲ To repair, update, and uninstall installed apps, use the Apps & Features window, which can also be found in the Settings app. The window also has a link to the Programs and Features window, which you can use to turn Windows features on or off.

▲ The System link opens the About page in the Settings app to display information about the system and gives links to many more tools to manage settings (see Figure 11-4). The About page replaces the System window of earlier versions of Windows, although you can still find the System window in Control Panel.

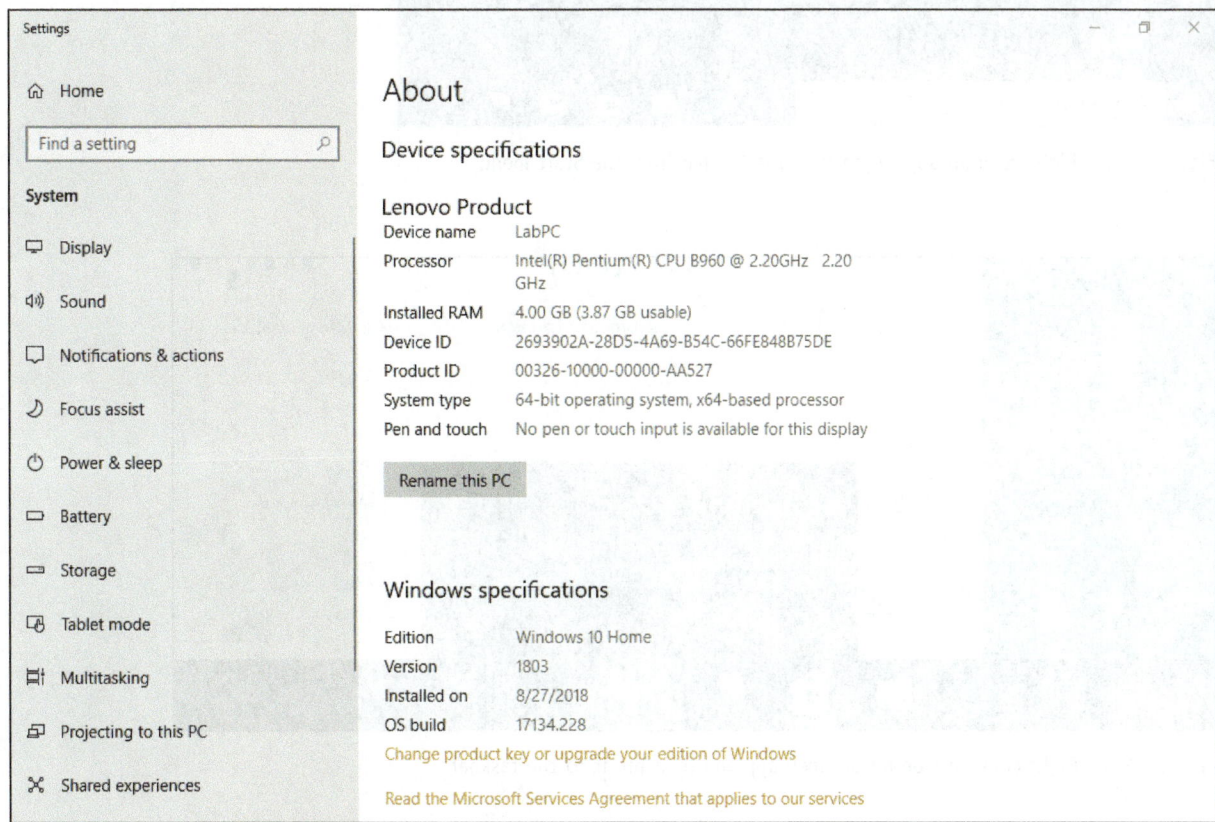

Figure 11-4 The About page in the Settings app displays the same information found in the System window

▲ Windows PowerShell and Windows PowerShell (Admin) provide a command-line interface where you can process small PowerShell programs called cmdlets. Earlier versions of Windows provided Command Prompt and Command Prompt (Admin) options on the Start menu, which open a command-line interface to enter Windows commands. You learn to use PowerShell and Command Prompt windows in Chapter 13.

▲ Notice the *Shut down or sign out* item near the bottom of the Quick Launch menu in Figure 11-3. When you point to it, you see submenu items that always include Shut down, Sign out, and Restart. Depending on your system configuration, you might also see Sleep or Hibernate.

▲ *Pin to taskbar.* For a program you use often, you can add its icon to the taskbar on the desktop, which is called pinning to the taskbar. Right-click an app on the Start menu to see the app's shortcut menu (see Figure 11-5). If necessary, click **More**, then click **Pin to taskbar**. You can also open a program, right-click the program's icon in the taskbar, and then click **Pin to taskbar** (see Figure 11-6).

11

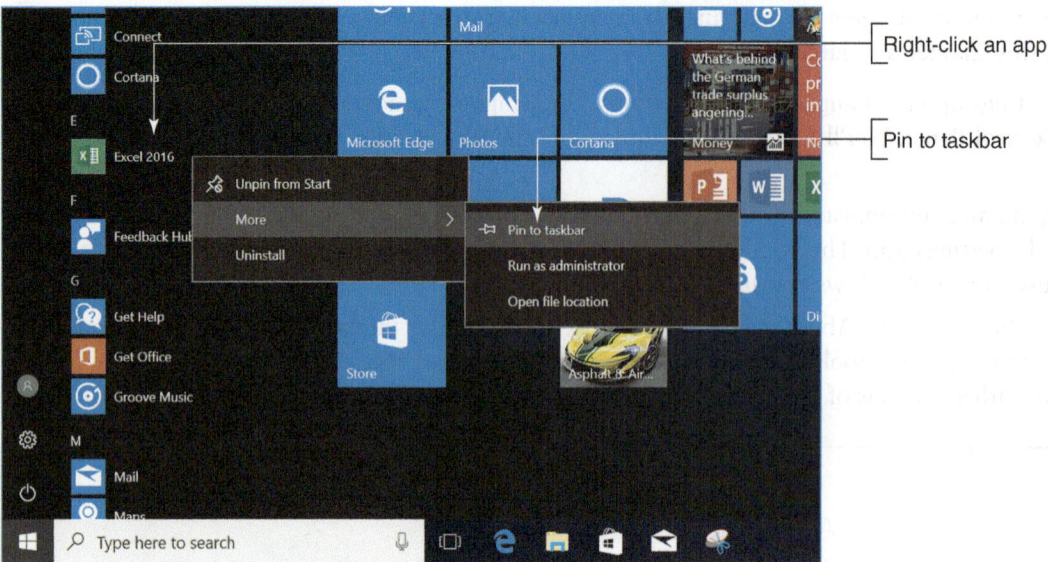

Figure 11-5 Right-click an app to pin it to the taskbar from the Start menu

Figure 11-6 Right-click an icon for an open app and then pin it to the taskbar

▲ ***Double-click the program file name in File Explorer.*** File Explorer allows you to view and manage files and folders on your computer or the network. To open File Explorer, click the **File Explorer** icon in the taskbar or the Quick Launch menu. You can launch a program by double-clicking the program file name in File Explorer.

▲ ***Shortcut on the desktop.*** You can place a shortcut to a program on the desktop and then double-click the shortcut to launch the program. You learn to create shortcuts later in this chapter.

▲ ***Run box or search box.*** If you know the name of the program file, you can open the Quick Launch menu and click **Run**. The Run box appears, as shown in Figure 11-7. Type the name of the program file and press **Enter**. For example, the program file name of the Notepad text editor is notepad.exe. When you type **notepad** in the Run box and press **Enter,** the Notepad window appears. (Windows assumes the file extension for a program is .exe, so it's not necessary to type the extension.) You can also enter **notepad** in the Windows 10 search box to launch the program.

Figure 11-7   Use the Run box to launch a program

Here are a few tips about managing windows on the desktop:

▲ Drag the title bar of a window to move the window. Use the buttons in the upper-right corner to resize, maximize, minimize, and close a window.

▲ Drag a window to the top of the screen to maximize it. Drag the window downward on the screen to return it to its original size. Drag a window to the right or left of the screen so that it snaps to the side of the screen and fills that half of it. Drag a window to a corner of the screen so that it snaps to a quarter-size of the screen in that corner.

▲ Press and shake (drag back and forth quickly) the title bar of a window to minimize all other windows except the one you shake. Shake again to restore the size of the other windows.

WINDOWS 10 FEATURES

Here's a brief list of Windows 10 features that apply mainly to the end user:

▲ *Action Center.* The new Action Center in Windows 10 is used to toggle several Windows features on and off, access the Settings app, and view notifications. In Windows 10, you open the Action Center by clicking the Action Center icon next to the date and time in the taskbar (see Figure 11-8). Windows 8 has an Action Center that is much more powerful than the Windows 10 Action Center. The Windows 10 version of the Windows 8 Action Center is called Security and Maintenance and can be found in the Windows 10 Control Panel.

11

Figure 11-8   The Action Center is used for accessing Security and Maintenance and other Windows features

▲ *Cortana*. Windows 10's digital assistant, Cortana, can learn your speech, handwriting patterns, and typing history to assist with user input. Access Cortana using the search box on the taskbar (see Figure 11-9). Cortana speaks using a woman's voice, so she is often referred to using a female pronoun. Cortana can, for example, help you search your computer for a file, compose an email, search the Internet, or even check the weather.

Click to activate Cortana's microphone

Figure 11-9   Access Cortana by typing or speaking to her

▲ *Snap Assist.* Windows 8 introduced Snap Assist, which makes it easy to snap windows to the left or right side of the screen, but this was a problem for Windows 8 modern apps that needed the entire screen. To allow for more flexibility, Snap Assist in Windows 10 allows for half and quadrant snapping, so a window can take up all of the screen, half of it, or only a quarter. Windows 10 apps are now contained in windows that float on the desktop and can be snapped to an edge or corner.

▲ *Task View.* To help organize applications opened on the desktop, Windows 10 uses Task View to create multiple virtual desktops so you can flip through to the desired desktop as needed (see Figure 11-10). For example, if you are paying bills, writing a paper, and surfing the Internet, you can put those three tasks on separate desktops. On desktop 1, you can open relevant web browsers and budgeting software. On desktop 2, open Microsoft Word, OneNote, and web browsers for research. On desktop 3, open web browsers to keep up with social media and news. To open a new desktop, click the **Task View** icon on the taskbar (refer back to Figure 11-2), and then click **New desktop**. The keyboard shortcut to toggle your open desktops is **Ctrl+Win+arrow left** or **arrow right**. To close a desktop, click the Task View icon and close its Desktop thumbnail in the pane just above the taskbar.

Figure 11-10   Use Task View to organize your open apps

APPLYING | CONCEPTS   SIGNING IN TO WINDOWS 10 AND USING THE WINDOWS 10 INTERFACE

Windows 10 is designed to flow between touch screen and desktop interfaces. Follow these steps to learn how to sign in to Windows 10 and manage apps:

1. When you start up a Windows 10 computer, you see the lock screen. Click anywhere on the screen and the sign-in screen appears (see Figure 11-11). To sign in, select a user account and enter the account password. The desktop appears.

(continues)

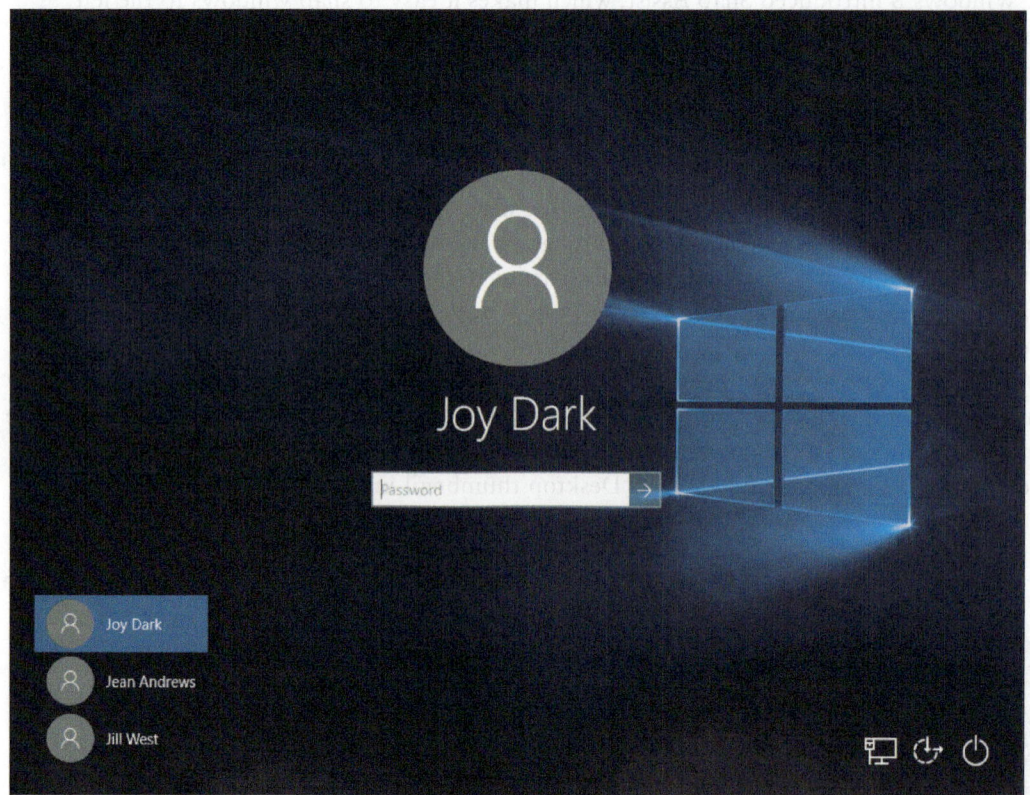

Figure 11-11 The Windows sign-in screen

> 📝 **Notes** These instructions assume you are using a mouse and keyboard. If you're using a touch screen, simply tap instead of clicking, press and hold instead of right-clicking, double-tap instead of double-clicking, and swipe to scroll the screen to the right, left, up, or down.

2. To open an app, click the **Start** icon, and then click the app tile on the Start menu.

3. Using the Start menu, open a second app.

> 📝 **Notes** In Windows, there are multiple ways to do the same thing. For example, to open the Start menu, (1) click the **Start** button or (2) press the Windows key on the keyboard.

4. Use Snap Assist to snap a window to the left or right side or a corner of the screen so a second window can share it. To snap a window, press and drag the title bar of the window to the left or right side of the screen. When you release the window, it snaps to the side, and then you can snap a second app to the other side of the screen. You can press and drag the vertical bar between the two windows to adjust the window sizes (see Figure 11-12).

> 📝 **Notes** To snap windows, your screen resolution must be at least 1024 × 768.

(continues)

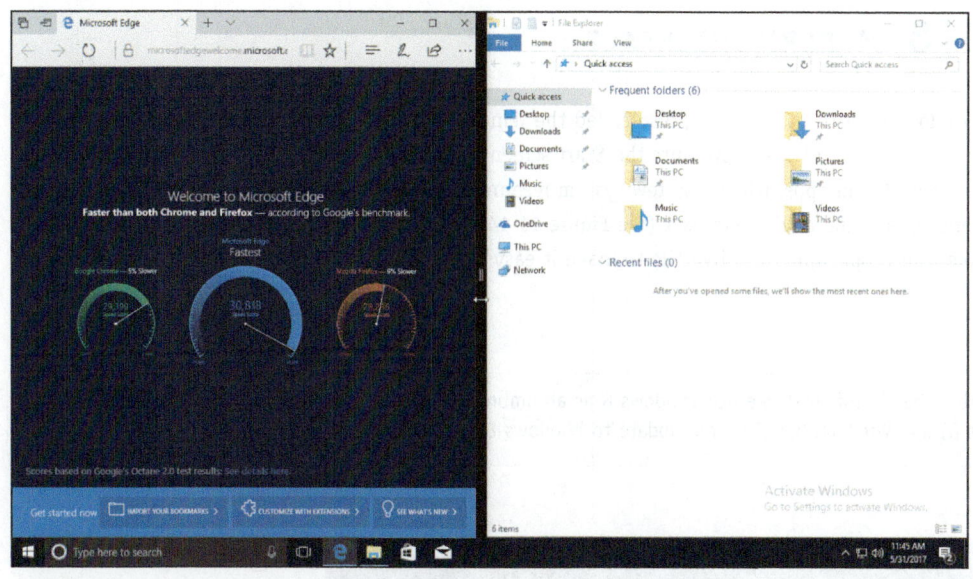

Figure 11-12   Two app pages on the screen

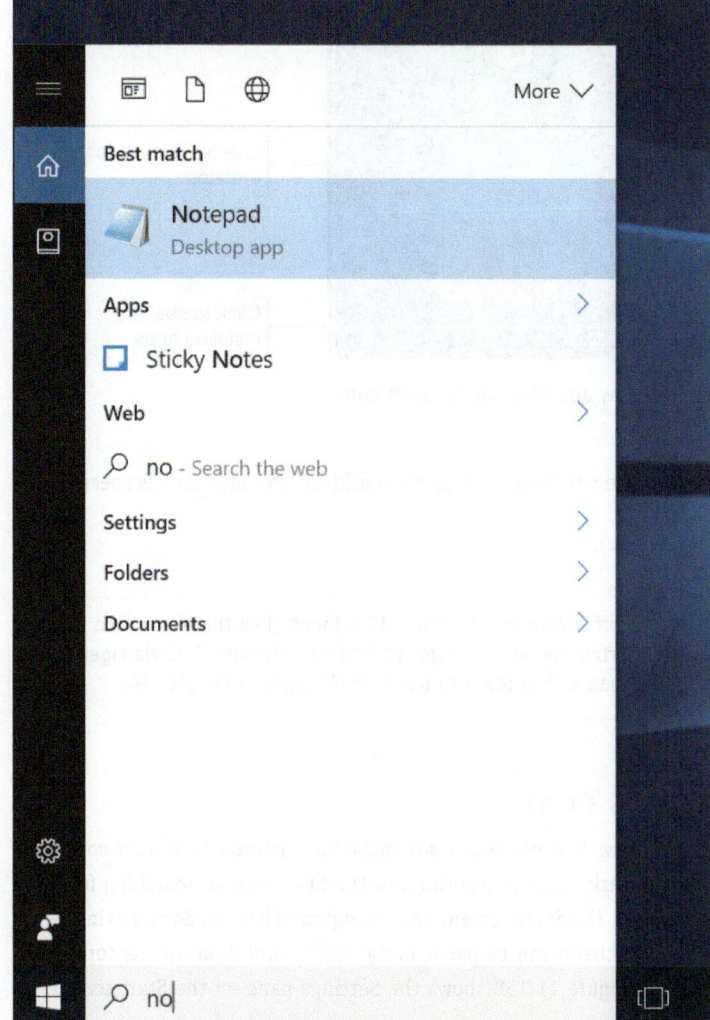

Figure 11-13   Use the Search bar to find and open apps and utilities

5. Open and close three other apps using these two methods:

   ◢ Open the Start menu and click a tile in the alphabetical list of programs on the left.

   ◢ In the Search bar, type the name of the app you want to open. As you type, search results appear above the Search bar. For example, when **no** is typed in the Search bar in Figure 11-13, Notepad appears as the best match. Other possible search results are also listed. You can click any app in the search results to open it. By default, the Search feature searches for apps, Windows settings, files, web images, and web videos. If you click an item under the *Web* heading, Edge opens to search online.

6. To see thumbnails of open apps that are not visible on the screen, click **Task View** in the taskbar (refer to Figure 11-10).

7. To close a selected app, move your pointer to the top of the screen. A menu bar appears if it was hidden. Click the red **X** on the far right of the menu bar.

8. Close all open apps.

11

WINDOWS | 8 MODERN INTERFACE

**A+
CORE 2
1.2**

The Windows 8 **modern interface**, also called the Windows 8 interface and formerly called the **Metro User Interface** or **Metro UI**, presents the Start screen to the user. The **Start screen** contains tiles that represent lean apps, which use few system resources and are designed for social media, social networking, and the novice end user (see Figure 11-14). Click a tile to open its app. Some apps use live tiles. For example, the People app has a live tile to make it easy to keep up with updates on Facebook, LinkedIn, and Twitter.

📝 **Notes** Remember that in this text, we use Windows 8 as an umbrella term to cover Windows 8.0 (the first release of Windows 8) and Windows 8.1 (the free update to Windows 8.0).

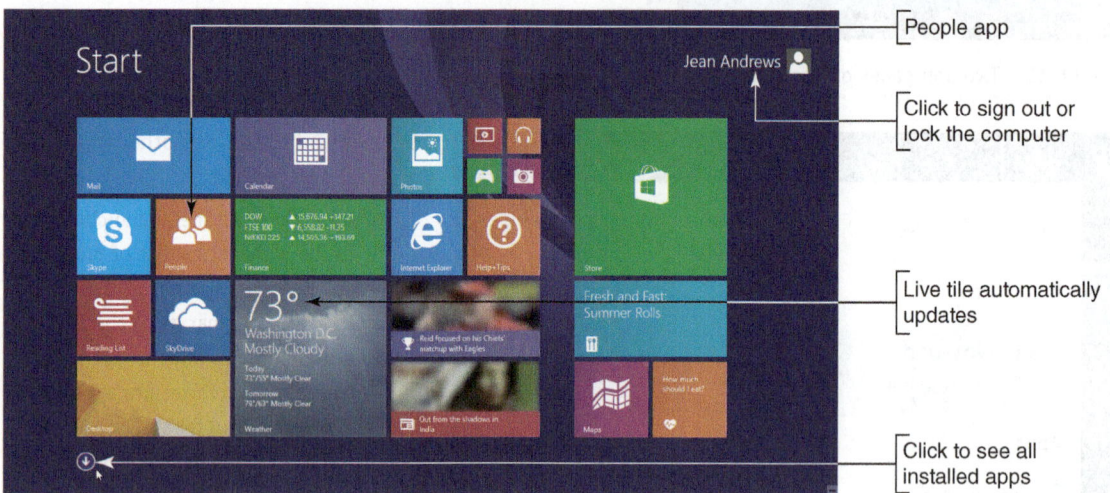

Figure 11-14 The Windows 8 Start screen is used to view app tiles and to open apps

The modern interface uses pages in comparison to the windows used on the desktop. The interface is specifically designed for touch screens.

📝 **Notes** To conserve system resources, you can turn off a Windows 10/8 live tile. Right-click the tile on the Start screen and then click **Turn live tile off** in the shortcut menu that appears. You can also use Task Manager to find out how the app is affecting overall system performance. You learn to use Task Manager in Chapter 14.

THE CHARMS BAR AND THE SETTINGS CHARM

The **charms bar** appears on the right side of any Windows 8 screen when you move your pointer to a right corner (see Figure 11-15A). It gives handy access to common tasks such as returning to the Start screen, searching for content, connecting to a wireless network, personalizing the Start screen, and changing other Windows settings. In the charms bar, click a **charm** to select it. The Settings charm can be particularly useful, and items at the top of the Settings pane can change depending on the situation. Figure 11-15B shows the Settings pane on the Start screen, and Figure 11-15C shows the Settings pane on the desktop.

(continues)

(A)　　　　　(B)　　　　　(C)

Figure 11-15 (A) The charms bar, (B) the Settings pane on the Start screen, and (C) the Settings pane on the desktop

> 📝 **Notes** With the first release of Windows 8, many users complained that important items like the charms bar were difficult to find and not intuitive to use. As a result, beginning with Windows 8.1, Microsoft added tips that randomly appear on screen to help users learn how to use the new interface.

THE POWER ICON

Use the Power icon in the upper-right corner of the Start screen to shut down or restart the computer. Click the **Power** icon, and then click an item in the menu that appears (see Figure 11-16). The items on this menu always include Shut down and Restart, and, depending on the configuration, might also include Sleep and Hibernate.

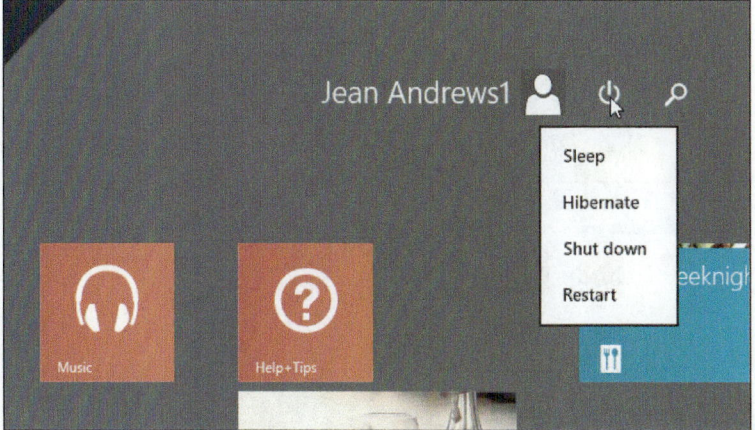

Figure 11-16 Use the Power icon at the top of the Start screen to shut down or restart the system

(continues)

WINDOWS 8 DESKTOP

To access the Windows 8 desktop, click the Desktop tile on the Start screen. When you move your pointer to a right corner of the desktop screen, the charms bar appears, as shown in Figure 11-17. Click the **Start** charm in the charms bar to return to the Start screen. Alternately, you can click the Start button in the taskbar to return to the Start screen.

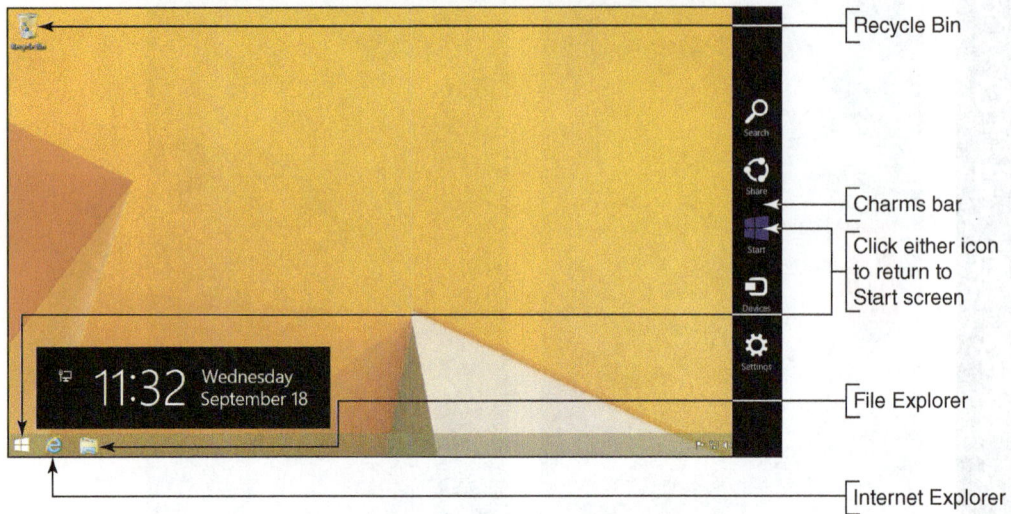

Recycle Bin

Charms bar

Click either icon to return to Start screen

File Explorer

Internet Explorer

Figure 11-17 The Windows 8 desktop with the charms bar in view

Notes According to Microsoft terminology, you *sign in* to Windows 10/8 and *log on* to Windows 7.

OS Differences The Windows 7 desktop provides a 3D user interface called the **Aero user interface** that gives a glassy appearance (see Figure 11-18). The Windows 7 desktop can have **gadgets**, which are mini-apps that provide information such as the time, date, news headlines, or weather. You can open programs by using the Start menu, shortcuts on the desktop, or icons in the taskbar. For example, to open Windows 7 Windows Explorer, click its icon in the taskbar. File Explorer in Windows 10/8 is called **Windows Explorer** in Windows 7.

Figure 11-18 The Windows 7 desktop using the Aero interface has a glassy, transparent look

CHOOSING A WINDOWS EDITION

A+ CORE 2 1.2

Microsoft offers several editions of each version of Windows. Here are the most important ones:

▲ Important Windows 10 editions for personal computers include Windows 10 Home, Windows 10 Pro, Windows 10 Enterprise, and Windows 10 Education. Home editions for Windows are intended for laptops and desktop computers in a home or small office. Pro, Enterprise, and Education editions are designed to work in large organizations and enterprises. Enterprise editions allow for volume licensing. Education editions are less expensive editions for those who can prove they qualify for the educational discounts.

▲ Windows 8 options are Windows 8.1 Core (the Home version), Windows 8.1 Pro, and Windows 8.1 Enterprise.

▲ Windows 7 options are Windows 7 Home Basic and Premium, Windows 7 Professional, and Windows 7 Enterprise.

> ★ **A+ Exam Tip** The A+ Core 2 exam expects you to be able to compare and contrast which version and edition of Windows is best in a given scenario, including Windows 10, Windows 8.1, Windows 8.0, and Windows 7 personal and corporate editions.

When deciding among Windows 10, Windows 8, or Windows 7 for a new installation, select Windows 10 if possible because Microsoft support for its latest OS will last longer, and Windows 10 improves in many ways on Windows 8 and Windows 7.

When faced with choosing an edition of Windows 10/8/7, consider the purposes for using Windows. Is the computer intended for corporate or personal use? Different editions offer different features. The professional editions have more features that are more useful in a corporate setting, which is why these editions are more expensive. Consider the following features that the user or organization might require; they are all available on the Windows 10/8/7 Pro, Education, Business, and Ultimate editions, but are not available in the Home editions:

▲ *Domain access.* If the computer connects to a corporate or educational network to access network resources, it requires access to a Windows domain, which manages resources on the network. How to join a domain is covered later in this chapter.

▲ *BitLocker.* BitLocker encrypts an entire volume on a drive to protect the data and can provide full hard drive encryption. This level of security is often required by corporations to secure a computer and its data and settings before the computer is allowed to connect to and access resources on a corporate network.

▲ *Encryption File System (EFS).* EFS encrypts files and folders to protect the data. Although not as secure as full drive encryption, EFS is sometimes required by individuals and corporations to protect the data on a computer's hard drive.

▲ *Branchcache.* Branchcache optimizes content access over a wide area network (WAN) by retrieving content from remote servers and caching it on local servers for better access. The feature is sometimes required to optimize accessing resources on remote corporate networks.

▲ *Media Center.* Media Center is a digital video recorder and media player originally offered as part of earlier editions of Windows, including Windows 7 Professional. It was also available as a paid add-on in Windows 8 Pro. However, it is deprecated (no longer available) starting with Windows 10.

Now that you're familiar with the Windows interfaces and editions, let's learn to use several tools that are helpful to both users and technicians.

11

WINDOWS TOOLS FOR USERS AND TECHNICIANS

> **A+**
> **CORE 2**
> **1.2, 1.3,**
> **1.5, 1.6,**
> **1.8**

All users need to know how to use File Explorer or Windows Explorer. In addition, a technician needs to know how to use the Control Panel, Power Options, System window, System Information window, and for Windows 8/7, the Action Center. All these tools are covered in this part of the chapter.

WINDOWS 10/8 FILE EXPLORER AND WINDOWS 7 WINDOWS EXPLORER

> **A+**
> **CORE 2**
> **1.6**

You open Windows 10/8 File Explorer or Windows 7 Windows Explorer in these ways:

◢ Click the yellow File Explorer or Windows Explorer icon in the taskbar. If an Explorer window is already open, it becomes the active window. To open an additional instance of Explorer, right-click the File Explorer icon and click **File Explorer**. Having two instances of Explorer open makes it easy to drag and drop files and folders from one location to another.

◢ For Windows 10, press **Win+X** or right-click the Start button to open the Quick Launch menu, and then click **File Explorer**. From the Windows 8 desktop, open the Quick Launch menu (press **Win+X**) and click **File Explorer** in the menu. For Windows 7, right-click **Start** and select **Open Windows Explorer** from the menu that appears. If an Explorer instance is already open, a new instance of Explorer is created.

◢ For Windows 10, enter **explorer** in the search box. For Windows 8, open the Quick Launch menu, click **Run,** and enter **explorer** in the Run box. For Windows 7, click **Start** and enter **explorer** in the search box. You can use this method to open multiple instances of Explorer.

◢ In Windows 10, click the **microphone** button in the search box on the taskbar. Tell Cortana to "**Open File Explorer.**" If an Explorer window is already open, it becomes the active window.

The Windows 10/8 File Explorer window has tabs near the top that open ribbons (see Figure 11-19). These tabs can change depending on the situation. You click a tab to see its ribbon or a drop-down menu that appears with more tools. The Home ribbon is shown in the figure. The left pane in Windows 10 is called the Quick access area; pin often-used folders in this area to quickly access them. In Windows 8/7, this area is called Favorites. The Windows 7 Windows Explorer window doesn't use ribbons (see Figure 11-20).

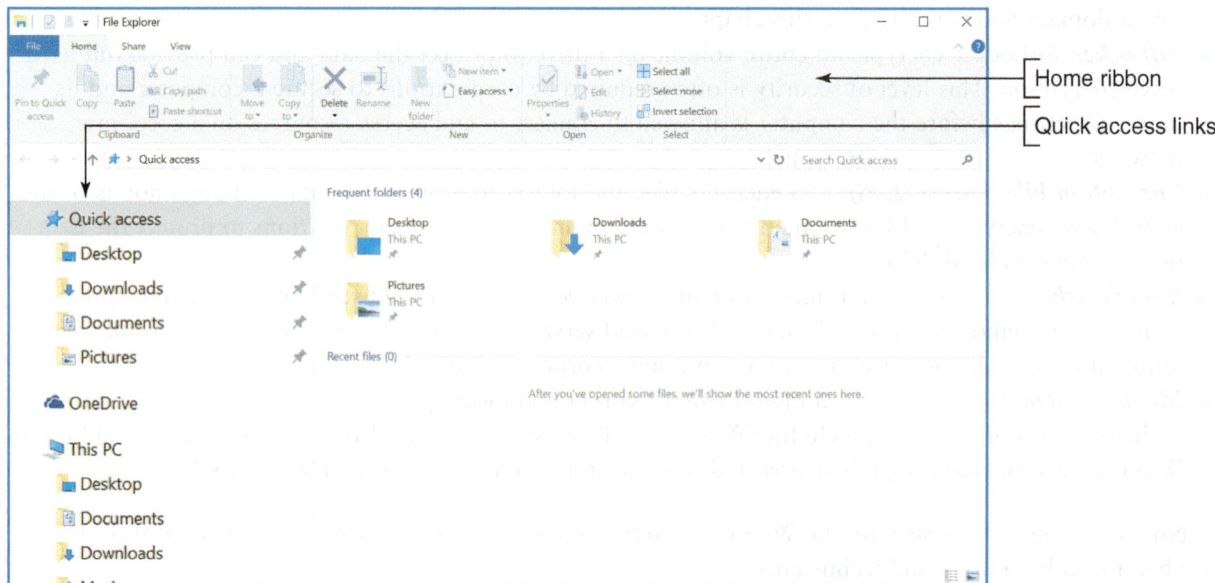

Figure 11-19 The Windows 10 File Explorer window with the Home ribbon shown

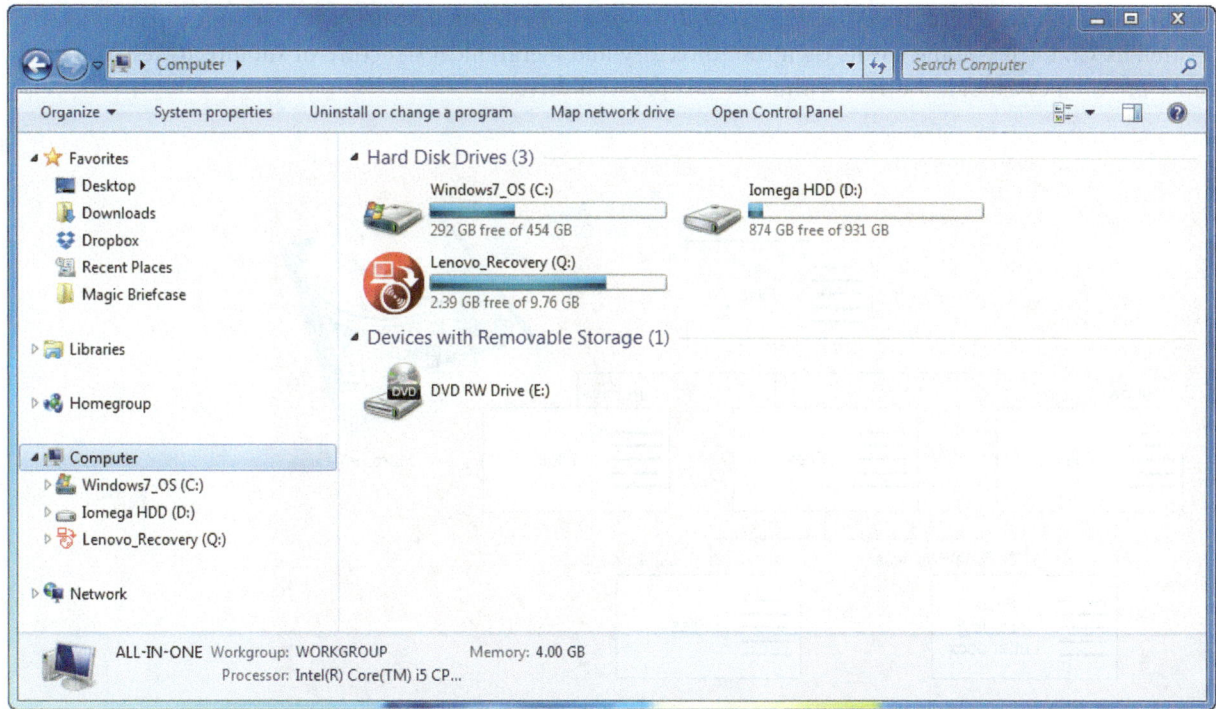

Figure 11-20 The Windows 7 Windows Explorer window with the Computer item selected in the left pane

11

APPLYING | CONCEPTS   USING QUICK ACCESS IN FILE EXPLORER

In Windows 10 File Explorer, shortcuts to Desktop, Downloads, Documents, and Pictures are pinned to the Quick access list by default. Pinned shortcuts remain in the list until you remove them. Shortcuts to recently used items appear in the list, and then disappear in time if they are no longer being used. If you want an item to remain in the Quick access list, you can pin it.

Follow these steps to pin a folder to the Quick access list:

1. Create a new folder on the desktop, and change the folder name to **Projects**. To create the folder, right-click the desktop, select **New** in the shortcut menu, and click **Folder**. You can then rename the folder.

2. Open **File Explorer**. Click **Quick access** in the left pane to view Quick access items in the main folder window. The top section lists frequently used folders (Frequent folders) and the bottom section lists recently used files (Recent files). Notice Frequent folders are also listed in the left pane of the File Explorer window.

3. Drag and drop the Projects folder into the Quick access Frequent folders section. Notice that a shortcut to the Projects folder now appears under *Quick access* in the left pane, with a pin icon next to its name.

4. Right-click the **Projects** folder under Quick access in the left pane or in the Quick access view and select **Unpin from Quick access**.

Let's see how to use the Explorer windows to manage files and folders and other system resources.

FILES AND DIRECTORIES

Every OS manages a hard drive, optical drive, USB drive, or other type of drive by using directories (also called folders), subdirectories, and files. The drive is organized with a single root directory at the top of the hierarchical structure of subdirectories, as shown in Figure 11-21. The exception to this rule is a hard drive because it can be divided into partitions that can have more than one volume, such as drive C: and drive D:, on the same physical hard drive (see Figure 11-22). For a volume, such as drive C:, the root directory is written as C:. Each volume has its own root directory and hierarchical structure of subdirectories. You can think of volumes as logical drives within the one physical drive.

Figure 11-21 Storage devices such as a USB drive, DVD, or hard drive are organized into directories and subdirectories that contain files

Figure 11-22 A hard drive can be divided into one or more partitions that can each contain a volume such as drive C: or drive D:

As shown in Figure 11-21, the root directory can hold files or other directories, which can have names such as C:\Data. These directories, called subdirectories, child directories, folders, or subfolders can have other directories listed in them in turn. Any directory can have files and other subdirectories listed in it; for example, Figure 11-21 shows that one file on drive C: is C:\Data\Business\Letter.docx. In this path to the file, the C: identifies the volume and is called the drive letter. Drive letters used for a hard drive, CD, USB drive, or DVD are C:, D:, E:, and so forth.

✎ Notes Technicians tend to call a directory a folder when working in File Explorer or Windows Explorer, but when working with a command-line interface, they call a directory a directory.

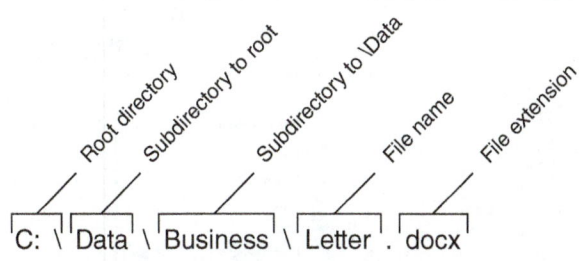

C: \ Data \ Business \ Letter . docx

Figure 11-23 The complete path to a file includes the volume letter, directories, file name, and file extension; the colon, backslashes, and period are required to separate items in the path

When you refer to a drive and directories that are pointing to the location of a file, as in C:\Data\Business\Letter.docx, the drive and directories are called the path to the file (see Figure 11-23). The first part of the name before the period is called the file name (Letter), and the part after the period is called the file extension (.docx). A file extension indicates how the file is organized or formatted, the type of content in the file, and what program uses the file. For example, the .docx file extension identifies the file type as a Microsoft Word document file. By default, Windows does not display file extensions in Explorer. How to display these extensions is coming up.

NAVIGATE THE FOLDER STRUCTURE

When working with the File Explorer or Windows Explorer window, these tips can make your work easier:

▲ Click or double-click items in the left pane, called the navigation pane, to drill down into these items. The folders or subfolders appear in the right pane. You can also double-click folders in the right pane to drill down. When you click the arrow on the left side of a folder in the navigation pane, its subfolders are listed underneath it in the pane.

▲ To control how files and subfolders appear in the right pane of Windows 10/8, click one of the icons in the lower-right corner to select Thumbnail view or Details view (see Figure 11-24A). For Windows 7, click the View icon in the menu bar and select your view (see Figure 11-24B).

11

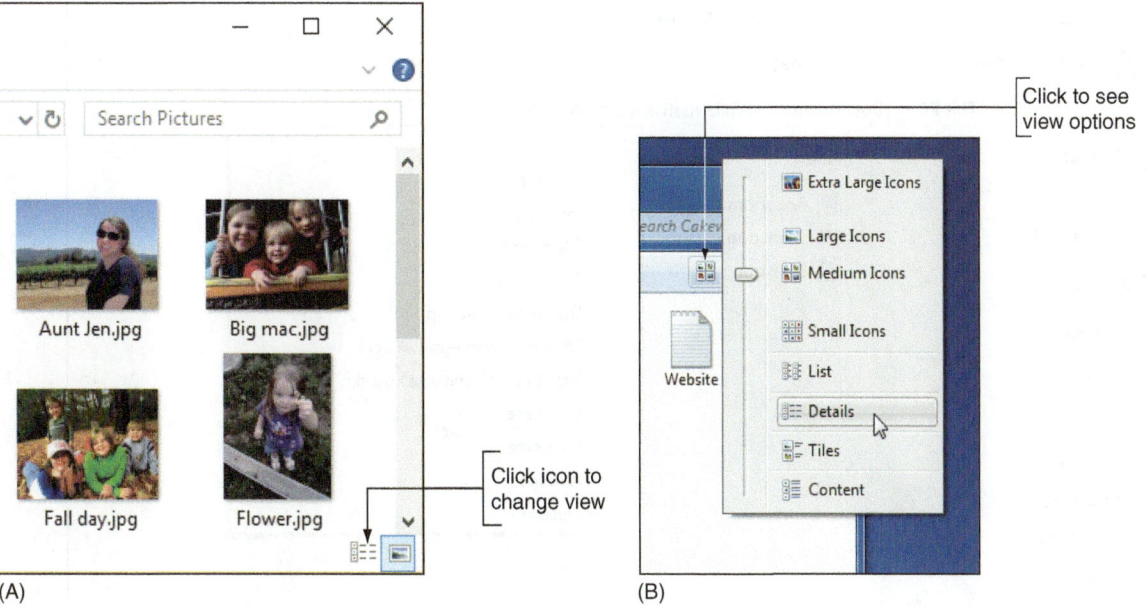

(A)

(B)

Figure 11-24 Click the View icon to change how files and folders display in the right pane of (A) Windows 10/8 File Explorer or (B) Windows 7 Windows Explorer

◢ To control the column headings that appear in Details view, right-click a column heading and select the headings that you want to appear (see Figure 11-25). To control which column is used to sort items in Details view, click a column heading.

Figure 11-25 Right-click a column heading to select columns to display in Details view

◢ To search for a folder or file, use the search box in the upper-right corner of the window.
◢ Use the forward and back arrows in the upper-left corner to move forward and backward to previous views.
◢ Click a right arrow in the path displayed in the address bar at the top of the Explorer window to see a drop-down list of subfolders (see Figure 11-26). Click one to move to the subfolder.

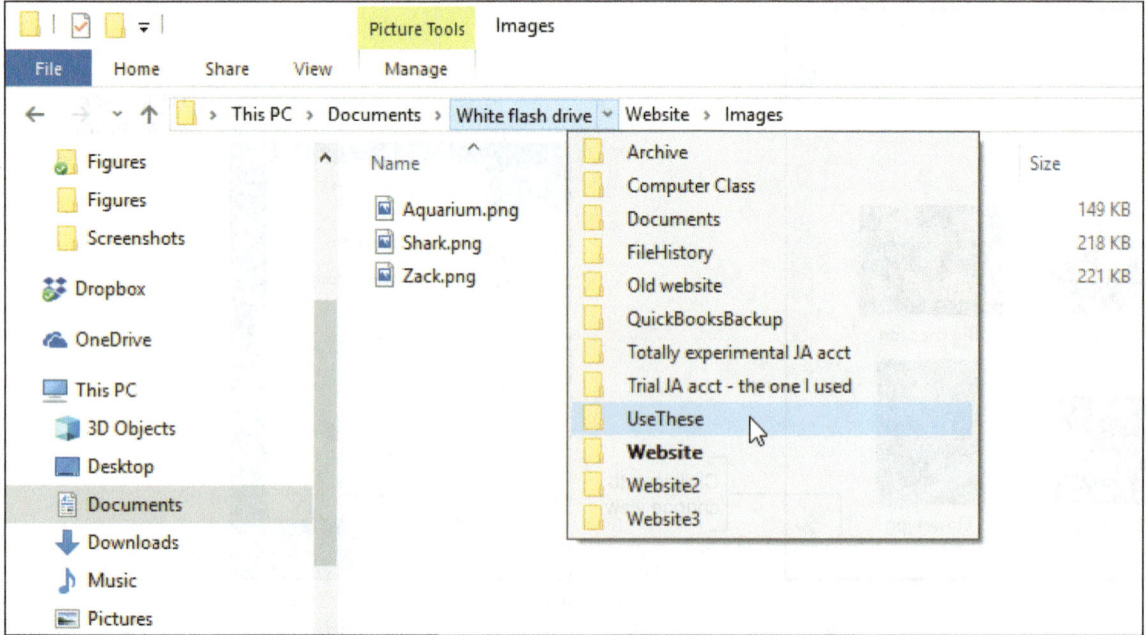

Figure 11-26 Click a right arrow in the address bar to move up the folder tree and down to a new folder

CREATE A FOLDER

To create a folder, first select the folder you want to use as the parent folder. (Remember that a parent folder contains the child folder.) Next, use one of these methods to create the new folder:

▲ In Windows 10/8, select the **Home** ribbon and click **New folder**. In Windows 7, click **New folder** on the menu bar.

▲ Right-click in the white area of the right pane and point to **New** in the shortcut menu. The menu in Figure 11-27 appears. Click **Folder** to create a regular folder or click **Compressed (zipped) Folder** to create a compressed folder.

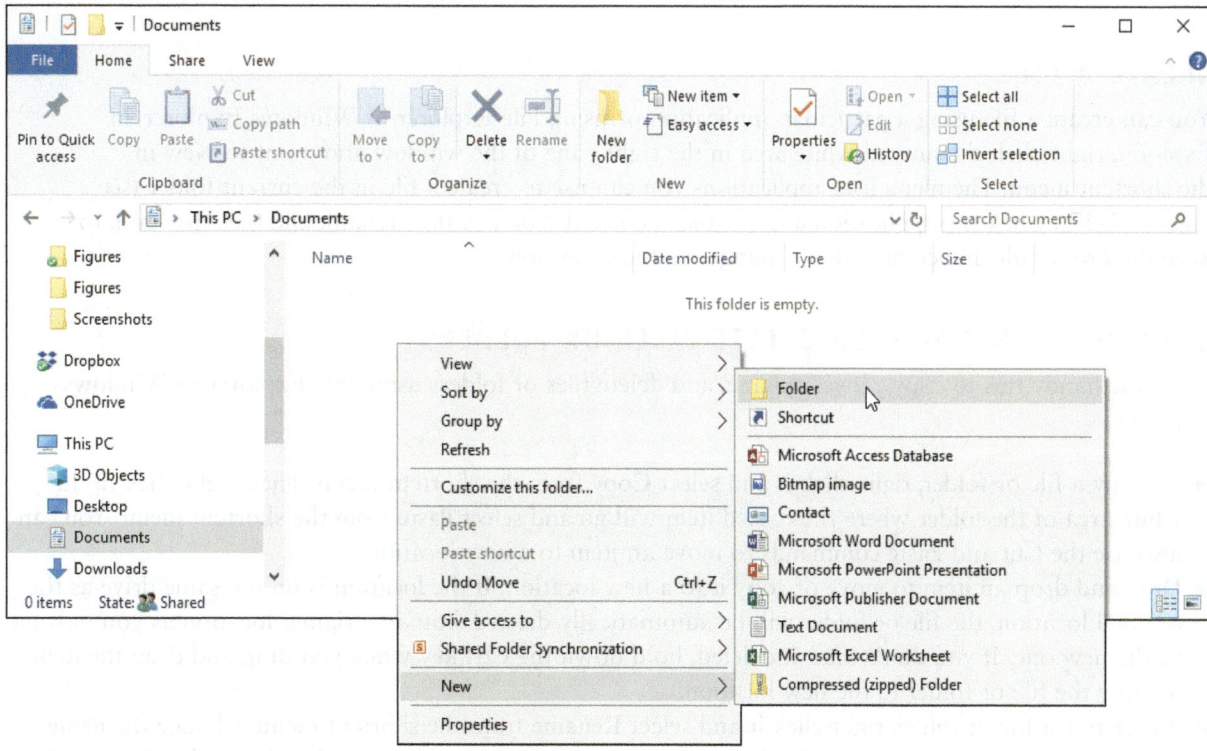

Figure 11-27   Create a new file, folder, or compressed folder

---

📝 **Notes** A **compressed (zipped) folder** has a .zip extension. Any file or folder that you put in this folder will be compressed to a smaller size than normal. A compressed folder is often used to make files smaller so they can more easily be sent by email. When you remove a file or folder from a compressed folder, the file or folder is uncompressed back to its original size. In general, Windows treats a compressed folder more like a file than a folder.

After Windows creates the folder, the folder name is highlighted so that you can rename it (see Figure 11-28).

📝 **Notes** The Windows desktop is itself a folder and is located at C:\Users*username*\Desktop. For example, if the user, Anne, creates a folder named Downloads on her desktop, the folder is located at C:\Users\Anne\Desktop\Downloads.

Figure 11-28 Edit the new folder's name

CREATE A FILE

You can create a file using a particular application or using File Explorer or Windows Explorer. In Explorer, right-click the unused white area in the right pane of the window and point to **New** in the shortcut menu. The menu lists applications you can use to create a file in the current folder (see Figure 11-27). Click the application and the file is created. You can then rename the file. However, to keep the proper file association, don't change the file extension.

COPY, MOVE, RENAME, OR DELETE FILES OR FOLDERS

Use these handy tips to copy, move, rename, and delete files or folders using File Explorer or Windows Explorer:

◢ To copy a file or folder, right-click it and select **Copy** from the shortcut menu. Then right-click in the white area of the folder where the copied item will go and select **Paste** from the shortcut menu. You can also use the Cut and Paste commands to move an item to a new location.

◢ Drag and drop an item to move or copy it to a new location. If the location is on the same drive as the original location, the file or folder will be automatically deleted from its original location as you move it to the new one. If you don't want it deleted, hold down the **Ctrl** key while you drag and drop the item to copy the file or folder to the new location.

◢ To rename a file or folder, right-click it and select **Rename** from the shortcut menu. Change the name and click off the file or folder to deselect it. You cannot rename a data file when an application has the file open, and you can't rename a program file when the program is running; first close the data file or program and then rename it.

◢ To delete a file or folder, select the item and press the **Delete** key, or right-click the item and select **Delete** from the shortcut menu. The deleted file or folder and all its contents, including subfolders, is sent to the Recycle Bin.

◢ To select multiple items to delete, copy, or move at the same time, hold down the **Shift** or **Ctrl** key as you click. To select several adjacent items in a list, click the first item and **Shift-click** the last item. To select nonadjacent items in a list, hold down the **Ctrl** key as you click each item.

Files deleted from the hard drive are stored in the Recycle Bin on the desktop. Emptying the Recycle Bin will free up your disk space by permanently deleting the files. To empty the Recycle Bin, right-click the bin and select **Empty Recycle Bin** from the shortcut menu.

> ✎ **Notes** In this chapter, you use File Explorer or Windows Explorer to create, copy, move, delete, and rename files and folders. In Chapter 13, you will learn that you can do the same tasks using commands from a command prompt.

CREATE A SHORTCUT

To create a shortcut on the Windows desktop to a data file or program, use File Explorer or Windows Explorer to locate the data file or program file, right-click it, and click **Create shortcut** in the menu that appears. For example, in Figure 11-29, you can see that a shortcut to the C:\Windows\System32\notepad.exe program is about to be placed on the Windows desktop.

Figure 11-29 Place a shortcut to a program file on the Windows desktop

CONTROL PANEL

A+
CORE 2
1.2, 1.6

Control Panel is a window containing several small utility programs called applets that are used to manage hardware, software, users, and the system. (In general, a utility program is used to maintain a system or fix a computer problem.) To access Control Panel in Windows 10, type **Control Panel** in the search box on the taskbar. In Windows 8, right-click **Start** and click **Control Panel**. In Windows 7, click **Start** and click **Control Panel**.

By default, Control Panel appears in **Category view** where utilities are grouped by category. To switch to **Classic view**, click **Category** and select either Large icons or Small icons. Figure 11-30 shows the Windows 10 Control Panel in Small icons view. Use the search box in the title bar to help find information and utilities in Control Panel.

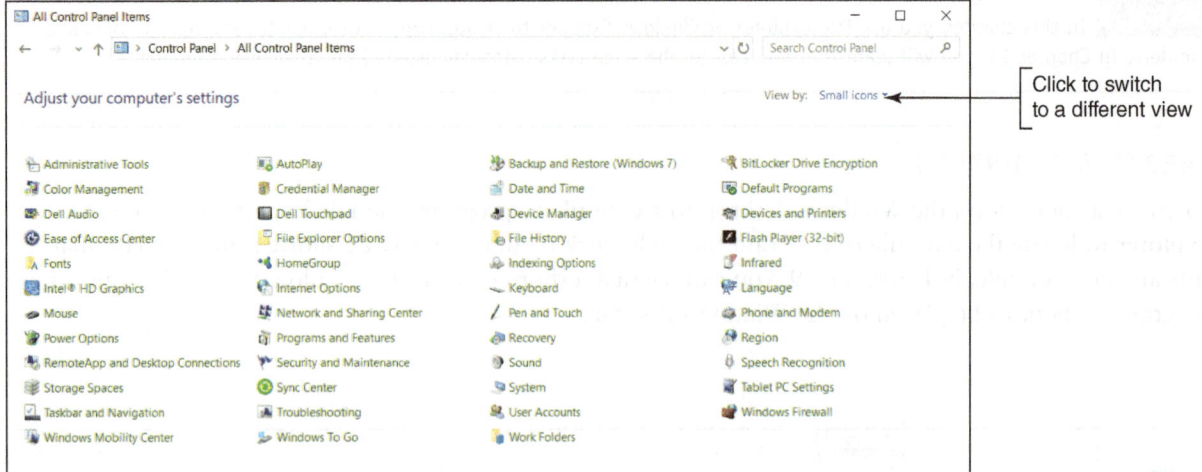

Figure 11-30   Many technicians prefer to use Control Panel in Classic view to more easily access utilities

Here is a short list of some of the applets in Control Panel. Later in the text, you learn about other Control Panel applets:

◢ The Sound applet is used to select a default speaker and microphone and adjust how Windows handles sounds. To control volume, recall you can use the volume icon in the taskbar.

◢ The Network and Sharing Center is a tool for viewing basic network information and setting up connections.

◢ HomeGroup is in the Windows 8/7 Control Panel but is not supported by Windows 10. A homegroup allows Windows 8/7 computers on a small network to share resources.

◢ The Power Options applet is used to select or customize a power plan for your computer.

◢ The Windows 10 File Explorer Options applet or Windows 8/7 Folder Options applet lets you change how files and folders are displayed in File Explorer or Windows Explorer.

★ **A+ Exam Tip**   The A+ Core 2 exam expects you to be able to use Control Panel utilities such as Folder Options, System, Power Options, HomeGroup, and the Network and Sharing Center when given a scenario.

WINDOWS 10 FILE EXPLORER OPTIONS OR WINDOWS 8/7 FOLDER OPTIONS

A+ CORE 2 1.6   The Windows 10 File Explorer Options applet or the Windows 8/7 Folder Options applet in Control Panel can be used to view and change options assigned to folders. These options control how users view the files in the folder and what they can do with these files. In File Explorer or Windows Explorer, Windows has an annoying habit of hiding file extensions if it knows which application is associated with a file extension. For example, just after installation, it hides .exe, .com, .sys, and .txt file extensions, but does not hide .docx, .pptx, or .xlsx file extensions until the software to open these files has been installed. Also, Windows really doesn't want you to see its own system files, and it hides these files from view until you force it to show them.

APPLYING | CONCEPTS   CHANGING FILE EXPLORER OPTIONS

A technician is responsible for solving problems with system files (files that belong to the Windows operating system) and file extensions. To fix problems with these files and extensions, you need to see them first. To change File Explorer options so you can view system files and file extensions in Windows 10/8/7, do the following:

1. Open **Control Panel** and, if necessary, change the view to **Small icons** view. For Windows 10, click **File Explorer Options**. For Windows 8/7, click **Folder Options**. The File Explorer Options or Folder Options dialog box appears. Even though the name is different, the dialog box works the same in Windows 10 and Windows 8/7. Figure 11-31A shows the box for Windows 10 with the General tab selected. On the General tab, you can change settings for how Explorer navigates folders and handles the navigation pane.

> 🖊 **Notes** In Windows, the difference between a window and a dialog box is that a window can be resized, but a dialog box cannot.

2. Click the **View** tab. Scroll down in the Advanced settings group and make these selections to show hidden information about files, folders, and drives, as shown in Figure 11-31B:

   ◢ Select **Show hidden files, folders, and drives**.
   ◢ Uncheck **Hide extensions for known file types**.
   ◢ Uncheck **Hide protected operating system files (Recommended)** and respond to the Warning box.

 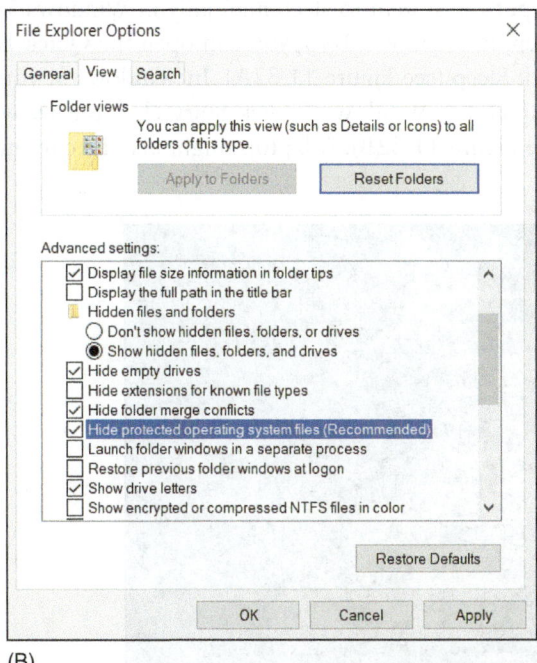

(A)   (B)

Figure 11-31   Use the File Explorer Options or Folder Options box to control how Explorer works and displays files and folders

3. To save your changes and close the File Explorer Options or Folder Options box, click **OK**.

⭐ **A+ Exam Tip**   The A+ Core 2 exam expects you to know how to view hidden files and file extensions in File Explorer and Windows Explorer.

POWER OPTIONS

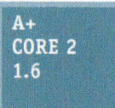

The Power Options applet of Control Panel can help you conserve power and increase the amount of time before a battery pack on a laptop needs recharging. Power is managed by putting the computer into varying degrees of suspend or sleep modes.

> ⭐ **A+ Exam Tip** The A+ Core 2 exam might give you a scenario and expect you to know which power options to change to solve a problem, including using power plans and sleep (suspend), hibernate, and standby modes.

Here are the different power-saving states:

▲ *Sleep mode.* Using Windows 10/8/7, you can put the computer into sleep mode, also called standby mode or suspend mode, to save power when you're not using the computer. If applications are open or other work is in progress, Windows first saves the current state, including open files, to memory and saves some of the work to the hard drive. Then everything is shut down except memory and enough of the system to respond to a wake-up. In sleep mode, the power light on the laptop might blink from time to time. (A laptop generally uses about 1 to 2 percent of battery power for each hour in sleep mode.) To wake up the computer, press the power button; for some computers, you press a key or touch the touch pad. Windows wakes up in about two seconds. When Windows is in sleep mode, it can still perform Windows updates and scheduled tasks. Windows can be configured to go to sleep after a period of inactivity, or you can manually put it to sleep.

To put the system to sleep manually in Windows 10, click **Start**, then click the power icon and select **Sleep**. In Windows 10/8, you can open the **Quick Launch** menu, point to **Shut down or sign out**, and click **Sleep** (see Figure 11-32A). In Windows 8, you can use the charms bar, as you learned earlier in the chapter. For Windows 7, click **Start**, click the arrow to the right of Shut down, and then click **Sleep** (see Figure 11-32B). A laptop might also be configured to go to sleep when you close the lid.

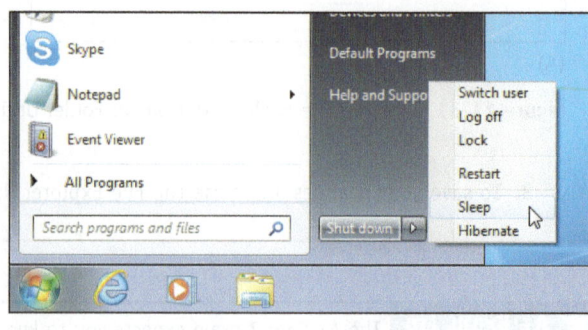

(A)   (B)

Figure 11-32 Put Windows to sleep using the (A) Windows 10/8 Quick Launch menu or (B) Windows 7 Start menu

▲ *Hibernation*. Hibernation saves all work to the hard drive and powers down the system. When you press the power button, Windows reloads its state, including all open applications and documents. When Windows is in sleep mode on a laptop and senses the battery is critically low, it will put the system into hibernation.

> **✎ Notes** Recall that hard drives are permanent or nonvolatile storage and memory is temporary or volatile storage. A hard drive does not require power to hold its contents, but memory, on the other hand, is volatile and loses its contents when it has no power. In hibernation, the computer has no power and everything must therefore be stored on the hard drive.

APPLYING | CONCEPTS   CONFIGURING WINDOWS POWER PLANS

Follow these steps to configure power plans in Windows 10:

1. Open Control Panel in Classic view and click **Power Options**. The Power Options window opens. Figure 11-33 shows the window for one laptop. The plans might be different for other laptops.

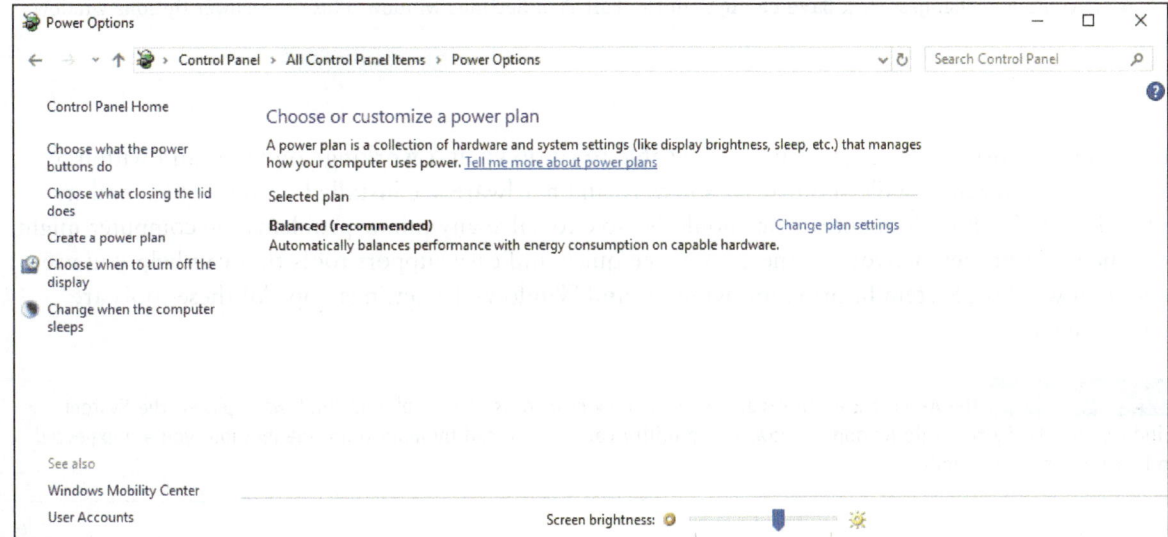

Figure 11-33   Power plans in Windows 10

2. You can customize each plan. For example, under Balanced (recommended), click **Change plan settings**. The Edit Plan Settings window appears (see the left side of Figure 11-34). Notice in the figure the various times of inactivity required before the computer goes into sleep mode; these are called sleep timers.

3. To see other changes you can make, click **Change advanced power settings**. Using the Power Options window (see the right side of Figure 11-34), you can control the number of minutes before the hard drive turns off; control what happens when you close the lid, press the sleep button, or press the power button; and set the brightness level of the LCD panel to conserve power. You can also use this box to set what happens when the battery gets low or critically low. Make your changes and click **OK** to close the box.

(continues)

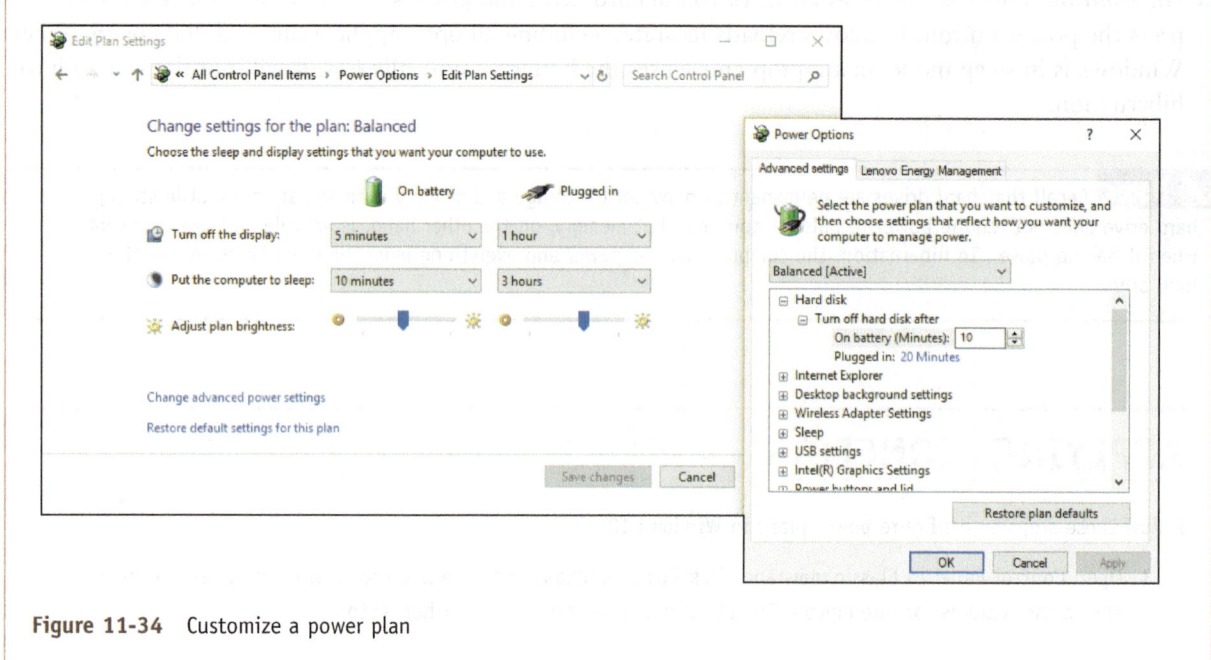

Figure 11-34 Customize a power plan

4. If you made changes, click **Save changes** in the Edit Plan Settings window. Close the Power Options window.

As an IT support technician, you need to be able to sit down at a working computer and within 5 or 10 minutes find the details about what software and hardware are installed on the system and its general health. Within 20 minutes, you should be able to solve any minor problems the computer might have, such as a broken network connection. Some quick and easy support tools that can help you are the System window, System Information window, and Windows 10 Settings app. All these tools are discussed next.

> ★ **A+ Exam Tip** The A+ Core 2 exam expects you to know how to use File Explorer, Windows Explorer, the System window, and the System Information window. If the utility can be accessed by more than one method, you are expected to know all of the methods.

SYSTEM WINDOW

A+
CORE 2
1.6

The System window is your friend. It can give you a quick look at what hardware and software are installed and can get you to other useful Windows tools. To open the System window in Windows 10, open **Control Panel** and click **System**. In Windows 8, open the Quick Launch menu (press **Win+X**) and click **System**. In Windows 7, click **Start**, right-click **Computer**, and select **Properties** from the shortcut menu. (Alternately, you can open **Control Panel** and click **System**.) Figure 11-35 shows the resulting System window for one Windows 10 laptop.

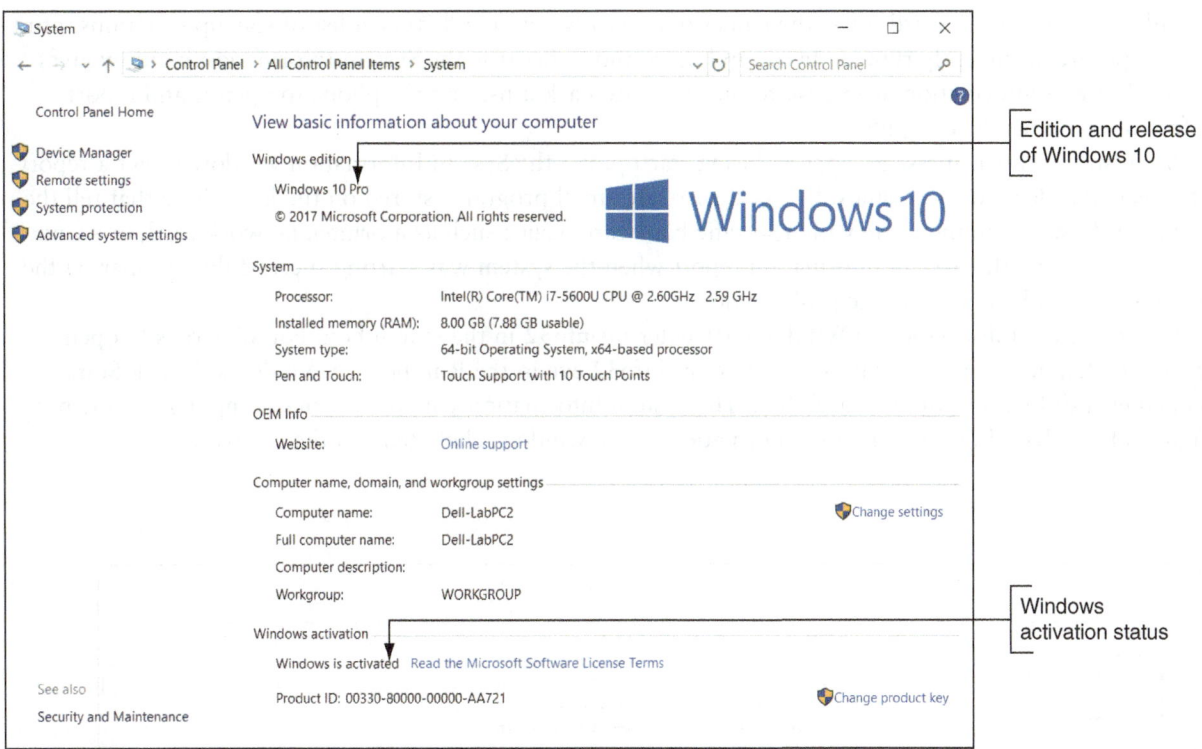

Figure 11-35   The System window reports Windows 10 Pro is installed

So what technical information are you looking at? Here is the rundown:

◢ Windows 10/8/7 comes in several editions; you can see this system has the Windows 10 Pro edition installed.

◢ The type of OS installed is a 64-bit OS. A 32-bit operating system processes 32 bits at a time, and a 64-bit operating system processes 64 bits at a time. Most editions of Windows 10/8/7 come in either 32-bit or 64-bit versions. A 64-bit OS performs better than a 32-bit OS, but requires more memory. A 32-bit OS can support up to 4 GB of memory, and a 64-bit OS can support much more. The details of how much memory each edition of Windows can support are covered in Chapter 12.

◢ The processor installed is the Intel Core i7-5600U, and 8 GB of RAM is installed.

◢ You can also see that Windows 10 is activated. (If it is not, refer to Chapter 12 to learn how to activate Windows.)

> **✎ Notes**   Windows 8/7 relies on the Control Panel applets to manage most settings. Windows 10 introduced the Settings app for settings a user might need to change, but settings a technician might change are still done with Control Panel applets. In Windows 10, you often find the same setting in both locations. For example, the About page (refer back to Figure 11-4) in the Settings app gives information similar to that shown in the System window in Control Panel.

That's a lot of useful information for a first look at a computer.

SYSTEM INFORMATION WINDOW

Turn to the System Information window (msinfo32.exe) for more details about a system, including installed hardware and software, the current system configuration, and currently running programs. For example, you can use the window to find out what BIOS/UEFI version is installed on the motherboard, how much RAM is installed, the directory where the OS is installed, the size of the hard drive, the names of currently running drivers, a list of startup programs, print jobs in progress, currently running tasks, and much more. Because the System Information window gives so much useful information, help-desk technicians often ask a user on the phone to open it and report information about the computer.

When strange error messages appear during startup, use the System Information window to get a report of drivers that loaded successfully. Device drivers are small programs stored on the hard drive that tell the computer how to communicate with a specific hardware device such as a printer, network card, or scanner. If you have saved the System Information report when the system was starting successfully, comparing the two reports can help identify the problem device.

To run System Information in Windows 10, enter **msinfo32** in the search box. For Windows 8, open the **Quick Launch** menu, click **Run**, and enter **msinfo32.exe** in the Run box. In Windows 7, click **Start** and enter **msinfo32.exe** in the search box. The System Information window for one computer is shown in Figure 11-36. To drill down to more information in the window, click items in the left pane.

Figure 11-36   Use the System Information utility to examine details about a system

WINDOWS 10 SETTINGS APP

The Windows 10 Settings app is a user-friendly interface to access numerous Windows settings. You can open the Settings app from the Start menu, the Quick Launch menu, or by pressing the hotkeys **Win+I**. On the Start menu, click **Start** and then click the **Settings** icon on the far-left side of the menu (see Figure 11-37).

Click to open the Settings app

Figure 11-37 Access the Settings app from the Start menu

The Settings app includes links to Control Panel and has a search box near the top that makes it easy to jump straight to a setting you want to adjust (see Figure 11-38). For example, suppose you want to configure Windows to use a different language. When you type **language** in the search box, several actions appear in the drop-down list, including *Add a language to this device*. The primary menu includes settings for the following:

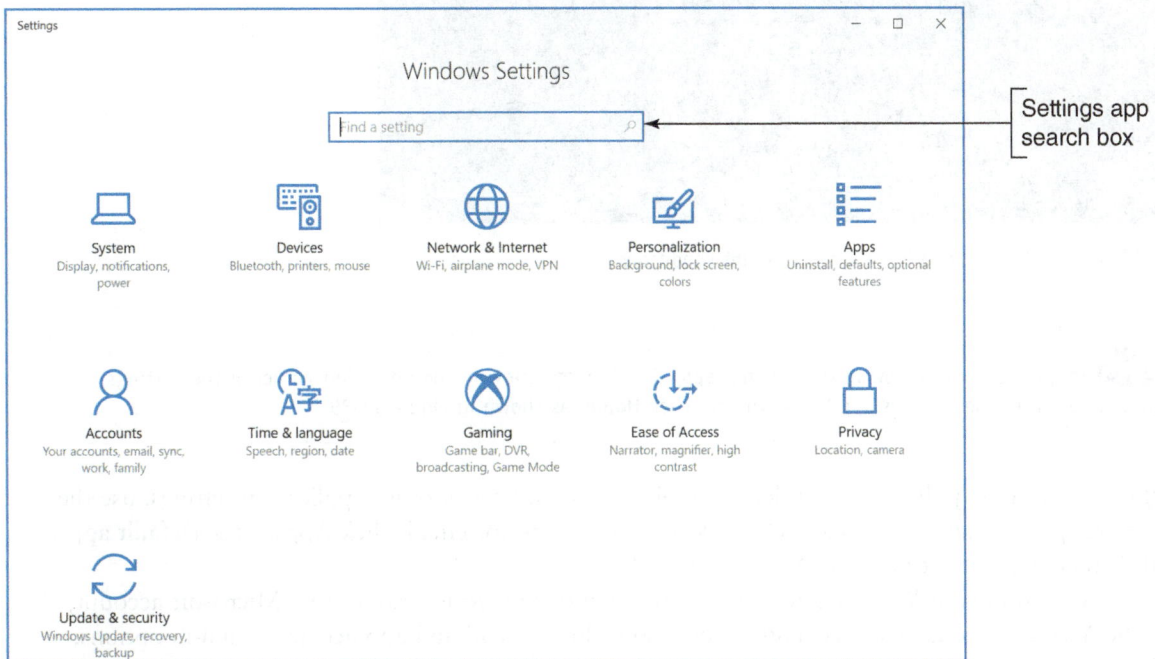

Settings app search box

Figure 11-38 The new Windows 10 Settings app

> ✎ **Notes** Some items in the Settings app may be unavailable if you are logged in with a Standard account. Use an account with administrative privileges to view all available settings.

- ▲ *System.* The catchall for information and settings that affect the function of your computer is the System group. Go here to adjust display, notification, power, sleep, storage, and tablet-mode settings.
- ▲ *Devices.* The Devices group includes settings for printers and scanners, connected devices, Bluetooth, mouse and touch pad devices, typing, AutoPlay, and USB.

11

◢ *Network & Internet.* The Network & Internet group provides network status, data usage information, and settings for different connections, including Wi-Fi, Ethernet, dial-up, VPN, and mobile hotspots. Go here to set up new connections. Airplane mode and proxy settings are also available for mobile devices. The link to the Network and Sharing Center takes you to more connection settings.

◢ *Personalization.* The Personalization group is where you find settings for the background, colors, lock screen, themes, Start menu, and taskbar. For example, to adjust your screen for working in low-light conditions, click **Personalization**, click **Colors** in the left pane, scroll down to **Choose your app mode**, and then click **Dark** (see Figure 11-39).

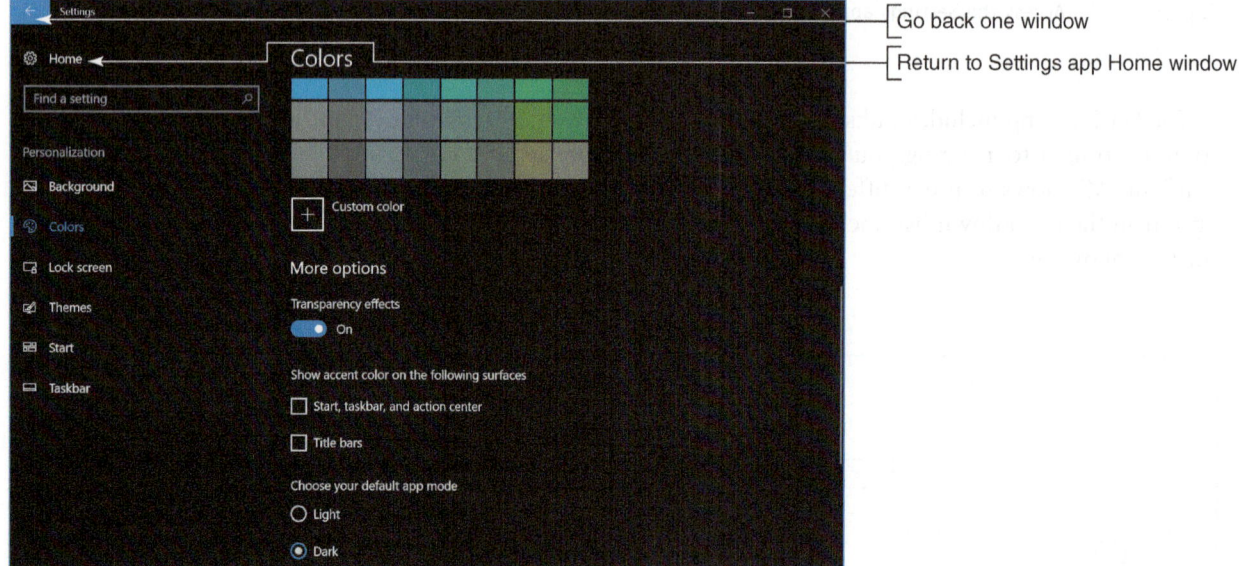

Figure 11-39 Dark app mode is ideal for low-light conditions

✎ Notes To go back one window in the Settings app, click the left arrow in the upper-left corner of the Settings window. To return to the Settings app Home window, click **Home**, as shown in Figure 11-39.

◢ *Apps.* To uninstall applications, set default applications, and check other application settings, use the Apps group. For example, to make Outlook the default app for email, click **Apps**, click **Default apps**, and then change the setting from Mail to Outlook.

◢ *Accounts.* To find your Windows account information or link your account to a Microsoft account, use the Accounts group. The Accounts group also includes email and app accounts, sign-in options, Microsoft account sync settings, options to sign in to work or school networks, and options to add new user accounts to the computer. You will learn more about accounts later in this text.

◢ *Time & language.* The Time & language group provides settings for date and time, region and language, and speech.

◢ *Gaming.* The Gaming group contains settings for the Game bar, Game DVR, broadcasting, and Game Mode. When you turn on Game Mode, Windows improves the gaming experience by prioritizing system resources for the game being played on the computer.

◢ *Ease of Access.* This group provides all the standard access settings, such as narrator, magnifier, closed captions, and more.

◢ *Privacy.* Find the settings to restrict or allow app access to your information in the Privacy group. You can limit app access and use of your location, camera, microphone, notifications, speech, inking, typing, account information, contacts, calendar, call history, email, messaging, radios, and other devices. The

Privacy group is also where you adjust settings for feedback, diagnostic, and usage data that is sent to Microsoft. You can also choose which apps are allowed to run in the background.

▲ *Update & security*. The Windows update status and settings, as well as the Windows Defender settings, are found in the Update & security group. Here you also find settings for backups, recovery, and activation, and links to Find My Device if you lose your connected devices, such as a phone. Finally, you find settings for developers, such as device discovery, remote desktop, and PowerShell.

WINDOWS | 8 ACTION CENTER

The Windows 8/7 Action Center is the tool to use when you want to make a quick jab at solving a computer problem. If a hardware or application problem is easy to solve, the Action Center can probably do it in a matter of minutes because it lists errors and issues that need attention and proposed solutions. The Action Center flag appears in the notification area of the taskbar. If the flag has a red X beside it, as shown in Figure 11-40, Windows considers the system to have an important issue that needs resolving immediately. When you click the flag, you can see a brief report of issues, as shown in the figure.

Figure 11-40 A red X on the Windows 8 Action Center flag in the taskbar indicates a critical issue needs resolving

To open the Action Center, you can click the red flag in the taskbar and then click **Open Action Center**. Alternately, you can open **Control Panel** and click **Action Center**. The Action Center window for one Windows 8 computer is shown in Figure 11-41. (The Windows 7 Action Center is similar.) Notice the colored bar to the left of a problem. A red bar indicates a critical problem that needs immediate attention. In this example, antivirus software is not running on the system. An orange bar indicates a less critical problem, such as apps running in the background that might be slowing down the system or no backups scheduled. Click the button to the right of a problem to find a recommended solution.

(continues)

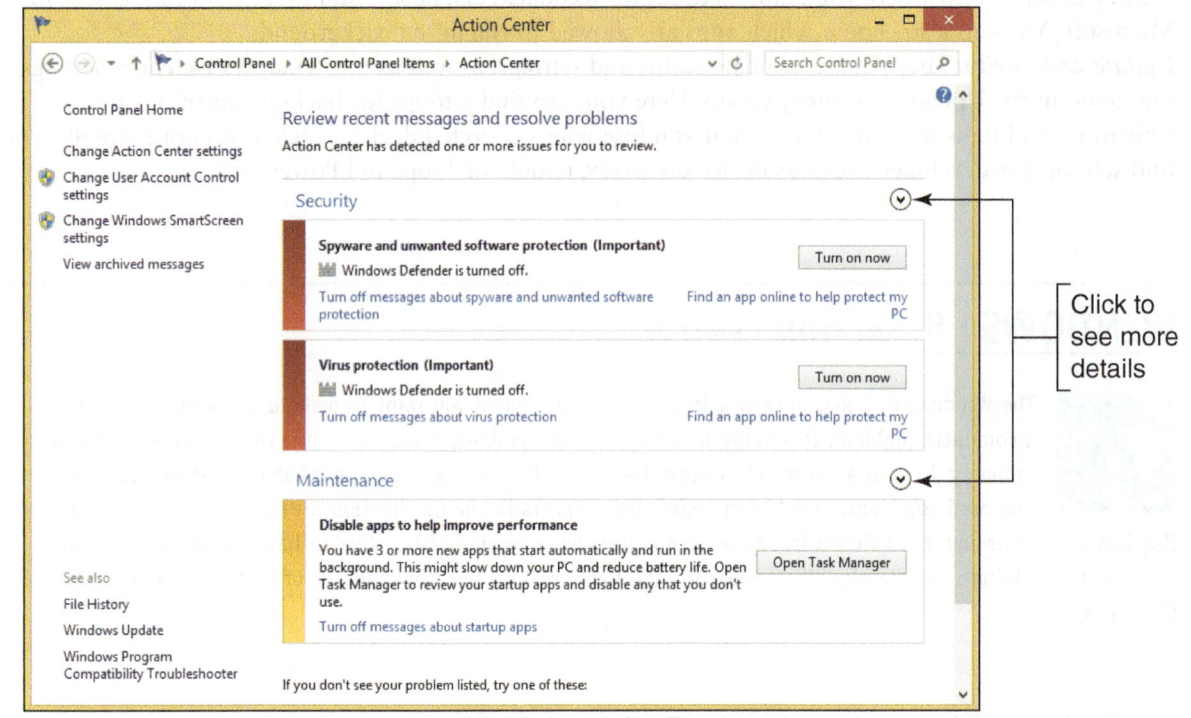

Figure 11-41 The Action Center shows a critical problem that needs a resolution

To see other information available under the Security or Maintenance group, click the down arrow to the right of a group. For example, when you click the arrow to the right of Security, detailed information appears for Windows Firewall, Windows Update, and other security settings.

To see a complete list of past and current problems on a computer, click **View archived messages** in the left pane of the Action Center. This report helps you understand the history of problems on a computer that you are troubleshooting. The problems in this list might or might not have a solution.

HOW WINDOWS CONTROLS ACCESS TO NETWORK RESOURCES

A+
CORE 2
1.8

An essential task of IT technicians is to connect computers to a wired or wireless network and support these connections, as you learned in Chapter 7. Once a computer is connected to a network, you need to look at the ways Windows accesses resources on the network. If a network is public, such as a public hotspot at a local coffee shop or airport, resources on the network aren't shared. However, private networks often share their data files, printers, and other resources. In this part of the chapter, you learn how Windows can access resources on a network using a Windows workgroup, homegroup, or domain, and you learn about options that Windows uses to secure a network connection.

WINDOWS WORKGROUP AND HOMEGROUP

A+
CORE 2
1.8

A network that doesn't have centralized control, such as one in a small office or home office (SOHO), is called a peer-to-peer (P2P) network. Windows can access resources on a P2P network by using file shares and/or a workgroup; Windows 8/7 can use a homegroup. (Windows 10 does not support homegroups.) Workgroups and homegroups can form a logical group of computers and users that share resources (see Figure 11-42), where administration, resources, and security on a workstation are controlled by that workstation.

Figure 11-42   A Windows workgroup is a type of peer-to-peer network where no single computer controls the network and each computer controls its own resources

> ✎ **Notes**   When looking at the diagrams in Figure 11-42 and later in Figure 11-43, know that the connecting lines describe the logical connections between computers and not the physical connections. Both networks might be physically connected the same way, but logically, resources are controlled by each computer on the network or by using a centralized database. In network terminology, the arrangement of physical connections between computers is called the **physical topology**. The logical way the computers connect on a network is called the **logical topology**.

In a Windows **workgroup**, each computer maintains a list of users and their rights on that particular computer. The computer allows a user on the network to access local resources based on the rights she has been given. In a **homegroup**, each computer shares files, folders, libraries, and printers with other computers in the homegroup. (In Windows 10/8/7, a **library** is a collection of folders.) A homegroup provides less security than a workgroup because any user of any computer in the homegroup can access homegroup resources. For this reason and others, the homegroup feature was removed from Windows 10 in the March 2018 update.

> ★ **A+ Exam Tip**   The A+ Core 2 exam expects you to be able to contrast a workgroup, homegroup, and domain and know which to use in a given scenario. You also need to know that homegroups only apply to Windows 8/7, and no longer to Windows 10.

WINDOWS DOMAIN

A+
CORE 2
1.8

A Windows **domain** is implemented on a larger, private network, such as a corporate or college network. The domain forms a logical group of networked computers that share a centralized directory database of user account information and security (see Figure 11-43). A Windows domain is a type of **client/server** network, which is a network where resources are managed by centralized computers. A computer making a request from another is called the client, and the computer answering the request is called the server. Using the client/server model, the directory database is controlled by a network operating system (NOS). Examples of network operating systems are Windows Server and various forms of Linux such as Ubuntu Server and Red Hat Enterprise Linux (RHEL).

Figure 11-43 A Windows domain is a type of client/server network where security on each computer or other device is controlled by a centralized database on a domain controller

> 🖉 **Notes** Windows Home editions do not support joining a domain. If you plan to join a domain on your network, install Windows 10 Professional, Enterprise, or Education edition; Windows 8.1 Professional or Enterprise edition; or Windows 7 Professional, Enterprise, or Ultimate edition.

Windows 10/8 allows three types of accounts to sign in to Windows: a local account, which applies only to the local computer and is also called an offline account; a Microsoft account (always an email address); and a network ID. Windows 7 uses local accounts and network IDs but does not use Microsoft accounts. A Microsoft account signs you in to the local computer and to Microsoft resources in the cloud, such as OneDrive. A network ID signs you in to a Windows domain to which the local computer belongs.

Figure 11-44 Active Directory and Azure AD are two Microsoft options for managing a domain

Microsoft offers two options for managing a domain—Active Directory and Azure Active Directory (see Figure 11-44):

▲ **Active Directory**. Windows Server controls a network using the directory database called Active Directory (AD). Each user on the network must have his own domain-level account, the most common of which is called a domain user account or network ID. These accounts are kept in AD and assigned by the network or system administrator. If you are connecting a computer to a domain, the administrator will tell you the network ID and password to the domain that you can use to sign in to the network. Active Directory normally manages a domain for users on company premises. Remote users can join the domain using a VPN or DirectAccess connection. Recall that a VPN is a security technique that encrypts data transmitted between a private network and a computer somewhere on the Internet. Windows DirectAccess was designed to eliminate the need for a VPN.

▲ **Azure Active Directory**. Azure Active Directory (Azure AD) manages users in the cloud and creates a virtual network of users connected through the Internet. Whereas AD is managed by Windows Server installed on private computers on company premises, Azure AD runs in the cloud from 28 Microsoft data centers around the world that offer Azure AD as a public service. Windows 10 professional and business editions allow work-owned devices and personal devices to join Azure AD. Windows 10 home editions and all editions of Windows 8/7 do not support Azure AD.

Windows 10 offers three ways to authenticate a user so that the computer can join a domain:

▲ **Domain join**. This method is used in Windows 10/8/7 to join an Active Directory domain maintained by a corporation or school. This is the traditional way employees on company premises access resources on the corporate network.

▲ **Azure AD join**. This method is primarily intended as a way for work-owned devices to access cloud resources, such as Office 365, from anywhere on the Internet. For example, a company might provide company-owned laptops to its sales force that work from many remote locations to access company resources in the cloud. Azure AD uses email addresses as account names.

▲ **Bring your own device (BYOD) experience**. Microsoft calls joining a personal device to Azure AD the BYOD experience. When a personal device joins Azure AD, you can access corporate resources, such as corporate databases, while still accessing personal resources, such as your personal OneDrive. The process works by using a personal account to sign in to Windows, followed by a secondary sign-in to authenticate to Azure AD. A school might use the BYOD experience to allow students to access school resources using their personal devices via the Internet.

Here is how to join a domain using each of the three methods:

1. Sign in to Windows using an administrator account. Open the **Settings** app. Click the **Accounts** group, and then click **Access work or school**.

2. Under *Connect to work or school*, click **Connect**. See Figure 11-45.

11

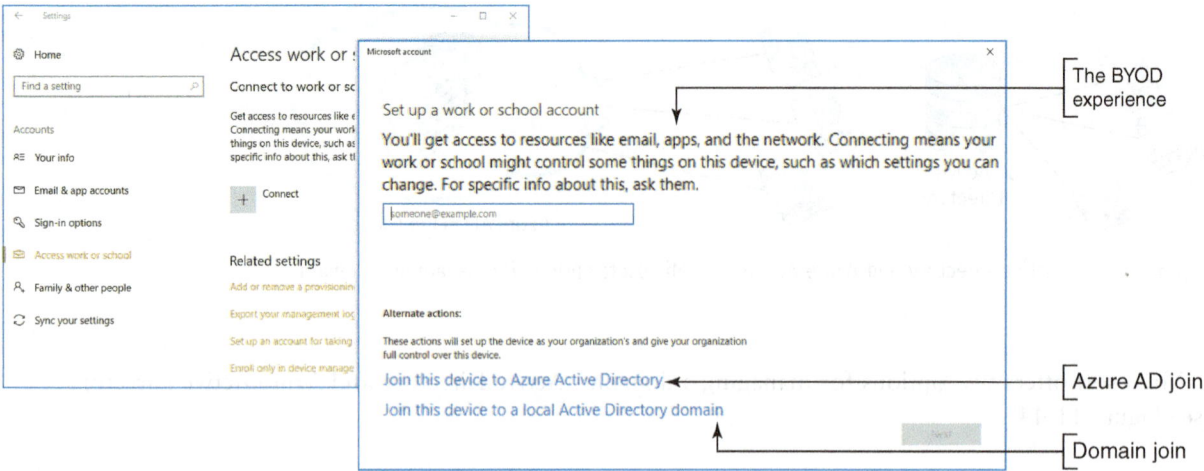

Figure 11-45 Three ways to join a domain

3. Do one of the following:

▲ For a domain join, click **Join this device to a local Active Directory domain**. Enter the domain name and click **Next**. Follow the on-screen directions. The next time you sign in to Windows, use your network ID on the domain.

▲ For an Azure AD join, click **Join this device to Azure Active Directory**. Enter the email address for the work or school account you are accessing and click **Next**. Follow the on-screen directions. The next time you sign in to Windows, use the same email address.

▲ For the BYOD experience, enter your Azure AD email address and click **Next**. Follow the on-screen directions. You will then have access to organizational resources using SSO (Single Sign On) as well as access to your personal resources, such as your personal OneDrive. The next time you sign in to Windows, use your personal account. You will automatically be signed in to Azure AD.

> 🖉 **Notes** If your computer is part of a domain, press **Ctrl+Alt+Del** when Windows starts to display a sign-in screen, and then enter your network ID and password.

DOMAIN SETUP

**A+
CORE 2
1.8**

If a computer is already connected to a physical network, you have signed in to Windows with a local user account, and you want to access resources controlled by a Windows domain on the network, you'll need to change the way Windows connects to the network. To make the change, you'll need the network ID and password to the domain provided by the network administrator. Open the System window (see Figure 11-46). Under *Computer name, domain, and workgroup settings*, click **Change settings**. In the System Properties box that appears, click **Network ID** and follow the directions on screen. The next time you restart the computer, you can sign in with your network ID and password to authenticate to the domain.

Figure 11-46 Set up Windows to join a domain

Now let's look at the different ways that Windows handles public and private network connections.

PUBLIC AND PRIVATE NETWORKS

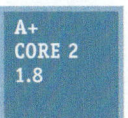

When you connect a Windows computer to a network the first time, Windows asks how you want to secure the network connection. When connecting to a public network, such as when you connect your laptop to a public wireless network at a local airport, you always want to ensure that your computer is protected from outside hackers and malware. Windows 10/8 offers three ways to secure a network connection:

▲ *Public network*. When using Public network security, Windows configures strong firewall settings, the computer is hidden from other devices on the network, and you can't share files or printers. This option is the most secure.

▲ *Private network*. When using Private network security, the computer is discoverable and you can share files and printers. In Windows 8/7, you can join a homegroup. Windows 10/8/7 computers can join a workgroup.

▲ *Domain network*. When the computer is set up to join a Windows domain, it yields control for authenticating users and sharing files, folders, and printers to settings in Active Directory or Azure Activity Directory managing the domain.

Windows 7 offers four network security options, which have different names and slightly different default settings:

▲ *Public network*. Network Discovery is turned off and you cannot join a homegroup or workgroup. This option is the most secure.

▲ *Home network*. Network Discovery is turned on and you can join a homegroup or workgroup.

▲ *Work network*. Network Discovery is turned on and you can join a workgroup, but you cannot join a homegroup.

▲ *Domain network*. When the computer is set up to join a Windows domain, it yields control for authenticating users and sharing its resources to Active Directory managing the domain.

If you want to change the setting that controls how Windows secures a network connection, open the **Network and Sharing Center** and click **Change advanced sharing settings**. In the Advanced sharing settings window (see Figure 11-47), you can change the public, private, home, or work status of a network connection, and you can turn network discovery and file and printer sharing on or off. You learn how to manage all these settings in Chapter 16.

Figure 11-47   Change the security setting for a Windows network connection

WHAT CUSTOMERS WANT: BEYOND TECHNICAL KNOW-HOW

**A+
CORE 2
4.7**

Probably the most significant indication that an IT technician is doing a good job is that customers are consistently satisfied. In your career as an IT support technician, commit to providing excellent service and to treating customers as you would want to be treated in a similar situation. One of the most important ways to achieve customer satisfaction is to do your best by being prepared, both technically and personally. Being prepared includes knowing what customers want, what they don't like, and what they expect from an IT technician.

Equally important to being prepared technically is knowing how to work effectively with people in a technical world, which is one of the most sought-after skills in today's service-oriented work environments. An employer once told me, "It's not hard to find technically proficient people these days. But it's next to impossible to find people who know how to get along with others and can be counted on when managers are not looking over their shoulders." I could sense his frustration, but I also felt encouraged to know that good social skills and good work ethics can take you far in today's world. My advice to you is to take this part of the chapter seriously. It's important to be technically proficient, but the skills learned in this part of the chapter just might be the ones that make you stand out above the crowd to land that new job or promotion.

> **✎ Notes** People respond in kind to the position of your facial muscles. Try smiling when you greet someone and see what happens.

BECOMING A COMPETENT AND HELPFUL SUPPORT TECHNICIAN

**A+
CORE 2
4.7**

The following traits distinguish a competent and helpful technician from a technician who is incompetent or unhelpful in the eyes of the customer:

▲ *Be dependable and reliable*. Customers appreciate and respect those who keep their word. If you promise to be back at 10:00 the next morning, be there on time. If you cannot keep your appointment, never ignore your promise. Call, apologize, let the customer know what happened, and reschedule your appointment. Also, do your best to return phone calls the same day and return email within two days.

> **✎ Notes** Quote from R.C., an employer: "When I choose a person to work for me, in a lot of cases, I choose based on his or her past dependability or attendance. I am less concerned about a person's ability because I can train anyone to do a specific job. I cannot, however, train anyone to do anything if he or she is not present for me to train. Being dependable and reliable has a profound impact on customer relationships as well."

▲ *Keep a positive and helpful attitude*. This helps establish good customer relationships. You communicate your attitude in your tone of voice, the words you choose, how you use eye contact, your facial expressions, how you dress, and in many other subjective and subtle ways. Generally, your attitudes toward your customers stem from how you see people, how you see yourself, and how you see your job. Your attitude is a heart issue, not a head issue. To improve your attitude, you must do it from your heart. That's pretty subjective and cannot be defined with a set of rules, but it always begins with a decision to change. As you work with customers or users, make it a habit not to patronize or talk down to them. Don't make customers or users feel inferior. People appreciate it when they feel your respect for them, even when they have made a mistake or are not knowledgeable. If a problem is simple to solve, don't make other people feel they have wasted your time. Your customer or user should always be made to feel that the problem is important to you.

11

APPLYING | CONCEPTS CUSTOMER SERVICE

Josie walked into a computer parts store and wandered over to the cleaning supplies looking for Ace monitor wipes. She saw another brand of wipes, but not the ones she wanted. Looking around for help, she noticed Mary stocking software on the shelves in the next aisle. She walked over to Mary and asked for help finding Ace monitor wipes. Mary put down her box, walked over to the cleaning supply aisle without speaking, picked up a can of wipes, and handed them to Josie, still without speaking a word. Josie explained she was looking for Ace wipes. Mary yelled over three aisles to a coworker in the back room, "Hey, Billy! This lady says she wants Ace monitor wipes. We got any?" Billy came from the back room and said, "No, we only carry those," pointing to the wipes in Mary's hand, and returned to the back room. Mary turned to Josie and said, "We only carry these," and then put the wipes back on the shelf. She turned to walk back to her aisle when Josie said to Mary, "Well, those Ace wipes are great wipes. You might want to consider carrying them." Mary said, "I'm only responsible for software." Josie left the store.

(continues)

Discuss this situation in a small group of students and answer the following questions:

1. If you were Josie, how would you feel about the service in this store?

2. What would you have expected to happen that did not happen?

3. If you were Mary, how could you have provided better service?

4. If you were Billy, is there anything more you could have done to help?

5. If you were the store manager, what principles of good customer service would you want Billy and Mary to know that would have helped them in this situation?

© iStockphoto.com/Sportstock

Figure 11-48   Learn to listen before you decide what a user needs or wants

▲ *Listen without interrupting your customer*. When you're working with or talking to a customer, focus on him or her. Don't assume you know what your customer is about to say. Let her say it, listen carefully, and don't interrupt (see Figure 11-48). Make it your job to satisfy this person, not just your organization, your boss, your bank account, or the customer's boss.

▲ *Use proper and polite language*. Speak politely and use language that won't confuse your customer. Avoid using slang or jargon, which is technical language that only technical people understand. Avoid acronyms (initial letters that stand for words). For example, don't say to a nontechnical customer, "I need to ditch your KVM switch," when you could explain yourself better by saying, "I need to replace that small switch box on your desk that controls your keyboard, monitor, and mouse."

▲ *Show sensitivity to cultural differences*. Cultural differences happen because we are from different countries and societies. Culture can cause us to differ in how we define or judge good service. For example, culture can affect our degree of tolerance for uncertainty. Some cultures are willing to embrace uncertainty, and others strive to avoid it. Those who tend to avoid uncertainty can easily get upset when the unexpected happens. For these people, you need to make special efforts to communicate early and often when things are not going as expected.

▲ *Express patience and honor to those with physical disabilities*. For the physically disabled, especially the hearing- or sight-impaired, communication can be more difficult. It's your responsibility in these situations to do whatever is necessary to find a way to communicate. It's especially important to have an attitude that expresses honor and patience, which you will unconsciously express in your tone of voice, your choice of words, and your actions.

✎ **Notes** Employers look for technicians with good social skills and work ethics because they realize that technicians with these skills are good for business.

▲ *Take ownership of the problem*. Taking ownership of the customer's problem means to accept the problem as your own. Doing that builds trust and loyalty because the customer knows you can be counted on. Taking ownership of a problem also increases your value in the eyes of your coworkers and boss. People who don't take ownership of the problem at hand are likely to be viewed as lazy, uncommitted, and uncaring. One way to take ownership of a problem is not to engage your boss in unproductive discussions about a situation he expects you to handle on your own.

APPLYING | CONCEPTS   SELF-CONTROL

Jack had a bad day on the phones at the networking help desk in Atlanta. An electrical outage coupled with a generator failure had caused servers in San Francisco to be down most of the day. The entire help-desk team had been fielding calls all day explaining to customers why they did not have service and giving expected recovery times. The servers were finally online, but it was taking hours to get everything reset and functioning. No one had taken a break all afternoon, but the call queue was still running about 20 minutes behind. Todd, the boss, had asked the team to work late until the queue was empty. It was Jack's son's birthday and his family was expecting Jack home on time. Jack moaned as he realized he might be late for Tyler's party. Everyone pushed hard to empty the queue. As Jack watched the last call leave the queue, he logged off, stood up, and reached for his coat.

And then another call comes. Jack is tempted to ignore it, but decides it has to be answered. It's Lacy, the executive assistant to the CEO (chief executive officer over the entire company). When Lacy calls, all priorities yield to her, and Lacy knows it. The CEO is having problems printing to the laser printer in his office. Would Jack please walk down to his office and fix the problem? Jack asks Lacy to check the simple things: "Is the printer turned on? Is it plugged in?" Lacy gets huffy and says, "Of course, I've checked that. Now come right now. I need to go." Jack walks down to the CEO's office, takes one look at the printer, and turns it on.

He turns to Lacy and says, "I suppose the on/off button was just too technical for you." Lacy glares at him in disbelief. Jack says, "I'll be leaving now." As he walks out, he begins to form a plan as to how he'll defend himself to his boss in the morning, knowing the inevitable call to Todd's office will come.

In a group of two or four students, one student should play the role of Jack and another the role of Todd. Discuss these questions:

1. Todd is informed the next morning of Jack's behavior, and calls Jack into his office. He likes Jack and wants him to be successful in the company. Jack is resistant and feels justified in what he did. As Todd, what do you think is important that Jack understand? How can you explain this to Jack so he can accept it? What would you advise Jack to do?

2. Switch roles or switch team members and replay the roles.

3. What are three principles of relating to people that would be helpful for Jack to keep in mind?

▲ *Portray credibility*. Convey confidence to your customers. Don't allow yourself to appear confused, afraid, or befuddled. Troubleshoot the problem in a systematic way that portrays confidence and credibility. Get the job done and do it with excellence. Credible technicians also know when the job is beyond their expertise and when to ask for help.

▲ *Work with integrity and honesty*. Don't try to hide your mistakes from your customer or your boss. Everyone makes mistakes, but don't compound them by a lack of integrity. Accept responsibility and do what you can to correct the error.

▲ *Know the law with respect to your work*. For instance, observe the laws concerning the use of software. Don't use or install pirated software.

▲ *Dress and behave professionally*. A professional at work knows not to allow his emotions to interfere with business relationships. If a customer is angry, allow the customer to vent, keeping your own professional distance. (You do, however, have the right to expect a customer not to talk to you in an abusive way.) Dress appropriately for the environment. Take a shower each day and brush your teeth after each meal. Use mouthwash. Iron your shirt. If you're not in good health, try as best you can to take care of the problem. Your appearance matters. And finally—don't use rough language; it is *never* appropriate.

> ✏️ **Notes** Your customers might never remember what you said or did, but they will always remember how you made them feel.

PLANNING FOR GOOD SERVICE

Your customers can be "internal," meaning you work for the same company and might consider the customers colleagues, or they can be "external" (they come to you or your company for service). Customers can be highly technical or technically naive, represent a large company or simply own a home computer, be prompt or slow at paying their bills, want only the best (and be willing to pay for it) or be searching for bargain service, be friendly and easy to work with or demanding and condescending. In each situation, the key to success is always the same: Don't allow circumstances or personalities to affect your commitment to excellence, and treat the customer as you would want to be treated.

> ⭐ **A+ Exam Tip** The A+ Core 2 exam expects you to know that when serving a customer, you should be on time, avoid distractions, set and meet expectations and timelines, communicate the status of the solution with the customer, and deal appropriately with customers' confidential materials.

Most good service for customers of IT support begins with entries in call tracking software, so let's start there.

CALL TRACKING SOFTWARE

Your organization is likely to use call tracking software to track support calls and give technicians a place to keep their call notes. Figure 11-49 shows a window in *everything HelpDesk* software, which is a popular call tracking application.

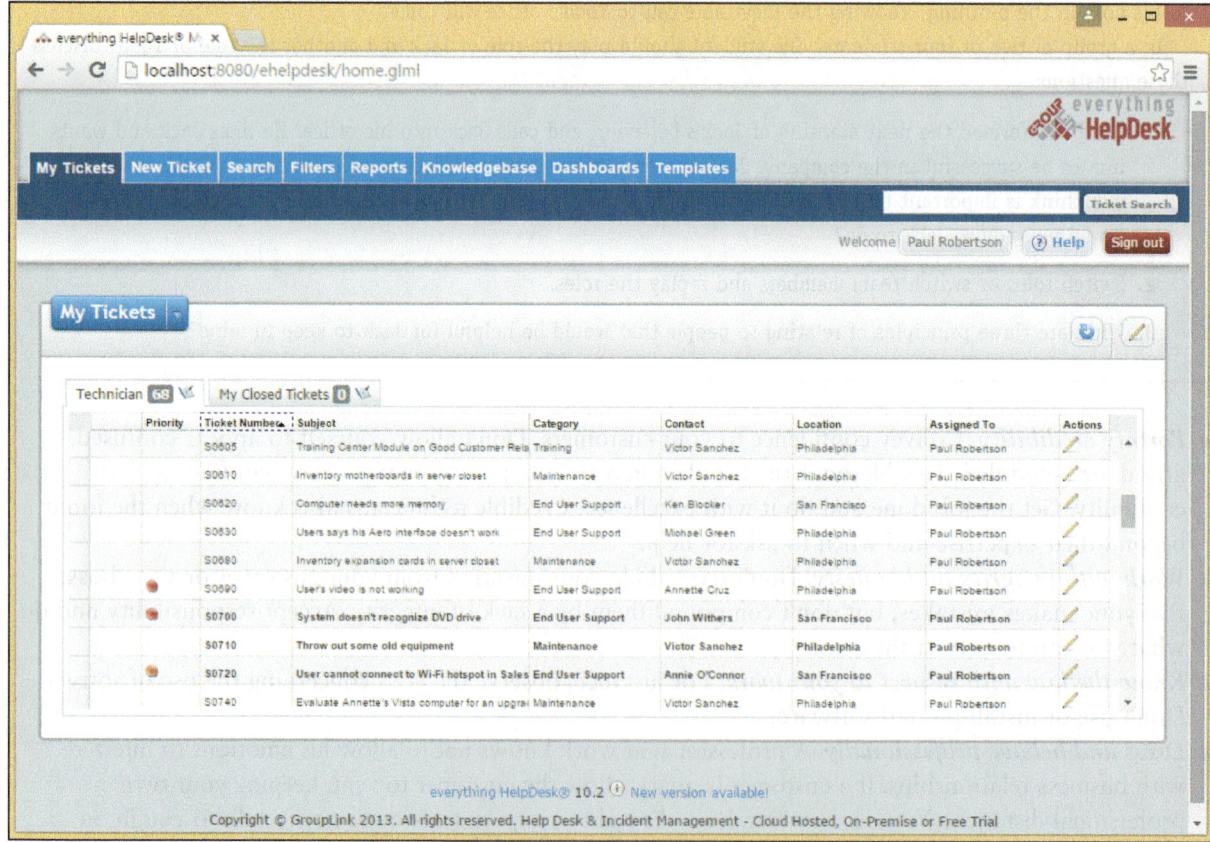

Figure 11-49 Call tracking software allows you to create, edit, and close tickets used by technicians

When someone initiates a call for help, whoever receives the call starts the process by creating a ticket (sometimes called an incident), which is a record of the request and what is happening to resolve it. The call tracking software might track: (1) the date, time, and length of help-desk or on-site calls, (2) causes of and solutions to problems already addressed, (3) who is currently assigned to the ticket and who has already worked on it, (4) who did what and when, and (5) how each call was officially resolved. The ticket is entered into the call tracking system and stays open until the issue is resolved. Support staff assigned to the ticket document their progress under this ticket in the call tracking system. As an open ticket ages, more attention and resources are assigned to it, and the ticket might be escalated (passed on to someone more experienced or who has more resources available) until the problem is finally resolved and the ticket closed. Help-desk personnel and managers acknowledge and sometimes even celebrate those who consistently close the most tickets!

As you support customers and solve computer problems, it's very important to include detailed information in your call notes so that you have the information as you solve the problem or when faced with a similar problem later. Sometimes another person must pick up your open ticket, and she should not have to waste time finding out information you already knew. Also, tracking-system notes are sometimes audited.

INITIAL CONTACT WITH A CUSTOMER

Your initial contact with a customer might be when the customer comes to you, such as in a retail setting, when you go to the customer's site, when the customer calls you on the phone, when the customer reaches you by chat or email, or when you are assigned a ticket already entered in a call tracking system. In each situation, always follow the specific guidelines of your employer. Let's look at some general guidelines for handling first contact with customers.

When you answer the phone, identify yourself and your organization. (Follow the guidelines of your employer on what to say.) Follow company policies to obtain specific information when answering an initial call, such as name (get the right spelling), phone number, and business name. For example, your company might require that you obtain a licensing or warranty number to determine whether the customer is entitled to receive your support. After you have obtained the information you need and confirmed you are authorized to help the customer, open up the conversation for the caller to describe the problem.

Prepare for on-site visits by reviewing information given to you by the person who took the call. Know the problem you are going to address, the urgency of the situation, and what computer, software, and hardware need servicing. Arrive with a complete set of equipment appropriate to the visit, which might include a toolkit, flashlight, multimeter, ESD strap and mat, and bootable media.

When you arrive at the customer's site, greet the customer in a friendly manner and shake his or her hand (see Figure 11-50). Use terms such as Mr. or Ms. and Sir or Ma'am when addressing the customer, unless you are certain the customer expects you to use his or her first name. If the site is a residence, you should *not* remain there when only a minor is present. If a minor

© iStockphoto.com/killerb10

Figure 11-50 If a customer permits it, begin each new relationship with a handshake

11

child answers the door, ask to speak with an adult and don't allow the adult to leave the house with only you and the child present.

After initial greetings, the first thing you should do is listen and ask questions. As you listen, it's fine to take notes, but don't start the visit by filling out your paperwork. Save the paperwork for later, or have the essentials already filled out before you reach the site.

INTERVIEW THE CUSTOMER

Troubleshooting begins by interviewing the user. As you ask the user questions, take notes and keep asking questions until you thoroughly understand the problem. Have the customer reproduce the problem, and carefully note each step taken and its results. This process gives you clues about the problem and the customer's technical proficiency, which helps you know how to communicate with the customer.

> ⭐ **A+ Exam Tip** The A+ Core 2 exam expects you to be able to clarify customer statements by asking open-ended questions to narrow the scope of the problem and by restating the issue or question.

Use diplomacy and good manners when you work with a user to solve a problem. For example, if you suspect that the user dropped the computer, don't ask, "Did you drop the laptop?" Put the question in a less accusatory manner: "Could the laptop have been dropped?"

SET AND MEET CUSTOMER EXPECTATIONS

A professional technician knows that it is her responsibility to set and meet expectations with a customer. It's important to create an expectation of certainty with customers so that they are not left hanging and don't know what will happen next.

Part of setting expectations is to establish a timeline with your customer for the completion of a project. If you cannot solve the problem immediately, explain to the customer what needs to happen and the timeline that he should expect for a solution. Then keep the customer informed about the progress of the solution. For example, you can say to a customer, "I need to return to the office and research the cost of parts that need replacing. I'll call you tomorrow before 10:00 a.m. with an estimate." If you later find out you need more time, call the customer before 10:00 a.m., explain your problem, and give him a new time to expect your call. This kind of service is very much appreciated by customers and, if you are consistent, you will quickly gain their confidence.

Another way to set expectations is to give customers an opportunity to make decisions about repairs to their equipment. When explaining to the customer what needs to be done to fix a problem, offer repair or replacement options if they apply (see Figure 11-51). Don't make decisions for your customer. Explain the problem and what you must do to fix it, giving as many details as the customer wants. When a customer must make a choice, state the options in a way that does not unfairly favor the most lucrative solution for you as the technician or for your company. For example, if you must replace a motherboard (a costly repair in parts and labor), explain to the customer the total cost of repairs and then help him decide if it's better to purchase a new system or repair the existing one.

© iStockphoto.com/Dean Mitchell

Figure 11-51 Advise and then allow a customer to make repair or purchasing decisions

WORK WITH A CUSTOMER ON SITE

As you work with a customer on site, avoid distractions. Don't accept personal calls or texts on your cell phone, and definitely don't check social media sites when you're on the job. Most organizations require that you answer calls from work, but keep them to a minimum. Be aware that the customer might be listening, so be careful not to discuss problems with coworkers, the boss, or other situations that might put the company, its employees, or products in a bad light with the customer. If you absolutely must excuse yourself from the on-site visit for personal reasons, explain the situation to the customer and return as soon as possible.

When working at a user's desk, follow these general guidelines:

1. As you work, be as unobtrusive as possible. Consider yourself a guest in the customer's office or residence. Don't make a big mess. Keep your tools and papers out of the customer's way. Don't pile your belongings and tools on top of the user's papers, books, and so forth.

2. Protect the customer's confidential and private materials. For example, if you are working on the printer and discover a budget report in the out tray, quickly turn it over so you can't read it, and hand it to the customer. If you notice a financial spreadsheet is displayed on the customer's computer screen, step away and ask the user if she wants to first close the spreadsheet before you work with the computer. If sensitive documents are on the customer's desk, you might let him know and ask if he would like to put them out of your view or in a safe place.

3. Don't take over the mouse or keyboard from the user without permission.

4. Ask permission again before you use the printer or other equipment.

5. Don't use the phone without permission.

6. Accept personal inconvenience to accommodate the user's urgent business needs. For example, if the user gets an important call while you are working, don't allow your work to interfere. You might need to stop work and perhaps leave the room.

7. Also, if the user is present, ask permission before you make a software or hardware change, even if the user has just given you permission to interact with the computer.

8. Don't disclose information about a customer on social media sites, and don't use those public outlets to complain about difficulties with a customer.

In some IT support situations, it is appropriate to consider yourself a support to the user as well as to the computer. Your goals can include educating the user as well as repairing the computer. If you want users to learn something from a problem they caused, explain how to fix the problem and walk them through the process if necessary. Don't fix the problem yourself unless they ask you to do so. It takes a little longer to train the user, but it is more productive in the end because the user learns more and is less likely to repeat the mistake (see Figure 11-52).

WORK WITH A CUSTOMER ON THE PHONE

Phone support requires more interaction with customers than any other type of IT support. To understand the problem and give clear instructions, you must be able to visualize what the customer sees at his or her computer. Patience is required if the customer must be told each key to press or command button to click. Help-desk support requires excellent communication skills, good phone manners, and lots of patience (see Figure 11-53). As your

© iStockphoto.com/Sportstock

Figure 11-52 Teaching a user how to fix her problem can prevent it from reoccurring

11

help-desk skills improve, you will learn to think through the process as though you were sitting in front of the computer yourself. Drawing diagrams and taking notes as you talk can be very helpful. In some cases, help-desk support personnel might have software that enables the remote control of customers' computers. Examples of this type of software are GoToAssist by Citrix at *netviewer.com* and LogMeIn Rescue by LogMeIn at *secure.logmeinrescue.com*. Always communicate clearly with customers when using this type of software, so that they understand what type of access they are allowing you to have on their computers.

© iStockphoto.com/mediaphotos

Figure 11-53 Learn to be patient and friendly when helping users

If your call is accidentally disconnected, call back immediately. Don't eat or drink while on the phone. If you must put callers on hold, tell them how long it will be before you get back to them. Speak clearly and don't talk too fast. Don't complain about your job, your boss, coworkers, your company, or other companies or products to your customers. A little small talk is okay and is sometimes beneficial in easing a tense situation, but keep it upbeat and positive.

DEAL WITH DIFFICULT CUSTOMERS

Most customers are polite and appreciate your help. If you make it a habit to treat others as you want to be treated, you'll find that most of your customers will tend to treat you well, too. However, occasionally you'll have to deal with a difficult customer. In this part of the chapter, you learn how to work with customers who are not knowledgeable, who are overly confident, and who complain.

WHEN THE CUSTOMER IS NOT KNOWLEDGEABLE

When on site, you can put a computer in good repair without depending on a customer to help you. But when you are trying to solve a problem over the phone, with a customer as your only eyes, ears, and hands, a computer-illiterate user can present a challenge. Here are some tips for handling this situation:

◢ Be specific with your instructions. For example, instead of saying, "Open File Explorer," say, "Using your mouse, right-click the Start button, and click File Explorer from the menu."

◢ Don't ask the customer to do something that might destroy settings or files without first having the customer back them up carefully. If you think the customer can't handle your request, ask for some on-site help.

◢ Frequently ask the customer what is displayed on the screen to help you track the keystrokes and action.

- Follow along at your own computer. It's easier to direct the customer keystroke by keystroke if you are doing the same things.
- Give the customer plenty of opportunity to ask questions.
- Genuinely compliment the customer whenever you can to help the customer gain confidence.
- If you determine that the customer cannot help you solve the problem without a lot of coaching, you might need to tactfully request that the caller have someone with more experience call you. The customer will most likely breathe a sigh of relief and have someone take over the problem.

> **✎ Notes** When solving computer problems in an organization other than your own, check with technical support within that organization instead of working only with the user. The user might not be aware of policies that have been set on his computer to prevent changes to the OS, hardware, or applications.

WHEN THE CUSTOMER IS OVERLY CONFIDENT

Sometimes customers might want to give advice, take charge of a call, withhold information they think you don't need to know, or execute commands at the computer without letting you know, so that you don't have enough information to follow along. A situation like this must be handled with tact and respect for the customer. Here are a few tips:

- When you can, compliment the customer's knowledge, experience, or insight.
- Slow the conversation down. You can say, "Please slow down. You're moving too fast for me to follow. Help me catch up."
- Don't back off from using problem-solving skills. You must still have the customer check the simple things, but direct the conversation with tact. For example, you can say, "I know you've probably gone over these simple things already, but could we just do them again together?"
- Be careful not to accuse the customer of making a mistake.
- Even though the customer might be using technical jargon, keep to your policy of not using jargon back to the customer unless you're convinced he truly understands you.

> **★ A+ Exam Tip** The A+ Core 2 exam expects you to know that it is important not to minimize a customer's problem and not to be judgmental toward a customer.

WHEN THE CUSTOMER COMPLAINS

When you are on site or on the phone, a customer might complain to you about your organization, products, or service or the service and product of another company. Consider the complaint to be helpful feedback that can lead to a better product or service and better customer relationships. Here are a few suggestions that can help you handle complaints and defuse customer anger:

- Be an active listener, and let customers know they are not being ignored. Look for the underlying problem. Don't take complaints or anger personally.
- Give the customer a little time to vent and apologize when you can. Then start the conversation by asking questions, taking notes, and solving problems. Unless you must have the information for problem solving, don't spend a lot of time finding out exactly who the customer dealt with and what happened to upset the customer.
- Don't be defensive. It's better to leave the customer with the impression that you and your company are listening and willing to admit mistakes. No matter how much anger is expressed, resist the temptation to argue or become defensive.
- Know how your employer wants you to handle a situation where you are verbally abused. For example, you might say something like this in a calm voice: "I'm sorry, but my employer does not require me to accept this kind of talk."

11

⬧ If the customer is complaining about a product or service that is not from your company, don't start by saying, "That's not our problem." Instead, listen to the customer complain. Don't appear as though you don't care.

⬧ If the complaint is against you or your product, identify the underlying problem if you can. Ask questions and take notes. Then pass these notes on to people in your organization who need to know.

⬧ Sometimes simply making progress or reducing the problem to a manageable state reduces the customer's anxiety. As you are talking to a customer, summarize what you have both agreed on or observed so far in the conversation (see Figure 11-54).

© iStockphoto.com/Kameleon007

Figure 11-54 When a customer is upset, try to find a place of agreement

⬧ Point out ways that *you* think communication could be improved. For example, you might say, "I'm sorry, but I'm having trouble understanding what you want. Could you please slow down, and let's take this one step at a time?"

APPLYING | CONCEPTS   CULTURE OF HONOR

Andy is one of the most intelligent and knowledgeable support technicians in his group at CloudPool, Inc. He is about to be promoted to software engineer and today is his last day on the help desk. Sarah, a potential customer with little computer experience, calls asking for help in accessing the company website. Andy says, "The URL is www dot cloud pool dot com." Sarah responds, "What's a URL?" Andy's patience grows thin. He's thinking to himself, "Oh, help! Just two more hours and I'm off these darn phones." He answers Sarah in a tone of voice that says, hey, I really think you're an idiot! He says to her, "You know, lady! That address box at the top of your browser. Now enter www dot cloud pool dot com!" Sarah gets flustered and intimidated and doesn't know what to say next. She really wants to know what a browser is, but instead she says, "Wait. I'll just ask someone in the office to help me," and hangs up the phone.

Discuss the situation with others in a small group and answer these questions:

1. If you were Andy's manager and overheard this call, how would you handle the situation?

2. What principles of working with customers does Andy need to keep in mind?

Two students sit back-to-back, one playing the role of Andy and the other playing the role of Sarah. Play out the entire conversation. Others in the group can offer suggestions and constructive criticism.

THE CUSTOMER DECIDES WHEN THE WORK IS DONE

When you think you've solved the problem, allow the customer to decide if the service is finished to his or her satisfaction. For remote support, the customer generally ends the call or chat session, not the technician. If you end the call too soon and the problem is not completely resolved, the customer can be frustrated, especially if it is difficult to contact you again.

For on-site work, after you have solved the problem, complete these tasks before you close the call:

1. If you changed anything on the computer after you booted it, reboot one more time to make sure you have not caused a problem with the boot.

2. Allow the customer enough time to be fully satisfied that all is working. Does the printer work? Print a test page. Does the network connection work? Can the customer sign in to the network and access data on it?

3. If you backed up data before working on the problem and then restored the data from backups, ask the user to verify that the data is fully restored.

4. Review the service call with the customer. Summarize the instructions and explanations you have given during the call. This is an appropriate time to fill out your paperwork and explain to the customer what you have written. Then ask if she has any questions.

5. Explain preventive maintenance to the customer, such as deleting temporary files from the hard drive or cleaning the mouse. Most customers don't have preventive maintenance contracts for their computers and appreciate the time you take to show them how to take better care of their equipment. One technician keeps a pack of monitor wipes in his toolkit and ends each call by cleaning the customer's monitor screen.

To demonstrate a sincere concern for your customer's business and that you have owned the problem, it's extremely important to follow up later with the customer, ask if he is still satisfied with your work, and ask if he has any more questions. For example, you can say to the customer, "I'll call you on Monday to make sure everything is working and you're still satisfied with the work." On Monday, make that call. As you do, you're building customer loyalty.

> ★ **A+ Exam Tip** The A+ Core 2 exam expects you to know to follow up with the customer at a later date to verify his or her satisfaction.

SOMETIMES YOU MUST ESCALATE A PROBLEM

You are not going to solve every computer problem you encounter. Knowing how to escalate a problem properly so it is assigned to people higher in the support chain is one of the first things you should learn on a new job. Know your company's policy for escalation. What documents or entries in the call tracking software do you use? Who do you contact? How do you pass the problem on—do you use email, a phone call, or an online entry in a database? Do you remain the responsible "support" party, or does the person now addressing the problem become the new contact? Are you expected to keep in touch with the customer and the problem, or are you totally out of the picture?

When you escalate, let the customer know. Tell the customer you are passing the problem on to someone who is more experienced or has access to more extensive resources. If you check back with the customer only to find out that the other support person has not called or followed through to the customer's satisfaction, don't lay blame or point fingers. Just do whatever you can to help within your company guidelines. Your call to the customer will go a long way toward helping the situation.

WORK WITH COWORKERS

Learn to be a professional when working with coworkers. A professional at work is someone who puts business matters above personal matters (see Figure 11-55). In big bold letters, I can say **the key to being professional is to learn not to be personally offended when someone lets you down or does not please you**. Remember, most people do the best they can considering the business and personal constraints they're up against. Getting offended leads to becoming bitter about others and about your job. Learn to keep negative opinions to yourself, and to expect the best of others. When a coworker starts to gossip, try to politely change the subject.

Know your limitations and be willing to admit when you can't do something. For example, Larry's boss stops by his desk and asks him to accept one more project. Larry already is working many hours overtime just to keep up. He needs to politely say to his boss, "I can accept this new project only if you relieve me of some of these tasks."

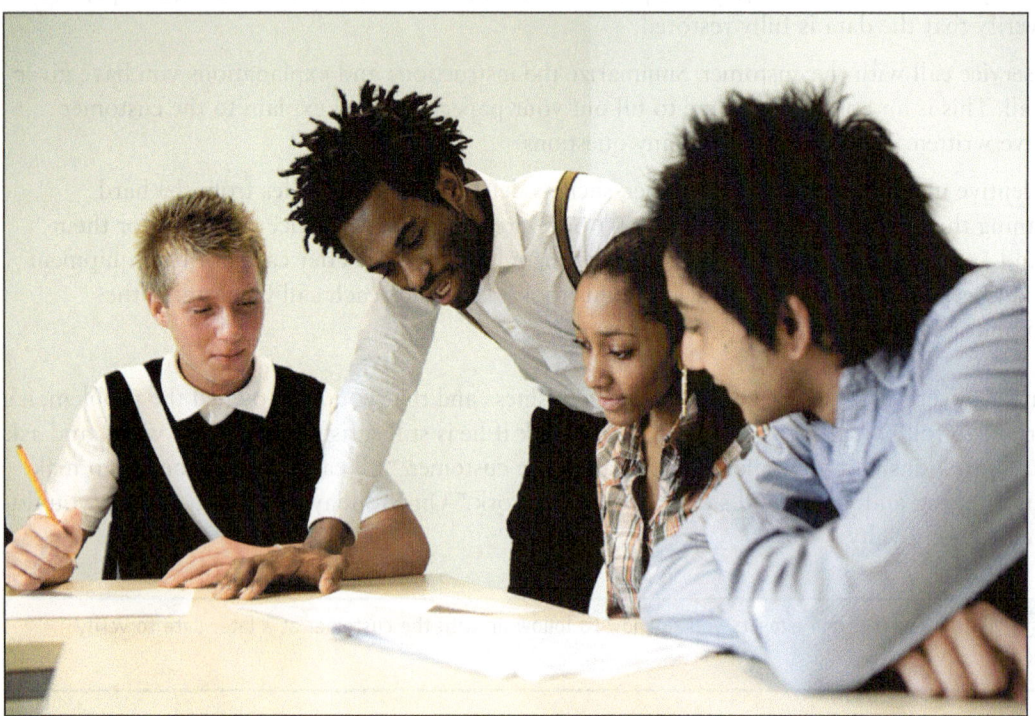

© iStockphoto.com/Chris Schmidt

Figure 11-55   Coworkers who act professionally are fun to work with

APPLYING | CONCEPTS   ACTIVE LEARNING

Ray was new at a corporate help desk that supported hospitals across the nation. He had only had a couple of weeks of training before he was turned loose on the phones. He was a little nervous the first day he took calls without a mentor sitting beside him. His first call came from Fernanda, a radiology technician who was trying to sign in to the network to start the day. When Fernanda entered her network ID and passcode, an error message stated her user account was not valid. She told Ray she had tried signing in several times on two different computers. Ray checked his database and found her account, which appeared to be in good order. He asked her to try again. She did and got the same results. In his two weeks of training, this problem had never occurred. He told her, "I'm sorry, I don't know how to solve this problem." She said, "Okay, well, thank you anyway," and hung up. She immediately called the

(continues)

help-desk number back and the call was answered by Jackie, who sits across the room from Ray. Fernanda said, "The other guy couldn't fix my problem. Can you help me?"

"What other guy?" Jackie asked.

"I think his name was Ray."

"Oh, him! He's new and he doesn't know much, and besides that, he should have asked for help. Tell me the problem." Jackie reset the account and the problem was solved.

In a group of three or more students, discuss and answer the following questions:

1. What mistake did Ray make? What should he have done or said?

2. What mistake did Jackie make? What should she have done or said?

3. What three principles of relating to customers and coworkers would be helpful for Ray and Jackie to keep in mind?

>> CHAPTER SUMMARY

Windows Interfaces

▲ An operating system manages hardware, runs applications, provides an interface for users, and stores, retrieves, and manipulates files.

▲ Windows 10 offers two graphical user interfaces: the desktop and Tablet mode. Windows 8 offers two GUIs: the modern interface and the Windows 8 desktop. The Windows 7 desktop offers the Aero user interface.

▲ Ways to launch a program from the Windows 10 desktop include using the Start menu, the search box, the Quick Launch menu, an icon pinned to the taskbar, File Explorer, a shortcut on the desktop, and the Run option on the Quick Launch menu.

▲ Ways to launch a program from the Windows 8 desktop include using the Start screen, the Quick Launch menu, an icon pinned to the taskbar, File Explorer, a shortcut on the desktop, and the Run option on the Quick Launch menu.

▲ Ways to launch a program from the Windows 7 desktop include using the Start menu, the search box, an icon pinned to the taskbar, Windows Explorer, or a shortcut on the desktop.

Windows Tools for Users and Technicians

▲ Windows 10/8 File Explorer and Windows 7 Windows Explorer are used to manage files and folders on storage devices. Folders are organized in a top-down hierarchical structure of subfolders.

▲ The file extension indicates how file contents are organized and formatted and what program uses the file.

▲ Control Panel gives access to a group of utility programs used to manage the system. Technicians generally prefer the Classic view for Control Panel.

▲ The Windows 10 File Explorer Options and Windows 8/7 Folder Options applets in Control Panel change the way files and folders are displayed in Explorer.

▲ The Sound applet in Control Panel controls audio, including default speakers and microphones.

▲ The Power Options applet in Control Panel manages power settings on a computer.

▲ The System window gives a quick overview of the system, including which edition and version of Windows is installed and the amount of installed memory.

11

◢ The System Information window gives much more information about the computer than the System window, including information on hardware, device drivers, the OS, and applications.

◢ The Settings app is a centralized location for users to access common Windows 10 settings.

How Windows Controls Access to Network Resources

◢ Windows 10/8/7 supports workgroups and domains to manage resources on a private network. In addition, Windows 8/7 supports homegroups to manage resources on a private network. Workgroups are more secure than homegroups.

◢ Windows 10/8 supports public and private settings to secure a network connection, and Windows 7 supports public, home, and work settings to secure a network connection.

◢ Join a Windows computer to a domain using one of these methods: (1) use a network ID when you sign in to Windows to authenticate the user to Active Directory on the local network or through some type of VPN; (2) use an email address and password when you sign in to Windows to authenticate the user to Azure AD in the cloud; or (3) use an email address and password to authenticate to Azure AD in the cloud as a secondary login after you have already signed in to Windows with your personal user account.

◢ Use the Settings app to set up a computer to connect to a workgroup or to authenticate a user so that the computer can join a domain.

◢ Use the Network and Sharing Center to change the security settings for a Windows network connection.

What Customers Want: Beyond Technical Know-How

◢ Customers want more than just technical know-how. They want a positive and helpful attitude, respect, good communication, sensitivity to their needs, ownership of their problem, dependability, credibility, integrity, honesty, and professionalism.

◢ Customers expect their first contact with you to be professional and friendly, and expect that listening to their problem or request will be your first priority.

◢ Know how to ask penetrating questions when interviewing a customer about a problem or request.

◢ Set and meet customer expectations by using good communication about what you are doing or intending to do and allowing the customer to make decisions where appropriate.

◢ Deal confidently and gracefully with customers who are difficult, including those who are not knowledgeable, are overly confident, or complain.

◢ When you first start a new job, find out how to escalate a problem you cannot solve.

>> KEY TERMS

For explanations of key terms, see the Glossary for this text.

32-bit operating system	BYOD experience	compressed (zipped) folder	File Explorer Options
64-bit operating system	call tracking software	Control Panel	applet
Action Center	Category view	Cortana	file extension
Active Directory (AD)	charm	device drivers	file name
Aero user interface	charms bar	domain	Folder Options applet
Azure Active Directory	child directories	domain user account	folders
(Azure AD)	Classic view	escalate	gadgets
Branchcache	client/server	File Explorer	

graphical user interface (GUI)
hibernation
homegroup
library
live tiles
logical topology
Media Center
Metro UI
Metro User Interface
modern interface
navigation pane

Network and Sharing Center
Notepad
notification area
operating system (OS)
path
peer-to-peer (P2P)
physical topology
pinning
Power Options applet
Recycle Bin
root directory

service
Settings app
sleep mode
sleep timers
Sound applet
standby mode
Start screen
subdirectories
suspend mode
System Information
system tray

System window
systray
taskbar
Task View
ticket
volume
Windows 8.1
Windows 10
Windows Explorer
workgroup

>> THINKING CRITICALLY

These questions are designed to prepare you for the critical thinking required for the A+ exams and may use content from other chapters and the web.

1. When Kristy recently started a photography business, she downloaded Photoshop to her computer to edit her photos. She notices her computer freezes when she is using Photoshop, so she asks you to help her fix the problem. Your research discovers that Photoshop requires a lot of RAM to run smoothly, and you need to know how much RAM Kristy's computer has to see if that is the problem. Which Windows tools from the following list can you use to know how much RAM is installed on a system? Select all that apply.

   a. System window

   b. Power Options applet

   c. System Information window

   d. Network and Sharing Center

2. John is traveling for work and is spending a week at a new branch. He needs to print an email, but he isn't able to add the network printer to his computer. He is using a Windows 10 Pro laptop, is connected to the network, and can access the Internet. What is a likely and easy fix to John's problem?

   a. The computer is not set to find resources shared on the network; use the Settings app to fix the problem.

   b. The computer is not set to find resources shared on the network; use the Network and Sharing Center to fix the problem.

   c. John did not correctly authenticate to the Windows domain; use the Settings app to fix the problem.

   d. The drivers for the network printer need to be updated. Use Device Manager to fix the problem.

3. Mary wants her 32-bit installation of Windows 7 Professional to run faster. She has 4 GB of memory installed on the motherboard. She decides more memory will help. She installs an additional 2 GB of memory for a total of 6 GB, but does not see any performance improvement. What is the problem and what should you tell Mary?

   a. She should use Control Panel to install the memory in Windows 7. After it is installed, performance should improve. Tell Mary how to open Control Panel.

   b. A 32-bit OS cannot use more than 4 GB of memory. Tell Mary she has wasted her money.

   c. A 32-bit OS cannot use more than 4 GB of memory. Tell Mary to upgrade her system to the 64-bit version of Windows 7 Professional.

   d. A 32-bit OS cannot use more than 4 GB of memory. Explain the problem to Mary and discuss the possible solutions with her.

11

4. Jack needs to email two documents to a friend, but the files are so large his email server bounced them back as undeliverable. What is your advice?

   a. Tell Jack to open the documents, break each of them into two documents, and then email the four documents separately.

   b. Tell Jack to put the two documents in a compressed folder and email the folder.

   c. Tell Jack to put each document in a different compressed folder and email each folder separately.

   d. Tell Jack to put the documents on a USB drive and snail mail the drive to his friend.

5. Jawana has been working on a paper for her Anatomy class for weeks. One day her little brother was on her computer and accidentally deleted her paper from the Documents folder. How can Jawana recover her deleted paper?

6. A technician needs to be prepared to launch programs even when utility windows or the Windows desktop cannot load. What is the program name for the System Information utility? What is the program name for the Remote Desktop utility?

7. Suppose you are a customer who wants to have a computer repaired. List five main characteristics that you would want to see in your computer repair person.

8. When you receive a phone call requesting on-site support, what is one thing you should do before you make an appointment?

9. You make an appointment to do an on-site repair, but you are detained and find out that you will be late. What is the best thing to do?

10. When making an on-site service call, what should you do before making any changes to software or before taking the case cover off a computer?

11. What should you do after finishing your computer repair?

12. What is a good strategy to follow if a conflict arises between you and your customer?

13. You have exhausted your knowledge of a problem and it still is not solved. Before you escalate it, what else can you do?

14. If you need to make a phone call while on a customer's site and your cell phone is not working, what do you do?

15. What is one thing you can do to help a caller who needs phone support and is not a competent computer user?

16. Describe what you should do when a customer complains to you about a product or service that your company provides.

17. Robert works in a call center and receives a call from Kathy. Kathy says she can no longer access the online reporting application for her weekly reports through her web browser. You ask your boss, and he tells you that the server team changed the application's URL during an upgrade over the weekend. He asks you to make sure all the other technicians are aware of this change. What is the best way to share this information?

   a. Print a flyer with the new URL and post it on the wall in the call center.

   b. Send out a mass email with the new URL to all the technicians.

   c. Update the knowledge base article that contains the application's URL in the call tracking application.

   d. Yell the new URL to all technicians sitting in the call center.

Hands-On | Project 11-1 Practicing Using the Quick Launch Menu

Do the following to practice using the Quick Launch menu:

1. Click the **Power** icon on the Start menu. What are the options on the Power icon menu?

2. Open the **Quick Launch** menu, and practice using several options on the menu. What are the submenu items that appear when you point to *Shut down or sign out*?

3. Click **Power Options** on the Quick Launch menu. The Settings app opens to the Power & sleep page. Sometimes you need to use links in the Settings app to navigate to the control panel applets and find more options. Find the settings in the Power Options window that allow you to change the options available in the *Shut down or sign out* menu.

4. Go to the **Start** menu. Click your account icon on the left side of the Start menu. What options appear in the drop-down menu? Try the Lock and Sign out options, and describe what each option does.

Hands-On | Project 11-2 Creating Shortcuts

Do the following to practice creating shortcuts on the Windows desktop:

1. Open Windows 10/8 File Explorer or Windows 7 Windows Explorer and create a folder called **Temp** under the root directory of the hard drive. List the steps you took.

2. Add a subfolder to Temp called **MyFiles**. List the steps you took.

3. Create a text file named **Text1.txt** in the MyFiles folder. List the steps you took.

4. Create a shortcut to the Text1.txt file on the Windows desktop. List the steps you took.

5. In the MyFiles folder, rename the file **Text2.txt**.

6. Double-click the shortcut on the desktop. Did that cause an error? Did the shortcut name change when you changed the name of the original file? Did it open the correct file?

7. The program file for Microsoft Paint is mspaint.exe. Use Windows Explorer to locate the program file and launch the Microsoft Paint program.

8. Create a shortcut to Microsoft Paint on the Windows desktop. Launch Microsoft Paint using the shortcut.

9. To clean up after yourself, delete the Temp folder and the shortcuts. Close the two Paint windows.

Hands-On | Project 11-3 Using the System Information Utility

Do the following to run the System Information utility and gather information about your system:

1. Use the **msinfo32.exe** command to launch the System Information window.

2. Browse through the different levels of information in this window and answer the following questions:
   a. What OS and OS version are you using?
   b. What is your CPU speed?
   c. What is your BIOS manufacturer and version?
   d. How much video RAM is available to your video adapter card? Explain how you got this information.
   e. What is the name of the driver file that manages your network adapter? Your optical drive?

11

Hands-On | Project 11-4 Installing and Uninstalling Windows 10/8 Apps

Windows 10/8 apps are installed from the Windows Store. Follow these steps to install an app and then uninstall it:

1. Open the Start menu.

> **⟳ OS Differences** In Windows 8, you must have a Microsoft account to get apps from the Windows Store. If you don't already have an account, you can get one free at *live.com*.

2. To install an app, click the **Microsoft Store** tile. Next, scroll through the apps in the Store or use its search box to find an app (see Figure 11-56). Click a free one, such as Windows Help+Tips, and follow the directions on screen to install it. If you did not sign in to Windows using a Microsoft account, you are asked to sign in so that you can apply this app to all your devices using this Microsoft account; in Windows 10, you can decline and install this app only on the local machine.

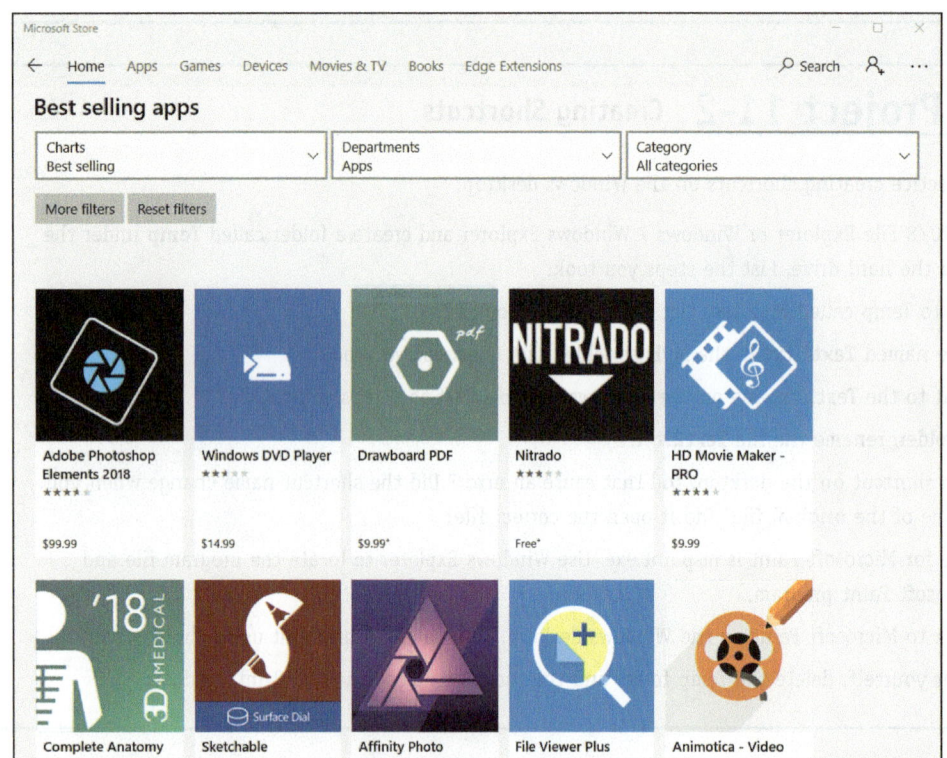

Figure 11-56 Search the Windows Store for apps to install

3. Launch the app and practice using it to make sure it works.

4. To uninstall the app, right-click the app tile on the Start menu. Click **Uninstall** and follow the directions on screen.

>> REAL PROBLEMS, REAL SOLUTIONS

REAL PROBLEM 11-1 Using Windows Help and Support

The best IT support technicians are the ones who continually teach themselves new skills. You can teach yourself to use and support Windows by using the web, a couple of apps in Windows 10 called Get Help and Tips, or the Windows Help and Support utility in Windows 8/7. To start the apps in Windows 10, type **get help** in the search box or type **tips** in the search box. In Windows 8, type **Help and Support** on the Start screen. In Windows 7, click **Start** and then click **Help and Support**. If you are connected to the Internet, clicking links can take you to the Microsoft website, where you can find information and watch videos about Windows.

Do the following to research a topic so you can become an independent learner about Windows:

1. The Windows 10/8/7 Snipping Tool can help you take screenshots of the Windows desktop. These screenshots are useful when documenting computer problems and solutions. Use Get Help or Windows Help and Support to find out how to use the Snipping Tool. Use it to take a screenshot of your Windows desktop. Save the screenshot into a file on a USB flash drive or on the hard drive. Print the file contents.

2. Access the *support.microsoft.com* website for Windows support. Save or print one article from the Knowledge Base that addresses a problem when installing Windows 10/8/7.

3. Search the web to learn the purpose of the pagefile.sys file. What website did you use to find your answer? Why is the Microsoft website considered the best source for information about the pagefile.sys file?

REAL PROBLEM 11-2 Documenting How to Use Windows

This problem requires a microphone, and a webcam would also be useful. Make a screen recording with a voiceover to teach end users how to use Windows. Do the following:

1. Screencast-O-Matic offers free software to make a screen recording with voice and video. Go to *screencast-o-matic.com* and launch the online video recording software. You might be required to download and install the software.

2. Select a Windows feature to explain. For example, you can explain how to open and close an app, install or uninstall an app, create a shortcut, empty the Recycle Bin, or use the Start menu. You or your instructor might have other ideas.

3. Use the Screencast-O-Matic software to make a screen recording that explains how to use the Windows feature you selected. The recording should be no longer than three minutes. Explain the steps as you go. The software records your screen movements, your voice if a microphone is detected, and video if a webcam is detected.

4. View the video. If you see a problem, record it again. When you're satisfied with your video, save it as an MP4 file.

REAL PROBLEM 11-3 Learning a New App Available in Windows 10

Sometimes you might encounter an application that you are not familiar with, yet you might be asked to help a user answer questions about the app. In that case, you can search for the information you need in the application's Help system. In this Real Problem, you use the Help system and online tutorials for Sway, a new app available for free in Windows 10. Perform the following steps, looking up Help information as

11

necessary to learn how to proceed. If you are already familiar with Sway, pretend you are not and rely on Help information instead. To practice using Sway, complete the following tasks:

1. Create a new Sway story.

2. Choose a design and layout.

3. Add a title, photographs, and text.

4. Add focus points on photographs.

5. Share the URL to your Sway story with another person and have her watch what you created using a web browser.

REAL PROBLEM 11-4 Installing and Using the Mouse Without Borders App

This Real Problem requires two computers on the same network, both with Internet access. Install the free Microsoft app Mouse Without Borders on both computers. This app allows one computer's mouse and keyboard to control up to four computers. The app is very useful when you frequently switch between two different computers, even when you are using both Windows 10 and Windows 8. Complete the following tasks:

1. Open Edge and search for the Mouse Without Borders download. Make sure your system meets the minimum system requirements.

2. Download and install the app from the Microsoft Download Center webpage.

3. Use Mouse Without Borders to connect two computers on the same network.

4. On the first computer, use the mouse and keyboard to control the second computer by opening an app on it without touching its mouse or keyboard.

CHAPTER 12

Installing Windows

After completing this chapter, you will be able to:

- Plan a Windows installation
- Install Windows 10, Windows 8.1, and Windows 7
- Configure Windows settings after the installation
- Describe special concerns when installing Windows in a large enterprise

Windows 10, 8, and 7 all share the same basic Windows architecture, and all have similar characteristics. Windows 10 includes free upgrades called builds. Windows 8 includes a free upgrade to Windows 8.1 via the Windows Store. Windows 10 is available for purchase directly from Microsoft, but you can no longer purchase Windows 8 or 7. (However, Windows 8.1 and 7 can be purchased from other vendors.)

This chapter discusses how to plan a Windows installation and the steps to perform a Windows 10, Windows 8.1, or Windows 7 installation in various scenarios, including what to do after the OS is installed. You also learn what to expect when installing Windows on computers in a large enterprise.

> ✎ **Notes** In the text, we use the term "Windows 8" to refer to Windows 8.0 and Windows 8.1.

HOW TO PLAN A WINDOWS INSTALLATION

As an IT support technician, you can expect to be called on to install Windows in a variety of situations. You might need to install Windows on a new hard drive, after an existing Windows installation has become corrupted, or to upgrade from one OS to another. Many decisions need to be made before the installation, and most of these decisions apply to any Windows operating system.

CHOOSING THE EDITION, LICENSE, AND VERSION OF WINDOWS

When buying a Windows operating system, know that the price is affected by the Windows edition and type of license you purchase. You learned about the different editions in Chapter 11. You also need to decide between 32-bit and 64-bit architecture. In this part of the chapter, you learn about your options when purchasing Windows and how to make sure your computer qualifies for the version and edition you've selected.

OEM OR RETAIL LICENSE

When buying Windows, you can purchase a retail license or an Original Equipment Manufacturer (OEM) license. Options for both types of licenses include 32-bit and 64-bit. Here are the key differences between an OEM license and a retail license:

◢ The OEM license is for builders and manufacturers of computers and can be installed only on a new computer. You can purchase and download a Windows 10 OEM license from a third party such as Amazon at *amazon.com* or Newegg at *newegg.com*.

◢ An OEM license allows all hardware upgrades except for an upgrade to a different model of motherboard.

◢ An OEM license costs less than a retail license. Microsoft generally refers technical support for an OEM license to the computer manufacturer or builder.

◢ Retail licenses can be purchased from the Microsoft online store at *microsoftstore.com*. Microsoft sells Windows 10 as either a download or on a boxed USB flash drive (sometimes called an Install Stick) that's shipped to you with the installation files. Whether you're doing a clean install of Windows 10 or an upgrade from Windows 8/7 to Windows 10, the retail license costs the same.

◢ The benefit of a retail license over an OEM license is that it can be transferred to a different computer, and you get Microsoft direct support from Microsoft support personnel.

When you download the Windows 10 setup files from Microsoft, you start by downloading the Media Creation Tool. After you install and launch the tool, you use it to download Windows setup files; you also have the option to create a bootable DVD or USB flash drive. You learn how to use the Media Creation Tool later in this chapter.

> ✎ **Notes** The Media Creation Tool and Windows setup files can be downloaded for free from Microsoft. Therefore, when you purchase Windows 10, you are really only purchasing a **product key**, which is required to activate a license to use Windows 10. The product key is emailed to your Microsoft account email address.

32-BIT OR 64-BIT ARCHITECTURE

Recall that an operating system can process 32 bits or 64 bits at a time. A 64-bit installation of Windows generally performs better than a 32-bit installation if you have enough RAM. (Table 12-1 shows how much RAM is supported by popular editions of Windows.) Also, 64-bit installations of Windows can support 64-bit applications, which run faster than 32-bit applications. Even though you can install 32-bit applications in a 64-bit OS, always choose 64-bit applications for best performance. Keep in mind that 64-bit installations of Windows require 64-bit device drivers.

Operating System	32-Bit Architecture	64-Bit Architecture
Windows 10 Home Windows 8.1	4 GB	128 GB
Windows 10 Pro Windows 10 Enterprise Windows 8.1 Pro Windows 8.1 Enterprise	4 GB	512 GB
Windows 7 Home Premium	4 GB	16 GB
Windows 7 Professional Windows 7 Enterprise Windows 7 Ultimate	4 GB	192 GB

Table 12-1 Maximum memory supported by Windows 10, 8.1, and 7 editions and versions

Notes All processors (CPUs) used in personal computers today are hybrid processors and can handle a 32-bit or 64-bit OS. However, the Intel Itanium and Xeon processors used in high-end workstations and servers are true 64-bit processors and require a 64-bit OS.

Notes How much memory or RAM you can install in a computer depends not only on the OS installed, but also on how much memory the motherboard can hold. To know how much RAM a motherboard can support, see the motherboard documentation.

VERIFYING THAT YOUR SYSTEM QUALIFIES FOR WINDOWS

**A+
CORE 2
1.1, 1.3**

The minimum hardware requirements for Windows 10/8/7 are listed in Table 12-2. (These minimum requirements are also the Microsoft recommended requirements.) Beginning with Windows 8, in addition to the requirements listed, Microsoft requires three technologies used by the processor (NX, PAE, and SSE2). All processors built in the last 10 years use these technologies, so the move was intended to prevent a new edition of Windows from being installed on a system that was more than 10 years old. Know, however, that Microsoft occasionally changes the minimum and recommended requirements for its OSs.

Hardware	For 32-Bit Windows	For 64-Bit Windows
Processor	1 GHz or faster; for Windows 10/8, must support NX, PAE, and SSE2	
Memory (RAM)	1 GB	2 GB
Free hard drive space	16 GB	20 GB
Video device and driver	DirectX 9 device with WDDM 1.0 or higher driver	

Table 12-2 Minimum and recommended hardware requirements for Windows 10/8/7

Notes The three processor technologies are NX (Never Execute or No Execute), which prevents malware from hiding in the data storage area of another program; PAE (Physical Address Extension), which was originally intended to allow 32-bit processors to use more than 4 GB of RAM but is no longer used for that purpose because it gave device drivers a big headache; and SSE2 (Streaming SIMD Extensions 2), which allows a processor to execute a single instruction multiple times.

★ A+ Exam Tip The A+ Core 2 exam may give you a scenario and ask you to demonstrate hardware compatibility requirements for a Windows installation.

MBR OR GPT PARTITIONING SYSTEM

You need to be aware of the partitioning method you will use on the hard drive. A hard drive is divided into one or more partitions. Windows can use one of two methods to partition a hard drive: The Master Boot Record (MBR) method is older, allows for four partitions, and is limited to 2.2-TB drives. The GUID Partition Table (GPT) method is newer, allows for any size of hard drive, and for Windows can have up to 128 partitions on the drive. GPT is required for drives larger than 2.2 TB.

When an MBR or GPT partition is formatted with a file system and assigned a drive letter (such as drive C:), it is called a volume. A file system is the overall structure an OS uses to name, store, and organize files on a volume; Windows is always installed on a volume that uses the NTFS file system. For most installations, you install Windows on the only hard drive in the computer and allocate all the space on the drive to one partition that Windows setup calls drive C:. Windows is installed in the C:\Windows folder. You learn more about partitions and file systems in Chapter 13.

BIOS/UEFI FIRMWARE ON THE MOTHERBOARD

To understand if your system qualifies for Windows 10/8/7, it helps to understand how Windows relates to hardware by using device drivers and firmware on the motherboard, as shown in Figure 12-1. (In the figure, the kernel is the part of Windows responsible for relating to hardware.)

Figure 12-1 Windows relates to hardware by way of device drivers and system BIOS/UEFI

When a computer is first turned on, it uses some devices such as the keyboard, monitor, and hard drive before the OS starts up. The motherboard BIOS/UEFI is contained on a chip on the motherboard (see Figure 12-2) and manages these essential devices. This chip is called a firmware chip because it holds programs.

Coin battery

Firmware chips

Figure 12-2 A chip on a motherboard contains BIOS/UEFI used to start the computer, hold motherboard settings, and run essential devices. The chip retains power from a nearby coin battery when the computer is turned off.

All modern motherboards use firmware called UEFI (Unified Extensible Firmware Interface). UEFI is a much improved replacement for BIOS (basic input/output system) and offers legacy support for BIOS compatibility. BIOS stores its setup information on the motherboard, while UEFI stores its setup information and some drivers on the motherboard and the hard drive. The motherboard BIOS/UEFI provides three main functions:

▲ The system BIOS/UEFI contains instructions for running essential hardware devices before an operating system is started. After the OS is started, it might continue to use system BIOS/UEFI or use device drivers to communicate with these devices.

▲ The startup BIOS/UEFI starts the computer and finds a boot device that contains an operating system. Boot devices that a system might support include an internal or external hard drive, CD or DVD drive, bootable USB flash drive, and the network. After it finds a boot device, the firmware turns the startup process over to the OS.

> **Notes** When choosing a boot device, consider that solid-state drives are faster than magnetic hard drives because they have no moving parts. USB flash drives are also solid-state devices. Some hard drives might be hot-swappable, which means they are inserted into an easily accessible hot-swap bay and can be exchanged without powering down the system.

▲ The setup BIOS/UEFI is used to change motherboard settings. You can use it to enable or disable a device on the motherboard (for example, the network port, video port, or USB ports), change the date and time that is later passed to the OS, and select the order of boot devices for startup BIOS/UEFI to search when looking for an operating system to load. This order of boot devices is called the boot priority order.

Most computers today give you the option of booting the system in UEFI mode or the legacy BIOS mode, which is called UEFI CSM (Compatibility Support Module) mode. You must select which firmware mode you will use *before* you install Windows. Here are points to help you decide:

▲ UEFI mode is required if the hard drive is larger than 2.2 TB or is using the GPT partitioning system. (However, a hard drive manufacturer might provide device drivers to allow a drive larger than 2.2 TB to use the MBR partitioning system and legacy BIOS.)

12

> ✎ **Notes** Seagate offers its DiscWizard device drivers that you can install on Seagate's 3-TB hard drive so you can install the hard drive in a system that only has legacy BIOS. DiscWizard creates two MBR virtual hard drives and presents them to BIOS; they appear to BIOS to be two physical MBR hard drives.

▲ UEFI and the GPT partitioning system for the hard drive work only with 64-bit versions of Windows 10/8/7. A 32-bit version of Windows 10/8/7 can read and write to a GPT disk but not boot from it.

▲ UEFI has a security system called Secure boot, which helps to prevent malware from hijacking a system during or before the operating system load. UEFI mode and Windows work together to ensure that no unsecured device driver, application, or OS component is loaded during startup. If you want to enable Secure boot, you must use UEFI, GPT, and a 64-bit edition of Windows.

▲ Ultimately, the only times you might select the CSM mode are when you use a legacy MBR hard drive or install a 32-bit version of Windows 10/8/7.

APPLYING | CONCEPTS   SELECTING THE FIRMWARE MODE AND BOOT PRIORITY ORDER

You can use BIOS/UEFI setup to change the firmware mode and boot priority order. See the motherboard documentation to find out how to access and use BIOS/UEFI setup. Here are steps for one system:

1. To access BIOS/UEFI setup, press a key such as **Del** or **F2** early in the boot process before Windows starts to load. When the BIOS/UEFI setup screen appears, look for a screen to manage the boot. For example, the Boot screen for one motherboard's firmware is shown in Figure 12-3.

Source: American Megatrends, Inc.

Figure 12-3 The Boot screen for BIOS/UEFI setup

2. To use CSM mode, which requires the MBR partitioning system:
   a. Click **CSM (Compatibility Support Module)** and make sure that CSM is enabled (see Figure 12-4).

(continues)

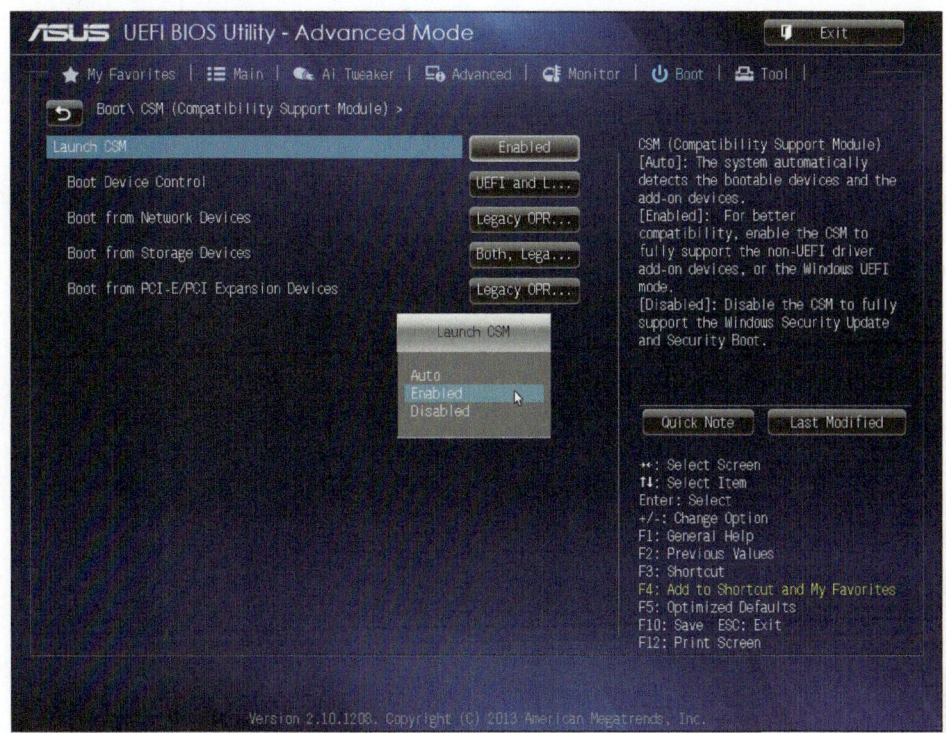

Source: American Megatrends, Inc.

Figure 12-4 Enable or disable CSM mode

    b. On the Boot screen (see Figure 12-3), click **Secure Boot**. In the Secure Boot menu, select **Other OS** for the OS Type (see Figure 12-5).

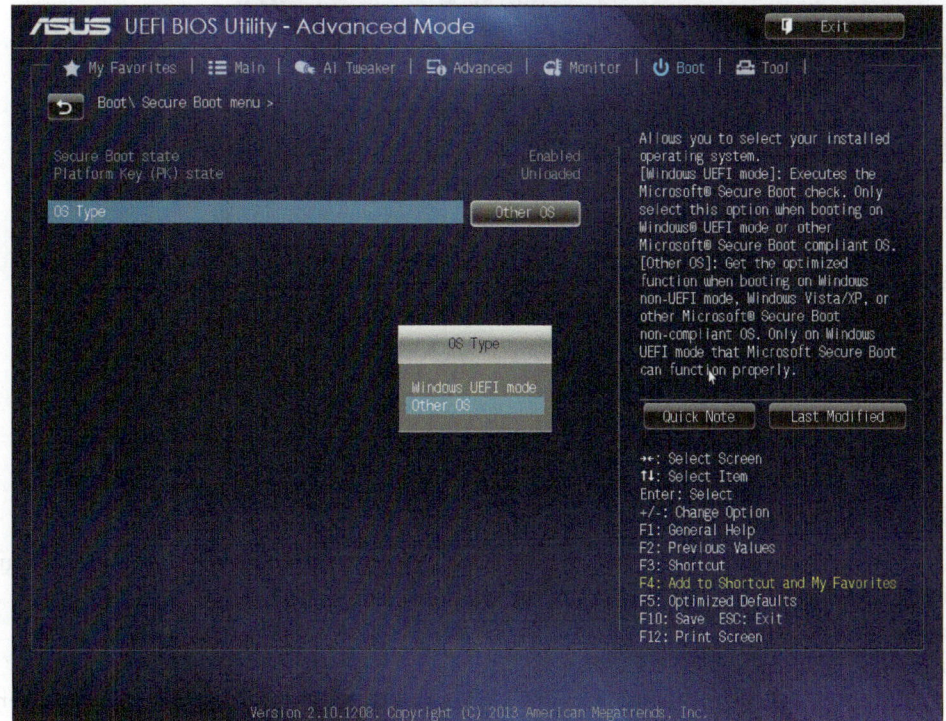

Source: American Megatrends, Inc.

Figure 12-5 Select Other OS to allow Windows to install on an MBR hard drive

3. To use UEFI mode and the GPT partitioning system, use the same screens from the previous step to disable **CSM** (see Figure 12-4) and set the OS Type to **Windows UEFI mode** (see Figure 12-5).

4. Normally, BIOS/UEFI is set to boot first from the internal hard drive. If you plan to install Windows by booting from a DVD, USB flash drive, or external hard drive connected to a USB port, you need to change the boot priority order. To make the change, look for a Boot screen or menu. For the system shown in Figure 12-6, boot options are the DVD drive, hard drive, and network port. Also, know that sometimes the DVD drive is labeled CD-ROM in BIOS/UEFI setup.

Source: American Megatrends, Inc.

Figure 12-6   Set the boot order in BIOS/UEFI setup

In a corporate or enterprise environment, automated methods might be in place to install a fresh copy of Windows on a workstation from deployment servers on the network. To use this method, you configure BIOS/UEFI setup to boot from the network and locate a deployment server to install Windows. How to do that is covered later in this chapter.

APPLICATION AND HARDWARE COMPATIBILITY

Verify that the applications you already have installed will work in a new OS you are about to install. You can go to the application manufacturer's website to check for compatibility with the new OS.

Device drivers are small programs stored on the hard drive that tell the computer how to communicate with a specific hardware device such as a printer, network card, or scanner. These drivers are installed on the hard drive when the OS is first installed or when new hardware is added to the system. A device driver is written to work for a specific OS, such as Windows 10, 8.1, or 7. In addition, a 32-bit OS requires 32-bit drivers and a 64-bit OS requires 64-bit drivers.

Windows provides some device drivers and the manufacturer of the hardware device provides others. When you purchase a printer, video card, digital camera, scanner, or other hardware device, a CD that contains the device drivers is usually bundled with the device along with a user manual (see Figure 12-7). You can also download the drivers for a device from the manufacturer's website. Be sure you have the correct Windows device drivers for all your critical devices, such as your network card or motherboard.

Figure 12-7   A device such as this video card comes packaged with its device drivers stored on a CD

If you are not sure your devices will work with Windows 10/8/7, one solution is to set up a dual boot. A dual boot, also called a multiboot, allows you to install the new OS without disturbing the old one so you can boot to either OS. After the installation, you can test your software or hardware. If they work under the new OS, you can delete the old one. If they don't work, you can still boot to the old OS and use it. How to set up a dual boot is covered later in this chapter.

CHOOSING THE TYPE OF INSTALLATION: IN-PLACE UPGRADE, CLEAN INSTALL, OR DUAL BOOT

A+
CORE 2
1.3

If you are installing Windows on a new hard drive, you must perform a clean install. If an OS is already installed on the hard drive, you have three choices:

▲ *Clean install.* You can perform a clean install, overwriting the existing operating system and applications. In the Windows setup program, a clean install is called a custom installation. The main advantage of a clean install is that problems with the old OS are not carried forward and you get a fresh start. During the installation, you will have the option to reformat the hard drive, erasing everything on it. If you don't format the drive, data will still be on it. The previous operating system settings and user profiles are collectively stored in the Windows.old folder that setup creates on the hard drive. After Windows is installed, you will need to install the applications. After you're sure the new installation is working as expected, you can delete the Windows.old folder to save space on the drive. Windows 10 automatically deletes most of the content of this folder 28 days after the installation.

▲ *In-place upgrade.* If the upgrade path allows it, you can perform an in-place upgrade installation. An in-place upgrade is a Windows installation that is launched from the Windows desktop and carries forward user settings and installed applications from the old OS to the new one. A Windows OS is already *in place* before you begin the new installation. An in-place upgrade is faster than a clean install and is appropriate if the system is generally healthy and does not have problems. To perform an in-place upgrade, Microsoft requires that certain editions and versions of Windows be installed already and running the latest version of either Windows 8.1 or Windows 7 with Service Pack 1 installed. These qualifying OSs are called upgrade paths. Table 12-3 outlines the acceptable upgrade paths for Windows 10 compatibility.

Windows 8		Windows 7	
From OS	To OS	From OS	To OS
Windows 8.1	Windows 10 Home	Windows 7 Starter	Windows 10 Home
		Windows 7 Home Basic	
		Windows 7 Home Premium	
Windows 8.1 Pro	Windows 10 Pro	Windows 7 Professional	Windows 10 Pro
Windows 8.1 Pro for Students		Windows 7 Ultimate	

Table 12-3 In-place upgrade paths to Windows 10

> **Notes** You can upgrade from Windows 10 Home to Windows 10 Pro by using the Settings app within Windows. If you have already purchased a Windows 10 Pro product key, simply change the product key on the Activation page in the Settings app and then follow the on-screen instructions. Alternately, you can go to the Microsoft Store app, purchase Windows 10 Pro, then follow the on-screen instructions. The upgrade is easy and does not require going through the entire upgrade process.

▲ *Multiboot*. You can install Windows in a second partition on the hard drive and create a dual-boot situation with the other OS, or even install three OSs, each in its own partition in a multiboot environment. Don't create a dual boot unless you need two operating systems, such as when you need to verify that applications and hardware work under Windows 10 before you delete the old OS. Windows 10/8/7 all require that they be the only operating system installed on a partition, so to set up a dual boot, you'll need at least two partitions on the hard drive or a second hard drive.

In addition to the information in Table 12-3, keep these tips in mind:

▲ A 64-bit version of Windows can only be upgraded to a 64-bit OS. A 32-bit OS can only be upgraded to a 32-bit OS.

▲ If you want to install a 64-bit version of Windows on a computer that already has a 32-bit OS installed, you must perform a clean install.

> **Notes** If your current installation of Windows is corrupted, you might be able to repair the installation rather than reinstalling Windows. Chapter 15 covers how to fix a corrupted Windows installation.

UNDERSTANDING THE CHOICES YOU'LL MAKE DURING THE INSTALLATION

While Windows is installing, you must choose which drive and partition to install Windows in, the size of a new partition, and how Windows will connect to the network. Next, you'll learn how to decide on the size of the Windows partition and how Windows will connect to the network.

THE SIZE OF THE WINDOWS PARTITION

For a clean install or dual boot, you can decide not to use all the available space on the drive for the Windows partition. Here are reasons not to use all the available space:

◢ *You plan to install more than one OS on the hard drive, creating a dual-boot system.* For example, you might want to install Windows 8 on one partition and leave room for another partition where you intend to install Windows 10, so you can test software under both operating systems. (When setting up a dual boot, always install the older OS first.)

◢ *Some people prefer to use more than one partition or volume to organize data on their hard drives.* For example, you might want to install Windows and all your applications on one partition and your data on another. Having your data on a separate partition makes backing up easier. In another situation, you might want to set up a volume on the drive that is used exclusively to hold data backups on another computer on the network. The size of the partition that will hold Windows 10/8/7 and its applications should be at least 16 GB for a 32-bit install and 20 GB for the 64-bit install, but a larger volume is nearly always preferred.

> ⚡ **Caution** It's convenient to back up one volume to another volume on a different hard drive. However, *don't* back up one volume to another volume on the same hard drive; if the drive fails, all volumes on the drive might be damaged and you could lose both your data and your backup.

In Chapter 13, you learn to use the Disk Management utility after Windows is installed to create partitions from unallocated space and to resize, delete, and split existing partitions.

NETWORK CONFIGURATION

Recall from Chapter 11 that all editions of Windows 10/8/7 can join a workgroup, Windows 8/7 computers can join a homegroup, and professional editions of Windows 10/8/7 can join a Windows domain. (Windows 10 does not support homegroups.) To join a domain, you'll need the name of the domain and the network ID and password assigned to you by the private network's administrator. To join a homegroup, you'll need its password. To use a workgroup, you configure each computer to share its folders and files to specific people on the local network. You can connect to a homegroup or domain during the installation, or you can wait and make the connection after the installation is complete. How to share folders and files on a local network is covered in Chapter 16.

You also need to know that the Windows installation process usually has no problems connecting to the network and the Internet without your help. However, you might need to know how the IP address is assigned. An IP address uniquely identifies a computer on the network, and it might be assigned dynamically (by a server each time the workstation connects to the network) or statically (permanently assigned to the workstation). If the network is using static IP addressing, you need the IP address for the workstation. How to change IP address assignments is covered in Chapter 7.

FINAL CHECKLIST BEFORE BEGINNING THE INSTALLATION

A+
CORE 2
1.1, 1.3

Before you begin the installation, complete the final checklist shown in Table 12-4 to verify that you are ready.

Questions to Answer	Further Information
Does the computer meet the minimum or recommended hardware requirement?	CPU: RAM: Hard drive partition size: Free space on the partition:
Do you have the Windows device drivers for your hardware devices and application setup CDs?	List hardware and software that need to be upgraded:
Do you have the product key available? (It might not be required if you are reinstalling Windows 10.)	Product key:
How will users be recognized on the network?	Homegroup password (for Windows 8/7): Domain name: Computer name: Network ID: Network password:
How will the computer be recognized on the network?	Static or dynamic IP addressing: IP address (for static addressing):
Will you do an upgrade or a clean install?	Current operating system: Does the old OS qualify for an upgrade?
For a clean install, will you set up a dual boot?	List reasons for a dual boot: Size of the second partition: Free space on the second partition:
Have you backed up important data on your hard drive?	Location of backup:

Table 12-4 Checklist to complete before installing Windows

Before getting into the step-by-step instructions for installing an OS, here are some general tips for installing Windows:

▲ Verify that you have all application software CDs or DVDs available and all device drivers.

▲ Back up all important data on the drive. How to perform backups is covered in Chapter 13.

▲ For upgrade installations and clean installs in which you do not plan to reformat the hard drive, run antivirus/anti-malware software to make sure the drive is free from malware. If Windows will not start or you suspect malware is present, perform a clean installation of Windows. If you suspect the hard drive is damaged, you can use the format command to scan the drive for bad sectors before you begin the installation. This process is discussed later in the chapter and in Chapter 13.

▲ If you want to begin the installation by booting from the Windows USB flash drive or DVD, use BIOS/ UEFI setup to verify that the boot sequence is first USB or the optical drive, and then the hard drive.

▲ In BIOS/UEFI setup, disable any virus protection setting that prevents the boot area of the hard drive from being altered.

▲ Set BIOS/UEFI to use UEFI mode (which uses GPT and possibly Secure boot) or UEFI CSM mode (which uses MBR partitions on the hard drive). Know that Windows will install on a GPT drive only when CSM mode is disabled and will install on an MBR drive only when CSM mode is enabled.

▲ For a laptop computer, connect the AC adapter and use this power source for the complete OS installation, updates, and installation of hardware and applications. You don't want the battery to fail in the middle of the installation.

📝 **Notes** In general, it's best not to upgrade an OS on a laptop unless you want to use some feature the new OS offers. For laptops, follow the general rule, "If it ain't broke, don't fix it." Many hardware components in a laptop are proprietary, and the laptop manufacturer is the only source for these drivers. If you are considering upgrading a laptop to Windows 10, check the laptop manufacturer's website for advice and to download Windows 10 drivers, which are called **third-party drivers** because they are not included in BIOS/UEFI or Windows. It's very important to have a Windows 10 driver for your network port without having to depend on the network or Internet to get one after Windows 10 is installed. Also know that many Windows 8/7 drivers work with Windows 10.

VERIFY THAT YOU HAVE THE WINDOWS 10 PRODUCT KEY

Typically, you'll purchase Windows 10 online, with the product key emailed to the Microsoft account used to make the purchase. If you purchased Windows 10 on a USB flash drive, look for the product key printed on the cover of the flash drive case, on a card inside the case, or affixed to the back of the Windows documentation booklet.

However, keep in mind that the product key might not be required to reinstall Windows. After Windows 10 is activated the first time with a valid product key, Windows assigns a digital license to the machine and stores it along with information about the computer's physical hardware (called the hardware signature) on Microsoft activation servers. If Windows is installed later, it can retrieve this information from Microsoft servers rather than requesting that you re-enter the product key.

In addition, for a laptop, all-in-one, or other brand-name computer, the computer manufacturer might have stored the Windows product key on motherboard firmware. When reinstalling Windows, setup can retrieve this product key from firmware. Either way, the new Windows installation is assigned a digital license and you don't have to enter the product key during the installation.

> **Notes** To determine if Windows was activated using a product key or digital license, open the Settings app, click **Update & security**, and click **Activation** (see Figure 12-8).

Figure 12-8 This installation of Windows was activated using a digital license stored on Microsoft activation servers

---

APPLYING | CONCEPTS

USING THE MEDIA CREATION TOOL TO CREATE A BOOTABLE WINDOWS SETUP DVD OR FLASH DRIVE

To create the installation media, you'll need a blank DVD, 4-GB or larger USB flash drive, or at least 4 GB of free space on your hard drive. Use a blank flash drive because any data on it will be lost. To use the Media Creation Tool to download Windows setup files and create a bootable DVD or USB flash drive, follow these steps:

1. To download and install the Media Creation Tool, use a working computer, go to the website *microsoft. com/en-us/software-download/windows10*, and click **Download tool now**. Save the file and then run **MediaCreationTool1803.exe**.

(continues)

2. Accept the license terms. On the next window shown in Figure 12-9, select **Create installation media (USB flash drive, DVD, or ISO file) for another PC** and click **Next**.

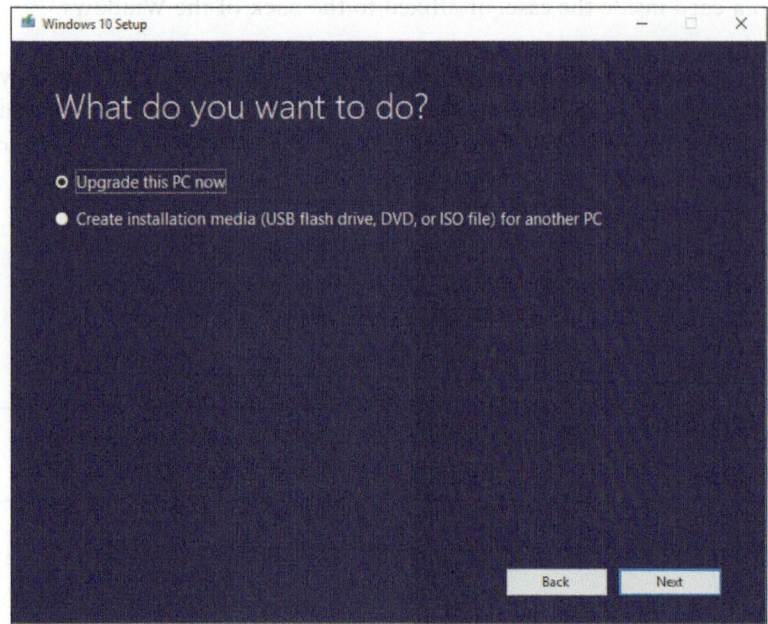

Figure 12-9 The Media Creation Tool can be used to upgrade a computer or to create installation media

3. Select a language and architecture (64-bit or 32-bit), as shown in Figure 12-10. (The only edition available to select is Windows 10.) Alternatively, if you're creating installation media as a troubleshooting tool for the computer you're using, check **Use the recommended options for this PC**. Click **Next**.

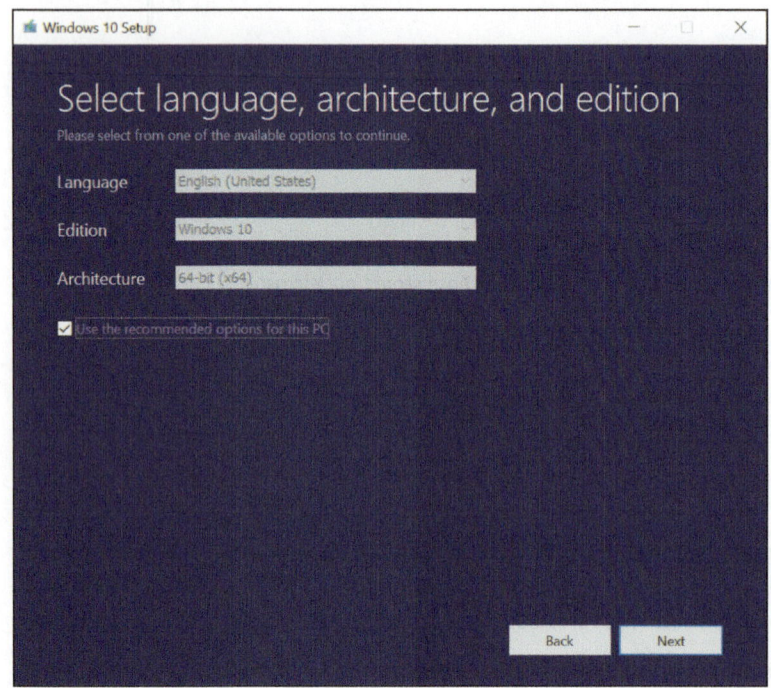

Figure 12-10 The installation medium is bit specific: Choose 32-bit for a 32-bit computer and 64-bit for a 64-bit computer

(continues)

> **Notes** The best practice is to save the Windows setup files to a USB flash drive or ISO image. You never know when you'll need the files later to repair a corrupted Windows installation.

4. On the next screen, select **USB flash drive** or **ISO file**, which you can later burn to a DVD. If you choose *USB flash drive*, the tool searches for the drive. If you choose *ISO file*, the tool asks for the location to save the file (see Figure 12-11). Navigate to the location, click **Save**, and follow the on-screen instructions. After the download completes, if you chose to save an ISO file, you will be given the opportunity to insert a DVD in the disk drive, right-click the ISO file, and click **Burn disc image**.

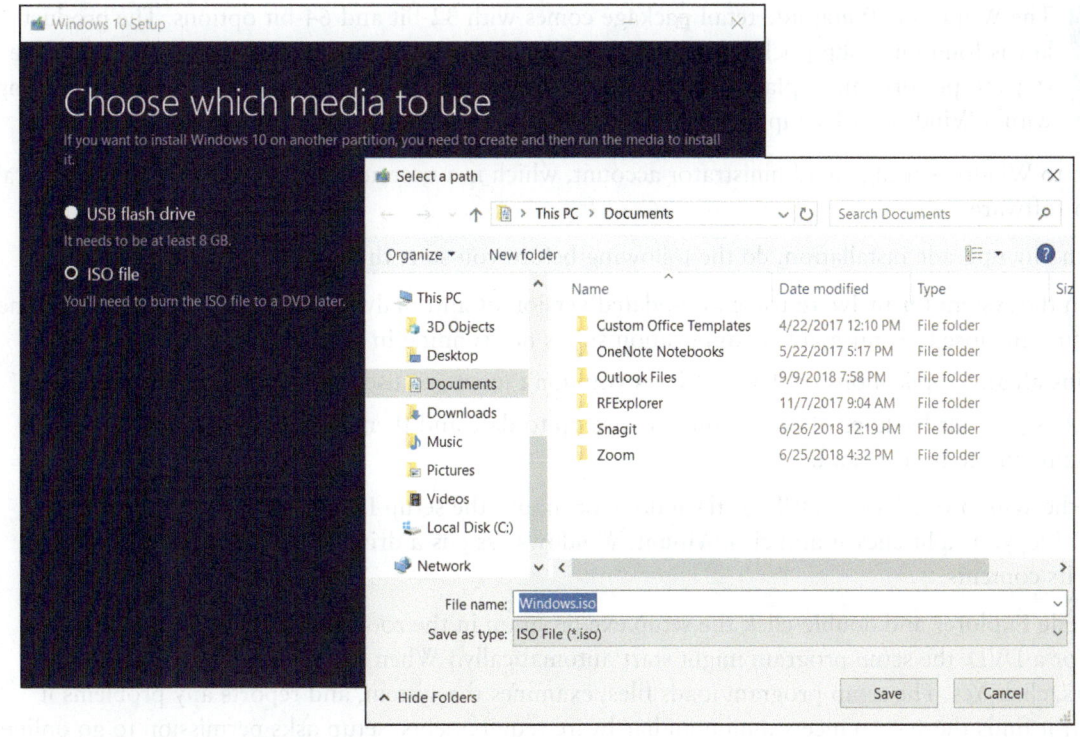

Figure 12-11 Select a location to save the ISO file

Here's some useful information about an ISO file:

- An ISO file, also called an ISO image or disc image, is an image of an optical disc, including its file system and all its files and folders. An ISO (International Organization for Standardization) file has an .iso file extension.
- To see the contents of an ISO file, open File Explorer or Windows Explorer, right-click the file, and click **Mount**. The ISO file is assigned a drive letter and you can drill down into its contents.
- If you have an optical drive that can write to DVDs and you want to burn a DVD from an ISO file, insert a blank DVD in your optical drive and double-click the ISO file. Follow the on-screen directions and Windows does the rest.
- Later in the chapter, you learn how to mount an ISO file to a virtual DVD drive in a virtual machine and use it to install Windows in the VM, as you would with a physical DVD installed in a physical computer.

INSTALLING WINDOWS 10, WINDOWS 8.1, AND WINDOWS 7

In this part of the chapter, you learn the steps to install Windows as an in-place upgrade, clean install, and dual boot. You also learn how to handle the special situation of using a Windows upgrade product key to install Windows on a new hard drive. Later in the chapter, you learn to install Windows 10 on a virtual machine. As you install and configure software, be sure to document what you do. This documentation will be helpful for future maintenance and troubleshooting. In a project at the end of this chapter, you will develop a documentation template.

Let's begin with how to perform an in-place upgrade of Windows 10.

WINDOWS 10 IN-PLACE UPGRADE

The Windows 10 upgrade retail package comes with 32-bit and 64-bit options. The product key is found in a slip pocket inside the box or is included in the emailed receipt. Here are the steps to perform an in-place upgrade from Windows 8.1 to Windows 10 when you're working with a Windows 10 setup DVD or USB flash drive:

1. Sign in to Windows using an administrator account, which is a user account that has the right to install system software.

2. As with any upgrade installation, do the following before you start the upgrade:

   ◢ Scan the system for malware using an updated version of anti-malware software. When you're done, be sure to close the anti-malware application so it's not running in the background.

   ◢ Uninstall any applications or device drivers you don't intend to use in the new installation.

   ◢ Make sure your backups of important data are up to date and then close any backup software running in the background.

3. Insert the Windows 10 setup DVD or flash drive or mount the setup ISO file. Recall that to mount an ISO file, you right-click it and click **Mount**. Windows assigns a drive letter to the file and you can access its contents.

4. Open **File Explorer** and double-click the **setup.exe** program in the root of the device or mounted ISO file. (For a DVD, the setup program might start automatically.) When the User Account Control box appears, click **Yes**. The setup program loads files, examines the system, and reports any problems it finds. If it finds the system meets minimum hardware requirements, setup asks permission to go online for updates (see Figure 12-12). Make your selection and click **Next**.

5. The next window requests the product key (see Figure 12-13). Enter the product key; Windows verifies that the key is valid. If the computer is connected to the Internet, setup will automatically activate Windows during the installation. Click **Next**.

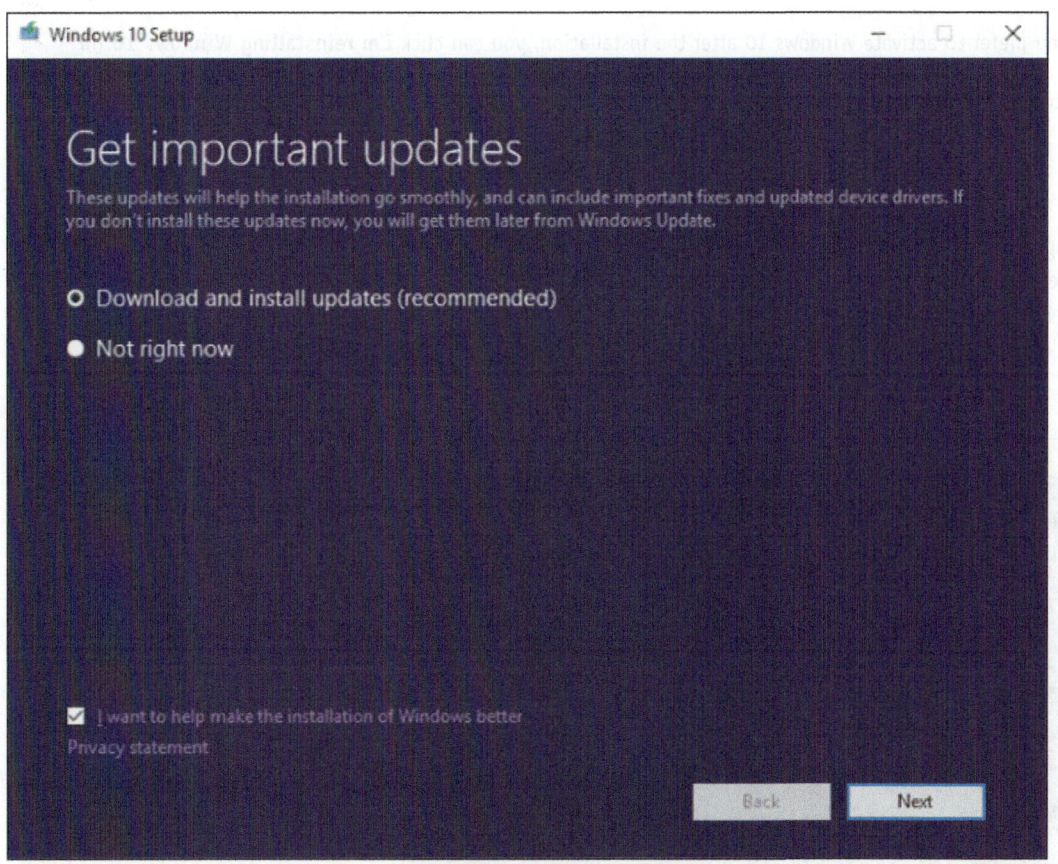

Figure 12-12 Decide how you will handle updates during the setup process

12

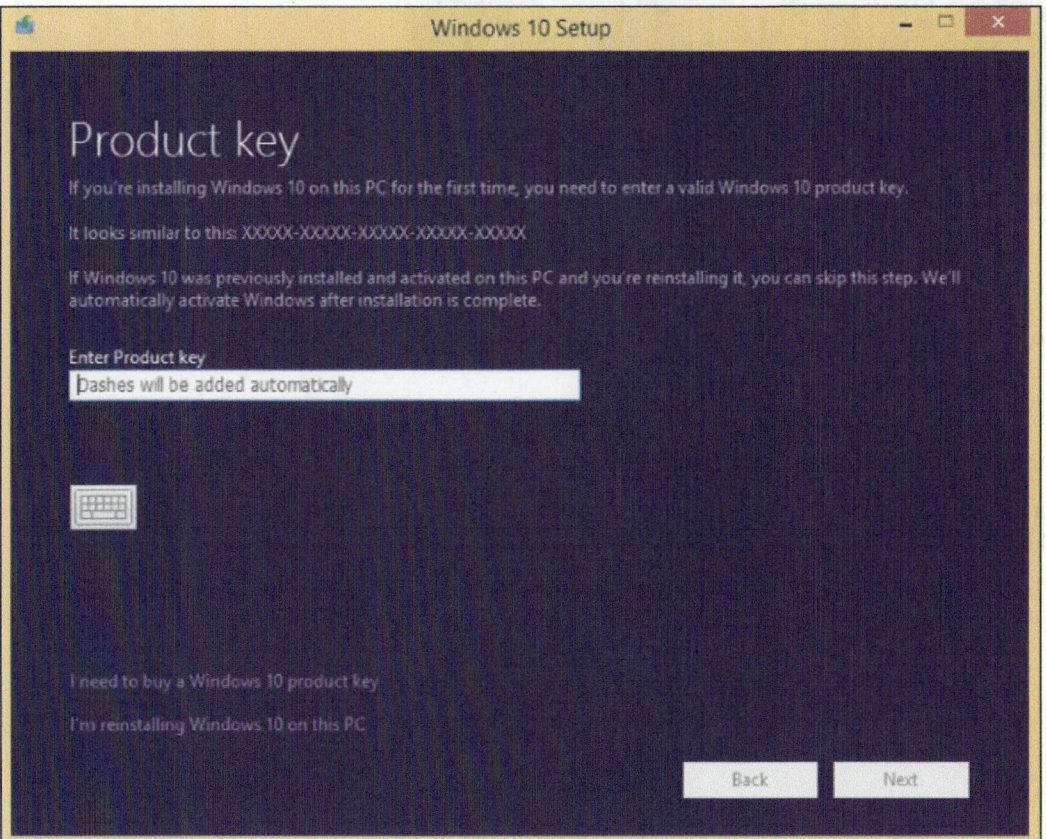

Figure 12-13 The product key is verified as valid during the setup process

> **✎ Notes** If you prefer to activate Windows 10 after the installation, you can click **I'm reinstalling Windows 10 on this PC**, which allows you to proceed without a product key and install Windows 10 although it's not yet activated. This is a good way to practice Windows installations.

6. The *License terms* window appears. Click **Accept**.

7. Wait for updates to download. Then, in the *Ready to install* window, verify that **Keep personal files and apps** is selected. To specify what you want to retain from the previous installation, click **Change what to keep** (see Figure 12-14).

Figure 12-14   Windows is ready to install as an upgrade, but you can still change what to keep

8. In the *Choose what to keep* window (see Figure 12-15), decide what you want to do with Windows settings, personal files, and apps:

   ◢ The first two options perform upgrades to Windows 10.

   ◢ The Nothing option performs a clean install of Windows 10.

   In this example, you are doing an in-place upgrade installation, so select **Keep personal files and apps**, and then click **Next**. The *Ready to install* window appears again.

Figure 12-15 Decide what to keep of the old installation

9. On the *Ready to install* window, verify the choices listed and click **Install** to begin the installation.

10. During the installation, setup might restart the system several times. When the *Welcome to Windows 10!* screen appears showing your user name, click **Next**.

11. On the *Choose privacy settings for your device* screen, select the privacy settings for location, speech recognition, diagnostics, tailored experiences with diagnostic data, and relevant ads, and then click **Accept**.

> 📝 **Notes** You might need to scroll down to view all the privacy settings on this screen.

12. On the *Meet Cortana* screen, you can decide to give Microsoft permission to use your information to personalize your experience with Cortana. To read more about the type of information Microsoft collects for Cortana, click **Learn more**. Click **Not now** or **Use Cortana** to move to the next screen.

13. The *New apps for the new Windows* screen appears. Review the new apps built into Windows 10. Click **Next**.

14. Settings are applied and the Windows 10 sign-on screen appears. You can now use the new upgrade to Windows 10.

WINDOWS 10 CLEAN INSTALL

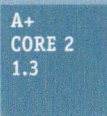
A+
CORE 2
1.3

Recall that a clean install is the best option to use if the current installation is sluggish or causing problems, the currently installed OS does not allow for an in-place upgrade, or you're installing Windows 10 on a new hard drive or new desktop computer you're building.

If you have a Windows 8/7 installation that qualifies for a Windows 10 upgrade and you need to do a clean install, follow these steps:

1. Begin by starting the installation from the Windows desktop as you would for an upgrade.

2. Follow the previous steps for an in-place upgrade to enter the product key, accept license terms, and download updates.

3. When you get to the *Ready to install* window (refer back to Figure 12-14), click **Change what to keep**.

4. On the *Choose what to keep* window (refer back to Figure 12-15), click **Nothing** and click **Next**. Then continue with the installation. The contents of the volume holding the previous version of Windows is deleted. If the hard drive has other volumes, they are left unchanged.

Use the following steps to perform a clean install on a newly installed hard drive, on a new computer you're building, or on a computer that has a corrupted Windows installation that refuses to start:

1. Boot from the Windows setup DVD or USB flash drive. Recall that you first might need to change the boot priority order in BIOS/UEFI. In the Windows Setup screen (see Figure 12-16), select the language and regional preferences and click **Next**. On the next screen, click **Install now**.

Figure 12-16 Decide on language and keyboard preferences

2. Enter your product key on the next screen (see Figure 12-17). Click **Next**. Setup verifies that the key is a valid product key, which then determines the version of Windows to install.

Notes If you prefer to enter the product key after you have installed Windows, click **I don't have a product key**. On the next screen, select the version of Windows you want to install.

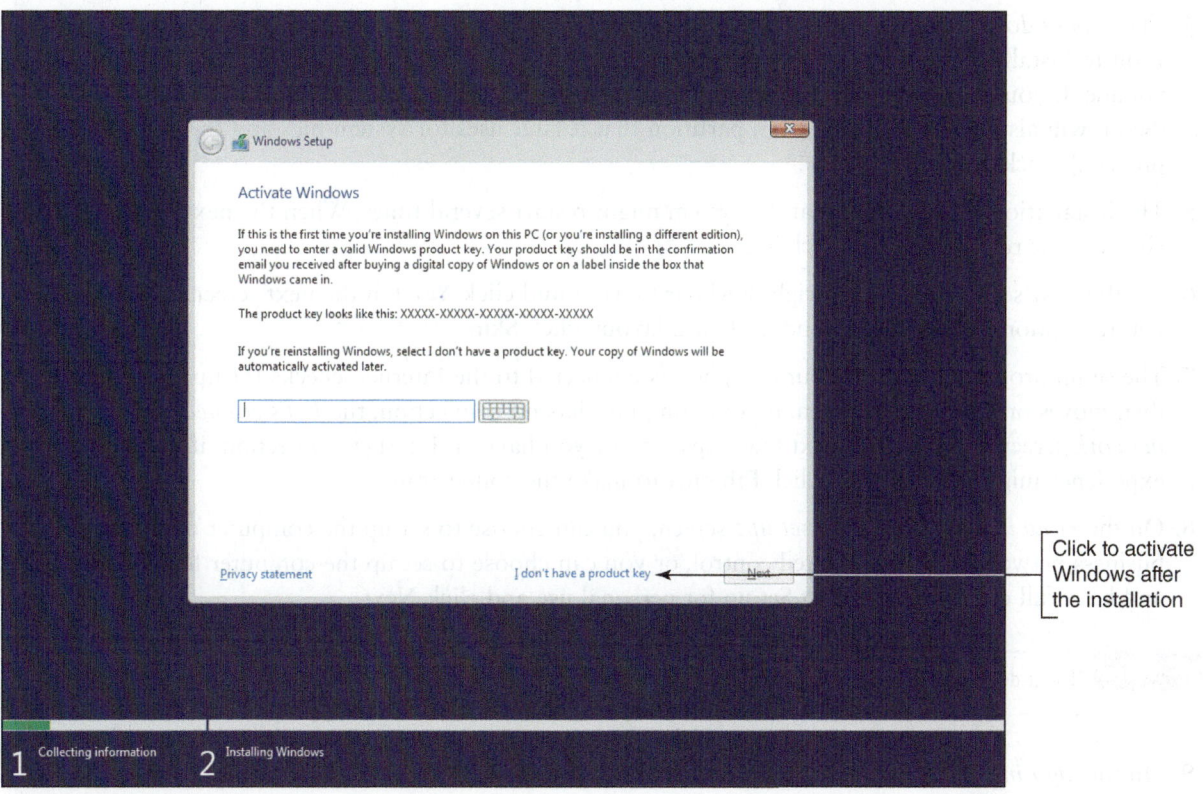

Figure 12-17 Enter a valid product key

3. Accept the license agreement on the next screen and click **Next**. On the next screen (see Figure 12-18), click **Custom: Install Windows only (advanced)**.

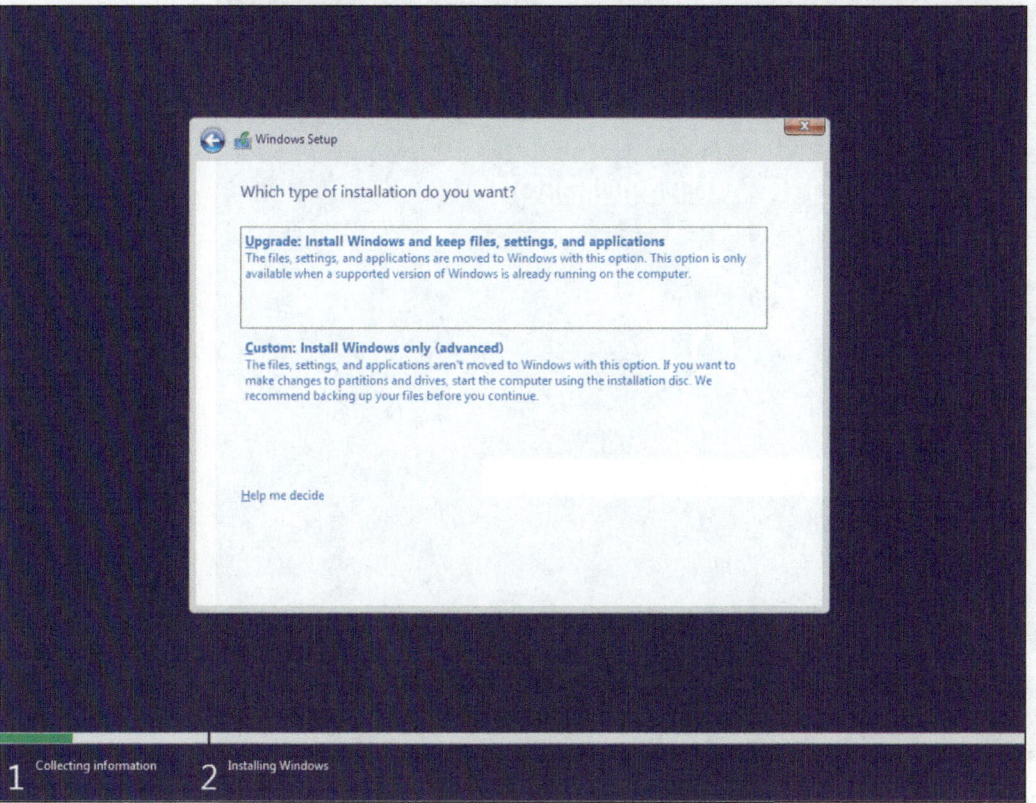

Figure 12-18 Decide between an upgrade and a clean installation

12

4. The *Where do you want to install Windows?* screen appears. Select the drive and volume where you want to install Windows. By default, setup will use the entire unallocated space for the Windows volume. If you want to use only a portion of the space, click **New** and enter the size of the volume. (Setup will also create a small system partition that it later uses for system files and the startup process.) Click **Next** to continue.

5. The installation begins. Note that the system might restart several times. When the next screen appears, choose your region and then click **Yes**.

6. On the next screen, choose the right keyboard layout and click **Yes**. On the next screen, which gives you the option of adding a second keyboard layout, click **Skip**.

7. The setup program detects if your computer is connected to the Internet, checks for updates, and then moves on to the next screen. If your computer has no connection, the *Let's connect you to a network* screen appears. The next few steps assume you have an Internet connection; if you don't, your experience might be different. Click **Ethernet** to make the connection.

8. On the *How would you like to set up?* screen, you can choose to set up the computer on a school or business network and have limited control, or you can choose to set up the computer for personal use and have full control of it. Select **Set up for personal use** and click **Next**.

> 🖊 **Notes** If you do not have a network connection set up, Windows has you use an offline, local account by default.

9. On the *Sign in with Microsoft* screen, you can choose to use an existing Microsoft account, create a new Microsoft account, or create an offline account (see Figure 12-19). To create a local, offline account, click **Offline account**.

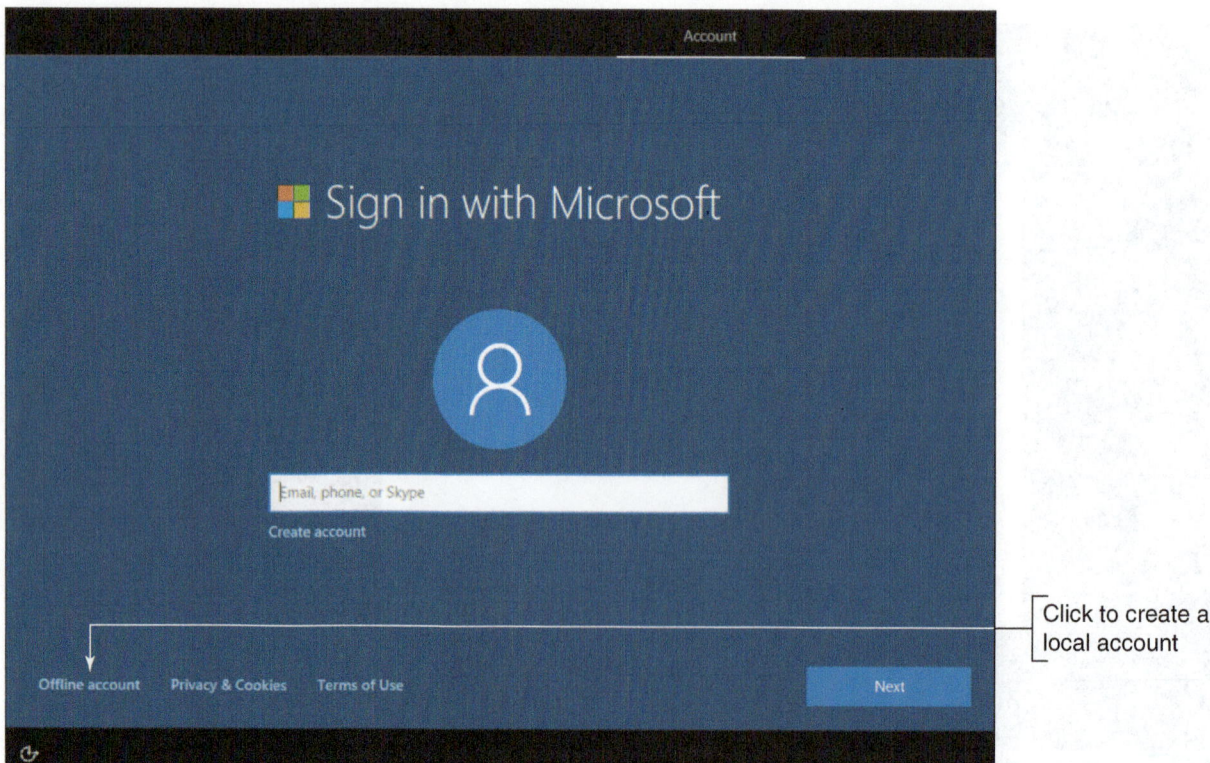

Figure 12-19 Choose the type of account to set up

10. On the *Sign in with Microsoft Instead?* screen, Microsoft again encourages you to use a Microsoft account instead of an offline account (see Figure 12-20). To continue creating an offline account, click **No**.

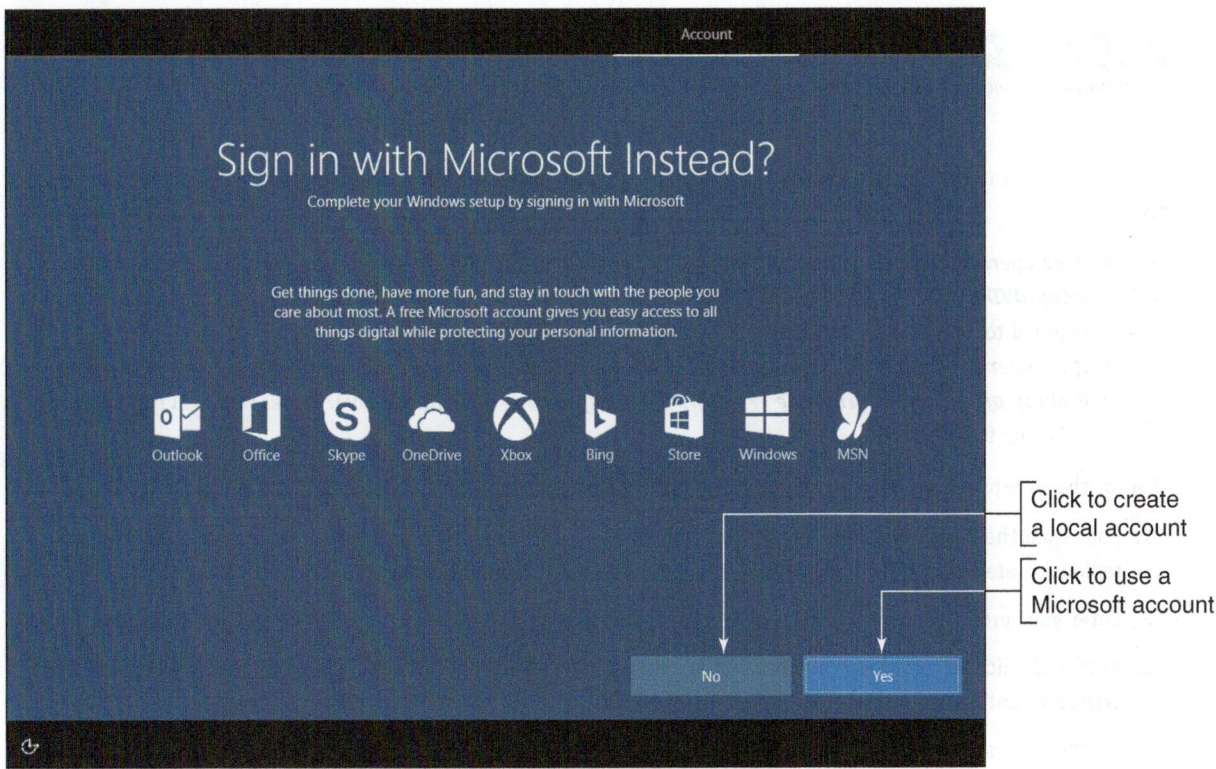

Click to create a local account

Click to use a Microsoft account

Figure 12-20   During setup, Microsoft strongly encourages the use of a Microsoft account and not a local account

11. On the next screen, enter the name for the user of the local account. (Again you see at the bottom of the screen that Microsoft is still encouraging you to use a Microsoft account.) Click **Next**, enter a password for the offline account, click **Next**, confirm the password, click **Next**, create a password hint, and then click **Next**.

12. On the *Make Cortana your personal assistant?* screen, you can give Microsoft permission to use your information to personalize your experience with Cortana. To read more about the type of information Microsoft collects for Cortana, click **Learn more**. To accept Cortana, click **Yes**.

13. On the next screen, select the device's privacy settings for location, speech recognition, diagnostics, tailored experiences with diagnostic data, and relevant ads, and then click **Accept**.

14. The installation continues, settings are applied, and the Windows desktop appears. You can now use the new installation of Windows 10.

WINDOWS | 8   STEPS TO PERFORM A WINDOWS 8.1 CLEAN INSTALL

**A+
CORE 2
1.3**

Recall that a clean install is the best option to use if the current installation is sluggish or giving problems, the currently installed OS does not allow for an in-place upgrade, or you're installing Windows 8.1 on a new hard drive.

If you have a Windows 7 installation that qualifies for a Windows 8.1 upgrade and you need to do a clean install, begin by starting the installation from the Windows desktop as you would for an upgrade. When

(continues)

you get to the window shown earlier in Figure 12-15, click **Nothing** and continue with the installation. The volume holding the old Windows installation is formatted and everything on the volume is lost. If the hard drive has other volumes, they are left unchanged.

> **◯ OS Differences** The steps and screenshots for a clean install in this section are for Windows 8.1. The steps for Windows 8.0 work about the same way.

To perform a clean install of Windows 8.1, you can begin the installation from the Windows 8.1 DVD or USB flash drive:

▲ *If no operating system is installed on the PC, begin the installation by booting from the Windows 8.1 setup DVD or USB flash drive.* Using this method, you will not be using the upgrade option, but will be required to do a Custom installation, also called a clean install.

▲ *If an operating system is already installed on the PC, you can begin the installation from the* Windows *desktop or by booting from the Windows 8.1 setup DVD or USB flash drive.* Either way, you can perform a Custom installation.

Follow these steps to begin the installation by booting from the Windows 8.1 setup DVD or USB flash drive:

1. Boot from the Windows setup DVD or USB flash drive. In the Windows Setup screen, select the language and regional preferences and click **Next**. On the next screen, click **Install now**.

2. Enter your product key on the next screen. Setup verifies that the key is a valid product key. Click **Next**.

3. Accept the license agreement on the next screen and click **Next**. On the next screen, click **Custom: Install Windows only (advanced)**.

4. On the next screen, select the drive and volume where you want to install Windows. By default, setup will use the entire unallocated space for the Windows volume. If you want to use only a portion of the space, click **New** and enter the size of the volume. (Setup will also create a small reserved partition that it later uses for system files and the startup process.) Click **Next** to continue.

> **✎ Notes** If you don't see the *New* link on the *Where do you want to install Windows?* screen, click **Drive options (advanced)** to see it and other links you can use to manage the space on the hard drive.

5. The installation begins, and the system might restart several times. You can select a screen color and enter the PC name. Next, the Settings screen appears.

6. After you have made your choices on the Settings screen, the *Sign in to your Microsoft account* screen appears. (Microsoft *really* encourages you to use a Microsoft account.) As with an in-place upgrade, you can sign in using an existing Microsoft account or create a new Microsoft account. In addition, you can create a new local account.

   If you want to create a new local account, click **Create a new account**. On the next screen, click **Sign in without a Microsoft account**. On the Your account screen, enter the local account name, password, and password hint, and then click **Finish**.

7. The installation continues, settings are applied, and the Start screen appears. You can now use the new installation of Windows 8.1.

> **◯ OS Differences** A clean install of Windows 7 works about the same as a Windows 8.1 installation. Boot from the Windows 7 setup DVD and follow the on-screen instructions.

MULTIBOOT INSTALLATIONS

A+
CORE 2
1.3

You can install two or more operating systems on the same computer in a multiboot situation—for example, Windows 10 and Ubuntu Desktop. Each OS must have its own hard drive partition and each partition must have enough free space to hold the OS, with room for applications, data, and OS working space. Recall that Windows 10/8/7 needs *at least* 16 GB (32-bit) or 20 GB (64-bit) of free space for the OS. Also know you cannot boot more than one OS at a time. To create a multiboot environment, always install Windows operating systems in order from older to newer.

> ✎ **Notes** If an OS is already installed, you might need to shrink a partition to make room for a second partition to hold the next OS. For Windows, use Disk Management to shrink a partition, create a new partition, or format a partition. Windows requires the NTFS file system. How to use Disk Management is covered in Chapter 13.

Here are the steps to set up a dual-boot system with two operating systems (using Windows 8.1 and 10 as examples):

1. Install Windows 8.1. If you plan to install Windows 10 on the same hard drive as Windows 8.1, leave some unallocated space for the Windows 10 partition. (See the setup screen in Figure 12-21, which works the same in Windows 8.1 as in Windows 10.) On this screen, click **New**. You can then specify how much of the total unallocated space you want to use for the Windows 8.1 installation.

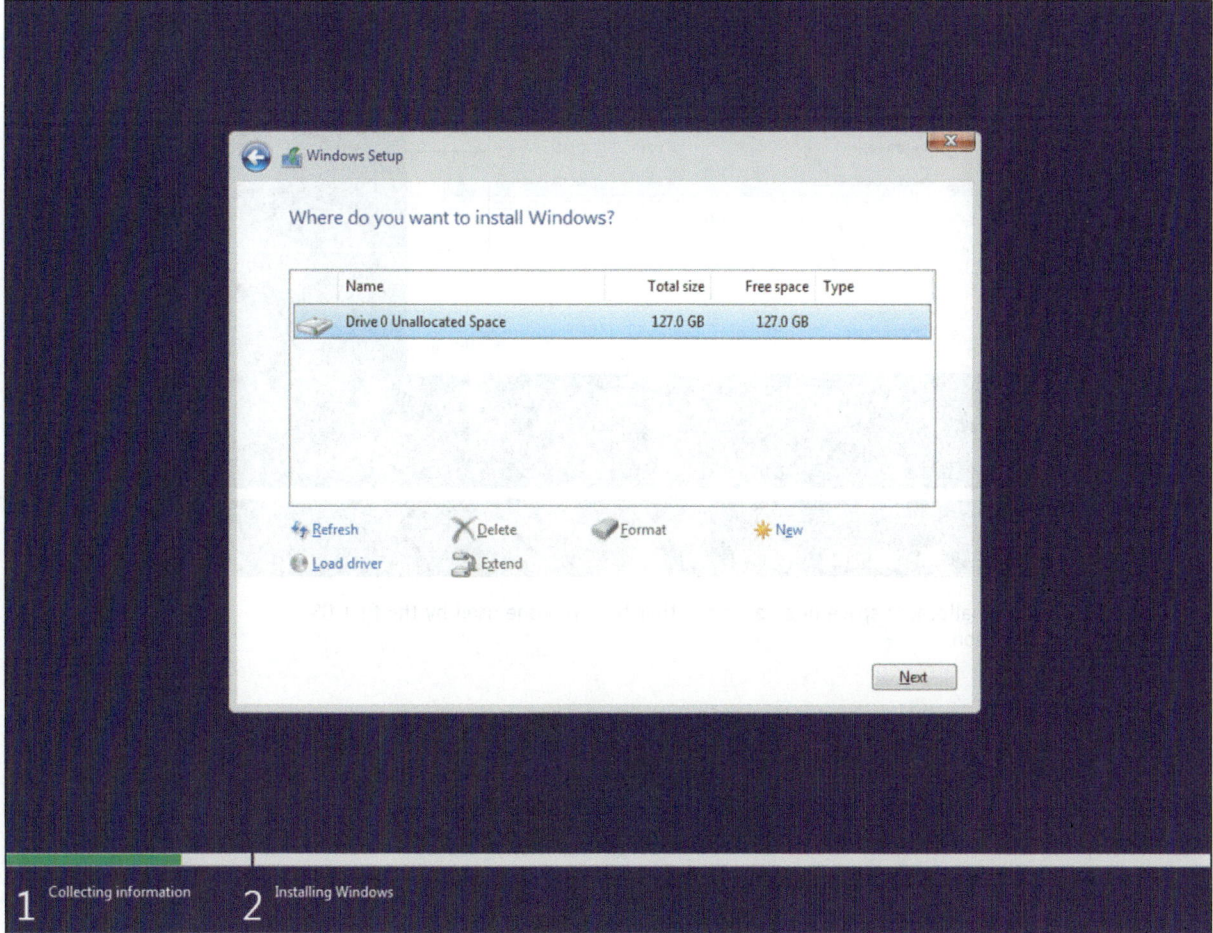

Figure 12-21 This hard drive has not yet been partitioned

2. To install Windows 10, first make sure you have (a) a second partition with enough free space to hold the Windows 10 installation, (b) enough unallocated space on the drive to create a new partition while installing Windows 10, or (c) a second hard drive to hold the Windows 10 installation.

3. Start the Windows 10 installation by booting from the Windows 10 setup DVD or USB flash drive. The Windows Setup screen appears. Follow the steps given earlier in this chapter to perform a clean install.

4. When you're asked where to install Windows, select the partition or unallocated space to hold the installation. For example, select **Unallocated Space** to hold the Windows 10 installation, as shown in Figure 12-22. Don't select the partition where the older operating system is already installed; doing so causes the setup program to install Windows 10 in place of the older OS. Continue on to complete the clean install.

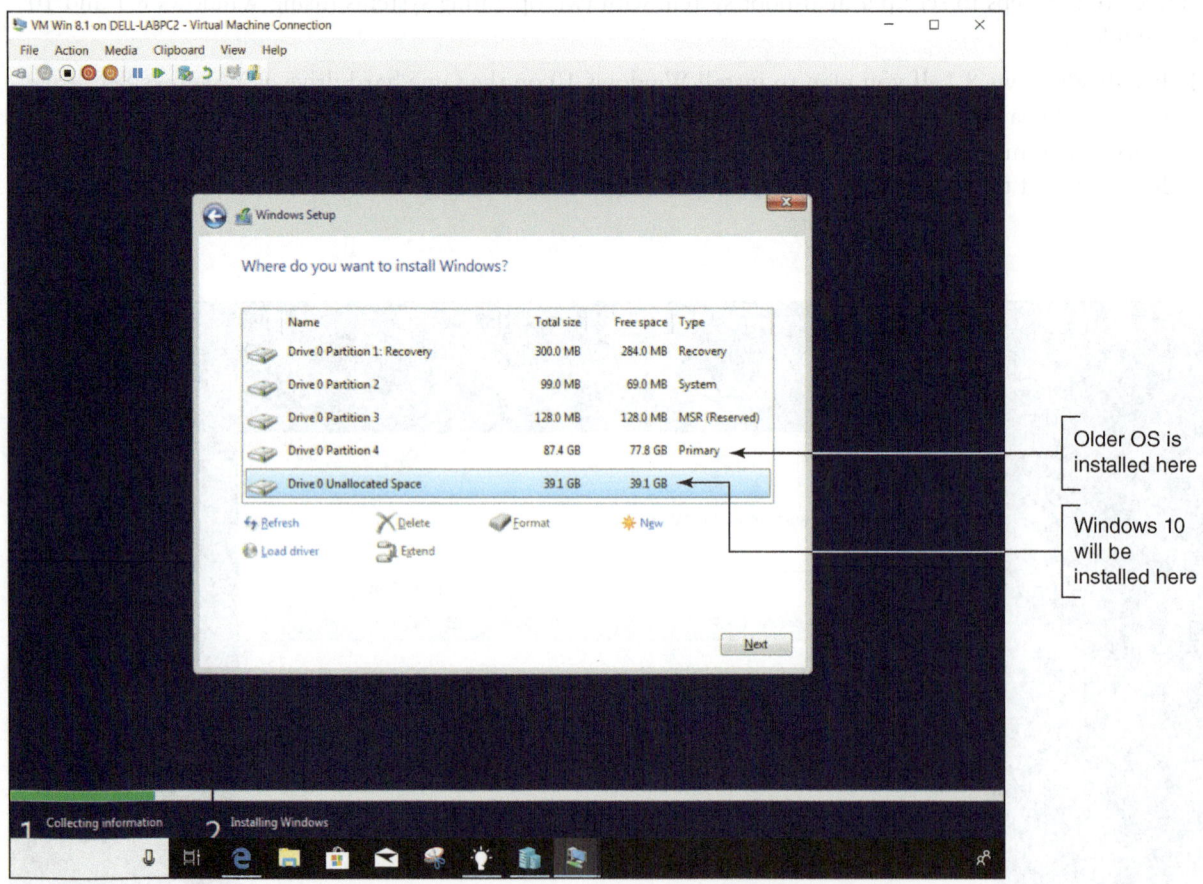

Figure 12-22 Select unallocated space or a partition other than the one used by the first OS installation

After the installation, when you boot with a dual boot, the boot loader menu automatically appears and asks you to select an operating system, as shown in Figure 12-23.

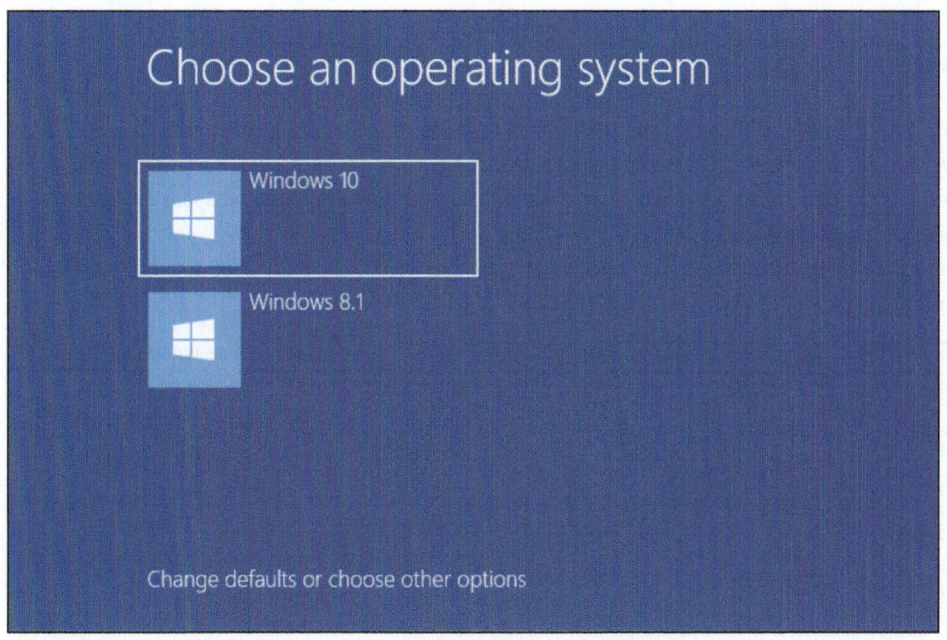

Figure 12-23   The boot loader menu in a dual-boot environment

When using a dual boot, you can execute an application while one OS is loaded even if the application is installed under the other OS, as long as each OS is using the same architecture (32-bit or 64-bit). If the application is not listed on the Windows 10 Start menu or the Windows 8.1 Start screen, locate the program file in File Explorer. Double-click the application to run it.

SOLVING PROBLEMS WITH INSTALLATIONS

**A+
CORE 2
1.3**

In this part of the chapter, we look at a few special situations you might encounter when installing Windows and what to do about them, including how to use an upgrade product key with a new hard drive and problems that require preparing a hard drive before the installation.

USE AN UPGRADE PRODUCT KEY ON A NEW HARD DRIVE

Suppose a Windows upgrade license has been used to install Windows on a computer and later the hard drive fails. You replace the hard drive with a new one, and now you need to reinstall and activate Windows. Microsoft doesn't sell a Windows 10 upgrade product key, but it did offer a free upgrade to Windows 10 from Windows 8.1 or 7 for a short time. These first free releases of Windows 10 can be activated using Windows 8.1, 8, or 7 product keys. Starting with the 1607 release of Windows 10, Windows began to use digital licenses that are linked to a Microsoft account. If you do not have a valid product key or did not link your Windows activation to a Microsoft account, you must buy a new Windows license with a product key. If you used a Microsoft account and Version 1607 or later, you can reinstall Windows 10 by simply logging in with your Microsoft account and activating Windows using the Activation troubleshooter in the Settings app. When you launch the Activation troubleshooter, click **I changed hardware on this device recently**. You will be required to use a Microsoft account to proceed.

In a situation where a Windows 7 system was upgraded to Windows 8.0 and then updated to Windows 8.1:

1. Reinstall Windows 7. You don't need to enter the product key during the installation or to activate Windows 7.

2. Reinstall Windows 8.0 using the upgrade product key and make sure Windows 8 is activated after the installation.

3. Download and install the free Windows 8.1 upgrade from the Windows Store.

12

APPLYING CONCEPTS CONVERTING AN MBR DRIVE TO GPT

Suppose you want to use a 64-bit version of Windows and UEFI firmware mode, thus requiring you to use the GPT partitioning system. However, your hard drive has already been partitioned with the MBR system. The error won't show up until you get to the step in the installation where you select the partition or unallocated space on the hard drive to hold the Windows installation (see Figure 12-24).

Follow these steps to use the **diskpart** command to wipe the partition system off the hard drive. All data on the drive will be destroyed and then you can convert the drive to GPT:

1. Restart the computer from the Windows setup DVD and select your language and regional preferences. Click **Next**. On the next screen, select **Repair your computer** (see Figure 12-25).

Figure 12-24 An error appears when Windows is in UEFI mode and requires the GPT partitioning system

Figure 12-25 Use the Windows setup DVD to launch a command prompt

(continues)

2. On the next screen, click **Troubleshoot**. On the Advanced options screen, click **Command Prompt**. A command prompt window appears. Type **diskpart** and press **Enter**. The DISKPART> prompt appears, as shown in Figure 12-26.

3. At the DISKPART> prompt, use the commands shown in Table 12-5 and Figure 12-26 to select the hard drive, clean it, and convert it to a GPT drive:

Command	Description
list disk	**List the hard drives installed. If you have more than one hard drive, use the size of the drive to determine which one you want to clean. Most likely, you will have one hard drive identified as Disk 0.**
select disk 0	**Make Disk 0 the selected hard drive.**
clean	**Clean the partition table and all partitions from the drive.**
convert gpt	**Convert the partitioning system to GPT.**
exit	**Exit the diskpart utility.**

Table 12-5 Diskpart commands to convert an MBR drive to GPT

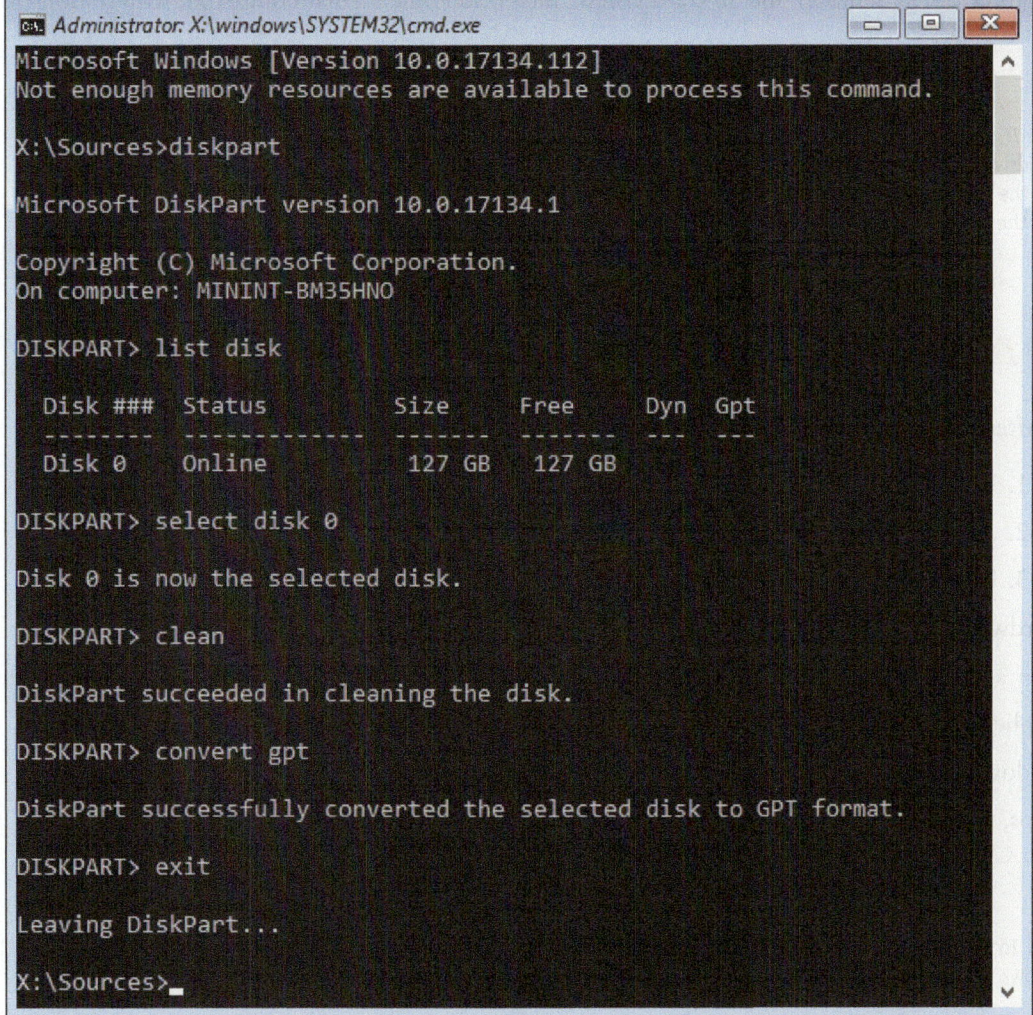

Figure 12-26 The command prompt window with diskpart running

(continues)

4. Enter one more **exit** command to close the command prompt window. On the setup screen that appears, click **Turn off your PC**.

5. You can now restart the system and install Windows in UEFI mode, which uses the GPT partitioning system.

REPAIR A DAMAGED HARD DRIVE

Besides diskpart, you can also use the format command in the command prompt window available from Windows setup media. Two types of formats are:

▲ Quick format, which creates an empty root directory for a volume, effectively resulting in all data being deleted from the volume. When Windows installs and formats the hard drive, it uses a quick format to save time.

▲ Full format, which creates an empty root directory, checks each sector on the volume for errors, and marks bad sectors so they will not be used by the file system.

If you suspect the hard drive is damaged and Windows will not start, launch the command prompt window from the Windows setup media and perform a full format. How to use the format command is covered in Chapter 13. In addition, the diskpart commands include the format command, with options for a quick or full format.

> ⚡ **Caution** If sensitive data is on the hard drive, know that a quick or full format will not actually erase this data from the drive; hackers have been known to be able to read such data even after the volume is formatted. To actually erase the data, you can use a zero-fill utility available from hard drive manufacturers. This software overwrites everything on the drive with zeroes. You learn more about zero-fill utilities in Chapter 17.

WHAT TO DO AFTER A WINDOWS INSTALLATION

After you have installed Windows, you need to do the following:

1. Verify that you have network access.

2. Activate Windows.

3. Install updates for Windows and verify update settings and anti-malware settings.

4. Install hardware.

5. Set up user accounts and transfer or restore user data and preferences from backups to the new system.

6. Install applications.

7. Turn Windows features on or off.

8. For laptops, use Control Panel to configure power-management settings. Power management was covered in Chapter 11.

> ⚡ **Caution** To protect your computer from malware, don't surf the web for drivers or applications until you have updated Windows and verified that anti-malware software is providing real-time protection from malware.

VERIFYING NETWORK ACCESS

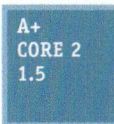
A+
CORE 2
1.5

Do the following to verify network and Internet access:

1. To make a wired connection to a network when using Windows, simply plug in the network cable and let Windows do the rest. To create a wireless connection, click the network icon in the taskbar and select the wireless network. You might need to enter a password to the Wi-Fi network.

2. To verify access to the local network, open File Explorer or Windows Explorer and verify that you can see other computers on the network (see Figure 12-27). Try to drill down to see shared resources on these computers.

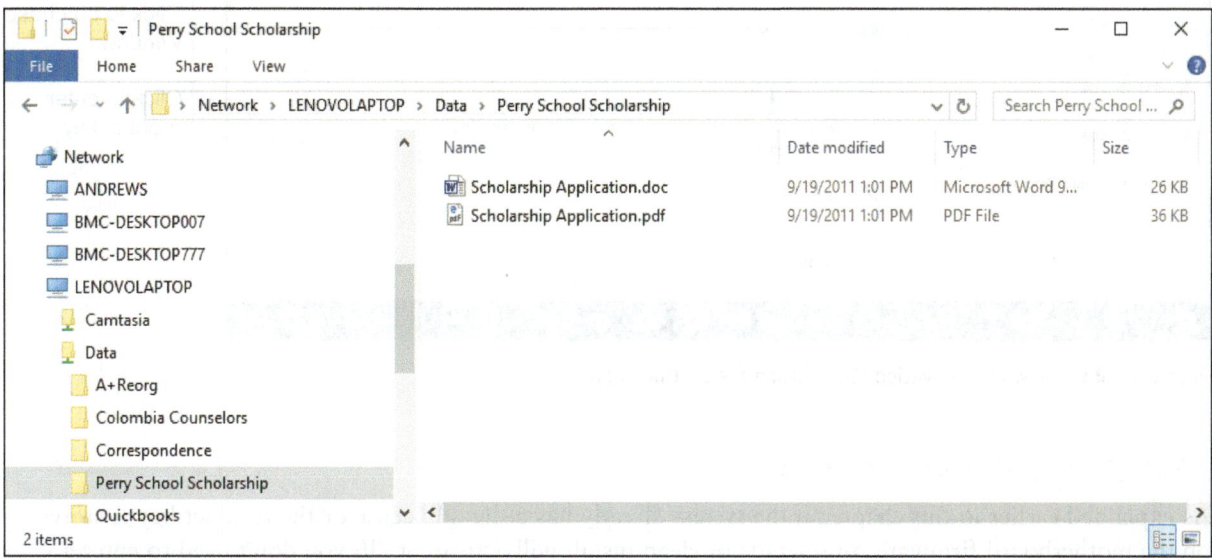

Figure 12-27   Use File Explorer to access resources on your network

3. To verify Internet access, open Internet Explorer and try to navigate to a couple of websites.

If a problem arises, the problem might be that you need to install the drivers for the motherboard, including the drivers for the onboard network port. Also, the IP address, wireless network, or network security settings might be wrong. How to configure network settings and troubleshoot network connections is covered in Chapter 7.

ACTIVATING WINDOWS

A+
CORE 2
1.3

To make sure a valid Windows license has been purchased for each installation of Windows, Microsoft requires product activation. If you entered a product key during the installation, Windows is already activated.

To view the activation status, open the **Settings** app, select the **Update & security** group, and then select **Activation**. Figure 12-28 shows the Activation window for a system that is not activated. To activate, you have a couple of options. First, make sure you're connected to the Internet. If you need to purchase Windows 10, click **Go to Store**. If you already have a product key, click **Change product key**.

12

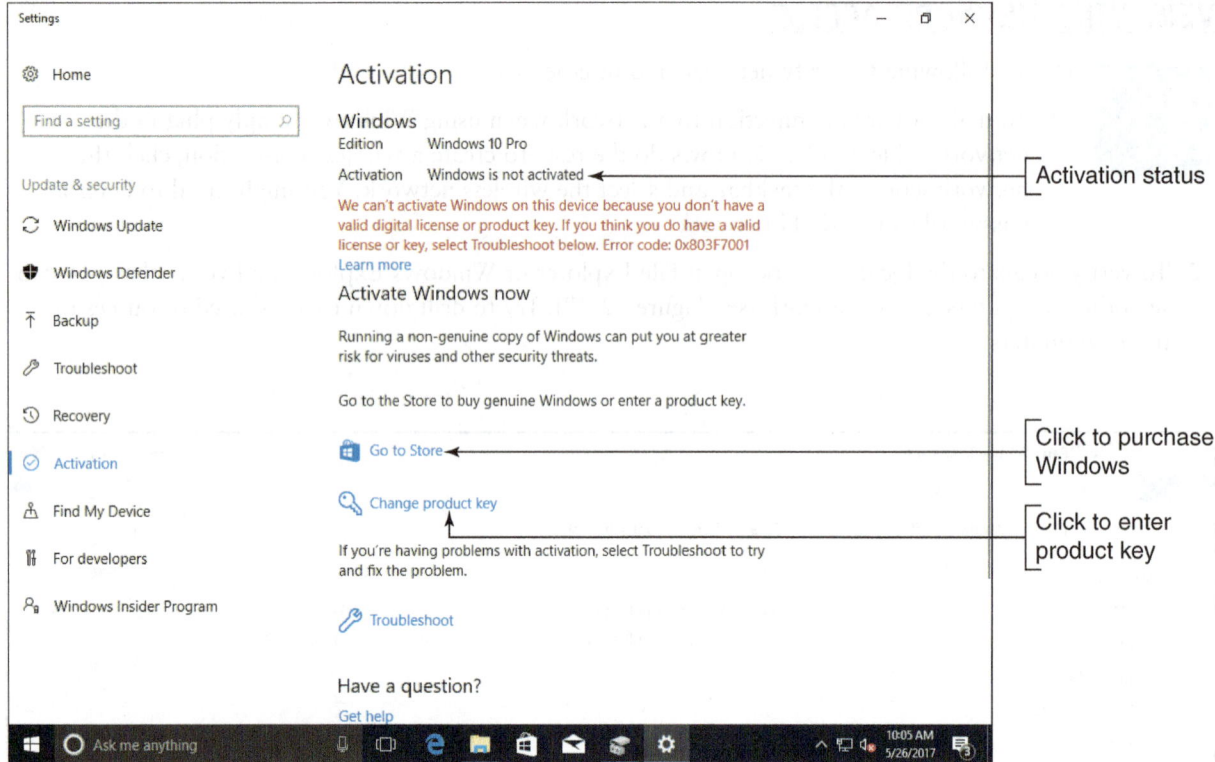

Figure 12-28   View the activation status using the Settings app

PROBLEMS WITH ACTIVATION

As explained earlier in this chapter, if the system already has a digital license or the product key is stored on the motherboard firmware, an upgrade or clean install will activate itself; you don't need to enter a product key. Here are some situations that might cause trouble when activating Windows:

▲ *Replacing a failed hard drive.* If you replace a failed hard drive with a new drive, you should still be able to perform a clean install of Windows 10 on the new hard drive and rely on the digital license, with no need to enter the product key. During setup, don't enter a product key. After Windows is installed, open the **Settings** app, select the **Activation** group, and verify that Windows is activated. If it is not, click **Troubleshoot** in the Activation window. Windows troubleshoots the problem and offers solutions. For example, when you click **I changed hardware on this device recently** in Figure 12-29, the troubleshooter gives you the opportunity to communicate with Microsoft and verify that the computer has a license to use Windows.

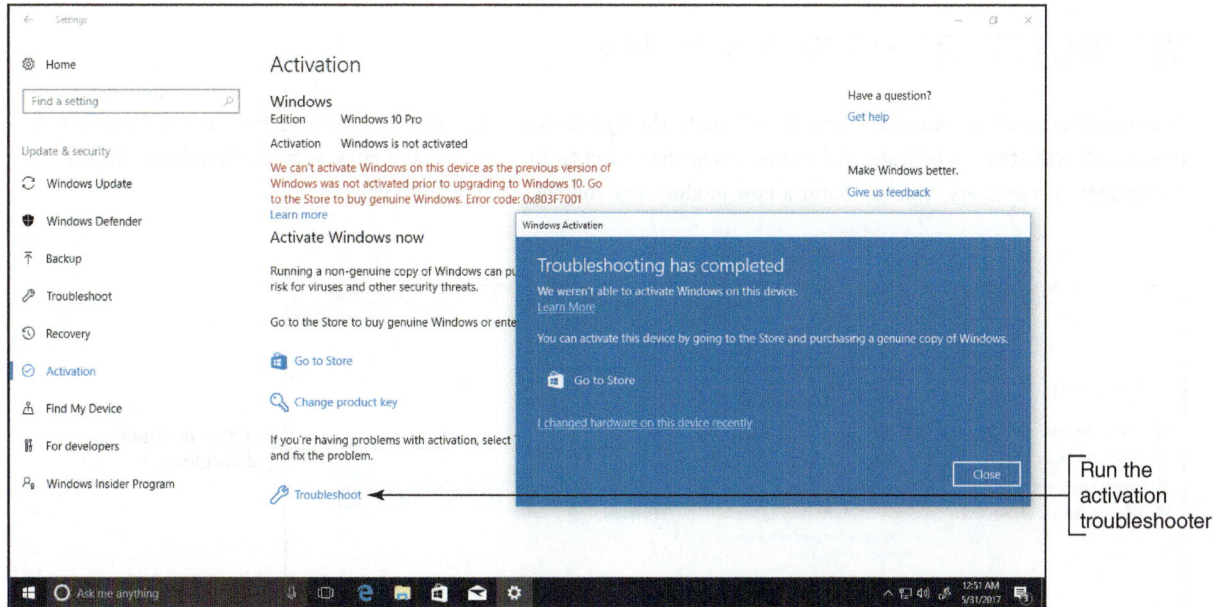

Figure 12-29   The activation troubleshooter resolves activation problems and might lead you to a chat window with Microsoft support

▲ *Upgrading the motherboard.* If the system is working, be sure to associate your Microsoft account with the Windows installation before you upgrade the motherboard. To do so, add the account and sign in to Windows using it. This will associate the digital license and hardware signature stored on Microsoft activation servers with your Microsoft account.

Later, after you upgrade the motherboard, start Windows and sign in using your Microsoft account. The system should be activated when Microsoft servers recognize your Microsoft account and the machine. If the installation is not activated, open the **Settings** app, select the **Activation** group, and then click **Troubleshoot**.

▲ *Replacing a failed motherboard.* Suppose the motherboard fails and you replace it, but you have never signed in to Windows using the Microsoft account that purchased the product key. In that case, Windows might not activate automatically and the Activation troubleshooter might not be able to resolve the problem. In this situation, you most likely will need to talk with Microsoft support staff and explain the problem.

▲ *Upgrading from Windows 8 Home to Windows 10 Pro.* When upgrading from Windows 8 Home to Windows 10 Pro, the installation may automatically upgrade to Windows 10 Home without giving you the option to choose Pro. If this happens, go to the Activation window after the installation is complete and enter your new product key for Windows 10 Pro. The system should reactivate with Windows 10 Pro.

▲ *Reinstalling Windows 10 Pro.* Suppose Windows 10 Pro is activated on a system and then gets corrupted. You perform a clean install to fix the problem, but setup automatically installs and activates Windows 10 Home without asking for a product key. You can fix the problem by going to the Activation window and changing the product key to the default product key for Pro: VK7JG-NPHTM-C97JM-9MPGT-3V66T. The system should reactivate with Windows 10 Pro.

WINDOWS | 8 ACTIVATE WINDOWS

To view the activation status for Windows 8/7, go to the System window. Figure 12-30 shows the window for a system that is not activated. To activate, make sure you're connected to the Internet and click **Activate Windows**. On the next screen, if necessary, you can enter a new product key and then activate Windows.

Figure 12-30 Use the System window to activate Windows

INSTALLING WINDOWS UPDATES

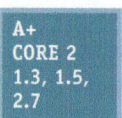

The Microsoft websites offer patches, fixes, and updates for known problems and have an extensive knowledge base that documents problems and their solutions. It's important to keep these updates current on your system to fix known problems and plug up security holes that might allow malware. Be sure to install updates before you attempt to install software or hardware.

Windows 10 updates automatically by default on a regular basis. To apply any pending Windows 10 updates, open the **Settings** app and click the **Update & security** group. In the Windows Update window (see Figure 12-31), you can view the update status and install any available updates. Depending on the situation, you might click **Restart now** to finish installing updates, click **Install now** to install available updates, or click **Check for updates** if no updates are available. Keep installing important updates and checking for more updates until no more are available. You might need to restart the system after certain updates are installed.

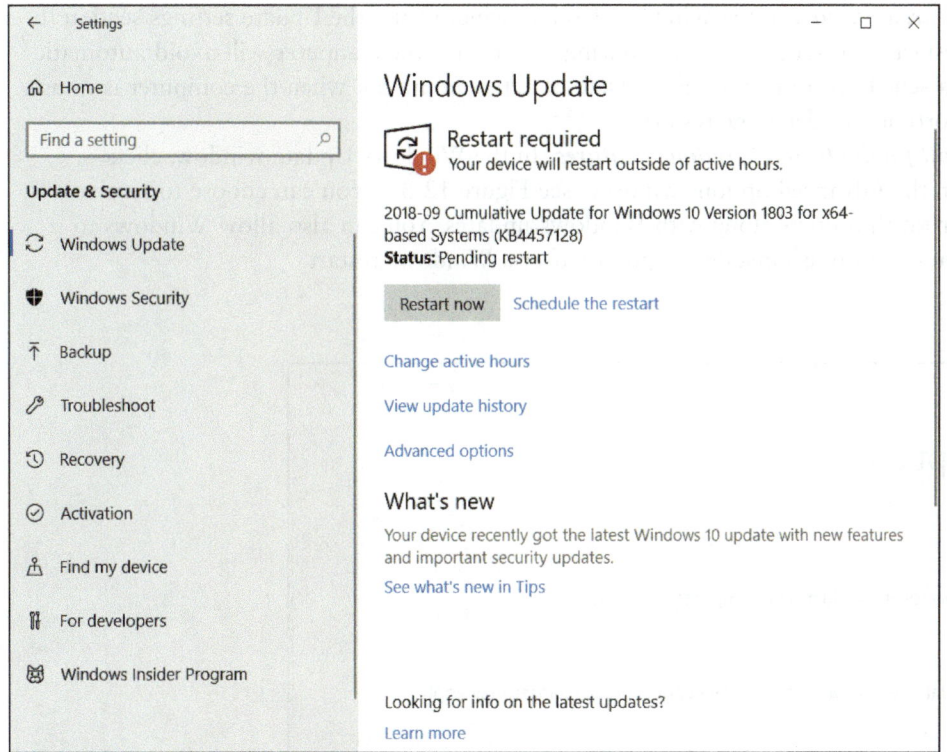

Figure 12-31 View and manage Windows 10 updates

Tools you can use to manage update settings include the Settings app, Group Policy, and the Registry Editor. Here's a brief list of your options for managing updates from the Settings app:

▲ **View or uninstall an update.** In the Settings app, click **Update & security** and then click **Windows Update** in the left pane. Click **View update history** to review recent updates and to uninstall updates that are available for uninstallation (see Figure 12-32).

Figure 12-32 Use the Settings app to manage Windows 10 updates

▲ *Schedule restarts and active hours.* In the Windows Update window, use the Update settings section to schedule a pending restart or to set active hours, during which time the computer will avoid automatic restarts. Note that if a scheduled restart occurs outside of active hours but when the computer is in use, you will have an opportunity to delay the restart.

▲ *Update other Microsoft products and Windows features.* In the Windows Update window, click **Advanced options**. On the Advanced options window (see Figure 12-33), you can choose to receive updates to other Microsoft products along with Windows updates. You can also allow Windows to automatically sign you in and finish installing updates after a Windows restart.

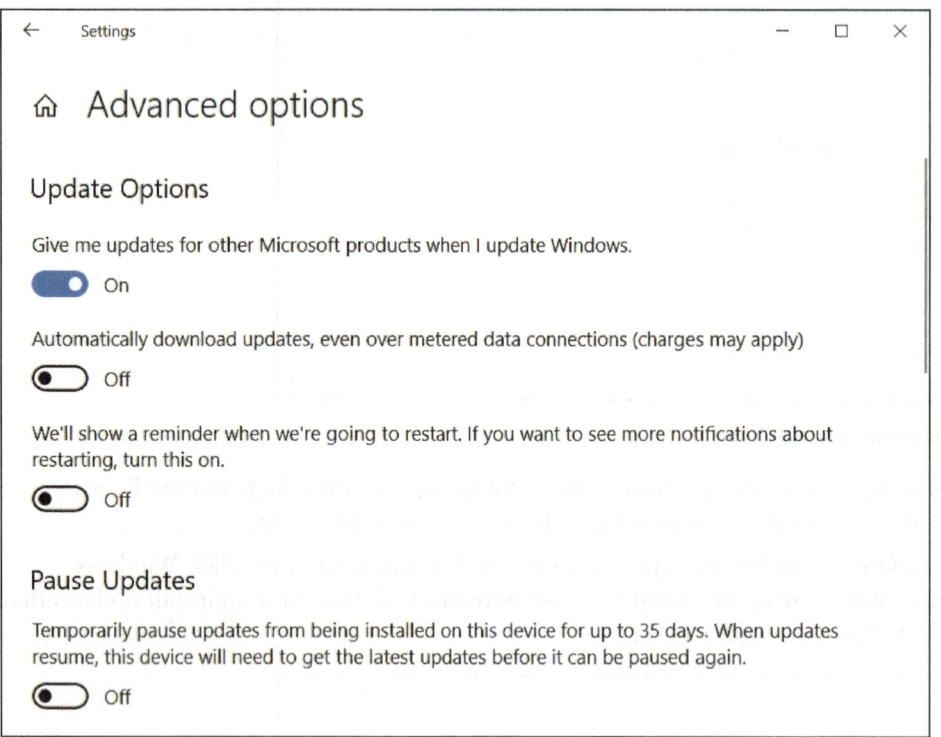

Figure 12-33   Control how updates to Windows and Microsoft apps are installed

▲ *Defer or pause updates.* For business and professional editions of Windows 10, you can open the Advanced options window and then choose when updates are installed or pause updates. Notice in Figure 12-33 that updates can be deferred for up to 35 days. You cannot defer or pause security updates in this window.

WINDOWS | 8 UPDATE WINDOWS 8

To view and manage Windows 8/7 update settings, open the **System** window and click **Windows Update** in the left pane. In the Windows Update window (see Figure 12-34), click **Check for updates** in the left pane. Don't forget to keep checking for and installing updates until there are no more to install. To change Windows Update settings, click **Change settings** in the Windows Update window and use the Change settings window.

Figure 12-34 View and manage Windows 8 updates

If Windows 8.0 is installed, you can update it to Windows 8.1 for free. Open the Windows Store app on the Start screen, select the Windows 8.1 update, and follow the on-screen directions to download and install it.

◇ OS Differences Recall that Windows 7 releases major updates as a service pack. On a Windows 7 system, if you see a service pack listed in the updates, install all the updates listed above it. Then install the service pack as the only update to install. It takes about 30 minutes and a reboot to download and install a service pack. Only the latest OS service pack will install because it includes all the content from previous service packs.

MALWARE PROTECTION

Windows includes its own preinstalled, anti-malware software called Windows Defender Antivirus in Windows 10 and Windows Defender in Windows 8/7. To verify that the utility is running in Windows 10, open **Control Panel,** click **Security and Maintenance,** and expand the Security group (see Figure 12-35).

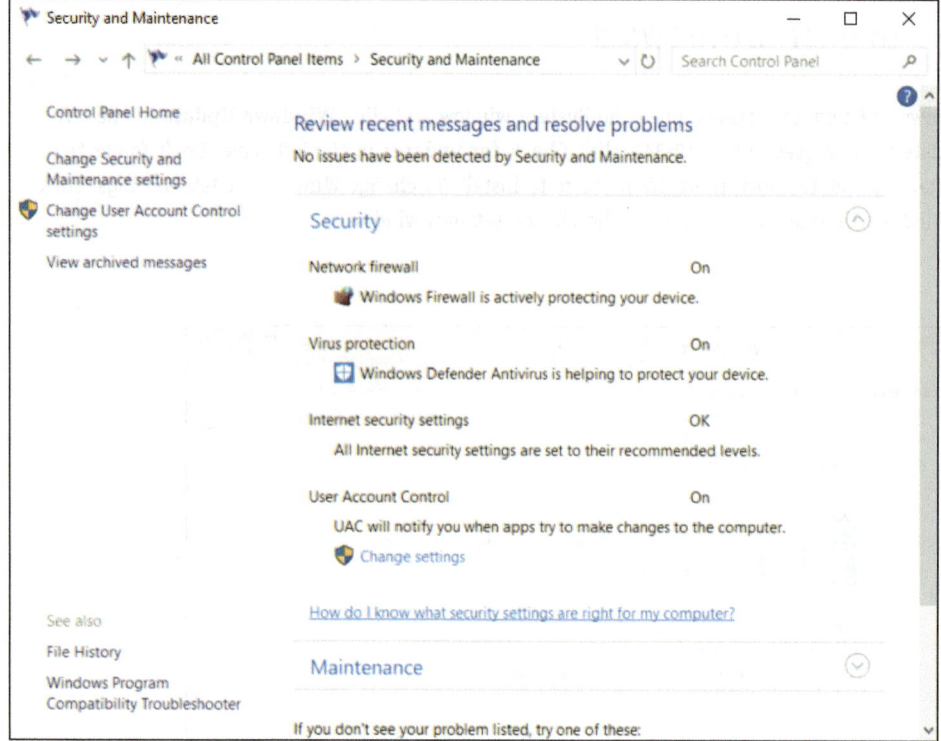

Figure 12-35 Verify that Windows Defender Antivirus is running

To verify protection in Windows 8, launch **Windows Defender** from the Start screen or menu. On the Settings tab, verify that **Real-time protection** is turned on.

> **OS Differences** In Windows 7, Windows Defender is not considered adequate protection against malware. For Windows 7, it's best to install third-party anti-malware software.

INSTALLING HARDWARE

A+ CORE 2 1.3, 1.5, 1.6

You're now ready to install the hardware devices that were not automatically installed during the Windows installation. Be sure to install 32-bit drivers for a 32-bit OS and 64-bit drivers for a 64-bit OS. Also, as much as possible, install drivers designed for the specific OS: Windows 10, Windows 8.1, or Windows 7. Sometimes drivers designed for an older OS will still work in the newer one. As you install each device, reboot and verify that the software or device is working before you move on to the next item. Most likely, you will need to do the following:

▲ *Install the drivers for the motherboard.* Motherboard drivers might come on a CD or DVD bundled with the motherboard, or you can download them from the motherboard manufacturer's website. To start the installation, double-click a setup program on the disc or that you downloaded and follow the on-screen directions.

▲ *Even though Windows has embedded video drivers, install the drivers that came with the video card so you can use all the features the card offers.* These drivers are on disc or are downloaded from the video card manufacturer's website.

▲ *Install printers.* To install a local USB printer, all you have to do is plug it in and Windows will install it automatically. For a network printer, you can run the setup program that came with the printer and the program will find and install the printer. Alternately, open Control Panel in Classic view and open the **Devices and Printers** window. Then click **Add a printer** and follow the on-screen directions.

◢ *For other hardware devices, always read and follow the manufacturer's directions for the installation.* Sometimes you are directed to install the drivers before you connect the device, and sometimes you will first need to connect the device.

If a problem arises while installing hardware in Windows 10, open Control Panel and click **Troubleshooting**. In the Troubleshooting app (see Figure 12-36), click **Hardware and Sound**. Windows will search for hardware installation problems and suggest solutions. If the problem persists, turn to Device Manager.

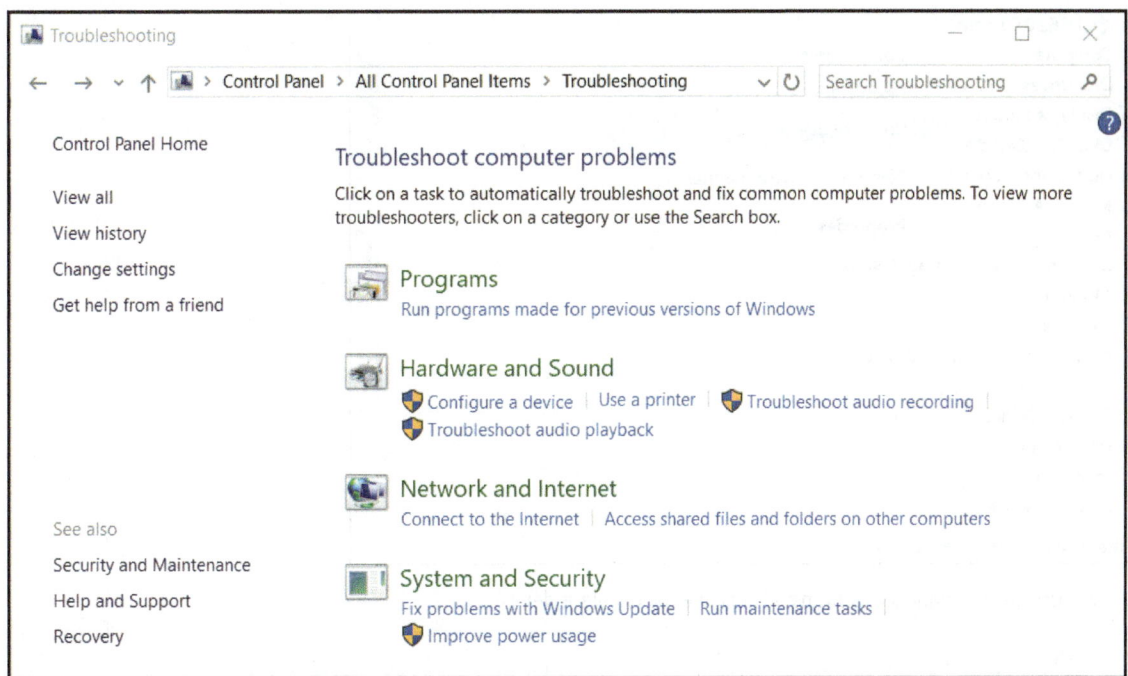

Figure 12-36   Use the Troubleshooting app in Control Panel to resolve hardware installation problems

---

◇ OS Differences If a problem occurs while Windows 8/7 is installing a device, it automatically launches the Action Center to help find a solution. Follow the on-screen directions to allow Windows to help you resolve the problem.

USE DEVICE MANAGER

Device Manager is your primary Windows tool for managing hardware. (Its program file is named devmgmt.msc.) It lists all installed hardware devices and the drivers they use. Using Device Manager, you can disable or enable a device, update its drivers, uninstall a device, and undo a driver update (called a driver rollback).

★ A+ Exam Tip The A+ Core 2 exam expects you to know which scenarios are appropriate for using Device Manager. You also need to know how to use the utility and how to evaluate its results.

To access Device Manager, use one of these methods:

◢ For Windows 10/8, right-click **Start** and select **Device Manager**.
◢ Open the System window and click **Device Manager**.
◢ Enter the **devmgmt.msc** command in the Windows 10/7 search box or the Windows 8 Run box.

A Device Manager window is shown in Figure 12-37.

Figure 12-37 Use Device Manager to uninstall, disable, or enable a device

Click an arrow to expand the view of an item or to collapse the view. Here are ways to use Device Manager to solve problems with a device:

◢ *Uninstall and reinstall the device*. To uninstall the device, right-click it and click **Uninstall device** on the shortcut menu, as shown in Figure 12-37. (Alternately, you can click **Properties** in the shortcut menu to open the Properties box and then click **Uninstall Device** on the Driver tab, as shown in Figure 12-38A.) Then reboot the system. Windows will recognize that the device is not installed and attempt to install the appropriate driver. Look for issues during the installation that point to the source of the problem. Sometimes, though, reinstalling a device is all you need to do. Notice in Figure 12-38B that the selected Device type is Cameras, and that the camera is connected through a USB interface. Sometimes USB devices are listed in Device Manager and sometimes they are not.

◢ *Look for error messages offered by Device Manager*. To get more information about a device, look for error messages that show up on the General tab of the Properties box (see Figure 12-38B). Some messages might suggest a solution.

◢ *Update or roll back the drivers*. Click the **Driver** tab (see Figure 12-38A) to update the drivers and roll back (undo) a driver update.

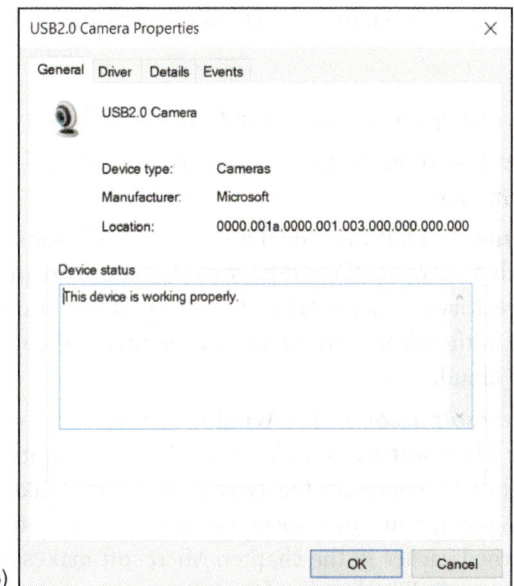

(A)   (B)

Figure 12-38   (A) Use the device's Properties box to uninstall a device and (B) solve problems with device drivers

APPLYING | CONCEPTS   UPDATING DEVICE DRIVERS

Follow these steps to use Device Manager to update device drivers:

1. For best results, locate and download the latest driver files from the manufacturer's website to your hard drive. Be sure to use 64-bit drivers for a 64-bit OS and 32-bit drivers for a 32-bit OS. If possible, use drivers specifically designed for Windows 10, Windows 8.1, or Windows 7.

2. Using Device Manager, right-click the device and select **Properties** from the shortcut menu. The Properties box for that device appears. Select the **Driver** tab and click **Update Driver**. The Update Driver Software box opens.

3. To search the Internet for drivers, click **Search automatically for updated driver software**. If you have already downloaded drivers to your computer, click **Browse my computer for driver software** and point to the downloaded files. Note that Windows is looking for an .inf file to identify the drivers. Continue to follow the on-screen directions to complete the installation.

✎ **Notes**   By default, Device Manager hides legacy devices that are not Plug and Play. To view installed legacy devices, click the **View** menu of Device Manager and check **Show hidden devices**.

SETTING UP USER ACCOUNTS

A+ CORE 2 1.7, 2.6

As you know, a user must sign in to Windows with a valid user account to gain access to the OS. When you install Windows as a clean installation, you create a user account and you can

12

create others later. Here's a brief overview of the types of user accounts and the privileges associated with them:

▲ *The scope of the account.* Windows offers three types of user accounts, each with a different scope:

  ▲ *Local account.* A local account is created on the local computer and is recognized only on the local computer.

  ▲ *Network ID.* Professional and business editions of Windows allow a user to sign in to Windows with a network ID and password that are created and maintained on a Windows domain in Active Directory or Azure Active Directory. When you sign in to Windows using this type of account, you are authenticated to the local computer and to the Windows domain on a corporate network or in the cloud.

  ▲ *Microsoft account.* For Windows 10/8, a Microsoft account is an email address initially set up at the Microsoft website, *live.com*. The account gives you access to several types of online accounts, including Microsoft OneDrive, Facebook, LinkedIn, Twitter, Skype, and *Outlook.com*. On a Windows computer, you can associate or link a Microsoft account to a local account or a network ID. As you learned earlier in the chapter, Microsoft makes every effort to encourage you to use a Microsoft account in Windows.

> ✎ **Notes** A Microsoft account is an example of a single sign-on (SSO) account, which accesses multiple, independent resources, systems, or applications after you sign in one time to one account.

▲ *Privileges for the account.* In Windows, there are two types of privileges assigned to a user account: those for an administrator account and for a standard account. An administrator account has more privileges than a standard account and is used by people responsible for maintaining and securing the system.

APPLYING | CONCEPTS   CREATING A LOCAL ACCOUNT

To create a new account, you can use the Windows 10 Settings app, the Windows 8 Settings charm, the Windows 7 User Accounts applet in Control Panel, or, for all editions of Windows, the Computer Management console in Control Panel. You have more control over creating and setting up an account when you use the Computer Management console, as you learn in Chapter 16. For now, let's use one of the other methods; follow these steps to create a local account:

1. Sign in to Windows with an administrator account.

2. Do one of the following to create an account:

   ▲ *Windows 10.* Open the **Settings** app. Click **Accounts**. Click **Family & other people** and click **Add someone else to this PC**. See Figure 12-39. Click **I don't have this person's sign-in information** and click **Add a user without a Microsoft account** (see the right side of Figure 12-39). Enter a user name, enter the password twice, and click **Next**.

(continues)

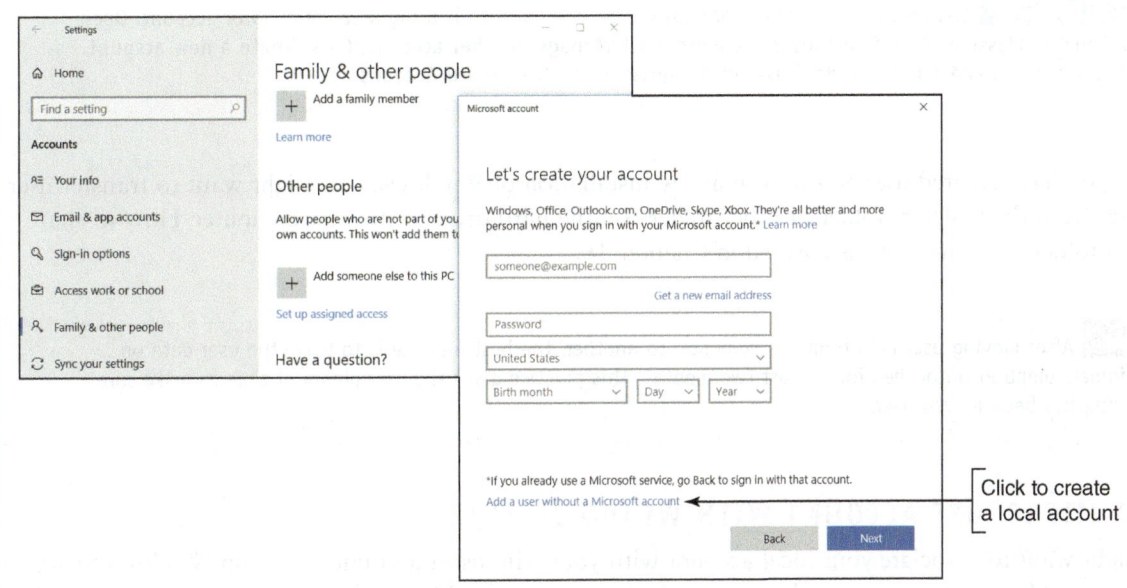

Figure 12-39 Bypass the Microsoft account and create a local account

▲ *Windows 8.* Open the **Settings** charm and click **Change PC settings**. On the PC settings screen, click **Accounts**. On the Accounts screen, click **Other accounts** (see Figure 12-40). Click **Sign in without a Microsoft account (not recommended)**, and click **Next**. Follow the on-screen directions to set up the account.

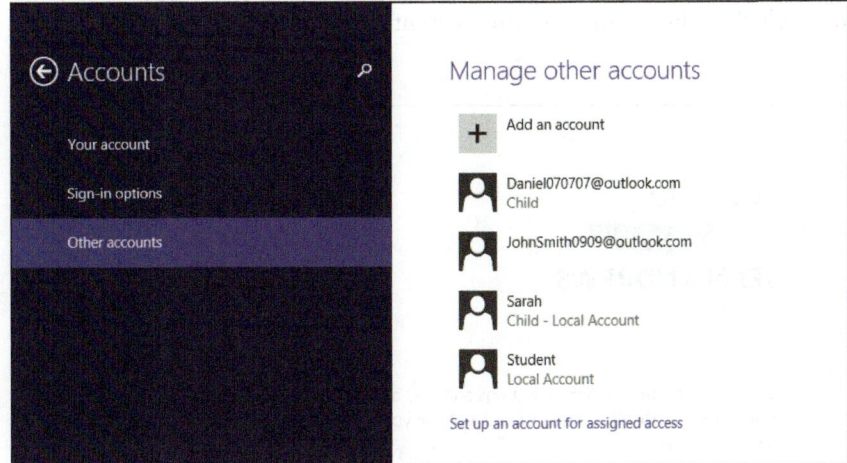

Figure 12-40 Set up a new user account

3. In Windows 10/8, the account created is a standard account. To change the account type to administrator, click the account and click **Change account type**. Then select **Administrator** and click **OK**. To remove the account, select it and click **Remove**.

The first time a user signs in to Windows with the account, user files and folders (called the user profile) are created in the C:\Users folder.

12

> **○ OS Differences** You create an account in Windows 7 by signing in to it using an administrator account. Open Control Panel in Classic view and click **User Accounts**. Click **Manage another account**. Click **Create a new account**. Enter the user name and select **Standard user** or **Administrator**. Click **Create Account**.

After you have created user accounts in a new installation of Windows, you might want to transfer user data files from the C:\Users folder or other folders on the hard drive to the new computer. How to share files and folders on a network is covered in Chapter 16.

> **✎ Notes** After moving user data from one computer to another, the best practice is to leave the user data on the original computer untouched for at least two months. This practice gives the user plenty of time to make sure everything has been moved over.

USE A MICROSOFT ACCOUNT WITH WINDOWS 10/8

You might want to associate your local account with your Microsoft account, or set up Windows to sign in with your Microsoft account so that you can get easy access to Microsoft resources in the cloud, such as OneDrive. However, know that anyone with administrative rights to the computer can access your Microsoft private settings, apps, online accounts, and OneDrive stored on the local computer. Therefore, you would only want to set up your Microsoft account on a computer where you trust people with administrative access to the computer. Here are the details of making the switch:

◢ *For Windows 10*. To connect an existing local account or network ID to a Microsoft account, open the **Settings** app, click **Users**, and then click **Sign in with a Microsoft account instead**. See Figure 12-41. Follow the on-screen directions, which include entering your current Windows password.

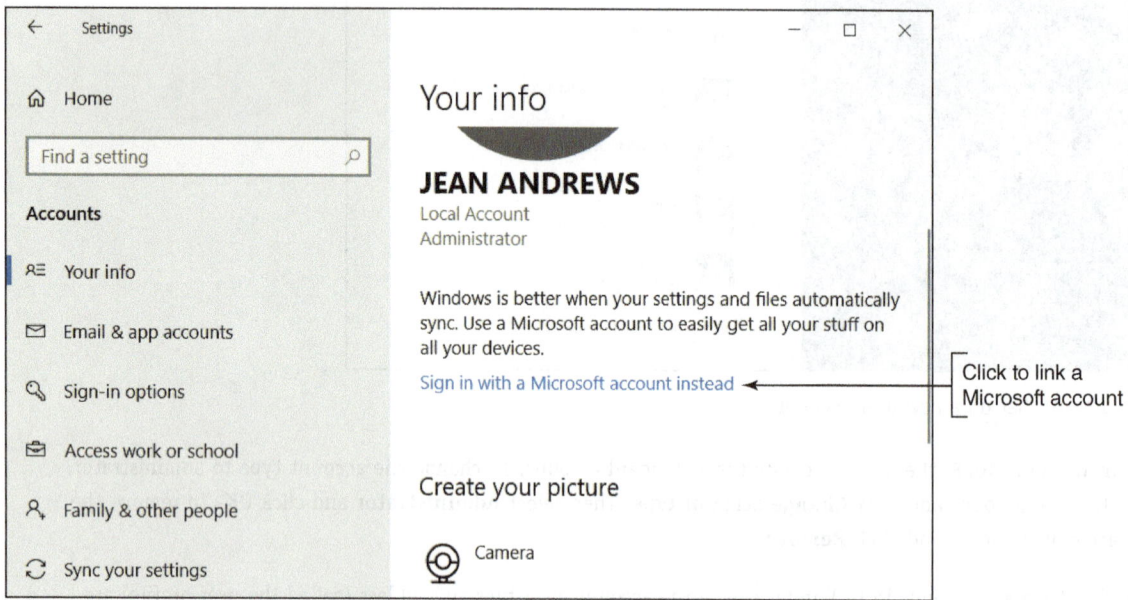

Figure 12-41 Associate a local account with a Microsoft account

◢ *For Windows 8*. Open the **charms** bar, select the **Settings** charm, select **Change PC settings**, and click **Accounts**. Select **Your account** and then click **Connect to a Microsoft account**. Follow the on-screen directions.

✎ Notes To connect a network ID on a domain to a Microsoft account, the Group Policies controlling the Windows domain must allow it. After the connection, the Microsoft account is used to authenticate to the domain.

If you want to switch the user account back to the local account, go back to your account settings, click **Your info**, and click **Sign in with a local account instead**. On a Windows 8 computer, go back to your account settings and click **Disconnect**.

Recall that you can sign in to Windows using a local account, network ID, or Microsoft account. As you ponder the differences among these accounts, consider where the account is authenticated:

◢ A local account is authenticated on the local computer and gives access to the local computer. An administrator local account has more access than a standard local account.

◢ A network ID is authenticated by a computer on the network, which gives you access to the local computer and other resources on the Windows domain.

◢ A Microsoft account is authenticated on the *live.com* website, which gives access to the local computer and online resources, such as OneDrive and *Facebook.com*. A Microsoft account can be a standard account or an administrator account. It can also be associated with a network ID so that you can sign in with the Microsoft account and be authenticated to the Windows network as well as to *live.com*.

USER ACCOUNT CONTROL DIALOG BOX

At some point while you are working with a computer to maintain or troubleshoot it, the User Account Control (UAC) dialog box will pop up (see Figure 12-42). If the UAC box appears and you are signed in as an administrator, all you have to do is click Yes to close the box and move on, as shown in Figure 12-42A. If the user account does not have administrative privileges, you'll have to enter the password of an administrative account to continue, as shown in Figure 12-42B.

(A)

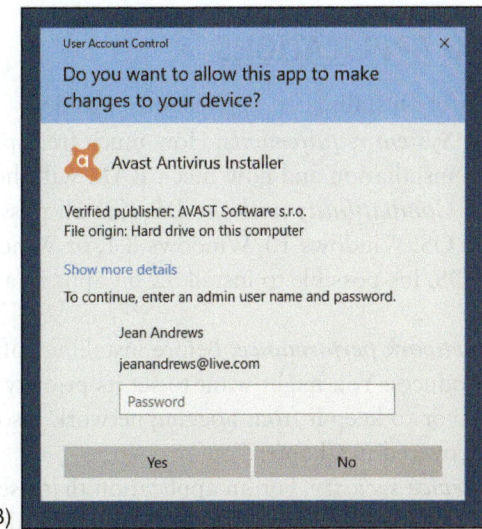

(B)

Figure 12-42 (A) The User Account Control box of an administrator does not require an administrative password; (B) the UAC box of a standard user requires an administrative password

The purposes of the UAC box are: (1) to prevent malicious background tasks from gaining administrative privileges when the administrator is signed in, and (2) to make it easier for an administrator to sign in using a less powerful user account for normal desktop activities, but still be able to perform administrative tasks while signed in as a regular user. The UAC box stands as a gatekeeper to malware installing behind your back because someone has to click the UAC box before the installation can proceed.

12

You can control how the UAC box works. In Control Panel, click **User Accounts** and click **Change User Account Control settings**. The User Account Control Settings window appears (see Figure 12-43). In the figure, the recommended setting is selected.

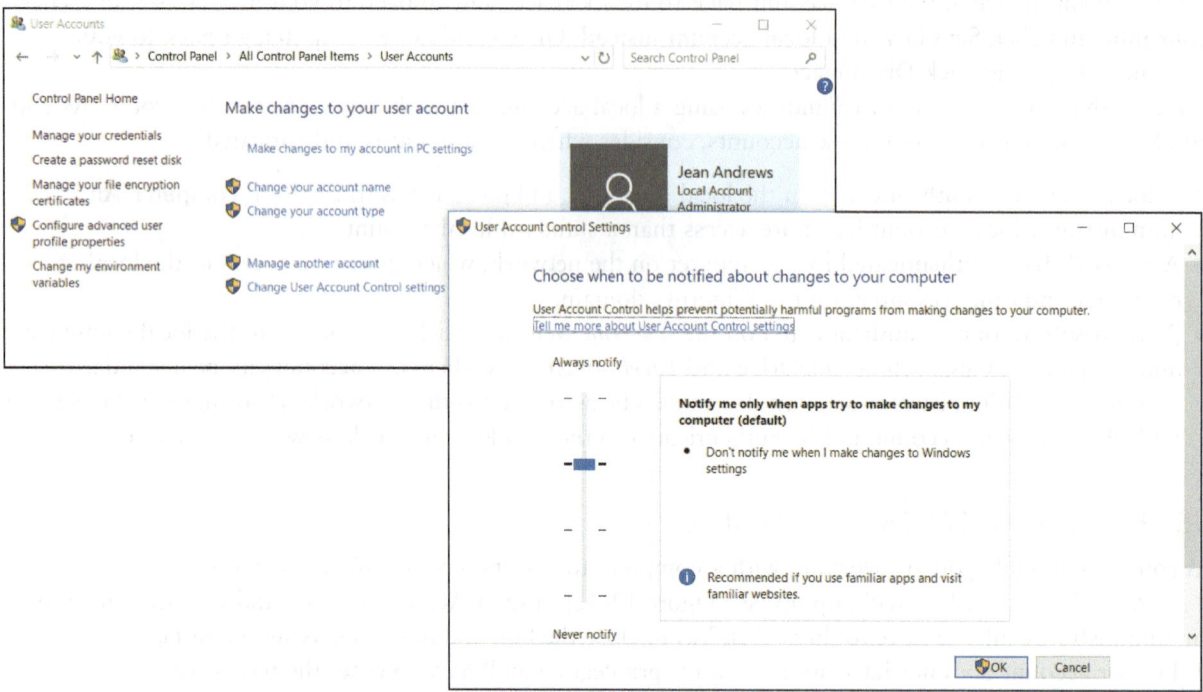

Figure 12-43 Windows provides options to control the UAC box

INSTALLING APPLICATIONS

A+
CORE 2
1.6, 1.7

Before installing an application, consider:

▲ *System requirements.* How much free space on the hard drive does the app need for the installation and how much RAM will the app use when running?

▲ *Compatibility with the OS.* If at all possible, install applications designed for the specific OS: Windows 10, Windows 8.1, or Windows 7. For best performance, install 64-bit apps in a 64-bit OS. It's possible to install 32-bit apps in a 64-bit OS, but you cannot install 64-bit apps in a 32-bit OS.

▲ *Impact to network performance.* Before installing software, research how much network activity the software produces. You might want to set its priority as high or low on the network to control its performance or to keep it from hogging network resources. How to prioritize applications on the network is covered in Chapter 7.

▲ *Impact to device security.* For an application that uses the Internet, consider if it will make the computer vulnerable to attack. Read manufacturer documentation and reviews about how to secure the application and the system, such as making changes to Windows Firewall or installing each app in its own secured virtual machine on the host computer.

▲ *Local user permissions.* Here are the situations you need to know when dealing with local user permissions:

　▲ A user account with administrator privileges has permission to install software for all users; this software is normally installed in the C:\Program Files folder or the C:\Program Files (x86) folder.

Both folders require administrator permissions to edit the folder's contents. For these installations, expect a UAC box to appear to verify the installation (refer back to Figure 12-42A).

▲ A user with standard privileges can install software that is designed to install in his C:/Users profile folder and does not make changes to protected areas of the Windows registry. (The registry is a database of Windows settings.) The software can only be used by this one user account.

▲ If a user signed in with a standard account attempts to install software, such as anti-malware software, that is designed to run under all user accounts, a UAC box appears (see Figure 12-42B). To continue with the installation, the user must enter the password for an administrator user account.

Applications can be installed in Windows 10/8/7 from CD, DVD, or USB flash drive, from a downloaded application file, directly from the web, from the Windows 10/8 Windows Store, or from a folder shared by another computer on the network.

To install applications from a disc, USB flash drive, or software downloaded from the Internet, open File Explorer or Windows Explorer, locate and double-click the setup program file, and follow the on-screen directions to launch the installation routine.

When installing a program directly from the web, click the link on the website to install the software and follow the on-screen directions. To install apps in the Windows Store, use the Store app on the Windows 10 taskbar or the Windows 8 Start screen. After an application is installed, you might also need to install any updates available for the application on the manufacturer's website.

> **✎ Notes** In Chapter 16, you learn that you can map a network drive to a folder that is shared by another computer on the network. For example, this shared folder can appear as drive Z: in your File Explorer window. It's common for administrators to put application setup programs in a shared folder for users on the network to install on their local computers. However, the setup program might give errors when you attempt to run it from the mapped network drive. The solution is to copy the setup program and other setup files to your computer and run it locally. In Chapter 14, you learn about other tasks you can try when an application fails to install.

12

UNINSTALL APPLICATIONS

If you need to uninstall an application, do one of the following:

▲ For Windows 10/8/7, open **Control Panel** and click **Programs and Features**.
▲ For Windows 10, right-click **Start** or press **Win+X**, and click **Apps and Features**.
▲ For Windows 8, right-click **Start** or press **Win+X**, and click **Programs and Features**.

Figure 12-44 shows the Programs and Features window. Using either the Programs and Features window or the Apps and Features window, select an app and click **Uninstall**. When you select an app in the Programs and Features window, the buttons at the top of the list will change based on the software. For example, in Figure 12-44, the Bonjour software offers the options to Uninstall and Repair the software. (Bonjour by Apple allows Windows to find resources on a network offered by Apple devices.)

> **✎ Notes** The new Windows Store apps can be uninstalled only in the Apps and Features window and not in the Programs and Features window. In Chapter 13, you learn how to use PowerShell to uninstall apps.

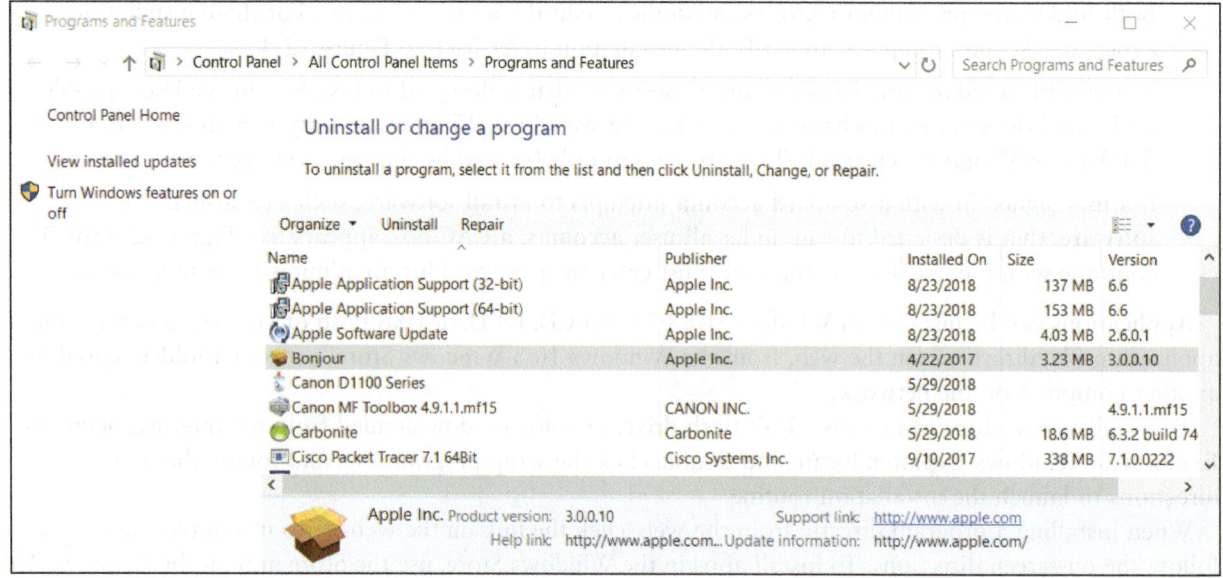

Figure 12-44 Select a program from the list to view your options to manage the software

Recall that you can also uninstall a Windows 10/8 app that provides a tile on the Start menu or Start screen. Right-click the app tile and then click **Uninstall**.

Figure 12-45 Turn Windows features on or off

TURNING WINDOWS FEATURES ON OR OFF

You can save on system resources by turning off Windows features you will not use, and you might need to turn on some features that are turned off by default. To control Windows features, open the Programs and Features window and click **Turn Windows features on or off** in the left pane (refer to Figure 12-44). The Windows Features box opens (see Figure 12-45). Check or uncheck the features you want or don't want and then click **OK**. Sometimes a restart is necessary for the changes to take effect.

The Windows installation, devices, user accounts, and applications should now be good to go. Restart the computer and make one last check that all is well. Now would be a good time to document what you did after the installation. A project at the end of this chapter will help you organize your documentation for each computer you support. Also consider making a backup of the entire Windows volume in the event of a hard drive failure or corrupted installation. How to make backups is covered in Chapter 13.

INSTALLATIONS IN A VIRTUAL MACHINE

**A+
CORE 2
1.3**

Another type of Windows installation is when you install Windows in a virtual computer. A virtual computer or virtual machine (VM) is software that simulates the hardware of a physical computer. Using this software, you can install and run multiple operating systems at the same time on a single computer, which is called the host machine. These multiple instances of operating systems can be used to train users, run legacy software, and support multiple operating systems. For example, help-desk technicians can run a virtual machine for each OS they support on a single computer and quickly switch from one OS to another by clicking a window. Another reason to use a virtual machine is that you can capture screenshots of the boot process in a virtual machine, which is how some screenshots were made for this text.

Software used to manage VMs installed on a workstation is called a hypervisor. Some popular hypervisors for Windows are Client Hyper-V and Virtual PC by Microsoft (*microsoft.com*), VirtualBox by Oracle (*virtualbox.org*), and VMware Player by VMware, Inc. (*vmware.com*). Client Hyper-V is embedded in Windows 10/8 Pro or Enterprise, but is not available for other Windows releases. Virtual PC is free for download in all other editions of Windows 10/8/7 except Windows 7 Starter. VirtualBox and VMware Player are freeware. Be aware that virtual machine programs require a lot of memory and might slow down your system. Figure 12-46 shows two virtual machines running under VirtualBox.

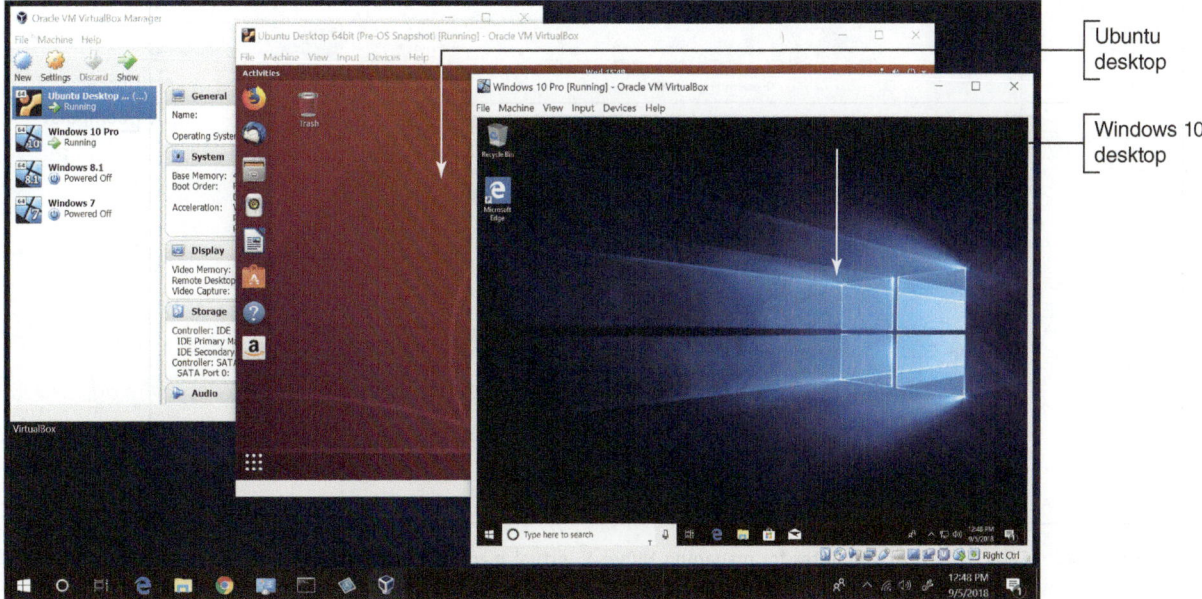

Ubuntu desktop

Windows 10 desktop

12

Source: VirtualBox (Oracle)

Figure 12-46   Two virtual machines running under VirtualBox

INSTALL WINDOWS IN A CLIENT HYPER-V VM

Client Hyper-V is the virtual machine (VM) manager that is part of 64-bit Windows 10 Pro. If your processor and motherboard support hardware-assisted virtualization (HAV), you can use Client Hyper-V to install and manage virtual machines on the desktop. Generation 1 VMs allow either a 32-bit or 64-bit installation of an OS in a VM. Generation 2 VMs require a 64-bit guest operating system. Hyper-V can connect a VM to the local network. Client Hyper-V supports dynamically expanding virtual hard drives and dynamically allocated memory. When using dynamically expanding virtual hard drives, the VM ties up only the portion of the host's hard drive that the VM's hard drive is actually using. When using dynamic memory, the VM ties up only the portion of allocated memory that it is actually using.

APPLYING | CONCEPTS   SETTING UP A VM

Here are the steps to set up a VM using Windows 10 Pro:

1. Go into BIOS/UEFI setup on your computer and make sure virtualization is enabled.

2. Hyper-V is disabled in Windows 10 Pro by default. To turn it on, open the **Settings** app, select the **Apps** group, select **Apps and features**, and click **Programs and Features**. In the Programs and Features window, click **Turn Windows features on or off**. Place a check mark by **Hyper-V** and click **OK**. You'll need to restart the system for the change to take effect.

3. To launch the Hyper-V Manager, open the search box, type **Hyper-V**, and then click **Hyper-V Manager**. The Hyper-V Manager window appears on the desktop. In the Hyper-V Manager pane on the left, select the host computer (see Figure 12-47).

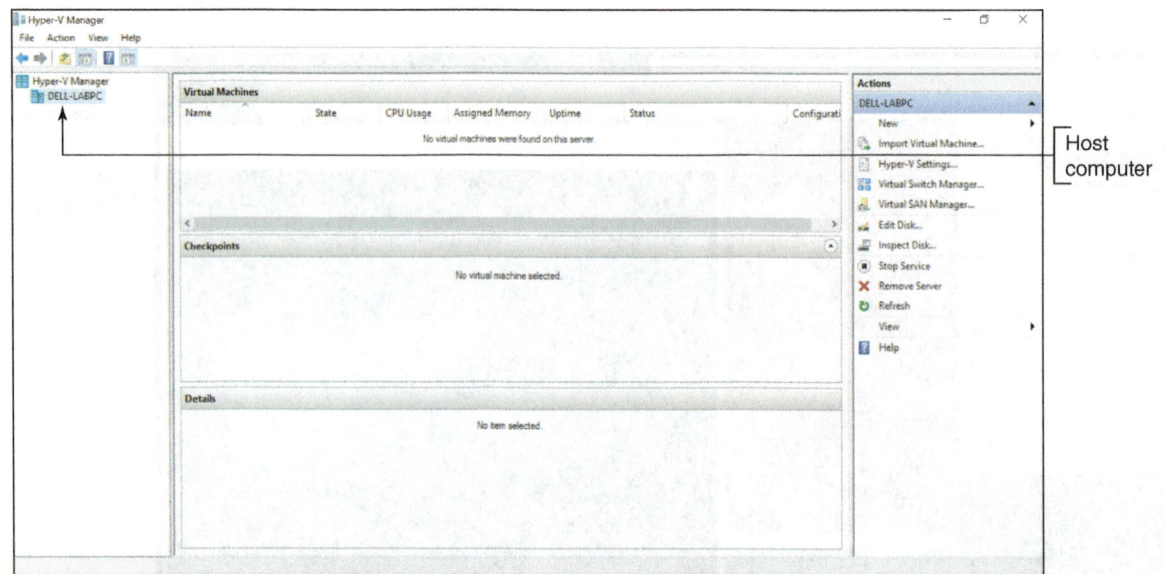

Figure 12-47   Select the host computer for managing Hyper-V virtual machines

4. To give your VMs access to the network or the Internet, you first need to install a virtual switch. To create a virtual switch, click **Virtual Switch Manager** in the Actions pane on the right side of the Hyper-V Manager window.

5. The Virtual Switch Manager window appears (see Figure 12-48). In the left pane, make sure **New virtual network switch** is selected. To bind the virtual switch to the physical network adapter so the VMs can access the physical network, click **External** in the right pane. Click **Create Virtual Switch**.

(continues)

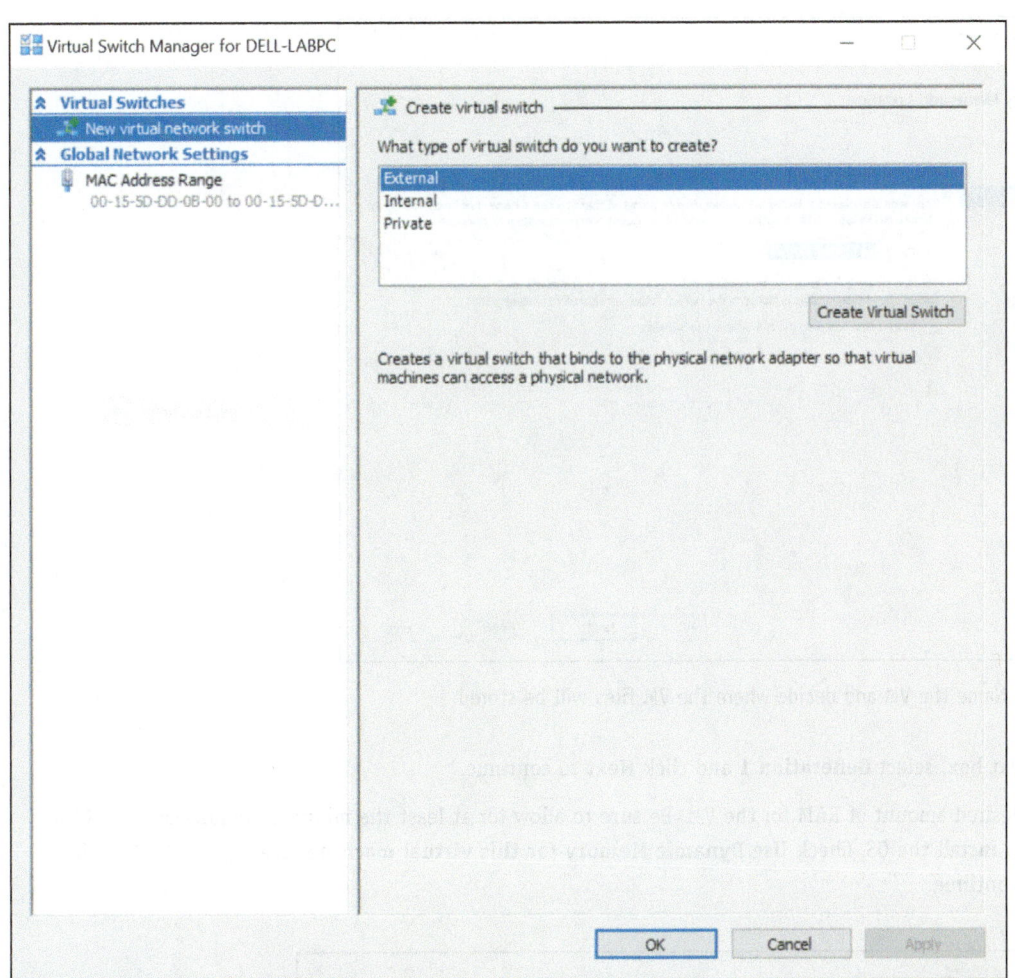

Figure 12-48 Create a virtual switch

6. The Virtual Switch Properties box appears; the new switch is shown in the right pane. In this pane, you can name the virtual switch or leave the default name. You can also select the network adapter to use for the switch. For most situations, that would be the wired Ethernet adapter. Make sure **Allow management operating system to share this network adapter** is checked, and then click **Apply**. Click **Yes** to create the virtual switch. Click **OK** to close the window.

7. You're now ready to create a VM. In the Actions pane, click **New**, and then click **Virtual Machine**. This opens the New Virtual Machine Wizard, where you can set the name and location of the VM files and configure memory and the virtual hard drive. Click **Next**. (Notice you can click **Finish** to accept default settings for the VM.)

8. Assign a name to the VM. If you want the VM files to be stored in a different location than the default, check **Store the virtual machine in a different location**, and browse to that location (see Figure 12-49). After you've selected the location, click **Next**.

(continues)

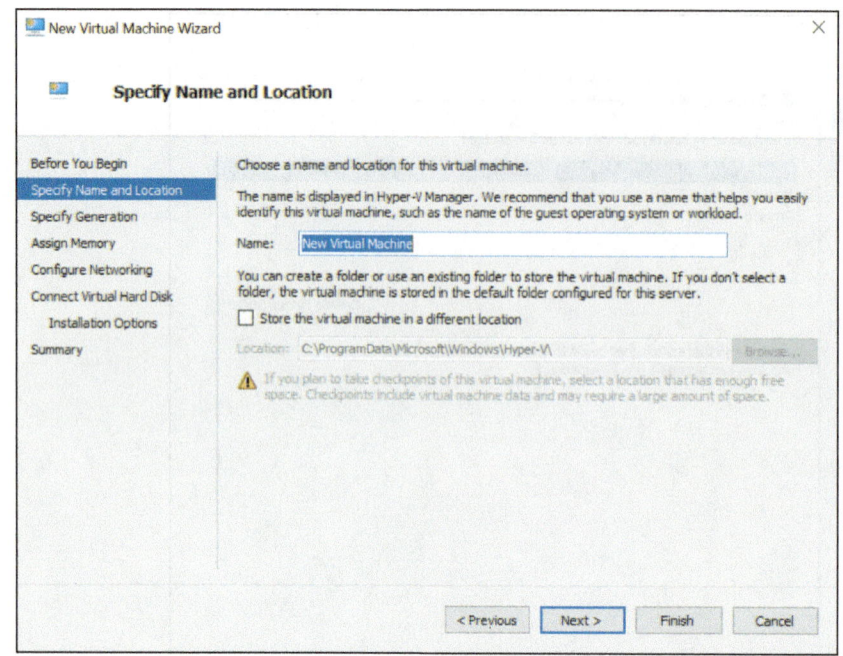

Figure 12-49   Name the VM and decide where the VM files will be stored

9. In the next box, select **Generation 1** and click **Next** to continue.

10. Set the desired amount of RAM for the VM. Be sure to allow for at least the minimum requirement of RAM needed to install the OS. Check **Use Dynamic Memory for this virtual machine** (see Figure 12-50). Click **Next** to continue.

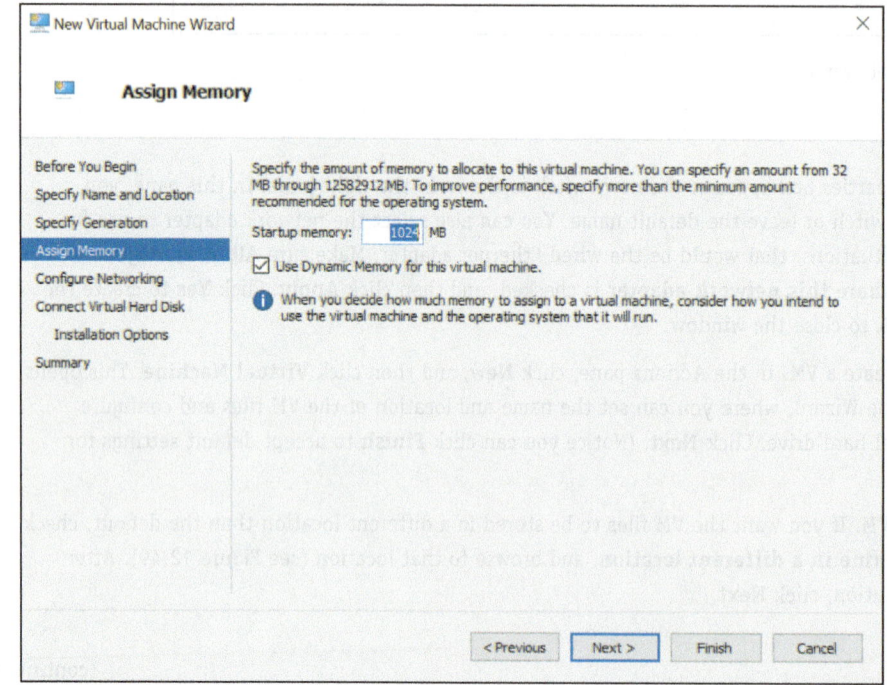

Figure 12-50   Use dynamic memory to conserve memory on the host computer

(continues)

11. In the Configure Networking dialog box, select the virtual switch you created earlier and click **Next**.

12. In the Connect Virtual Hard Disk dialog box, select **Create a virtual hard disk** and click **Next**.

13. The Installation Options dialog box appears (see Figure 12-51). To install Windows from the ISO file you downloaded earlier using the Media Creation Tool, select **Install an operating system from a bootable CD/DVD-ROM**. Select **Image file (.iso)**. Click **Browse** and select the ISO file for the Windows installation. Click **Next** to continue. The last dialog box in the New Virtual Machine Wizard shows a summary of your selections. Click **Finish** to create the VM. The new VM is listed in the Virtual Machines pane in the Hyper-V Manager window.

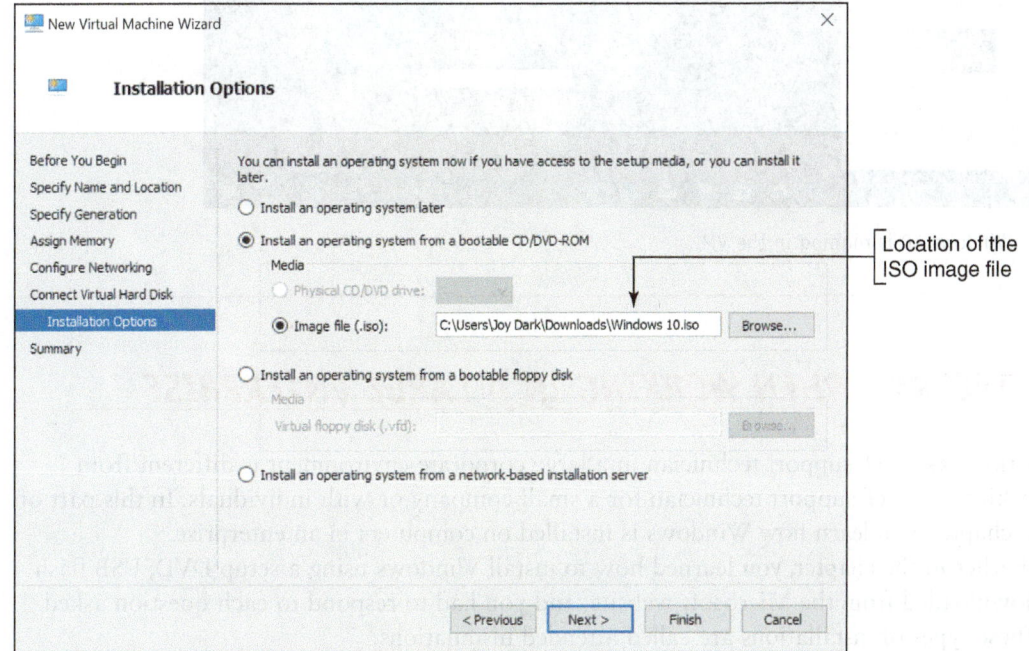

Figure 12-51 Decide how an OS will be installed in the VM

14. To manage the VM's virtual hardware, select the VM in Hyper-V Manager and click **Settings** near the bottom of the Actions pane. The Settings dialog box for the VM appears. Select the hardware in the left pane and apply your settings in the right pane.

15. To install Windows, you need to boot from the virtual DVD drive. Click **BIOS** in the left pane and select **Boot from CD** in the right pane.

16. Close the **Settings** box. To start the VM, select it and click **Start** in the Actions pane. The VM boots up and Windows setup starts. A thumbnail of the VM appears in the bottom-middle pane of the Hyper-V Manager window. To see the VM in a separate window, double-click the thumbnail. Figure 12-52 shows the VM window at the beginning of the OS installation. Notice in the figure that several VMs have been created, and three of them are currently running.

> ✎ **Notes** If you are trying to install an OS in a new VM and you get an error after the Product Key screen, try shutting down and restarting the VM. Then start the install again.

(continues)

VMs created

VM open

Figure 12-52 Windows 10 is running in the VM

SPECIAL CONCERNS WHEN WORKING IN A LARGE ENTERPRISE

**A+
CORE 2
1.3, 1.4**

Working as an IT support technician in a large corporate environment is different from working as an IT support technician for a small company or with individuals. In this part of the chapter, you learn how Windows is installed on computers in an enterprise.

Earlier in the chapter, you learned how to install Windows using a setup DVD, USB flash drive, or files downloaded from the Microsoft website, and you had to respond to each question asked during setup. These types of installations are called attended installations.

If, however, you were responsible for installing Windows on several hundred computers in a large corporation, you might want a less time-consuming method. These methods are called deployment strategies. As an IT support technician in a large corporation, most likely you would not be involved in choosing or setting up the deployment strategy. However, you need to be aware of the different strategies so you have a general idea of what will be expected when you are asked to provide desk-side or help-desk support as Windows is being deployed in your organization or a desktop OS that has failed needs to be refreshed.

Beginning with Windows 10, Microsoft expanded the methods it offers to deploy Windows in an enterprise. These methods are listed in Table 12-6. Some methods were designed to work with on-premises domains controlled by Active Directory (AD) and others work with Azure Active Directory (AAD) in the cloud.

Category	Method	Description
Modern deployments: Use these methods with AD or AAD domains.		
	Windows Autopilot	Streamlines the OOBE (out-of-box experiences) for devices preregistered with the enterprise. When a user receives a new device, turns it on, connects to the Internet, and enters his user name and password, the device is automatically joined to AAD and configured with settings and content specific for the organization without further user input.

Table 12-6 Deployment strategies for Windows 10 (continues)

Category	Method	Description
	In-place upgrade	Automates an in-place upgrade from Windows 8/7 to Windows 10 using a setup created by a system administrator with tools in the Microsoft Deployment Toolkit (MDT).
Dynamic deployments: Use these methods with AAD domains.		
	Subscription activation	Used to upgrade Windows 10 Pro to Windows 10 Enterprise. When a user signs in to AAD, the Windows upgrade happens automatically without user input or a restart. Product keys and Windows licensing information are kept in AAD, not on the local computer. This method creates a Windows subscription.
	Azure Active Directory join with MDM	MDM (Mobile Device Management) is software that forces devices to comply with corporate policies when they join an AAD domain.
	Provisioning packages	When a device joins AAD and MDM is not implemented, a provisioning package containing settings, apps, and data specific for the enterprise is downloaded to the device and applied with minimal input from the user. This package is easier to set up than an image, which is used in traditional deployments.
Traditional image deployments: Use these methods for on-premises AD domains when older deployment strategies are already established in the enterprise.		
	Bare metal	Also called wipe and load deployment, a standard image is created that contains the OS, drivers, applications, settings, and data specific for the enterprise. The image can be deployed on a new, empty hard drive or the drive can first be wiped clean.
	Refresh	Also called wipe and load deployment, user settings and data are saved and the hard drive is wiped clean before the standard image is applied. Then the image is applied and the user state is reinstalled.
	Replace	Used to replace an old device with a new one. After the standard image is applied to the new computer, the user state is copied from the old computer and applied to the new one.

Table 12-6 Deployment strategies for Windows 10 (continued)

METHODS TO DEPLOY A STANDARD IMAGE

A+
CORE 2
1.3

A standard image contains the entire Windows volume in a single Windows Imaging (WIM) file, which has a .wim file extension. Installing Windows on a computer via a standard image is called image deployment. Here are a few details about image deployments:

▲ A standard image is hardware independent, meaning it can be installed on any computer. (In Chapter 13, you learn to create other types of images that can only be used on the computer that created them.)

▲ A standard image is created in a process called drive imaging. Microsoft provides several tools you can use to image a drive; many are included in the MDT.

▲ Deploying a standard image always results in a clean install rather than an upgrade.

Image deployment can be started using one of these methods:

▲ *Local installation*. Your company might provide you with a bootable flash drive or DVD that contains the image. When you boot from the device, Windows Preinstallation Environment (Windows PE) is launched; this is a minimum operating system used to start the installation. Follow the on-screen instructions.

◢ *Network installation.* To boot to the network and deploy the image from a server, first go to BIOS/ UEFI setup and configure it to boot from a network device. You might need to search the motherboard documentation for help; in general, you'll need to change the following or similar settings, which are likely to be on an Advanced screen or Boot screen:

◢ Enable the Network Stack (see Figure 12-53). For the LAN controller, enable the PXE option.

◢ Disable Secure boot, Fast boot, and Quiet mode.

◢ Enable CSM support. In the CSM group, enable Boot from network devices.

◢ Change the boot priority so that an IPv4 Network boot is listed first. If you don't see it as an option, reboot after making the changes in the previous three bullets. The Network boot option should then be available.

◢ Select the Network boot option to have the computer launch the Preboot eXecution Environment or Pre-Execution Environment (PXE). The identification for the Network boot option might include IPv4 and the name of the network adapter, as shown in Figure 12-54. PXE searches for a server on the network to provide a bootable operating system (Windows PE on the deployment server).

◢ *Push automation.* A technician does not start the image deployment; rather, the installation uses push automation when a user is not likely to be sitting at the computer. The entire remote network installation is automated and no user intervention is required. The process can turn on a computer that is turned off and even works when no OS is installed on the computer or the current OS is corrupted.

Figure 12-53 Configure BIOS/UEFI setup to boot to the network

Source: American Megatrends, Inc.

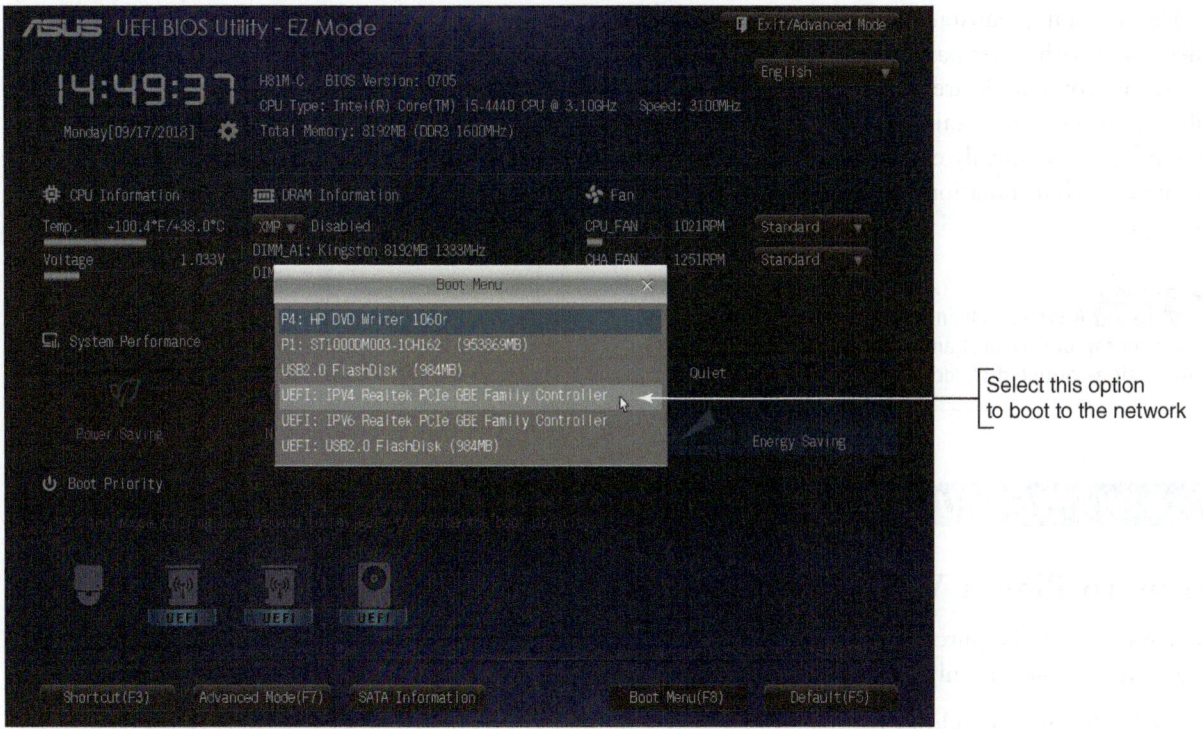

Source: American Megatrends, Inc.

Figure 12-54 When you click IPV4 Realtek PCIe GBE Family Controller, this system reboots to the network

Depending on how the system administrator has set up the deployment, you might be required to respond to questions as the installation progresses. An unattended installation does not require any responses, such as the administrator password or domain name, because these responses are stored in an answer file. After the installation completes, the User State Migration Tool might be used to transfer user settings, user data files, and application settings to the new installation.

The degree of work required by a technician to deploy an image is called high-touch, lite-touch, or zero-touch. The less involved the technician or user is, the more work is required by the system administrator to set up the deployment. For this reason, lite-touch or zero-touch deployments are only used in very large organizations.

> **Notes** IT support technicians find that large enterprises appreciate quick and easy solutions to desktop or laptop computer problems. Technicians quickly learn that their marching orders are almost always "replace or reimage." Little time is spent trying to solve the underlying problem when hardware can quickly be replaced or a Windows installation can quickly be reimaged.

USING USMT SOFTWARE

A+
CORE 2
1.3, 1.4

The User State Migration Tool (USMT) can be used when deploying Windows in a Windows domain to copy user files and settings from one computer to another. Let's look briefly at what to expect when using the following three commands, which are part of the USMT software:

▲ scanstate copies user settings and files from the source computer to a safe location.
▲ loadstate applies these settings and files to the destination computer.
▲ usmtutils provides encryption options and hard drive management.

The scanstate, loadstate, and usmtutils command lines can be lengthy and include references to .xml files along with other parameters. The details of these command lines are not covered in this text. Most likely, the commands are stored in batch files provided by the system administrator. A batch file has a .bat file extension and contains a list or batch of OS commands that are executed as a group. These batch files might be automatically executed as part of a zero-touch installation or manually executed in a lite-touch or high-touch installation. To manually execute a batch file, you type the name of the file at a command prompt.

> **✎ Notes** A system administrator uses the DISM (Deployment Image Servicing and Management) commands to initially capture (create) and manage a standard image. The DISM command also comes with Windows 10; you can use it to repair a corrupted Windows installation. You learn to use some DISM commands in Chapter 14.

>> CHAPTER SUMMARY

How to Plan a Windows Installation

▲ Windows can be purchased as a less expensive OEM version or a more expensive retail version. The OEM version can only be installed on a new computer.

▲ Each edition of Windows 10, Windows 8, and Windows 7 (except Windows 7 Starter) is available in either 32- or 64-bit versions. A 32-bit OS cannot address as much memory as a 64-bit OS. A 64-bit OS performs better and requires more memory than a 32-bit OS.

▲ Before purchasing Windows, make sure your system meets the minimum hardware requirements and that all the hardware and applications will work under the OS. A 64-bit OS requires 64-bit drivers.

▲ A hard drive contains one or more partitions or volumes and can use the MBR or GPT partitioning system. To use UEFI Secure boot, the partitioning system must be GPT and the Windows installation must be 64-bit.

▲ Normally, Windows is installed on the C: volume in the C:\Windows folder. The volume in which Windows is installed must use the NTFS file system.

▲ A computer might have legacy BIOS installed on the motherboard or have the newer UEFI firmware installed. Most UEFI firmware offers the option to support legacy BIOS when in UEFI CSM mode.

▲ Windows can be installed as an in-place upgrade, a clean installation, or in a multiboot environment with another OS.

▲ Windows can be installed from the setup DVD, a USB flash drive, files downloaded from the Internet via the Media Creation Tool, or in a virtual machine.

Installing Windows 10, Windows 8.1, and Windows 7

▲ A technician needs to know how to perform an in-place upgrade, a clean install, or a multiboot with Windows.

▲ The steps for installing or upgrading Windows 8.1 are about the same as those for Windows 10.

▲ A clean install is the best option to use if the current installation is sluggish or giving problems, or if you're installing Windows on a new desktop computer that you're building.

▲ In a multiboot, each OS must be installed on its own partition. Make sure you have enough free space on a partition before installing Windows on it, and make sure it doesn't currently hold an OS.

What to Do After a Windows Installation

▲ After a Windows installation, verify network access, activate Windows, install any Windows updates or Windows 7 service packs, verify that automatic updates are configured correctly, install hardware and applications, create user accounts and transfer or restore user data and preferences from backups, and turn Windows features on or off.

▲ Virtual machine software can provide multiple instances of operating systems for training users, running legacy software, and supporting multiple operating systems.

Special Concerns When Working in a Large Enterprise

▲ Three types of deployments for installing Windows in a large enterprise are modern deployments, dynamic deployments, and traditional image deployments. Modern deployments are done using Active Directory or Azure Active Directory, dynamic deployments use AAD, and traditional deployments use AD.

▲ Zero-touch deployments require the most time to set up, but do not require a technician to be at the computer when the installation happens.

>> KEY TERMS

For explanations of key terms, see the Glossary for this text.

active hours
administrator account
answer file
batch file
BIOS (basic input/output system)
boot loader menu
boot priority order
clean install
custom installation
default product key
device drivers
Device Manager
digital license
diskpart
DISM (Deployment Image Servicing and Management)
drive imaging
driver rollback
dual boot
file system

full format
GUID Partition Table (GPT)
hardware signature
hot-swappable
hypervisor
image deployment
in-place upgrade
ISO file
ISO image
loadstate
local account
Master Boot Record (MBR)
Media Creation Tool
Microsoft account
Microsoft Deployment Toolkit (MDT)
multiboot
Original Equipment Manufacturer (OEM) license

Preboot eXecution Environment
Pre-Execution Environment (PXE)
product activation
product key
Programs and Features
provisioning package
push automation
quick format
remote network installation
scanstate
Secure boot
service pack
setup BIOS/UEFI
single sign-on (SSO)
solid-state drive
standard account
standard image
startup BIOS/UEFI
system BIOS/UEFI

third-party drivers
UEFI (Unified Extensible Firmware Interface)
UEFI CSM (Compatibility Support Module) mode
unattended installation
upgrade paths
User Account Control (UAC) dialog box
User State Migration Tool (USMT)
usmtutils
virtual machine (VM)
volume
Windows Defender Antivirus
Windows.old folder
Windows Preinstallation Environment (Windows PE)

>> THINKING CRITICALLY

These questions are designed to prepare you for the critical thinking required for the A+ exams and may use content from other chapters and the web.

1. You are planning an upgrade from Windows 8.1 to Windows 10. Your system uses a network card that you don't find on the Microsoft Windows 10 list of compatible devices. What do you do next?

a. Abandon the upgrade and continue to use Windows 8.1.

b. Check the website of the network card manufacturer for a Windows 10 driver.

c. Buy a new network card.

d. Install a dual boot for Windows 8.1 and Windows 10 and only use the network when you have Windows 8.1 loaded.

2. You have just installed Windows 10 and now want to install your favorite game that worked fine under Windows 8.1. When you attempt the installation, you get an error. What is your best next step?

a. Purchase a new version of your game—one that is compatible with Windows 10.

b. Download any updates to Windows 10.

c. Reinstall Windows 8.1.

d. Install a VM running Windows 8.1.

3. You have 32-bit Windows 8.1 installed on your computer, and you purchase a license for Windows 10 Pro. You want to install Windows 10 using the 64-bit architecture. In which way(s) can you install Windows 10?

a. You can perform an upgrade, but not a clean install.

b. You can perform an upgrade or a clean install.

c. You can perform a clean install, but not an upgrade.

d. None of the above

4. A laptop reports that it has made a wireless network connection but cannot access the network or the Internet. Arrange the following steps in the best order to troubleshoot the problem:

a. Use Device Manager to uninstall the wireless adapter and install it again.

b. Disable and enable the wireless network adapter.

c. Disconnect the connection and connect again to the wireless network.

d. Use Device Manager to update the wireless adapter drivers.

5. Which installation of Windows 10 requires you to enter a product key during the install process?

a. You are replacing a failed hard drive that already had Windows 10 installed.

b. You are replacing a failed motherboard on a system with Windows 10 installed and a Microsoft account was not used to sign in to Windows.

c. You are replacing a failed motherboard on a system with Windows 10 installed and a Microsoft account had been used to sign in to Windows.

d. Windows 10 has become corrupted and you decide to perform a clean install to recover the OS.

6. Which of the following methods can you use to install Windows 10 in a VM? Select all that apply.

a. Clean install from an ISO image

b. Clean install from a USB flash drive

c. Upgrade from Windows 8 using an ISO image

d. Clean install from a setup DVD

7. Suppose you want to boot a VM from its virtual DVD drive, but it boots to the VM's hard drive. Which of the following could be the source of this problem? Select all that apply.

a. There is no DVD or ISO file mounted to the virtual DVD drive.

b. The virtual DVD drive is not enabled.

c. The boot sequence is not correct in the VM's BIOS/UEFI settings.

d. The hard drive does not have an OS installed.

8. You are setting up a Windows 10 desktop computer that requires 4 TB of storage. Which options work (select all that apply)? Which option is the recommended best practice?

a. Install one 3-TB hard drive with the MBR partitioning system and 64-bit Windows 10.

b. Install two 1.5-TB hard drives with the GPT partitioning systems and 32-bit Windows 10.

c. Install two 1.5-TB hard drives with the MBR partitioning systems and 64-bit Windows 10.

d. Install two 1.5-TB hard drives with the GPT partitioning systems and 64-bit Windows 10.

9. If you suspect a computer is infected with a virus and you are ready to upgrade from Windows 8 to Windows 10, what is your best practice?

a. Perform a clean install of Windows 10 rather than an upgrade.

b. Scan the system for malware before you perform the Windows 10 upgrade.

c. Install Windows 8 as an in-place upgrade to remediate the system and then upgrade to Windows 10.

d. Completely erase the hard drive with a full format and then install Windows 10.

10. After setting up a dual-boot installation with Windows 8 and Windows 10, how do you boot the system into Windows 8?

a. Start the system as normal; the oldest OS automatically loads.

b. Start the system as normal; the newest OS automatically loads.

c. Start the system and select the OS in the boot loader menu.

d. Go into BIOS/UEFI setup and set the boot priority order to start with Windows 8.

11. After a Windows installation, what is the easiest way to determine that you have Internet access?

a. Open the Network and Sharing Center and verify that Wi-Fi is turned on and shows no errors.

b. Open Internet Explorer and browse to a website.

c. Open Device Manager and check the network adapter for errors.

d. Verify that the local router has lights blinking to indicate connectivity.

12. After installing the device drivers for a video adapter, you still are not able to use the special features of the adapter. What is your next step?

a. Open Device Manager and check for errors.

b. Uninstall the adapter and try the installation again.

c. Update Windows.

d. Check the website of the video adapter's manufacturer for guidance.

13. The PXE programming code is used to boot a computer when it is searching for an OS on the network. Where is this code stored?

a. On the deployment server

b. On the motherboard

    c. On the Windows volume of the local hard drive

    d. In the cloud in Azure Active Directory

14. What is an advantage of using a dynamic hard drive in a VM?

15. Ming is building an inexpensive computer to use for her online classes, and needs to purchase Windows. What is the most cost-effective way Ming can purchase and activate a selected version of Windows?

>> HANDS-ON PROJECTS

Hands-On | Project 12-1   Installing 64-Bit Windows 10 Pro

Use the Media Creation Tool to download Windows 10 setup files, and then install 64-bit Windows 10 Pro on your lab computer. If you need help with the installation, see the directions in the chapter. Set up Windows to use a local account to sign in to Windows. Write down each decision you have to make as you perform the installation. If you get any error messages during the installation, write them down and list the steps you took to recover from them. How long did the installation take?

Hands-On | Project 12-2   Using the Internet for Problem Solving

Access the *support.microsoft.com* website for Windows 10 support. Print one article from the Knowledge Base that addresses a problem when installing Windows 10. In your own words, write a paragraph describing the problem and a paragraph explaining the solution. If you don't understand the problem or the solution from this article, do a search online for additional information so that you can give a well-rounded description of both the problem and the solution.

Hands-On | Project 12-3   Installing Windows 8.1 in a VM

This project assumes you already have 64-bit Windows 10 Pro installed on a computer. Do the following:

    1. Enable Client Hyper-V and set up a VM in it.

    2. Using the Media Creation Tool, create an ISO file to install Windows 8.1 in the VM.

    3. Verify that you can use Internet Explorer in the VM to surf the web.

Hands-On | Project 12-4 Installing Windows 10 in a VM as a Dual Boot

This project assumes you already have 64-bit Windows 10 Pro installed and a VM with Windows 8.1 installed on a computer. Do the following:

1. Using the Media Creation Tool, create an ISO file to install Windows 10 in the VM.

2. Open the VM you already created with Windows 8.1 installed and create a second partition with at least 16 GB.

3. Mount the Windows 10 ISO file to the VM. In the Settings app for the Windows 8.1 VM, change the firmware settings to boot from a file. Restart the Windows 8.1 VM and install Windows 10 as a dual boot on the partition you just created.

4. Verify that you can use Microsoft Edge in the VM to surf the web.

Hands-On | Project 12-5 Recommended Updates

On a Windows 10 system connected to the Internet, open the **Settings** app and click the **Update & security** group. Under *Looking for info on the latest updates?*, click **Learn more**. Windows Update opens the Microsoft website and recommends Windows updates. Print the webpage showing a list of recommended updates. Then, on a Windows 8.1 system connected to the Internet, open the System window and click **Windows Update**. Windows Update searches the Microsoft website and recommends Windows updates. Print the webpage showing a list of recommended updates. For a lab computer, don't perform the updates unless you have your instructor's permission.

12

Hands-On | Project 12-6 Creating a Documentation Form

Support technicians are expected to maintain documentation for each computer for which they are responsible. Create a document that a technician can use when installing Windows and performing all the chores mentioned in the chapter that are needed before and after the installation. The document needs a checklist of what to do before the installation and a checklist of what to do after the installation. It also needs a place to record decisions made during the installation, the applications and hardware devices installed, user accounts created, and any other important information that might be useful for future maintenance or troubleshooting. Don't forget to include a way to identify the computer, the name of the technician doing the work, and when the work was done.

>> REAL PROBLEMS, REAL SOLUTIONS

REAL PROBLEM 12-1 Recovering Data from a Corrupted Windows Installation

As an IT support technician for a small organization, it's your job to support the computers, the small network, and the users. One of your coworkers, Jason, comes to you in a panic. His Windows 10 system won't boot, and he has lots of important data files in several locations on the drive. He has no idea which folders hold the files. Besides the application data he's currently working on, he's especially concerned about losing email addresses, email, and his Internet Explorer Favorites links.

After trying everything you know about recovering Windows 10, you conclude the OS is corrupted beyond repair. You decide there might be a way to remove the hard drive from Jason's computer and connect it to another computer so that you can recover the data. Search the Internet and find a device that you can use to connect Jason's hard drive to another computer through one of its USB ports. The hard drive uses a SATA hard drive interface. Print the webpage showing the device and its price.

REAL PROBLEM 12-2 Troubleshooting an Upgrade

Your friend, Thomas, has upgraded his Windows 8.1 desktop to Windows 10. After the installation, he discovers his media card reader does not work. He calls you on the phone and asks you what to do. Do the following to plan your troubleshooting approach:

1. List the questions you should ask Thomas to help diagnose the problem.

2. List the steps you would take if you were sitting at the computer solving the problem.

3. What do you think is the source of the problem? Explain your answer.

CHAPTER

13

Maintaining Windows

After completing this chapter, you will be able to:

- Set up and perform scheduled preventive maintenance tasks to keep Windows healthy

- Prepare for disaster by keeping good backups of user data, the Windows volume, and Windows system files

- Use Windows tools, including Disk Management, to manage hard drives

- Use commands to manage files, folders, and hard drives

- Connect to remote computers for screen and file sharing

E arlier in the text, you learned how to install Windows. This chapter takes you to the next step in learning how to support a Windows operating system: maintaining the OS after it is installed. Most Windows problems stem from poor maintenance. If you are an IT support technician responsible for the ongoing support of several computers, you can make your work easier and your users happier by setting up and executing a good maintenance plan for each computer you support. A well-maintained computer gives fewer problems and performs better than one that is not maintained. In this chapter, you learn how to schedule regular maintenance tasks, prepare for disaster by setting up backup routines for user data and system files, use Windows tools and commands to manage files, folders, and hard drives, and remotely access computers so that you can share screens and files.

This text covers Windows 10, 8.1, 8.0, and 7. As you read, you might consider following the steps in the chapter using a Windows 10 system, and then going through the steps again using a Windows 8 or Windows 7 system.

SCHEDULING PREVENTIVE MAINTENANCE

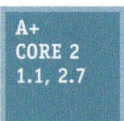

Regular preventive maintenance can keep a Windows computer performing well for years. At least once a month, you need to verify critical Windows settings and clean up the hard drive. These skills are covered in this part of the chapter. If you notice the system is slow as you do this maintenance, you need to dig deeper to improve Windows performance, which is covered in Chapter 14.

> ✎ **Notes** When you're responsible for a computer, be sure to keep good records of all that you do to maintain, upgrade, or fix it. When performing preventive maintenance, take notes and include them in your documentation. The Computer Inventory and Maintenance document available at *cengage.com* can help you organize your notes.

VERIFYING CRITICAL WINDOWS SETTINGS

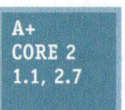

The Windows settings discussed here are critical for keeping the system protected from malware and hackers. Users sometimes change these settings without realizing their importance. Check the following settings; if you find they are incorrect, take time to explain to the computer's primary user how important they are. Here are the critical Windows settings you need to verify:

- ▲ *Windows updates.* Install any important Windows updates or Windows 7 service packs that are waiting to be installed and verify that Windows Update is configured to automatically allow updating. These updates may include updates to Windows, applications, device drivers, and firmware. You learned how to configure Windows Update in Chapter 12.
- ▲ *Antivirus/anti-malware software.* To protect a system against a malicious attack, you need to verify that anti-malware software is configured to scan the system regularly and that it is up to date. If you discover it is not scanning regularly, take the time to do a thorough scan for viruses. For Windows 10/8, Windows Defender is running in the background. To verify this, follow the directions in Chapter 12.
- ▲ *Network security setting.* To secure the computer against attack from the network, use the Network and Sharing Center to check that the network security type is set correctly for the optimum firewall settings. The network types are public and private in Windows 10/8, and public, work, and home in Windows 7. How to verify the network type was covered in Chapter 11. Further details of configuring network security in Windows are discussed in Chapter 16.
- ▲ *Backups of user data, the Windows volume, and system files.* Following directions given later in the chapter, verify that backup routines are running as expected to protect data and software from loss or corruption.

To keep Windows performing well, do the following:

- ▲ *Uninstall software you no longer need.* This helps overall performance by reducing the number of startup processes running in the background. To uninstall software, use the Windows 10/8 Apps & Features window or the Windows 10/8/7 Programs and Features window. Also, for Windows 10/8, turn off live tiles you don't watch.
- ▲ *Clean up the hard drive.* A hard drive needs at least 15 percent free space on drive C:, where Windows is installed. Later in the chapter, you learn how to use Disk Cleanup to erase unnecessary files on drive C:. You can also move data on the drive to other media.

> ✎ **Notes** Don't forget that what you learn about maintaining Windows also applies to Windows in a VM. When maintaining a VM, make sure Windows in a VM is updated, anti-malware software is installed and running, and network settings are secure.

PATCH MANAGEMENT

When researching a problem, suppose you discover that Microsoft or a manufacturer's website offers a fix or patch for Windows, a device driver, or an application. To download and apply compatible software, you need to make sure you get a 32-bit patch for a 32-bit installation of Windows, a device driver, or an application. For a 64-bit installation of Windows, make sure you get a 64-bit device driver. An application installed in a 64-bit OS might be a 32-bit application or a 64-bit application.

The documentation on the Microsoft website or other sites might be cryptic about the type of patch. Follow these guidelines when reading error messages or documentation:

◢ The term *x86* refers to 32-bit CPUs or processors and to 32-bit operating systems. For example, the Microsoft website might say a patch to fix a problem with a USB device applies to a Windows 10, x86-based version. This means the patch is for a 32-bit version of Windows 10.

◢ The term *x64* refers to 64-bit operating systems. For example, Microsoft offers two versions of Windows 10: the x86 version and the x64 version.

◢ All CPUs installed in personal computers today are hybrid processors that can process either 32 bits or 64 bits. The term *x86-64* refers to these processors, such as the Intel Core i5 or an AMD Ryzen processor. (AMD64 refers specifically to these hybrid AMD processors.) The term x86-64 can also refer to a 64-bit OS. For example, a Windows message might read, "You are attempting to load an x86-64 operating system." Take that to mean you are attempting to load a 64-bit OS on a computer that has a hybrid 32-bit/64-bit processor installed, such as the Ryzen 5 1500x or Intel Core i5-7500.

◢ The term *IA64* refers specifically to 64-bit Intel processors such as the Xeon or Itanium, which is used in servers or high-end workstations.

> ★ **A+ Exam Tip** The A+ Core 2 exam expects you to know the difference between 32-bit and 64-bit operating systems and, when given a scenario, to select compatible software for patch management.

Now let's look at how to perform on-demand backups and how to schedule routine backups.

BACKUP PROCEDURES

A backup is an extra copy of a data file or software file that you can use if the original file is damaged or destroyed. Losing data due to system failure, a virus, file corruption, or some other problem really makes you appreciate the importance of having backups.

> ✎ **Notes** With data and software, here's a good rule of thumb: If you can't get along without it, back it up.

APPLYING | CONCEPTS   BACKUPS PAY OFF

Dave was well on his way to building a successful career as an IT support technician. His IT tech support shop was doing well, and he was excited about his future. But one bad decision changed everything. He was called to repair a server at a small accounting firm. The call was on the weekend when he was normally off, so he was in a hurry to get the job done. He arrived at the accounting firm and saw that the problem was an easy one to fix, so he decided not to do a backup before working on the system. During his repairs, the hard drive crashed and all data on the drive was lost—four million dollars' worth! The firm sued, Dave's business license was stripped, and he was ordered to pay the money the company lost. A little extra time to back up the system would have saved his whole future. True story!

13

Because most of us routinely write data to the hard drive, this section focuses on backing up from the hard drive to other media. However, when you store important data on any medium—such as a flash drive, external hard drive, CD, or in the cloud—always keep a copy of the data on another device or in the cloud. Never trust important data to only one location.

In this part of the chapter, you learn how to make a disaster recovery plan and then learn how to use Windows to back up user data, entire volumes, and critical Windows system files.

PLANNING FOR DISASTER RECOVERY

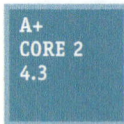

The time to prepare for disaster is before it occurs. If you have not prepared, the damage from a disaster will most likely be greater than if you had made and followed disaster recovery plans. Suppose the hard drive on your computer stopped working and you lost all its data. What would be the impact? Are you prepared for this to happen? Here are decisions you need to make for your backup and recovery plans:

▲ *Decide on the type of backup.* Different backup types include different kinds of data:

   ▲ You might back up single files or folders, in which case you might also have access to previous versions of a file; this is called a file-level backup and allows granular control over which content is included in the backup and which content can be recovered on a file-by-file basis. File-level backups are appropriate for backing up user data, but generally are not considered good options for backing up applications and Windows.

   ▲ You might back up an entire volume of a drive, called an image-level backup. Restoring from an image-level backup would also restore your OS installation, applications, user account settings, and user data. However, the process restores the entire backup image and does not allow selecting portions of the backup separately.

   ▲ You might need a separate backup plan for critical applications, which are any applications required to keep a business functioning while other backup solutions are being used to recover from any data loss. Consider cloud solutions or virtualization options as backups for critical applications such as email, databases, or office productivity software.

▲ *Decide on the backup destination.* For example, for a personal computer or small network, options include backup to a cloud, network drive, CD, DVD, Blu-ray, SD card, USB flash drive, external hard drive, or other media. Here are points to keep in mind:

   ▲ A cloud storage backup service such as Carbonite (*carbonite.com*), Backblaze (*backblaze.com*), Amazon Drive (*amazon.com/amazondrive*), Google Drive (*drive.google.com*), or iCloud Drive (*icloud.com*) is the easiest, most reliable, and most expensive solution. You pay a yearly subscription for the service, and it guarantees your backups, which are automatically done when your computer is connected to the Internet. If you decide to use one of these services, be sure to restore files from backup occasionally to make sure your backups are happening as you expect and that you can recover a lost file.

   ▲ Local storage backups are relatively inexpensive and convenient, in that data is easily accessible at your location. This method might present a problem, however, if a catastrophic event, such as a fire or flood, destroys the building where your original data and backups are all located. For this reason, always keep backups at an off-site location.

   ▲ Even though it's easy to do, don't make the mistake of backing up your data to another volume or folder on the same hard drive. When a hard drive crashes, most likely all volumes go down together and you will lose your data and your backup. Back up to another device and, for extra safety, store it at an off-site location.

> ✎ **Notes** For individuals or small networks, backups to the cloud are generally more expensive than backing up to a local server or external hard drive. For large networks, storing data in the cloud, such as Google Cloud or Amazon Web Services, can save money over buying and maintaining backup storage solutions on location.

◢ *Decide on the backup software.* Windows offers one or more backup utilities. However, you can purchase third-party backup software that might offer more features. Read reviews about the software and consider:

   ◢ Hard drive manufacturers often bundle backup software with a new hard drive or you can download the software from the manufacturer's website.

   ◢ What does the software back up? Files or the entire image of a volume?

   ◢ Does the software provide a way to boot from backup media so you can easily access the backups when the hard drive crashes?

   ◢ Can you schedule when backups occur?

   ◢ Does the software support backing up to a remote location, such as a different branch office where you can easily access the backups?

◢ *Decide how simple or complex your backup strategy needs to be.* A backup and recovery plan for individuals or small organizations might be very simple. However, large organizations might require that backups be documented each day and scheduled at certain times of the day or night, and recovery plans might have to be tested on a regular basis. Know the requirements of your organization when creating a backup and recovery plan. As a general rule of thumb, back up data for at least every 4 to 6 hours of data entry. This might mean a backup needs to occur twice a day, daily, weekly, or monthly. Find out the data entry habits of workers before making your backup schedule and deciding on the folders or volumes to back up.

◢ *Consider ways of ensuring business continuity.* Not all disasters are directly related to data loss. A loss of power or Internet connection can also interfere with business productivity, and physical or electrical damage to computer or network hardware is another significant concern. Plugging a computer's power cord into a surge protector can protect against voltage spikes by blocking or grounding excessive voltage. An uninterruptible power supply (UPS) can be strategically placed on the network to supply power when voltage drops during brownouts or short-term blackouts and ensure that routers, switches, and servers keep running during a power outage. See Figure 13-1. Also consider physical security to protect against theft or vandalism. You can learn more about surge protectors and UPS devices in Appendix A, and you'll learn more about physical security in Chapter 17.

13

Figure 13-1 A UPS protects a desktop computer, server, or network devices from low voltages and blackouts

Source: amazon.com

After you have a backup plan working, test the recovery plan. In addition, you need to occasionally retest the recovery plan to make sure all is still working as you expect. Do the following:

◢ *Test the recovery process.* Erase a file on the hard drive, and use the recovery procedures to verify that you can re-create the file from the backup. This test also verifies that the backup medium works, that the recovery software is effective, and that you know how to use it. After you are convinced that the recovery works, document how to perform it.

◢ *Keep backups in a safe place and routinely test them.* Don't leave a backup DVD or other media lying around for someone to steal. Backups of important and sensitive data should be kept under lock and key at an off-site location. In case of fire, keep enough backups off-site so that you can recover data even if the entire building is destroyed. Routinely verify that your backups are good by performing a test recovery of a backed-up file or folder. Backups are useless if the data on the backup is corrupted.

> ✏️ **Notes** One reason that organizations use cloud solutions, such as Microsoft Azure, Google Cloud, and Amazon Web Services, is that work can be done from any location by signing in to the online service where applications and data are kept in the cloud. Cloud computing greatly eliminates the need for an organization to maintain its own backups and still be protected against local catastrophic events.

Now let's see how to back up user data, the entire Windows volume, and important Windows system files.

BACKING UP USER DATA AND THE SYSTEM IMAGE

A+ CORE 2 4.3

Here are the tools offered by Windows 10/8/7 for backups:

- ◢ Windows 10 offers File History or Backup and Restore to back up user data and create a system image.
- ◢ Windows 8 uses File History but not Backup and Restore. In addition, Windows 8 offers the recimg command to create a custom refresh image, which is a type of system image.
- ◢ Windows 7 offers Backup and Restore to back up user data and to create a system image.

A system image is a backup of the entire Windows volume, including the Windows installation, applications, user settings, and data. The best time to create the image is right after you've installed Windows, hardware, applications, and user accounts and customized Windows settings. The image is stored in a single file with a .wim file extension. The WIM file uses the Windows Imaging File (WIM) format and is a compressed file that contains many related files.

Next, let's see how these backup tools work.

WINDOWS 10/8 FILE HISTORY

Windows 10/8 File History backs up user data stored in the Documents, Music, Pictures, Videos, and Desktop folders, as well as offline OneDrive files (for Microsoft accounts) and other folders as determined by the user. When the backup is enabled, it first makes a full backup to another medium. By default, it scans for file and folder changes every hour and keeps as many generations of backups as free space allows on the storage device.

Follow these steps to use File History on a Windows 10 computer:

1. First connect your backup device. In the Settings app, click **Update & Security**, then click **Backup**. When you click **Add a drive**, Windows searches for a usable drive. Select the drive or click **Show all network locations** to find and select a drive on the network. File History connects to the drive and turns on.

2. To manage these backups, click **More options**. On the Backup options window shown in Figure 13-2, you can set how often backups are made (every 10 minutes up to daily), how long old backups should be kept (forever, until space is needed, 1 month, 1 year, and so forth), and which folders to back up.

Figure 13-2 Backup options for File History

File History can also be accessed through Control Panel (see Figure 13-3). Click items in the left pane to turn File History on or off, change File History settings, and restore files from backup. Using the File History window in Control Panel, you can click System Image Backup (see Figure 13-3) to start the process of creating a system image.

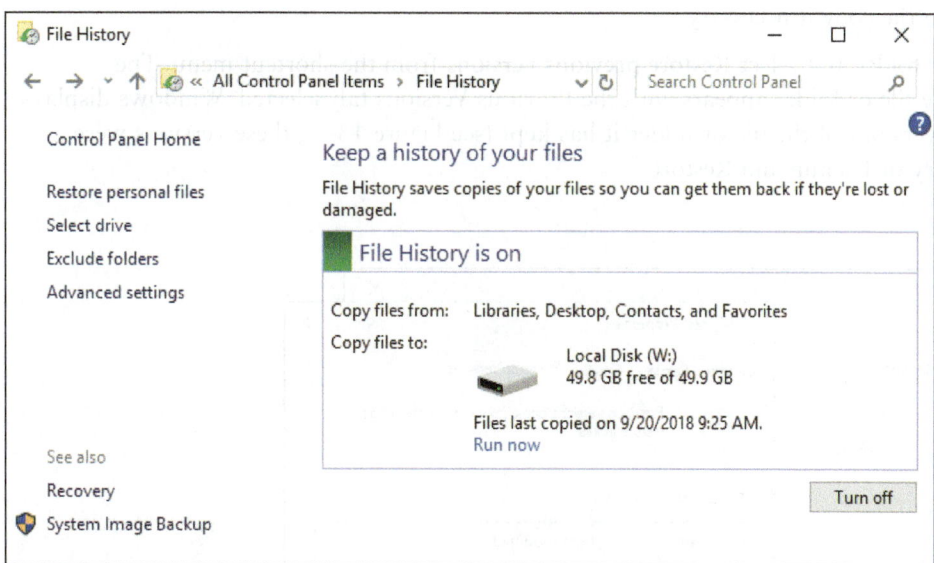

Figure 13-3   Control File History settings and restore files from backup

★ A+ Exam Tip   The A+ Core 2 exam might give you a scenario that expects you to create, use, and test backups.

RESTORE FILES AND FOLDERS IN FILE HISTORY

To restore a file or folder from backup, open the **File History** window from Control Panel and click **Restore personal files**. You can view and recover items from the backups (see Figure 13-4). Use the left and right arrow keys on either side of the green **Restore** button at the bottom of the window to select a backup, and then drill down into the backup to find the file or folder you need. Select an item to see a preview, and then click the **Restore** button to restore the item. If you prefer to save the previous version in a different location so as not to overwrite the newest version of the file, right-click the **Restore** button and click **Restore to**. Navigate to the location where you want to save the previous version and then click **Select Folder**.

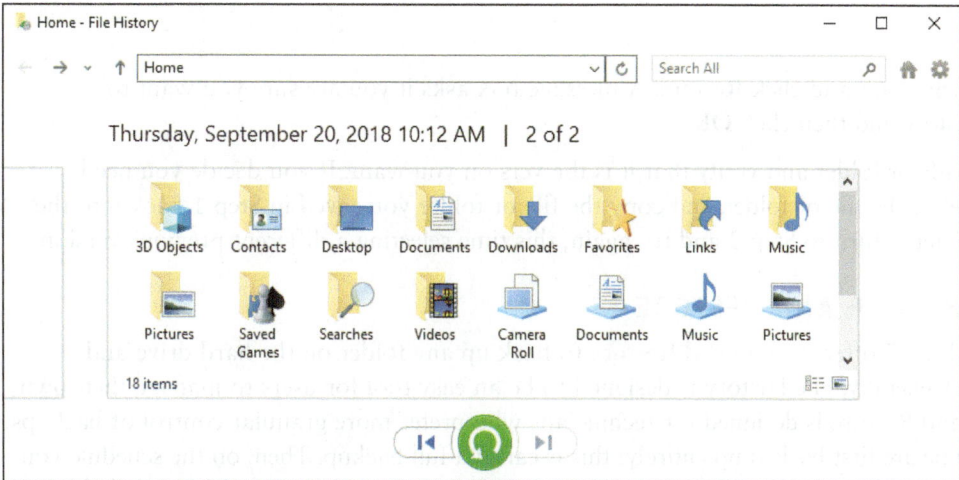

Figure 13-4   Drill down into backups to find what you want to restore

Another way to restore a file or folder from backup is to use File Explorer or Windows Explorer. Follow these steps:

1. When you restore a file or folder to a previous version, the current file or folder can be overwritten by the previous version. To keep the original, first copy—not move—the folder or file to a new location so that you can revert to the copy if necessary.

2. Right-click the file or folder and select **Restore previous versions** from the shortcut menu. The Properties box for the file or folder appears with the Previous Versions tab selected. Windows displays a list of all previous versions of the file or folder it has kept (see Figure 13-5); these versions were created by File History or Backup and Restore.

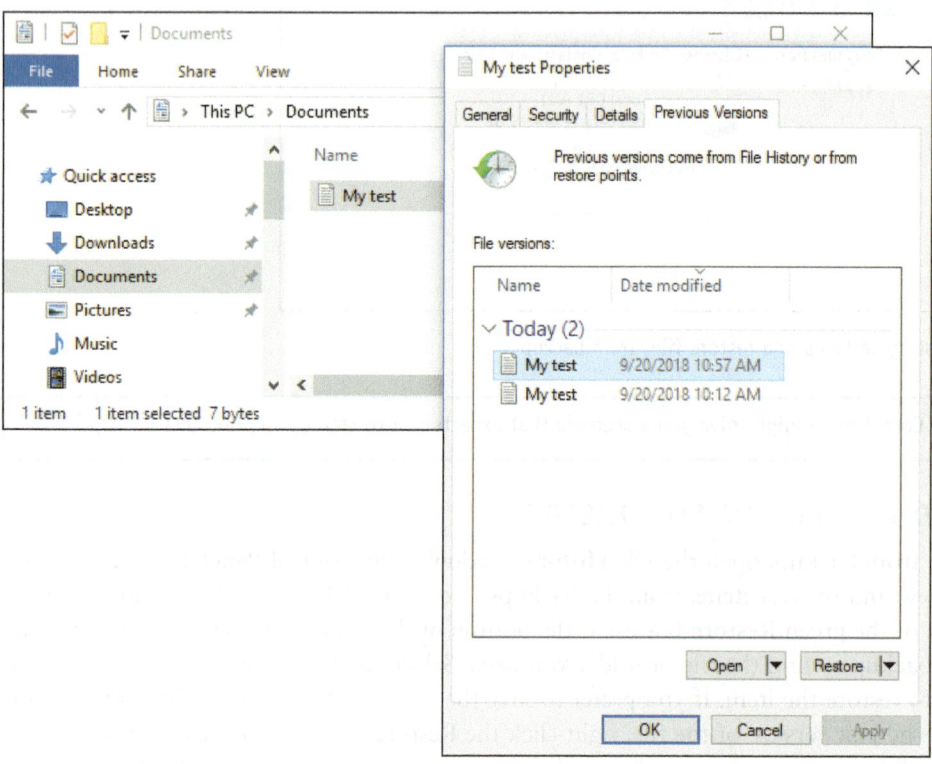

Figure 13-5   Restore a file or folder from a previous version

3. Select the version you want and click **Restore**. A message box asks if you are sure you want to continue. Click **Restore** and then click **OK**.

4. Open the restored file or folder and verify that it is the version you want. If you decide you need another version, delete the file or folder, and copy the file or folder you saved in Step 1 back into the original location. Then return to Step 2 and try again, this time selecting a different previous version.

WINDOWS 10/7 BACKUP AND RESTORE

Windows 10 and Windows 7 offer Backup and Restore to back up any folder on the hard drive and create a system image. Generally, File History is designed to be an easy tool for users to manage their own backups, and Backup and Restore is designed for technicians who prefer more granular control of backups.

The folders and volume are first backed up entirely; this is called a full backup. Then, on the schedule you set, any file or folder is backed up if it has changed or been created since the last backup. This is called an incremental backup. Occasionally, Windows does another full backup. If you've established a backup schedule in File History on a Windows 10 machine, those settings will appear in the Backup and Restore window.

Follow these steps to save a backup and set up an ongoing backup schedule using Backup and Restore in Windows 10:

1. Open Control Panel in Classic view, and click **Backup and Restore**. If no backup has ever been scheduled on the system, the window will look like the one shown in Figure 13-6. Click **Set up backup**.

Figure 13-6   Use the Backup and Restore window to schedule backups

2. In the next dialog box, select the device or location to hold the backup. All Windows 10 editions and Windows 7 Professional, Ultimate, and Enterprise editions allow you to save the backup to a network location. To use a shared folder on the network for the backup destination, click **Save on a network**. In the resulting box, click **Browse** and point to the folder. See Figure 13-7. Also enter the user name and password on the remote computer that the backup utility will use to authenticate to that computer when it makes the backup. You cannot save to a network location when using Windows 7 Home editions. For these editions, the *Save on a network* button is missing in the window where you select the backup destination.

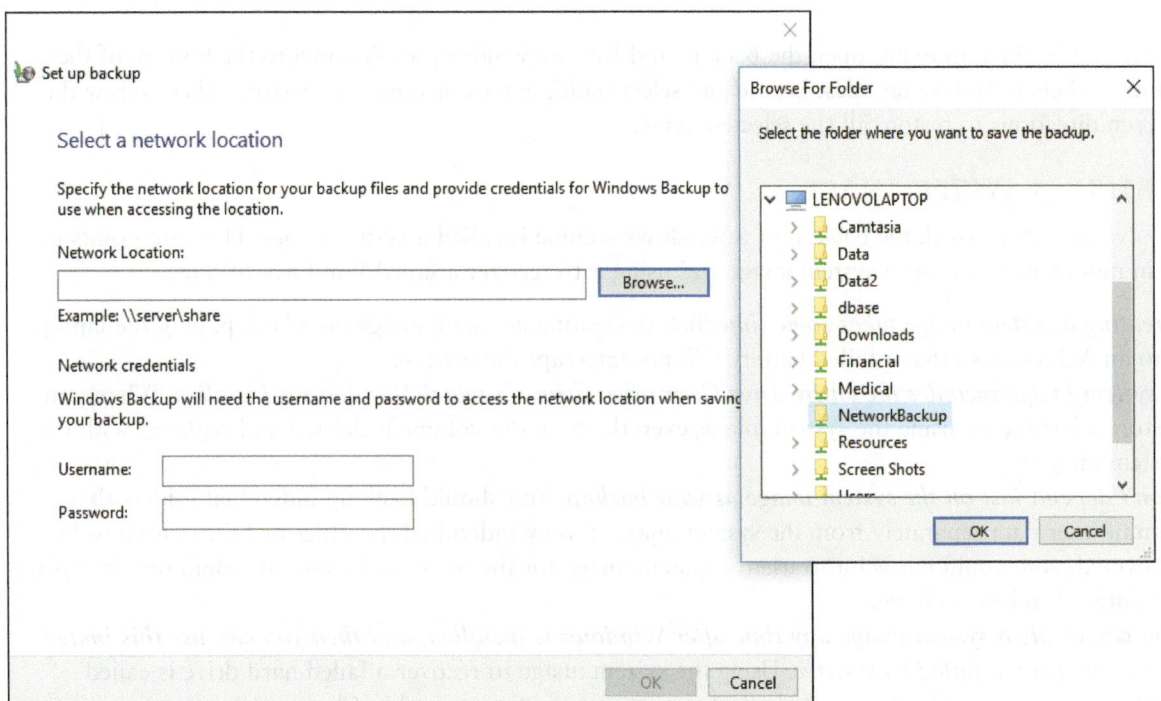

Figure 13-7   Point to a shared folder on the network to hold the backups

13

3. In the next box, you can allow Windows to decide what to back up or choose for yourself. Select **Let me choose** so that you can select the folders to back up. Click **Next**.

4. In the next box, make your selections. If the backup medium can hold the system image, the option to include the image is selected by default. If you don't want to include the image, uncheck the option. Click **Next** to continue. Here are folders that might contain important user data:

   ◢ Application data is usually found in C:\Users*username*\AppData.

   ◢ Internet Explorer favorites are in C:\Users*username*\Favorites.

   ◢ Better still, back up the entire user profile at C:\Users*username*.

   ◢ Even better, back up all user profiles at C:\Users.

5. In the next box, you can verify that the correct items are selected. To change the default schedule, click **Change schedule**. In the next box, you can choose to run the backup daily, weekly, or monthly and select the time of day. Make your selections and click **OK**.

6. Review your backup settings, and click **Save settings and run backup**. The backup proceeds. A shadow copy is made of any open files so that they are included in the backup.

Later, you can return to the Backup and Restore window to change the backup settings or to turn off the backup.

> ✎ **Notes** One limitation of Windows File History and Backup and Restore is that you can have only one scheduled backup routine.

> ✎ **Notes** After Windows does a full backup, it only backs up files that have changed since the last full backup. Occasionally, it does another full backup. Each full backup is called a backup period. Windows keeps as many backup periods as it has space on the backup device. As free space fills, it deletes the oldest backup periods. To see how space is used on your backup media, click **Manage space** in the Backup and Restore window. In the Manage Windows Backup disk space, you can click **View backups** to delete a backup period, but be sure to keep the most recent backup periods.

To recover backed-up items, open the Backup and Restore window, scroll down to the bottom of the window, and click **Restore my files**. Locate and select multiple files or folders to restore. Then follow the on-screen directions to restore all the selected items.

MAINTAIN A SYSTEM IMAGE

As you've already learned, the backup of a Windows volume is called a system image. Here are points to keep in mind when creating a system image and using it to recover a failed Windows volume:

◢ *Creating a system image takes some time*. Before creating a system image on a laptop, plug the laptop into an AC outlet so that a failed battery will not interrupt the process.

◢ *A system image includes the entire drive C: or other drive on which Windows is installed*. When you restore a hard drive using the system image, everything on the volume is deleted and replaced with the system image.

◢ *Don't depend just on the system image as your backup*. You should back up individual folders that contain user data separately from the system image. If only individual data files or folders need to be recovered, you would not want to use the system image for the recovery because it would totally replace the entire Windows volume.

◢ *You can create a system image any time after Windows is installed, and then you can use this image to recover from a failed hard drive*. Using the system image to recover a failed hard drive is called reimaging the drive. The details of how to reimage a drive are covered in Chapter 15.

WINDOWS | 8 CUSTOM REFRESH IMAGE

A **custom refresh image** was intended to replace the Windows 7 system image. However, it was not as popular, so the recimg command used to create a custom refresh image is not included in Windows 10.

Here are the steps to create a Windows 8 custom refresh image:

1. Open an elevated command prompt window. One way to do so is to press **Win+X** and click **Command Prompt (Admin)**. Respond to the UAC box. The Administrator: Command Prompt window opens.

2. Enter the following command, substituting a drive and folder for the sample path shown:

   `recimg /createimage D:\MyImage`

Creating the image takes some time, and then the image and its location are registered as the **active recovery image**. The image is stored in a large .wim file that you can view using File Explorer. You can create as many refresh images as you like, but only one is designated as the active recovery image, and it's the one that will be used when you refresh the Windows 8 installation. How to perform a Windows 8 refresh is covered in Chapter 15.

The recimg command can also be used to manage refresh images. The parameters for the command are listed in Table 13-1.

Command	Result
recimg /createimage <path>	Creates the refresh image and registers its location as the active refresh image
recimg /showcurrent	Displays the location of the active refresh image
recimg /deregister	Deregisters the active recovery image; during the refresh process, Windows will not find an image and will revert to a hidden recovery partition on the hard drive or the Windows 8 setup files for the refresh
recimg /setcurrent <path>	Registers a refresh image in the path given; the image at this location is now the active refresh image

Table 13-1 The recimg command and parameters

Suppose you've created multiple refresh images and you want to select a particular image for a refresh. Figure 13-8 shows the commands you can use to change the active refresh image from the one stored in the D:\MyImage folder to one stored in the D:\MyImage2 folder.

Notes Because a refresh image must be named CustomRefresh.wim, you must store each image in a separate folder.

(continues)

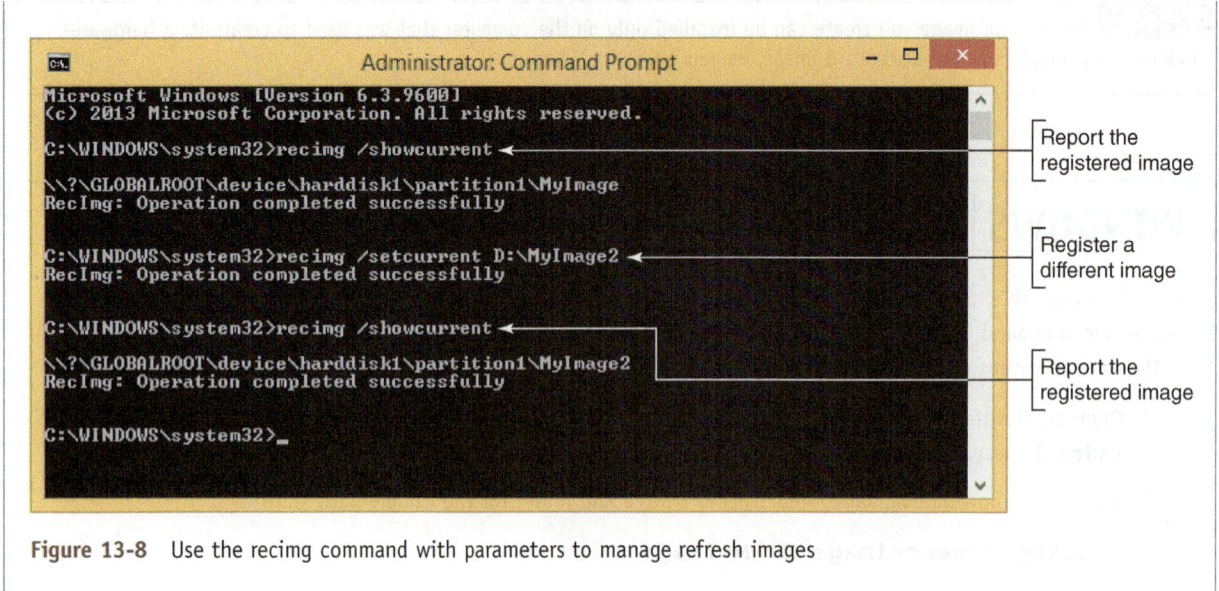

Figure 13-8   Use the recimg command with parameters to manage refresh images

BACKING UP WINDOWS SYSTEM FILES WITH SYSTEM PROTECTION

A+
CORE 2
4.3

When the System Protection utility is turned on, it automatically backs up system files and stores them on the hard drive at regular intervals and just before you install software or hardware. These snapshots of the system are called restore points and include Windows system files that have changed since the last restore point was made. A restore point does not contain all user data, and you can manually create a restore point at any time. System Restore (rstrui.exe) restores the system to its condition at the time a restore point was made. If you restore the system to a previous restore point, user data on the hard drive will not be altered, but you can affect installed software and hardware, user settings and passwords, and OS configuration settings. You'll learn how to use System Restore in Chapter 14.

ENABLE SYSTEM PROTECTION

System Protection is turned off by default in Windows 10. To enable System Protection, open **Control Panel** and open the **System** window. In the System window, click **System protection**. The System Protection tab of the System Properties box appears (see the left side of Figure 13-9). Make sure protection is turned on for the drive containing Windows, which indicates that restore points are created automatically. In Figure 13-9, protection for drive C: is on and other drives are not being protected. To make a change, click **Configure**. The System Protection box appears, as shown on the right side of the figure. If you make a change to this box, click **Apply** and then click **OK**.

Figure 13-9 Make sure System Protection is turned on for the volume on which Windows is installed

Restore points are normally kept in a folder named C:\System Volume Information, which is not accessible to the user. Restore points are taken at least every 24 hours, and they can use up to 15 percent of disk space. If disk space gets very low, restore points are no longer made, which is one more good reason to keep at least 15 percent or more of the hard drive free.

MANUALLY CREATE A RESTORE POINT

To manually create a restore point, use the System Protection tab of the System Properties box, as shown on the left side of Figure 13-9. Click **Create**. In the System Protection box, enter a name for the restore point, such as "Before I tested software," and click **Create**. The restore point is created.

MANAGING FILES, FOLDERS, AND STORAGE DEVICES

In this part of the chapter, you learn how files, folders, and volumes on a hard drive are organized, how to manage hard drive partitions and volumes using the Disk Management utility, and how to improve hard drive performance. Let's begin the discussion with how partitions and file systems work in Windows.

HOW PARTITIONS AND FILE SYSTEMS WORK

Recall that a hard drive is organized into partitions, volumes, and file systems. Total capacities for today's drives are measured in GB (gigabytes, roughly one million bytes) or TB (terabytes, roughly one trillion bytes). Before a hard drive leaves the factory, a process called low-level formatting organizes the space in a long series of logical blocks; this is called Logical Block

Addressing (LBA). When you first prepare a new hard drive for use, the drive is further organized into one or more partitions using one of two partitioning systems:

▲ *MBR partitions*. The Master Boot Record (MBR) partitioning system keeps a map of partitions in a partition table stored at the beginning of the hard drive called the MBR. Recall that the MBR system is required when a computer is using a 32-bit operating system or legacy BIOS. The MBR partition table can track up to four partitions on a drive. A drive can have one, two, or three primary partitions, also called volumes. The fourth partition is called an extended partition and can hold one or more volumes called logical drives, which are tracked in their own partition table separately from the primary partitions. Figure 13-10 shows how an MBR hard drive is divided into three primary partitions and one extended partition.

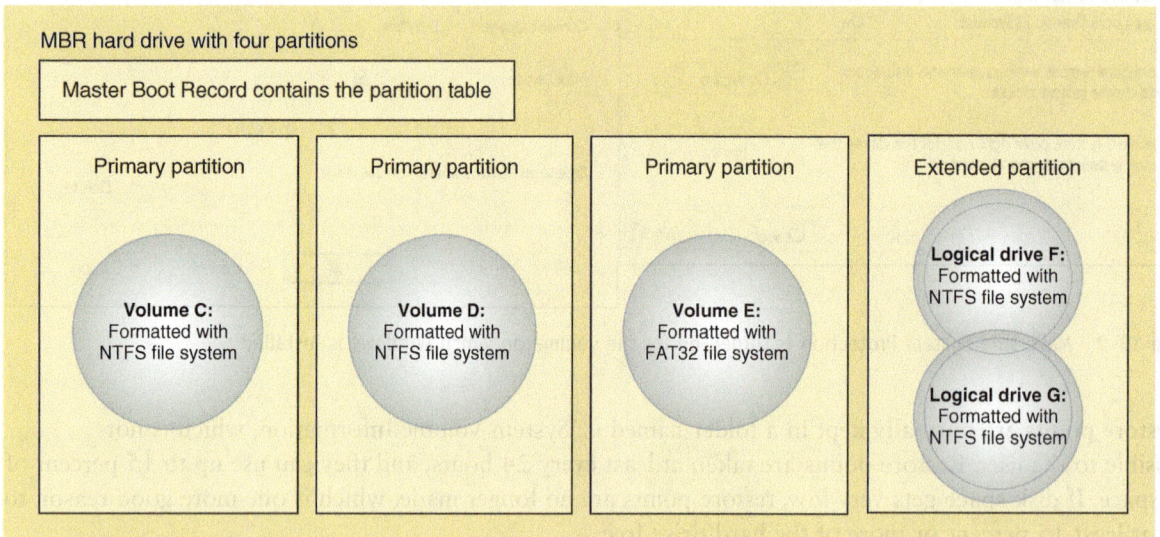

Figure 13-10 A hard drive with four partitions; the fourth partition is an extended partition

★ **A+ Exam Tip**   The A+ Core 2 exam expects you to know the difference between a primary and extended partition and between a volume and logical drive on an MBR hard drive.

▲ *GPT partitions*. The Globally Unique Identifier Partition Table (GUID or GPT) system can support up to 128 partitions and is required for drives larger than 2.2 TB. Recall that GPT requires a 64-bit operating system and UEFI firmware and is needed to use Secure boot, a feature of UEFI and the OS. Most new computers sold today use the GPT system.

The first sector in a GPT system contains the protective MBR, which provides information to legacy software that doesn't recognize GPT systems so that the legacy software will not attempt to repair or install an MBR system on the drive. GPT tracks all partitions in a single partition table, which it stores in the GPT header immediately following the protective MBR. GPT systems also back up the partition table at the end of the disk (see Figure 13-11).

Figure 13-11 A hard drive using GPT partitioning

WINDOWS FILE SYSTEMS

Before a partition or drive can be accessed, it must be assigned a drive letter such as C: or D: and formatted using a file system. Recall that the file system is the overall structure an OS uses to name, store, and organize files and folders on a drive. Installing a drive letter, file system, and root directory on a volume is called formatting the drive or high-level formatting. This formatting can happen during the Windows installation.

> **Notes** In most Microsoft documentation, a partition is called a partition until it is formatted with a file system and assigned a drive letter. Then it is called a volume.

Here is a list of file systems supported by Windows:

◢ *NTFS.* For most editions of Windows, NTFS (New Technology file system) is required for the volume on which Windows is installed. NTFS was designed to replace the older FAT32 file system; it is more reliable, efficient, and secure than FAT32. NTFS supports encryption, disk quotas (limiting the hard drive space available to a user), and file and folder compression. If you boot the system from another boot medium such as a DVD, you can access a volume using a FAT file system. If the volume uses NTFS, an administrator password is required to gain access.

◢ *ReFS.* The latest file system by Microsoft is the Resilient File System (ReFS), which is designed to improve on the NTFS file system by offering better performance. ReFS also offers fault tolerance, which protects data when sectors on the hard drive fail, eliminating the need for repairs using chkdsk, and it offers compatibility with virtualization and data redundancy in a RAID system. (RAID joins multiple hard drives into one virtual hard drive space.) ReFS is included in Windows 10 Pro for Workstations, but not with Windows 10 Pro or other editions of Windows 10.

13

◢ *NFS*. The NFS (Network File System) is a client/server file system that supports file sharing over a network across platforms. For example, a Linux-hosted NFS server can serve up file shares to Windows workstations on the network. Windows 10 supports NFS client connections.

◢ *exFAT*. Choose the exFAT file system for large external storage devices that you want to use with other operating systems. For example, you can use a smart card formatted with exFAT in a Mac or Linux computer or in a digital camcorder, camera, or smartphone. exFAT uses the same structure as the older FAT32 file system, but with a 64-bit-wide file allocation table (FAT). exFAT does not use as much overhead as the NTFS file system and is designed to handle very large files, such as those used for multimedia storage.

◢ *FAT32*. Use FAT32 for small hard drives or USB flash drives because it does not have as much overhead as NTFS and is supported by Linux and other OSs.

◢ *CDFS and UDF*. CDFS (Compact Disc File System) is an older file system used by optical discs (CDs, DVDs, and BDs), and is being replaced by the newer UDF (Universal Disk Format) file system.

> ★ **A+ Exam Tip** The A+ Core 2 exam expects you to know about the FAT32, exFAT, NTFS, CDFS, and NFS file systems, including which is appropriate to use in a given scenario.

> 🖊 **Notes** Windows installs on an NTFS volume, but if a second volume on the drive is formatted using the FAT32 file system, you can convert that volume to NTFS. For large drives, NTFS is more efficient, and converting might improve performance.

HOW PARTITIONS ARE USED DURING THE BOOT

With MBR hard drives, one of the primary partitions is designated the active partition, which is the bootable partition that startup BIOS/UEFI turns to when searching for an operating system to load. In GPT systems, this bootable partition is called the EFI System Partition (ESP); UEFI turns to it to find and start the operating system. The OS program it looks for in this partition is called the boot loader or boot manager.

In Windows, the MBR active partition or the GPT EFI System Partition is called the system partition. For Windows 10/8/7, the boot manager program is named BootMgr (with no file extension). The boot manager turns to the volume that is designated the boot partition, where the Windows operating system is stored, and continues the process of starting Windows.

> 🖊 **Notes** Don't be confused by the terminology here. It is really true that, according to Windows terminology, the Windows OS is on the boot partition and the boot manager is on the system partition, although that might seem backward. The computer starts or boots from the system partition and loads the Windows operating system from the boot partition. Typically, the boot partition and folder where Windows is stored is C:\Windows.

USING DISK MANAGEMENT TO MANAGE HARD DRIVES

A+ CORE 2 1.3, 1.5

The primary tool for managing hard drives is Disk Management. In Chapter 12, you learned how to install Windows on a new hard drive. This installation process initializes, partitions, and formats the drive. After Windows is installed, you can use Disk Management to install and manage drives. In this part of the chapter, you learn to use Disk Management to manage partitions on a drive, prepare a new drive for first use, mount a drive, use Windows dynamic disks, and troubleshoot problems with the hard drive.

APPLYING | CONCEPTS EXAMINING HARD DRIVES USING DISK MANAGEMENT

Let's use Disk Management (diskmgmt.msc) to view the hard drives in two systems:

1. To open the Disk Management window, use one of these methods:

   ◢ For Windows 10/8, right-click **Start** and click **Disk Management**. You can find Disk Management in the Windows 7 Start menu.

   ◢ Press **Win+R** and enter **diskmgmt.msc** in the Windows 10/7 search box or the Windows 8 Run box.

   In Figure 13-12, you can see an example of the Disk Management window showing three MBR hard drives in a system. In this computer, Windows is installed on Disk 0; Disk 1 is an unformatted drive, and Disk 2 is formatted using the NTFS file system. On Disk 0, the first partition is the System Reserved partition, which is designated the active partition and the Windows system partition. The boot partition is drive C:, where Windows is stored.

2. To see the Disk 0 Properties box, right-click **Disk 0** on the left side of the Disk Management window and click **Properties**. The Properties box appears, as shown in Figure 13-12. Select the **Volumes** tab to find out the partitioning system for the disk.

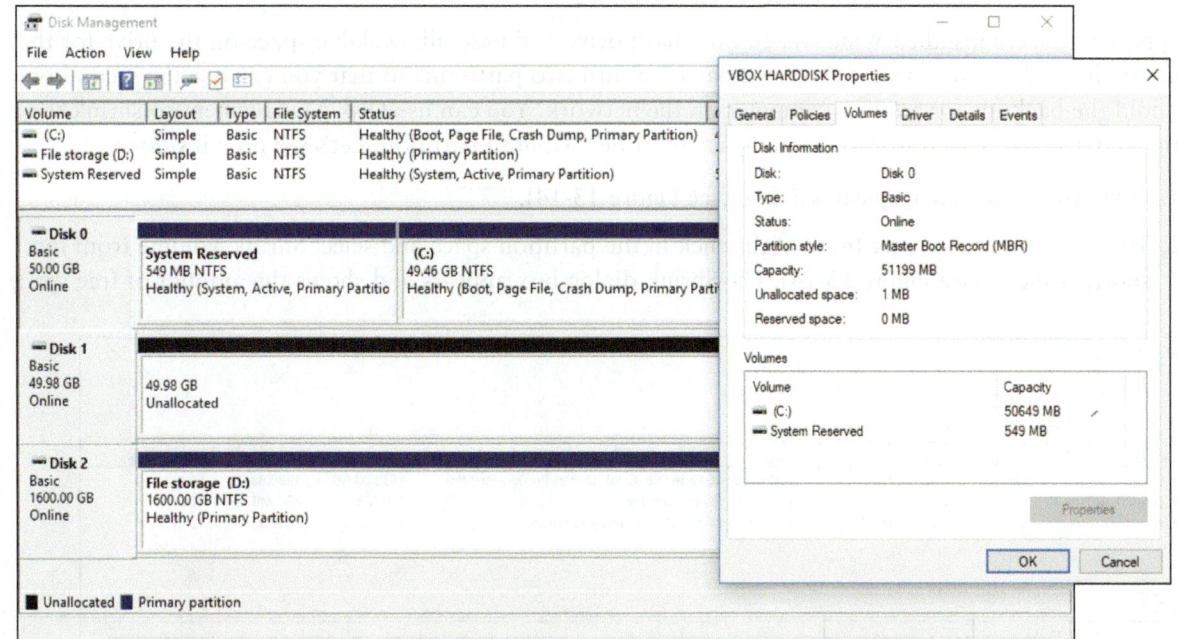

Figure 13-12 Three MBR disks with Windows 10 installed on Disk 0

Figure 13-13 shows another computer that has a single GPT hard drive installed. Among other partitions, it contains an OEM recovery partition, the EFI System Partition, and drive C:, which is designated the boot partition and holds the Windows 10 installation.

(continues)

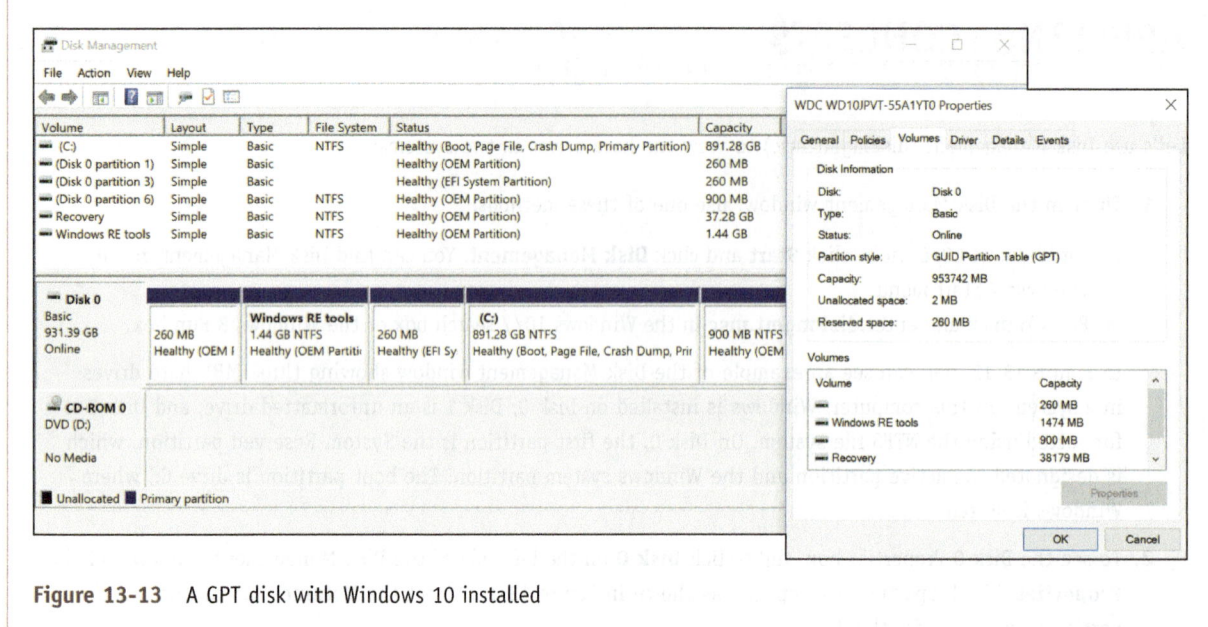

Figure 13-13   A GPT disk with Windows 10 installed

RESIZE, CREATE, AND DELETE PARTITIONS

Suppose you have installed Windows 10 on a hard drive and used all available space on the drive for the one partition. Now you want to split the partition into two partitions so that you can use the second one to hold the backups for another computer on the network. You can use Disk Management to shrink the original partition, which frees up some space for a new Ubuntu partition. Let's see how it's done:

1. Open the Disk Management window (see Figure 13-14).

2. To shrink the existing partition, right-click in the partition space and select **Shrink Volume** from the shortcut menu (see Figure 13-14). The Shrink dialog box appears and shows the amount of free space

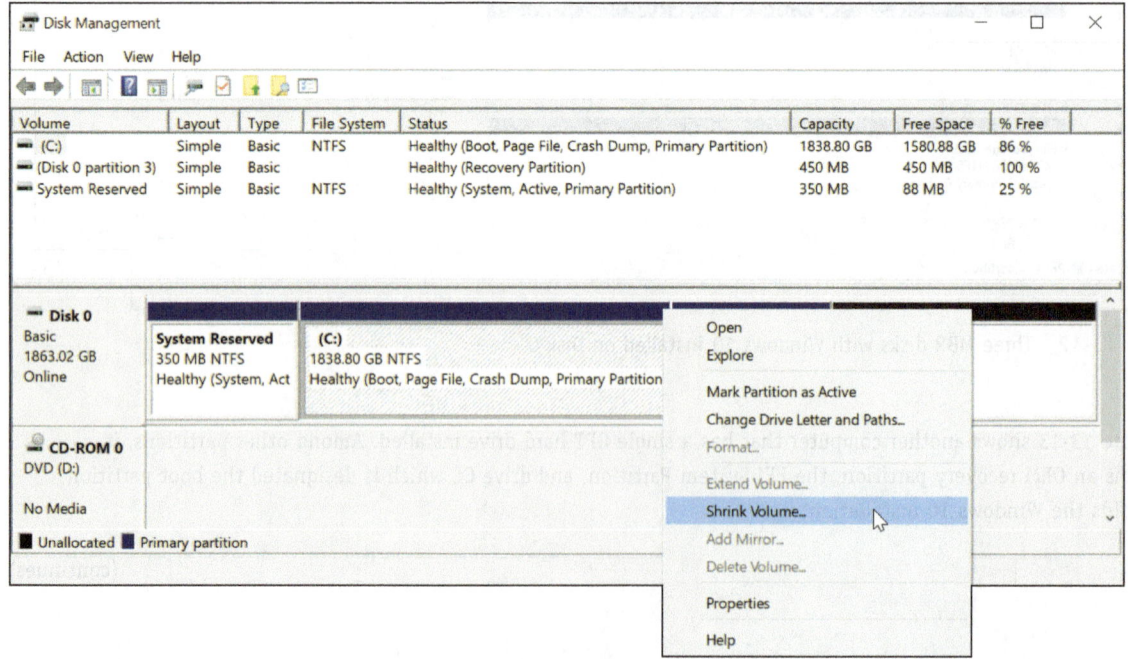

Figure 13-14   Shrink a volume to make room for a new partition

on the partition. Enter the amount in MB to shrink the partition; this amount cannot be more than the available amount of free space so that no data on the partition will be lost. (For best performance, be sure to leave at least 20 percent free space on the existing partition.) Click **Shrink**. The disk now shows unallocated space.

3. To create a new partition in the unallocated space, right-click in that space and select **New Simple Volume** from the shortcut menu (see Figure 13-15). The New Simple Volume Wizard opens.

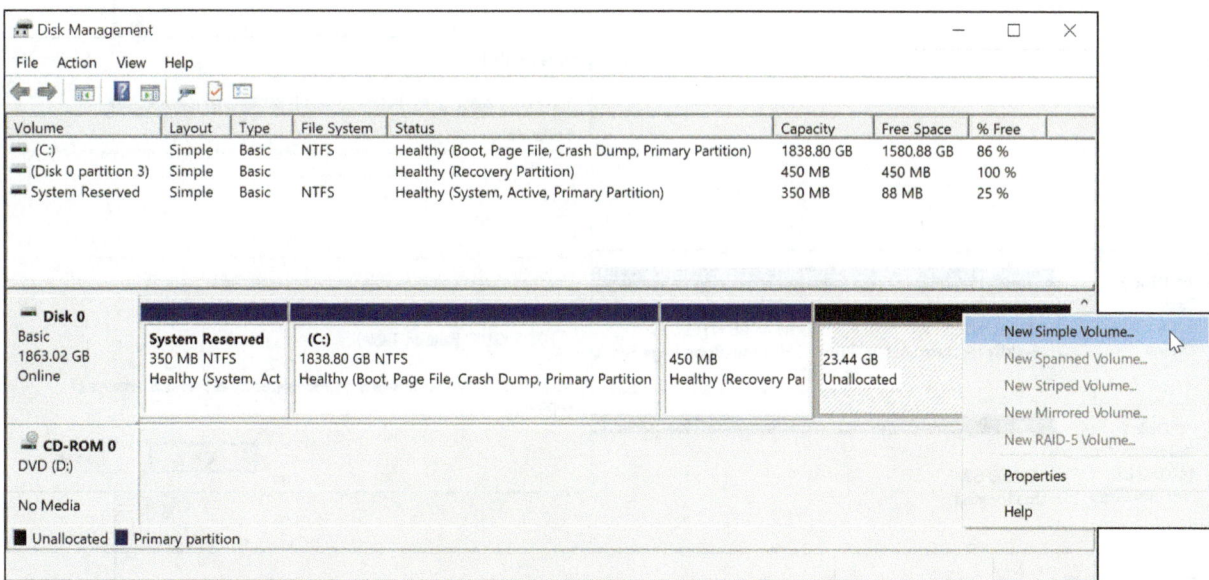

Figure 13-15   Use unallocated space to create a new partition

4. Follow the on-screen directions to enter the size of the volume in MB, select a drive letter for the volume, and select a file system. Leave the Allocation unit size at Default. You can also enter a Volume label and decide to do a quick format. (A quick format does not check the volume for bad sectors.) The partition is then created and formatted with the file system you chose. When you open Explorer, you should see the new volume listed.

Notice in Figure 13-14 the options on the shortcut menu for this MBR system, where you can make the partition the active partition (the one BIOS/UEFI looks to for an OS), change the drive letter for a volume, format the volume (which erases all data on it), extend the volume (increase its size), and shrink or delete the volume. An option that is not available for the particular volume and situation is grayed out.

> ★ **A+ Exam Tip**   The A+ Core 2 exam expects you to know how to use Disk Management to extend, split, and shrink partitions and configure a new hard drive in a system.

PREPARE A DRIVE FOR FIRST USE

When you install a new, second hard drive in a computer, use Disk Management to prepare the drive for use. This happens in a two-step process:

1. *Initialize the disk.* When the disk is initialized, Windows identifies it as a basic disk. A basic disk is a single hard drive that works independently of other hard drives. When you first open Disk Management after you have installed a new hard drive, the Initialize Disk box automatically appears (see Figure 13-16). Select the partitioning system (MBR or GPT) and click **OK**. Disk Management now reports the hard drive as a Basic disk.

13

Figure 13-16   Use the Initialize Disk box to set up a partitioning system on new hard drives

---

✎ Notes After installing a new hard drive, if you don't see the Initialize Disk box when you first open Disk Management, right-click in the Disk area and select **Initialize Disk** from the shortcut menu. The Initialize Disk box will appear.

---

2. *Create a volume and format it with a file system*. As you learned to do earlier, you can now create a New Simple Volume in unallocated space on the disk.

HOW TO MOUNT A DRIVE

A mounted drive is a volume that can be accessed by way of a folder on another volume so that the folder has more available space. A mounted drive is useful when a folder is on a volume that is too small to hold all the data you want in the folder. In Figure 13-17, the mounted drive gives the C:\Projects folder a capacity of 20 GB. The C:\Projects folder is called the mount point for the mounted drive.

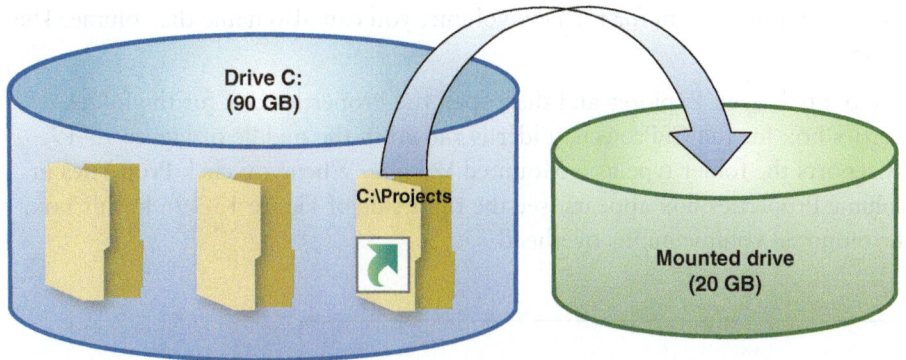

Figure 13-17 The C:\Projects folder is the mount point for the mounted drive

Follow these steps to mount a drive:

1. Make sure the volume that will host the mounted drive uses the NTFS file system. The folder on this volume, called the mount point, must be empty. You can also create the folder during the mount process. In this example, we are mounting a drive to the C:\Projects folder.

2. Using Disk Management, right-click in the unallocated space of a disk. In our example, we're using Disk 3 (the fourth hard drive). Select **New Simple Volume** from the shortcut menu. The New Simple Volume Wizard launches. Using the wizard, specify the amount of unallocated space you want to devote to the volume. Our example uses 20 GB, although the resulting size of the C:\Projects folder will only show about 19 GB because of overhead.

3. As you follow the wizard, the box shown on the left side of Figure 13-18 appears. Select **Mount in the following empty NTFS folder**, and then click **Browse**. In the Browse for Drive Path box that appears (see the right side of Figure 13-18), you can drill down to an existing folder or click **New Folder** to create a new folder on drive C:.

Figure 13-18 Select the folder that will be the mount point for the new volume

4. Complete the wizard by selecting a file system for the new volume; you can also name the volume. The volume is created and formatted.

5. To verify that the drive is mounted, open Explorer and then open the Properties box for the folder. In our example, the Properties box for the C:\Projects folder is shown in the middle of Figure 13-19. Notice the Properties box reports the folder type as a Mounted Volume. When you click **Properties** in the Properties box, the volume Properties box appears (see the right side of Figure 13-19). In this box, you can see the size of the mounted volume minus overhead.

Figure 13-19 The mounted drive in Explorer appears as a very large folder

You can think of a mount point, such as C:\Projects, as a shortcut to a volume on a second hard drive. If you look closely at the left window in Figure 13-19, you can see the shortcut icon beside the Projects folder.

WINDOWS DYNAMIC DISKS

A basic disk works independently of other hard drives, but a dynamic disk can work with other hard drives to hold data. Volumes stored on dynamic disks are called dynamic volumes. Several dynamic disks can work together to collectively present a single dynamic volume to the system.

When dynamic disks work together, data to configure each hard drive is stored in a disk management database that resides in the last 1 MB of storage space on each hard drive. Note that Home editions of Windows do not support dynamic disks.

Here are three uses of dynamic disks:

▲ *For better reliability, you can configure a hard drive as a dynamic disk and allocate the space as a simple volume.* This is the best reason to use dynamic disks and is a recommended best practice. Because of the way a dynamic disk works, the simple volume is considered more reliable than when it is stored on a basic disk. A volume that is stored on only one hard drive is called a simple volume.

▲ *You can implement dynamic disks on multiple hard drives to extend a volume across these drives (called spanning).* This volume is called a spanned volume.

▲ *Dynamic disks can be used to piece data across multiple hard drives to improve performance and/or provide fault tolerance (protecting data against loss).* The technology to configure two or more hard drives to work together as an array of drives is called RAID (redundant array of inexpensive disks or redundant array of independent disks).

    ▲ Joining hard drives together to improve performance is called striping or RAID 0. The volume is called a striped volume (see Figure 13-20). RAID 0 can improve performance because the work is shared between two hard drives. However, RAID 0 does not provide fault tolerance (if one drive fails, the data is lost).

    ▲ Copying one hard drive to another as a backup is called mirroring or RAID 1. The volume is called a mirrored volume. RAID 1 improves fault tolerance because if one drive fails, you have another copy of the data. RAID 1 can reduce performance because the drives operate at the speed of the slowest drive.

When RAID is implemented in this way using Disk Management, it is called software RAID. A more reliable way of configuring RAID is to use BIOS/UEFI setup on a motherboard that supports RAID, which is called hardware RAID.

Figure 13-20 A simple volume is stored on a single disk, but a striped volume or a mirrored volume is stored on an array of dynamic disks

> ★ **A+ Exam Tip** The A+ Core 2 exam expects you to select which RAID type is appropriate to use in a given scenario.

    You can use Disk Management to convert two or more basic disks to dynamic disks. Then you can use unallocated space on these disks to create a simple volume or a Windows array of disks using a spanned, striped, or mirrored volume. To convert a basic disk to dynamic, right-click the Disk area and select **Convert to Dynamic Disk** from the shortcut menu (see Figure 13-21). Then right-click free space on the disk and select **New Simple Volume, New Spanned Volume, New Striped Volume,** or **New Mirrored Volume** from the shortcut menu. If you were to select spanning or striping in Figure 13-21, you could make Disk 1 and Disk 2 dynamic disks that hold a single volume. The size of the volume would be the sum of the space on both hard drives. If you were instead using mirroring in Figure 13-21, you could make Disk 2 mirror the volume on Disk 1 as a backup copy. The size of the volume would be the space both hard drives have in common—which means it would be the size of the smaller of the two disks.

Figure 13-21 Convert a basic disk to a dynamic disk

> 📝 **Notes** When Windows implements RAID, know that you cannot install an OS on a spanned or striped volume that uses software RAID. You can, however, install Windows on a hardware RAID drive.
>   Also, after you have converted a basic disk to a dynamic disk, you cannot revert it to a basic disk without losing all data on the drive.

Now for some serious cautions about software RAID where you use Windows for spanning, striping, and mirroring: Microsoft warns that when Windows is used for software RAID, the risk of catastrophic failure increases and can lead to data loss. Microsoft suggests you only use Windows spanning, striping, or mirroring when you have no other option. In other words, spanning, striping, and mirroring in Windows aren't very safe. Instead, use a mounted drive or use hardware RAID to expand the size of a volume or to copy a volume to another drive.

WINDOWS STORAGE SPACES

Storage Spaces in Windows 10/8 is a potential replacement for traditional Windows software RAID. With Storage Spaces, you can create a storage pool using any number of internal or external backup drives that use interfaces such as SATA (Serial ATA), SAS (Serial Attached SCSI), or even USB. Then you create one or more virtual drives, called spaces, from this pool, which appear as normal drives in File Explorer. Drives used for Storage Spaces can be formatted with the NTFS or ReFS file system.

Storage Spaces is designed for resiliency, which resists data loss in the event of drive failure. The following storage options offer varying degrees of resiliency in Storage Spaces:

- ◢ *Simple*. A simple storage space combines multiple physical drives into a single logical drive with no built-in data backup. This option offers no resiliency.
- ◢ *Two-way mirroring*. A logical drive can be mirrored, which means the data is duplicated across multiple physical drives used to create the space.

▲ *Three-way mirroring*. In three-way mirroring, data is stored in triplicate to provide additional resiliency against data loss, although this feature requires that at least five physical drives be used to create the storage pool.

▲ *Parity*. To provide even greater resiliency, parity spaces maintain multiple copies of data (depending on the configuration) plus parity checking, which is a way to check backed-up data for any loss and re-create compromised data through parity calculations.

A single storage pool can be divided into multiple spaces, and each space can be configured with different resiliency settings. As pool capacity is depleted, more drives can be added to increase the available space without reconfiguring the space. In fact, the space can be configured as if it has more virtual storage than the physical drives actually offer by using a feature called thin provisioning. For example, in Figure 13-22, you can see the total of storage spaces presented to users is 12 TB; however, the physical hard drive capacities add up to only 8 TB. As the space actually used approaches 8 TB, the administrator is prompted to add more physical storage to the pool, which can eventually meet the 12-TB maximum capacity.

Figure 13-22 Thin provisioning allows for additional physical devices as needed without reconfiguring space available to users

To set up a system to use Storage Spaces, do the following:

1. Attach any drives to the computer that you intend to use for your storage pool. These can include SATA, SAS, or certain USB devices, and they do not have to match in capacity. Make sure the drives are identified as basic disks. All data on the storage drives will be lost during formatting, so be sure to back up anything important first.

2. In Classic view of Control Panel, click **Storage Spaces**. Click **Create a new pool and storage space**. Respond to the UAC box.

3. Any drives that are compatible with Storage Spaces will be listed. Select the drives to format. All data on the selected drives will be lost. Click **Create pool** to prepare the drives.

4. After the drives are ready, use the Create a storage space window (see Figure 13-23) to assign a name and drive letter for the storage space and select a file system. File system options include NTFS; for Windows 10 Pro Workstation, ReFS is an option.

13

Figure 13-23 Define the resiliency type for the new storage space

5. Select a resiliency type. Options include simple (no resiliency), two-way mirror, three-way mirror, and parity. Then, if you plan to use thin provisioning, adjust the maximum size of the storage pool. Sizes can be set in GB or TB. Notice that you can set a maximum size well beyond the actual sizes of the disks in the pool, and you'll be notified when you need to add more drives to provide that space. Click **Create storage space**. The storage space is created and formatted.

6. After the storage space is created, you can return to the Storage Spaces window to change the name, drive letter, and size of an existing storage space.

USE DISK MANAGEMENT TO TROUBLESHOOT HARD DRIVE PROBLEMS

Notice in Figure 13-21 that the system has four hard drives (Disk 0, Disk 1, Disk 2, and Disk 3), and information about the disks and volumes is shown in the Disk Management window. When you are having a problem with a hard drive, it helps to know what the information in the window means. Here are the disk and volume statuses you might see in this window:

▲ *Healthy*. The healthy volume status shown in Figure 13-21 indicates that the volume is formatted with a file system and that the file system is working without errors.

▲ *Failed*. A failed volume status indicates a problem with the hard drive or that the file system has become corrupted. To try to fix the problem, make sure the hard drive data cable and power cable are secure. Data on a failed volume is likely to be lost. For dynamic disks, if the disk status is Offline, try bringing the disk back online. (Details are covered later in this list.)

▲ *Online*. An online disk status indicates the disk has been sensed by Windows and can be accessed by either reading or writing to the disk.

▲ *Active*. One volume on an MBR system will be marked as Active. This is the volume that startup BIOS/ UEFI looks to for an OS boot manager to load.

▲ *EFI System Partition*. In GPT systems, one volume will be marked as the EFI System Partition. BIOS/ UEFI looks to this volume to find an OS boot manager to load an OS.

▲ *Unallocated*. Space on the disk is marked as unallocated if it has not yet been partitioned.

▲ *Formatting*. This volume status appears while a volume is being formatted.

▲ *Basic*. When a hard drive is first sensed by Windows, it is assigned the Basic disk status. A basic disk can be partitioned and formatted as a stand-alone hard drive.

▲ *Dynamic*. The following status indicators apply only to dynamic disks:

   ▲ *Offline*. An offline disk status indicates a dynamic disk has become corrupted or is unavailable. The problem can be caused by a corrupted file system, loose drive cables, a failed hard drive, or another hardware problem. If you believe the problem is corrected, right-click the disk and select **Reactivate Disk** from the shortcut menu to bring the disk back online.

   ▲ *Foreign drive*. If you move a hard drive that has been configured as a dynamic disk on one computer to another computer, it will report the disk as a foreign drive. To fix the problem, you need to import the foreign drive. Right-click the disk and select **Import Foreign Disks** from the shortcut menu. You should then be able to see the volumes on the disk.

   ▲ *Healthy (At Risk)*. The dynamic disk can be accessed, but I/O errors have occurred. Try returning the disk to online status. If the volume status does not return to healthy, back up all data and replace the drive.

If you are still having problems with a hard drive, volume, or mounted drive, check Event Viewer for events about the drive that might have been recorded there. These events might help you understand the nature of the problem and what to do about it. How to use Event Viewer is covered in Chapter 14.

IMPROVING HARD DRIVE PERFORMANCE

**A+
CORE 2
1.5, 3.1**

For best performance, Windows needs at least 15 percent free space on the hard drive that it uses as working space, so it's important to uninstall software you no longer need and delete unneeded files occasionally. Disk Management includes a Disk Cleanup (cleanmgr.exe) utility that deletes temporary files on the drive. In addition, a hard drive can be optimized to improve performance; how that's done depends on the type of hard drive.

Two types of hard drives are magnetic hard disk drives (HDDs), which contain spinning platters, and solid-state drives (SSDs), which contain flash memory. For magnetic hard drives, Windows automatically defragments the drive once a week, and for SSDs, Windows automatically trims the drive weekly. Let's look at what each of these operations accomplishes:

▲ *Magnetic hard drives*. To defragment is to rearrange fragments or parts of files on the drive so each file is stored on the drive in contiguous clusters. Each platter on a magnetic hard drive is divided into tracks, which are divided into sectors (see Figure 13-24). In a file system, a cluster, also called a file allocation unit, is a group of whole sectors. The number of sectors in a cluster is fixed and is determined when the file system is first installed. A file is stored in whole clusters, and the unused space at the end of the last cluster, called slack, is wasted free space. As files are written and deleted from an HDD, clusters are used,

One sector

One track

Figure 13-24 A magnetic hard drive is divided into concentric circles called tracks, and tracks are divided into sectors

13

released, and used again. New files written on the drive can be put in available clusters spread over the drive. Over time, drive performance is affected when the moving read/write arm of a magnetic drive must move over many areas of the drive to collect all the fragments of a file. Defragmenting a drive rewrites files in contiguous clusters and improves drive performance.

▲ *Solid-state drives.* Defragmenting an SSD can reduce the life of the drive and is not recommended—Windows disables defragmenting for solid-state drives. However, data on an SSD still needs trimming. To trim an SSD is to erase a block on the drive that is filled with unused data. Recall that SSDs are organized in blocks, and each block contains many pages. A file can spread over several pages in various blocks. Each time a new page is written to the drive, the entire block to which it belongs must be read into a buffer, erased, and then rewritten with the new page included. When a file is deleted, information about the file is deleted, but the actual data in the file is not erased. This can slow down SSD performance because the unused data must still be read and rewritten in its block. To improve performance, Windows sends the trim command to an SSD drive to erase a block that no longer contains useful data so that a write operation does not have to manage the data.

> ↻ **OS Differences** Windows 7 does not support optimizing an SSD.

APPLYING | CONCEPTS   CLEANING AND OPTIMIZING HARD DRIVES

To delete unneeded files on a drive and verify that the drive is being automatically defragged or trimmed, use the Disk Cleanup utility (cleanmgr.exe) and the Defragment and Optimize Drives (dfrgui.exe) utility. Do the following when starting the utilities from Explorer:

1. To delete unneeded files, open Explorer, right-click drive **C:**, and click **Properties**. On the General tab of the drive Properties box, click **Disk Cleanup** to calculate how much space can be cleaned up. Select the file types to delete (see Figure 13-25) and click **OK**.

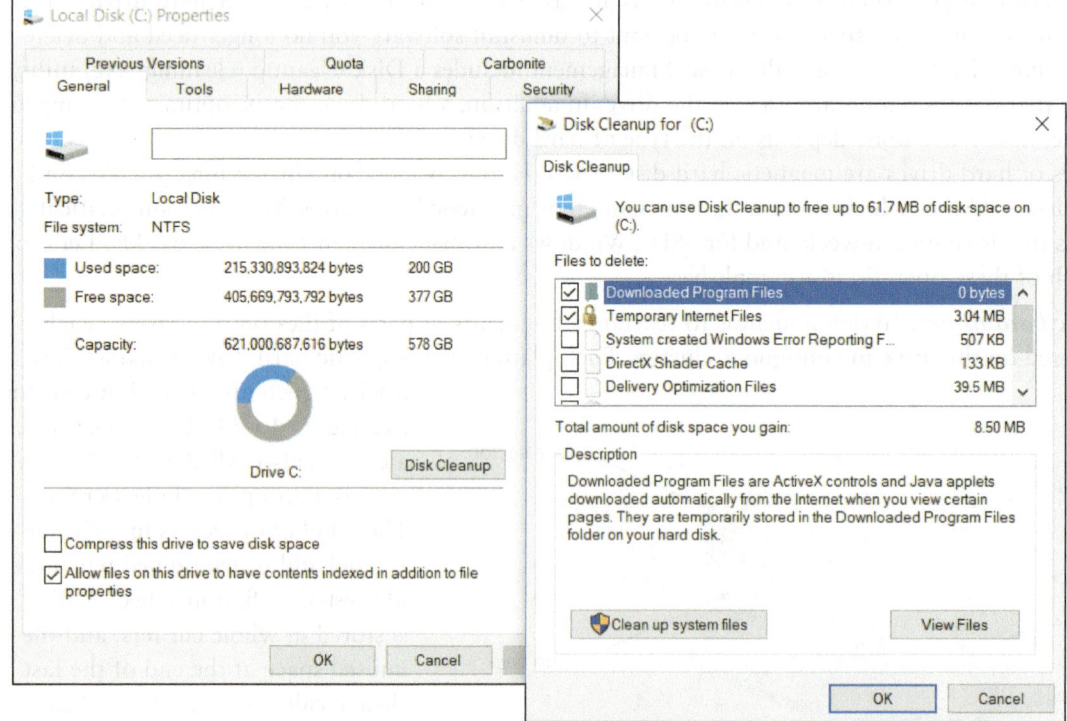

Figure 13-25   Delete unneeded files on a hard drive to free up space

(continues)

2. To optimize the hard drive, select the **Tools** tab in the drive Properties box and click **Optimize**. The Optimize Drives box appears (see Figure 13-26). This system has two hard drives installed. Drive C: is an SSD and drive F: is a magnetic HDD.

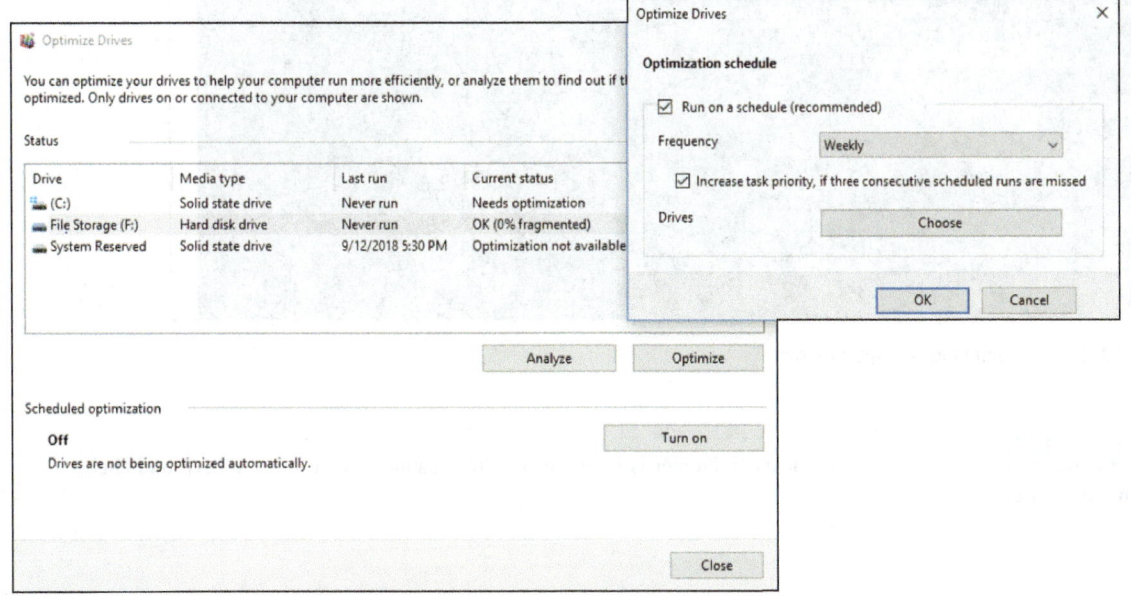

Figure 13-26 Windows is set to automatically defragment a magnetic hard drive once a week

3. Here are tasks you can do:

◢ For a magnetic drive, click **Analyze** for Windows to tell you if a drive needs defragmenting. To defrag the drive, click **Optimize**. The process can take a few minutes to several hours. If errors occur while the drive is defragmenting, check the hard drive for errors and try to defragment again.

◢ For a solid-state drive, click **Optimize** to trim the SSD.

◢ Near the bottom of Figure 13-26, you can see optimization is turned off. To turn it on, click **Turn on**. In the box that appears (see the right side of the figure), check **Run on a schedule (recommended)** and select **Weekly** for the Frequency. Click **OK**.

Throughout this chapter, you've learned a lot about Windows maintenance tasks, backup procedures, and how to manage hard drives. The next part of this chapter discusses ways to perform many related tasks from a command-line interface.

USING A COMMAND-LINE INTERFACE (CLI)

A+
CORE 2
1.3, 1.4

IT support technicians find it is much faster to manipulate files and folders and perform other tasks by using commands in a command prompt window than by using Explorer and other graphical tools. In some troubleshooting situations, you have no other option but to use a command prompt window.

Windows has two levels of command prompt windows: a standard window and an elevated window. In a standard window, the default directory is the currently signed-in user's folder and commands have the same permissions as that user. Commands issued in an elevated command prompt window have administrative privileges and the default directory is C:\Windows\System32.

To open a standard command prompt window (see Figure 13-27), enter **command** or **cmd** in the Windows 10/7 search box or the Windows 8 Run box, and then click **Command Prompt**.

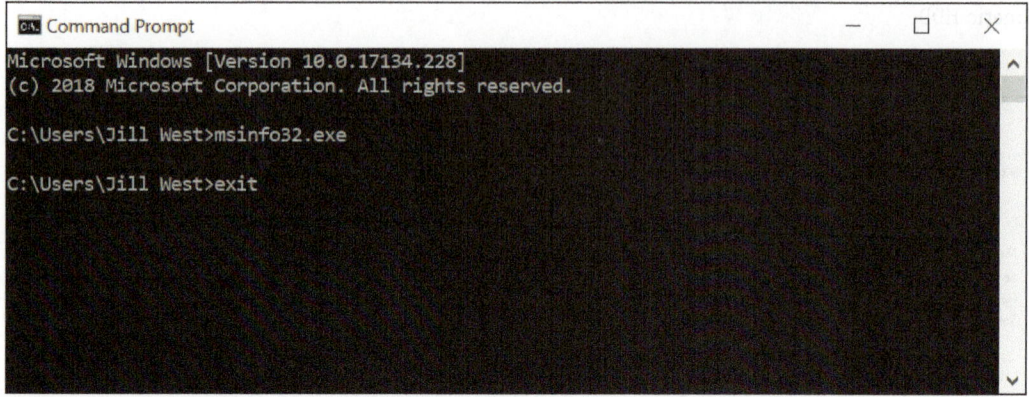

Figure 13-27 A command prompt window

> **OS Differences** For Windows 8, Command Prompt is listed in the Quick Launch menu. Press **Win+X** and click **Command Prompt**.

To open an elevated command prompt window, type **cmd** or **command** in the Windows 10/7 search box or the Windows 8 Run box, right-click **Command Prompt**, and click **Run as administrator**. Then respond to the UAC box. The Administrator: Command Prompt window is shown in Figure 13-28. Notice the word *Administrator* in the title bar, which indicates the elevated window, and the default directory, which is the C:\WINDOWS\system32 folder.

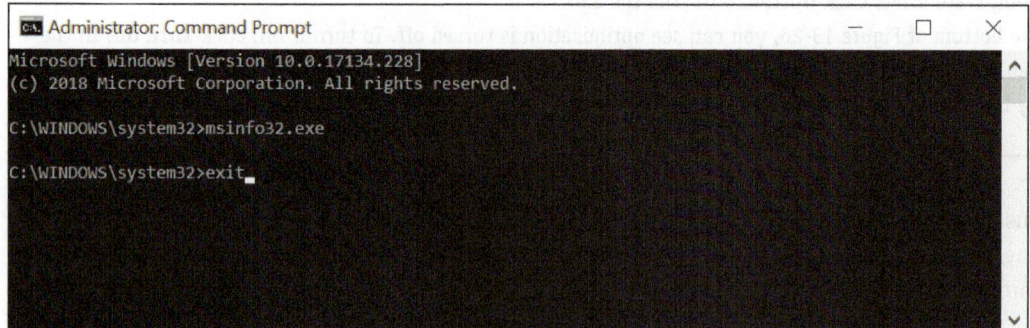

Figure 13-28 An elevated command prompt window has administrative privileges

> **OS Differences** To get an elevated command prompt window in Windows 8, press **Win+X**, click **Command Prompt (Admin)**, and respond to the UAC box. In Windows 7, click **Start**, **All Programs**, **Accessories**, and right-click **Command Prompt**. Then select **Run as administrator** from the shortcut window and respond to the UAC box.

Here are some tips for working in a command prompt window:

- Type **cls** and press **Enter** to clear the window.
- To retrieve the last command you entered, press the up arrow. To retrieve the last command line one character at a time, press the right arrow.
- To terminate a command before it is finished, press **Ctrl+C**, **Ctrl+Break**, or **Ctrl+Pause**.
- To access settings for the command prompt window, right-click the title bar and click **Properties**. You can change the background color, font, font color, and font size so you can better read the text in the window, adjust opacity so you can see what's behind the window as you work, and access Ctrl key shortcuts.
- To close the window, type **exit** (see Figure 13-28) and press **Enter**.

> ✎ **Notes** Many of the commands you learn about in this section can also be used in the Windows Recovery Environment (Windows RE), which can be loaded from within Windows during troubleshooting. When Windows refuses to start, you can load Windows RE from Windows setup media or a USB or DVD recovery drive. How to use the Recovery Environment is covered in Chapters 14 and 15.

COMMANDS TO MANAGE FILES AND FOLDERS

A+ CORE 2 1.3, 1.4

If the command you are using applies to files or folders, the path to these files or folders is assumed to be the default drive and directory. The default drive and directory, also called the current drive and directory, shows in the command prompt. For example, in Figure 13-27, the default drive is C: and the default path is C:\Users\Jill West. If you use a different path in the command line, the path you use overrides the default path. Also know that Windows makes no distinction between uppercase and lowercase in command lines (however, Linux does).

Now let's look at the file-naming conventions you will need to follow when creating files, wildcard characters you can use in command lines, and several commands useful for managing files and folders.

FILE-NAMING CONVENTIONS

When using the command prompt window to create a file, keep in mind that file name and file extension characters can be the letters *a* through *z*, the numbers *0* through *9*, and the following characters:

```
_ ^ $ ~ ! # % & – { } ( ) @ ' `
```

In a command prompt window, if a path or file name has spaces in it, it is sometimes necessary to enclose the path or file name in double quotation marks.

WILDCARD CHARACTERS IN COMMAND LINES

As you work at the command prompt, you can use wildcard characters in a file name to apply the command to a group of files or to abbreviate a file name if you do not know the entire name. The question mark (?) is a wildcard for one character, and the asterisk (*) is a wildcard for one or more characters. For example, if you want to find all file names in a directory that start with *A* and have a three-letter file extension, you would use the following command:

```
dir a*.???
```

> ★ **A+ Exam Tip** The A+ Core 2 exam expects you to know how to use the dir, cd, copy, xcopy, robocopy, chkdsk, format, /?, and shutdown commands, which are all covered in this chapter. Other commands also required for the A+ Core 2 exam are covered in other chapters.

13

> **✎ Notes** Many commands can use parameters in the command line to affect how the command will work. Parameters (also called options, arguments, or switches) often begin with a slash or a hyphen followed by a single character. In this chapter, you learn about the basic parameters used by a command for the most common tasks. For a full listing of the parameters available for a command, use the help command. Another way to learn about commands is to follow this link on the Microsoft website: *docs.microsoft.com/en-us/windows-server/administration/windows-commands/windows-commands*.

HELP OR *<COMMAND NAME>* /?

Use the help command to get help about any command. You can enter help followed by the command name or enter the command name followed by /?. Table 13-2 lists some sample applications of this command.

Command	Result
`help xcopy` `xcopy /?`	**Gets help information about the xcopy command**
`help`	**Lists all commands**
`help xcopy	more`	**Lists information about the xcopy command one screen at a time; press Space to see the next screen, or Enter to advance one line at a time**

Table 13-2   Sample help commands

> **✎ Notes** Windows commands are not case sensitive. You can type help, Help, or HELP and you'll get the same result.

> **★ A+ Exam Tip** The A+ Core 2 exam does not give you access to /? or the help command and expects you to know how to structure each command and its parameters covered in this and other chapters.

DIR [*<FILENAME>*] [/P] [/S] [/W]

Use the dir command to list files and directories. In Microsoft documentation about a command (also called the command syntax), the brackets [ ] in a command line indicate the parameter is optional. In addition, the parameter included in < >, such as *<filename>*, indicates that you can substitute any file name in the command. This file name can include a path or file extension. Table 13-3 lists some examples of the dir command.

Command	Result
`dir /p`	**Lists one screen at a time**
`dir /w`	**Presents information using wide format, where details are omitted and files and folders are listed in columns on the screen**
`dir *.txt`	**Lists all files with a .txt file extension in the default path**
`dir d:\data\*.txt`	**Lists all files with a .txt file extension in the D:\data\ folder**
`dir myfile.txt`	**Checks that a single file, such as myfile.txt, is present**
`dir /s`	**Includes subdirectory entries**

Table 13-3   Sample dir commands

CD [<DRIVE>:\[<PATH>]] OR CD..

The cd (change directory) command changes the current default directory. You enter cd followed by the drive (a volume letter, such as C:) and the entire path that you want to be current, like so:

```
C:\> cd C:\game\chess
```

The command prompt now looks like this:

```
C:\game\chess>
```

To move up from a child directory to its parent directory, use the .. (dot, dot) variation of the command:

```
C:\game\chess> cd..
```

The command prompt now looks like this:

```
C:\game>
```

Remember that .. (dot, dot) always indicates the parent directory. You can move from a parent directory to one of its child directories simply by stating the name of the child directory:

```
C:\game> cd chess
```

The command prompt now looks like this:

```
C:\game\chess>
```

Remember not to put a backslash in front of the child directory name; doing so tells the OS to go to a directory named chess that is directly under the root directory.

> **✎ Notes** Two commands closely related to cd are md (make directory), which creates a subdirectory under a directory, and rd (remove directory), which removes an empty directory.

13

COPY [/V] [/Y] <SOURCE> [<DESTINATION>]

The copy command copies a single file or group of files. The original files are not altered. To copy a file from one drive to another, use a command similar to this one:

```
E:\> copy C:\Data\Myfile.txt E:\mydata\Newfile.txt
```

The drive, path, and file name of the source file follow the copy command. The drive, path, and file name of the destination file follow the source file name. If you don't specify the file name of the destination file, the OS assigns the file's original name to this copy. If you omit the drive or path of the source or the destination, then the OS uses the current default drive and path.

To copy the file myfile.txt from the root directory of drive C: to drive E:, use the following command:

```
C:\> copy myfile.txt E:
```

Because the command does not include a drive or path before the file name myfile.txt, the OS assumes that the file is in the default drive and path. Also, because there is no destination file name specified, the file written to drive E: will be named myfile.txt.

To copy all files in the C:\Docs directory to the USB flash drive designated drive E:, use the following command:

```
C:\> copy c:\docs\*.* E:
```

To make a backup file named system.bak of the SYSTEM registry hive file in the \Windows\System32\config directory of the hard drive, use the following command:

```
C:\Windows\system32\config> copy system system.bak
```

If you use the copy command to duplicate multiple files, the files are assigned the names of the original files. When you duplicate multiple files, the destination portion of the command line cannot include a file name.

Here are two parameters that are useful with the copy command:

▲ */v.* When the /v switch is used, the size of each new file is compared with the size of the original file. This slows down the copying but verifies that the copy is done without errors.

▲ */y.* When the /y switch is used, a confirmation message does not ask you to confirm before overwriting a file.

> 📝 **Notes** When trying to recover a corrupted file, you can sometimes use the copy command to copy the file to new media, such as from the hard drive to a USB drive. If the copy command reports a bad or missing sector during the copying process, choose the option to ignore that sector. The copying process then continues to the next sector. The corrupted sector will be lost, but others can likely be recovered. The recover command can be used to accomplish the same thing.

XCOPY <SOURCE> [<DESTINATION>] [/S] [/E] [/C] [/Y] [/D:[DATE]]

The **xcopy** command is more powerful than the copy command. It follows the same general command-source-destination format as the copy command, but it offers several more options. Table 13-4 shows some of these options.

Command	Result
xcopy C:\docs*.* E: /s	Uses the /s parameter to include subdirectories in the copy; this command copies all files in the directory C:\docs, as well as all subdirectories under \ docs and their files, to drive E:, unless the subdirectory is empty
xcopy C:\docs*.* E: /e	Works the same as /s but empty subdirectories are included in the copy
xcopy C:\docs*.* E: /d: 03-14-19	Uses the /d switch to examine the date; this command copies all files from the directory C:\docs created or modified on or after March 14, 2019
xcopy C:\docs*.* E: /y	Uses the /y switch to overwrite existing files without prompting
xcopy C:\docs*.* E: /c	Uses the /c switch to keep copying even when an error occurs

Table 13-4 Sample xcopy commands

ROBOCOPY <SOURCE> <DESTINATION> [/S] [/E] [/LOG:<LOGFILE>] [/LOG+:<LOGFILE>] [/MOVE] [/PURGE]

The **robocopy (robust file copy)** command is similar to the xcopy command. It offers more options than xcopy and is intended to replace xcopy. A few options for robocopy are listed in Table 13-5.

Command	Result
robocopy C:\docs*.* E: /s	Uses the /s switch to include subdirectories in the copy but does not include empty directories
robocopy C:\docs*.* E: /e	Uses the /e switch to include subdirectories, even the empty ones
robocopy C:\docs*.* E: /log:Mylog.txt	Records activity to a log file and overwrites the current log file
robocopy C:\docs*.* E: /log+:Mylog.txt	Appends a record of all activity to an existing log file
robocopy C:\docs*.* E: /move	Moves files and directories, deleting them from the source
robocopy C:\docs*.* E: /purge	Deletes files and directories at the destination that no longer exist at the source

Table 13-5 Sample robocopy commands

COMMANDS TO MANAGE HARD DRIVES

Several commands can be used to manage hard drives either when setting up a new hard drive, refreshing a hard drive, or during troubleshooting. Sometimes these commands are easier than digging through menus for a needed utility. If you're restricted to the Windows Recovery Environment during troubleshooting, these commands might be your only means of accessing some of these tools.

CHKDSK [<*VOLUME*>:] [/F] [/R]

The chkdsk (check disk) command fixes file system errors and recovers data from bad sectors. Recall that a file is stored on the hard drive as a group of clusters. The FAT32 and exFAT file systems use a FAT (file allocation table) to keep a record of each cluster that belongs to a file. In Figure 13-29, you can see that each cell in the FAT represents one cluster and contains a pointer to the next cluster in a file. The NTFS file system uses a database called the master file table (MFT) to hold similar information.

Figure 13-29 Lost and cross-linked clusters

> ✎ **Notes** For an interesting discussion of how the FAT works, see the document FAT Details.pdf on the companion website for this text at *cengage.com*. See the Preface for more information.

Used with the /f parameter, chkdsk searches for and fixes two types of file system errors made by the FAT or MFT:

▲ *Lost clusters (also called lost allocation units).* Lost clusters are clusters that are marked as used in the FAT or MFT, but they do not belong to any file. In effect, the data in these clusters is lost.
▲ *Cross-linked clusters.* Cross-linked clusters are marked in the FAT or MFT as belonging to more than one file.

Used with the /r parameter, chkdsk checks for lost clusters, cross-linked clusters, and bad sectors on the drive. The FAT and MFT keep a table of bad sectors that they normally do not use. However, over time, a sector might become unreliable. If chkdsk determines that a sector is unreliable, it attempts to recover the data from the sector and marks the sector as bad so that the FAT or MFT will not use it again.

Used without any parameters, the chkdsk command only reports information about a drive and does not make any repairs.

An elevated command prompt is required to use the chkdsk command. In the following sample commands, the command prompt is not shown because the default drive and directory are not important. To check the hard drive for file system errors and repair them, use this command:

```
chkdsk C:/f
```

To redirect a report of the findings of the chkdsk command to a file that you can later print, use this command:

```
chkdsk C:>Myfile.txt
```

Use the /r parameter of the chkdsk command to fix file system errors and examine each sector of the drive for bad sectors, like so:

```
chkdsk C:/r
```

If chkdsk finds data that it can recover, it asks you for permission to do so. If you give permission, it saves the recovered data in files that it stores in the root directory of the drive.

> 🖊 **Notes** Use either the /f or /r parameter with chkdsk, but not both. Using both parameters is redundant. For the most thorough check of a drive, use /r.

The chkdsk command will not fix anything unless the drive is locked, which means the drive has no open files. If you attempt to use chkdsk with the /f or /r parameter when files are open, chkdsk tells you of the problem and asks permission to schedule the run the next time Windows is restarted. Know that the process will take plenty of time.

> 🖊 **Notes** The chkdsk command is also available from the Windows Recovery Environment.

DEFRAG [<VOLUME>:] [/C]

The Disk Defragmenter defrag command examines a magnetic hard drive for fragmented files and rewrites these files to the drive in contiguous clusters. Use this command to optimize a magnetic hard drive's performance. Table 13-6 shows two examples of the command. Recall that it's not a good idea to defrag solid-state storage devices such as an SSD, flash drive, or smart card. Doing so can shorten the life of the drive.

Command	Result
defrag C:	**Defrags volume C:**
defrag /C	**Defrags all volumes on the computer, including volume C:**

Table 13-6 Sample defrag commands

The defrag command requires an elevated command prompt window in Windows. It is not available under the Windows Recovery Environment.

FORMAT <VOLUME:>[/Q] [FS:<FILESYSTEM>]

You can format a hard drive or other storage device using Disk Management. In addition, you can use the format command from a command prompt window and from the Windows Recovery Environment. This high-level format installs a file system on the device and *erases all data on the volume*. Table 13-7 lists various sample uses of the format command.

Command	Result
format D:	Performs a full format of volume D: using the default file system for the volume type
format D: /q	Performs a quick format of volume D: by re-creating an empty root directory; use it to quickly format a previously formatted disk that is in good condition; /q does not read or write to any other part of the disk
format D: /fs:NTFS	Formats volume D: using the NTFS file system
format D: /fs:FAT32	Formats volume D: using the FAT32 file system
format D: /fs:EXFAT	Formats volume D: using the extended FAT file system

Table 13-7 Sample format commands

SHUTDOWN [/I] [/R] [/S] [/M \\<COMPUTERNAME>] [/T XX]

Use the shutdown command to shut down the local computer or a remote computer. You must be signed in with an administrator account to use this command. By default, the command gives users a 30-second warning before shutdown. To shut down a remote computer on the network, you must have an administrator account on that computer and be signed on the local computer with that same account and password. Table 13-8 lists some shutdown commands.

Command	Result
shutdown /r	Restarts the local computer
shutdown /s /m \\bluelight	Shuts down the remote computer named \\bluelight
shutdown /s /m \\bluelight /t 60	Shuts down the \\bluelight computer after a 60-second delay
shutdown /i	Displays the Remote Shutdown dialog box so you can choose computers on the network to shut down

Table 13-8 Sample shutdown commands

13

WINDOWS 10 POWERSHELL AND UBUNTU BASH INTERFACES

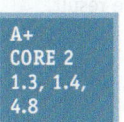

A+ CORE 2 1.3, 1.4, 4.8

As you become more comfortable with command-line interfaces, you'll find they can be more flexible and convenient than a graphical interface, especially for commands you use frequently. Microsoft continues to make significant improvements to command-line options in Windows, including increased emphasis on PowerShell and the addition of a Linux shell. The three command-line interfaces (CLI) offered by Windows 10 are the Command Prompt, PowerShell, and Linux shell interfaces. First, let's explore PowerShell cmdlets, and then we'll see how the Linux shell works in Windows 10.

POWERSHELL

Windows PowerShell is designed to replace the command prompt utility for providing a command-line interface. Windows PowerShell processes objects called cmdlets (pronounced "command-lets") that essentially run prebuilt programs, similar to batch files. Windows PowerShell contains thousands of cmdlets so that users don't have to build their own. Technicians or programmers who program their own cmdlets can build customized objects using existing cmdlets as building blocks.

PowerShell skills are becoming increasingly important for all IT technicians. In this part of the chapter, we look at some basic PowerShell cmdlets as a starting point to help you warm up to PowerShell.

POWERSHELL CMDLET SYNTAX

Native PowerShell cmdlet syntax almost always starts with a verb followed by a noun and connected with a hyphen, as in *verb-noun*. For example, consider the cmdlet Get-ChildItem. The *Get* verb defines the action and the *ChildItem* noun defines the object of that action. "Get" simply means to retrieve something; an item is a file or folder, and "ChildItem" is any item within another item. So, the cmdlet Get-ChildItem retrieves items in one or more specified locations, similar to how dir works at the command prompt.

Some cmdlets have parameters, such as the -Depth parameter in the Get-ChildItem cmdlet. This parameter allows you to specify how many layers to search in the targeted location to retrieve child items. To use this parameter, you must also use the -Recurse parameter, which instructs PowerShell to retrieve items within child items (such as files within folders) at the targeted location. For example, Get-ChildItem -Recurse -Depth 2 delivers a list of items in the current folder, that folder's child folders, and folders within those child folders, but the list goes no deeper than two child layers of folders. In a project at the end of this chapter, you get some practice using the Get-ChildItem cmdlet with parameters.

Set, Copy, and Remove are other verb options for cmdlets. Other noun options include Help, Location, Content, Process, and Service. With this information, you can deduce the names of several helpful cmdlets, as shown in Table 13-9.

Cmdlet	Description
Get-Item	Retrieves files and folders
Get-Process	Retrieves the processes running on a computer
Set-Location	Changes the current working location to a specified location
Copy-Item	Copies an item to a specified location
Remove-Item	Deletes an item
Get-Verb	Shows a list of all cmdlet verbs
Get-Verb *-Location	Shows a list of all cmdlet verbs available for a specific noun, where the asterisk is a wildcard in place of any verb attached to the noun *Location*
Get-Command	Shows a list of all available cmdlets

Table 13-9 Common PowerShell cmdlets

> ✎ **Notes** PowerShell cmdlets are not case sensitive. You can type Get-Item or get-item and you'll get the same result.

APPLYING | CONCEPTS   USING POWERSHELL

Let's learn to use PowerShell by looking at an example of how helpful and powerful it can be. Even a clean copy of Windows comes with several apps that you might not want and that cannot be removed through the Apps & features window or the Programs and Features window. For example, you might not want Xbox installed on a computer you use for work. You can use PowerShell to uninstall unwanted apps.

Complete the following steps to install an app from the Windows Store and then remove it using PowerShell:

1. Open the **Windows Store** and find a simple app to install, such as Dropbox. Click **Get** to download and install the app. Close the Windows Store.

2. Open the **Settings** app and click **Apps**.

3. Scroll down to the app you just installed. In most cases, you can use this window to remove the app, but some apps can't be uninstalled from here. For example, as shown in Figure 13-30, the Uninstall button is grayed out for the Maps app.

(continues)

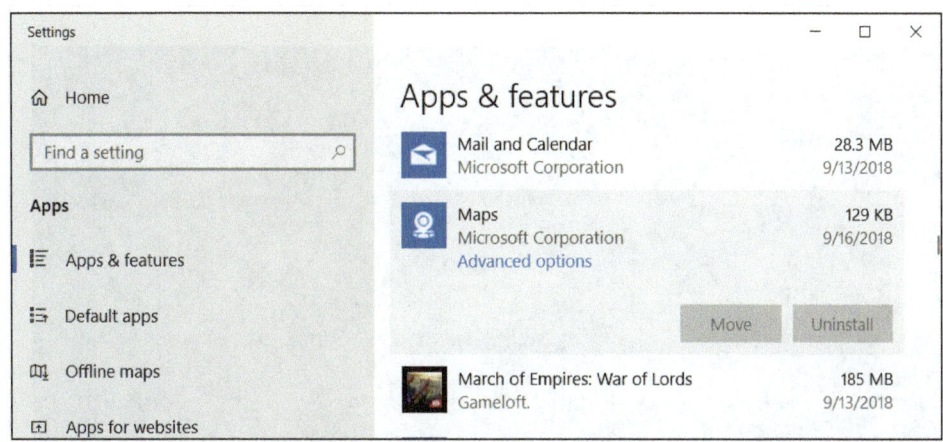

Figure 13-30 Some apps cannot be uninstalled through the Apps & features window

4. Let's use PowerShell to uninstall an app. PowerShell offers a standard PowerShell window and an elevated PowerShell window. Use one of these methods to open an elevated PowerShell window:

   ▲ For Windows 10, press **Win+X** and click **Windows PowerShell (Admin)**.

   ▲ For Windows 8, open the Start screen and type **powershell**. Right-click **Windows PowerShell** and click **Run as administrator**.

   ▲ For Windows 7, click **Start**, **All Programs**, **Accessories**, and **Windows PowerShell**. In the folder, right-click **Windows PowerShell** and click **Run as administrator**.

5. If needed, click **Yes** in the UAC dialog box.

6. Enter **Get-AppxPackage** to see a list of all apps installed for the current user. Wade through and find the entry for the app you just installed. (It's most likely at the bottom of the list because you just installed it.) For example, Figure 13-31 shows Dropbox installed on the system.

```
Administrator: Windows PowerShell                                              —   □   ×

Name               : C27EB4BA.Dropbox
Publisher          : CN=852D08DC-3DFB-4331-AD77-990D03FE9E36
Architecture       : X64
ResourceId         :
Version            : 4.5.3.0
PackageFullName    : C27EB4BA.Dropbox_4.5.3.0_x64__xbfy0k16fey96
InstallLocation    : C:\Program Files\WindowsApps\C27EB4BA.Dropbox_4.5.3.0_x64__xbfy0k16fey96
IsFramework        : False
PackageFamilyName  : C27EB4BA.Dropbox_xbfy0k16fey96
PublisherId        : xbfy0k16fey96
IsResourcePackage  : False
IsBundle           : False
IsDevelopmentMode  : False
Dependencies       : {Microsoft.VCLibs.140.00_14.0.24123.0_x64__8wekyb3d8bbwe,
                     Microsoft.NET.Native.Framework.1.3_1.3.24201.0_x64__8wekyb3d8bbwe,
                     Microsoft.NET.Native.Runtime.1.4_1.4.24201.0_x64__8wekyb3d8bbwe,
                     C27EB4BA.Dropbox_4.5.3.0_neutral_split.scale-150_xbfy0k16fey96}


PS C:\WINDOWS\system32>
```

Figure 13-31 Find the app you just installed

7. Select and copy the text for the PackageFullName field of the app to be removed. Enter the command **Remove-AppxPackage** <*PackageFullName*>, as shown in Figure 13-32.

(continues)

Figure 13-32 The text for the PackageFullName field must be typed exactly; therefore, it's easiest to copy and paste

8. Enter the command **Get-AppxPackage** to confirm the app was removed. Also check the Settings app to make sure the app is no longer listed there.

9. Enter **exit** to close the PowerShell session.

> **Notes** By default, Windows 10 lists Windows PowerShell in the Quick Launch menu. You can change this setting so Command Prompt is listed. Open the **Settings** app, click **Personalization,** and click **Taskbar.** Scroll down and turn the slider button to **Off** under *Replace Command Prompt with Windows PowerShell in the menu when I right-click the start button or press Windows key+X.*

Here are some other basic cmdlet features you should know:

▲ *Aliases for command prompt commands.* An alias is a nickname or shortcut for a cmdlet. For convenience, many of the commands you're accustomed to using in a command prompt window also work in PowerShell. These commands are defined as aliases for native PowerShell cmdlets. For example, one default alias for Get-ChildItem is dir. Therefore, you can enter dir in PowerShell to execute the Get-ChildItem cmdlet. Note that an alias applies only to the referenced command and does not include parameters or values (such as a file name) that might be used by the command.

> **Notes** You can create your own aliases using the Set-Alias and New-Alias cmdlets. For example, **Set-Alias show Get-ChildItem** assigns the alias *show* to the cmdlet *Get-ChildItem.*

▲ *List of aliases.* The cmdlet **Get-Alias** shows all the available aliases in the current session, including the default aliases and other aliases you created during the session.

▲ *Help.* To find the cmdlet assigned to a specific alias, use the Help cmdlet (also called Get-Help). For example, enter **help dir** to see the output shown in Figure 13-33. Here you can see that dir is an alias for Get-ChildItem.

> **Notes** At the bottom of Figure 13-33, a message informs the user that the Help files for the cmdlet are not available on the computer. You must install the PowerShell help files to access them; open an elevated PowerShell window, type **Update-Help,** and press **Enter.** The process will take a few minutes. When you return to the PowerShell prompt, enter **help dir** again to see how much additional information you can access.

```
Windows PowerShell                                              —    □    ×

Windows PowerShell
Copyright (C) Microsoft Corporation. All rights reserved.

PS C:\Users\Jean Andrews> help dir

NAME
    Get-ChildItem

SYNTAX
    Get-ChildItem [[-Path] <string[]>] [[-Filter] <string>] [-Include <string[]>] [-Exclude <string[]>
] [-Recurse]
    [-Depth <uint32>] [-Force] [-Name] [-UseTransaction] [-Attributes {ReadOnly | Hidden | System | Di
rectory |
    Archive | Device | Normal | Temporary | SparseFile | ReparsePoint | Compressed | Offline | NotCont
entIndexed |
    Encrypted | IntegrityStream | NoScrubData}] [-Directory] [-File] [-Hidden] [-ReadOnly] [-System]
    [<CommonParameters>]

    Get-ChildItem [[-Filter] <string>] -LiteralPath <string[]> [-Include <string[]>] [-Exclude <string
[]>] [-Recurse]
    [-Depth <uint32>] [-Force] [-Name] [-UseTransaction] [-Attributes {ReadOnly | Hidden | System | Di
rectory |
    Archive | Device | Normal | Temporary | SparseFile | ReparsePoint | Compressed | Offline | NotCont
entIndexed |
    Encrypted | IntegrityStream | NoScrubData}] [-Directory] [-File] [-Hidden] [-ReadOnly] [-System]
    [<CommonParameters>]


ALIASES
    gci
    ls
    dir


REMARKS
    Get-Help cannot find the Help files for this cmdlet on this computer. It is displaying only partia
l help.
        -- To download and install Help files for the module that includes this cmdlet, use Update-Hel
p.
        -- To view the Help topic for this cmdlet online, type: "Get-Help Get-ChildItem -Online" or
           go to https://go.microsoft.com/fwlink/?LinkID=113308.




PS C:\Users\Jean Andrews>
```

Figure 13-33   dir, gci, and ls are all aliases for Get-ChildItem

UBUNTU BASH ON WINDOWS

In response to customer feedback, Microsoft built a Linux shell into Windows 10 that provides a shell prompt to enter Linux commands. Note that this shell is not a VM, and it's not a fully separate operating system; rather, it's a shell that allows users to interact with underlying Windows functions and system files. The new shell requires a Windows component, Windows Subsystem for Linux (WSL), to support it. WSL installs a subset of the Ubuntu distribution of Linux, which is one of the most popular distributions. By default, Ubuntu provides Bash, which is its most popular shell. This shell is called Bash on Ubuntu on Windows, Bash on Windows, or Ubuntu Bash. (It's possible to install other Ubuntu shells by using switcher software in PowerShell.) Many Linux commands work in WSL running Ubuntu Bash.

WSL runs on any 64-bit Windows 10 system with the Anniversary Update build 14393 or later. You must first turn on Developer Mode and then enable the Windows Subsystem for Linux (Beta) feature. As its name suggests, this feature is still in beta as Microsoft continues to resolve many bugs and gaps in compatibility.

13

APPLYING | CONCEPTS   ENABLING WINDOWS SUBSYSTEM FOR LINUX (WSL) AND INSTALLING UBUNTU BASH

Complete the following steps to enable Windows Subsystem for Linux and install Ubuntu Bash on a Windows 10 system:

1. First, turn on Developer Mode.
   a. Open the **Settings** app and click **Update & Security**. In the left pane, scroll down and click **For developers**.
   b. Select **Developer mode**, as shown in Figure 13-34. Click **Yes** to turn on Developer Mode and close the Settings app.

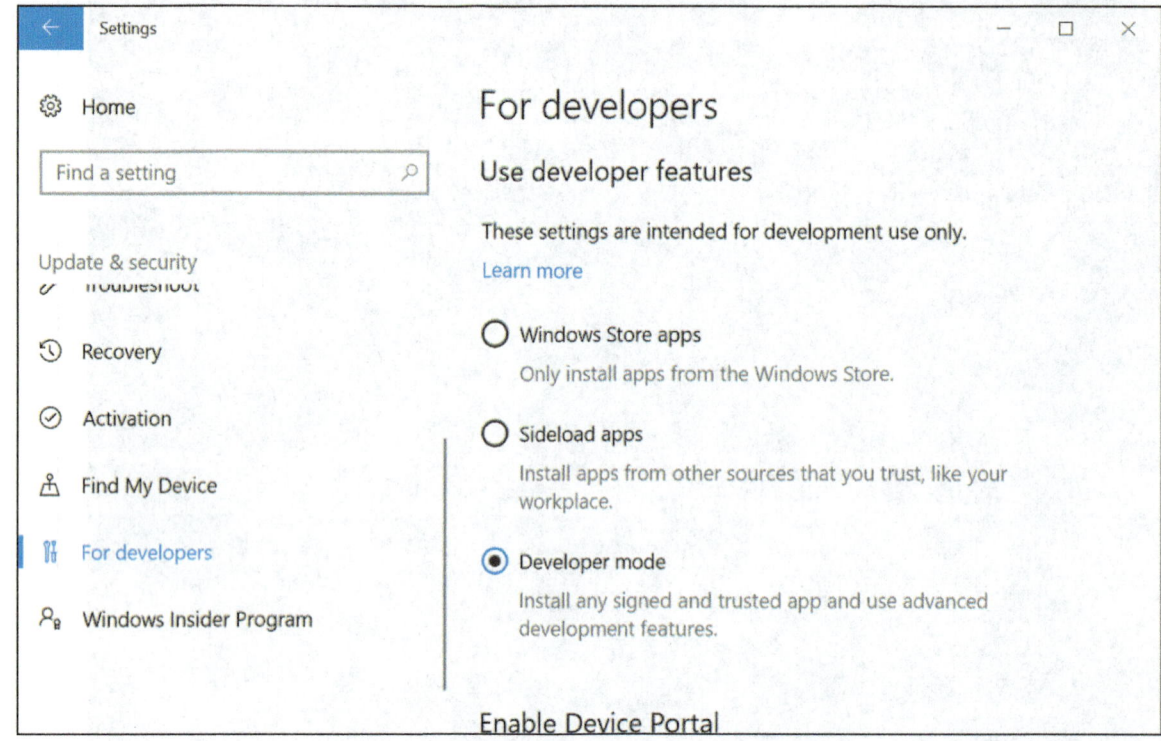

Figure 13-34   Turn on Developer Mode from the Settings app

2. Enable Windows Subsystem for Linux.
   a. Open **Control Panel** and click **Programs and Features**. In the left pane, click **Turn Windows features on or off**.
   b. Scroll down and click **Windows Subsystem for Linux (Beta)**, as shown in Figure 13-35. Click **OK**.

(continues)

Figure 13-35 Turn on the Windows Subsystem for Linux (Beta) feature

   c. Restart the computer when the changes are complete to finish enabling Windows Subsystem for Linux.

3. Install and run Bash on Ubuntu on Windows from the command prompt.
   a. Open a command prompt window and enter **bash** (see Figure 13-36). Note that the first time you enter the bash command, Windows downloads and installs Ubuntu on Windows.

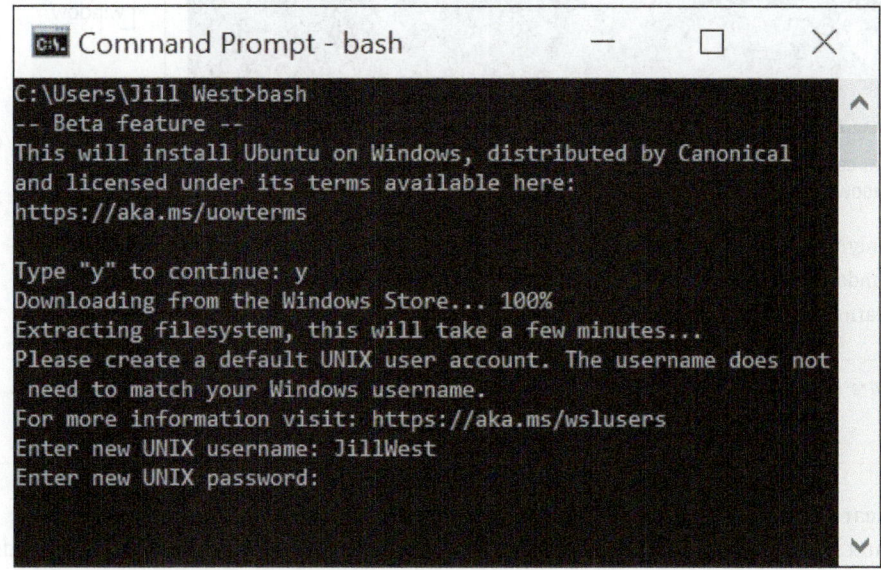

Figure 13-36 The first time you enter the bash command, Windows will download and install Ubuntu on Windows

b. Enter **y** to accept the installation terms. Bash on Ubuntu on Windows downloads from the Windows Store, and then is extracted and installed. This might take several minutes.

c. Enter a new UNIX user name at the prompt. This user name can be different from your Windows user name.

d. Enter a password at the next prompt. The cursor will not move as you type the password. Re-enter the password at the next prompt.

e. After the installation is complete, Windows switches to the Bash on Ubuntu environment with its shell prompt within the command prompt window.

4. You can continue to interact with Ubuntu Bash from the command prompt window, or you can open Bash on Ubuntu on Windows in a separate window. To do this, click **Start** and then click **Bash on Ubuntu on Windows** in the Start menu. You can also open Bash from within PowerShell. See Figure 13-37 to compare the three windows.

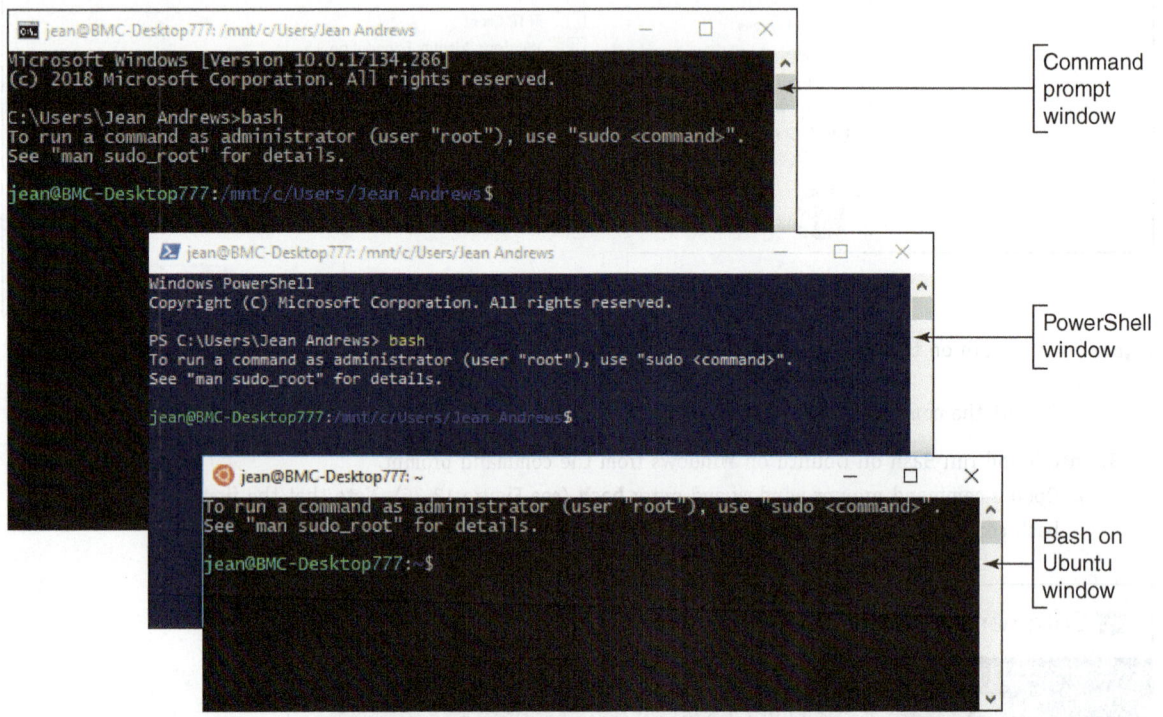

Figure 13-37 Bash on Ubuntu can be accessed from the command prompt, PowerShell, or its own app, Bash on Ubuntu on Windows

At this point, most commonly used Linux commands will work as usual at the Ubuntu shell prompt. The commands interact with the underlying Windows system files, and changes to those files can be monitored through other Windows tools. You'll learn more about Linux commands in Chapter 18.

> ✎ **Notes** Linux commands *are* case sensitive. If you enter Ifconfig, you'll get an error message.

It might seem like you're learning three different languages when you try switching among Command Prompt, PowerShell, and Linux. Table 13-10 provides a quick look at some of the most familiar commands in Command Prompt, allowing you to compare them to similar commands in PowerShell and Linux. Keep in mind that each command will function differently in its respective environment and will also offer various options and limitations. What's really interesting is to explore the extent of these differences and learn how a command in one environment might offer options that another environment does not. What other commands would you add to this list?

Command Prompt	PowerShell	Ubuntu Bash
dir	Get-ChildItem	ls
ipconfig	Get-NetIPConfiguration Get-NetIPAddress	ifconfig iwconfig
ping	Test-NetConnection	ping
cd	Set-Location	cd
tasklist	Get-Process	ps
help *command* *command* /?	Get-Help *command*	*command* -help
exit	Exit	exit

Table 13-10   Common commands in three CLIs

REMOTE CONNECTIONS

A+
CORE 2
1.5, 1.6,
1.8, 4.9

You might find it handy to access your Windows desktop from a remote location, and technicians are sometimes called upon to assist users remotely. Windows 10/8/7 offers Remote Desktop Connection (RDC) for screen and file sharing and Remote Assistance to assist users by screen sharing. In Windows 10, you have a new option to remotely assist a user: Quick Assist. Finally, if using a Windows feature isn't your preferred method, you can also use third-party software for a remote connection.

REMOTE DESKTOP CONNECTION (RDC)

A+
CORE 2
1.5, 1.6,
1.8, 4.9

Remote Desktop Connection (RDC), commonly called Remote Desktop, gives a user access to a Windows desktop from anywhere on the Internet. As a software developer, I find Remote Desktop extremely useful when I work from a remote location (my home office) and need to access a corporate network to support software on that network. Using the Internet, I can access a file server on these secured networks to make my software changes. Remote Desktop is easy to use and relatively safe for the corporate network. To use Remote Desktop, the computer you want to remotely access (the server) must be running business or professional editions of Windows 10/8/7, but the computer you're using to access it (the client) can be running any version of Windows.

> 🖉 **Notes** In Chapter 8, you learned that Remote Desktop Protocol (RDP) is used by the Windows Remote Desktop and Remote Assistance services and that these services listen at port 3389.

> ⭐ **A+ Exam Tip** The A+ Core 2 exam expects you to know how to use Remote Desktop and Remote Assistance and to know which is appropriate in a given scenario.

13

APPLYING | CONCEPTS CONFIGURING REMOTE DESKTOP ON TWO COMPUTERS

A+ CORE 2 1.5, 1.6, 1.8, 4.9

In this section, you see how to set up Remote Desktop for first use, and then you learn how to use it.

How to Set Up Remote Desktop for First Use

The host or server computer is the computer that serves up Remote Desktop to client computers that can "remote in to" (remotely access) the server. To prepare your host computer, you need to configure it for static IP addressing and configure the Remote Desktop service. Here are the steps needed:

1. Configure the computer for static IP addressing. How to assign a static IP address is covered in Chapter 7.

2. If your computer is behind a firewall, configure the router for port forwarding and allow incoming traffic on port 3389. Forward that traffic to the IP address of your desktop computer. You learned how to set up port forwarding in Chapter 7.

3. To turn on the Remote Desktop service, open the **System** window in Control Panel and click **Remote settings** in the left pane. The System Properties box appears with the Remote tab selected (see Figure 13-38). In this window, you can control settings for Remote Assistance and Remote Desktop. In the Remote Desktop area, check **Allow remote connections to this computer**. Leave the box checked for *Allow connections only from computers running Remote Desktop with Network Level Authentication (recommended)*.

Figure 13-38 Configure a computer to run the Remote Desktop service

◇ OS Differences To enable Remote Desktop on a Windows 7 computer, go to the Remote Desktop area on the Remote tab in the System Properties box, and check **Allow connections from computers running any version of Remote Desktop (less secure).**

(continues)

Notes Server applications such as Remote Desktop listen for network activity from clients. If you want these server applications to be available at all times, you can set your network adapter properties to Wake-on-LAN, which you learned about in Chapter 7.

4. Users who have administrative privileges are allowed to use Remote Desktop by default, but other users need to be added. If you need to add a user, click **Select Users** and follow the on-screen directions. Then close all windows.

5. To verify that Windows Firewall is set to allow Remote Desktop activity on this computer, open **Control Panel** and click **Windows Defender Firewall**. (Click **Windows Firewall** in Windows 8.) The Windows Defender Firewall window appears (see Figure 13-39). In the left pane, click **Allow an app or feature through Windows Defender Firewall**.

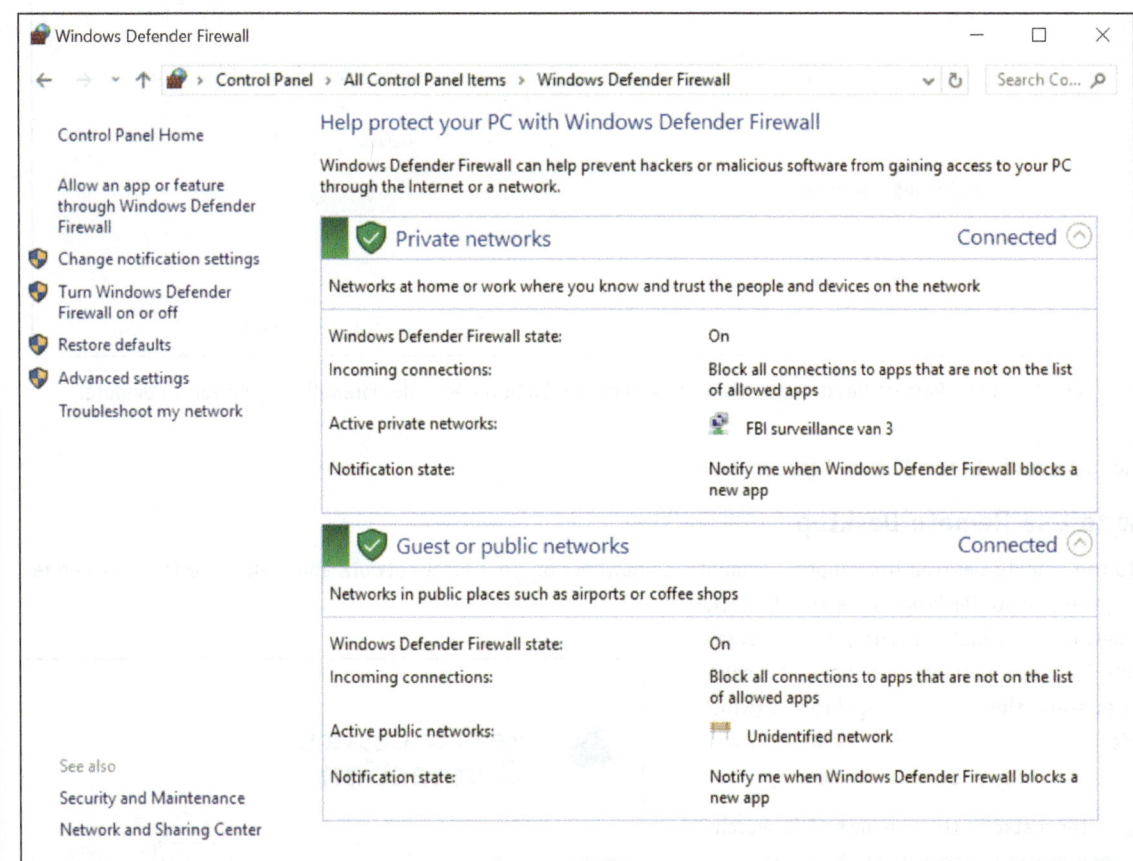

Figure 13-39 Windows Defender Firewall can block or allow activity on the network to your computer

OS Differences To allow Remote Desktop activity on a Windows 7 computer, open the Windows Firewall window and click **Allow a program or feature through Windows Firewall**.

6. The Allowed apps window appears. Scroll down to Remote Desktop and adjust the settings as needed (see Figure 13-40). Click **OK** to apply any changes.

(continues)

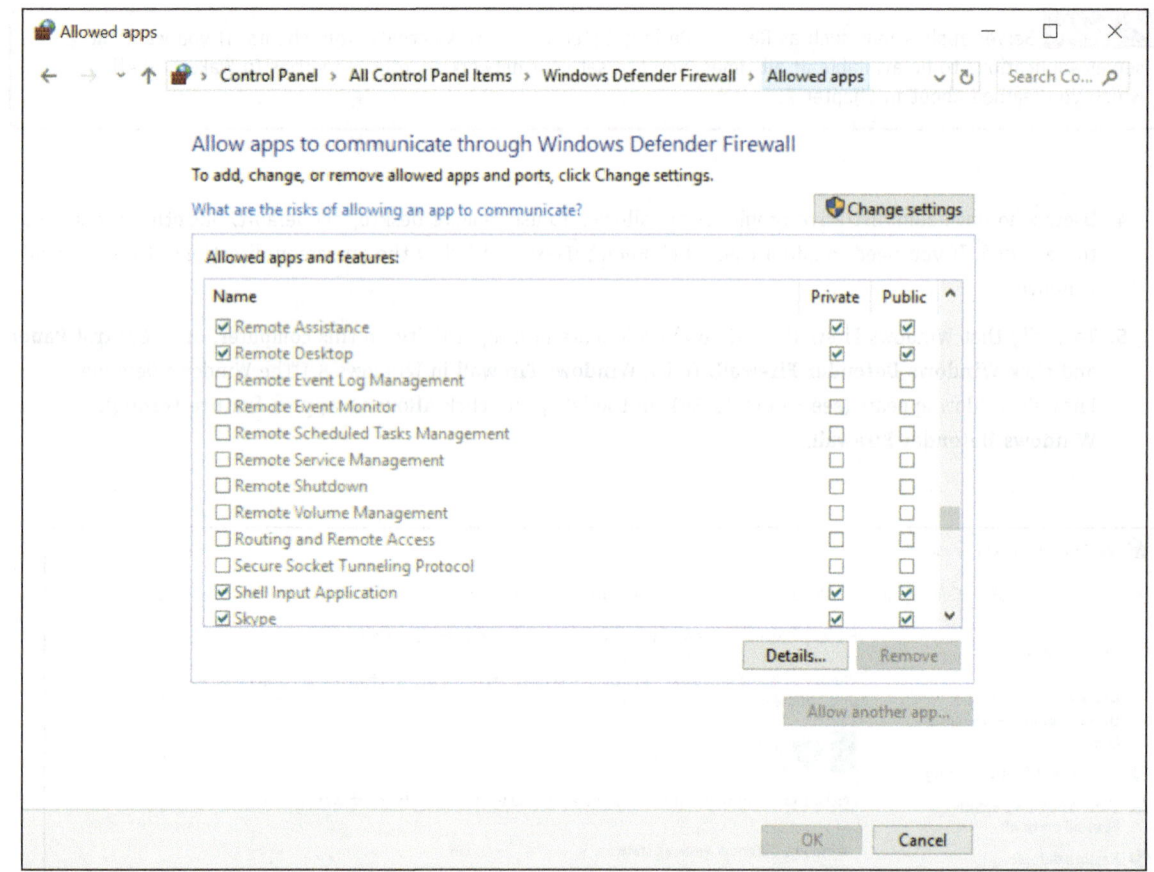

Figure 13-40 Allow Remote Desktop communication through Windows Defender Firewall on your local computer

You are now ready to test Remote Desktop.

How to Use Remote Desktop

Try to use Remote Desktop from another computer somewhere on your local network and make sure it works before testing the Remote Desktop connection from the Internet. On the client computer, you can start Remote Desktop to remote in to your host computer by using the **mstsc.exe** application (which stands for **Microsoft Terminal Services Client**). Follow these steps to use Remote Desktop:

1. Enter **mstsc** in the Windows 10/7 search box or the Windows 8 Run box. The Remote Desktop Connection box opens (see Figure 13-41).

2. Enter the IP address or the host name of the computer to which you want to connect. If you decide to use a host name, begin the name with two backslashes, as in *CompanyFileServer*.

Figure 13-41 The IP address of the remote computer can be used to connect to it

(continues)

3. If you plan to transfer files from one computer to the other, click **Show Options** for Windows 10/8 or **Options** for Windows 7, and then click the **Local Resources** tab, as shown on the left side of Figure 13-42. Click **More** to see the box on the right side of the figure. Check **Drives** and click **OK**. Click **Connect** to make the connection. If a warning box appears, click **Connect** again. If another warning box appears, click **Yes**.

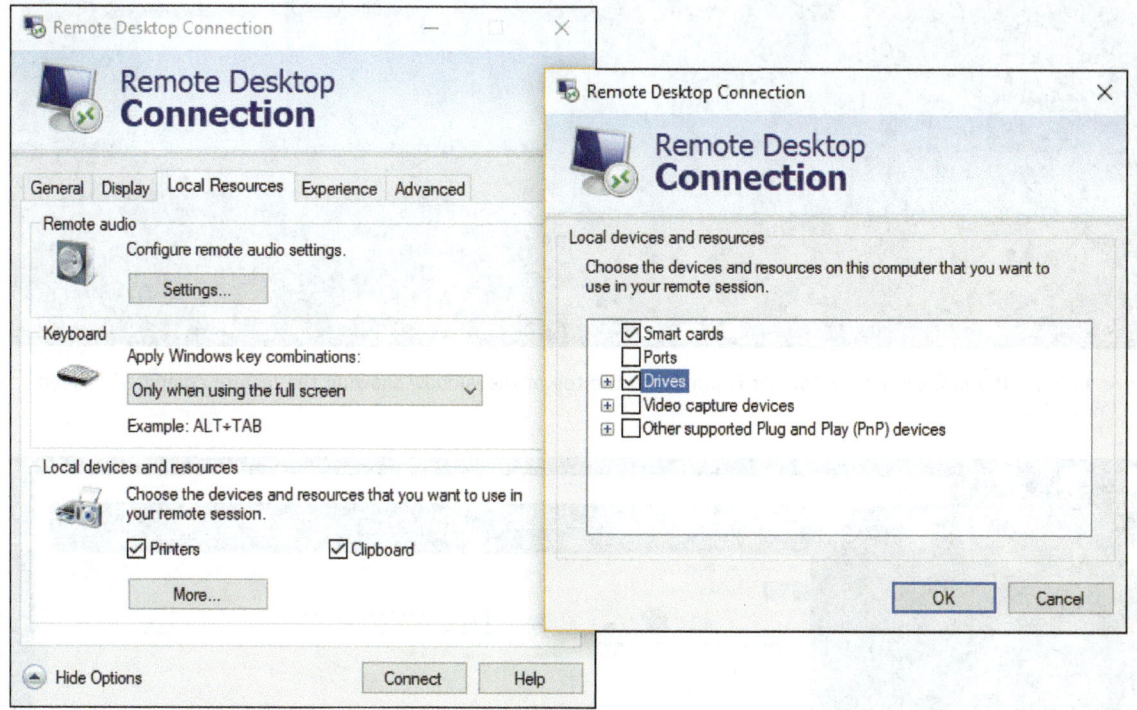

Figure 13-42 Allow drives and other devices to be shared using the Remote Desktop Connection

4. A Windows security box is displayed by the remote computer (see Figure 13-43). Sign in with a user name and password for the remote computer. If a warning box reports that the remote computer might not be secure, click **Yes** to continue the connection.

5. The desktop of the remote computer appears with a toolbar at the top of the screen, as shown in Figure 13-44. Click **Restore Down** to show both the remote desktop and the local desktop on the same screen, as shown in Figure 13-45.

Figure 13-43 Enter your user name and password on the remote computer

(continues)

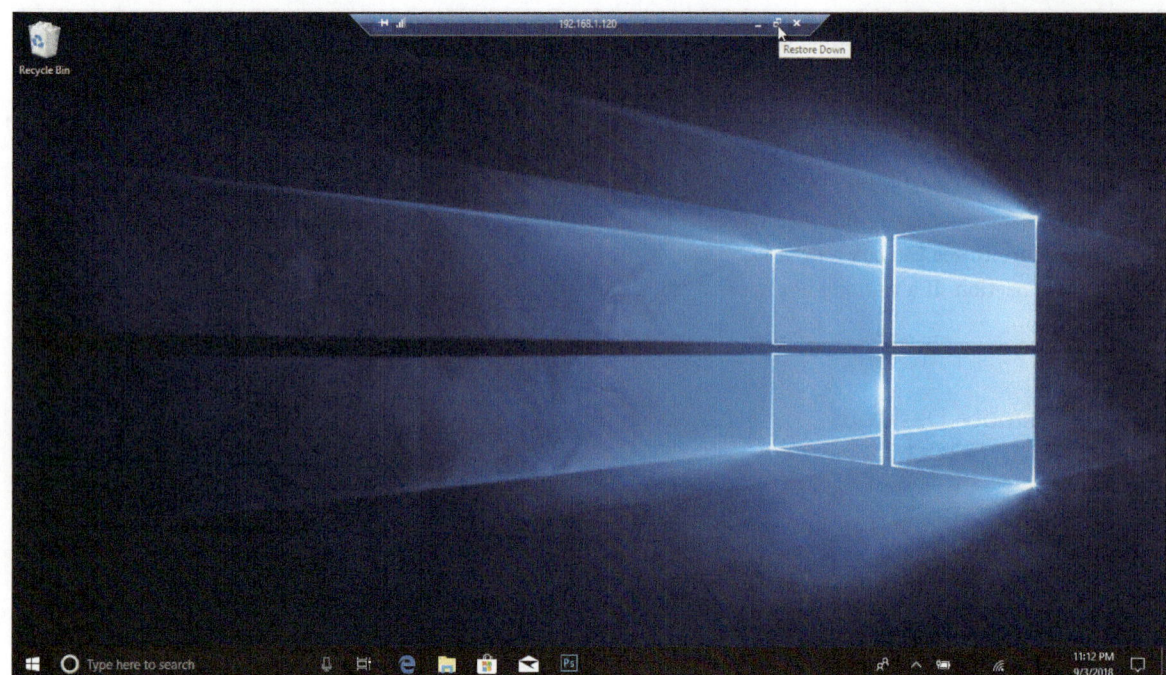

Figure 13-44 The RDC connection toolbar is pinned to the top of the window showing the remote computer's screen

Figure 13-45 The desktop of the remote computer is available on your local computer

📝 **Notes** When a remote desktop connection is made, the user sitting at the remote computer will see it return to the sign-on screen.

6. When you click in the remote desktop's window, you can work with the remote computer just as if you were sitting in front of it, except response time is slower. To move files back and forth between computers, use File Explorer or Windows Explorer on the remote computer. Files on your local computer and on the remote computer will appear in the Explorer window on the remote computer. Specifically, the files will appear in the This PC group in Windows 10/8 or the Windows 7 Computer group. For example, you can see drive C: on each computer labeled in Figure 13-45. To close the connection to the remote computer, sign out from the remote computer or close the desktop window.

> ✏️ **Notes** Even though Windows normally allows more than one user to be signed in at the same time, this is not the case with Remote Desktop. When a Remote Desktop session is opened, all local users on the remote computer must sign out after receiving a warning, as shown in Figure 13-46.

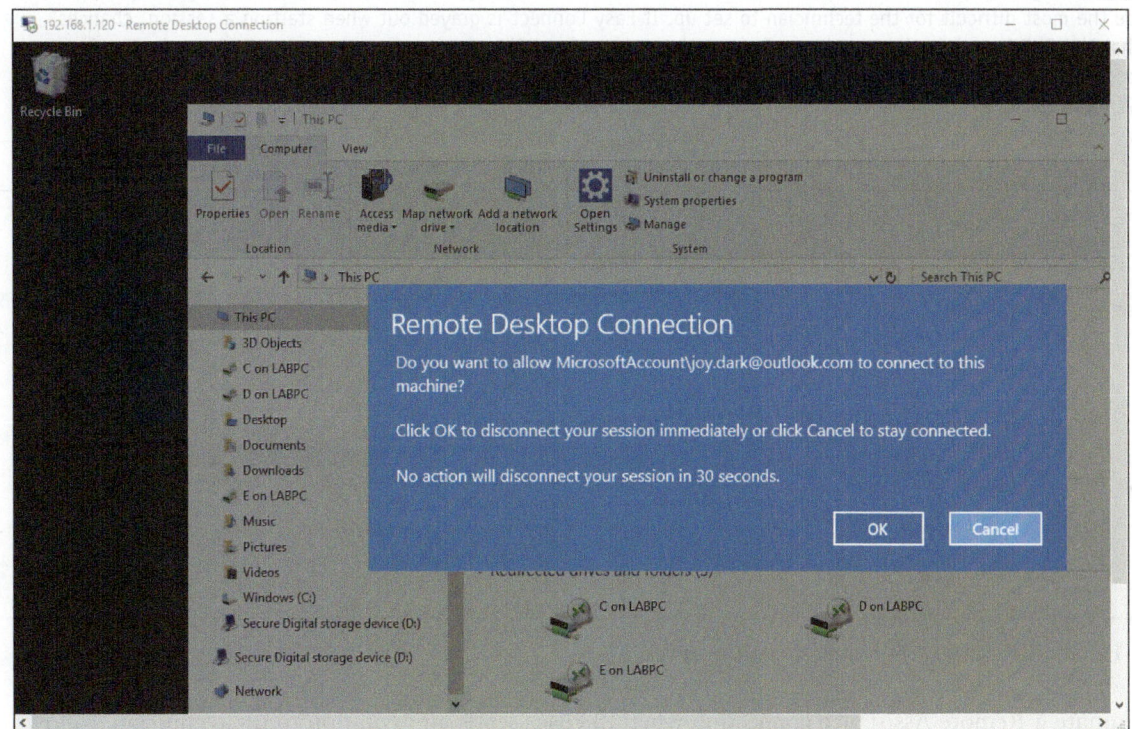

Figure 13-46 Local users must sign out before a Remote Desktop Connection can happen

Is your host computer as safe as it was before you set it to serve up Remote Desktop and enabled port forwarding to it? Actually, no, because a port has been opened, so take this into account when you decide to use Remote Desktop.

REMOTE ASSISTANCE

**A+
CORE 2
1.5, 1.6**

Remote Assistance differs from Remote Desktop in that a user on the server computer can remain signed in during the remote session, retains control of the session, and can see the screen. This is helpful when troubleshooting problems on a computer. The user who needs your help sends you an invitation by email or chat to connect to her computer using Remote Assistance. When you respond to the invitation, you can see the user's desktop just as she sees it; if the user gives you permission, you can take control of her computer to change settings or do whatever else is needed to fix her problem or show her how to perform a task. Think of Remote Assistance as a way to provide virtual desk-side support.

13

There are several ways to initiate a Remote Assistance session. The first method listed is the most reliable:

◢ The user saves an invitation file and then sends that file to the technician. The file can be sent by any method, including email, chat, or posting to a shared folder on the network.

◢ The user can send an automated email through the Remote Assistance app. This option only works if the system is configured with a compatible email program.

◢ The user can use Easy Connect, which is the easiest method to start a Remote Assistance connection but only works if both computers used for the connection are using Windows. Also know that some routers don't support the Peer Name Resolution Protocol (PNRP), which is the protocol Easy Connect uses to establish a Remote Assistance connection.

◢ The technician can initiate a session. This method is the most difficult to use; it requires that Group Policies be applied on the technician's computer. You learn more about Group Policy later in the text.

> ✎ **Notes** Easy Connect is the easiest method for the user when initiating a Remote Assistance connection but it can be the most difficult for the technician to set up. If Easy Connect is grayed out when starting a session, chances are that the PNRP service might be down. To start the service, enter the **services.msc** command to open the Services console (see Figure 13-47). Select **Peer Name Resolution Protocol** and click **Start**. You learn more about services and the Services console in Chapter 14.

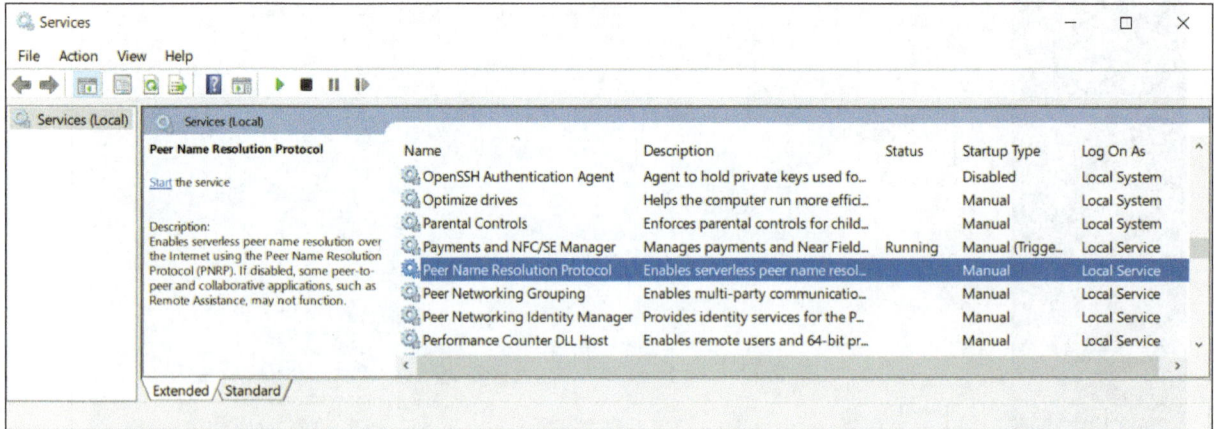

Figure 13-47   Use the Services console to start a service

To initiate a Remote Assistance connection when the user sends an invitation to the technician, follow these steps:

1. To allow Remote Assistance sessions on the user's computer, called the host computer, open the **System** window in Control Panel and click **Remote settings** in the left pane. If the user does not have administrative permissions, he must respond to the UAC box by entering an administrator password. The System Properties box appears with the Remote tab selected (refer back to Figure 13-38).

2. In the Remote Assistance area, check **Allow Remote Assistance connections to this computer**, and then click **OK**.

3. In the search box, type **remote assistance**, then click **Invite someone to connect to your PC and help you, or offer to help someone else**. The Windows Remote Assistance box appears, as shown in Figure 13-48.

> ↻ **OS Differences** To launch Remote Assistance in Windows 8, open **Control Panel** in Category view. Click **System and Security**. Under System, click **Launch remote assistance**. (Alternately, you can press **Win+S** to open the search box and type **Invite**, then click **Invite someone to connect to your PC and help you**.)
>
> To launch Remote Assistance in Windows 7, click **Start**, type **Remote Assistance** in the search box, and then click **Windows Remote Assistance**.

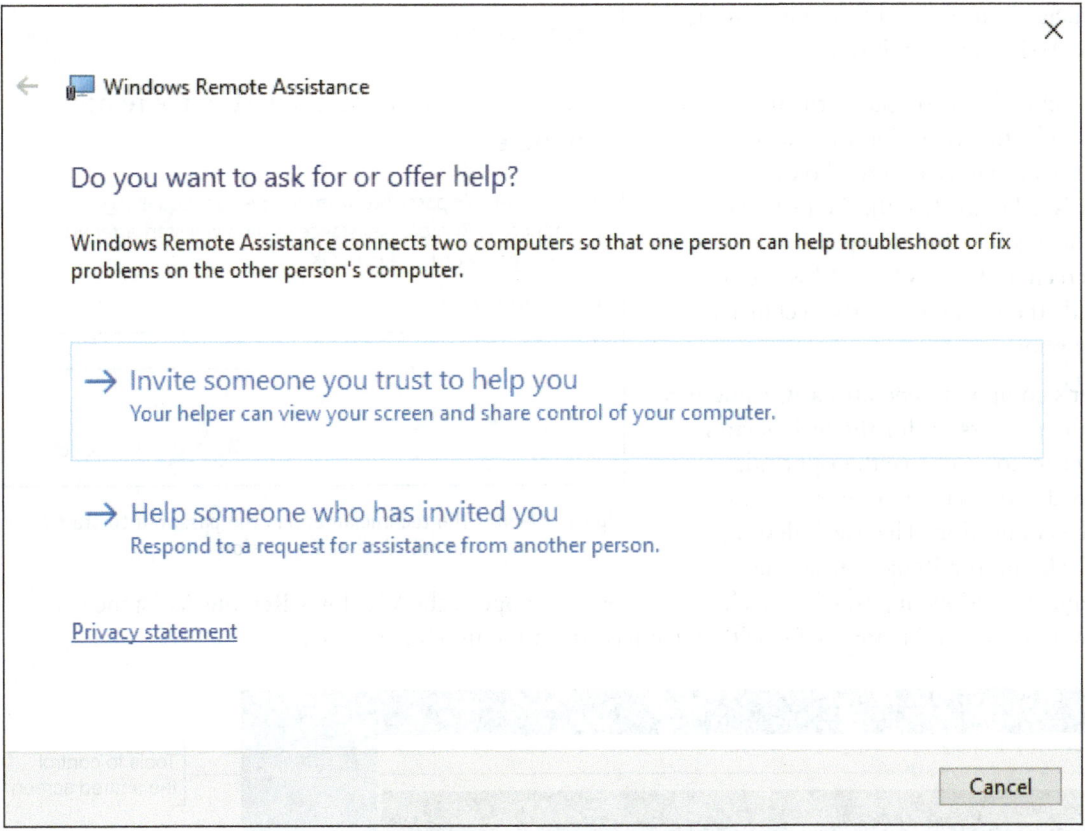

Figure 13-48 Create or respond to an invitation to connect

13

4. Click **Invite someone you trust to help you,** then click **Save this invitation as a file.** Point to a location to save the file and click **Save.** Remote Assistance provides a password for the user to give the technician in order to create the connection (see the left side of Figure 13-49). The user can send the invitation file to the technician as an email attachment or by other means.

Figure 13-49 The user's computer shows a password the technician must enter to connect Remote Assistance

The technician can respond to the invitation into Remote Assistance as follows:

1. On the technician's computer, the technician double-clicks the invitation file she has received from the user. In the box that appears (see Figure 13-50), the technician enters the password that appeared on the user's screen and clicks **OK**. (Most often, the user reads the password to the technician over the phone.)

2. The user's computer generates a warning box requesting permission for the technician's computer to connect (see the right side of Figure 13-49). The user clicks **Yes** to allow the connection. The user's desktop turns black and the Remote Assistance management window appears. The technician's computer opens the Windows Remote Assistance window, as shown in Figure 13-51, with a live feed from the user's computer.

Figure 13-50 The technician enters the password to start a Remote Assistance session

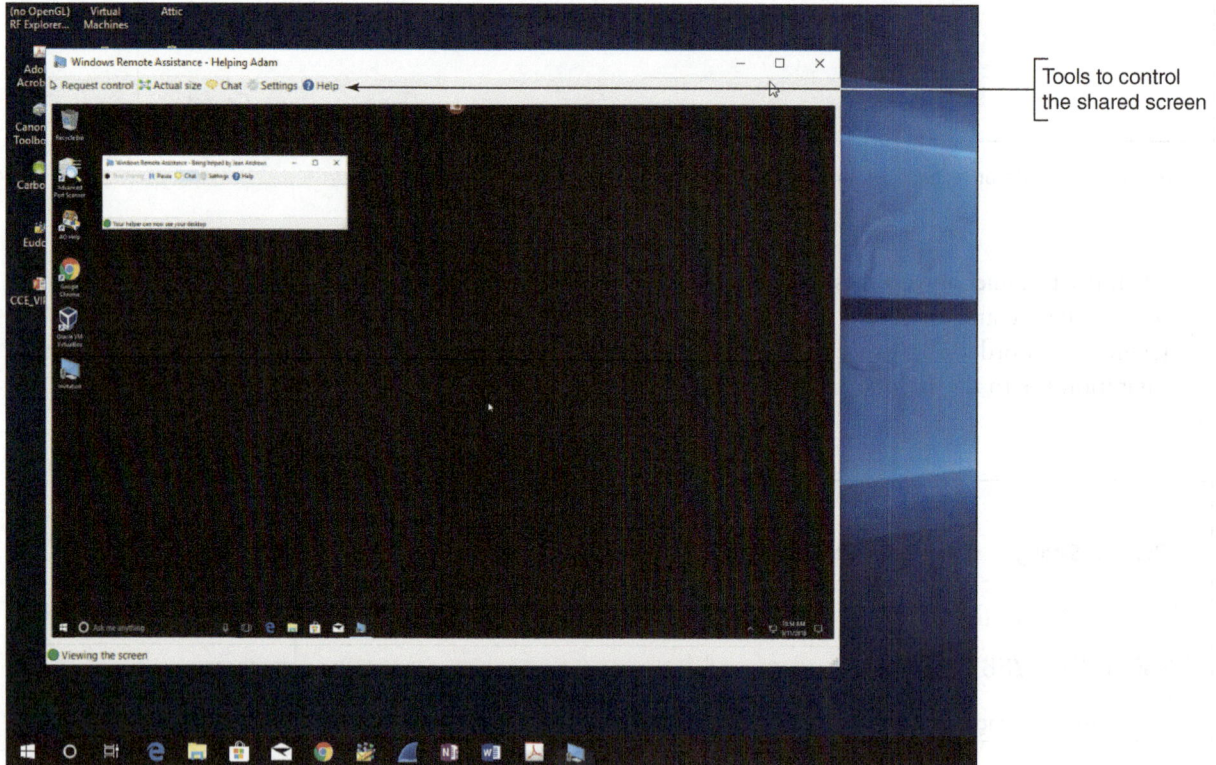

Tools to control the shared screen

Figure 13-51 Control the shared screen using the toolbar options at the top

Using Remote Desktop, you can share files between computers, but Remote Assistance does not allow for file sharing. Here are some things you can do during a Remote Assistance session:

▲ To open a chat session with the user, click the **Chat** icon. A chat pane appears in the Remote Assistance window on both desktops.

▲ To ask the user if you can take control of his desktop, click **Request control** in the Remote Assistance control window. When the user accepts the request, you can control his computer. The user can stop sharing control by clicking **Stop sharing**.

◢ The user can hide his desktop from you at any time by clicking **Pause** in the control window.

◢ Either of you can disconnect the session by closing the control window.

◢ A log file is kept of every Remote Assistance session in the C:\Users*username*\Documents\Remote Assistance Logs folder. The file includes the chat session. If you type instructions during the chat session that will later help the user, he can use the log file to remind him of what was said and done.

◢ If an invitation created by a user is not used within six hours, the invitation expires. This time frame can be changed by clicking **Advanced** in the Remote Assistance section on the Remote tab of the System Properties dialog box.

If you have problems making the connection, do the following:

1. Windows Firewall on the user's computer might be blocking Remote Assistance. Verify that Remote Assistance is checked as an exception to blocked apps in the Windows Firewall window.

2. If you are outside the user's local network, the hardware firewall protecting his network might be blocking Remote Assistance. Verify that port forwarding on that hardware firewall is enabled for Remote Assistance. Remote Assistance uses port 3389, the same RDP port used by Remote Desktop.

> 🖊 **Notes** Because Remote Assistance can be difficult to set up, Windows 10 offers Quick Assist, which is more universally compatible with existing network hardware configurations. For Quick Assist to work, both computers must be running Windows 10, the technician providing assistance must have a Microsoft account, and the person receiving the connection must agree to it by entering a code generated by the technician's client computer.

THIRD-PARTY REMOTE ACCESS

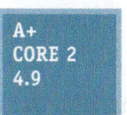

Remote Desktop and Remote Assistance require you to open a port to your network, which is a security risk. Third-party remote access software executed from a browser window is more secure because the browser initiates communication outside the protected network and open listening ports are not required. Examples of this type of software, some of which are free, are TeamViewer (*teamviewer.com*), GoToMyPC by Citrix (*gotomypc.com*), LogMeIn (*logmein.com*), and Zoom (*zoom.us*). When evaluating third-party remote access applications, consider the following:

◢ Where is software installed? On the host, on the client, or on both computers?

◢ How secure is the connection? Are you required to open incoming ports?

◢ How are live screens shared? For example, is a live screen shared only by the host computer or can it be shifted to another computer in the same screen sharing session?

◢ Can files be shared in one or both directions during the same screen sharing session?

>> CHAPTER SUMMARY

Scheduling Preventive Maintenance

◢ Regular preventive maintenance includes verifying Windows Update, anti-malware, and network security settings, uninstalling software you no longer need, and cleaning up and optimizing the hard drive.

◢ Apply 32-bit patches to 32-bit applications and OSs. Apply 64-bit patches to 64-bit applications and OSs.

Backup Procedures

◢ You need a plan for disaster recovery in the event the hard drive fails. This plan needs to include routine backups of data files, the entire Windows volume, critical applications, and system files.

◢ You can back up to local storage or to the cloud. Test your backups to make sure you can restore from them.

▲ Windows 10/8 File History and Windows 10/7 Backup and Restore can be used to schedule routine backups of user data files. Both tools can back up a system image.

▲ The best time to create a system image is right after you've installed Windows, hardware, applications, and user accounts and customized Windows settings.

▲ A Windows 8 custom refresh image backs up the entire Windows volume.

▲ System Protection creates restore points, which include Windows system files that have changed since the last restore point was made.

Managing Files, Folders, and Storage Devices

▲ The MBR partitioning system can support only three primary partitions and one extended partition.

▲ The GPT partitioning system can support up to 128 partitions and hard drives larger than 2.2 TB. A GPT hard drive contains a protective MBR for compatibility with legacy software.

▲ Windows file systems include NTFS, ReFS, NFS, exFAT, FAT32, CDFS, and UDF.

▲ An MBR hard drive has a designated active partition and GPT drives have a designated EFI System Partition that contains the Windows boot manager program that starts Windows. In Windows, this partition is called the system partition.

▲ Use Disk Management to manage hard drives and partitions. Use it to create, delete, and resize partitions, mount a drive, manage dynamic disks, and solve problems with hard drives.

▲ Windows Storage Spaces is expected to replace the Windows solution for software RAID and can support thin provisioning, which allows for physical hard drives to be added to the storage pool as need demands.

▲ To improve hard drive performance, use the Disk Cleanup tool and the Defragment and Optimize Drives tool to clean and optimize the drive.

Using a Command-Line Interface (CLI)

▲ Commands used to manage files, folders, and storage media include help, dir, cd, copy, xcopy, robocopy, chkdsk, defrag, format, and shutdown.

▲ The PowerShell command-line interface uses cmdlets with parameters and is intended to ultimately replace the command prompt window.

▲ Using the Ubuntu Bash interface, you can enter Linux commands in a Windows shell and interact with the Windows system.

Remote Connections

▲ Remote Desktop gives you access to your Windows desktop and file sharing from anywhere on the Internet. Remote Assistance lets you provide remote support to users but does not allow file sharing.

▲ When using Remote Assistance, the user on the host computer can remain signed in during the remote session, retains control of the session, and can see the screen.

▲ When evaluating third-party remote access applications, consider how screens and files are shared and the security of the connection.

>> KEY TERMS

For explanations of key terms, see the Glossary for this text.

active partition
active recovery image
alias
array
Backup and Restore
Bash on Ubuntu on Windows
basic disk
BootMgr
boot partition
cd (change directory)
CDFS (Compact Disc File System)
chkdsk (check disk)
cluster
cmdlets
copy
critical applications
custom refresh image
defrag
defragment
Defragment and Optimize Drives
dir
Disk Cleanup

dynamic disk
dynamic volume
EFI System Partition (ESP)
elevated command prompt window
exFAT
extended partition
FAT (file allocation table)
FAT32
fault tolerance
file allocation unit
File History
file-level backup
formatting
Globally Unique Identifier Partition Table (GUID or GPT)
hardware RAID
help
high-level formatting
image-level backup
logical drives
low-level formatting
Master Boot Record (MBR)

master file table (MFT)
Microsoft Terminal Services Client
mirroring
mount point
mounted drive
mstsc.exe
NFS (Network File System)
NTFS (New Technology file system)
partition table
PowerShell
primary partitions
quick format
RAID (redundant array of inexpensive disks or redundant array of independent disks)
RAID 0
RAID 1
Remote Assistance
Remote Desktop Connection (RDC)
resiliency

Resilient File System (ReFS)
restore points
robocopy (robust file copy)
shutdown
simple volume
slack
software RAID
Storage Spaces
striping
surge protector
system image
system partition
System Protection
System Restore
thin provisioning
trim
UDF (Universal Disk Format)
uninterruptible power supply (UPS)
wildcard
Windows Subsystem for Linux (WSL)
xcopy

>> THINKING CRITICALLY

These questions are designed to prepare you for the critical thinking required for the A+ exams and may use content from other chapters and the web.

1. Order the following routine maintenance tasks from most to least important when securing a computer.

   a. Verify anti-malware settings.

   b. Verify file sharing settings.

   c. Verify Windows Update settings.

   d. Verify that hard drives are being optimized weekly.

2. While verifying Windows settings, you discover defragmenting is turned off for the hard drive. What do you do next?

   a. Immediately defrag the drive.

   b. Turn on defragmenting.

   c. Analyze the drive for errors.

   d. Check the type of hard drive installed.

3. What are reasons to uninstall software you no longer use? Select all that apply.

   a. To prevent Windows errors

   b. To speed up Windows performance

   c. To free up hard drive space

   d. To clean the system of malware

4. What type of storage media must be used to create a Windows system image? Select all that apply.

   a. DVDs

   b. Internal hard drive

   c. External hard drive

   d. Network drive

5. Which Windows utilities are used to create previous versions of files that can be recovered from the file properties dialog box? Select all that apply.

   a. Windows 10/8 File History

   b. Windows 10/7 Backup and Restore

   c. Disk Management

   d. Windows 8 Custom Refresh Image

6. Sarah is setting up Backup and Restore and wants to create a system image. She has discovered that drive E: in the system has plenty of free space for the image. What is the next thing she should check before she creates the image?

   a. Does the Windows volume have enough free space to perform the procedure?

   b. Is there a drive on the network she can use? Network drive images are faster to create.

   c. Is drive E: on the same hard drive as drive C:?

   d. Ask the user which folders on drive C: are the most important and need backing up.

7. Linda works from home occasionally and needs to set up her computer at work so she can remote in from her home office. Which tools should she use?

   a. System Protection

   b. Remote Assistance

   c. Ubuntu Bash

   d. Remote Desktop

8. You suspect malware might have infected restore points saved on the computer and you want to delete them all. What is your next step?

   a. Turn off System Protection.

   b. Run anti-malware software to scan the system for malware.

   c. Harden the Windows Firewall, closing all open ports.

   d. Update Windows.

9. You suspect the hard drive is corrupted. Which window do you open to repair the drive?

   a. Command prompt window to use chkdsk

   b. Elevated command prompt window to use chkdsk

c. Disk Management

d. File Explorer

10. You are planning to install Windows 10 on a computer in a dual-boot configuration. The computer already has Windows 8 installed. You open Disk Management and discover there is one hard drive with an EFI System Partition, a primary partition with plenty of free space, and no unallocated space. In Disk Management, how can you prepare the drive to hold the Windows 10 installation?

   a. There's nothing more to do in Disk Management. Close the windows and begin the installation.

   b. Shrink the EFI System Partition and create a new partition for Windows 10.

   c. Shrink the primary partition and create a simple volume for Windows 10.

   d. Shrink the primary partition and create a new basic disk for Windows 10.

11. Your friend is setting up a computer and plans to use Windows RAID striping. He asks you how many hard drives he should install in the system. What do you tell him?

   a. At least three drives: one to hold the Windows installation and two for the array

   b. At least two drives: the striped array can install on two drives and it can also hold the Windows installation

   c. Only one drive is necessary. He can create extra partitions on the drive; the first can hold Windows and the other two can hold the array.

   d. Suggest to your friend that he use hardware RAID, which is more stable.

12. A family member calls and wants to copy the Notepad text editor to a folder she has just created in the root of drive C:. She asks you to help her construct the command line. Which is the correct command?

   a. `Copy C:\notepad.exe C:\Windows`

   b. `Copy C:\Windows\Notepad.exe C:\`

   c. `Copy C:\Windows\System32\Notepad.exe C:\`

   d. `Copy notepad.exe C:\`

13. Without changing the default folder, what is the command to list all files in the C:\Linda\test2 folder that have file extensions of only two characters?

   a. `Dir C:\Linda\test2\*.??`

   b. `Dir *.*`

   c. `Dir C:\Linda\test2\********.**`

   d. `Dir C:\*.*`

14. You are trying to clean up a slow Windows 8 system that was recently upgraded from Windows 7, and you discover that the 75-GB hard drive has only 5 GB of free space. The entire hard drive is taken up by the Windows volume. What is the best way to free up some space?

   a. Compress the entire hard drive.

   b. Move the /Program Files folder to an external hard drive.

   c. Delete the Windows.old folder.

   d. Uninstall several applications.

15. Which is the best first step to protect important data on your hard drive?

   a. Use dynamic disks to set up a striped volume so that the data has redundancy.

   b. Back up the data to another device.

13

   c. Compress the folder that holds the data.

   d. Put password protection on the data folder.

16. Adam frequently calls your help desk asking for instructions on how to use Windows 10. What is the best way to help Adam?

   a. Open a chat session with Adam over Facebook and talk with him about Windows 10.

   b. Use Remote Assistance to show Adam how to use Windows 10 and point him to the log file created.

   c. Explain to Adam that a help desk is not the place to go to learn to use new software, and he needs to look elsewhere for help.

   d. Email Adam some links to online video tutorials about Windows 10.

17. Remote Desktop and Remote Assistance require a technician to change port settings and firewall settings, but third-party apps such as GoToMyPC do not. Why is this?

   a. Microsoft makes its apps more secure than third-party apps.

   b. GoToMyPC and other third-party apps use ports already left open for web browsing and don't require incoming connections.

   c. Remote Desktop and Remote Assistance allow incoming connections at the same port 80 that is already left open for web browsing.

   d. GoToMyPC and other third-party apps are not concerned about security because they depend on Windows to secure a network connection.

18. Christos is traveling on vacation. On his server at home, he has several movies that he bought and downloaded. He wants to remotely connect with his server at home and watch the movies on his laptop in the hotel. Which remote connection would be best for this purpose and why?

   a. Remote Assistance

   b. Remote Desktop Connection

   c. TeamViewer

   d. Quick Assist

19. Carrie works on a help desk and is assigned a ticket that was automatically generated by a server because of an error. The error message states that the server has run out of storage space because logs were not set to delete at a certain age. Rather than going to the data center to physically access that server on the rack, what Windows tool might Carrie use to troubleshoot the server?

>> HANDS-ON PROJECTS

Hands-On | Project 13-1   Performing Routine Maintenance

Sign in to a Windows system using a standard user account. Step through the process described in the chapter to do the following routine maintenance. As you work, note which chores you cannot perform unless you know the password to an administrator account. Do the following:

   1. Verify critical Windows settings in Windows Update, anti-malware software, and the Network and Sharing Center.

(continues)

2. Open Windows File Explorer or Windows Explorer and view the Properties box of drive C:. What percentage of the volume is free space? Click **Disk Cleanup**. Is the Windows.old folder available for deletion? How much space will Disk Cleanup free?

3. Click **Clean up system files**. How much space will Disk Cleanup free when system files are included in the cleanup? To understand what types of files are selected for deletion, highlight an item and read its description. Don't include files in the cleanup that you think you might need later (for example, previously installed device drivers).

4. Clean the drive. After cleanup, what percentage of the volume is free space?

5. Find out the brand and model of the hard drive that holds Windows. What is the brand and model? Is the drive a magnetic or solid-state drive? How do you know?

6. Check hard drive optimization settings and change them as necessary. Analyze the hard drive and determine if it needs defragmenting or optimizing. If so, optimize the drive.

7. Check the hard drive for errors.

Hands-On | Project 13-2 Using System Restore

Do the following to find out how System Restore works and how it can affect a system:

1. Create a restore point.

2. Make a change to the display settings.

3. Change the desktop background.

4. Create a new text file in your Documents folder.

5. Restore the system using System Restore.

Is the text file still in your Documents folder? Are the other changes still in effect? Why or why not?

13

Hands-On | Project 13-3 Using Disk Management on a Virtual Machine

In a project in Chapter 12, you used Client Hyper-V software to install Windows in a virtual machine. Use this VM to practice using Disk Management. Do the following:

1. Open Hyper-V Manager, but do not open the virtual machine.

2. With the virtual machine selected, click **Settings**. Use the Settings box to add a new hard drive to the VM: Click **IDE Controller 0** in the left pane, click **Hard Drive** in the right pane, and then click **Add**. The Settings box to add a hard drive appears (see Figure 13-52). With **Virtual hard disk** selected, click **New**.

(continues)

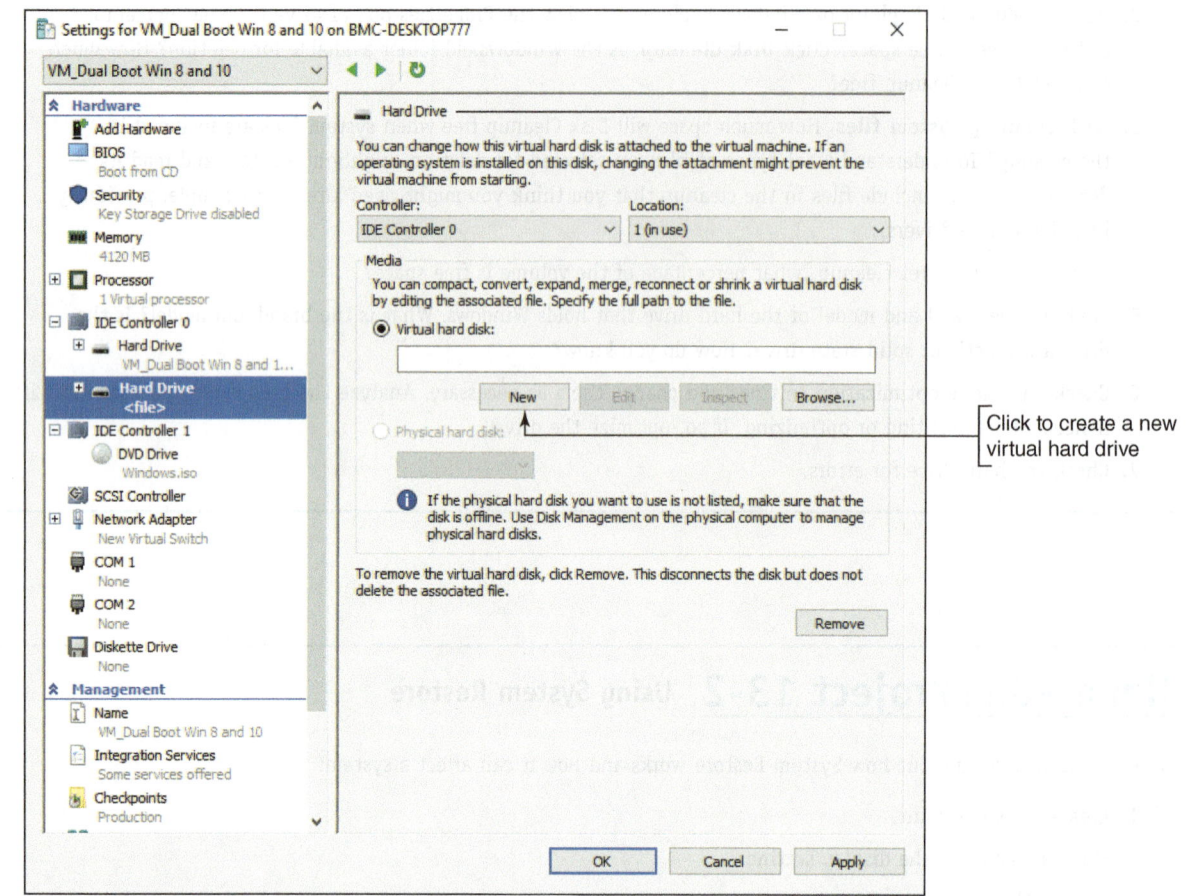

Figure 13-52 Add a new virtual hard drive to IDE Controller 0

3. The New Virtual Hard Disk Wizard starts. Step through the wizard using these values:
   a. For the format type, select **VHDX**.
   b. For the type of virtual hard drive, select **Dynamically expanding**.
   c. Name the virtual hard drive: **HDD2**.
   d. To specify the location of the virtual hard drive, click **Browse** and point to the same folder where the VM is stored.
   e. Leave all other settings at their default values.

4. Click **Finish** to create the virtual hard drive. The wizard closes.

5. In the Settings box, click **Apply** to save your changes. Close the Settings box.

6. Start up the VM, sign in to Windows 10, and open **Disk Management**.

7. Use Disk Management to initialize the new disk and partition it. Create two partitions on the disk: one formatted using the NTFS file system and one using the FAT32 file system.

8. View the new volumes using File Explorer.

9. Create and save a snip of your screen showing the virtual machine with the new volumes created. Email the snip to your instructor.

Hands-On | Project 13-4 **Using a Batch File**

A file with a .bat file extension is called a batch file. You can use a batch file to execute a group of commands, sometimes called a script, from a command prompt. Do the following to learn to use a batch file:

1. Make sure you have at least two files in your Documents folder (My Documents in Windows 7), not including subfolders. Using a command prompt window, copy the files in your Documents folder to a folder named \Save on a USB flash drive. Don't include subfolders in the copy. Create a new subfolder named \Save\Myfiles on the flash drive. Copy (don't move) the two files in your \Save folder to the \Save\Myfiles folder.

2. Using Notepad, create a batch file named MyBatch.bat on the USB flash drive that contains the commands to do the following:
   a. Create the C:\Data folder on your hard drive.
   b. Use xcopy to copy the \Save folder and subfolder to your C:\Data folder.
   c. List the contents of the C:\Data\Save\Myfiles folder.
   d. Delete the C:\Data\Save folder.
   e. Create a new folder named \Save\Newfolder on your flash drive.
   f. Use the robocopy command to copy the \Save folder and both subfolders to the C:\Data folder, creating a log file of the command results on your flash drive. Name the log file Mylog.txt.

3. Using a command prompt window, execute the MyBatch.bat file and fix any problems you see. What happens when you execute the batch file and the C:\Data\Save folder already exists?

Hands-On | Project 13-5 **Exploring the Get-ChildItem Cmdlet**

13

Complete the following steps to practice using parameters with the Get-ChildItem cmdlet:

1. Open a standard PowerShell window. By default, you begin at the home directory of your user account.

2. Enter the cmdlet **Get-ChildItem**. This produces a list of files and folders in your user's home directory.

3. By adding the -recurse parameter, you can retrieve a list of files and folders that also shows the contents of those folders. To do this, enter the cmdlet **Get-ChildItem -recurse**. If you have many files and folders stored in your user account, it might take a while for this output to scroll by on your screen. Press **Ctrl+C** to stop the output.

4. Instead of listing all the contents of all the folders in your user account, you might want to limit the depth of that information to only one or two layers. Here's where the -depth parameter comes in. Enter the cmdlet **Get-ChildItem -recurse -depth 1** and compare the output this time to the extensive output you received in the previous step.

5. You can also limit the search to only certain types of files in a particular location. Here, let's combine the -recurse parameter with the -include parameter to list all the .jpg and .png files in your Pictures folder. Using your own user name, enter the cmdlet **Get-ChildItem -recurse C:\users***username***\Pictures*.* -include *.jpg,*.png**, as shown in Figure 13-53. This instructs Windows to search the Pictures folder and its subfolders for files of any name and type, but to list only those files with the .jpg or .png file type. (The -exclude parameter would show all file types *except* those listed in the cmdlet.)

(continues)

Figure 13-53 The -recurse parameter shows the contents of the listed folder, and the -include parameter limits the output to only the file types given in the cmdlet

6. The output of a cmdlet can be piped, or fed for immediate use, into another cmdlet in the same entry. Suppose you want to sort the picture files in the previous step by size rather than by file name. Enter the cmdlet **Get-ChildItem -recurse c:\users***username***\Pictures*.* -include *.jpg,*.png | Sort-Object length**. By default, this shows the files in ascending order.

7. To sort in descending order instead, specify the -descending parameter: **Get-ChildItem -recurse c:\ users***username***\Pictures*.* -include *.jpg,*.png | Sort-Object length -descending**.

>> REAL PROBLEMS, REAL SOLUTIONS

REAL PROBLEM 13-1 Researching the WinSxS Folder

While cleaning up a hard drive, you begin to look for folders that are excessively large and discover the C:\Windows\WinSxS folder is more than 7 GB. That's almost half the size of the entire C:\Windows folder on this drive. Use the web to research the purpose of the WinSxS folder. What goes in this folder and how does it get there? How can the size of the folder be reduced without causing major trouble with the OS? Write a one-page paper about this folder and cite at least three articles you find on the web about it.

REAL PROBLEM 13-2 Cleaning Up a Sluggish Windows System

Do you have a Windows system that is slow and needs optimizing? If not, talk with family and friends and try to find a slow system that can use your help. Using all the tools and techniques presented in this chapter, clean up this sluggish Windows system. Take detailed notes as you go, listing what you checked before you started to solve the problems, describing what you did to solve the problems, and describing the results of your efforts. What questions did you have along the way? Bring these questions to class for discussion.

REAL PROBLEM 13-3 Creating a Virtual Hard Drive

You can use the Disk Management tool or the diskpart command to create a virtual hard drive (VHD) on a physical computer. The VHD is a file that takes up some free space on the physical hard drive, but to the

Windows interface, it appears as a second hard drive. You can store data in folders and files on the VHD and even install Windows in the VHD. Follow these steps to create a VHD:

1. In Disk Management, click **Action** in the menu bar and click **Create VHD**. Follow the on-screen directions to create the VHD, specifying its location on the hard drive and its size. You can make the size dynamically expanding. The VHD is listed as a Disk in the Disk Management window.

2. Right-click the new disk and click **Initialize Disk**. Use the GPT partitioning system for the disk.

3. To format the disk, right-click the unallocated space on the disk and click **New Simple Volume**. The VHD is now ready for use and appears in File Explorer or Windows Explorer as a new volume.

Discuss in your class and research online how a VHD might be useful. What are two uses of a VHD in which it offers advantages over using a physical hard drive?

13

Troubleshooting Windows After Startup

In previous chapters, you learned about the tools and strategies to install and maintain Windows and about the importance of keeping good backups. This chapter takes you one step further as an IT support technician so that you can solve problems with Windows, applications, and hardware using Windows tools and methods. This chapter is about problems that occur after startup. Troubleshooting Windows startup is covered in Chapter 15. We begin the chapter by learning about the Windows concepts and tools you'll need to optimize and troubleshoot Windows. Then we turn our attention to general steps you can follow when solving Windows, applications, and hardware problems, and finally move on to specific problems you might encounter and how to solve them. As you read the chapter, you might consider following along using a Windows 10/8/7 system.

> ✎ **Notes** Windows installed in a virtual machine is an excellent environment to use when practicing the skills in this chapter.

CONCEPTS AND WINDOWS TOOLS FOR SOLVING PROBLEMS WITH WINDOWS, APPLICATIONS, AND HARDWARE

> **A+**
> **CORE 2**
> **1.4, 1.5,**
> **1.6**

Knowledge is power when it comes to supporting Windows. In this part of the chapter, you learn more about how Windows works and how it is structured. We also survey several Windows tools that are useful when solving a problem with Windows, applications, Windows users, networks, and hardware. In later parts of the chapter, you learn to use these tools to solve typical problems you might encounter as an IT technician supporting Windows.

WHAT ARE THE SHELL AND THE KERNEL?

> **A+**
> **CORE 2**
> **1.4, 1.5,**
> **1.6**

It might sound like we're talking about a grain of wheat, but Windows has a shell and a kernel, and you need to understand what they are and how they work so you can solve problems with each. A shell is the portion of an OS that relates to the user and to applications. The kernel is responsible for interacting with hardware. Figure 14-1 shows how the shell and kernel relate to users, applications, and hardware. In addition, the figure shows a third component of an OS, the configuration data. For Windows, this data is primarily contained in the registry.

Figure 14-1   Inside an operating system, different components perform various functions

THE WINDOWS SHELL

The shell provides tools such as File Explorer or the Windows desktop as a way for the user to do such things as select music to burn to a CD or launch an application. For applications, the shell provides commands and procedures that applications can call on to do such things as print a document, read from a storage device, or display a photograph on the screen.

The shell is made up of several subsystems that all operate in user mode, which means these subsystems have only limited access to system information and can access hardware only through other OS services. One of these subsystems, the Win32 security subsystem, provides sign-in to the system and other security functions, including privileges for file access. All applications relate to Windows by way of the Win32 subsystem.

THE WINDOWS KERNEL

The kernel, or core, of the OS is responsible for interacting with hardware. Because the kernel operates in kernel mode, it has more power to communicate with hardware devices than the shell has. Applications operating under the OS cannot get to hardware devices without the shell passing those requests to the kernel. This separation of tasks provides for a more stable system and helps to prevent a wayward application from destabilizing the system.

The kernel has two main components: (1) the HAL (hardware abstraction layer), which is the layer closest to the hardware, and (2) the executive services interface, which is a group of services that operate in kernel mode between the user mode subsystems and the HAL. Executive services contained in the ntoskrnl.exe program file manage memory, I/O devices, file systems, some security, and other key components directly or by way of device drivers.

> **Notes** In Task Manager, the Windows processes group on the Processes tab shows that the Windows kernel process ntoskrnl.exe appears as System.

When Windows is first installed, it builds the HAL based on the type of CPU installed. The HAL cannot be moved from one computer to another, which is one reason you cannot copy a Windows installation from one computer to another.

14

DIRECTORY STRUCTURES

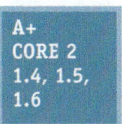
A+
CORE 2
1.4, 1.5,
1.6

Folder or directory locations you need to be aware of include those for user files, program files, and Windows data. In the folder locations given in this discussion, we assume Windows is installed on drive C:.

USER PROFILE NAMESPACE

When a user first signs in to Windows, a user profile is created. This collection of user data and settings consists of two general items:

- ◢ *A user folder together with its subfolders.* These items are created under the C:\Users folder—for example, C:\Users\Jean Andrews. This folder contains a group of subfolders collectively called the user profile namespace. (In general, a namespace is a container to hold data—for example, a folder.)
- ◢ *NTUSER.DAT.* NTUSER.DAT is a hidden file stored in the C:\Users*username* folder that contains user settings. Each time the user signs in, the contents of this file are copied to a location in the registry.

PROGRAM FILES

Here is where Windows stores program files unless you select a different location when a program is installed:

◢ Program files are stored in C:\Program Files for 32-bit versions of Windows. Only 32-bit applications can be installed in a 32-bit installation of Windows.

◢ In 64-bit versions of Windows, 64-bit programs are stored in the C:\Program Files folder, and 32-bit programs are stored in the C:\Program Files (x86) folder. (For best performance, when you have the option, install 64-bit applications in a 64-bit installation of Windows.)

Here are folders that applications and some utilities use to launch programs at startup:

◢ A program file or shortcut to a program file stored in the C:\Users*username*\AppData\Roaming\ Microsoft\Windows\Start Menu\Programs\Startup folder launches at startup for an individual user.

◢ A program file or shortcut to a program file stored in the C:\ProgramData\Microsoft\Windows\Start Menu\Programs\Startup folder launches at startup for all users.

FOLDERS FOR WINDOWS DATA

An operating system needs a place to keep hardware and software configuration information, user preferences, and application settings. This information is used when the OS is first loaded and when needed by hardware, applications, and users. Windows uses a database called the registry for most of this information. In addition, Windows keeps some data in text files called initialization files, which often have an .ini or .inf file extension.

Here are some important folder locations used for the registry and other Windows data:

◢ *Registry location.* The Windows registry is stored in the C:\Windows\System32\config folder.

◢ *Backup of the registry.* A backup of the registry is stored in the C:\Windows\System32\config\RegBack folder.

◢ *Fonts.* Fonts are stored in the C:\Windows\Fonts folder.

◢ *Temporary files.* These files, which are used by Windows when it is installing software and performing other maintenance tasks, are stored in the C:\Windows\Temp folder.

◢ *Offline files.* Offline files are stored in the CSC (client-side caching) folder, which is C:\Windows\CSC. The folder is managed by Sync Center, an applet in Control Panel, which syncs files in a shared folder on the network with the \CSC folder on the local computer. Users can work with the \CSC folder when the computer is offline; later, when the computer is connected to the network, Sync Center can sync up the files with those on the network share. How to use Sync Center is covered in Chapter 16.

✎ **Notes** Most often, Windows is installed on drive C:, although in a dual-boot environment, one OS might be installed on C: and another on a different drive. For example, Windows 8 can be installed on C: and Windows 10 installed on E:. Also, drive C: for one OS in a dual-boot system is likely to have a different drive letter in the other OS.

If the drive letter of the Windows volume is not known, it is written in Microsoft documentation as *%SystemDrive%*. For example, the location of the Program Files folder is written as *%SystemDrive%*\Program Files.

HOW WINDOWS MANAGES APPLICATIONS

A+
CORE 2
1.4, 1.5,
1.6

When an application is first installed, its program files are normally stored on the hard drive. When the application is launched, the program is copied from the hard drive into memory and there it is called a process. A process is a program that is running under the authority of the shell, together with the system resources assigned to it. System resources might include other programs the process has started and memory addresses to hold its data. When the process makes a request for resources, this request is made to the Win32 subsystem and is called a thread. A thread is a single task, such as the task of printing a file that the process requests from the kernel. Figure 14-2 shows two threads in action, which is possible because the process and Windows support multithreading. Sometimes a process is called an instance, such as when you say to a user, "Open two instances of Internet Explorer." Technically, you are saying to open two Internet Explorer processes.

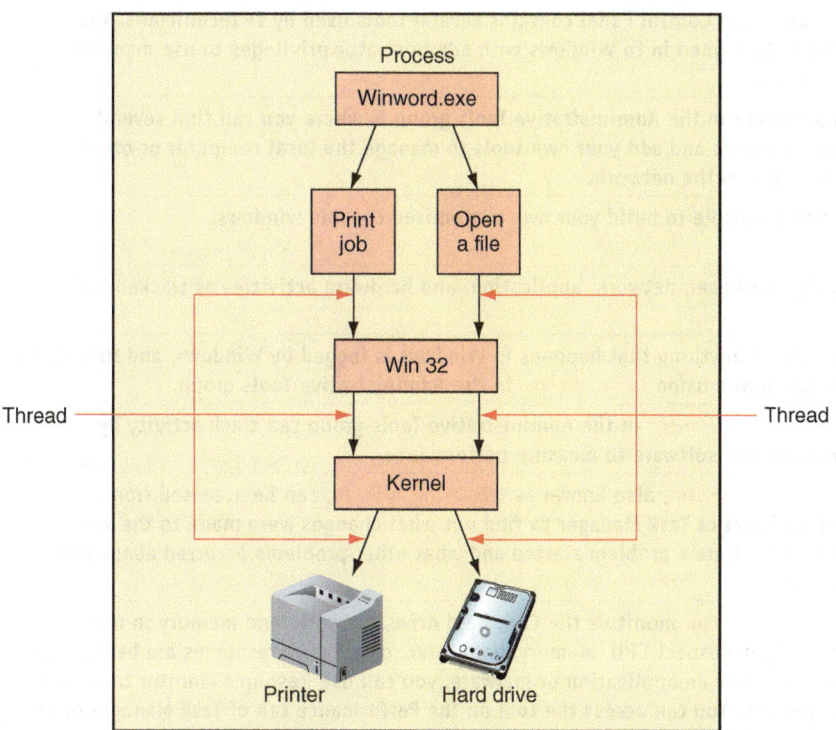

Figure 14-2 A process with more than one thread is called multithreading

SURVEY OF WINDOWS TOOLS AND TECHNIQUES

A+
CORE 2
1.4, 1.5,
1.6

With an understanding of how Windows is structured, let's turn our attention to useful tools and techniques for managing and troubleshooting Windows, applications, users, hardware, and networks. Table 14-1 lists many of these tools. As you read through the list, try to form a context for how you might use a tool to help you solve a Windows-related problem. To get started, launch each tool and take a look at how its window is organized, the basic functions available, and what is on each tab in a window. Later in the chapter, you learn how to apply each tool as you address many typical Windows problems.

⭐ **A+ Exam Tip** The A+ Core 2 exam gives you a scenario with possible alternatives toward a solution. It expects you to know which Windows tool to use and how to use it to resolve a problem. These Windows tools include Computer Management, Performance Monitor, the Services console, System Configuration, Data Sources, Print Management, Event Viewer, Task Manager, the Registry Editor, MMC, and DxDiag. All of these tools are discussed in this chapter.

⭐ **A+ Exam Tip** In performance-based questions on the A+ Core 2 exam, you are expected to know how to access a Windows tool using more than one method. It's a good idea to know the command that launches a given tool.

14

Tool	Description
Use these tools to conveniently access and manage other Windows tools:	
Control Panel	Control Panel is a collection of small programs, called applets, that are used to manage many Windows settings. To open Control Panel in Windows 10/7, enter Control Panel in the search box. For Windows 8, right-click Start and click Control Panel.
Administrative Tools	This applet in Control Panel contains several tools used by IT technicians. You need to be signed in to Windows with administrator privileges to use many of these tools.
Computer Management (compmgmt.msc)	This console in the Administrative Tools group is where you can find several Windows tools and add your own tools to manage the local computer or other computers on the network.
Microsoft Management Console (MMC, mmc.exe)	Use this console to build your own customized console windows.
Use these tools to observe Windows, Windows user, network, application, and hardware activities as tracked and logged by Windows:	
Event Viewer (eventvwr.msc)	Just about anything that happens in Windows is logged by Windows, and these logs can be viewed using Event Viewer in the Administrative Tools group.
Performance Monitor (perfmon.msc)	Performance Monitor in the Administrative Tools group can track activity by hardware and software to measure performance.
Reliability Monitor	Reliability Monitor, also known as reliability history, can be accessed from Control Panel or Task Manager to find out what changes were made to the system around the time a problem started and what other problems occurred about that same time.
Resource Monitor (resmon.exe)	Resource Monitor monitors the CPU, hard drive, network, and memory in real time. If you suspect CPU, memory, hard drive, or network resources are being used excessively by an application or malware, you can use Resource Monitor to identify the process. You can access the tool on the Performance tab of Task Manager or in the Administrative Tools group.
Solve Windows, application, networking, and Windows user problems with these tools:	
Task Manager (taskmgr.exe)	Task Manager lets you view the applications and processes running on your computer as well as information about process and memory performance, network activity, and user activity. Use Task Manager to end a process causing trouble and to enable or disable programs that launch at Windows startup. One way to access Task Manager is to press Ctrl+Alt+Del and click Task Manager.
System Configuration (msconfig.exe)	Use the System Configuration utility (commonly called "*M-S-config*") in the Administrative Tools group to temporarily disable programs from launching at startup in order to troubleshoot a startup problem.
Services console (services.msc)	Use the Services console in the Administrative Tools group to control Windows and third-party services installed on a system.
Troubleshooting	Use the Troubleshooting applet in Control Panel to automatically troubleshoot and fix many common Windows problems involving applications, hardware, sound, networking, Windows updates, and maintenance tasks.
Group Policy (gpedit.msc)	Group Policy is used on a Windows domain to secure and manage the domain; it can control what users can do and how Windows clients in the domain can be used.
Local Group Policy (gpedit.msc)	Local Group Policy is a limited version of Group Policy included in business and professional editions of Windows (not home editions) and applies to the local computer. Use it to control a variety of application, user, and Windows settings.
Registry Editor (regedit.exe)	Use the Registry Editor to back up and edit the Windows registry.

Table 14-1 Tools and techniques to solve Windows-related problems (continues)

Tool	Description
Solve Windows problems using these tools:	
System File Checker (sfc.exe)	Use System File Checker (SFC) to verify and replace Windows system files. It keeps a cache of current system files in case it needs to refresh a damaged file.
DISM (dism.exe)	Use DISM (Deployment Image Servicing and Management) to repair corrupted Windows system files when SFC cannot do the job or Windows Update is corrupted.
Windows Updates	Use Windows Updates to download and apply the latest Windows updates to solve problems with Windows, applications, and hardware. In Windows 10, open Windows Updates in the Settings app. For Windows 8/7, use the System window to find Windows Updates.
Clean boot	A clean boot disables all third-party software that has been added to the Windows startup process. To clean boot, use System Configuration and Task Manager to disable all but Microsoft services launched at startup. You learn how to do this later in the chapter.
Safe Mode, aka Safe boot	Safe Mode goes beyond a clean boot; it not only eliminates third-party software from Windows startup, it also reduces startup to only the Windows minimum configuration necessary to start the OS. It can create a stable environment when the Windows system or device drivers become corrupted. First try a clean boot. If that doesn't resolve a problem, try Safe Mode. To do so, use System Configuration to restart the computer in Safe boot.
System Restore (rstrui.exe)	Use System Restore to revert the system back to a previously saved restore point before a problem started.
Solve application errors or crashes with these tools:	
Programs and Features (appwiz.cpl)	Use the Programs and Features tool in Control Panel to repair and uninstall applications and enable and disable Windows features.
tasklist	The tasklist command reports the process identifier (PID), which is a number that identifies each running process.
taskkill	The taskkill command uses the process ID to kill the task or process. Use taskkill to end a process when Task Manager is unable to do so.
Component Services	Use Component Services (also called COM+) in the Administrative Tools group to register components in the Windows registry so that an application can access the component. This resolves a problem that happens when a component is not correctly registered to the application when it is first installed or the connection between the two gets broken.
Secondary logon	Use a secondary logon to run an application using administrator privileges that refused to run under the authority of a standard user. Use the Properties dialog box of the application program file to perform a secondary logon.
Compatibility mode	To solve an incompatibility problem with the OS, try running the application in compatibility mode by using the Properties dialog box of the application program file.
Digital signature	A digital signature verifies that the application is not a rogue application and that it is certified as Windows-compatible by Microsoft. Verify a digital signature using the Properties dialog box of the application program file.
Data Sources	Use Data Sources, also called ODBC Data Sources (Open Database Connectivity Data Sources), to create a connection between a local application and a remote database so that the application can manage the database. Data Sources can be accessed in the Administrative Tools group.
Task Scheduler (taskschd.msc)	Use Task Scheduler in the Administrative Tools group to schedule a program to run at a future time, including at startup.

14

Table 14-1 Tools and techniques to solve Windows-related problems (continues)

Tool	Description
Manage and solve problems with hardware using these tools:	
Device Manager (devmgmt.msc)	Recall Device Manager in Control Panel is the go-to tool to make sure Windows has correctly installed a hardware device and to solve problems with a device.
Print Management (printmanagement.msc)	Use Print Management in the Administrative Tools group to monitor and manage printer queues for all printers on the network.
Display applet (desk.cpl)	Use the Display applet to manage display settings. In Windows 10, access Display settings in the Settings app. For Windows 8/7, use Control Panel.
DxDiag (dxdiag.exe)	Use the DxDiag (DirectX Diagnostic Tool) command to diagnose problems with DirectX. DirectX is Microsoft's interface between video and sound hardware and the applications that use these devices. Some gaming applications or other apps that rely heavily on graphics and sound require the latest version of DirectX. DxDiag can tell you which version of DirectX is installed; you can download the latest version from *Microsoft.com*.
Memory Diagnostics (mdsched.exe)	Use Memory Diagnostics in Administrative Tools to test memory before or after Windows is launched.
chkdsk	The chkdsk command checks the hard drive for a corrupted file system and bad sectors on the drive. Use this command to check drive C: and recover data: `chkdsk c: /r`
Disk Defragmenter (defrag.exe)	Defrag a magnetic hard drive to improve drive performance.

Table 14-1   Tools and techniques to solve Windows-related problems (continued)

✎ **Notes** If you have not already used a tool listed in Table 14-1, open the tool's window and take a good look at its features and menus before you continue with the chapter. If you can, open each tool using more than one method. Try to remember at least one way to open it. Don't worry if you don't know how to use the tool—that's coming up.

★ **A+ Exam Tip** If an often-used Windows utility can be launched from a command prompt, the A+ Core 2 exam expects you to know the program name of that utility.

APPLYING │ CONCEPTS   USING WINDOWS TOOLS TO MANAGE TOOLS

Windows offers several windows and consoles to help access and organize Windows tools. Take a quick look at each to get familiar with how a window or console works and the tools each one contains:

◢ *Control Panel*. Control Panel is a collection of applets used to manage most Windows settings. By default, Control Panel opens in Category view, but applets are easier to find in Classic view, also called icon view. To switch to Classic view, click **Category** and select either Large icons or Small icons. Also, the search box in the upper-left corner of Control Panel can help you quickly find an applet.

◢ *Administrative Tools*. In Classic view of Control Panel, click **Administrative Tools** to see a group of tools used by technicians and developers to support Windows. Figure 14-3 shows the Administrative Tools window for Windows 10 Pro. The Home editions of Windows don't include several of these tools.

◢ *Computer Management*. Computer Management (compmgmt.msc) contains several tools that can be used to manage the local computer or other computers on the network. The window is called a console because it consolidates several Windows administrative tools. To use most of these tools, you must be signed in as an administrator, although you can view certain settings in Computer Management if you are signed in with lesser privileges. The Computer Management window is shown in Figure 14-4.

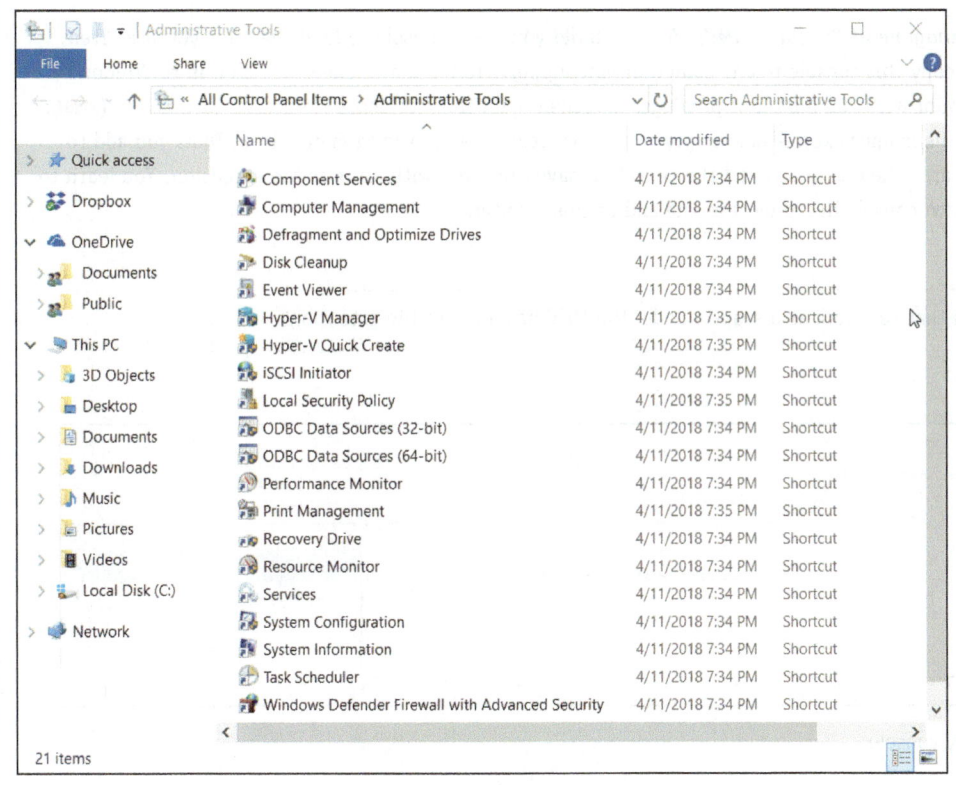

Figure 14-3 Administrative tools available in Windows 10 Pro

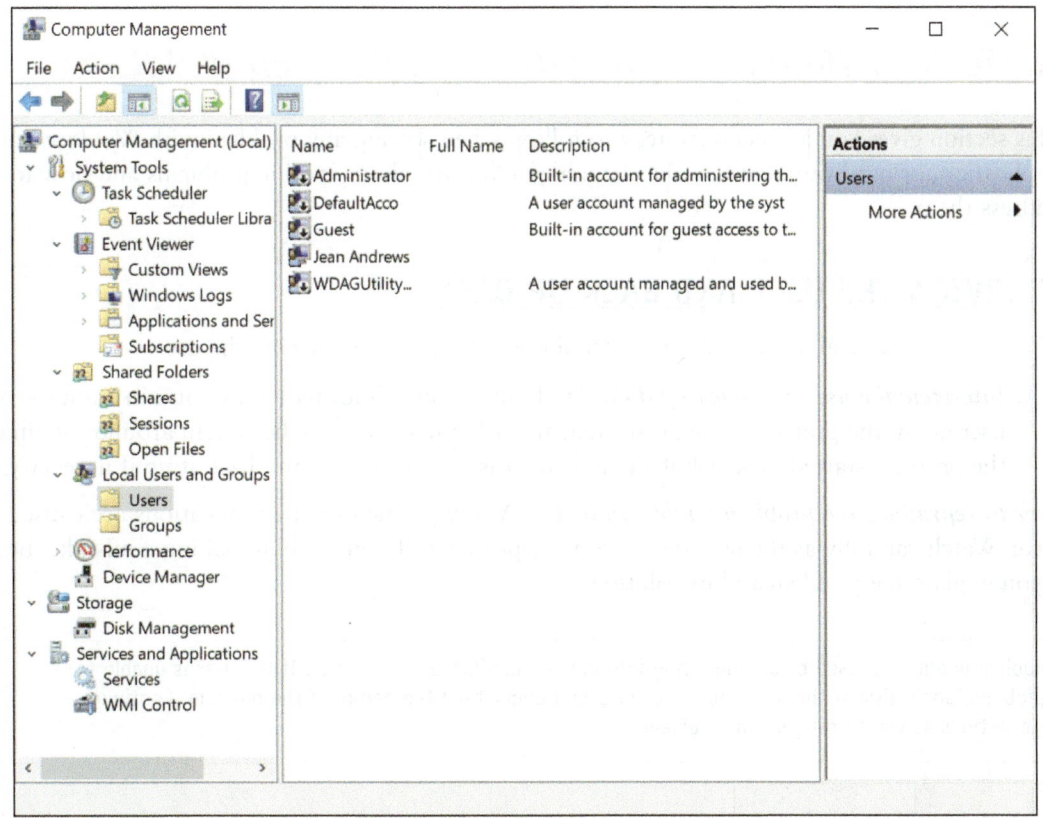

Figure 14-4 Windows Computer Management combines several administrative tools into a single, easy-to-access window

14

(continues)

⊿ *Microsoft Management Console (MMC)*. You can build your own console to hold the tools you use often, and you can copy this console to any computer you support. To build a console, first sign in to Windows using an account with administrator privileges and then open the Microsoft Management Console (MMC; the program file is mmc.exe). A new empty console is created, as shown in Figure 14-5. Tools you add to your console are called snap-ins and the console is saved in a file with an .msc file extension. You learn to create your own console in a project at the end of this chapter.

> ✎ **Notes** A program that can work as a snap-in under the MMC has an .msc file extension.

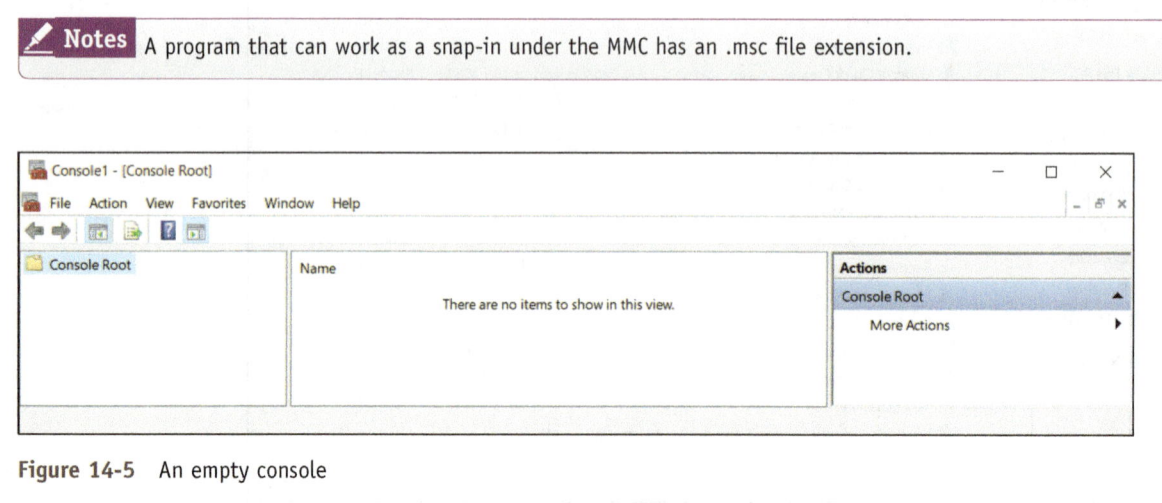

Figure 14-5   An empty console

BEST PRACTICES TO TROUBLESHOOT WINDOWS-RELATED PROBLEMS

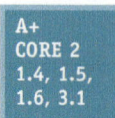
A+
CORE 2
1.4, 1.5,
1.6, 3.1

This section gives you a general strategy to follow when solving any problem with Windows, an application, or hardware. Later in the chapter, you'll learn about specific problems and how to address them.

STEP 1: INTERVIEW THE USER AND BACK UP DATA

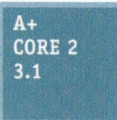
A+
CORE 2
3.1

When the user is available, always start troubleshooting by interviewing the user:

1. *Interview the user and back up data.* Find out as much information as you can from the user about the problem, when it started, and what happened to the system around the time the problem started. Also ask if valuable data is on the system, and back it up if necessary.

2. *Ask the user to reproduce the problem while you watch.* Many problems with applications are caused by user error. Watch carefully as the user shows you the problem. If you see him making a mistake, be tactful as you explain the problem and its solution.

> ✎ **Notes** A problem might be caused by an underlying intermittent conflict or other issue. If the user is unable to reproduce the problem, don't dismiss the user's ability to help you understand the nature of the problem. Continue asking the user questions as you investigate the problem.

3. *Try a reboot.* Reboots solve a lot of application problems and one might be a shortcut to your solution. If it doesn't work, no harm is done and you're ready to begin investigating the system. (Before you restart the system, be sure to ask the user if she needs to save her work.)

STEP 2: ERROR MESSAGES, THE WEB, COWORKERS, AND LOGS MIGHT HELP

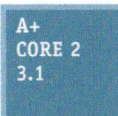

**A+
CORE 2
3.1**

Windows might display an error message and offer a solution. Logs kept by Windows can offer clues. Following are a few examples of how to get help from Windows, the web, and coworkers.

USE EVENT VIEWER AND RELIABILITY MONITOR TO LOOK FOR CLUES

The Event Viewer logs might give clues about hardware or network failure, OS error messages, a device or service that has failed to start, or general protection faults, which can cause Windows to lock up or hang. Use Reliability Monitor to look for errors with applications or with key hardware components such as the hard drive.

Here are general steps to use Event Viewer:

1. Open Event Viewer in the Administrative Tools group or by using the command **eventvwr.msc.** To see events, select a log in the left pane and then drill down into subcategories of these logs. For example, Figure 14-6 shows events in the Administrative Events log. Select an event to see more about it. In the figure, the selected event is that the computer was not able to lease an IP address from the DHCP server.

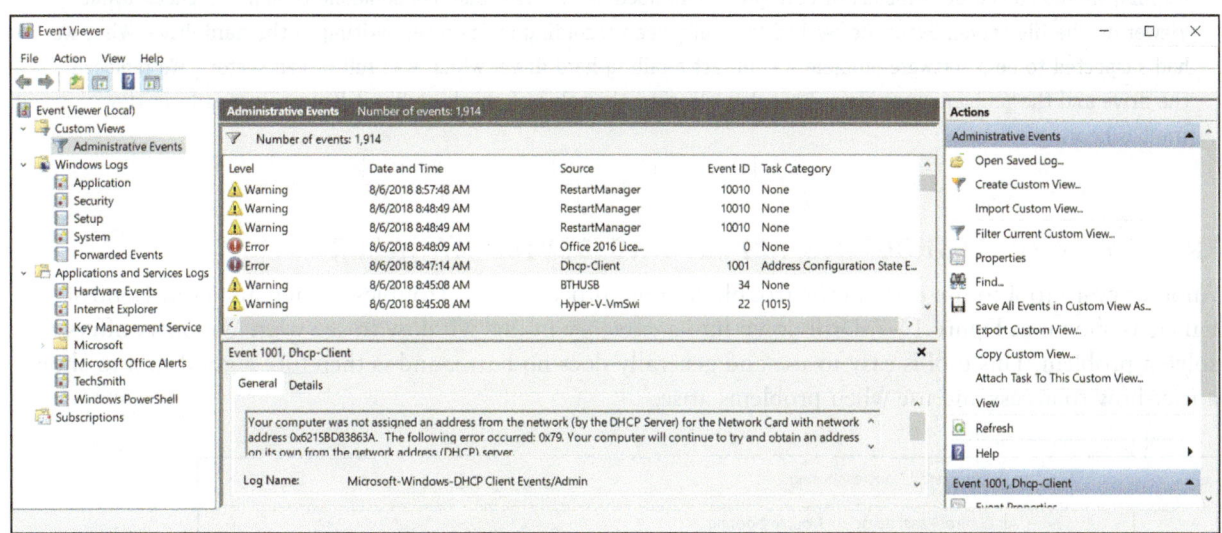

Figure 14-6   Use Event Viewer to see logs about hardware, Windows, security, and application events

2. To sort a list of events, click a column heading in the middle pane. After you have selected an event, click the Details tab to show more information about the event.

The types of events are Critical, Error, Warning, Information, and Audit Success. Error events are the most important and indicate something went wrong with the system, such as a scheduled backup failing to work. Warning events indicate failure might occur in the future, and Critical events indicate a problem occurred with a critical Windows process.

Here are the logs that are the most useful:

▲ *Administrative Events log.* This filtered log shows only Critical, Error, and Warning events intended for the administrator. This log is in the Custom Views category and is selected in Figure 14-6.
▲ *Application log.* In the Windows Logs group, look in the Application log for events recorded by an application. This log might help you identify why an application is causing problems.
▲ *Security log.* Events in the Security log are called audits and include successful and unsuccessful sign-ins to a user account and attempts from another computer on the network to access shared resources on this computer.
▲ *Setup log.* Look in the Setup log for events recorded at the time applications are installed.

14

▲ *System log.* Look in the System log to find events triggered by Windows components, such as a device driver failing to load or a problem with hardware.

▲ *Forwarded Events log.* This log receives events that were recorded on other computers and sent to this computer.

When you first encounter a Windows, hardware, application, or security problem, get in the habit of checking Event Viewer as one of your first steps toward investigating the problem. To save time, first check the Administrative Events log because it filters out all events except Critical, Error, and Warning events.

APPLYING CONCEPTS EVENT VIEWER SOLVES A MYSTERY

A+
CORE 2
1.4, 1.5,
1.6, 3.1

Event Viewer can be useful in solving intermittent hardware problems. For example, I once worked in an office where several people updated Microsoft Word documents stored on a file server. For weeks, people complained about these Word documents getting corrupted. We downloaded the latest patches for Windows and Microsoft Office and scanned for viruses, thinking that the problem might be with Windows or the application. Then we suspected a corrupted template file for building the Word documents. But nothing we did solved our problem of corrupted Word documents. Then one day someone thought to check Event Viewer on the file server. Event Viewer had faithfully been recording errors when writing to the hard drive. What we had suspected to be a software problem was in fact a failing hard drive, which was full of bad sectors. We replaced the drive and the problem went away. That day I learned the value of checking Event Viewer very early in the troubleshooting process.

TRY THE TROUBLESHOOTING APPLET AND DEVICE MANAGER

Another go-to tool to use early in the troubleshooting process is the Troubleshooting applet in Control Panel, as shown in Figure 14-7. Drill down into a category in this window to see what Windows offers to solve a problem. This tool is easy to use and generally does no harm, and is therefore a good tool to show a user how to access and use when problems arise.

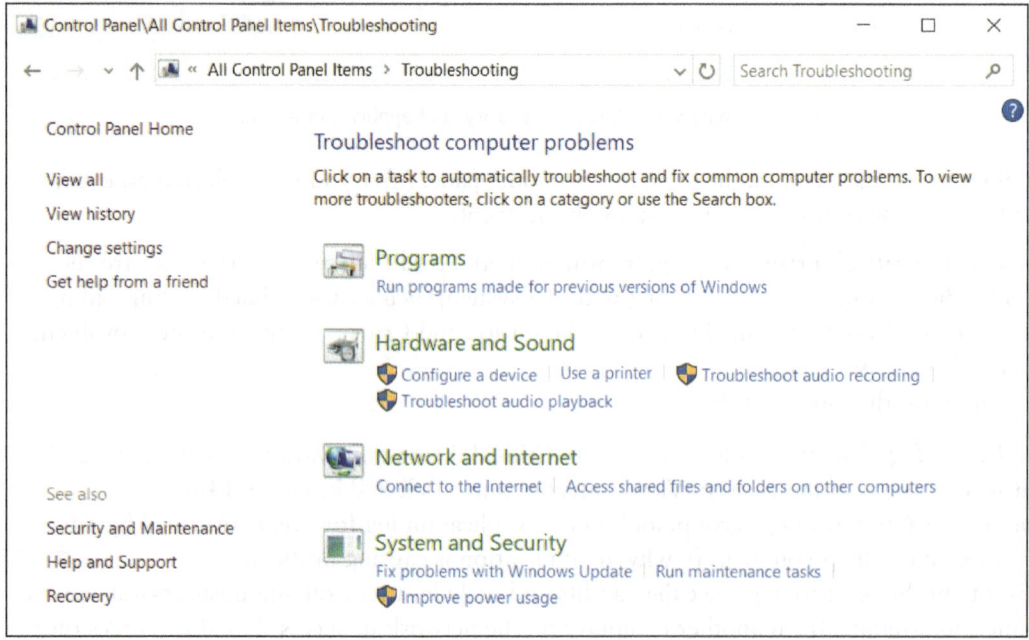

Figure 14-7 Use the Troubleshooting applet early in the troubleshooting process to solve simple Windows, application, hardware, network, and security problems

When the problem is hardware-related, check Device Manager. Sometimes using Device Manager to uninstall a device and then reinstalling the device solves the problem.

FIND AND ASK FOR HELP

For Windows problems, search for the error message or description of the problem on the web. When you perform a Google search, add **site:microsoft.com** to the end of the search text to target your search to Microsoft websites. For problems with hardware and applications, try searching the website of the manufacturer for support and help. Also, search the web on the error message, application, or description of the problem. Look for forums where others have posted the same problem with the same app or device. Someone else has likely posted a solution. However, be careful and don't take the advice unless you trust the website. After you've made a reasonable effort to find help on your own, ask for help from coworkers who are more experienced.

> ✎ **Notes** Working while a customer looks over your shoulder can be awkward. A customer needs her IT support technician to appear confident and in charge. To maintain your customer's confidence in your technical abilities, you might want to find privacy when searching the web or talking with coworkers.

STEP 3: CONSIDER THAT THE DATA OR THE APPLICATION MIGHT BE CORRUPTED

Now that you've interviewed the user, backed up important data, examined the system, and investigated the problem, it's time to come up with a theory as to the cause of the problem. For general problems with applications, consider and do these things:

▲ *Consider data corruption.* For applications such as Microsoft Office that use data files, it might appear that the application, Windows, or hardware has a problem when the problem is really a corrupted data file. Try creating an entirely new data file. If that works, then suspect that previous errors might be caused by corrupted data. You might be able to recover part of a corrupted file by changing its file extension to .txt and importing it into the application as a text file.

▲ *Check application settings and logs for errors.* Maybe a user has made one too many changes to the application settings, which can cause a problem with missing toolbars and other functions. Write down each setting the user has changed and then restore all settings back to their default values. If the problem is solved, restore each setting to the way the user had it until you find the one causing the problem. The process will take some time, but users can get upset if you change their application settings without justification.

▲ *Repair the application.* The application setup might have the option to repair the installation. Look for it in the Programs and Features window, on the setup disc for the application, or on the manufacturer's website.

▲ *Uninstall and reinstall the application.* Do so with caution because you might lose any customized settings, macros, or scripts. Also know this still might not solve a problem with a corrupted application because registry entries might not be properly reset during the uninstall process.

> ⚡ **Caution** When researching a problem, suppose you discover that Microsoft or a manufacturer's website offers a fix or patch you can download and apply. To get the right patch, recall you need to make sure you get a 32-bit patch for a 32-bit installation of Windows, a device driver, or an application. For a 64-bit installation of Windows, make sure you get a 64-bit device driver. An application installed in a 64-bit OS might be a 32-bit application or a 64-bit application.

STEP 4: CONSIDER OUTSIDE INTERFERENCE

The problem could be caused by a virus, Windows, applications other than the one that presented the initial symptoms, or hardware.

14

MALWARE IS AT WORK

Scan the system for malware using up-to-date anti-malware software. In Chapter 17, you learn more about symptoms that indicate malware is at work and how to scan for and remove malware.

FAULTY MEMORY

Errors with memory are often difficult to diagnose because they can appear intermittently and might be mistaken as application errors, user errors, or other hardware component errors. Sometimes these errors cause the system to hang, a BSOD (blue screen of death) error might occur, or the system continues to function with applications giving errors or data being corrupted. You can quickly identify a problem with memory or eliminate memory as the source of a problem by using the Windows Memory Diagnostics (mdsched.exe) tool. It works before Windows is loaded to test memory for errors and can be used on computers that don't have Windows installed. Use one of these two methods to start the utility:

▲ *Use the mdsched.exe command.* After Windows has started, enter the **mdsched.exe** command. A dialog box appears and asks if you want the tool to immediately restart the system and run the test or wait until the next restart.

▲ *Boot from Windows setup media.* If Windows is not the installed operating system or you cannot boot from the hard drive, boot the computer from the Windows setup USB drive or DVD to test memory for errors. Follow these steps:

1. If necessary, change the boot priority order in BIOS/UEFI setup to boot first from the optical drive or USB drive. Boot from the Windows setup DVD or USB drive.

2. On the opening screen for Windows 10/8, select your language and click **Next**. On the next screen (see Figure 14-8), click **Repair your computer**. Next choose **Troubleshoot**. For Windows 10, the Advanced options screen appears; for Windows 8, you must click **Advanced options** to see this screen.

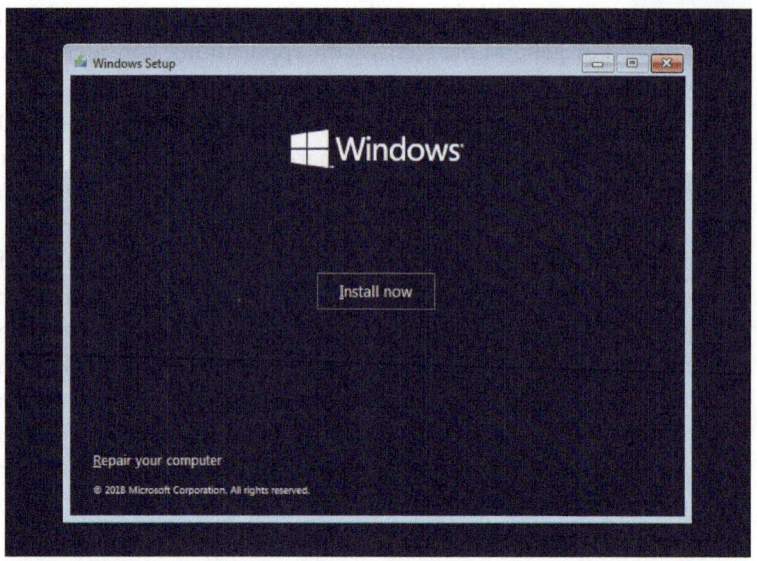

Figure 14-8 The opening menu when you boot from Windows 10 setup media

3. On the Advanced options screen (see Figure 14-9), choose **Command Prompt**. In the command prompt window, enter the **mdsched.exe** command.

> ↻ **OS Differences** For Windows 7, after booting from the Windows 7 setup DVD, select the Windows installation to repair. On the System Recovery Options screen, click **Windows Memory Diagnostic**. For Windows 7, it is not necessary to open a command prompt window to test memory.

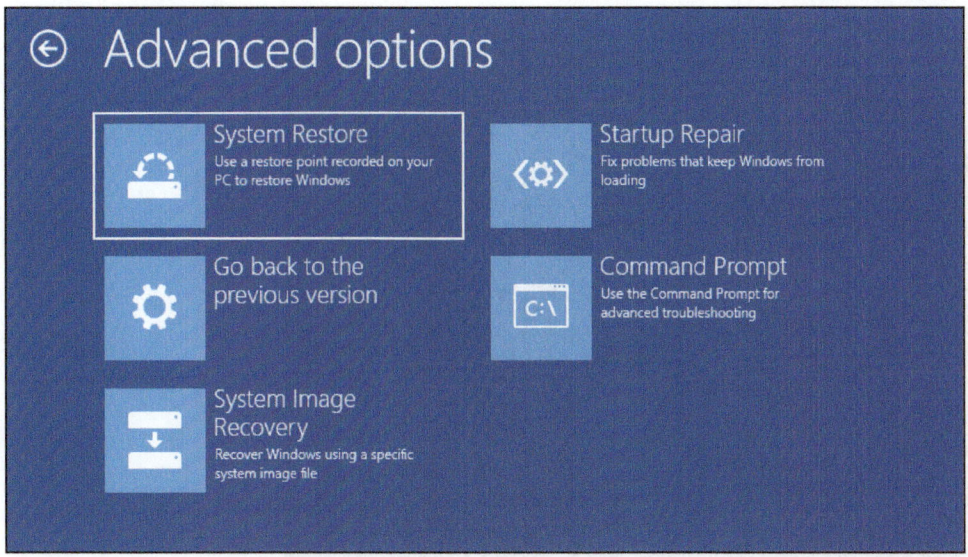

Figure 14-9 The Windows 10 Advanced options screen launched from Windows 10 setup media

If the tool reports memory errors, replace all memory modules installed on the motherboard.

CORRUPTED HARD DRIVE

To eliminate the hard drive as the source of a Windows or application error, use the **chkdsk c: /r** command to check the drive. The error-checking utility searches for bad sectors on a volume and recovers the data from them if possible. It then marks the sector as bad so that it will not be reused. Also check Event Viewer for warnings or errors regarding the hard drive.

LOW ON SYSTEM RESOURCES

Malware, applications, background services, device drivers, or Windows might be hogging system resources to slow down the system and/or prevent an application from working or cause Windows errors.

Use Task Manager to verify that a process is not using excessive system resources. Several ways to access Task Manager are:

- ▲ Press **Ctrl+Alt+Del**. Depending on your system, the security screen (see Figure 14-10) or Task Manager appears. If the security screen appears, click **Task Manager**. This method works well when the system has a problem and is frozen.
- ▲ Press **Ctrl+Shift+Esc**.
- ▲ For Windows 10/8, press **Win+X** and click **Task Manager** in the Quick Launch menu. For Windows 7, click **Start**, enter **taskmgr.exe** in the search box, and press **Enter**.

> 🖉 **Notes** When working with a virtual machine, you cannot send the Ctrl+Alt+Del keystrokes to the guest operating system in the VM because these keystrokes are always sent to the host operating system. To send the Ctrl+Alt+Del keystrokes to a VM in Windows Client Hyper-V, click the **Action** menu in the VM window and click **Ctrl+Alt+Delete** (see Figure 14-11).
>
> To send the Ctrl+Alt+Del keystrokes to a VM in Oracle VirtualBox, click **Input** in the menu bar at the top of the VM window. For the system shown in Figure 14-12A, you can see the keystrokes to press for Ctrl+Alt+Del are Host+Del. By default, the Host key in VirtualBox is the right Ctrl key. To verify the Host key for your installation of VirtualBox, look in the bottom-right corner of the VM window (see Figure 14-12B).

14

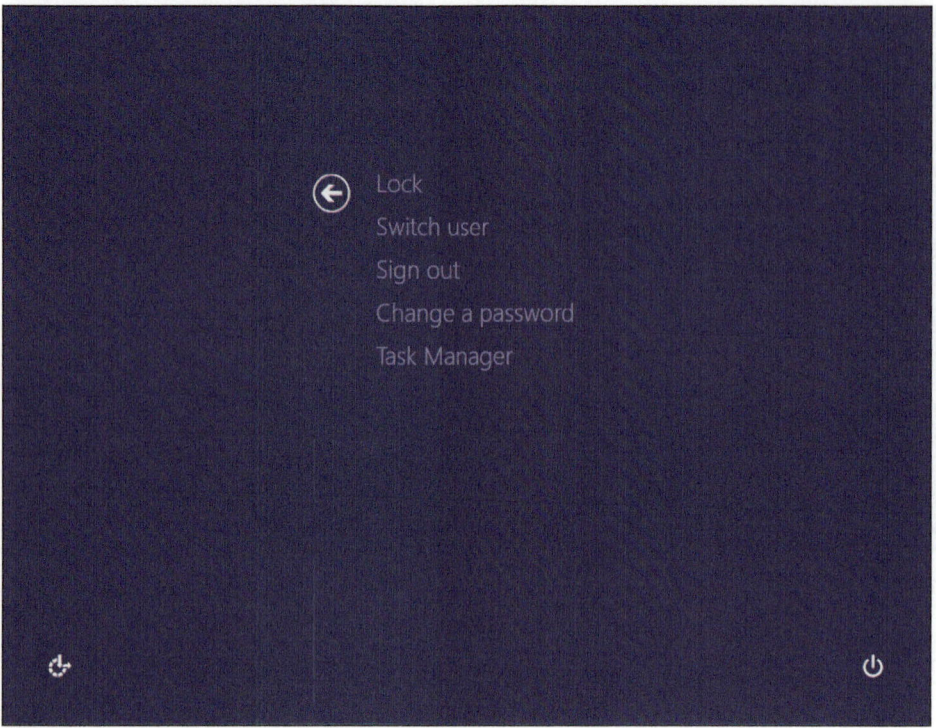

Figure 14-10   Use the security screen to launch Task Manager

Figure 14-11   Send the Ctrl+Alt+Del keystrokes to a VM managed by Windows 10 Pro Client Hyper-V

The Windows 10 Task Manager window is shown in Figure 14-13. If you see very limited information in the window, click **More details** to see the details shown in the figure.

Here are important details about each tab in Task Manager:

▲ *Processes tab and Details tab*. The Processes tab shows running processes organized by Apps, Background processes, and Windows processes. Right-click a process and click **Go to details** (see Figure 14-13) to jump to the Details tab, where you see the name of the program file and other details about the running program. On the Details tab (see Figure 14-14), a hung process is reported as Not Responding. To end the task, select it and click **End task**. The application will attempt a normal shutdown; if data has not been saved, you are given the opportunity to save it.

✎ **Notes**   If your desktop locks up, you can use Task Manager to refresh it. To do so, press **Ctrl+Alt+Del** and open **Task Manager**. Click the **Processes** tab. In the Windows processes group, select **Windows Explorer** and click **Restart**. (Yes, Windows 10/8 Task Manager really does call Explorer "Windows Explorer.")

In Windows 7, click the Processes tab and select and end the **explorer.exe** process. Then click **File** in the menu bar and click **New Task (Run)**. Enter **explorer.exe** in the Create New Task box, and click **OK**. Your desktop will be refreshed and any running programs will still be open.

Figure 14-12 For Oracle VirtualBox, (A) send the Ctrl+Alt+Del keystrokes to a VM, and (B) verify the Host key for the VM

Figure 14-13 The Windows 10 Task Manager window with the Processes tab selected

Figure 14-14 Use the Details tab to end a task that is not responding

If you want to end a process and all related processes, click the **Details** tab, right-click the process, and select **End Process Tree** from the shortcut menu. Be careful not to end critical Windows processes; ending these might crash your system.

> **OS Differences** The Windows 7 Task Manager window has six tabs: Applications, Processes, Services, Performance, Networking, and Users. The Applications tab of Task Manager is used to view a list of running processes. You can end a process that is not responding on this tab or end it on the Processes tab.

> ★ **A+ Exam Tip** The A+ Core 1 exam expects you to understand the purposes of each tab in Task Manager and know when to use a tab to resolve a problem in a given scenario.

▲ *Performance tab*. The Performance tab of Task Manager (see Figure 14-15) allows you to monitor performance of key devices in the system and network connections. For example, Figure 14-15 shows the CPU selected, where you can monitor what percentage of CPU resources are in use. You can also see whether Hardware-assisted Virtualization is enabled. Also notice the link to open the Resource Monitor, which can identify each process using system resources. Check for such a process if you suspect malware might be at work in a denial-of-service (DoS) attack.

> **OS Differences** In Windows 7, the Performance tab of Task Manager monitors performance of the CPU and memory and gives you access to the Resource Monitor. To monitor the performance of network connections, see the Networking tab of Task Manager. Alternately, you can use the Windows 7 Resource Monitor to monitor the performance of the CPU, memory, hard drive, and network connections.

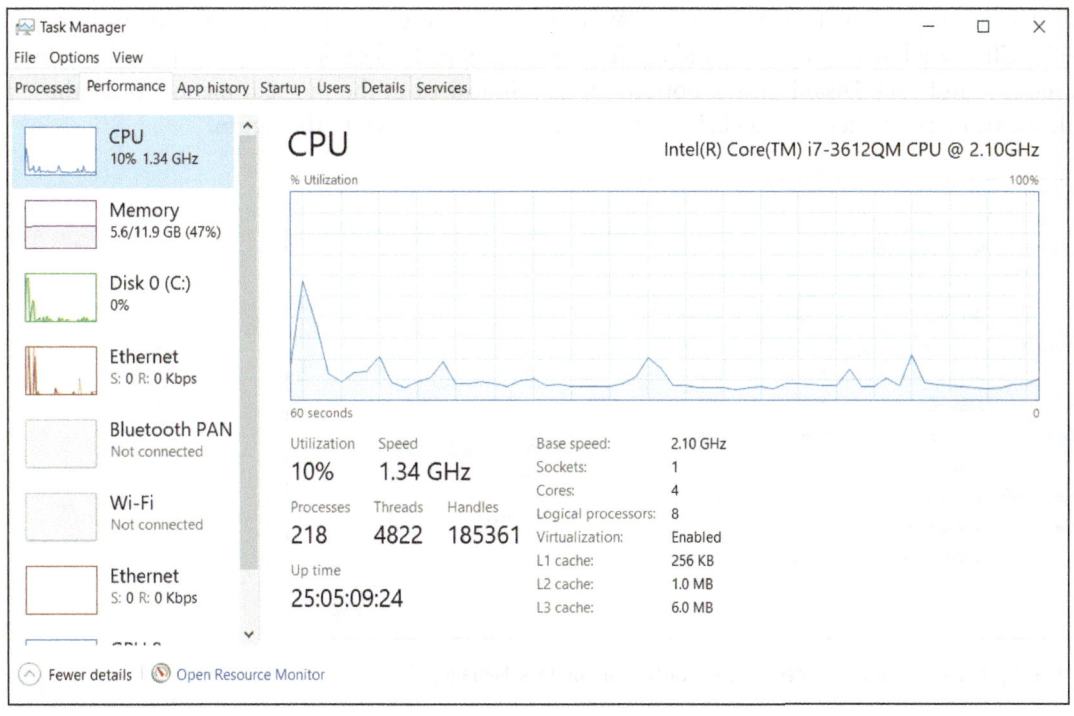

Figure 14-15   Use the Performance tab to view system resource usage

▲ *App history tab*. The App history tab (see Figure 14-16) shows the resources that a program is using. For example, it's useful when deciding if a live tile or other app is using too much CPU time or network resources.

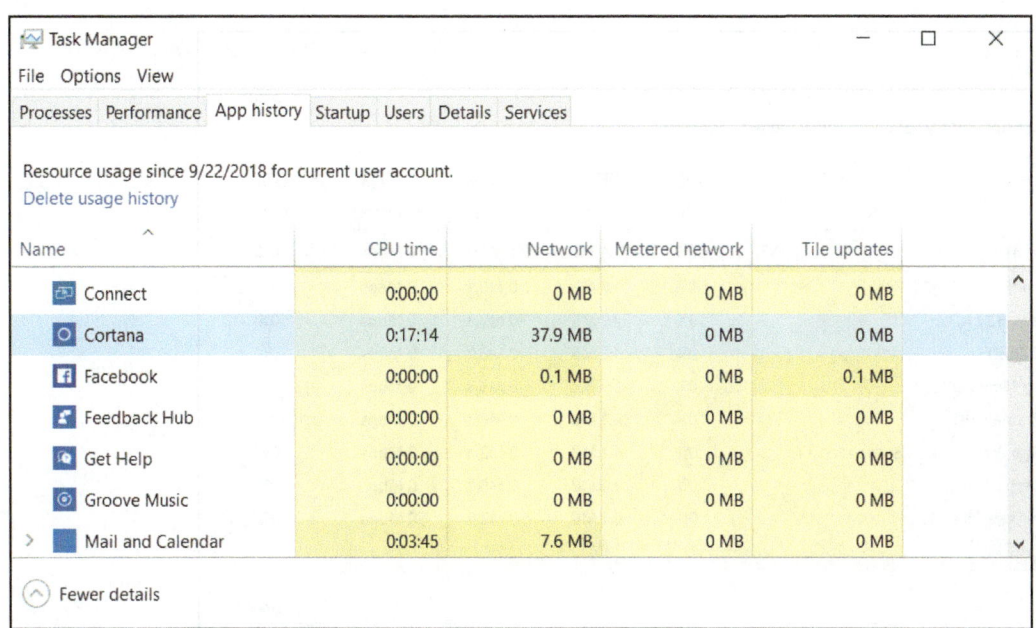

Figure 14-16   The App history tab can help you decide if a background program is hogging system resources

> ✎ **Notes**   To conserve resources, you can disable a live tile on the Windows 10 Start menu or Windows 8 Start screen from updating itself. Go to the **Start** menu or screen, right-click the tile, and click **Turn live tile off** in the shortcut menu.

14

▲ *Startup tab*. The Startup tab of Task Manager in Windows 10/8 is used to manage startup items (see Figure 14-17). Click a white arrow to expand the items in a group. To disable a program from launching at startup, select it and click **Disable** at the bottom of the window or in the shortcut menu. To see the program file location, right-click it and click **Open file location,** as shown in the figure.

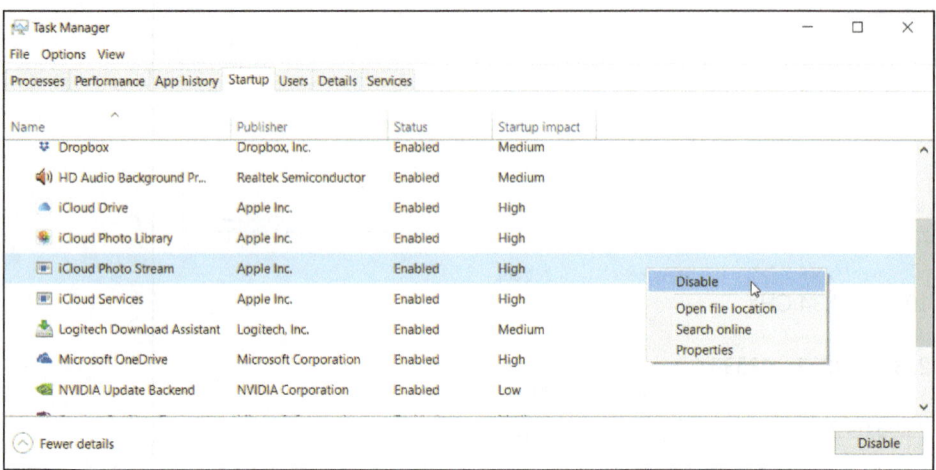

Figure 14-17 Startup processes are managed on the Startup tab of Task Manager

▲ *Users tab*. The Users tab (see Figure 14-18) lists currently signed-in users. Expand the list for a user to show processes started by the user that might be affecting overall system performance. Notice that the statuses of some programs on this tab are listed as Suspended. If certain apps remain idle for a short time, they're suspended so they don't require the attention of the CPU. When the app is used again, it automatically comes out of suspension, and the CPU once again begins servicing it. To disconnect a remote user or sign out a local user from the system, select the user and click **Disconnect** or **Sign out** at the bottom of the screen.

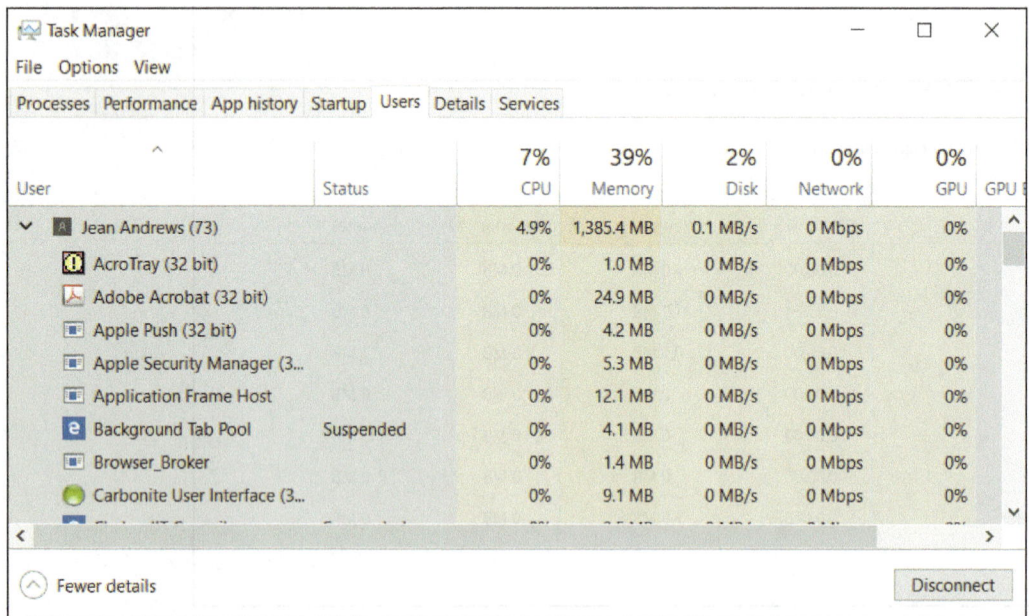

Figure 14-18 The Users tab shows system resources used by each signed-in user

▲ *Services tab*. The Services tab (see Figure 14-19) lists the services currently installed along with the status of each service. You can stop, start, or restart a service by right-clicking it and selecting the action in the shortcut menu. Services can also be managed from the Services console, as discussed later in this chapter.

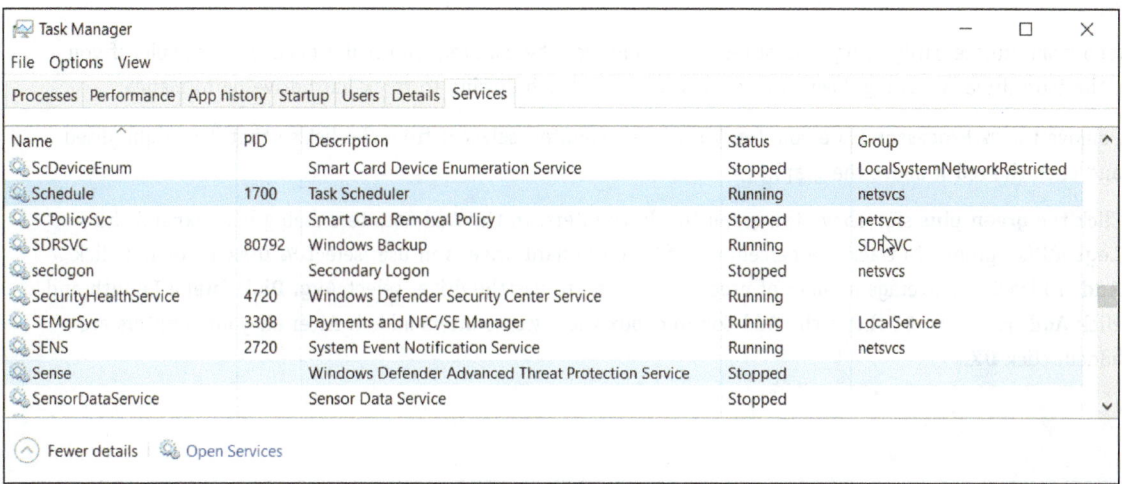

Figure 14-19 The Services tab of Task Manager gives the current status of all installed services

The system might be slow because the OS does not have the hardware resources it needs. Use System Information (msinfo32.exe) to find the model and speed of the installed processor and hard drive and the amount of memory installed. Compare all these values with the minimum and recommended requirements for Windows listed in Chapter 12. If you suspect that the processor, hard drive, or memory is a bottleneck, use Performance Monitor to get more information. If the bottleneck appears to be graphics, the problem might be solved by updating the graphics drivers or video adapter.

APPLYING | CONCEPTS — OBSERVING HARDWARE ACTIVITY USING PERFORMANCE MONITOR

Performance Monitor (perfmon.msc) tracks activity by hardware and software to measure performance. It can monitor in real time and can save collected data in logs for future use. Software developers might use this tool to evaluate how well their software is performing and to identify software and hardware bottlenecks.

To open Performance Monitor, enter the **perfmon.msc** command or open it from the Administrative Tools group in Control Panel. Performance Monitor offers hundreds of counters used to examine many aspects of the system related to performance. The Windows default setting is to show the % Processor Time counter the first time you open the window (see Figure 14-20). This counter appears as a red line in the graph and tracks activity of the processor.

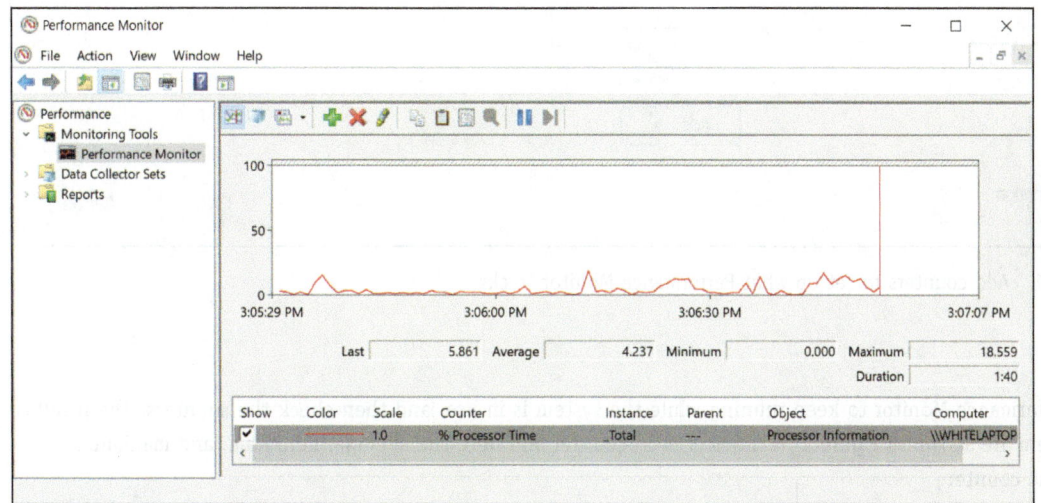

Figure 14-20 Performance Monitor uses counters to monitor various activities of hardware and software

(continues)

To keep from unnecessarily using system resources, only use the counters you really need. For example, if you suspect the hard drive is slowing down the entire system, do the following to track hard drive performance:

1. Remove the **% Processor Time** counter. To delete a counter, select it from the list so that it is highlighted and click the red **X** above the graph.

2. Click the **green plus** sign above the graph to add counters. In the Add Counters dialog box, expand the **LogicalDisk** group. To track the percentage of time the hard drive is in use, select **% Disk Time** and click **Add**. To track the average number of processes waiting to use the drive, select **Avg. Disk Queue Length** and click **Add**. Figure 14-21 shows the Add Counters box with two counters added. After all your counters are added, click **OK**.

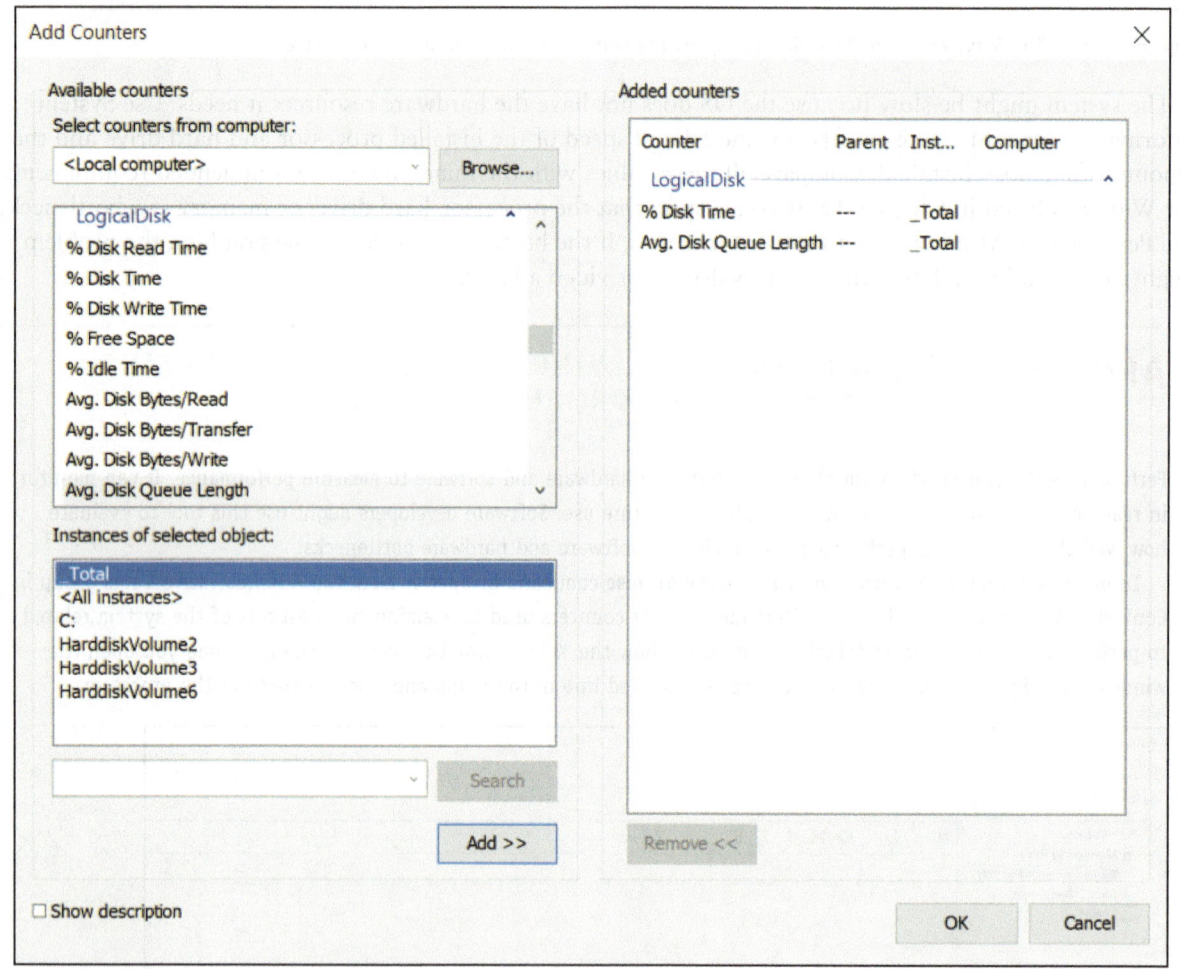

Figure 14-21 Add counters to set up what Performance Monitor tracks

Allow Performance Monitor to keep running while the system is in use, and then check the counters. The results for one system are shown in Figure 14-22. Select each counter and note the average, minimum, and maximum values for the counter.

(continues)

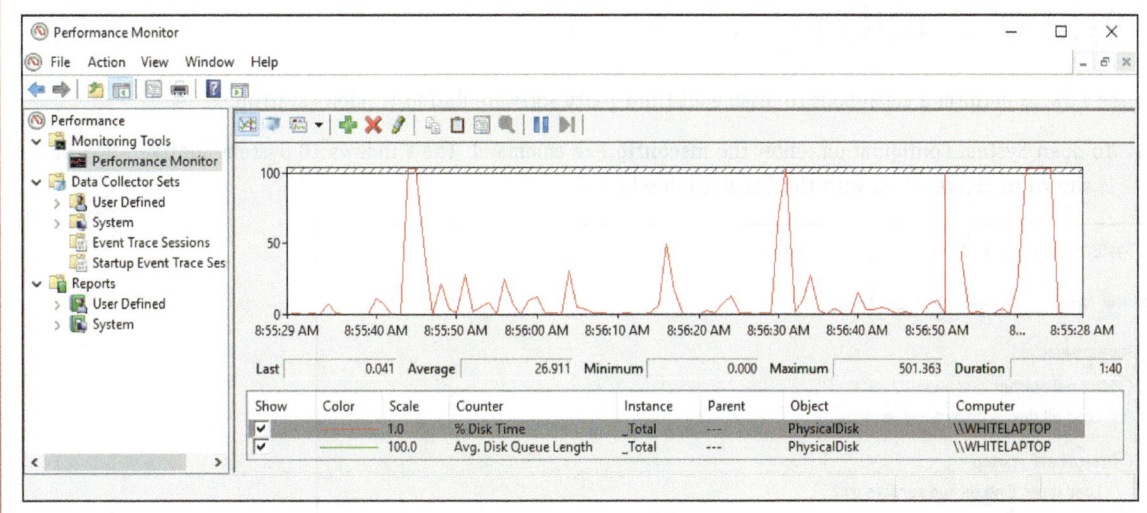

Figure 14-22 Two counters can measure hard drive performance

If the % Disk Time is more than 80 percent and the Avg. Disk Queue Length is above two, you can conclude that the hard drive is working excessively hard and processes are slowed down waiting on the drive. Anytime a process must wait to access the hard drive, you are likely to see degradation in overall system performance.

> ✎ **Notes** To find out which counters to use to measure specific performances, search the Microsoft website or perform a general web search.

If you find that the system is slow because of a hardware component, discuss the situation with the user. You might be able to upgrade the hardware or OS or remove background processes drawing on hardware resources.

> ↻ **OS Differences** The Windows 7 Aero interface might be slowing down the system as it uses computing power. If disabling it improves performance, you can keep it disabled or upgrade memory and/or the video card to support it. To disable the Aero interface, right-click the desktop, select **Personalize** from the shortcut menu, and click **Windows 7 Basic**.

INCOMPATIBLE APPLICATIONS OR THIRD-PARTY SERVICES

Sometimes you can't install or run an application without errors because there is a conflict or compatibility issue with other software. To eliminate these conflicts, run the application causing problems after a clean boot. A clean boot eliminates third-party software from starting during the boot and is done using System Configuration and Task Manager. If a clean boot allows the application to run without errors, you need to methodically zero in on the third-party program until you discover the one in conflict. Try disabling half of these programs. If the problem persists, disable the other half. Continue disabling half of the half until you find the program in conflict.

> ⚡ **Caution** Don't depend on System Configuration or Task Manager to be a permanent fix to disable a startup program or service. Once you've decided you want to make the change permanent, use other methods to permanently remove that process from Windows startup. For example, you might uninstall a program, remove it from a startup folder, or use the Services console to disable a service.

14

APPLYING CONCEPTS PERFORMING A CLEAN BOOT

Let's see how to perform a clean boot to disable all third-party software during Windows startup:

1. To open System Configuration, enter the **msconfig.exe** command. The Windows 10 System Configuration box is shown in Figure 14-23 with the General tab selected.

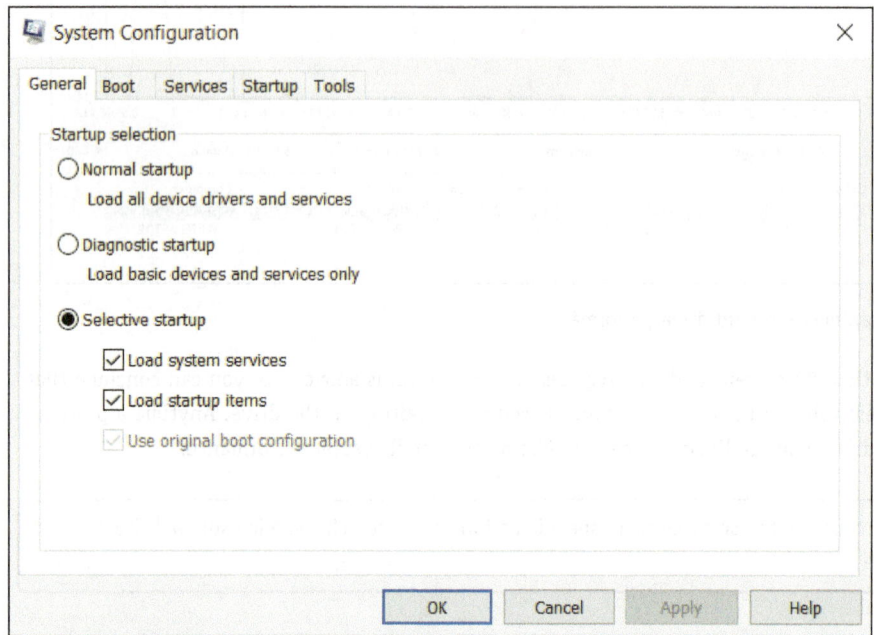

Figure 14-23   Use the General tab to control how Windows starts

2. Click the **Services** tab and check **Hide all Microsoft services**. The list now shows only services put there by third-party software (see Figure 14-24). Click **Disable all**.

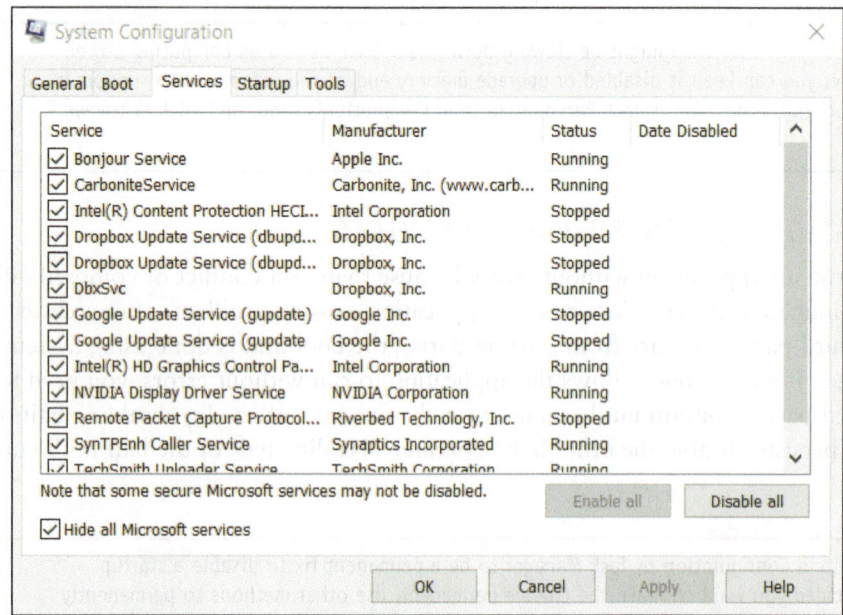

Figure 14-24   Use the Services tab of System Configuration to view and control services launched at startup

3. Click the **General** tab and notice that Selective startup is now selected. Click **Apply** and close the System Configuration box.

4. Open **Task Manager** and select the **Startup** tab (refer back to Figure 14-17). For each startup item, select it and click **Disable**. Close the Task Manager window and restart Windows.

Verify that the problem is solved in a clean boot environment. If the problem involves an application that will not install, install it now; then you can return the system to a normal startup. If the problem involves an application giving errors, you need to disable half the startup items and continue to disable half until you discover the startup program that is in conflict.

Here's how to return to a normal Windows startup:

1. Open the **System Configuration** box. On the General tab, click **Normal startup**. On the Services tab, uncheck **Hide all Microsoft services**. Verify that all services are now checked.

2. Open **Task Manager**. In the Task Manager window, select each startup item and enable it. Close all windows and restart the system.

> **○ OS Differences** In Windows 10/8, the Startup tab in System Configuration is used only to open Task Manager, where startup items can be enabled and disabled. However, in Windows 7, startup items are managed on the Startup tab in System Configuration.

The Tools tab in the System Configuration box gives you quick access to other Windows tools you might need during a troubleshooting session (see Figure 14-25).

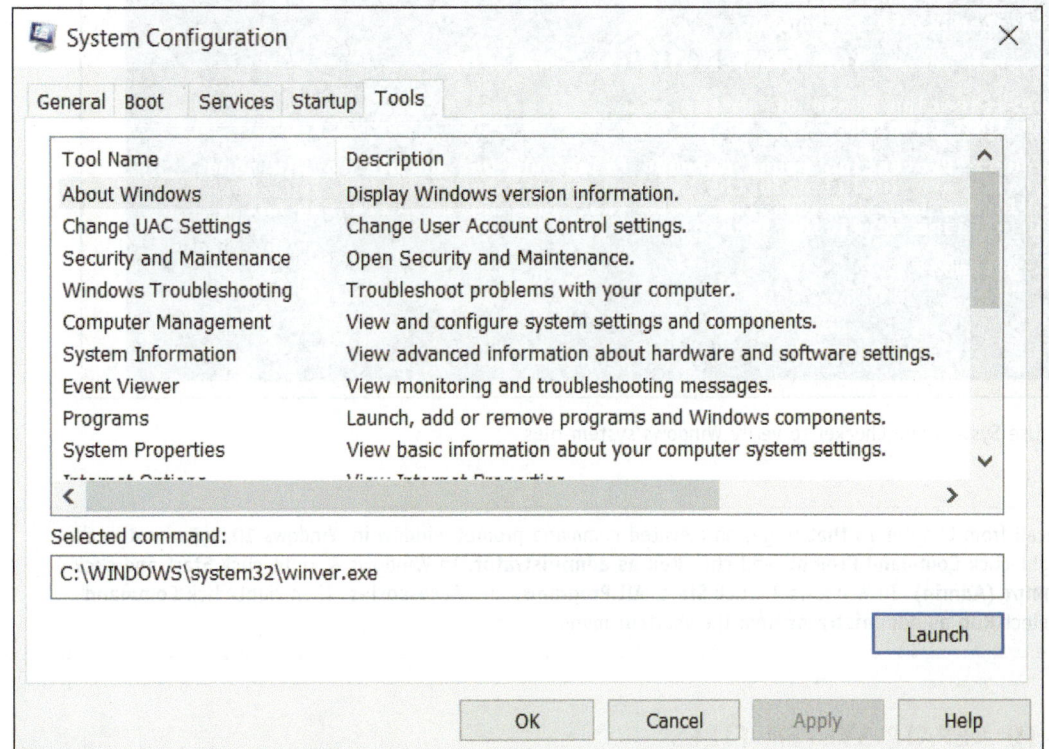

Figure 14-25 The Tools tab makes it easy to find troubleshooting tools

> **✎ Notes** System Configuration reports only what it is programmed to look for when listing startup programs and services. It looks only in certain registry keys and startup folders, and sometimes does not report a startup process. Therefore, don't consider its list of startup processes to be complete.

STEP 5: CONSIDER THAT WINDOWS MIGHT BE THE PROBLEM

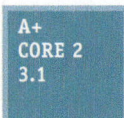

An application or device might be giving problems because Windows system files are missing or corrupted. Here's what to do.

UPDATE WINDOWS

Make sure all critical and important Windows updates are installed. Microsoft Office and other Microsoft application updates are included in Windows updates.

USE SYSTEM FILE CHECKER

For essential hardware devices, use the System File Checker (SFC) to verify and replace system files, which include device drivers for many hardware devices. To run SFC, close all applications, open an elevated command prompt window, and enter the **sfc /scannow** command (see Figure 14-26). If corrupted system files are found, you might need to use Windows setup media to restore the files.

If you have problems running the SFC utility, boot the computer into Safe boot and run the sfc /scannow command again in Safe Mode. If you still have problems, know that you will learn more about repairing system files in Chapter 15.

Figure 14-26   Use System File Checker to verify Windows system files

> ✎ **Notes**   Recall from Chapter 13 that to get an elevated command prompt window in Windows 10, type **cmd** in the search box, right-click **Command Prompt**, and click **Run as administrator**. In Windows 8, right-click **Start** and click **Command Prompt (Admin)**. In Windows 7, click **Start**, **All Programs**, and **Accessories**. Then right-click **Command Prompt** and select **Run as administrator** from the shortcut menu.

USE DISM TO REPAIR SYSTEM FILES

In Chapter 12, you learned that DISM commands are used to create, manage, and deploy standard system images. You can also use the commands to repair an existing Windows installation, which sometimes works when SFC does not work. SFC depends on Windows Update to download the system files it needs to replace corrupted ones, but if Windows Update is not working, SFC cannot complete the repairs. DISM, on the other hand, gets new copies of system files from a Windows standard image available on the local machine or network. When troubleshooting a corrupted Windows installation, first try SFC; if that doesn't work, turn to DISM.

When using the DISM commands, know that a standard image is normally stored in the install.wim file and is called an offline image, and a running installation of Windows is called an online image. In addition, a virtual hard drive with a .vhd file extension that contains an installation of Windows is considered an offline image. Let's look at a few DISM commands, listed in the most likely order that you will use them:

1. To scan the current Windows installation for corrupted system files, use this command, which takes some time:

   ```
   dism /online /cleanup-image /scanhealth
   ```

2. To report if system files in the Windows image have been flagged as corrupted, use this command:

   ```
   dism /online /cleanup-image /checkhealth
   ```

3. Use this command to search for and replace corrupted system files, using Windows Update to find new system files:

   ```
   dism /online /cleanup-image /restorehealth
   ```

4. If Windows Update is not working, you can use the system files stored in a standard image to replace corrupted files. Use the DISM command with the /source parameter to point to the image and the /limitaccess parameter to not use Windows Update to find replacement files:

   ```
   dism /online /cleanup-image /restorehealth /source:install.wim /limitaccess
   ```

This last DISM command assumes the install.wim file is in the C:\Windows\System32 folder. You can add a path to a different location in the command line. If you don't have a standard image available, you can extract one from the Windows setup files, as you'll see in a project at the end of this chapter. Also know that DISM keeps a log file of what it did at C:\Windows\Logs\DISM\dism.log.

BOOT WINDOWS IN SAFE MODE

Safe Mode, also called Safe boot, loads Windows with a minimum configuration and can create a stable environment when Windows gets corrupted. There are several ways to start Safe Mode, which you learn about in Chapter 15. One way is to open System Configuration, click the **Boot** tab, and check **Safe boot** (see Figure 14-27). If the application in question needs the Internet to work, select **Network**. Click **OK** and restart the system.

14

If the application works in Safe Mode, you can assume the problem is not with the application but with the operating system or device drivers. Try System Restore, which is discussed next, to repair the system. To return the system to a normal startup, open System Configuration again and click **Normal startup** on the General tab.

USE SYSTEM RESTORE

If you know the approximate date the error started and that date is in the recent past, use System Restore (rstrui.exe)

Figure 14-27 Restart Windows in a Safe boot with minimal Windows configuration to restore the system to a point just before the problem started. Reverting to a restore point can solve problems with corrupted registry entries used by applications, device driver updates, or other Windows problems. However, System Restore can cause problems of its own, so use it with caution. Keep these points in mind:

▲ System Restore might make many changes to a system. If you know which change caused a problem, try to undo that particular change first. The idea is to use the least invasive solution first. For example, if updating a driver has caused a problem, first use Device Manager to perform a driver rollback and undo that change.

▲ System Restore won't help you if you don't have restore points to use. System Protection must be turned on so that restore points are automatically created.

▲ Restore points replace certain keys in the registry but cannot completely rebuild a totally corrupted registry. Therefore, System Restore can recover from errors only if the registry is somewhat intact.

▲ The restore process cannot remove a virus or worm infection. However, it might help you start a system that is infected with a virus that launches at startup. After Windows has started, you can then use anti-malware software to remove the infection.

▲ System Restore might create a new problem. Often when using a restore point, anti-malware software gets out of whack and sometimes even needs reinstalling. Therefore, use restore points sparingly.

▲ Restore points are kept in a hidden folder on the hard drive. If that area of the drive is corrupted, the restore points are lost. Also, if a user turns System Protection off, all restore points are lost.

▲ Viruses and other malware sometimes hide in restore points. To completely clean an infected system, you need to delete all restore points by turning System Protection off and back on.

▲ If Windows will not start, you can launch System Restore using startup recovery tools, which are covered in Chapter 15.

★ **A+ Exam Tip** The A+ Core 2 exam gives you a scenario and expects you to know when and how to use System Restore to solve a Windows, hardware, or application problem within that scenario.

Here's how to use System Restore:

1. Enter the **rstrui.exe** command. The System Restore box appears and shows the most recent restore point selected (see Figure 14-28).

2. Do one of the following:

   ▲ For most situations, select the most recent restore point to make the least possible changes to your system, and then click **Next**.

   ▲ To see other restore points, select **Choose a different restore point** and click **Next**. Select a restore point and click **Next**.

3. Click **Finish**. The system restarts and the restore point is applied.

Figure 14-28 Select a restore point

Now that you understand the general approach to take when troubleshooting problems with Windows, applications, and hardware, let's look at some specific problems you might face and what to do about them.

SLOW STARTUP AND SLOW PERFORMANCE

 A+ CORE 2 1.4, 1.5, 1.6, 3.1

If Windows starts slowly (sometimes called a slow startup or slow boot) or performs slowly, use the following steps to clean up the startup process and improve performance. We're assuming Windows starts with no errors. If Windows refuses to start or starts with errors, use the tools and techniques described in Chapter 15.

> ★ **A+ Exam Tip** The A+ Core 2 exam expects you to know how to troubleshoot and solve problems with slow system performance.

STEP 1: OBSERVE STARTUP

 A+ CORE 2 3.1

To get a benchmark of how fast Windows starts and see what might be causing the problem of a slow startup, do the following:

1. Use a stopwatch or a watch with a second hand to time a normal startup from the moment you press the power button until the wait icon on the Windows desktop disappears.

2. Follow the steps given earlier in the chapter to set up a clean boot. Time the boot again, this time using a clean boot. Note the differences.

If there is no difference, you can assume startup processes are not the source of the problem. If the difference is significant, follow the steps in this part of the chapter to reduce Windows startup to essentials. If the performance problem still exists after a clean boot, you can assume that the problem is with hardware or Windows settings. You can then look for bottlenecks with hardware and consider that Windows might be corrupted, using the tools presented earlier in the chapter.

STEP 2: BACK UP USER DATA

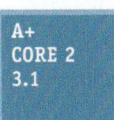 **A+ CORE 2 3.1**

As always, if valuable data is not backed up, back it up before you apply any of the fixes in this chapter. You don't want to risk losing the user's data.

> ✎ **Notes** If you are able to interview the user to find out when slow performance began, use Reliability Monitor (called reliability history in Windows 10) to discover what changes were made to the system around that time and what other problems occurred.

STEP 3: PERFORM ROUTINE MAINTENANCE

 A+ CORE 2 1.4, 1.5, 1.6, 3.1

It might seem pretty mundane, but the first things you need to do to improve Windows performance are the routine maintenance tasks that you learned in Chapter 13. These tasks are summarized here:

▲ *Verify critical Windows settings.* Make sure Windows updates are current. Verify that antivirus software is updated and set to routinely scan for viruses. Make sure the network connection is secured and backups are happening as you expect. If the system is experiencing a marked decrease in performance, suspect a virus and use up-to-date antivirus software to perform a full scan of the system.

14

▲ *Uninstall software you no longer need and optimize the hard drive.* Make sure drive C: has at least 15 percent free space and the hard drive is being defragged or optimized weekly. If you suspect hard drive problems, use chkdsk to check the hard drive for errors and recover data.

STEP 4: INVESTIGATE AND ELIMINATE STARTUP PROGRAMS

To speed up startup, search for unnecessary startup programs you can eliminate. Tools that can help are System Configuration (msconfig.exe), startup folders, and Task Manager. Follow these steps to investigate startup:

1. Open the **Startup** tab in Windows 10/8 Task Manager or the **Startup** tab in Windows 7 System Configuration. In the list of startup items, look for a specific startup program you don't want. If you're not sure of the purpose of a program, right-click it in Windows 10/8 and click **Search online** in the shortcut menu. (For Windows 7, scroll to the right in the Command column to see the location and name of the startup program file, and use that information for a web search.) Then search the web for information on this program. Be careful to use only reliable sites for credible information.

> ⚡ **Caution**   A word of caution is important here: Many websites will tell you a legitimate process is malicious so that you will download and use their software to get rid of the process. However, their software is likely to be adware or spyware that you don't want. Make sure you can trust a site before you download from it or take its advice.

2. If you want to find out whether disabling a startup entry gives problems or improves performance, temporarily disable it using Windows 10/8 Task Manager or Windows 7 System Configuration. To permanently disable a startup item, it's best to uninstall the software or remove the entry from a startup folder. See Appendix B for a list of startup folders.

> ✎ **Notes**   The startup folder for all users is hidden by default. In Chapter 11, you learned how to "unhide" folders that are hidden.

3. As you research startup processes, Task Manager can tell you what processes are currently running. Open Task Manager and select the **Processes** tab. If you see a process and want to know its program file location, right-click the process in Windows 10/8 and click **Open file location**. File Explorer opens at the program file's location.

> ↻ **OS Differences**   For Windows 7, you can find out the file location by clicking **View** and clicking **Select Columns**. In the Select Process Page Columns box, check **Image Path Name** and click **OK**. The Image Path Name column is added to the Processes tab.

For extremely slow systems that need a more drastic fix, set Windows for a clean boot. Then restart the system and see what problems you have if a program you really need is disabled. Enable just the services and programs you decide you need.

Regardless of the method you use, be sure to restart the system after each change and note what happens. Do you get an error message? Does a device or application not work? If so, you have probably disabled a service or program you need.

Has performance improved? If performance does not improve by disabling services or startup programs, go back and enable them again. If a non-Microsoft service or startup program didn't cause the problem, turn your attention to Microsoft services or startup programs. Start disabling them one at a time.

> ★ **Caution** You might be tempted to disable all Microsoft services. If you do, however, you are disabling Networking, Event Logging, Error Reporting, Windows Firewall, Windows Installer, Windows Backup, Print Spooler, Windows Update, System Protection, and other important services. These services should be disabled only when testing for performance problems and then immediately enabled when the test is finished. Also, know that if you disable the Volume Shadow Copy service, all restore points kept on the system will be lost. If you intend to use System Restore to fix a problem with the system, don't disable this service. If you are not sure what a service does, read its description in the Services console before you change its status.

Remember that you don't want to permanently leave System Configuration or Task Manager in control of startup. After you have used these tools to identify the problem, use other tools to permanently remove the problem service or program from startup. Use the Services console to disable a service, use the Programs and Features window to uninstall software, and remove program files from startup folders. After the problem is fixed, return System Configuration and/or Task Manager to a normal startup.

Don't forget to restart the computer after making a change to verify that all is well.

STEP 5: CHECK FOR UNWANTED SCHEDULED TASKS

A+ CORE 2 1.5, 3.1

When applications install, they often schedule tasks to check for and download their program updates, and malware sometimes hides as a scheduled task. Scheduled tasks might be unnecessary and can slow a system down. The best way to uninstall a scheduled task is to uninstall the software that is responsible for the task. Open the Task Scheduler window and search through tasks to find those you think are unnecessary or causing trouble. Research the software the task works with and then decide if you want to uninstall the software or disable the task.

APPLYING | CONCEPTS USING TASK SCHEDULER TO MANAGE STARTUP PROGRAMS

To get familiar with Task Scheduler and use it to remove unnecessarily scheduled tasks from Windows startup, do the following:

1. Task Scheduler stores tasks in files and subfolders in the C:\Windows\System32\Tasks folder. Open Windows 10/8 **File Explorer** or Windows 7 **Windows Explorer** and drill down into this folder to see the list of scheduled task files. One example is shown in Figure 14-29.

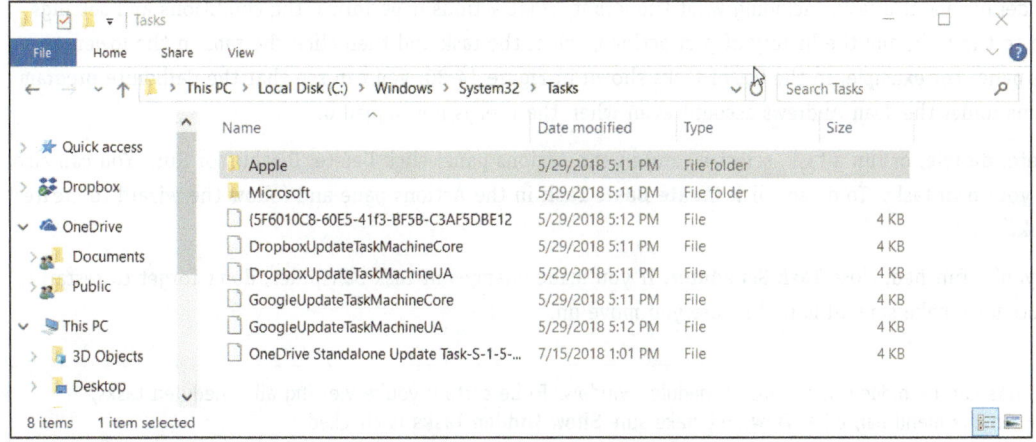

Figure 14-29 The Tasks folder contains tasks managed by Task Scheduler

14

(continues)

2. To open Task Scheduler, enter the **taskschd.msc** command or double-click **Task Scheduler** in the Administrative Tools group. The Task Scheduler window is shown in Figure 14-30.

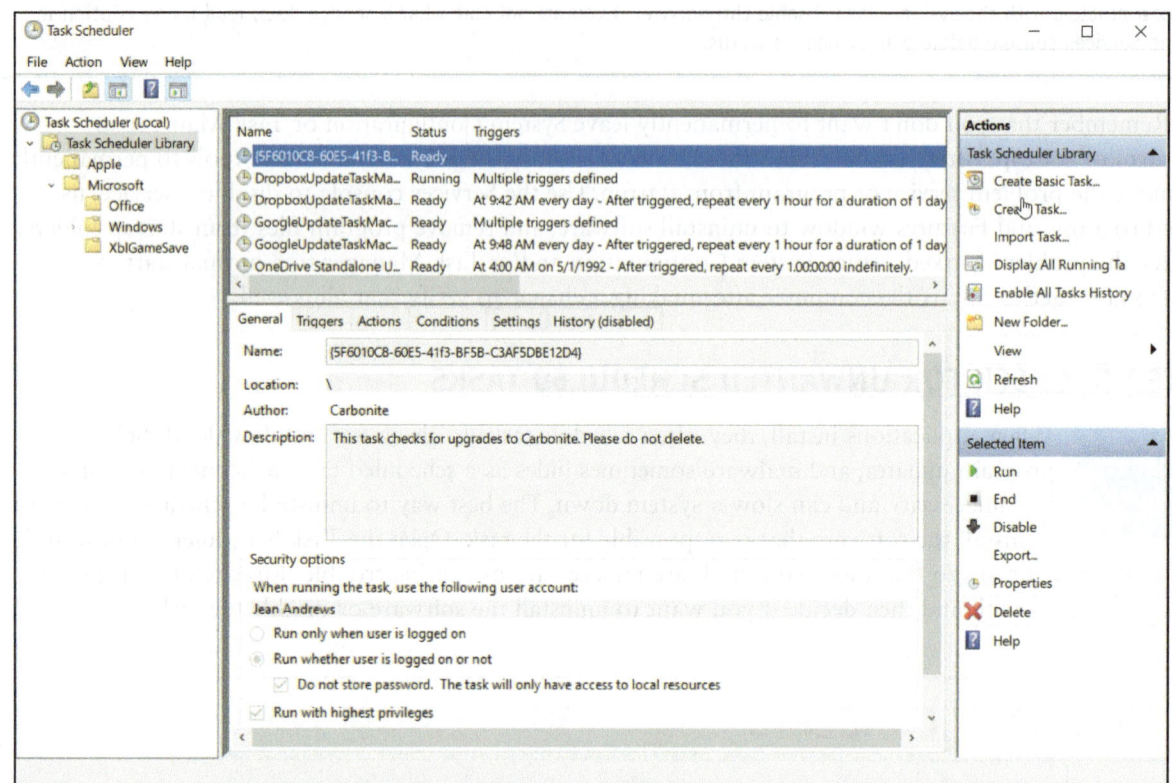

Figure 14-30 View and manage tasks from the Task Scheduler window

3. To explore tasks, drill down into groups and subgroups in the left pane. Notice in the left pane of Figure 14-30 that the groups and subgroups match up with the folder structure in the Tasks folder of Explorer. Tasks in a group are listed in the middle pane.

4. To see details about a task, including what triggers it, what actions it performs, the conditions and settings related to the task, and the history of past actions, select the task and then click the tabs in the lower-middle pane. For example, in the list of tasks shown in Figure 14-30, you can see that the Carbonite program task runs under the Jean Andrews account even when the user is not logged on.

5. To delete, disable, or run a task, select it, and in the Actions pane, click Delete, Disable, or Run. You can also create your own tasks. To do so, click **Create Basic Task** in the Actions pane and follow the wizard to create the task.

6. When you're finished, close **Task Scheduler**. If you made changes in Task Scheduler, don't forget to restart the system to make sure all is well before you move on.

> 🖉 **Notes** Tasks can be hidden in the Task Scheduler window. To be certain you're viewing all scheduled tasks, unhide them. In the menu bar, click **View** and make sure **Show Hidden Tasks** is checked.

STEP 6: CHECK FOR LOW SYSTEM RESOURCES

**A+
CORE 2
1.4, 1.5,
1.6, 3.1**

Follow directions in the "Low on System Resources" section earlier in this chapter to check a hardware component that might be a bottleneck. Also, you might be able to improve performance by moving the virtual memory file, pagefile.sys; Windows uses this file in the same way it uses memory to enhance the amount of RAM in a system. Normally, pagefile.sys is a hidden file stored in the root directory of drive C:. To save space on drive C:, you can move pagefile.sys to another volume on the same hard drive or to a different hard drive, but don't move it to a different hard drive unless you know that drive is at least as fast as the current one. If the drive is as fast as the one on which Windows is installed, performance should improve. Also, make sure the new volume has plenty of free space to hold the file—at least three times the amount of installed RAM.

★ **A+ Exam Tip**   The A+ Core 2 exam expects you to know how to configure virtual memory for optimal performance.

APPLYING | CONCEPTS   CHANGING THE LOCATION OF PAGEFILE.SYS

To change the location of pagefile.sys, follow these steps:

1. Open the System window and click **Advanced system settings** in the left pane. The System Properties box appears with the Advanced tab selected (see Figure 14-31).

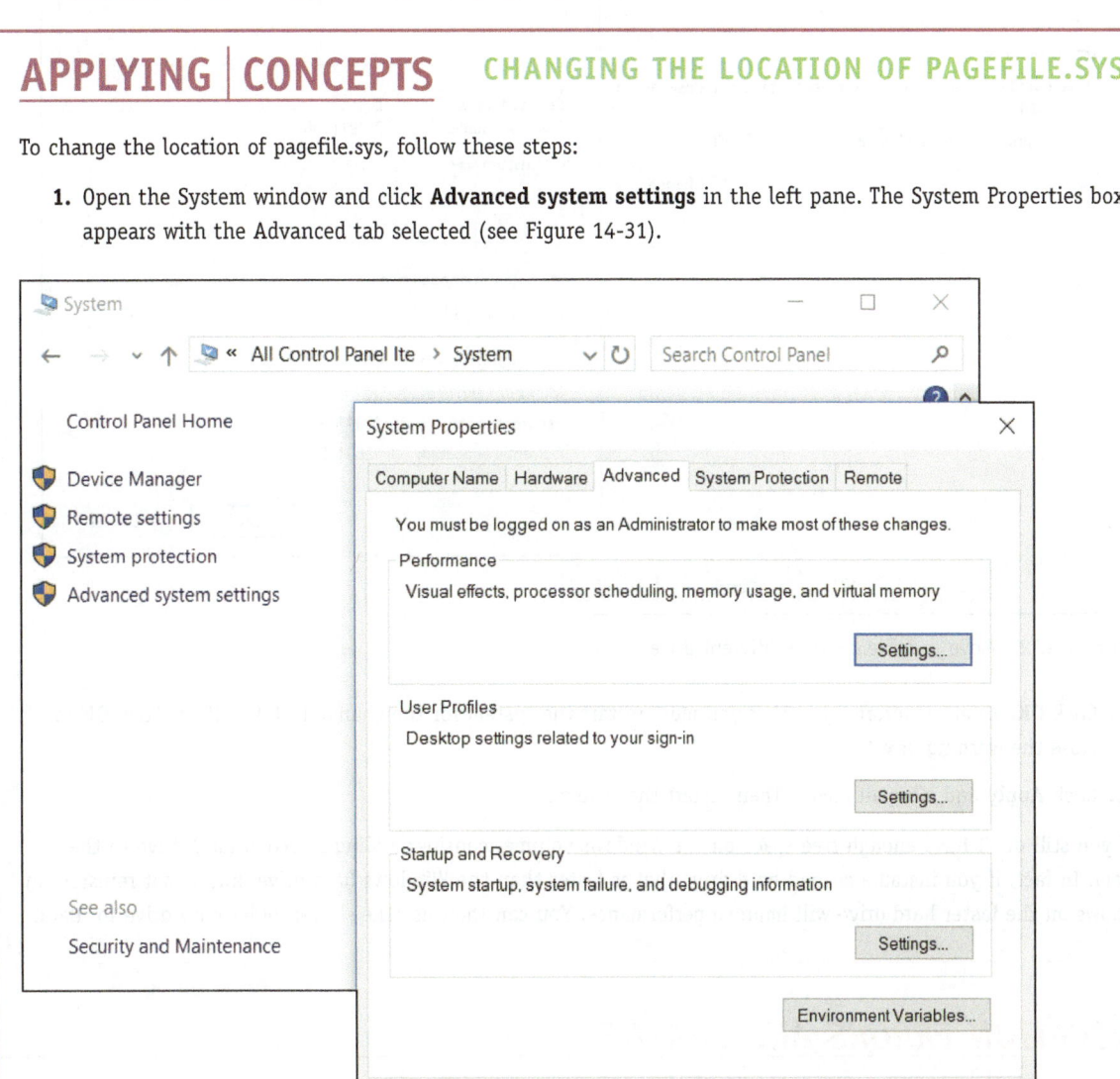

Figure 14-31   Manage virtual memory using the System Properties box

14

(continues)

2. In the Performance section, click **Settings**. In the Performance Options box, select the **Advanced** tab and click **Change**. The Virtual Memory dialog box appears.

3. Uncheck **Automatically manage paging file size for all drives** (see Figure 14-32). Select the drive where you want to move the paging file. For best performance, allow Windows to manage the size of the paging file. If necessary, select **System managed size** and click **Set**.

Figure 14-32   Move pagefile.sys to a different drive

4. Click **OK**. Windows informs you that you must restart the system for the change to take effect. Click **OK** to close the warning box.

5. Click **Apply** and close all boxes. Then restart the system.

If you still don't have enough free space on the Windows volume, consider adding a second hard drive to the system. In fact, if you install a second hard drive that is faster than the Windows hard drive, know that reinstalling Windows on the faster hard drive will improve performance. You can then use the slower, older hard drive for data.

APPLICATION ERRORS AND CRASHES

A+
CORE 2
1.4, 1.5,
1.6, 3.1

In this part of the chapter, you learn to deal with specific application errors and crashes.

✎ **Notes** If you are troubleshooting a problem and make a change to the system, be sure to restart Windows and check to see if the problem is resolved before you move on to the next fix.

APPLICATION HANGS

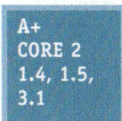

If an application is locked up and not responding, use Task Manager to end it. If Task Manager can't end a process, use the tasklist and taskkill commands. The tasklist command returns the process identifier (PID), which is a number that identifies each running process. The taskkill command uses the process ID to kill the process. Here's how to use the commands, using Notepad as our sample application:

1. Open a command prompt window and start Notepad with the **notepad.exe** command. Be sure the Notepad window and the command prompt window are positioned so both are visible on your screen.

2. Use the **tasklist | more** command to see a list of processes currently running (press the Spacebar to scroll to the next page). Note the PID of the Notepad process—for example, 7132. (You can also view PIDs on the Details tab of Task Manager.)

3. Enter the command **taskkill /f /pid:7132**, substituting the PID you noted in Step 2. The /f parameter forcefully kills the process. Be careful using this command; it is so powerful that you can end critical system processes that will cause the system to shut down.

SLOW-PERFORMING APPLICATION

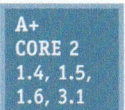

Each application running on your computer is assigned a priority level, which determines its position in the queue for CPU resources. You can use Task Manager to change the priority level for an application that is already open. If an application performs slowly, increase its priority. You should only do this with very important applications because giving an application higher priority than certain background system processes can sometimes interfere with the operating system.

To use Task Manager to change the priority level of an open application, do the following:

1. In Task Manager, click the **Processes** tab, right-click the application, and click **Go to details**.

2. On the Details tab, right-click the selected program and point to **Set priority**. Set the new priority to **Above normal** (see Figure 14-33). If that doesn't give satisfactory performance, try **High**.

Remember that any changes you make to an application's priority level affect only the current session.

14

Figure 14-33   Change the priority level of a running application

> **OS Differences** For Windows 7, you can set the priority for a process in Task Manager by beginning with the **Applications** tab. Right-click the application and select **Go To Process**. On the Processes tab, right-click the selected process and point to **Set Priority**. You can then set the new priority.

SERVICE FAILS TO START

**A+
CORE 2
1.5, 3.1**

An error results when an application expects a background service to be running but it failed to start. Research the application documentation and find out if the app relies on a service to work. To manage services, enter the **services.msc** command to open the Services console. If the Extended tab at the bottom of the window is not selected, click it (see Figure 14-34). This tab gives a description of a selected service.

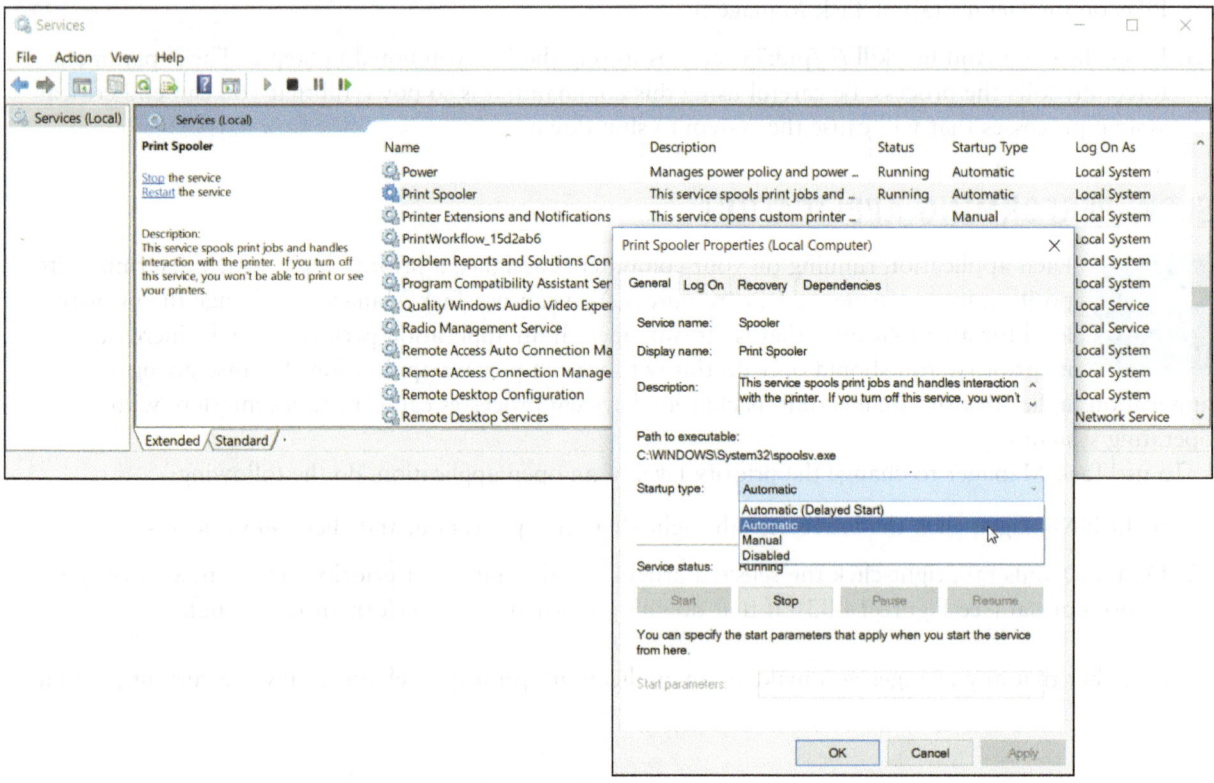

Figure 14-34   The Services console is used to manage Windows services

When you click a service to select it and the description is missing, most likely it's a third-party service put there by an installed application; in fact, it might be malware. To get more information about a service or to stop or start a service, right-click its name and select **Properties** from the shortcut menu. In the Properties box (see Figure 14-34), the startup types for a service are:

▲ *Automatic (Delayed Start).* Starts shortly after startup and after the user signs in, so as not to slow down the startup process
▲ *Automatic.* Starts when Windows loads
▲ *Manual.* Starts as needed
▲ *Disabled.* Cannot be started

Use the Services console to make sure the service an application requires has started. If the service has failed to start, make sure it has an Automatic or Manual setting. If problems with the service or application persist, you might need to reinstall the service or the application that uses the service.

Other problems with a service can sometimes be resolved by stopping and restarting the service. For example, stopping and restarting the Spooler service might solve a problem with print jobs not moving on to the printer. To stop or restart, right-click the service and use the shortcut menu.

Notes If you suspect a Windows system service is causing a problem, you can use System Configuration to disable the service. If this works, try replacing the service file with a fresh copy from Windows setup media.

FILE FAILS TO OPEN

A+ CORE 2 3.1

Windows depends on the file extension to associate a data file with an application used to open it; this is called the file association. An application associated with a file extension is called its default program. When you double-click a data file and Windows examines the file extension but doesn't know which application to call on to open the file, it displays an error message. The solution to this problem is to change the file association for the file extension.

APPLYING | CONCEPTS   SOLVING FILE ASSOCIATION PROBLEMS

A+ CORE 2 3.1

In our example, the Transact.dbf file shown in Figure 14-35A is a legacy database file created by dBASE, and the error box in Figure 14-35A appeared when the user double-clicked the file.

(A)

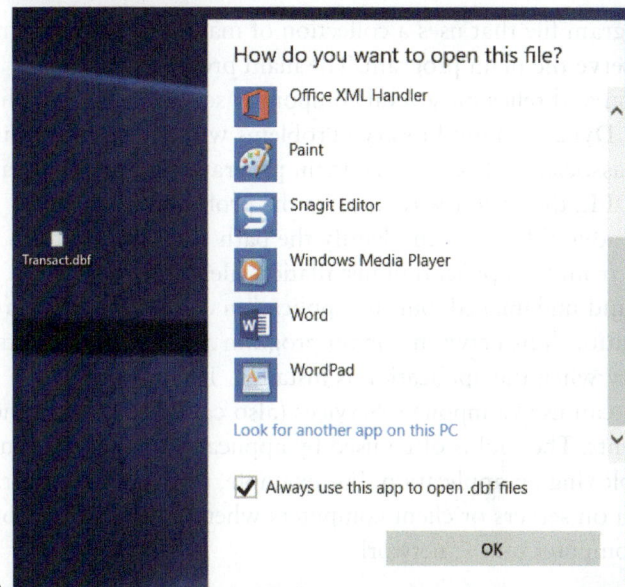

(B)

Figure 14-35 Windows does not know which application to use to open the data file

Follow these steps to instruct Windows to use Microsoft Excel to open files with a .dbf file extension:

1. When Windows displays an error message asking which application it should use to open a file, click **More apps**, as shown in Figure 14-35A. (For Windows 8/7, click **More Options**.) At the bottom of the box (see Figure 14-35B), click **Look for another app on this PC**. (For Windows 7, click **Select a program from a list of installed programs**.)

2. The *Open with* window appears. Locate the program file for Microsoft Excel, as shown in Figure 14-36, and click **Open**. (If you don't know an application's program file and location, launch the application and then open Task Manager. On the Processes tab of Task Manager, right-click the application and click **Open file location**. File Explorer or Windows Explorer opens and highlights the program file. You can see the path to the program file at the top of the Explorer window.)

14

(continues)

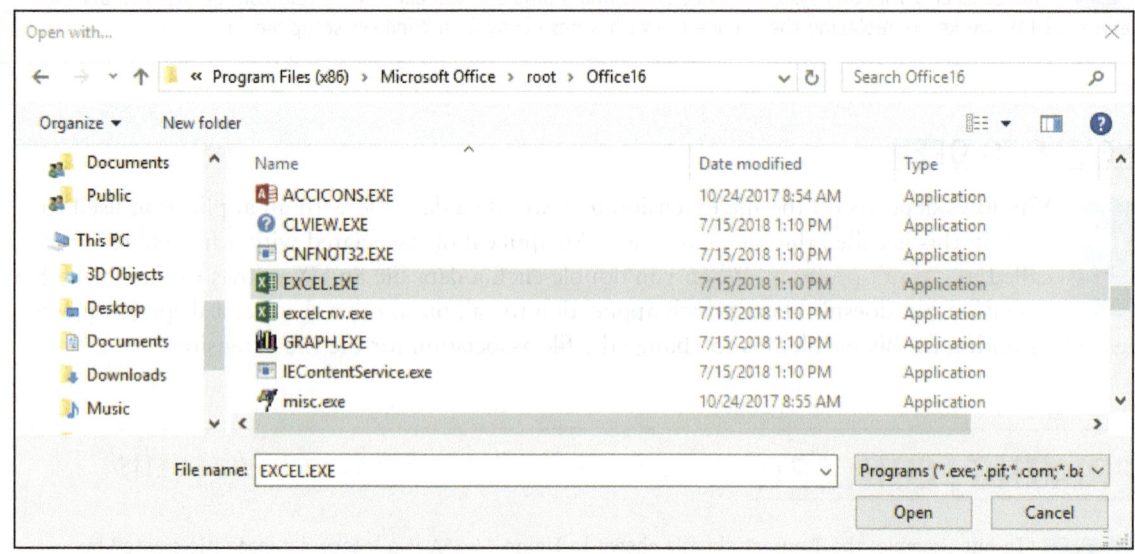

Figure 14-36   Locate and select the EXCEL.EXE application program file

3. When you double-click the **Transact.dbf** file, the file opens in an Excel window. Also, the icon used for the file on the desktop is now the Excel icon.

You might need to change the program associated with a file extension. For example, suppose you tried to associate the Transact.dbf file with Microsoft Access, and when you opened the file, Access gave an error. To change a file association, right-click the file in Explorer and click **Open with**. Next, for Windows 10, click **Choose another app**, check **Always use this app to open files**, and then find and select the new application. (For Windows 8/7, click **Choose default program** and find the new application to associate with the file extension.)

MISSING DLL OR COMPONENT NOT REGISTERED

A+
CORE 2
1.5, 1.6,
3.1

Most applications have a main program file that uses a collection of many smaller programs called components or objects that serve the main program. The main program for an application has an .exe file extension and relies on several component services that often have .dll file extensions. (DLL stands for Dynamic Link Library.) Problems with applications can be caused by a missing DLL program or a broken association between the main program and a component.

If you get an error message about a missing DLL, the easiest way to solve the problem might be to reinstall the application. However, if that is not advisable, you can identify the path and name of the missing DLL file and recover it from backup or from the application installation files.

On the other hand, the file might be present and undamaged, but the application cannot find it because the relationship between the two is broken. Relationships between a main program and its components are normally established by entries in the registry when the application is installed. The process is called registering a component. In addition, you can use Component Services (also called COM+) in the Administrative Tools group to register components. The tool is often used by application developers and system administrators when developing and deploying an application. For example, a system administrator might use COM+ when installing an application on servers or client computers where an application on one computer calls an application on another computer on the network.

⭐ **A+ Exam Tip**   The A+ 220-902 exam expects you to know how to handle missing DLL errors and to know when it's appropriate to use the Component Services tool.

As an IT support technician, you might be asked by a system administrator or software provider to use the COM+ tool to help solve a problem with an application giving errors. Suppose you get this error when installing an application:

$$\text{Error 1928 "Error registering COM+ application."}$$

When you contact the help desk of the application provider, you might be instructed to use the COM+ tool to solve the problem. To open the tool, open Control Panel and click **Administrative Tools**, then double-click **Component Services**. The Component Services window is shown in Figure 14-37. To learn how to use the tool, click **Help** in the menu bar. The application provider should be able to step you through the process of registering one of their components.

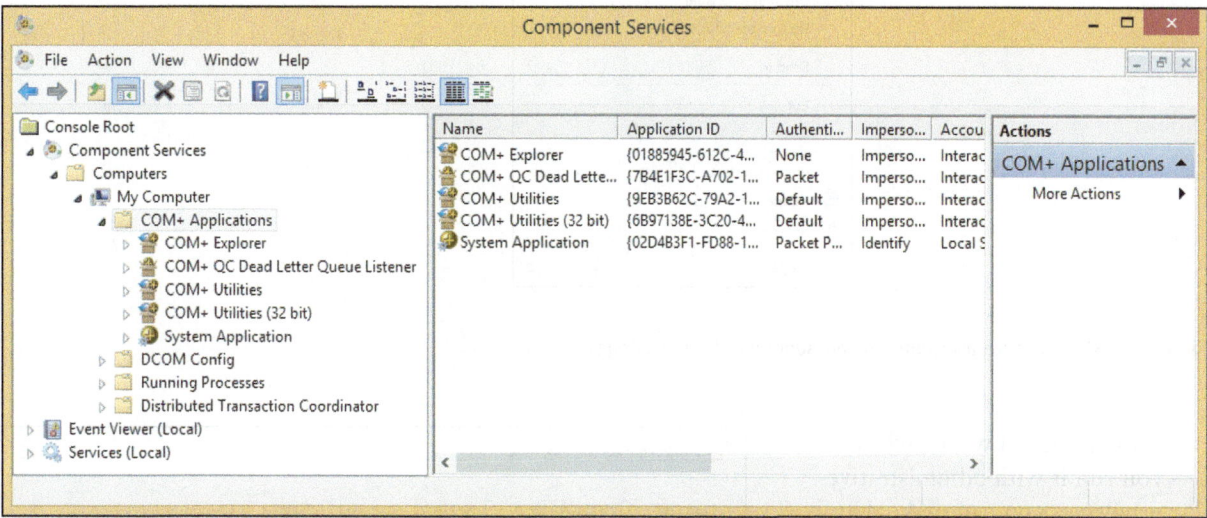

Figure 14-37 Use the Component Services window to register components used by an application

14

APPLICATION HAS NEVER WORKED

A+
CORE 2
1.5, 1.6,
3.1

If an application has never worked or stops working after the OS has been upgraded, follow these steps:

1. *Update Windows and search the web.* Installing all important and critical Windows updates can sometimes solve a problem with an application that won't install. Also check the website of the software manufacturer and the Microsoft support site (*support.microsoft.com*) for solutions. Search on the application name or the error message you get when you try to run it. Verify that the application is approved by its manufacturer to work in the installed OS.

2. *Run the installation program or application as an administrator.* The program might require that the user have privileges not assigned to the current user account. Try running the application with administrator privileges, which Windows calls a secondary logon. Use Explorer to locate the executable program file in a subfolder of the Program Files or Program Files (x86) folder. Right-click the file and select **Run as administrator** from the shortcut menu (see Figure 14-38).

> **Notes** To run a program from a user account other than administrator, hold down the Shift key and right-click the program file. Then select **Run as different user** from the shortcut menu. You must then enter the user name and password of another user account in the Windows Security box.

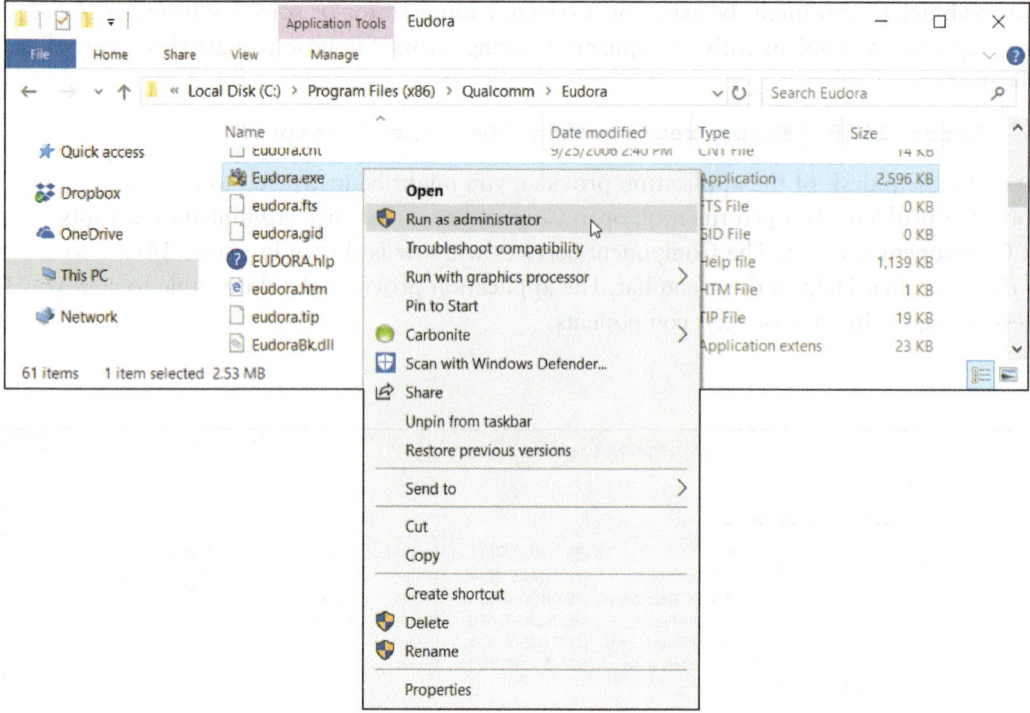

Figure 14-38 Execute a program using administrative privileges

If the program works when you run it with administrative privileges, you can make that setting permanent. To do so, right-click the program and select **Properties** from the shortcut menu. Then click the **Compatibility** tab and check **Run this program as an administrator** (see Figure 14-39). Click **Apply** and then close the Properties box.

3. *Consider whether an older application is having compatibility problems with Windows.* Some older applications cannot run under Windows 10/8 or they run with errors. In the Properties box shown in Figure 14-39, click **Run compatibility troubleshooter**. Windows makes its recommendations, such as enabling Compatibility mode for Windows XP programs. Test the program and click **OK** to make the change permanent.

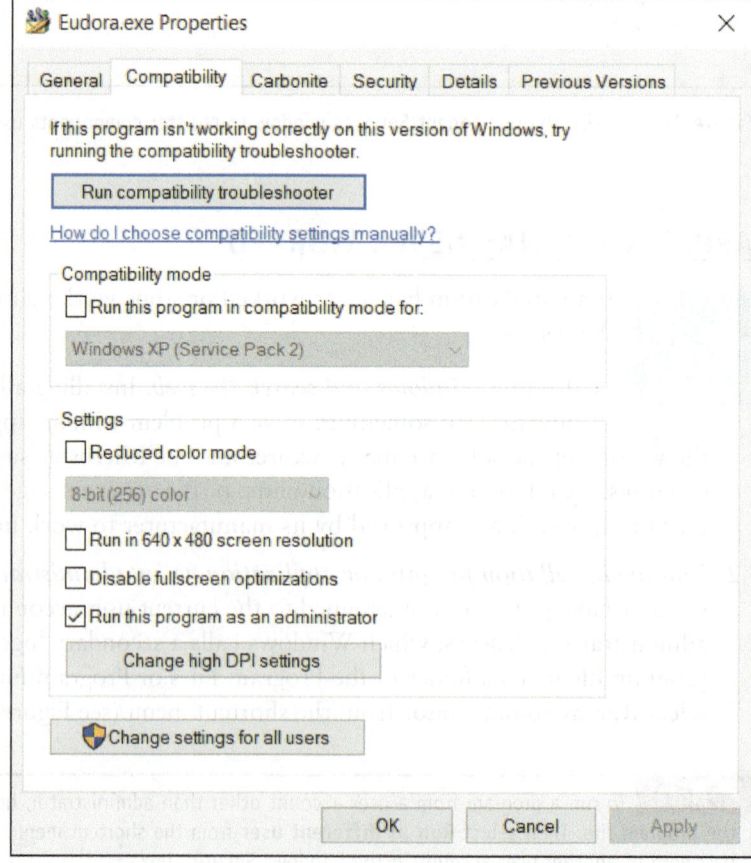

Figure 14-39 Permanently change the privilege level of an application

4. ***Verify that the application is digitally signed.*** Although applications that are not digitally signed can still run on Windows, a digital signature does verify that the application is not a rogue application and that it is certified as Windows-compatible by Microsoft. To view the digital signature, select the **Digital Signatures** tab of the program file's Properties box. Select a signer in the list and click **Details** (see Figure 14-40). If the Digital Signatures tab is missing, the program is not digitally signed.

Figure 14-40   This program is digitally signed

ODBC DATA SOURCES

As an IT technician, you might be called on to help set up a local computer on a corporate network to connect to a remote database stored on a company database server. For example, suppose Microsoft Access is installed on the local computer and you want to configure it to connect to a Microsoft SQL Server database on a server. Open Database Connectivity (ODBC) is the technology used to create the data source, which provides access to the database and includes the drivers required to interface between Access and the data (see Figure 14-41). Drivers for Microsoft SQL Server must be installed on the local computer (Windows has SQL drivers installed by default). Then you can use the ODBC Data Sources tool in the Administrative Tools group of Control Panel to configure the data source.

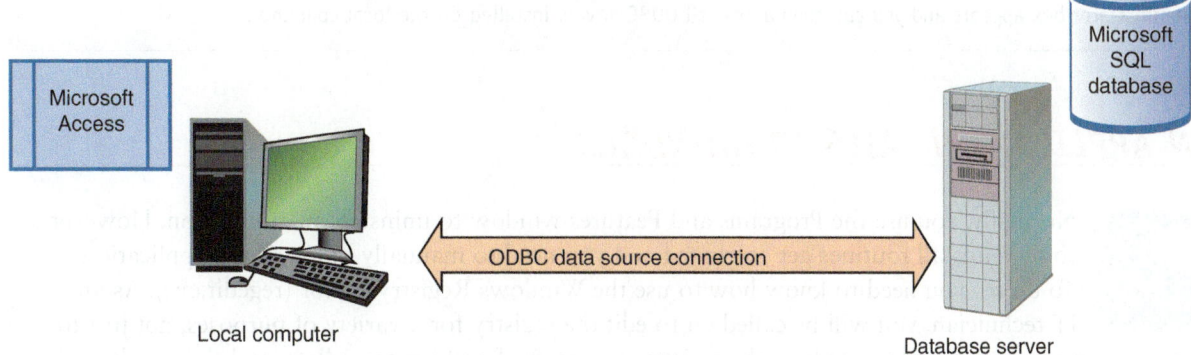

Figure 14-41   Microsoft Access connects to an ODBC data source on a corporate network

14

Do the following to create a new data source for Microsoft Access so that it can work with a remote Microsoft SQL Server database:

1. For Windows 10/8, you need to know whether Access is installed as a 32-bit or 64-bit application. One easy way to find out is to look on the Processes tab of Task Manager when the application is open. You'll see "32 bit" or "64 bit" listed in the application name.

2. Open the **Administrative Tools** group. For Windows 10/8, click either **ODBC Data Sources (32-bit)** or **ODBC Data Sources (64-bit)**, depending on the version of Access that's installed. For Windows 7, click **Data Sources (ODBC)**. The ODBC Data Source Administrator box opens (see the left side of Figure 14-42).

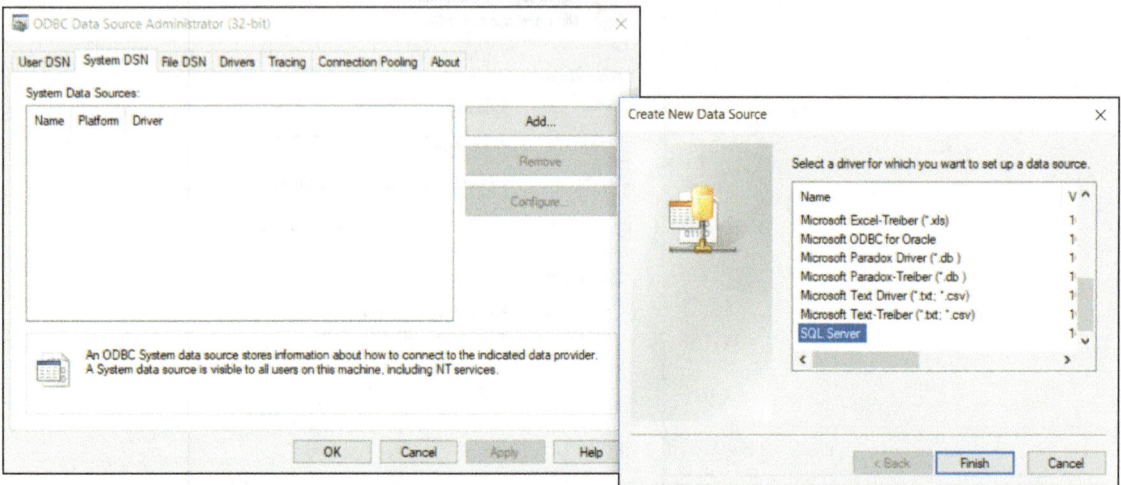

Figure 14-42 Use the Data Sources tool to create a connection between a foreign data source and an application

3. To make the data source apply to all users of the system, click the **System DSN** tab. (DSN stands for Data Source Name; the **User DSN** tab applies only to the current user.) Click **Add**. The Create New Data Source box appears (see the right side of Figure 14-42). Scroll down, select **SQL Server**, and click **Finish**. Follow the on-screen directions to enter the name of the SQL Server computer on the network and the sign-in ID and password to SQL Server. The database administrator in your organization can supply this information.

> ✎ **Notes** If you don't see the driver you need in the Create New Data Source box, close all windows and use Explorer to locate the C:\Windows\SysWOW64\Odbcad32.exe program file. When you double-click this file, the ODBC Data Source Administrator box appears and you can then access all ODBC drivers installed on the local computer.

AN APPLICATION FAILS TO UNINSTALL

| A+ |
| CORE 2 |
| 1.5, 1.6, |
| 3.1 |

Normally, you use the Programs and Features window to uninstall an application. However, some uninstall routines get corrupted and you need to manually uninstall the application. To do so, you need to know how to use the Windows Registry Editor (regedit.exe). As an IT technician, you will be called on to edit the registry for a variety of purposes, not just to remove software. Let's first look at how the registry is organized and how to edit it, and then we'll explore the details of manually removing software.

REGISTRY EDITOR

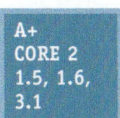

A+
CORE 2
1.5, 1.6,
3.1

Many actions, such as installing application software or hardware, can result in changes to items in the registry, called keys, which are assigned values. Changes to the registry can include adding or removing keys and their values or editing the values assigned to existing keys. For a few difficult problems, you might need to edit the values assigned to a key or remove a registry key. This part of the chapter looks at how the registry is organized, which keys might hold entries causing problems, and how to back up and edit the registry using the Registry Editor. Let's first look at how the registry is organized.

HOW THE REGISTRY IS ORGANIZED

The registry is the most important Windows component that holds information for Windows. The registry is a database designed with a treelike structure (called a hierarchical database) that contains configuration information for Windows, users, software applications, and installed hardware devices. During startup, Windows builds the registry in memory and keeps it there until Windows shuts down. During startup, after the registry is built, Windows reads from it to obtain information to complete the startup process. After Windows is loaded, it continually reads from many of the subkeys in the registry.

Windows builds the registry from the current hardware configuration and from information it takes from the following files:

▲ Five files stored in the C:\Windows\System32\config folder; these files are called hives, and they are named the SAM (Security Accounts Manager), SECURITY, SOFTWARE, SYSTEM, and DEFAULT hives. (Each hive is backed up with a log file and a backup file, which are also stored in the C:\Windows\System32\config folder.)

▲ C:\Users*username*\Ntuser.dat file, which holds the preferences and settings of the currently signed-in user.

After the registry is built in memory, it is organized into five high-level keys (see Figure 14-43). Each key can have subkeys, and subkeys can have more subkeys and can be assigned one or more values. The way data is organized in the hive files is different from the way it is organized in registry keys. Figure 14-44 shows the relationship between registry keys and hives. For example, notice that the HKEY_CLASSES_ ROOT key contains data that comes from the SOFTWARE and DEFAULT hives, and some of this data is also stored in the larger HKEY_LOCAL_MACHINE key.

14

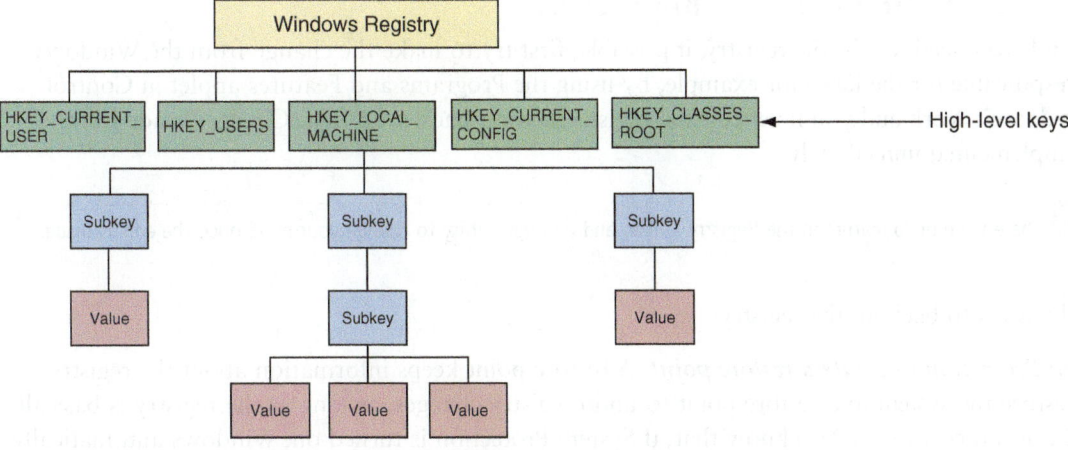

Figure 14-43 The Windows registry is logically organized in five keys with subkeys

Here are the five keys, including where they get their data and their purposes:

◢ **HKEY_LOCAL_MACHINE (HKLM)** is the most important key and contains hardware, software, and security data. The data is taken from four hives: the SAM hive, the SECURITY hive, the SOFTWARE hive, and the SYSTEM hive. In addition, the HARDWARE subkey of HKLM is built when the registry is first loaded, based on data collected about the current hardware configuration.

◢ **HKEY_CURRENT_CONFIG (HKCC)** contains information that identifies each hardware device installed on the computer. Some of the data is gathered from the current hardware

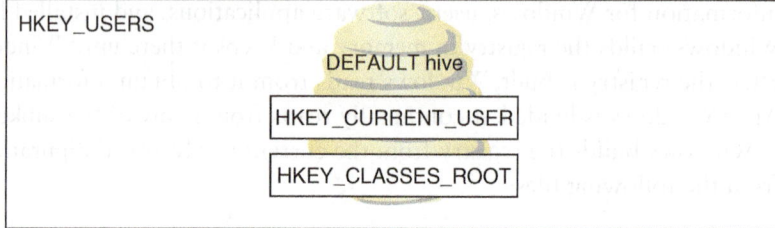

Figure 14-44   The relationship between registry keys and hives

configuration when the registry is first loaded into memory. Other data is taken from the HKLM key, which got its data primarily from the SYSTEM hive.

◢ **HKEY_CLASSES_ROOT (HKCR)** stores information that determines which application to open when the user double-clicks a file. This file association relies on the file's extension. Data for this key is gathered from the HKLM key and the HKCU key.

◢ **HKEY_USERS (HKU)** contains data about all users and is taken from the DEFAULT hive.

◢ **HKEY_CURRENT_USER (HKCU)** contains data about the current user. The key is built when a user signs in using data kept in the HKEY_USERS key and in the Ntuser.dat file of the current user.

> ✎ **Notes** Device Manager reads data from the HKLM\HARDWARE key to build the information it displays about hardware configurations. You can consider Device Manager to be an easy-to-view presentation of this HARDWARE key data.

BEFORE YOU EDIT THE REGISTRY, BACK IT UP!

When you think you need to edit the registry, if possible, first try to make the change from the Windows tool that is responsible for the key—for example, by using the Programs and Features applet in Control Panel. If that doesn't work and you must edit the registry, always back it up first. Changes made to the registry are implemented immediately.

> ⚡ **Caution**   There is no undo feature in the Registry Editor, and no opportunity to change your mind once the edit is made.

Here are the ways to back up the registry:

◢ *Use System Protection to create a restore point.* A restore point keeps information about the registry. You can restore the system to a restore point to undo registry changes, as long as the registry is basically intact and not too corrupted. Also know that, if System Protection is turned on, Windows automatically makes a daily backup of the registry hive files to the C:\Windows\System32\Config\RegBack folder.

▲ *Back up a single registry key just before you edit the key.* This method, called exporting a key, should always be used before you edit the registry. How to export a key is explained in the following steps.

▲ *Make an extra copy of the C:\Windows\System32\config folder.* This is what I call the old-fashioned shotgun approach to backing up the registry. This backup will help if the registry gets totally trashed. You can boot from Windows setup media and use the Windows Recovery Environment to get a command prompt window that you can use to restore the folder from your extra copy. This method is drastic and not recommended except in severe cases. Still, just to be on the safe side, you can make an extra copy of this folder just before you start any serious digging into the registry.

In some situations, such as when you're going to make drastic changes to the registry, you'll want to play it safe and use more than one backup method. Extra registry backups are always a good thing! Now let's look at how to back up an individual key in the registry, and then you'll learn how to edit the registry.

BACK UP, EDIT, AND RESTORE INDIVIDUAL KEYS

A less time-consuming method of backing up the registry is to back up a particular key that you plan to edit. However, know that if the registry gets corrupted, having a backup of only a particular key most likely will not help you much when trying a recovery. Also, although you could use this technique to back up the entire registry or an entire tree within the registry, it is not recommended.

To back up a registry key along with its subkeys, follow these steps:

1. To open the Registry Editor, enter the **regedit** command and respond to the UAC box. Figure 14-45 shows the Registry Editor with the five main keys and several subkeys listed. Click the triangles on the left to see subkeys. When you select a subkey, such as KeyboardClass in the figure, the names of the values in that subkey are displayed in the right pane along with the data assigned to each value.

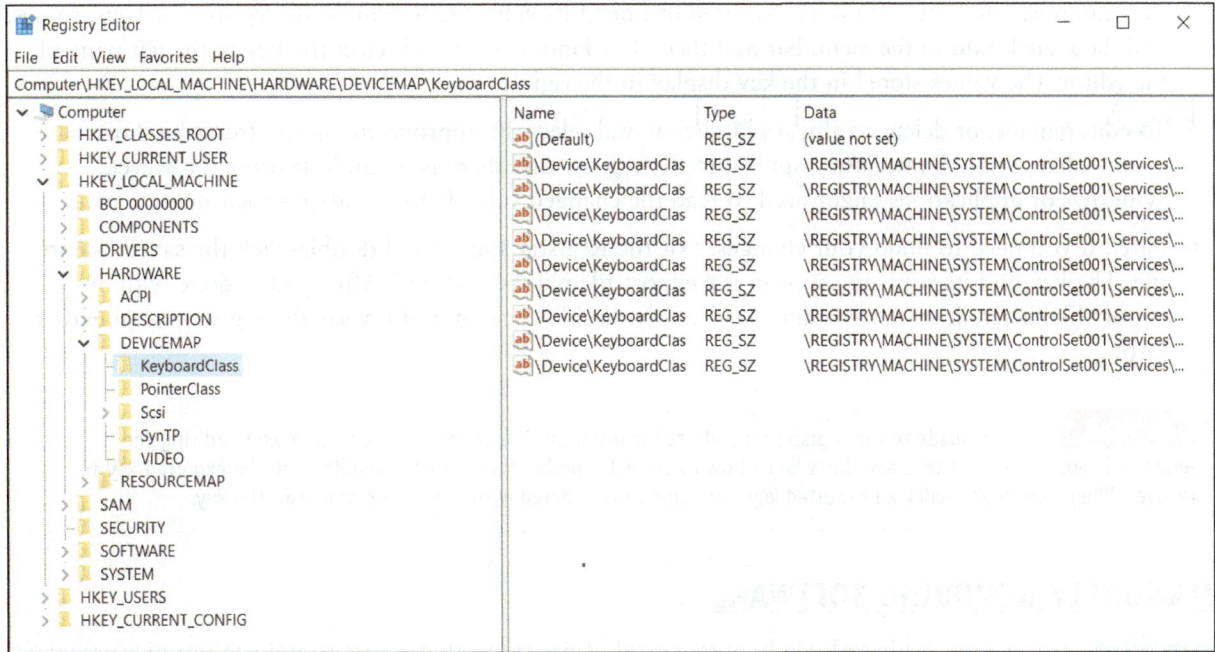

Figure 14-45 The Registry Editor showing the five main keys, subkeys, values, and data

14

✎ **Notes** The full path to a selected key displays in the bar at the top of the Windows 10 editor window and at the bottom of the Windows 8/7 editor window. If the bar is missing, click **View** in the menu bar. For Windows 10, make sure **Address Bar** is checked. For Windows 8/7, make sure **Status Bar** is checked.

2. Suppose we want to back up the registry key that contains a list of installed software, which is HKLM\
SOFTWARE\Microsoft\Windows\CurrentVersion\Uninstall. (HKLM stands for HKEY_LOCAL_
MACHINE.) First click the appropriate triangles to navigate to the key. Next, right-click the key and
select **Export** from the shortcut menu, as shown in Figure 14-46. The Export Registry File dialog box
appears.

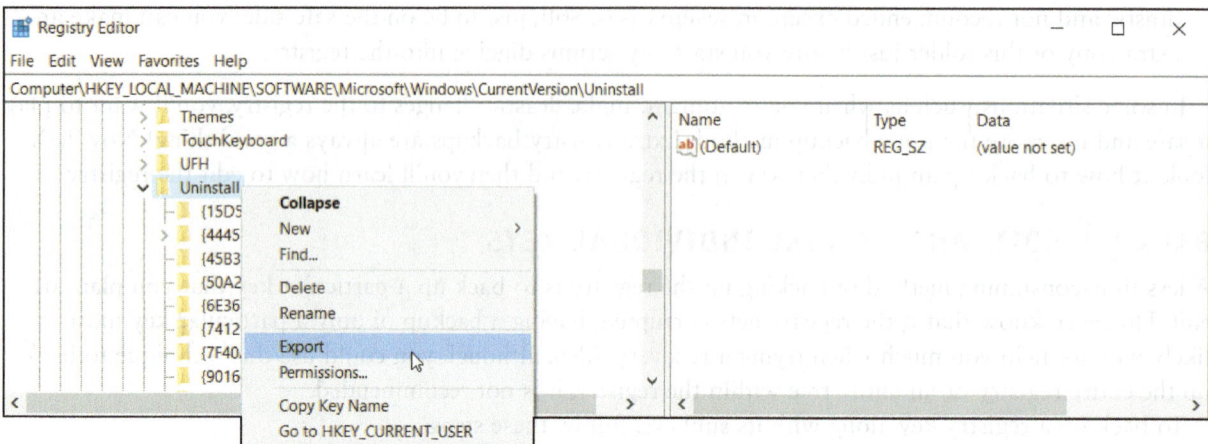

Figure 14-46 Using the Registry Editor, you can back up a key and its subkeys with the Export command

3. Select the location to save the export file and name the file. The desktop is a convenient place to store
an export file while you edit the registry. Click **Save** when done. The saved file will have a .reg file
extension.

4. You can now edit a key you have exported or one of its subkeys. To search the registry for keys, values,
and data, click **Edit** in the menu bar and then click **Find**. Locate and select the key in the left pane of
the editor. The values stored in the key display in the right pane.

5. To edit, rename, or delete a value, right-click it and select the appropriate option from the shortcut
menu. Changes are immediately applied to the registry and there is no undo feature. (However,
Windows or applications might need to read the changed value before it affects their operations.)

6. Later, if you need to undo your changes, exit the Registry Editor and double-click the saved export
file. The key and its subkeys saved in the export file will be restored. After you're done with an
export file, delete it so that no one accidentally double-clicks it and reverts the registry to an earlier
setting.

> ⚡ **Caution** Changes made to the registry take effect immediately. Therefore, take extra care when editing the
> registry. If you make a mistake and don't know how to correct a problem you create, double-click the exported key to
> recover. When you double-click an exported key, the registry is updated with the values stored in the key.

MANUALLY REMOVING SOFTWARE

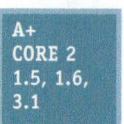

A+
CORE 2
1.5, 1.6,
3.1

You're now ready to learn how to get rid of programs that refuse to uninstall or give errors
when uninstalling. Doing so often causes problems later, so use the methods discussed in this
section only as a last resort after normal uninstall methods have failed.
Here are the high-level steps:

1. First try to locate and use an uninstall routine provided by the software. If this works, you are done
and can skip the next steps.

2. Delete the program folders and files that hold the software.

3. Delete the registry entries used by the software.

4. Remove the entries in the Start menu and delete any shortcuts on the desktop.

5. Remove any entries that launch processes at startup.

> **✏ Notes** Before uninstalling software, make sure it's not running in the background. For example, antivirus software cannot be uninstalled if it's still running. You can use Task Manager to end all processes related to the software, and you can use the Services console to stop services related to the software. Then remove the software.

Now let's step through the process of manually removing software.

STEP 1: FIRST TRY THE UNINSTALL ROUTINE

Most programs written for Windows have an uninstall routine that can be accessed from the Programs and Features window or launched from the Windows 10/7 Start menu or Windows 8 Start screen. First, try one of these methods before moving on to Step 2.

STEP 2: DELETE PROGRAM FILES

If the uninstall routine is missing or does not work, the next step is to delete the program folders and files that contain the software. In our example, we'll delete the RegServe software without using its uninstall routine. (RegServe is utility software that can clean the registry of unused keys.) Follow these steps:

1. If you have not already done so, close the application.

2. Look for the program folder in the C:\Program Files or C:\Program Files (x86) folder. In Figure 14-47, you can see the RegServe folder under the C:\Program Files (x86) folder. Keep in mind, however, the program files might be in another location that was set by the user when the software was installed.

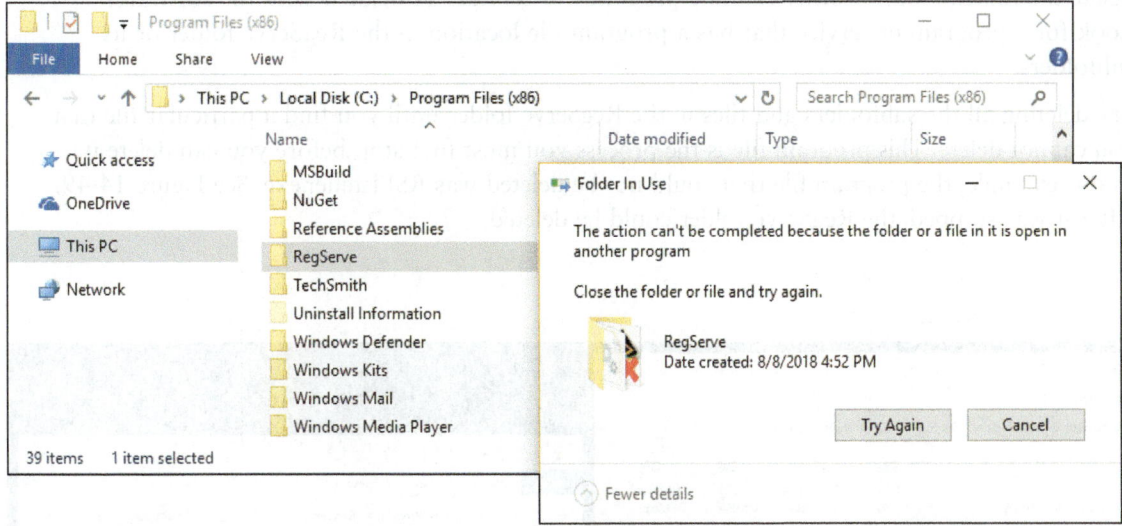

Figure 14-47 Program files are usually found in the Program Files or Program Files (x86) folder

3. Delete the **RegServe** folder and all its contents. As you do, the *Folder In Use* box shown on the right side of Figure 14-47 might report the program is in use. In this situation, do the following:

   a. Look for the program file reported on the **Processes** tab of Task Manager. If you see it listed, end the process (see Figure 14-48).

14

Figure 14-48 Task Manager shows a process is running and needs to be stopped before the program files can be deleted

b. If you don't find the program on the Processes tab, check the **Services** tab. If you find it there, select it and stop the service.

c. After the program or service is stopped, try to delete the program folder again. If you still cannot delete the folder, look for other running programs or services associated with the software. Look for a program or service that has a program file location in the RegServe folder or its subfolders.

d. Try deleting all the subfolders and files in the RegServe folder until you find a particular file that you cannot delete. This program file is the process you must first stop before you can delete it. In our example, the program file that could not be deleted was RSListener.exe. See Figure 14-49. After it was stopped, the RegServe folder could be deleted.

Figure 14-49 A running process prevents the RegServe folder and its running process from being deleted

STEP 3: DELETE REGISTRY ENTRIES

Editing the registry can be dangerous, so do it with caution and be sure to back up first! Do the following to delete registry entries that cause a program to be listed as installed software in the Programs and Features window of Control Panel:

1. To be on the safe side, back up the entire registry using one or more of the methods discussed earlier in the chapter.

2. Open the Registry Editor by entering the **regedit** command.

3. Locate a key that contains the entries that make up the list of installed software. Use the following criteria to decide which key to locate:

   ◢ For a 32-bit program installed in a 32-bit OS or for a 64-bit program installed in a 64-bit OS, locate this key:

      HKEY_LOCAL_MACHINE\Software\Microsoft\Windows\CurrentVersion\Uninstall

   ◢ For a 32-bit program installed in a 64-bit OS, locate this key:

      HKEY_LOCAL_MACHINE\SOFTWARE\Wow6432Node\Microsoft\Windows\CurrentVersion\Uninstall

   ✎ **Notes** Recall that 32-bit programs normally install in the \Program Files (x86) folder on a 64-bit system. These 32-bit programs normally use the Wow6432Node subkey in the registry of a 64-bit OS. However, occasionally you'll see a 32-bit app in the Uninstall key tree for 64-bit apps.

4. Back up the Uninstall key to the Windows desktop so that you can backtrack, if necessary. To do that, right-click the **Uninstall** key and select **Export** from the shortcut menu (see Figure 14-46 earlier in the chapter).

5. In the Export Registry File dialog box, select **Desktop**. Enter the file name as **Save Uninstall Key**, and click **Save**. You should see a new file icon named Save Uninstall Key.reg on your desktop.

6. The Uninstall key can be a daunting list of all the programs installed on your computer. When you expand the key, the left pane shows a long list of subkeys, which might have meaningless names that won't help you find the program you're looking for. Select the first subkey in the Uninstall key and watch as its values and data are displayed in the right pane. Step down through each key, watching for a meaningful name of a subkey in the left pane or meaningful details in the right pane until you find the program you want to delete. If you don't find the application in the Uninstall key for 32-bit apps, check the Uninstall key for 64-bit apps. Occasionally you'll see a 32-bit app in the 64-bit Uninstall key tree.

7. To delete the key, right-click it and select **Delete** from the shortcut menu. Confirm the deletion, as shown in Figure 14-50. Be sure to search through all the keys in this list because the software might have more than one key. Delete them all and exit the Registry Editor.

14

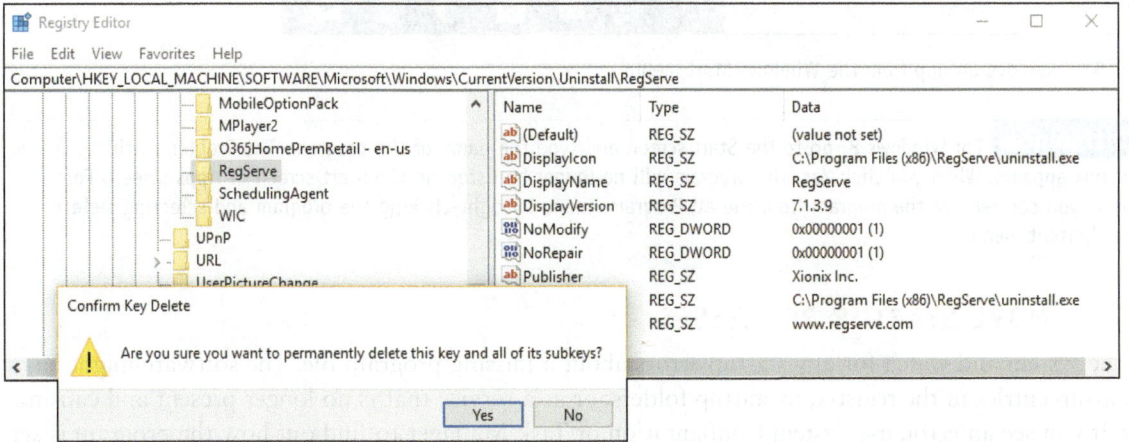

Figure 14-50 Select a subkey under the Uninstall key to display its values and data in the right pane and to delete the subkey

8. Open the Programs and Features window and verify that the list of installed software is correct and the software you are uninstalling is no longer listed.

9. If the list of installed software is not correct, restore the Uninstall registry key by double-clicking the **Save Uninstall Key.reg** icon on your desktop.

10. As a last step when editing the registry, clean up after yourself by deleting the Save Uninstall Key.reg file on your desktop. Right-click the icon and select **Delete** from the shortcut menu.

STEP 4: REMOVE PROGRAM SHORTCUTS

For Windows 10, you can remove the app from the **Start** menu by opening the menu, right-clicking the app, and clicking **More**. Then click **Remove from this list**. See Figure 14-51. If the program has shortcuts on the desktop, delete them.

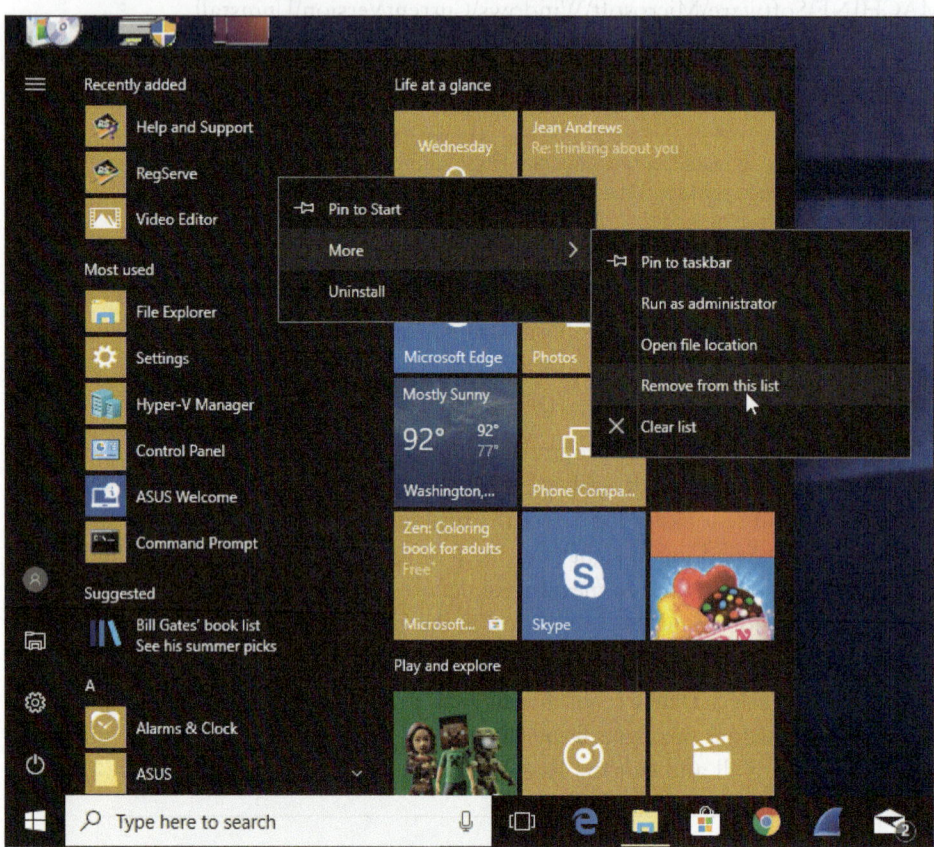

Figure 14-51 Remove an app from the Windows Start menu

⟳ OS Differences For Windows 8, go to the Start screen and type the name of the program. The Problem with Shortcut box appears. When you click **Yes**, the program will no longer be listed on the Start screen or Apps screen. For Windows 7, you can remove the program from the All Programs menu by right-clicking the program and selecting **Delete** from the shortcut menu.

STEP 5: REMOVE STARTUP PROCESSES

Restart the system and watch for any startup errors about a missing program file. The software might have stored startup entries in the registry, in startup folders, or as a service that is no longer present and causing an error. If you see an error, use System Configuration or Task Manager to find out how the program is set to start. This entry point is called an orphaned entry. You'll then need to delete this startup entry by editing the registry, deleting a shortcut in a startup folder, or disabling a service using the Services console.

It's unlikely you will be able to completely remove all keys in the registry that the software put there. A registry cleaner can help you find these orphaned keys, but if no errors appear at startup, you can just leave these keys untouched. Also, an installation might put program files in the C:\Program Files\Common Files folder or the C:\Program Files (x86)\Common Files folder. Most likely you can just leave these untouched as well. Address all error messages you encounter and stop there.

TROUBLESHOOTING HARDWARE PROBLEMS IN WINDOWS

Now we're ready to discuss dealing with display problems, network printing problems, and limited network connectivity.

DISPLAY SETTINGS AND GRAPHICS SOFTWARE

For Windows 10, you can access the display settings by right-clicking the desktop and clicking **Display settings**. Alternately, you can click **Display** in the Settings window. The Display window is shown in Figure 14-52. For a dual-monitor setup, select the display you want to adjust, as shown in the figure.

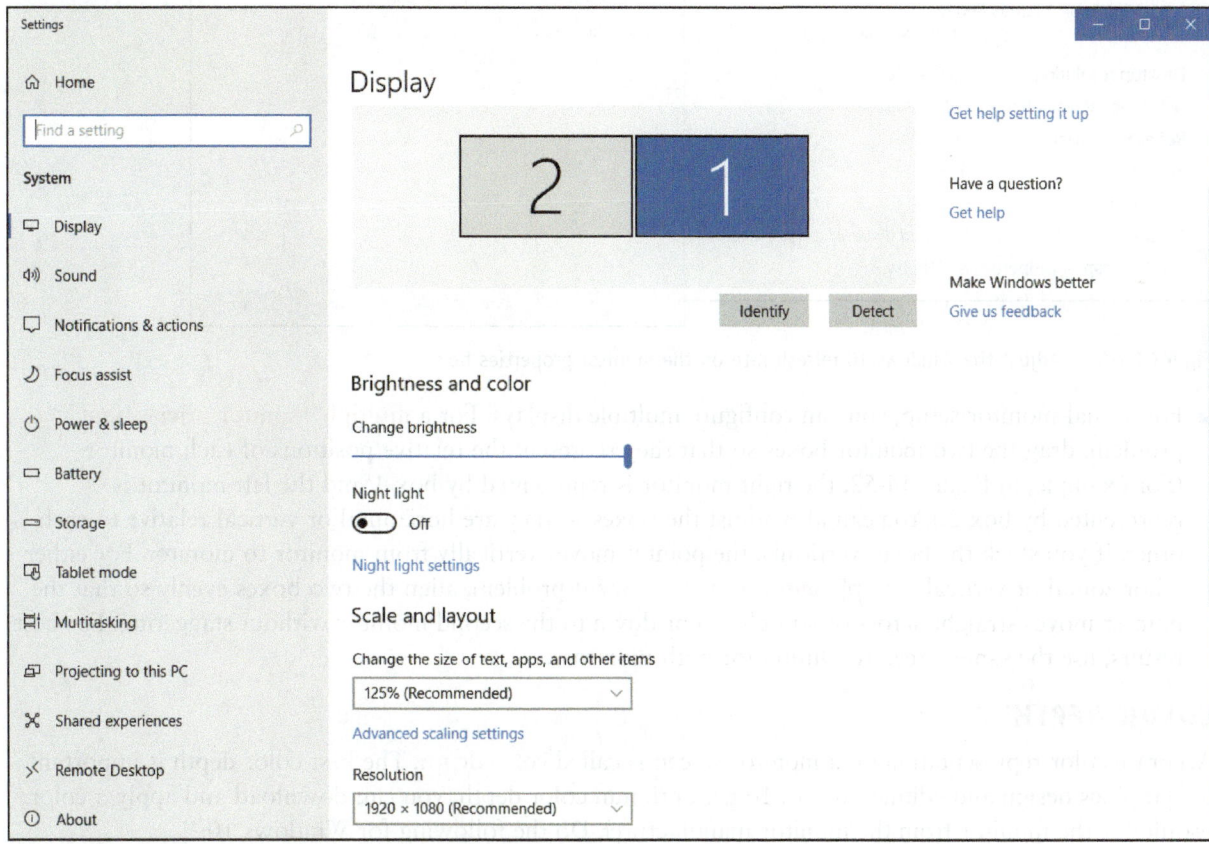

Figure 14-52 Adjust Windows 10 display settings

Here are a few basic display settings:

▲ To adjust resolution (the number of horizontal and vertical pixels used to build one screen), click the Resolution drop-down menu and select the highest or recommended resolution. The recommended resolution is usually the native resolution, which is the optimal resolution the monitor was designed to support.

◢ The refresh rate is the number of times the monitor refreshes the screen in one second. To set the rate, scroll down and click **Advanced display settings**. Click **Display adapter properties for Display** for the display device you want to configure. The video adapter properties box for that display appears. Click the **Monitor** tab and select the highest value available under Screen refresh rate (see Figure 14-53).

Figure 14-53 Adjust the Windows 10 refresh rate on the monitor properties box

◢ For a dual-monitor setup, you can configure multiple displays. For a multiple monitor orientation problem, drag the two monitor boxes so that they represent the relative positions of each monitor. (For example, in Figure 14-52, the right monitor is represented by box 1 and the left monitor is represented by box 2.) You can also adjust the boxes so they are horizontal or vertical relative to each other. If you stack the boxes vertically, the pointer moves vertically from monitor to monitor. For either a horizontal or vertical multiple monitor misalignment problem, align the two boxes evenly so that the pointer moves straight across or straight up or down to the second monitor without staggering. For best results, use the same screen resolution for both monitors.

COLOR DEPTH

Accurate color representation on a monitor screen is called color depth. The best color depth is important for graphics design and editing photos. To get optimum color depth, you can download and apply a color profile for the monitor from the monitor manufacturer. Do the following for Windows 10:

1. Look on the front or rear of the monitor for its brand and model.

2. Go to the monitor manufacturer's website and download the latest drivers for the monitor model (not the video adapter) and the version of Windows installed. The color profile file, which has an .icm file extension, should be in the downloaded package. To find the file, you might need to unzip a downloaded zipped folder or execute a downloaded executable file.

3. Open the video adapter properties box shown earlier in Figure 14-53 and select the **Color Management** tab. Then click **Color Management**. The Color Management box appears. See Figure 14-54.

4. In the drop-down menu, select the monitor and check **Use my settings for this device**. To add a new profile, click **Add** and click **Browse**. Then point to the .icm file you downloaded. Click **Add**.

5. In the Color Management box, select the added profile and click **Set as Default Profile**. You should notice colors on the screen change slightly after applying a new color profile.

6. There's one more color adjustment you can make. On the Color Management box, click the **Advanced** tab, click **Calibrate display,** and follow the on-screen directions to calibrate brightness and contrast settings.

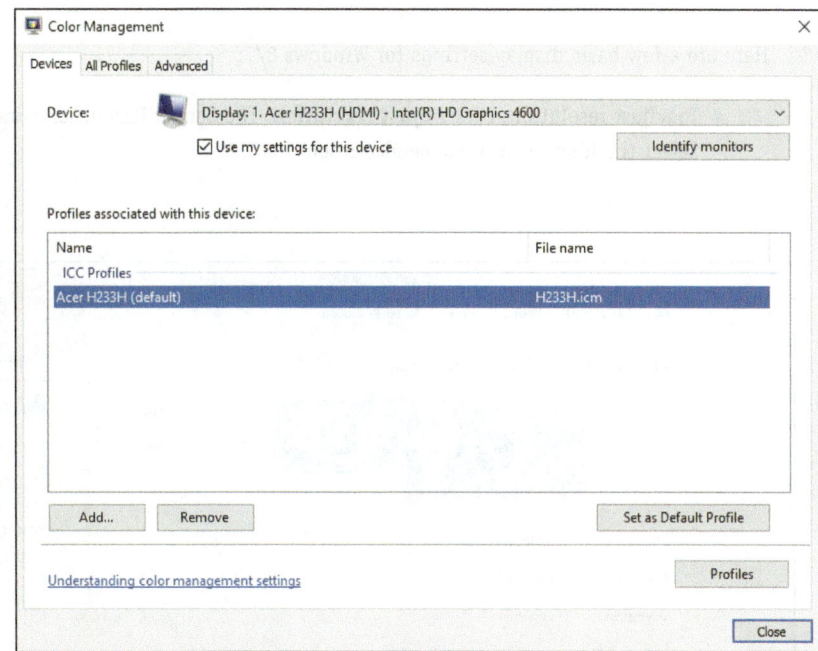

Figure 14-54 Use the Color Management box to apply a color profile

WINDOWS | 8 DISPLAY SETTINGS FOR WINDOWS 8

**A+
CORE 2
1.5, 1.6, 3.1**
For Windows 8/7, use the Display applet in Control Panel to manage display settings. The Display window for Windows 8 is shown in Figure 14-55.

14

Figure 14-55 Adjust Windows 8 display settings

(continues)

Here are a few basic display settings for Windows 8/7:

◢ To adjust resolution, click **Adjust resolution**. The Screen Resolution window shown in Figure 14-56 appears. Select the highest or recommended resolution.

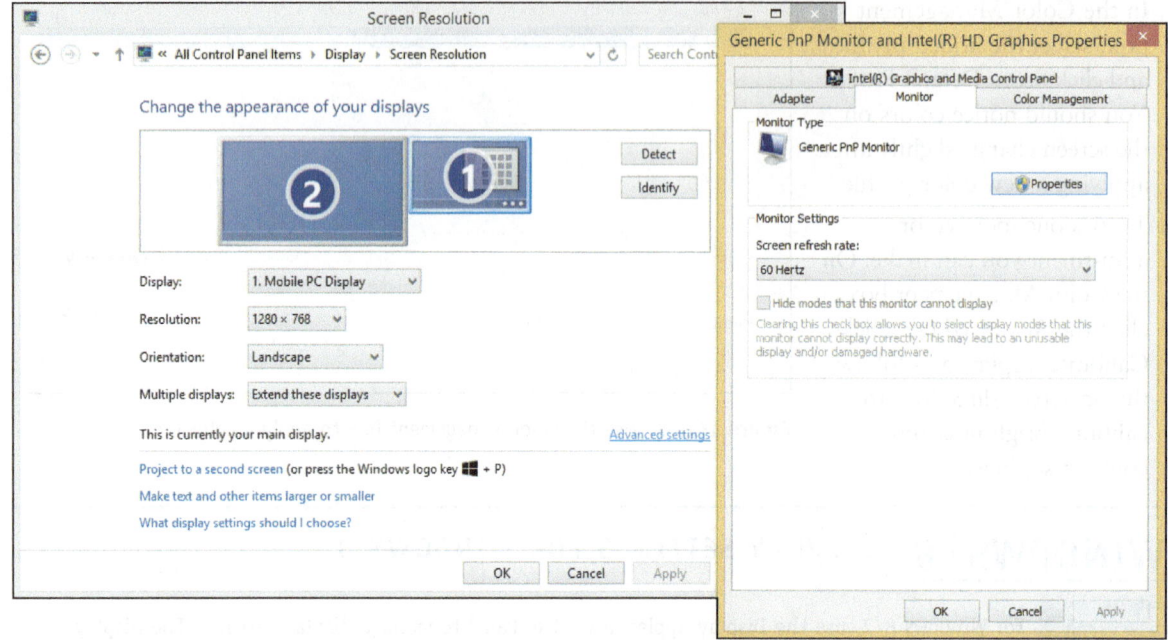

Figure 14-56 Adjust the Windows 8/7 refresh rate on the monitor properties box

◢ To set the refresh rate, click **Advanced settings** on the Screen Resolution window. The video adapter properties box appears. Click the **Monitor** tab and select the highest value available under Screen refresh rate (see Figure 14-56).

◢ To adjust color depth by applying a color profile for the monitor, select the **Color Management** tab on the monitor properties box (see Figure 14-56).

◢ To calibrate color, click **Calibrate color** on the Display window (see Figure 14-55) and follow the on-screen directions.

UPDATE DIRECTX

Recall from Chapter 12 that Windows requires the video adapter and drivers to support DirectX 9. DirectX is a Microsoft software development tool that developers can use to write multimedia applications, such as games, video-editing software, and computer-aided design software. The video firmware on the video card or motherboard chipset can interpret DirectX commands to build 3D graphics.

If an application such as a game or desktop publishing app that relies heavily on graphics is not performing well or giving errors, the problem might be the version of DirectX the system is using. You can use the dxdiag.exe command to display information about hardware and diagnose problems with DirectX. The first time you execute the **dxdiag.exe** command, a message box appears and asks if you want to check whether your drivers are digitally signed. When you click **Yes**, the opening window appears, as shown in Figure 14-57. Look for the version of DirectX that's installed (version 12 in the figure).

Figure 14-57 The DirectX Diagnostic tool reports information about DirectX components

To find out the latest version of DirectX published by Microsoft, go to *microsoft.com* and search on "DirectX End-User Runtime Web Installer." You can use a link on the page to download and install a new version of DirectX.

PRINT MANAGEMENT

A+
CORE 2
1.5, 1.6,
3.1

Windows professional and business editions offer the Print Management (printmanagement.msc) console in the Administrative Tools group of Control Panel. (Home editions don't provide the Print Management tool.) It comes in handy when you're responsible for managing several printers and users. Rather than having to walk over to a computer that has an installed printer with a problem, you can manage the computer's printer queue and other print issues while sitting at your own workstation. In Print Management, each computer on the network that has installed printers is considered a print server.

APPLYING | CONCEPTS   LEARNING TO USE PRINT MANAGEMENT

A+
CORE 2
1.5, 1.6,
3.1

Follow these steps to learn to use Print Management:

1. Open **Control Panel** and **Administrative Tools**. Double-click **Print Management**. The Print Management window appears.

2. In the Print Servers group, drill down to your local computer and click **Printers**. The list of printers installed on your computer appears, as shown in Figure 14-58.

(continues)

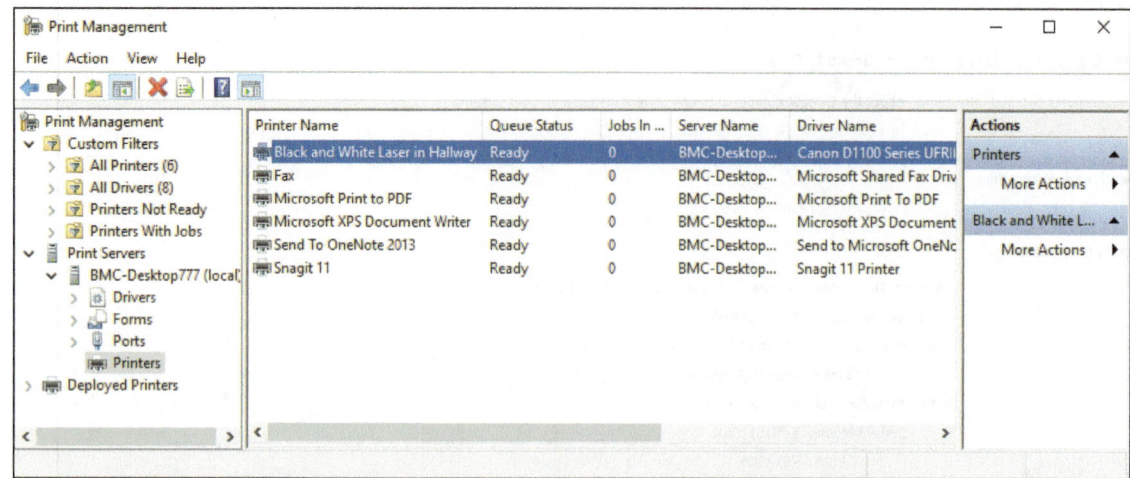

Figure 14-58 Use Print Management to monitor and manage printers on the network

3. You can manage printers installed on other computers on the network by adding each computer as a print server. To add other print servers to the list, right-click **Print Servers** in the left pane and click **Add/Remove Servers**. In the Add/Remove Servers box (see the left side of Figure 14-59), click **Browse**. Locate the computer (see the right side of Figure 14-59) and click **Select Server**. The computer is now listed under Add servers in the Add/Remove Servers box. Click **Add to List**. The computer is listed in the Print servers area. Click **OK** to close the Add/Remove Servers box.

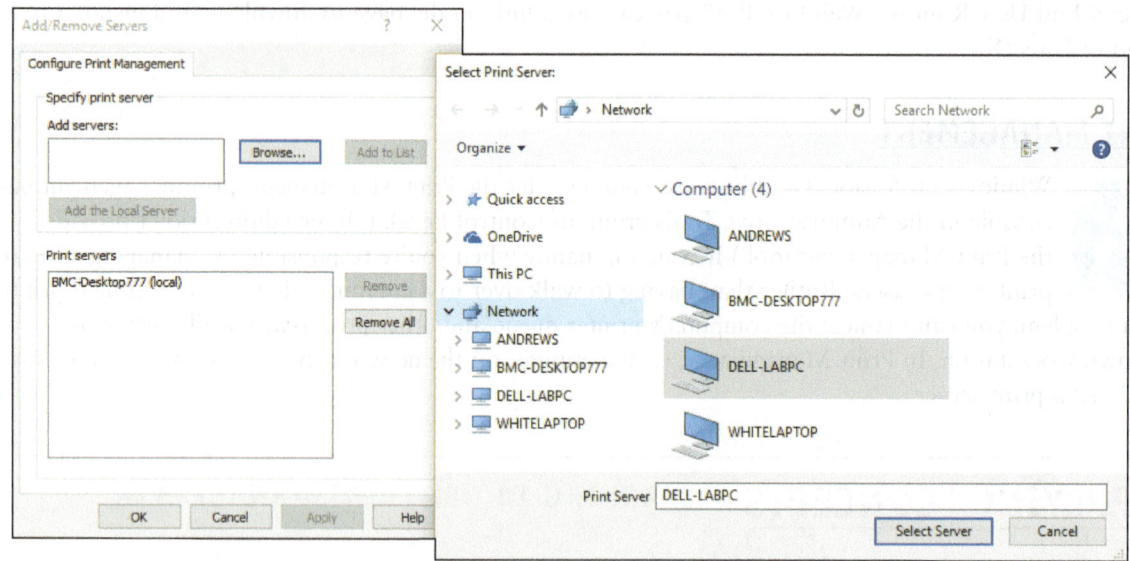

Figure 14-59 Select a print server to monitor and manage

4. The computer is now listed as a print server in the left pane of the Print Management window. Notice in Figure 14-60 that you can view a computer on the network that has its printer offline. Right-click this printer to see a menu with options that you can use to manage the printer and its printer queue.

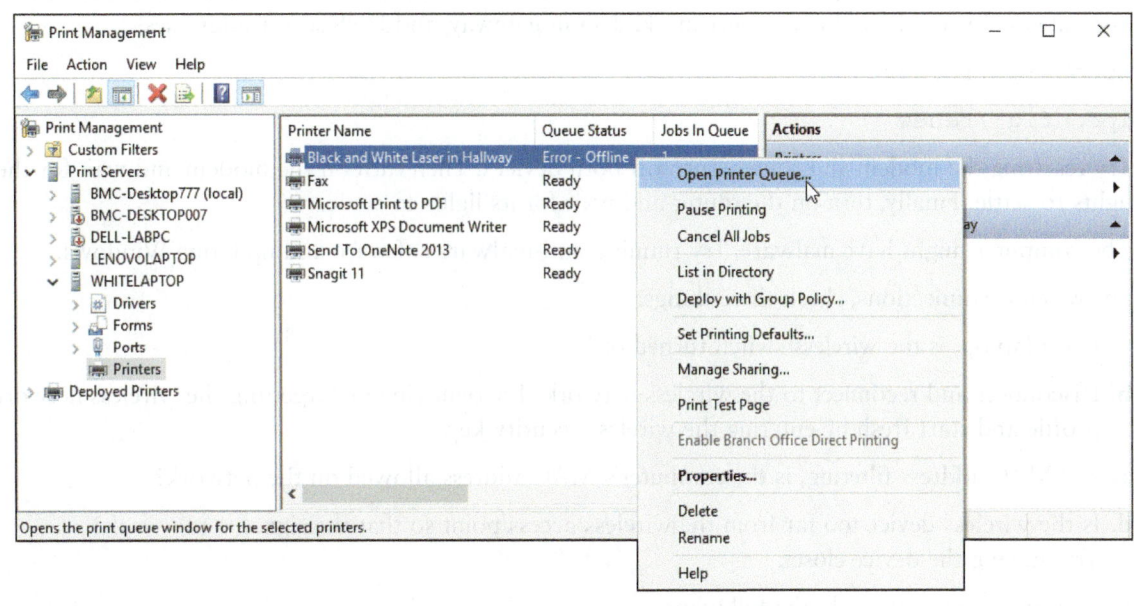

Figure 14-60 Manage print servers, printers, and printer queues on the network

> **✎ Notes** If printers you know to be installed on a remote computer don't show up in the console, the problem might be that DNS on the network cannot find the remote computer. For Windows domains, configure DNS for forward lookups by adding a DNS 'A' record for the client computer that is running Print Management. For peer-to-peer networks, try adding the remote computer and its IP address to the hosts file of the client that is running Print Management. For this last method to permanently work, the remote computer must have a static IP address. You learned to use the hosts file in Chapter 7. Configuring DNS is beyond the scope of this text.

14

LIMITED CONNECTIVITY

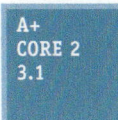

IT technicians are often asked to help when the local network has no connectivity or limited connectivity. Here is a brief list of what to do to solve these types of problems:

1. Verify that the network cable between the computer and the router or wall jack is not damaged and is securely connected at both ends.

2. For SOHO routers, connect the cable to a different port on the router. You know you have connectivity when the port LED lights are blinking. If the power LED light on the router is blinking, the problem is with the router and the router firmware might be corrupted. If LED lights don't indicate connectivity, consider the problem is hardware-related. You might need to replace the network adapter.

3. Go to Device Manager on the computer and disable then enable the network adapter. Update the device drivers.

4. As you learned to do in Chapter 7, go to the TCP/IP Properties box and verify the TCP/IP configuration for the connection. Most likely the correct option is *Obtain an IP address automatically.* Verify that the computer is getting a unique IP address from the router. When two computers on the network have the same IP address, connectivity errors occur. Have two computers been assigned the same static IP address? An administrator needs to check all static IP address assignments for duplicated addresses.

5. Update the network settings. Try using the following two commands to release and renew the DHCP assignments for the IP address, subnet mask, default gateway, and DNS server addresses:

```
ipconfig /release
```

```
ipconfig /renew
```

6. Try resetting the modem and router. Turn off both devices. Then turn on the modem and wait for the lights to settle. Finally, turn on the router and wait for its lights to settle.

7. The computer might have malware. Try running anti-malware software and updating Windows.

8. For wireless connections, check these things:

   a. For a laptop, is the wireless switch turned on?

   b. Disconnect and reconnect to the wireless network. Try removing or forgetting the wireless network profile and start fresh by entering the wireless security key.

   c. For MAC address filtering, is the computer's MAC address allowed on the network?

   d. Is the wireless device too far from the wireless access point so that the signal is too weak? Try moving the device closer.

9. For Internet connectivity, do the following:

   a. To eliminate DNS as the problem, try this command:

   ```
   ping www.cengage.com
   ```

   b. If you are unable to access a particular computer on the Internet, try using the tracert command. For example:

   ```
   tracert www.cengage.com
   ```

   c. If you can access resources on the local network but don't have Internet connectivity, contact your ISP and ask them to reset the connection at their end.

For more information about troubleshooting network connectivity problems, see Chapters 7 and 8.

>> CHAPTER SUMMARY

Concepts and Windows Tools for Solving Problems with Windows, Applications, and Hardware

▲ The Windows OS is made up of two main components: the shell and the kernel. The shell provides an interface for users and applications. The kernel is responsible for interacting with hardware.

▲ A process is a program running under the shell, together with all the resources assigned to it. A thread is a single task that a process requests from the kernel.

▲ Windows tools that conveniently access and manage other Windows tools are Control Panel, Administrative Tools, Computer Management, and Microsoft Management Console (MMC).

▲ Tools to observe, track, and log Windows, user, network, application, and hardware activities are Event Viewer, Performance Monitor, Reliability Monitor, and Resource Monitor.

▲ Tools for solving Windows, application, networking, and Windows user problems are Task Manager, System Configuration, the Services console, the Troubleshooting applet, Group Policy, Local Group Policy, and the Registry Editor.

- Other tools for solving Windows problems are System File Checker, DISM, Windows Updates, a clean boot, Safe Mode (Safe boot), and System Restore.

- Tools for solving application errors and crashes are Programs and Features, tasklist, taskkill, Component Services, secondary logons, Compatibility mode, digital signatures, Data Sources, and Task Scheduler.

- Tools for solving problems with hardware are Device Manager, Print Management, the Display applet, DxDiag, Memory Diagnostics, chkdsk, and Disk Defragmenter.

Best Practices to Troubleshoot Windows-Related Problems

- General steps to solve Windows-related problems are to (1) interview the user and back up data, (2) get help from error messages, the web, coworkers, and event logs, (3) consider that the data or the application might be corrupted, (4) consider outside interference such as malware, faulty memory, a corrupted hard drive, low system resources, and incompatible applications or third-party services, and (5) consider that Windows might be corrupted.

Slow Startup and Slow Performance

- General steps to solve problems with slow performance or slow startup are to (1) get a benchmark by using a stopwatch or watch to time startup to the point the Windows desktop loads and observe any errors that appear in the startup process, (2) back up user data, (3) perform routine maintenance, (4) investigate and eliminate unwanted startup programs, (5) eliminate unwanted scheduled tasks, and (6) check for low system resources.

Application Errors and Crashes

- The commands taskkill and tasklist can be used to forcefully end an application that is hung.

- Task Manager can change the priority level to improve performance of an application.

- The Services console is used to change the way a background service is started.

- In Explorer, use the shortcut menu for a data file to create a file association so that Windows knows which application is associated with the given data file. This solves the problem of a file that fails to open.

- Use Component Services to solve the problem that causes an error message to appear for an unregistered component or missing DLL. The tool creates the association between the DLL or component and its application in the Windows registry.

- When an application has never worked, update Windows, search the web for help, try running the application in compatibility mode or as an administrator using a secondary logon, and verify that the application is legitimate with a digital signature.

- To solve a problem when connecting a local database application to a database source online, use ODBC Data Sources to connect the application with the database server.

An Application Fails to Uninstall

- When an application fails to uninstall, you might need to manually edit the Windows registry using the Registry Editor.

- Always back up registry keys before editing them.

- To manually remove software, (1) try the uninstall routine, (2) delete program files, (3) delete registry entries, (4) remove program shortcuts, and (5) remove startup processes.

14

Troubleshooting Hardware Problems in Windows

▲ Use Display settings to adjust the resolution, refresh rate, multiple monitor orientation, and color depth for monitors.

▲ Use the dxdiag command to determine which version of DirectX is installed. DirectX is Microsoft software that works with graphics software and graphics adapter video drivers.

▲ Print Management makes it easy to manage network printers and their connections with workstations on the network.

▲ Limited network connectivity problems can be solved by verifying network cable connections, network port activity, NIC device drivers, TCP/IP configuration (network settings), cable or DSL modem connectivity to the ISP, wireless connectivity and access, and DNS name resolution.

>> KEY TERMS

For explanations of key terms, see the Glossary for this text.

Administrative Tools	dxdiag.exe	Microsoft Management Console (MMC)	Safe Mode
Aero interface	Event Viewer	multiple monitor	secondary logon
chkdsk	executive services	misalignment	Services console
clean boot	file association	multiple monitor	shell
color depth	Group Policy	orientation	snap-in
compatibility mode	HAL (hardware	native resolution	System Configuration
Component Services (COM+)	abstraction layer)	Open Database Connectivity (ODBC)	System File Checker (SFC)
Computer Management	HKEY_CLASSES_ROOT (HKCR)	pagefile.sys	System Restore
console	HKEY_CURRENT_ CONFIG (HKCC)	Performance Monitor	taskkill
data source	HKEY_CURRENT_USER (HKCU)	Print Management	tasklist
Data Sources	HKEY_LOCAL_ MACHINE (HKLM)	process	Task Manager
default program		Programs and Features	Task Scheduler
digital signature	HKEY_USERS (HKU)	refresh rate	thread
DirectX	initialization files	registry	Troubleshooting applet
DISM (Deployment Image Servicing and Management)	kernel	Registry Editor	user mode
	kernel mode	reliability history	user profile
DxDiag (DirectX Diagnostic Tool)	Local Group Policy	Reliability Monitor	user profile namespace
	Memory Diagnostics	resolution	virtual memory
		Resource Monitor	

>> THINKING CRITICALLY

These questions are designed to prepare you for the critical thinking required for the A+ Core 2 exam and may use information from other chapters or from the web.

1. A user complains that her computer is performing slowly. She tells you the problem started about a week ago when new database software was installed. The software runs in the background to update a database synced between the user's workstation and database server. Which is the best tool or method to use to determine if the new software is hogging computer resources?

   a. Uninstall the database software and see if performance improves.

   b. Use Performance Monitor and Process counters to observe performance.

    c. Use the Performance tab of Task Manager to observe database software activity.

    d. Install more memory to improve system resources to handle the new software.

2. You have exhausted your knowledge of a problem and it still is not solved. Before you escalate it, what else can you do?

    a. Go back through the problem one more time, looking for what you overlooked.

    b. Explain to the user that you cannot solve his problem but you will find someone who can.

    c. Ask a knowledgeable coworker for help.

    d. Interview the user one more time to make sure you correctly understand the problem.

3. You are having difficulty uninstalling freeware a user accidentally installed while surfing the web. You look online and see the software is designed to work in an x86-based version of Windows. In which folder should you expect to find the program files for the software?

    a. C:\Windows

    b. C:\Program Files (x86)

    c. C:\Program Files

    d. It depends on the version of Windows installed.

4. You are troubleshooting an application problem and want to eliminate faulty memory as a source of the problem. Which command do you use?

    a. Mdsched.exe

    b. Taskmgr.exe

    c. Msconfig.exe

    d. Sfc /scannow

5. When a user, Belinda Lim, signs in to Windows, she cannot see her Documents folder in File Explorer and some of her Windows user settings are lost. You suspect her user profile is corrupted. Which tool or method should you use first to investigate and/or solve the problem? Second?

    a. Check the C:\User\Belinda Lim\Documents folder.

    b. Check the C:\Users\Belinda Lim\Documents folder.

    c. Use the chkdsk command.

    d. Use the sfc command.

6. An application is frozen and you cannot close its application window. What is the first thing you should do to end the process? Second thing?

    a. Use the tasklist command.

    b. Use Task Manager.

    c. Reboot the system.

    d. Use the taskkill command.

7. How can you eliminate the possibility that an application error is caused by another application or service running in the background?

8. How does Windows know which application to use to open a file when you double-click the file in File Explorer or Windows Explorer?

9. When Windows first starts and the user signs in, a message about a missing DLL appears. Which tool or method should you use first to solve the problem? Second?

14

    a. Use Task Manager to identify the startup process.

    b. Use the Services console to stop the process that needed the DLL.

    c. Search the web on the error message to better understand the problem.

    d. Use Component Services to register the DLL.

10. If an application works when the system is loaded in Safe Mode, but does not work when Windows is loaded normally, what can you assume?

11. A user tells you that Microsoft Word gives errors when saving a file. What should you do next?

    a. Install Windows updates that also include patches for Microsoft Word.

    b. Ask the user when the problem first started.

    c. Ask the user to save the error message as a screenshot the next time the error occurs and email it to you.

    d. Use Task Manager to end the Microsoft Word program.

12. When trying to improve performance of a slow system, you notice in Task Manager that the superfetch service is using a high percentage of CPU time. What is your next best step?

    a. Disable superfetch to improve performance.

    b. Update Windows to improve superfetch performance.

    c. Superfetch is an essential Windows process and should not be disabled. Move on to other solutions to improve performance.

    d. Ask the user if he uses the superfetch service. If he doesn't, uninstall it.

13. You need to install a customized console on 10 computers. What is the best way to do that?

    a. When installing the console on the first computer, write down each step to make it easier to do the same chore on the other nine.

    b. Create the console on one computer and copy the .mmc file to the other nine.

    c. Create the console on one computer and copy the .msc file to the other nine.

14. What is the name of the program file that you can enter in the Windows search or Run box to execute Event Viewer? What process is running when Event Viewer is displayed on the screen? Why do you think the running process is different from the program file name?

15. When cleaning up the startup process, which of these should you do first?

    a. Use the Registry Editor to look for keys that hold startup processes.

    b. Run System Configuration to see what processes are started.

    c. After you have launched several applications, use Task Manager to view a list of running tasks.

    d. Run the Defrag utility to optimize the hard drive.

16. Using the Internet, investigate each of the following startup processes. Identify the process and write a one-sentence description.

    a. Acrotray.exe

    b. Ieuser.exe

17. Using Task Manager, you discover an unwanted program that is launched at startup. Of the items listed below, which ones might lead you to the permanent solution to the problem? Which ones would not be an appropriate solution to the problem? Explain why they are not appropriate.

a. Look at the registry key that launched the program to help determine where in Windows the program was initiated.

b. Use Task Manager to disable the program.

c. Search Task Scheduler for the source of the program being launched.

d. Use System Configuration to disable the program.

e. Search the startup folders for the source of the program.

18. List the program file name and path for the following utilities. (*Hint*: You can use Explorer or a Windows search to locate files.)

a. Task Manager

b. System Configuration

c. Services Console

d. Microsoft Management Console

e. Registry Editor

19. A customer reports that his recently purchased computer does not consistently run his old applications. Application errors occur intermittently, and data files get corrupted. He has tried uninstalling and reinstalling the apps, and the problems persist. As you troubleshoot the problem, you reboot the system and get a BSOD error. The customer tells you the BSOD has occasionally appeared. Which subsystem is most likely causing the problem? What is the next best step?

a. Windows is corrupted; reinstall Windows.

b. Windows Update is not working; use System Restore.

c. Memory is faulty; run Memory Diagnostics.

d. Applications are faulty; uninstall and reinstall the applications causing errors.

14

>> HANDS-ON PROJECTS

Hands-On | Project 14-1 Using the Microsoft Management Console

Using the Microsoft Management Console, create a customized console. Put two snap-ins in the console: Device Manager and Event Viewer. Store your console on the Windows desktop. Copy the console to another computer and install it on the Windows desktop.

Hands-On | Project 14-2 Using Event Viewer

Event Viewer can be intimidating to use but is really nothing more than a bunch of logs to search and manipulate. If you have Microsoft Office installed, open a Word document, make some changes in it, and close it without saving your changes. Now open Event Viewer and look in **Applications and Services Logs** and **Microsoft Office Alerts**. What event is recorded about your actions?

Hands-On | Project 14-3 Launching Programs at Startup

Do the following to practice launching programs at startup, listing the steps you took for each activity:

1. Configure Scheduled Tasks to launch Notepad each time the computer starts and any user signs in. List the steps you took.

2. Put a shortcut in a startup folder so that any user launches a command prompt window at startup. See Appendix B for a list of startup folders.

3. Restart the system and verify that both programs are launched. Did you receive any errors?

4. Remove the two programs from the startup process.

Hands-On | Project 14-4 Editing and Restoring the Registry

When you install Windows on a new computer, Windows setup gives you the opportunity to enter the computer's registered owner and registered organization. Practice editing and restoring the registry by doing the following to change the registered owner name:

1. Enter the command **winver.exe**, which displays the About Windows box. Who is the registered owner and registered organization of the computer?

2. Using the Registry Editor, export the registry key HKEY_LOCAL_MACHINE\SOFTWARE\Microsoft\Windows NT\ CurrentVersion to an export file stored on the desktop.

3. With the HKEY_LOCAL_MACHINE\SOFTWARE\Microsoft\Windows NT\CurrentVersion key selected in the left pane, double-click the **RegisteredOwner** value in the right pane. The Edit String box appears (see Figure 14-61). Change the Value data, which is highlighted in the box, and click **OK**.

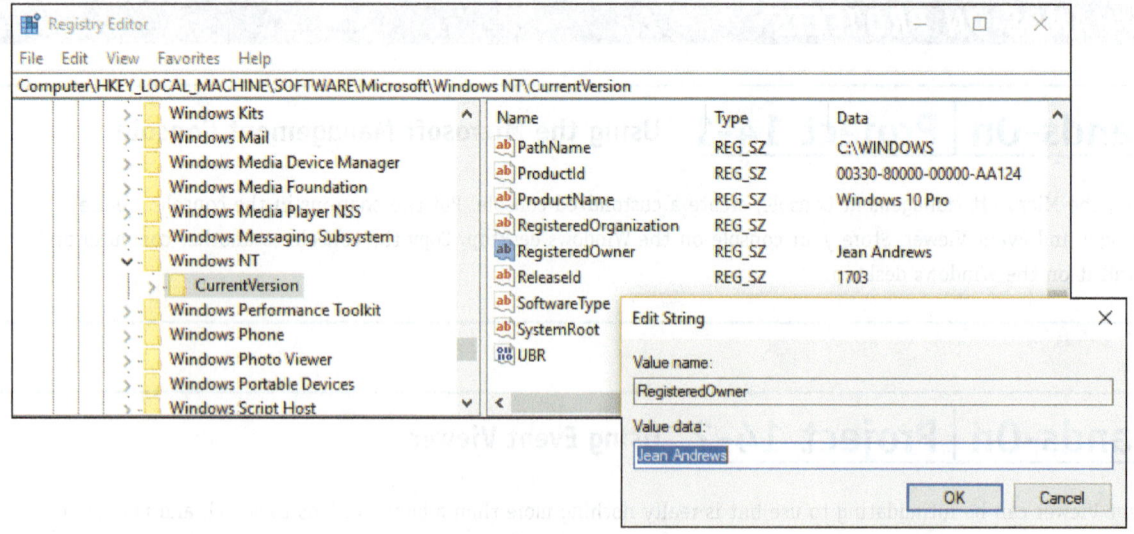

Figure 14-61 Change the name of the registered owner of Windows

4. Use the **winver** command again to display the About Windows box. Did the new name appear as the registered owner? Close the box.

5. Close the Registry Editor window. To restore the Value data to its original name, double-click the exported key on your desktop. Once again, use the **winver** command to display the About Windows box and verify that the original name is restored. Close the box.

6. Delete the exported registry key stored on the desktop.

Hands-On | Project 14-5 Finding Lost Downloaded Files

Your friend is using Internet Explorer to send and receive email using her Hotmail account. She received a Word document attached to an email message from a business associate. She double-clicked the Word attachment and spent a couple of hours editing it, saving the document as she worked. Then she closed the document. But where's the document now? When she later needed it, she searched her email account online and the Documents folder on her hard drive, but she could not find the document. She called you in a panic asking you to help her find her lost document.

Hint: In what folders does Internet Explorer store its temporary files? What are the paths to these folders on the hard drive?

> ✎ **Notes** As an IT technician, it's helpful to be familiar with the locations of temporary folders that might contain lost files. However, a shortcut to finding a lost Word document is to open Word, click **File**, click **Open**, and then search through the Recent Documents list.

14

>> REAL PROBLEMS, REAL SOLUTIONS

REAL PROBLEM 14-1 Cleaning Up Startup

Using a computer that has a problem with a sluggish startup, apply the tools and procedures you learned in this chapter to clean up the startup process. Take detailed notes of each step you take and its results. (If you are having a problem finding a computer with a sluggish startup, consider offering your help to a friend, a family member, or a nonprofit organization.)

REAL PROBLEM 14-2 Manually Removing Software

To practice manually removing software, install WinPatrol from *winpatrol.com*. (WinPatrol monitors Windows and alerts you when an application attempts to add a startup process.) Following the directions in the chapter, manually remove the software, listing the steps you used. (Do not use the uninstall routine provided by WinPatrol.) After you have manually removed the software, reboot the system. Did you get any error messages?

REAL PROBLEM 14-3 Using DISM to Repair Windows

When SFC cannot fix a problem with a corrupted Windows 10 installation, you can use DISM commands to repair system files. The following steps extract a standard image from the Windows setup files and use the image to repair a Windows installation. Follow these steps:

1. Follow directions in Chapter 12 to download the Windows setup ISO file from the Microsoft website.

2. In File Explorer, right-click the ISO file and click **Mount**. The ISO file is mounted and assigned a drive letter. You can now drill down into the file.

3. Copy the **install.esd** file in the \sources folder of the ISO drive to the root of drive C:.

4. Use this command to examine the install.esd file and to see the images in it.

   ```
   dism /get-wiminfo /wimfile:C:\install.esd
   ```

   What is the index number for Windows 10 Pro? In our example in Figure 14-62, the number is 6.

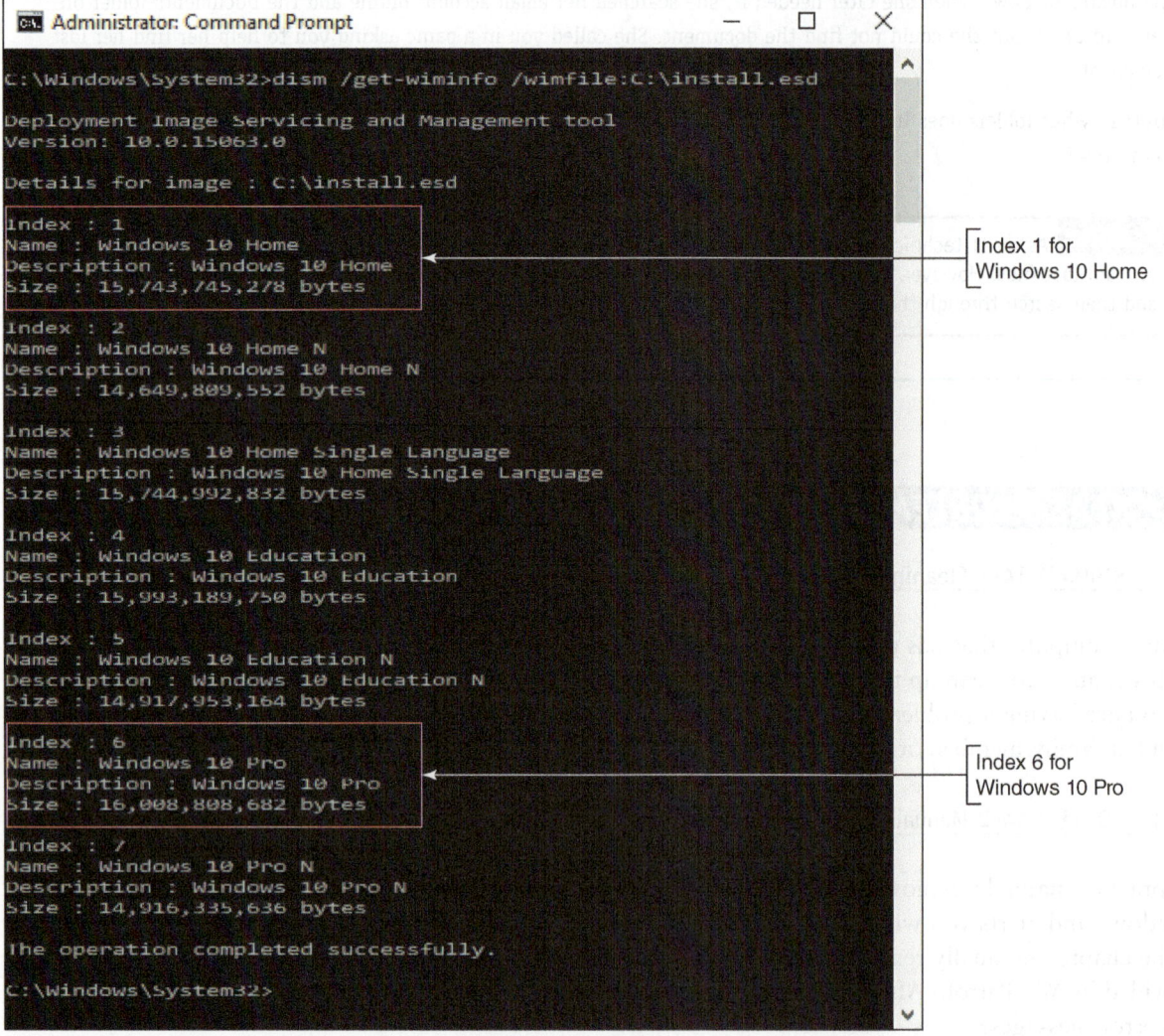

Figure 14-62 Examine the install.esd file for image indexes

5. Extract the install.wim file from install.esd for Windows 10 Pro. The install.wim file will be stored in the C:\Windows\System32 folder. Use the index number from Step 4 in this command:

```
dism /export-image /sourceimagefile:C:\install.esd /sourceindex:6 /
destinationimagefile:install.wim /compress:max /checkintegrity
```

6. Use this command to repair Windows system files using the files from the install.wim image you just extracted:

```
dism /online /cleanup-image /restorehealth /source:install.wim /
limitaccess
```

7. To save space on your hard drive, you can delete the C:\install.esd file. However, you might want to leave install.wim in the C:\Windows\System32 folder in case you need it to later repair the Windows installation.

14

Troubleshooting Windows Startup

After completing this chapter, you will be able to:

- Describe the boot process from the time you press the power button until the Windows desktop or Start screen loads

- Create bootable media and backups to prepare for Windows startup problems

- Implement appropriate Windows tools to solve Windows startup problems

- Implement appropriate Windows tools to reimage or reload Windows

- Troubleshoot Windows startup problems

You've already learned how to deal with application and hardware problems, and Windows problems after the OS has started. In this chapter, you take your troubleshooting skills one step further by learning to deal with startup problems caused by Windows. When Windows fails to start, it can be stressful if important data has not been backed up or the user has pressing work to do with the computer. What helps more than anything else is to have a good understanding of Windows startup and a good plan for approaching startup problems.

We begin the chapter with a discussion of what happens when you first turn on a computer and Windows starts. The more you understand about startup, the better your chances of fixing startup problems. Then you learn about Windows tools specifically designed to handle startup problems. Finally, you learn about strategies for solving startup problems.

UNDERSTANDING THE BOOT PROCESS

A+
CORE 2
3.1

Knowledge is power. The better you understand what happens when you first turn on a computer until Windows is loaded and the Windows desktop or Start screen appears, the more likely you will be able to solve a problem when Windows cannot start. Let's begin by noting the differences between a hard boot and a soft boot.

> 🖊 **Notes** Most techies use the terms *boot* and *startup* interchangeably. However, in general, the term *boot* refers to the hardware phase of starting up a computer. Microsoft consistently uses the term *startup* to refer to how its operating systems are booted—I mean, started.

DIFFERENT WAYS TO BOOT

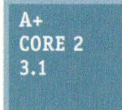
A+
CORE 2
3.1

The term **booting** comes from the phrase "lifting yourself up by your bootstraps" and refers to the computer bringing itself up to a working state without the user having to do anything but press the On button. Two fundamental ways to boot a computer are:

▲ A **hard boot**, or **cold boot**, involves turning on the power with the on/off switch.
▲ A **soft boot**, or **warm boot**, involves using the operating system to reboot. In Windows, a soft boot is called a restart.

A hard boot takes more time than a soft boot because a hard boot requires the initial steps performed by BIOS/UEFI. Most desktop cases have three power buttons, which for one system are shown in Figure 15-1.

Figure 15-1 This computer case has two power buttons on the front and one power switch on the rear

Here's how the buttons work:

▲ The power button in front can be configured as a "soft" power button, causing a Windows restart.
▲ The reset button initializes the CPU so that it restarts at the beginning of the BIOS/UEFI startup program. The computer behaves as though the power were turned off and back on and then goes through the entire boot process.

▲ The switch on the rear of the case simply turns off the power abruptly and is a "hard" power button. If you use this switch, wait 30 seconds before you press the power button on the front of the case to boot the system. This method gives you the greatest assurance that memory will clear. However, if Windows is abruptly stopped, it might give an error message when you reboot.

How the front two buttons work can be controlled in BIOS/UEFI setup. Know, however, that different cases offer different options.

When Windows hangs, first try a restart. If that doesn't work, try a shutdown and then power the system back up. Windows shutdown closes all open applications, user sessions, services, devices, and system processes and then powers down the computer. If a shutdown does not work, press the reset button on the front of the case. If that doesn't work, turn off the power switch on the rear of the case, wait 30 seconds, turn it back on, and then press the power button on the front of the case.

STEPS TO BOOT THE COMPUTER AND START WINDOWS

**A+
CORE 2
3.1**

Recall that BIOS/UEFI is responsible for getting a system up and going and finding an OS to load. Table 15-1 lists the components and files stored on the hard drive that are necessary to start Windows. The table can serve as a guide as you study the steps to see what happens from the time power is turned on until Windows is started. In these steps, we assume the OS is loaded from the hard drive.

Component or File	Partition and Path*	Description
BIOS systems using MBR partitioning		
MBR	The first sector of the hard drive is called the Master Boot Record (MBR)	BIOS looks to the partition table in the MBR to locate the active partition.
System partition	Also called the active partition or System Reserved partition	The system partition holds the Boot Manager, Boot Configuration Data (BCD) store, and other files and folders needed to begin Windows startup. For Windows, these files are stored in the root and \Boot directory of the hidden system partition.
Boot Manager	In the root of the system partition	Windows Boot Manager, bootmgr (with no file extension), accesses the BCD store and locates the Windows Boot Loader.
BCD store	\Boot directory on the system partition	The Boot Configuration Data (BCD) store is a database file named BCD (no file extension) and is organized the same as a registry hive. It contains boot settings that control the Boot Manager and can be viewed and edited with the bcdedit command.
UEFI systems using GPT partitioning		
GPT partition table	At the beginning of the hard drive and a backup copy at the end of the drive	UEFI looks to the GPT partition table to locate the EFI System Partition.
System partition	The EFI System Partition (ESP) is normally 100 MB to 200 MB in size.	The system partition holds the Windows Boot Manager, BCD, and other supporting files. For Windows, the Boot Manager is bootmgfw.efi and is stored in \EFI\Microsoft\Boot. A backup copy of bootmgfw.efi is at \EFI\Boot\bootx64.efi.

Table 15-1   Software components and files needed to start Windows (continues)

15

Component or File	Partition and Path*	Description
Boot Manager	For Windows, \EFI\Microsoft\ Boot on the ESP	Bootmgfw.efi loads EFI applications based on variables stored in onboard RAM and reads the BCD store to find out other boot parameters (such as a dual boot).
BCD store	\EFI\Microsoft\Boot on the ESP	Entries in the BCD store point the Windows Boot Manager to the location of the Windows Boot Loader program.
All Windows BIOS and UEFI systems		
Windows Boot Loader	C:\Windows\System32*	Windows Boot Manager turns control over to the Windows Boot Loader, which loads and starts essential Windows processes. Two versions of the program file are: winload.exe (BIOS) winload.efi (UEFI)
Resume from hibernation	C:\Windows\System32	This Windows Boot Loader is used when Windows resumes from hibernation: winresume.exe (BIOS) winresume.efi (UEFI)
Ntoskrnl.exe	C:\Windows\System32	Windows kernel
Hal.dll	C:\Windows\System32	Dynamic Link Library handles low-level hardware details
Smss.exe	C:\Windows\System32	Sessions Manager program responsible for starting user sessions
Csrss.exe	C:\Windows\System32	Win32 subsystem manages graphical components and threads
Winlogon.exe	C:\Windows\System32	Logon process
Services.exe	C:\Windows\System32	Service Control Manager starts and stops services
Lsass.exe	C:\Windows\System32	Authenticates users
System registry hive	C:\Windows\System32\Config	Holds data for the HKEY_LOCAL_MACHINE key of the registry
Device drivers	C:\Windows\System32\Drivers	Drivers for required hardware

*It is assumed that Windows is installed in C:\Windows.

Table 15-1   Software Components and Files Needed to Start Windows (continued)

A successful boot depends on essential hardware devices, BIOS/UEFI, and the operating system all performing without errors. Let's look at the steps to start a Windows computer. Several of these steps are diagrammed in Figures 15-2 and 15-3 to help you visually understand how the steps work.

BIOS/UEFI checks essential hardware (POST)

No ← Did error occur? → Yes

Is video active?

No   Yes

UEFI

Loads UEFI Boot Manager

Loads EFI device drivers and enforces Secure Boot

Follows boot file path

Loads bootmfw.efi

Reads BCD store

BIOS

Checks BIOS RAM to find OS

Consults MBR

Searches for active partition

Loads bootmgr

Reads BCD store

Sends error message as beeps or speech

Displays error message on-screen

Normal startup

Dual-boot system or Windows 7 user presses Spacebar

User presses F8

Windows previously stopped abruptly

Windows Boot Loader

Windows Boot Manager screen

Advanced Boot Options screen

Error Recovery screen

1. Loads OS kernel (ntoskrnl.exe)

2. Loads HAL

3. Loads System registry hive

4. Reads registry and, for BIOS systems, loads device drivers

5. Starts memory paging process

6. Turns over startup to OS kernel (ntoskrnl.exe)

Figure 15-2 Steps to booting the computer and loading Windows

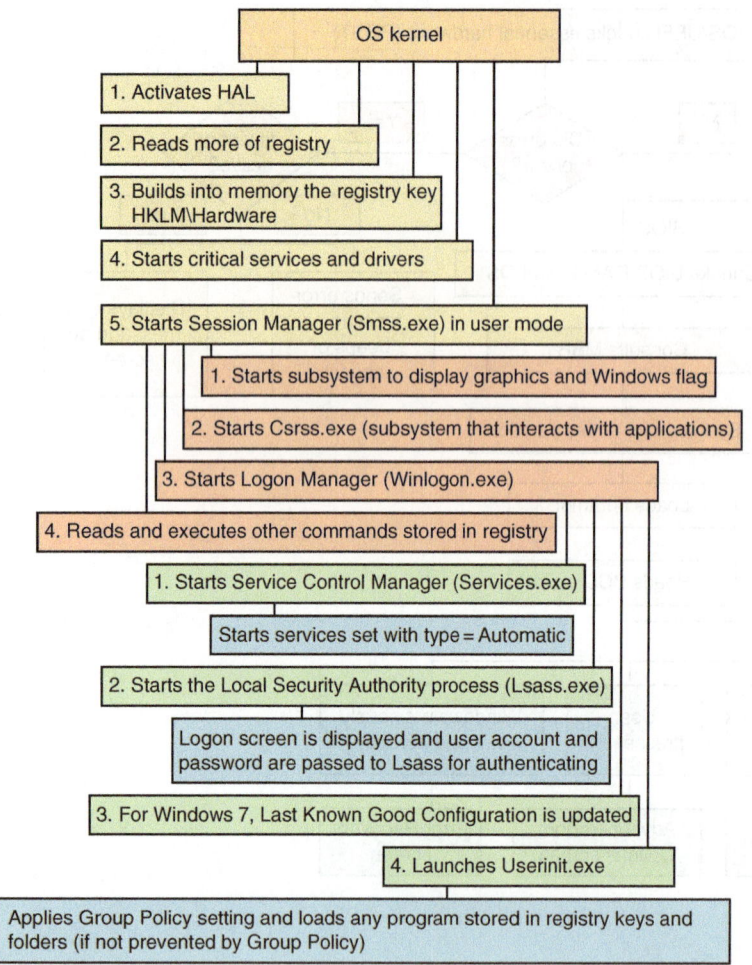

Figure 15-3 Steps to complete loading Windows

Study these steps carefully because the better you understand startup, the more likely you'll be able to solve startup problems:

1. Startup BIOS/UEFI is responsible for the early steps in the boot process. Onboard RAM accessible to BIOS/UEFI holds an inventory of hardware devices, hardware settings, security passwords, date and time, and startup settings. Startup BIOS/UEFI reads this information and then surveys the hardware devices it finds present, comparing it with the list kept in its RAM.

> ✎ **Notes** Onboard RAM, also called onboard memory, nonvolatile RAM, or NVRAM, is used by BIOS/UEFI to hold configuration data and keeps its data even when power is turned off. Onboard RAM is different from system memory or RAM, which holds programs and data only while the system is turned on.

2. Startup BIOS/UEFI runs POST (power-on self test), which is a series of tests to find out if the firmware can communicate correctly with essential hardware components required for a successful boot. Any errors are indicated as a series of beeps, recorded speech, or error messages on the screen (after video is checked). If the key is pressed to request BIOS/UEFI setup, the BIOS/UEFI setup program runs.

3. Based on information kept in onboard RAM, startup UEFI loads the UEFI boot manager and device drivers. BIOS/UEFI then turns to the hard drive or other boot device to locate and launch the Windows Boot Manager. If BIOS/UEFI cannot find a Windows Boot Manager or cannot turn over operation to it, one of these error messages appears:

```
Missing operating system
Error loading operating system
Windows failed to load
Invalid partition table
```

4. The Windows Boot Manager does the following:

   a. It reads the settings in the BCD.

   b. The next step depends on entries in the BCD and these other factors:

   ▲ *Option 1.* For normal startups that are not dual booting, no menu appears and Boot Manager finds and launches the Windows Boot Loader program.

   ▲ *Option 2.* If the computer is set up for a dual-boot environment, Boot Manager displays the *Choose an operating system* screen, as shown in Figure 15-4.

   ▲ *Option 3.* If Windows was previously stopped abruptly or another error occurs, the Windows Startup Menu appears (see Figure 15-5) to give you the option to troubleshoot the problem.

Figure 15-4   In a dual-boot setup, Windows Boot Manager provides a choice of operating systems

15

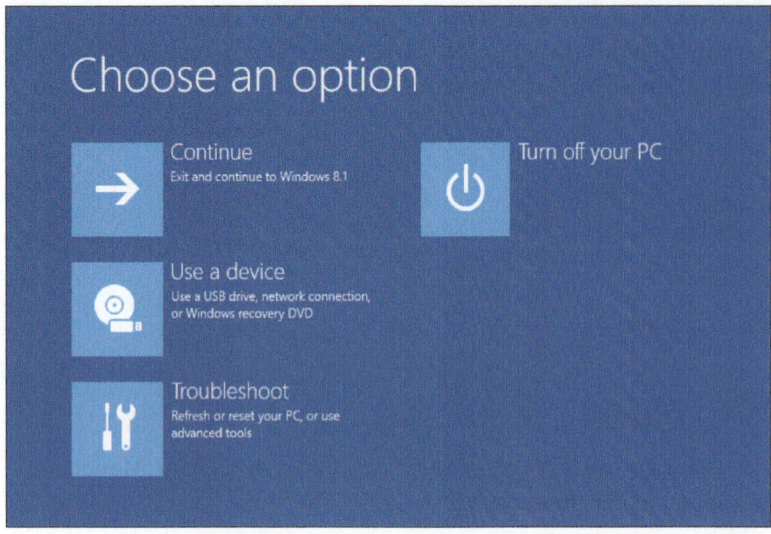

Figure 15-5 The Windows Startup Menu offers the opportunity to troubleshoot a problem with startup

5. Windows Boot Loader (winload.exe or winload.efi) is responsible for loading Windows components. It does the following:

   a. For normal startups, Boot Loader loads into system memory the OS kernel, Ntoskrnl.exe, but does not yet start it. Boot Loader also loads into memory the hardware abstraction layer (Hal.dll), which will later be used by the kernel.

   b. Boot Loader loads into memory the system registry hive (C:\Windows\System32\Config\System).

   c. Boot Loader then reads the registry key just created, HKEY_LOCAL_ MACHINE\SYSTEM\Services, looking for and loading into memory the device drivers that must be launched at startup. The drivers are not yet started.

   d. Boot Loader starts up the memory paging process and then turns over startup to the OS kernel (Ntoskrnl.exe).

6. The kernel (Ntoskrnl.exe) does the following:

   a. It activates the HAL, reads more information from the registry, and builds into memory the registry key HKEY_LOCAL_ MACHINE\HARDWARE, using information that has been collected about the hardware.

   b. The kernel then starts critical services and drivers that are configured to be started by the kernel during the boot. Recall that drivers interact directly with hardware and run in kernel mode, while services interact with drivers. Most services and drivers are stored in C:\Windows\System32 or C:\Windows\System32\Drivers and have an .exe, .dll, or .sys file extension.

   c. After the kernel starts all services and drivers configured to load during the boot, it starts the Session Manager (Smss.exe), which runs in user mode.

7. The Session Manager (Smss.exe) loads the graphical interface and starts the client/server run-time subsystem (csrss.exe), which also runs in user mode. Csrss.exe is the Win32 subsystem component that interacts with applications.

8. Smss.exe starts the Logon Manager (winlogon.exe) and reads and executes other commands stored in the registry, such as a command to replace system files placed there by Windows Update.

9. Winlogon.exe does the following:

   a. It starts the Service Control Manager (services.exe). Services.exe starts all services listed with the startup type of Automatic in the Services console.

   b. Winlogon.exe starts the Local Security Authority process (lsass.exe). The sign-in screen appears (see Figure 15-6), and the user account and password are passed to the lsass.exe process for authenticating.

   c. Winlogon.exe launches userinit.exe. For Windows 10/7, the desktop is launched. For Windows 8, the Start screen is launched.

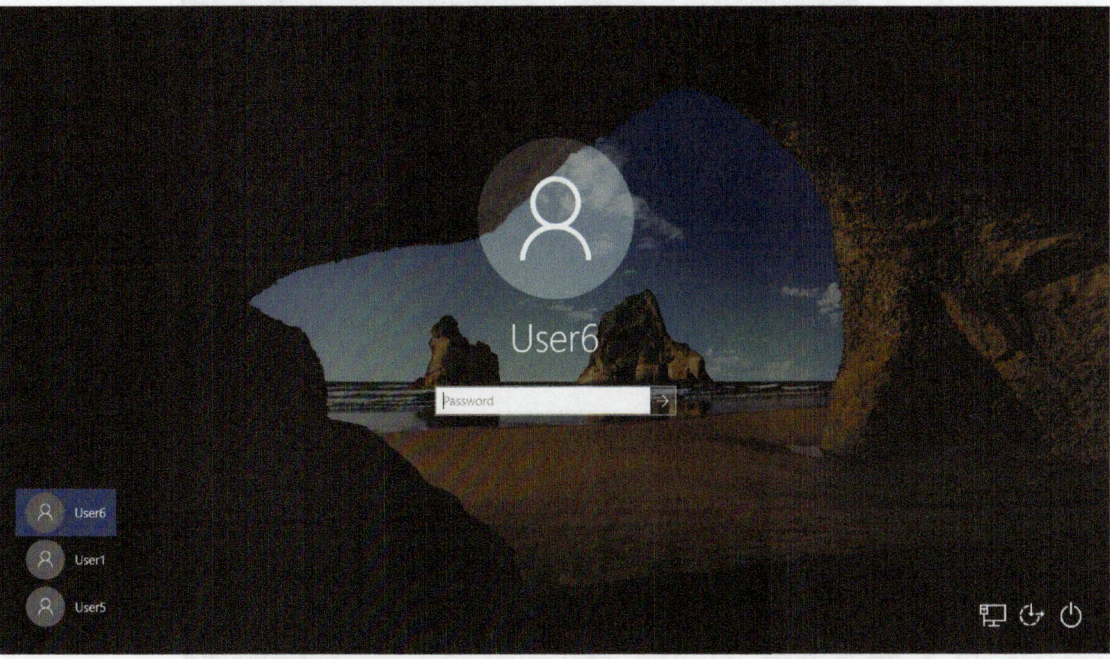

Figure 15-6   The Windows sign-in screen

15

10. Userinit.exe applies Group Policy settings and any programs not trumped by Group Policy that are stored in startup folders and startup registry keys. See Appendix B for a list of these folders and registry keys.

The Windows startup is officially completed when the Windows desktop or Start screen appears and the pinwheel wait icon disappears.

> ◊ **OS Differences** For Windows 7, if the OS encounters an error during startup, the Windows 7 Error Recovery screen appears (see Figure 15-7). Also, Windows 7 can be controlled by keystrokes entered during startup: If the user presses the Spacebar near the beginning of startup, the Windows 7 Boot Manager screen appears, which allows the user to run Windows Memory Diagnostics. If the user presses F8 at startup, the Windows 7 Advanced Boot Options screen appears (see Figure 15-8).

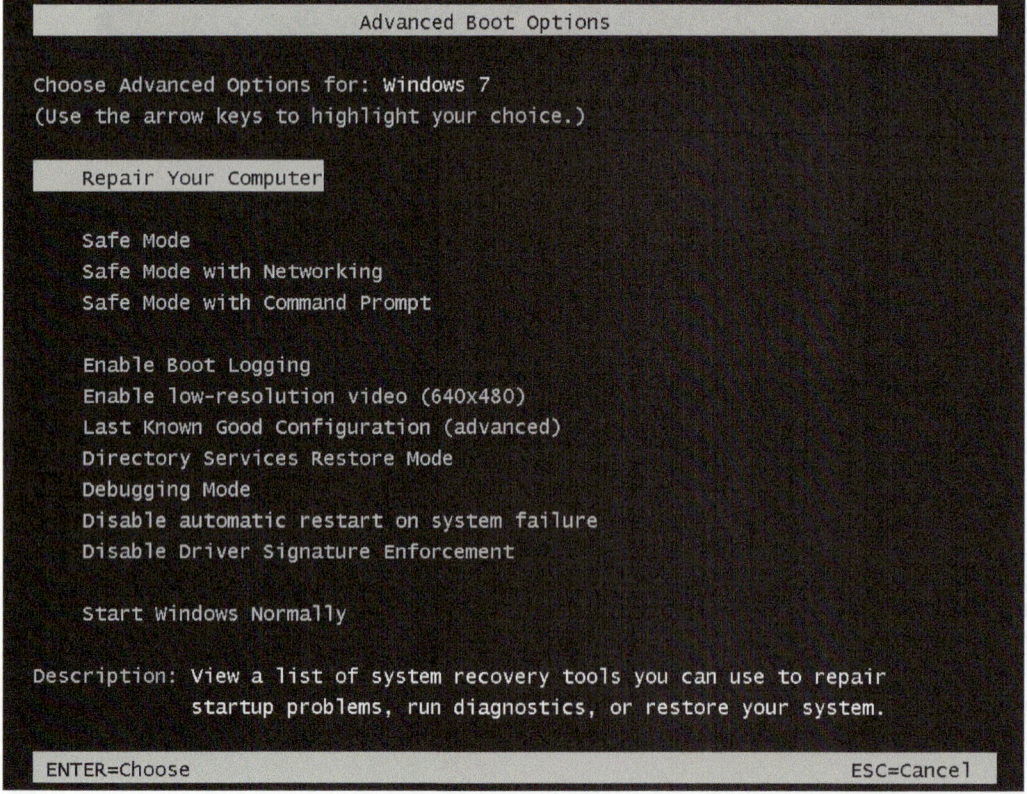

```
                              Windows Error Recovery

Windows did not shut down successfully. If this was due to the system not
responding, or if the system was shut down to protect data, you might be
able to recover by choosing one of the Safe Mode configurations from the
menu below:
(Use the arrow keys to highlight your choice.)


    Safe Mode
    Safe Mode with Networking
    Safe Mode with Command Prompt


    Start Windows Normally


Seconds until the highlighted choice will be selected automatically: 23
Description: Start Windows with its regular settings.










 ENTER=Choose
```

Figure 15-7 The Windows Error Recovery screen appears if Windows 7 has been abruptly stopped

```
                              Advanced Boot Options

Choose Advanced Options for: Windows 7
(Use the arrow keys to highlight your choice.)

    Repair Your Computer


    Safe Mode
    Safe Mode with Networking
    Safe Mode with Command Prompt

    Enable Boot Logging
    Enable low-resolution video (640x480)
    Last Known Good Configuration (advanced)
    Directory Services Restore Mode
    Debugging Mode
    Disable automatic restart on system failure
    Disable Driver Signature Enforcement


    Start Windows Normally


Description: View a list of system recovery tools you can use to repair
             startup problems, run diagnostics, or restore your system.

 ENTER=Choose                                                   ESC=Cancel
```

Figure 15-8 Press F8 during the boot to launch the Windows 7 Advanced Boot Options menu

With this basic knowledge of the boot in hand, let's turn our attention to what you can do to prepare for problems when Windows refuses to load.

WHAT TO DO BEFORE A PROBLEM OCCURS

A+ CORE 2 3.1

When troubleshooting startup, it helps to have a road map, which is the purpose of the diagram in Figure 15-9. It can help you organize in your mind the various ways to boot the system and the menus and procedures available to you depending on how the boot happens.

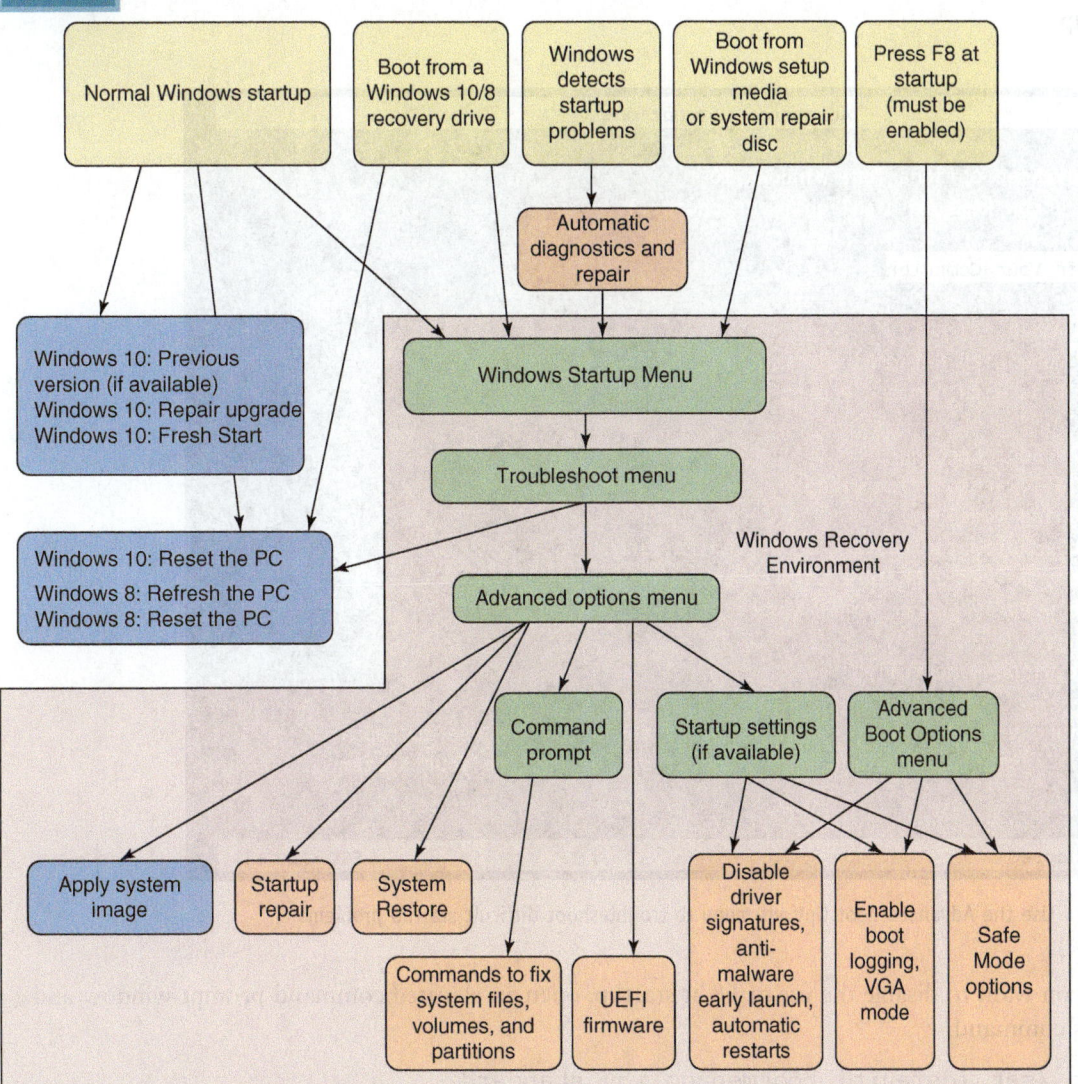

Figure 15-9 Methods to boot the system, menus that appear, and tools available on menus used to troubleshoot startup problems

As you learn to use each tool, keep in mind that you want to use the tool that makes as few changes to the system as possible to fix the problem. Good preparation will make troubleshooting startup problems much simpler and more successful. When you are responsible for a computer and while the computer is still healthy, be sure to complete the following tasks:

▲ *Keep good backups.* Chapter 13 covers methods to back up data, applications, and user settings.

▲ *Create a system image.* Recall that a Windows 10/7 system image or a Windows 8 custom refresh image should be created right after you've installed Windows, hardware, applications, and user accounts, and

15

customized Windows settings. The image can be updated periodically. You learned to create a Windows 10/7 system image and Windows 8 custom refresh image in Chapter 13.

▲ *Configure Windows 10/8 to use the F8 key at startup*. The F8 key gives you access to the Advanced Boot Options menu in Windows, which you'll learn about later in this chapter. Windows 10/8 has the feature disabled by default, and Windows 7 has it enabled. To enable the F8 key at startup, open an elevated command prompt window and enter this command:

```
bcdedit /set {default} bootmenupolicy legacy
```

Figure 15-10 shows the Advanced Boot Options screen that appears when you press F8 during Windows 10 startup.

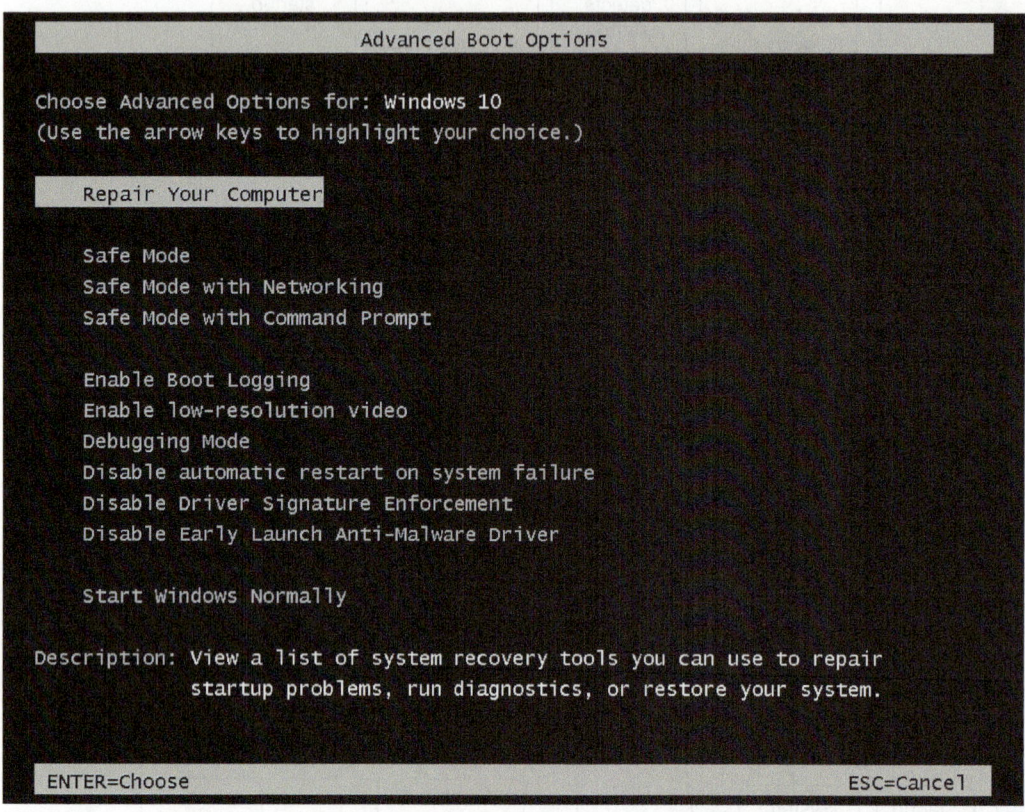

```
                            Advanced Boot Options


Choose Advanced Options for: Windows 10
(Use the arrow keys to highlight your choice.)


   Repair Your Computer


   Safe Mode
   Safe Mode with Networking
   Safe Mode with Command Prompt


   Enable Boot Logging
   Enable low-resolution video
   Debugging Mode
   Disable automatic restart on system failure
   Disable Driver Signature Enforcement
   Disable Early Launch Anti-Malware Driver


   Start Windows Normally


Description: View a list of system recovery tools you can use to repair
            startup problems, run diagnostics, or restore your system.



ENTER=Choose                                              ESC=Cancel
```

Figure 15-10 Use the Advanced Boot Options menu to troubleshoot difficult startup problems

Later, if you want to disable the use of F8 at startup, open an elevated command prompt window and enter this command:

```
bcdedit /set {default} bootmenupolicy standard
```

> ⚡ **Caution** As you learn to troubleshoot Windows 10/8 startup, don't depend on the F8 key to work during the boot because you never know when you'll work on a computer that has it disabled. All the tools available on the Advanced Boot Options screen are also available on the Startup Settings screen, which you can access without using F8. You learn about the Startup Settings screen later in this chapter.

▲ *Create recovery boot media*. If Windows can't boot from the hard drive, you may be able to repair the Windows installation using tools available in the **Windows Recovery Environment (Windows RE)**. Windows RE is normally stored on a hidden partition on the hard drive and is a lean operating system that can be launched to solve Windows startup problems. It provides both a graphical and command-line interface. Figure 15-9 shows Windows RE as a pink background. Menus in Windows RE are in green, tools are in blue and purple, and ways to launch Windows RE are in yellow boxes. Notice in the figure you can launch Windows RE after a normal Windows startup. However, if Windows won't start, you'll need other recovery boot media to launch it. Although it's possible to use recovery media created on a different computer than the one you are troubleshooting, the process is simplified if you already have these tools on hand. Figure 15-9 shows the three types of recovery boot media:

▲ Windows 10/7 DVD system repair disc

▲ Windows 10/8 USB recovery drive

▲ Windows 10 setup media created by the Media Creation Tool

The key to using a system repair disc or recovery drive is to create the disc or drive *before* it is needed. Let's look at each of the three recovery boot media.

> ✎ **Notes** All boot media are bit-specific. Use 32-bit media to repair a 32-bit Windows installation and 64-bit media to repair a 64-bit installation. Also, use Windows 10 recovery boot media to repair Windows 10 systems. Use Windows 8 recovery boot media for Windows 8 installations, and Windows 7 recovery boot media to repair Windows 7 installations.

WINDOWS 10/7 SYSTEM REPAIR DISC

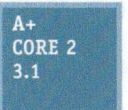

A+
CORE 2
3.1

A system repair disc is a bootable DVD with Windows repair tools that can start the system and fix problems. Using the DVD requires an optical drive. For Windows 10/7, open Control Panel and go to the **Backup and Restore (Windows 7)** window (see Figure 15-11). Click **Create a system repair disc**. A 32-bit Windows installation will create a 32-bit version of the repair disc, and a 64-bit Windows installation will create a 64-bit version of the repair disc. Windows 8 has the option to create a system repair disc, but it is hidden. To use a system repair disc, boot the system from the disc and select your keyboard layout. Then Windows RE is launched.

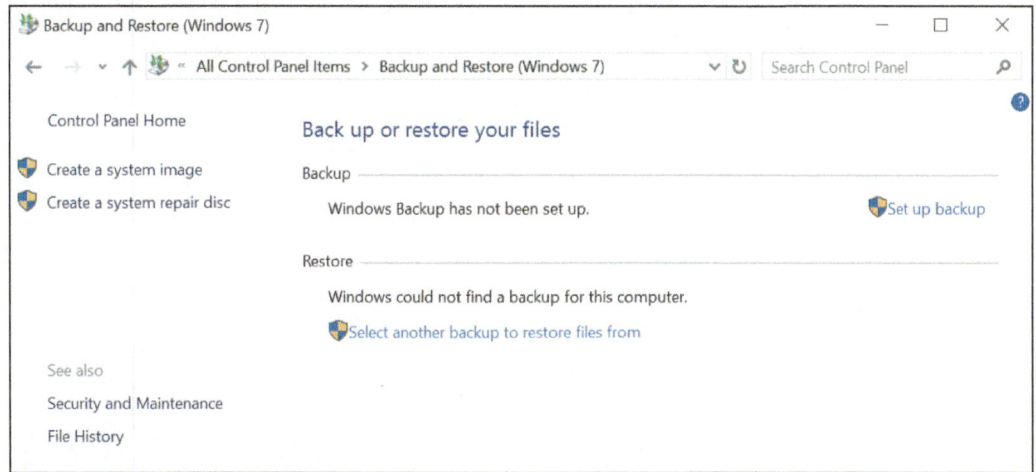

Figure 15-11 Create a system image or a system repair disc from Control Panel

WINDOWS 10/8 RECOVERY DRIVE

A+
CORE 2
3.1

Suppose the hard drive in a laptop completely fails. You can purchase a new hard drive for the system, but a problem might arise when you install Windows on the new drive. Most laptops, all-in-one, and other brand-name computers include an OEM recovery partition on the hard drive that contains the drivers specific for the computer. Before a problem occurs, you can

15

back up this OEM recovery partition to a Windows recovery drive. A recovery drive is a bootable USB flash drive that can access Windows 10/8 repair tools; in addition to holding an OEM recovery partition, it is handy when you need to repair a computer that doesn't have an optical drive.

> ✎ **Notes** A recovery drive is bit-specific: Use a 32-bit recovery drive to repair a 32-bit Windows installation and a 64-bit recovery drive to repair a 64-bit installation.

If you include the system files on the recovery drive, you have the option of reinstalling Windows from the recovery drive. As you can see in Figure 15-9, a recovery drive can be used to perform a Windows 10 reset or a Windows 8 refresh or reset. You learn to use these tools later in the chapter. You can use a recovery drive to repair a computer other than the one on which it was created. However, system files included on a recovery drive may not be compatible with all computers.

Do the following to create a recovery drive:

1. Open **Control Panel** in Classic view and click **Recovery**. Click **Create a recovery drive**, and respond to the UAC dialog box.

2. Choose whether to include system files (see Figure 15-12), which will copy the OEM recovery partition to the recovery drive. If the computer doesn't have an OEM recovery partition, the check box on this dialog box is gray and not available. Click **Next** to continue.

Figure 15-12 Back up system files to the recovery drive so you can reinstall Windows later

3. Windows reports the size of the USB flash drive needed (see Figure 15-13.) Plug in a USB flash drive that is large enough. Know that the entire USB flash drive will be formatted and everything on the drive will be lost.

![Recovery window with Advanced recovery tools showing "Create a recovery drive" option, overlaid by a Recovery Drive window titled "Connect a USB flash drive" with text "The drive must be able to hold at least 8 GB, and everything on the drive will be deleted." and Next/Cancel buttons]

Figure 15-13 Windows reports the size of the USB flash drive needed to hold the recovery drive

15

4. Windows inspects the size of the drive; if it is large enough, you see it listed among available devices. Be careful to select the USB flash drive because everything on the drive will be lost. Click **Next**. Click **Create** to begin the process. It will take a while to complete. Then click **Finish**.

Be sure to label the flash drive well and put it in a safe place. For example, you can put it in an envelope, label it "Recovery drive for John Hawkins 64-bit Windows 10 Sony laptop," and store it in the computer's documentation file.

> 🖊 **Notes** If you copied the OEM recovery partition to the USB flash drive and are short on hard drive space on the computer, you can use Disk Management to delete the recovery partition and free up some space, and then expand the Windows volume.

WINDOWS 10 MEDIA CREATION TOOL

You can launch Windows RE from a Windows setup DVD or flash drive. For Windows 10, recall you can use the Media Creation Tool on a working computer to create a bootable Windows setup ISO file, DVD, or flash drive. You learned how to use the Media Creation Tool in Chapter 12.

TOOLS FOR LEAST INVASIVE SOLUTIONS

Looking back at the diagram in Figure 15-9, tools to diagnose and repair Windows are shown in purple boxes. In this part of the chapter, we discuss several tools that are easy to use and don't make major changes to Windows system files or user settings, including several options on the Windows advanced startup screens.

If Windows works well enough to get to the Windows desktop, you can use one of the following methods to launch Windows RE:

▲ **Windows 10 Settings app.** Open the **Settings** app and click **Update & security**. In the left pane, click **Recovery**. Under *Advanced startup*, click **Restart now**. See Figure 15-14.

> 🖉 **Notes** The Advanced startup option is not available on the Recovery window when you are using a remote connection to the computer or Windows 10 is installed in a VM.

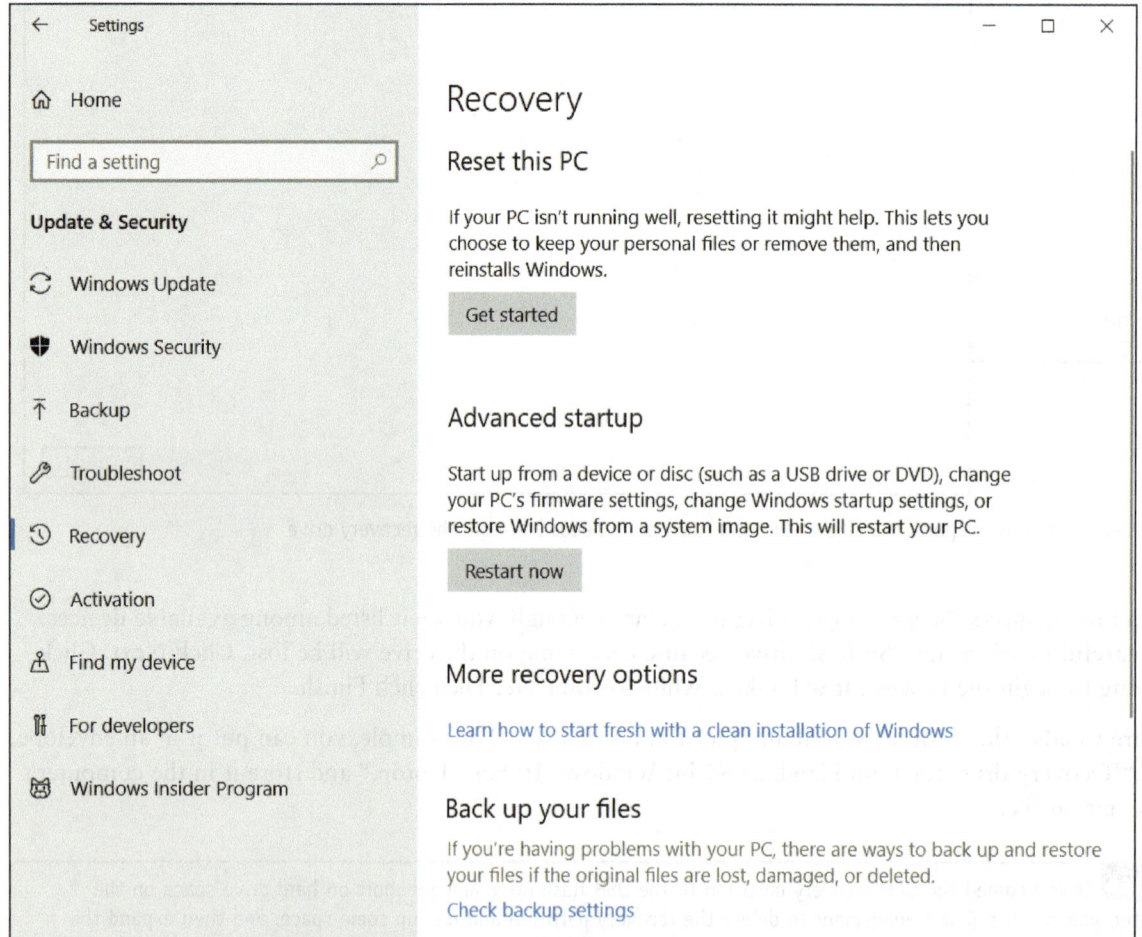

Figure 15-14   The Windows 10 Recovery page in the Settings app

> ↻ **OS Differences**   For Windows 8, you can launch Windows RE after a normal startup by opening the charms bar and clicking **Settings**. In the Settings pane, click **Change PC settings**. In the left pane of the PC settings window, click **Update and recovery**. In the Update and recovery pane, click **Recovery** and click **Restart now** (see Figure 15-15).
>   For Windows 7, press **F8** at startup and click **Repair Your Computer** on the Advanced Boot Options screen (refer back to Figure 15-10).

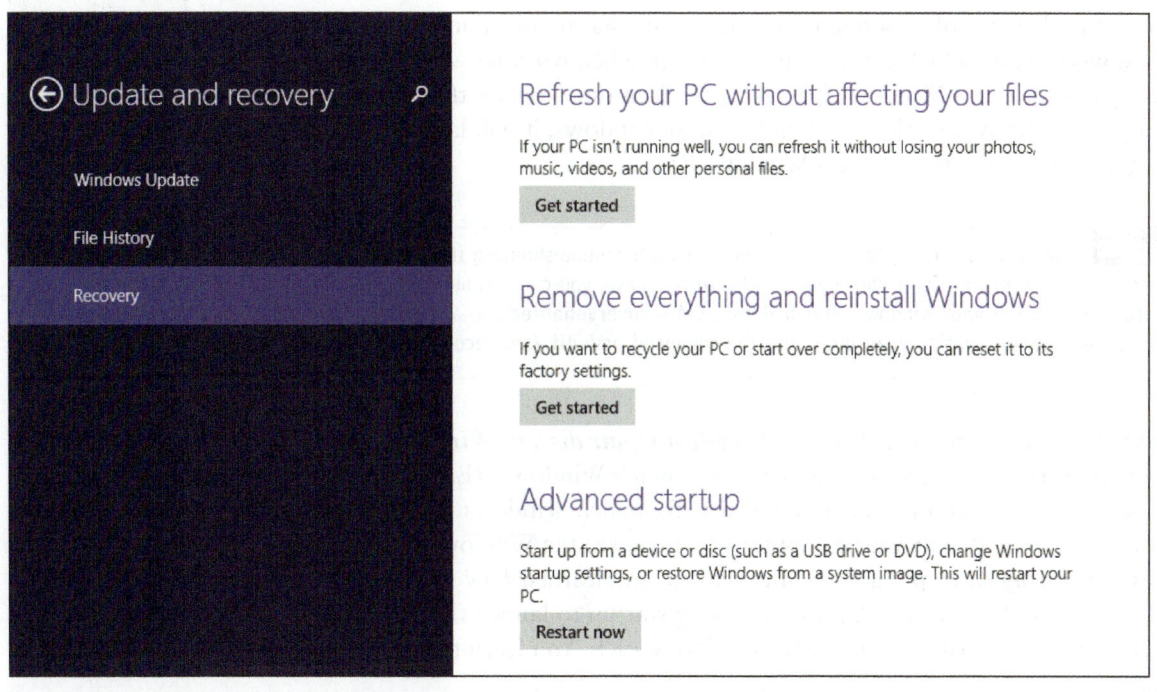

Figure 15-15 Refresh or reset a Windows 8 computer or restart the computer in advanced startup mode

▲ *Shift + Restart*. From the Windows 10/8 Start menu, click the **Power** icon. Press and hold the **Shift** key and click **Restart**.

▲ *Command prompt*. In a Windows 10/8/7 command prompt window, enter **shutdown /r /o**. The /r parameter instructs the computer to restart, and the /o parameter opens Windows RE after the restart.

> **Notes** You can also use the shutdown command to remotely shut down computers over the network.

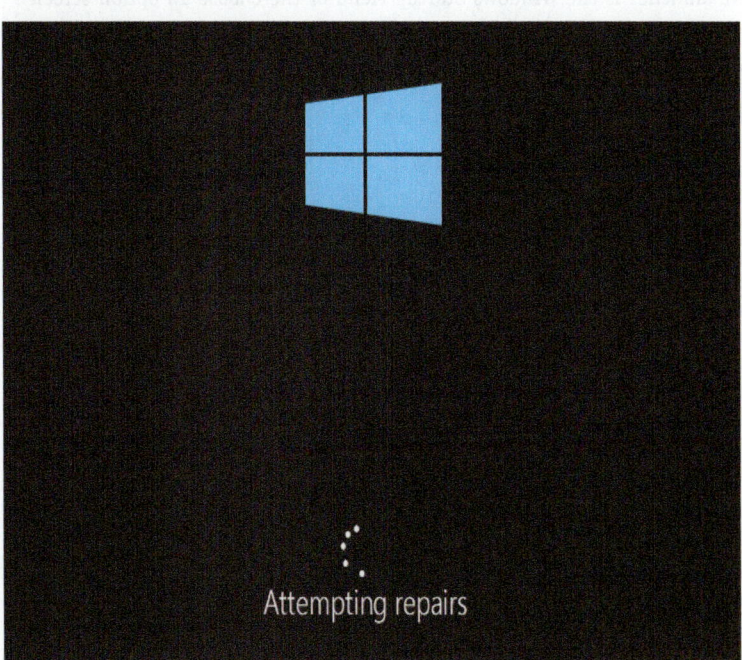

Figure 15-16 Windows automatically launches diagnostic and repair procedures after several restarts within a few minutes

Here are the methods to launch Windows RE when Windows cannot start normally:

▲ *Windows detects startup problems and launches automatic diagnostics and repairs*. If you restart the computer several times within a few minutes or Windows detects errors during startup, it automatically launches diagnostics (see Figure 15-16) and takes you through steps to attempt to repair the system. The process, called Automatic Repair or Startup Repair, includes running both Check Disk and System File Checker.

If Automatic Repair fails, you're given the option to boot into Windows RE, where you have

15

access to other troubleshooting tools. Also know that if you cannot launch Windows RE after a normal Windows startup, which can sometimes happen when working with a Windows 10 installation in a VM, you can restart Windows several times. Each time you see the Windows flag appear, turn off the computer. After two or three attempts to start Windows, it will launch Automatic Repair on the next startup, and then you can access Windows RE.

> ✎ **Notes** When you are trying to restart a computer while troubleshooting it yourself, you might find that Automatic Repair slows down or interferes with your efforts. In this case, you can disable Automatic Repair as follows: Open an elevated command prompt window, enter **bcdedit /set recoveryenabled no**, and then perform your own repair steps. You can reenable Automatic Repair later with the command **bcdedit /set recoveryenabled yes**.

▲ *Boot from a USB recovery drive, DVD system repair disc, or Windows setup DVD or USB drive.* These boot recovery media give you the option to launch Windows RE. You might have to adjust BIOS/UEFI settings to boot from these alternate media. To launch Windows RE from a Windows setup DVD or flash drive, click **Repair your computer** when you see the Windows Setup screen.

▲ *Press F8 during startup.* Earlier in the chapter, you learned how to configure Windows 10/8 to enable F8 at startup. If it is enabled, press **F8** during startup to launch the Advanced Boot Options menu (refer back to Figure 15-10), which is part of Windows RE. You learn to use the tools on this menu later in the chapter.

APPLYING | CONCEPTS — EXPLORING WINDOWS RE MENUS AND OPTIONS

**A+
CORE 2
3.1**

Let's explore the menu screens in Windows RE, which are shown in green boxes in Figure 15-9. Follow these steps to explore Windows RE menus:

1. Start Windows and use one of the methods listed earlier to launch Windows RE. The first screen you see after Windows RE launches is the Windows Startup Menu or the *Choose an option* screen (see Figure 15-17).

Figure 15-17 The Windows Startup Menu is the first screen you see after launching Windows RE

(continues)

2. Click **Troubleshoot** to see the **Troubleshoot** menu screen. Figure 15-18A shows the Windows 10 Troubleshoot screen, and Figure 15-18B shows the Windows 8 Troubleshoot screen.

 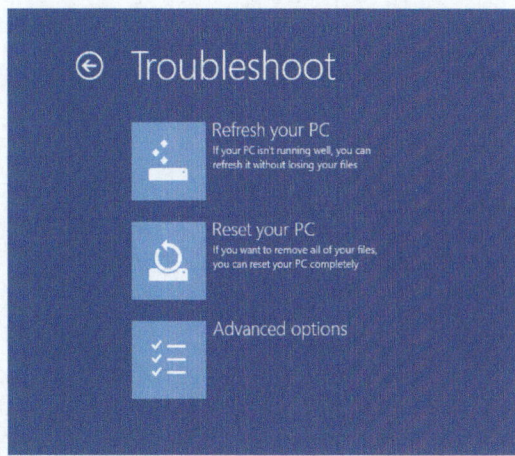

(A)   (B)

Figure 15-18   (A) Windows 10 reset or (B) Windows 8 refresh and reset are available on the Troubleshoot screen

3. Click **Advanced options** to see the Advanced options screen in Figure 15-19.

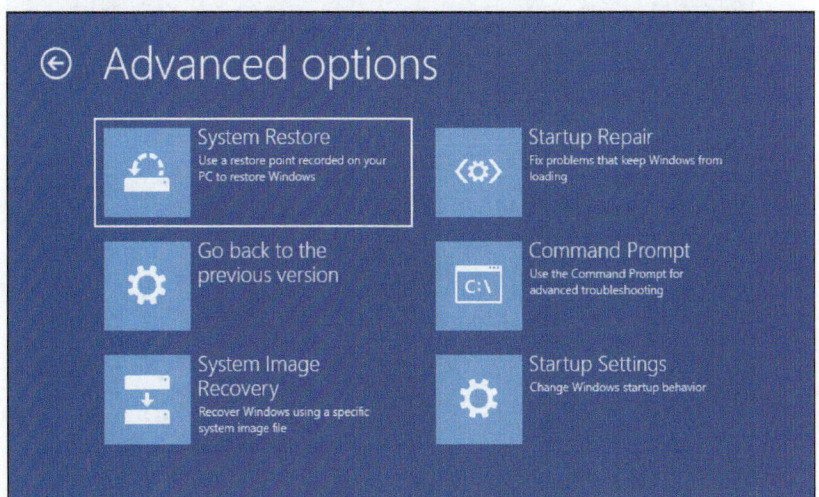

Figure 15-19   The option to go back to a previous version is available because this computer recently received a major Windows update

> 📝 **Notes** Depending on the situation, you might see a seventh option on the Advanced options screen, which is UEFI Firmware Settings. Use this option to change settings in a computer's UEFI firmware.

4. To get a command prompt, click **Command Prompt**. Here you can enter various commands to troubleshoot and solve problems. To exit the command prompt, enter the **exit** command. You are returned to the Advanced options screen.

5. The Startup Settings option is available on the Advanced options screen shown in Figure 15-19 because Windows RE was launched after a normal Windows startup. Click **Startup Settings** to see the startup options shown in Figure 15-20.

15

(continues)

Restart to change Windows options such as:

- Enable low-resolution video mode
- Enable debugging mode
- Enable boot logging
- Enable Safe Mode
- Disable driver signature enforcement
- Disable early-launch anti-malware protection
- Disable automatic restart on system failure

Restart

Figure 15-20   The Startup Settings menu gives options for how Windows starts up

6. Click **Restart**. After the restart, another Startup Settings screen appears (see Figure 15-21), which has more options than the first one. Press numbers or function keys F1 through F9 to launch the tools on this screen. The tools listed on this screen are the same as those listed on the Advanced Boot Options screen (refer back to Figure 15-10) that appears when you press F8 at startup.

7. To return to the Windows Startup Menu shown earlier in Figure 15-17, press **F10**. On the *Choose an option* screen, click **Continue** to reload Windows 10.

Startup Settings

Press a number to choose from the options below:

Use number keys or functions keys F1-F9.

1) Enable debugging
2) Enable boot logging
3) Enable low-resolution video
4) Enable Safe Mode
5) Enable Safe Mode with Networking
6) Enable Safe Mode with Command Prompt
7) Disable driver signature enforcement
8) Disable early launch anti-malware protection
9) Disable automatic restart after failure

Press F10 for more options
Press Enter to return to your operating system

Figure 15-21   Press a function key or number to restart the system in a given mode

Next, we discuss some tools to repair Windows, including Startup Repair, Startup Settings, System Restore, and commands entered in a command prompt window.

STARTUP REPAIR

A+ CORE 2 3.1

When addressing startup problems, the first tool to try is startup repair, which is a built-in diagnostic and repair tool. It can fix Windows system files without changing Windows settings, user data, or applications. You can't cause additional problems with the tool and it's easy to use.

To run startup repair in Windows RE, drill down to the Advanced options screen (refer back to Figure 15-19) and click **Startup Repair**. Windows RE examines the system, fixes problems, reports what it did, and might offer suggestions for further fixes. A log file of the process can be found at C:\Windows\ System32\LogFiles\SRT\SRTTrail.txt.

> ↻ **OS Differences** For Windows 7, after you launch Windows RE, the Advanced Boot Options screen appears (refer back to Figure 15-8). Click **Repair Your Computer** and enter an administrator password. The System Recovery Options box appears (see Figure 15-22). Click **Startup Repair** to launch the startup repair process.

Figure 15-22 Recovery tools in Windows RE for a Windows 7 installation

CHANGING STARTUP SETTINGS

A+ CORE 2 3.1

The Startup Settings option on the Advanced options screen shown in Figure 15-19 is available only when Windows RE is launched from the hard drive rather than other media. Following directions given earlier, launch Windows RE and drill down to the Startup Settings screen shown earlier in Figure 15-21. Here's a quick rundown of what these tools can do.

PRESS 1 OR F1: ENABLE DEBUGGING

This tool moves system boot logs from the failing computer to another computer for evaluation. The computers must be connected by way of a serial port.

15

PRESS 2 OR F2: ENABLE BOOT LOGGING

Windows loads normally and all files used during the load process are recorded in a log file, C:\Windows\Ntbtlog.txt (see Figure 15-23). Use this option to see what did and did not load during the boot. For instance, if you have a problem getting a device to work, check Ntbtlog.txt to see what driver files loaded. Boot logging is much more effective if you have a copy of Ntbtlog.txt that was made when everything worked as it should. Then you can compare the good load with the bad load, looking for differences.

> ✎ **Notes** The Ntbtlog.txt file is also generated when you boot into Safe Mode.

```
ntbtlog.txt - Notepad                                          —   □   ×
File  Edit  Format  View  Help
Microsoft (R) Windows (R) Versi 8  4 2015 09:14:41.352
BOOTLOG_LOADED \SystemRoot\system32\ntoskrnl.exe
BOOTLOG_LOADED \SystemRoot\system32\hal.dll
BOOTLOG_LOADED \SystemRoot\system32\kd.dll
BOOTLOG_LOADED \SystemRoot\system32\mcupdate_GenuineIntel.dll
BOOTLOG_LOADED \SystemRoot\System32\drivers\werkernel.sys
BOOTLOG_LOADED \SystemRoot\System32\drivers\CLFS.SYS
BOOTLOG_LOADED \SystemRoot\System32\drivers\tm.sys
BOOTLOG_LOADED \SystemRoot\system32\PSHED.dll
BOOTLOG_LOADED \SystemRoot\system32\BOOTVID.dll
BOOTLOG_LOADED \SystemRoot\system32\CI.dll
BOOTLOG_LOADED \SystemRoot\System32\drivers\msrpc.sys
BOOTLOG_LOADED \SystemRoot\System32\drivers\Wdf01000.sys
```

Figure 15-23 A sample C:\Windows\Ntbtlog.txt log file

> ✎ **Notes** If Windows hangs during the boot, try booting using the Enable Boot Logging option. Then look at the last entry in the Ntbtlog.txt file. This entry might be the name of a device driver causing the system to hang.

PRESS 3 OR F3: ENABLE LOW-RESOLUTION VIDEO (640 × 480)

Use this option when the video settings don't allow you to see the screen well enough to fix a bad setting (for example, black fonts on a black background or a corrupted video driver). Booting in this mode gives you a very plain, standard video in VGA mode. You can then go to **Display settings**, correct the problem, and reboot normally. For problems with video drivers, open Device Manager and update, roll back, or uninstall and reinstall the video drivers.

PRESS 4 OR F4: ENABLE SAFE MODE

With this option, the Safe Mode desktop appears (see Figure 15-24) after the system restarts and you sign in to Windows. Launching Safe Mode and then restarting the system again can sometimes solve a startup problem. You can also go to the Windows desktop in Safe Mode and launch anti-malware software to scan the system for malware. You can open Event Viewer to find events that are helpful in troubleshooting the system, run the System File Checker command (**sfc /scannow**) to restore system files, use Device Manager to roll back a driver, use Memory Diagnostics (**mdsched.exe**) to verify memory, use the **chkdsk /r** command to check for file system errors, configure Windows for a clean boot on the next restart, and perform other troubleshooting tasks. Recall from Chapter 14 that you can also launch Safe Mode from the Boot tab on the System Configuration window, where Safe Mode is called Safe boot.

> ★ **A+ Exam Tip** The A+ Core 2 exam gives you a scenario and expects you to know when and how to use Safe Mode to help resolve a Windows startup problem.

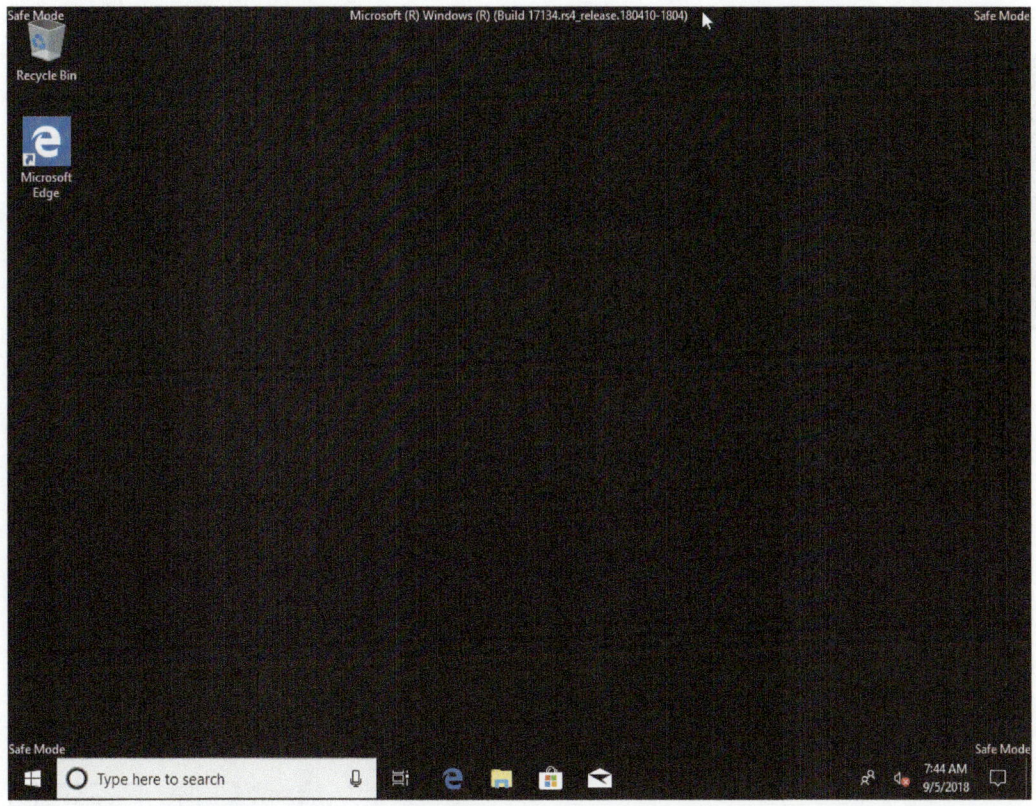

Figure 15-24 The Windows 10 Safe Mode desktop

PRESS 5 OR F5: ENABLE SAFE MODE WITH NETWORKING

Use this option when you need access to the network to solve the problem. For example, you might need to download updates to your anti-malware software. Also use this mode when the Windows installation files are available on the network, rather than Windows setup media, and you need to access those files.

PRESS 6 OR F6: ENABLE SAFE MODE WITH COMMAND PROMPT

If Safe Mode can't start, try Safe Mode with Command Prompt, which doesn't attempt to load the graphical interface. At the command prompt, use the **sfc /scannow** command to verify system files (see Figure 15-25). If the problem is still not solved, you can use the **rstrui** command to launch System Restore and then follow the on-screen directions to select a restore point. However, as Figure 15-26 shows, if restore points have not been previously made, System Restore cannot help. As you learn later in the chapter, you can also use this command prompt to restore a corrupted Windows registry from backups.

Figure 15-25 SFC finds and attempts to repair corrupted system files

15

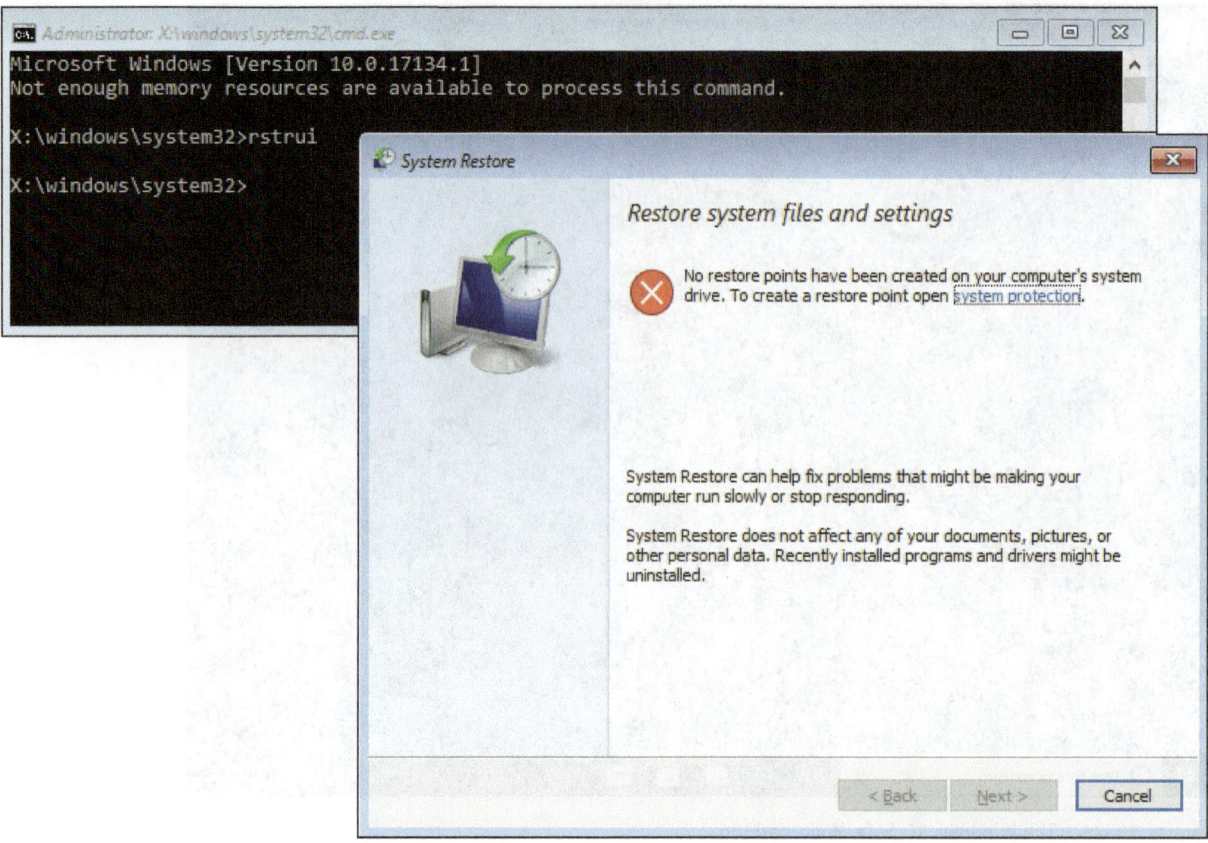

Figure 15-26 Use System Restore after booting to Safe Mode with Command Prompt

PRESS 7 OR F7: DISABLE DRIVER SIGNATURE ENFORCEMENT

All 64-bit editions of Windows require that kernel-mode drivers be digitally signed. Developers disable driver signature enforcement when they test kernel-mode device drivers that are not yet digitally signed. Don't use this option for troubleshooting Windows startup because doing so might allow malware drivers to load.

PRESS 8 OR F8: DISABLE EARLY LAUNCH ANTI-MALWARE DRIVER

Windows 10/8 allows anti-malware software to launch a driver before any third-party drivers are launched so it can scan these drivers for malware. Unless you're sure a driver is the problem, don't disable this security feature. (Windows 7 doesn't offer this option on its Advanced Boot Options screen.)

PRESS 9 OR F9: DISABLE AUTOMATIC RESTART ON SYSTEM FAILURE

By default, Windows automatically restarts immediately after a blue screen of death (BSOD) stop error, which is described in more detail later in this chapter. The error can cause the system to continually reboot rather than shut down. Press **F9** to disable automatic restarts and stop the rebooting.

> **Notes** To permanently disable automatic restarts, go to **Control Panel**, open the **System** window, and click **Advanced system settings**. In the Startup and Recovery group of the System Properties box, click **Settings**. In the Startup and Recovery box, uncheck **Automatically restart** (see Figure 15-27). Click **OK** twice and close the System window.

Figure 15-27   Permanently disable automatic restarts

PRESS F10: RETURN TO THE STARTUP SETTINGS SCREEN

Press F10 to return to the Windows Startup Menu screen shown previously in Figure 15-17.

> **Notes** As you use these startup settings tools, be sure to reboot after each attempt to fix the problem to make sure it has not been resolved before you try another tool. To exit Windows RE and relaunch Windows, press **Enter** on the Startup Settings screen.

> **OS Differences** Windows 7 offers an option on the Advanced Boot Options menu called the Last Known Good Configuration, which is not available in Windows 10/8. The Windows 7 **Last Known Good Configuration** settings are saved in the registry each time the user successfully logs on to the system. If your problem is caused by a bad hardware or software installation, using the Last Known Good can, in effect, undo the bad installation. Try the Last Known Good option early in the troubleshooting session before a bad Last Known Good overwrites a good one. (However, know that if you sign in to Safe Mode, the Last Known Good is not saved.)

SYSTEM RESTORE

**A+
CORE 2
3.1**

Windows gives you several opportunities during the startup troubleshooting process to use System Restore to restore the system to an earlier point in time when a restore point was made. You can select System Restore from the Windows RE Advanced options screen (refer back to Figure 15-19) or the Windows 7 System Recovery Options screen (refer back to Figure 15-22). You can also perform System Restore in Safe Mode or from a command prompt with the **rstrui** command.

15

System Restore can cause problems of its own because Windows updates and updates to anti-malware software can be lost, and hardware devices and applications might need to be reinstalled. System Restore won't help if the file system is corrupted or the registry is trashed. In these situations, the command prompt might help.

THE COMMAND PROMPT WINDOW IN WINDOWS RE

A+
CORE 2
3.1

Use the command prompt window in Windows RE when the graphical interface is missing or corrupted or you want to use a specific command to fix a problem when Windows refuses to start. Using this command prompt, you have administrator privileges and full read and write access to all files on all drives. Many commands you learned about in Chapter 13 can be used at this command prompt. To access the Windows RE command prompt, click **Command Prompt** on the Windows 10/8 Advanced options screen (refer back to Figure 15-19) or the Windows 7 System Recovery Options screen (refer back to Figure 15-22).

Next are some examples of how to use the Windows RE command prompt to repair a system.

MANAGE DATA FILES AND SYSTEM FILES

As you learned in Chapter 14, you can use the SFC or DISM commands to restore critical Windows system files. Use the cd, copy, rename, and delete commands to manage data files and system files. For example, if key registry files are corrupted or deleted, the system will not start. You can restore registry files using files saved in the C:\Windows\System32\config\RegBack folder. This RegBack folder contains partial backups of the registry files put there after a successful boot. Use the commands in Table 15-2 to restore the registry files. In the table, we assume Windows is installed on drive C:. However, know that Windows RE is likely to assign a different drive letter to the Windows volume.

Command Line	Description
1. c:	Makes drive C: the current drive. The default directory is root.
2. dir	Examines the contents of drive C:. If this is not your Windows volume, try a different drive letter.
3. cd \windows\system32\config	Makes the Windows registry folder the current folder.
4. ren default default.save **5.** ren sam sam.save **6.** ren security security.save **7.** ren software software.save **8.** ren system system.save	Renames the five registry files.
9. cd regback	Makes the registry backup folder the current folder.
10. copy system c:\windows\system32\config	For hardware problems, first try copying just the System hive from the backup folder to the registry folder and then reboot.
11. copy software c:\windows\system32\config	For software problems, first try copying just the Software hive to the registry folder and then reboot.
12. copy system c:\windows\system32\config **13.** copy software c:\windows\system32\config **14.** copy default c:\windows\system32\config **15.** copy sam c:\windows\system32\config **16.** copy security c:\windows\system32\config	If the problem is still not solved, try copying all five hives to the registry folder and reboot.

Table 15-2 Steps to restore the registry files

After you try each fix, reboot the system to see if the problem is solved before you try the next fix.

REPAIR THE HARD DRIVE FILE SYSTEMS AND PARTITIONS

A corrupted file system or partition can cause a failure to boot. To repair the file system, first try the chkdsk /r command. If you decide the hard drive is so corrupted you must start over with a fresh installation of Windows, you can use the diskpart command to totally wipe the hard drive clean of everything, including the partitioning system, before you install Windows again using Windows setup media. You learned to use diskpart in Chapter 12; a project at the end of this chapter gives you more practice with diskpart. Diskpart and chkdsk can also be used in a normal command prompt window.

ENABLE NETWORKING

Networking is not normally available from the Windows RE command prompt. Use the wpeinit command to enable networking. The wpeinit command initializes Windows PE. Recall from Chapter 12 that Windows PE is the preinstallation-environment operating system that is launched prior to installing Windows in a clean install and includes networking components.

USE BOOTREC AND BCDEDIT TO REPAIR THE FILE SYSTEM AND KEY BOOT FILES

A failure to boot can be caused by a corrupted BCD. If startup repair does not fix the problem, you can use the bootrec command to repair the BCD and boot sectors. Use the bcdedit command to manually edit the BCD. (Be sure to make a copy of the BCD before you edit it.) Use the bootsect command to repair a dual-boot system. To get helpful information about these commands, enter the command followed by /?, such as bcdedit /?. Some examples of the bootrec and bcdedit commands are listed in Table 15-3.

Command Line	Description
bootrec /scanOS	Scans the hard drive for Windows installations not stored in the BCD
bootrec /rebuildBCD	Scans for Windows installations and rebuilds the BCD
bootrec /fixboot	Repairs the boot sector of the system partition
bootrec /fixmbr	Repairs the MBR for hard drives using the MBR partitioning system
bcdedit /enum	Displays the contents of the BCD

Table 15-3   Bootrec and bcdedit commands to repair system files and the file system

Although a startup repair should solve the problem when you get an error message at startup that "Bootmgr is missing," rebuilding the BCD store should also be able to resolve the same problem on a legacy BIOS and MBR system.

OPTIONS TO REINSTALL WINDOWS

A+ CORE 2 1.3, 3.1
After you have made reasonable efforts to repair a Windows installation, your next option is to reinstall Windows. The startup troubleshooting tools discussed in this part of the chapter affect the entire Windows installation on a computer rather than a few files or settings. Look back at Figure 15-9 and notice that these tools to reinstall Windows are shown in blue boxes; you can also see how to reach each tool. Some of these options allow you to keep personal data, and other options remove that data; the tools are listed here starting with the least intrusive solution:

1. *Windows 10/8 previous version*. Undo a recent Windows 10/8 update.

2. *Windows 10 repair upgrade*. Install Windows 10 as an upgrade over the existing installation, keeping personal data, apps, and Windows settings.

3. *Windows 10 Fresh Start.* Do a clean installation of the most recent version of Windows 10. User data, some Windows settings, and a few apps can be kept.

4. *Windows 10 reset.* Do a clean Windows 10 installation from recovery media or the recovery partition on the hard drive. User data, some Windows settings, and a few apps can be kept.

5. *Windows 8 refresh.* Restore Windows 8 from a custom refresh image with the option to keep user data and some apps.

6. *Apply a Windows 10/7 system image.* Use a system image to replace everything on the Windows volume. Current user data, Windows settings, and apps are lost.

7. *Windows 8 reset.* The hard drive is reformatted and a clean installation of Windows is done. If an OEM recovery partition is available, it is used for the Windows installation.

8. *Install Windows 10/8/7 from the OEM recovery partition.* Laptops and brand-name computers may have an OEM recovery partition on the hard drive that can be used to restore the system to factory state. Some manufacturer procedures allow user data to be kept.

9. *Windows 10/8/7 clean install from setup media.* This method is covered in Chapter 12 and may allow you to keep user data on the hard drive.

Let's see how the Windows previous version, repair upgrade, Fresh Start, reset, and refresh work.

WINDOWS 10 PREVIOUS VERSION

**A+
CORE 2
3.1**

Minor updates to Windows are distributed on the second Tuesday of each month (called "Patch Tuesday"). Major updates, called versions, come along once or twice a year. Recall that you can look up your computer's current Windows 10 version by opening the **Settings** app, clicking **System,** and then clicking **About**. For Windows 10/8/7, you can also enter the **winver** command in the Windows search box or Run box. The About Windows box that appears reports the current version and build of Windows. See Figure 15-28.

Figure 15-28 Version and build numbers can identify the major and minor Windows updates installed

✎ **Notes** A Windows 10 version, such as the April 2018 Update, is assigned a version number, which appears as Version 1803 in Figure 15-28. A build number identifies updates to the current version. The major portion of the build number (such as 17134 for build 17134.228, shown in Figure 15-28) appears to be somewhat arbitrary and is notoriously unpredictable for future releases. However, the minor portion of the build number is more specific, in that these decimal places increment with each minor update.

A version includes all previous updates, so even minor updates are reinstalled when you install the next version. If a new version is giving problems, you can revert your system back to the earlier version as long as (1) the version was installed within the last 10 days; (2) you have not reset your computer during this time; and (3) the Windows.old folder has not been deleted.

To roll back Windows updates, including device drivers that come with Windows updates, do one of the following to revert your system to a previous version:

◢ *From the Windows desktop*. Open the **Settings** app, click **Update & security**, and then click **Recovery**. Under *Go back to the previous version of Windows 10*, click **Get started**. If this button is grayed out, the time limit for reverting to the previous version has already passed or the Windows.old folder is missing.

◢ *From Windows RE*. If the option is available, you can see it on the Advanced options screen in Windows RE, shown earlier in Figure 15-19. Use this method when a new version has caused the system to fail to start, such as when a critical driver is corrupted.

WINDOWS 10 REPAIR UPGRADE

If you're having problems with Windows updates or basic Windows functionality but you can still boot into Windows, you might consider performing a repair upgrade, also known as a repair install or an in-place upgrade. A repair upgrade is a nondestructive installation of Windows 10 over an existing Windows installation. This is not the same as a full reinstall because the Windows volume will not be reformatted. Just as with an upgrade from Windows 8 to Windows 10, you can keep personal files, apps, and Windows settings. Essentially, you trick the machine into thinking it's being upgraded while potentially repairing the Windows installation.

Keep these points in mind when doing a repair upgrade:

◢ Create Windows setup media, either on DVD or USB, or save an ISO file on the local hard drive.

◢ Make sure that you can fully boot into Windows 10. If you can't, you'll have to use a different troubleshooting tool.

◢ Even though all data, apps, and settings should be protected in a repair upgrade, make a backup just in case.

◢ Gather all product keys for all installed apps to make reinstallation of these apps easier should it become necessary.

> **✎ Notes** Belarc Advisor (*belarc.com*) is a free tool that is quick and easy to use. It will produce a list of all installed apps along with their product keys if that information is available. Print a copy of the report and keep it in a safe place.

15

APPLYING | CONCEPTS   PERFORMING A REPAIR UPGRADE

The easiest way to perform a repair upgrade is to start with an ISO file created by the Media Creation Tool, as described in Chapter 12. Complete the following steps:

1. Sign in to Windows using an administrator account. Back up all personal data using one of the methods you learned about in Chapter 13.

2. Following steps in Chapter 12, download the correct ISO file for the Windows installation you're currently using on the computer to be repaired.

3. In File Explorer, double-click the ISO file that you created with the Media Creation Tool. This mounts the image and shows the included files.

4. Double-click **setup.exe**, as shown in Figure 15-29. Click **Yes** in response to the UAC dialog box.

(continues)

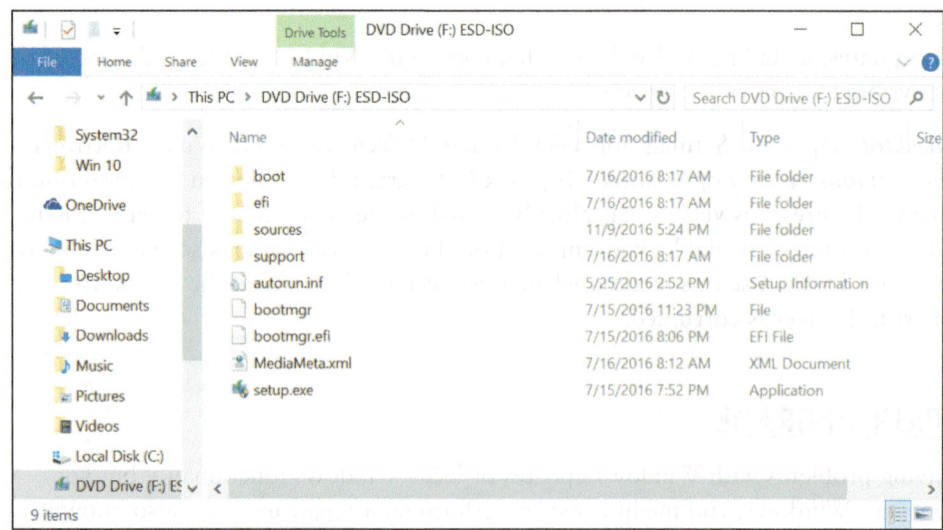

Figure 15-29   To begin the repair upgrade, double-click setup.exe on the virtual DVD in Explorer

5. On the first Windows 10 Setup window, make sure **Download and install updates (recommended)** is selected, and then click **Next**. Setup examines the system.

6. Click **Accept** on the Applicable notices and license terms window. Windows 10 Setup checks for and downloads updates.

7. If the *Choose what to keep* window appears, decide whether to keep personal files and apps, personal files only, or nothing. Sometimes setup makes these decisions for you and skips directly to the *Ready to install* window.

8. On the *Ready to install* window, make sure **Keep personal files and apps** appears and is checked, as shown in Figure 15-30. If not, click **Change what to keep** and select **Keep personal files and apps**, and then click **Next** to return to the *Ready to install* window. Click **Install** to begin the installation process, which will take a while and require several restarts. Enjoy a cup of tea or coffee while you wait.

9. When the lock screen appears, sign in to Windows. Once you see the desktop, all your files, apps, and settings should still be in place.

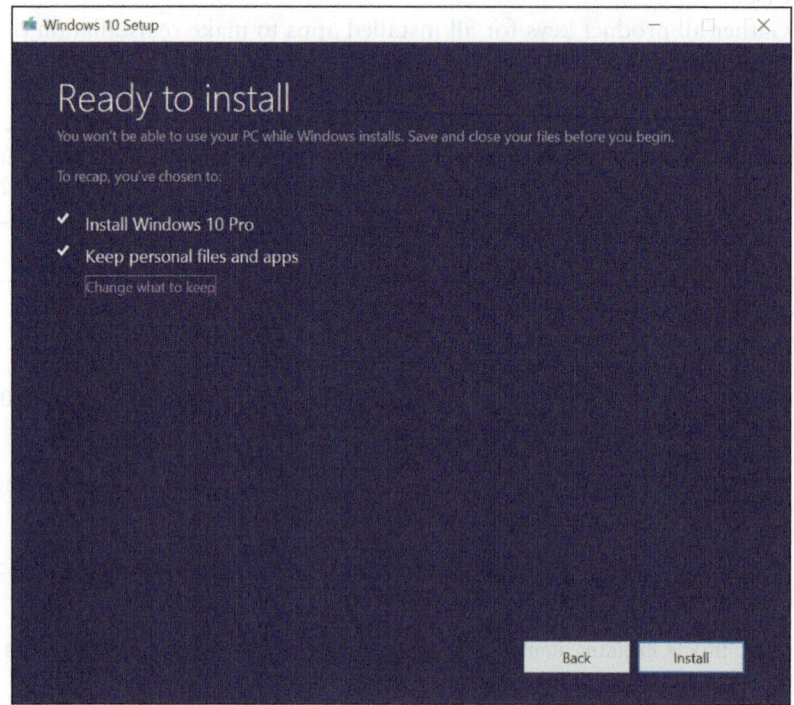

Figure 15-30   You can keep user data and settings and third-party apps during a repair upgrade

WINDOWS 10 FRESH START

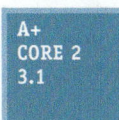

A+
CORE 2
3.1

A Fresh Start performs a clean installation of the most recent version of Windows 10 and is often used to remove manufacturer bloatware. Here's what is installed, kept, and not kept with a Fresh Start:

▲ *Installed*. The latest generic copy of Windows, free from manufacturer bloatware, is downloaded directly from the Microsoft website.
▲ *Kept*. User accounts, their settings, and personal data are kept as well as some Windows settings. Microsoft apps that are natively integrated in Windows and Microsoft store apps installed by the computer manufacturer are also kept.
▲ *Not kept*. All apps are removed, except as stated above. A list of removed apps is displayed on the desktop after the Fresh Start completes. Be aware that you also lose any manufacturer drivers or OEM system files.

To install a fresh copy of Windows 10, first make sure you're connected to the Internet and that you have sufficient storage space for the Windows image (about 3 GB). Open the Settings app, click **Update & security,** and then click **Recovery**. Under *More recovery options* (see Figure 15-31), click **Learn how to start fresh with a clean installation of Windows**. Then click **Yes** to switch to the Fresh start page, which is shown on the right side of Figure 15-31. Click **Get started** to begin the process. The tool downloads and performs a clean installation of Windows 10. Sign in to complete setup.

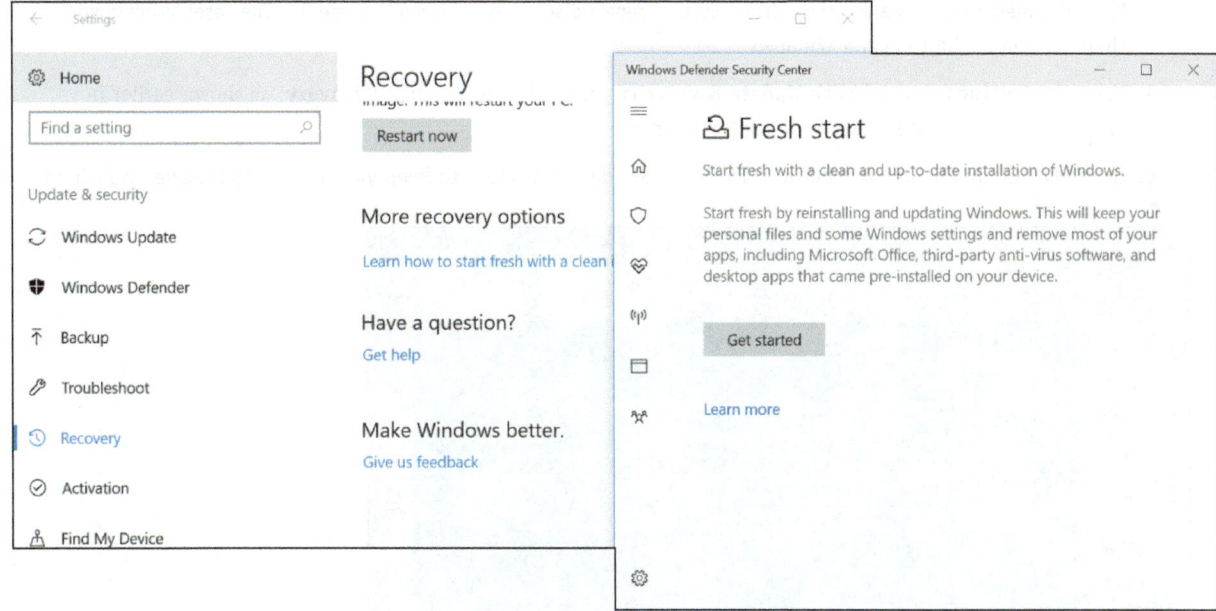

Figure 15-31 Personal files are kept when executing a Fresh Start for Windows 10

WINDOWS 10 RESET

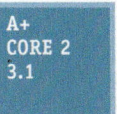

A+
CORE 2
3.1

A Windows 10 reset reinstalls Windows with the option of keeping user accounts, some Windows settings, and all personal data files. If you decide to remove data files, you can also choose to clean the drive. During a reset, any apps or drivers that were installed from third-party providers will be removed, and some changes made to Windows settings will be lost. Also, if your computer has received a major update within the past 10 days, you will lose the ability to revert to a previous version of Windows. If you're using a Microsoft account, you can choose to have many Windows settings automatically resynced to the device.

15

✏️ **Notes** The basic difference between a Windows 10 reset and Fresh Start is the source of the Windows installation files. A reset uses files taken from recovery media or the recovery partition on the hard drive, whereas a Fresh Start downloads a pristine, up-to-date copy of Windows from the Microsoft website. Fresh Start therefore gives you a cleaner reinstall or fresher start than a reset. On the other hand, a reset installs original manufacturer drivers and OEM system files, which may be needed for a customized system. Both methods are capable of retaining personal files.

✏️ **Notes** Before performing a reset, you might want to back up any desktop apps that you've customized or use frequently. Then you can restore the backed-up versions rather than installing fresh copies. To do this, store a copy of selected apps on a flash drive using a third-party app such as CloneApp (*Mirinsoft.com*), and then restore the apps along with their customized settings after the Windows reset is complete.

APPLYING | CONCEPTS   RESETTING A WINDOWS 10 COMPUTER

**A+
CORE 2
3.1**

If you are not able to start Windows, you can use Windows 10 setup media or a recovery drive to launch Windows RE. Drill down to the Troubleshoot screen (refer back to Figure 15-18) and click **Reset this PC** to start the reset.

Here are the steps in Windows 10 to reset a computer using the Settings app:

1. Sign in to Windows using an administrator account. If possible, first back up all personal files.

2. If a recovery partition is present, it will be used for the reset. If there's no recovery partition, insert bootable Windows media such as a recovery drive, system repair disc, or Windows setup media. The reset process will then use the media to install Windows.

3. Open the **Settings** app and click **Update & security**. In the left pane, click **Recovery**, as shown earlier in Figure 15-14. Under *Reset this PC*, click **Get started**.

4. In the *Choose an option* box, shown in Figure 15-32, decide whether to keep your files or to remove everything.

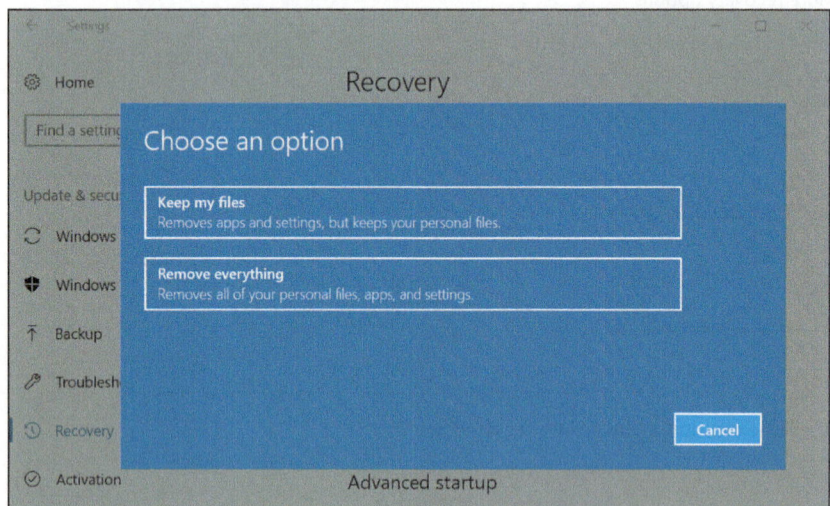

Figure 15-32 Keep your files or remove everything

✏️ **Notes** For a laptop, all-in-one, or other brand-name computer with a recovery partition present, you might see a third option on the *Choose an option* box: Restore factory settings. This option reinstalls the version of Windows that your computer came with (for example, Windows 8.1) and removes your personal files.

(continues)

5. If you click **Keep my files**, you're given a list of all apps that will be removed. If you've recently updated your computer, you might see a warning that you will not be able to undo the update. Click **Next** and then click **Reset** to begin.

6. If you click **Remove everything**, you're given the option to clean only the Windows volume or all volumes on the hard drive. Make your selections and click **Reset** to begin.

APPLYING A WINDOWS 10/7 SYSTEM IMAGE

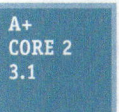

You learned how to create a system image in Chapter 13. System image recovery tends to be an all-or-nothing recovery option where you replace the entire contents of a hard drive with whatever operating system state and personal data are saved in the system image. It recovers all personal files, system files, and installed apps that were in place at the time the system image was most recently created or updated. If your system image is updated regularly, this option could work very well for you when repairing or replacing hardware, such as a failed hard drive. However, if a software-related problem has been building for a while, a recently updated system image won't necessarily fix the root of the problem.

To recover Windows 10/8 using a system image file, reboot the computer into Windows RE, drill down to the **Advanced options** screen (refer back to Figure 15-19), and select **System Image Recovery**. For Windows 7, select **System Image Recovery** on the **System Recovery Options** screen shown earlier in Figure 15-22.

WINDOWS | 8 REFRESHING AND RESETTING A WINDOWS 8 COMPUTER

Windows 8 offers a refresh process that's not available in Windows 10 or Windows 7. In addition, a Windows 8 reset works differently than a Windows 10 reset. Let's see how to perform a Windows 8 refresh and then a reset.

REFRESH A WINDOWS 8 COMPUTER

In Chapter 13, you learned that Windows 8 prefers to use a custom refresh image of the Windows volume rather than the traditional system image. To solve a problem with a corrupted Windows 8 installation, you can perform a refresh in Windows 8. The refresh can use a custom refresh image that has been designated as the active recovery image, a hidden OEM recovery partition on the hard drive, or the Windows 8 setup DVD.

When you refresh a computer, the refresh saves installed apps that use the Windows 8 interface and current user settings and data. Unless you're working with a custom refresh image, Windows settings and desktop applications are lost during a refresh. Here's how to perform a refresh:

1. Because the system will restart a couple of times during the refresh, remove any discs in the optical drive and unplug any bootable external hard drives or USB flash drives. For a laptop, plug in the AC adapter so you don't lose battery power during the refresh. If the computer doesn't have a recovery partition and you haven't made a custom refresh image, insert the Windows setup DVD in the optical drive, which the refresh will use to perform a partial in-place upgrade of Windows 8.

2. Do one of the following, depending on the health of the Windows installation:

   ◢ If you can launch Windows, open the **charms bar**, click **Settings**, click **Change PC settings**, click **Update and recovery**, and click **Recovery**. Click **Get started** under *Refresh your PC without affecting your files* (refer back to Figure 15-15). A warning message appears (see Figure 15-33). Click **Next**. Click **Refresh**.

(continues)

15

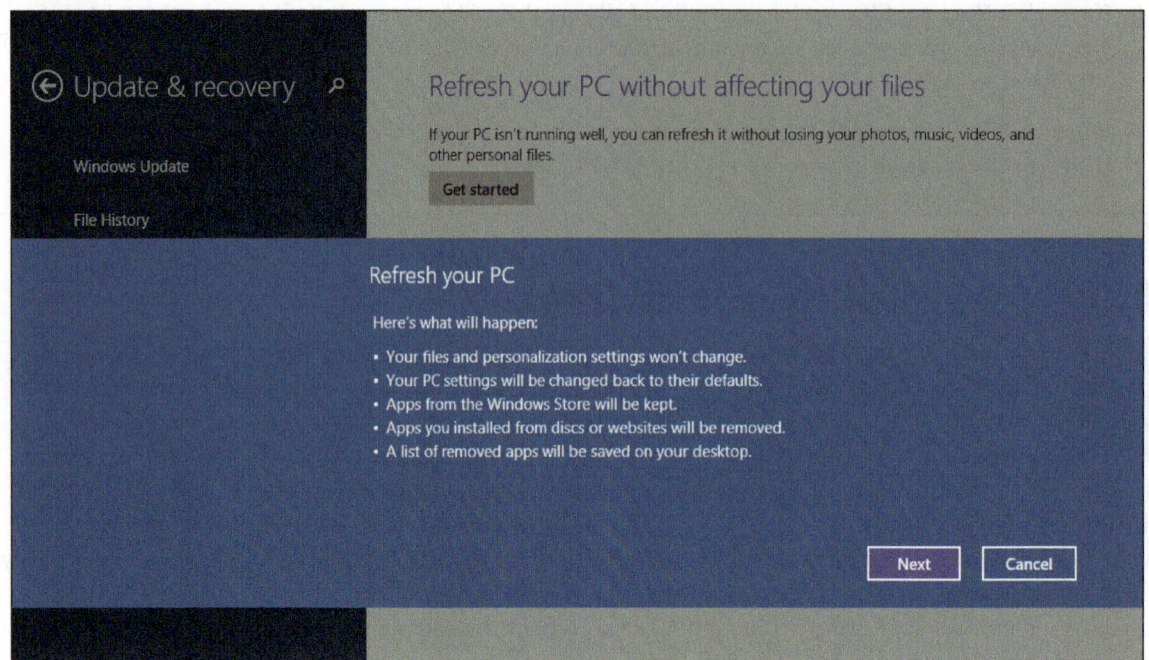

Figure 15-33 Windows lists what to expect from a refresh

> ▲ If you cannot launch Windows, boot from the Windows 8 setup DVD or a recovery drive to launch Windows RE. Drill down to the **Troubleshoot** screen (refer back to Figure 15-18B) and click **Refresh your PC**.

3. Windows verifies there's enough free space on the hard drive to perform the refresh. A lot of space is needed (as much as half the space on the Windows volume) because Windows will store the old Windows installation in a Windows.old folder and will also need space to back up apps and data. If there's not enough space, an error occurs, and you'll need to delete files or folders or move them to a different location to free up enough space, and then start the refresh again.

4. Another warning message appears. Click **Refresh** to continue. Next, user settings, user data, and Windows 8 apps are backed up, and Windows searches for media or an image to use to reinstall Windows. It uses this order for the search:

   a. *It checks for a custom refresh image.* If a custom refresh image was previously made and registered with the system, this image is used to refresh the system. (If desktop applications were included in the image, they are included in the refresh. Any desktop applications that were installed after the refresh image was created are lost and must be manually reinstalled.)

   b. *If no custom refresh image is found, Windows checks for an OEM recovery partition.* If it finds an OEM recovery partition, the image on the partition is used to refresh the computer to its factory state.

   c. *If no image or recovery partition is found, Windows requests the Windows setup DVD if it's not already available.* The refresh process will use the Windows setup DVD to perform a partial in-place upgrade of Windows 8.

5. The system restarts and the refresh begins. Progress is reported as a percentage of completion. The Windows volume is formatted, and Windows is reinstalled from an image or from the Windows setup files. User settings, data, and Windows 8 apps are restored from backup, and the system restarts.

(continues)

Options to Reinstall Windows and

6. The names of desktop applications lost during the refresh are stored in a file named *Removed Apps.html* on the Windows desktop (see Figure 15-34). Open the file to see the list of applications. You'll need to reinstall these applications.

Figure 15-34   View a list of desktop applications lost during the refresh

7. The refresh created a Windows.old folder containing the old Windows installation. After you're sure you don't need anything in it, you can delete the folder to free up the disk space.

RESET A WINDOWS 8 COMPUTER

You might want to perform a Windows 8 reset when you're about to give away a computer, recycle it, or totally want to start over. The Windows volume is formatted and Windows is reinstalled. If an OEM recovery partition is present, the system is reset to its factory state. If there's no recovery partition, the process requests the Windows 8 setup DVD, which it uses to reinstall Windows. All user data and settings and installed apps are lost. You can use the recovery methods provided by the manufacturer (for example, press F12 or F10 at startup) or you can use Windows 8 to reset the system.

Here are the steps to reset a computer in Windows 8:

1. If a recovery partition is present, it will be used for the reset. If there's no recovery partition, insert the Windows setup DVD in the optical drive, which the reset process uses to perform a clean install of Windows.

2. Do one of the following:

   ◢ If you can launch Windows, go to the **Update and recovery** screen and click **Get started** under *Remove everything and reinstall Windows* (refer back to Figure 15-15). A warning message appears. Click **Next**.
   ◢ If you cannot launch Windows, boot from the Windows setup DVD or a recovery drive and make your way to the Troubleshoot screen shown earlier in Figure 15-18B. Click **Reset your PC**.

3. If the system contains more than one volume or hard drive, Windows asks if you want to format all drives or just the Windows volume. Click a box to make your selection.

4. On the next screen (see Figure 15-35), you're asked to decide between a quick format and a thorough format. A thorough format makes it less likely someone can recover data on the drive. Make your selection by clicking a box.

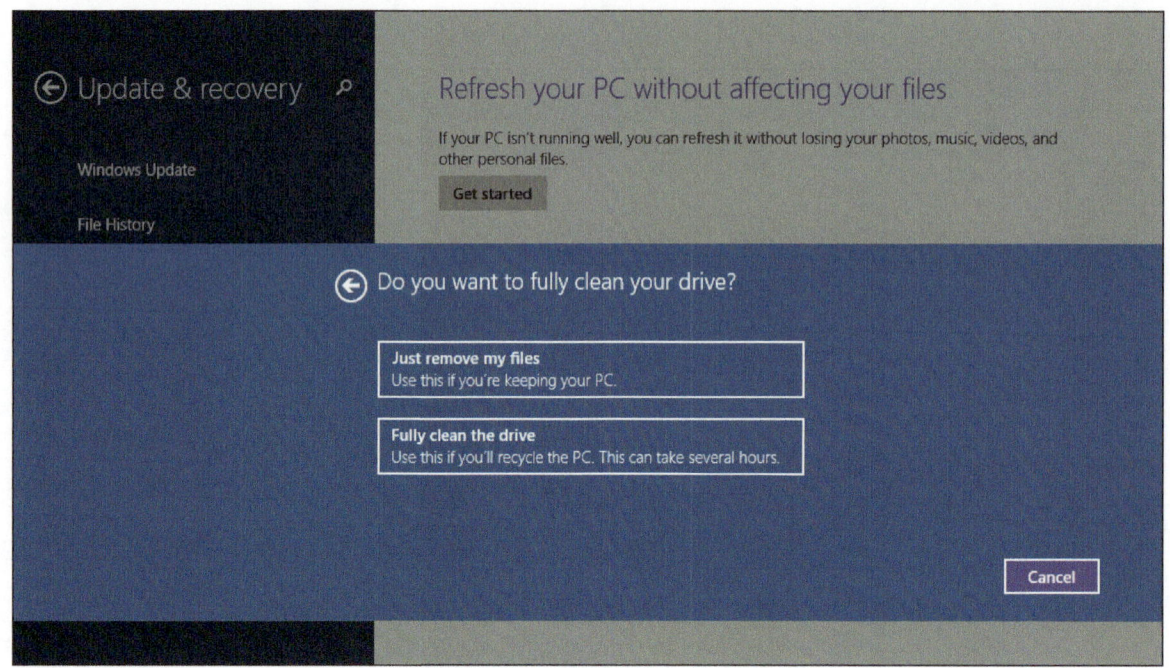

Figure 15-35 Decide what type of format the reset will use

5. On the next screen, another warning appears. Click **Reset** to start the process. The system restarts and resetting begins. After another restart, you can step through the process of preparing Windows for first use.

OEM FACTORY RECOVERY PARTITION

Laptops, all-in-one computers, and brand-name desktops come with the OS preinstalled at the factory. This OEM (original equipment manufacturer) build of the OS is likely to be customized, and for laptops, the drivers might be specific to proprietary devices installed in the laptops.

The laptop or brand-name computer is likely to have a recovery partition on the hard drive that contains a copy of the OS build, device drivers, diagnostics programs, and preinstalled applications needed to restore the system to its factory state. This partition might or might not be hidden. For example, Figure 15-36 shows the Disk Management information for a hard drive on one laptop that has a 16.38-GB recovery partition.

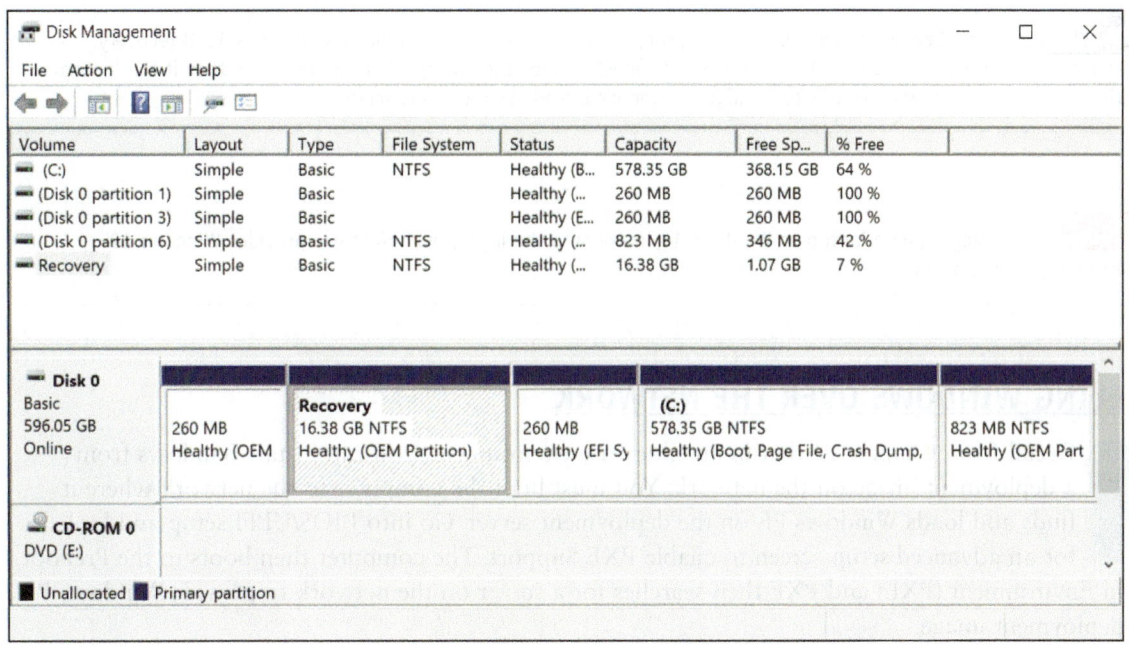

Figure 15-36 This laptop hard drive has a 16.38-GB recovery partition that can be used to recover the system

To know how to access the recovery tools stored on a recovery partition, see the manufacturer's website or look for a message at the beginning of the boot, such as "Press ESC for diagnostics" or "Press F12 to recover the system." For one Sony laptop, you press the red **Assist** button during the boot (see Figure 15-37). When you press the key or button, a menu appears with options to diagnose the problem, to repair the current OS installation, or to completely rebuild the entire hard drive to its factory state.

Figure 15-37 For this laptop, press the Assist button during the boot to launch programs on the recovery partition

If the laptop doesn't have a recovery partition or the partition is corrupted, look for the option to download recovery media from the manufacturer's website and use it to create a bootable USB flash drive or DVD. You can then use the media to install Windows to its factory state.

15

> ✎ **Notes** When you first become responsible for a laptop, use a USB flash drive to make a Windows 10/8 recovery drive that includes the OEM recovery partition in case you must replace the laptop's hard drive. Know that if the laptop is more than three years old, the manufacturer might no longer provide the recovery media.

> ⚡ **Caution** Before upgrading a laptop to Windows 10, make sure the laptop manufacturer provides Windows 10 drivers for laptop components.

INSTALLING WINDOWS OVER THE NETWORK

Recall from Chapter 12 that in an enterprise environment, you can install Windows from a deployment image on the network. You must boot the computer to the network where it finds and loads Windows PE on the deployment server. Go into BIOS/UEFI setup and look for an advanced setup screen to enable PXE Support. The computer then boots to the Preboot eXecution Environment (PXE) and PXE then searches for a server on the network to provide Windows PE and the deployment image.

> ★ **A+ Exam Tip** The A+ Core 2 exam expects you to know how to use a preinstallation environment and a recovery image to help resolve a Windows startup problem.

TROUBLESHOOTING SPECIFIC WINDOWS STARTUP PROBLEMS

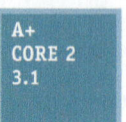

And now the fun begins! With your understanding of the boot process and Windows tools for troubleshooting startup in hand, let's work through a bunch of errors and problems that can affect Windows startup and see what can be done about them. When troubleshooting a startup problem, follow procedures to interview the user, back up important data or verify that you have current backups, research and identify any error messages, and determine what has just changed that might be the source of the problem.

When you know the source of the problem, decide which tool will be the least invasive to use yet still fix the problem. If that doesn't work, move on to the next tool. Remember that tools are described earlier in the chapter from least to most invasive.

IMPORTANT DATA ON THE HARD DRIVE

Troubleshooting a computer problem should always start with the most important question: Is there important data on the hard drive that's not backed up? Even if data is lost or corrupted, you might be able to recover it using Windows tools, third-party file recovery software, or commercial data recovery services. One good product is GetDataBack by Runtime Software (*runtime.org*), which can recover data and program files even when Windows cannot recognize the drive.

For less than $30, you can purchase a SATA-to-USB converter kit (see Figure 15-38) that includes a data cable and power adapter. You can use one of these kits to temporarily connect a desktop or laptop hard drive to a USB port on a working computer. Set the drive beside your computer and plug one end of the data cable into the drive and the other into the USB port. The AC adapter supplies power to the drive. While power is getting to the drive, be careful not to touch the circuit board on the drive.

Figure 15-38 Use a SATA-to-USB converter to recover data from a drive using a SATA connector

Using File Explorer or Windows Explorer, you can browse the drive and copy data to other media. After you have saved the data, you can use diagnostic software from the hard drive manufacturer to examine the drive and possibly repair it or return the drive to its own computer and start troubleshooting there.

ERROR MESSAGES AND PROBLEMS

A+ CORE 2 3.1, 4.3

Problems that prevent Windows from booting can be caused by hardware, device drivers, services, applications, or Windows. This section covers what to do when error messages appear on a black or blue screen or when Windows gets corrupted.

STARTUP ERROR MESSAGES ON A BLACK SCREEN

Generally, problems that present as white text on a black screen are caused by hardware. Here are some possible error messages:

- No OS found
- A disk read error occurred
- Invalid boot disk
- Hard drive not found
- Disk boot failure
- No boot device found

Here is what's happening and what to do about it:

1. Start with the error message. Research the text shown on the screen so that you understand the problem and get solutions from trusted websites.

2. If you see spinning white dots on a black screen, Windows may be installing updates before it launches. Wait. It may take some time for the update installations to complete. If the system hangs indefinitely, the updates might be causing a problem. If a reboot doesn't solve the problem, boot into Windows RE and return to a previous version of Windows.

3. Consider that startup BIOS/UEFI might not be able to communicate with the hard drive. Check BIOS/UEFI setup for the boot sequence. Update the boot order so that you can try booting from another device.

15

4. For Windows 10/8, try going into BIOS/UEFI setup and disabling any quick boot features. This causes BIOS/UEFI to do a more thorough job of POST and reports more information on the screen as it performs POST.

5. Windows might halt and show a black screen when it encounters a video problem at startup. Try restarting the system in Safe Mode, as you learned to do earlier in the chapter. Then check Event Viewer for clues, update Windows, and use Device Manager to roll back drivers or disable or uninstall the video adapter. If you cannot boot into Safe Mode, launch Windows RE and use Startup Repair, Memory Diagnostics, and the chkdsk /r command to check Windows, memory, and the hard drive.

6. The hard drive might be failing. To recover data from the drive, move it to another computer and install it as a second hard drive.

PROBLEMS WITH USER PROFILES

If Windows bogs down right after the user signs in, the problem might be with loading the user profile. For a slow profile load, the user might see a black screen with spinning dots for several minutes. To fix the problem, try these tasks listed in the least invasive order:

1. Try the Windows Troubleshooting applet that you learned about in Chapter 14. Go to **Control Panel** and click **Troubleshooting**. On the Troubleshooting page, click **Run maintenance tasks** and follow the on-screen directions.

2. Make sure Windows updates are applied.

3. Run **sfc /scannow** to fix problems with system files.

4. Reduce startup items. Compare the time to load a user profile when starting Windows normally and during a clean boot.

5. Apply a restore point that was created before the problem started.

6. For Windows 10, try a repair upgrade.

7. Create a new user profile. You can copy user data files from the old profile into the new user profile namespace. (Locations of these files are given in Chapter 14.)

If the user profile gets corrupted, it might not load at all and you might see the error message, "The User Profile Service failed the logon." To rebuild the user profiles, do the following to repair Windows system files that affect the corrupted profiles:

◢ Do as many of the above steps as you can do when a single user profile is slow to load.
◢ Following directions given in Chapter 14, use the DISM commands to repair corrupted Windows system files.
◢ For Windows 10, perform a reset. Be sure to back up data before you do a reset.

Sometimes you can recover a user account by deleting it without deleting its files and then creating a new one with the same name.

To delete the account and keep its files, open Control Panel, click **User Accounts**, select the account, and click **Delete the account**. In the Delete Account window (see Figure 15-39), click **Keep Files** and then click **Delete Account**. The files are stored in a folder on your desktop and the account and its settings are deleted. Create a new account with the same name. Then you can copy the files saved to your desktop folder to the new user profile namespace.

Figure 15-39 Delete a user account and its settings and keep the files in the user profile

If this doesn't work, you can edit the registry to delete an old profile or repair a corrupted one:

1. Launch the Registry Editor and back up this registry key:

   HKEY_LOCAL_MACHINE\SOFTWARE\Microsoft\Windows NT\CurrentVersion\ProfileList

2. Drill down into each S-1-5 folder in the above key until you find the correct user profile in the ProfileImagePath subkey (see Figure 15-40).

3. If the profile has a State subkey, set it to 0, as shown in the figure. If the profile has a RefCount subkey, set it to 0.

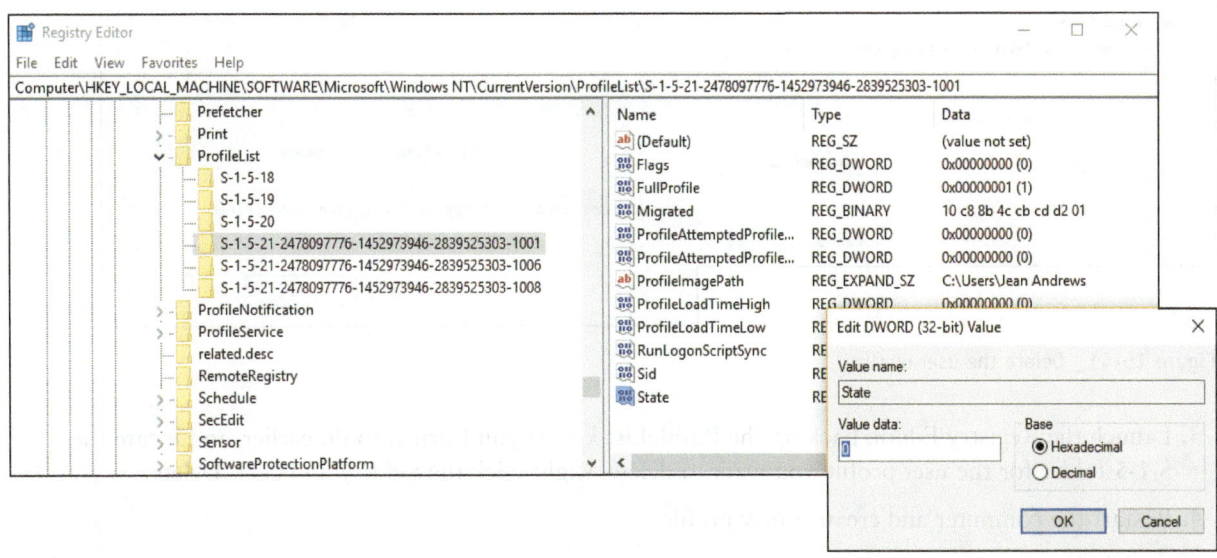

Figure 15-40 Set the State subkey value to 0

4. Close the Registry Editor and restart the computer.

> **Notes** If you're searching for the correct S-1-5 folder and it has .bak in the name, remove .bak from the folder name. To rename a folder, right-click it and click **Rename**.
>
> If you see two S-1-5 folders with the same name, except one has .bak at the end, you must switch the names: First rename the folder that does not contain .bak to .hold. Then remove the .bak from the other folder name. Next, rename the .hold folder to .bak. Then edit the S-1-5 folder that does not have .bak in the name.

If you still have problems with a user profile, you can follow these steps to delete the profile:

1. Manually copy any important data files in the user profile namespace to a new location. Recall that you can find these files in the C:\Users*username* subfolders.

2. Go to **Control Panel** and open the **System** window. Click **Advanced system settings**. In the System Properties box, select the **Advanced** tab and click **Settings** under User Profiles. See Figure 15-41. In the list of user profiles, select the profile and click **Delete**.

Figure 15-41 Delete the user profile

3. Launch the Registry Editor, back up the **ProfileList** key as you learned to do earlier, and locate the **S-1-5** folder for the user profile you want to delete. Right-click the **Sid** key and click **Delete**.

4. Restart the computer and create a new profile.

ERROR MESSAGES ON A BLUE SCREEN

Hardware and software errors can present as error messages on a Windows blue screen of death (BSOD) and are called stop errors. Also, sometimes Windows hangs with the pinwheel spinning, continuously restarts, or does an abrupt and improper shutdown. A BSOD, or stop error, happens when processes running in kernel mode encounter a problem and Windows must stop the system. Figure 15-42 shows an example of a Windows 8 blue screen with the stop error at the top and the specific number of the error near the bottom of the screen. Windows 10 blue screens may be much simpler, such as the one shown in Figure 15-43.

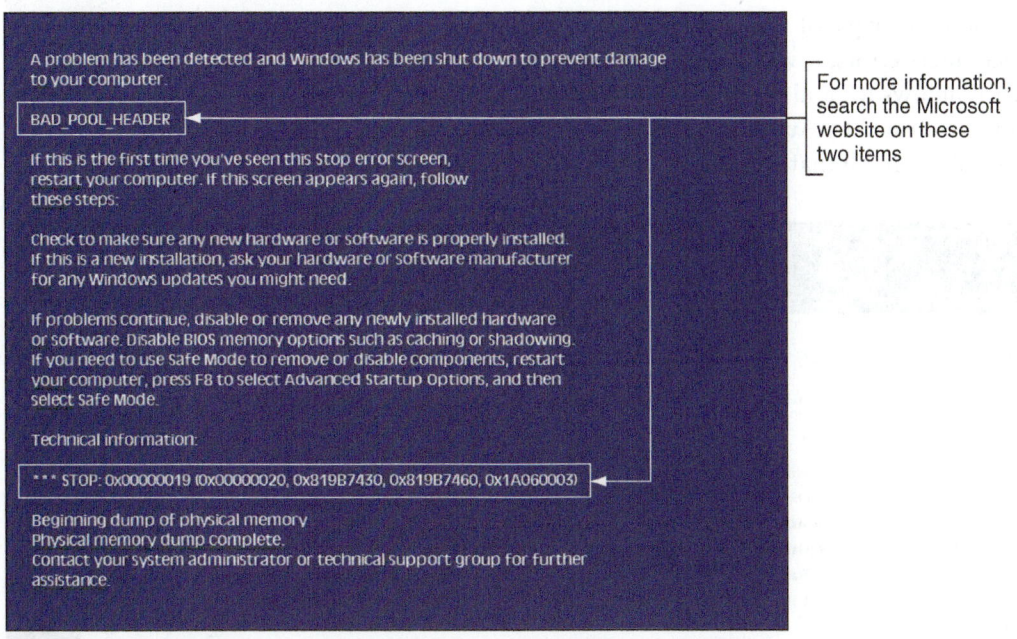

For more information, search the Microsoft website on these two items

Figure 15-42 A blue screen of death (BSOD) is definitively not a good sign; time to start troubleshooting

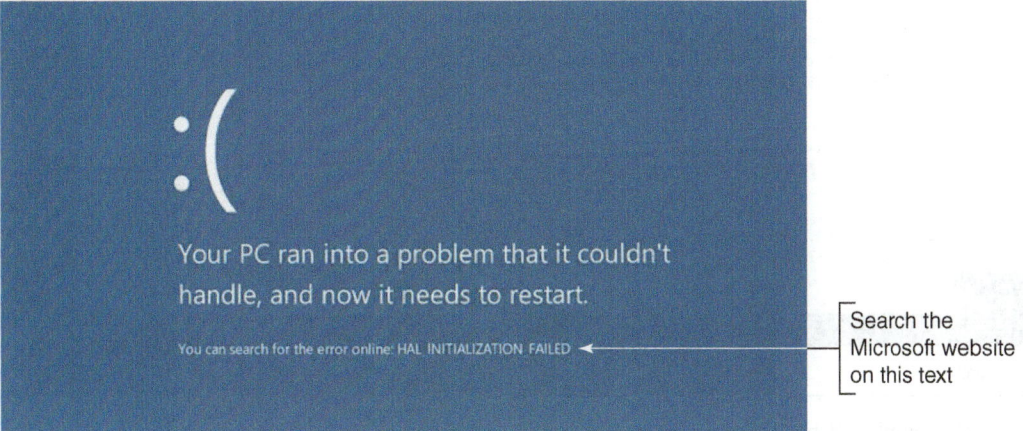

Search the Microsoft website on this text

Figure 15-43 The Windows 10 stop error screen

A stop error can be caused by a corrupted Windows update, a corrupted registry, a system file that is missing or damaged, a device driver that is missing or damaged, bad memory, or a corrupted or failing hard drive. Stop errors can occur during or after startup. Here's what to do when you get a stop error:

1. As for the tools that are useful in solving stop errors, put the web at the top of your list! (But don't forget that some sites are unreliable and others mean you harm.) Search the Microsoft websites on the items labeled in Figure 15-42 or Figure 15-43.

2. Disconnect any peripheral devices that might be causing trouble, such as a docking station, USB device, projector, or extra monitor.

3. Reboot the system. Immediately after a reboot following a stop error, Windows displays an error message box or bubble with useful information. Follow the links in the box.

4. If possible, restart the system and enable boot logging. Check the C:\Windows\Ntbtlog.txt file to see if the correct driver files loaded.

5. Restart the computer a couple of times. Sometimes that's all you need to do to solve a problem. If Windows encounters errors, it will launch an automatic repair. If that doesn't fix the problem, you can launch Windows RE and restart Windows in **Safe Mode with Networking**. In Safe Mode, examine the log file created by Automatic Repair at C:\Windows\System32\LogFiles\Srt\SrtTrail.txt. See Figure 15-44. Also, recall that Safe Mode creates its own log file at C:\Windows\Ntbtlog.txt.

Figure 15-44   Examine the log file left by Automatic Repair

> ✎ **Notes** If the stop error prevents Windows from loading the desktop and F8 has not yet been enabled at startup, you can force automatic repair by turning off the computer a couple of times as Windows launches.

ERRORS WITH HARDWARE AND DEVICE DRIVERS

If the blue screen names a device or device driver that caused the problem, do the following:

1. If the driver has been recently updated and the Safe Mode desktop is loaded, open **Device Manager** and roll back the driver.

2. Consider that the device driver might have been updated along with a Windows update. For recent Windows updates, try to return to a previous version of Windows.

3. A Windows update might fix the problem. Open the Settings app and update Windows.

4. Use Device Manager to uninstall the device. When given the option, select **Delete the driver software for this device**. Then reboot the system.

5. If the stop error does not identify the device but names a program file, open File Explorer or Windows Explorer on a working computer to locate the program file. Driver files are stored in the C:\Windows\System32\drivers folder. Right-click the file and select **Properties** from the shortcut menu. The Details tab of the Properties box tells you the purpose of the file (see Figure 15-45). You can then reinstall the device or program that caused the problem.

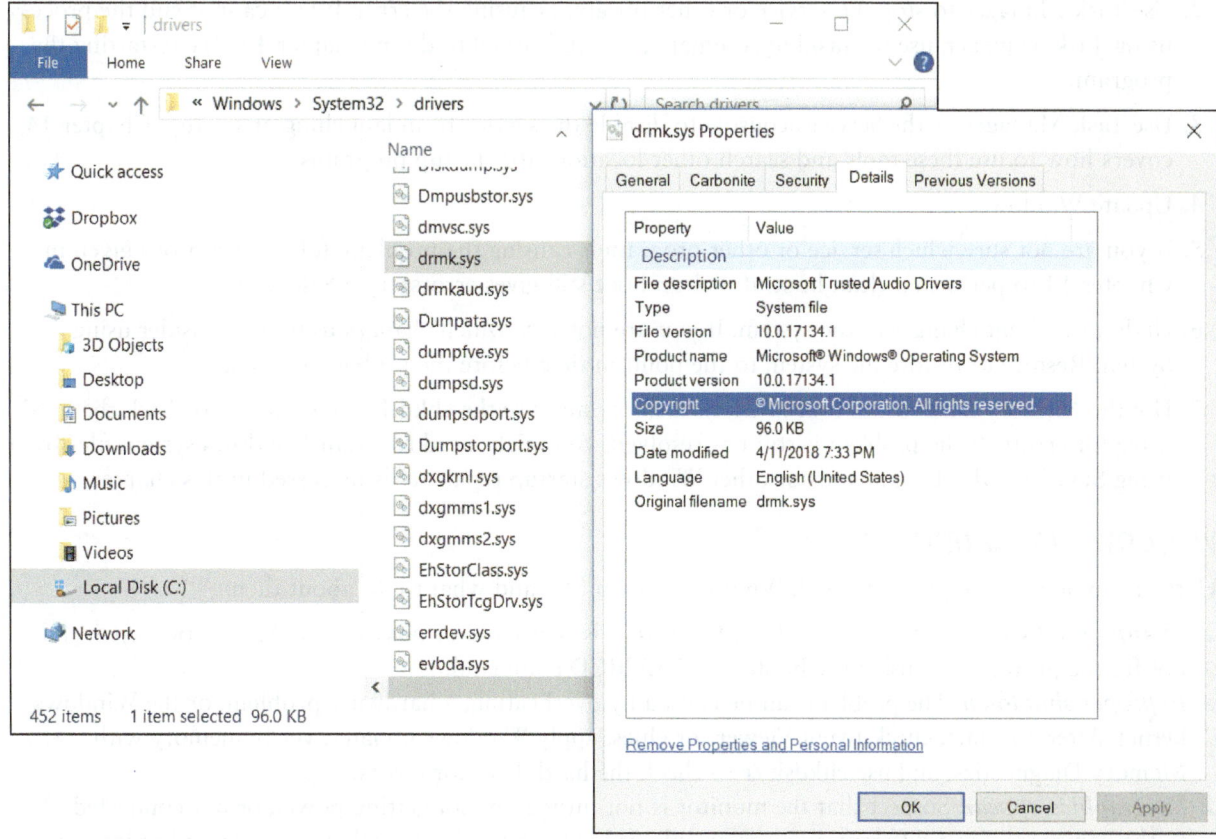

Figure 15-45 Use the Details tab of a driver's Properties box to identify the purpose of the driver

6. If you cannot start Windows in Safe Mode, use Windows RE to open a command prompt window. Then back up the registry and open the Registry Editor using the **regedit** command. Drill down to the service or device key. The key that loads services and drivers can be found in this location:

HKEY_LOCAL_MACHINE\System\CurrentControlSet\Services

Disable the service or driver by changing the Start value to 0x4. Close the Registry Editor and reboot. If the problem goes away, use the copy command to replace the service or driver program file, and restart the service or driver.

> ⚡ **Caution**   Consider that the device might be physically damaged. If you feel excessive heat coming from the computer case or a peripheral device, immediately unplug the device or power down the system. Don't turn the device or system back on until the problem is solved; you don't want to start a fire! Other symptoms that indicate potential danger are strong electrical odors, unusual noises, no noise (such as when the fan is not working to keep the system cool), liquid spills on a device, and visible damage such as a frayed cable, melted plastic, or smoke. In these situations, turn off the equipment immediately.

15

ERRORS WITH SERVICES OR OTHER PROGRAMS

Applications don't generally cause stop errors because they all run in user mode rather than kernel mode. When a blue screen with a stop error identifies a service or other program that failed to start or is causing problems, do the following:

1. Check Event Viewer, which might provide events it has logged. Recall that critical errors and warnings are recorded in the Administrative Events log.

2. Use Task Manager to stop the service or other program causing the error. If you cannot end the process using Task Manager, use the taskkill command, as you learned to do in Chapter 14. Try restarting the program.

3. Use Task Manager or the Services console to disable the service from launching at startup. Chapter 14 covers how to use these tools and search other locations for startup programs.

4. Update Windows.

5. If you are not sure which service or other program is causing the problem, follow directions given in Chapter 14 to perform a clean boot. If a clean boot still gives errors, try a Safe boot.

6. Undo any recent changes to the system. If you are not sure which changes to undo, consider using System Restore to restore the system to the point in time before the problem started.

7. Use the Memory Diagnostics tool to check memory and use the **chkdsk /r** command to check the hard drive for errors. If the problem is still not resolved, you might need to repair Windows system files by using SFC and DISM commands or other Windows startup repair tools discussed in this chapter.

WINDOWS IS CORRUPTED

Here are some possible problems with Windows system files and what to do about them:

- *Missing Boot Configuration Data*. If the BCD store is corrupted or missing and Automatic Repair did not fix the problem, try using the **bootrec /rebuildBCD** command.
- *Improper shutdown*. The problem can be caused by overheating, a hardware problem, or the Windows kernel. After a restart, check Event Viewer for clues, apply Windows updates, verify memory with Memory Diagnostics, and use **chkdsk /r** to check the hard drive for errors.
- *No graphics appear*. Suspect that the monitor is not turned on, not getting power, or not connected to the computer. Try a different monitor or onboard video port. Try launching a command prompt in Windows RE and use it to perform a System Restore.

After you have done your best to back up user data and troubleshoot problems with hardware and applications, you may decide the Windows installation is beyond repair and it's time to reimage or reload Windows. As you learned in this chapter, the tools to use to reimage or reload Windows, listed in the least intrusive order, are the Windows 10 previous version (if available), a Windows 10 repair upgrade, Windows 10 Fresh Start, a Windows 10 reset, and applying a system image. For Windows 8, your options are a refresh and a reset. For Windows 7, your option is applying a system image. As a last resort, you can perform a clean installation of Windows 10/8/7, as you learned in Chapter 12. After you have Windows up and running again, you can restore the user data from backups.

>> *CHAPTER SUMMARY*

Understanding the Boot Process

- When you first turn on a system, startup BIOS/UEFI on the motherboard takes control and performs POST to examine hardware components and then find an operating system to load.

- Windows startup is managed by the Windows Boot Manager. For a BIOS system, the program is bootmgr. For a UEFI system, the program is bootmgfw.efi. The Windows Boot Loader is winload.exe or winload.efi. The Boot Configuration Data (BCD) store contains Windows startup settings.

What to Do Before a Problem Occurs

◢ Before a startup problem occurs, you can keep good backups, create a system image, configure the F8 key at startup, and create recovery boot media.

Tools for Least Invasive Solutions

◢ The Windows Recovery Environment (Windows RE) can be started from within Windows, from the Windows setup DVD or flash drive, from a recovery drive, or from a system repair disc. For Windows 7, press F8 at startup to launch Windows RE.

◢ Tools for startup troubleshooting include startup repair, startup settings, System Restore, Safe Mode, enabling boot logging, SFC, and the chkdsk, diskpart, bootrec, and bootsect commands.

Options to Reinstall Windows

◢ Tools that can be used to reinstall Windows are the Windows 10 previous version, a repair upgrade, Fresh Start, and a reset. Windows 8 tools are a refresh and a reset. With Windows 10/7, you can apply a system image. Some manufacturers offer a recovery partition on the hard drive to restore a computer to factory state. You can also reinstall Windows from Windows setup media.

Troubleshooting Specific Windows Startup Problems

◢ If a hard drive contains valuable data but will not boot, you might be able to recover the data by installing the drive in another system as the second, nonbooting hard drive.

◢ Use the web to research stop errors by the error title and error number listed on a black or blue screen.

◢ Improper shutdowns are most likely hardware related. Event Viewer might record failures. Use Memory Diagnostics and chkdsk to check memory and the hard drive. Consider overheating as a source of the problem.

◢ When a device or service causes the system to hang during a normal boot, boot into Safe Mode or perform a clean boot and disable the device or service. System Restore can return the system to a previously saved restore point before the problem occurred.

>> KEY TERMS

For explanations of key terms, see the Glossary for this text.

bcdedit	bootsect	recovery drive	warm boot
blue screen of death (BSOD)	cold boot	recovery partition	Windows 8 reset
	Fresh Start	refresh	Windows Boot Loader
Boot Configuration Data (BCD) store	hard boot	repair upgrade	Windows Recovery Environment (Windows RE)
booting	Last Known Good Configuration	soft boot	
bootrec	POST (power-on self test)	startup repair	wpeinit
		system repair disc	

>> THINKING CRITICALLY

These questions are designed to prepare you for the critical thinking required for the A+ exams and may use content from other chapters and the web.

1. As a computer starts up, you see an error message about the HAL. At what point in startup does this error occur?

    a. When BIOS/UEFI is searching for an OS using devices listed in the boot priority order

    b. When Windows attempts to load the user profile

15

    c. When Windows attempts to launch critical device drivers

    d. When Windows attempts to launch the Windows kernel

2. Which Windows program must be running before a user can sign in to Windows?

    a. Kernel.exe

    b. Userinit.exe

    c. Explorer.exe

    d. Lsass.exe

    e. All of the above

3. As a computer starts up, you see an error message about a missing operating system. At what point in startup does this error occur?

    a. When BIOS/UEFI is searching for an OS using devices listed in the boot priority order

    b. When Windows attempts to load the user profile

    c. When Windows attempts to launch critical device drivers

    d. When Windows attempts to launch the Windows kernel

4. Your friend sees an error message during Windows startup about a corrupted bootmgr file. He has another computer with a matching configuration and decides to copy the bootmgr file from the working computer to the computer with the problem. Where can he locate the bootmgr file?

    a. C:\Boot\bootmgr

    b. System Reserved\Boot\bootmgr

    c. System Reserved\bootmgr

    d. All of the above

5. In question 4 above, your friend is having problems finding the bootmgr file and asks for your help. What is your best response?

    a. Use diskpart commands to "unhide" and locate the file.

    b. Use the File Explorer options applet to unhide the hidden bootmgr file.

    c. Explain to your friend that performing a startup repair is a better option.

    d. Explain to your friend that he can use the bootrec command to fix the bootmgr file without having to copy another file to the computer.

6. You are seeing multiple errors about device drivers failing to launch at startup. Of the following, which is the best option to try first? Second?

    a. Restore the SYSTEM hive from backup.

    b. Restore the SAM hive from backup.

    c. Perform a startup repair.

    d. Perform a Windows 10 reset.

7. A stop error halts the Windows 10 system while it is booting, and the booting starts over in an endless loop of restarts. How can you solve this problem?

    a. Use the Windows Startup Settings screen to disable automatic restarts.

    b. Press F8 at startup and then disable automatic restarts.

    c. Launch Windows 10 from setup media and perform a Windows 10 reset.

    d. Press F9 at startup and then disable automatic restarts.

8. If you are having a problem with a driver, which of the following should you try first? Second?

   a. Update the driver.

   b. Use System Restore to apply a restore point.

   c. Update Windows.

   d. Perform a clean boot.

9. When error messages indicate that the Windows registry is corrupted and you cannot boot from the hard drive, what tool or method is the first best option to fix the problem? The second best option?

   a. Use bootable media to launch Windows RE and use System Restore to apply a restore point.

   b. Use bootable media to launch Windows RE and perform a startup repair.

   c. Use bootable media to launch Windows RE and then use commands to recover the registry from backup.

   d. Refresh Windows using a system image or custom refresh image.

10. Your Windows system boots to a blue screen stop error and no Start screen or desktop. What do you do first?

    a. Reinstall Windows.

    b. Use the web to research the stop error messages and numbers.

    c. Attempt to boot into Windows RE using the Windows setup DVD or a recovery drive.

    d. Verify that the system is getting power.

11. You have important data on your hard drive that is not backed up and your Windows installation is so corrupted you know that you must refresh the entire installation. What do you do first?

    a. Use System Restore to apply a restore point.

    b. Make every attempt to recover the data.

    c. Perform an in-place upgrade of Windows.

    d. Reformat the hard drive and reinstall Windows.

12. Your computer displays the error message "A disk read error occurred." You try to boot from the Windows setup DVD and you get the same error. What is most likely the problem?

    a. The Windows setup DVD is scratched or damaged in some way.

    b. The hard drive is so damaged the system cannot read from the DVD.

    c. Both the optical drive and the hard drive have failed.

    d. The boot device order is set to boot from the hard drive before the optical drive.

13. When a driver is giving problems in Windows 10, which tool offers the least intrusive solution?

    a. Device Manager

    b. Windows Update

    c. System Restore

    d. Registry Editor

14. An error message is displayed during Windows startup about a service that has failed to start, and then the system locks up. You try to boot into Safe Mode, but get the same error message. What do you try next?

    a. Use the command prompt to edit the registry.

    b. Boot to Windows RE and enable boot logging.

    c. Perform an upgrade repair of Windows 10.

    d. Boot to Windows RE and perform a startup repair.

15

15. Stop errors happen when which type of processes encounter an error?

    a. Processes created by applications

    b. Processes created by Windows components running in user mode

    c. Processes created by Windows components running in kernel mode

    d. Processes created by anti-malware software

16. What is the command to use the System File Checker to immediately verify and repair system files?

17. What is the path and name of the log file created when you enable boot logging on the Windows 10/8 Startup Settings menu?

18. What information is contained in the C:\Windows\System32\LogFiles\SRT\SRTTrail.txt file?

>> HANDS-ON PROJECTS

Hands-On | Project 15-1 Using Boot Logs and System Information to Research Startup

Boot logs can be used to generate a list of drivers that were loaded during a normal startup and during a Safe Mode startup. Do the following to use boot logs to research startup:

1. Boot to the normal Windows desktop with boot logging enabled. Save the boot log just created to a different name or location so it will not be overwritten on the next boot.

2. Reboot the system in Safe Mode, which also creates a boot log. Compare the two logs, identifying differences in drivers loaded during the two boots. You can print both files and lay them side by side for comparison. An easier method is to compare the files using the Compare tool in Microsoft Word.

3. Use the System Information utility or other methods to identify the hardware devices loaded during normal startup but not loaded in Safe Mode. Which devices on your system did not load in Safe Mode?

As you identify the drivers not loaded during Safe Mode, these registry keys might help with your research:

▲ Lists drivers and services loaded during Safe Mode: HKLM\System\CurrentControlSet\Control\SafeBoot\ Minimal

▲ Lists drivers and services loaded during Safe Mode with Networking: HKLM\System\CurrentControlSet\ Control\SafeBoot\Network

Hands-On | Project 15-2 Taking Ownership and Replacing a Windows System File

In Chapter 14, you learned to use SFC and DISM commands to find and replace corrupted Windows system files. SFC keeps a log of its actions at C:\Windows\Logs\CBS\CBS.log, and DISM keeps a log at C:\Windows\Logs\DISM\dism. log. Sometimes these logs or BSOD error screens reveal the name and location of corrupted system or device driver files that Windows tools cannot replace. In this situation, you can manually replace the file. To do so, you can use the takeown command to take ownership of a file and the icacls command to get full access to the file. The Microsoft Knowledge Base Article 929833 at *support.microsoft.com* explains how to use these two commands.

(continues)

Do the following to practice manually replacing a system file:

1. Boot the computer into Safe Mode with Command Prompt.

2. Take ownership and gain full access to the C:\Windows\System32\jscript.dll file. What commands did you use?

3. Rename the jscript.dll file to jscript.dll.hold. Run the **sfc /scannow** command. Did SFC restore the jscript.dll file? What is the path and file name of the log file that lists repairs?

4. SFC restores a file using files accessed from Windows Update or stored on the Windows setup DVD or other folders on the hard drive. If SFC cannot restore a file, you might find a fresh copy in the C:\Windows\winsxs folder or its subfolders. Search these folders. Did you find a version of jscript.dll that is the same file size as the one in C:\Windows\System32? Other than the C:\Windows\winsxs folder, where else can you find a known good copy of a corrupted system file or device driver file?

> ✏️ **Notes** To use a command prompt window to search for a file in a folder and its subfolders, use the **dir /s** command.

Hands-On | Project 15-3   Viewing the BCD Store

On two or more computers, open an elevated command prompt window and use the bcdedit /enum command to view the BCD store. One BCD store is shown in Figure 15-46.

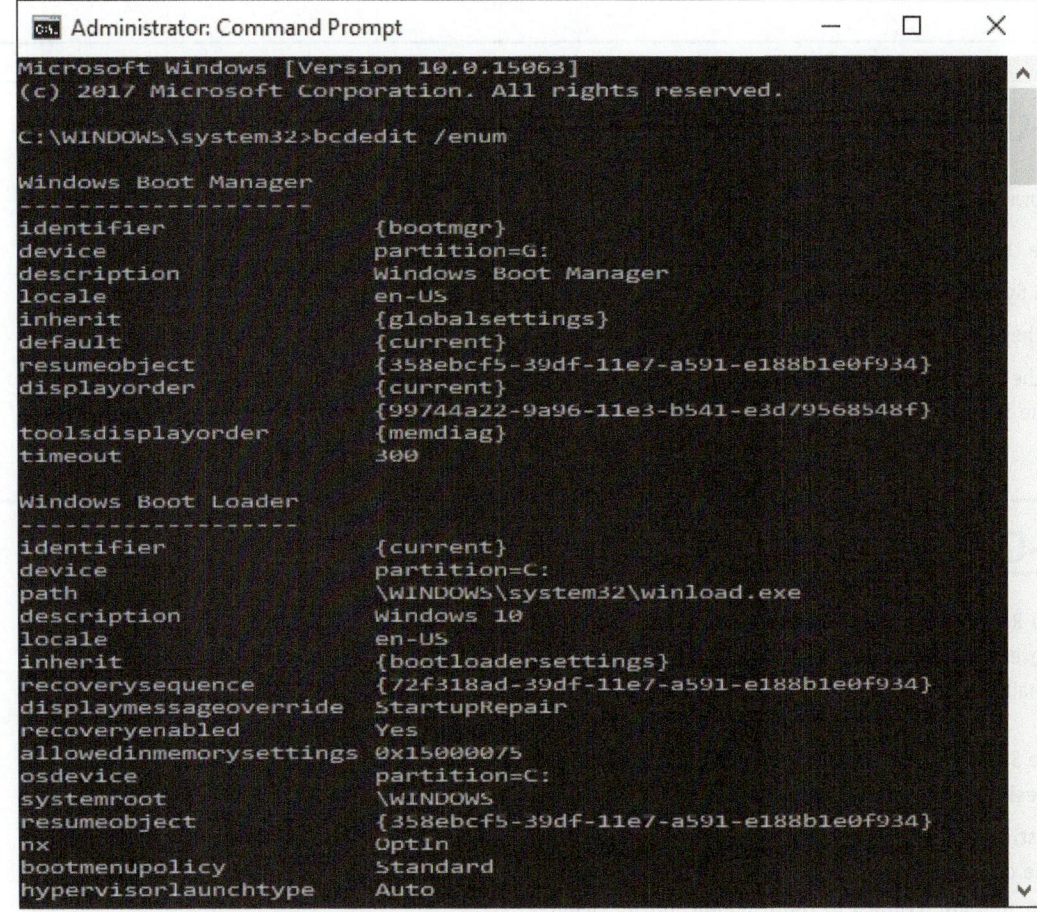

Figure 15-46 A BCD store on a computer that uses the GPT partitioning system

15

(continues)

Answer the following questions:

1. Can you view the BCD store and determine if the system is using the MBR or GPT partitioning system? Why or why not?

2. Explain how you can look at the BCD store and tell if the system is a single boot or multiboot system.

Hands-On | Project 15-4   **Researching Laptop Online Resources**

Suppose the hard drive in a laptop has failed and you must replace the hard drive with a new one and then install Windows on the new drive. What online resources can help you? Do the following to find a service manual and recovery files for a laptop to which you have access, such as one you or a friend owns:

1. What are the brand, model, and serial number of the laptop?

2. What is the website of the laptop manufacturer? Print a webpage on that site that shows you what recovery files you can download to install Windows on a new hard drive for the laptop.

3. If the website provides a service manual, download the manual and print the pages that show how to replace the hard drive.

4. Based on what you have learned about online support for this laptop, what backups or recovery media do you think need to be created now, before a hard drive crash occurs?

Hands-On | Project 15-5   **Practicing Using System Recovery Options**

Launch Windows RE and do the following:

1. Execute the startup repair process. What were the results?

2. Launch System Restore. What is the most recent restore point? (Do not apply the restore point.)

3. Using the command prompt window, open the Registry Editor. What command did you use? Close the editor.

4. Using the command prompt window, copy a file from your Documents folder to a flash drive. Were you able to copy the file successfully? If not, what error message(s) did you receive?

Hands-On | Project 15-6   **Using Startup Repair**

When Startup Repair attempts to fix a system, it creates a log file with information about the steps taken during the repair process. If Startup Repair doesn't fix the system, you can use the log file to investigate the problem and perhaps manually fix it. Do the following to practice using Startup Repair and examine its log file:

1. Use the Settings app in Windows to launch Windows RE. From the initial Windows Startup Menu, click **Troubleshoot**, **Advanced options**, and then **Startup Repair**.

2. Diagnostics of the system are made and the location of the log file appears. Note the path and name of the file. The default location of the log file is C:\Windows\System32\LogFiles\SRT\SRTTrail.txt. Click **Advanced options**. You are returned to the Windows Startup Menu.

(continues)

3. To view the log file from the Windows RE command prompt, click **Troubleshoot** and click **Command Prompt**.

4. In the command prompt window, enter the command **c:** to access the hard drive. (You might need to use a different drive depending on the log file location reported in Step 2.)

5. Use the following command to go to the directory where the log file is located:

   `cd \Windows\System32\LogFiles\SRT`

6. To use Notepad to view the file contents, enter the following command:

   `notepad.exe SRTTrail.txt`

7. In the log file, look for information about a failed test.

>> REAL PROBLEMS, REAL SOLUTIONS

REAL PROBLEM 15-1 Sabotaging a Windows System

In a lab environment, follow these steps to find out if you can corrupt a Windows system so that it will not boot, and then repair the system. (This problem can be done using a Windows installation in a virtual machine.) Don't forget about the takeown and icacls commands discussed in this chapter.

1. Rename or move one of the program files listed in Table 15-1. Which program file did you select? In what folder did you find it?

2. Restart your system. Did an error occur? Check in Explorer. Is the file restored? What Windows feature repaired the problem?

3. Try other methods of sabotaging the Windows system, but carefully record exactly what you did to sabotage the boot. Can you make the boot fail?

4. Now recover the Windows system. List the steps you took to get the system back to good working order.

REAL PROBLEM 15-2 Creating a Stop Error

This project is more difficult than it might first appear. Using a VM with Windows 10 installed, create a BSOD or stop error. Take a screenshot of the BSOD. List the steps you took to make Windows 10 crash. Tip: Search the web on **Windows 10 stop error** and try to reproduce the problem.

REAL PROBLEM 15-3 Recovering Data from a Hard Drive

To practice recovering data from a hard drive that won't boot, create a folder on a VM with Windows 10 installed. Put data files in the folder. What is the name of your folder? Move the hard drive to another working VM and install it as a second hard drive in the system. Copy the data folder to the primary hard drive in this second VM. Now return the hard drive to the original VM and verify that the VM starts with no errors. List the steps you used in this project.

REAL PROBLEM 15-4 Preparing a Corrupted Hard Drive for a Clean Windows Installation

You can use a VM to practice using the diskpart command to prepare a corrupted hard drive for a clean installation of Windows. Do the following:

1. Using a VM you have already created in this course, add a second hard drive to the VM. Start the VM and open an elevated command prompt window.

15

2. Enter the diskpart command. At the diskpart prompt, enter the commands shown in Table 15-4 to clean all partitions off the drive, create a new partition, and format it using the NTFS file system. Then open File Explorer in your VM and verify that the second hard drive is present and available for use.

Diskpart Command	Description
list disk	List the hard drives installed. Select the one to clean based on the size of the drive.
select disk 1	Make Disk 1 the selected hard drive.
clean	Clean the partition table and all partitions from the drive.
convert gpt	Install the GPT partitioning system.
create partition primary	Create the primary partition.
list partition	List the partitions. Note the number of the primary partition.
select partition 2	Select the primary partition.
format fs=ntfs quick	Format using the NTFS file system.
Assign letter W	Assign a drive letter to the volume.
detail partition	Display partition details.
detail volume	Display volume details.
exit	Exit diskpart.

Table 15-4 Diskpart commands to partition and format a GPT hard drive

Notes For a complete list of diskpart commands, go to the Microsoft support site (*technet.microsoft.com*) and search on "Diskpart Command-Line Options."

CHAPTER 16

Securing and Sharing Windows Resources

After completing this chapter, you will be able to:

- Secure a Windows personal computer using Windows tools on the local computer

- Share and secure files and folders on a network

- Support network resources using Active Directory

In this chapter, you learn about some tools and techniques to secure the resources on a personal computer, small network, and Windows domain. Later in your career as a support technician, you can build on the skills learned in this chapter to implement even more security, such as controlling how Windows stores its passwords. However, keep in mind that even the best security will eventually fail. As a thief once said, "Locks are for honest people," and a thief will eventually find a way to break through. Security experts tell us that security measures basically make it more difficult and time consuming for a thief to break through so that she gets discouraged and moves on to easier targets.

This chapter also explains how to lock down a personal computer from unauthorized access. Because security is always a huge concern when dealing with networks, you learn how to share resources on the network while protecting them from people who should not have access. Finally, you'll learn how to use Active Directory to manage users and resources on a network.

SECURING A WINDOWS PERSONAL COMPUTER

**A+
CORE 2
1.4, 1.5,
1.6, 1.8,
2.2, 2.6,
2.7**
When you have a choice in the security measures that you use, keep in mind two goals, which are sometimes in conflict. One goal is to protect resources, and the other goal is not to interfere with the functions of the system. A computer or network can be so protected that no one can use it, or so accessible that anyone can do whatever they want with it. The trick is to provide enough security to protect resources while still allowing users to work unhindered (see Figure 16-1). Also, too much security can sometimes force workers to find insecure alternatives. For example, if you require users to change their passwords weekly, more of them might start writing their passwords down to help remember them.

> ✎ **Notes** The best protection against attacks is layered protection. If one security method fails, the next might stop an attacker. When securing a workstation, use as many layers of protection as you reasonably can that are justified by the value of the resources you are protecting. These layers of defense are collectively called **defense in depth**.

Source: iStock.com/ojogabonitoo

Figure 16-1 Security measures should protect resources without hindering how users work

USING WINDOWS TO AUTHENTICATE USERS

**A+
CORE 2
1.4, 1.5,
1.6, 2.2,
2.5, 2.6,
2.7**
Access to computer resources is controlled by authenticating and authorizing a user or process. A user is authenticated when he proves he is who he says he is. When a computer is on a Windows domain, Active Directory (AD) is responsible for authentication. For a peer-to-peer network, authentication must happen at the local computer. Normally, Windows authenticates a user with a Windows password.

As an administrator, when you first create an account, be sure to assign it a password. It's best to give the user the ability to change the password at any time. In this part of the chapter, you learn how to create strong passwords and how to use Local Group Policy and Local Security Policy to control how users can authenticate to Windows.

CREATE STRONG PASSWORDS

A password needs to be a strong password, which means it should not be easy to guess either by people or by computer programs using various methods, including a simple brute force attack, which tries every single combination of characters until it discovers your password.

A strong password, such as *y*3Q1693pEWJaTz1!*, meets all of the following criteria:

▲ Use 16 or more characters, which is the best protection against a password attack.
▲ Combine uppercase and lowercase letters, numbers, and symbols.
▲ Use at least one symbol in your password.
▲ Don't use consecutive letters or numbers, such as "abcdefg" or "12345."
▲ Don't use adjacent keys on your keyboard, such as "qwerty."
▲ Don't use your sign-in name in the password.

◢ Don't use words in any language. Don't even use numbers or symbols for letters (as in "p@ssw0rd") because programs can easily guess those as well.

◢ Don't use the same password for more than one system.

Studies have proven that the most secure criterion of those listed above is the length of the password. Passwords of 16 characters or more that use letters, numbers, and symbols are the most difficult to crack.

> 🖊 **Notes** How secure is a password? Go to *howsecureismypassword.net* and find out how long it will take a computer to crack the password.

In some situations, a blank Windows password might be more secure than an easy-to-guess password such as "1234." That's because you cannot authenticate to a Windows computer from a remote computer unless the user account has a password. A criminal might be able to guess an easy password and authenticate remotely. For this reason, if a computer is always in a protected room such as a home office and the user doesn't intend to access it remotely, she might choose not to use a password. However, if the user travels with a laptop, always recommend that the user create a strong password.

Although it's not recommended you write your password down, if you do write it down, keep it in as safe a place as you would the data you are protecting. Don't send your passwords over email or chat. Change your passwords regularly, and don't type them on a public computer. For example, computers in hotel lobbies or Internet cafés should only be used for web browsing—not for signing in to your email account or online banking account. These computers might be running keystroke-logging software put there by criminals to record each keystroke. Several years ago, while on vacation in a foreign country, I entered credit card information on a computer in a hotel lobby. Months later, I was still protesting $2 or $3 charges to my credit card from that country. Trust me. Don't do it—I speak from experience.

> 🖊 **Notes** Rather than writing down passwords, consider storing your passwords with a password manager app such as Dashlane (*dashlane.com*), Sticky Password (*stickypassword.com*), or LastPass (*lastpass.com*). These apps can keep your passwords in the cloud or on your own device, and the passwords they create are longer and stronger than those you would be able to memorize.

Next, let's see how Local Group Policy and Local Security Policy tools can be used to enforce security best practices on a workstation.

LOCAL GROUP POLICY AND LOCAL SECURITY POLICY EDITORS

You need to be aware of three tools for policies that control what users and computers can do with a system or network:

◢ **Group Policy** works in Active Directory on a Windows domain to control the privileges of computers and users on the domain. You learn more about Group Policy and Active Directory later in this chapter.

◢ **Local Group Policy** (gpedit.msc) contains a subset of policies in Group Policy; this subset applies only to the local computer or local user.

◢ **Local Security Policy** (secpol.msc) contains a subset of policies in Local Group Policy, which apply only to the local computer's Windows security settings. Local Security Policy is an Administrative Tools snap-in in Control Panel.

The Local Group Policy and Local Security Policy editors are available with business and professional editions of Windows. Figure 16-2 shows the Local Group Policy Editor window on the left and the Local Security Policy window on the right. Notice that the Local Group Policy editor contains two major categories of policies: Computer Configuration and User Configuration. The list of policy groups selected are for the computer configuration for Windows security settings. Compare this list with the one in the Local Security Policy window; they are the same list of policies. In short, when you are working with the computer configuration in the Windows security settings group of the Local Group Policy editor, know you are working with the same group of policies you can edit when using the Local Security Policy editor.

16

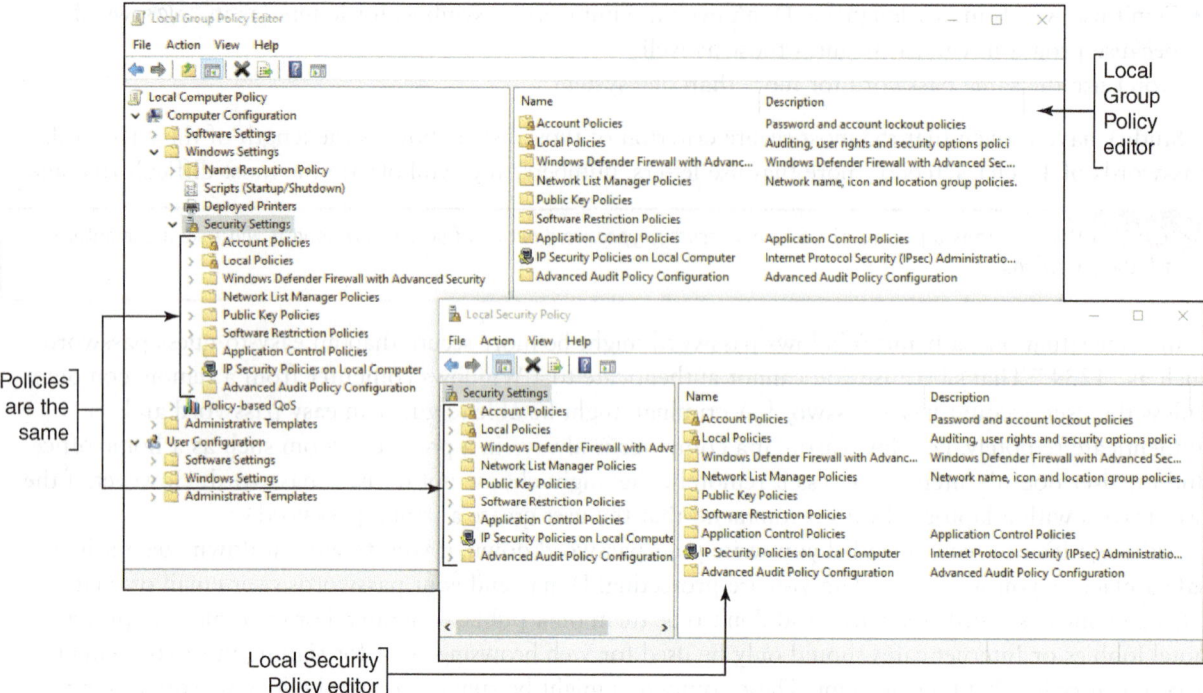

Figure 16-2 The Local Security Policy editor allows you to edit a subset of policies available in the Local Group Policy editor

Now let's see how you can use the Local Group Policy editor to secure a workstation. For example, you can set policies to require all users to have passwords. Once you have enabled a policy, a standard user of the workstation would be required to comply and would not be able to change the policy.

APPLYING | CONCEPTS   APPLYING LOCAL SECURITY POLICIES

Follow these steps to set a few important policies to secure a workstation:

1. Sign in to Windows using an administrator account on a system that uses Windows 10 Pro or Enterprise, Windows 8/8.1 Professional or Enterprise, or Windows 7 Professional, Ultimate, or Enterprise.

2. To start Local Group Policy, enter the **gpedit.msc** command in the Windows 10/7 search box or the Windows 8 Run box. The Local Group Policy Editor console opens.

3. To change a policy, first use the left pane to drill down into the appropriate policy group and then use the right pane to view and edit a policy. Here are important policies you can use to secure a workstation:

   ◢ ***Require user passwords and password expiration.*** To require that all user accounts have passwords, drill down to the **Computer Configuration, Windows Settings, Security Settings, Account Policies, Password Policy** group (see the left side of Figure 16-3). Use the **Minimum password length** policy and set the minimum length to at least eight characters (see the right side of Figure 16-3). Additionally, reduce the password expiration time frame so users must create new passwords frequently. Use the **Maximum password age** policy to require users to reset their password every 60 days. (The best practice is to set the Maximum password age in the range of 30 to 90 days.)

(continues)

Figure 16-3 Require that each user account have a password by setting the minimum password length policy

- ▲ **Screen lock timeout.** Windows can monitor for inactivity and run the screen saver after a set amount of time, locking the session. This prevents another person from continuing a Windows session after the user has stepped away from the computer. Drill down to the **Computer Configuration**, **Windows Settings**, **Security Settings**, **Local Policies**, **Security Options** group. Use the **Interactive logon: Machine inactivity limit** policy to set the number of seconds of inactivity before the screen saver runs and locks the workstation until a user signs in.
- ▲ **Set failed logon restrictions.** Windows can be configured to lock a user account if too many incorrect logons are attempted. Drill down to the **Computer Configuration**, **Windows Settings**, **Security Settings**, **Account Policies**, **Account Lockout Policy** group. Use the **Account lockout threshold** policy to set the number of invalid logon attempts. When the number is exceeded, the account will be locked.

> **✎ Notes** The Properties box for many policies offers the Explain tab. Use this tab to read more about a policy and how it works.

- ▲ **Disable the Guest account.** For best security, the Guest account should stay disabled; you don't want a user to accidentally enable it. To set a policy to disable the Guest account, first use the left pane to navigate to the **Computer Configuration**, **Windows Settings**, **Security Settings**, **Local Policies**, **Security Options** group. In the Security Options group, right-click **Accounts: Guest account status**, and select **Properties**. Change the status to **Disabled** and click **OK**.
- ▲ **Change default user names.** A hacker is less likely to hack into the built-in Administrator account or Guest account if you change the names of these default accounts. To change the name of the Administrator

(continues)

16

account, drill down to the **Computer Configuration**, **Windows Settings**, **Security Settings**, **Local Policies**, **Security Options** group (see the left side of Figure 16-4). In the right pane, double-click **Accounts: Rename administrator account**. In the Properties box for this policy (see the right side of Figure 16-4), change the name and click **OK**. To change the name of the Guest account, use the policy **Accounts: Rename guest account**.

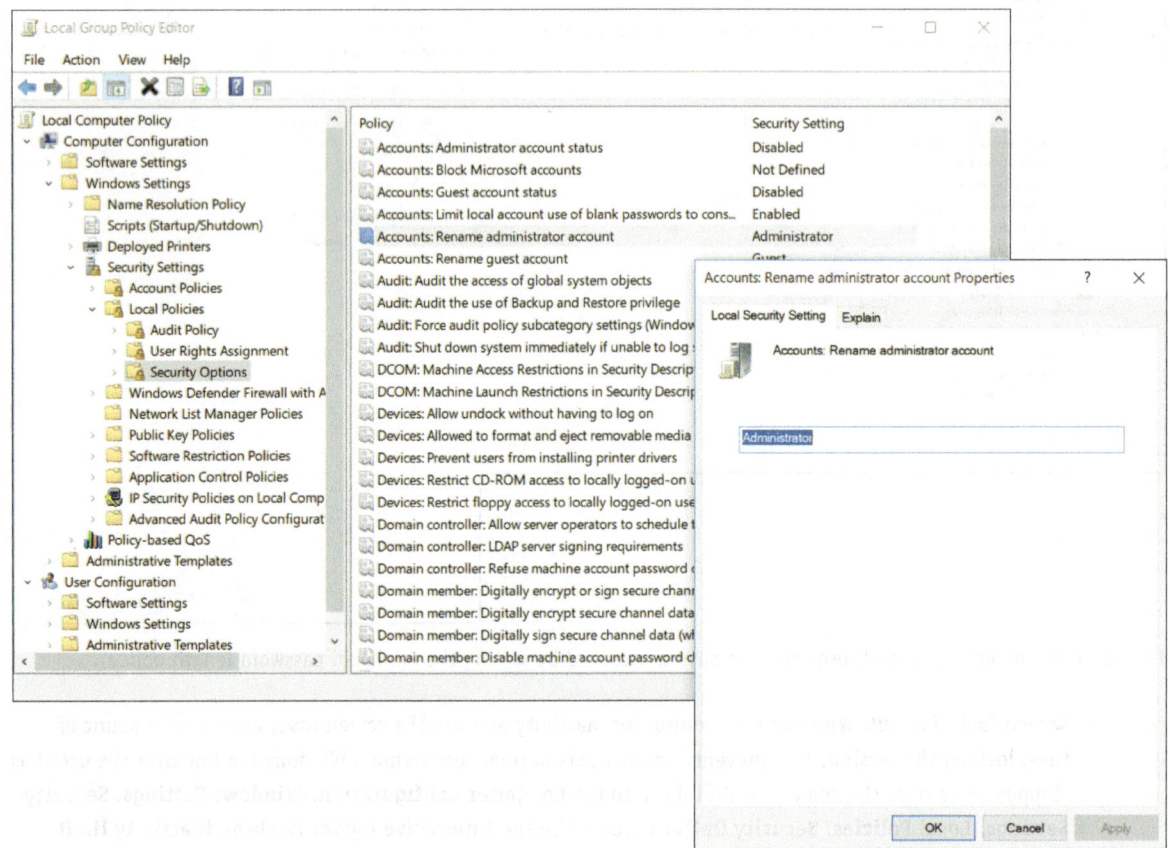

Figure 16-4　Use Group Policy to rename a default user account

---

✎ **Notes**　The Administrator account is a built-in account that you might need in an emergency when other user accounts fail. Be sure to create a password for this account. One way to do that is to open an elevated command prompt window and enter the following command:

```
net user Administrator <password>
```

For added security, open the Computer Management console and change the name of the Administrator account. Because this account and password are extremely valuable and not used very often, don't trust your memory—keep the user account name and password in a protected and secure place.

▲ *Audit logon failures.* Group Policy offers several auditing policies that monitor and log security events. You can then review these Security logs using Event Viewer. For example, to set an audit policy to monitor a failed logon event, drill down to the **Computer Configuration**, **Windows Settings**, **Security Settings**, **Local Policies**, **Audit Policy** group. Use the **Audit logon events** policy. You can audit logon successes and failures. To keep the log from getting too big, you can select **Failure** to log only these events.

(continues)

All the previous policies are also found in the Local Security Policy console. The following policies are available only in Local Group Policy:

▲ **Logon time restrictions.** In many cases, users should only be allowed access to a workstation during specific hours, such as during office hours. The schedule for a user's or group's logon hours is set through Active Directory on the domain. When logon hours set by Active Directory have expired, individual workstations can be configured to disconnect, lock, or log off the user, or to allow the user to continue the current session. To configure what happens when a user's logon hours have expired, drill down to the **User Configuration**, **Administrative Templates**, **Windows Components**, **Windows Logon Options** group. Double-click **Set action to take when logon hours expire**. Select **Enabled** and then choose Lock, Disconnect, or Logoff. If the policy is not enabled, the user's session will continue, but the user will not be able to log on outside of the assigned logon hours once the current session has been terminated.

▲ **Disable Microsoft account resources.** Recall that a Microsoft account is a single sign-on (SSO) account, which means it provides authentication to multiple services and resources. When a user signs in to a Windows 10/8 computer with a Microsoft account, she has access to online resources such as OneDrive and OneNote and can sync settings on the computer with other computers that use the same Microsoft account. Settings include Start screen tiles, desktop personalization, installed apps and app settings, web browser favorites, and passwords to apps, websites, and networks.

> 🖊 **Notes** To see and edit the sync settings available for a Microsoft account, open the Windows 10 **Settings** app, click the **Accounts** group, and select **Sync your settings** in the left pane. In Windows 8, open the charms bar, click **Settings**, click **Change PC settings**, click **OneDrive**, and click **Sync settings**.

Depending on your company's policy, you might need to restrict access to online resources and sync settings that are linked to a user's Microsoft account. To disable OneDrive, for example, drill down to the **Computer Configuration**, **Administrative Templates**, **Windows Components**, **OneDrive** group. Enable the **Prevent the usage of OneDrive for file storage** policy to prevent users and programs from accessing OneDrive. Additionally, in the **Windows Components** submenu, click the **Sync your settings** group and use these policies to disable syncing apps, app settings, passwords, and other Windows settings (see Figure 16-5).

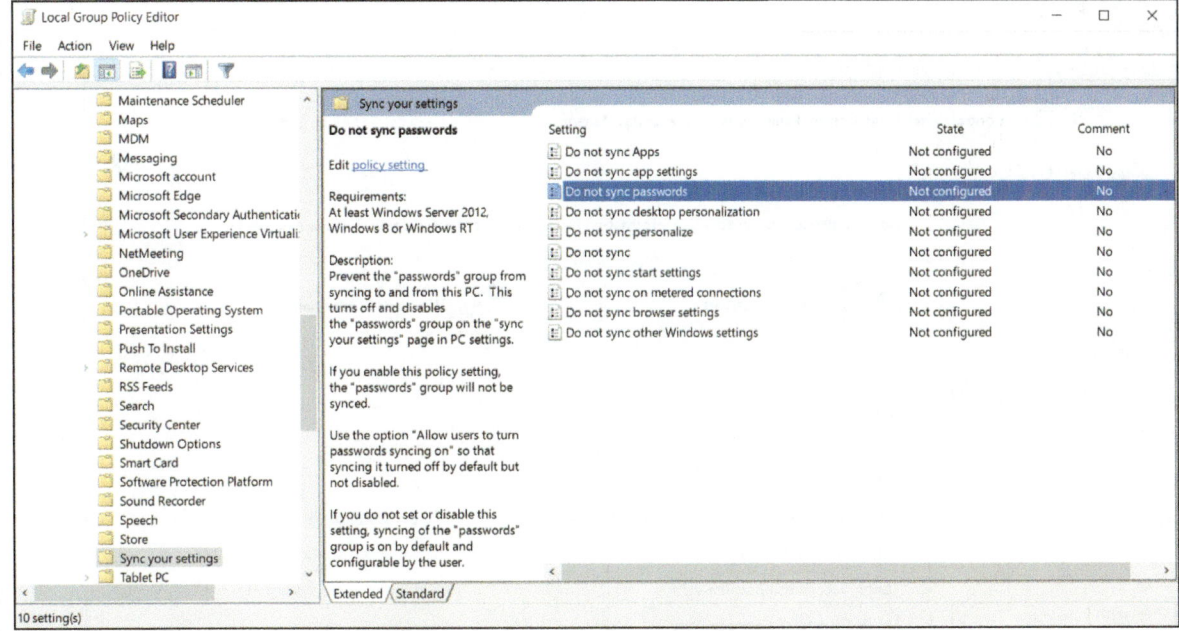

Figure 16-5   Restrict SSO authentication to online resources associated with a Microsoft account

(continues)

◢ *Disable AutoRun and AutoPlay.* When you attach a USB flash drive or external hard drive or insert a disc in the optical drive, Windows automatically accesses the storage media and then requests instructions for what to do next. Media files can be played automatically, which is called AutoPlay. Executable files can be run automatically, which is called AutoRun. You can disable both of these features to add yet another layer of security protection. To disable AutoPlay, drill down to the **Computer Configuration**, **Administrative Templates**, **Windows Components**, **AutoPlay Policies** group. Enable the **Turn off Autoplay** policy. To disable AutoRun, enable **Set the default behavior for AutoRun** and use the **Disabled** option.

4. When you finish setting your local security policies, close the Local Group Policy Editor console. To put your changes into effect, restart the system or open a command prompt window and enter the command **gpupdate /force**. The command might request that you restart the computer for all policies to take effect. The gpupdate command refreshes local group policies as well as group policies set in Active Directory on a Windows domain.

★ **A+ Exam Tip** The A+ Core 2 exam expects you to know how to secure a workstation in a given scenario, including setting a strong password and configuring a workstation so that passwords will expire, knowing that a screen saver requires a password to unlock the workstation, that a logon time is restricted, and that the system locks when sign-in attempts have failed.

MANAGE USER CREDENTIALS

A user might need help managing the passwords and digital certificates stored on a Windows computer. To manage these user credentials, open the **Credential Manager** applet in Control Panel. The tool allows you to manage web credentials and Windows credentials (see Figure 16-6). When you select a website under Web Credentials, you can edit or delete the user name and password to access the site. When you click **Windows Credentials**, you can edit and delete Windows user names, passwords, and digital certificates installed on the system. You can also use this window to install a new digital certificate in Windows.

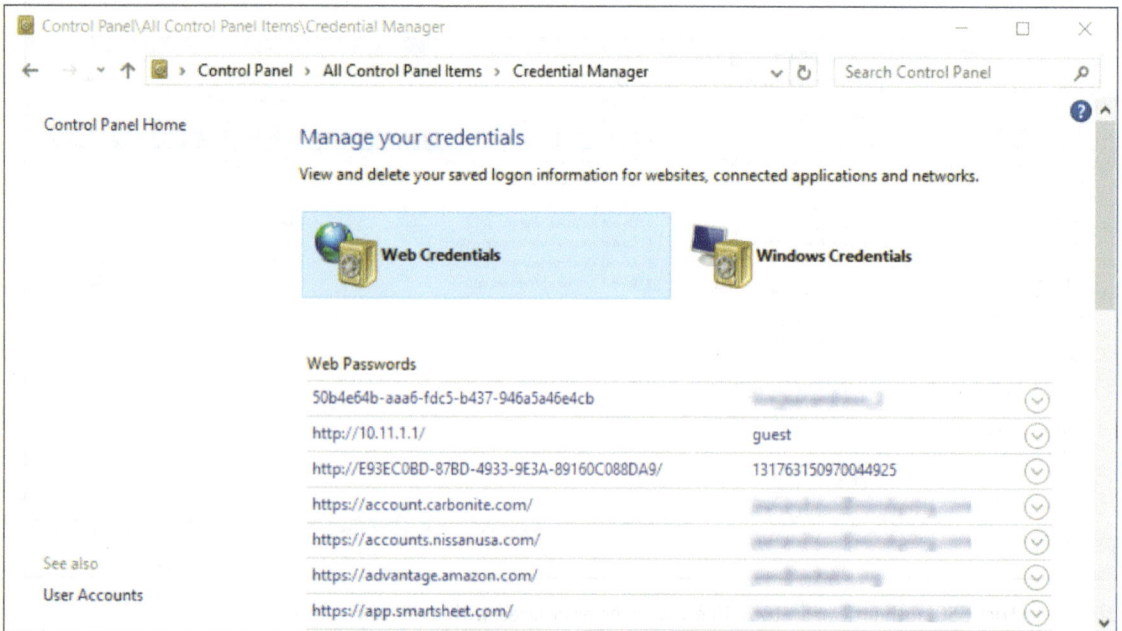

Figure 16-6 Manage passwords and digital certificates in Credential Manager

USING BIOS/UEFI PASSWORDS TO AUTHENTICATE USERS

**A+
CORE 2
2.7**

BIOS/UEFI firmware on the motherboard offers power-on passwords, which include an administrator or supervisor password (required to change BIOS/UEFI setup) and a user password (required to use the system or view BIOS/UEFI setup). Some firmware may also offer a drive lock password, which is required to access the hard drive. The drive lock password is stored on the hard drive so that it will still control access if the drive is removed from the computer and installed on another system. Figure 16-7 shows a BIOS/UEFI setup Security screen where you can set the Administrator and User passwords.

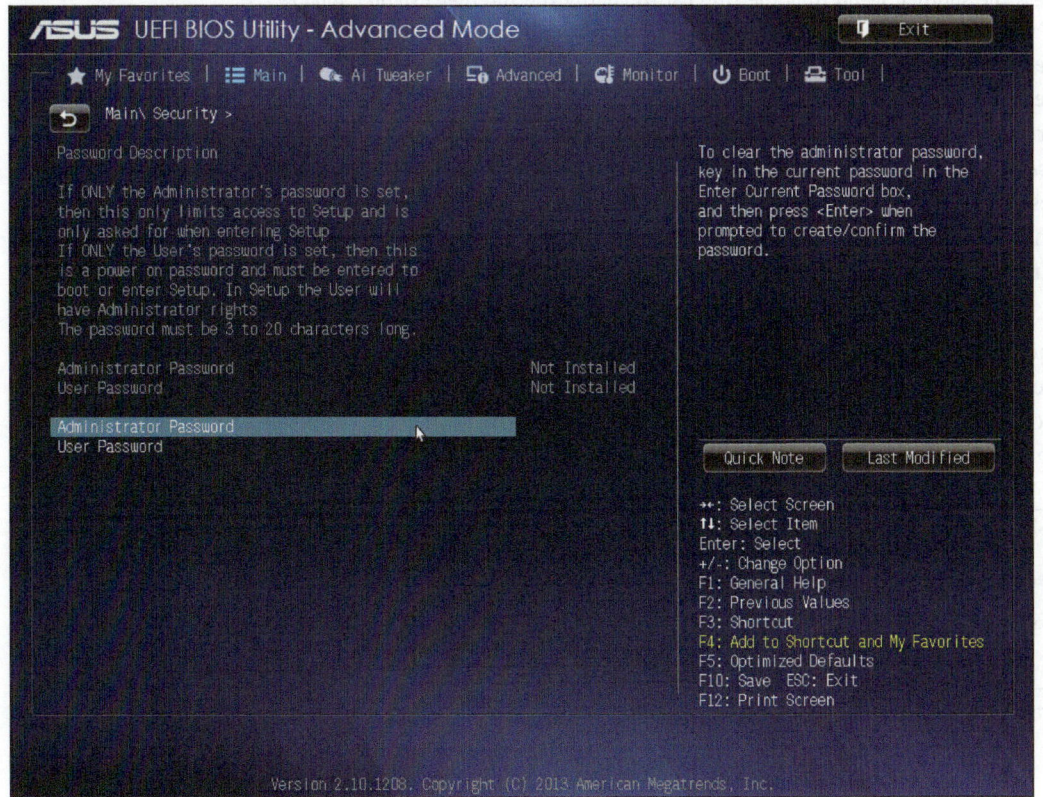

Source: American Megatrends, Inc.

Figure 16-7   BIOS/UEFI passwords can control access to BIOS/UEFI setup and to boot the system

16

SECURING INTERNET EXPLORER

**A+
CORE 2
1.6**

The Internet Options dialog box can be used to secure Internet Explorer, a browser included with Windows 10/8/7. The latest release of Internet Explorer is version 11, although Windows 10 features a new browser called Microsoft Edge to eventually replace Internet Explorer. Current releases of Windows 10/8/7 come with Internet Explorer 11 installed; for an old installation of Windows, open Windows Update and find and install the Internet Explorer 11 update. You can also go to the *microsoft.com* website and follow links to download and install Internet Explorer 11.

Here are some tips about using Internet Explorer 11:

▲ *Menu bar.* To open the Internet Explorer menu bar, press the **Alt** key or right-click a blank area in the title bar and check **Menu bar** in the shortcut menu. Notice in Figure 16-8 that you can also add the command bar to the Internet Explorer window.

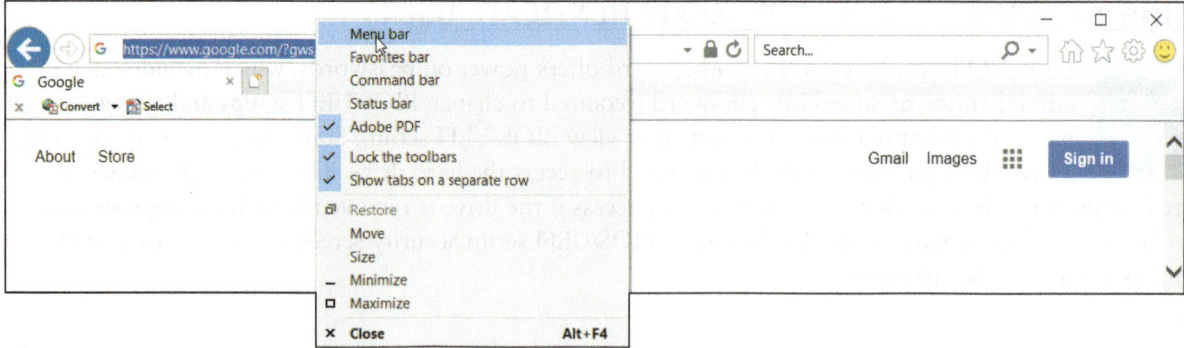

Figure 16-8 Access the shortcut menu from the title bar to control the Internet Explorer window

▲ *HTTP Secure.* Some web servers use HTTP with the SSL or TLS protocols (called HTTP Secure or HTTPS) to secure transmissions to and from the web server. Look for *https* and a padlock icon in the browser address box when HTTPS is used. Click the padlock to get information about the site security.

▲ *Repair or disable.* If you have a problem with Internet Explorer 11, try installing Windows updates, applying a restore point, or refreshing Windows 10/8. If you prefer to use a different browser, you can disable Internet Explorer 11. Open the **Programs and Features** window in Control Panel and click **Turn Windows features on or off**. In the Windows Features box, uncheck **Internet Explorer 11** and click **OK**.

Now let's see how you can use the Internet Options box to secure Internet Explorer. To open the box, click the **Tools** icon on the right side of the Internet Explorer title bar and click **Internet options**. Another method is to press **Alt** to display the menu bar, click **Tools** in the menu, and click **Internet options**. A third method is to click **Internet Options** in the Classic view of Control Panel. The Internet Options box is shown in Figure 16-9.

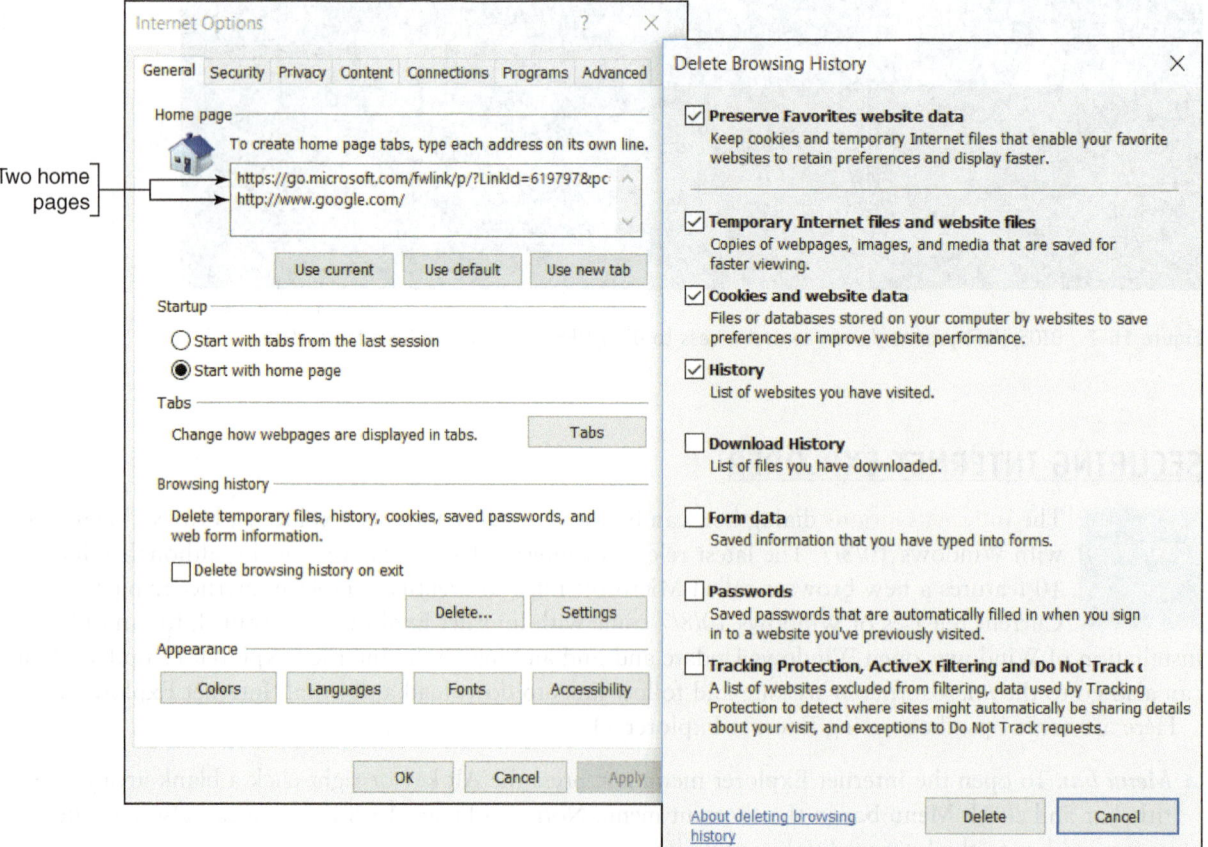

Figure 16-9 Use the General tab of the Internet Options box to delete your browsing history

★ A+ Exam Tip The A+ Core 2 exam expects you to know how to use the General, Security, Privacy, Connections, Programs, and Advanced tabs in the Internet Options box.

Here are the more important tabs in the Internet Options box and how to use them:

▲ *General tab.* Using the General tab, you can change the home page or add a second home page tab. You can also protect your identity and surfing records:

  ▲ To delete what Internet Explorer has kept about your former browsing, click **Delete**. In the Delete Browsing History box (see the right side of Figure 16-9), uncheck the first item and check all other items. (If you want to keep cookies used by websites in your Favorites list, check the first item, **Preserve Favorites website data**.) Click **Delete**.

  ▲ For future browsing sessions, you can delete your browsing history each time you close Internet Explorer by checking **Delete browsing history on exit** on the General tab of the Internet Options box.

  Internet Explorer holds a cache containing previously downloaded content in case it is requested again. The cache is stored in several folders named Temporary Internet Files. On the General tab, click **Settings** to change the maximum allowed space used for temporary Internet files and control the location of these files.

▲ *Security tab.* You can set a zone security level on the Security tab. For the Internet, medium-high is the default value; at this level, Internet Explorer prompts before downloading content and does not download ActiveX controls that are not signed by Microsoft. An ActiveX control is a small app or add-on that can be downloaded from a website along with a webpage and is executed by Internet Explorer to enhance the webpage (for example, to add animation to the page). A virus can sometimes hide in an ActiveX control, but Internet Explorer is designed to catch them by authenticating each ActiveX control it downloads. To customize security settings, click **Custom level**. In the Security Settings box, you can decide exactly how you want to handle downloaded content. For example, you can disable file downloads.

▲ *Privacy tab.* Use the Privacy tab to block cookies that might invade your privacy or steal your identity. You can also use this tab to control the Pop-up Blocker, which prevents annoying pop-ups as you surf the web. To allow a pop-up from a particular website, click **Settings** and enter the URL of the website in the Pop-up Blocker Settings box. See Figure 16-10. Some pop-ups are useful, such as when you're trying to download a file from a website and the site asks permission to complete the download.

▲ *Connections tab.* The Connections tab allows you to configure proxy server settings and create a VPN connection. Many large corporations and ISPs use proxy servers to speed up Internet access. A web browser does not have to be aware that a proxy server is in use. However, one reason you might need to configure Internet Explorer to be aware of and use a proxy server is when you are on a corporate network and are having a problem connecting to a secured website (one using HTTP over SSL or another encryption protocol). The problem might be caused by Windows trying to connect using the wrong proxy server on the network. Check with your network administrator to find out if a specific proxy server should be used to manage secure website connections.

★ A+ Exam Tip The A+ Core 2 exam expects you to know how to configure proxy settings on a client desktop.

16

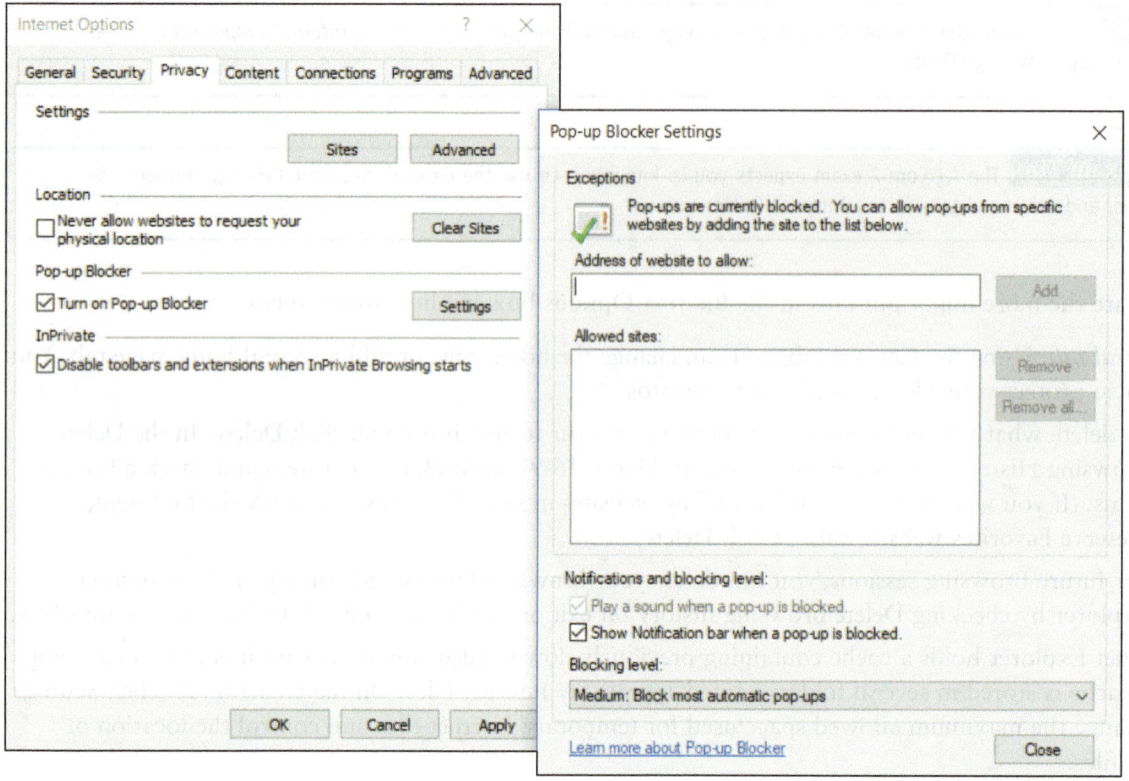

Figure 16-10 Use the Privacy tab to control pop-ups and cookies

If you need to configure Internet Explorer to use a specific proxy server, open the **Connections** tab and click **LAN settings**. In the settings box, check **Use a proxy server for your LAN** and enter the IP address of the proxy server (see Figure 16-11). If your organization uses more than one proxy server, click **Advanced** and enter IP addresses for each type of proxy server on your network (see the right side of Figure 16-11). You can also enter a port address for each server, if necessary. If you are trying to solve a problem of connecting to a server using HTTP over SSL or another secured protocol, use the Secure field to enter the IP address of the proxy server that is used to manage secure connections.

Figure 16-11 Configure Internet Explorer to use one or more proxy servers

▲ *Programs tab.* The Programs tab is used to manage add-ons, also called plug-ins, which are small apps that help Internet Explorer to display multimedia content, manage email, translate text, or other actions. On the Programs tab, click **Manage add-ons** to open the Manage Add-ons box. See Figure 16-12. Here's what you can do with this box:

    ▲ *View all add-ons.* In the left pane under Show, you can select all add-ons installed on the computer, as shown in the figure.

    ▲ *Enable or disable an add-on.* Select an add-on listed in the right pane to see information about it in the lower pane. To enable or disable a selected add-on, click **Enable** or click **Disable**.

    ▲ *Delete an add-on.* Downloaded ActiveX controls can be uninstalled using this window. Select a downloaded ActiveX add-on and click **More information** in the lower pane. If the add-on has been downloaded and can be removed, the Remove button on the More information box will be available. You can also uninstall downloaded add-ons using the Programs and Features window in Control Panel.

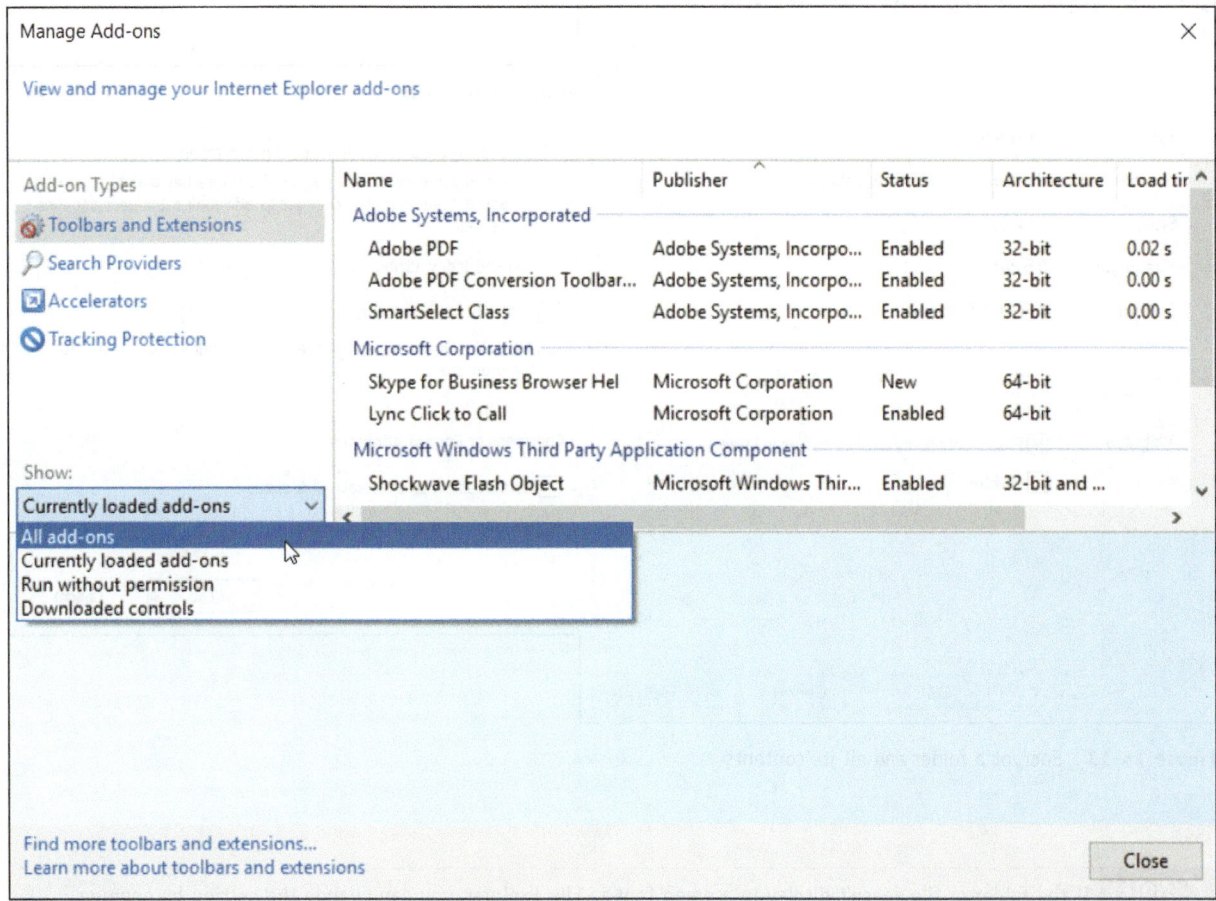

Figure 16-12 Manage Internet Explorer add-ons

> **✎ Notes** If you use Control Panel to open the Internet Options box and open the Manage Add-ons box from there, the *Currently loaded add-ons* option is missing in the drop-down list under Show.

▲ *Advanced tab.* The Advanced tab contains several miscellaneous settings used to control Internet Explorer. If you suspect problems are caused by wrong settings, use this tab to reset Internet Explorer to all default settings.

Now let's turn our attention to securing another resource on the network: folders and files.

16

FILE AND FOLDER ENCRYPTION

**A+
CORE 2
2.6**

In Windows, files and folders can be encrypted using the Windows Encrypting File System (EFS). This encryption works only with the NTFS file system and business and professional editions of Windows. If a folder is marked for encryption, every file created in the folder or copied to the folder will be encrypted. An encrypted file remains encrypted if you move it from an encrypted folder to an unencrypted folder on the same or another NTFS volume. To encrypt a folder or file, right-click it and open its Properties box (see Figure 16-13). On the General tab, click **Advanced**. In the Advanced Attributes box, check **Encrypt contents to secure data** and click **OK**. In File Explorer or Windows Explorer, encrypted file and folder names are displayed in green by default.

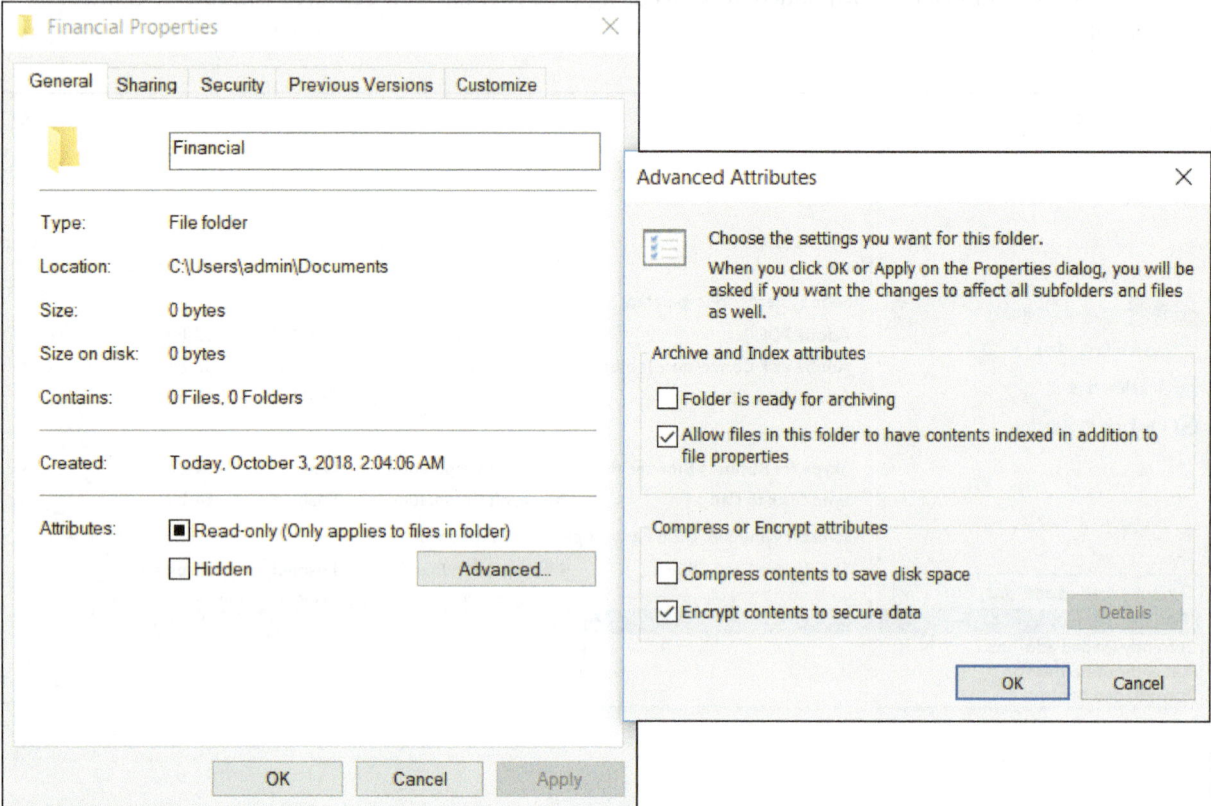

Figure 16-13   Encrypt a folder and all its contents

Notes   If the folder or file doesn't display in a green font in File Explorer, you can change the setting by opening **Control Panel** and clicking **File Explorer Options**. On the View tab, check **Show encrypted or compressed NTFS files in color**. Click **OK**.

Caution   A user sometimes forgets a password, and an administrator can reset the forgotten password. However, know that if an administrator resets a user password, the user will lose all his EFS encrypted folders and files, personal digital certificates, and passwords stored on the computer. To reset a user password, you can use the Network Places Wizard tool (netplwiz.exe), as shown in Figure 16-14. Select the user and click **Reset Password**.

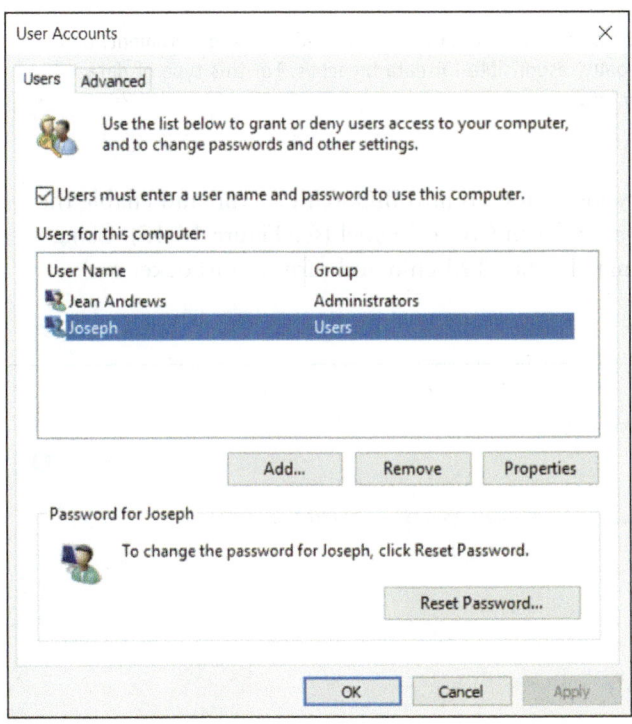

Figure 16-14 Reset a user password

BITLOCKER ENCRYPTION

A+
CORE 2
1.6, 2.6

BitLocker Drive Encryption in Windows professional and business editions locks down a hard drive by encrypting the entire Windows volume and any other volume on the drive and restricts access by requiring one or two encryption keys. A similar feature, BitLocker To Go, encrypts data on a USB flash drive and restricts access by requiring a password. You need to be aware of the restrictions and possible risks before you decide to use BitLocker. It's intended to work in partnership with file and folder encryption to provide data security.

⭐ **A+ Exam Tip** The A+ Core 2 exam expects you to know when it is appropriate to use BitLocker Drive Encryption and BitLocker To Go in a given scenario.

The three ways you can use BitLocker Drive Encryption depend on the type of protection you need and the computer hardware available:

▲ *Computer authentication*. Many laptop computers have a chip on the motherboard called the TPM (Trusted Platform Module) chip. The TPM chip holds the BitLocker encryption key (also called the startup key). If the hard drive is stolen from the laptop and installed in another computer, the data would be safe because BitLocker would not allow access without the startup key stored on the TPM chip. Therefore, this method authenticates the computer. However, if the motherboard fails and is replaced, you'll need a backup copy of the startup key to access data on the hard drive. (You cannot move the TPM chip from one motherboard to another.)

▲ *User authentication*. For computers that don't have TPM, the startup key can be stored on a USB flash drive (or other storage device the computer reads before the OS is loaded), and the flash drive must be installed before the computer boots. This method authenticates the user. For this method to be the most secure, the user must never leave the flash drive stored with the computer. (Instead, the user might keep the USB startup key on his key ring or a lanyard.)

▲ *Computer and user authentication*. For *best* security, a password can be required at every startup in addition to TPM. Using this method, both the computer and the user are authenticated. This practice is an example of multifactor authentication (MFA), which uses more than one method to authenticate.

BitLocker Drive Encryption provides great security, but security comes with a price. For instance, you risk the chance your TPM will fail or you will lose all copies of the startup key. In these events, recovering the data can be messy. Therefore, use BitLocker only if the risks of using it do not outweigh the risks of stolen data. And, if you decide to use BitLocker, be sure to make extra copies of the startup key and/or password and keep them in a safe location.

16

> ⚡ **Caution** In Chapter 17, you learn that some data, such as health-care data, is regulated by the government, and organizations that are negligent to protect it can be held legally responsible for data breaches. For this type of data, encryption and other security measures may be mandated by law.

To start the process of using BitLocker Drive Encryption, first go into BIOS/UEFI setup and enable the TPM chip. Then open the **BitLocker Drive Encryption** applet in Control Panel (see Figure 16-15). Using this window, you can click **TPM Administration** to manage the TPM chip and turn on BitLocker or BitLocker To Go.

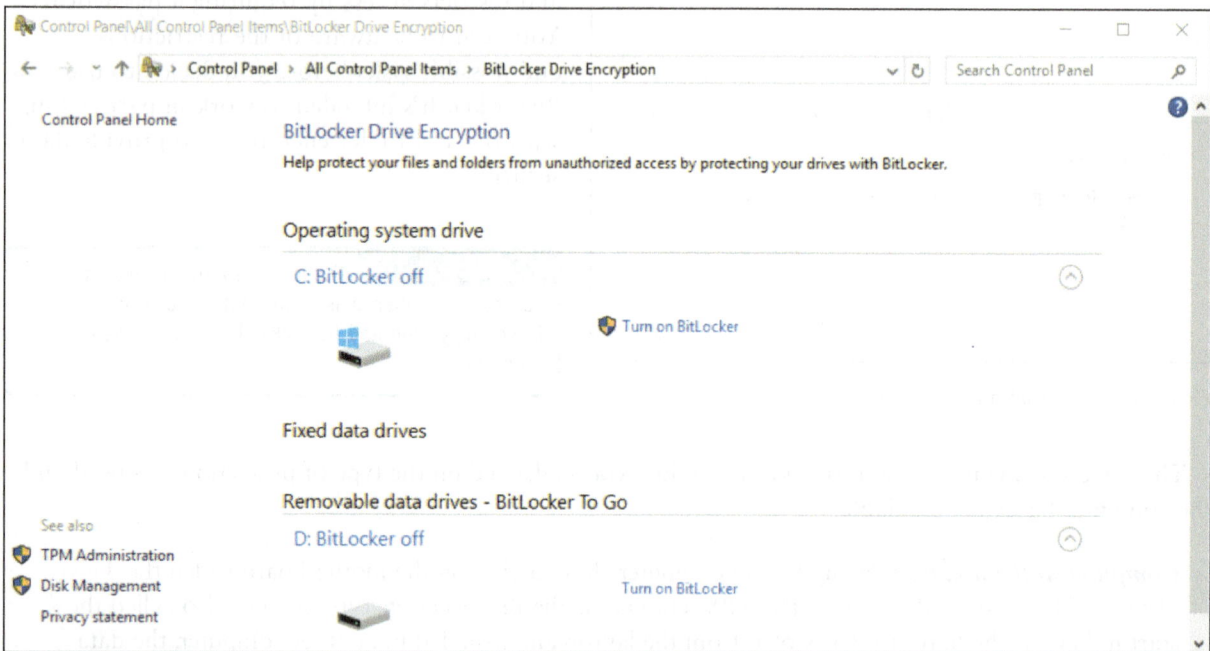

Figure 16-15 Manage BitLocker Drive Encryption, the TPM chip, and BitLocker To Go

> 📝 **Notes** For detailed instructions on how to set up BitLocker Drive Encryption, see the Microsoft Windows IT Pro Center article "BitLocker" at *docs.microsoft.com/en-us/windows/security/information-protection/bitlocker/bitlocker-overview.*

WINDOWS FIREWALL SETTINGS

**A+
CORE 2
1.5, 1.6,
1.8**

Recall from Chapter 7 that a SOHO router can serve as a hardware firewall to protect its network from attack over the Internet. Recall that the best protection from attack is layered protection (see Figure 16-16). In addition to a network hardware firewall, a large corporation might use a software firewall, also called a corporate firewall, installed on a computer that stands between the Internet and the network to protect the network. This computer has two network cards installed, and the installed software firewall filters the traffic between the two cards.

A personal firewall, also called a host firewall or application firewall, is software installed on a personal computer to protect it. A personal firewall provides redundant protection from attacks over the Internet, filters inbound traffic to protect a computer from attack from other computers on the same network, and filters outbound traffic to prevent attacks on other computers on the same network. When setting up a SOHO network or a personal computer, configure a personal firewall on each computer.

Windows Firewall is a personal firewall that protects a computer from intrusion and from attacking other computers; it is automatically configured when you set up your security level for a new network

Figure 16-16   Three types of firewalls used to protect a network and individual computers on the network

connection. To set the security for a network connection, open the **Network and Sharing Center** in Control Panel and click **Change advanced sharing settings**. The resulting Windows 10 Advanced sharing settings window is shown in Figure 16-17. (Recall that for Windows 10/8, the options are private and public security, and for Windows 7, the options are home, work, and public security.)

Figure 16-17   Configure the security level for network connections

Later in the chapter, you learn how to share folders and printers on a private network. For folder and printer sharing to work, you need to use the Advanced sharing settings window to turn on network discovery and file and printer sharing so that Windows Firewall allows this type of network traffic.

APPLYING | CONCEPTS   CONFIGURING WINDOWS FIREWALL

You can use the Windows Firewall window to configure even more firewall settings. Follow these steps to find out how:

1. Use one of these methods to open Windows Firewall:

   ◢ Open the **Network and Sharing Center**. For Windows 10, click **Windows Defender Firewall** in the lower part of the left pane. For Windows 8/7, click **Windows Firewall**.
   ◢ Open Control Panel in Classic view and click **Windows Defender Firewall**. For Windows 8/7, click **Windows Firewall**.

   The Windows Defender Firewall window is shown in Figure 16-18. Although the Windows 8/7 Windows Firewall window looks slightly different, the windows work basically the same way.

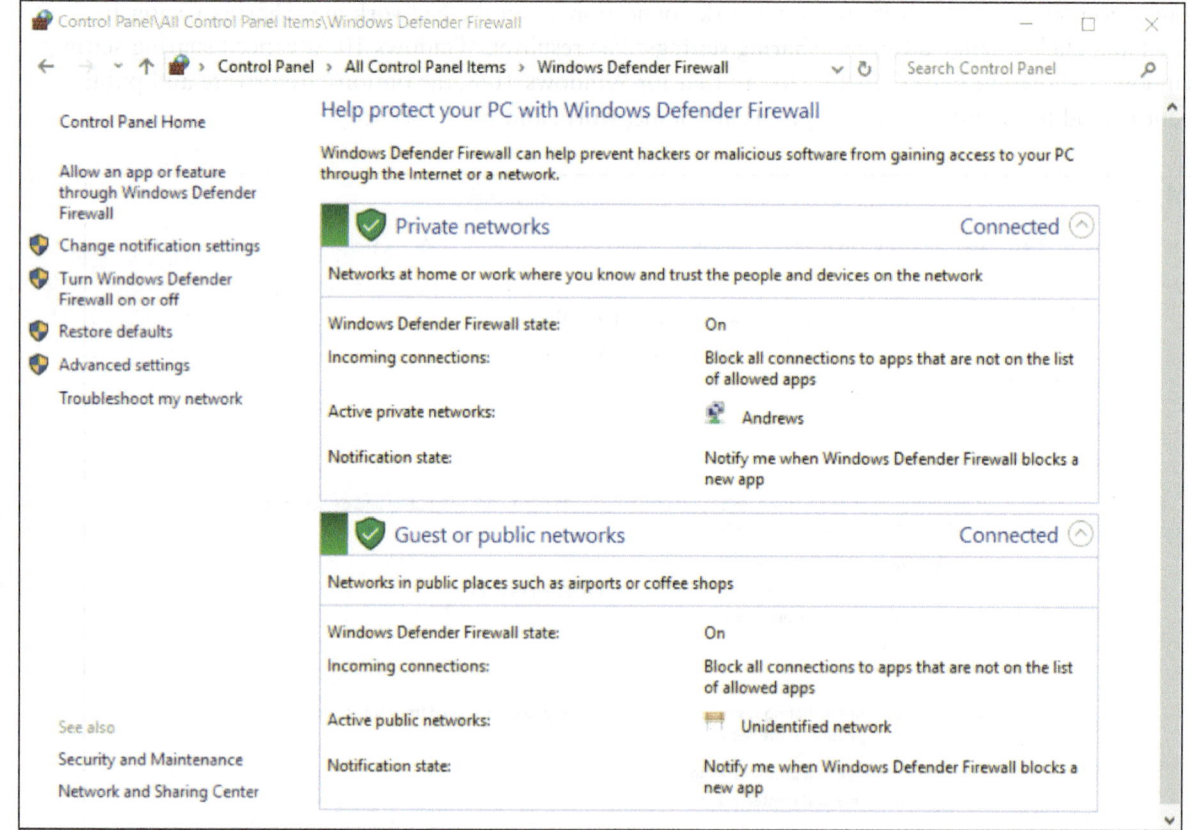

Figure 16-18   Windows Defender Firewall shows the firewall is turned on to protect private and public networks

(continues)

2. In general, Windows Firewall works by allowing or denying network traffic on incoming or outgoing ports. Recall that a port is a number an application on the computer uses to connect to another application on the network or Internet. Here are some basic settings you can configure in Windows Firewall:

a. Use the left pane to turn Windows Firewall on or off. When Windows Firewall is disabled (not a good idea), all traffic is allowed to pass and your computer is unprotected.

b. When Windows Firewall is enabled, all traffic is stopped unless you have specified an exception. To allow or deny a specific app access to the computer, click **Allow an app or feature through Windows Defender Firewall**. You can then select the app from a list of apps and decide how it can use the network connection.

c. To allow or deny all other types of traffic, not just those related to apps, click **Advanced settings**. On the Advanced Security window (see Figure 16-19), you can click Inbound Rules or Outbound Rules to create or edit an inbound or outbound rule and control traffic. A rule can specify how port numbers, TCP/IP protocols, programs, services, computers, and remote users can use the network connection. A rule can apply to public, private, and domain networks.

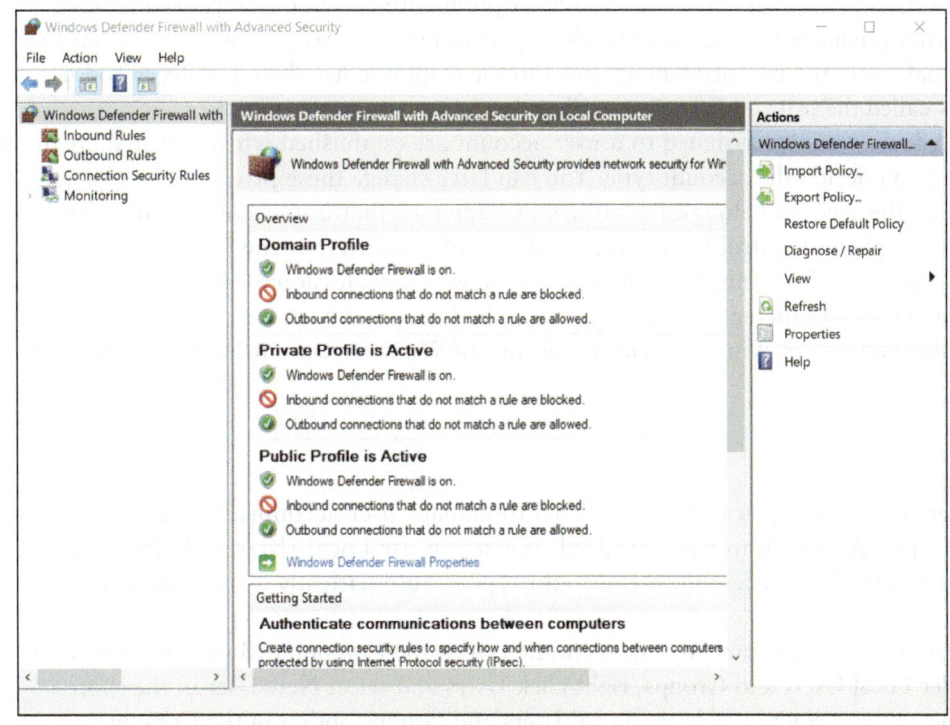

Figure 16-19 Customize an inbound or outbound rule to control exactly what incoming or outgoing traffic is allowed through the firewall

CONTROLLING ACCESS TO FOLDERS AND FILES

Responsibility for a peer-to-peer network or domain can include controlling access to folders and files for users of a local computer and for remote users accessing shared resources over the network. Managing shared resources is accomplished by (1) assigning privileges to user accounts and (2) assigning permissions to folders, files, and printers.

> ✎ **Notes**   In Windows, the terms *privileges* and *permissions* have different meanings. **Privileges** (also called rights) refer to the tasks an account is allowed to do in the system, such as installing software or changing the system date and time. **Permissions** refer to which user accounts or user groups are allowed access to data files and folders. *Privileges are assigned to an account, and permissions are assigned to data files and folders.*

Let's first look at the strategies used for controlling privileges to user accounts and controlling permissions to folders and files. Then you learn the procedures in Windows for assigning these privileges and permissions.

CLASSIFYING USER ACCOUNTS AND USER GROUPS

> **A+ CORE 2 1.8, 2.2, 2.6**

Computer users should be classified to determine the privileges they need to do their jobs. For example, some users need the privilege to sign in to a system remotely and others do not. Other privileges granted to users might include the right to install software or hardware, change the system date and time, change Windows Firewall settings, and so forth. Generally, when a new employee begins work, that employee's job description with exceptions approved by his supervisor determine what privileges the employee needs to perform his job. You, as the support technician, will be responsible to make sure the user account assigned to the employee has these privileges and no more. This approach is called the principle of least privilege.

In Windows, the privileges or rights assigned to a user account are established when you first create the account, which is when you decide the account type. You can later change these privileges by changing the user groups to which the account belongs. Recall from Chapter 12 that user accounts can be created using the User Accounts applet in Control Panel (in any edition of Windows) or the Local Users and Groups utility in the Computer Management console (in business and professional editions of Windows). User accounts can be assigned to different user groups using the Computer Management console in business and professional editions of Windows. Home editions of Windows cannot be used to manage user groups.

TYPE OF USER ACCOUNT

When you use the User Accounts applet in Control Panel to manage user accounts, you can choose between two account types: Administrator or Standard. When you use Local Users and Groups in Computer Management to create an account, the account type is automatically a standard user account.

To create a user account using Computer Management, first open the Computer Management console (compmgmt.msc). Under **Local Users and Groups**, right-click **Users** and select **New User** in the shortcut menu. (Windows Home editions don't include the Local Users and Groups option in the Computer Management console.) Enter information for the new user and click **Create** (see Figure 16-20).

> ★ **A+ Exam Tip**   The A+ Core 2 exam expects you to be able to compare privileges assigned to the administrator, standard user, power user, and guest user groups.

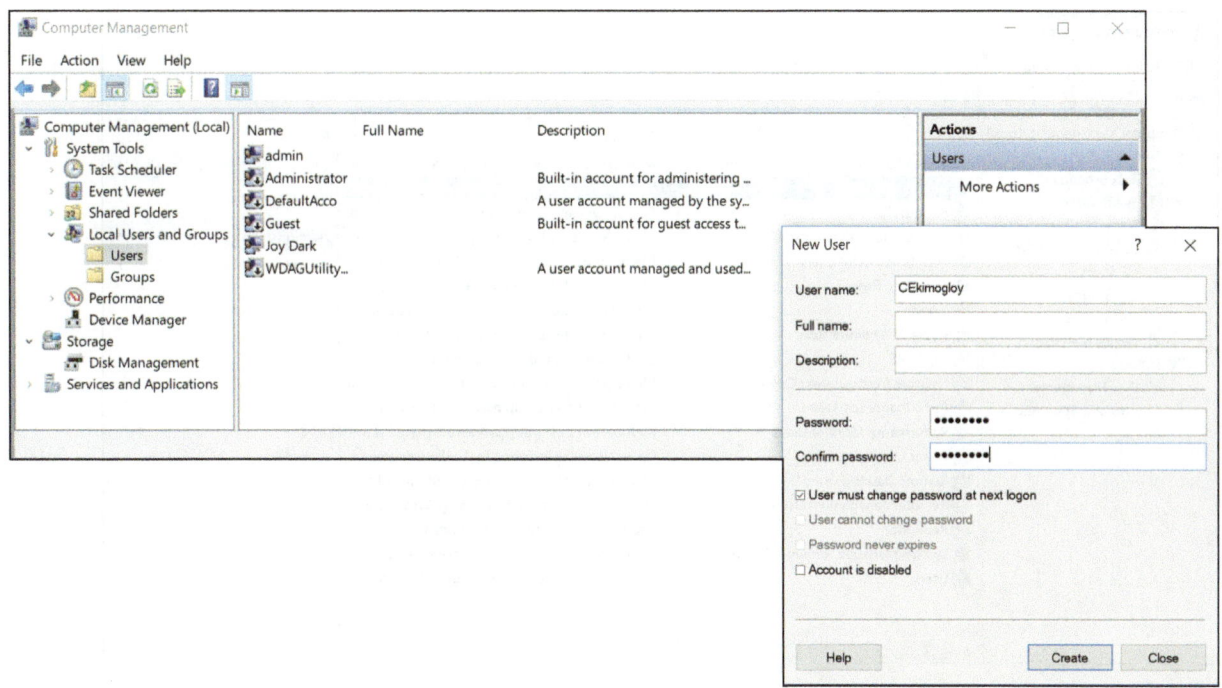

Figure 16-20 Create a new user

BUILT-IN USER GROUPS

A user account can belong to one or more user groups. Windows offers several built-in user groups and you can create your own. Here are important built-in user groups:

▲ *Administrators and Users groups.* By default, administrator accounts belong to the Administrators group, and standard user accounts belong to the Users group. If you want to give administrator privileges to a standard user account, use the Computer Management console to add the account to the Administrators group.

▲ *Guests group.* The Guests group has limited privileges on the system and is given a temporary profile that is deleted when the user signs out. Windows automatically creates one account in the Guests group named the Guest account, which is disabled by default.

▲ *Power Users group.* Older editions of Windows have a Power Users group that can read from and write to parts of the system other than its own user profile folders, install applications, and perform limited administrative tasks. Windows 10/8/7 offers a Power Users group only for backward compatibility with legacy applications.

To view user groups installed on a system, open the Computer Management console. Under Local Users and Groups, click **Groups** (see Figure 16-21).

16

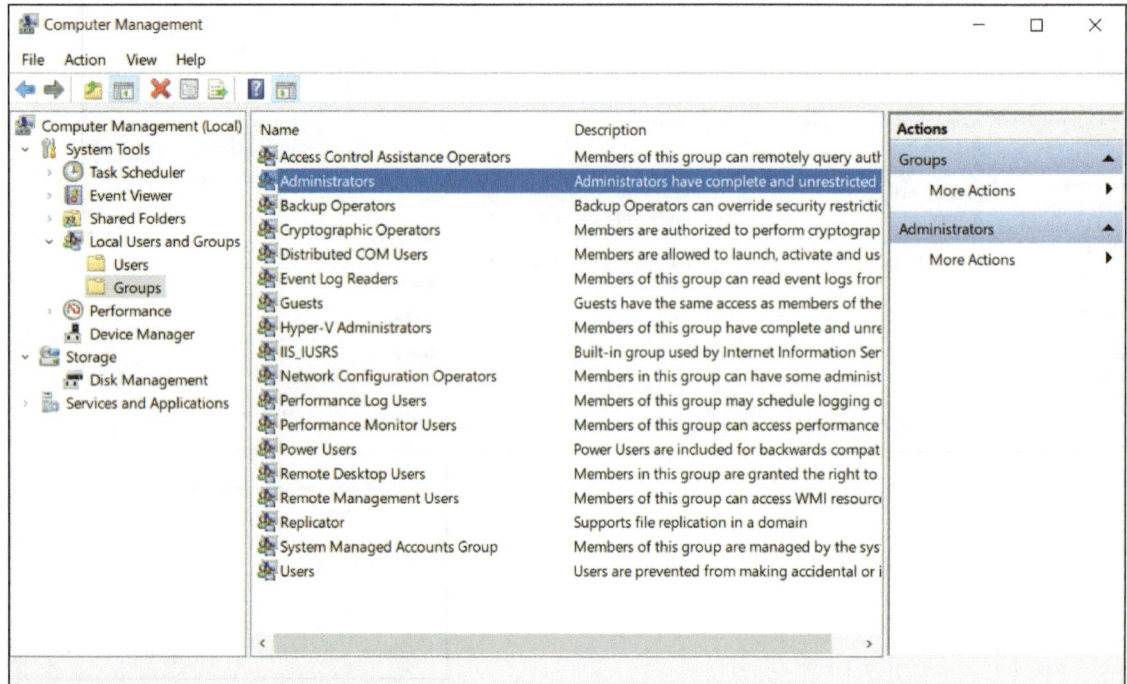

Figure 16-21 User groups installed on a system

To change the groups a user account is in, click **Users** under Local Users and Groups. The list of user accounts appears in the right pane of the console window (see the left side of Figure 16-22). Right-click the user account and select **Properties** in the shortcut menu. In the user account Properties box, click the **Member Of** tab (see the middle of Figure 16-22). Click **Add** and enter the user group name. You must type the user group name exactly as it appears in the list of user groups that you saw earlier (see Figure 16-21). To verify that the group name is correct, click **Check Names**. A verified name is underlined. (Alternately, you can click **Advanced**, click **Find Now**, and select the group name from the list of groups that appears.) Click **OK** twice to close both boxes.

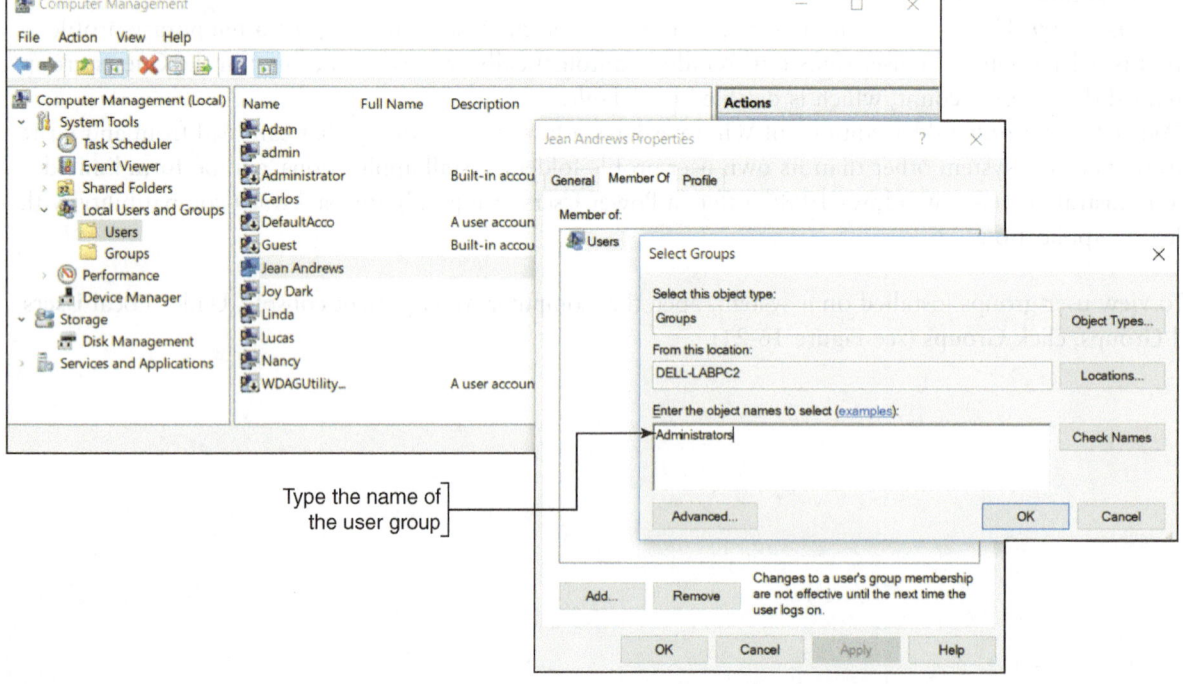

Figure 16-22 Add a user account to a user group

In addition to the groups you can assign to an account, Windows might automatically assign one of these built-in user groups to an account when it is determining permissions assigned to a file or folder:

- The Authenticated Users group includes all user accounts that can access the system except the Guest account. These accounts include domain accounts (used to sign in to the domain) and local accounts (used to sign in to the local computer). The accounts might or might not require a password. When you create a folder or file that is not part of your user profile, Windows gives access to all Authenticated Users by default.
- The Everyone group includes the Authenticated Users group as well as the Guest account. When you share a file or folder on the network (or to a homegroup in Windows 8/7), Windows gives access to the Everyone group by default.
- Anonymous users are users who have not been authenticated on a remote computer. If you sign in to a computer using a local account and then attempt to access a remote computer, you must be authenticated on the remote computer. You will be authenticated if your user account and password match on both computers. If you signed in to your local computer with an account and password that do not match an account and password on the remote computer, you are considered an anonymous user on the remote computer. As an anonymous user, you might be allowed to use File Explorer or Windows Explorer to view shared folders and files on the remote computer, but you cannot access them.

CUSTOMIZED USER GROUPS

Use the Computer Management console or the Local Users and Groups console (lusrmgr.msc) in business and professional editions of Windows to create and manage your own user groups. When managing several user accounts, it's easier to assign permissions to user groups rather than to individual accounts. First create a user group and then assign permissions to this user group. Any user account that you put in this group then acquires or inherits the same permissions.

User groups work especially well when several users need the same permissions. For example, you can set up an Accounting group and a Medical Records group for a small office. Users in the Accounting department and users in the Medical Records department go into their respective user groups. Then you only need to manage the permissions for two groups rather than multiple user accounts.

METHODS TO ASSIGN PERMISSIONS TO FOLDERS AND FILES

A+
CORE 2
2.2, 2.6

There are two general strategies for managing shared files and folders, also called directories, in Windows:

- *Workgroup sharing.* With workgroup sharing, all privileges and permissions are set up on each local computer so that each computer manages access to its files, folders, and printers shared on the peer-to-peer network. The local user decides which users on the network have access to which shared folder and the type of access they have.
- *Domain controlling.* If a Windows computer belongs to a domain instead of a workgroup or homegroup, all security should be managed by the network administrator for the entire network. Although individual users on workstations can share files and folders with other users in the domain, this is not considered a security best practice.

16

> ↻ **OS Differences** For Windows 8/7, when all users on a small network require the same access to all resources, you can use a homegroup. Folders, libraries, files, and printers shared with the homegroup are available to all users on the network whose computers have joined the homegroup. After the homegroup is set up, you can share a file or folder with the homegroup using the Sharing Wizard. To do so, right-click the item and select **Share with** in the shortcut menu. The wizard lists three general options for sharing followed by a list of specific people (see Figure 16-23). Click **Homegroup (view)** or **Homegroup (view and edit)** to assign this permission to the homegroup.
>
> Because of the lack of control over who can access a particular file or folder in a homegroup, Windows 10 Version 1803 and higher does not support homegroups.

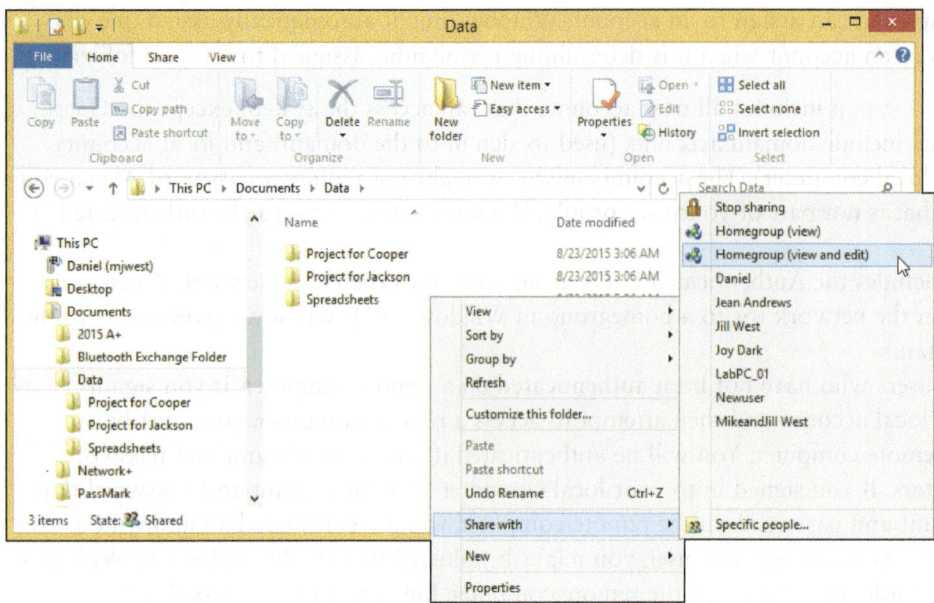

Figure 16-23   Share a folder with the homegroup

On a Windows peer-to-peer network, each workstation shares its files and folders with others in the workgroup, or files and folders on a file server are shared. Here are some tips about which folders to use to hold shared data on a file server or personal computer:

▲ Private data for an individual user is best kept in the C:\Users folder for that user. User accounts with limited or standard privileges cannot normally access these folders because they belong to another user account. However, accounts with administrative privileges do have access.

▲ The C:\Users\Public folder is intended to be used for folders and files that all users share. It is not recommended that you use this folder for controlled access to data.

▲ For best security, create a folder that's not in the C:\Users folder and assign permissions to that folder and its subfolders. You can allow all users access or only certain users or user groups.

Some applications can be shared with others on the network. If you share a folder that has a program file in it, a user on another computer can double-click the program file and execute it remotely on his or her desktop. This is a handy way for several users to share an application that is installed on a single computer. However, know that not all applications are designed to work this way.

Regardless of whether you are sharing to a workgroup or domain, Windows offers two methods to share a folder over the network:

▲ *Share permissions.* Share permissions grant permissions only to network users, and these permissions do not apply to local users of a computer. Share permissions work on NTFS, FAT32, and exFAT volumes and are configured using the Sharing tab in a folder's Properties box. Share permissions apply to a folder and its contents, but not to individual files.

▲ *NTFS permissions.* NTFS permissions apply to local users and network users and apply to both folders and individual files. NTFS permissions work on NTFS volumes only and are configured using the Security tab in a file or folder's Properties box. (The Security tab is missing on the Properties box of a folder or file on a FAT volume.)

Here are some tips when implementing share permissions and NTFS permissions:

▲ If you use both share permissions and NTFS permissions on a folder, the more restrictive permission applies. For NTFS volumes, use only NTFS permissions because they can be customized better. For FAT volumes, your only option is share permissions.

▲ If NTFS permissions are conflicting—for example, when a user account has been given one permission and the user group to which this user belongs has been given a different permission—the more liberal permission applies.

▲ Permission propagation is when permissions are passed from parent object to child. Inherited permissions are permissions that are attained from a parent. For example, when you create a file or folder in a parent folder, the new object takes on the permissions of the parent folder.

▲ When you move or copy an object to a folder, the object takes on the permissions of that folder. The exception to this rule is when you move (not copy) an object from one location to another on the same volume. In this case, the object retains its permissions from the original folder.

> ✎ **Notes** You can use the xcopy or robocopy command with parameters to change the rules for how inherited permissions are managed when copying and moving files. For more information, see the Microsoft Knowledge Base article cc733145 at *https://technet.microsoft.com/en-us/library/cc733145*.

> ★ **A+ Exam Tip** The A+ Core 2 exam expects you to compare NTFS and share permissions, including how allow and deny conflicts are resolved with each and what happens to permissions when you move or copy a file or folder.

HOW TO SHARE FOLDERS AND FILES

A+
CORE 2
1.5, 1.6,
2.2, 2.6

Now that you know about the concepts and strategies for sharing folders and files, let's look at the details of how to use Windows to manage user privileges and file and folder permissions.

APPLYING | CONCEPTS   CREATING USER ACCOUNTS WITH DATA ACCESS

Nicole is responsible for a peer-to-peer network at a medical doctor's office. Four computers are connected to the small company network; one of these computers acts as the file server for the network. Nicole has created two classifications of data, Financial and Medical. Two workers (Nancy and Adam) require access to the Medical data, and two workers (Linda and Carlos) require access to the Financial folder. In addition, the doctor, Lucas, requires access to both categories of data. Nicole must do the following to set up the users and data:

1. Create folders named Financial and Medical on the file server. Create five user accounts, one each for Lucas, Nancy, Adam, Linda, and Carlos. All the accounts belong to the Windows standard user group. Create two user groups, Financial and Medical.

2. Using NTFS permissions, set the permissions for the Financial and Medical folders on the file server so that only the members of the appropriate group can access each folder.

3. Test access to both folders using test data and then copy all real data into the two folders and subfolders. Set up a backup plan for the two folders, as you learned to do in Chapter 13.

Let's look at how each of these three steps is done.

(continues)

16

STEP 1: CREATE FOLDERS, USER ACCOUNTS, AND USER GROUPS

Follow these steps to create the folders, user accounts, and user groups on the file server computer that is using Windows 10 Pro:

1. Sign in to the system as an administrator.

2. Using an NTFS volume, create these two folders: **C:\Medical** and **C:\Financial**.

3. Open the Computer Management console or the Local Users and Groups console and create user accounts for **Lucas**, **Nancy**, **Adam**, **Linda**, and **Carlos**. The account types are automatically standard user accounts.

4. To create the Medical user group, right-click **Groups** under Local Users and Groups and select **New Group** in the shortcut menu. The New Group box appears. Enter the name of the group (**Medical**) and its description (**Users have access to the Medical folder**), as shown in Figure 16-24.

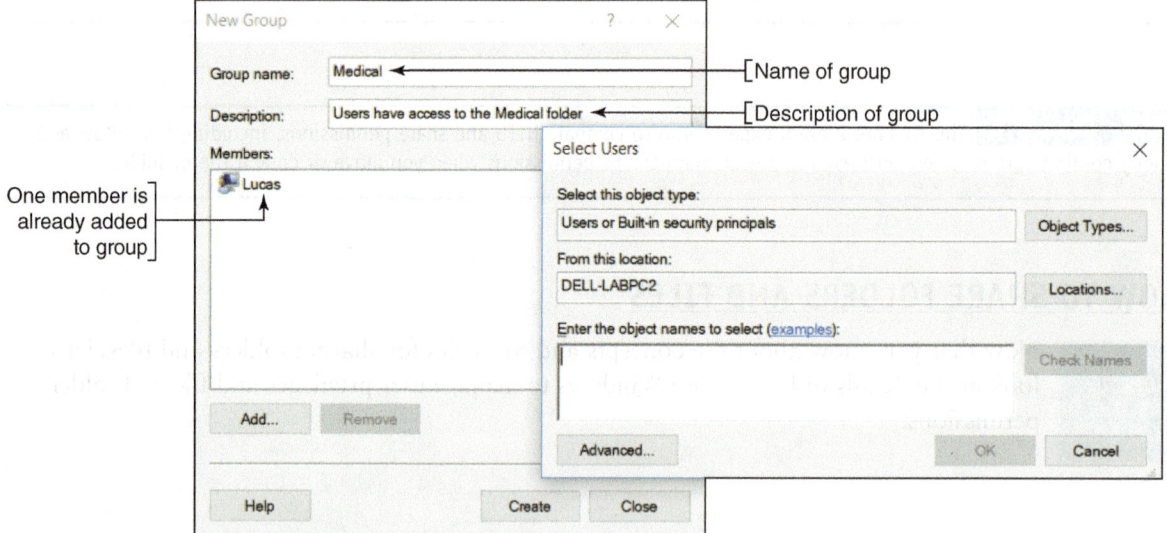

Figure 16-24 Setting up a new user group

5. Add all the users who need access to medical data (Lucas, Adam, and Nancy). To add members to the Medical group, click **Add**. The Select Users box opens, as shown on the right side of Figure 16-24. Under *Enter the object names to select*, enter the name of a user. Click **Check Names** to verify the user. Click **OK**. As each user is added, his or her name appears under Members in the New Group box, as shown in Figure 16-24. To create the group, click **Create** in the New Group box.

6. In the same way, create the Financial group and add Lucas, Linda, and Carlos to the group. Later, you can use the Computer Management console to add or remove users from either group.

7. Close the Computer Management console.

> ★ **A+ Exam Tip** The A+ Core 2 exam expects you to be able to set up a user account or group and know how to change the group to which an account is assigned.

STEP 2: SET NTFS FOLDER PERMISSIONS FOR USER GROUPS

Follow these steps to set the NTFS permissions for the two folders:

1. Open File Explorer or Windows Explorer, right-click the **Medical** folder, and select **Properties** in the shortcut menu. The Properties box for the folder appears.

(continues)

2. Click the **Security** tab (see Figure 16-25). Notice in the box that Authenticated Users, SYSTEM, Administrators, and Users all have access to the C:\Medical folder. When you select a user group, the type of permissions assigned to that group appears in the *Permissions* area. Table 16-1 explains the more significant types of permission. Note that the Administrators group has full control of the folder. Also notice the checks under Allow are dimmed. These permissions are dimmed because they have been inherited from the parent object. In this case, the parent object is Windows default settings.

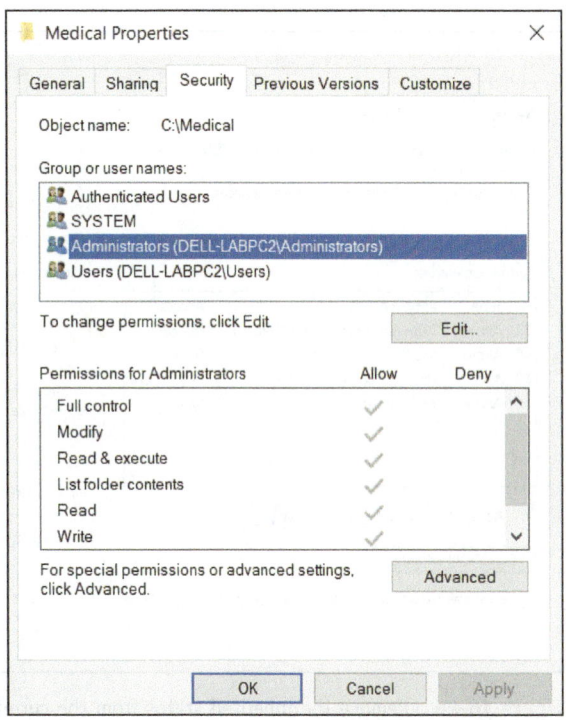

> ✏️ **Notes** For a thorough discussion of how permissions work, see the Microsoft Knowledge Base article cc783530 at *https://technet.microsoft.com/en-us/library/Cc783530(v=WS.10).aspx*.

> ⭐ **A+ Exam Tip** The A+ Core 2 exam expects you to know that NTFS permissions can be customized better than share permissions.

Figure 16-25 Permissions assigned to the Medical folder

Permission Level	Description
Full control	Can read, change, delete, and create files and subfolders, read file and folder attributes, read and change permissions, and take ownership of a file or folder.
Modify	Can read, change, and create files and subfolders. Can delete the folder or file but cannot delete subfolders and their files. Can read and change attributes. Can view permissions but not change them. Cannot take ownership.
Read & execute	Can read folders and contents and run programs in a folder. (Applies to both files and folders.)
List folder contents	Can read folders and contents and run programs in a folder. (Applies only to folders.)
Read	Can read folders and contents.
Write	Can create a folder or file and change attributes but cannot read data. This permission is used for a drop folder, where users can drop confidential files that can only be read by a manager. For example, an instructor can receive student homework in a drop folder.

Table 16-1 Permission levels for files and folders

3. To remove the inherited status from these permissions so you can change them, click **Advanced**. The Advanced Security Settings box appears (see the left side of Figure 16-26). Click **Disable inheritance**. The Block Inheritance box appears (see the right side of Figure 16-26). To keep the current permissions but remove the inherited status placed on them, click **Convert inherited permissions into explicit permissions on this object**. Click **Apply**.

> 🔁 **OS Differences** To remove the inherited status of folder permissions in Windows 7, open the Advanced Security Settings box and click **Change Permissions**. In the new Advanced Security Settings box, you can now uncheck **Include inheritable permissions from this object's parent**. A Windows Security warning box appears. To keep the current permissions but remove the inherited status placed on them, click **Add**.

16

(continues)

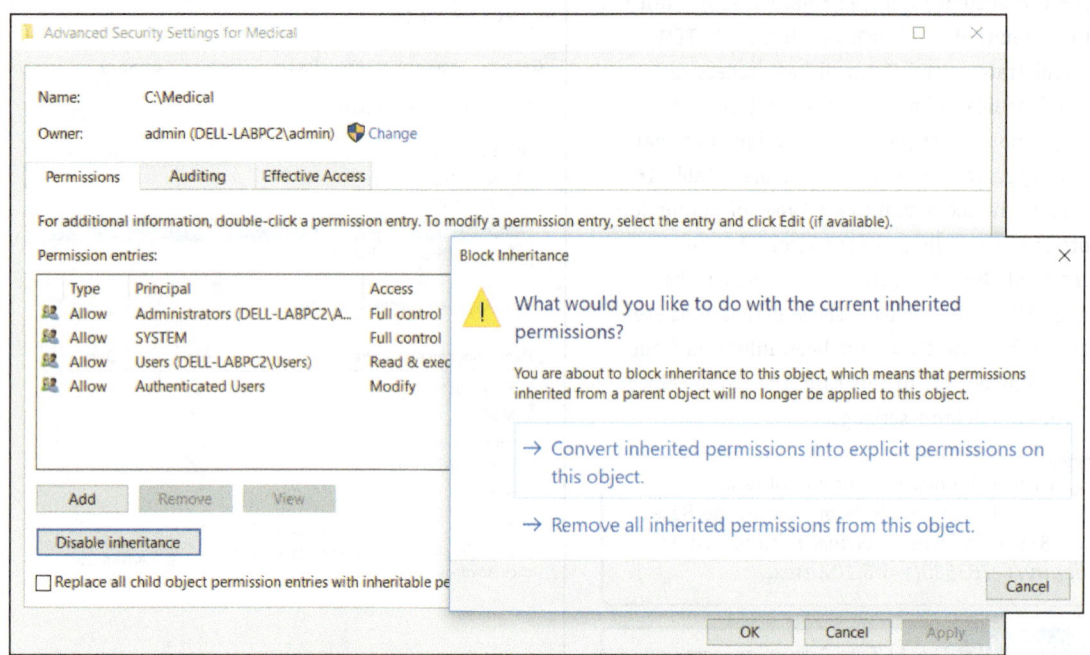

Figure 16-26 Remove the inherited status from the current permissions

4. Close the Advanced Security Settings box.

5. In the Medical Properties box, notice the permissions are now checked in black, indicating they are no longer inherited permissions and can be changed. Click **Edit** to change these permissions.

6. The Permissions box opens (see Figure 16-27). Select the **Authenticated Users** group and click **Remove**. Also remove the **Users** group. Don't remove the SYSTEM group, which gives Windows the access it needs. Also, don't remove the Administrators group. You need to leave that group as is so that administrators can access the data.

7. To add a new group, click **Add**. The Select Users or Groups box opens. Under *Enter the object names to select*, type **Medical**, as shown in Figure 16-28. Click **Check Names** to verify the group. Click **OK**. The Medical group is added to the list of groups and users for this folder.

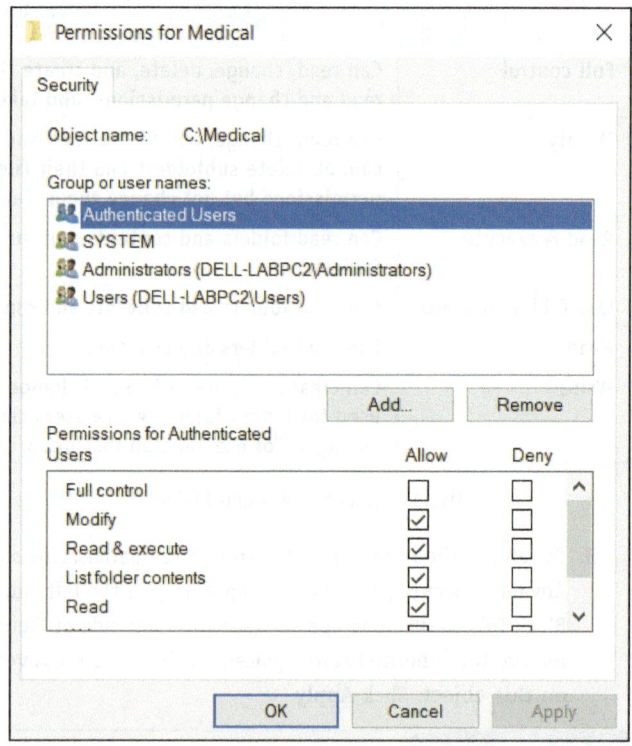

Figure 16-27 Change the permissions to a folder

(continues)

8. In the Permissions box, make sure the **Medical** group is selected. Under *Permissions for Medical*, check **Allow** under *Full control* to give that permission to this user group. Click **OK** twice to close the Properties box.

9. In a similar way, change the permissions of the C:\Financial folder so that Authenticated Users and Users are not allowed access and the Financial group is allowed full control.

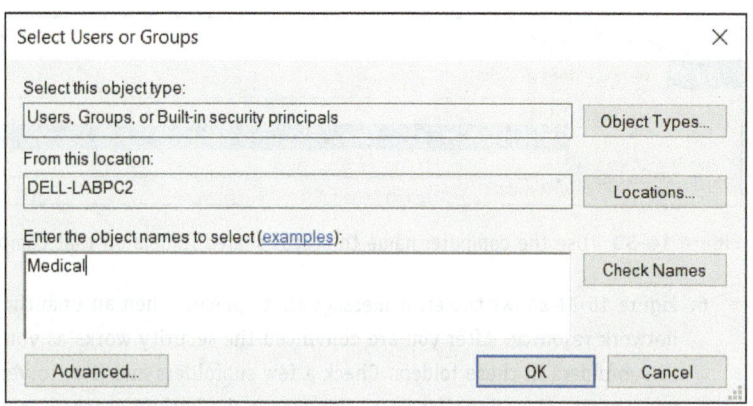

Figure 16-28 Add a user or group to shared permissions

STEP 3: TEST, SET SHARE PERMISSIONS, AND GO LIVE

It's now time to test your security measures. Do the following to test the NTFS permissions and implement your shared folders:

1. Test a user account in each user group to make sure the user can read, write, and delete in the folder he needs but cannot access the other folder. Put some test data in each folder. Then sign in to the system using an account you want to test and try to access each folder. Figure 16-29 shows the box that appears when an unauthorized user attempts to access a local folder. When you click **Continue**, entering an administrator password in the resulting UAC box gives you access.

Figure 16-29 Access to a folder is controlled

2. Now that NTFS permissions are set correctly for each local and network user, you are ready to allow access over the network. To do that, both NTFS and share permissions must allow network access. (Share permissions apply only to network access, not local access.) The best practice is to allow full access using share permissions and restrictive access using NTFS permissions. Remember that the most restrictive permissions apply. To allow full access using share permissions, click the **Sharing** tab of each folder's properties box, and click **Advanced Sharing**.

3. In the Advanced Sharing box, check **Share this folder** if it is not already checked. Then click **Permissions**. To add a new group, click **Add**. The Select Users or Groups box opens. Under *Enter the object names to select*, type **Everyone** and click **OK**. The Everyone group is added to the list of groups and users for this folder.

4. With **Everyone** selected, check **Allow** under *Full control* to give that permission to the Everyone user group. Click **OK** twice and then close the Properties box.

5. Now that you have the security settings in place for one computer, go to each computer on the network and create the user accounts that will be using this computer. Then test the security and make sure each user can or cannot access the \Financial and \Medical folders as you intend. To access shared folders, you can drill down into the Network group in File Explorer or Windows Explorer. Another method is to type the IP address (for example, **\\192.168.1.112**) or computer name (for example, **\\DELL-LABPC2**) in the address bar of the Explorer window, as shown in Figure 16-30.

16

(continues)

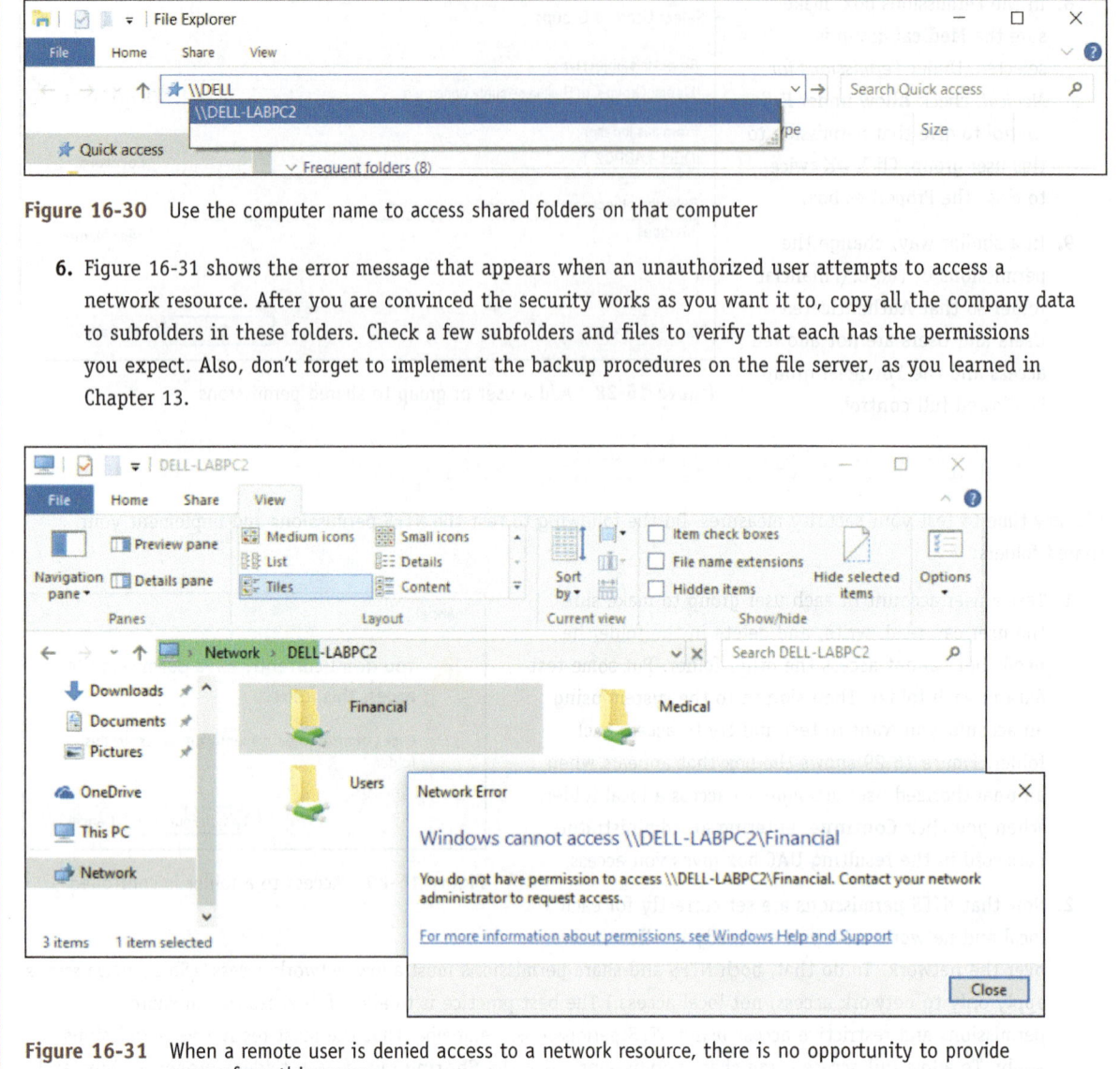

Figure 16-30 Use the computer name to access shared folders on that computer

6. Figure 16-31 shows the error message that appears when an unauthorized user attempts to access a network resource. After you are convinced the security works as you want it to, copy all the company data to subfolders in these folders. Check a few subfolders and files to verify that each has the permissions you expect. Also, don't forget to implement the backup procedures on the file server, as you learned in Chapter 13.

Figure 16-31 When a remote user is denied access to a network resource, there is no opportunity to provide access from this screen

USER AND GROUP INFORMATION WITH THE GPRESULT COMMAND

You can pull a list of all the groups a user belongs to with the gpresult command. This information can be helpful when troubleshooting user group issues or Group Policy problems; the command displays user groups a user belongs to and all the currently applied policies set by Group Policy. To retrieve information about a user other than the one signed in, open an elevated command prompt window and enter the command **gpresult /scope user /user** *username* **/r**. Figure 16-32 shows output for the user Adam; you can verify that he belongs to the Medical group. You learn more about the gpresult command later in this chapter.

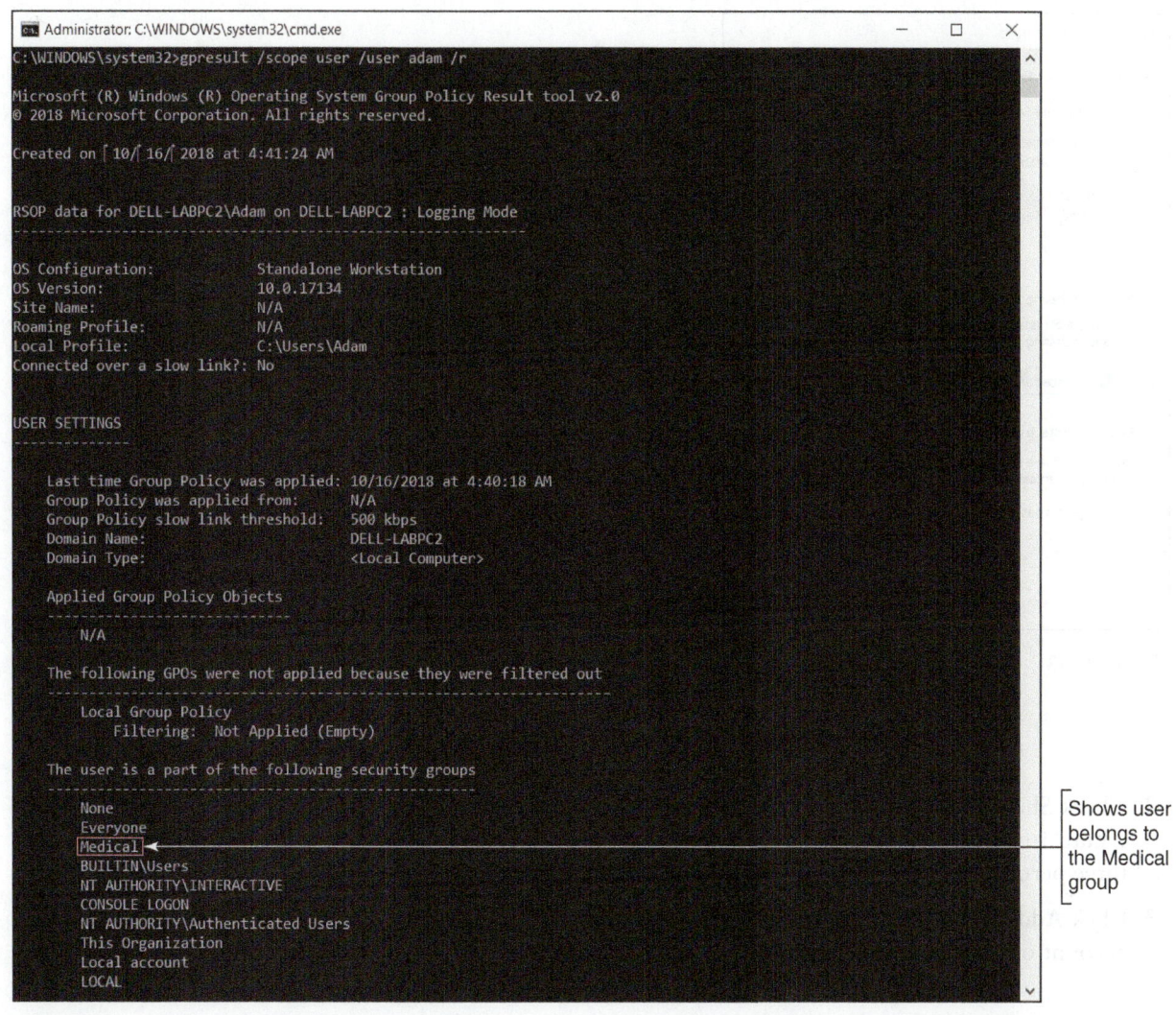

Figure 16-32   The /r parameter requests a summary of the gpresult information instead of more verbose (/v) output

HOW TO USE SHARE PERMISSIONS

Although you can mix NTFS permissions and share permissions on the same system, life is simpler if you use one or the other. For NTFS volumes, NTFS permissions are the way to go because they can be customized better than share permissions. However, you must use share permissions on FAT volumes. To do so, follow these steps:

1. Open the Properties box for the folder (*Personnel* in this case). Notice in Figure 16-33 that the Security tab is missing because the folder is on a FAT volume. Select the **Sharing** tab and click **Advanced Sharing**. The Advanced Sharing box opens (see the right side of Figure 16-33).

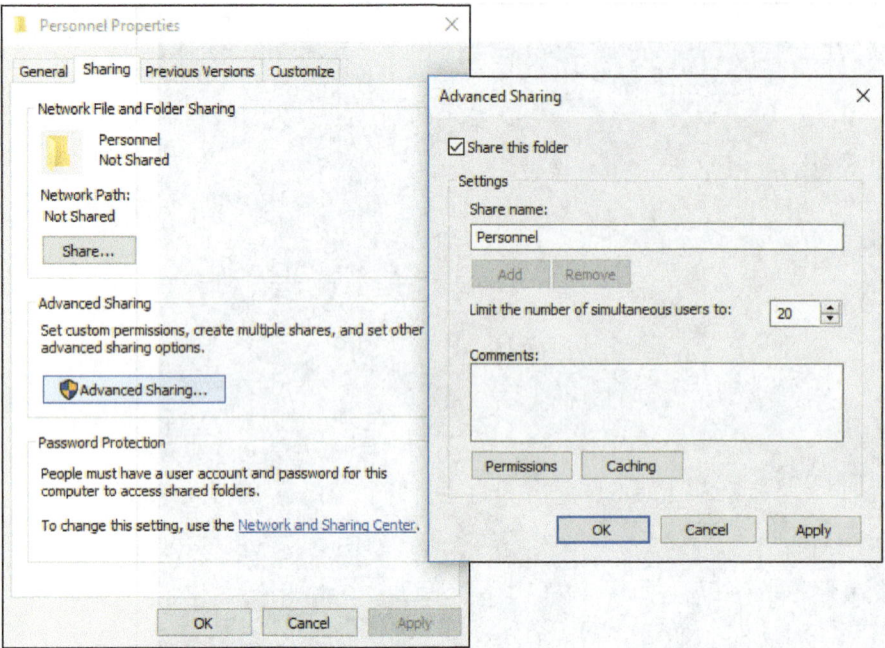

Figure 16-33   Use the Sharing tab of a folder Properties box to set up share permissions
on a FAT volume

2. Check **Share this folder**. Then click **Permissions**. The Permissions box opens (see the left side of Figure 16-34). Initially, the folder is shared with Everyone. Also notice that share permissions offer only three permission levels: Full Control, Change, and Read.

3. Click **Add**. The Select Users or Groups box appears (see the right side of Figure 16-34). Enter a user account or user group and click **OK**.

Figure 16-34   Add a user or user group to assign share permissions

4. To delete the Everyone group, select it in the Permissions box and click **Remove**. Click **OK** to close each open box in turn.

SUPPORT AND TROUBLESHOOT SHARED FOLDERS AND FILES

You have just seen how to set up user groups and folder permissions assigned to these groups. If you have problems accessing a shared resource, follow these steps:

1. Windows might be able to solve the problem for you. In Control Panel, click **Troubleshooting**. The Troubleshooting window presents a list of troubleshooters for addressing problems in the categories of Programs, Hardware and Sound, Network and Internet, or System and Security. Click **Access shared files and folders on other computers** and walk through the Shared Folders troubleshooter.

2. Open the Network and Sharing Center. Make sure your network location is set to Private (Home or Work for Windows 7).

3. In the left pane, click **Change advanced sharing settings**. The Advanced sharing settings window opens (refer back to Figure 16-17).

4. Verify that the settings here are the default settings for a Private network profile:

   ◢ Select **Turn on network discovery** and make sure **Turn on automatic setup of network connected devices** is checked.

   ◢ Select **Turn on file and printer sharing**.

> ★ **A+ Exam Tip** The A+ Core 2 exam expects you to know the difference between a shared printer and a network printer. A printer installed locally on a computer can be shared with other computers. This is different from a network printer, which is accessed by each networked computer directly through the network.

> ◯ **OS Differences** If you want a Windows 8/7 computer to access Homegroup resources, select **Allow Windows to manage homegroup connections (recommended)** under HomeGroup connections.
> If you are using NTFS permissions along with less restrictive share permissions to share resources on a network, disable homegroup sharing, which can cause conflicts.

   ◢ If you want to share the Public folder to the network, go to the Public folder sharing section under All Networks and select **Turn on sharing so anyone with network access can read and write files in the Public folders.**

   ◢ If you want the added protection of requiring that all users on the network must have a valid user account and password on this computer, select **Turn on password protected sharing**.

   After you have made your changes, click Save changes at the bottom of the window.

5. In the Network and Sharing Center, click **Change adapter settings**. The Network Connections window appears. Right-click the network connection icon and select **Properties** in the shortcut menu. In the Properties box, verify that **File and Printer Sharing for Microsoft Networks** is checked (see Figure 16-35).

16

Figure 16-35 Verify that the properties for the network connection are set for sharing resources over the connection

6. The user account name and password on the remote computer must match the user account and password on the host computer. If these accounts and passwords don't match, the user is considered an anonymous user and is denied access to resources shared on the remote computer. To verify that account names and passwords match, open the Computer Management console, where you can view user account names, create new accounts, and set passwords.

Here are a few tips about managing shared folders and files:

◢ *Use advanced permissions settings.* If you need further control of the permissions assigned to a user or group, click **Advanced** on the Security tab of a folder's Properties box. The Advanced Security Settings box appears (see Figure 16-36A). You can see that the Medical user group was given full control. To change these permission details, double-click the user group. In this example, the Medical group is being edited. The Permission Entry box opens (see Figure 16-36B). On Windows 10/8 systems only, click **Show advanced permissions**.

Detailed permissions can now be changed. For example, to prevent users in the Medical group from deleting the Medical folder, its subfolders, and its files, uncheck **Delete subfolders and files** and uncheck **Delete**. Click **OK** to close each box. The resulting change means that users of the Medical group cannot delete or move a file or folder. (They can, however, copy the file or folder.)

★ **A+ Exam Tip** The A+ Core 2 exam expects you to be able to implement permissions so that a user can copy but not move a file or folder and understand how to apply Allow and Deny permissions.

(A)

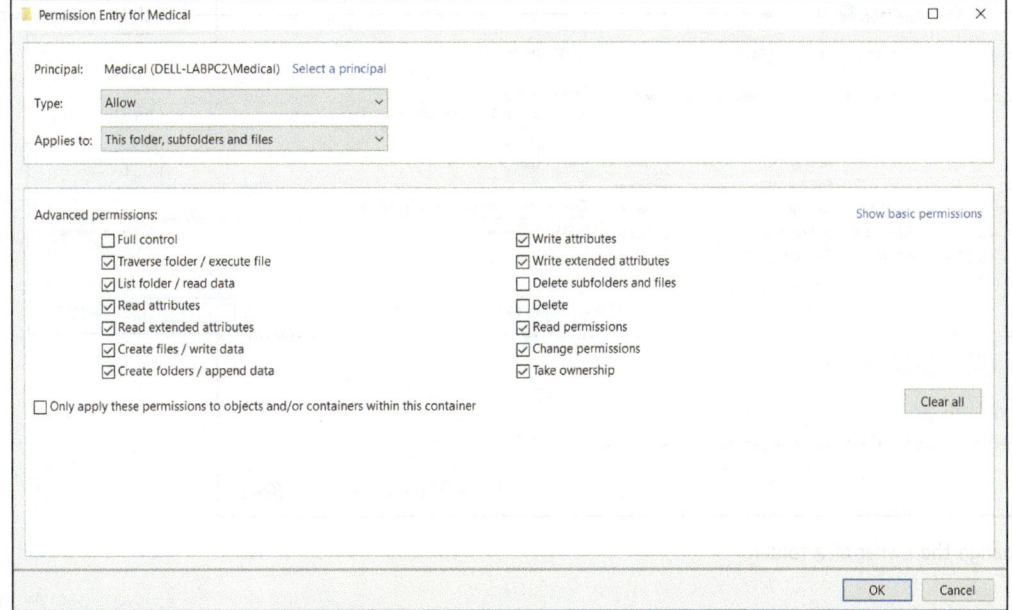

(B)

Figure 16-36 Advanced permissions settings

▲ *Manage permissions using the parent folder.* When a subfolder is created, it is assigned the permissions of the parent folder. Recall that these inherited permissions appear dimmed. The best way to change inherited permissions is to change the permissions of the parent object. In other words, to change the permissions of the C:\Financial\QuickBooks folder, change the permission of the C:\Financial folder. Changing permissions of a parent folder affects all its subfolders.

16

▲ *Check the effective permissions.* Permissions manually set for a subfolder or file can override inherited permissions. Permissions that are manually set are called explicit permissions. When a folder or file has inherited an explicit permission set, it might be confusing to know exactly which permissions are in effect for the file or folder. To find out, see the Advanced Security Settings box. (Look back at Figure 16-36A.) NTFS permissions are reported on the Permissions tab and share permissions are reported on the Share tab. Use the Effective Access tab (for Windows 7, the tab is called Effective Permissions) to get a detailed report of resources available to a particular user.

▲ *Take ownership of a folder.* The owner of a folder always has full permissions for the folder. If you are having a problem changing permissions and you are not the folder owner, try taking ownership of the folder. To do that, click **Advanced** on the Security tab of the folder's Properties box. The Advanced Security Settings box appears. Next to the name of the owner, click **Change**. You can then enter the name of the new owner (see Figure 16-37). Click **Check Names** to confirm the name is entered correctly and click **OK** twice.

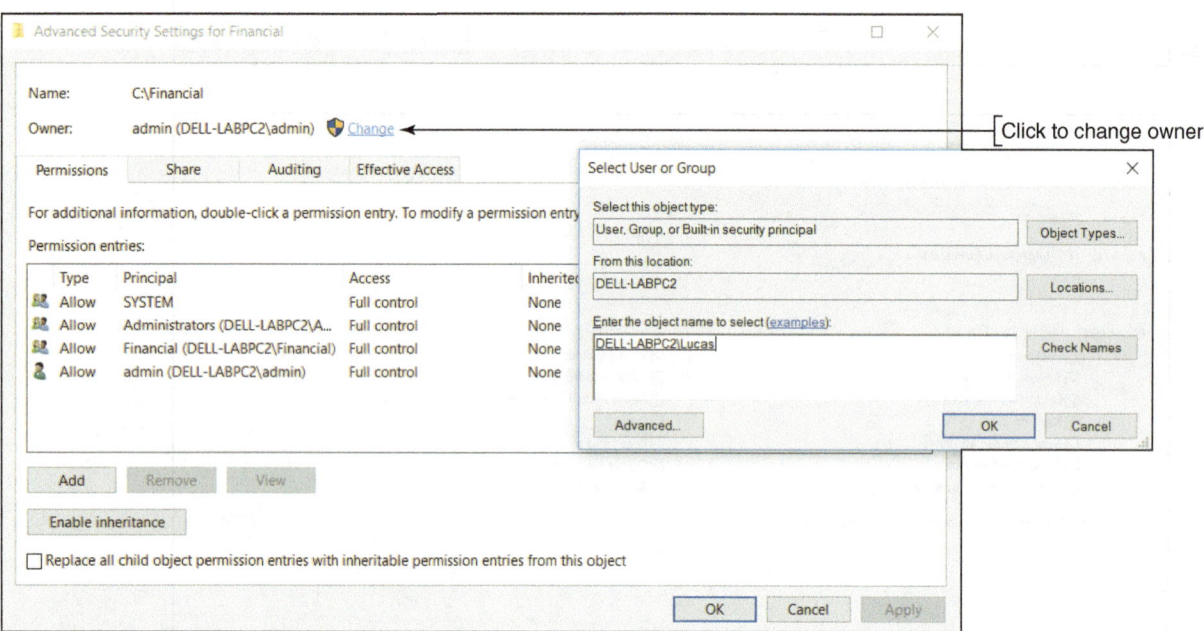

Figure 16-37   Change the owner of a folder

○ **OS Differences** To change the owner of a folder in Windows 7, open the Advanced Security Settings box, click the **Owner** tab, then click **Edit**. Select a user from the *Change owner to* list (see Figure 16-38) and click **Apply** to make that user the new owner. If a user is not listed, click **Other users or groups** and add the user. Close the Advanced Security Settings box and the Properties box, and reopen the Properties box for the change to take effect.

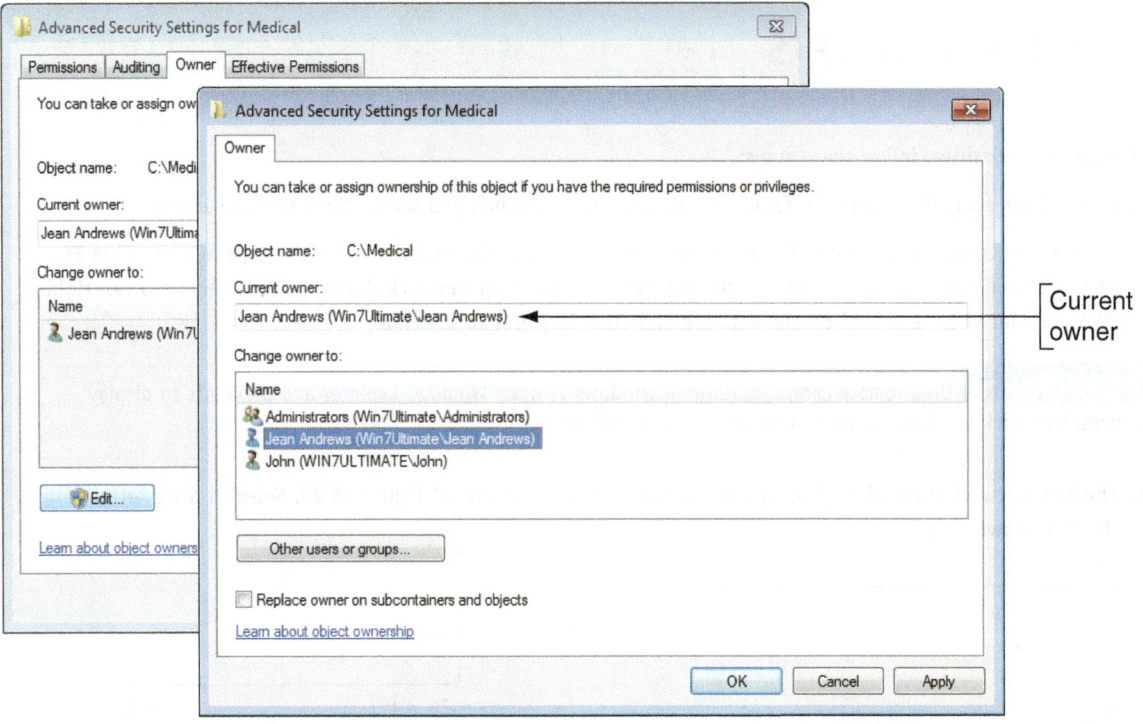

Figure 16-38 Change the owner of a folder in Windows 7

◢ *Use only one workgroup.* It is not necessary that all computers belong to the same workgroup in order to share resources. However, performance improves when they are all in the same workgroup.

◢ *Require passwords for all user accounts.* Don't forget that for best security, each user account needs a password. In a workgroup, the policy to require that all accounts have passwords is set using Local Group Policy. On a domain, Group Policy is used.

◢ *Use a mapped network drive.* For the convenience of remote users, map network drives for shared folders that are heavily used. How to do that is coming up next.

HOW TO MAP A NETWORK DRIVE OR NETWORK PRINTER

A **network share** is one of the most powerful and versatile methods of communicating over a network. A network share makes one computer (the client) appear to have a new hard drive, such as drive E:, that is really hard drive space on another host computer (the server). The client computer creates and saves a shortcut associated with a drive letter that points to the host computer's shared folder or drive. This is called **mapping** the drive. This client/server arrangement is managed by a Windows component, the **Network File System (NFS)**, which makes it possible for files on the network to be accessed as easily as if they are stored on the local computer. NFS is a type of distributed file system (DFS), which is a system that shares files on a network. Even if the host computer uses a different OS, such as macOS or Linux, the network share still functions. In addition to mapping a network drive, you can also map a network printer to a computer.

> ✎ **Notes** A network-attached storage (NAS) device provides hard drive storage for computers on a network. Computers on the network can access this storage using a mapped network drive.

16

APPLYING | CONCEPTS   MAPPING A NETWORK DRIVE AND NETWORK PRINTER

To set up a network drive, follow these steps:

1. On the host computer, share the folder or entire volume to which you want others to have access.

2. On the remote computer that will use the network drive, open File Explorer. In the left pane, click **This PC**. At the top of the window, click the **Computer** tab and click **Map network drive**. (Alternately, you can right-click a folder you see shared on the network and click **Map network drive**.)

> **OS Differences** On a remote computer running Windows 7, open Windows Explorer and press **Alt** to display the menu bar. Click the **Tools** menu and select **Map network drive**.

3. The Map Network Drive dialog box opens, as shown on the left side of Figure 16-39. Select a drive letter from the drop-down list.

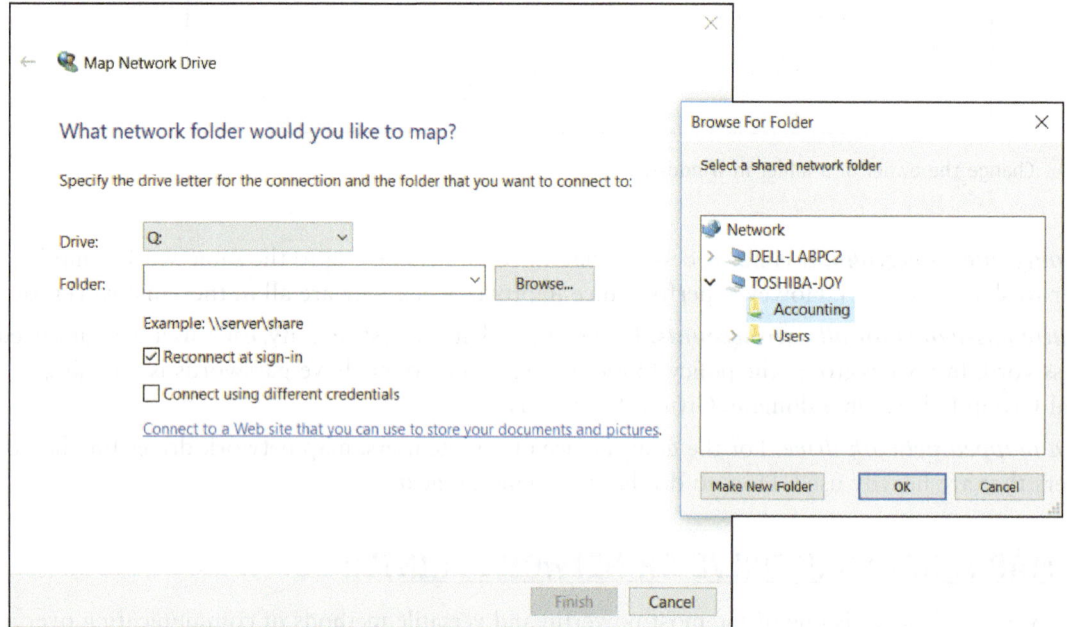

Figure 16-39   Mapping a network drive to a host computer

4. Click the **Browse** button and locate the shared folder or drive on the host computer (see the right side of Figure 16-39). Click **OK** to close the Browse For Folder dialog box, and click **Finish** to map the drive. The folder on the host computer now appears as one more drive in Explorer on your computer.

> **Notes** When mapping a network drive, you can type the path to the host computer rather than clicking the Browse button to navigate to the host. To enter the path, open the Map Network Drive dialog box and use two backslashes followed by the name of the host computer, followed by a backslash and the drive or folder to access on the host computer. For example, to access the Projects folder on the computer named Win8, enter **\\Win8\Projects** and then click **Finish**.

If a network drive does not work, go to the Network and Sharing Center and verify that the network connection is good. You can also use the net use command to solve problems with mapped network drives. You learned about the net use command in Chapter 7.

(continues)

> ✏️ **Notes** A host computer might be in sleep mode or powered down when a remote computer attempts to make a mapped drive connection at startup. To solve this problem, configure the host computer for Wake-on-LAN, as you learned in Chapter 7.

Recall from Chapter 14 that you can connect a network printer to a server and the server can share the printer on the network. The Print Management console can be used to manage all shared printers on the network from a single workstation. You can also map a network printer directly to your computer, eliminating a print server or printer sharing from the process. Here's how:

1. In Windows 10, open the **Settings** app, select the **Devices** group, and then click **Printers & scanners**. A list of installed printers and scanners appears. Click **Add a printer or scanner**. Windows searches for available printers and scanners, but probably will not find the network printer. Click **The printer that I want isn't listed**. In the Add Printer box (see Figure 16-40), select **Add a printer using a TCP/IP address or hostname** and click **Next**.

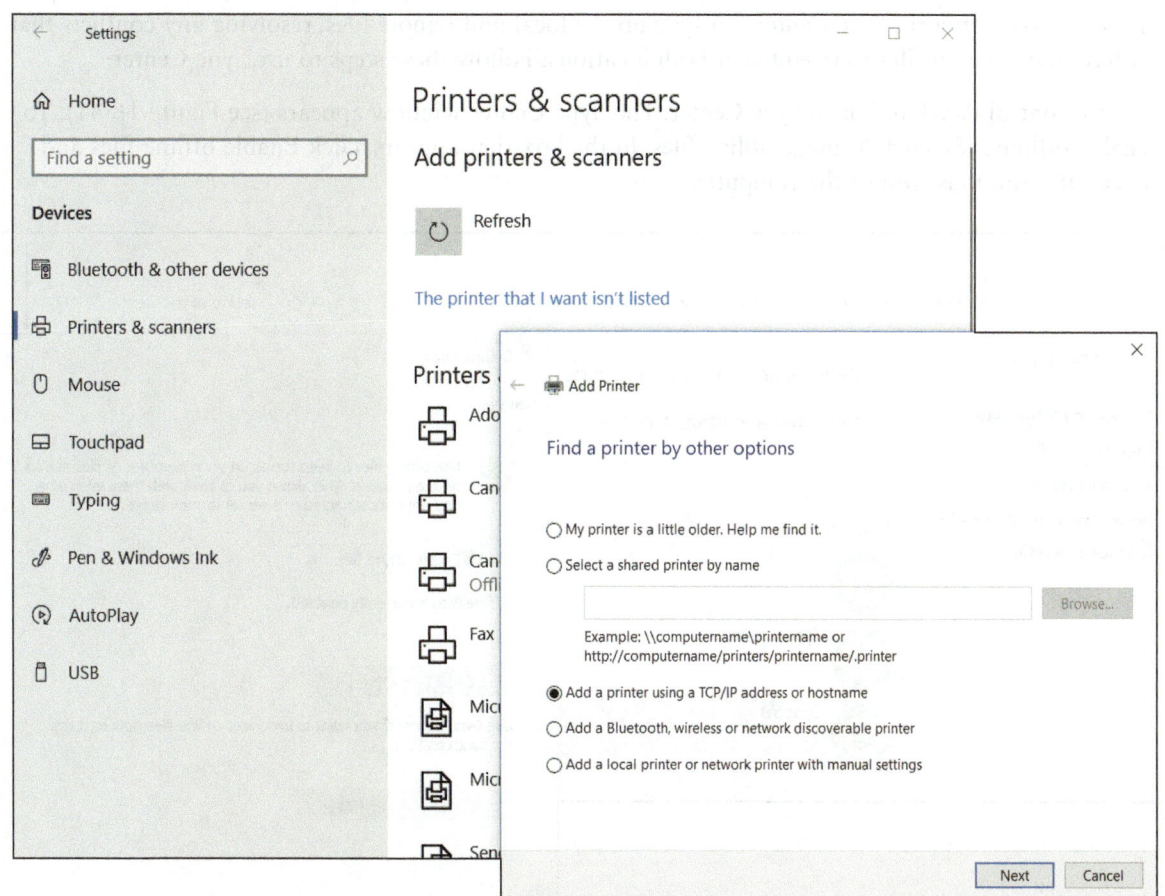

Figure 16-40 Select a network printer identified by its IP address or host name

2. Enter the printer's IP address and click **Next**. Windows searches the network for the printer. If it finds the printer, the installation proceeds and you can select the printer manufacturer and model. Alternately, you can provide printer drivers that you can download to your computer. After the printer is installed, be sure to print a test page.

(continues)

> **⟳ OS Differences** To install a network printer for Windows 8/7 systems, open **Control Panel** in Classic view and click **Devices and Printers**. Click **Add a printer**. Windows 8/7 will most likely find and list the network printer. Be sure to select a printer that shows its IP address; otherwise, you are connecting to a computer that has shared the printer to the network. If the printer doesn't appear in the list, click **The printer that I want isn't listed**, enter the name of the printer or its IP address, and click **Next**.

If you have problems mapping to a network printer, download the printer drivers from the website of the printer manufacturer and follow the manufacturer's directions to install the printer.

SYNC CENTER AND OFFLINE FILES

A+
CORE 2
1.6

Sync Center, an applet in Control Panel, allows two computers to sync the contents of a shared folder or volume. When you set up a folder to work offline, your computer can work with the folder even when your computer is not connected to the remote computer that holds the share because Sync Center keeps a copy of the files on the local computer. Later, when the computer reconnects to the network, Sync Center can sync up the local and remote files, resolving any conflicts that might have happened if files were edited at both locations. Follow these steps to use Sync Center:

1. Go to **Control Panel** and open **Sync Center**. The Sync Center window appears (see Figure 16-41). To enable offline files, click **Manage offline files**. In the box that appears, click **Enable offline files** and click **OK**. You must restart the computer.

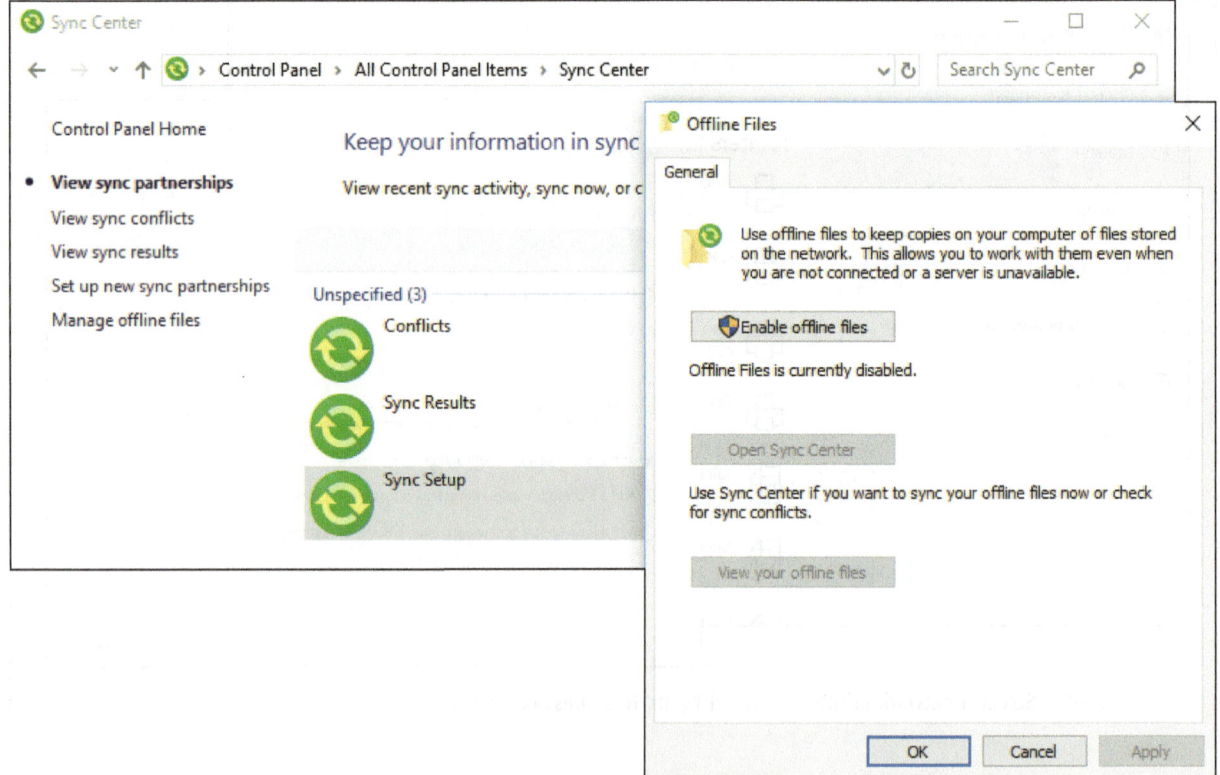

Figure 16-41 Enable offline files so you can use Sync Center

2. Using File Explorer or Windows Explorer, right-click a shared folder on the network and click **Always available offline** (see Figure 16-42). Alternately, you can select the folder, open the **Home** menu, click **Easy access**, and click **Always available offline**.

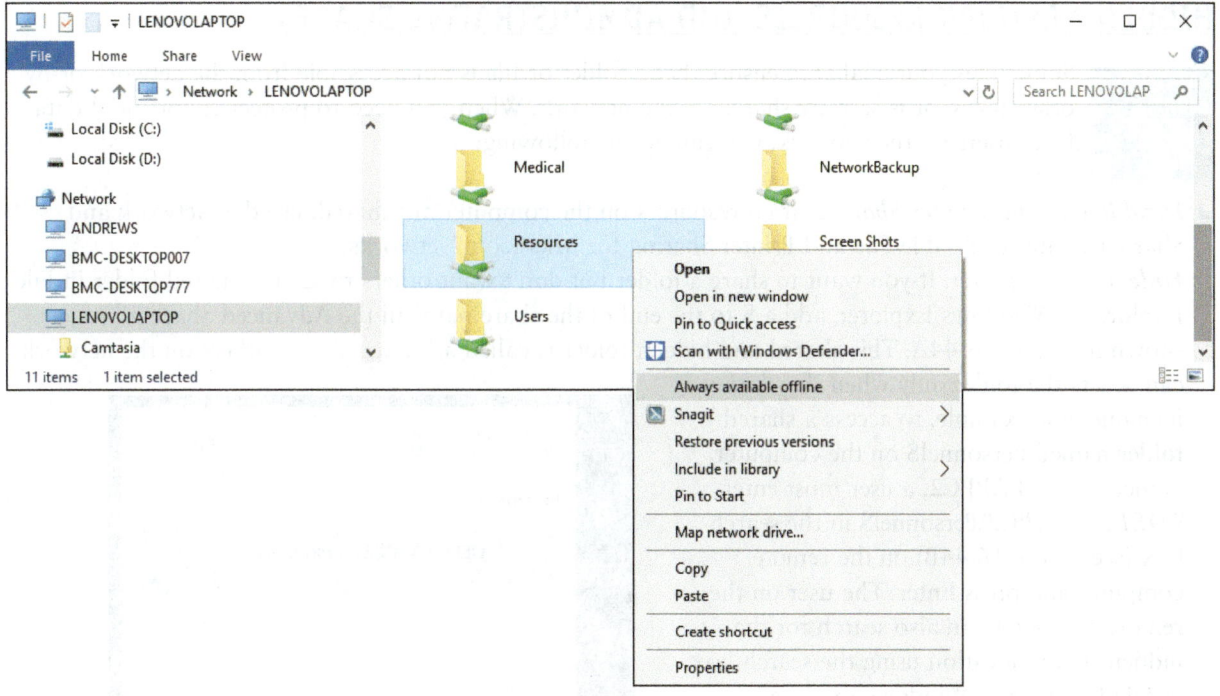

Figure 16-42 Configure a network share as an offline folder

3. The folder will sync on your computer and the remote computer. (On your computer, offline files are stored in the C:\Windows\CSC folder.) When your network connection is slow or disconnected, you can continue to use the folder on your computer.

4. Later, when your computer and the remote computer are connected, you can force a manual sync of the files in the folder. In File Explorer, select the folder, open the **Home** menu, click **Easy access**, and click **Sync**. See Figure 16-43.

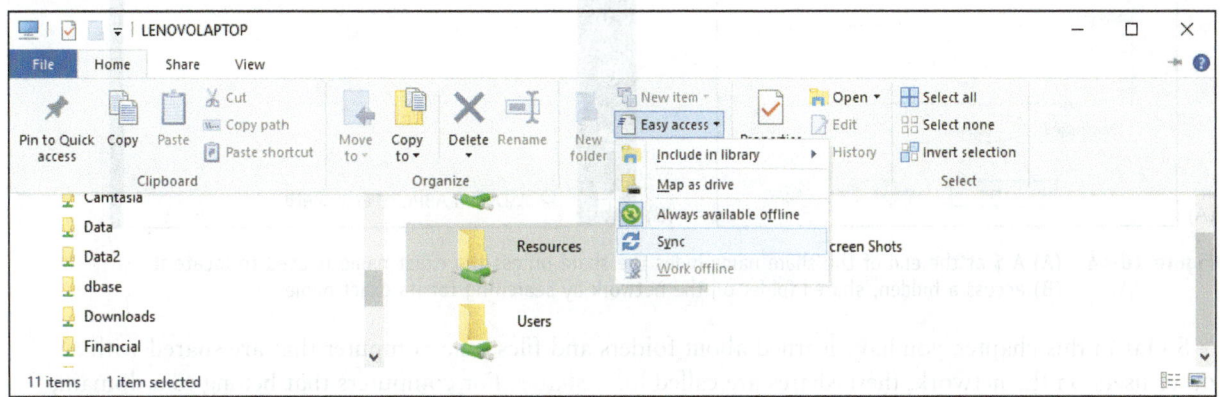

Figure 16-43 Manually force an offline folder to sync with the network share

> ✎ **Notes** OneDrive is cloud storage associated with your Microsoft account and stored in the Microsoft Cloud. To make OneDrive folders available offline when you are not connected to the Internet, right-click a folder in OneDrive and click **Always available offline**.

16

HIDDEN NETWORK RESOURCES AND ADMINISTRATIVE SHARES

**A+
CORE 2
1.8, 2.6**

Sometimes your goal is to ensure that a folder or file is not accessible from the network or by other users, or is secretly shared on the network. When you need to protect confidential data from users on the network, you can do the following:

▲ *Disable File and Printer Sharing.* If no resources on the computer are shared, use the Network and Sharing Center to disable File and Printer Sharing for Microsoft Networks.

▲ *Hide a shared folder.* If you want to share a folder but don't want others to see the shared folder in File Explorer or Windows Explorer, add a $ to the end of the share name in the Advanced Sharing box, as shown in Figure 16-44A. This shared and hidden folder is called a hidden share. Others on the network can access the folder only when they know its name. For example, to access a shared folder named Personnel$ on the computer named DELL-LABPC2, a user must enter *\\DELL-LABPC2*Personnel$ in the search box (see Figure 16-44B) on the remote computer and press **Enter**. The user on the remote computer can also search for the hidden share's location using the search box in File Explorer or Windows Explorer.

(A)   (B)

Figure 16-44   (A) A $ at the end of the share name hides the share unless the exact name is used to locate it; (B) access a hidden, shared folder on the network by searching for its exact name

So far in this chapter, you have learned about folders and files on a computer that are shared with other users on the network; these shares are called local shares. For computers that belong to a domain, you need to be aware of another way folders are shared, called administrative shares. Administrative shares are folders shared by default that administrator accounts at the domain level can access. You don't need to manually share these folders because Windows automatically does so by default. Two types of administrative shares are:

▲ *The %systemroot% folder.* Enter the path *computername*\admin$ to access the *%systemroot%* folder (most likely the C:\Windows folder) on a remote computer in order to work with that computer's system folders and files. For example, to connect to the ws14 workstation shown in Figure 16-45, the entry in the Explorer address bar is **\\ws14**_admin$_. The authenticate box appears; enter **Administrator** as the user name and the password to the Administrator account. The admin$ administrative share is called the Remote Admin share.

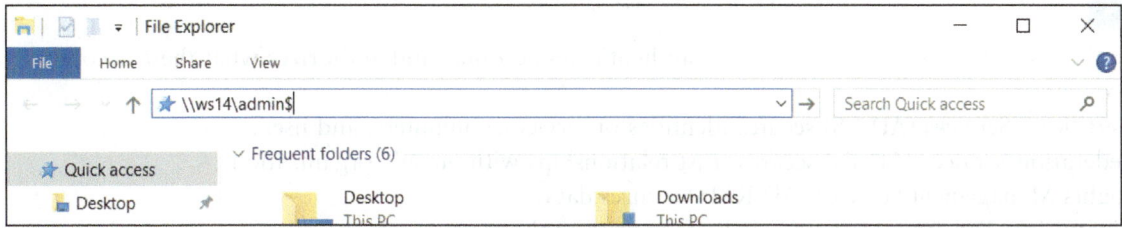

Figure 16-45 Access an administrative share on a domain

▲ *Any volume or drive.* To access the root level of any volume or drive on the network, enter the computer name and drive letter followed by a $—for example, **\\ws14\\C$**.

> ⭐ **A+ Exam Tip** The A+ Core 2 exam expects you to understand the difference between administrative shares and local shares.

> ✏️ **Notes** To see a list of all shares on a computer, open the Computer Management console and drill down to **System Tools**, **Shared Folders**, **Shares** (see Figure 16-46).

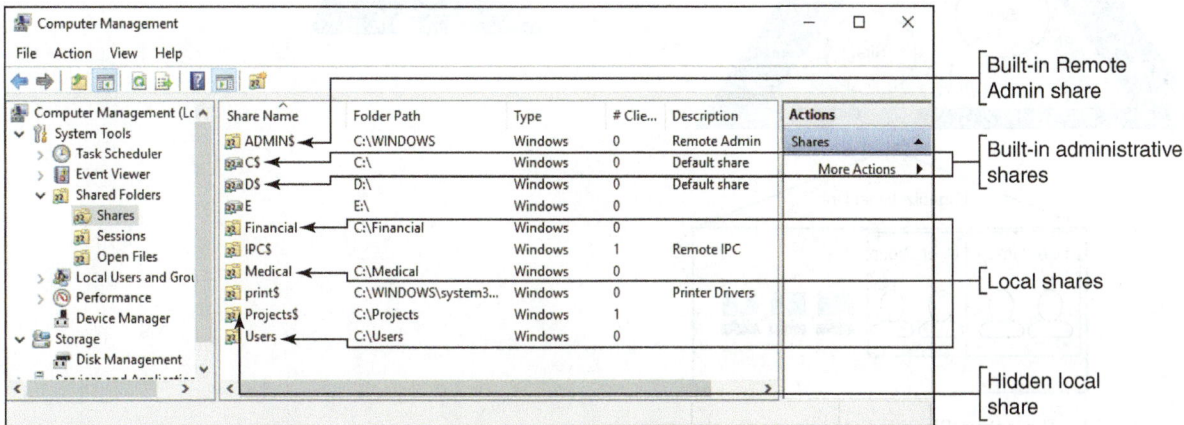

Figure 16-46 Use the Computer Management console to view all shares

> ⚡ **Caution** When supporting a workgroup, you might be tempted to share all the drives on all computers so that you can have easy access remotely. However, using local shares in this way is not a good security practice. Don't share the \Windows folder or an entire drive or volume on the network. These local shares appear in everyone's Explorer window. You don't want your system files and folders exposed like this.

16

USING ACTIVE DIRECTORY DOMAIN SERVICES

Active Directory (AD) is a suite of services and databases provided by Windows Server that is used to manage Windows domains, including access to the domain and what users and computers can do in the domain. AD incorporates five groups of services:

▲ **Active Directory Domain Services (AD DS)** authenticates accounts and authorizes what these accounts can do.
▲ AD Certificate Services (AD CS) secures identities of services, computers, and users.
▲ AD Federation Services (AD FS) secures trust relationships with outside organizations.
▲ AD Rights Management Services (AD RMS) secures data.
▲ AD Lightweight Directory Services (AD LDS) secures applications.

Active Directory organizes resources in a top-down hierarchical structure, as shown in Figure 16-47. Users and resources of a company or school managed by AD are organized into a **forest** (the entire enterprise), which contains a domain (for example, *mycompany.com*). For a few very large enterprises, domains can contain subdomains (for example, *mycompany.com* and *mycompany-dev.com*), but in most situations, a forest contains only a single domain. Domains can contain sites (for example, a New York branch office and a San Francisco branch). Domains are also organized into organizational units and sub-organizational units.

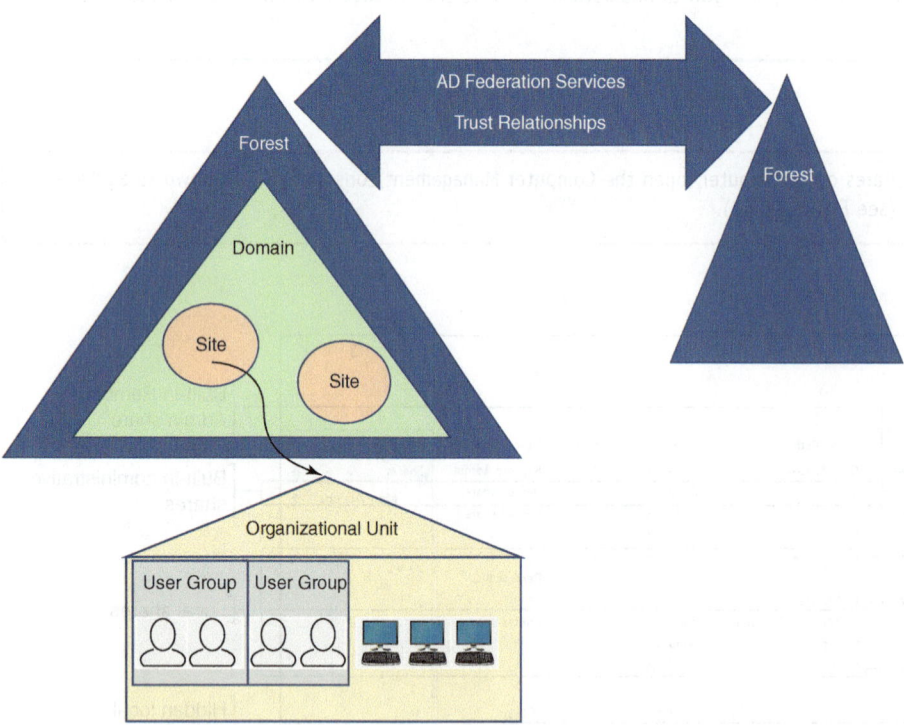

Figure 16-47   The Active Directory organizational structure

An **organizational unit (OU)** is created to make it easier for technicians to assign privileges to users and computers in the OU; privileges are assigned using policies created by Group Policy. These policies are contained in **Group Policy Objects (GPOs)** that are applied to each user and computer in the OU.

An OU also can contain user groups, which contain users. Permissions assigned to folders work much the same way as they do in Windows 10/8/7. NTFS and share permissions are assigned to a folder on a server in the domain by assigning permissions to a user group, and the users in this group inherit these assigned permissions. In summary, managing resources in AD revolves around the tools shown in Figure 16-48.

Figure 16-48 Group policies apply to OUs, and NTFS and share permissions apply to folders to control access to the resources in a domain

In this chapter, we focus on the skills an IT technician needs to manage user accounts with Active Directory Domain Services, including creating, resetting, unlocking, enabling, and disabling user accounts and resetting user account passwords. You also learn how Group Policy can be used to assign privileges to an OU and the groups and users in the OU.

CREATING AND MANAGING USER ACCOUNTS IN AD

A+ CORE 2 2.2, 2.7

Before we discuss how to manage a user account on a Windows domain, let's pause to see how you can access Domain Services on the domain controller to get to the tools you need. You'll need a local administrator account for a Windows Server computer that is a domain controller. Then you can use one of these methods to access the domain controller:

◢ *Sitting at the computer.* While physically seated at the Windows Server computer, sign in to Windows Server with an administrator account. Then click **Start** and click **Server Manager** in the Start menu. The Server Manager console is shown in Figure 16-49 with the Tools menu open. The Server Manager console contains the tools used to manage Active Directory and is included in Windows Server. It can also be installed in Windows 10.

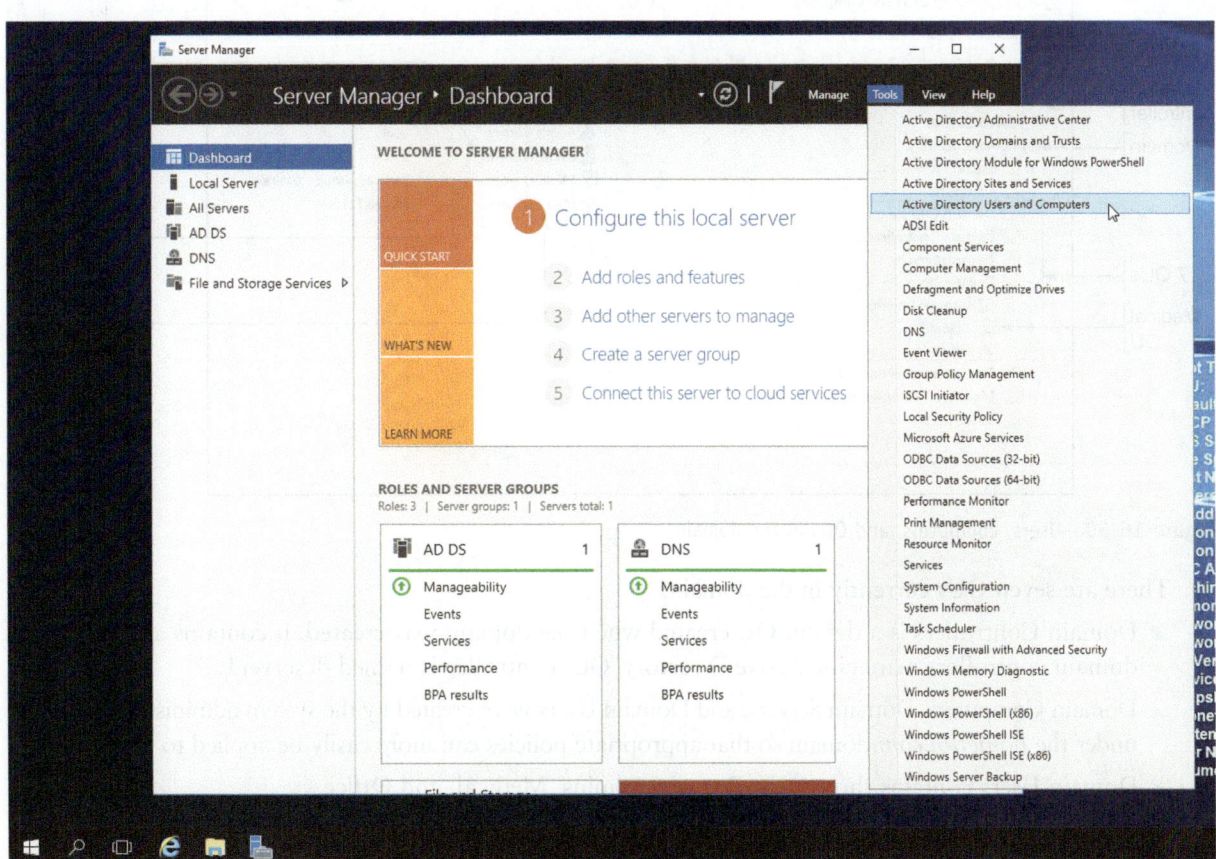

Figure 16-49 The Windows Server desktop with the Server Manager console showing the Tools menu

▲ *Remote access to Windows Server.* You can use Remote Desktop from anywhere on the Internet to connect to a Windows Server computer, sign in, and open Server Manager. How to use Remote Desktop is covered in Chapter 13. Recall that Remote Desktop requires the host computer to have a static IP address; you can expect a domain controller to have one.

▲ *AD Administrative Center and PowerShell.* Administrative Center is an interface for managing Active Directory. In Windows 10/8/7, you can download and install Remote Server Administrative Tools (RSAT) from *microsoft.com*. Administrative Center is one of the tools in this package. Many PowerShell cmdlets apply to Active Directory. To use PowerShell to manage Active Directory, you must first execute the cmdlet **Import-Module ActiveDirectory**, which installs the AD cmdlets.

> ✎ **Notes** If you don't have access to Active Directory and a Windows domain to practice the skills in this part of the chapter, you can follow the steps in Real Problem 16-2 at the end of this chapter to set up your own Windows domain in Windows Server using the free Google Cloud Platform at *cloud.google.com*.

USE SERVER MANAGER AND CREATE A NEW USER

Let's get started learning to use Server Manager. In Server Manager, follow these steps to view the OU structure and create a new user:

1. Sign in to Windows Server with an administrator account and open **Server Manager**.

2. Click **Tools** (refer back to Figure 16-49) and click **Active Directory Users and Computers**. (The utility is also available in Control Panel under Administrative Tools.) The Active Directory Users and Computers window displays. Figure 16-50 shows the sample domain *homerun.com*, which belongs to our fictitious company, Homerun Sports Medicine, Inc.

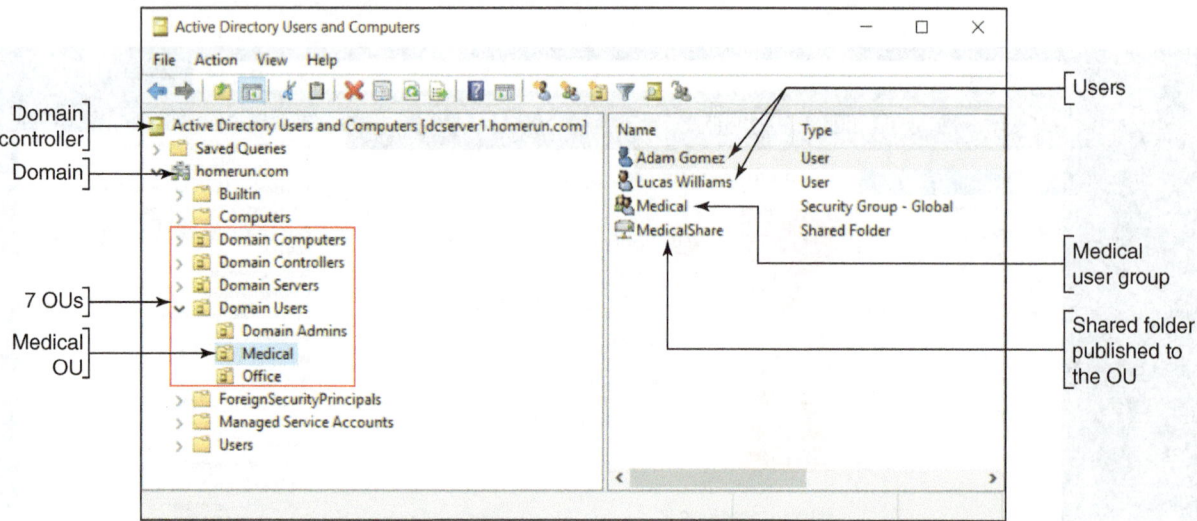

Figure 16-50 Users, computers, and OUs in the domain

There are seven OUs currently in the domain:

▲ Domain Controllers is a default OU created when the domain was created. It contains all the domain controllers managing Active Directory. Our controller is named dcserver1.

▲ Domain Computers, Domain Servers, and Domain Users were created by the system administrator directly under the *homerun.com* domain so that appropriate policies can more easily be applied to these OUs.

▲ Domain Users contains three OUs: Domain Admins, Medical, and Office.

▲ The Medical OU is selected, and you can see it contains two users, one user group, and one shared folder. (If you drill down into the Medical user group, you can see that Adam Gomez and Lucas Williams are members of the group.) It's okay to give a user group the same name as an OU, but it can sometimes get confusing, depending on the situation.

> **✎ Notes** To share a folder in Active Directory, first set the folder's NTFS and share permissions for the user group, as you learned to do earlier in the chapter. Then, to publish the folder in AD, right-click the OU to which you want to include the folder, click **New**, click **Folder**, and point to the folder. The folder is published in AD and can be found by users signed in to the domain on client computers.

3. To add a new user, right-click the OU to which you want to add the user, point to **New**, and click **User** (see Figure 16-51).

Figure 16-51 Right-click the OU to create a new user

4. Enter the user's first name, last name, and user name (see Figure 16-52A). Click **Next**. On the next screen, decide how to handle the password (see Figure 16-52B).

(A)　　　　　　　　　　　　　　　　(B)

Figure 16-52 To create a new user, (A) enter a name and logon name, and (B) decide how to handle the password

16

Here are the best practices for these password options:

◢ Always require a password.

◢ By default, the password you enter must meet AD's complexity requirements: It must have at least eight lowercase and uppercase letters, numbers, and symbols, and it cannot contain any three consecutive letters in the user name or display name.

◢ The best practice is to require the user to change the password at next logon.

◢ Don't check *Password never expires*. It's a good idea for the user to occasionally change the password.

◢ Notice you can select *Account is disabled*. This might be appropriate when you are setting up an account well in advance of the account actually being used.

5. Click **Next** and click **Finish**. The account is created. To confirm that the account is created in the correct OU, click the OU; the account should be listed in the right pane.

6. After the account is created, you can add it to an existing user group. Right-click the user account and click **Add to a group** (see Figure 16-53).

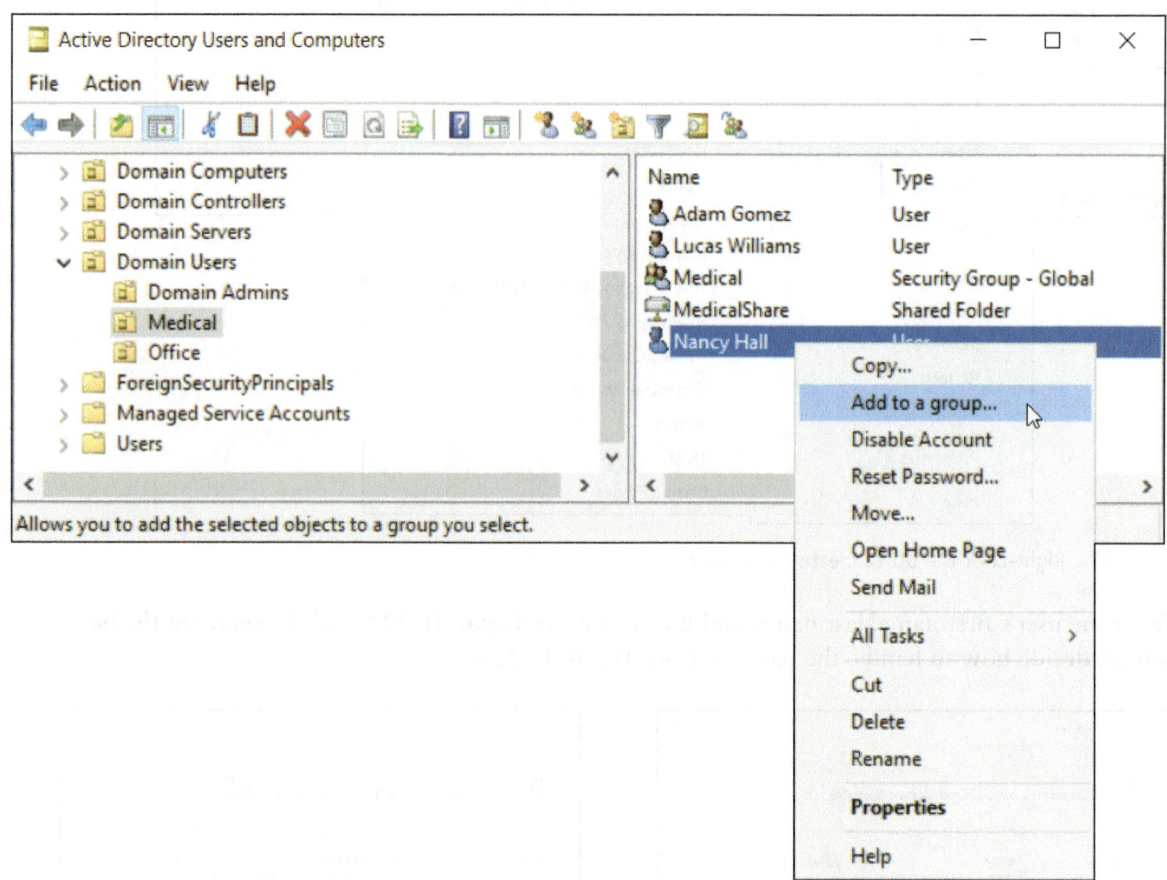

Figure 16-53   Add the user account to an existing user group

7. Type the group name and click **Check Names**. Windows verifies the name of the group and confirms it by underlining the name. Click **OK** (see Figure 16-54).

> ✎ **Notes**   To create a new user group, right-click the OU where you want to add the group, click **New**, and click **Group**. You can then name the group.

Figure 16-54 Type the user group name and click Check Names

Recall that users belong to user groups and users and user groups belong to OUs. When a policy is applied to an OU, it is applied to all users and user groups in the OU. When folder permissions are assigned to a user group, they are assigned to all users in the user group.

MANAGE ACCOUNTS AND PASSWORDS

An account might get locked after too many failed attempts to sign in. If the user says she knows the password but the account is locked, do the following to unlock the account:

1. An enterprise domain is likely to have hundreds if not thousands of user accounts. Do one of the following to locate the account:

   ◢ If you don't know where to find the account, you can use the search utility. Click the search icon in the Active Directory Users and Computers window (see Figure 16-55).

16

Figure 16-55 Search for a user account

At the top of the Find Users, Contacts, and Groups box, notice you can filter the search using the drop-down menus. Enter the name of the account and click **Find Now**. Double-click the account in the list of matches that appears. The account's Properties box appears.

◢ If you know where to find the account, drill down to it, right-click it, and select **Properties**.

2. In the Properties box for the account, select the **Account** tab (see Figure 16-56), check **Unlock account**, and click **Apply**. The user should then be able to sign in.

Follow these steps to reset a forgotten password and disable, enable, or delete an account:

1. Locate the account and right-click it. In the shortcut menu, click **Reset Password** (refer back to Figure 16-53). In the Reset Password box (see Figure 16-57), enter a new password twice. It's a good idea to leave the *User must change password at next logon* box checked. If the account has been locked, check **Unlock the user's account**. Click **OK**.

2. In the account's shortcut menu in Figure 16-53, note the options to disable and delete an account. When you click **Disable Account**, the user cannot sign in, but the account's user profile still exists and you can later enable the account using the same shortcut menu. Click **Delete** to delete the account, which deletes the user profile. You can also disable and enable an account and designate when an account will expire using options on the Account tab of the user's Properties box.

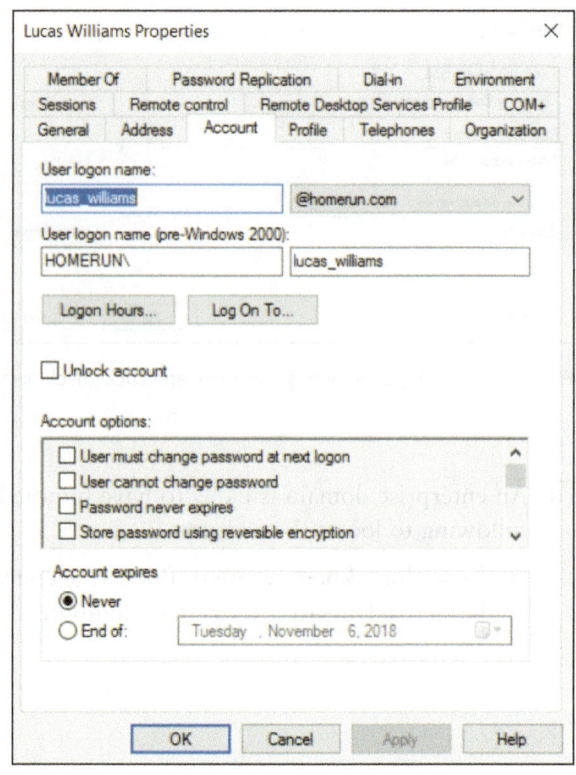

Figure 16-56 Unlock a locked account

> ✎ **Notes** The user account is considered an object in Active Directory. When you delete an AD object, it goes to the Active Directory Recycle Bin, where it can be recovered until the Recycle Bin is emptied.

Figure 16-57 Reset the user password

Here are a few other tips to help you manage accounts in Active Directory:

◢ *Disable the Guest account*. In Active Directory, the Guest account is disabled by default. For best security, leave the account disabled. If you find the Guest account enabled, right-click it and select **Disable Account**.

◢ *Logon time restrictions*. By default, a user can sign in to AD at any time. Suppose, however, that midnight to 8:00AM every Sunday is restricted for routine maintenance. To set logon time restrictions, open the user's Properties box, select the **Account** tab, and click **Logon Hours** (see Figure 16-58). Click an hour and then click **Logon Denied**. Notice that in Figure 16-58, midnight to 8:00AM on Sunday is denied.

Figure 16-58 Logon time restrictions

- *Timeout and screen lock.* On the Sessions tab of the user's Properties box, you can limit how long a session remains disconnected before it ends (never or up to 2 days), how long an active session stays up (never or up to 2 days), and how long an idle session stays up. After you have made your selections, click **Apply** to save changes.

- *Administrator password.* Before AD Domain Services can be configured to be a domain controller on the network, the Administrator account on its computer must have a strong password (including lowercase and uppercase letters, numbers, and symbols). To manage the properties of the Administrator account, open **Users** in the **Active Directory Users and Computers** window, right-click **Administrator**, and click **Properties**. See Figure 16-59. To change the password of the Administrator account, you can use the following command in an elevated command prompt window in Windows Server:

```
net user Administrator <password>
```

- *Home folder.* The Home folder is the default folder that is presented to the user whenever she is ready to save a file. On a peer-to-peer network, the Home folder in Windows is normally the Documents folder in the user profile at C:\Users*username*\Documents. Active Directory is able to change this Home folder location to a share on the network, which is called folder redirection. Two reasons to apply folder redirection to the Home folder are:

  - On a domain, a user might sign in to different computers. When his Home folder is stored on the network, it's always available and does not need to be copied to each computer he uses.

  - It's easier for backups to be maintained when all Home folders are on a network server rather than on individual workstations. In an organization, individual workstations are generally not backed up regularly, but servers on the network are backed up at least every night.

16

Figure 16-59 Manage the properties of the Administrator account

To see if a user's Home folder is on his local computer or on the network, select the **Profile** tab of the user's Properties box (see Figure 16-60). For this user, the Home folder is in a network share.

> ✎ **Notes** Many corporations are beginning to use cloud services rather than managing data on their premises. One way to do this is to set up OneDrive in the Microsoft cloud for each user in the Windows domain. Users are then encouraged to use their OneDrive for personal files rather than their Home folders stored on a network share.

▲ *Logon scripts.* A logon script is a list of commands stored in a script file that is performed each time a user signs in to Windows. In Active Directory, logon scripts are normally stored on the domain controllers in a network share named Netlogon. Types of logon scripts supported by Active Directory include Windows batch files (.bat file extension), VBScript files (.vbs file extension), and PowerShell scripts (.ps2 file extension). After the script file is stored in the Netlogon share, select the **Profile** tab in the user's Properties box. See Figure 16-60. Under Logon script, enter the name of the script file along with its file extension.

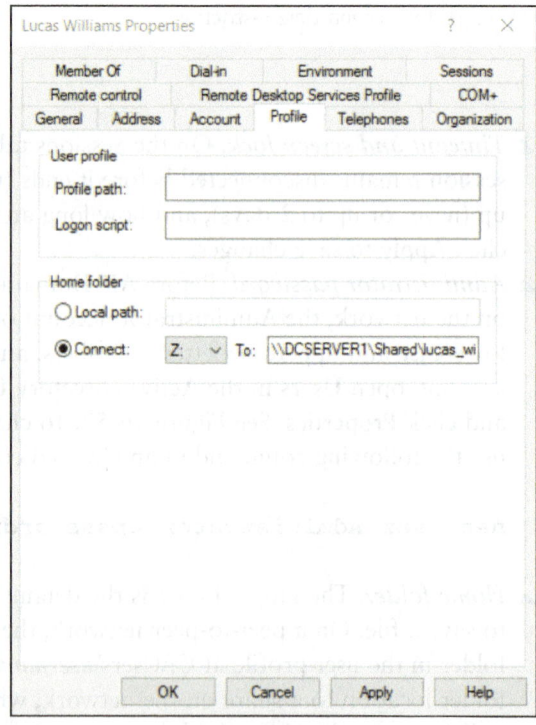

Figure 16-60 This user's Home folder is contained in a network share

Normally, when you want to change a setting for a single user, you use the user's Properties box, as just explained. If you need to change settings for all the users in an OU, the best tool to use is Group Policy because these policies affect multiple users.

GROUP POLICY OBJECTS

A+
CORE 2
2.2, 2.7

Group Policy can be used on the domain controller to create Group Policy Objects, which contain policies that apply to an OU. These OU policies apply to users, computers, shared folders, and printers in the OU.

Using Group Policy to manage GPOs is beyond the scope of this text. However, let's take a quick look at how you would get started to create and edit a GPO.

CREATE AND EDIT A GPO

You learned earlier that you can use the user account Properties box to set a logon script for a single user. Here is how to create a GPO to set a policy to run a startup script for all users in the domain or an OU:

1. In the Server Manager window, click **Tools** and click **Group Policy Management**. (The tool is also available in Administrative Tools in Control Panel.)

2. In the Group Policy Management window (see Figure 16-61), drill down into the OUs to find the one to which you want to apply the GPO. Right-click the OU and click **Create a GPO in this domain, and Link it here**. You can then name the GPO, as shown in the figure, and click **OK**.

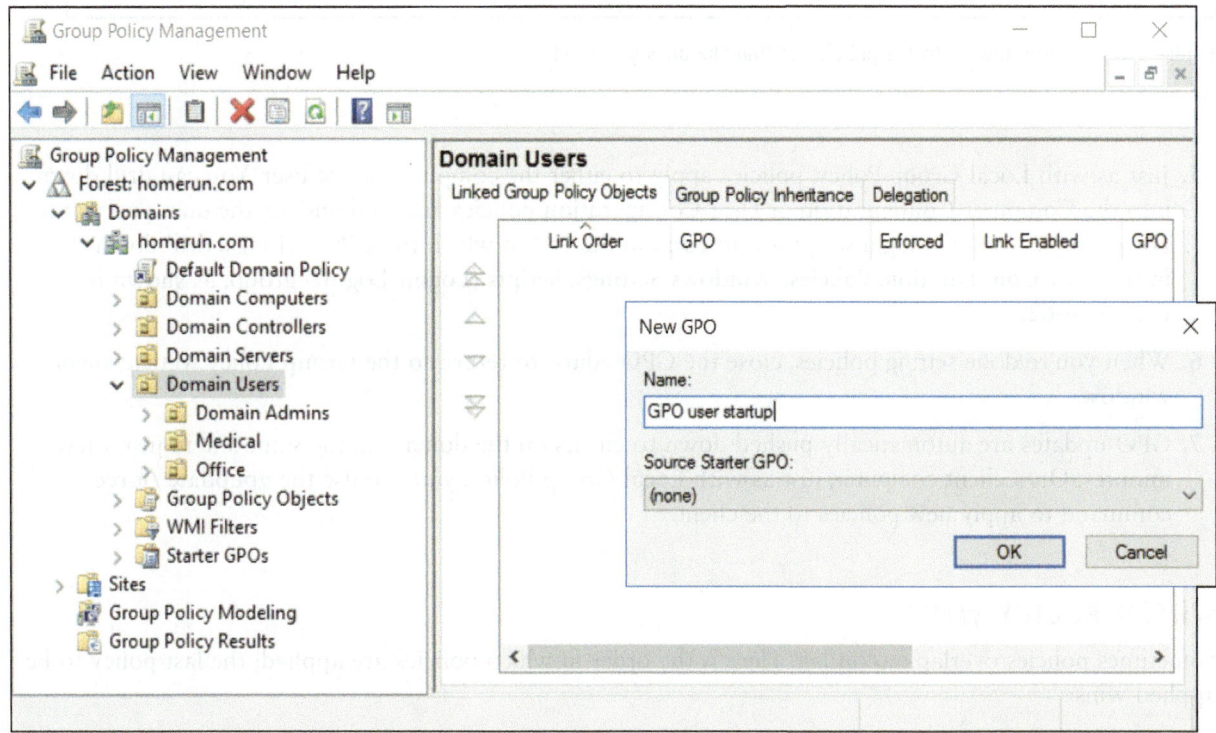

Figure 16-61 Create a new GPO for the Domain Users OU

3. The new GPO appears in the list under the OU and in the Group Policy Objects list. To display details about the GPO, click it and click **OK**. The GPO details display in the right pane with the Settings tab selected.

4. To edit a GPO, right-click it in the left pane and click **Edit**. The Group Policy Management Editor window opens so you can edit the GPO. You can see the GPO name at the top of the left pane of the editor (see Figure 16-62).

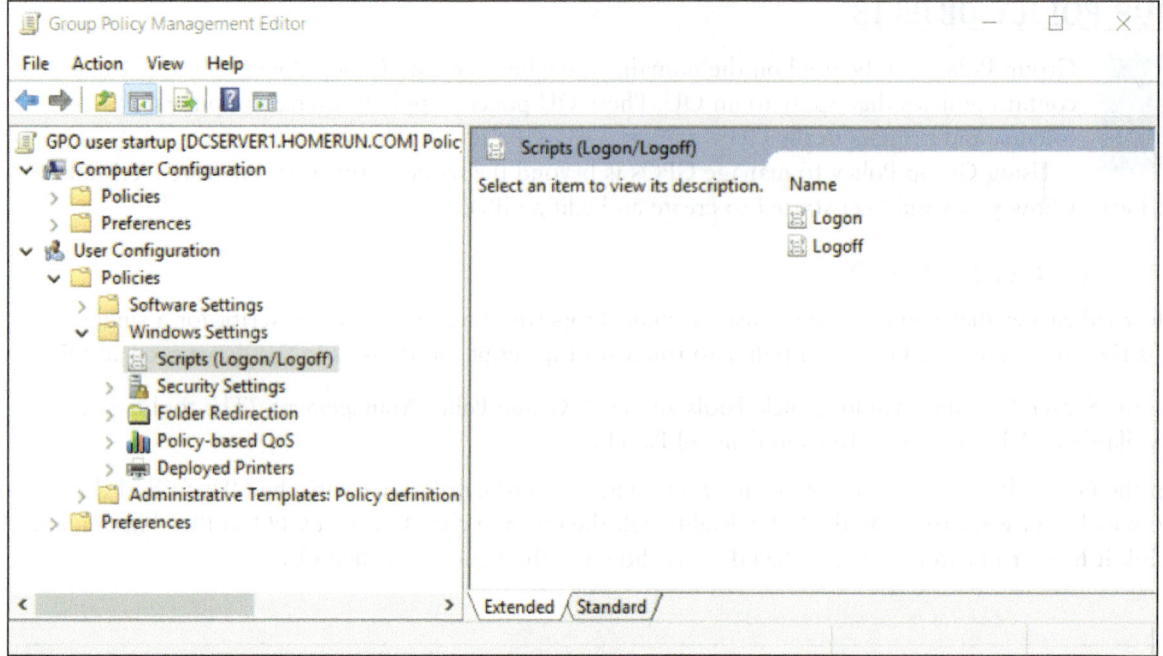

Figure 16-62 Drill down into the policies to find the ones you need

5. Just as with Local Group Policy, policies apply to either the computer or the user. You can drill down into the Computer Configuration or User Configuration policies and find and set the ones you want. For example, to add a login script for all users in the OU to which the GPO belongs, drill down in the **User Configuration, Policies, Windows Settings, Scripts (Logon/Logoff)** group, as shown in Figure 16-62.

6. When you're done setting policies, close the GPO editor to return to the Group Policy Management window.

7. GPO updates are automatically pushed down to clients on the domain in the same site in just a few minutes. On a client computer, just as with Local Group Policy, you can use the **gpupdate /force** command to apply new policies to the client.

WHICH POLICY WINS

Sometimes policies overlap or conflict. Here is the order in which policies are applied; the last policy to be applied wins:

1. *Local*. All local policies are applied first. As you learned earlier, Local Group Policy on the local computer can create policies that apply to the local computer or users.

2. *Site*. Policies for sites are applied next.

3. *Domain*. Policies for a domain are applied next.

4. *OU*. Policies for an OU are applied next and then policies for sub-OUs are applied next.

5. *Enforced*. Policies that are tagged as Enforced policies are applied last and always win over other policies.

> ✎ **Notes** To tag a GPO as Enforced, right-click the GPO in the Group Policy Management window and click **Enforced**.

Where there is a conflict of policies, the last policy applied wins. It's important to remember the order in which policies are applied, and the acronym LSDOE (usually pronounced "LS-doe") can help: Local, Site, Domain, OU, and Enforced.

Figure 16-63 shows what can happen when there are conflicting policies. In the figure, you see that policies A, B, C, and D are applied; to understand which policy is applied at each level, follow the diagram from left to right. First, notice that local policy A wins because policy A does not exist at the site, domain, OU, or enforced level. For policy B, domain policy B wins over site policy B. For policy C, site policy C wins over local policy C. Although OU policy D would have won over local policy D, the OU policy D was not applied because it was overridden by enforced policy D. Therefore, the resultant policies are local policy A, domain policy B, site policy C, and enforced policy D.

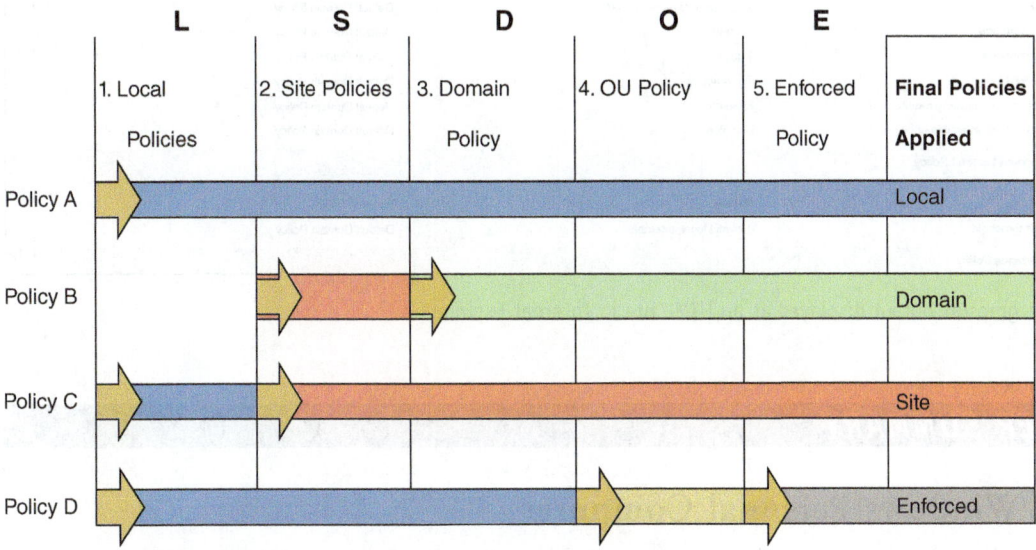

Figure 16-63 Resulting policies applied when conflicting policies exist

To find out the resulting policies for the computer or user, do one of the following:

- In a command prompt window, enter the **rsop.msc** command. The Resultant Set of Policy (RSoP) window opens, where you can drill down to see the policies set for the computer or user. For example, Figure 16-64 shows the RSoP for the Password Policy.

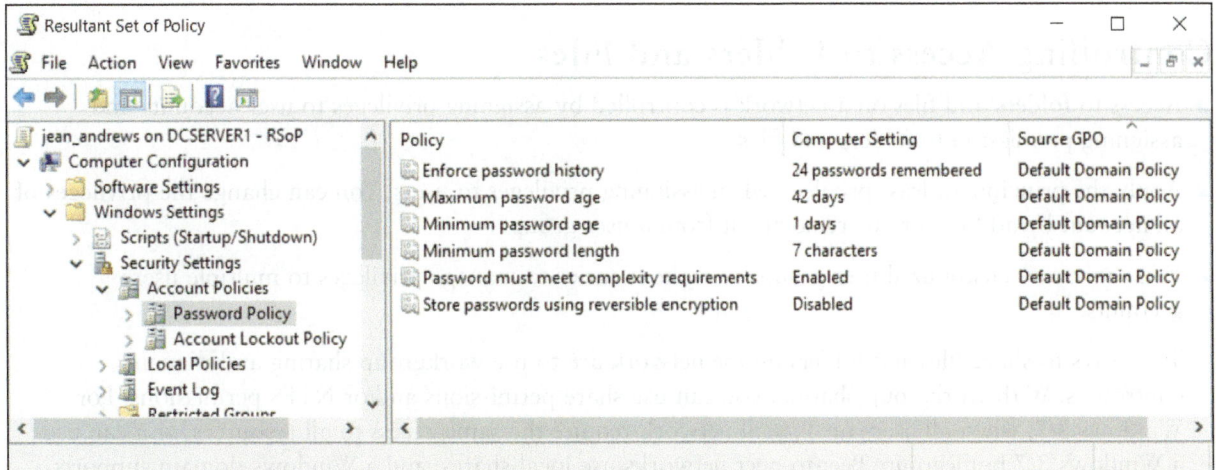

Figure 16-64 The Resultant Set of Policy for the Password Policy

16

◢ In a command prompt window, enter the **gpresult /v** command, which displays the policies currently applied to the computer and user. The report is very long; you can save it to an HTML file so you can later search it. For example, use this command: **gpresult /h C:\myfile.html**. To view the file, double-click it in File Explorer. The HTML file opens in Internet Explorer. Figure 16-65 shows a snip of the file that includes the Password Policy.

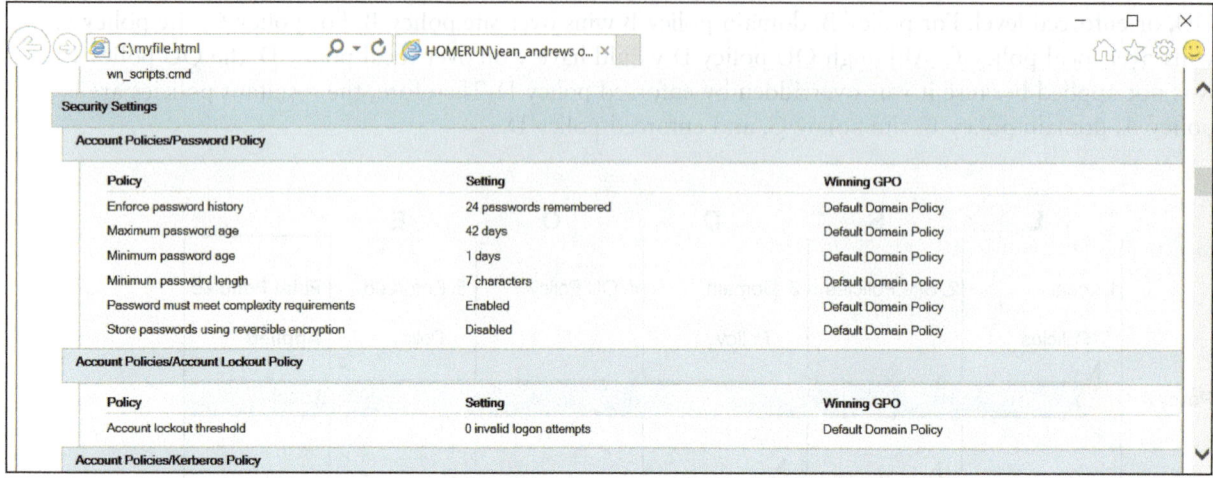

Figure 16-65   The gpresult output displayed as an HTML file in Internet Explorer

>> *CHAPTER SUMMARY*

Securing a Windows Personal Computer

◢ A long password is a strong password.

◢ Use Local Group Policies (gpedit.msc) and Local Security Policies (secpol.msc) to secure a Windows computer.

◢ The Internet Options dialog box is used to manage many Internet Explorer settings. Proxy settings are managed using the Connections tab, and add-ons are managed using the Programs tab.

◢ Encrypting File System (EFS) encrypts files and folders on an NTFS file system. BitLocker Drive Encryption encrypts an entire volume on a hard drive. Both are available on business and professional editions of Windows.

Controlling Access to Folders and Files

◢ Access to folders and files on a network is controlled by assigning privileges to user accounts and assigning permission to folders and files.

◢ Apply the principle of least privilege when assigning privileges to users. You can change the privileges of an account by adding it to or removing it from a user group.

◢ You can create customized user groups to make it easier to manage privileges to multiple user accounts.

◢ Two ways to share files and folders on the network are to use workgroup sharing and domain controllers. With workgroup sharing, you can use share permissions and/or NTFS permissions. For Windows 8/7, when all users on a small network require the same access to all resources, you can use a Windows 8/7 homegroup. Peer-to-peer networks use local shares, and a Windows domain supports administrative shares. You can also hide network resources so that a user must know the name of the resource to access it.

◢ A mapped network drive makes it easier for users to access drives and folders on the network.

Using Active Directory Domain Services

◢ Active Directory (AD) is a suite of services and databases provided by Windows Server that is used to manage Windows domains.

◢ Active Directory organizes resources in a top-down hierarchical structure. A forest contains a domain. Domains can contain sites. Domains are also organized into organizational units (OUs) and sub-organizational units.

◢ Managing resources in AD revolves around the OU, user groups, and NTFS and share permissions. Group Policies apply to OUs, and NTFS and share permissions apply to folders to control access to the resources in a domain.

◢ Active Directory is able to change the Home folder location to a share on the network, which is called folder redirection.

◢ The order in which group policies are applied are: local, site, domain, OU, and enforced. Where there is a conflict in policies, the last policy applied wins.

>> KEY TERMS

For explanations of key terms, see the Glossary for this text.

Active Directory (AD)	Everyone group	Local Security Policy	principle of least privilege
Active Directory Domain Services (AD DS)	folder redirection	local shares	privileges
	forest	Local Users and Groups	Remote Admin share
ActiveX control	gpresult	mapping	Resultant Set of Policy
administrative shares	gpupdate	multifactor authentication	(RSoP)
Administrators group	Group Policy	(MFA)	Server Manager
Anonymous users	Group Policy Object	Network File System (NFS)	share permissions
Authenticated Users group	(GPO)	Network Places Wizard	strong password
BitLocker Drive Encryption	Guests group	network share	Sync Center
BitLocker To Go	hidden share	NTFS permissions	TPM (Trusted Platform
brute force attack	Home folder	organizational unit (OU)	Module)
defense in depth	inherited permissions	permission propagation	Users group
Encrypting File System	Internet Options	permissions	Windows Firewall
(EFS)	Local Group Policy	Power Users group	

>> THINKING CRITICALLY

These questions are designed to prepare you for the critical thinking required for the A+ exams and may use content from other chapters and the web.

1. Your organization has set up three levels of classification for data accessed by users on a small network:
   ◢ Low security: Data in the C:\Public folder
   ◢ Medium security: Data in a shared folder that some, but not all, user groups can access
   ◢ High security: Data in a shared and encrypted folder that requires a password to access. The folder is shared only to one user group.

Classify each of the following sets of data:

a. Directions to the company's Fourth of July party

b. Details of an invention made by the company president that has not yet been patented

c. Résumés presented by several people applying for a job with the company

d. Payroll spreadsheets

e. Job openings at the company

2. You work in the Accounting department and have been using a network drive to post Excel workbook files to your file server as you complete them. When you attempt to save a workbook file to the drive, you see the error message: "You do not have access to the folder 'J:\'. See your administrator for access to this folder." What should you do first? Second? Explain the reasoning behind your choices.

a. Ask your network administrator to give you permission to access the folder.

b. Check File Explorer to verify that you can connect to the network.

c. Save the workbook file to your hard drive.

d. Using File Explorer, remap the network drive.

e. Reboot your PC.

3. Which type of server can function as a firewall?

a. Mail server

b. Proxy server

c. Print server

d. FTP server

4. What is the command to launch each of the following tools?

a. Local Group Policy

b. Local Security Policy

c. Computer Management console

d. Local Users and Groups console

e. Resultant Set of Policy (RSoP)

5. What hardware component is needed to set up BitLocker Encryption so that you can authenticate the computer?

6. Where in Group Policy can you locate the policy that requires a smart card to be used to authenticate a user to Windows?

a. Computer Configuration, Windows Settings, Security Settings, Local Policies, Biometrics

b. Computer Configuration, Administrative Templates, System, Logon

c. Computer Configuration, Windows Settings, Security Settings, Local Policies, Security Options

d. User Configuration, Administrative Templates, System, Logon

7. You open a folder Properties box to encrypt the folder, click Advanced, and discover that *Encrypt contents to secure data* is dimmed. What is the most likely problem?

a. Encryption has not been enabled. Use the Computer Management console to enable it.

b. You are not using an edition of Windows that supports encryption.

c. Most likely a virus has attacked the system and is disabling encryption.

d. Encryption applies only to files, not folders.

8. You have shared a folder, C:\DenverCO, with your team. The folder contains information about your company branch in Denver, Colorado. Your company decides to reorganize into zones, so you move the folder as a subfolder in the folder G:\Zone3. When your team members try to access G:\Zone3\DenverCO, they get an error message saying they have been denied access. What happened to the permissions when you moved the folder to its new location?

9. What command do you enter in the Explorer search box to access the Remote Admin share on the computer named Fin?

10. In your organization, each department has a folder on a shared drive. Your boss frequently copies the folder to his local computer to run reports. You have noticed that the folder for your department keeps disappearing from the shared drive. You discover that the folder isn't being deleted and often gets moved into a random, nearby folder. You suspect that coworkers in other departments are being careless with their mouse clicks while accessing their own folders on the shared drive and are dragging and dropping your department folder into other folders without noticing. How can you prevent this folder from being moved, but still allow it to be copied? What steps do you take?

11. If you are having a problem changing the permissions of a folder that was created by another user, what can you do to help solve the problem?

12. When setting up OUs in a new domain, why might it be useful to put all computers in one OU and all users in another?

    a. It will be easier to inventory computers in the domain.

    b. It will help organize users into user groups.

    c. An OU must contain either users or computers, but not both.

    d. Policies generally apply to either computers or users.

13. You have set up a user group named Accounting and have put all employees in the Accounting department in this group, which has been given permission to use the Financial folder on a file server. You are now asked to create a subfolder under Financial named Payroll. Megan, the payroll officer, is the only employee in the Accounting department allowed to access this folder. What is the best way to configure the new share?

    a. Assign Megan read/write permissions to the Payroll folder, and explain to your boss that it is not a best practice to give only one employee access to an important folder.

    b. Assign Megan read/write permissions to the Payroll folder.

    c. Create a new user group named Payroll, put Megan in the group, and assign the group read/write permissions to the Payroll folder.

    d. Ask your boss to allow you to put the folder outside of the Financial folder so you can assign a new user group read/write permissions to this folder that will not conflict with the Accounting user group.

14. Which of the following is true about NTFS permissions and share permissions? Select all that apply.

    a. Share permissions do not work on an NTFS volume.

    b. NTFS permissions work only on an NTFS volume.

    c. If share permissions and NTFS permissions are in conflict, NTFS permissions win.

    d. If you set NTFS permissions but do not set share permissions, NTFS permissions apply.

15. Which security features are available on Windows 10 Home? Select all that apply.

    a. Local Group Policy

    b. NTFS permissions

    c. Active Directory

    d. Internet Options

16

>> HANDS-ON PROJECTS

Hands-On | Project 16-1 Exploring Password Management Software

Password management software, also called password vault software, such as KeePass (*keepass.info*), LastPass (*lastpass.com*), and Dashlane (*dashlane.com*), can hold your passwords safely so that you don't forget them or have to write them down. Choose two of these programs and a third of your own selection that interests you, then answer the following questions about each one:

1. Which platforms are supported?
2. Which web browsers are supported?
3. From how many competitors can the program import passwords?
4. What types of authentication are supported (e.g., master password, fingerprint, etc.)?
5. Where are the passwords stored? Are they synced across devices? How is the information protected?
6. What are some of the differences between the free edition of each program and the paid versions?
7. What happens to the user's account if the user dies or is incapacitated?

Hands-On | Project 16-2 Using Group Policy to Secure a Workstation

Using Windows 10/8 Professional or Enterprise, or Windows 7 Professional, Ultimate, or Enterprise, set local security policies to require a password for each account, to audit failed logon events, and to create a logon script that displays the message, "The Golden Pineapple Was Here!" when anyone signs in to the system. Test your policies by verifying that a password is required, your script executes when you sign in, and a failed sign-in event using an invalid password is logged and can be viewed in Event Viewer. Answer the following questions:

1. Which policies did you set and what setting was applied to each policy?
2. What software did you use to create your script? What is the exact path and file name (including the file extension) to your script?
3. Which log in Event Viewer shows the logon failure event?
4. List three more policies you find in Group Policy that can make a workstation more secure but are not discussed in this chapter.

Hands-On | Project 16-3 Using Google Chrome

Internet Explorer is not the only browser available, and many users prefer others such as Mozilla Firefox (*mozilla.org*) or Google Chrome (*google.com*). Go to the Google website and download and install Google Chrome. Use it to browse the web. How does it compare with Internet Explorer? What do you like better about it? What do you not like as well? When might you recommend that someone use Chrome rather than Internet Explorer? What security features does Google Chrome offer? What are the steps to import your favorites list from Internet Explorer into Chrome?

Hands-On | Project 16-4 Researching a Laptop with a TPM Chip

Many laptops sold today have a TPM chip, and some have encryption-enabled hard drives that don't require encryption software such as BitLocker. Research the web for a laptop that offers a TPM chip and answer these questions:

1. What is the brand and model of laptop that has the TPM chip? Print the webpage that lists the laptop specifications for the chip.
2. Is the chip optional? If so, what is the cost of including the chip?
3. Does the laptop have an encryption-enabled hard drive?
4. Does the laptop come bundled with encryption software? If so, what is the name of the software?
5. Does the laptop offer a drive lock password?
6. What is the cost of the laptop, including the TPM chip?

Hands-On | Project 16-5 Sharing and Securing a Folder

Using two computers networked together, do the following to practice sharing and securing folders using Windows:

1. Create a user account named **User1** on Computer 1. In the My Documents folder for that account, create a folder named **Folder1**. Create a text file named **File1** in the folder. Edit the file and add the text **Golden Egg**.
2. On Computer 2, create a user account named **User2**. Try to read the Golden Egg text in File1 on Computer 1. What is the result?
3. Configure the computers so that User1 signed in to Computer 2 can open File1 and edit the text "Golden Egg," but User2 cannot view or access the contents of Folder1. List the steps you took to share and secure the folder and to test this scenario to make sure it works.
4. Now make the folder private so that it cannot be seen from Computer 2 in File Explorer or Windows Explorer but can be accessed if User1 knows the folder name. Describe how you did that.

16

>> REAL PROBLEMS, REAL SOLUTIONS

REAL PROBLEM 16-1 Recovering a Windows Password

You can use freeware to discover a forgotten Windows password, and hackers can use the software to steal a password. The stronger the password, the more difficult it is to discover. Follow these steps to learn more:

1. Create three user accounts on a system and assign the accounts an easy password (use only lowercase letters), a moderately easy password (use lowercase letters and numbers, but no symbols), and a strong password (see the rules given earlier in the chapter for strong passwords).
2. Go to **ophcrack.sourceforge.net** by Geeknet, Inc., and download the free ISO file that contains ophcrack Vista/7 LiveCD. (The software works in Windows 10/8/7.) Use the ISO file to burn the ISO image to a CD-R. Label the CD.

3. Boot from the CD. As it boots, it automatically searches for and lists the user accounts and passwords on the system. Answer the following questions:

   a. What is the name of the operating system the ophcrack software uses on the CD?

   b. Which user account passwords did ophcrack discover?

   c. If ophcrack did not discover a password, perhaps another freeware utility can. List three other password-cracking products that receive positive online reviews.

   Keep the ophcrack LiveCD in your computer repair toolkit in case a client in the field asks you to help recover a forgotten Windows password.

REAL PROBLEM 16-2 Setting Up a Windows Domain in Google Cloud

In Chapter 10, you used Google Cloud Platform to create a VM with Windows Server installed. To use that VM or a new VM to create a Windows domain, do the following:

1. Go to **cloud.google.com**. If you have not already set up a free trial, click **Try free**. You will need to sign in using a Google account. If you don't have an account, you can create one with any valid email address. When you first set up an account, you must enter payment information, which Google promises not to use during your free trial period. Create an individual account type, enter your information, and click **START MY FREE TRIAL**. Google automatically sets up your first project, aptly named My First Project.

2. In the left pane of the Google Cloud Platform page, click **Compute Engine**. If you don't already have a VM created with Windows Server, do the following:

   a. Click **CREATE INSTANCE** in the VM instances menu to create a VM.

   b. Use the default settings, except:
      ◢ Change the name of the VM to **dcserver**.
      ◢ Change the Boot disk to **Windows Server 2016 Datacenter**.

   c. Click **Create** and then wait for Google to create the instance.

3. In the VM instances list, click the **dcserver** instance, which takes you to the VM instance details page. Click **Set Windows password** and assign a user name to your VM instance. Note the user name and click **SET**. Google Cloud assigns a password, which displays on the screen. Copy the password, save it somewhere safe, then click **CLOSE**.

4. A domain controller needs a static IP address on the domain. To set the Primary internal IP address to a static address, follow these steps:

   a. On the VM instance details page, in the *Network interfaces* group under *Network*, click **default**. The VPC network details page appears.

   b. Click **Static internal IP addresses**. Then click **Reserve static address**.

   c. Under Name, enter **dcserver**. Click **RESERVE**.

5. To return to the list of VM instances, click the back arrow to the left of *VPC network details*. The VM instance details page appears. In the left pane, under *Compute Engine*, click **VM instances**. Your list of VMs appears.

6. For the dcserver VM instance, write down the Internal IP and External IP addresses.

7. You are now ready to use Remote Desktop with screen and file sharing to access your VM. Follow these steps:

   a. Enter the **mstsc** command in the Windows 10/7 search box or the Windows 8 Run box. In the Remote Desktop Connection box, enter the External IP address of your VM, which is its public IP address available on the Internet. Click **Connect**.

b. In the *Enter your credentials* box, your Windows user name appears. If your VM's user name is not the same as your Windows user name, click **More choices** and then click **Use a different account**. You can then enter the VM's user name and password. Click **OK** to connect.

8. The Windows Server desktop appears in the Remote Desktop window with the Server Manager window open. In the Networks pane on the right, click **Yes** to turn on network discovery.

9. You are now ready to set up your Windows domain. Follow these steps:

   a. In the Server Manager window, under *Configure this local server*, click **Add roles and features**. The Add Roles and Features Wizard opens. Click **Next**.

   b. On the *Select destination server* page, accept the default values and click **Next**.

   c. Under *Select server roles*, check **Active Directory Domain Services** and click **Add Features**.

   d. Under *Select server roles*, check **DNS Server** and click **Add Features**. A warning message appears. Click **Continue**. (The message was caused by Google Cloud handling tasks that the domain controller would normally handle.)

   e. Click **Next** four times to step through pages in the wizard, accepting default values. The *Confirm installation selections* page appears. Click **Install**. Wait while the installation happens. You can click the flag in the upper-right corner of the Server Manager window to view the progress. See Figure 16-66.

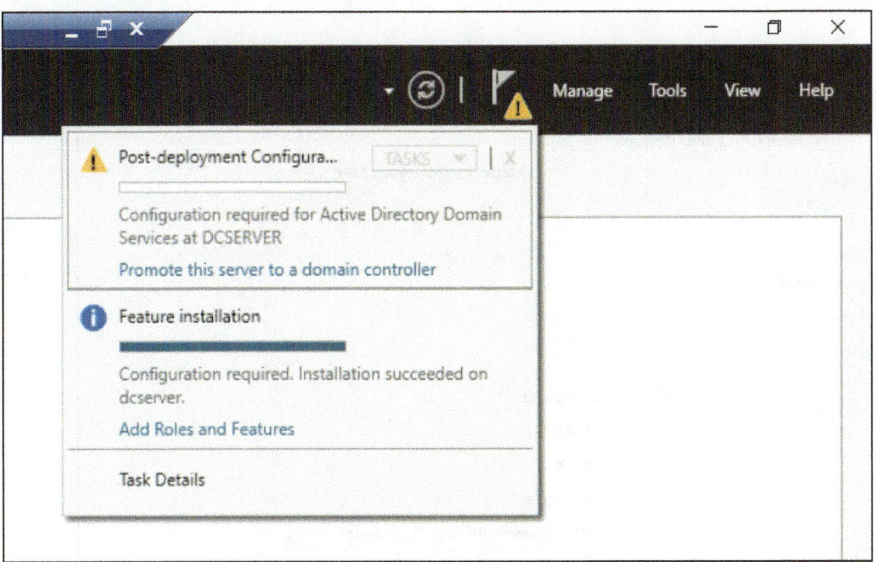

Figure 16-66   The notification flag reports installation progress

10. Although AD Domain Services is now installed, you cannot promote the server to a domain controller until you first set a password for the all-powerful Administrator account. (Recall that this account is different from your user name account, which has Administrative privileges.) To set the password, do the following:

    a. To open an elevated command prompt window, right-click **Start** and click **Command Prompt** (**Admin**). Click **Yes**.

    b. Use a password that satisfies AD complexity requirements. For example, in the command prompt window, enter this command:

    ```
    net user Administrator Passw0rd /passwordreq:yes
    ```

    c. Close the command prompt window.

11. Click the notification flag in the Server Manager window and then click **Promote this server to a domain controller**. The *Deployment Configuration* window appears. Select **Add a new forest**. Enter your root domain name. You can use **homerun.com** or another domain name. Click **Next**.

12. Wait while the Domain Controller Options window loads—it can take some time. Then enter a password twice and click **Next**. Ignore any warning messages and click **Next** several times to step through the wizard. Finally, click **Install**.

13. After the system reboots, you will need to connect again through Remote Desktop. At this point, you have a working domain controller and can practice the skills you learned in this chapter to manage Active Directory. Here is how to get started:

    a. If Server Manager is not already open, click **Start** and click **Server Manager**.

    b. The Server Manager window appears. To manage OUs, user groups, and users, click **Tools** and then click **Active Directory Users and Computers**. Refer back to Figure 16-50.

    c. By default, your domain has one OU: Domain Controllers. To create another OU directly under the domain, right-click the domain name, point to **New**, and click **Organizational Unit** (see Figure 16-67). You can then name the OU.

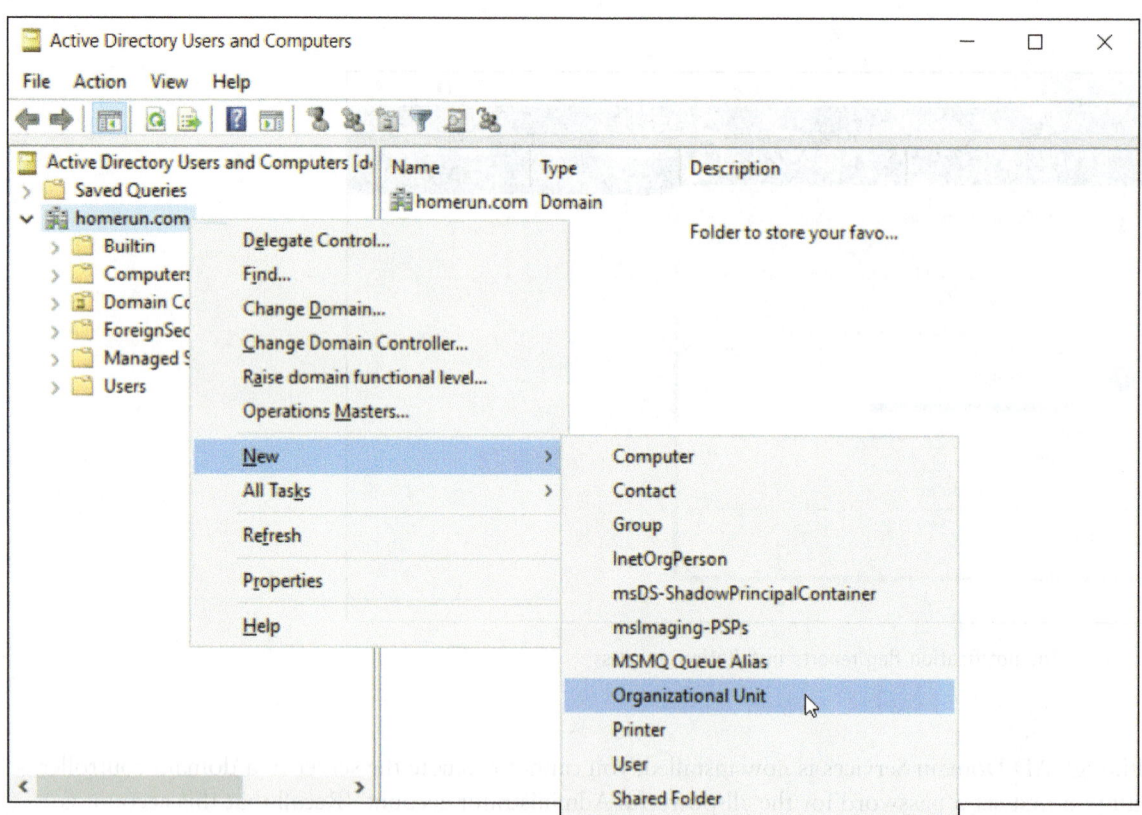

Figure 16-67   Create an OU directly under the domain

14. Have fun poking around and learning to use Active Directory! Every great IT technician needs to have a working knowledge of AD, and you have started that in this chapter. When you're finished working with AD, avoid accumulating any charges against your free quota by shutting down the server VM in the Remote Desktop Connection box.

> **Notes** You will use the Google Cloud Platform service for another project in Chapter 18. Do not disable your Google Cloud Platform account until after you have completed that project.

REAL PROBLEM 16-3 Using Chrome Remote Desktop

Chrome Remote Desktop by Google lets users sign in to remote computers through a Chrome browser. This blend of cloud computing technology and remote desktop access can be handy when you need to support computers that use operating systems other than Windows. Complete the following steps to install and use Chrome Remote Desktop:

1. On Computer 1, download and install Google Chrome, and sign in. Then add the Chrome Remote Desktop add-in.

2. Configure Chrome Remote Desktop to allow access to your computer over the Internet. Run the Chrome Remote Desktop Host Installer after it is downloaded. Be sure to record your PIN in a safe place.

3. On Computer 2, download and install Google Chrome, and sign in. Then add the Chrome Remote Desktop add-in.

4. Configure Chrome Remote Desktop to allow access to your computer over the Internet. Run the Chrome Remote Desktop Host Installer after it is downloaded. Be sure to record your PIN in a safe place.

5. Use Chrome Remote Desktop to create a remote connection to Computer 2. Can you use the utility to view the desktop of Computer 2? Can you control Computer 2 from Computer 1? Can you control Computer 2 directly from its own desktop? What options are available from the Remote Desktop menu on Computer 1?

6. What other operating systems will Chrome Remote Desktop work with?

7. List three reasons why a user might find Chrome Remote Desktop useful. Be sure to consider the advantages of using it with Google Cloud Platform.

16

Security Strategies and Documentation

In Chapter 16, you learned the concepts and principles of securing Windows resources on workstations and networks by classifying users and data, and you learned how to protect resources by applying appropriate permissions so that only authorized users can access the data. In this chapter, you learn about additional tools and techniques to secure the resources on a personal computer and network. You also learn how to recognize that a personal computer is infected with malware and how to clean an infected system and keep it clean. Finally, you learn what your employer might expect of you when dealing with issues of change management, regulated data, software licensing, incident response, and data destruction and disposal.

Chapter 16 and this chapter give you the basics of securing a personal computer or network. Later in your career as a support technician, you can build on the skills learned in these chapters to implement even more security, such as controlling how Windows stores its passwords.

PROTECTING NETWORK RESOURCES

A+
CORE 2
2.1, 2.2,
2.3, 2.4,
2.10, 4.1

In this part of the chapter, you learn both physical and logical methods of protecting computer resources, securely authenticate users on a large network, and educate users to understand their roles to protect and secure network resources by carefully following established best practices.

PHYSICAL SECURITY AND ACCESS CONTROLS

A+
CORE 2
2.1, 2.2

Physically protecting access to a computer's resources is often seen by security experts as the most important—and most overlooked—form of security. Here are some best practices for physical security:

▲ *If the data is really private, keep it behind a locked door or under lock and key*. You can use all kinds of security methods to encrypt, password protect, and hide data, but if it really is that important, one obvious thing you can do is to keep the computer behind a locked door. Sounds simple, but it works. You can also store the data on a removable storage device such as an external hard drive and, when you're not using the data, put the drive in a fireproof safe. (And, of course, keep two copies that are stored in different locations.) Don't forget that printouts of sensitive documents should be kept under lock and key, as well as any passwords you might have written down. Door locks and safes come in several types, including keyed locks, combination locks, and biometric locks. Biometric locks require special input called biometric data to identify a person by her fingerprint, handprint, face, retina, iris, voice, or handwritten signature. Figure 17-1 shows a biometric input device: a fingerprint scanner. Many mobile devices, such as iPads and some laptops, have fingerprint scanners built in.

▲ *Use server locks or cable locks*. Some computer cases allow you to add a lock so that you can physically prevent others from opening the case (see Figure 17-2A). These locks, called server locks, might be used on computers that hold corporate data. You can also use a cable lock, or Kensington lock, to secure a laptop or other computer to a table so someone can't walk away with it (see Figure 17-2B). Most laptops have a security slot on the case to connect the cable lock; this slot is called a Kensington Security Slot or K-Slot. Many thefts occur in private offices or hotel rooms, so even if you're not sitting in a public area with your laptop, consider keeping it locked to a nearby table or post. Be sure to choose a cable lock that resists tampering with pliers or cable cutters.

Source: iStockphoto.com/viiwee

Figure 17-1 This access control device accepts typed code, fingerprint, or smart card input

(A)   (B)

Figure 17-2 To physically secure a computer, (A) use a computer case lock and key for a desktop to prevent intrusion, or (B) use a cable lock system for a laptop to prevent theft

▲ *Secure ports with port locks*. Any exposed port on a device, such as an RJ-45 port or a USB port, can be used to access the device and compromise its security. USB ports in particular are security risks due to the ease of uploading malware or downloading sensitive data using a small flash drive carried in someone's pocket. If you can't restrict access to the device itself, you might install a port lock to restrict physical access to the exposed ports. The USB lock by PadJack, Inc., consists of three pieces, as shown in Figure 17-3. The smaller two pieces are inserted into the USB port, sealed into place with the wire loop, and cannot be removed without damaging the port or destroying the lock. Other port lock designs can lock a cable into the port so it can't be easily removed.

RJ-45 lock

USB locks

Wire loop seal

Source: PadJack.com

Figure 17-3 These port locks are reusable, but the wire loop seal can be used only once

17

▲ *Use privacy screens.* To keep other people from viewing a monitor screen, you can install a privacy screen, also called a privacy filter, that fits over the screen to prevent it from being read from a wide angle. This is especially useful in tight quarters, such as on an airplane, bus, or subway, or other exposed locations such as a receptionist's desk.

▲ *Install a theft-prevention plate.* As an added precaution, physically mark a computer case or laptop so it can be identified if it is later stolen. You can embed a theft-prevention plate into the case and engrave or tattoo your ID information into it. The numbers or barcode identify you as the owner and can clearly establish to police that the laptop has been stolen. Two sources of theft-

Ownership Permanently Monitored Police Traceable Tattoo Beneath

To Return to Rightful Owner Please Call Toll Free
Within the US: 1-800-473-7867
Outside the US: +800-473-7867-7
or Visit www.stoptheft.com

U S I 8 4 7 0 1

Source: computersecurity.com/stop/

Figure 17-4 The security plate and the tattoo beneath it serve as an asset management tag and theft-prevention plate

prevention plates and cable locks are Flexguard Security System (*flexguard.com*) and Computer Security Products, Inc. (*computersecurity.com*). See Figure 17-4. To further help you identify stolen equipment, record serial numbers and model numbers in a safe place separate from the equipment. This information can also be included in an inventory management system.

▲ *Use a mantrap and security guard.* The ultimate in physical security is a mantrap, which consists of two doors on either end of a small entryway where the first door must close and/or lock before the second door can open. A separate form of identification might be required for each door, such as a badge for the first door and a fingerprint scan for the second door. A security guard might also maintain an entry control roster, which is a list of people allowed into the restricted area and a log of any approved visitors.

LOGICAL SECURITY AND ACCESS CONTROLS

**A+
CORE 2
2.2, 2.10**

Software, such as Windows Firewall, can make up a significant portion of your defense resources. Other types of software-based security measures include:

▲ *Antivirus/anti-malware.* Antivirus software or anti-malware software monitors a device for activity that is recognized to be harmful to data or other resources. The software then attempts to block the activity, identify the source of the problem, and remove any malicious files that have infected the computer. You'll learn more about viruses, malware, and antivirus/anti-malware software later in this chapter.

▲ *Email filtering.* Email providers often offer email filtering to filter out suspicious messages based on databases of known scams, spammers, and malware. Corporations might route incoming and outgoing email through a proxy server for filtering with the following goals in mind:

  ▲ Incoming email is inspected for scams or spam that might trick an employee into introducing malware into the corporate network.

  ▲ Outgoing email from employees might be filtered for inappropriate content. This lawful interception is intended to verify that an employee is complying with privacy laws (for example, laws that protect confidential medical records) and is not accidentally or intentionally leaking corporate data and secrets. Email filtering software used in this way is an example of data loss prevention (DLP) software, which helps protect against leaking corporate data.

▲ *Trusted software sources.* It's important to download software only from trusted publishers and providers. Even software from a trusted publisher can be filled with destructive extras if the software is obtained from an untrusted provider. Also know that a website might be trying to trick you into thinking you're downloading applications, software updates, or drivers from a trusted source when you're actually downloading malware. Be careful which sites you use for software downloads.

▲ *Access control lists.* An access control list (ACL) includes which user, device, or program has access to a particular resource, such as a printer, folder, or file, on a corporate network or computer. As you learned in Chapter 16, larger corporate networks manage access control through Active Directory on a Windows domain, and, on smaller peer-to-peer networks, each computer controls access to its own resources. For both types of networks, Group Policy can control user rights, and NTFS permissions and share permissions control access to files and folders.

▲ *Port security and MAC address filtering.* Recall that a switch has multiple Ethernet ports for devices to connect to the network. See Figure 17-5. By default, any device can connect to any port; however, you can enable port security to control which devices can use any port or a specific port on the switch. Most managed switches (switches that can be configured through a web-based utility) can provide MAC address filtering, which allows you to specify how many MAC addresses a port can accept or to provide a whitelist of MAC addresses the switch will accept. Because it's so easy to spoof, or counterfeit, a legitimate MAC address, MAC address filtering is not considered a recommended best practice as your only layer of defense against attack.

Source: cisco.com/c/en/us/support/switches/catalyst-2960s-48lps-l-switch/model.html

Figure 17-5 This managed switch by Cisco allows for MAC address filtering on its Ethernet ports

17

✎ **Notes** MAC address filtering can also be implemented on a SOHO router, and can easily be hacked as part of your defenses against attack. Therefore, MAC address filtering should only serve as one layer of defense among many. These various layers of defense are collectively called defense in depth.

▲ *VPN.* Recall from Chapter 7 that a VPN (virtual private network) protects data by encrypting it over a remote connection to a private network. When you set up a VPN, the VPN software (for example, OpenVPN at *openvpn.net* and *privatetunnel.com*) creates a virtual tunnel between the client computer and a VPN server behind the private network's firewall. Network packets are encrypted at one end of the tunnel and decrypted as they exit the tunnel. VPN connections are used for telecommuters to securely connect to their corporate networks (see Figure 17-6) or for individuals to securely surf the web. In the latter use, all transmissions are sent between the client computers and web servers through a VPN service center that manages the VPN connection. Managed switches, including the one shown earlier in Figure 17-5, sometimes have VPN services embedded in their firmware so they can provide VPN connections for remote users of the private network to which they belong.

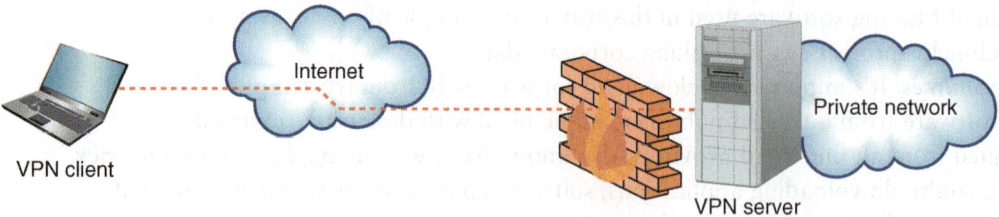

Figure 17-6 A VPN connection secures all traffic between the VPN client and VPN server on the private network

▲ *Mobile device management.* Corporate or personal mobile devices present a particular set of security challenges because they hold sensitive company data while traveling outside of the company network's physical perimeter. Mobile device management (MDM) software provides tools for tracking mobile devices—even when they're turned off—and managing the data on those devices. MDM policies typically include:

  ▲ Security policy enforcement, such as applying patches or enforcing password requirements

  ▲ Data encryption requirements, to protect data on the mobile device even if it falls into the wrong hands

  ▲ Remote wipe capabilities, to erase all data on the device

To do all this, MDM installs a small app called an agent on a managed mobile device, which communicates through various Wi-Fi or cellular connections back to the MDM server in the company data center. The initial installing of the agent and the agent checking the device for security compliance is called on-boarding. The reverse process when the mobile device is removed from the MDM fleet is called off-boarding. You learned more about BYOD (Bring Your Own Device) security in a corporate environment in Chapter 9.

USER AUTHENTICATION

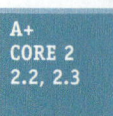

In Chapter 16, you learned that the first line of defense to protect a network is user authentication. Besides Windows authenticating a user with a Windows password, you can increase authentication security using these methods:

▲ Enforce a password policy, which is a set of rules that defines the minimum length of a password, complexity requirements, and how frequently a password must be reset, for example.

▲ Enforce multifactor authentication, which requires at least one more factor or action to authenticate beyond the single-factor password. Two-factor authentication (2FA) is most often used, and the two factors normally involve what the user:

  ▲ Knows (such as a Windows or Facebook password)

  ▲ Possesses, which is called a token (such as a smart card or key fob)

  ▲ Does (such as typing a certain way)

  ▲ Is, which is called biometric data (such as a fingerprint)

One warning to keep in mind is that factors such as a smart card or biometric data should be used in addition to, and not as a replacement for, a Windows password on a personal computer or domain.

Next, let's look at hardware and software security tokens and authentication services that can work together to provide multifactor authentication.

HARDWARE SECURITY TOKENS

Two types of hardware security tokens are a smart card and a key fob:

▲ *Smart card.* A smart card used as a security token has an embedded microprocessor, which is usually installed on the card under a small gold plate. For example, most current credit cards have a gold plate and microprocessor and are smart cards, as opposed to earlier credit cards that used only a magnetic strip with no internal processor. The microprocessor contains information that is read by a smart card reader or badge reader when the device is inserted into the reader or transmitted wirelessly. See Figure 17-7. At the same time, most smart cards can receive information from the card reader to confirm that the reader is authentic. This is called mutual authentication, which occurs when authentication goes in both directions at the same time and both entities confirm the identity of the other. Because a smart card contains a microprocessor and data, it's considered both a hardware token and a software token.

Source: istock.com/humonia

Figure 17-7 A smart card is read by a wireless smart card reader

> **✎ Notes** A common use of mutual authentication is sending a confirmation code by text to your smartphone using a phone number the server already has on file. This gives you reassurance that the server to which you're authenticating is what it says it is.

▲ *Key fob.* A key fob is a hardware token that fits conveniently on a keychain, such as the one shown in Figure 17-8. The number on the key fob changes every 60 seconds. When a user signs in to the network, he must enter the number on the key fob, which is synchronized with the network

Source: iStockphoto.com/David Clark

Figure 17-8 A security token such as this key fob is used to authenticate a user gaining access to a secured network

17

authentication service. Entering the number proves that the user has the key fob in hand. Because the device doesn't actually make physical contact with the system, it is called a contactless token or disconnected token.

SOFTWARE SECURITY TOKENS

Software tokens can be security tokens stored as an app or digital certificate. Here's how each works:

◢ *Software token apps.* These apps, sometimes called authenticator apps, are installed on your smartphone or other computing device and can perform the same service as a key fob, providing a counter or number generator that serves as one factor in multifactor authentication. The app is synchronized with the same calculations on the server so that the app and the server expect the same number at the same time. Software token providers for 2FA include Google Authenticator (*google.com*), Twilio Authy (*authy.com*), and LastPass Authenticator (*lastpass.com/auth*). Many online accounts, such as banking accounts, Facebook, Google, and Amazon, can be set to use 2FA and software tokens. For example, the Authy app by Twilio can be used to require 2FA to sign in to Facebook (see Figure 17-9).

In general, to set up 2FA with an online account, you would:

1. Sign up for and configure the 2FA service with a 2FA provider such as Twilio. You'll need to download and install its authenticator app to your phone or computer.

2. Enable 2FA with a Facebook, Google, banking, or other account you want to secure.

3. Configure the account to use the 2FA service.

4. Now, each time you sign in to the account, you must provide your password and the number generated by the authenticator app.

Source: https://authy.com/features/setup/ by Twilio, Inc.

Figure 17-9 When you sign in to your account, Facebook requests the token generated by the 2FA app

◢ *Digital certificates.* Think of a digital certificate as a digital signature that proves a person or entity, such as a web server, is who they say they are; it's a small file that holds information about the identity of the person or entity. In addition, a public encryption key is used to prove the certificate is legitimate, and is similar to a notary verifying that a signature is legitimate. The digital certificate and public encryption key are assigned by a Certificate Authority (CA) that has confirmed your identity in a separate process. VeriSign (*verisign.com*) and GlobalSign (*globalsign.com*) are two well-known CAs. You purchase a digital certificate from a CA and then install it on your desktop, laptop, or other computing device; in some cases, you can install it on a smart card or flash drive that you can use on any computer.

Digital certificates are used to authenticate individuals (such as to digitally sign and encrypt email or to connect to a corporate network via a VPN), software (Windows can require that device drivers be digitally signed), or server applications (many web servers are digitally signed). For example, to see a web server's digital certificate, navigate to the webpage in your browser and then click the lock icon, as shown in Figure 17-10. Click **View certificate**.

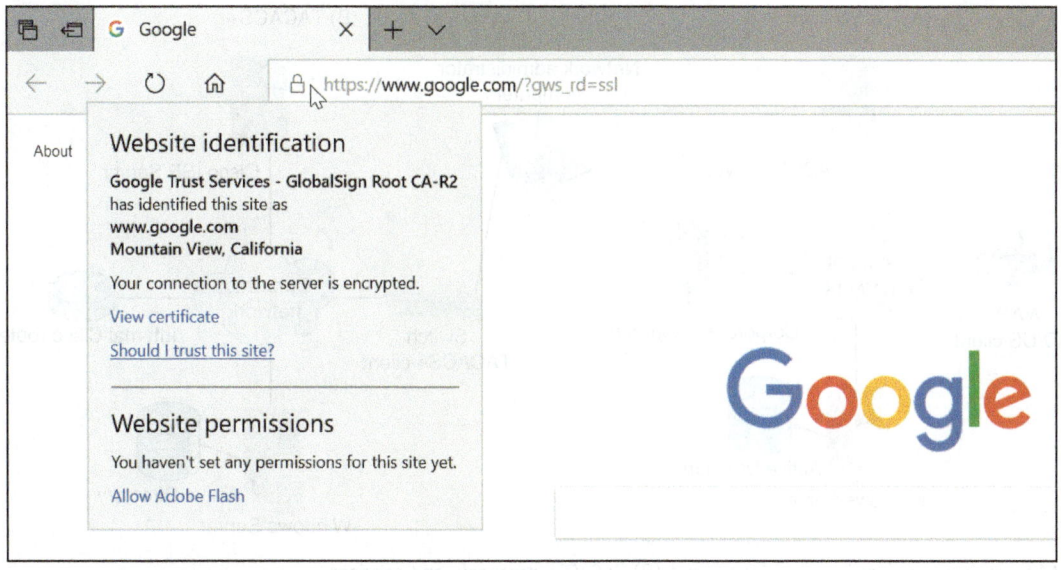

Source: google.com

Figure 17-10 Google's digital certificate is provided by GlobalSign, Inc.

AUTHENTICATION SERVICES

For large networks, you learned in Chapter 16 that Active Directory on a Windows domain is used to authenticate users to the domain and authorize what users can do with domain resources. For added security, everything users attempt to do or do once they are authenticated to the network can be tracked or logged for future auditing. These three security measures are generally known in networking as AAA (authenticating, authorizing, and accounting) or triple A. Two popular solutions to provide AAA services for large networks are RADIUS and TACACS+:

◢ RADIUS (Remote Access Dial-In User Service) was originally developed to authenticate end users accessing resources on a network through dial-up connections and has evolved to other types of connections to a network, including wired, wireless, and VPN.

◢ TACACS+ (Terminal Access Controller Access Control System Plus) was developed by Cisco to improve on RADIUS for AAA services specifically designed for network administrators and technicians to remotely connect to a network to configure and manage Cisco network devices, such as routers, switches, and firewalls.

RADIUS and TACACS+ each can work with Active Directory or some other type of directory server to authenticate and authorize users, and sometimes both services are used on the same network. RADIUS and TACACS+ can each support wireless, wired, and VPN connections. Notice in Figure 17-11 the similarities of how each service works; both use a client, server, and user directory:

◢ *Client*. A RADIUS or TACACS+ client can be a wireless access point (WAP) or switch that receives the initial connection from the user's laptop or other device. The client is responsible for querying the RADIUS or TACACS+ server to authenticate the user before allowing the user on the network.

◢ *Server*. A RADIUS or TACACS+ server authenticates the user by querying a user directory. Cisco calls its TACACS+ server the Identify Service Engine server (ISE server).

◢ *User directory*. The RADIUS to ISE server queries a user directory or database, where user credentials are stored. Active Directory is the most popular user directory for today's large networks.

> ✎ **Notes** Often, a basic WAP isn't smart enough to act as the RADIUS or TACACS+ client. In an enterprise environment, many WAPs are connected to a wireless controller device in the data closet, which in turn does the work of managing client requests to the RADIUS or ISE server.

17

Figure 17-11 AAA services provided by (A) RADIUS and (B) TACACS+ protocols and services

In summary, Table 17-1 compares RADIUS and TACACS+.

Characteristic	RADIUS	TACACS+
Primary use	Intended for end-user network access	Intended for Cisco network device administrative access
Encryption	Encrypts user passwords only	Encrypts every message
Underlying protocol	The RADIUS protocol uses UDP, which does not guarantee transmissions over the corporate network	The TACACS+ protocol uses TCP to guarantee transmissions over the corporate network
Network types	Works on wireless, wired, and VPN network connections	Works on wireless, wired, and VPN network connections

Table 17-1 RADIUS and TACACS+ characteristics

USER EDUCATION

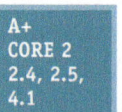

A+
CORE 2
2.4, 2.5,
4.1

Generally speaking, people are the weakest link in setting up security in a computer environment. That's because people can often be tricked into giving out private information. Even with all the news and hype about identity theft and criminal websites, it's amazing how well they still work. Many users naively download a funny screen saver, open an email attachment, or enter credit card information on a website without regard to security. In the IT arena, social engineering is the practice of tricking people into giving out private information or allowing unsafe programs into the network or computer.

A good support technician is aware of the criminal practices used, and is able to teach users how to recognize and avoid this mischief. A document that can help educate users is an acceptable use policy (AUP), which explains what users can and cannot do on the corporate network or with company data, and explains the penalties for violations. The AUP might also describe how these measures help protect the network's security. Important security measures that users need to follow to protect passwords and the computer system are:

▲ Never give out your passwords to anyone, not even a supervisor or tech support person who calls and asks for it.

▲ Don't store your passwords on a computer unless you use company-approved password vault software (for example, KeePass or LastPass). Some organizations even forbid employees from writing down their passwords.

- Don't use the same password on more than one computer, network, application, or website.
- Be aware of shoulder surfing, which is when other people secretly peek at your monitor screen as you work. A privacy filter can help.
- Lock down your workstation each time you step away from your desk.
- Users need to be on the alert for tailgating, which is when an unauthorized person follows an employee through a secured entrance to a room or building. Another form of tailgating is when a user steps away from a computer that's not properly locked and another person continues to use the Windows session.

Hackers might obtain information or trick people into giving information that can be used to hack a computer or network by:

- *Dumpster diving*. Dumpster diving is looking for useful information in someone's trash to help create a convincing impersonation of an individual or company to aid in a malicious attack. Even something that might appear harmless, such as an organizational chart, can help a thief create a convincing email hoax message. For best security, shred all papers and printouts before recycling and educate users about the importance of shredding.
- *Phishing, spear phishing, impersonation, and spoofing*. Phishing (pronounced "fishing") is a type of identity theft in which the sender of an email hoax scams you into responding with personal data about yourself. Even more plausible is spear phishing, where the email appears to come from companies you already do business with. The scam artist baits you by asking you to verify personal data on your bank account, ISP account, credit card account, or something of that nature. Often a convincing impersonation of an individual or company tricks you into responding to the email or clicking a link in the email message, which takes you to an official-looking site complete with corporate or bank logos, where you are asked to enter your user ID and password to enter the site. This tactic is called spoofing, which means the scam artist makes both the email and website look like the real thing. For example, when the user who received the email shown in Figure 17-12 scanned the attached file using antivirus software, the software reported that the file contained malware.

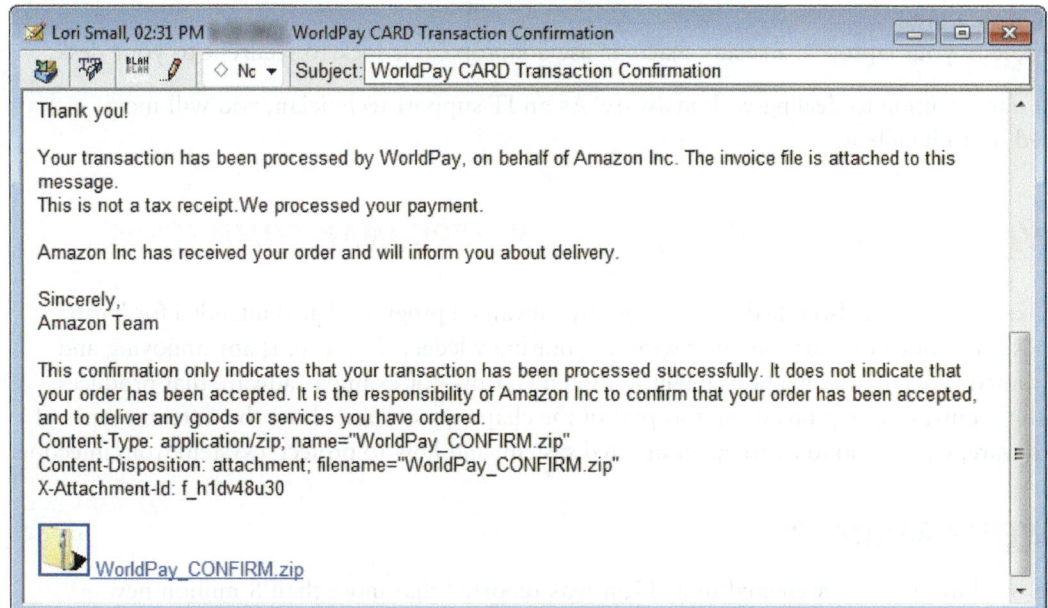

Figure 17-12 This phishing technique using an email message with an attached file is an example of social engineering

An email message might contain a link that leads to a malicious script. If you think an email is legitimate, be on the safe side and don't click the link. To keep a script from running, type the website's home page into your browser address bar and navigate to the relevant page on the website.

Good sites to help you debunk a virus hoax or email hoax are:

◢ *snopes.com* by Barbara and David Mikkelson
◢ *securelist.com* by Kaspersky Lab
◢ *virusbtn.com* by Virus Bulletin, Ltd

Don't forward an email hoax. If you get a hoax from a person you know, do us all a favor and send that person some of the preceding links!

> 📝 **Notes** A helpful tool to combat phishing attacks is a **Secure DNS** service (sometimes written as SecureDNS), which monitors requests for websites and redirects your browser when it attempts to visit a known malicious site. Popular providers include the free SecureDNS service by Comodo (*comodo.com*) and the enterprise-grade SecureDNS service by RiskAnalytics (*riskanalytics.com*). To use Secure DNS on a personal computer, go to the Network Connections window, open the active connection's TCP/IPv4 properties box, and change the DNS server settings so your computer uses Secure DNS server addresses listed on the provider's website.

> ⭐ **A+ Exam Tip** The A+ Core 2 exam expects you to recognize and distinguish among examples of social engineering situations that might compromise security, such as tailgating, phishing, spear phishing, impersonation, shoulder surfing, and dumpster diving.

A study by Dell showed that 65 percent of business travelers have not secured the corporate data on their hard drives, and 42 percent don't back up that data. Here are some commonsense rules to help protect a laptop when traveling:

◢ When traveling, always know where your laptop is. If you're standing at an airport counter, tuck your laptop case securely between your ankles. At security checkpoints, pay attention to your belongings; tell yourself to stay focused. When flying, never check your laptop as baggage, and don't store it in airplane overhead bins; keep it at your feet.
◢ Never leave a laptop in an unlocked car. If you leave your laptop in a hotel room, use a laptop cable lock to secure it to a table.
◢ When at work, lock your laptop in a secure place or use a laptop cable lock to secure it to your desk.

Next, we turn our attention to dealing with malware. As an IT support technician, you will most certainly be called on to handle it.

DEALING WITH MALICIOUS SOFTWARE ON PERSONAL COMPUTERS

Malicious software, also called **malware**, is any unwanted program that is intended for harm and is transmitted to your computer without your knowledge. **Grayware** is any annoying and unwanted program that might or might not intend harm—for example, adware that produces all those unwanted pop-up ads. In this part of the chapter, you learn about the different types of malware and grayware, what to do to clean up an infected system, and how to protect a system from infection.

WHAT ARE WE UP AGAINST?

You need to know your enemy! In 2017, it was reported that more than 8 million new malware programs were discovered. Different categories of malware and scamming techniques are listed next:

◢ *Viruses*. A **virus** is a program that replicates by attaching itself to other programs. The infected program must be executed for a virus to run. The program might be an application, a macro in a document, a Windows system file, or a boot loader program.

◢ *Spyware*. Spyware spies on you to collect personal information that it transmits over the Internet to web-hosting sites. An example of spyware is a keylogger that tracks all your keystrokes and can be used to steal your identity, credit card numbers, Social Security number, bank information, passwords, email addresses, and so forth.

◢ *Worms*. A worm is a program that copies itself throughout a network or the Internet without a host program. A worm creates problems by overloading the network as it replicates and can even hijack or install a server program such as a web server.

◢ *Trojans*. A Trojan does not need a host program to work; rather, it substitutes itself for a legitimate program. In most cases, a user launches it thinking she is launching a legitimate program. A Trojan is often embedded in the files of legitimate software that is downloaded from an untrustworthy website, or a user is tricked into opening an email attachment (refer back to Figure 17-12).

◢ *Rootkits*. A rootkit loads itself before the OS boot is complete. It can hide in boot managers, boot loader programs, or kernel mode device drivers. UEFI secure boot is especially designed to catch rootkits that launch during the boot. Because a rootkit is already loaded when most anti-malware software loads, it is sometimes overlooked by the software. A rootkit can hide folders that contain software it has installed, cause Task Manager to display a different name for its process, hide registry keys, and can operate in user mode or kernel mode. This last trick helps it remain undetected (see Figure 17-13).

Figure 17-13   A rootkit can run in user mode or kernel mode

A rootkit running in user mode intercepts the API calls between the time the API retrieves the data and when it is displayed in a window. A rootkit running in kernel mode actually interferes with the Windows kernel and substitutes its own information in place of the raw data read by the Windows kernel. Because most anti-malware software to one degree or another relies on Windows tools and components to work, the rootkit is not detected or cannot be deleted if the Windows tools themselves are infected.

> ⚡ **Caution**   If anti-malware software reports that a rootkit is present but cannot delete it, the best solution is to immediately disconnect the computer from the network (if you have not already done so), back up your important data, format your hard drive, and reinstall Windows.

17

▲ *Ransomware*. Ransomware holds your computer system hostage until you pay money. For example, the CryptoLocker Trojan program that did damage in 2014 was embedded in email attachments and was known to work on Windows, Android, and even some iOS systems. When the user clicked the attachment, the program encrypted the computer's personal files. If the user didn't pay within a 24-hour period, all the files were lost. Many users who did not have backups of their data chose to pay the ransom. A computer infected with ransomware can infect all computers on the network and even cloud servers to which the computer connects.

> ⚡ **Caution** The best defense against ransomware is to keep backups of data file versions in a location that is not accessible from File Explorer. A ransomware attack can infect any storage device connected or mapped to your computer, and a single layer of data file backups might be replaced with the encrypted files before you're able to clean your computer and restore the backed-up data. Use a backup method that retains multiple file versions (indefinitely, if possible) and that is not directly accessible from your computer. Many cloud backup services meet these requirements, such as Carbonite (*carbonite.com*), Backblaze (*backblaze.com*), or IDrive (*idrive.com*). After a ransomware attack, you can wipe the computer, reinstall software from original sources, and restore unaffected file versions from your online backups.

▲ *Zero-day attack*. A zero-day attack can happen in two ways: a hacker discovers a security hole in software that is unknown to the developer of the software, or a hacker takes advantage of a recently reported gap in software security before users apply patches released by the developer. The race is on for the vendor to provide a patch to the software and for users to apply those patches before hackers have even one day to use the hole to infect systems and steal user data. Microsoft normally publishes security patches on the second and fourth Tuesday of each month (known as patch Tuesday), but sometimes releases patches off schedule so that hackers have less time to attack customers.

▲ *Man-in-the-middle attack*. In a man-in-the-middle attack, the attacker intercepts communication between two parties and reads and/or alters the content of messages. The attacker can impersonate a legitimate website, network, FTP site, or person in a chat session. For example, a user might connect to an "evil twin" Wi-Fi hotspot, thinking it's a legitimate hotspot, and attempt to start a chat session with a business associate. The attacker pretends to be the business associate and continues the chat with the intention of obtaining private information. The best protection against man-in-the-middle attacks is to use digital certificates to identify a person or service before transmitting sensitive information.

▲ *Denial of service*. A denial-of-service (DoS) attack overwhelms a computer or network with requests or traffic until new connections can no longer be accepted. A distributed denial-of-service (DDoS) attack happens when multiple computers are involved in the attack. DDoS attacks are sometimes performed by botnets, which are described next.

▲ *Zombies and botnets*. A zombie is a computer that has been hacked, and the hacker is using the computer to run repetitive software in the background without the knowledge of its user. For example, the zombie might be email spamming or performing DDoS attacks. A hacker might build an entire network of zombies, which is called a botnet (a network of robots). The CryptoLocker Trojan program was distributed by a botnet and ultimately isolated when the botnet was taken down.

▲ *Dictionary attack*. A dictionary attack can be used to crack a password by trying words in a dictionary. Password cracker software might combine a brute force attack (systematically trying every possible combination of letters, numbers, and symbols) with a dictionary attack to guess the password. A dictionary attack is usually more efficient than using brute force.

▲ *Rainbow tables*. A rainbow table contains a long list of plaintext passwords, just as users would enter, and the password hash list (after it is encrypted). Organizations store only hashed passwords and not plaintext passwords. When a hacker obtains a stolen list of hashed passwords, she can compare this list with those in her rainbow tables to find a match. When two hashed passwords match, she can use the plaintext password in the rainbow table to sign in to the system, impersonating the user.

Rainbow tables make cracking passwords faster than dictionary cracking or brute force cracking. The best defenses against rainbow table attacks are for an organization to use the very best hashing techniques to encrypt their passwords and to add extra characters to the password hash (called *salting the passwords*).

▲ *Noncompliant systems and violations of security best practices.* A system administrator needs techniques in place to routinely scan BYOD and corporate-owned smartphones, tablets, laptops, desktops, and servers for noncompliant systems that violate security best practices, such as out-of-date anti-malware software or cases where it's not installed. One software product designed to scan devices for noncompliance is System Center Configuration Manager by Microsoft, which works with Microsoft Intune. Intune focuses specifically on mobile devices that connect to a corporate network.

> ★ **A+ Exam Tip** The A+ Core 2 exam might give you a scenario that requires you to detect, remove, or prevent viruses, Trojans, worms, spyware, keyloggers, ransomware, rootkits, and botnet software. You also need to identify and describe zero-day attacks, man-in-the-middle attacks, zombies, dictionary attacks, brute force attacks, phishing, spear phishing, impersonation, shoulder surfing, tailgating, dumpster diving, DoS/DDoS attacks, rainbow tables, spoofing, and noncompliant systems.

STEP-BY-STEP ATTACK PLAN

> A+
> CORE 2
> 3.3

This section is a step-by-step attack plan to clean up an infected system. We use anti-malware software, also called antivirus software, to remove all types of general malware, including viruses, spyware, worms, and rootkits. Then we'll use some Windows tools to check out the system, making sure all remnants of malware have been removed and the system is in tip-top order.

> ⚡ **Caution** If a system is highly infected and will later hold sensitive data, a fresh start might be in order. In fact, Microsoft recommends reinstalling Windows as the safest way to deal with highly infected systems. If you have recent backups of data, format the hard drive, reinstall or reimage Windows, and restore data from backups.
>
> If you don't have recent backups for a Windows 10 system, you can try a repair upgrade, a fresh start, or a reset without losing user data. For Windows 8, a refresh can be an excellent option if you have a recent custom refresh image. For Windows 7, consider applying a system image. In Chapter 15, you learned about all of these options to reinstall Windows.

17

STEP 1: IDENTIFYING AND RESEARCHING MALWARE SYMPTOMS

> A+
> CORE 2
> 3.3

An IT support technician needs to know how to recognize that a system is infected. Here are some warnings that suggest malicious software is at work:

▲ *Pop-up ads and browser redirection.* Basically, a user is losing control of his system. For example, Figure 17-14 shows the desktop immediately after a user signed in. Pop-up ads are randomly appearing and the browser home page has changed. A browser might also have an uninvited toolbar. Security alerts—real or spoofed—regularly interrupt the user's activity.

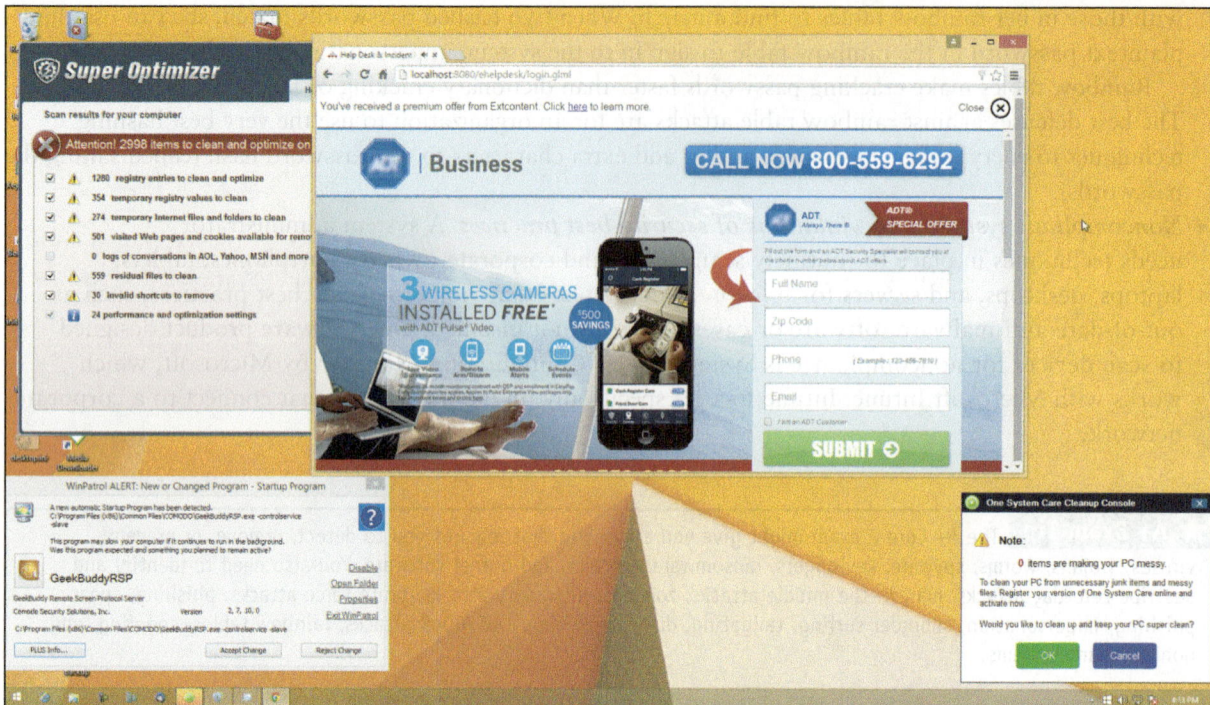

Figure 17-14 A hijacked home page, security alerts, and pop-up ads indicate an infected system

▲ *Rogue antivirus software*. When the user tries to run Windows Defender (anti-malware software embedded in Windows 8), it refuses to run. She opens the Action Center to find that Defender has been disabled because other antivirus software she did not install is running. See Figure 17-15.

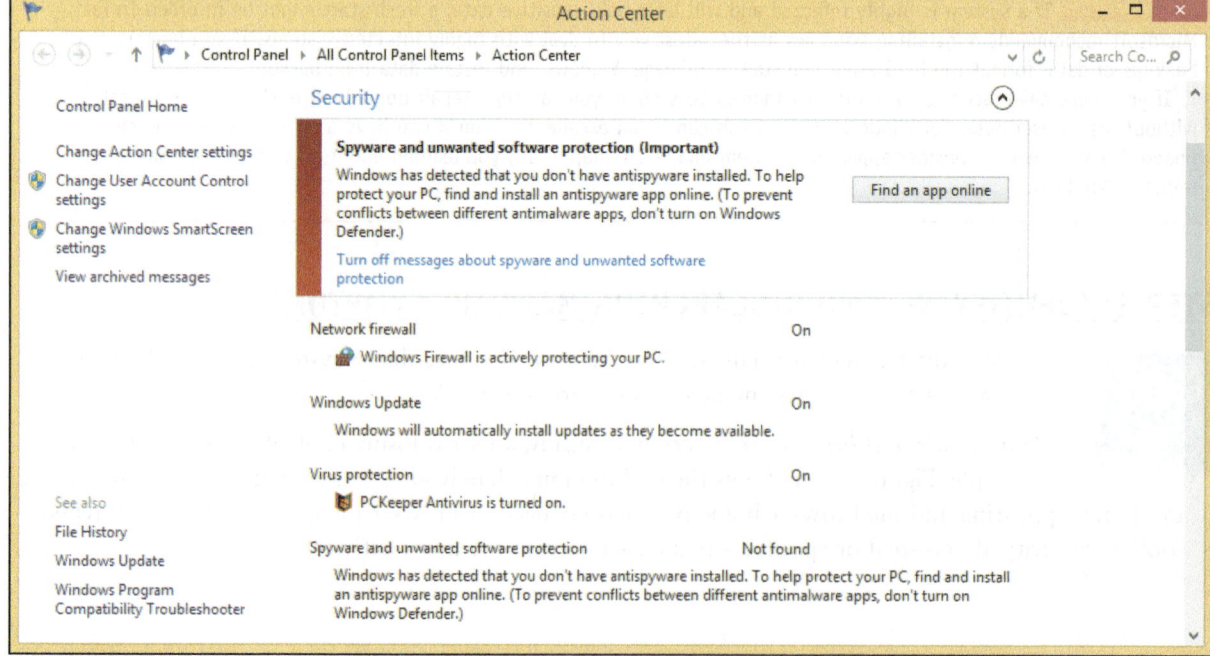

Figure 17-15 Action Center reports Windows Defender has been disabled and rogue antivirus software is running

Windows allows only one anti-malware product to run at a time. You can use Task Manager to stop the rogue antivirus software and then start Windows Defender.

- ▲ *Slow performance or lockups*. Generally, the system works much slower than before. Programs take longer than normal to load. Strange or bizarre error messages appear. Programs that once worked now give errors. Task Manager shows unfamiliar processes running. The computer's operating system might lock up.
- ▲ *Internet connectivity issues, application crashes, and OS update failures*. These types of problems seem to plague the system with no reasonable explanation that is specific to the network, application, or Windows update.
- ▲ *System and application log errors*. The Administrative Events logs in Event Viewer report system and application errors, system crashes, application crashes, and failed OS updates.
- ▲ *Problems with files*. File names now have weird characters or their file sizes seem excessively large. Executable files have changed size or file extensions change without reason. Files mysteriously disappear or appear. Windows system files are renamed. Files constantly become corrupted. Files you could once access now give access-denied messages, and file permissions change.
- ▲ *Email problems*. You receive email messages from other users saying you have sent someone spam or an infected message, or you receive automated replies indicating you sent email you didn't know about. This type of attack indicates that your email address or email client software on your computer has been hijacked. Extra spam you're not accustomed to seeing shows up.
- ▲ *Problems updating your anti-malware software*. Even though you can browse to other websites, you cannot access anti-malware software sites such as *symantec.com* or *mcafee.com*, and you cannot update your anti-malware software.
- ▲ *Invalid digital certificates*. An OS is responsible for validating certificates used to secure communication. For Windows, Microsoft maintains a database of trusted root certificates issued by Certificate Authorities (CAs). A root certificate is the original certificate issued by the CA. When a Windows system opens a secure email or visits a secure website and encounters a new digital certificate, it requests Microsoft's trusted root certificate, which is downloaded to the computer. The download happens seamlessly without the user's knowledge unless there's a problem. If Windows cannot obtain the root certificate to validate the email or website, it displays an error (see Figure 17-16). Don't trust websites or email whose certificates have expired or been revoked.

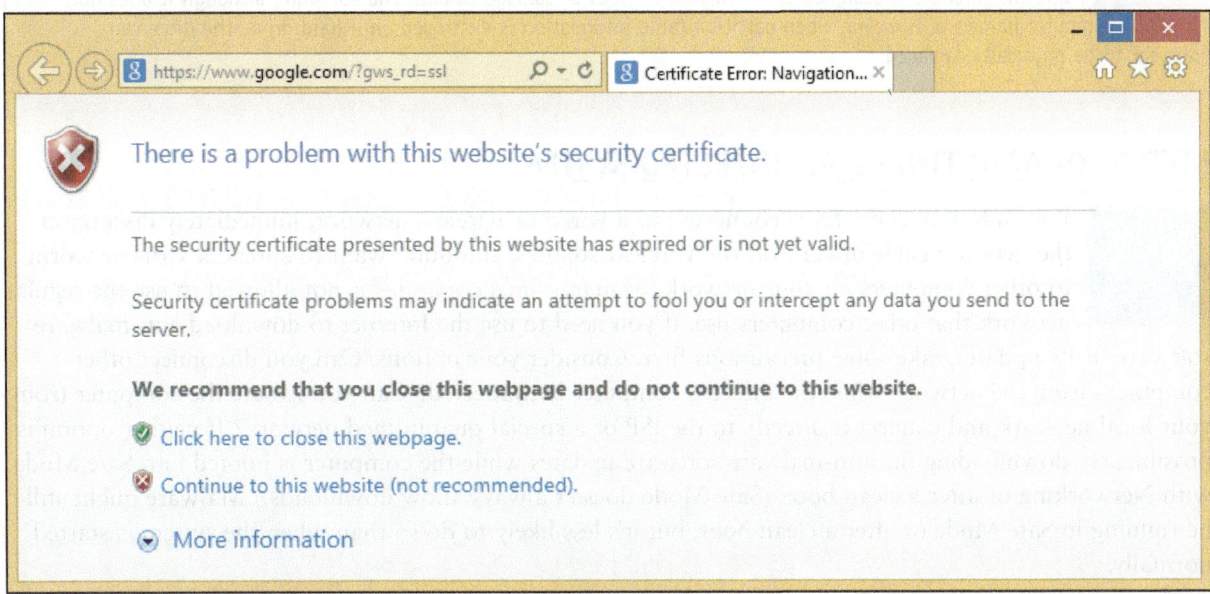

Figure 17-16 Windows reports a problem with a digital certificate

> ✏️ **Notes** If a computer gives invalid certificate errors, check that the Windows date is correct. A wrong Windows date before the certificate was issued can cause the problem.

You can use the Certificate Manager (*certmgr.msc*) to view and delete root certificates, as shown in Figure 17-17. For example, the Superfish virus injects a rogue root certificate into the Microsoft store of trusted certificates on the local computer so that it can perform a man-in-the-middle attack to display adware on secure websites a user visits. If you see a Superfish certificate listed among trusted root certificates, be sure to delete it.

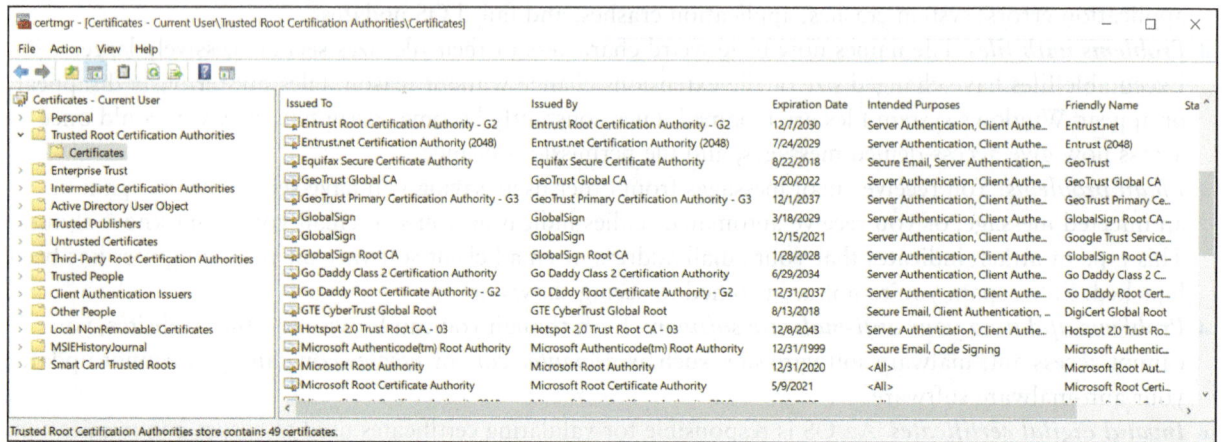

Figure 17-17 Windows Certificate Manager can be used to view and delete root certificates kept in the store of trusted certificates

> ⭐ **A+ Exam Tip** The A+ Core 2 exam might give you a scenario that requires you to recognize the common symptoms of malware listed previously and know how to quarantine and remediate an infected system.

> ✏️ **Notes** Malicious software is designed to do varying degrees of damage to data and software, although it does not damage computer hardware. However, when partition table information is destroyed on a hard drive, the drive can appear to be physically damaged.

STEP 2: QUARANTINING AN INFECTED SYSTEM

A+
CORE 2
3.3

If an infected computer is connected to a wired or wireless network, immediately disconnect the network cable or turn off the wireless adapter. You don't want to spread a virus or worm to other computers on your network. A quarantined computer is not allowed to use the regular network that other computers use. If you need to use the Internet to download anti-malware software or its updates, take some precautions first. Consider your options. Can you disconnect other computers from the network while the infected computer is connected? Can you isolate the computer from your local network and connect it directly to the ISP or a special quarantined network? If neither option is possible, try downloading the anti-malware software updates while the computer is booted into Safe Mode with Networking or after a clean boot. (Safe Mode doesn't always allow downloads.) Malware might still be running in Safe Mode or after a clean boot, but it's less likely to do so than when the system is started normally.

Always keep in mind that data on the hard drive might not be backed up. Before you begin cleaning up the system, back up data to another media.

STEP 3: DISABLING SYSTEM RESTORE

In Windows, some malware hides its program files in restore points stored in the System Volume Information folder that's maintained by System Protection. If System Protection is on, anti-malware software can't clean this protected folder. To get rid of the malware, turn off System Protection so that anti-malware software can clean the System Volume Information folder (see Figure 17-18). Realize that when you turn off System Protection, all your restore points are lost, so first consider whether you might need those restore points to troubleshoot the malware infection before you disable System Protection.

Source: McAfee VirusScan

Figure 17-18   Malware found in a restore point

> ⚡ **Caution**   Some highly infected systems will not allow anti-malware software to run. In this situation, you can boot the computer into Safe Mode and use System Restore to apply a restore point that was taken before the infection. Applying a restore point cannot be counted on to completely remove an infection, but it might remove startup entries the malware is using, making it possible to run the anti-malware software from the normal Windows desktop or to run the software in Safe Mode. Consider that you might need to apply a restore point before you disable System Protection, which deletes all your restore points.

To turn off System Protection, go to **Control Panel**, open the **System** window, and click **System protection**. Later, when you are sure the system is clean, turn System Protection back on and create a new restore point that you can use in the future if problems arise.

STEP 4: REMEDIATING THE INFECTED SYSTEM

Table 17-2 lists popular anti-malware software for personal computers and the programs' websites, which also provide information about malware. Before selecting a product, be sure to read some reviews about it and check out some reliable websites that rate anti-malware software.

Anti-Malware Software	Website
Maximum, Internet, or Antivirus+ Security by Trend Micro (for home use)	*trendmicro.com*
Avast Ultimate, Premium, or Free Antivirus (for home use)	*avast.com*
Bitdefender Antivirus Plus, Internet Security, or Total Security	*bitdefender.com*
ClamWin Free Antivirus (open source and free)	*clamwin.com*
F-Secure Total, Safe, Anti-Virus, or Online Scanner (Online Scanner is free)	*f-secure.com*
Kaspersky Internet Security, Anti-Virus, or Security Cloud (Security Cloud is free)	*kaspersky.com*
Malwarebytes for Windows (free version available)	*malwarebytes.com*
McAfee Total Protection	*mcafee.com*
Symantec Endpoint Protection	*symantec.com*
Panda Dome Essential, Advanced, or Complete	*pandasecurity.com*
SUPERAntiSpyware (free edition available)	*superantispyware.com*
Windows Defender (included in Windows 10/8), Microsoft Security Essentials (free for Windows 7)	*microsoft.com*

Table 17-2   Anti-malware software and websites

17

> ⚡ **Caution** Beware of websites that appear as sponsored links at the top of search results for anti-malware software. These sites might appear to be the home site for the software, but they are really trying to lure you into downloading adware or spyware.

> ✏️ **Notes** Windows Defender anti-malware software is embedded in Windows 10/8 and can be accessed through the Windows 10 Settings app or Windows 8 Control Panel. Windows 7 includes Windows Defender, but the Windows 7 version finds only spyware, not viruses and other malware. For Windows 7, you can download and install Microsoft Security Essentials, which is free anti-malware software.

Now let's look at different situations you might encounter when attempting to run anti-malware software.

WHEN AN INFECTED COMPUTER WILL NOT BOOT

If an infected computer will not boot, the boot manager, boot loaders, or kernel mode drivers launched at startup might be infected or damaged. Launch the computer into Windows Recovery Environment (Windows RE) and use the Startup Repair process to repair the system. Chapter 15 gives more information about solving boot problems. You can also install the hard drive as a second drive in another system and use that system to scan the drive for malware.

UPDATE AND RUN ANTI-MALWARE SOFTWARE THAT'S ALREADY INSTALLED

If anti-malware software is already installed on a system and you suspect an infection, update the software and perform a full scan on the system. Do the following:

1. Make sure the anti-malware software is up to date. These updates download the latest malware definitions, also called malware signatures, which the software uses to define or detect new malware as it gets into the wild (becomes available on the Internet).

2. Use the anti-malware software to perform a full scan of the system. As it scans, the software might ask you what to do with an infected program, or it might log the event in an event viewer or history log it keeps. For example, Windows Defender reports a threat, as shown in Figure 17-19. When you click **Clean PC**, you can decide what to do with the threat. In most situations, select **Remove** to delete the program.

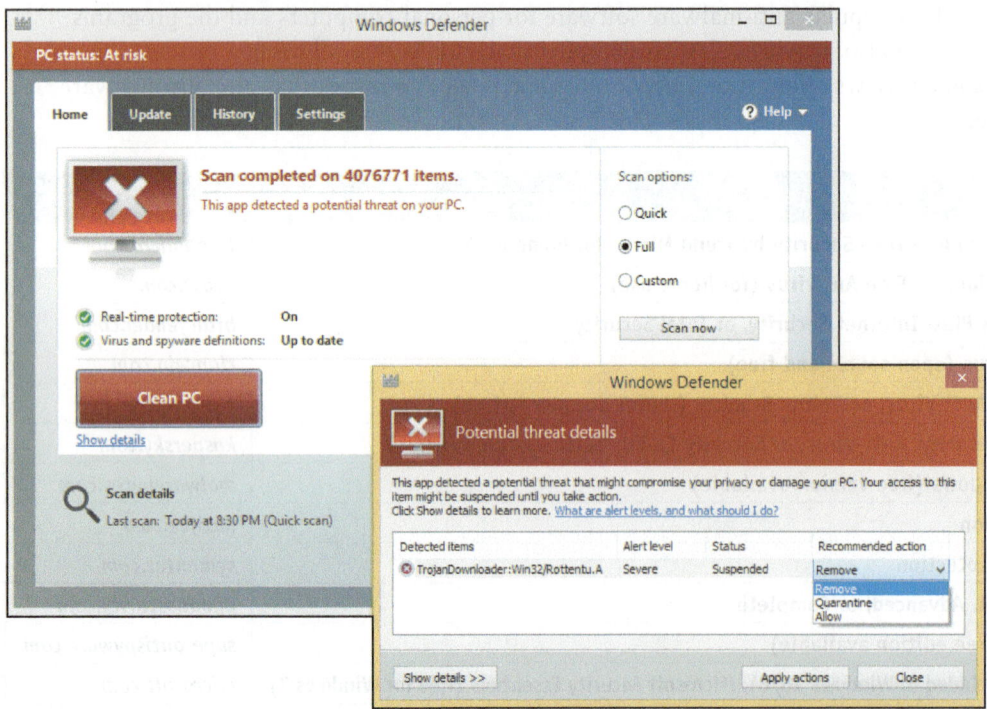

Figure 17-19 Decide what to do with a program that Windows Defender has identified as a severe threat to the system

3. After the scan is complete and you have decided what to do with each suspicious file, reboot the system, allow the software to update itself again, and then scan the system again. Most likely, some new malware will be discovered. Keep rebooting and rescanning until a scan comes up clean.

> **Notes** If you ever encounter a virus that your updated anti-malware software did not find, be sure to let the manufacturer of the software know so they can research the problem.

RUN ANTI-MALWARE SOFTWARE FROM A NETWORKED COMPUTER

If anti-malware software is not already installed, the most effective way to clean the computer is to run the software from another computer. Follow these steps:

1. Make sure the remote computer has its software firewall set for maximum protection and its installed anti-malware software is up to date and running.

2. Network the two computers and share drive C: on the infected computer. (Don't connect the infected computer to the entire network. If necessary, you can connect the two computers using a crossover cable or using a small switch and network cables.)

3. To make your work easier, you can map a network drive from the remote computer to drive C: on the infected computer.

4. Perform an anti-malware scan on the remote computer, pointing the scan to drive C: on the infected computer.

INSTALL AND RUN ANTI-MALWARE SOFTWARE ON THE INFECTED COMPUTER

If you don't have another computer that you are willing to risk connecting to the infected computer, you can use another computer to purchase and download anti-malware software and then copy the downloaded files to a CD or flash drive that you can insert in the infected computer. Don't make the mistake of using the infected computer to purchase and download anti-malware software because keyloggers might be spying and collecting credit card information. During the installation process, the anti-malware software updates itself and performs a scan. You can also run free online anti-malware software without downloading and installing it, but be careful to use only reputable websites.

INSTALL AND RUN ANTI-MALWARE SOFTWARE IN SAFE MODE

Some malware prevents anti-malware software from installing or running. In this situation, try booting the system in Safe Mode or performing a clean boot and installing the anti-malware software. Some viruses still load in Safe Mode or after a clean boot, and some anti-malware programs will not install in Safe Mode. Recall that to launch Windows in Safe Mode, also called Safe boot, enter the **msconfig** command in the Windows 10/7 search box or the Windows 8 Run box. In the System Configuration box, click the **Boot** tab and check **Safe boot** (see Figure 17-20). To launch Safe Mode with Networking so that you can update your anti-malware software, select **Network** in the list of options. Then restart the system.

17

> **Notes** If viruses are launched even after you boot in Safe Mode and you cannot get the anti-malware software to work, try searching for suspicious entries in the Windows registry subkeys under HKLM\System\CurrentControlSet\Control\SafeBoot. Subkeys under this key control what is launched when you boot into Safe Mode. How to edit the registry is covered in Chapter 14.

Figure 17-20 Use the Safe boot option to boot the system in Safe Mode and prevent malware from launching at startup

RUN AN ANTI-MALWARE SCAN BEFORE WINDOWS BOOTS

Microsoft offers a specialized scanning utility called Windows Defender Offline (WDO) that loads before Windows and performs a scan in the Windows Preinstallation Environment (WinPE). WinPE is a limited version of Windows that can be used for customizing Windows installations, modifying the Windows installation while it's not running, or performing recovery tasks. WDO can be started from the Windows 10 Settings app:

1. Click **Update & Security, Windows Security,** and **Virus & threat protection**.

2. In the Windows Defender Security Center window that opens, click **Run a new advanced scan**. Select **Windows Defender Offline scan,** as shown in Figure 17-21. Make sure all apps and files are saved and closed, then click **Scan now**.

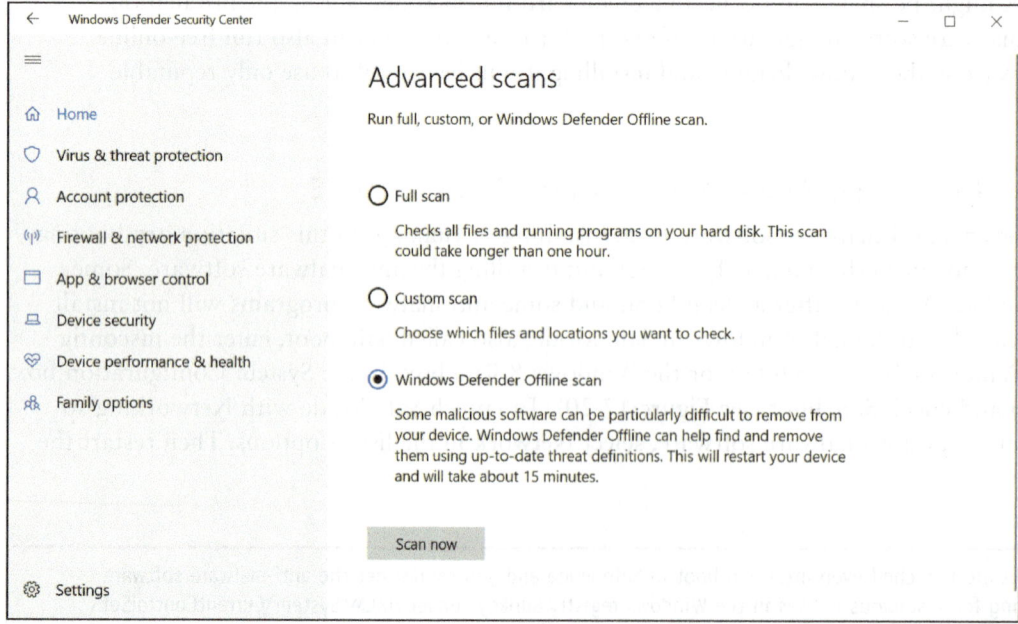

Figure 17-21 A WDO scan searches for and removes malware in the Windows Preinstallation Environment

3. After the scan completes, find information about the scan in the Virus & threat protection window by clicking **Threat history**.

If you're unable to boot into Windows 10, or if you're working with an earlier version of Windows, use an uninfected computer to create a bootable CD or flash drive with the WDO tool, and then boot from that device:

1. Depending on the architecture of the infected machine, download the 32-bit or 64-bit version of WDO from the Microsoft support website at the following link and save it to a CD or flash drive:

   support.microsoft.com/en-us/help/17466/windows-defender-offline-help-protect-my-pc

2. Boot from the WDO device, perform the scan, and check the results.

Other anti-malware companies, such as those listed in Table 17-2, offer preinstallation scanning tools, also called rescue disks or bootable antivirus tools. Two examples are the Bitdefender Rescue CD (*bitdefender.com*) and Kaspersky's Rescue Disk (*kaspersky.com*).

RUN MORE THAN ONE SCAN OF ANTI-MALWARE SOFTWARE

After you've scanned the system using one of the methods just discussed, reboot and install anti-malware software on the hard drive. Update the software, and then keep scanning and rebooting until the scan report is clean.

If a second or third scan doesn't remove all symptoms of malware, consider installing and running a second anti-malware program. What one anti-malware program cannot detect or remove, another one might. For example, Windows Defender on one system removed malware it detected, but did not detect or remove the downloader *dnsatlantic.exe*, which hijacked a browser and is still running in the background (see Figure 17-22).

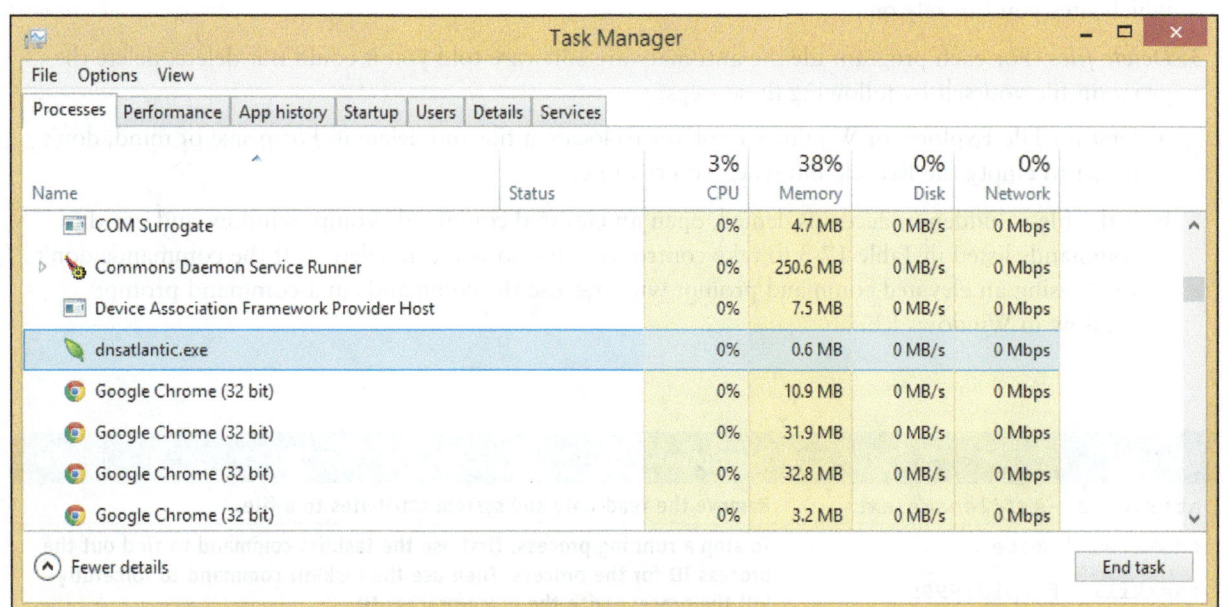

Figure 17-22 The malware downloader *dnsatlantic.exe* is still running after multiple scans of anti-malware software

In this situation, try another anti-malware program. For example, Microsoft Safety Scanner (*docs.microsoft.com/en-us/windows/security/threat-protection/intelligence/safety-scanner-download*) is not designed for ongoing malware prevention but can sometimes remove malware that Windows Defender did not find. Download and run the latest version of the software.

CLEAN UP WHAT'S LEFT OVER

Next, you'll need to clean up anything the anti-malware software left behind. Sometimes anti-malware software tells you it is not able to delete a file, or it deletes an infected file but leaves behind an orphaned entry in the registry or startup folders. If the anti-malware software tells you it was not able to delete or clean a file, first check the anti-malware software website for any instructions you might find to manually clean things up. Here are some general actions you can take to clean up what the software left behind:

1. *Respond to any startup errors.* On the first boot after anti-malware software has declared a system clean, you might still find some startup errors caused by incomplete removal of the malware. Use System Configuration and/or Task Manager to find out how a startup program is launched. If the program is launched from the registry, you can back up and delete the registry key. If the program is launched from a startup folder, you can move or delete the shortcut or program in the folder. See Chapter 14 for the details of how to remove unwanted startup programs.

2. *Research malware types and program files.* Your anti-malware software might alert you to a suspicious program file that it quarantines, and then ask you to decide if you want to delete it. Also, Task Manager and other tools might find processes you suspect are malware. The web is your best tool to use when making your decision about a program. Here are some websites that offer malware encyclopedias that are reliable and give you symptoms and solutions for malware:

   ◢ Process Library by ProcessLibrary at *processlibrary.com*

   ◢ DLL Library by Uniblue Systems Limited at *liutilities.com*

   ◢ All the anti-malware software sites listed earlier in the chapter in Table 17-2

   Beware of using other sites! Much information on the web is written by people who are just guessing, and some of the information is put there to purposefully deceive. Check things out carefully, and learn which sites you can rely on.

3. *Delete files.* For each program file the anti-malware software told you it could not delete, delete the program file yourself by following these steps:

   a. First try File Explorer or Windows Explorer to locate a file and delete it. For peace of mind, don't forget to empty the Recycle Bin when you're done.

   b. If the file is hidden or access is denied, open an elevated command prompt window and use the commands listed in Table 17-3 to take control of a file so you can delete it. If the commands don't work using an elevated command prompt window, use the commands in a command prompt window in Windows RE.

Command	Description
`attrib -r -s filename.ext`	**Remove the read-only and system attributes to a file.**
`tasklist	more` `taskkill /f /pid:9999`	**To stop a running process, first use the tasklist command to find out the process ID for the process. Then use the taskkill command to forcefully kill the process with the given process ID.**
`takeown /f filename.ext`	**Take ownership of a file.**
`icacls filename.ext /grant administrators:f`	**Take full access of a file.**

Table 17-3 Commands used to take control of a malware file so you can delete it

c. To get rid of other malware files, delete all Internet Explorer temporary Internet files. Use the Disk Cleanup process in the Drive C: properties box, or delete the browsing history using the Internet Options box.

d. Delete all subfolders and files in the C:\Windows\Temp folder. Figure 17-23 shows where Windows Defender lists potentially unwanted programs (PuPs) that a Trojan downloader put in this folder.

Figure 17-23 A Trojan downloader put programs in the C:/Windows/Temp folder, which must be manually deleted

4. *Clean the registry.* Appendix B lists folders and registry keys that can affect startup. You can search these folders and keys and delete entries you don't want. After you have finished cleaning startup folders and the registry, don't forget to restart the system and make sure all is well before you move on.

5. *Clean up your browsers and uninstall unwanted programs.* Adware and spyware might install add-ons to a browser (including toolbars you didn't ask for), install cookie trackers, and change your browser security settings. Anti-malware software might have found all these items, but as a good defense, take a few minutes to find out for yourself. Chapter 16 covered how to use the Internet Options box to search for unwanted add-ons and delete ActiveX controls. You can uninstall unwanted toolbars, plug-ins, and other software using the Programs and Features window (see Figure 17-24).

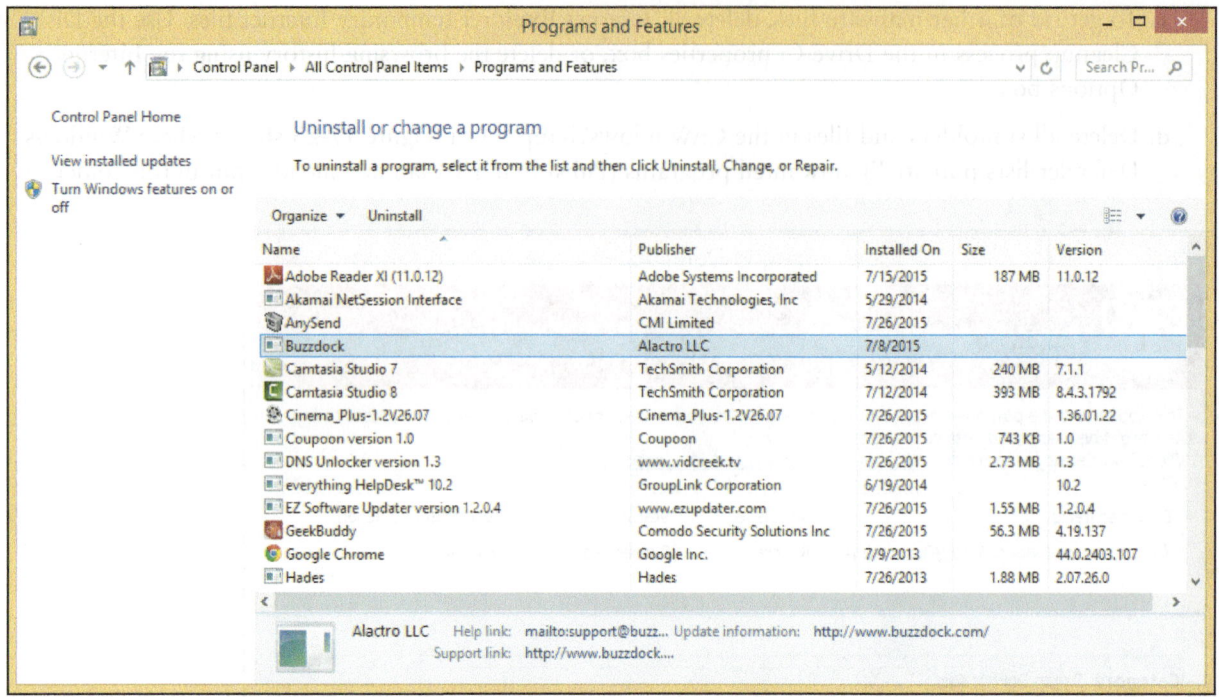

Figure 17-24 A Trojan downloader installed several unwanted programs, which must be uninstalled

STEP 5: PROTECTING THE SYSTEM WITH SCHEDULED SCANS AND UPDATES

A+
CORE 2
3.3

Once your system is clean, you'll certainly want to keep it that way. The three best practices to protect a system against malware are:

▲ *Use anti-malware software.* Install and run anti-malware software and keep it current. Configure the software so that it (1) runs in the background in real time to alert users of malware that attempts to run or install, (2) automatically scans incoming email attachments, and (3) performs scheduled scans of the system and automatically downloads updates to the software. To find out what anti-malware software is installed and turned on, open the Windows 10 Security and Maintenance window in Control Panel (see Figure 17-25).

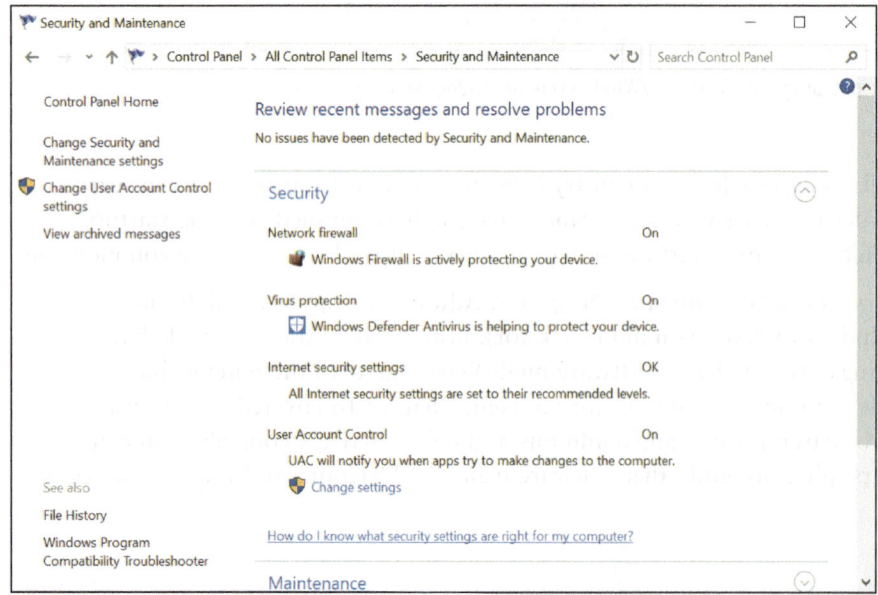

Figure 17-25 Check which apps are providing security protections for your computer

> **◯ OS Differences** In Windows 8/7, open the Action Center to see what anti-malware software is installed and running.

- ◢ *Always use a software firewall.* Never, ever connect your computer to an unprotected network without using a firewall. Windows Firewall is turned on by default. Recall that you can configure Windows Firewall to allow no uninvited communication or to allow the exceptions that you specify.
- ◢ *Keep Windows updates current.* Microsoft continually releases updates to plug vulnerable entrances in Windows where malware might attack and updates to Windows Defender and Microsoft Security Essentials. Recall that you can verify Windows Update settings in the Settings app (Windows 10 only) or by clicking **Windows Update** in the System window in Control Panel (Windows 8/7).

STEP 6: ENABLING SYSTEM PROTECTION AND CREATING A RESTORE POINT

Now that the system is clean, you can turn System Protection back on if necessary and create a restore point. You learned how to do this in Chapter 13.

STEP 7: EDUCATING THE END USER

Now would be a good time to sit down with the user and go over the tips presented earlier in this chapter to keep the system free from malware. Sometimes the most overlooked step in preventing malware infections is to educate the user. Even with all your security measures in place, a user can still download and execute a Trojan, which can install more malware in the system.

> **★ A+ Exam Tip** The A+ Core 2 exam might give you a scenario that requires you to perform one or more of the seven steps to remove malware. Memorize these seven steps and know how to use them in the correct order.

BEST PRACTICES FOR DOCUMENTATION AND SECURITY POLICIES

Well-run IT departments rely on good documentation and security policies to set expectations and standards for security in the entire organization. In this part of the chapter, you learn about the types of documentation and security policies you might encounter in your IT career and what is generally expected of you as an IT technician to follow these best practices and policies.

17

TYPES OF DOCUMENTATION

Earlier in this text, you learned about ticketing software that tracks, manages, and documents customer service in an IT organization, acceptable use policies (AUP) that document what users can and cannot do with corporate resources, and password policies that document how to create strong passwords. Other types of documentation and documentation software an IT technician might encounter in an organization are described next:

- ◢ *Knowledge base.* A knowledge base is a collection of articles containing text, images, or video that give information about a network, product, or service. Here are two examples of how a knowledge base might be used:
  - ◢ *Customer service.* To better support customers, a company might publish a knowledge base about its products or services on its website. Technical support specialists usually have access to a knowledge base to aid in helping customers during support calls; the knowledge base might be integrated into a ticketing system.

◢ *IT training and troubleshooting.* As IT personnel install, configure, and troubleshoot devices and software, the information they learn can be documented in the IT department's knowledge base so it's readily available for future troubleshooting and for training new IT personnel.

◢ *Inventory management.* Inventory management documents inventory, including end-user devices, network devices, IP addresses, software licenses, and related licenses. Hardware inventory might track equipment by using asset tags and theft-prevention plates, as you learned earlier in the chapter. These tags and plates contain barcodes that are easily read by a laser scanner. See Figure 17-26. Asset tracking software can scan the barcodes to report on existing inventory, track equipment, report needed maintenance, and help with identifying and returning stolen property.

Source: MyAssetTag.com

Figure 17-26 The print on this tag is embedded under a protective surface so it can't be easily damaged

◢ *Password policy.* In Chapter 16, you learned what is required to create a strong password and best practices for passwords (for example, allowing one to expire so that the user must occasionally change it). These requirements are sometimes documented as a password policy.

◢ *Network topology diagrams.* Network documentation should contain a map of a network's topology, which is called a network topology diagram. In networking, topology refers to the pattern in which devices on a network are connected with each other. For example, devices connected in a line are using a bus topology, and devices connected to a single, centralized device are using a star topology. Recall from Chapter 8 that most Ethernet networks today use a design called a star bus topology, which means that nodes are connected to one or more centralized devices that are connected to each other (see Figure 17-27).

Figure 17-27 A star bus network formed by nodes connected to multiple switches

A network topology diagram might show how nodes on a network are physically connected, such as the one in Figure 17-27, or it might show the logical network topology. For example, the diagram shown earlier in Figure 17-11 shows the logical connection among clients and servers to indicate how data flows among them.

On small networks, a network topology diagram can be hand drawn, but for larger networks, inventory data is usually compiled automatically through network scans. For example, Spiceworks (*spiceworks.com*) offers a free Network Inventory product that probes devices on the network and presents a list of detected devices along with any information gathered about them, such as IP addresses, installed operating systems, and shared folders.

You learn about other types of documentation, such as that involved with change management, later in this chapter.

> ★ **A+ Exam Tip** The A+ Core 2 exam requires you to understand the similarities and differences between various types of documentation, including network topology diagrams, knowledge base articles, incident documentation, regulatory and compliance policies, acceptable use policies, and inventory management documentation. All are discussed in this chapter.

CHANGE MANAGEMENT

A+ CORE 2 4.2

As an IT support technician, you will undoubtedly be involved in new projects, such as installing hardware or software, upgrading networks, moving IT operations from onsite services to cloud-based services, rolling out virtualized desktops across the organization, implementing a VoIP communication platform, and much more. A project is temporary—it has a beginning, an end, and a singular, well-defined goal. A successful project depends on expert project management to direct a project team through specific tasks and deliver results on time, within the agreed-to budget, and with complete customer satisfaction.

When a project is implemented, change happens. Change managed well means that people affected by the change can make a smooth transition from their current state to the project goal or end result. In most situations, change management is closely integrated with project management and often involves the same teams. For example, a project manager works with a team to plan, develop, test, and implement new software. A change manager might work with the same team to define how the software will affect people and manage all communication, scheduling, training, and support required so that affected people are satisfied, embracing and accepting the end result.

> ★ **A+ Exam Tip** The A+ Core 2 exam will give you a scenario and expect you to apply the basic principles of change management, including documenting business processes, purpose of change, scope of change, risk analysis, end-user acceptance, change boards, back-out plans, and the need to document change.

A high-level change process is diagrammed in Figure 17-28. Know, however, that change processes vary widely. Let's look at the basic elements of change management and how they might relate to you as an IT support technician.

DOCUMENTED BUSINESS PROCESSES

A business is complex and well-run organizations know they must understand and document their core business goals and processes. Documented business processes are related activities that lead to a desired business goal, such as an efficient and cost-effective service, excellent customer satisfaction, or a superior product. For example, if customer satisfaction is a defined business goal, IT operational processes might describe how customers are taken care of, support tickets are documented, and customer satisfaction is measured.

Figure 17-28 The general flow of change management

17

As change happens, be aware of how this change affects documented business processes. For example, suppose help-desk software is changed so that the customer's electronic signature is required when a ticket is closed. If you forget the electronic signature, your company may not be able to collect payment or follow up with the customer for a satisfaction survey.

PURPOSE OF CHANGE

The starting point for every proposed change is a clear and concise purpose for the change. What will change? What is the current situation and expected outcome? Why is the change needed? What happens if the organization does not initiate this change? How will the success of the change be measured?

> ✎ **Notes** IT technicians often communicate with people impacted by change. Therefore, it's important that you have a firm understanding of the purpose for the change so that you can maintain a positive, helpful attitude.

A proposed change is formally submitted using a change request process. A change request states what needs to be updated or changed but does not indicate how the change will be executed. A simple change request might require only preapproval from a manager. Complex changes, with higher impact and risks, are submitted to a change advisory board. The change advisory board (CAB) meets on a regular basis to assess, prioritize, authorize, and schedule changes. The change manager and other representatives approve changes based on the recommendations of the change advisory board.

CHANGE PLAN AND SCOPE

The change plan defines the scope of change, which may outline:

▲ Key components of the change and how they will be addressed
▲ Skill sets, tasks, and activities required to carry out the change
▲ Individuals or departments that will participate in the change
▲ How the success of change is measured and when the change is completed

The scope of change defines your responsibilities in the change plan. It's important that you understand exactly your assignment for planning, implementing, and supporting the change and then work within these boundaries, which is called working "in scope." The scope of change might evolve through the feedback process of change management, but until the scope changes, it's important to work in scope. Although it might be tempting to perform yet one more step while implementing a change, don't make "out of scope" modifications, which might result in major disruption.

RISK ANALYSIS

Change almost always involves risk, which refers to a problem (event, situation, or condition) that may or may not occur as a result of the change. For example, a change might be half-finished when the change manager realizes the budget is inadequate. Other risks are alienating customers, not finishing on time, or not delivering the intended results. Risk analysis is the process of identifying potential problems so there are no surprises or crisis situations once the change begins. For each potential problem identified, the team attempts to determine the likelihood it may occur, its impact, and what to do if it does occur. As an IT technician, you need to be aware of the risks involved and how to execute the response plan if the problem actually happens.

BACK-OUT PLAN

What if a change goes bad—really bad? Suppose all users lose network connectivity for hours or all database servers that log all online sales orders spontaneously crash. The back-out plan defines the activities needed to recover to the original state in the event of an aborted or failed change implementation.

The back-out plan is created and sometimes tested even before the change starts, and includes detailed steps to restore service to users. Obviously, you need to be aware of the back-out plan prior to implementing a change.

END-USER ACCEPTANCE

Recall that change management is responsible for people impacted by change being able to make a smooth transition during the change. End-user acceptance to change often fails because the focus of the change is on the technical side rather than the people side. To gain end-user acceptance, users must know:

1. The purpose of the change, especially the business reasons for the change

2. That the leadership of the company agrees with the change

3. How the change will affect them and their job

4. How to get their individual concerns and questions answered and how their voices will be heard

5. That they will receive end-user training for the changes that impact them

Before a change begins, an organization might request user feedback to the change in a request for comments (RFC). Technical users often have valuable input in the RFC process that may affect the entire change process. IT technicians often play a major role in end-user acceptance. Users who struggle with change will appreciate your empathetic and positive outlook. When a proposed change has been clearly communicated and the user understands "what's in it for me," you have made a significant contribution to a successful change.

DOCUMENT CHANGES

No part of change management should rely on spoken communication. Everything related to changes must be documented, including how the change management process itself works. Change plans are documented and updated throughout the entire change management process. Many larger organizations use change management software, such as Alloy Software (*alloy-software.com*), to manage all stages of change management from the change request form to the final close report. Smaller organizations may manually document change using MS Word or Excel documents or database software. Regardless of the size of the organization, you will be expected to maintain proper documentation for all stages of a change in which you participate.

REGULATED DATA, LICENSING, AND SECURITY POLICIES

An IT technician is expected to follow company security policies for regulated data and software licensing. You also need to know what to do when you discover an incident where these policies have been violated.

REGULATORY AND COMPLIANCE POLICIES

Certain types of data are protected by special governmental regulations and are called regulated data. Each industry must comply with a variety of regulations, policies, and laws, which are collectively called regulatory and compliance policies. For example, in the health-care industry, patient data is highly regulated, and most hospitals employ one or more regulatory and compliance officers to ensure that the hospital is compliant. Other regulated industries include the copyright laws regulated by the U.S. Copyright Office, workplace safety regulated by the Occupational Safety and Health Administration (OSHA), and consumer protection regulated by the Federal Trade Commission (FTC). Many of these policies directly affect IT operations. When you're first hired by a company, you should receive training on how these issues affect your work and what is expected of you.

17

Let's look at some specific types of regulated data:

◢ *Personal identity.* PII (personally identifiable information) is a legal term to describe data that can uniquely identify a person, including a Social Security number, email address, physical address, birthdate, birth place, mother's maiden name, marital status, phone numbers, race, and biometric data. Some PII is more sensitive than other information and should be protected more vigilantly.

◢ *Health information.* PHI (protected health information) includes any data about a person's health status or health care. This data is protected by regulations defined by HIPAA (the Health Insurance Portability and Accountability Act), passed in 1996. HIPAA gives patients the rights to monitor and restrict the sharing of their medical information. Hospitals, medical personnel, and other entities covered by HIPAA regulations risk steep penalties for privacy breaches.

◢ *Credit card data.* The Payment Card Industry (PCI) standards were defined to help prevent credit card fraud and are backed by all the major credit card brands (Visa, MasterCard, and others). PCI standards apply to how credit card data is transmitted (such as when receiving payments) and stored (such as when keeping records for recurring billing) by vendors, retailers, and financial institutions.

◢ *Citizens of the EU.* The GDPR (General Data Protection Regulation) is a group of regulations implemented in 2018 in the European Union (EU) to protect personal data of EU citizens, giving them more control over how their data is collected, stored, and shared. The GDPR also includes requirements for how individuals should be notified in the event their data is hacked. Covered personal data includes name, address, photos, IP address, genetic information, and biometric data that uniquely identifies a person.

> ✎ **Notes** Organizations and individuals who have access to regulated data are at risk legally and financially if they do not comply with the legal requirements regarding the security of this data. When you work in an organization that handles regulated data, ensure your own protection by making certain you understand and comply with all laws regarding this data.

SOFTWARE LICENSING

As an IT support technician, you need to be especially aware of the issues surrounding software licensing. As you have learned, open source software can be freely distributed and installed, but closed source software is owned by the creator (developer) and a license is required to use the software. When someone purchases software from a software developer, that person or organization has only purchased a commercial license for the software, which is the right to use it. The buyer does not legally *own* the software and therefore does not have the right to distribute it. The right to copy the work, called a copyright, belongs to the creator of the work or others to whom the creator transfers this right. Copyrights are intended to legally protect the intellectual property rights of organizations or individuals to creative works, which include books, images, and software. Your rights to use or copy software are clearly stated in the End User License Agreement (EULA) that you agree to when you install the software (see Figure 17-29).

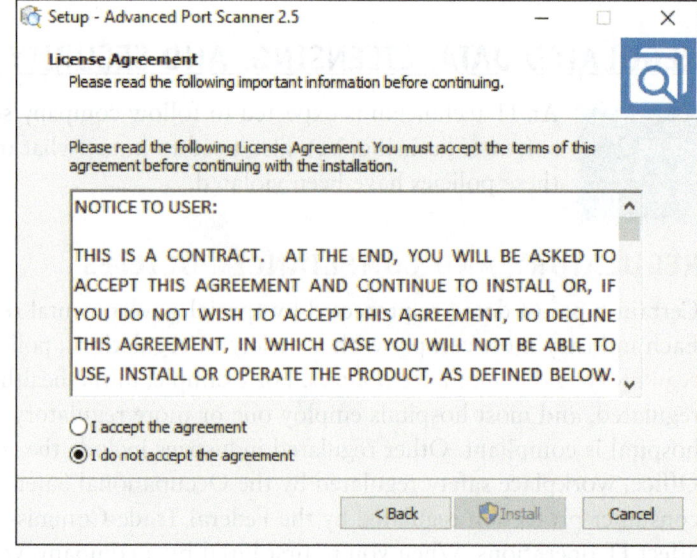

Source: Famatech Corp.

Figure 17-29   Agreeing to the EULA is required before software installs

Making unauthorized copies of original software violates the Federal Copyright Act of 1976 and is called software piracy or, more officially, software copyright infringement. (This act allows for one backup copy of software to be made.) Making a copy of software and then selling it or giving it away is a violation of the law. Normally, only the employee who violates the copyright law is liable for infringement; however, in some cases, an employer or supervisor is also held responsible, even when the copies were made without the employer's knowledge.

> **✎ Notes** When an individual or organization purchases the right to install one instance of software, the license is called a personal license. By purchasing a site license, also called an enterprise license, a company can obtain the right to multiple installations of software.

Many software companies, including Microsoft, have implemented measures to control the use of their software, which is called digital rights management (DRM). For example, recall that the retail release of Windows 10 requires a valid product key or a digital license for activation, and Microsoft carefully verifies and monitors that this product key is used only in one installation.

INCIDENT RESPONSE FOR PROHIBITED CONTENT AND ACTIVITIES

As you know, employees in an organization are often asked to agree to an acceptable use policy (AUP) that documents a code of conduct when using corporate resources. For example, the AUP may prohibit an employee from accessing pornographic material on company computers, using company computers and time for personal shopping, or installing pirated software on these computers.

An incident is when an employee or other person has negatively affected safety or corporate resources, violated the code of conduct for the organization, or committed a crime. When you start a new job, ask your employer what procedures you follow for an incident response. If you're the first person to discover an incident, such as use of prohibited content or other activities, you're responsible to perform certain first response duties. Here are some things you need to know:

▲ *Identify and go through proper channels*. When you identify what you believe to be an infringement of the law or the company's code of conduct, where do you turn to report the issue? Make sure you go only through proper channels; don't spread rumors or accusations.

▲ *Preserve data and devices*. What data or device should you immediately preserve as evidence for what you believe has happened? For example, if you believe you have witnessed a customer or employee using a company computer for a crime, should you remove and secure the hard drive from the computer, or should you remove and secure the entire computer?

▲ *Incident documentation*. Incident documentation surrounding the evidence of an incident is important to prevent future incidents and crucial to a criminal investigation. What documentation are you expected to submit and to whom is it submitted? This documentation might track the chain of custody for the evidence, which includes exactly what, when, and from whom it was collected, the condition of this evidence, and how the evidence was secured while it was in your possession. It also includes a paper trail of each person to whom the evidence has been passed on and when. For example, suppose you suspect that a criminal act has happened and you hold a flash drive that you believe contains evidence of this crime. You need to carefully document exactly when and how you received the flash drive. Also, don't pass it on to someone else in your organization unless you have the person's signature on a chain-of-custody document so that you can later prove you handled the evidence appropriately. You don't want the evidence to be disallowed in a court of law because you have been accused of misconduct or tampering with the evidence. Also know that more information than a signature, such as a copy of a driver's license, might be required to identify people in the chain of custody.

17

> ⭐ **A+ Exam Tip** The A+ Core 2 exam expects you to be able to explain the process of an incident response, which includes reporting prohibited content or activity through the proper channels, preserving relevant data and evidence, and tracking evidence through an appropriate chain-of-custody document.

DATA DESTRUCTION AND DISPOSAL

**A+
CORE 2
2.9**

Besides dumpster diving, consider the impact of digital dumpster diving. You need to totally destroy data before you throw out a hard drive, flash drive, CD, DVD, tape, or other media that might have personal or corporate data on it, unless you know the data can't be stolen off the device. Trying to wipe a drive clean by deleting files or even by using Windows to format the drive does not completely destroy the data. Here are some ways to destroy printed documents and sanitize storage devices:

◢ *Overwrite data on the drive.* A drive needs to be wiped clean before you recycle or repurpose it. With older magnetic hard drives, an end user could perform a low-level format of a drive to redefine the sector marks on the drive's platters, making the existing data inaccessible. (This is different from a standard Windows format that configures a file system on the drive.) Today's devices receive a low-level format at the factory that can't be changed later. However, end users can wipe the drive using a zero-fill utility that overwrites all data on the drive with zeroes; sometimes this is inaccurately called a low-level format. You can download a zero-fill utility or so-called low-level format utility from many hard drive manufacturers' websites. This method works for most low-security situations, but professional thieves know how to break through it. If you use one of these utilities, run it multiple times to write zeroes on top of zeroes. Data recovery has been known to reach 14 levels of overwrites because each bit is slightly offset from the one under it.

> ✏️ **Notes** An app called a file shredder can permanently delete an individual file or folder by overwriting it multiple times. Check the reviews before downloading and using one of these apps.

◢ *For solid-state devices, use a Secure Erase utility.* As required by government regulations for personal data privacy, the American National Standards Institute (ANSI) developed the ATA Secure Erase standards to wipe clean a solid-state device such as a USB flash drive or SSD. You can download a Secure Erase utility from the manufacturer of the device and run it to sanitize the drive, or you can securely erase all data on the device and then reuse or dispose of it.

◢ *Physically destroy the storage media.* Use a drill to drill many holes all the way through the drive housing. Break CDs and DVDs in half and do similar physical damage with a hammer to flash drives or tapes, even to the point of setting them on fire to incinerate them. Again, expert thieves can still recover some of the data.

◢ *For magnetic devices, use a degausser.* A degausser exposes a storage device to a strong electromagnetic field to *completely* erase the data on a magnetic hard drive or tape drive (see Figure 17-30). A degaussed drive can't be reused, but for the best destruction, use the degausser and

Figure 17-30 Use a degausser to sanitize a magnetic hard drive or tape drive

physically destroy the drive. Degaussing does not erase data on a solid-state hard drive or other flash media because these devices don't use magnetic surfaces to hold data.

▲ *Use a shredder*. Recall you can use a paper shredder to destroy all documents that contain sensitive data. The best paper shredders apply multiple passes to cross-cut the paper instead of strip-cutting; this cuts the paper into smaller pieces that can't be easily reassembled. Many paper shredders can handle credit cards or thin cardboard. Multimedia shredders can also destroy optical discs. Disk drive shredders, such as the one shown in Figure 17-31 from Whitaker Brothers (*whitakerbrothers.com*), can destroy magnetic hard drives, solid-state drives, flash drives, optical discs, and even mobile devices such as smartphones or small tablets.

▲ *Use a secure data-destruction service*. For the very best data destruction, consider a secure data-destruction service. To find a service, search the web for "secure data destruction." However, don't use a service unless you have thoroughly checked its references and guarantees of legal compliance that your

Source: whitakerbrothers.com

Figure 17-31 This drive shredder pulverizes small storage devices such as hard drives, flash drives, and smartphones

organization is required to meet. The service should provide you with a digital certificate of destruction, which verifies that the data has been destroyed beyond recovery. Paper certificates can be forged, but digital certificates produced by the software that performs the destruction will provide auditable results of the destruction process.

★ **A+ Exam Tip** The A+ Core 2 exam might give you a scenario that requires you to implement data-destruction techniques, including using a shredder, degausser, incineration, drill, hammer, and recycling or repurposing techniques (low-level formats, overwriting, and drive wipes).

17

>> CHAPTER SUMMARY

Protecting Network Resources

▲ Physical security can include a locked door, a server lock and cable lock, port lock, privacy filter, theft-prevention plate, mantrap, and security guard.

▲ Logical security can include anti-malware software, a VPN connection, email filtering, qualifying software distributors, an access control list, MAC address filtering, and mobile device management.

◢ Large networks might require additional user authentication other than a Windows password, which can include a password policy and multifactor authentication using hardware or software tokens.

◢ AAA (authenticating, authorizing, and accounting) services include RADIUS and TACACS+.

◢ Security methods include educating users against social engineering and protecting a laptop when traveling.

Dealing with Malicious Software on Personal Computers

◢ Malware includes viruses, spyware, keyloggers, worms, Trojans, rootkits, ransomware, zero-day attacks, man-in-the-middle attacks, DoS attacks, DDoS attacks, zombies, and botnets. Attacks on passwords include dictionary, brute force, and rainbow table attacks. Noncompliant systems open a network up to attack.

◢ Symptoms that indicate malware is present include pop-up ads, slow performance, error messages and logs, file errors, email problems, and invalid digital certificates.

◢ Some systems become so highly infected that the only solution is to format the hard drive, reinstall Windows, and restore data from backups.

◢ To clean up an infected system, (1) know how to identify common malware symptoms, (2) quarantine the infected system, (3) disable System Restore, (4) remediate the system, (5) protect the system with scheduled scans and updates, (6) enable System Protection and create a restore point, and (7) educate the end user.

Best Practices for Documentation and Security Policies

◢ Types of security documentation include ticketing software to document customer service, a knowledge base, acceptable use policies, password policies, inventory management, network topology diagrams, and the documentation needed for change management.

◢ Change management includes identifying the purpose and scope of change, developing a change plan and back-out plan, getting approval from a change board, acquiring end-user acceptance, performing a risk analysis, and documenting the entire change process.

◢ Regulatory and compliance policies help protect regulated data, which can include PII, PHI, PCI, and GDPR data regulated by governmental agencies.

◢ Commercial licensing of software can be a personal license or enterprise license. Terms of the licensing agreement are found in the EULA.

◢ A chain-of-custody document is part of incident documentation and provides a paper trail of the evidence in response to an incident that is suspected to be criminal.

◢ Data can be partly or completely destroyed using a paper shredder, multimedia shredder, low-level format, zero-fill utility, drill, hammer, incinerator, or degausser.

◢ Professional data destruction services may provide a certificate of destruction for legal purposes.

>> KEY TERMS

For explanations of key terms, see the Glossary for this text.

AAA (authenticating, authorizing, and accounting)	access control list (ACL)	ATA Secure Erase	biometric data
	agent	back-out plan	biometric lock
acceptable use policy (AUP)	anti-malware software	badge reader	botnet
	antivirus software	barcode	brute force

cable lock
Certificate Authority (CA)
certificate of destruction
chain of custody
change advisory board (CAB)
change management
commercial license
copyright
data loss prevention (DLP)
defense in depth
degausser
denial-of-service (DoS)
dictionary attack
digital certificate
digital rights management (DRM)
disk drive shredders
distributed denial-of-service (DDoS)
documented business processes
dumpster diving
email filtering
email hoax
End User License Agreement (EULA)
enterprise license
entry control roster
first response

GDPR (General Data Protection Regulation)
grayware
impersonation
incident
incident documentation
incident response
inventory management
Kensington lock
Kensington Security Slot
key fob
keylogger
knowledge base
low-level format
MAC address filtering
malicious software
malware
malware definitions
malware encyclopedias
malware signatures
man-in-the-middle attack
mantrap
MDM policies
mobile device management (MDM)
multifactor authentication
multimedia shredders
mutual authentication
network topology diagram
noncompliant systems
off-boarding

on-boarding
password policy
Payment Card Industry (PCI)
personal license
PHI (protected health information)
phishing
PII (personally identifiable information)
port lock
port security
privacy filter
privacy screen
quarantined computer
RADIUS (Remote Access Dial-In User Service)
rainbow table
ransomware
regulated data
regulatory and compliance policies
request for comments (RFC)
risk analysis
root certificate
rootkit
scope of change
Secure DNS
server lock
shoulder surfing
shredder

site license
smart card
smart card reader
social engineering
software piracy
software token
spear phishing
spoofing
spyware
TACACS+ (Terminal Access Controller Access Control System Plus)
tailgating
topology
triple A
Trojan
two-factor authentication (2FA)
USB lock
virus
VPN (virtual private network)
Windows Defender
Windows Defender Offline (WDO)
Windows Preinstallation Environment (WinPE)
worm
zero-day attack
zero-fill utility
zombie

>> THINKING CRITICALLY

These questions are designed to prepare you for the critical thinking required for the A+ exams and may use content from other chapters and the web.

1. Why is PINE963$&apple not a strong password?

2. What type of employee badge does not have to be swiped by a card reader in order to allow the employee through a door?

   a. RFID badge

   b. Smart card badge

   c. A badge containing a digital certificate

   d. Key fob

3. What tool is best to use when destroying data on an SSD?

   a. Zero-fill utility

   b. Low-level format

   c. Degausser

   d. ATA Secure Erase

17

4. What device can be installed on a laptop to prevent shoulder surfing?

5. Define and explain the differences between a virus, worm, and Trojan.

6. What is the best way to determine if an email message warning about a virus is a hoax?

   a. Check websites that track virus hoaxes.

   b. Scan the message for misspelled words or grammar errors.

   c. Open the message and see what happens.

   d. Scan your email inbox for malware.

7. What is the first thing you should do when you discover a computer is infected with malware? The second thing?

   a. Turn off system protection.

   b. Update installed anti-malware software.

   c. Format the hard drive.

   d. Quarantine the computer.

8. What does anti-malware software look for to determine that a program or a process is a virus?

9. What registry key keeps information about services that run when a computer is booted into Safe Mode?

10. What folder is used by Windows to hold restore points?

11. What must you do to allow anti-malware software to scan and delete malware it might find in the data storage area where restore points are kept?

12. A virus has attacked your hard drive. Instead of seeing the Windows Start screen when you start up Windows, the system freezes and you see a blue screen of death. You have important document files on the drive that are not backed up and you cannot afford to lose. What do you do first? Explain why this is your first choice.

   a. Try a data-recovery service even though it is expensive.

   b. Remove the hard drive from the computer case and install it in another computer.

   c. Try GetDataBack by Runtime Software (*runtime.org*) to recover the data.

   d. Use Windows utilities to attempt to fix the Windows boot problem.

   e. Run antivirus software to remove the virus.

13. You sign in to your personal computer with your Microsoft account and then you want to set up your computer as a trusted device to make changes to the account settings. Microsoft sends a code to your cell phone in a text message. You enter the code on a Windows screen. This type of authentication is called:

   a. Multifactor authentication

   b. Mutual authentication

   c. Biometric authentication

   d. None of the above

14. At a restaurant, you overhear people discussing an interesting case they treated while working in a dental office that day. Which type of regulated data policies are most likely to have been violated?

a. PII

b. PHI

c. PCI

d. GDPR

15. As a bank employee, you often work from home and remotely access a file server on the bank's network to correct errors in financial data. Which of the following services is most likely the one you are using to authenticate to the network and track what you do on the network?

a. RADIUS

b. Secure DNS

c. Active Directory

d. TACACS+

16. Among the following, which is the best protection against ransomware?

a. Windows File History

b. Carbonite

c. Keylogger software

d. Authy by Twilio

17. Your boss asks you to work through the weekend to install new software on the applications server that serves up applications to 20 users. The following Monday, all users report they cannot open their data files. After speaking with technical support for the new application, you discover it is not compatible with the old data files. Which type of documentation should you refer to first to address this problem?

a. Risk analysis documents

b. Back-out plan documents

c. Change management documents

d. Scope of change documents

>> HANDS-ON PROJECTS

Hands-On | Project 17-1   Creating and Using an Anti-Malware Software Rescue Disc

When an infected computer does not have anti-malware software installed, one method to clean the infection is to create and use an anti-malware rescue disc. Select anti-malware software that offers a free download to create a bootable USB flash drive or CD. For example, you can use Windows Defender Offline or Bitdefender Rescue CD. Create a bootable USB flash drive or CD and use it to scan a computer. Answer the following questions:

1. What is the URL where you found the download to create a rescue disc or drive?

2. List the files in the root directory of the USB flash drive or CD that the software created.

3. Describe the menu or screen that appeared when you booted from the rescue media.

Hands-On | Project 17-2   Downloading and Using Anti-Malware Software

A free trial of AVG Protection software is available on the AVG site at *avg.com*. Do the following to download, install, and run the software:

1. Download the free trial version of AVG Protection software from *avg.com* and install the software.
2. Update the software with the latest malware signatures.
3. Perform a complete scan of the system. Were any suspicious programs found?
4. Set the software to scan the system daily.
5. Set the software to scan incoming email.

Hands-On | Project 17-3   Using the Web to Learn About Malware

One source of information about malware on the web is F-Secure Corporation. Go to the website *f-secure.com* and find information about the latest malware threats. Answer the following questions:

1. Name and describe a recent Trojan downloader. How does the Trojan install and what is its payload (the harm it does)?
2. Name and describe a recent rootkit. How does the rootkit install and what is its payload?
3. Name a recent worm. How does it get into the network and what is its payload?

Hands-On | Project 17-4   Scanning a Network for Connected Devices

To help document devices connected to your network, you can use Advanced IP Scanner. Do the following to install and use the software:

1. Go to **advanced-ip-scanner.com** and then download and install Advanced IP Scanner by Famatech Corp. The software launches automatically.
2. Make sure the range of IP addresses includes all the IP addresses on your network. Click **Scan**. Figure 17-32 shows the results of one scan. Notice the software reports nodes on the network, their IP addresses, services they are running, and shared folders.

(continues)

Figure 17-32 Scan for nodes on a local network and information about each host

Source: Famatech Corp.

>> REAL PROBLEMS, REAL SOLUTIONS

REAL PROBLEM 17-1 Using a Port Scanner

Port scanning software can be used to find out how vulnerable a computer is with open ports. This project requires the use of two computers on the same network to practice using port scanning software. Do the following:

1. On Computer 1, download and install Advanced Port Scanner by Famatech at **advanced-port-scanner.com**. (Be careful not to accept other software offered while downloading.)

2. If your Computer 2 is a Windows 10/8 system, open the **Network and Sharing Center**, click **Change advanced sharing settings,** and turn off network discovery and file and printer sharing. (For Windows 7, open the **Network and Sharing Center** and click the network location to change the settings.)

3. On Computer 1, start Advanced Port Scanner and make sure that the range of IP addresses includes the IP address of Computer 2. Change the default port list to 0 through 6000. Then click **Scan**.

4. Browse the list and find Computer 2. List the number and purpose of all open ports found on Computer 2.

17

5. On Computer 2, turn on network discovery and file and printer sharing. Open the **System** window, click **Remote settings,** and allow Remote Assistance connections to this computer. Close all windows.

6. On Computer 1, rescan and list the number and purpose of each port now open on Computer 2. Figure 17-33 shows the results for one computer, but yours might be different.

Source: Advanced Port Scanner by Famatech Corp.

Figure 17-33 Advanced Port Scanner shows open ports on networked computers

REAL PROBLEM 17-2 Implementing More Security for Remote Desktop

When Jacob travels on company business, he finds it's a great help to be able to access his office computer from anywhere on the road using Remote Desktop. However, he wants to make sure his office computer and the corporate network are as safe as possible. One way you can help Jacob add more security is to change the listening port that Remote Desktop uses. Knowledgeable hackers know that Remote Desktop uses port 3389, but if you change this port to a secret port, hackers are less likely to find the open port. Search the Microsoft Knowledge Base articles (*support.microsoft.com* and *technet.microsoft.com*) for a way to change the port that Remote Desktop uses. Practice implementing this change by doing the following:

1. Set up Remote Desktop on a computer using a business or professional edition of Windows. This computer is your host computer. Use another computer (the client computer) to create a Remote Desktop session to the host computer. Verify that the session works by transferring files in both directions.

2. Next, change the port that Remote Desktop uses on the host computer to a secret port. Save or print a screenshot showing how you made the change. Use the client computer to create a Remote Desktop session to the host computer using the secret port. Print a screenshot showing how you made the connection using the secret port. Verify that the session works by transferring files in both directions.

3. What secret port did you use? What link on the Microsoft websites gave you the information you needed?

macOS, Linux, and Scripting

In this chapter, you learn about two more operating systems for desktops and laptops other than Windows: macOS and Linux. As you will see, understanding Windows gives you a solid foundation to approach learning and supporting other operating systems. IT technicians are expected to be familiar with a variety of operating systems and operating environments, and this chapter equips you for these skills. In addition, you learn the fundamentals of scripting used in all scripting software and environments. IT technicians customarily use scripts to automate repetitive tasks.

macOS FOR MACINTOSH COMPUTERS

**A+
CORE 2
1.1, 1.3,
1.9**

macOS, formally called Mac OS X, is a proprietary operating system that is only available for Macintosh computers by Apple Inc. (*apple.com*). Like Linux, macOS is built on a UNIX foundation and has been evolving and improving since its original release in 1984. (UNIX is a popular OS used to control networks and to support server applications available on the Internet.) At the time of this writing, macOS Mojave was just released, and some users are converting to it from the last release, macOS High Sierra.

The Mac keyboard has some special keys. See Figure 18-1. However, don't depend on these special keys because a customer might have a regular keyboard connected via a USB port. The touch pad on a Mac laptop is called the trackpad, and is a touch pad on steroids; you can use multiple fingers and actions called gestures, which you learn about as you read through this part of the chapter.

Figure 18-1 Special keys on a Mac keyboard

Now let's get to know the macOS interface, including the desktop with its dock and Apple menu, Finder, Launchpad, System Preferences, Spotlight, Mission Control, multiple desktops, iCloud Drive, Keychain, Screen Sharing, Remote Disc, and Terminal.

GETTING TO KNOW THE macOS DESKTOP

The macOS desktop, with its major components labeled, is shown in Figure 18-2. The Finder application, which can help you find applications and data files, is open and active. Because Finder is the currently active application, the menu bar for the Finder window is displayed at the top of the screen. The menu bar provides drop-down menus that contain options for working with applications, files, and the interface.

Source: Apple Inc.

Figure 18-2 The macOS desktop with a Finder window showing the Applications pane

By default, the dock appears at the bottom of the desktop. It contains shortcut icons to access frequently used applications. To open an application from its icon in the dock, click it once. The icons in the dock that represent open applications have a small, black dot underneath them. The macOS desktop can also include shortcuts that provide quick access to files, folders, and applications.

When a window is open, three circles in the upper-left corner (see Figure 18-3A) let you manipulate the window. The red circle closes the window, the yellow circle minimizes the window to the dock in the lower-right corner of the screen (see Figure 18-3B), and the green circle maximizes the window to full-screen size. To restore a maximized window to its original size, move your pointer to the top of the screen. When the circle icons appear, click the green circle.

18

Source: Apple Inc.

Figure 18-3 (A) Close, minimize, or expand a window; (B) this Finder window has been minimized, but the app is still running and is easily accessible in the dock

Closing an app's window does not close the app. To quit an app that is active, click the name of the app in the menu bar and click **Quit** at the bottom of the drop-down menu. See Figure 18-4.

Source: Apple Inc.

Figure 18-4   To close an app, select Quit in the app's menu

FINDER

The Finder window, shown earlier in Figure 18-2 and again in Figure 18-5, functions something like File Explorer in Windows; use it to find and access files, applications, and macOS utility programs. To open the Finder window, click it in the dock. Note that the Finder is always running; you can close the Finder window, but you can't end the Finder utility. Here are useful things you can do with Finder:

▲ *Files and folders.* To open files and folders, click **Documents** or some other storage location, such as iCloud Drive or Downloads. Double-click a folder to drill down into it and double-click a document file to open it. You can drag and drop a file or folder into and out of a folder or location window.

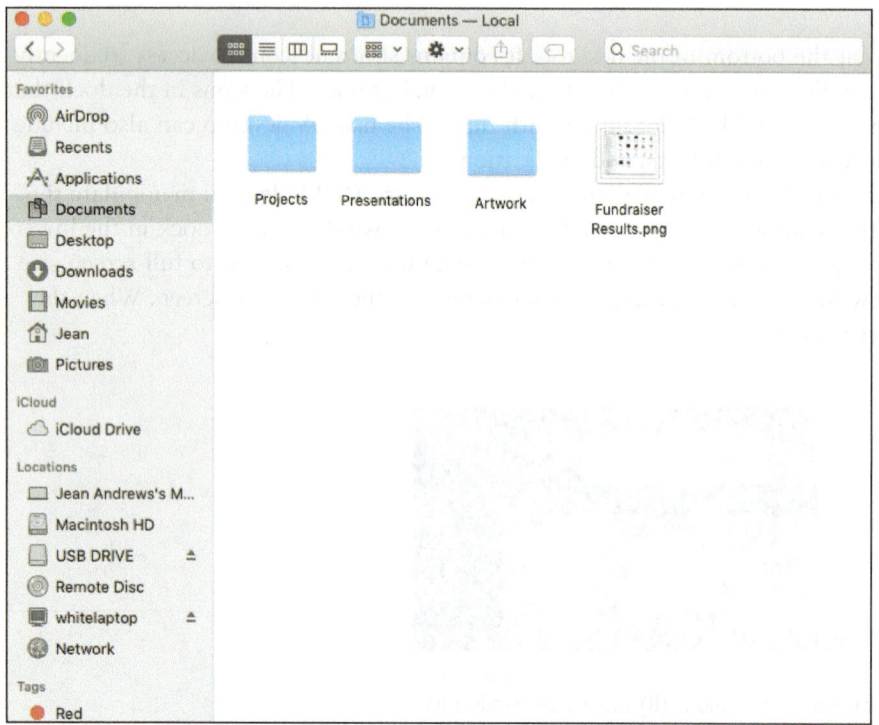

Figure 18-5   The Finder window showing the Documents folder contents   Source: Apple Inc.

- ◢ *Applications*. To open an app, click **Applications** in the sidebar, scroll to the app, and click it. You can also open apps from Launchpad.
- ◢ *macOS utilities*. macOS offers several utility programs that are accessed from the Finder window. Click **Applications**, scroll down to the **Utilities** folder, and click it. See Figure 18-6. You learn to use several of these utilities later in this chapter.

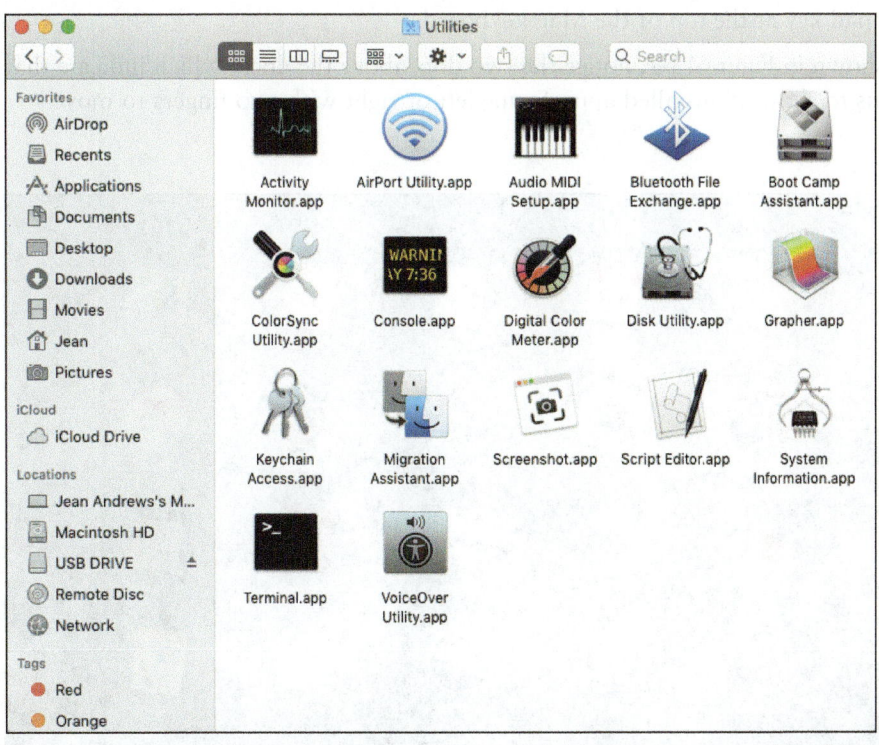

Source: Apple Inc.

Figure 18-6 Utilities to support a Mac are in the Utilities folder under Applications in the Finder window

- ◢ *Locations*. As shown on the left side of Figure 18-6, available locations are the Mac, the internal hard drive (Macintosh HD), a USB drive, Remote Disc, and the network. Drill down into any of these locations to see available resources. When you drill down into Network, you see network devices and their shared resources. When you drill down into Remote Disc, you can see a shared optical drive that has been shared by another computer on the network.
- ◢ *Finder menu bar*. To use the Finder menu bar to list devices and other resources, click **Go** in the Finder menu bar and click **Computer**. The Computer window shows all locations and storage devices, and you can drill down into them. To control what appears in the Finder sidebar or on the desktop, click **Finder** in the menu bar and then click **Preferences**.
- ◢ *Tags*. Tags are used to assign a tag or color to a file or folder to make it easier to find later. For example, you can secondary-click a file and use the shortcut menu to assign it a blue tag. (A secondary-click is a tap of the trackpad with two fingers.) Later, click the blue tag in the left column of Finder to see all items with blue tags.

18

🖉 **Notes** If you use an app frequently, such as GarageBand, you can add it to the dock or desktop. In Finder, click **Applications** and then click and drag the app's icon to the dock or desktop. To remove an icon from the dock or desktop, click and drag the icon to the Trash icon.

LAUNCHPAD

Launchpad (see Figure 18-7), which is somewhat similar to a combination of the Windows Start menu and Programs and Features window, shows all apps installed on the computer. Use one of these methods to open Launchpad:

▲ *Use the dock.* Click the Launchpad icon in the dock.

▲ *Use a gesture.* Pinch with three fingers and your thumb on the trackpad.

▲ *Use a key.* Press the Launchpad key at the top of the Mac keyboard.

In the Launchpad window shown in Figure 18-7, notice the two dots above the dock, which indicate that Launchpad requires two screens to show all installed apps. Swipe left or right with two fingers to move through the screens.

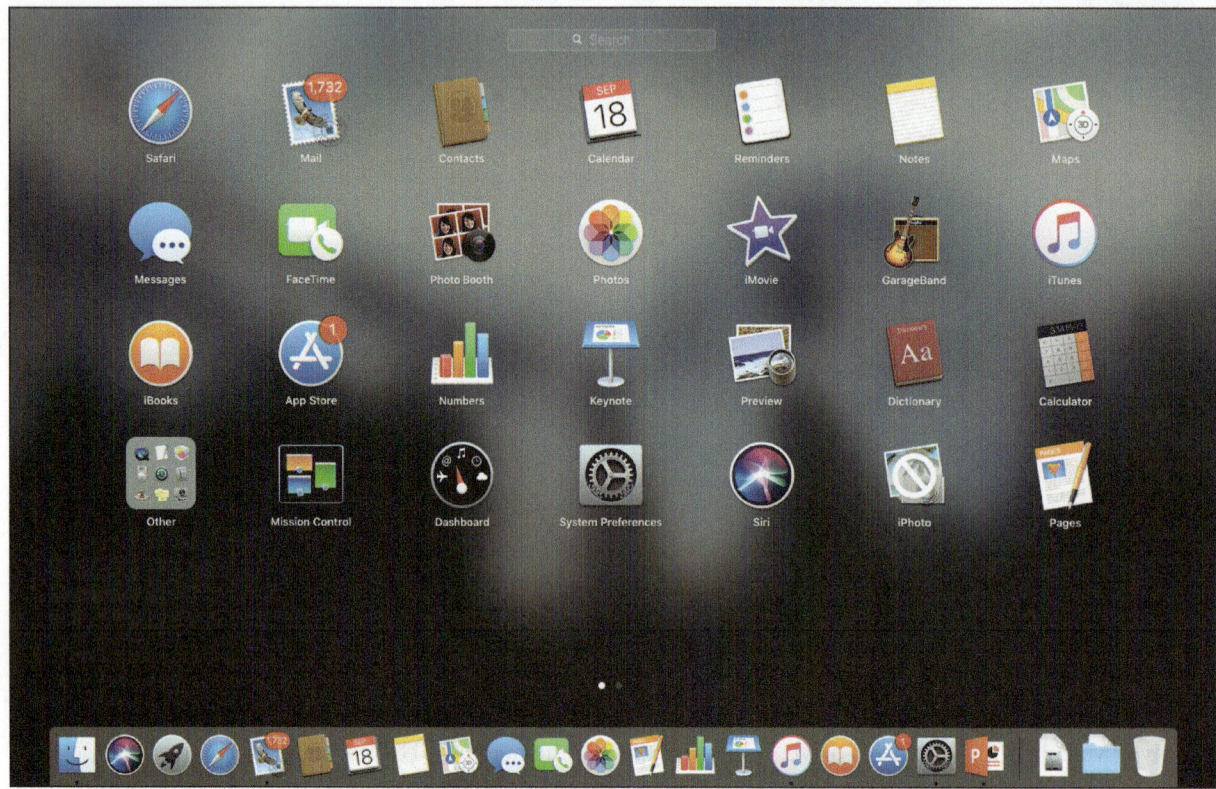

Source: Apple Inc.

Figure 18-7   View all installed apps in Launchpad; when more apps are installed, Launchpad creates additional screens to the side

Here are tips on how to use Launchpad:

▲ Click an app to open it, which also closes Launchpad.

▲ To uninstall an app, press and hold the **option** key, which causes the app icons to jiggle. Click an **X** on an icon to uninstall its app. You can also rearrange jiggling icons, similar to how an iPad and iPhone work. Release the option key when you're done.

▲ To close Launchpad and return to the desktop, use a pinch gesture with three fingers and your thumb spread apart.

APPLE MENU

The menu at the top of the macOS screen changes with each application that is active except for the Apple icon, which is always shown at the far left of the menu bar. The Apple menu (see Figure 18-8) opens when you click the Apple icon. Use the Apple menu to put the computer to sleep, log out, restart, or shut down the system.

Source: Apple Inc.

Figure 18-8 The Apple menu is always available no matter which application is active

The Apple menu also provides access to system information, system preferences, the App Store, recent items, and the Force Quit option. Similar to ending a task from Task Manager in Windows, you can force quit an app by clicking **Force Quit**. In the Force Quit Applications window (see Figure 18-9), select the app and click **Force Quit**. The application closes. You can also access the Force Quit Applications window by pressing **command (⌘)-option-esc**.

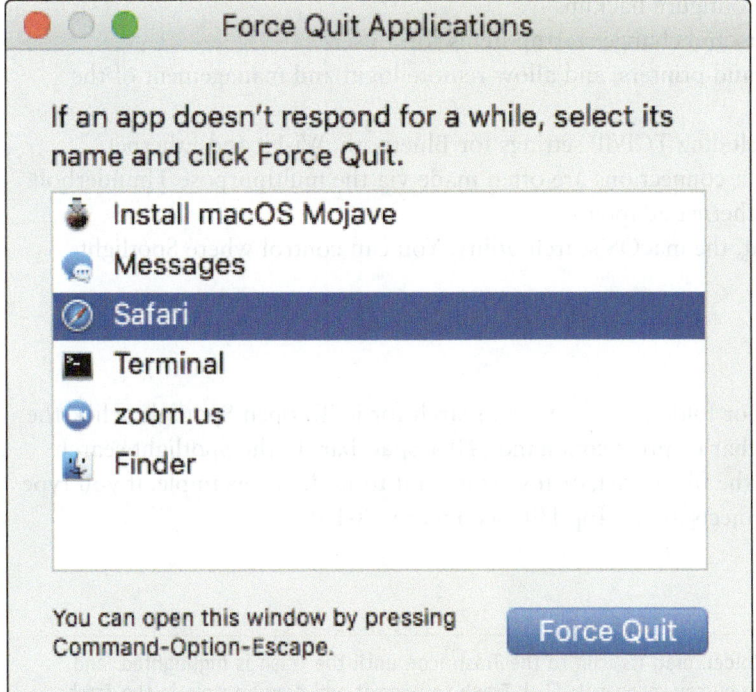

Source: Apple Inc.

Figure 18-9 Force Quit can be used to close an app that is not responding

SYSTEM PREFERENCES

The System Preferences window is used to change and customize macOS settings and is similar to the Settings app in Windows 10. It can be opened from the Apple menu (refer back to Figure 18-8) or from the System Preferences icon in the dock (see Figure 18-10). The System Preferences window is shown in Figure 18-11.

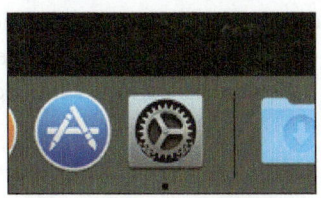

Source: Apple Inc.

Figure 18-10 The System Preferences icon in the dock shows the app is open

18

Click at any time to return to this screen in System Preferences

Source: Apple Inc.

Figure 18-11 The System Preferences window is used to customize the macOS interface

Click an icon in System Preferences to change settings for that tool, feature, or app. As an IT technician, here are a few important tools you might use in System Preferences:

- ◢ *Trackpad*. Click Trackpad to adjust trackpad gestures.
- ◢ *iCloud*. Set up an iCloud account on this computer, choose what content to sync to iCloud and iCloud Drive, and adjust account details.
- ◢ *Time Machine*. Use Time Machine to configure backups.
- ◢ *Users & Groups*. Add and remove users and change startup items for a user.
- ◢ *Sharing*. Share the Mac's screen, files, and printers, and allow remote login and management of the computer.
- ◢ *Network*. Change network settings, including TCP/IP settings for Bluetooth, Wi-Fi, and Ethernet connections. (For Mac laptops, Ethernet connections are often made via the multipurpose Thunderbolt port using a Thunderbolt to Gigabit Ethernet adapter.)
- ◢ *Spotlight*. Change settings for Spotlight, the macOS search utility. You can control where Spotlight searches and its keyboard shortcuts.

SPOTLIGHT

If you're having a problem locating a file or folder, Spotlight can search for it. To open Spotlight, click the search icon on the right side of the menu bar or press **command** (⌘) + **spacebar**. In the Spotlight search box (see Figure 18-12), type the name of the file, folder, or text you want to find. For example, if you type **Projects**, Spotlight lists a folder named Projects as the Top Hit (see Figure 18-13).

✎ **Notes** When you no longer need a file or folder, drag its icon to the Trash icon until the Trash is highlighted, and release the icon. When an item is in the Trash, you can recover it: Click **Trash** to open it and drag an item in the Trash to another location. To empty the trash, click **Finder** in the menu bar and click **Empty Trash**.

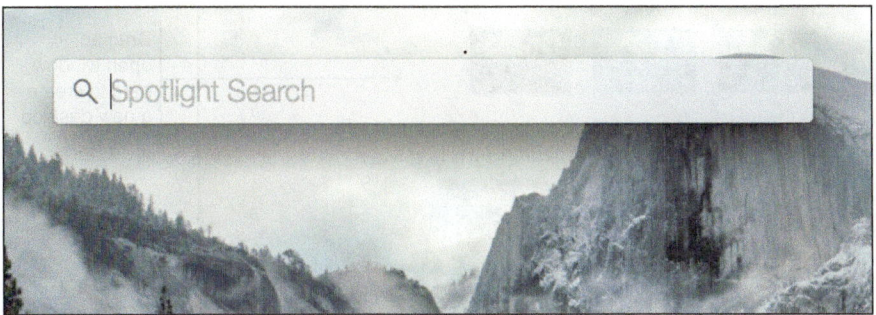

Figure 18-12 Spotlight searches the local computer and online resources
Source: Apple Inc.

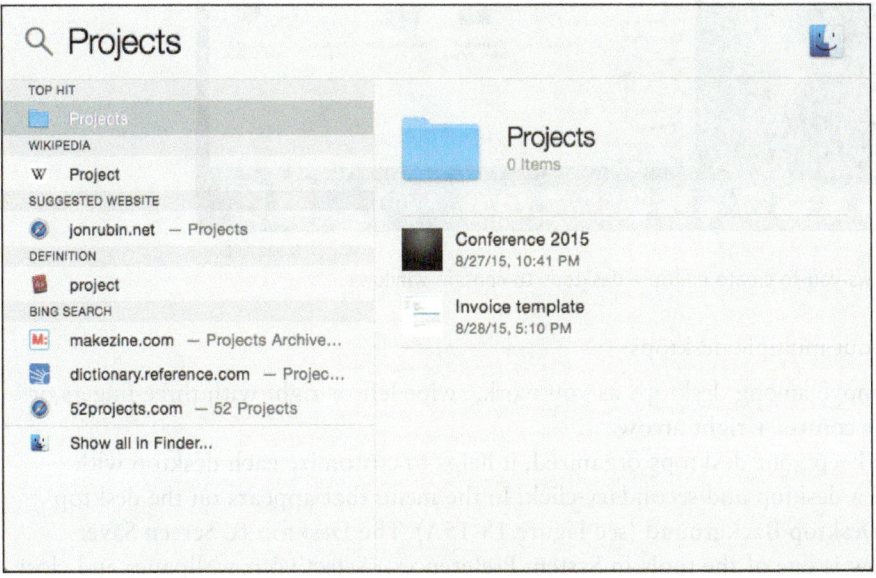

Figure 18-13 Use Spotlight to search for files and folders
Source: Apple Inc.

MISSION CONTROL AND MULTIPLE DESKTOPS

Mission Control gives you a quick view of all open windows and desktops and lets you switch among them. The macOS includes a feature called multiple desktops, which as its name indicates, is several desktop screens, each with its own collection of open windows. Suppose you're working with several windows for a school project, and you have a few more windows open for a project at work. You can place the school project windows on one desktop, called a Space, and place the work project windows on a separate desktop or Space.

To accomplish this, first open Mission Control using one of these methods:

◢ Press the Mission Control key.
◢ Click **Mission Control** in the Launchpad window.
◢ Swipe up with three or four fingers on your trackpad.

A Mission Control window is shown in Figure 18-14. Three desktops have been created on the system, as you can see in the Spaces bar at the top of the window. Also, when an app is in full-screen mode, it acts as a separate Space and shows up in the Spaces bar along with desktops. To create a new desktop, drag an open window into the Spaces bar or click + on the right side of the Spaces bar. To delete a desktop, hover over it in the Spaces bar and click the X. Desktop configurations apply to each user and remain in place even when the computer is rebooted.

18

Drag an
open window
here to create
a new desktop

Source: Apple Inc.

Figure 18-14   Mission Control allows you to create multiple desktops to contain windows

Here are a few more tips about multiple desktops:

◢ *Move among desktops*. To move among desktops as you work, swipe left or right with three fingers or press **control + left arrow** or **control + right arrow**.

◢ *Organize desktops*. To help keep your desktops organized, it helps to customize each desktop with a different wallpaper. Go to a desktop and secondary-click. In the menu that appears on the desktop background, click **Change Desktop Background** (see Figure 18-15A). The Desktop & Screen Saver window opens. (This window is one of the tools in System Preferences.) Select your wallpaper and close the window. Wallpaper settings in other existing desktops won't be affected.

(A)

(B)

Source: Apple Inc.

Figure 18-15   (A) Set a different background for each desktop, and (B) assign different apps in the dock of each desktop

◢ *Organize apps in desktops*. To help keep your apps organized, you can assign an app to a specific desktop. Go to that desktop and secondary-click the app's icon in the dock (see Figure 18-15B). Select **Options** and then click **This Desktop**. Later, when you open the app, the selected desktop will appear with the app's open window.

iCLOUD AND iCLOUD DRIVE

Looking back at the Finder window shown earlier in Figure 18-5, notice that iCloud Drive is listed in the sidebar along with other storage locations such as Desktop, Documents, and Downloads. When a user signs in to macOS for the first time, she is given the opportunity to set up iCloud with her Apple ID, or the setup can be done later in System Preferences. In System Preferences, you can also control which apps store their data in iCloud (see Figure 18-16).

Source: Apple Inc.

Figure 18-16 Choose what content to sync with iCloud

To open iCloud Drive, click it in the Finder window or in Launchpad. Drag and drop files in and out of the iCloud Drive window. The contents are synced with any iPhone, iPad, or Windows desktop that has the iCloud Drive app installed, or with another device that is set up with your Apple ID. (On iPhone and iPad, recall that you can manage iCloud Drive using the Files app.) You can also access your iCloud content, including iCloud Drive, from any device with a browser by going to *icloud.com* and signing in with your Apple ID.

KEYCHAIN

Keychain is the macOS built-in password manager. To open Keychain, go to the Finder window, drill down into the **Applications** list, and then click **Utilities** (refer back to Figure 18-6). Double-click **Keychain Access app**. From the Keychains window (see the left side of Figure 18-17), you can view, edit, and remove accounts for applications, websites, and servers. You can also manage personal accounts that you've added, such as credit card and bank accounts.

18

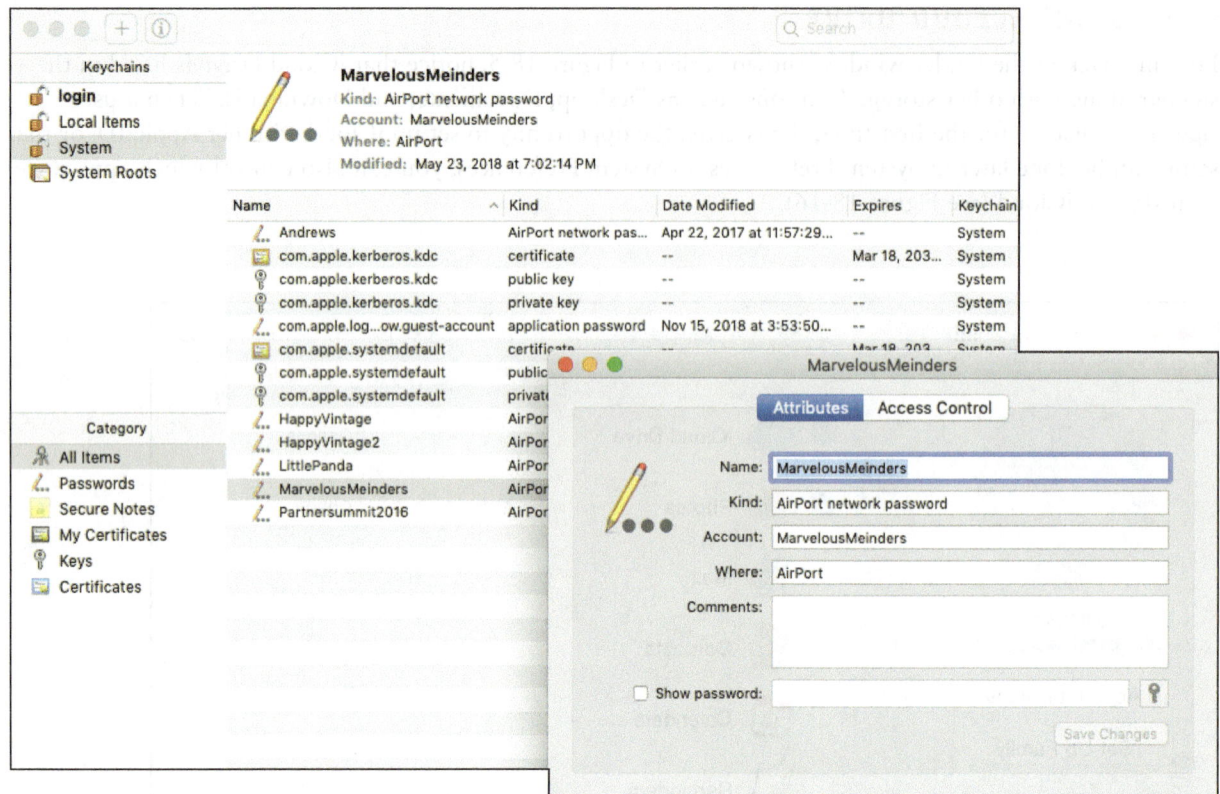

Source: Apple Inc.

Figure 18-17 The data stored in Keychain is encrypted

If you have problems with Keychain, you can delete all saved passwords and restore from backup. In the **Keychain Access** menu, click **Preferences**. In the Preferences box, click **Reset My Default Keychains**. New, empty Login and Local Items keychains are created. If you have Time Machine backups, try to restore the keychains from backup.

SCREEN SHARING

In System Preferences, click **Sharing** to open the Sharing window, where you can set up file and folder sharing on the network, printer sharing, remote access, and screen sharing. Screen Sharing works like Remote Desktop in Windows. In the Sharing window (see Figure 18-18), turn on Screen Sharing and set it up to allow all users or only certain users that you add.

To use screen sharing, a user of another Mac on the network should be able to see your shared Mac in his Finder window in the Shared group. He can click your computer and then click **Share Screen**. He then has the opportunity to sign in to your computer with a user name and password recognized by your computer. Using screen sharing, he can move files and folders between the two computers.

Notes Screen Sharing uses incoming port 5900. To access a Mac from the Internet, set up port forwarding on your router to allow incoming traffic on port 5900.

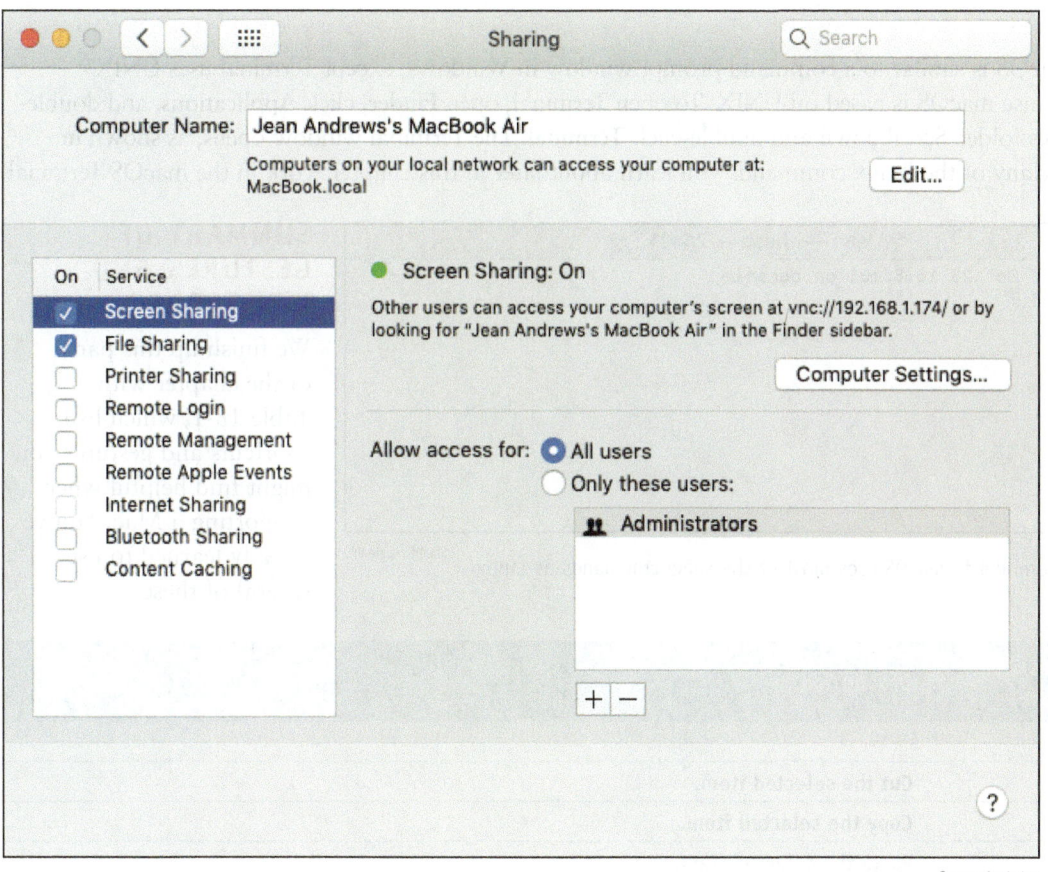

Source: Apple Inc.

Figure 18-18 Screen Sharing makes it easier to collaborate on projects or to help other users with their computers

How secure is macOS screen sharing? Some of the content moved between computers is encrypted and some is not, and you must open an incoming port on your router. Therefore, macOS screen sharing is not as secure as other types of remote access software. Also, as you'll recall from Chapter 13, third-party remote access apps that use a browser are considered more secure than OS tools that open ports for incoming traffic initiated from the Internet. Two examples of apps that use browsers and provide encrypted communication are join.me (*join.me*) and Zoom (*zoom.us*).

REMOTE DISC

If your Mac has an optical drive, the Sharing window includes the option *DVD or CD Sharing*. This feature, called Remote Disc, gives other Mac computers on the network access to the computer's optical drive. Remote Disc is especially useful when you need to install software or drivers from a disc on a Mac that doesn't have an optical drive. After you turn on *DVD or CD Sharing* on a Mac that has an optical drive, go to the Mac that doesn't have an optical drive and open **Finder**. In Finder, click **Remote Disc** in the sidebar under Locations (refer back to Figure 18-5).

18

> ✎ **Notes** You can enable remote disc sharing on a Windows computer. To share a Windows computer's optical drive with Macs on your network, download and install **DVD or CD Sharing Update 1.0 for Windows**, which is available at *support.apple.com/kb/DL112?locale=en_US*.

TERMINAL

Terminal in macOS is similar to a command prompt window in Windows, except Terminal uses UNIX commands because macOS is based on UNIX. To open Terminal, open **Finder**, click **Applications**, and double-click the **Utilities** folder. Scroll down and double-click **Terminal**. The Terminal window opens, as shown in Figure 18-19. Many of the Linux commands you learn about later in this chapter work in the macOS Terminal.

Source: Apple Inc.

Figure 18-19 Terminal in macOS uses most of the same commands as Linux

SUMMARY OF GESTURES AND KEYSTROKES

We finish up this part of the chapter with Table 18-1, which lists shortcuts and gestures you might find helpful when supporting a Mac. You've already learned to use several of these.

Keystrokes, Substitute Keys, and Gestures	Description
Keystrokes	
command-x	Cut the selected item.
command-c	Copy the selected item.
command-v	Paste the selected item.
command-a	Select all items.
option-command-esc	Force quit an app.
command-spacebar	Open Spotlight.
shift-command-5	Take a screenshot of the entire screen or part of the screen. By default, screenshots are saved to the desktop.
Substitute keys when using a regular keyboard instead of a Mac keyboard	
command key	The Windows logo key or Control key is the substitute.
option key	The Alt key is the substitute.
Gestures (gesture actions can be changed in the trackpad app's System Preferences)	
Secondary-click	Tap the trackpad with two fingers. Optional actions are: ◢ Tap the bottom-right corner of the trackpad. ◢ Tap the bottom-left corner of the trackpad. ◢ With a mouse, right-click.
Swipe	Swipe left or right with three fingers to move among desktops. On a keyboard, press control + right arrow and control + left arrow.
Scroll	Swipe up or down with two fingers.
Zoom	Pinch in or out with two fingers.
Pinch	Pinch in with three fingers and thumb to show Launchpad. Do a spread-apart pinch with three fingers and thumb to return to the desktop. If you are already on the desktop, a spread-apart pinch pushes all open windows to the edges to clear the desktop.

Table 18-1 Useful keystrokes, substitute keys, and gestures

MAINTAINING AND SUPPORTING macOS

A+
CORE 2
1.3, 1.9

In addition to working with files and applications, you also need to know how to support and maintain macOS, including updates, backups, and hard drive maintenance. This section will give you a good foundation for these skills. To dig deeper into how to support a Mac, search the documentation on the Apple website (*support.apple.com*).

> ⚡ **Caution** Many Apple computers are covered by an Apple Care warranty, which provides excellent coverage for Macs. Always be absolutely certain that a Mac is not covered by Apple Care before opening the case or doing anything else that might void the warranty.

macOS DIRECTORY STRUCTURES

You need to be familiar with the directory structure in macOS so you know where to look for what. Here are some tips:

◢ To see the directory structure, click **Go** on the Finder menu bar and then click **Computer**. In the Finder window, click the hard drive, which is labeled Macintosh HD in most systems. In Figure 18-20, you can see the five folders at the root level. (Other folders in the root are hidden.) User data is in the Users folder.

Source: Apple Inc.

Figure 18-20 Folders visible in the root of the hard drive

18

◢ Notice the vm folder is selected, and it contains a single file, swapfile0. This swapfile is used to hold virtual memory, similar to pagefile.sys in Windows.
◢ You can also browse the directory structure using the Terminal and Linux commands. In **Finder**, open **Applications**, open **Utilities**, and double-click **Terminal**. Use the cd command to move through the directory structure and the ls command to list files and directories. For example, Figure 18-21 shows the root directory of the Macintosh HD. Compare Figure 18-20 with Figure 18-21 and notice that some folders that appear in the Terminal window are hidden in the Finder window. You learn more about these directories later in this chapter.

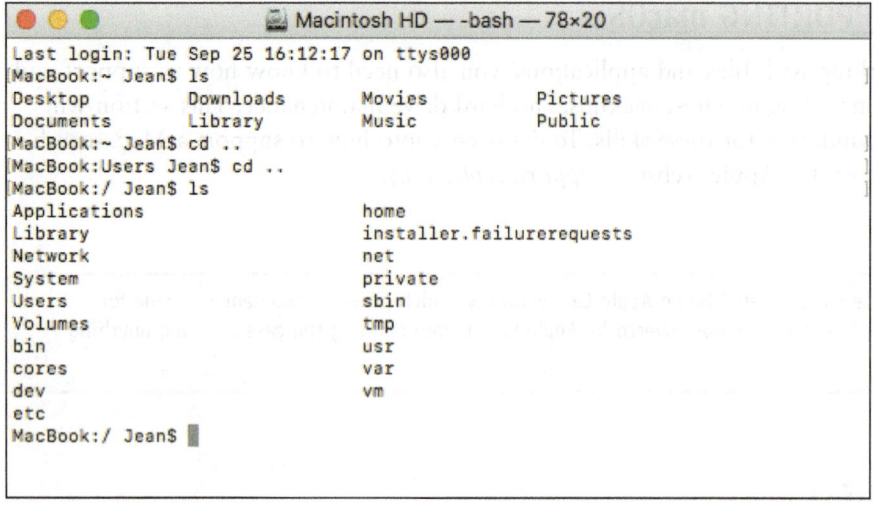

Figure 18-21 Contents of the root directory on a Mac hard drive

Source: Apple Inc.

UPDATE macOS, DRIVERS, AND FIRMWARE

Just like Windows, macOS needs regular updates. Updates often address zero-day vulnerabilities, which makes these updates important to maintaining a healthy system. However, sometimes the updates themselves introduce bugs, which is why many Mac experts advise against setting macOS updates to install automatically. Instead, wait a few days after a macOS update is released before manually installing the update; this gives you a chance to see if the update introduces any significant issues.

macOS updates come from the App Store. To manually update macOS, click the **App Store** icon in the dock, then click **Updates** in the left pane. See Figure 18-22. Any available OS updates will be shown near the top of the screen. Additional updates to apps might also be available in this window.

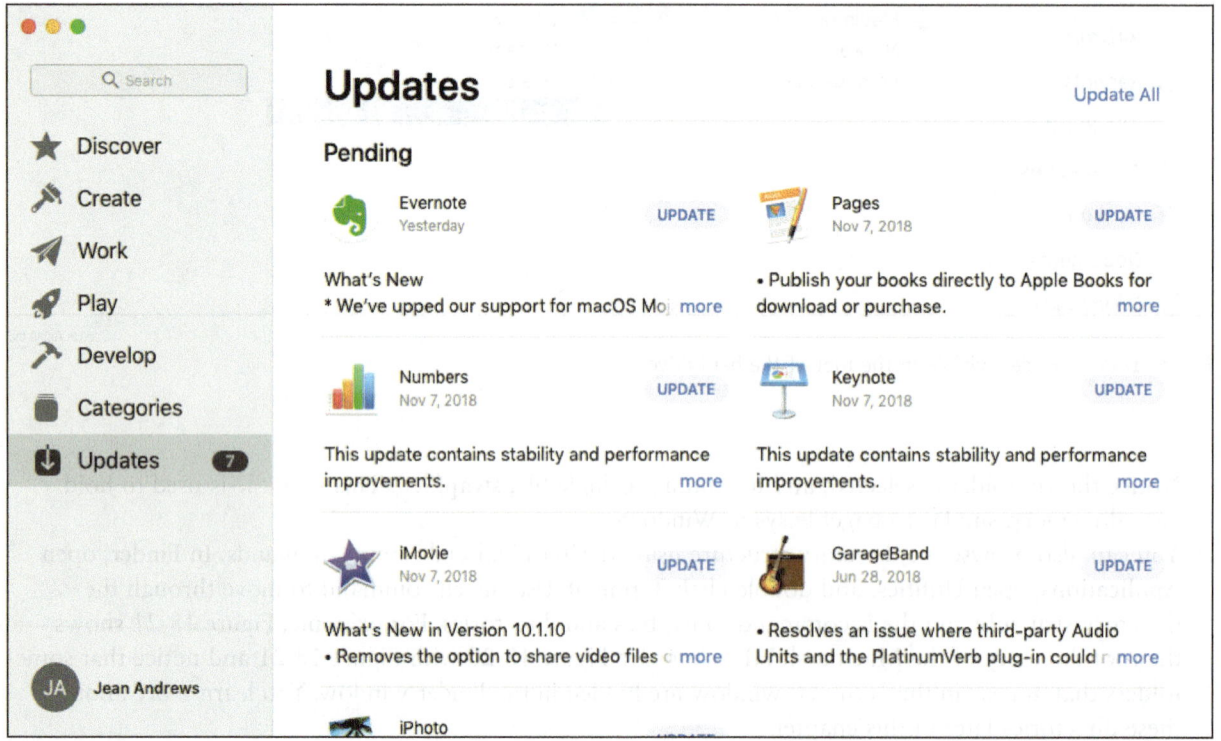

Figure 18-22 The Updates window shows available updates and recently installed updates

Source: Apple Inc.

> **✎ Notes** Printer, scanner, and graphics driver updates are usually included in macOS updates. Other devices that require drivers, if not included in macOS, can be downloaded from the manufacturer's website and installed. These drivers will not be updated through macOS updates. If any problems are encountered with these devices, you'll need to check the manufacturer's website for updates.

To change the settings for automatic updates, open **System Preferences** and click **Software Update**. The OS checks for and reports available updates. For automatic updates, check **Automatically keep my Mac up to date**. To change detailed update settings, click **Advanced** (see Figure 18-23). Here is an explanation of each option:

▲ *Check for updates*. Automatically check for updates.
▲ *Download new updates when available*. Download updates without installing them.
▲ *Install macOS updates*. Install all updates to the operating system without first requiring user approval.
▲ *Install app updates from the App Store*. Install all updates to App Store applications without first requiring user approval.
▲ *Install system data files and security updates*. Install critical system patches that address known vulnerabilities.

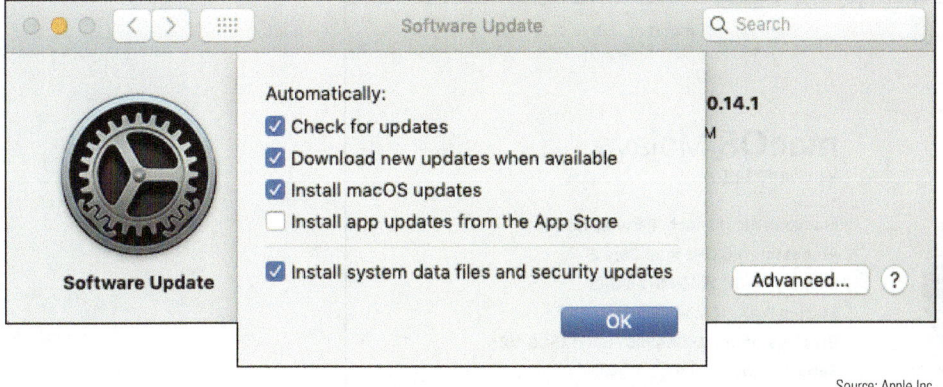

Source: Apple Inc.

Figure 18-23 Manage how automatic updates are handled

Usually any needed firmware updates are included in the macOS update. Occasionally, however, Apple has released a firmware update as a stand-alone installation. You can find a list of available firmware updates in the Apple Knowledge Base Article at *support.apple.com/en-us/HT201518*.

To determine whether a Mac computer needs a firmware update, first check the current firmware version on the computer. This and a great deal more information is available in the System Information app. Open **Finder**, navigate to the **Utilities** folder, and double-click **System Information**. In the System Information window (see Figure 18-24), select **Hardware** in the sidebar and look under Hardware Overview for the *Model Identifier, Boot ROM Version*, and *SMC Version (system)*. Compare the information in the System Information window with the information for the latest firmware update available on the *support.apple.com* website. Install a firmware update only if the version listed on Apple's website is newer than what's installed on the computer.

> **✎ Notes** The System Information app can also be opened from the Apple menu. Click the **Apple** icon, then click **About This Mac**, which gives an overview of the computer's system information, as shown in Figure 18-25. Then click **System Report** to open the System Information window that you saw in Figure 18-24.

18

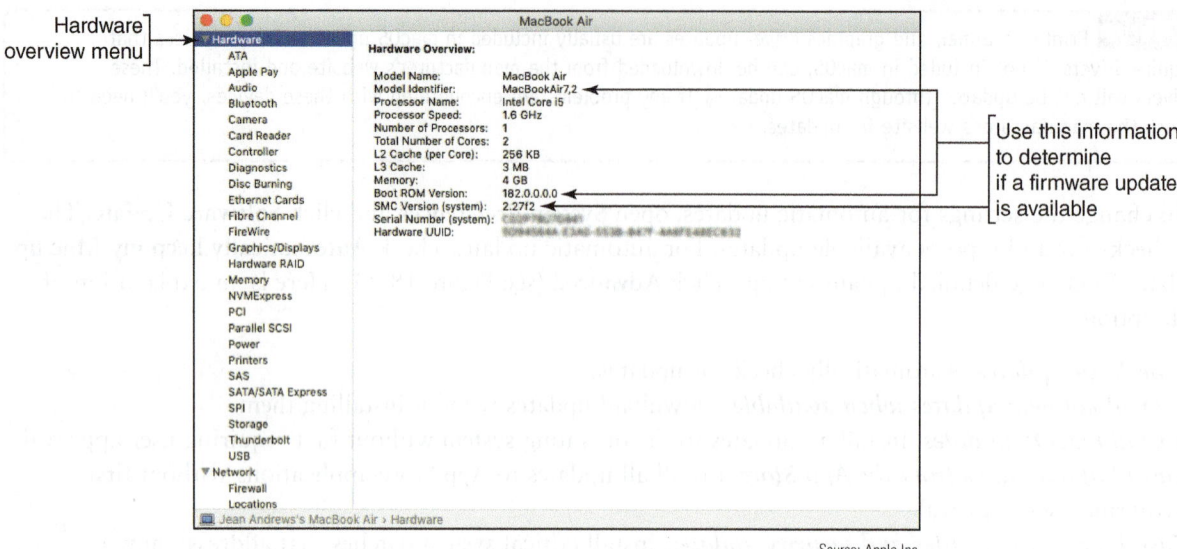

Hardware overview menu

Use this information to determine if a firmware update is available

Source: Apple Inc.

Figure 18-24 The System Information window gives detailed information about the computer

Source: Apple Inc.

Figure 18-25 Click System Report to go to the System Information window for more detailed information

---

Notes Although Macs are not attacked by malware as often as Windows systems, it's still important to protect a Mac by installing and maintaining anti-malware software. Products to consider are Avast Free Mac Security (*avast.com*), Sophos Home Premium for Mac (*sophos.com*), and Trend Micro Antivirus for Mac (*trendmicro.com/mac*).

BACK UP AND RESTORE WITH TIME MACHINE

Like iOS mobile devices, Mac computers can use iCloud Drive to store files and folders in the cloud and sync this content across all of your devices. Unlike the mobile devices you learned about in Chapter 9, iCloud is not sufficient for backing up a Mac. For this purpose, macOS includes Time Machine, which is a built-in backup utility that automatically backs up user-created data, applications, and the entire macOS system. You can back up to:

◢ An external USB or Thunderbolt hard drive or a USB flash drive
◢ Another Mac on the local network
◢ Network-attached storage (NAS) devices that support Time Machine

Once Time Machine is set up, backups are updated in the background. Depending on the space available on the backup drive, Time Machine keeps hourly backups for 24 hours, daily backups for a month, and weekly backups until the disk is full. The oldest backups are deleted to make space for new backups. You can also set up multiple backup schedules to more than one backup device.

To set up Time Machine in macOS, open **System Preferences** and click **Time Machine**. The Time Machine window appears, as shown in Figure 18-26.

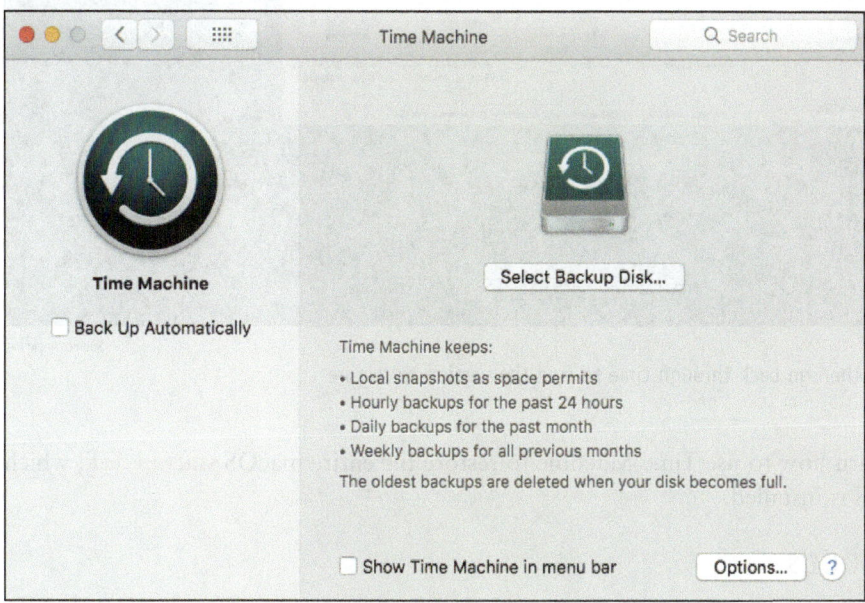

Source: Apple Inc.

Figure 18-26 Configure Time Machine backups

Follow the on-screen directions to select a backup disk and configure backup options. Everything on the disk will be erased. The original backup will be at least 20 GB, includes the entire macOS volume, and takes some time to complete.

> **✏ Notes** When your Mac is not connected to the backup disk, Time Machine stores backup copies, called local snapshots, of created, modified, or deleted files on the hard drive. When you reconnect the computer to the backup disk, the local snapshots are copied to the backup disk. Local snapshots stay on the hard drive as long as they don't take up too much space, and can be restored from the hard drive if needed. Time Machine saves one snapshot each day and one weekly snapshot for each week the backup disk is disconnected.

You can use the backups to recover files, folders, or the entire macOS volume. To recover a file or folder from Time Machine, open **Finder**. In the **Applications** group, double-click **Time Machine**. The timeline and available backups in Finder appear (see Figure 18-27). Use the Finder window to locate the file or folder. Then go back through time to find the version of the file or folder you want to restore. To move through time, you can use the timeline on the right, the arrow buttons, or click a Finder window in the stack of available windows. Select the item and click **Restore**.

18

Source: Apple Inc.

Figure 18-27 Locate an item and then go back through time to find the version to restore

Later in this chapter, you learn how to use Time Machine to restore the entire macOS startup disk, which is the volume on which macOS is installed.

DRIVE MAINTENANCE TOOLS

Hard drives in Mac computers require very little maintenance. However, performing a few simple tasks on a regular basis can help keep things running smoothly:

▲ **Empty the trash.** To empty the Trash, click the **Trash** icon in the dock. Trash contents appear in a Finder window (see Figure 18-28). Click **Empty** and then click **Empty Trash** in the warning box. Items are permanently deleted.

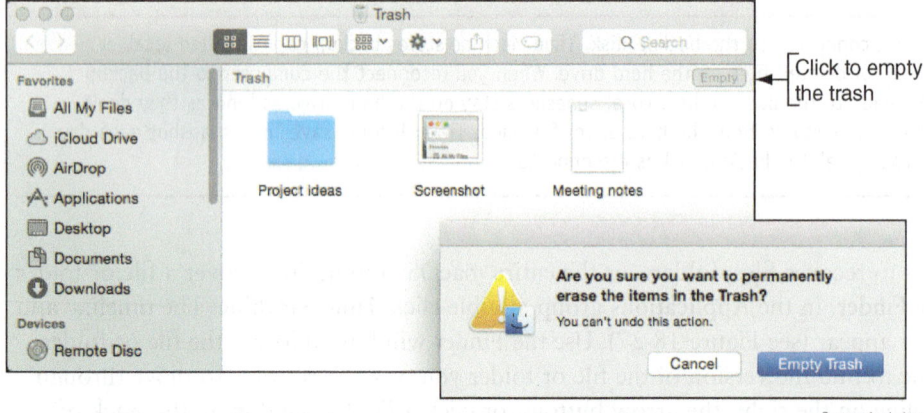

Source: Apple Inc.

Figure 18-28 Check the contents of the Trash Can before emptying it

▲ *Free up space*. Maintain at least 15–20 percent free space on the hard drive for optimal performance. To see how much free space is available on the drive, open the Apple menu, click **About This Mac**, and then click the **Storage** tab, as shown in Figure 18-29.

Source: Apple Inc.

Figure 18-29 Maintain at least 15 percent free space on the hard drive

▲ *Install updates*. Regularly check for and install macOS and app updates, which you learned to do earlier in this chapter.

▲ *Verify no startup items*. Programs that automatically launch at startup are called startup items and programs that automatically launch after a user logs in are called login items. Apple discourages the use of startup items because they slow down the startup process and items in the startup folder might be malware. You can verify that the system doesn't have startup items by looking in two directories that can contain them: /Library/StartupItems and /System/Library/StartupItems (see Figure 18-30).

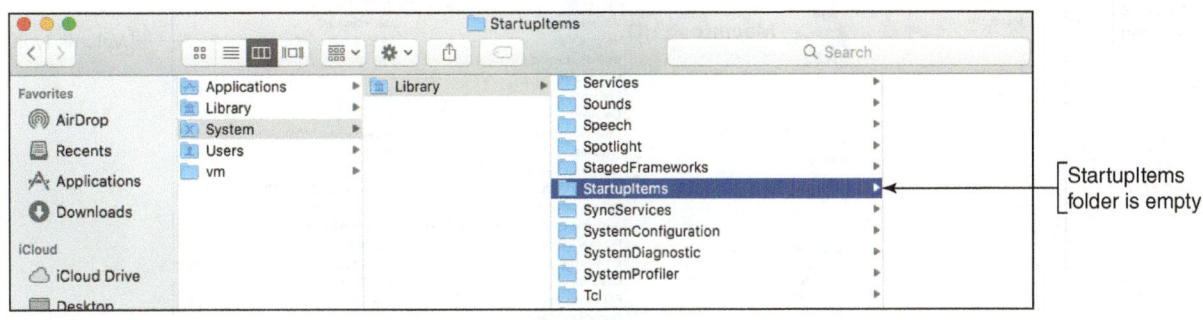

Source: Apple Inc.

Figure 18-30 For best performance, the StartupItems folder should remain empty

▲ *Remove login items*. Launching too many programs at login slows down the boot process and uses up valuable RAM. To adjust login items, open **System Preferences** and click **Users & Groups**. Select a user account in the sidebar, and then click the **Login Items** tab (see Figure 18-31). Use the + and – buttons at the bottom of the items list to add or remove login items.

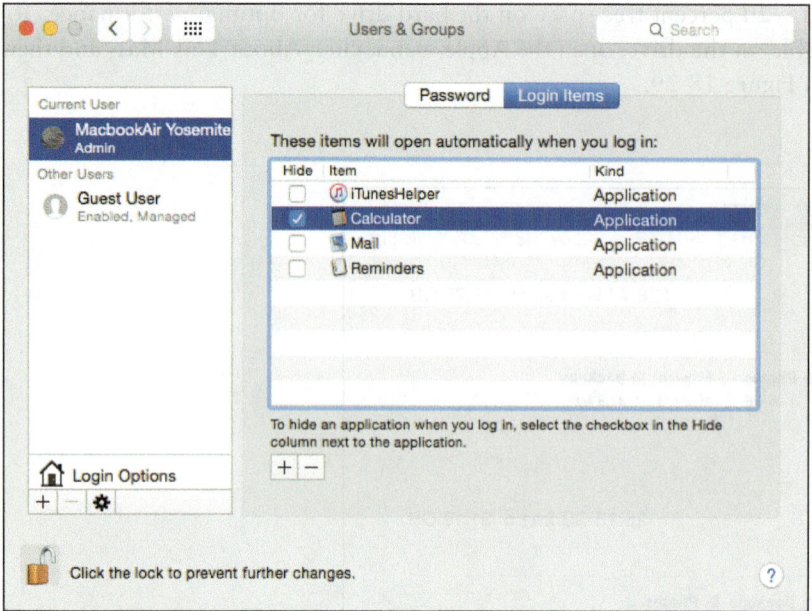

Figure 18-31 A list of login items applies to each user

Source: Apple Inc.

◢ *Restart the computer.* Power cycle the computer at least once a week. A quick way to do so is to click **Restart** in the Apple menu (refer back to Figure 18-8).

◢ *Uninstall unneeded apps.* Uninstall apps you no longer need. Apps obtained from the App Store are uninstalled from Launchpad. For apps installed from other sources besides the App Store, locate the app in Finder and drag the app to the Trash. Empty the trash to complete the uninstall.

REPAIRS USING THE DISK UTILITY APP

The Disk Utility app can be used to repair file system errors and hard drive corruptions. To open Disk Utility, open **Finder** and navigate to the **Utilities** folder. Double-click **Disk Utility**. In the sidebar, select **Macintosh HD** (see Figure 18-32) and click **Info** in the menu bar to view information about the drive.

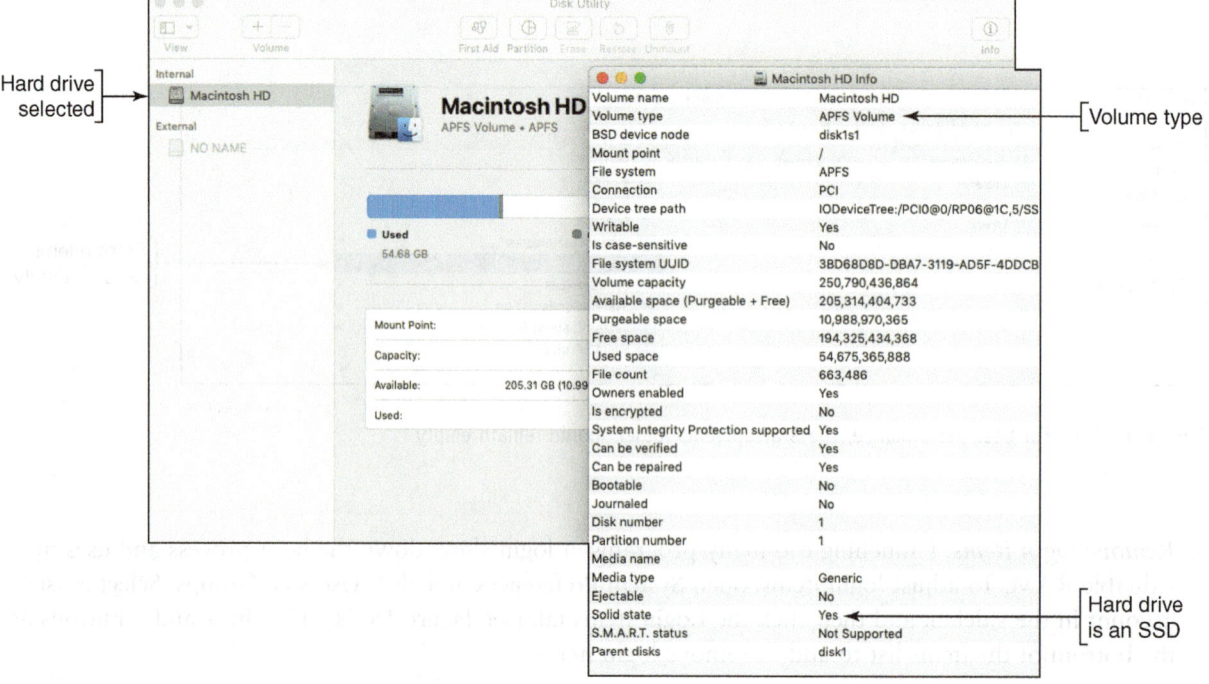

Figure 18-32 Manage drives from the Disk Utility app

Source: Apple Inc.

In the Info box shown on the right side of Figure 18-32, you can see the drive is using the APFS file system. Here are the file systems macOS supports:

- **APFS (Apple File System)** is the default file system for SSDs and can also be used for magnetic hard drives. APFS allocates free space as needed for each volume on the drive. APFS uses the GUID (also called GPT) partitioning system.
- **Mac OS Extended** file system, also called **HFS+ (Hierarchical File System Plus)**, is an older file system in macOS 10.12 and earlier versions that uses a proprietary Apple partitioning system. If the Mac OS Extended file system is installed on an SSD and the system is upgraded to High Sierra, the upgrade converts the file system to APFS because it better manages an SSD. When upgrading to Mojave, the file system is always upgraded to APFS. However, APFS is not compatible with some earlier versions of macOS.
- The FAT32 and exFAT file systems are supported for compatibility with Windows and Linux.

Notes Windows cannot read from storage devices that are using the APFS or Mac OS Extended file system unless third-party drivers are installed in Windows. For example, HFS Explorer can be installed to allow Windows to read a volume using the Mac OS Extended (also called HFS) file system.

You can use **First Aid** in Disk Utility to scan the hard drive for file system errors and repair them. In Disk Utility, select the drive in the sidebar, click **First Aid**, and click **Run** in the box that appears. A warning box reports that apps will be frozen while the drive is repaired. Click **Continue**. The process can take some time. Click **Done** when it completes.

Notes If you plug in an external hard drive and macOS does not recognize the drive, you can use Disk Utility to fix the problem. In the Disk Utility window, select the drive and click **Mount**. If the mount does not work, click **First Aid** and then try to mount the drive again. When you mount a drive, it can be viewed by the OS, the drive is listed in the sidebar of the Finder window, and its icon appears on the desktop.

TROUBLESHOOTING macOS STARTUP

When you have problems with macOS startup, use the options discussed in this part of the chapter to diagnose and fix the problems. These options are summarized in Table 18-2. Turn on the Mac and press certain keys at startup to launch tools or boot from other media. Release the keys as soon as you see the Apple logo.

Keys to Press as a Mac Boots	Tools Launched
Hold down shift key	Boots into Safe Mode
Hold down option key	Displays the Startup Manager so you can choose to boot from different media (for example, the external hard drive, USB flash drive, or network locations)
Hold down d key	Launches Apple Diagnostics to perform tests on hardware
Hold down command+r	Launches macOS Recovery to reinstall macOS from a Time Machine backup or the Internet

Table 18-2 Keys to press to access Mac startup options

> ✏ **Notes** Many of these same steps can also help when troubleshooting kernel panics. A **kernel panic** is similar to a BSOD in Windows. It might be caused by something simple, such as a crashed app or a network communication issue, or it might result from a corrupted macOS installation. macOS restarts automatically when experiencing a kernel panic. If the kernel panic continues to prompt restarts, macOS will stop trying after five attempts and shut down the computer.

SAFE MODE

Starting the computer in Safe Mode can solve problems when the computer won't start due to file system errors or corrupted startup or login items. Safe Mode in macOS loads essential kernel components, prevents startup items and login items from launching, and loads a minimum of user processes. It also verifies the startup disk and repairs any file system errors it finds.

To boot into Safe Mode, hold down the **shift** key as a Mac starts up. To verify that the computer booted into Safe Mode, open **System Information**. In the Software group, look for Boot Mode, which should report Safe (see Figure 18-33).

Source: Apple Inc.

Figure 18-33 Boot Mode indicates the computer is booted into Safe Mode

Do these things in Safe Mode:

◢ When Safe Mode starts, it automatically attempts to fix many problems. Restart the computer normally and see whether the problem is solved.
◢ Delete startup and login items that you suspect are causing a problem.

macOS RECOVERY

Using the macOS Recovery tools, you can reinstall macOS from a Time Machine backup or from the Internet. You can also erase the hard drive before you perform the image recovery. Turn on the Mac and press and hold **command+r** until you see the Apple logo. macOS Recovery launches and you see the macOS Utilities menu (see Figure 18-34).

Figure 18-34   Boot into macOS Recovery to reinstall macOS

After you select an option, click **Continue**. Here are the options you'll see:

- ◢ *Restore From Time Machine Backup*. Plug in the external hard drive that holds the Time Machine backup, then select this option and follow the on-screen directions.
- ◢ *Reinstall macOS*. The latest macOS that was installed on the computer is downloaded from the Internet and reinstalled. As you follow the on-screen directions, the computer will reboot several times. If errors occur during the process, try erasing the hard drive and reinstalling again. After the new installation of macOS boots up, any data backed up with Time Machine can be restored.
- ◢ *Disk Utility*. If you need to erase the hard drive (for example, before you give away a Mac), select **Disk Utility** and follow the on-screen directions.

Suppose you are attempting to reinstall macOS from the Internet and you are not able to get an Internet connection through Wi-Fi or Ethernet. In this situation, you can use another Mac to create a bootable installation device and use it to reinstall macOS. This bootable device is created using commands in the Terminal window and is not covered in this text. The commands and process can be found at *support.apple.com/en-us/HT201372*.

18

STARTUP MANAGER AND NETBOOT

When you press the option key at startup, the Startup Manager screen appears and allows you to select your boot device. See Figure 18-35.

Source: *https://support.apple.com/en-us/HT202796*

Figure 18-35   Startup Manager allows you to select a startup disk or network startup

If you want to boot to a deployment server on the network to reinstall macOS from a disk image, you will use the Apple technology called NetBoot. NetBoot searches for a disk image stored in a DMG file on the server. A DMG file is a disk image file for a Mac and is similar to WIM or ISO files in Windows. In addition to storing clones of the macOS, DMG files are often used to hold app installers, as are EXE files in Windows.

BOOT CAMP

Notice in Figure 18-35 the option to start the computer using Boot Camp, which is an Apple technology that allows you to install and run Windows on a Mac. If the hard drive on a Mac is using a single partition with at least 40 GB of free space, Boot Camp can split the partition and install Windows in the new partition for a dual boot. Access the Boot Camp Assistant through the Utilities folder; Figure 18-36 shows the first screen, which includes a warning to first back up your disk before installing Windows on a Mac. After Windows is installed, you can choose which OS to use as your default for the computer, or you can press and hold the **option** key when starting the computer to reach the Startup Manager, which lets you choose from the installed operating systems. (Although you can install Windows on a Mac, you cannot install macOS on a non-Apple computer.)

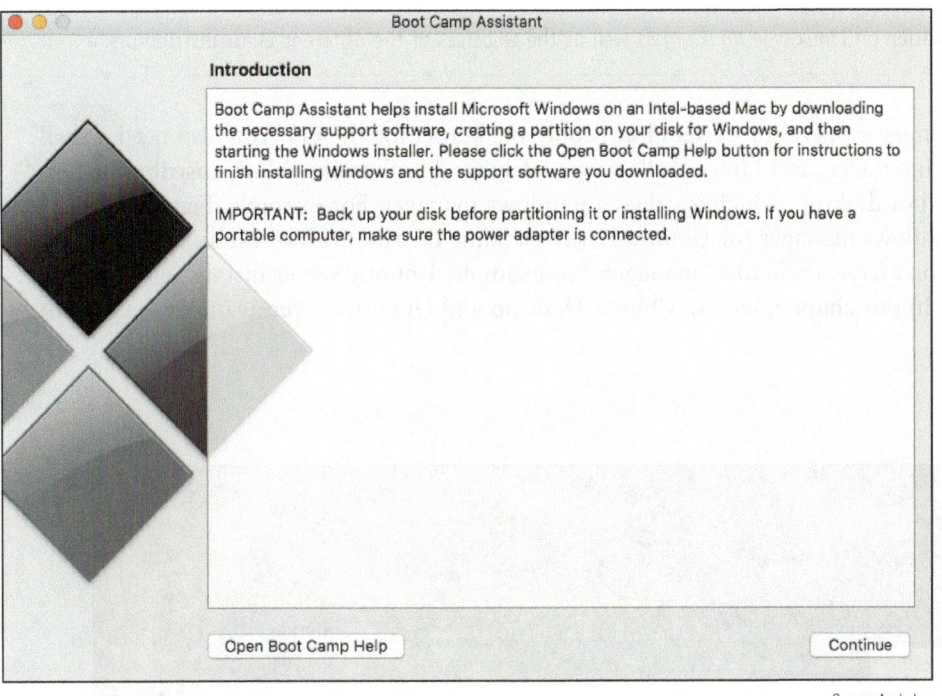

Source: Apple Inc.

Figure 18-36 Use Boot Camp Assistant to install Windows on a Mac and manage the Windows installation

LINUX OPERATING SYSTEM

A+ CORE 2 1.3, 1.9, 4.9 A variation of UNIX is Linux (pronounced "Lih-nucks"), an OS created by Linus Torvalds when he was a student at the University of Helsinki in Finland. Basic versions of this OS are open source, and all the underlying programming instructions (called source code) are freely distributed. Linux is popular because it's inexpensive and very stable (it seldom crashes). Linux is used as an OS for desktops, servers, mobile devices, and IoT devices. It's the most popular OS for server applications such as web servers and email servers. In addition, Android and Chrome OS for mobile devices are based on Linux, and bootable CDs and flash drives that contain utility software often use Linux. Versions of Linux are called distributions or flavors; the more popular ones for desktops and servers are listed in Table 18-3. Hardware requirements for Linux vary widely by distribution.

Name	Comments	Website
Arch Linux	Arch Linux must be manually configured. It has excellent online documentation and community support, and Linux professionals appreciate its simplicity.	*archlinux.org*
Fedora	Fedora has been around for a long time and is backed by a stable company. When updates are released, they tend to work well without errors. It's a great distribution for just about any OS purpose.	*getfedora.org*
Linux Mint	Linux Mint is based on Ubuntu with several features added.	*linuxmint.com*
openSUSE	openSUSE is made for servers, desktops, and mobile devices. Applications install without a hassle; go to *software.opensuse.org*, select an app, and perform a Direct Install.	*opensuse.org*
Red Hat Enterprise Linux	Designed for enterprise use on servers and workstations, this commercial distribution is stable and comes with long-term support. The free version of Red Hat Enterprise is CentOS, which comes with no support.	*redhat.com*
Ubuntu	Ubuntu is one of the most popular distributions of Linux for desktops and servers, and it comes with tons of online tutorials and help.	*ubuntu.com*

Table 18-3 Popular Linux distributions for desktops and servers

18

> ✎ **Notes** For more information on Linux, see *linux.org* as well as the websites of the different Linux distributors.

Linux itself is not a complete operating system but is only the kernel for the OS. You also need a shell for user and application interfaces, and Linux shells vary widely by distributions. Many distributions of Linux include a GUI shell or desktop, which is called a windows manager. For example, Figure 18-37 shows the desktop or windows manager for Ubuntu Desktop. Some distributions of Linux designed for server applications don't have a windows manager. For example, Ubuntu Server installs with only a command-line interface. In this chapter, we use Ubuntu Desktop and Ubuntu Server as our sample Linux distributions.

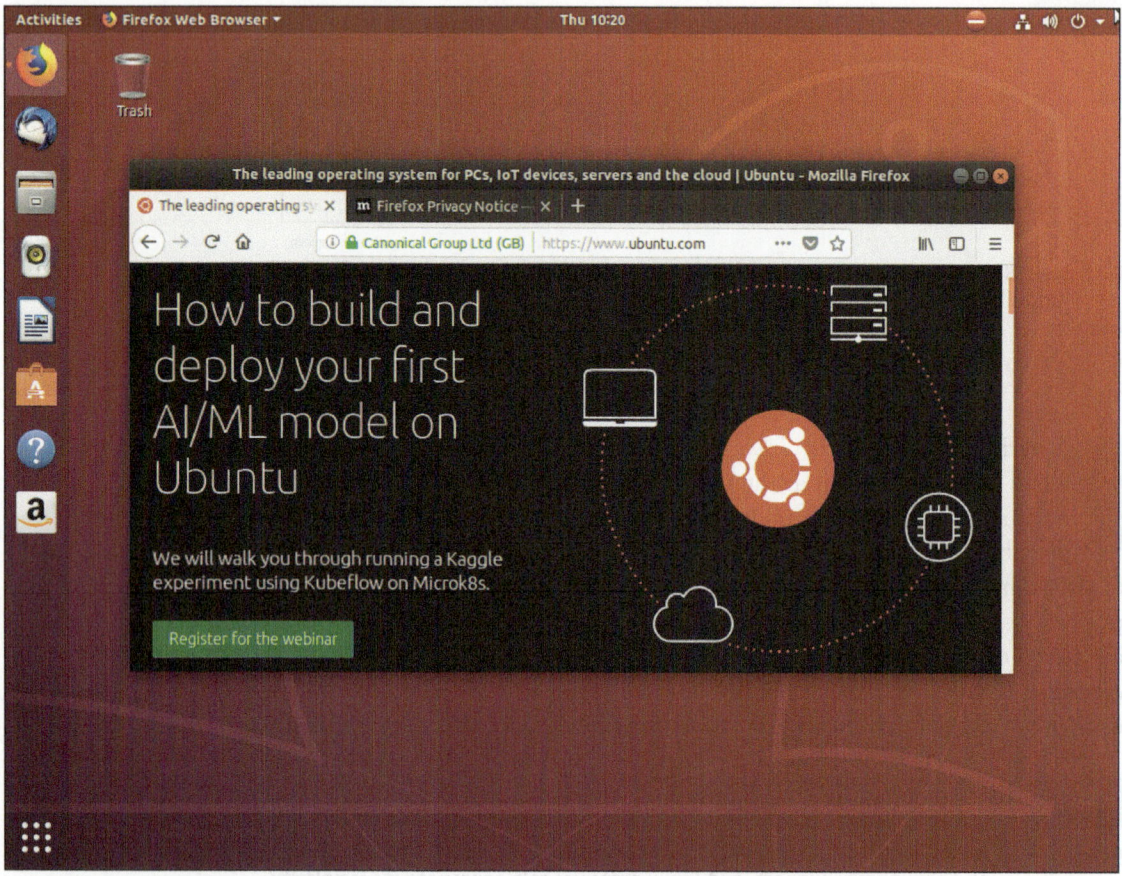

Source: Canonical Ltd.

Figure 18-37 Ubuntu Desktop with the Mozilla Firefox browser window open

You can install Ubuntu Desktop or Ubuntu Server in a VM or on a hard drive, CD, or USB flash drive. When you install Ubuntu on a CD or USB flash drive, it is called a **Live CD** or **Live USB**. A Live CD or USB can boot up a live version of Linux, complete with Internet access and all the tools you normally have available in a hard drive installation of Linux, but without installing the OS on the hard drive. In Chapter 5, you created a Live USB that can be used to test a computer when it cannot boot from the hard drive where Windows is installed.

Let's first install and explore Ubuntu Desktop with its graphical interface, and then you'll learn to install and use Ubuntu Server with its command-line interface.

APPLYING | CONCEPTS   INSTALLING UBUNTU DESKTOP IN A VM

Follow these steps to install Ubuntu Desktop in a VM:

1. Recall that you learned how to install a hypervisor and create a VM in Chapter 12. If you don't already have a hypervisor installed, install one that you can use to manage VMs. For example, in 64-bit Windows 10 Pro, you can use the Programs and Features window to enable Client Hyper-V, which comes embedded in the OS. Alternately, you can download and install one of these free hypervisors:

   ◢ Oracle VirtualBox at *virtualbox.org/wiki/Downloads*
   ◢ Windows Virtual PC at *microsoft.com/en-us/download/details.aspx?id=3702*
   ◢ VMware Workstation Player at *my.vmware.com/web/vmware/free#desktop_end_user_computing/vmware_workstation_player/12_0*

2. Go to **ubuntu.com/download/desktop** and download the free Ubuntu Desktop OS to your hard drive. The file that downloads is an ISO file.

> 🖊 **Notes** Ubuntu Desktop is only available as a 64-bit OS. To install a 64-bit guest OS in a VM, the host OS must also be 64-bit.

3. Open the Hyper-V Manager, Oracle VM VirtualBox, Virtual PC Manager, or VMware Workstation Player manager. Create a new VM with at least 2 GB of RAM and at least a 25-GB virtual hard drive capacity. Mount the ISO file that contains the Ubuntu Desktop download to a virtual DVD in your VM.

4. Start up the VM and install Ubuntu Desktop in the VM, accepting all default settings. Be sure to write down the name of the VM and your Ubuntu host name, Ubuntu user name, and password. When given the option, decline to install any extra software bundled with the OS. If needed, the software can be installed later.

> 🖊 **Notes** If you need help learning to use your hypervisor of choice, try searching for some tutorial videos at *youtube.com* or on the hypervisor manufacturer's website.

5. When asked to restart the VM, first dismount (remove) the ISO file from the optical drive so that the VM boots to the hard drive. After Ubuntu Desktop launches, log in with your user name and password. Figure 18-38 shows the desktop with the Settings window active and the Network setting selected. To open this window, click the **Apps** button and then click **Settings**. When a window is active, its menu appears at the top of the screen. Also notice the System menu is displayed. To open the System menu, click the system icons area in the upper-right corner of the screen.

6. Take a few minutes to poke around the desktop. You'll see how it resembles macOS in many ways. For example, to open a Terminal window where you can enter Linux commands, click **Activities** and type **terminal** in the search box. Then click **Terminal** in the list that appears. Using the Terminal, you can enter Linux commands to manage and support the OS.

7. To shut down Ubuntu Desktop, click the system icons area in the upper-right corner of the screen. The System menu opens. Click the **Power** icon and click **Power Off**.

To learn more about using Ubuntu Desktop, an excellent source of information is the Ubuntu Desktop Guide at *help.ubuntu.com/stable/ubuntu-help/*.

18

(continues)

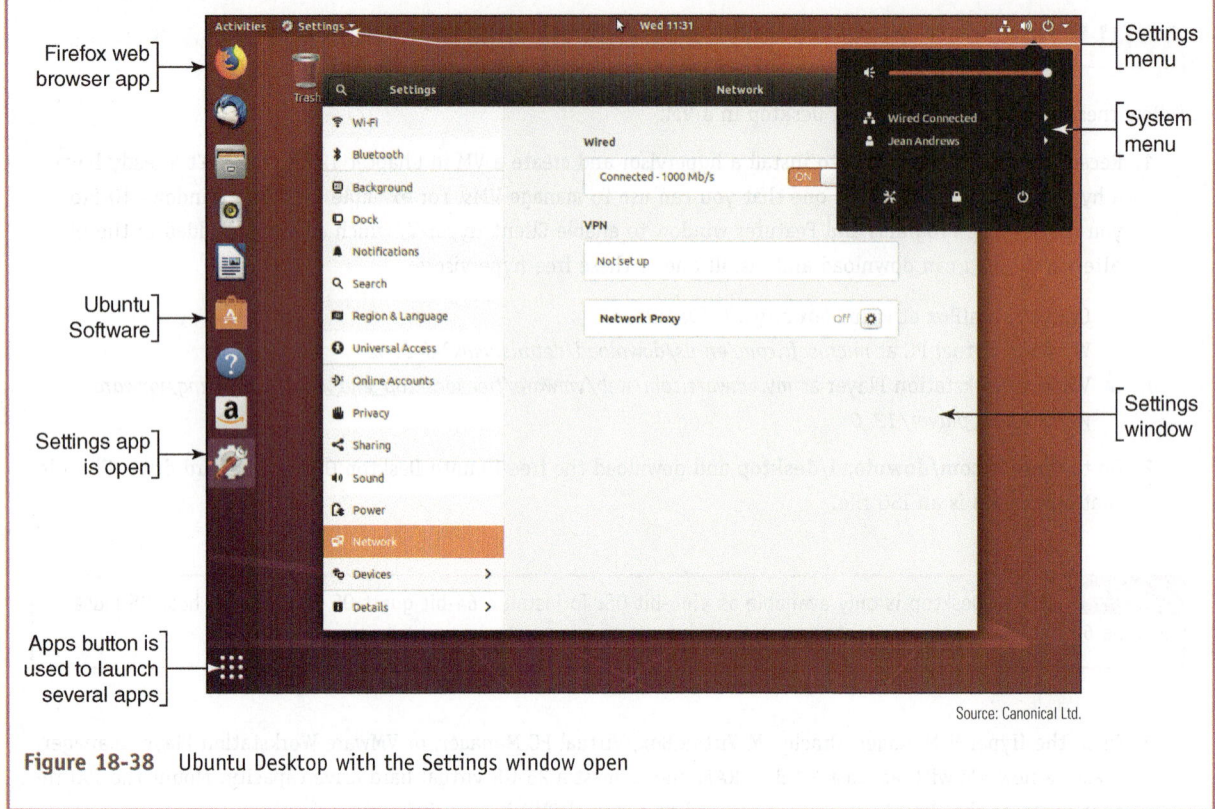

Firefox web browser app

Ubuntu Software

Settings app is open

Apps button is used to launch several apps

Settings menu

System menu

Settings window

Source: Canonical Ltd.

Figure 18-38   Ubuntu Desktop with the Settings window open

LINUX INSTALLS, UPDATES, AND BACKUPS

A+
CORE 2
1.3, 1.9,
4.9

When supporting a Linux system, an IT technician needs to know how to install software, update the OS and apps, and create and maintain scheduled backups. Here are a few details to get you started:

◢ *Install software*. To install software, click the **Ubuntu Software** button. Ubuntu Desktop software appears. Click an item and then click **Install** to start its installation. You can also install an app by clicking a setup file you have downloaded from the web.

◢ *Update Ubuntu and apps*. To update, click **Updates** in the Ubuntu Software window. Updates for Ubuntu are listed first, followed by app updates. Click **Install** beside the updates you want to install. Figure 18-39 shows that no updates are available.

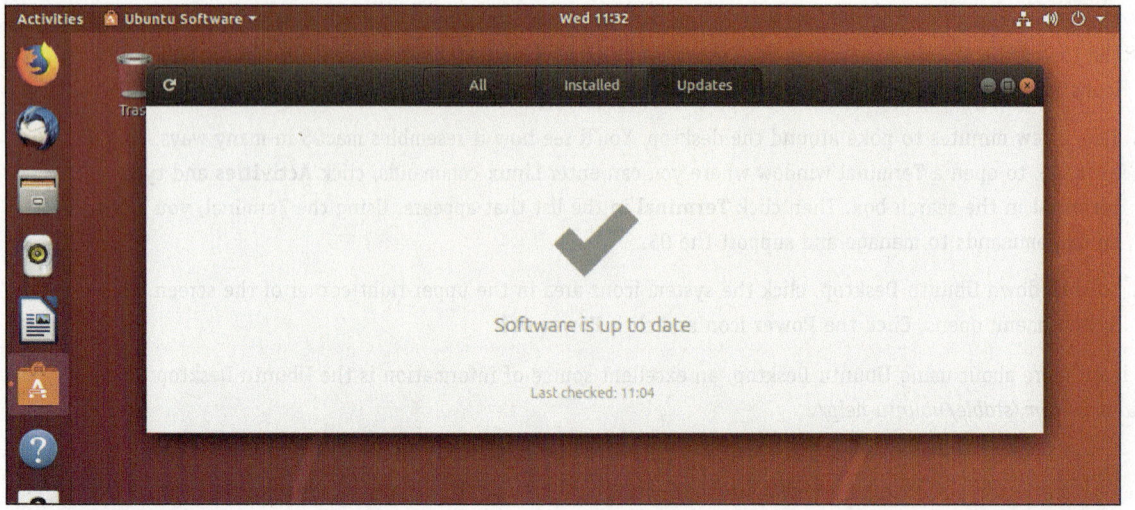

Source: Canonical Ltd.

Figure 18-39   Ubuntu Desktop is up to date

▲ *Change update settings*. To change update settings, open the **Software & Updates** menu and click **Software & Updates** in the drop-down list. Then click the **Updates** tab in the Software & Updates window (see Figure 18-40).

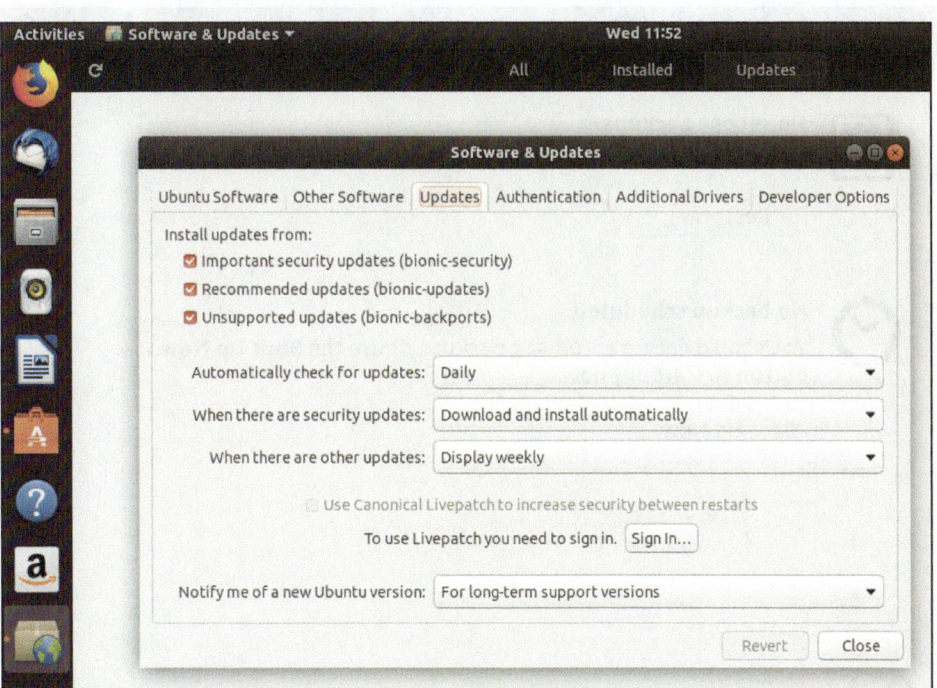

Figure 18-40 Change how Ubuntu Desktop handles updates

Source: Canonical Ltd.

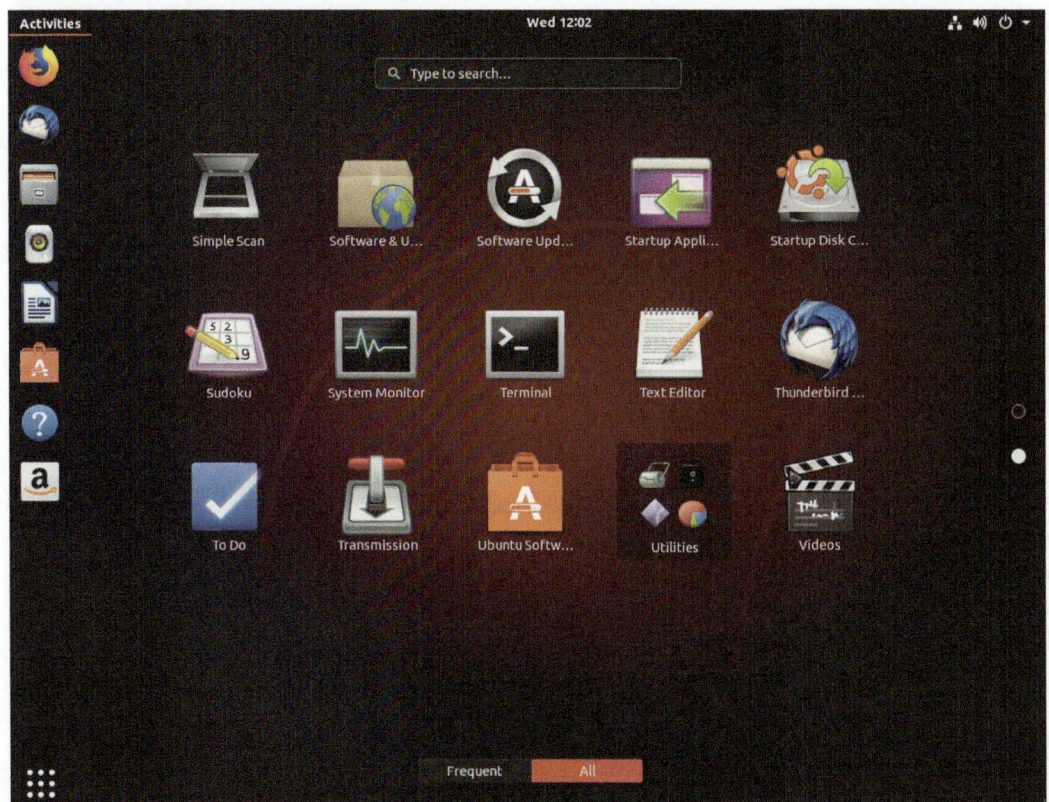

Figure 18-41 Ubuntu Desktop utilities

Source: Canonical Ltd.

◢ *Configure backups*. Click the **Apps** button. In the list of apps, scroll down and click **Utilities** (see Figure 18-41). Click the **Backups** utility. Using the Backups window (see Figure 18-42), you can schedule backups, decide where the backups are stored, and select which items are included in the backup.

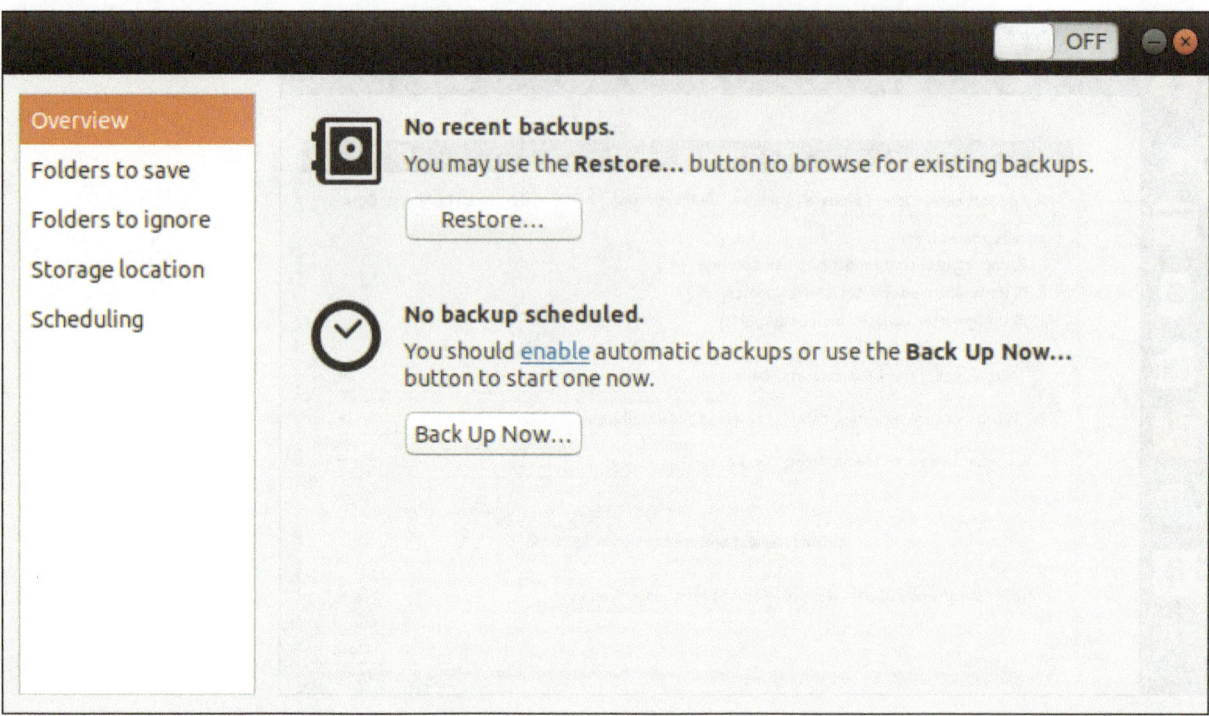

Source: Canonical Ltd.

Figure 18-42 Schedule an Ubuntu Desktop backup

Now that you know about Ubuntu Desktop, let's turn our attention to Ubuntu Server.

INSTALLING AND EXPLORING UBUNTU SERVER

**A+
CORE 2
1.3, 1.9,
4.9**

Ubuntu Server does not include a windows manager but uses a command-line interface called the **terminal**. The default shell for the terminal is the **Bash shell**, which stands for "Bourne Again Shell" and takes the best features from two previous shells, the Bourne and Korn shells. In this chapter, we use Ubuntu Server and its default Bash shell. In Linux, a command prompt in the terminal is called a **shell prompt**.

📝 **Notes** To find out what shell is the default shell for the Linux system, enter the **echo $SHELL** command. To find out which shell you are currently using, enter the **echo $0** command.

As an IT support technician, you should know a little about Linux and its command-line interface. In this chapter, you learn about root and user accounts, file structure, some common commands, and how to use the vi text editor. As you work, be aware that the organization of files and directories and the way each command works might be slightly different with the distribution and version of Linux you are using.

📝 **Notes** As you learn to use Ubuntu, know that the *help.ubuntu.com* website contains a wealth of information about Ubuntu and links to even more help.

APPLYING | CONCEPTS   INSTALLING UBUNTU SERVER IN A VM

To practice Linux skills covered in this chapter, you need an installation of Ubuntu Server. Before you continue with this chapter, follow these steps to install Ubuntu Server in a VM on a Windows computer:

1. Go to **ubuntu.com/download/server** and download the Ubuntu Server OS to your hard drive. The file that downloads is an .iso file.

2. Open the Hyper-V Manager, Oracle VM VirtualBox, Virtual PC Manager, or VMware Workstation Player manager, and then create a new VM. For Ubuntu Server, you'll need at least 2 GB of RAM and at least a 25-GB virtual hard drive. Mount the ISO file that contains the Ubuntu Server download to a virtual DVD in your VM.

3. Start up the VM and install Ubuntu Server, accepting all default settings until you get to the Filesystem setup screen (see Figure 18-43). To improve Ubuntu performance, you can set up a swap partition, which is used to hold virtual memory. In Linux, a swapfile or swap partition can hold virtual memory, but a swap partition yields better performance. Select **Manual**, as shown in the figure, so that you can create two partitions on the hard drive.

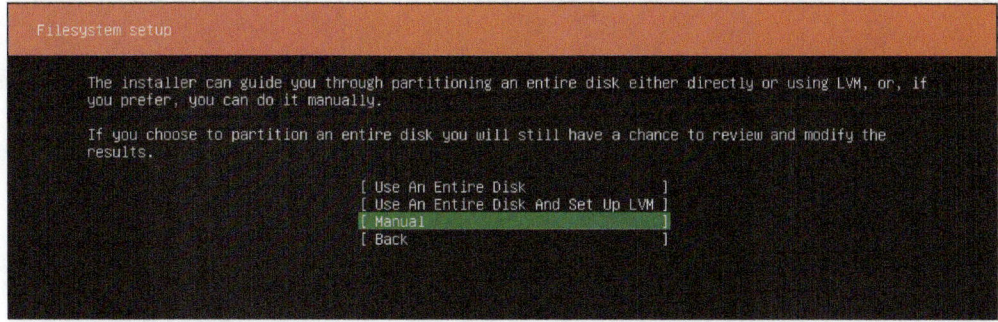

Figure 18-43   Partition the hard drive to include a swap partition

Source: Canonical Ltd.

> ✎ **Notes**   When installing Ubuntu, use the arrow keys to navigate menus and press **Enter** to make a selection. The **Esc** key takes you back one level in a menu.

4. On the next screen, under AVAILABLE DEVICES, point to the local disk and press **Enter**. In the drop-down menu, select **Add Partition**, as shown in Figure 18-44.

Figure 18-44   Create a new partition on the drive

Source: Canonical Ltd.

18

(continues)

5. In the Adding partition box, enter the size of the boot partition (at least 50 GB) and select the file system type **ext4**, as shown in Figure 18-45.

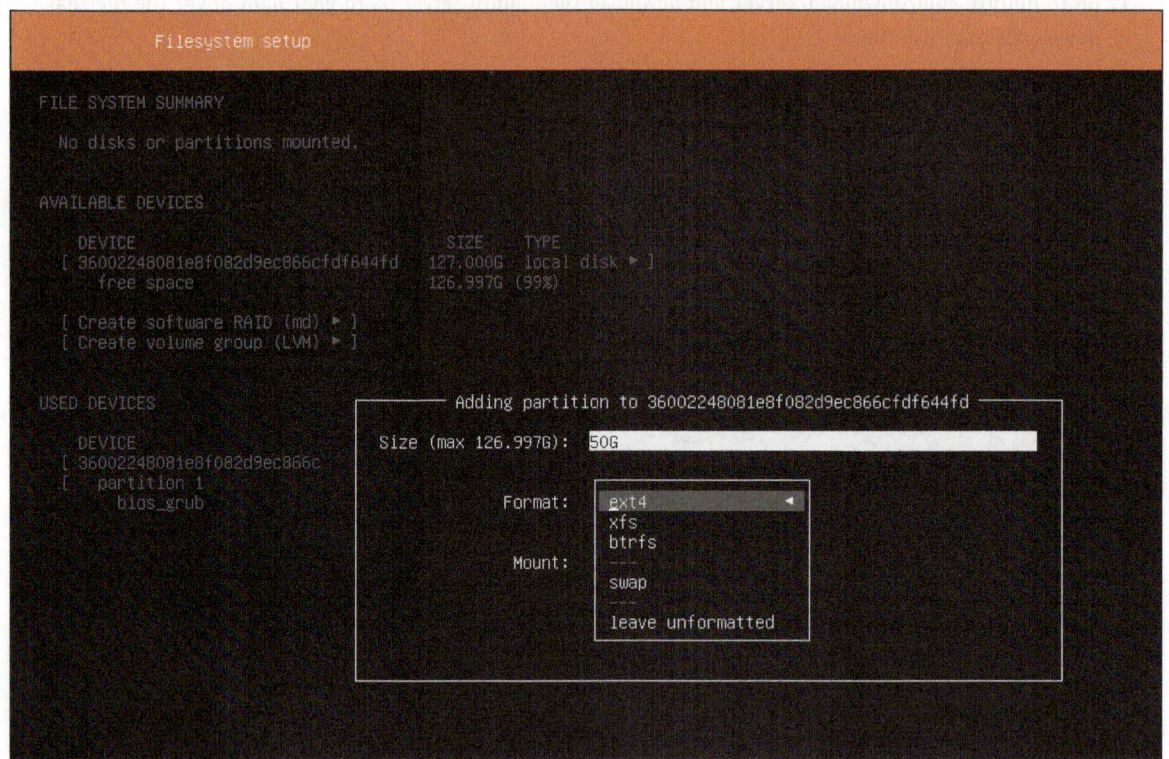

Source: Canonical Ltd.

Figure 18-45   Select ext4 for the file system of the new Ubuntu partition

6. Add a second partition and select **swap** as the file system type. Make the partition size a little larger than the amount of installed memory. Figure 18-46 shows the resulting Filesystem setup screen with three partitions created. Notice that not all of the hard drive is partitioned in our example:

   ▲ **Partition 1**. The small bios_grub partition is automatically created and is used to boot the system in a dual-boot environment. **GRUB (GR and Unified Bootloader)** is a boot loader used to manage dual-boot systems.

   ▲ **Partition 2**. The 50-GB partition that will hold the OS uses the ext4 file system.

   ▲ **Partition 3**. The 4-GB swap partition is used to hold virtual memory. A swap partition does not have a file system installed.

7. Select **Done** to complete the installation, accepting all defaults. Be sure to write down the name of the VM and your Ubuntu host name, Ubuntu user name, and password. When given the option, decline to install any extra software bundled with the OS. Notice this software includes add-ons to be used when Ubuntu Server is installed in the cloud at Amazon Web Services or Google Cloud. If needed, the software can be installed later.

8. After the VM restarts, Ubuntu Server launches, and you should see the terminal shell in the VM. See Figure 18-47.

(continues)

Figure 18-46 Partitions are created to hold the Ubuntu installation

Figure 18-47 When you log in to Ubuntu Server, available updates are listed

9. You might need to press **Enter** to see the shell prompt. Then enter your user name and password, and you're logged in to Ubuntu Server. In the figure, the server is named spock and the logged-in user is jean. Notice Ubuntu reports that 37 packages can be updated. In Ubuntu, a **package** is the collection of files needed to install software.

10. Whenever you're ready to shut down Ubuntu Server, use the **sudo shutdown now** command.

Normally, the shell prompt includes the user name, host name, and the current directory, followed by a $. For example, in Figure 18-47, the shell prompt shows the user name is jean, the host name is spock, and the ~ character indicates the user's home directory, which for the jean account is /home/jean. When you first log in to Linux, the current directory is always the home directory of the logged-in user. (In Linux, directories in a path are separated with forward slashes, in contrast to the backward slashes used by Windows.)

It's easiest to install a swap partition when you install Ubuntu. If Ubuntu is installed on a single partition on the hard drive and you want to improve performance later, you can shrink the Ubuntu partition and create a swap partition in the free space. How to do that is not covered in this text.

⭐ **A+ Exam Tip** The A+ Core 2 exam expects you to know that a swap partition improves performance and that you can create one during or after the installation. You also need to know about the ext4 and ext3 file systems.

Recall that each OS has file systems it can support. Linux file systems include:

▲ *ext4*. The current Linux file system is **ext4 (fourth extended file system)**.
▲ *ext3*. The **ext3** file system was the first to support journaling, which is a technique that tracks and stores changes to the hard drive and helps prevent file system corruption.
▲ *FAT32 and NTFS*. The FAT32 and NTFS file systems are supported for compatibility with Windows and macOS. Windows can use either FAT32 or NTFS, and macOS can use FAT32. Ubuntu should not be installed on a FAT32 or NTFS volume.

✎ **Notes** On a local network or in a dual boot with Windows and Linux, you might want to access files in either volume from either OS. Know that Linux can access the NTFS file system on the Windows volume, but Windows cannot access the ext4 file system on the Linux volume. You can, however, install third-party software, such as Paragon ExtFS for Windows (*paragon-software.com*), to access the ext4 volume.

As you read along and learn about Linux commands, you can use your Ubuntu VM to practice these commands.

DIRECTORY STRUCTURES

Table 18-4 lists some important directories that are created in the root during a typical Linux installation. (Some distributions of Linux modify the directory structure.) Not all directories in the root are listed in the table.

Directory	Description
/bin	Contains programs and commands necessary to boot the system and perform other system tasks not reserved for the administrator, such as shutdown and reboot
/boot	Consists of components needed for the boot process, such as boot loaders
/dev	Holds device names, which consist of the type of device and a number identifying the device; actual device drivers are located in the /lib/modules /[*kernel version*]/ directory
/etc	Contains system configuration data, including configuration files and settings and their subdirectories; these files are used for tasks such as configuring a user account, changing system settings, and configuring a domain name resolution service
/home	Contains user data; every user of the system has a directory in the /home directory, such as /home/jean or /home/scott, and when a user logs in, that directory becomes the current working directory
/lib	Stores common libraries used by applications so that more than one application can use the same library at one time; an example is the library of C programming code, without which only the kernel of the Linux system could run
/lost+found	Stores data that is lost when files are truncated or when an attempt to fix system errors is unsuccessful
/opt	Contains installations of third-party applications such as web browsers that do not come with the Linux OS distribution
/root	Serves as the home directory for the root user and contains only files specific to the root user; don't confuse this directory with the root, which contains all the directories listed in this table
/sbin	Stores commands required for system administration
/tmp	Stores temporary files, such as the ones that applications use during installation and operation
/usr	Contains executable programs, libraries, and shared resources that are not critical to the Ubuntu system
/var	Holds variable data such as logs, email, news, print spools, and administrative files

Table 18-4 Important directories in a typical Linux root directory

APPLYING | CONCEPTS   EXPLORING DIRECTORIES AND FILES

Let's learn a few Linux commands that we can use to explore directories and files. As shown in Figure 18-48, use these commands:

1. Use the **clear** command to clear the screen of all its clutter.

2. Use the **pwd** command (print working directory) to display the full path to the current directory, which is /home/jean in the figure.

3. Use the **cd ..** command to move up one directory to /home. (There's a space after d.)

4. Use the **ls** command to display the list of files and subdirectories in the /home directory. Notice in the figure that the one subdirectory in the /home directory is jean.

5. Use the **ls -l** command to display the results using the long format. (There's a space after the s.) As you can see in the figure, the results are:

```
drwxr-xr-x 4 jean jean 4096 Sep 12 16:56 jean
```

18

(continues)

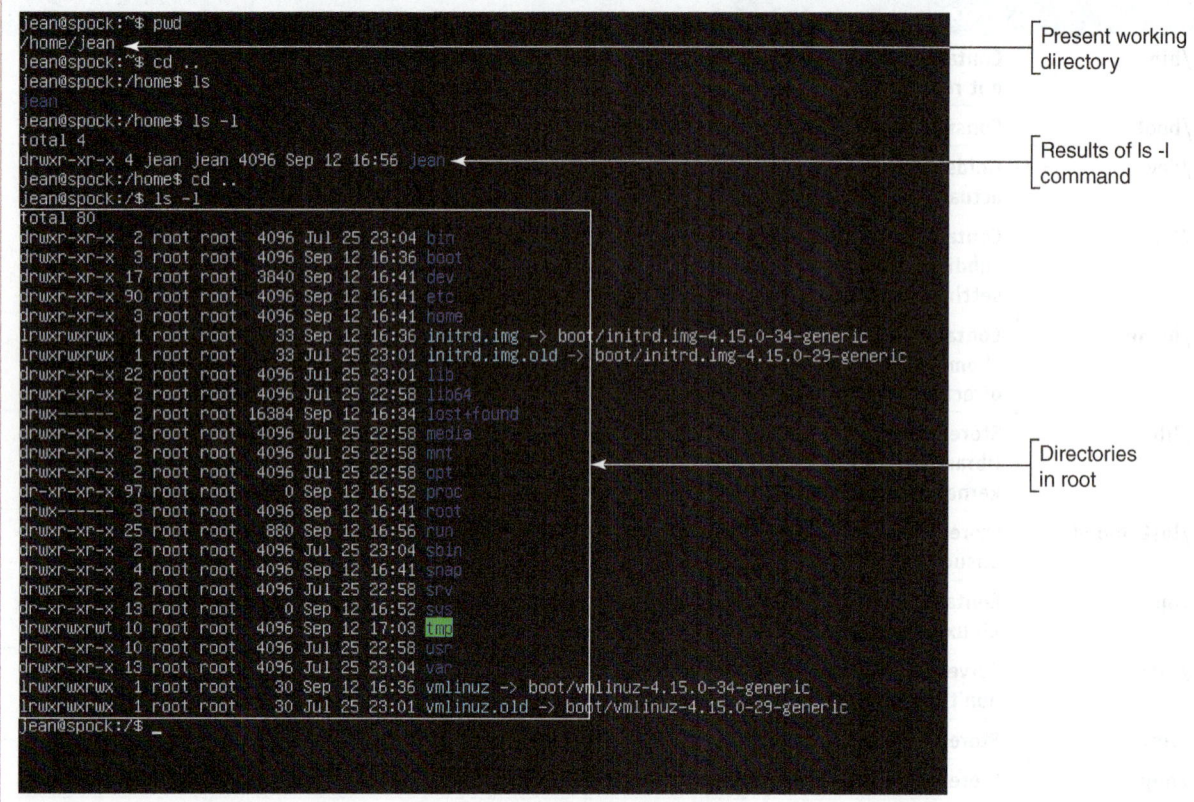

Source: Canonical Ltd.

Figure 18-48 Directories in the root

Here is an explanation of the types of information in the list:

▲ *Attributes*. The first 10 characters (`drwxr-xr-x`) define the file or directory attributes. The first character identifies the type of item: A d is a directory, a - is a regular file, and a 1 indicates the item is a link to another location. The other nine characters (`rwxr-xr-x`) define the read, write, and execute permissions assigned to the file or directory; these permissions are explained in detail later in the chapter.

▲ *Links*. The second column lists the number of links the item has, which is 4 in our example. In Linux, a link is similar to a Windows shortcut to a file or directory.

▲ *Owners*. The third column lists the user owner and the fourth column lists the group that owns the file or directory. In Figure 18-48, the owner is jean and the owner group is also jean.

▲ *Size, date, and name*. The last columns list the size of the file or directory in bytes, the date the item was last modified, and the name of the file or directory. The name of directory jean is listed in blue.

6. When you use the **cd ..** command again, you move up to the main directory in Linux, called the root directory, which is indicated with a forward slash. The **ls -l** command lists the files and subdirectories in the root.

ROOT ACCOUNT AND USER ACCOUNTS

A Linux system administrator is responsible for installing updates to the OS (called patches), managing backups, installing software and hardware, setting up user accounts, resetting passwords, and generally supporting the OS and users. To accomplish this, she requires root privileges or access to all the functions of the OS. Two ways Linux allows for root privileges are:

▲ *Superuser*. The principal user account is called the root account. Notice in Figure 18-48 that all the directories and files in the root directory belong to the root account. When logged in to the root account, the user is called the superuser. Because the root account is so powerful, Ubuntu disables login to this account by default. The root account is similar to the Windows Administrator account.

◢ *Regular user account with root privileges*. Any user account can be assigned root privileges. If the user has root privileges, she can execute any command that requires root access by adding sudo to the beginning of the command line. An account with root privileges is similar to a Windows account that has been assigned Administrative rights.

The command to switch users is su. For a user to switch to the root account, she uses the command **sudo su root**, as shown in Figure 18-49. Notice in the figure that the shell prompt changes to

root@spock:/#. The Linux command prompt for the root user is different from the command prompt for regular users. The root command prompt is #, and other users have the $ command prompt. To switch back to the jean account, use the command **su jean**. As a general practice, never log in to Linux as root unless you have no other option; you can do a lot of damage as root.

```
jean@spock:/$ sudo su root
[sudo] password for jean:
root@spock:/# su jean
jean@spock:/$ _
```

Source: Canonical Ltd.

Figure 18-49 The user account, host name, and current directory appear in the shell prompt along with a # or $ to indicate the root account or other account

LINUX COMMANDS

Table 18-5 describes some basic Linux commands, together with simple examples of how some are used. As you read along, be aware that all commands entered in Linux are case sensitive, meaning that uppercase and lowercase matter.

Command	Description
adduser	**Add a user to a system:** adduser `<username>`
apt-get	**Install and remove applications and other programs (called packages) in Linux. When you first install Linux, it installs with only a bare-bones set of commands and utilities and includes a library of packages that you can install as needed. For example, to install the SSH (Secure Shell) package so you can remote in to your Linux server, use this command:** sudo apt-get install ssh **The apt-get command requires root access, which means you must precede the command with sudo.**
cat	**View the contents of a file. Many Linux commands can use the redirection symbol > to redirect the output of the command. For example, use the redirection symbol with the cat command to copy a file:** cat /etc/shells > newfile **The content of the shells file is written to newfile.**
cd	**Change the directory.** **To change the directory to /etc:** cd /etc **To move up one level in the directory tree:** cd .. **To go to the root:** cd /
chmod	**Change modes (or permissions) for a file or directory. You'll see several examples of this command later in the chapter.**
chown	**Change the owner of a file or directory.**
clear	**Clear the screen. This command is useful when the screen has become cluttered with commands and data that you no longer need to view.**

18

Table 18-5 Some common Linux commands (continues)

Command	Description
cp	**Copy a file:** cp *\<source\>* *\<destination\>*
dd	**Copy and convert files, directories, partitions, and even entire DVDs or hard drives. It's a powerful command with many practical uses and parameters, and only a superuser can use it. The basic format of the command is:** dd if=*\<source\>* of=*\<destination\>* **For example, use this command to create an ISO file from the contents of a CD:** dd if=/dev/cdrom of=/tmp/cdimage.iso
deluser	**Remove a user from a system:** deluser *\<username\>* **Remove the user and his home directory:** deluser -remove-home *\<username\>*
df	**The command stands for** *disk filesystem* **and displays the amount of free space on the hard drive. To see the file system the drive is using:** df -T
echo	**Display information on the screen. You can also save the information to a file. For example, to create a new file that contains text, enter this command:** echo "Hello World" > myfile
exit	**Log out; the login shell prompt appears, where you can log in again.**
grep	**Search for a specific pattern in a file or in multiple files. This command is useful when searching through long log files:** grep *\<pattern\>* *\<file\>*
ifconfig	**Troubleshoot problems with TCP/IP network connections. This command can disable and enable network adapters and assign a static IP address to an adapter. For example, to show all configuration information:** ifconfig –a **To enable or disable an adapter, use the up or down parameter. For example, to enable eth0, the first Ethernet interface:** sudo ifconfig eth0 up **To assign a static IP address to the eth0 interface:** ifconfig eth0 192.168.1.90
iwconfig	**This command works like ifconfig but applies only to wireless networks. Use it to display information about the wireless adapter's configuration or to change the configuration. To set the wireless NIC to Ad-Hoc mode so that other devices within range can connect directly to it, use this command, where wlan0 identifies the wireless adapter:** iwconfig wlan0 mode Ad-Hoc **To force the NIC to use channel 3:** iwconfig wlan0 channel 3
kill	**Kill a process instead of waiting for it to terminate. Use the ps command to list process IDs. To end a process, use the kill command followed by the PID. For example, to kill the process with a PID of 984:** kill 984 **The command sends a signal to the process to end itself in an orderly way. If the process doesn't die peacefully, you can get the kernel involved to forcefully end the process; this is called a forced kill:** kill -kill 984

Table 18-5 Some common Linux commands (continues)

Command	Description
ls	Like the Windows dir command, ls displays a list of directories and files. For example, to list files in the /etc directory, use the long parameter for a complete listing: `ls -l /etc` **To include hidden files in the list:** `ls -la /etc` (In Linux, hidden files begin with a period.)
man	Display the online help manual, called man pages. For example, to get information about the echo command: `man echo` The manual program displays information about the command. To exit the manual program, type q.
mkdir	Make a new directory: `mkdir <directory>`

mv	Move a file or rename it, if the source and destination are the same directory:
	
	`mv <source> <destination>`
	
	To move myfile from the jean directory to the home directory:
	
	`sudo mv /home/jean/myfile /home/myfile`
	
	Because the /home directory is owned by the root account, the sudo command is required.

passwd	Change a password. When a user enters the command, he is asked for the old password and then can change it. The superuser can change the password for any account and does not need to enter the account's old password, making it possible to reset a forgotten password.
ping	Test network connections by sending a request packet to a host. If a connection is successful, the host will return a response packet. For example: `ping 192.168.1.100` The ping results continue until you manually stop the process. Press Ctrl+C to break out of the process. **To specify the number of pings:** `ping 192.168.1.100 -c 4`
ps	The command stands for *process status* and displays the process table so that you can identify process IDs for currently running processes. (Once you know the process ID, you can use the kill command to terminate a process.) **To list processes of the current user:** `ps` **To list processes owned by all users:** `ps aux`
pwd	Show the name of the current or present working directory. When you first log in to Linux, the directory is /home/*username*.
rm	Remove or delete the file or files that are specified: `rm <file>`
rmdir	Remove or delete an empty directory: `rmdir <directory>`
shutdown	Automatically shut down the system. **To shut down now:** `sudo shutdown now` **To warn users and then shut down:** `sudo shutdown -h +10 "Everyone log out now. The system will shut down in 10 minutes for maintenance."` **To reboot now:** `sudo shutdown -r now`

18

Table 18-5 Some common Linux commands (continues)

Command	Description
su	The command stands for *substitute user* or *switch user* and changes to a different user account. When switching to superuser, add sudo to the command. **To switch to the root account:** `sudo su root` **To switch back to the jean account:** `su jean`
sudo	The command stands for *substitute user to do the command* and is pronounced "sue-doe" or "sue-doo." When logged in as a normal user with an account that has the right to use root commands, you can start a command with sudo to run the command as the superuser. A user password may be required. **For example:** `sudo shutdown now`
touch	**Create a blank file in the current directory. For example:** `touch myfile`
vi	**Launch a full-screen editor that can be used to edit a file:** `vi <file>`

Table 18-5 Some common Linux commands (continued)

⭐ **A+ Exam Tip** The A+ Core 2 exam expects you to be familiar with these Linux commands: ls, grep, cd, shutdown, pwd, passwd, mv, cp, rm, chmod, chown, iwconfig, ifconfig, ps, su, sudo, apt-get, vi, dd, and kill.

Here are a few tips when using commands at a shell prompt:

◢ *Retrieve previous commands*. Press the arrow-up key to retrieve previously entered commands and then edit a command that appears.

◢ *Use wildcard characters*. Linux can use the * and ? wildcard characters in command lines, similar to Windows. For example, the ls *.??? command lists all files with a file extension of three characters. In addition, Linux provides a third wildcard: Brackets can give a choice of characters. For example, the ls *.[abc]* command lists all files whose file extension begins with a, b, or c.

◢ *Redirect output*. Normally, output from a command displays on the screen. To redirect that output to a file, use the redirection symbol >. For example, to redirect the output of the ifconfig command to myfile, use this command: **ifconfig > myfile**

◢ *Page the output*. Append |more to the end of a command line to display the results of the command on the screen one page at a time. For example, to page the ls command: **ls -l |more**

◢ *Use Ctrl+C*. To break out of a command or process, press **Ctrl+C**. Use it to recover after entering a wrong command or to stop a command that requires a manual halt.

THE VI EDITOR

The vi editor (visual editor) is a text editor that works in command mode (to enter commands) or in insert mode (to edit text). In this section, you learn how to create a text file in the vi editor, edit text, and save your changes. All vi commands are case sensitive.

Let's create and work with a file called mymemo:

1. You can save a file to your home directory because you own that directory. If you are not already in your home directory, use the cd command to go there. For example:

   `cd /home/jean`

2. To open the vi editor and create the new file, enter the command **vi mymemo**. The vi editor screen appears and the file name is shown at the bottom of the screen.

3. When you first open the vi editor, you are in command mode. Type **i** to switch to insert mode. When you are in insert mode, the word INSERT is shown at the bottom of the screen.

4. Type the contents of Step 3 as the text for your memo (see Figure 18-50). Use your arrow keys to move over the text to edit it. You can also use the Insert key to switch between inserting text and overwriting text.

When you first open the vi editor, you are in command mode. Type i to switch to Insert mode. When you are in Insert mode, the word INSERT is shown at the bottom of the screen.

INSERT   3,1   All

Source: Canonical Ltd.

Figure 18-50 The vi text editor in Insert mode

5. To switch back to command mode, first press the **Esc** key and then type a **:**. The colon command prompt appears and your pointer goes to the bottom of the screen. Type **wq** to save (write) the file and exit (quit) the editor.

Here is a list of enough vi commands to get you started with the editor. You can find other commands online:

:w   Save your changes but don't exit the editor.

:q   Exit the editor after you have just saved your changes with the :w command.

:wq   Save your changes and exit the editor.

:q!   Quit without saving your changes.

APPLYING | CONCEPTS   INSTALLING FTP SERVER IN UBUNTU

In the following steps, you learn to use several Linux commands to install and configure software and examine a log file. Follow these steps to set up an FTP server in Ubuntu:

1. Log in to Ubuntu Server with your user name and password.

2. To create a short file to test the FTP server, you can use the echo command with redirection. Create mymemo in your /home/*username* directory using this command:

   echo "my typing" > /home/*username*/mymemo

3. To install the FTP program named vsftpd, enter this command:

   sudo apt-get install vsftpd

4. Respond to the prompts and then wait for the package to install.

18

(continues)

5. Now you need to configure the FTP program by editing the /etc/vsftpd.conf text file. Before you edit the file, go to the /etc directory and make a backup copy of the file just in case you need it later. The sudo command is needed because files in the /etc directory belong to root:

```
cd /etc
sudo cp vsftpd.conf vsftpd.backup
```

6. Use the vi editor to edit the FTP configuration file:

```
sudo vi vsftpd.conf
```

7. Verify and/or change three lines in the file to create the settings listed below. Part of the file, including the three lines, is shown in Figure 18-51.

`anonymous_enable=NO`	**Disable anonymous logins.**
`local_enable=YES`	**If necessary, remove the # to uncomment the line and allow local users to log in.**
`write_enable=YES`	**If necessary, remove the # to uncomment the line and allow users to write to a directory.**

```
#listen_ipv6=YES
#
# Allow anonymous FTP? (Disabled by default)
anonymous_enable=NO
#
# Uncomment this to allow local users to log in.
local_enable=YES
#
# Uncomment this to enable any form of FTP write command.
write_enable=YES
#
# Default umask for local users is 077. You may wish to change this to 022,
# if your users expect that (022 is used by most other ftpd's)
#local_umask=022
#
# Uncomment this to allow the anonymous FTP user to upload files. This only
# has an effect if the above global write enable is activated. Also, you will
# obviously need to create a directory writable by the FTP user.
#anon_upload_enable=YES
#
# Uncomment this if you want the anonymous FTP user to be able to create
# new directories.
#anon_mkdir_write_enable=YES
#
```

Source: Canonical Ltd.

Figure 18-51 Part of the vsftpd.conf text file

8. Exit the vi editor, saving your changes. Restart the FTP service using this command:

```
service vsftpd restart
```

9. To find out the IP address of the server, type **ifconfig**.

10. On your host Windows computer, open a command prompt window and go to a directory on your Windows computer where you have a file stored. To test your FTP server, open an FTP session using the IP address of the server—for example, **ftp 192.168.1.110** (your IP address may be different). Then enter your user name and password. The ftp> prompt appears. See Figure 18-52.

(continues)

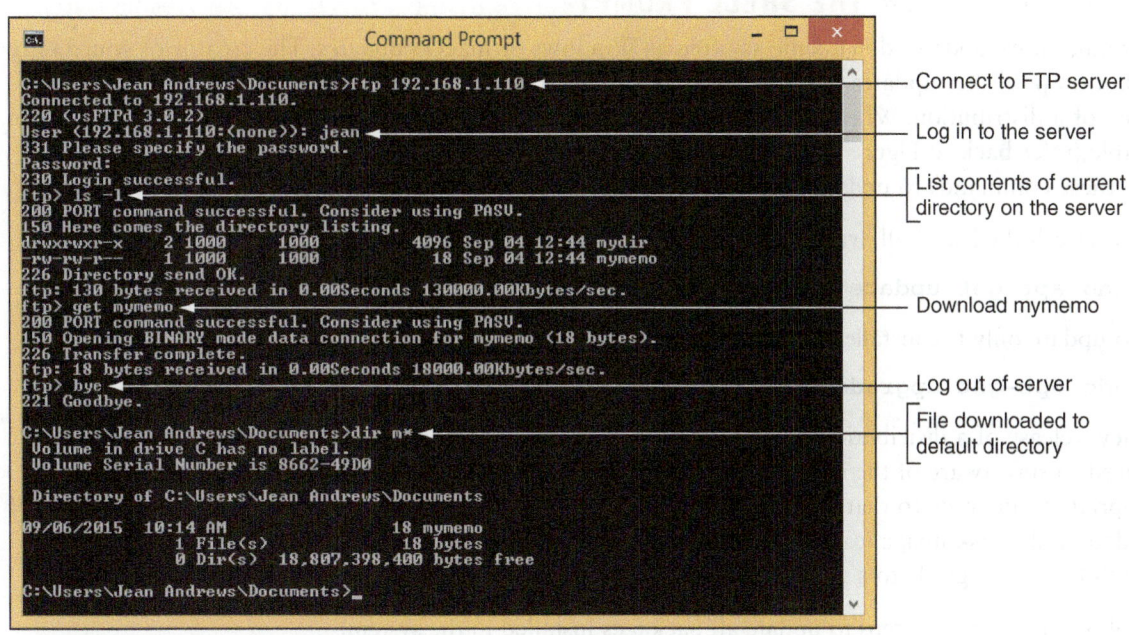

Figure 18-52 Use FTP to transfer files between a Windows and Ubuntu system

11. Next use the **ls -l** command to see a list of directories and files. You should see the file mymemo that you created in your /home/*username* directory earlier.

12. If you want to transfer files with FTP commands, use the **get** and **put** commands. To download the mymemo file, use the command **get mymemo**. To transfer a file from your Windows computer to your Ubuntu server, use the **put** command.

13. Type **bye** to disconnect from the FTP server. At the Windows command prompt, you can use the **dir m*** command, as shown in Figure 18-52, to verify that the file was received on the Windows computer.

14. Return to Ubuntu Server and examine the FTP log file, /var/log/vsftpd.log. Because the file is short, you can use the cat command to display the entire log. The sudo command is required because /var files belong to root:

    ```
    sudo cat /var/log/vsftpd.log
    ```

15. After much activity, log files can get quite long. The grep command can help you find a specific action, user, IP address, file name, or directory name. For example, to display lines in the log file that contain the text "LOGIN," use this grep command:

    ```
    sudo grep "LOGIN" /var/log/vsftpd.log
    ```

    The results of the cat and grep commands are shown in Figure 18-53.

18

```
jean@VM50:~$ cd /var/log
jean@VM50:/var/log$ sudo cat vsftpd.log
Fri Sep  4 12:42:29 2015 [pid 1420] CONNECT: Client "127.0.0.1"
Fri Sep  4 12:42:38 2015 [pid 1419] [jean] OK LOGIN: Client "127.0.0.1"
Fri Sep  4 12:45:48 2015 [pid 1428] CONNECT: Client "192.168.1.124"
Fri Sep  4 12:45:58 2015 [pid 1427] [jean] OK LOGIN: Client "192.168.1.124"
Fri Sep  4 12:46:24 2015 [pid 1429] [jean] OK DOWNLOAD: Client "192.168.1.124", "/home/jean/mymemo", 18 bytes, 19.93Kbyte/sec
jean@VM50:/var/log$ sudo grep "LOGIN" /var/log/vsftpd.log
Fri Sep  4 12:42:38 2015 [pid 1419] [jean] OK LOGIN: Client "127.0.0.1"
Fri Sep  4 12:45:58 2015 [pid 1427] [jean] OK LOGIN: Client "192.168.1.124"
jean@VM50:/var/log$ _
```

Source: Canonical Ltd.

Figure 18-53 The grep command can be used to search for specific text in log files

UPDATE LINUX FROM THE SHELL PROMPT

In general, Linux updates don't come as often as Windows or macOS updates. The creator of your Linux distribution publishes updates to packages in the current release of a distribution and publishes new releases of a distribution. When you first log in to the system, Linux reports the package updates that are available (refer back to Figure 18-47).

Use these commands to update the packages previously installed in your system:

1. To refresh the list of all available updates:

    sudo apt-get update

2. To update only the installed packages:

    sudo apt-get upgrade

A new release of a distribution contains all updates since the last release. As a Linux administrator, you need to stay aware of the latest release of the distribution you are using and decide when or if it's appropriate to upgrade to that release. Before you upgrade to a new release, be sure you have backups of your data and a disk image (called a clone) of the entire Linux partition.

Here's how to upgrade to a new release for Ubuntu Server:

1. Follow the previous steps to update all packages installed in the system.

2. To make sure the latest update manager program is installed:

    sudo apt-get install update-manager-core

3. To install the latest release of Ubuntu Server:

    sudo do-release-upgrade

If a new release is available, the last command reports it and you can follow directions to install it.

✎ Notes Ubuntu Server does not have an easy-to-use backup service. Normally, the system administrator installs third-party software, such as Bacula, to perform backups. Another option is to write your own shell scripts, which are similar to batch files, that include tar commands to create an archive of many files and copy it to other media or network storage. How to set up a backup process for Linux is not covered in this chapter.

ASSIGN PERMISSIONS AND OWNERSHIP OF FILES OR DIRECTORIES

A file or directory can have read, write, and/or execute permissions assigned to it. Permissions can be assigned to (a) the owner, (b) other users in the same group as the owner, and (c) all users. The chmod command is used to manage permissions for files and directories. To see current permissions, examine the 10 characters in the left column that display when you use the ls -l command. For example, suppose the output for the ls -l command on the /home/jean directory is that shown in Figure 18-54.

Figure 18-54 Information about the jean directory displayed by ls-l

Here is the explanation of these characters:

◢ The first character identifies the type of item (d is a directory; - is a regular file).

◢ Characters 2–4 show the permissions assigned to the user or owner (for example, rwx means the user has read, write, and execute permissions).

◢ Characters 5–7 show the permissions assigned to the group (for example, r-x means the group has read and execute permissions, but not write permission).

◢ Characters 8–10 show the permissions for others (for example, r-x means other users have read and execute permissions, but not write permission. By contrast, --- would mean others don't have read, write, or execute permission).

The chmod command changes these permissions. For example, in Figure 18-54, if the user jean wants to give read, write, and execute permissions to everyone (group and other), she can use this command:

```
chmod g=rwx,o=rwx /home/jean
```

The **g** assigns permission to the group and the **o** assigns permissions to others. (The **u** can assign permissions to the owner.) For a folder, you must move out of the folder before you change its permissions. Also, the command has no space before or after a comma.

Let's look at an example of when you might need to change the ownership of a directory or file. Suppose you are setting up an FTP server so that users who have accounts on the server can use FTP to upload files to their home directories. Table 18-6 lists commands that might be useful to set up the user directories.

Command	Description
`sudo adduser carlos`	**Creates the user account and its home directory**
`sudo mkdir /home/carlos/files`	**Creates a directory for carlos to store his files when using FTP; the sudo command is required to create the directory in another user's account, and this new directory belongs to root**
`sudo chown carlos:carlos /home/carlos/files`	**Makes carlos the owner of the files directory; the carlos group is also assigned to the files directory**
`sudo chmod g-w,o-w /home/carlos/files`	**Removes write permissions for the files directory for all but the carlos user (the g-w parameter removes write permissions and g+w adds write permissions)**

Table 18-6 Commands to set up user directories with appropriate write permissions

18

TELNET AND SSH FOR REMOTE ACCESS

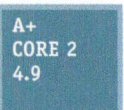

Recall that Windows uses Remote Desktop and macOS uses Screen Sharing to remotely access a computer with screen and file sharing. In Linux, the primary utilities for remote access at a shell prompt are Telnet and SSH (Secure Shell). Telnet does not encrypt transmissions, but SSH encrypts all transmissions. Therefore, SSH is more secure than Telnet and is the most common method to remotely access a Linux system. Use the commands in Table 18-7 to install Telnet and SSH in Linux.

Command	Description
sudo apt-add-repository universe	**Add the universe repository to the list of places Ubuntu can find apps. This is an official repository of apps, but it is not supported by Ubuntu. (Note that when you attempt to add the repository and it is already available, a message appears saying the component is already enabled.)**
sudo apt-get update	**Download and update all apps available to Ubuntu, including the ones in the universe repository.**
sudo apt-get install openssh-server	**Install and run the SSH server in Linux.**
sudo apt install telnetd	**Install and run the Telnet server.**

Table 18-7   Install and run Telnet and SSH in Linux

In Windows, SSH is enabled by default and Telnet Client can be turned on using the Windows Features window, which is available in the Programs and Features window. Here are the steps to remotely access a Linux system from a Windows or Linux computer:

1. For Windows, turn on **Telnet Client** in the **Windows Features** window.

2. At a Windows command prompt or Linux shell prompt, use the following command to open a Telnet session, substituting the IP address for the Linux system you want to remote in to:

   telnet 192.168.1.160

3. The Linux login prompt appears. Enter your user name and password. To close the session, use the **logout** command.

4. To use SSH to remote in, enter the following command, substituting your user name and IP address for the remote Linux system:

   ssh jean@192.168.1.160

5. Enter your password to log in to Linux. To close the session, use the **logout** command.

COMPARING WINDOWS, macOS, AND LINUX

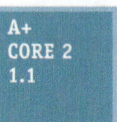

Now that you have learned how to use and support Windows, macOS, and Linux, let's take a step back and compare these three types of operating systems. As an IT technician, most likely you'll be called on to help a customer decide which type of OS to use in a given situation. Here are some tips to help you decide between Windows, macOS, and Linux:

▲ *User desktops and laptops.* Windows and macOS are well-suited for user desktops and laptops because each OS has a plethora of applications designed for it. Most often when deciding between the two, it comes down to what a company or individual prefers and knows how to use and support. Linux with a windows manager, on the other hand, comes up short in the number of desktop applications designed for it.

▲ *Server applications*. Linux is popular as a server OS for supporting many types of server applications, such as web servers, email servers, and DNS servers. However, Windows Server with Active Directory is more popular when it comes to controlling and securing access to a network in a corporate environment. Many IT departments use a combination of Windows Server to manage the Windows domain and Linux servers to manage server applications.

▲ *End-of-life vendor limitation*. In practice, computers and their operating systems might stay in service long after manufacturer support for the OS has ended. However, it's important that you know when an OS will no longer be supported by its manufacturer. Here is the rundown:

  ▲ *Windows*. In the past, Microsoft released a new version of Windows about every three years, but with Windows 10, it seems to be heading in the direction of Windows as a service. Microsoft has unofficially said that Windows 10 is its last version of Windows, meaning that it will continue to provide ongoing feature updates (about every six months) and minor updates weekly. Eventually, we expect to think of just Windows, not a particular version, which is the direction that Apple has taken.

  ▲ *macOS*. Over the past 20 years, Apple has released versions of Mac OS X about once a year; it was renamed macOS in 2016. The version a Mac can support depends on the age of the Mac. For example, a MacBook made in 2009 or later should support High Sierra, a current macOS release, and a MacBook made in 2012 or later should support Mojave, the latest macOS release.

  ▲ *Linux*. How long a Linux distribution will be supported depends on the developer. For example, Canonical (*canonical.com*), which makes Ubuntu Desktop and Ubuntu Server, releases a new distribution of Ubuntu about every two years and provides support of that release for about five years.

▲ *Compatibility between OSs*. When selecting an OS, consider how compatible it is with other OSs in the organization. Because macOS and Linux are both built on UNIX, they are more compatible with each other than with Windows. The FAT32 file system can be read and written by Linux, macOS, and Windows, and is therefore the file system of choice when you are concerned with compatibility. Linux can read and write to NTFS file systems used on Windows systems, but macOS cannot.

Now let's turn our attention to the last topic of the chapter, scripting.

SCRIPTING SOFTWARE AND TECHNIQUES

**A+
CORE 2
4.8**

In this text you've learned to use commands in a Windows command prompt window, cmdlets in a PowerShell window, and Linux commands in macOS and Linux terminals. When a technician finds himself repetitively entering the same group of commands, he might decide to store them in a text file and execute them as a batch. The text file containing the list of commands is called a script; using scripts can save time and assures consistency (fewer errors). In this part of the chapter, you learn about the various script file types and then explore the basics of reading and writing scripts, which will help get you started using scripts written by others or writing your own scripts.

SCRIPT FILE TYPES

**A+
CORE 2
4.8**

In Chapter 13, you learned to create a batch file that contains Windows commands. This and other script file types are listed in Table 18-8 with a description of the software that can read and interpret each command in a script file and execute these commands in a run-time environment.

18

Script File Extension	Description
.bat	A batch file contains a list of Windows commands that can be executed in a command prompt window.
.ps1	A PowerShell script contains cmdlets executed in Windows PowerShell. The script is written using dynamic type checking, which means each cmdlet is checked by the PowerShell interpreter as it is typed to verify that the command can be executed as it is added to the script file. Many scripting and programming applications support dynamic type checking.
.vbs	A .vbs script is written with VBScript, which is modeled after the more complex Visual Basic, a full-fledged programming language.
.sh	A UNIX or Linux script, also called a shell script, contains Linux commands and is executed in a UNIX or Linux shell.
.py	A Python script is a group of Python commands interpreted by Python. Python can also compile the commands into an executable program.
.js	A .js script written in JavaScript is a text file that contains commands normally used with webpages. These scripts can be embedded in an HTML file, which is downloaded from a web server to a browser and used to build an interactive webpage in the browser.

Table 18-8 Types of script files and scripting software

Scripts are simpler to write and use than programs. The difference between a script and a program is:

◢ *A script is interpreted.* A script is read, interpreted, and executed command by command directly from the script file by software called an interpreter. For example, a technician types commands into a script file, and the commands are verified to work by PowerShell or VBScript. When a technician executes the script, PowerShell or VBScript reads, interprets, and executes each command in the file.

◢ *A program is compiled.* A program is first written using a programming language such as Visual Basic or Python, which interprets the code to verify that it can be executed. Then the coding file is compiled by the Visual Basic or Python complier into a binary executable file that has an .exe file extension. The executable file can then be run or executed by an operating system.

BASICS OF SCRIPTING

A+
CORE 2
4.8

Ready to learn a little scripting? Let's get started with some key terms:

◢ An environmental variable (sometimes called a system variable) is information the OS makes available to a script. For example, the Windows and Linux PATH variable lists the paths (drives, directories, and subdirectories) the script can use. Another example is the TEMP variable, which tells a script where it can store its temporary files. To view and edit environmental variables in Windows, open the **System** window and click **Advanced system settings**. On the Advanced tab of the System Properties box, click **Environmental Variables**. See Figure 18-55.

◢ Comments are text you put in a script to document the script. They can include your name, the date, the purpose of the script, and documentation that might help someone understand command lines in the script. Comment syntax refers to how you tag the text as a comment so that it is not interpreted as a command. For example, in PowerShell, a line in the script file can hold a comment if you begin the line with a #.

◢ A basic loop executes the same commands multiple times until some condition is met.

◢ A variable is the name of an unknown data item and can be assigned a value, which is called initializing the variable. In PowerShell, a variable name is preceded by $. You can assign a value to a variable using the equal symbol (=).

◢ A data type determines what type of value a variable can be assigned. Two common data types are integers (whole numbers) and strings (text).

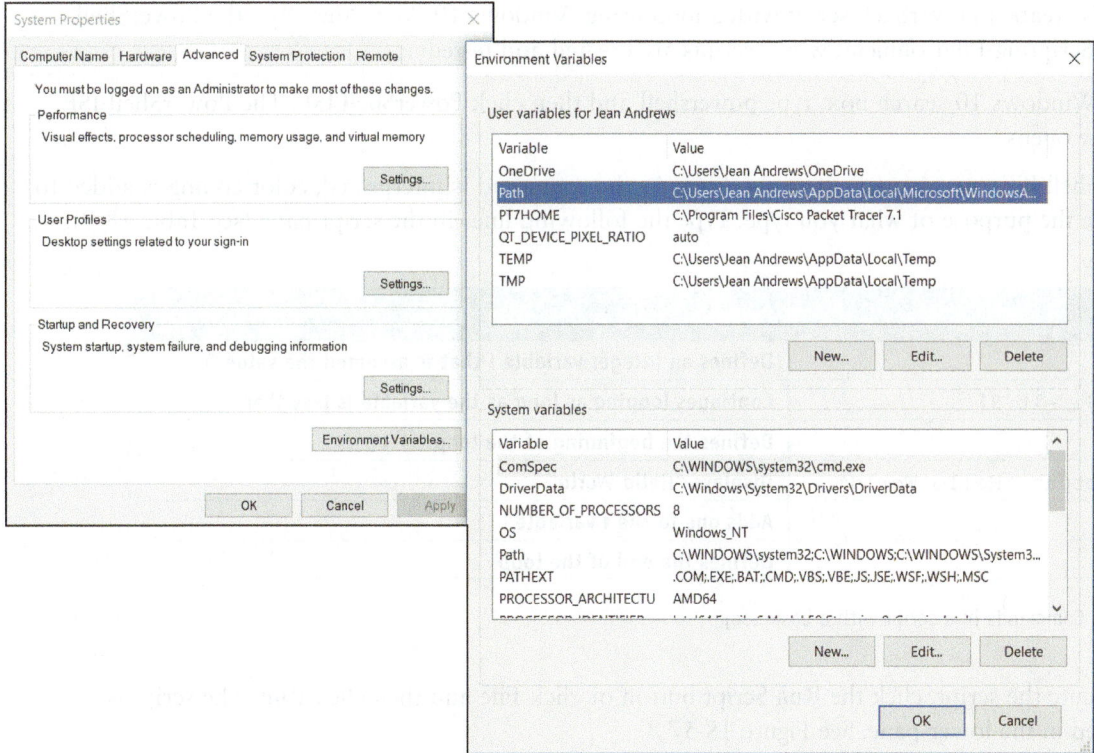

Figure 18-55 View, create, edit, and delete environmental variables

It's a commonly known fact in the world of scripting and programming that the very first script or program a person writes does nothing more than say "Hello World." This proves you know how to create, save, and execute a script. Let's create one in a shell script:

1. At an Ubuntu shell prompt, make sure the current directory is your home directory. Then enter this command, saving the .sh file in your home directory:

   echo "echo Hello World" > my-script.sh

2. To assign execute permission to the file, use this command:

   chmod u=rwx my-script.sh

3. To execute a shell script, type ./ before the script file name. Enter this command (see Figure 18-56):

   ./my-script.sh

```
jean@spock:~$ echo "echo Hello World" > my-script.sh          ⎤ Create the
jean@spock:~$ ls -l                                           ⎦ script
total 12
drwxrwxr-x 2 jean jean 4096 Sep 27 21:09 Hold
-rw-rw-r-- 1 jean jean   17 Sep 27 21:17 my-script.sh
-rw------- 1 jean jean    4 Sep 12 19:57 MyTestFile.txt
jean@spock:~$ chmod u=rwx my-script.sh
jean@spock:~$ ls -l
total 12
drwxrwxr-x 2 jean jean 4096 Sep 27 21:09 Hold
-rwxrw-r-- 1 jean jean   17 Sep 27 21:17 my-script.sh
-rw------- 1 jean jean    4 Sep 12 19:57 MyTestFile.txt
jean@spock:~$ ./my-script.sh                                  ⎤ Execute
Hello World                                                   ⎦ the script
jean@spock:~$ _
                                                              ⎤ Script
                                                              ⎦ results
```

18

Figure 18-56 A simple shell script is created and executed

Now let's create a PowerShell script with a loop using Windows 10 PowerShell ISE, the PowerShell Integrated Scripting Environment, where scripts are created and tested:

1. In the Windows 10 search box, type **powershell** and then click **PowerShell ISE**. The PowerShell ISE window opens.

2. PowerShell ISE does dynamic type checking. As the command is interpreted, color coding is added to indicate the purpose of what you type. Type the following lines in the script pane (see Table 18-9):

Command	Purpose
$i = 0	Defines an integer variable i that is assigned the value 0
While ($i -lt 3)	Continues looping as long as the variable is less than 3
{	Defines the beginning of the loop
Write-output "Hello World"	Displays "Hello World"
$i++	Adds one to the i variable
}	Defines the end of the loop

Table 18-9   Commands in a script with a basic loop

3. To execute the script, click the **Run Script** button or click **File** and then click **Run**. The script is executed in the lower pane. See Figure 18-57.

Figure 18-57   A PowerShell script with a basic loop is executed

4. To save your script, click **File**, click **Save**, and save the script to your desktop. Name the script **MyLoopScript**. By default, the .ps1 file extension is assigned to the file.

5. Close the **PowerShell ISE** window and open a standard **PowerShell** window.

6. By default, running PowerShell scripts is disabled. To set the execution policy so that scripts will run except those downloaded from the Internet without a valid digital signature, enter this cmdlet:

   Set-ExecutionPolicy RemoteSigned

7. Use this alias cmdlet to go to your Windows desktop folder:

   cd desktop

8. Use the **dir** alias cmdlet to list the contents of your desktop folder. You should see the script file listed.

9. To execute a PowerShell script, begin with ./. Use this cmdlet to execute your script:

   ./MyLoopScript

So that's the basics of scripting. I hope you love it and write many more scripts in your IT career.

CHAPTER SUMMARY

macOS for Macintosh Computers

▲ macOS is used only for Macintosh computers by Apple Inc. Like Linux, macOS is built on a UNIX foundation.

▲ The dock appears at the bottom of the desktop. The icons in the dock that represent open applications have a small, black circle underneath them.

▲ Important macOS tools used to manage and support a Mac include Finder, Launchpad, the Apple menu, System Preferences, Spotlight, Mission Control, Keychain, Screen Sharing, Remote Disc, Terminal, and gestures on a trackpad.

▲ For IT technicians, the most important tools in System Preferences are accessed through Time Machine, Users & Groups, and Sharing. Screen Sharing, one of the Sharing tools, works like Remote Desktop in Windows.

▲ macOS updates often address zero-day vulnerabilities, which makes these updates important to maintaining a healthy system.

▲ Time Machine is a built-in backup utility that automatically backs up user-created data, applications, and system files to an external hard drive that's attached either directly to the computer or through the local network.

▲ First Aid in Disk Utility can scan and repair file system errors on a hard drive.

▲ Tools to fix macOS startup problems include Safe Mode, macOS Recovery, Startup Manager, and NetBoot.

▲ Boot Camp is a macOS utility that allows you to install Windows on a Mac computer in a dual boot with macOS.

Linux Operating System

▲ Distributions of Linux provide a shell prompt in the Linux terminal and might also provide a desktop with a GUI. The default command-line shell for Linux is the Bash shell.

▲ Ubuntu Desktop with its windows manager offers Ubuntu software to install apps and update Ubuntu.

▲ The root account in Linux has access to all features of the OS. When logged in to the root account, the user is called the superuser.

18

◢ Important Linux commands include adduser, apt-get, cat, cd, chmod, chown, clear, cp, dd, deluser, df, echo, exit, grep, ifconfig, iwconfig, kill, ls, man, mkdir, mv, passwd, ping, ps, pwd, rm, rmdir, shutdown, su, sudo, touch, and vi.

◢ An app is normally configured in Linux by editing a text file in the /etc directory.

◢ Telnet and SSH can be used to remotely access a Linux computer. Telnet transmissions are not secured, but all SSH transmissions are encrypted.

◢ Windows and macOS are popular OSs for desktops and laptops, and Linux is popular as an application server OS. For compatibility, the FAT32 file system can be used by Windows, macOS, and Linux.

Scripting Software and Techniques

◢ Scripts are executed in a run-time environment without first being compiled, as are programs.

◢ Script file types include batch files, PowerShell scripts, VBScript, shell scripts (for Linux and UNIX), Python scripts, and JavaScript.

>> KEY TERMS

For explanations of key terms, see the Glossary for this text.

APFS (Apple File System)	First Aid	macOS	Spotlight
Apple menu	force quit	Mac OS Extended	SSH (Secure Shell)
apt-get	forced kill	Mission Control	startup disk
Bash shell	gestures	multiple desktops	startup items
basic loop	grep	NetBoot	strings
batch file	GRUB (GR and Unified	package	su (substitute user or
Boot Camp	Bootloader)	passwd	switch user)
chmod	HFS+ (Hierarchical File	PowerShell ISE	sudo
chown	System Plus)	PowerShell script	superuser
clone	ifconfig	Python script	swapfile
comment syntax	integers	Remote Disc	swap partition
dd	iwconfig	root account	System Preferences
DMG file	JavaScript	run-time environment	Telnet
dock	kernel panic	Screen Sharing	terminal
dynamic type checking	Keychain	script	Terminal
environmental variable	kill	secondary-click	Time Machine
ext3	Launchpad	shell prompt	variable
ext4 (fourth extended file	Linux	shell script	VBScript
system)	Live CD	snapshots	vi editor
Finder	Live USB	Space	Windows as a service
	login items		

>> THINKING CRITICALLY

These questions are designed to prepare you for the critical thinking required for the A+ exams and may use content from other chapters and the web.

1. Why is the scrollbar typically hidden from view in macOS?

2. Which app manages multiple desktop screens in macOS?

3. Which app provides tools for customizing the macOS interface?

4. A scanner connected to your Mac is giving problems and you suspect corrupted device drivers. What should you do first? Second?

   a. Download and install drivers from the scanner manufacturer.

   b. Back up the macOS startup disk using Time Machine.

   c. Update macOS.

   d. Uninstall the scanner and install it again.

5. How often does Time Machine create new backups, and how long are these backups kept?

6. Your macOS installation is corrupted and you want to boot from an external Thunderbolt hard drive to repair the installation. Which key(s) do you hold down at startup to boot from the external hard drive?

   a. d key

   b. command+r keys

   c. shift key

   d. option key

7. You are helping your friend troubleshoot a problem with his Linux server. You enter a common Linux command and discover it doesn't work exactly as you expected. What might be the problem and what do you do next?

   a. The Linux installation is corrupted; restore the system from backup.

   b. The Linux shell is not the one you expected; use the echo $SHELL command.

   c. You probably don't know how to use the Linux command; search the web for information about the command.

   d. The Linux shell is not the one you expected; use the echo $0 command.

8. What is the full path to the home directory of the user account lucio in Linux?

9. You are running a web server app in Ubuntu Server. Users complain that their browsers are loading webpages with errors. Where are you likely to find the log file where the web server reports its errors?

   a. /app/log

   b. /bin

   c. /var/log

   d. /root

10. In Linux, when logged in as a normal user with root privileges, which command must precede the apt-get command in the command line in order to install a program?

   a. sudo

   b. sudo user

   c. su

   d. root

11. Which file system does Linux currently use for the volume on which Linux is installed?

12. You have set up an FTP server in Ubuntu Server. Jason, a user, calls to say he gets an error when trying to put a file in his /home/jason/files directory. You look at the directory structure and see that you forgot to give the user ownership of the directory. Which command can fix the problem?

18

    a. chown jason:jason /home/jason/files

    b. sudo chmod u=rwx /home/jason/files

    c. sudo chown jason:jason /home/jason/files

    d. chmod u-rwx /home/jason/files

13. What is the Linux vi editor command to save your changes and exit the editor?

14. You are managing an FTP server installed in Ubuntu Server. The server has created a very large log file, vsftpd.log. Which command is appropriate to search the log file for activity of the user charlie?

    a. sudo cat /var/log/vsftpd.log

    b. grep "charlie" /var/log/vsftpd.log

    c. sudo grep "charlie" /var/log/vsftpd.log

    d. cat /var/log/vsftpd.log

15. Explain why most Linux commands work about the same on a Mac computer as they do on a Linux system.

16. You work at an IT help desk and have been asked to set up 25 new user accounts in Active Directory. Your boss tells you to save time by using a PowerShell script that's available on a network share. You look at several script files named CreateNewUsers that are stored on the drive. Which one is likely to be the one you want?

    a. The file with a .js file extension

    b. The file with a .bat file extension

    c. The file that is the largest

    d. The file with a .ps1 file extension

>> HANDS-ON PROJECTS

Hands-On | Project 18-1   Practicing Using the macOS Desktop

If you're not used to a Mac, the macOS desktop might feel strange compared with Windows, but with a little practice, you'll find all of the essential functions right at your fingertips. Complete the following steps to explore the macOS desktop:

    1. ***Confirm that you have a Wi-Fi connection.*** Look for the Wi-Fi icon in the upper-right corner of the screen. If there is no connection, the icon will look like an empty upside-down triangle (see Figure 18-58). Click the Wi-Fi icon, turn on Wi-Fi if necessary, and connect to the network.

    2. ***Install an app from the App Store.*** Click the App Store icon in the dock; sign in if necessary. Select a free app and install it. A good one to try is Evernote. After installation is complete, leave the App Store window open. Use Finder to open the app.

Source: Apple Inc.

Figure 18-58   Click to turn on Wi-Fi or click Open Network Preferences to set other options

(continues)

3. *Switch between windows with Exposé*. Open two more windows, such as Safari and Maps. On a laptop, swipe down with three fingers to open Exposé. On a desktop, press **control + down arrow**. In Exposé, press **tab** to switch between windows. Press **esc** to return to the desktop.

4. *See all open windows with Mission Control*. On a laptop, swipe up with three fingers to open Mission Control. On a desktop, open **Mission Control** by pressing **control + up arrow** or the **F3 Mission Control** key. Click a window to go to that window on the desktop.

5. *Uninstall the app you installed*. Close all open windows on the desktop. You might need to use the Evernote menu on the menu bar to close it, if that is the app you installed. Next, open Launchpad. On a laptop, use a trackpad gesture; on a desktop, press the **F4 Launchpad** key. In Launchpad, locate the icon for the app you installed. Press and hold the icon. All the icons jiggle. Some apps, such as Mission Control, are embedded in macOS and cannot be uninstalled; others that can be uninstalled have an X on the icon (see Figure 18-59). Click the **X** on the app you want to uninstall, then click **Delete** in the message bubble that appears, as shown in the figure. Click an open space on the screen to make the icons stop jiggling. Click the open space again to return to the desktop.

Source: Apple Inc.

Figure 18-59 Use Launchpad to uninstall an app

18

Hands-On | Project 18-2 Practicing Linux Commands

Practice the Linux commands listed in Table 18-10 using the Ubuntu Server you created earlier. As you do so, you'll examine the directory structure, create a new directory, and put a blank file in it.

(continues)

Task	Command	Description
1	`ls -l`	Lists files and directories in the current directory; in Linux, a directory is treated more like a file than it is in a Windows directory
2	`pwd`	Displays the full path to the current directory; when you first log in to a system, that directory is /home/*username*
3	`mkdir mydir`	Creates a directory named mydir; the directory is created in the current directory
4	`cd mydir`	Goes to the directory you just created in the /home/*username* directory
5	`touch myfile`	Creates a blank file named myfile in the current directory
6	`ls`	Lists the current directory's contents
7	`cd ..`	Moves up one level in the directory tree
8	`cd /etc`	Changes the directory to the /etc directory, where text files are kept for configuring installed programs
9	`ls`	Lists the contents of the /etc directory
10	`cd /home`	Changes the directory to the /home directory
11	`ping 127.0.0.1`	Pings the loopback address; pinging continues until you stop it by pressing Ctrl+C
12	`ifconfig`	Displays TCP/IP configuration data
13	`man ifconfig`	Displays the page from the Linux Manual about the ifconfig command; press q to exit
14	`df -T`	Displays free space on the hard drive and the file system used
15	`exit`	Logs out; the login shell prompt appears, where you can log in again

Table 18-10   Practice using Linux commands

Hands-On | Project 18-3   Changing Permissions for a Ubuntu Directory

Follow these steps to change permissions for your home directory and then create a new user account to test these permissions:

1. Create a new user account named **charlie**. Log in to Ubuntu Server as charlie and try to copy a file to your own home directory. For example, you can use this command to make a new copy of the mymemo file you created earlier:

   cp mymemo mymemo.charlie

   When you do so, permission is denied.

2. Log back in to Ubuntu Server with your own account.

3. To install the chmod command, use this command:

   sudo apt-get install coreutils

4. Use the chmod command to give full read, write, and execute permissions to everyone for your home directory.

5. Log out and log back in to the system as charlie, and verify that the user charlie can now copy a file to your home directory.

Hands-On | Project 18-4   Practicing macOS Commands

To practice using Terminal, repeat the steps in Hands-On Project 18-2 using the macOS Terminal window. (For the df –T command, don't use the –T parameter.) In macOS, the final command of that project, exit, will not produce the same results as it does in Linux. Do research online and answer the following questions about closing the macOS Terminal window:

1. What does the exit command do in the macOS Terminal window?
2. How can you adjust Terminal settings so that the exit command closes the Terminal window?
3. What keyboard shortcut can you use instead to close the Terminal window?

Notes Even if you don't have a Mac computer to use for completing this project, you can still research the answers to the questions above. The information is readily available online.

Hands-On | Project 18-5   Killing a Process in macOS

macOS Terminal is a powerful tool and can be used to kill a hung process or to kill a process you suspect to be malware. First, try to use Force Quit to end the process. If that doesn't work, use Terminal to end the process. Follow these general directions to practice this skill:

1. Once again, install the Evernote app, but don't launch it.
2. Open **Terminal**. Use the following command to list all running processes (the x option displays all processes, even those not started in this shell):

   `ps x`

3. Leave Terminal open. Launch the Evernote app. Return to the Terminal window and list all running processes again. What are the Evernote app process IDs? Of the two process IDs, which one represents the application itself, and which one represents a login item?
4. The pgrep command combines the functionality of ps and grep. Do research online to find the Apple man page for pgrep. What do the –f and –l options do?
5. Confirm the Evernote app's process IDs with the command **pgrep –f –l Evernote**. (Be sure to capitalize the E in Evernote.) Do the process IDs match the information you found earlier?
6. Use Terminal to kill the Evernote app (not the login item).
7. Return to the macOS desktop and uninstall Evernote.

18

Hands-On | Project 18-6   Using Telnet and SSH

Following directions given earlier in the chapter, install Telnet and SSH in Ubuntu Server in your VM. If you get an error, Ubuntu Server might need updating. Commands to update Ubuntu are also given in the chapter.

On your Windows host computer, turn on Telnet Client. Open a command prompt window and remote in to your Ubuntu Server VM using both Telnet and SSH.

>> REAL PROBLEMS, REAL SOLUTIONS

REAL PROBLEM 18-1 Using Google Cloud Platform to Create an Ubuntu VM

Recall that Google Cloud Platform is an example of PaaS that you can use to learn a new operating system or develop apps. To use the service to create an Ubuntu VM, do the following:

1. Go to **cloud.google.com** and click **Free Trial**. You will need to sign in using a Google account. If you don't have an account, you can create one with any valid email address.

2. In the Developers Console, create a new project. Then drill down into **Compute, Compute Engine,** and **VM instances**. Create a VM instance with the latest Ubuntu version (Ubuntu 18.04 LTS at the time of this writing) as the installed OS. Then wait several minutes for Google to create the instance.

3. Note the External IP assigned to the VM instance. Click **SSH**. In the drop-down menu that appears, click **Open in browser window** and remote in to your VM using the SSH utility. The VM opens in a separate window where you can use Ubuntu commands (see Figure 18-60).

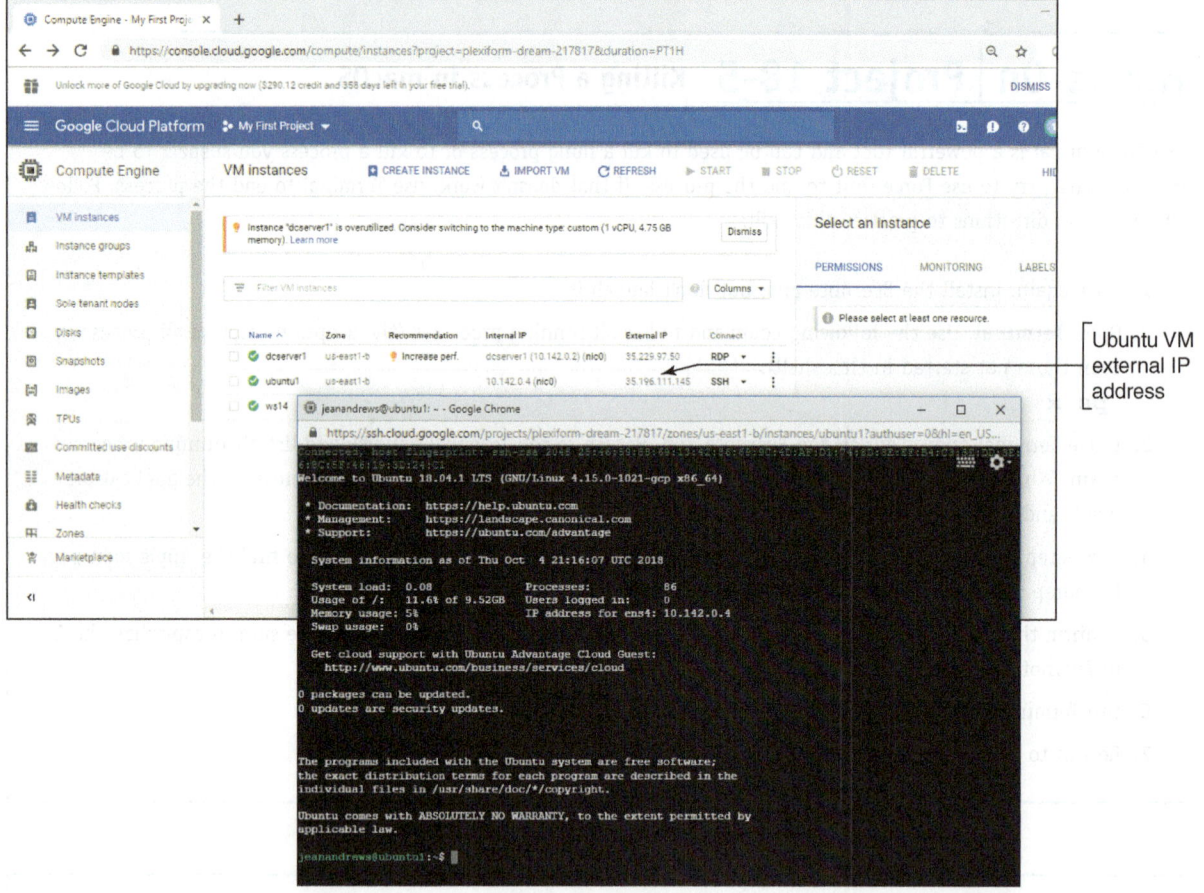

Sources: Google and Canonical Ltd.

Figure 18-60 Google Cloud Platform serves up an Ubuntu VM instance

> **Notes** When you set up your Google Cloud account, your credit card information was required. If you're now done with your Google Cloud 60-day free trial, close your billing account so that your credit card will not be accidentally charged at the end of your free trial period. Click the three-bar icon on the far-left side of the blue Google Cloud Platform menu bar and click **Billing**. Then click **CLOSE BILLING ACCOUNT**.

REAL PROBLEM 18-2 Sharing a Folder to the Network from a Mac Computer and Mapping the Drive on a Windows Computer

In Chapter 16, you shared a folder on the network and mapped a network drive. These tasks can also be done in macOS, which makes it easier to share files between computers of various operating systems. Complete the following steps to set up a network share from a Mac computer:

1. *Create a folder to share.* Use Finder to create a subfolder in the Documents folder and name the new folder **MeetingMinutes**.

2. *Set sharing options.* Open **System Preferences** and click **Sharing**. Select **File Sharing** in the sidebar and make sure it's turned on. Click the **Options** button and make sure that *Share files and folders using SMB* is checked. Under Windows File Sharing, check the box to turn on file sharing for your macOS user account with Windows computers. Enter your macOS user account password if necessary and click **OK**. Click **Done**.

3. *Share the folder.* Under Shared Folders, click **Documents** and click the **+** button below the Shared Folders list. Double-click the **MeetingMinutes** folder, which should then be added to the Shared Folders list. Click **MeetingMinutes** to select it. Under Users, make sure the **Everyone** group is set to **Read Only**. Return to the System Preferences main window.

4. *Enable shared folders for the guest account.* Click **Users & Groups**. Click the lock icon in the lower-left corner of the window so you can make changes to user settings, and sign in. Click the **Guest User** account in the sidebar. Check *Allow guest users to connect to shared folders* and return to the main System Preferences window.

5. *Set a static IP address.* In System Preferences, click **Network** and then click **Advanced**. Click the **TCP/IP** tab. Configure the IPv4 address with a manual address as directed by your instructor. Click **OK**.

6. *Map the network share on a Windows computer.* On your Windows computer, open **File Explorer**, right-click **This PC**, and click **Map network drive**. In the **Map Network Drive** box, enter the Mac's IP address and the name of the shared folder, as shown in Figure 18-61, adjusting the specific details to your situation. Check *Connect using different credentials* and then click **Finish**. When asked for a user name and password, enter **Guest** for the user name and leave the password blank. Explorer should open a new window that shows the mapped drive.

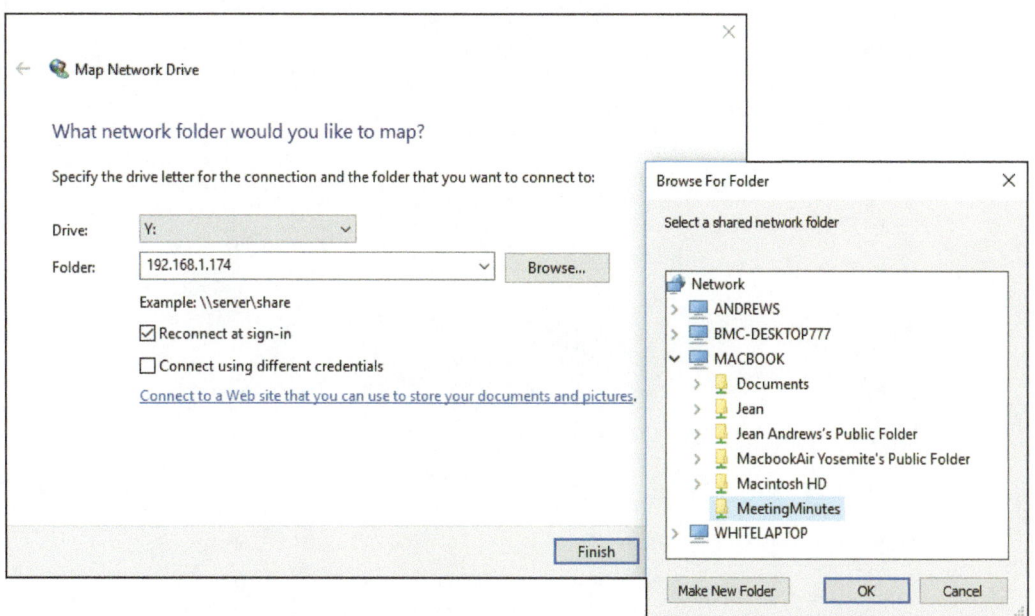

18

Figure 18-61   Folder information includes the IP address of the remote computer and the folder name

7. *Check the network share*. Create a file on the Mac computer and save it to the shared folder. Does it appear in the mapped network drive on the Windows computer? If not, troubleshoot and fix the problem. Create a file on the Windows computer and save it to the shared folder. Does the file appear in the shared folder on the Mac computer? What do you think went wrong? What setting do you need to change so you can add files to the shared folder from the Windows computer? Did it work? If not, troubleshoot and fix the problem.

8. *Change share permissions*. Currently the folder is shared with anyone on the network. This is fine in certain situations, but it's not a best practice for most corporate networks. What changes can you make to restrict the shared folder to a single user? To a group of users?

9. *Create a new user and a new group*. List the steps to create a new user and a new user group on the Mac computer. What types of user accounts are available? What did you name the new user account and the new user group? Add both the new user and your own user account to the new group. Change the share settings on the MeetingMinutes folder so that the new user group has read and write privileges, and the Everyone group has read-only privileges.

10. *Take a screenshot and share it*. With the sharing window showing the new settings, take a screenshot. Press **command + shift + 4** and then select the Sharing window. The screenshot is saved to the desktop. Drag it from the desktop to the shared folder and email the screenshot to your instructor.

REAL PROBLEM 18-3 Preparing for the A+ Core 2 Exam

Chapters 7, 9, and 11 through 18 of this text prepare you for the A+ Core 2 exam. Now that you have studied these chapters, you are ready to make your final review of the A+ Core 2 objectives and sit for the exam. Read through the objectives listed at the beginning of this text and make sure you understand each objective. Your instructor might suggest other exam-prep tasks. You can go to the CompTIA website at *comptia.org* to sign up for the exam or use another method suggested by your instructor. A+ Certification requires that you pass the A+ Core 1 and A+ Core 2 exams.

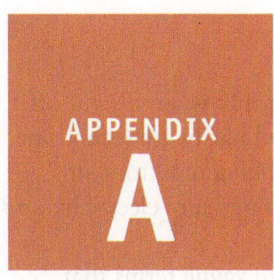

APPENDIX
A

Safety Procedures and Environmental Concerns

T his appendix covers how to stay safe and protect equipment and the environment as you perform the duties of an IT support technician. We begin by understanding the properties and dangers of electricity.

MEASURES AND PROPERTIES OF ELECTRICITY

A+ CORE 2 4.4, 4.5

In our modern world, we take electricity for granted, and we miss it terribly when it's cut off. Nearly everyone depends on it, but few really understand it. A successful hardware technician does not expect to encounter failed processors, fried motherboards, smoking monitors, or frizzed hair. To avoid these excitements, you need to understand how to measure electricity and how to protect computer equipment from its damaging power.

Let's start with the basics. To most people, volts, ohms, joules, watts, and amps are vague terms that simply mean electricity. All these terms can be used to measure some characteristic of electricity, as listed in Table A-1.

Unit	Definition	Computer Example
Volt (for example, 115 V)	Electrical force is measured in volts. The symbol for volts is V.	A power supply steps down the voltage from 115-V house current to levels of 3.3, 5, and 12 V that computer components can use.
Amp or ampere (for example, 1.5 A)	An amp is a measure of electrical current. The symbol for amps is A.	An LCD monitor requires about 5 A to operate. A small laser printer uses about 2 A. An optical drive uses about 1 A.
Ohm (for example, 20 Ω)	An ohm is a measure of resistance to electricity. The symbol for ohm is Ω.	Current can flow in typical computer cables and wires with a resistance of near zero Ω.
Joule (for example, 500 J)	A joule is a measure of work or energy. One joule (pronounced "jewel") is the work required to push an electrical current of 1 A through a resistance of 1 Ω. The symbol for joule is J.	A surge suppressor (see Figure A-1) is rated in joules—the higher the better. The rating determines how much work a device can expend before it can no longer protect the circuit from a power surge.
Watt (for example, 20 W)	A watt is a measure of the total electrical power needed to operate a device. One watt is one joule per second. Watts can be calculated by multiplying volts by amps. The symbol for watts is W.	The power consumption of an LCD computer monitor is rated at about 14 W. A DVD burner uses about 25 W when burning a DVD.

Table A-1 Measures of electricity

Rating is 720 joules

Figure A-1 A surge suppressor protects electrical equipment from power surges and is rated in joules

> **✏ Notes** To learn more about how volts, amps, ohms, joules, and watts measure the properties of electricity, see "Electricity and Multimeters" in the online content that accompanies this text at *cengage.com*. To find out how to access this content, see the Preface to this text.

Now let's look at how electricity gets from one place to another and how it is used in house circuits and computers.

AC AND DC

A+
CORE 2
4.4, 4.5

Electricity can be either AC or DC. Alternating current (AC) goes back and forth, or oscillates, rather than traveling in only one direction. House current in the United States is AC and oscillates 60 times in one second (60 hertz). Voltage in the system is constantly alternating from positive to negative, which causes the electricity to flow first in one direction and then in the other. Voltage alternates from +115 V to −115 V. AC is the most economical way to transmit electricity to our homes and workplaces. By decreasing current and increasing voltage, we can force alternating current to travel great distances. When alternating current reaches its destination, it is made more suitable for driving our electrical devices by decreasing voltage and increasing current.

Direct current (DC) travels in only one direction and is the type of current that most electronic devices require, including computers. A rectifier is a device that converts AC to DC, and an inverter is a device that converts DC to AC. A transformer is a device that changes the ratio of voltage to current. The power supply used in computers is both a rectifier and a transformer.

Large transformers reduce the high voltage on power lines coming to your neighborhood to a lower voltage before the current enters your home. The transformer does not change the amount of power in this closed system; if it decreases voltage, it increases current. The overall power stays constant, but the ratio of voltage to current changes, as illustrated in Figure A-2.

Figure A-2   A transformer keeps power constant but changes the ratio of current to voltage

Again, direct current flows in only one direction. Think of electrical current like a current of water that flows from a state of high pressure to a state of low pressure or rest. Electrical current flows from a high-pressure state (called hot) to a state of rest (called ground or neutral). For a power supply, a power line may be either +5 or −5 volts in one circuit or +12 or −12 volts in another circuit. The positive or negative value is determined by how the circuit is oriented, either on one side of the power output or the other. Several circuits coming from the power supply accommodate different devices with different power requirements.

HOT, NEUTRAL, AND GROUND

A+
CORE 2
4.4, 4.5

AC travels on a hot line from a power station to a building and returns to the power station on a neutral line. When the two lines reach the building and enter an electrical device, such as a lamp, the device controls the flow of electricity between the hot and neutral lines. If an easier path (one with less resistance) is available, the electricity follows that path. This can cause a short, a sudden increase in flow that can also create a sudden increase in temperature—enough to start a fire and injure both people and equipment. Never put yourself in a position where you are the path of least resistance between the hot line and ground!

> ⚡ **Caution**   It's very important that PC components be properly grounded. Never connect a PC to an outlet or use an extension cord that doesn't have the third ground plug. The third line can prevent a short from causing extreme damage. In addition, the bond between the neutral and ground helps eliminate electrical noise (stray electrical signals) within the PC that is sometimes caused by other nearby electrical equipment.

To prevent uncontrolled electricity in a short, the neutral line is grounded. Grounding a line means that the line is connected directly to the earth; in the event of a short, the electricity flows into the earth and not back to the power station. Grounding serves as an escape route for out-of-control electricity because the earth is always capable of accepting a flow of current. With computers, a surge suppressor can be used to protect them and their components against power surges.

> ⚡ **Caution**   Beware of the different uses of black wire. In desktop computers and in DC circuits, black is used for ground, but in home wiring and in AC circuits, black is used for hot!

The neutral line to your house is grounded many times along its way (in fact, at each electrical pole) and is also grounded at the breaker box where the electricity enters your house. You can look at a three-prong plug and see the three lines: hot, neutral, and ground (see Figure A-3).

Figure A-3   A polarized plug showing hot and neutral, and a three-prong plug showing hot, neutral, and ground

> ✎ **Notes** House AC voltage in the United States is about 110–120 V, but know that in other countries, this is not always the case. In many other countries, the standard is 220 V. Outlet styles also vary from one country to the next.

Now that you know about electricity, you will learn how to protect yourself against the dangers of electricity and other factors that might harm you as you work around computers.

PROTECTING YOURSELF

To protect yourself against electrical shock when working with any electrical device, including computers, printers, scanners, and network devices, disconnect the power if you notice a dangerous situation that might lead to electrical shock or fire. When you disconnect the power, do so by pulling on the plug at the AC outlet. To protect the power cord, don't pull on the cord itself. Also, don't just turn off the on/off switch on the device; you need to actually disconnect the power. Note that any of the following can indicate a potential danger:

- ◢ You notice smoke coming from the computer case or the case feels unusually warm.
- ◢ The power cord is frayed or otherwise damaged in any way.
- ◢ Water or other liquid is on the floor around the device or was spilled on it.
- ◢ The device has been exposed to excess moisture.
- ◢ The device has been dropped or you notice physical damage.
- ◢ You smell a strong electronics odor.
- ◢ The power supply or fans are making a whining noise.

SAFELY WORKING INSIDE COMPUTERS, PRINTERS, AND OTHER ELECTRICAL DEVICES

To stay safe, always do the following before working inside computers, printers, and other electrical devices:

- ◢ *Remove jewelry.* Remove any jewelry that might come in contact with components. Jewelry is commonly made of metal and might conduct electricity if it touches a component. It can also get caught in cables and cords inside computer cases.
- ◢ *Power down the system and unplug it.* For a computer, unplug the power, monitor, mouse, and keyboard cables, unplug any other peripherals or cables attached, and move them out of your way.
- ◢ *For a computer, press and hold down the power button for a moment.* After you unplug the computer, press the power button for about three seconds to completely drain the power supply. Sometimes when you do so, you'll hear the fans quickly start and go off as residual power is drained. Only then is it safe to work inside the case.

ELECTRICAL FIRE SAFETY

Never use water to put out a fire fueled by electricity because water is a conductor and you might get a severe electrical shock. A computer lab needs a fire extinguisher that is rated to put out electrical fires. Fire extinguishers are rated by the type of fires they put out:

- ◢ Class A extinguishers can use water to put out fires caused by wood, paper, and other combustibles.
- ◢ Class B extinguishers can put out fires caused by liquids such as gasoline, kerosene, and oil.
- ◢ Class C fire extinguishers use nonconductive chemicals to put out a fire caused by electricity. See Figure A-4.

A

Class C

Figure A-4 A Class C fire extinguisher is rated to put out electrical fires

PROPER USE OF CLEANING PADS AND SOLUTIONS

A+
CORE 2
4.4, 4.5

As a support technician, you'll find yourself collecting different cleaning solutions and cleaning pads to clean a variety of devices, including the mouse and keyboard, CDs, DVDs, Blu-ray discs and their drives, and monitors. Figure A-5 shows a few of these products. For example, the contact cleaner in the figure is used to clean the contacts on the edge connectors of expansion cards; a good cleaning can solve a problem with a faulty connection.

Figure A-5 Cleaning solutions and pads

Most of these cleaning solutions contain flammable and poisonous materials. Take care when using them so that they don't get on your skin or in your eyes. To find out what to do if you are accidentally exposed to a dangerous solution, look at the instructions printed on the can or check out the material safety data sheet (see Figure A-6). A material safety data sheet (MSDS) explains how to properly handle substances such as chemical solvents and how to dispose of them.

An MSDS includes information such as physical data, toxicity, health effects, first aid, storage, shipping, disposal, and spill procedures. The MSDS comes packaged with the chemical; you can also order one from the manufacturer or find one on the Internet (see *ilpi.com/msds*).

Figure A-6 Each chemical you use should have a material safety data sheet available

⭐ **A+ Exam Tip** The A+ Core 2 exam expects you to know how to use MSDS documentation to dispose of chemicals and help protect the environment. You also need to know that you must follow all local government regulations when disposing of chemicals and other materials dangerous to the environment.

If you have an accident with cleaning solutions or other dangerous products, your company or organization might require you to report the accident and/or fill out an incident report. Check with your organization to find out how to report these types of incidents.

MANAGING CABLES

People can trip over cables or cords left on the floor, so be careful that cables are in a safe place. If you must run a cable across a path or where someone sits, use a cable or cord cover that can be nailed or screwed to the floor. Don't leave loose cables or cords in a traffic area where people can trip over them; such objects are called trip hazards.

LIFTING HEAVY OBJECTS

Back injury caused by lifting heavy objects is one of the most common work injuries. Whenever possible, put heavy objects, such as a large laser printer, on a cart to move them. If you do need to lift a heavy object, follow these guidelines to keep from injuring your back:

1. Look at the object and decide which side of it to face so that the load will be the most balanced when you lift it.

2. Stand close to the object with your feet apart.

3. Keeping your back straight, bend your knees and grip the load.

A

4. Lift with your legs, arms, and shoulders, not with your back or stomach.

5. Keep the load close to your body and avoid twisting your body while you're holding the load.

6. To put the object down, keep your back as straight as you can and lower the object by bending your knees.

Don't try to lift an object that is too heavy for you. Because there are no exact guidelines for when heavy is too heavy, use your best judgment as to when to ask for help.

SAFETY GOGGLES AND AIR FILTER MASK

If you work in a factory environment where flying fragments, chips, or other particles are about, your employer might require that you wear safety goggles to protect your eyes. In addition, if the air is filled with dust or other contaminants, your employer might require you to wear an air-purifying respirator, commonly called an air filter mask, which filters out the dust and other contaminants. If safety goggles or a mask is required, your employer is responsible for providing one that is appropriate for your work environment.

PROTECTING THE EQUIPMENT

As you learn to troubleshoot and solve computer problems, you gradually begin to realize that many of them could have been avoided by good computer maintenance, which includes protecting the computer against environmental factors such as humidity, dust, and out-of-control electricity.

PROTECTING THE EQUIPMENT AGAINST STATIC ELECTRICITY OR ESD

Suppose you come indoors on a cold day, pick up a comb, and touch your hair. Sparks fly! What happened? Static electricity caused the sparks. Electrostatic discharge (ESD), commonly known as static electricity, is an electrical charge at rest. When you came indoors, this charge built up on your hair and had no place to go. An ungrounded conductor (such as wire that is not touching another wire) or a nonconductive surface (such as your hair) holds a charge until it is released. When two objects with dissimilar electrical charges touch, electricity passes between them until the dissimilar charges become equal.

To see static charges equalizing, turn off the lights in a room, scuff your feet on the carpet, and touch another person. Occasionally, you can see and feel the charge in your fingers. If you can feel the charge, you discharged at least 1500 volts of static electricity. If you hear the discharge, you released at least 6000 volts. If you see the discharge, you released at least 8000 volts of ESD. A charge of only 10 volts can damage electronic components! *You can touch a chip on an expansion card or motherboard, damage the chip with ESD, and never feel, hear, or see the electrical discharge.*

ESD can cause two types of damage in an electronic component: catastrophic failure and upset failure. A catastrophic failure destroys the component beyond use. An upset failure damages the component so that it does not perform well, even though it may still function to some degree. Upset failures are more difficult to detect because they are not consistent and not easily observed. Both types of failures permanently affect the device. Components are easily damaged by ESD, but because the damage might not show up for weeks or months, a technician is likely to get careless and not realize the damage he or she is doing.

Unless you are measuring power levels with a multimeter or power supply tester, *never* touch a component or cable inside a computer case while the power is on. The electrical voltage is not enough to seriously hurt you but is more than enough to permanently damage the component.

Before touching or handling a component (for example, a hard drive, motherboard, expansion card, processor, or memory modules), protect it against ESD by always grounding yourself first. You can ground yourself and the computer parts by using one or more of the following static control devices or methods:

▲ *ESD strap*. An ESD strap, also called a ground bracelet, antistatic wrist strap, or ESD bracelet, is a strap you wear around your wrist. The strap has a cord attached with an alligator clip on the end. Attach the clip to the computer case you're working on, as shown in Figure A-7. Any static electricity between you and the case will be discharged. Therefore, as you work inside the case, you will not damage the components with static electricity. The bracelet also contains a resistor that prevents electricity from harming you.

Figure A-7   A ground bracelet, which protects computer components from ESD, can clip to the side of the computer case and eliminate ESD between you and the case

⚡ **Caution**   When working on a laser printer, *don't* wear the ESD strap because you don't want to be the ground for these high-voltage devices.

▲ *Ground mats*. A ground mat, also called an ESD mat, dissipates ESD and is commonly used by bench technicians (also called depot technicians) who repair and assemble computers at their workbenches or in an assembly line. Ground mats have a connector in one corner that you can use to connect the mat to the ground (see Figure A-8). If you lift a component off the mat, it is no longer grounded and is susceptible to ESD, so it's important to use an ESD strap with a ground mat.

A

Figure A-8 An ESD mat dissipates ESD and should be connected to the ground

▲ *Static shielding bags.* New components come shipped in static shielding bags, also called antistatic bags. These bags are a type of Faraday cage, named after Michael Faraday, who built the first cage in 1836. A Faraday cage is any device that protects against an electromagnetic field. Save the bags to store other devices that belong in a computer but are not currently installed. As you work on a computer, know that a device is not protected from ESD if you place it on top of the bag; the protection is inside the bag (see Figure A-9).

Figure A-9 An antistatic bag helps protect components from ESD

> ⚡ **Caution** An older CRT monitor can also damage components with ESD. Don't place or store expansion cards on top of or next to a CRT monitor, which can discharge as much as 29,000 volts onto the screen.

The best way to guard against ESD is to use an ESD strap together with a ground mat. Consider an ESD strap essential equipment when working on a computer. However, if you are in a situation in which you must work without one, touch the computer case or the power supply before you touch a component in the case, which is called self-grounding. Self-grounding dissipates any charge between you and whatever you touch. Here are some rules that can help protect computer parts against ESD:

▲ When passing a circuit board, memory module, or other sensitive component to another person, ground yourself and then touch the other person before you pass the component.

▲ Leave components inside their protective bags until you are ready to use them.

▲ Work on hard floors, not carpet, or use antistatic spray on the carpet.

▲ Don't work on a computer if you or the computer has just come in from the cold because there is more danger of ESD when the atmosphere is cold and dry.

▲ When unpacking hardware or software, remove the packing tape and cellophane from the work area as soon as possible because these materials attract ESD.

▲ Keep components away from your hair and clothing.

> ★ **A+ Exam Tip** The A+ Core 2 exam emphasizes that you should know how to protect computer equipment as you work on it, including how to protect components against damage from ESD.

PHYSICALLY PROTECTING YOUR EQUIPMENT FROM THE ENVIRONMENT

A+ CORE 2 4.4, 4.5 When you protect equipment from ongoing problems with the environment, you are likely to have fewer problems later, and you will have less troubleshooting and repair to do. Here is how you can physically protect a computer:

▲ *Protect a computer against dust and other airborne particles.* When a computer must sit in a dusty environment, around those who smoke, or where pets might leave hair, you can:

  ▲ Use a plastic keyboard cover to protect the keyboard. When the computer is turned off, protect the entire system with a cover or enclosure.

  ▲ Install air filters over the front or side vents of the case where air flows in. Put your hand over the case of a running computer to feel where the air flows in. For most systems, air flows in from the front vents or vents on the side of the case that is near the processor cooler. The air filter shown in Figure A-10 has magnets that hold the filter to the case when screw holes are not available.

> ✎ **Notes** When working at a customer site, be sure to clean up any mess you created by blowing dust out of a computer case or keyboard.

  ▲ Use compressed air or an antistatic vacuum (see Figure A-11) to remove dust from inside the case, if you have the case cover open. Figure A-12 shows a case fan that jammed because of dust and caused a system to overheat. While you're cleaning up dust, don't forget to blow or vacuum out the keyboard.

Figure A-10 This air filter is designed to fit over a case fan, power supply fan, or panel vent on the case

A

Figure A-11 An antistatic vacuum is designed to work inside sensitive electronic equipment such as computers and printers

Figure A-12 This dust-jammed case fan caused a system to overheat

▲ *Allow for good ventilation inside and outside the system.* Proper air circulation is essential to keeping a system cool. Don't block air vents on the front and rear of the computer case or on the monitor. Inside the case, make sure cables are tied up and out of the way so as to allow for airflow and not obstruct fans from turning. Put covers on expansion slot openings at the rear of the case and put faceplates over empty bays on the front of the case. Don't set a tower case directly on thick carpet because the air vent on the bottom front of the case can be blocked. If you are concerned about overheating, monitor temperatures inside and outside the case.

★ **A+ Exam Tip** The A+ Core 2 exam expects you to know how to keep computers and monitors well ventilated and to use protective enclosures and air filters to protect the equipment from airborne particles.

▲ *High temperatures and humidity can be dangerous for hard drives.* I once worked in a basement with PCs, and hard drives failed much too often. After we installed dehumidifiers, the hard drives became more reliable. If you suspect a problem with room humidity, you can monitor it using a hygrometer. High temperatures can also damage computer equipment, and you should take precautions not to allow a computer to overheat.

> ✎ **Notes** A server room where computers stay and people don't stay for long hours is usually set to balance what is good for the equipment and to conserve energy. Low temperatures and moderate humidity are best for the equipment, although no set standards exist for either. Temperatures might be set from 65 to 70 degrees F, and humidity between 30 percent and 50 percent, although some companies keep their server rooms at 80 degrees F to conserve energy. A data center where both computers and people stay is usually kept at a comfortable temperature and humidity for humans.

▲ *Protect electrical equipment from power surges.* Lightning and other electrical power surges can destroy computers and other electrical equipment. If a house or office building does not have surge protection equipment installed at the breaker box, be sure to install a protective device at each computer. The least expensive device is a power strip that is also a surge suppressor, although you might want to use an uninterruptible power supply for added protection.

Lightning can also get to your equipment across network cabling coming in through an Internet connection. To protect against lightning, use a surge suppressor such as the one shown in Figure A-13 in line between the ISP device (for example, a DSL modem or cable modem) and the computer or home router to protect it from spikes across the network cables. Notice the cord on the surge suppressor, which connects it to ground.

Figure A-13 A surge protector by APC for Ethernet lines

An **uninterruptible power supply (UPS)** is a device that raises the voltage when it drops during **brownouts** or **sags** (temporary voltage reductions). A UPS also does double duty as a surge suppressor to protect the system against power surges or spikes. In addition, a UPS can serve as a battery backup to provide enough power for a brief time during a total blackout so you can save your work and shut down the system. A UPS is not as essential for a laptop computer as it is for a desktop because a laptop has a battery that can sustain it during a blackout. Also, consider using a UPS to protect power to a router, switch, or other essential network device.

A

A common UPS device is a rather heavy box that plugs into an AC outlet and provides one or more electrical outlets and perhaps Ethernet and USB ports (see Figure A-14). It has an on/off switch, requires no maintenance, and is very simple to install. Use it to provide uninterruptible power to your desktop computer, monitor, and essential network devices. It's best not to connect a UPS to nonessential devices such as a laser printer or scanner. The UPS shown in Figure A-14 has a USB port so that a computer can monitor power management and network ports to block harmful voltage on the network.

Source: dell.com

Figure A-14   The front and rear of an uninterruptible power supply (UPS)

> 🖉 **Notes** If a power outage occurs and you don't have a reliable power conditioner installed at the breaker box in your house or building, unplug all power cords to the computers, printers, monitors, and peripherals. Sometimes when the power returns, sudden spikes are accompanied by another brief outage. You don't want to subject your equipment to these surges. When buying a surge suppressor, look for one that guarantees against damage from lightning and that reimburses for equipment destroyed while the surge suppressor is in use.

PROTECTING THE ENVIRONMENT

**A+
CORE 2
4.4, 4.5**

IT support technicians need to be aware that they can do damage to the environment if they dispose of used computer equipment improperly. As a support technician, one day you're sure to face an assortment of useless equipment and consumables (see Figure A-15). Before you decide to trash it all, take a moment and ask yourself if some of the equipment can be donated or at least recycled. Think about fixing up an old computer and donating it to an underprivileged middle school student. If you don't have the time for that, consider donating to the local computer repair class. The class can fix up such computers as a class project and donate them to young students.

Figure A-15 Keep, trash, recycle, or donate?

When disposing of any type of equipment or consumables, make sure to comply with local government environmental regulations. Table A-2 lists some items and how to dispose of them.

Parts	How to Dispose of Them
Alkaline batteries, including AAA, AA, A, C, D, and 9-volt	Dispose of these batteries in the regular trash. First check to see if there are recycling facilities in your area.
Button batteries used in digital cameras and other small equipment; battery packs used in notebooks	These batteries can contain silver oxide, mercury, lithium, or cadmium and are considered toxic waste that require special toxic waste handling. Dispose of them by returning them to the original dealer or by taking them to a recycling center. To recycle, pack them separately from other items. If you don't have a recycling center nearby, contact your county for local disposal regulations.
Cell phones and tablets	Most cell phone carriers will buy back old cell phones to recycle or refurbish. If you can restore the device to factory state, donate it to charity. Before tossing it in the trash, check with local county or environmental officials for laws and regulations in your area that cover proper disposal of the item. E-waste recycling companies, such as Eco-Cell (*eco-cell.com*), receive cell phones for resale or recycling.
Laser printer toner cartridges	Return these to the manufacturer or dealer to be recycled.
Ink-jet printer cartridges, cell phones, tablets, computer cases, power supplies, other computer parts, monitors, chemical solvents, and their containers	Check with local county or environmental officials for laws and regulations in your area that cover proper disposal of these items. The county might have a recycling center that will receive the items. Discharge a CRT monitor before disposing of it. See the MSDS documents for chemicals to know how to dispose of them.
Storage media such as hard drives, CDs, DVDs, and BDs	Do physical damage to the device so it is not possible for sensitive data to be stolen. Then the device can be recycled or put in the trash. Your organization might have to meet legal requirements to destroy data. If so, make sure you understand these requirements and how to comply with them.

Table A-2 Computer parts and how to dispose of them

★ **A+ Exam Tip** The A+ Core 2 exam expects you to know how to follow environmental guidelines to dispose of batteries, laser printer toner, cell phones, tablets, CRT monitors, chemical solvents, and containers. If you're not certain how to dispose of a product, see its MSDS document.

A

Be sure a CRT monitor is discharged before you dispose of it. Most CRT monitors are designed to discharge after sitting unplugged for 60 minutes. They can be manually discharged by using a high-voltage probe with the monitor case opened. Ask a technician who's trained to service monitors to do this for you.

> **✎ Notes** Go to *youtube.com* and search on "discharge a CRT monitor" to see some interesting videos that demonstrate the charge inside a monitor long after it is turned off and unplugged. As for proper procedures, I'm not endorsing all these videos; just watch for fun.

>> KEY TERMS

For explanations of key terms, see the Glossary for this text.

air filter mask	electrostatic discharge	material safety data sheet	surge suppressor
alternating current (AC)	(ESD)	(MSDS)	transformer
amp	ESD mat	ohm	trip hazard
antistatic bag	ESD strap	rectifier	uninterruptible power
antistatic wrist strap	ground bracelet	safety goggles	supply (UPS)
brownout	ground mat	sag	volt
Class C fire extinguisher	inverter	self-grounding	watt
direct current (DC)	joule	static electricity	

>> HANDS-ON PROJECTS

Hands-On | Project A-1   Practicing Handling Computer Components

Working with a partner, you'll need some computer parts and the antistatic tools you learned about in this appendix. Practice touching and picking up the parts and passing them between you. As you do so, follow the rules to protect the parts against ESD. Have a third person watch as you work and point out any ways you might have exposed a part to ESD. As you work, be careful not to touch components on circuit boards or the gold "fingers" on the edge connector of an expansion card. When you are finished, store the parts in antistatic bags.

Hands-On | Project A-2   Safely Cleaning Computer Equipment

Practice some preventive maintenance tasks by following these steps to clean a computer:

1. Shut down the computer and unplug it. Press the power button to drain power.

2. Clean the keyboard, monitor, and mouse. For a wheel mouse, remove the ball and clean the wheels. Clean the outside of the computer case. Don't forget to clean the mouse pad.

3. Open the case and use a ground bracelet to clean the dust from the case. Make sure all fans move freely.

4. Verify that the cables are out of the way of airflow. Use cable ties as necessary.

5. Check that each expansion card and memory module is securely seated in its slot.

6. Power up the system and make sure everything is working.

7. Clean up around your work area. If you left dust on the floor as you blew it out of the computer case, be sure to clean it up.

Hands-On | Project A-3   Researching Disposal Rules

Research the laws and regulations in your community concerning the disposal of batteries and old computer parts. Answer these questions:

1. How do you properly dispose of a monitor in your community?

2. How do you properly dispose of a battery pack used by a notebook computer?

3. How do you properly dispose of a large box of assorted computer parts, including hard drives, optical drives, computer cases, and circuit boards?

A

Entry Points for Startup Processes

This appendix contains a summary of the entry points that can affect Windows 10/8/7 startup. The entry points include startup folders, Group Policy folders, the Scheduled Tasks folder, and registry keys. To see all the subfolders listed in this appendix, use File Explorer Options or Folder Options in Control Panel to unhide folders that don't normally display in File Explorer or Windows Explorer.

Programs and shortcuts to programs are stored in these startup folders:

▲ C:\Users*username*\AppData\Roaming\Microsoft\Windows\Start Menu\Programs\Startup
▲ C:\ProgramData\Microsoft\Windows\Start Menu\Programs\Startup

Startup and shutdown scripts used by Group Policy are stored in these folders:

▲ C:\Windows\System32\GroupPolicy\Machine\Scripts\Startup
▲ C:\Windows\System32\GroupPolicy\Machine\Scripts\Shutdown
▲ C:\Windows\System32\GroupPolicy\User\Scripts\Logon
▲ C:\Windows\System32\GroupPolicy\User\Scripts\Logoff

Scheduled tasks are stored in this folder:

▲ C:\Windows\System32\Tasks

To see a list of scheduled tasks, enter the **schtasks** command in a command prompt window.

These keys cause an entry to run once and only once at startup:

▲ HKLM\Software\Microsoft\Windows\CurrentVersion\RunOnce
▲ HKLM\Software\Microsoft\Windows\CurrentVersion\RunServiceOnce
▲ HKLM\Software\Microsoft\Windows\CurrentVersion\RunServicesOnce
▲ HKCU\Software\Microsoft\Windows\CurrentVersion\RunOnce

Group Policy places entries in the following keys to affect startup:

▲ HKCU\Software\Microsoft\Windows\CurrentVersion\Policies\Explorer\Run
▲ HKLM\Software\Microsoft\Windows\CurrentVersion\Policies\Explorer\Run

Windows loads many DLL programs from the following key, which is sometimes used by malicious software. Don't delete one unless you know it's causing a problem:

▲ HKLM\Software\Microsoft\Windows\CurrentVersion\ShellServiceObjectDelayLoad

Entries in the keys listed next apply to all users and hold legitimate startup entries. Don't delete an entry unless you suspect it to be bad:

▲ HKLM\Software\Microsoft\Windows\CurrentVersion\Run
▲ HKCU\Software\Microsoft\Windows NT\CurrentVersion\Windows
▲ HKCU\Software\Microsoft\Windows NT\CurrentVersion\Windows\Run
▲ HKCU\Software\Microsoft\Windows\CurrentVersion\Run

These keys and their subkeys contain entries pertaining to background services that are sometimes launched at startup:

▲ HKLM\Software\Microsoft\Windows\CurrentVersion\RunService
▲ HKLM\Software\Microsoft\Windows\CurrentVersion\RunServices

The following key contains a value named BootExecute, which is normally set to autochk. It causes the system to run a type of Chkdsk program to check for hard drive integrity if it was previously shut down improperly. Sometimes another program adds itself to this value, causing a problem. The Chkntfs utility can be used to exclude volumes from being checked by autochk. For more information about this situation, search for "CHKNTFS.EXE: What You Can Use It For" at *support.microsoft.com*.

▲ HKLM\System\CurrentControlSet\Control\Session Manager

Here is an assorted list of registry keys that have all been known to cause various problems at startup. Remember, before you delete a program entry from one of these keys, research the program file name so that you won't accidentally delete something you want to keep:

- HKCU\Software\Microsoft\Command
- HKCU\Software\Microsoft\Command Processor\AutoRun
- HKCU\Software\Microsoft\Windows\CurrentVersion\RunOnce\Setup
- HKCU\Software\Microsoft\Windows NT\CurrentVersion\Windows\load
- HKLM\Software\Microsoft\Windows NT\CurrentVersion\Windows\AppInit_DLLs
- HKLM\Software\Microsoft\Windows NT\CurrentVersion\Winlogon\System
- HKLM\Software\Microsoft\Windows NT\CurrentVersion\Winlogon\Us
- HKCR\batfile\shell\open\command
- HKCR\comfile\shell\open\command
- HKCR\exefile\shell\open\command
- HKCR\htafile\shell\open\command
- HKCR\piffile\shell\open\command
- HKCR\scrfile\shell\open\command

Finally, check out the subkeys in the following key; they apply to 32-bit programs installed in a 64-bit version of Windows:

- HKLM\Software\Wow6432Node

Other ways in which processes can be launched at startup:

- Services can be set to launch at startup. To manage services, use the Services console (services.msc).
- Device drivers are launched at startup. For a listing of installed devices, use Device Manager (devmgmt.msc) or the System Information utility (msinfo32.exe).

B

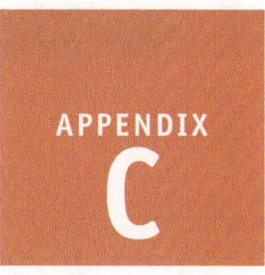

CompTIA Acronyms

CompTIA provides a list of acronyms that you need to know before you sit for the A+ exams. You can download the list from the CompTIA website at *comptia.org*. The list is included here for your convenience. However, CompTIA occasionally updates the list, so be sure to check the CompTIA website for the latest version.

Acronym	Spelled Out
AC	Alternating Current
ACL	Access Control List
ACPI	Advanced Configuration Power Interface
ADF	Automatic Document Feeder
ADSL	Asymmetrical Digital Subscriber Line
AES	Advanced Encryption Standard
AHCI	Advanced Host Controller Interface
AP	Access Point
APIPA	Automatic Private Internet Protocol Addressing
APM	Advanced Power Management
ARP	Address Resolution Protocol
ASR	Automated System Recovery
ATA	Advanced Technology Attachment
ATAPI	Advanced Technology Attachment Packet Interface
ATM	Asynchronous Transfer Mode
ATX	Advanced Technology Extended
AUP	Acceptable Use Policy
A/V	Audio Video
BD-R	Blu-ray Disc Recordable
BD-RE	Blu-ray Disc Rewritable
BIOS	Basic Input/Output System
BNC	Bayonet-Neill-Concelman
BSOD	Blue Screen of Death
BYOD	Bring Your Own Device
CAD	Computer-Aided Design
CAPTCHA	Completely Automated Public Turing test to tell Computers and Humans Apart
CD	Compact Disc
CD-ROM	Compact Disc-Read-Only Memory
CD-RW	Compact Disc-Rewritable
CDFS	Compact Disc File System
CERT	Computer Emergency Response Team
CFS	Central File System, Common File System, or Command File System
CGA	Computer Graphics and Applications
CIDR	Classless Interdomain Routing
CIFS	Common Internet File System
CMOS	Complementary Metal-Oxide Semiconductor
CNR	Communications and Networking Riser
COMx	Communication port (x = port number)
CPU	Central Processing Unit
CRT	Cathode-Ray Tube
DaaS	Data as a Service
DAC	Discretionary Access Control

Acronym	Spelled Out
DB-25	Serial Communications D-Shell Connector, 25 pins
DB-9	Serial Communications D-Shell Connector, 9 pins
DBaaS	Database as a Service
DC	Direct Current
DDoS	Distributed Denial of Service
DDR	Double Data Rate
DDR RAM	Double Data Rate Random Access Memory
DFS	Distributed File System
DHCP	Dynamic Host Configuration Protocol
DIMM	Dual Inline Memory Module
DIN	Deutsche Industrie Norm
DLP	Digital Light Processing or Data Loss Prevention
DLT	Digital Linear Tape
DMA	Direct Memory Access
DMZ	Demilitarized Zone
DNS	Domain Name Service or Domain Name Server
DoS	Denial of Service
DRAM	Dynamic Random Access Memory
DRM	Digital Rights Management
DSL	Digital Subscriber Line
DVD	Digital Versatile Disc
DVD-R	Digital Versatile Disc-Recordable
DVD-RAM	Digital Versatile Disc-Random Access Memory
DVD-ROM	Digital Versatile Disc-Read Only Memory
DVD-RW	Digital Versatile Disc-Rewritable
DVI	Digital Visual Interface
DVI-D	Digital Visual Interface–Digital
ECC	Error Correcting Code
ECP	Extended Capabilities Port
EEPROM	Electrically Erasable Programmable Read-Only Memory
EFS	Encrypting File System
EIDE	Enhanced Integrated Drive Electronics
EMI	Electromagnetic Interference
EMP	Electromagnetic Pulse
EPP	Enhanced Parallel Port
EPROM	Erasable Programmable Read-Only Memory
ERD	Emergency Repair Disk
eSATA	External Serial Advanced Technology Attachment
ESD	Electrostatic Discharge
EULA	End User License Agreement
EVGA	Extended Video Graphics Adapter/Array
exFAT	Extended File Allocation Table

C

Acronym	Spelled Out
Ext2	Second Extended File System
FAT	File Allocation Table
FAT12	12-bit File Allocation Table
FAT16	16-bit File Allocation Table
FAT32	32-bit File Allocation Table
FDD	Floppy Disk Drive
FPM	Fast Page Mode
FQDN	Fully Qualified Domain Name
FSB	Front-Side Bus
FTP	File Transfer Protocol
GDDR	Graphics Double Data Rate
GDI	Graphics Device Interface
GPS	Global Positioning System
GPT	GUID Partition Table
GPU	Graphics Processing Unit
GSM	Global System for Mobile Communications
GUI	Graphical User Interface
GUID	Globally Unique Identifier
HAL	Hardware Abstraction Layer
HAV	Hardware Assisted Virtualization
HCL	Hardware Compatibility List
HDCP	High-Bandwidth Digital Content Protection
HDD	Hard Disk Drive
HDMI	High Definition Media Interface
HIPS	Host Intrusion Prevention System
HPFS	High Performance File System
HTML	Hypertext Markup Language
HTPC	Home Theater PC
HTTP	Hypertext Transfer Protocol
HTTPS	Hypertext Transfer Protocol Secure
I/O	Input/Output
IaaS	Infrastructure as a Service
ICMP	Internet Control Message Protocol
ICR	Intelligent Character Recognition
IDE	Integrated Drive Electronics
IDS	Intrusion Detection System
IEEE	Institute of Electrical and Electronics Engineers
IIS	Internet Information Services
IMAP	Internet Mail Access Protocol
IMEI	International Mobile Equipment Identity
IMSI	International Mobile Subscriber Identity
IP	Internet Protocol

Acronym	Spelled Out
IPConfig	Internet Protocol Configuration
IPP	Internet Printing Protocol
IPS	Intrusion Prevention System
IPSec	Internet Protocol Security
IR	Infrared
IrDA	Infrared Data Association
IRP	Incident Response Plan
IRQ	Interrupt Request
ISA	Industry Standard Architecture
ISDN	Integrated Services Digital Network
ISO	International Organization for Standardization
ISP	Internet Service Provider
JBOD	Just a Bunch of Disks
KB	Knowledge Base
KVM	Kernel-based Virtual Machine
KVM	Keyboard-Video-Mouse
LAN	Local Area Network
LBA	Logical Block Addressing
LC	Lucent Connector
LCD	Liquid Crystal Display
LDAP	Lightweight Directory Access Protocol
LED	Light-Emitting Diode
LPD/LPR	Line Printer Daemon/Line Printer Remote
LPT	Line Printer Terminal
LVD	Low Voltage Differential
MAC	Media Access Control or Mandatory Access Control
MAN	Metropolitan Area Network
MAPI	Messaging Application Programming Interface
mATX	Micro Advanced Technology Extended
MAU	Media Access Unit or Media Attachment Unit
MBR	Master Boot Record
MBSA	Microsoft Baseline Security Analyzer
MDM	Mobile Device Management
MFA	Multifactor Authentication
MFD	Multifunction Device
MFP	Multifunction Product
MicroDIMM	Micro Dual Inline Memory Module
MIDI	Musical Instrument Digital Interface
MIME	Multipurpose Internet Mail Extension
MIMO	Multiple Input Multiple Output
MMC	Microsoft Management Console
MP3	Moving Picture Experts Group Layer 3 Audio

C

Acronym	Spelled Out
MP4	Moving Picture Experts Group Layer 4
MPEG	Moving Picture Experts Group
MSConfig	Microsoft Configuration
MSDS	Material Safety Data Sheet
MT-RJ	Mechanical Transfer Registered Jack
MUI	Multilingual User Interface
NaaS	Network as a Service
NAC	Network Access Control
NAS	Network-Attached Storage
NAT	Network Address Translation
NetBEUI	Networked Basic Input/Output System Extended User Interface
NetBIOS	Networked Basic Input/Output System
NFC	Near Field Communication
NFS	Network File System
NIC	Network Interface Card
NiCd	Nickel Cadmium
NiMH	Nickel Metal Hydride
NLX	New Low-profile Extended
NNTP	Network News Transfer Protocol
NTFS	New Technology File System
NTLDR	New Technology Loader
NTP	Network Time Protocol
NTSC	National Transmission Standards Committee
NVMe	Non-volatile Memory Express
OCR	Optical Character Recognition
OEM	Original Equipment Manufacturer
OLED	Organic Light-Emitting Diode
OS	Operating System
PaaS	Platform as a Service
PAL	Phase Alternating Line
PAN	Personal Area Network
PAT	Port Address Translation
PC	Personal Computer
PCI	Payment Card Industry
PCI	Peripheral Component Interconnect
PCIe	Peripheral Component Interconnect Express
PCIX	Peripheral Component Interconnect Extended
PCL	Printer Control Language
PCMCIA	Personal Computer Memory Card International Association
PE	Preinstallation Environment
PGA	Pin Grid Array
PGA2	Pin Grid Array 2

Acronym	Spelled Out
PGP	Pretty Good Protection
PHI	Personal Health Information
PII	Personally Identifiable Information
PIN	Personal Identification Number
PKI	Public Key Infrastructure
PnP	Plug and Play
PoE	Power over Ethernet
POP3	Post Office Protocol 3
PoS	Point of Sale
POST	Power-On Self-Test
POTS	Plain Old Telephone Service
PPM	Pages Per Minute
PPP	Point-to-Point Protocol
PPTP	Point-to-Point Tunneling Protocol
PRI	Primary Rate Interface
PROM	Programmable Read-Only Memory
PS/2	Personal System/2 connector
PSTN	Public Switched Telephone Network
PSU	Power Supply Unit
PVA	Patterned Vertical Alignment
PVC	Permanent Virtual Circuit
PXE	Preboot Execution Environment
QoS	Quality of Service
RADIUS	Remote Authentication Dial-In User Server
RAID	Redundant Array of Independent (or Inexpensive) Disks
RAM	Random Access Memory
RAS	Remote Access Service
RDP	Remote Desktop Protocol
RF	Radio Frequency
RFI	Radio Frequency Interference
RFID	Radio Frequency Identification
RGB	Red Green Blue
RIP	Routing Information Protocol
RIS	Remote Installation Service
RISC	Reduced Instruction Set Computer
RJ-11	Registered Jack Function 11
RJ-45	Registered Jack Function 45
RMA	Returned Materials Authorization
ROM	Read-Only Memory
RPO	Recovery Point Objective
RTC	Real-Time Clock
RTO	Recovery Time Objective

C

Acronym	Spelled Out
Saas	Software as a Service
SAN	Storage Area Network
SAS	Serial Attached SCSI
SATA	Serial Advanced Technology Attachment
SC	Subscription Channel
SCP	Secure Copy Protection
SCSI	Small Computer System Interface
SCSI ID	Small Computer System Interface Identifier
SD card	Secure Digital Card
SEC	Single Edge Connector
SFC	System File Checker
SFF	Small Form Factor
SFTP	Secure File Transfer Protocol
SIM	Subscriber Identity Module
SIMM	Single In-Line Memory Module
SLI	Scalable Link Interface, System Level Integration, or Scan-line Interleave
S.M.A.R.T.	Self-Monitoring, Analysis, and Reporting Technology
SMB	Server Message Block
SMTP	Simple Mail Transfer Protocol
SNMP	Simple Network Management Protocol
SoDIMM	Small Outline Dual Inline Memory Module
SOHO	Small Office/Home Office
SP	Service Pack
SPDIF	Sony-Philips Digital Interface Format
SPGA	Staggered Pin Grid Array
SRAM	Static Random Access Memory
SSD	Solid-State Drive
SSH	Secure Shell
SSID	Service Set Identifier
SSL	Secure Sockets Layer
SSO	Single Sign-on
ST	Straight Tip
STP	Shielded Twisted-Pair
SXGA	Super Extended Graphics Array
TACACS	Terminal Access Controller Access Control System
TCP	Transmission Control Protocol
TCP/IP	Transmission Control Protocol/Internet Protocol
TDR	Time Domain Reflectometer
TFTP	Trivial File Transfer Protocol
TKIP	Temporal Key Integrity Protocol
TLS	Transport Layer Security
TN	Twisted Nematic

Acronym	Spelled Out
TPM	Trusted Platform Module
UAC	User Account Control
UDF	User Defined Functions, Universal Disk Format, or Universal Data Format
UDP	User Datagram Protocol
UEFI	Unified Extensible Firmware Interface
UNC	Universal Naming Convention
UPnP	Universal Plug and Play
UPS	Uninterruptible Power Supply
URL	Uniform Resource Locator
USB	Universal Serial Bus
USMT	User State Migration Tool
UTM	Unified Threat Management
UTP	Unshielded Twisted-Pair
UXGA	Ultra Extended Graphics Array
VA	Vertical Alignment
VDC	Volts DC
VDI	Virtual Desktop Infrastructure
VESA	Video Electronics Standards Association
VFAT	Virtual File Allocation Table
VGA	Video Graphics Array
VLAN	Virtual LAN
VM	Virtual Machine
VNC	Virtual Network Computer
VoIP	Voice over Internet Protocol
VPN	Virtual Private Network
VRAM	Video Random Access Memory
WAN	Wide Area Network
WAP	Wireless Access Protocol or Wireless Access Point
WEP	Wired Equivalent Privacy
Wi-Fi	Wireless Fidelity
WINS	Windows Internet Name Service
WLAN	Wireless Local Area Network
WMN	Wireless Mesh Network
WPA	Wireless Protected Access
WPA2	Wi-Fi Protected Access 2
WPS	Wi-Fi Protected Setup
WUXGA	Wide Ultra Extended Graphics Array
WWAN	Wireless Wide Area Network
XGA	Extended Graphics Array
ZIF	Zero-Insertion-Force
ZIP	Zigzag Inline Package

C

GLOSSARY

100BaseT An Ethernet standard that operates at 100 Mbps and uses twisted-pair cabling up to 100 meters (328 feet). *Also called* Fast Ethernet. Variations of 100BaseT are 100BaseTX and 100BaseFX.

10-foot user interface Applications software used on large screens to control output display menus and other clickable items in fonts large enough to read at a distance of 10 feet.

20-pin P1 connector A connector used by an older ATX power supply and motherboard; it provided +3.3 volts, +5 volts, +12 volts, –12 volts, and an optional and rarely used –5 volts.

24-pin P1 connector A connector used by an ATX Version 2.2 power supply and motherboard; it provides additional power for PCI Express slots.

32-bit operating system A type of operating system that processes 32 bits at a time.

3D printer A printer that uses a plastic filament to build a 3D model of a digital image.

3G A third generation cellular wireless Internet connection standard used with CDMA or GSM mobile phone services that allows for transmitting data and video.

4G A fourth generation cellular wireless Internet connection standard typically used with LTE (Long Term Evolution) technology; 4G transmits data and video up to 1 Gbps.

4-pin 12-V connector An auxiliary motherboard connector used for extra 12-V power to the processor.

5G A fifth generation cellular wireless Internet connection standard expected to transmit 10–50 Gbps. 5G is not yet released.

64-bit operating system A type of operating system that processes 64 bits at a time.

802.11 a/b/g/n/ac The collective name for the IEEE 802.11 standards for local wireless networking, which is the technical name for Wi-Fi.

802.11a An outdated Wi-Fi standard that transmitted up to 54 Mbps.

802.11ac *See* IEEE 802.11ac.

802.11b An outdated Wi-Fi standard that transmitted up to 11 Mbps and experienced interference with cordless phones and microwaves.

802.11g An outdated Wi-Fi standard that was compatible with and replaced 802.11b.

802.11n *See* IEEE 802.11n.

8-pin 12-V connector An auxiliary motherboard connector used for extra 12-V power to the processor; it provides more power than the older 4-pin auxiliary connector.

A+ Certification A certification awarded by CompTIA (the Computer Technology Industry Association) that measures an IT technician's knowledge and skills.

AAA (authenticating, authorizing, and accounting) The three major methods used to secure a network and its resources. Authenticating controls access to the network, authorizing controls what a user or computer can do on the network, and accounting tracks what a user or computer has done on the network. *Also called* triple A.

AC adapter A device that converts AC to DC and can use regular house current to power a laptop computer.

accelerometer A type of gyroscope used in mobile devices to sense the physical position of the device.

acceptable use policy (AUP) A document that explains to users what they can and cannot do on the corporate network or with company data, and the penalties for violations.

access control list (ACL) A record or list of the resources (for example, a printer, folder, or file) that a user, device, or program has access to on a corporate network, server, or workstation.

Action bar On an Android device, an area at the bottom of the screen that can contain up to five custom software buttons, called Home touch buttons. The three default buttons are back, home, and overview.

Action Center A tool in Windows 8/7 that lists errors and issues that need attention.

Active Directory (AD) A suite of services and databases provided by Windows Server that is used to manage Windows domains, including five groups of services: Domain Services, Certificate Services, Federation Services, Rights Management, and Lightweight Directory Services.

Active Directory Domain Services (AD DS) A component of Active Directory that is responsible for authenticating accounts and authorizing what these accounts can do.

active hours The range of time during the day when Windows 10 avoids automatic restarts while applying updates.

active partition For MBR hard drives, the primary partition on the drive that boots the OS. Windows calls the active partition the system partition.

active recovery image In Windows 8, the custom refresh image of the Windows volume that will be used during a refresh of the Windows installation. *Also see* custom refresh image.

ActiveX control A small app or add-on that can be downloaded from a website along with a webpage and is executed by a browser to enhance the webpage.

ad hoc mode A peer-to-peer wireless network between computers where each wireless computer serves as its own wireless access point and is responsible for securing each connection.

adapter address *See* MAC (Media Access Control) address.

address reservation When a DHCP server assigns a static IP address to a DHCP client. For example, a network printer might require a static IP address so that computers on the network can find the printer.

ADF (automatic document feeder) scanner A component of a copier, scanner, or printer that can automatically pull individual items of paper, cards, or envelopes from a stack into a roller system for processing.

administrative shares The folders and volumes shared by default on a network that administrator accounts can access but are invisible to standard users. Use the fsmgmt.msc command to view a list of shared folders and volumes.

Administrative Tools A group of tools accessed through Control Panel and used to manage the local computer or other computers on the network.

administrator account In Windows, a user account that grants an administrator rights and privileges to all hardware and software resources, such as the right to add, delete, and change accounts and to change hardware configurations. *Compare with* standard account.

Administrators group A type of user group. When a user account is assigned to this group, the account is granted rights that are assigned to an administrator account.

Advanced Boot Options menu A Windows 7 menu that appears when you press F8 as Windows starts. The menu can be used to troubleshoot problems when loading Windows.

Aero user interface The Windows 7 interface that gives windows a transparent, glassy appearance. *Also called* Aero glass *or* Aero interface.

AES (Advanced Encryption Standard) An encryption standard used by WPA2; it is currently the strongest encryption standard used by Wi-Fi.

AFP (Apple Filing Protocol) An outdated file access protocol used by early editions of macOS by Apple; AFP is one protocol in the suite of AppleTalk networking protocols.

agent A small app installed on a client that communicates with a server. For example, MDM on-boarding might install an agent on a mobile device to verify that the device complies with security measures.

air filter mask A mask that filters the dust and other contaminants from the air for breathing safety. *Also called* air-purifying respirator.

AirDrop A feature of iOS whereby iPhones and iPads can transfer files between nearby devices. The devices use Bluetooth to detect nearby devices and Wi-Fi to establish connectivity and transfer files.

airplane mode A setting within a mobile device that disables the cellular, Wi-Fi, and Bluetooth antennas so the device cannot transmit signals.

AirPrint   A technology by Apple that allows Apple computers and mobile devices to print to an AirPrint-capable printer without first installing the printer.

alias   A nickname or shortcut for a cmdlet in Windows PowerShell. For example, dir is an alias for the Get-ChildItem cmdlet.

all-in-one computer   A computer that has the monitor and computer case built together and uses components that are common to both a notebook and a desktop computer.

alternate IP address   When configuring TCP/IP in Windows, the static IP address that Windows uses if it cannot lease an IP address from a DHCP server.

alternating current (AC)   Current that cycles back and forth rather than traveling in only one direction. In the United States, the AC voltage from a standard wall outlet is normally between 110 and 115 V. In Europe, the standard AC voltage from a wall outlet is 220 V.

AM3+   A type of pin grid array CPU socket used with AMD Piledriver and Bulldozer processors and the 9-series chipset. AM3+ is typically used in high-end gaming systems.

AM4   A type of CPU socket used with AMD Ryzen and Athlon processors and the AM4 family of chipsets, including the 970, 980G, and 990X chipsets. AM4 is typically used in mainstream desktop systems. The socket has 1331 pins in a pin grid array.

A-Male connector   A common type of USB connector that is flat and wide and connects an A Male USB port on a computer or USB hub.

amp (A)   A measure of electrical current.

analog   A continuous signal with infinite variations, as compared with digital, which is a series of binary values—1s and 0s.

Android   An operating system for mobile devices that is based on the Linux OS and supported by Google.

anonymous users   User accounts that have not been authenticated on a remote computer.

ANSI (American National Standards Institute)   A nonprofit organization dedicated to creating trade and communications standards.

answer file   A file of information that Windows requires in order to do an unattended installation.

anti-malware software   Utility software that can prevent infection, scan a system, and detect and remove all types of general malware, including viruses, spyware, worms, and rootkits.

antistatic bag   A static shielding bag that new computer components are shipped in.

antistatic wrist strap   *See* ESD strap.

antivirus software   Utility software that can prevent infection, scan a system, and detect and remove viruses.

anycast address   Using TCP/IP version 6, a type of IP address used by routers that identifies multiple destinations. Packets are delivered to the closest destination.

APFS (Apple File System)   In macOS, the default file system for SSDs; it can also be used for magnetic hard drives. APFS uses the GUID partitioning system.

APIPA (automatic private IP address)   *See* automatic private IP address (APIPA).

APK (Android Application Package)   The format used to distribute an Android app in a package of files wrapped into one file with an .apk file extension.

app drawer   An app embedded in the Android OS that lists and manages all apps installed on the device.

App Store   The app on an Apple device (iPad, iPhone, or iPod touch) that can be used to download content from the iTunes Store website (*itunes.apple.com*).

Apple ID   A user account that uses a valid email address and password and is associated with a credit card number that allows you to download iOS and macOS updates and patches, apps, and multimedia content.

Apple menu   In macOS, the menu that appears when the user clicks the Apple icon in the upper-left corner of the screen.

application streaming   A hybrid technique between a cloud-based application that is never installed on the local computer and an application that's downloaded and installed locally. An example is Android Instant Apps.

application virtualization   Using this virtualization, a virtual environment is created in memory for an application to virtually install itself.

G

Application Virtualization (App-V) Software by Microsoft used for application virtualization.

Apps Drawer An Android app that lists and manages all apps installed on the device. By default, this app's icon is in the favorites tray on an Android screen.

apt-get A Linux and macOS command to install and remove software packages and install OS updates.

AR (augmented reality) headset A Microsoft headset with native compatibility with Windows 10 that is a hybrid between a mobile and tethered VR headset.

array A group of hard drives that work together to provide a single storage volume.

artifact A horizontally torn image on a computer screen.

ATA Secure Erase Standards developed by the American National Standards Institute (ANSI) that dictate how to securely erase data from solid-state devices such as a USB flash drive or SSD in order to protect personal privacy.

ATAPI (Advanced Technology Attachment Packet Interface) An interface standard within the IDE/ATA standards that allows tape drives, optical drives, and other drives to be treated like an IDE hard drive by the system.

ATX (Advanced Technology Extended) The most common form factor for desktop computer cases, motherboards, and power supplies; it was originally introduced by Intel in 1995. ATX motherboards and cases make better use of space and resources than the earlier AT form factor.

ATX12V power supply An ATX Version 2.1 power supply that provides an extra 12-V power cord with a 4-pin connector and is used with the auxiliary 4-pin power connector on motherboards to provide additional power for processors.

audio port A port that can be used by microphone, audio in, audio out, and stereo audio out connections. *Also called* a sound port.

Authenticated Users group All user accounts that have been authenticated to access the system except the Guest account. *Compare with* anonymous users.

authentication server A server responsible for authenticating users or computers to the network so they can access network resources.

authenticator application An app installed on a smartphone to provide multifactor authentication—for example, Google Authenticator, Microsoft Authenticator, and Authy.

autodetection A feature of BIOS/UEFI that detects a new drive and automatically selects the correct drive capacity and configuration, including the best possible standard supported by both the hard drive and the motherboard.

automatic private IP address (APIPA) In TCP/IP version 4, an IP address in the address range 169.254.x.y, used by a computer when it cannot successfully lease an IP address from a DHCP server.

auto-switching A function of a laptop computer's AC adapter that enables it to automatically switch between 110-V and 220-V AC power.

Azure Active Directory (Azure AD) Microsoft domain services managed by Microsoft servers in the cloud. Windows 10 business and professional editions support joining an Azure domain.

back flash To revert to an earlier version of BIOS/UEFI after flashing BIOS/UEFI.

back-out plan A plan that defines the activities needed to recover to the original state in the event of an aborted or failed change implementation.

Backup and Restore The Windows utility used to create and update scheduled backups of user data and the system image.

Backup Operators group A type of Windows user account group. When a user account belongs to this group, it can back up and restore any files on the system, regardless of whether it has access to these files.

badge reader A device that can read the microchip or magnetic stripe on a card, such as a credit card, and transmit the information to a computer.

bandwidth In relation to analog communication, the range of frequencies that a communications channel or cable can carry. In general use, the term refers to the volume of data that can be transmitted on a bus or over a cable; bandwidth is stated in bits per second (bps), kilobits per second (Kbps), or megabits per second (Mbps). *Also called* data throughput *or* line speed.

barcode A pattern of numbers and variable-length lines that can be read by a machine; a barcode is often used to identify a manufacturer and product.

barcode reader A device used to scan barcodes on products at the points of sale or when taking inventory.

base station A fixed transceiver and antenna used to create one cell within a cellular network.

baseband update An update to radio firmware on a mobile device that manages cellular, Wi-Fi, and Bluetooth radios. Baseband updates may be included in OS updates.

Bash on Ubuntu on Windows A Windows 10 shell that uses Ubuntu Bash commands. Ubuntu is a popular distribution of Linux. *Also called* Bash on Windows *and* Ubuntu Bash.

Bash shell The default shell used by the terminal for many distributions of Linux.

basic disk The term Windows uses to describe a hard drive when it is a stand-alone drive in the system. *Compare with* dynamic disk.

basic loop A scripting or programming technique to execute the same group of commands multiple times until a condition is met.

batch file A script text file that has a .bat file extension and contains a series of Windows commands.

BCD (Boot Configuration Data) A small Windows database that is structured the same as a registry file and contains configuration information about how Windows is started. The file is stored in the \Boot directory of the hidden system partition.

bcdedit A Windows command used to manually edit the BCD.

BD (Blu-ray disc) An optical disc technology that uses the UDF version 2.5 file system and a blue laser beam, which is shorter than any red beam used by DVD or CD discs. The shorter blue laser beam allows Blu-ray discs to store more data than a DVD.

beamforming A technique supported by the IEEE 802.11ac Wi-Fi standard that can detect the location of connected devices and increase signal strength in that direction.

best-effort protocol *See* connectionless protocol.

biometric authentication To authenticate to a network, computer, or other computing device by means of biometric data, such as a fingerprint

or retinal data. Touch ID on an iPhone or face lock on an Android device can perform biometric authentication.

biometric data Data that identifies a person by a fingerprint, handprint, face, retina, iris, voice, or handwritten signature.

biometric device An input device that can identify biological data about a person's fingerprints, handprints, face, voice, eyes, and handwriting.

biometric lock A lock that can be opened by input of biometric data.

BIOS (basic input/output system) Firmware that can control much of a computer's input/output functions, such as communication with the keyboard and the monitor. *Compare with* UEFI.

BIOS setup The program in system BIOS that can change the values in CMOS RAM. *Also called* CMOS setup.

BitLocker Drive Encryption A utility in Windows 10/8/7 that is used to lock down a hard drive by encrypting the entire Windows volume and any other volume on the drive. *Also called* BitLocker Encryption.

BitLocker Encryption *See* BitLocker Drive Encryption.

BitLocker To Go A Windows utility that can encrypt data on a USB flash drive and restrict access by requiring a password.

bitmap Rows and columns of bits that collectively represent an image.

blacklist In filtering, a list of items that are not allowed—for example, a list of websites that computers on a local network are not allowed to access. *Compare with* whitelist.

blue screen of death (BSOD) A Windows error that occurs in kernel mode, is displayed against a blue screen, and causes the system to halt. The error might be caused by problems with devices, device drivers, or a corrupted Windows installation. *Also called* a stop error.

Bluetooth A short-range wireless technology used to connect two devices in a small personal network.

Bluetooth PIN code A code that may be required to complete the Bluetooth connection in a pairing process.

Blu-ray Disc (BD) *See* BD.

G

B-Male connector A USB connector that connects a USB 1.x or 2.0 device such as a printer.

BNC connector An outdated network connector used with thin coaxial cable. Some BNC connectors are T-shaped and are called T-connectors. One end of the T connects to the NIC, and the two other ends can connect to cables or end a bus formation with a terminator.

Bonjour An Apple program that is used to interface between computers and devices and share content and services between them. When iTunes is installed on a Windows computer, the installation includes Bonjour.

Boot Camp A utility in macOS that allows you to install and run Windows on a Mac computer.

Boot Configuration Data (BCD) store *See* BCD.

boot loader menu A startup menu in a dual-boot system that gives the user the choice of which operating system to load, such as Windows 10 or Windows 8. Multiples OSs are installed on a dual-boot system.

boot partition The hard drive partition where the Windows OS is stored. The system partition and the boot partition may be different partitions.

boot priority order A list of devices stored in firmware on the motherboard that BIOS/UEFI startup uses in the order listed to search for and load an operating system.

booting The process of starting up a computer and loading an operating system.

BootMgr The file name of the boot manager program responsible for loading Windows on a BIOS system. The file has no file extension.

bootrec A Windows command used to repair the BCD and boot sectors.

bootsect A Windows command used to repair a dual-boot system.

botnet A network of zombies or robots.

Branchcache A Windows feature to optimize content on a WAN by caching the content on local servers for better access.

bridge A networking device that stands between two segments of a network and manages traffic between them.

broadband A transmission technique that carries more than one type of transmission on the same medium, such as voice and DSL on a regular telephone line.

broadcast message A message sent over a local network to all devices on the network; the message does not contain recipient information.

brownout A temporary reduction in voltage that can sometimes cause data loss. *Also called* sag.

brute force Systematically trying every possible combination of letters, numbers, and symbols to crack a password.

brute force attack A method to hack or discover a password by trying every single combination of characters.

BSOD (blue screen of death) *See* blue screen of death (BSOD).

burn-in When a static image stays on a monitor for many hours, leaving a permanent impression of the image on the monitor.

bus The paths, or lines, on the motherboard on which data, instructions, and electrical power move from component to component.

BYOD (Bring Your Own Device) A corporate policy that allows employees or students to connect their own devices to the corporate network.

BYOD Experience A Microsoft feature that allows a personal device to join an Azure domain and access corporate resources on the domain.

cable Internet A broadband technology that uses cable TV lines and is always connected (always up).

cable lock A cable with a lock used to physically secure a laptop or computer to a table or other stationary device. *Also called* Kensington lock.

cable modem A device that converts a computer's digital signal to analog before sending it over cable TV lines and that converts incoming analog data to digital.

cable stripper A hand tool used to cut away the plastic jacket or coating around the wires of a network cable.

cable tester A tool used to test a cable to find out if it is good or to identify a cable that is not labeled.

calibration The process of checking and correcting the graduations of an instrument or device, such as an inkjet printer.

call tracking software A system that tracks the dates, times, and transactions of help-desk or on-site IT support calls, including the problem presented, the issues addressed, who did what, and when and how each call was resolved.

CAS Latency A method of measuring access timing to memory, which is the number of clock cycles required to write or read a column of data off a memory module. CAS stands for Column Access Strobe.

case fan A fan inside a computer case that's used to draw air out of or into the case.

cast A mobile device feature that allows the device to transmit its display to a television, monitor, or projector.

CAT-5 (Category 5) A rating used for UTP cables and rated for Fast Ethernet, but seldom used today.

CAT-5e (Category 5e) A popular rating used for UTP cables and rated for Fast Ethernet and Gigabit Ethernet.

CAT-6 (Category 6) A rating used for twisted-pair cables that have less crosstalk than CAT-5e cables. CAT-6 cables might contain a plastic cord down the center that helps to prevent crosstalk, but they are less flexible and more difficult to install than CAT-5e.

CAT-6a (Category 6a) A rating used for twisted-pair cables that are thicker and faster than CAT-6 and rated for 10GBase-T (10-Gigabit Ethernet).

CAT-6e (Category 6e) An unofficial name for CAT-6a.

CAT-7 (Category 7) A rating used for twisted-pair cables that have shielding to almost completely eliminate crosstalk and improve noise reduction.

Category view The default view in Control Panel that presents utilities grouped by category.

cd (change directory) The Windows command to change the current default directory.

CD (compact disc) An optical disc technology that uses a red laser beam and can hold up to 700 MB of data.

CDFS (Compact Disc File System) The 32-bit file system for CD discs and some CD-R and CD-RW discs. *Also see* Universal Disk Format (UDF).

CDMA (Code Division Multiple Access) A protocol standard used by cellular WANs and cell phones for transmitting digital data over cellular networks.

cellular network A network that can be used when a wireless network must cover a wide area. The network is made up of cells, each controlled by a base station. *Also called* a cellular WAN *or* wireless wide area network (WWAN).

cellular network analyzer Software and hardware that can monitor cellular networks for signal strength of cell towers, WAPs, and repeaters, which can help technicians better position antennas in a distributed antenna system (DAS).

central processing unit (CPU) The component where almost all processing of data and instructions takes place. The CPU receives data input, processes information, and executes instructions. *Also called* a microprocessor *or* processor.

Centrino A technology used by Intel whereby the processor, chipset, and wireless network adapter are all interconnected as a unit, which improves laptop performance.

Certificate of Authenticity A sticker that contains the Windows product key.

certificate of destruction Digital or paper documentation that assures customers their data has been destroyed beyond recovery by a secure service.

Certificate Authority (CA) An organization, such as VeriSign, that assigns digital certificates or digital signatures to individuals or organizations. *Also called* certification authority.

chain of custody Documentation that tracks all evidence collected and used in an investigation, including when and from whom the evidence was collected, the condition of the evidence, and how the evidence was secured while in possession of a responsible party.

change advisory board (CAB) The team in an organization charged with assessing, prioritizing, authorizing, and scheduling change.

change management The processes for successfully bringing people forward to an end result or goal.

channel A specific radio frequency within a broader frequency.

charging In laser printing, the process of placing a high electrical charge on the imaging drum to condition it before an image is exposed to the drum.

charm A Windows 8 shortcut that appears in the charms bar.

charms bar A menu that appears on the right side of any Windows 8 screen when you move your pointer to the right corner.

G

chassis A case for any type of computer.

chassis air guide (CAG) A round air duct that helps to pull and direct fresh air from outside a computer case to the cooler and processor.

child directory *See* subdirectory.

chip reader A device that reads the chip on a smart card or license to pull information from it.

chipset A group of chips on the motherboard that controls the timing and flow of data and instructions to and from the CPU.

chkdsk (check disk) A Windows command to verify that the hard drive does not have bad sectors that can corrupt the file system.

chmod A Linux and macOS command to change modes (or permissions) for a file or directory.

chown A Linux and macOS command to change the owner of a file or directory.

Chrome OS An OS by Google that is built on the open source Chromium OS and used on Google Chromebooks. The OS looks and works much like the Chrome browser and relies heavily on web-based apps and storage.

CIDR (Classless Interdomain Routing) notation A shorthand notation (pronounced "*cider notation*") for expressing an IPv4 address and subnet mask; the IP address is followed by a slash (/) and the number of bits in the IP address that identifies the network—for example, 15.50.35.10/20.

CIFS (Common Internet File System) A file access protocol and the cross-platform version of SMB used between Windows, Linux, macOS, and other operating systems. CIFS is a spinoff of the SMB2 protocol.

Class C fire extinguisher A fire extinguisher rated to put out electrical fires.

Classic view A view in Control Panel that presents utilities as small or large icons that are not grouped.

clean boot A process of starting Windows with a basic set of drivers and startup programs; a clean boot can be useful when software does not install properly.

clean install A process used to overwrite the existing operating system and applications when installing an OS on a hard drive.

client/server Two computers communicating using a local network or the Internet. One computer (the client) makes requests to the other computer (the server), which answers the request.

client/server application An application where a client program installed on one computer requests information from a server program installed on another computer on the network or Internet.

client-hosted desktop virtualization When a local computer is used to host a hypervisor and its virtual machines.

client-side desktop virtualization Using this virtualization, software installed on a desktop or laptop manages virtual machines used by the local user.

client-side virtualization Using this virtualization, a personal computer provides multiple virtual environments for applications.

clone In Linux and macOS, an image of the entire partition on which the OS is installed.

closed source Software owned by a vendor that requires a commercial license to install and use. *Also called* vendor-specific or commercial license software.

cloud computing A service where server-side virtualization is delegated to a third-party service, and the Internet is used to connect server and client machines.

cloud file storage service A way of storing files in the cloud. Examples are Google Drive, iCloud Drive, Dropbox, and OneDrive.

cloud printing Printing to a printer anywhere on the Internet from a personal computer or mobile device connected to the Internet.

cloud-based application An application installed on a server on the Internet; the user can access the software through a browser. The application is a type of SaaS.

cloud-based network controller A manager of network resources in the cloud through services that are also in the cloud. These network resources are managed through a browser and might include Wi-Fi access points, network servers, routers, switches, and firewalls. An example of a cloud-based network controller is CloudTrax (*cloudtrax.com*).

cluster On a magnetic hard drive, one or more sectors that constitute the smallest unit of space on the drive for storing data (also referred to as a file allocation unit). Files are written to a drive as groups of whole clusters.

cmdlets Prebuilt scripts (pronounced "*command-lets*") written for Windows PowerShell, a command-line interface expected to replace the command prompt window.

CMOS (complementary metal-oxide semiconductor) The technology used to manufacture microchips. CMOS chips require less electricity, hold data longer after the electricity is turned off, and produce less heat than earlier technologies. The configuration or setup chip is a CMOS chip.

CMOS battery The lithium coin-cell battery on the motherboard used to power the CMOS chip that holds BIOS setup data so that the data is retained when the computer is unplugged.

CMOS RAM Memory contained on the CMOS configuration chip.

coaxial (coax) cable A cable that has a single copper wire down the middle and a braided shield around it.

cold boot *See* hard boot.

color depth The accuracy of color representation on a monitor screen; color depth is important for editing photographs and in graphic design.

comment syntax The text in a script or program that tags a line as documentation so it is not interpreted as a command in the script or program.

commercial license When applied to software, the rights to use the software, as assigned to the user by the software vendor.

community cloud Online resources and services that are shared between multiple organizations but are not available publicly.

CompactFlash (CF) card A flash memory device that allows for sizes up to 137 GB, although current sizes range up to 64 GB.

compatibility mode A group of settings that can be applied to older drivers or applications so that they might work using a newer version of Windows than the one they were designed to use.

Compatibility Support Module (CSM) A feature of UEFI that allows it to be backward-compatible with legacy BIOS devices and drivers.

Component Services (COM+) A Microsoft Management Console snap-in that can be used to register components used by installed applications.

compressed (zipped) folder A folder with a .zip extension that contains compressed files. When files are put in the folder, they are compressed. When files are moved to a regular folder, they are decompressed.

computer infestation *See* malicious software.

Computer Management A Windows console (compmgmt.msc) that contains several administrative tools used by support technicians to manage the local computer or other computers on the network.

computer name *See* host name.

connectionless protocol A TCP/IP protocol such as UDP that works at the OSI Transport layer and does not guarantee delivery by first connecting and checking where data is received. It might be used for broadcasting, such as streaming video or sound over the web, where guaranteed delivery is not as important as fast transmission. *Also called* a best-effort protocol. *Also see* UDP (User Datagram Protocol).

connection-oriented protocol In networking, a TCP/IP protocol that confirms a good connection has been made before transmitting data to the other end, verifies that data was received, and resends data if it was not received. An example of a connection-oriented protocol is TCP.

console A window that consolidates several Windows administrative tools.

contrast ratio The contrast between true black and true white on a screen.

Control Panel A window containing several small utility programs called applets that are used to manage hardware, software, users, and the system.

controller hub A device that controls the smart devices in an IoT network to create an integrated smart home experience. *Also called* smart home hub.

cooler A cooling system that sits on top of a processor and consists of a fan and a heat sink.

copy The Windows command to copy a single file, a group of files, or a folder and its contents.

G

copyright   The right to copy a creative work; a copyright belongs to the creator(s) of the work or others to whom the creator transfers this right.

Cortana   A Windows 10 voice-enabled digital assistant and search feature.

CPU   *See* central processing unit (CPU).

crimper   A hand tool used to attach a terminator or connector to the end of a cable.

critical applications   Applications that are required to keep a business functioning and that require alternative solutions if they are not functioning.

crossover cable   A cable used to connect two like devices such as a hub to a hub or a computer to a computer (to make the simplest network of all). The transmit connectors at one end of the cable are wired as the receiving connectors at the other end of the cable and vice versa.

custom installation   In the Windows setup program, the option used to overwrite the existing operating system and applications, producing a clean installation of the OS. The main advantage is that problems with the old OS are not carried forward.

custom refresh image   In Windows 8, an image of the entire Windows volume, including the Windows installation. The image can be applied during a Windows 8 refresh operation.

data loss prevention (DLP)   Methods that protect corporate data from being exposed or stolen; for example, software that filters employee email to verify that privacy laws are not accidentally or intentionally being violated.

data source   A resource on a network that includes a database and the drivers required to interface between a remote computer and the data.

Data Sources   A connection between a local application and a remote database so that the application can manage the database. *Also called* ODBC Data Sources (Open Database Connectivity Data Sources).

data throughput   *See* bandwidth.

DB-15   *See* VGA (Video Graphics Array) port.

DB-9   *See* serial port.

DB15 port   *See* VGA (Video Graphics Array) port.

DB9 port   *See* serial port.

dd   In Linux and macOS, the command to copy and convert files, directories, partitions, and entire DVDs or hard drives. You must be logged in as a superuser to use the command.

DDR   *See* Double Data Rate SDRAM.

DDR2   Memory that is faster and uses less power than DDR.

DDR3   Memory that is faster and uses less power than DDR2.

DDR3L   Memory that is faster and uses less power than regular DDR3.

DDR4   Memory that is faster and uses less power than DDR3.

DE15 port   *See* VGA (Video Graphics Array) port.

dead pixel   A pixel on an LCD monitor that is not working and can appear as a small white, black, or colored spot on the screen.

default gateway   The gateway a networked computer uses to access another network unless it knows to specifically use another gateway for quicker access.

default printer   The designated printer to which Windows prints unless another one is selected.

default product key   A product key that can be used to fix a problem created when Windows 10 setup installs the wrong edition of the OS.

default program   A program associated with a file extension that is used to open the file.

defense in depth   Layered protection for a system or network so that, if one security method fails, the next might stop an attacker.

defrag   The Windows command that examines a magnetic hard drive for fragmented files and rewrites these files to the drive in contiguous clusters.

Defrag and Optimization tool (defrgui.exe)   A Windows utility that defragments a magnetic hard drive and trims an SSD to improve performance. *Also called* Defragment and Optimize Drives utility.

defragment   A drive maintenance procedure that rearranges fragments or parts of files on a magnetic hard drive so each file is stored on the drive in contiguous clusters.

Defragment and Optimize Drives   *See* Defrag and Optimization tool.

defragmentation tool   A utility or command to rewrite a file to a disk in one contiguous chain of clusters, thus speeding up data retrieval.

degausser   A machine that exposes a storage device to a strong magnetic field to completely erase the data on a magnetic hard drive or tape drive.

del   The Windows command to delete a file or group of files. *Also called* the erase command.

denial-of-service (DoS)   An attack that overwhelms a computer or network with incoming traffic until new connections can no longer be accepted.

deployment strategy   A procedure to install Windows, device drivers, and applications on a computer; it can include the process to transfer user settings, application settings, and user data files from an old installation to the new installation.

desktop case   A computer case that lies flat and sometimes serves double duty as a monitor stand. A tower case is sometimes called a desktop case.

destination network address translation (DNAT)   When a firewall using NAT allows uninitiated communication to a computer behind the firewall through a port that is normally closed. *Also see* port forwarding.

device driver   A small program stored on the hard drive and installed in Windows that tells Windows how to communicate with a specific hardware device such as a printer, network, port on the motherboard, or scanner.

Device Manager   The primary Windows tool (devmgmt.msc) for managing hardware.

DHCP (Dynamic Host Configuration Protocol)   A protocol used by a server to assign a dynamic IP address to a computer when it first attempts to initiate a connection to the network and requests an IP address.

DHCP client   A computer or other device (such as a network printer) that requests an IP address from a DHCP server.

DHCP server   A computer or other device that provides an IP address from a pool of addresses to a client computer that requests an address.

DHCPv6 server   A DHCP server that serves up IPv6 addresses.

dictionary attack   A method to discover or crack a password by trying words in a dictionary.

digital   A signal consisting of a series of binary values—1s and 0s. *Compare with* analog.

digital assistant   A service or app, such as Apple's Siri and Microsoft's Cortana, that responds to a user's voice commands with a personable, conversational interaction to perform tasks and retrieve information. *Also called* personal assistant.

digital certificate   Encrypted data that serves as an electronic signature to authenticate the source of a file or document or to identify and authenticate a person or organization sending data over a network. The data is assigned by a certificate authority such as VeriSign and includes a public key for encryption. *Also called* digital ID *or* digital signature.

digital license   A Windows 10 license assigned to a computer after Windows 10 has been activated on the machine.

digital rights management (DRM)   Software and hardware security limitations meant to protect digital content and prevent piracy.

digital signature   *See* digital certificate.

digitizer   *See* graphics tablet.

digitizing tablet   *See* graphics tablet.

DIMM (dual inline memory module)   A miniature circuit board installed on a motherboard to hold memory.

dir   The Windows command to list files and directories.

direct current (DC)   Current that travels in only one direction (the type of electricity provided by batteries). Computer power supplies transform AC to low DC.

direct thermal printer   A type of thermal printer that burns dots onto special coated paper, as older fax machines did.

DirectX   A Microsoft software development tool that developers can use to write multimedia applications such as games, video-editing software, and computer-aided design software.

disc image   *See* ISO image.

discolored capacitor   An indicator of a failing motherboard; such capacitors might have bulging heads or crusty corrosion at their base.

Disk Cleanup   A Windows utility to delete temporary files and free up space on a drive.

disk cloning   *See* drive imaging.

disk drive shredder   A device that can destroy magnetic hard drives, SSDs, flash drives, optical discs, and mobile devices so that sensitive data on the device is also destroyed.

diskpart A Windows command to manage hard drives, partitions, and volumes.

DISM (Deployment Image Servicing and Management) A set of commands to create, capture, and manage a Windows 10 standard image. The commands can also be used to repair a corrupted Windows 10 installation.

DisplayPort A port that transmits digital video and audio (not analog transmissions) and can be used in the place of VGA and DVI ports on personal computers.

distorted geometry Images that are stretched inappropriately on a monitor.

distributed denial-of-service (DDoS) A DoS attack performed by multiple computers and sometimes by botnets, even when users of the botnet computers are not aware of the attack.

distribution server A file server holding Windows setup files that are used to install Windows on computers networked to the server.

distribution share The collective files in an installation that include Windows, device drivers, and applications. The package of files is served up by a distribution server.

DMG file In macOS, a disk image file similar to WIM or ISO files in Windows.

DMZ (demilitarized zone) A computer or network that has limited or no firewall protection within a larger organization of protected computers and networks.

DNS (Domain Name System or Domain Name Service) A distributed pool of information (called the namespace) that keeps track of assigned host names and domain names and their corresponding IP addresses. DNS also refers to the system that allows a host to locate information in the pool and the protocol the system uses.

DNS client When Windows queries the DNS server for name resolution, which means to find an IP address for a computer when the fully qualified domain name is known.

DNS server A Domain Name Service server that uses a DNS protocol to find an IP address for a computer when the fully qualified domain name is known. An Internet service provider is responsible for providing access to one or more DNS servers as part of the service it provides for Internet access.

dock (1) For the Android OS, the area at the bottom of the Android screen where up to four apps can be pinned. (2) For macOS, a bar that appears by default at the bottom of the screen and contains program icons and shortcuts to files and folders.

docking port A connector on the bottom of the laptop that connects to a port replicator or docking station.

docking station A device that receives a laptop computer and provides additional secondary storage and easy connection to peripheral devices.

documented business processes Stated goals of a business, including how the business achieves these goals.

domain In Windows, a logical group of networked computers, such as those on a college campus, that share a centralized directory database of user account information and security.

domain account *See* global account.

domain name A name that identifies a network and appears before the period in a website address, such as *microsoft.com*. A fully qualified domain name is sometimes loosely called a domain name. *Also see* fully qualified domain name.

domain user account An account assigned to a user by Active Directory that identifies the user and defines user rights on the domain. *Also called* network ID.

Double Data Rate SDRAM (DDR SDRAM) A type of memory technology used on DIMMs that runs at twice the speed of the system clock, has one notch, and uses 184 pins. *Also called* DDR SDRAM, SDRAM II, *and* DDR.

double-sided A DIMM feature whereby memory chips are installed on both sides of a DIMM.

drive imaging Making an exact image of a hard drive, including partition information, boot sectors, operating system installation, and application software, to replicate the hard drive on another system or recover from a hard drive crash. *Also called* disk cloning *or* disk imaging.

driver rollback To undo a device driver update by returning to the previous version.

driver store The location where Windows stores a copy of the driver software when first installing a device.

DSL (Digital Subscriber Line) A telephone line that carries digital data from end to end and is used as a type of broadband Internet access.

DSL modem A device that converts a computer's digital signal to analog before sending it over telephone lines and converts incoming analog data to digital.

dual boot The ability to boot using either of two different OSs, such as Windows 10 and Windows 7. *Also called* multiboot.

dual channels A motherboard feature that improves memory performance by providing two 64-bit channels between memory and the chipset. DDR, DDR2, DDR3, and DDR4 DIMMs can use dual channels.

dual processors Two processor sockets on a server motherboard.

dual rail A power supply with a second +12 V circuit or rail used to ensure that the first circuit is not overloaded.

dual ranked Double-sided DIMMs that provide two 64-bit banks. The memory controller accesses one bank and then the other. Dual-ranked DIMMs do not perform as well as single-ranked DIMMs.

dual voltage selector switch A switch on the back of the computer case where you can change the input voltage to the power supply to 115 V (in the United States) or 220 V (in other countries).

dumb terminal *See* zero client.

dump In Linux, a collection of data that is copied to backup media.

dumpster diving Looking for useful information in someone's trash to help create an impersonation of an individual or company to aid in a malicious attack.

duplex printer A printer that is able to print on both sides of the paper.

duplexing assembly In a duplex printer, an assembly of several rollers that enables printing on both sides of the paper.

DVD (digital versatile disc or digital video disc) A technology for optical discs that uses a red laser beam and can hold up to 17 GB of data.

DVD-ROM Stands for DVD read-only memory.

DVD-RW Stands for DVD rewriteable memory.

DVD-RW DL Stands for DVD rewriteable memory, dual layers. It doubles storage capacity.

DVI (Digital Video Interface) port A port that transmits digital or analog video.

DVI-A A DVI (Digital Video Interface) video port that only transmits analog data.

DVI-D A DVI video port that works only with digital monitors.

DVI-I A DVI video port that supports both analog and digital monitors.

DXDiag (DirectX Diagnostics Tool) A Windows command (dxdiag.exe) used to display information about hardware and diagnose problems with DirectX. The command returns the version of DirectX installed.

dxdiag.exe *See* DXDiag (DirectX Diagnostics Tool).

dynamic disk A way to partition one or more hard drives so that they can work together to increase space for data storage or to provide fault tolerance or improved performance. *Also see* RAID. *Compare with* basic disk.

dynamic IP address An IP address assigned by a DHCP server for the current session only, and leased when the computer first connects to a network. When the session is terminated, the IP address is returned to the list of available addresses. *Compare with* static IP address.

dynamic RAM (DRAM) The most common type of system memory; it requires refreshing every few milliseconds.

dynamic type checking A technique in scripting and programming whereby each command line is checked by the command interpreter software to verify that the command can be executed.

dynamic volume A volume type used with dynamic disks by which you can create a single volume that uses space on multiple hard drives.

ECC (error-correcting code) A chipset feature on a motherboard that checks the integrity of data stored on DIMMs or RIMMs and can correct single-bit errors in a byte. More advanced ECC schemas can detect, but not correct, double-bit errors in a byte.

EFI (Extensible Firmware Interface) The original version of UEFI, which was first developed by Intel.

EFI System Partition (ESP) For a GPT hard drive, the bootable partition used to boot the OS; ESP contains the boot manager program for the OS.

electrostatic discharge (ESD) Another name for static electricity, which can damage chips and destroy motherboards, even though it might not be felt or seen with the naked eye.

elevated command prompt window A Windows command prompt window that allows commands requiring administrator privileges.

email filtering To search incoming or outgoing email messages for matches kept in databases that can identify known scams and spammers and protect against social engineering.

email hoax An email message that tries to tempt you to give out personal information or tries to scam you.

embedded MMC (eMMC) Internal storage used instead of an SSD in mobile devices such as cell phones, tablets, and laptops.

emergency notifications Government alerts, such as AMBER alerts, that are sent to mobile devices in an emergency.

emulator A virtual machine that emulates hardware, such as the hardware buttons on a smartphone.

Encrypting File System (EFS) A way to use a key to encode a file or folder on an NTFS volume and protect sensitive data. Because it is an integrated system service, EFS is transparent to users and applications.

End User License Agreement (EULA) A digital or printed statement of your rights to use or copy software, which you agree to when the software is installed.

end-of-life limitation The point when the manufacturer of software or hardware stops providing updates or patches for its product.

endpoint device A computer, laptop, smartphone, printer, or other host on a network.

endpoint management server A server that monitors various endpoint devices on the network to ensure that endpoints are compliant with security requirements such as anti-malware and that OS updates are applied.

enterprise license A license to use software that allows an organization to install multiple instances of the software. *Also called* site license.

entry control roster A list of people allowed into a restricted area and a log of approved visitors; the roster is used and maintained by security guards.

environmental variable Data the OS makes available to a script or program for use during its execution. *Also called* a system variable.

EoP (Ethernet over Power) The technology that allows Ethernet transmissions over power lines in a building. A powerline adapter is plugged into the electrical circuit(s) at both ends and the adapters connect to the Ethernet network. Because the transmissions are not contained, encryption is required for security. *Also called* powerline networking.

erase *See* del.

e-reader A mobile device that holds digital versions of books, newspapers, magazines, and other printed documents, which are usually downloaded to the device from the web.

eSATA (external SATA) A standard and port used to connect external SATA drives to a computer. eSATA uses a special shielded SATA cable up to 2 meters long.

escalate To assign a problem to someone higher in the support chain of an organization. This action is normally recorded in call tracking software.

ESD mat A mat that dissipates ESD and is commonly used by technicians who repair and assemble computers at their workbenches or in an assembly line. *Also called* ground mat.

ESD strap A strap worn around your wrist and attached to a computer case, ground mat, or another ground so that ESD is discharged from your body before you touch sensitive components inside a computer. *Also called* antistatic wrist strap *or* ground bracelet.

Ethernet over Power (EoP) *See* powerline networking.

Ethernet port *See* network port.

Event Viewer A Windows tool (Eventvwr.msc) useful for troubleshooting problems with Windows, applications, and hardware. It displays logs of significant events, such as a hardware or network failure, OS failure, OS error messages, a device or service that has failed to start, and General Protection Faults.

Everyone group In Windows, the Authenticated Users group as well as the Guest account. When you share a file or folder on the network, Windows gives access to the Everyone group by default.

Exchange Online An email service provided by Microsoft that is hosted on Microsoft servers.

executive services In Windows, a group of components running in kernel mode that interfaces between the subsystems in user mode and the HAL.

exFAT   A file system suitable for large external storage devices and compatible with Windows, macOS, and Linux.

expand   The Windows command that extracts files from compressed distribution files, which are often used to distribute files for software installation.

expansion card   A circuit board inserted into a slot on the motherboard to enhance the capability of the computer. *Also called* an adapter card.

expert system   Software that uses a database of known facts and rules to simulate a human expert's reasoning and decision-making processes.

ext3   The Linux file system that was the first to support journaling, which is a technique that tracks and stores changes to the hard drive and helps prevent file system corruption.

ext4 (fourth extended file system)   The current Linux file system, which replaced the ext3 file system.

extended partition   On an MBR hard drive, the only partition that can contain more than one logical drive. In Windows, a hard drive can have only a single extended partition. *Compare with* primary partition.

extender   A device that amplifies and retransmits a wireless signal to a wider coverage area and retains the original network name.

extension magnet brush   A long-handled brush made of nylon fibers that are charged with static electricity to pick up stray toner inside a laser printer.

external enclosure   A housing designed to store hard drives outside the computer.

external SATA (eSATA) port   A port for external drives based on SATA that uses a special, external shielded SATA cable up to 2 meters long.

F connector   A connector used with an RG-6 coaxial cable for connections to a TV; it has a single copper wire.

factory default   The state of a mobile device or other computer at the time of purchase. The operating system is reinstalled and all user data and settings are lost.

Fast Ethernet   *See* 100BaseT.

FAT (file allocation table)   A table on a hard drive or other storage device used by the FAT file system to track the clusters used to contain a file.

fat client   *See* thick client.

FAT32   A file system suitable for low-capacity hard drives and other storage devices and supported by Windows, macOS, and Linux.

fault tolerance   The degree to which a system can tolerate failures. Adding redundant components, such as disk mirroring or disk duplexing, is a way to build in fault tolerance.

favorites tray   On Android devices, the area above the Action bar that contains up to seven apps or groups of apps. These apps stay put as you move from home screen to home screen.

ferrite clamp   A clamp installed on a network cable to protect against electrical interference.

fiber optic   As applied to Internet access technologies, a dedicated, leased line that uses fiber-optic cable from the ISP to a residence or place of business.

fiber-optic cable   Cable that transmits signals as pulses of light over glass or plastic strands inside protected tubing.

field replaceable unit (FRU)   A component in a computer or device that can be replaced with a new component without sending the computer or device back to the manufacturer. Examples include a power supply, DIMM, motherboard, and hard disk drive.

file allocation unit   *See* cluster.

file association   The association between a data file and an application to open the file; this association is determined by the file extension.

file attributes   The properties assigned to a file. Examples of file attributes are read-only and hidden status.

File Explorer   The Windows 10/8 utility used to view and manage files and folders.

File Explorer Options applet   The Windows 10 applet used to determine how files and folders are displayed in File Explorer. In Windows 8/7, the applet is called Folder Options.

file extension   A portion of the file name that indicates how the file is organized or formatted, the type of content in the file, and what program uses the file. In command lines, the file extension follows the file name and is separated from it by

G

a period—for example, in Msd.exe, exe is the file extension.

File History A Windows 10/8 utility that can schedule and maintain backups of data. It can also create a system image for backward compatibility with Windows 7.

file name The first part of the name assigned to a file, which does not include the file extension. In Windows, a file name can be up to 255 characters.

file server A computer dedicated to storing and serving up data files and folders.

file system The overall structure that an OS uses to name, store, and organize files on a disk. Examples of file systems are NTFS and FAT32. Windows is always installed on a volume that uses the NTFS file system.

file-level backup A process that backs up and restores individual files.

Finder The macOS utility used to find and view applications, utilities, files, storage devices, and network resources available to macOS. Finder is similar to Windows File Explorer.

firewall Hardware and/or software that blocks unwanted Internet traffic from a private network and can restrict Internet access for local computers.

firmware Software that is permanently stored in a chip. The BIOS on a motherboard is an example of firmware.

First Aid A macOS tool in the Disk Utility group of tools that scans a hard drive or other storage device for file system errors and repairs them.

first response The duties of the person who first discovers an incident, which may include identifying and going through proper channels to report the incident, preserving data or devices, and documenting the incident.

fitness monitor A wearable computer device that can measure heart rate, count pool laps or miles jogged or biked, and a host of other activities.

flashing BIOS/UEFI The process of upgrading or refreshing the programming stored on a firmware chip.

flatbed scanner A scanner with a flat, glass surface that holds paper to be scanned. The scan head moves under the glass and the scanner might have feeders to scan multiple copies.

flat-panel monitor *See* LCD (liquid crystal display) monitor.

folder *See* subdirectory.

Folder Options applet In Windows 8/7, an applet accessed through Control Panel that manages how files and folders are displayed in File Explorer or Windows Explorer. *Compare with* File Explorer Options applet.

folder redirection The technique in Active Directory of using a shared folder on the network instead of a user's Home folder on the local computer.

force quit In macOS, to abruptly end an app without allowing the app to go through its close process.

forced kill In Linux, to abruptly end an app without allowing the app to go through its close process.

forest The entire enterprise of users and resources that is managed by Active Directory.

form factor A set of specifications for the size, shape, and configuration of a computer hardware component such as a case, power supply, or motherboard.

format The Windows command to prepare a hard drive volume, logical drive, or USB flash drive for use (for example, format d:). This process erases all data on the device.

formatting *See* format.

FPC (flexible printed circuit) connectors Flat and flexible ZIF and non-ZIF connectors used for tight locations in electronic equipment.

FQDN (fully qualified domain name) A host name and domain name that identifies a computer and the network to which it belongs. For example, *joesmith.mycompany.com* is an FQDN. An FQDN is sometimes loosely referred to as a domain name.

fragmented file A file that has been written to different portions of the disk so that it is not in contiguous clusters.

Fresh Start The Windows 10 process to perform a clean installation of the OS using the most recent version of Windows 10 available from Microsoft.

front panel connector A group of wires running from the front or top of the computer case to the motherboard.

front panel header A group of pins on a motherboard that connect to wires at the front panel of the computer case.

Front Side Bus (FSB) *See* system bus.

FRU (field replaceable unit) *See* field replaceable unit (FRU).

FTP (File Transfer Protocol) A TCP/IP protocol and application that uses the Internet to transfer files between two computers.

FTP server A server using the FTP or Secure FTP protocol to download or upload files to remote computers.

full device encryption A process that encrypts all the stored data on a device, such as a smartphone or tablet.

full duplex Communication that happens in two directions at the same time.

full format The process of creating an empty root directory, checking each sector for errors, marking bad sectors so they will not be used by the file system, and installing a file system and drive letter to a storage device or volume.

fully qualified domain name (FQDN) *See* FQDN (fully qualified domain name).

fuser assembly A component in laser printing that uses heat and pressure to fuse the toner to paper.

gadget A mini-app that appears on the Windows 7 desktop.

gateway Any device or computer that network traffic can use to leave one network and go to a different one.

GDPR (General Data Protection Regulation) A group of regulations implemented by the European Union (EU) to protect personal data of EU citizens.

geotracking A mobile device's routine reporting of its position to Apple, Google, or Microsoft at least twice a day, making it possible for these companies to track your device's whereabouts.

gesture An action performed on the Mac trackpad using one or more fingers.

ghost cursor A trail on the screen left behind when you move the mouse.

Gigabit Ethernet A version of Ethernet that supports rates of data transfer up to 1 gigabit per second.

gigahertz (GHz) One thousand MHz, or one billion cycles per second. *Also see* hertz *and* megahertz.

global account An account used at the domain level, created by an administrator, and stored in the SAM (security accounts manager) database on a Windows domain controller. *Also called* a domain account *or* network ID. *Compare with* local account.

global address *See* global unicast address.

global unicast address In TCP/IP version 6, an IP address that can be routed on the Internet. *Also called* global address.

Globally Unique Identifier Partition Table (GUID or GPT) *See* GUID Partition Table (GPT).

Gmail An email service provided by Google at *mail.google.com*.

Google account A user account identified by a valid email address that is registered on the Google Play website (*play.google.com*) and used to download content to an Android device.

Google Play The official source for Android apps (also called the Android marketplace), at *play.google.com*.

gpresult The Windows command to find out which group policies are currently applied to a system for the computer or user.

GPS (Global Positioning System) A receiver that uses the system of 24 or more satellites orbiting Earth. The receiver locates four or more of these satellites and uses their locations to calculate its own position in a process called triangulation.

gpupdate The Windows command to refresh local group policies as well as group policies set in Active Directory on a Windows domain.

graphical user interface (GUI) An interface that uses graphics as opposed to a command-driven interface.

graphics processing unit (GPU) A processor that manipulates graphic data to form the images on a monitor screen. A GPU can be embedded on a video card, on the motherboard, or integrated within the processor.

graphics tablet An input device that can use a stylus to hand draw. It works like a pencil on the tablet and uses a USB port. *Also called* digitizing tablet *and* digitizer.

grayware A program that is potentially harmful or potentially unwanted.

grep A Linux and macOS command to search for and display a specific pattern of characters in a file or multiple files.

ground bracelet *See* ESD strap.

G

ground mat *See* ESD mat.

Group Policy A console (gpedit.msc) available in Windows Server and Windows 10/8/7 professional and business editions that is used to control what users can do and how the local and network computers on the Windows domain can be used.

Group Policy Object (GPO) A named set of policies that have been created by Group Policy and are applied to an OU.

GRUB (GRand Unified Bootloader) The current Linux boot loader, which can handle dual boots with another OS installed on the system.

GSM (Global System for Mobile Communications) An open standard for cellular WANs and cell phones that uses digital communication of data and is accepted and used worldwide.

Guests group A type of user group in Windows. User accounts that belong to this group have limited rights to the system and are given a temporary profile that is deleted after the user logs off.

GUID Partition Table (GPT) A method for partitioning hard drives that allows for drives of any size. For Windows, a drive that uses this method can have up to 128 partitions. The GPT partitioning system is required to use a Secure boot with UEFI firmware.

gyroscope A device that contains a disc that can move and respond to gravity as the device is moved.

HAL (hardware abstraction layer) The low-level part of Windows, written specifically for each CPU technology, so that only the HAL must change when platform components change.

half duplex Communication between two devices whereby transmission takes place in only one direction at a time.

Handoff A technique of Apple devices and computers that lets you start a task on one device, such as an iPad, and then pick up that task on another device, such as a Mac desktop or laptop.

hard boot A restart of the computer by turning off the power or pressing the Reset button. *Also called* a cold boot.

hard disk drive (HDD) *See* hard drive.

hard drive The main secondary storage device of a computer. Two technologies are currently used by hard drives: magnetic and solid state. *Also called* hard disk drive (HDD).

hard reset (1) For Android devices, a factory reset, which erases all data and settings and restores the device to its original factory default state. (2) For iOS devices, a forced restart similar to a full shutdown, followed by a full clean boot of the device.

hardware address *See* MAC (Media Access Control) address.

hardware RAID One of two ways to implement RAID. Hardware RAID is more reliable and performs better than software RAID, and is implemented using BIOS/UEFI on the motherboard or a RAID controller card.

hardware signature Information kept on Microsoft activation servers along with a digital license to identify a machine that has activated a Windows installation.

hardware-assisted virtualization (HAV) A processor feature that can provide enhanced support for hypervisor software to run virtual machines on a system. The feature must be enabled in BIOS/UEFI setup.

HAV (hardware-assisted virtualization) *See* hardware-assisted virtualization (HAV).

HD15 port *See* VGA (Video Graphics Array) port.

HDMI (High Definition Multimedia Interface) port A digital audio and video interface standard currently used on desktop and laptop computers, televisions, and other home theater equipment. HDMI is often used to connect a computer to home theater equipment.

HDMI connector A connector that transmits both digital video and audio and is used on most computers and televisions.

HDMI mini connector A smaller type of HDMI connector used for connecting devices such as smartphones to a computer. *Also called* mini-HDMI connector.

header On a motherboard, a connector that consists of a group of pins that stick up on the board.

heat sink A piece of metal with cooling fins that can be attached to or mounted on an integrated chip package (such as the CPU) to dissipate heat.

help A Windows command that gives information about any Windows command.

hertz (Hz) A unit of measurement for frequency calculated in terms of vibrations or cycles per second. For example, for 16-bit stereo sound, a frequency of 44,000 Hz is used. *Also see* megahertz *and* gigahertz.

HFS+ (Hierarchical File System Plus) An older macOS file system for macOS 10.12 and earlier versions that uses a proprietary Apple partitioning system. *Also called* the Mac OS Extended file system.

hibernation A power-saving state that saves all work to the hard drive and powers down the system.

hidden share A folder whose folder name ends with a $ symbol. When you share the folder, it does not appear in the File Explorer or Windows Explorer window of remote computers on the network.

high-level formatting A process performed by the Windows Format program (for example, FORMAT C:/S), the Windows installation program, or the Disk Management utility. The process creates the boot record, file system, and root directory on a hard drive volume or other storage device. *Also called* formatting, OS formatting, *or* operating system formatting. *Compare with* low-level formatting.

high-touch using a standard image A strategy to install Windows that uses a standard image for the installation. A technician must perform the installation on the local computer. *Also see* standard image.

high-touch with retail media A strategy to install Windows where all the work is done by a technician sitting at the computer using Windows setup files. The technician also installs drivers and applications after the Windows installation is finished.

HKEY_CLASSES_ROOT (HKCR) A Windows registry key that stores information to determine which application is opened when the user double-clicks a file.

HKEY_CURRENT_CONFIG (HKCC) A Windows registry key that contains information about the hardware configuration that is used by the computer at startup.

HKEY_CURRENT_USER (HKCU) A Windows registry key that contains data about the current user. The key is built when a user logs on

using data kept in the HKEY_USERS key and data kept in the Ntuser.dat file of the current user.

HKEY_LOCAL_MACHINE (HKLM) An important Windows registry key that contains hardware, software, and security data. The key is built using data taken from the SAM hive, the Security hive, the Software hive, the System hive, and from data collected at startup about the hardware.

HKEY_USERS (HKU) A Windows registry key that contains data about all users and is taken from the Default hive.

Home button A hardware button on the bottom of Apple's iPhone or iPad.

Home folder The default folder presented to a user when she is ready to save a file. On a peer-to-peer network, the Home folder is normally the Documents folder in the user profile.

Home Theater PC (HTPC) A PC that is designed to play and possibly record music, photos, movies, and video on a television or extra-large monitor screen.

homegroup In Windows 8/7, a type of peer-to-peer network where each computer shares files, folders, libraries, and printers with other computers in the homegroup. Access to the homegroup is secured using a homegroup password. Windows 10 does not support a homegroup, as it is considered a security risk.

host A device, such as a desktop computer, laptop, or printer, on a network that requests or serves up data or services to other devices.

host name A name that identifies a computer, printer, or other device on a network; the host name can be used instead of the computer's IP address to address the computer on the network. The host name together with the domain name is called the fully qualified domain name. *Also called* computer name.

Hosts file A file in the C:\Windows\System32\ drivers\etc folder that contains computer names and their associated IP addresses on the local network. The file has no file extension.

hot-plugging Plugging in a device while the computer is turned on. The computer will sense the device and configure it without rebooting. In addition, the device can be unplugged without an OS error. *Also called* hot-swapping.

hotspot A small area that offers connectivity to a wireless network, such as a Wi-Fi network.

hot-swappable The ability to plug in or unplug devices without first powering down the system. USB devices are hot-swappable.

hot-swapping *See* hot-plugging.

HTTP (Hypertext Transfer Protocol) The TCP/IP protocol used for the World Wide Web and used by web browsers and web servers to communicate.

HTTPS (HTTP secure) The HTTP protocol working with a security protocol such as Secure Sockets Layer (SSL) or Transport Layer Security (TLS) to create a secured socket that includes data encryption. TLS is better than SSL.

hub A network device or box that provides a central location to connect cables and distributes incoming data packets to all other devices connected to it. *Compare with* switch.

hybrid cloud A combination of public, private, and community clouds used by the same organization. For example, a company might store data in a private cloud but use a public cloud email service.

hybrid hard drive (H-HDD) A hard drive that uses both magnetic and SSD technologies. The bulk of storage uses the magnetic component, and a storage buffer on the drive is made of an SSD component. Windows ReadyDrive supports hybrid hard drives.

HyperTransport The AMD technology that allows each logical processor within the processor package to handle an individual thread in parallel; other threads are handled by other processors within the package.

HyperThreading The Intel technology that allows each logical processor within the processor package to handle an individual thread in parallel; other threads are handled by other processors within the package.

hypervisor Software that creates and manages virtual machines on a server or on a local computer. *Also called* virtual machine manager (VMM).

I/O shield A plate installed on the rear of a computer case that provides holes for I/O ports coming off the motherboard.

IaaS (Infrastructure as a Service) A cloud computing service that provides only hardware, which can include servers, storage devices, and networks.

iCloud A website by Apple (*www.icloud.com*) used to sync content on Apple devices in order to provide a backup of the content.

iCloud Backup A feature of an iPhone, iPad, or iPod touch that backs up the device's content to the cloud at *icloud.com*.

iCloud Drive Storage space at *icloud.com* that can be synced with files stored on any Apple mobile device or any personal computer, including a macOS or Windows computer.

IDE (Integrated Drive Electronics or Integrated Device Electronics) A hard drive whose disk controller is integrated into the drive, eliminating the need for a controller cable and thus increasing speed as well as reducing price.

IDS (intrusion detection system) Software that monitors all network traffic and creates alerts when suspicious activity happens. IDS software can run on a UTM appliance, router, server, or workstation.

IEEE 802.11ac The latest Wi-Fi standard; it supports up to 7 Gbps (actual speeds are currently about 1300 Mbps) and uses 5.0-GHz radio frequency and beamforming.

IEEE 802.11n A Wi-Fi standard that supports up to 600 Mbps, uses 5.0-GHz or 2.4-GHz radio frequency, and supports MIMO.

ifconfig (interface configuration) A Linux and macOS command similar to ipconfig that displays details about network interfaces and can enable and disable an interface. When affecting the interface, the command requires root privileges.

image deployment Installing a standard image on a computer.

image-level backup A process that backs up and restores everything on a device, such as a hard drive, smartphone, or tablet. The restore process restores the device to a previous state.

imaging drum An electrically charged rotating drum found in laser printers.

IMAP4 (Internet Message Access Protocol, version 4) A TCP/IP protocol used by an email server and client that allows the client to manage email stored on the server without downloading the email. *Compare with* POP3.

IMEI (International Mobile Equipment Identity) A unique number that identifies a mobile phone or tablet device worldwide. The number can usually be found imprinted on the device or reported in the About menu of the OS.

impact paper Paper used by impact printers that comes in a box of fanfold paper or in rolls (used with receipt printers).

impact printer A type of printer that creates a printed page by using a mechanism that touches or hits the paper.

impersonation Pretending to be another individual or company to aid in a malicious attack.

IMSI (International Mobile Subscriber Identity) A unique number that identifies a cellular subscription for a device or subscriber, along with its home country and mobile network. Some carriers store the number on a SIM card installed in the device.

incident When an employee or other person has negatively affected safety or corporate resources, violated the code of conduct for an organization, or committed a crime.

incident documentation Documentation, including chain-of-custody documents, surrounding the evidence of an incident that may be used to prevent future incidents and as evidence in a criminal investigation.

incident response Predefined corporate procedures that are to be followed when an incident occurs.

Infrared (IR) An outdated wireless technology that has been mostly replaced by Bluetooth to connect personal computing devices.

infrastructure mode A mode in which Wi-Fi devices connect to a Wi-Fi access point, such as a SOHO router, which is responsible for securing and managing the wireless network.

inherited permissions Permissions assigned by Windows that are obtained from a parent object.

initialization files Text files that keep hardware and software configuration information, user preferences, and application settings and are used by the OS when first loaded and when needed by hardware, applications, and users.

ink cartridge A cartridge in inkjet printers that holds different colors of ink.

inkjet printer A type of ink dispersion printer that uses cartridges of ink. The ink is heated to a boiling point and then ejected onto the paper through tiny nozzles.

in-place upgrade A Windows installation that is launched from the Windows desktop. The installation carries forward user settings and installed applications from the old OS to the new one. A Windows OS is already in place before the installation begins.

In-Plane Switching (IPS) A class of LCD monitor that offers truer color images and better viewing angles, although it is expensive and has slower response times.

integer In scripting and programming, a type of data that is a whole number.

integrated print server A printer feature that allows it to connect to a network, manage print jobs from multiple computers, monitor printer maintenance tasks, and perhaps send email alerts when a problem arises.

interface In TCP/IP version 6, a node's attachment to a link. The attachment can be a physical attachment (for example, when using a network adapter) or a logical attachment (for example, when using a tunneling protocol). Each interface is assigned an IP address.

interface ID In TCP/IP version 6, the last 64 bits or 4 blocks of an IP address that identify the interface.

internal components The main components installed in a computer case.

Internet Options A dialog box used to manage Internet Explorer settings.

Internet service provider (ISP) *See* ISP (Internet service provider).

intranet Any private network that uses TCP/IP protocols. A large enterprise might support an intranet that is made up of several local networks.

inventory management In an IT organization, the methods used to track end-user devices, network devices, IP addresses, software licenses, and other software and hardware equipment.

inverter An electrical device that converts DC to AC.

iOS The operating system owned and developed by Apple and used for their various mobile devices.

IoT (Internet of Things) Any device that can connect to the Internet for a specific purpose, such as a smart thermostat or door lock.

IP (Internet Protocol) The primary TCP/IP protocol, used by the Internet layer, that is

G

responsible for getting a message to a destination host. In the OSI model, the Internet layer is called the Network layer.

IP address A 32-bit or 128-bit address used to uniquely identify a device or interface on a network that uses TCP/IP protocols. Generally, the first numbers identify the network; the last numbers identify a host. An example of a 32-bit IP address is 206.96.103.114. An example of a 128-bit IP address is 2001:0000:B80::D3:9C5A:CC.

iPad A handheld tablet developed by Apple.

ipconfig (IP configuration) A Windows command that displays TCP/IP configuration information and can refresh TCP/IP assignments to a connection, including its IP address.

iPhone A smartphone developed by Apple.

IPS (intrusion prevention system) Software that monitors and logs suspicious activity on a network and can prevent the threatening traffic from burrowing into the system. *Compare with* IDS (intrusion detection system).

IPv4 (Internet Protocol version 4) Version 4 of the TCP/IP protocols and standards that define 32-bit IP addresses and how they are used.

IPv6 (Internet Protocol version 6) Version 6 of the TCP/IP protocols and standards that define 128-bit IP addresses and how they are used.

IR (infrared) A wireless connection that requires an unobstructed line of sight between transmitter and receiver and uses light waves just below the visible red-light spectrum.

ISATAP In TCP/IP version 6, a tunneling protocol that has been developed for IPv6 packets to travel over an IPv4 network; ISATAP stands for Intra-Site Automatic Tunnel Addressing Protocol.

ISDN (Integrated Services Digital Network) A broadband telephone line that can carry data at about five times the speed of regular telephone lines. Two channels (telephone numbers) share a single pair of wires. ISDN has been replaced by DSL.

ISO file *See* ISO image.

ISO image A file format that has an .iso file extension and holds an image of all the data that is stored on an optical disc, including the file system. ISO stands for International Organization for Standardization.

ISP (Internet service provider) An organization, such as Charter, that provides individuals and organizations access to the Internet via a technology such as cable Internet, DSL, or cellular.

iTunes Software by Apple installed on a Mac or Windows computer to sync an iPhone or iPad to iOS updates downloaded from *itunes.com* and to troubleshoot problems with the Apple device.

iTunes Store The Apple website at *itunes.com* and the Apple app on an Apple mobile device, where apps, music, TV shows, movies, books, podcasts, and iTunes U content can be purchased and downloaded to a device.

iTunes U Content at the iTunes Store website (*itunes.com*) that contains lectures and even complete courses from many schools, colleges, and universities.

ITX *See* Mini-ITX.

iwconfig A Linux and macOS command similar to ifconfig that applies only to wireless networks. Use it to display information about a wireless interface and configure a wireless adapter.

jailbreaking A process to break through the restrictions that only allow apps for an iOS device to be downloaded from the iTunes Store at *itunes.com*. Jailbreaking gives the user root or administrator privileges to the operating system and the entire file system, and complete access to all commands and features.

JavaScript A scripting language normally used to create scripts for webpages; the scripts are embedded in an HTML file to build an interactive webpage in a browser.

joule A measure of work or energy. One joule of energy produces 1 watt of power for one second.

jumper Two small posts or metal pins that stick up side by side on a motherboard or other device and are used to hold configuration information. The jumper is considered closed if a cover is over the wires and open if the cover is missing.

Kensington lock *See* cable lock.

Kensington Security Slot A security slot on a laptop case to connect a cable lock. *Also called* K-Slot.

kernel The portion of an OS that is responsible for interacting with the hardware.

kernel mode A Windows "privileged" processing mode that has access to hardware components.

kernel panic A Linux or macOS error from which it cannot recover, similar to a blue screen of death in Windows.

key fob A device, such as a type of smart card, that can fit conveniently on a key chain.

keyboard backlight A feature on some keyboards where the keys light up.

Keychain In macOS, a built-in password manager utility.

Key-enrollment Key (KEK) *See* Key-exchange Key (KEK).

Key-exchange Key (KEK) A Secure boot database that holds digital signatures provided by OS manufacturers.

keylogger A type of spyware that tracks your keystrokes, including passwords, chat room sessions, email messages, documents, online purchases, and anything else you type on your computer. Text is logged to a text file and transmitted over the Internet without your knowledge.

keystone RJ-45 jack A jack that is used in an RJ-45 wall jack.

kill A Linux and macOS command used to forcefully end or kill a process.

knowledge base A collection of articles containing text, images, or video that give information about a network, product, or service.

KVM (Keyboard, Video, and Mouse) switch A switch that allows you to use one keyboard, mouse, and monitor for multiple computers. Some KVM switches also include sound ports so that speakers and a microphone can be shared among multiple computers.

LAN (local area network) A network bound by routers or other gateway devices that usually covers only a small area, such as one building.

land grid array (LGA) A socket that has blunt protruding pins in uniform rows that connect with lands or pads on the bottom of the processor. *Compare with* pin grid array (PGA).

laptop A portable computer that is designed for travel and mobility. Laptops use the same technology as desktop computers, with modifications for conserving voltage, taking up less space, and operating while on the move. *Also called* a notebook computer.

laser printer A type of printer that uses a laser beam to control how toner is placed on the page and then uses heat to fuse the toner to the page.

Last Known Good Configuration In Windows 7, registry settings and device drivers that were in effect when the computer last booted successfully. These settings are saved and can be restored during the startup process to recover from errors during the last boot.

latency Delays in network transmissions that result in slower network performance. Latency is measured by the round-trip time it takes for a data packet to travel from source to destination and back to the source.

launcher The Android graphical user interface (GUI) that includes multiple home screens and supports windows, panes, and 3D graphics.

Launchpad The macOS utility used to launch and uninstall applications.

LC (local connector) connector A fiber-optic cable connector that can be used with either single-mode or multimode fiber-optic cables and is easily terminated; it is smaller than an SC connector.

LCD (liquid crystal display) monitor A monitor that uses LCD technology. LCD produces an image using a liquid crystal material made of large, easily polarized molecules. *Also called* a flat-panel monitor.

LDAP (Lightweight Directory Access Protocol) A TCP/IP protocol used by client applications to query and receive data from a database. The LDAP protocol does not include encryption.

LED (Light-Emitting Diode) A technology used in an LCD monitor that requires less mercury than earlier technologies.

Level 1 cache (L1 cache) Memory on the processor die used as a cache to improve processor performance.

Level 2 cache (L2 cache) Memory in the processor package but not on the processor die. The memory is used as a cache or buffer to improve processor performance. *Also see* Level 1 (L1) cache.

Level 3 cache (L3 cache) Cache memory that is further from the processor core than Level 2 cache but still in the processor package.

LGA1150 A CPU socket for Intel processors that works with 4th and 5th generation chipsets and

G

processors. The socket uses a land grid array and 1150 pins.

LGA1151 A CPU socket for Intel processors that uses a land grid array and 1151 pins. Two versions of the socket currently exist; the older version works with 6th and 7th generation chipsets and processors, and the newer version works with 8th generation chipsets and processors. The two sockets are not compatible because the pins are used differently on each version of the socket.

library A collection of one or more folders that can be stored on different local drives or on the network.

Lightning *See* Lightning port.

Lightning port The proprietary Apple connector used on Apple iPhones, iPods, and iPads for power and communication.

Lightweight Directory Access Protocol (LDAP) *See* LDAP (Lightweight Directory Access Protocol).

line-of-sight wireless connectivity A type of connection used by satellites that requires an unobstructed path free of mountains, trees, and tall buildings from the satellite dish to the satellite.

link (local link) In TCP/IP version 6, a local area network or wide area network bounded by routers. *Also called* local link.

link local address *See* link local unicast address.

link local unicast address In TCP/IP version 6, an IP address used for communicating among nodes in the same link; this IP address is not allowed on the Internet. *Also called* local address *and* link local address.

Linux An OS based on UNIX that was created by Linus Torvalds of Finland. Basic versions of this OS are open source, and all the underlying programming instructions are freely distributed.

lite-touch, high-volume deployment A strategy that uses a deployment server on the network to serve up a Windows installation after a technician starts the process at the local computer.

lithium ion Currently the most popular type of battery for notebook computers; it is more efficient than earlier types. Sometimes abbreviated as "Li-Ion" battery.

Live CD In Linux, a CD, DVD, or flash drive that can boot up a live version of Linux,

complete with Internet access and all the tools you normally have available in a hard drive installation of Linux; however, the OS is not installed on the hard drive.

live sign in A way to sign in to Windows 8 using a Microsoft account.

live tiles On the Windows 10 Start menu or the Windows 8 Start screen, tiles used by some apps to offer continuous real-time updates.

Live USB In Linux, a live CD stored on a USB flash drive. *Also see* Live CD.

loadstate A command used by the User State Migration Tool (USMT) to copy user settings and data temporarily stored at a safe location to a new computer. *Also see* scanstate.

local account A Windows user account that applies only to the local computer and cannot be used to access resources from other computers on the network. *Compare with* global account.

local area network (LAN) *See* LAN (local area network).

Local Group Policy A console (gpedit.msc) available in Windows 10/8/7 professional and business editions that applies only to local users and the local computer. *Also see* Group Policy.

local link *See* link.

local printer A printer connected to a computer by way of a port on the computer. *Compare with* network printer.

Local Security Policy A Windows Administrative Tools snap-in in Control Panel that can manage the Security Settings group of policies. This same group can also be found in Group Policy in the Local Computer Policy/Computer Configuration/Windows Settings group.

local shares Folders on a computer that are shared with others on the network by using a folder's Properties box. Local shares are used with a workgroup and not with a domain.

Local Users and Groups For business and professional editions of Windows, a Windows utility console (lusrmgr.msc) that can be used to manage user accounts and user groups.

location data Data that a device can routinely report to a website so that the device can be located on a map.

location independence A function of cloud computing whereby customers generally don't know the geographical locations of the physical devices providing cloud services.

locator application An app on a mobile device that can be used to locate the device on a map, force the device to ring, change its password, or remotely erase all data on the device.

logical drive On an MBR hard drive, a portion or all of a hard drive's extended partition that is treated by the operating system as though it were a physical drive or volume. Each logical drive is assigned a drive letter, such as drive F, and contains a file system. *Compare with* volume.

logical topology The logical way computers connect on a network.

login item In macOS, a program that automatically launches after a user logs in. Login items are managed in the Users & Groups utility in System Preferences.

LoJack A technology by Absolute Software that tracks the whereabouts of a laptop computer and, if the computer is stolen, locks down access to it or erases data on it. The technology is embedded in the BIOS/UEFI of many laptops.

Long Term Evolution (LTE) *See* LTE (Long Term Evolution).

loopback address An IP address that indicates your own computer and is used to test TCP/IP configuration on the computer.

loopback plug A device used to test a port in a computer or other device to make sure the port is working; it might also test the throughput or speed of the port.

low-level format A type of formatting, usually done at the factory, where sector marks are added to the platters of a magnetic hard drive.

low-level formatting A process (usually performed at the factory) that electronically creates the hard drive tracks and sectors and tests for bad spots on the disk surface. *Compare with* high-level formatting.

LPT (Line Printer Terminal) Assignments of system resources that are made to a parallel port and used to manage a print job. Two possible LPT configurations are referred to as LPT1: and LPT2:.

LPT port *See* parallel port.

LTE (Long Term Evolution) In telecommunications, a set of wireless communication standards that

define data and voice transmissions over cellular networks; LTE is expected to replace GSM and CDMA.

M.2 connector A motherboard or expansion card slot that connects to a mini add-on card. The slot uses a PCIe, USB, or SATA interface with the motherboard chipset, and several variations of the slot exist. *Also called* a Next Generation Form Factor (NGFF) connector.

MAC (Media Access Control) address A 48-bit (6-byte) hardware address unique to each NIC or onboard network controller; the address is assigned by the manufacturer at the factory and embedded on the device. The address is often printed on the adapter as hexadecimal numbers. An example is 00 00 0C 08 2F 35. *Also called* a physical address, an adapter address, *or a* hardware address.

MAC address filtering A technique used by a router or wireless access point that allows computers and devices to access a private network if their MAC addresses are on a list of approved addresses.

Mac OS Extended *See* HFS+ (Hierarchical File System Plus).

macOS The proprietary desktop operating system by Apple. macOS is based on UNIX and used only on Apple computers. macOS was formerly called Mac OS X.

magnetic hard drive One of two technologies used by hard drives where data is stored as magnetic spots on disks that rotate at a high speed. *Compare with* solid-state drive (SSD).

magnetic stripe reader A device that can read the magnetic stripe on a card, such as a credit card, and transmit the information to a computer.

main board *See* motherboard.

malicious software Any unwanted program that is transmitted to a computer without the user's knowledge and that is designed to do varying degrees of damage to data and software. Types of infestations include viruses, Trojan horses, worms, adware, spyware, keyloggers, browser hijackers, dialers, and downloaders. *Also called* malware, infestation, *or* computer infestation.

malware *See* malicious software.

malware definition Information about malware that allows anti-malware software to detect and define malware. *Also called* a malware signature.

malware encyclopedias   Lists of malware, including symptoms and solutions, often maintained by manufacturers of anti-malware software and made available on their websites.

malware signatures   *See* malware definition.

MAN (metropolitan area network)   A type of network that covers a large city or campus.

managed switch   A switch that has firmware that can be configured to monitor, manage, and prioritize network traffic.

man-in-the-middle attack   An attack that pretends to be a legitimate website, network, FTP site, or person in a chat session in order to obtain private information.

mantrap   A physical security technique of using two doors on either end of a small entryway where the first door must close before the second door can open. A separate form of identification might be required for each door, such as a badge for the first door and a fingerprint scan for the second door. In addition, a security guard might monitor people as they come and go.

mapping   A process in which the client computer creates and saves a shortcut (called a network drive) to a folder or drive shared by a remote computer on the network. The network drive has an associated drive letter that points to the network share.

Master Boot Record (MBR)   A partitioning system used by hard drives with a capacity less than 2 TB. On an MBR hard drive, the first sector is called the MBR; it contains the partition table and a program motherboard that firmware uses to boot an OS from the drive.

master file table (MFT)   The database used by the NTFS file system to track the contents of a volume or logical drive.

Material Safety Data Sheet (MSDS)   A document that explains how to properly handle substances such as chemical solvents; it includes information such as physical data, toxicity, health effects, first aid, storage, disposal, and spill procedures.

mATX   *See* microATX.

MBR (Master Boot Record)   *See* Master Boot Record (MBR).

md (make directory)   The Windows command to create a directory.

MDM policies   Policies that establish compliance standards used by MDM and may include various forms of security enforcement, such as data encryption requirements and remote wipes.

measured service   When a cloud computing vendor offers services that are metered for billing purposes or to ensure transparency between vendors and customers.

Media Center   In some editions of Windows 8/7, a digital video recorder and media player; it is not available in Windows 10.

Media Creation Tool   Software downloaded from the Microsoft website and used to download Windows setup files, which in turn are used to create setup media or to install Windows.

megahertz (MHz)   One million Hz, or one million cycles per second. *Also see* hertz *and* gigahertz.

memory bank   The memory a processor addresses at one time. Today's desktop and laptop processors use a memory bank that is 64 bits wide.

Memory Diagnostics   A Windows 10/8/7 utility (mdsched.exe) used to test memory.

Metro User Interface (Metro UI)   *See* modern interface.

micro USB   A smaller version of the regular USB connector.

Micro-A connector   A USB connector that has five pins and is smaller than the Mini-B connector. It is used on digital cameras, cell phones, and other small electronic devices.

microATX (mATX)   A smaller version of the ATX form factor. MicroATX addresses some technologies that were developed after the original introduction of ATX. *Also called* mATX.

Micro-B connector   A USB connector that has five pins and a smaller height than the Mini-B connector. It is used on digital cameras, cell phones, and other small electronic devices.

microprocessor   *See* central processing unit (CPU).

Microsoft account   For Windows 10/8, an email address registered with Microsoft that allows access to several types of online accounts, including Microsoft OneDrive, Facebook, LinkedIn, Twitter, Skype, and Outlook.

Microsoft Assessment and Planning (MAP) Toolkit   Software that can be used by a system administrator from a network location to query hundreds of computers in a single scan and determine if a computer qualifies for a Windows upgrade.

Microsoft Deployment Toolkit (MDT)   A suite of Microsoft tools that can automate a Windows installation.

Microsoft Exchange   A popular server application used by large corporations for employee email, contacts, and calendars.

Microsoft Management Console (MMC)   A Windows utility to build customized consoles. These consoles can be saved to a file with an .msc file extension.

Microsoft Store   The official source for Windows apps at *microsoftstore.com*.

Microsoft Terminal Services Client   *See* mstsc (Microsoft Terminal Services Client).

MIDI (musical instrument digital interface)   A set of standards that are used to represent music in digital form. A MIDI port is a 5-pin DIN port that looks like a keyboard port, only larger.

MIMO (multiple input/multiple output)   *See* multiple input/multiple output (MIMO).

Mini DisplayPort   A smaller version of DisplayPort that is used on laptops or other mobile devices.

Mini PCI   The PCI industry standard for desktop computer expansion cards; it is applied to a much smaller form factor for notebook expansion cards.

Mini PCI Express (Mini PCIe)   A standard used for a notebook's internal expansion slots that follows the PCI Express standards. *Also called* Mini PCIe.

Mini PCIe   *See* Mini PCI Express (Mini PCIe).

Mini-B connector   A USB connector that has five pins and is often used to connect small electronic devices, such as a digital camera, to a computer.

minicartridge   A tape drive cartridge that is only 3¼ × 2½ × 3/5 inches. It is small enough to allow two drives to fit into a standard 5-inch drive bay of a PC case.

Mini-DIN-6 connector   A 6-pin variation of the S-Video port that looks like a PS/2 connector; it is used by a keyboard or mouse.

mini-HDMI connector   *See* HDMI mini connector.

Mini-ITX   A smaller version of the microATX form factor. *Also called* ITX *and* mITX.

miniUSB   A smaller version of the regular USB connector; it is also smaller than microUSB.

Miracast   A wireless display-mirroring technology that requires a Miracast-capable screen or dongle in order to mirror a smartphone's display to a TV, a wireless monitor, or a wireless projector.

mirrored volume   The term used by Windows for the RAID 1 level that duplicates data on one drive to another drive and is used for fault tolerance. *Also see* RAID 1.

mirroring   Copying one hard drive to another as a backup. *Also called* RAID 1.

Mission Control   In macOS, a utility and screen that gives an overview of all open windows and thumbnails of the Dashboard and desktops.

mITX   *See* Mini-ITX.

mobile device management (MDM)   Software that includes tools for tracking mobile devices and managing the security of data on the devices according to established MDM policies.

mobile hotspot   A location created by a mobile device so that other devices or computers can connect by Wi-Fi to the device and to the Internet.

mobile payment service   An app that allows you to use your smartphone or other mobile device to pay for merchandise or services at a retail checkout counter.

modem port   A port used to connect dial-up phone lines to computers.

modern interface   In Windows 10/8, an interface that presents the Windows 10 live tiles and their apps or the Windows 8 Start screen to the user. In Windows 8, it was called the Metro User Interface or Metro UI.

Molex connector   A 4-pin power connector used to provide power to a PATA hard drive, optical drive, or other internal component.

motherboard   The main board in the computer. The CPU, ROM chips, DIMMs, and interface cards are plugged into the motherboard. *Also called* the system board.

mount point   A folder that is used as a shortcut to space on another volume, which effectively increases the size of the folder to the size of the other volume. *Also see* mounted drive.

G

mounted drive A volume that can be accessed by way of a folder on another volume so that the folder has more available space. *Also see* mount point.

mstsc (Microsoft Terminal Services Client) A command (mstsc.exe) that allows you to remote in to a host computer using Remote Desktop Connection.

MT-RJ (mechanical transfer registered jack) connector A type of connector that can be used with either single-mode or multimode fiber-optic cables and is more difficult to connect than the smaller LC connector.

multiboot *See* dual boot.

multicast address In TCP/IP version 6, an IP address used when packets are delivered to a group of nodes on a network.

multicasting In TCP/IP version 6, the transmission of messages from one host to multiple hosts, such as when the host transmits a videoconference over the Internet.

multicore processing A processor technology whereby the processor housing contains two or more processor cores that operate at the same frequency but independently of each other.

multifactor authentication (MFA) The use of more than one method to authenticate access to a computer, network, or other resource.

multimedia shredder A device that can destroy optical discs, flash drives, SSDs and other devices so that sensitive data stored on the device is also destroyed.

MultiMediaCard (MMC) A compact storage card that looks like an SD card, but the technology is different and they are not interchangeable. Generally, SD cards are faster than MMC cards.

multimeter A device used to measure the various attributes of an electrical circuit. The most common measurements are voltage, current, and resistance.

multiple desktops A feature of Mission Control in macOS, where several desktop screens, each with its own collection of open windows, are available to the user.

multiple input/multiple output (MIMO) A feature of the IEEE 802.11n/ac standards for wireless networking whereby two or more antennas are used at both ends of transmissions to improve performance.

multiple monitor misalignment When the display is staggered across multiple monitors, making the display difficult to read. Fix the problem by adjusting the display in the Windows Screen Resolution window.

multiple monitor orientation The aligned orientation of dual monitor screens. When the display does not accurately represent the relative positions of multiple monitors, use the Windows Screen Resolution window to move the display for each monitor so they are oriented correctly.

multiplier The factor by which the bus speed or frequency is multiplied to get the CPU clock speed.

multiprocessing Two processing units installed within a single processor; it was first used by the Pentium processor.

multiprocessor platform A system that contains more than one processor. The motherboard has more than one processor socket and the processors must be rated to work in this multiprocessor environment.

multitouch A touch screen on a computer or mobile device that can handle a two-finger pinch.

mutual authentication To authenticate in both directions at the same time as both entities confirm the identity of the other.

name resolution The process of associating a character-based name with an IP address.

NAND flash memory The type of memory used in SSDs. NAND stands for "Not AND" and refers to the logic used when storing a 1 or 0 in the grid of rows and columns on the memory chip.

NAS (network attached memory) A group of hard drives inside an enclosure that connects to a network via an Ethernet port and is used for storage on the network.

NAT (Network Address Translation) A technique that substitutes the public IP address of the router for the private IP address of a computer on a private network when the computer needs to communicate on the Internet.

native resolution The actual (and fixed) number of pixels built into an LCD monitor. For the clearest display, always set the resolution to the native resolution.

navigation pane In File Explorer or Windows Explorer, a pane on the left side of the window where devices, drives, and folders are listed. Double-click an item to drill down into it.

nbtstat (NetBIOS over TCP/IP Statistics) A Windows TCP/IP command that is used to display statistics about the NetBT protocol.

Near Field Communication (NFC) *See* NFC.

neighbors In TCP/IP version 6, two or more nodes on the same link.

net localgroup A Windows TCP/IP command that adds, displays, or modifies local user groups.

net use A Windows TCP/IP command that connects or disconnects a computer from a shared resource or can display information about connections.

net user A Windows TCP/IP command used to manage user accounts.

NetBIOS A legacy suite of protocols used by Windows before TCP/IP.

netbook A low-end, inexpensive laptop with a 9- or 10-inch screen and no optical drive that is generally used for web browsing, email, and word processing by users on the go.

NetBoot A technology that allows a Mac to boot from the network and then install macOS on the machine from a clone DMG file stored on a deployment server.

NetBT (NetBIOS over TCP/IP) A feature of Server Message Block (SMB) protocols that allows legacy NetBIOS applications to communicate on a TCP/IP network.

netdom (network domain) A Windows TCP/IP command that allows administrators to manage Active Directory domains and trust relationships for Windows Server from the command prompt on the server or remotely from a Windows 8/7 workstation.

netstat (network statistics) A Windows TCP/IP command that displays statistics about TCP/IP and network activity and includes several parameters.

network adapter *See* network interface card (NIC).

Network and Sharing Center The primary Windows 10/8/7 utility used to manage network connections.

Network Attached Storage (NAS) A device that provides multiple bays for hard drives and an Ethernet port to connect to the network. The device is likely to support RAID.

network drive map Mounting a drive to a computer, such as drive E:, that is actually hard drive space on another host computer on the network.

Network File System (NFS) *See* NFS (Network File System).

network ID The leftmost bits in an IP address. The rightmost bits of the IP address identify the host.

network interface card (NIC) An expansion card that plugs into a computer's motherboard and provides a port on the back of the card to connect a computer to a network. *Also called* a network adapter.

network multimeter A multifunctional tool that can test network connections, cables, ports, and network adapters.

Network Places Wizard *See* User Accounts.

network port A port used by a network cable to connect to the wired network. *Also called* an Ethernet port.

network printer A printer that any user on the network can access, either through the printer's own network card and connection to the network, through a connection to a stand-alone print server, or through a connection to a computer as a local printer that is shared on the network.

network share A networked computer (the client) that appears to have a hard drive, such as drive E:, which is actually hard drive space on another host computer (the server). *Also see* mapping.

network topology diagram A documented map of network devices that includes the patterns or design used to connect the devices, either physically or logically.

next-generation firewall (NGFW) A firewall that combines firewall software with anti-malware software and other software that protects resources on a network.

NFC (Near Field Communication) A wireless technology that establishes a communication link between two NFC devices (for example, two smartphones or a smartphone and an NFC tag) that are within 4 inches (10 cm) of each other.

G

NFS (Network File System)   A client/server distributed file system that supports file sharing over a network across platforms. For example, a Linux-hosted NFS server can serve up file shares to Windows workstations on the network. Windows 10 supports NFS client connections.

NIC (network interface card)   *See* network interface card (NIC).

node   Any device that connects to the network, such as a computer, printer, or router.

noncompliant system   A system that violates security best practices, such as out-of-date anti-malware software or cases where it's not installed.

nonvolatile RAM (NVRAM)   Flash memory on the motherboard that UEFI firmware uses to store device drivers and information about Secure boot. Contents of NVRAM are not lost when the system is powered down.

North Bridge   The portion of the chipset hub that connects faster I/O buses (for example, the video bus) to the system bus. *Compare with* South Bridge.

notebook   *See* laptop.

Notepad   A text editing program.

notification area   An area to the right of the taskbar that holds the icons for running services; these services include the volume control and network connectivity. *Also called* the system tray *or* systray.

notifications   Alerts and related information about apps and social media sent to mobile devices and other computers.

nslookup (namespace lookup)   A TCP/IP command that lets you read information from the Internet namespace by requesting information about domain name resolutions from the DNS server's zone data.

NTFS (New Technology file system)   A file system that supports encryption, disk quotas, and file and folder compression; it is required for the volume that holds a Windows installation.

NTFS permissions   A method to share a folder or file over a network; these permissions can be applied to local users and network users. The folder or file must be on an NTFS volume. *Compare with* share permissions.

NVMe (Non-Volatile Memory Express or NVM Express)   An interface standard used to connect an SSD to the system and that uses the PCI Express ×4 interface to communicate with the processor. NVMe is about five times faster than SATA3.

octet   In TCP/IP version 4, each of the four numbers that are separated by periods and make up a 32-bit IP address. One octet is 8 bits.

off-boarding   The established process used when a mobile device is removed from the MDM fleet of devices allowed to connect to a corporate network and its resources. *Compare with* on-boarding.

Offline Files   A utility that allows users to work with files in a designated folder when the computer is not connected to the corporate network. When the computer is later connected, Windows syncs up the offline files and folders with those on the network.

ohm (Ω)   The standard unit of measurement for electrical resistance. Resistors are rated in ohms.

OLED (organic light-emitting diode) monitor   A type of monitor that uses a thin LED layer or film between two grids of electrodes and does not use backlighting.

onboard NIC   A network port embedded on the motherboard.

onboard port   A port that is directly on the motherboard, such as a built-in keyboard port or onboard network port.

on-boarding   The established process used when a mobile device is added to the MDM fleet of devices allowed to connect to a corporate network and its resources. *Compare with* off-boarding.

on-demand   A service that is available to users at any time. On-demand cloud computing means the service is always available.

OneDrive   A file hosting service from Microsoft that offers free and purchased storage space in the cloud.

Open Database Connectivity (ODBC)   A technology that allows a client computer to create a data source so that the client can interface with a database stored on a remote (host) computer on the network. *Also see* data source.

open source   Source code for an operating system or other software that is available for free; anyone can modify and redistribute the source code.

operating system (OS)   Software that controls a computer. An OS controls how system resources are used, and it provides a user interface, a way of managing hardware and software, and ways to work with files.

optical connector   A connector used with a fiber-optic cable.

organizational unit (OU)   An object that defines a collection of user groups and/or computers in Active Directory.

Original Equipment Manufacturer (OEM) license   A Microsoft Windows license available for purchase only by manufacturers or builders of personal computers and intended to be installed only on a computer for sale.

OS X   *See* macOS.

OSI (Open Systems Interconnection) Model   A model for understanding and developing computer-to-computer communication that divides networking functions among seven layers: Physical, Data Link, Network, Transport, Session, Presentation, and Application.

overclocking   Running a processor at a higher frequency than that recommended by the manufacturer. Overclocking can result in an unstable system, but it is a popular practice when a computer is used for gaming.

overheat shutdown   When a device, such as a projector, overheats and automatically powers off. Allow it to cool down before powering it up again.

PaaS (Platform as a Service)   A cloud computing service that provides hardware and an operating system and is responsible for updating and maintaining both.

package   A collection of files needed to install software.

packet   A message sent over a network as a unit of data; the information at the beginning of the packet identifies the type of data, where it came from, and where it's going. *Also called* data packet *or* datagram.

pagefile.sys   The Windows swap file used to hold virtual memory, which enhances physical memory installed in a system.

paired   When two Bluetooth devices have established connectivity and are able to communicate.

pairing   The process of two Bluetooth devices establishing connectivity.

PAN (personal area network)   A small network consisting of personal devices at close range; the devices can include smartphones, PDAs, and notebook computers.

parallel ATA (PATA)   An older IDE cabling method that uses a 40-pin flat or round data cable or an 80-conductor cable and a 40-pin IDE connector. *Also see* serial ATA.

parallel port   An outdated female 25-pin port on a computer that transmitted data in parallel, 8 bits at a time, and was typically used with a printer. Parallel ports have been replaced by USB ports. *Also called* an LPT1 port, LPT2 port, *and* LPT port.

parity   An older error-checking scheme used with SIMMs in which a ninth, or "parity," bit is added. The value of the parity bit is set to either 0 or 1 to provide an even number of 1s for even parity and an odd number of 1s for odd parity.

parity error   An error that occurs in parity error-checking when the number of 1s in the byte is not in agreement with the expected number.

partition   A division of a hard drive that can hold a volume. MBR drives can support up to four partitions on one hard drive. In Windows, GPT drives can have up to 128 partitions.

partition table   A table that contains information about each partition on the drive. For MBR drives, the partition table is contained in the Master Boot Record. For GPT drives, the partition table is stored in the GPT header and a backup of the table is stored at the end of the drive.

passive CPU cooler   *See* fanless CPU cooler.

passwd   A Linux and macOS command to change a password. A superuser can change the password for another user.

password policy   A set of rules that defines the minimum length of a password, complexity requirements, and how frequently the password must be reset.

patch   A minor update to software that corrects an error, adds a feature, or addresses security issues. *Also called* an update. *Compare with* service pack.

patch cable   *See* straight-through cable.

G

patch panel   A device that provides multiple network ports for cables that converge in one location such as an electrical closet or server room.

path   A drive and list of directories pointing to a file, such as C:\Windows\System32.

Payment Card Industry (PCI)   Regulated credit card and debit card data and the standards that regulate how this data is transmitted and stored to help prevent fraud; PCI applies to vendors, retailers, and financial institutions.

PCI (Peripheral Component Interconnect)   A bus common to personal computers that uses a 32-bit wide or 64-bit data path. Several variations of PCI exist. On desktop systems, one or more notches on a PCI slot keep the wrong PCI cards from being inserted in the slot.

PCI Express (PCIe)   An evolution of PCI that is not backward-compatible with earlier PCI slots and cards. PCIe slots come in several sizes, including PCIe ×1, PCIe ×4, PCIe ×8, and PCIe ×16.

PCIe 6/8-pin connector   A power cord connector used by high-end video cards with PCIe ×16 slots to provide extra voltage to the card; the connector can accommodate a 6-hole or 8-hole port.

PCI-X   The second evolution of PCI, which is backward-compatible with conventional PCI slots and cards, except 5-V PCI cards. PCI-X is focused on the server market.

PCL (Printer Control Language)   A printer language developed by Hewlett-Packard that communicates instructions to a printer.

PCMCIA card   A card used with older laptops that was one or more variations of a PC Card to add memory to the laptop or provide ports for peripheral devices—for example, modem cards, network cards for a wired or wireless network, sound cards, SCSI host adapters, FireWire controllers, USB controllers, flash memory adapters, TV tuners, and hard disks.

PDU (protocol data unit)   A message on a TCP/IP network. A PDU might be called a packet or frame, depending on the complexity of the PDU.

peer-to-peer (P2P)   As applied to networking, a network of computers that are all equals, or peers. Each computer has the same amount of authority, and each can act as a server to the other computers.

Performance Monitor   A Microsoft Management Console snap-in that can track activity by hardware and software to measure performance.

permission propagation   When Windows passes permissions from parent objects to child objects.

permissions   Varying degrees of access assigned to a folder or file and given to a user account or user group. Access can include full control, write, delete, and read-only.

personal license   A license that gives a user the right to install and use one or two instances of software.

PHI (protected health information)   Regulated data about a person's health status or health care as defined by HIPAA (the Health Insurance Portability and Accountability Act), which includes steep penalties and risks for noncompliance.

phishing   Sending an email message with the intent of getting the user to reveal private information that can be used for identity theft. *Also see* spear phishing.

physical address   *See* MAC (Media Access Control) address.

physical topology   The physical arrangement of connections between computers.

pickup roller   A part in a printer that pushes a sheet of paper forward from the paper tray.

PII (personally identifiable information)   Regulated data that identifies a person, including a Social Security number, email address, physical address, birthdate, birth place, mother's maiden name, marital status, phone numbers, race, and biometric data.

pin grid array (PGA)   A socket that has holes aligned in uniform rows around it to receive the pins on the bottom of the processor. *Compare with* land grid array (LGA).

ping (Packet InterNet Groper)   A TCP/IP command used to troubleshoot network connections. It verifies that the host can communicate with another host on the network.

pinning   Making a frequently used application more accessible by adding its icon to the taskbar on the desktop.

pixel   A small spot on a fine horizontal scan line. Pixels are illuminated to create an image on the monitor.

pixel pitch   The distance between adjacent pixels on the screen.

plasma monitor   A type of monitor that provides high contrast with better color than LCD monitors. It works by discharging xenon and neon plasma on flat glass, and it doesn't contain mercury.

platform   The hardware, operating system, runtime libraries, and modules on which an application runs.

Platform Key (PK)   A digital signature that belongs to the motherboard or computer manufacturer. The PK authorizes turning Secure boot on or off and updating the KEK database.

plenum   The area between floors of a building.

PoE injector (Power over Ethernet)   A device that adds power to an Ethernet cable so the cable can provide power to a device.

POP or POP3 (Post Office Protocol, version 3)   The TCP/IP protocol that an email server and client use when the client requests the downloading of email messages. The most recent version is POP version 3. *Compare with* IMAP4.

port   (1) As applied to services running on a computer, a number assigned to a process on a computer so that the process can be found by TCP/IP. *Also called* a port address *or* port number. (2) A physical connector, usually at the back of a computer, that allows a cable to be attached from a peripheral device, such as a printer, mouse, or modem.

port address   *See* port.

port filtering   To open or close certain ports so they can or cannot be used. A firewall uses port filtering to protect a network from unwanted communication.

port forwarding   A technique that allows a computer on the Internet to reach a computer on a private network using a certain port when the private network is protected by NAT and a firewall that controls the use of ports. *Also called* port mapping.

port lock   A physical lock, such as a USB lock, that prevents use of a computer port.

port mapping   *See* port forwarding.

port number   *See* port.

port replicator   A nonproprietary device that typically connects to a laptop via a USB port

and provides ports to allow the laptop to easily connect to peripheral devices, such as an external monitor, network, printer, keyboard, mouse, or speakers. *Also called* a universal docking station.

port security   Controlled access to ports on a managed switch, which is usually done through MAC address filtering for one or more ports.

port triggering   When a firewall opens a port because a computer behind the firewall initiates communication on another port.

POST (power-on self test)   A self-diagnostic program used to perform a simple test of the CPU, RAM, and various I/O devices. The POST is performed by startup BIOS/UEFI when the computer is first turned on.

POST card   A test card installed in a slot on the motherboard or plugged in to a USB port that is used to help discover and report computer errors and conflicts that occur when a computer is first turned on and before the operating system is launched.

POST diagnostic card   *See* POST card.

PostScript   A printer language developed by Adobe Systems that tells a printer how to print a page.

Power Options applet   An applet accessed through Control Panel that manages power settings to conserve power.

Power over Ethernet (PoE)   A feature that might be available on high-end wired network adapters that allows power to be transmitted over Ethernet cable to remote devices.

power supply   A box inside the computer case that receives power and converts it for use by the motherboard and other installed devices. Power supplies provide 3.3, 5, and 12 volts DC. *Also called* a power supply unit (PSU).

power supply tester   A device that can test the output of each power cord coming from a power supply.

power supply unit (PSU)   *See* power supply.

Power Users group   A type of user account group. Accounts assigned to this group can read from and write to parts of the system other than their own user profile folders, install applications, and perform limited administrative tasks.

powerline networking   *See* EoP (Ethernet over Power).

G

PowerShell A command-line interface (CLI) that processes objects called cmdlets, which are pre-built programs built on the .NET Framework, rather than processing text in a command line.

PowerShell ISE Software used to create, edit, and test PowerShell scripts. ISE stands for Integrated Scripting Environment.

PowerShell script A text file of PowerShell commands that can be executed as a batch.

Preboot eXecution Environment (PXE) Programming contained in the BIOS/UEFI code on the motherboard that is used to start up the computer and search for a server on the network to provide a bootable operating system. *Also called* Pre-Execution Environment (PXE).

Pre-Execution Environment (PXE) *See* Preboot eXecution Environment (PXE).

presentation virtualization Using this virtualization, a remote application running on a server is controlled by a local computer.

PRI (Product Release Instructions) Instructions about an update to an OS or other software published by the product manufacturer to alert users about what to expect from the update.

primary partition A hard disk partition that can be designated as the active partition. An MBR drive can have up to three primary partitions. In Windows, a GPT drive can have up to 128 primary partitions. *Compare with* extended partition.

principle of least privilege An approach where computer users are classified and the rights assigned are the minimum rights required to do their job.

print head The part in an inkjet or impact printer that moves across the paper, creating one line of the image with each pass.

Print Management A utility in the Administrative Tools group of Windows professional and business editions that allows you to monitor and manage printer queues for all printers on the network.

print server Hardware or software that manages the print jobs sent to one or more printers on a network.

print spooler A queue for print jobs.

printer maintenance kit A kit purchased from a printer manufacturer that contains the parts, tools, and instructions needed to perform routine printer maintenance.

printer self-test page A test page that prints by using controls at the printer. The page allows you to eliminate a printer as a problem during troubleshooting and usually includes test results, graphics, and information about the printer, such as its resolution and how much memory is installed.

printui The Windows Printer User Interface command, which is used by administrators to manage printers on local and remote computers.

privacy filter *See* privacy screen.

privacy screen A device that fits over a monitor screen to prevent other people from viewing it from a wide angle. *Also called* privacy filter.

private cloud Services on the Internet that an organization provides on its own servers or that are established virtually for a single organization's private use.

private IP address In TCP/IP version 4, an IP address used on a private network that is isolated from the Internet.

privileges The access to data files and folders given to user accounts and user groups. *Also called* rights.

PRL (Preferred Roaming List) A list of preferred service providers or radio frequencies your carrier wants a mobile device to use; it is stored on a Removable User Identity Module (R-UIM) card installed in the device.

process A program that is running under the authority of the shell, together with the system resources assigned to it.

processor *See* central processing unit (CPU).

processor frequency The speed at which the processor operates internally, usually expressed in GHz.

processor thermal trip error A problem when the processor overheats and the system restarts.

product activation The process that Microsoft uses to prevent software piracy. For example, once Windows 10 is activated for a particular computer, it cannot be legally installed on another computer.

product key A series of letters and numbers assigned by Microsoft that is required to activate a license to use Windows.

Product Release Instructions (PRI) Information published by the manufacturer of an operating system that describes what to expect from a published update to the OS.

profile security requirements A set of policies and procedures that define how a student or employee's profile settings are configured for security purposes. For example, a policy might require encryption and backup software to be installed on the student or employee's personal devices that connect to the organization's network.

Programs and Features A Control Panel applet that lists the programs installed on a computer; you can use it to uninstall, change, or repair programs.

projector A device used to shine a light that projects a transparent image onto a large screen; a projector is often used in classrooms or with other large groups.

protocol A set of rules and standards that two entities use for communication. For example, TCP/IP is a suite or group of protocols that define many types of communication on a TCP/IP network.

provisioning package A package of settings, apps, and data specific to an enterprise that is downloaded and installed on a device when it first joins Azure Active Directory.

proxy server A computer that intercepts requests that a client (for example, a browser) makes of a server (for example, a web server). A proxy server can serve up the request from a cache it maintains to improve performance or it can filter requests to secure a large network.

PS/2 port A round 6-pin port used by an older keyboard or mouse.

public cloud Cloud computing services provided over the Internet to the general public. Google or Yahoo! email services are examples of public cloud deployment.

public IP address In TCP/IP version 4, an IP address available to the Internet.

pull automation A Windows installation from a deployment server that requires the local user to start the process. *Compare with* push automation.

punchdown tool A hand tool used to punch individual wires from a network cable into their slots to terminate the cable.

push automation An installation automatically pushed by a server to a computer when a user is not likely to be manning the computer. *Compare with* pull automation.

PVC (polyvinyl chloride) The product used to cover Ethernet cables; it is not safe to be used in a plenum because it gives off toxic fumes when burned.

Python script A text file of Python commands that can be executed as a batch.

QoS (Quality of Service) *See* Quality of Service (QoS).

quad channels Technology used by a motherboard and DIMMs that allows the memory controller to access four DIMMS at the same time. DDR3 and DDR4 DIMMs can use quad channels.

Quality of Service (QoS) A feature used by Windows and network hardware devices to improve network performance for an application. For example, VoIP requires a high QoS.

quarantined computer A computer that is suspected of infection and not allowed to use the network, is put on a different network dedicated to such computers, or is allowed to access only certain network resources.

quick format A format procedure for a hard drive volume or other drive that doesn't scan the volume or drive for bad sectors; use it only when a drive has been previously formatted and is in healthy condition. *Compare with* full format.

Quick Launch menu The menu that appears when the Windows Start button is right-clicked.

QuickPath Interconnect (QPI) The technology used first by the Intel X58 chipset for communication between the chipset and the processor; it uses 16 serial lanes, similar to PCI Express. QPI replaced the 64-bit wide Front Side Bus used by previous chipsets.

radio firmware Firmware on a device that manages wireless communication, such as cellular, Wi-Fi, and Bluetooth radio communication.

radio frequency (RF) The frequency of waves generated by a radio signal, which are electromagnetic frequencies above audio and below light. For example, Wi-Fi 802.11n transmits using a radio frequency of 5 GHz and 2.4 GHz.

RADIUS (Remote Access Dial-in User Service) A standard to authenticate and authorize users to wired, wireless, and VPN network connections. Authentication is made to a user database such as Active Directory.

G

RAID (redundant array of inexpensive disks or redundant array of independent disks) Several methods of configuring multiple hard drives to store data to increase logical volume size and improve performance, or to ensure that if one hard drive fails, the data is still available from another hard drive.

RAID 0 Using space from two or more physical disks to increase the disk space available for a single volume. Performance improves because data is written evenly across all disks. Windows calls RAID 0 a striped volume. *Also called* striping *or* striped volume.

RAID 1 A type of drive imaging that duplicates data on one drive to another drive and is used for fault tolerance. Windows calls RAID 1 a mirrored volume. *Also called* mirrored volume.

RAID 1+0 *See* RAID 10.

RAID 10 A combination of RAID 1 and RAID 0 that requires at least four disks to work as an array of drives and provides the best redundancy and performance.

RAID 5 A technique that stripes data across three or more drives and uses parity checking, so that if one drive fails, the other drives can re-create the data stored on the failed drive. RAID 5 drives increase performance and provide fault tolerance. Windows calls these drives RAID-5 volumes.

RAID-5 volume The term used by Windows for RAID 5. *See* RAID 5.

rainbow table A list of plaintext passwords and matching password hashes (encrypted passwords) used by hackers for reverse lookup. When the password hash is known, a hacker can find the plaintext password and use it to hack into a computer or network.

RAM (random access memory) Memory modules on the motherboard that contain microchips used to temporarily hold data and programs while the CPU processes both. Information in RAM is lost when the computer is turned off.

ransomware Malware that holds your computer system hostage with encryption techniques until you pay money or a time period expires and the encrypted content is destroyed.

rapid elasticity A cloud computing service that is capable of scaling up or down as a customer's need level changes.

raw data Data sent to a printer without any formatting or processing.

RCA connector A connector used with composite and component cables that is round and has a single pin in the center.

rd (remove directory) The Windows command to delete a directory (folder) or group of directories (folders).

RDP (Remote Desktop Protocol) *See* Remote Desktop Protocol (RDP).

read/write head A sealed, magnetic coil device that moves across the surface of a disk in a hard disk drive (HDD), either reading data from or writing data to the disk.

ReadyBoost A Windows utility that uses a flash drive or secure digital (SD) memory card to boost hard drive performance.

recover The Windows command that can recover a file when part of it is corrupted.

recovery drive A Windows 10/8 bootable USB flash drive that can be used to recover the system when startup fails; the drive can be created using the Recovery applet in Control Panel. The drive can hold an OEM recovery partition copied from the hard drive.

recovery partition A partition on a hard drive that contains a recovery utility and installation files.

Recovery System In macOS, a lean operating system that boots from a hidden volume on the macOS startup disk and is used to troubleshoot macOS when startup errors occur.

rectifier An electrical device that converts AC to DC. A computer power supply contains a rectifier.

Recycle Bin A location on the hard drive where deleted files are stored.

refresh A Windows 8 technique to recover from a corrupted Windows installation using a custom refresh image, a recovery partition, or the Windows setup DVD. Depending on the health of the system, the user settings, data, and Windows 8 apps might be restored from backup near the end of the refresh operation.

refresh rate As applied to monitors, the number of times in one second the monitor can fill the screen with lines from top to bottom. *Also called* vertical scan rate.

registry A database that Windows uses to store hardware and software configuration information, user preferences, and setup information.

Registry Editor The Windows utility (Regedit.exe) used to edit the Windows registry.

Regsvr32 A utility for registering component services used by an installed application.

regulated data Data that is protected by special governmental laws or regulations; industry must comply with these regulations or face penalties.

regulatory and compliance policies The governmental policies or rules that an industry must follow to protect regulated data.

reliability history *See* Reliability Monitor.

Reliability Monitor A Windows utility that provides information about problems and errors that happen over time. *Also called* reliability history.

Remote Admin share A default share that gives the Administrator user account access to the Windows folder on a remote computer in a Windows domain.

remote application An application that is installed and executed on a server and is presented to a user working at a client computer.

Remote Assistance A Windows tool that allows a technician to remote in to a user's computer while the user remains signed in, retains control of the session, and can see the screen. This is helpful when a technician is troubleshooting problems on a computer.

remote backup application A cloud backup service on the Internet that backs up data to the cloud and is often used for laptops, tablets, and smartphones.

Remote Desktop Connection (RDC) A Windows tool that gives a user access to a Windows desktop from anywhere on the Internet.

Remote Desktop Protocol (RDP) The Windows protocol used by Remote Desktop and Remote Assistance utilities to connect to and control a remote computer.

Remote Disc A feature of macOS that gives other computers on the network access to the Mac's optical drive.

remote network installation An automated installation where no user intervention is required.

remote printing Printing from a computer or mobile device to a printer that is not connected directly to the computer or device.

remote wipe An operation that remotely erases all contacts, email, photos, and other data from a device to protect your privacy.

ren (rename) The Windows command to rename a file or group of files.

repair upgrade A nondestructive installation of Windows 10 over an existing Windows installation; the upgrade can repair the existing installation.

repeater A networking device that amplifies and retransmits a wireless signal to a wider coverage area and uses a new network name for the rebroadcast.

request for comments (RFC) Feedback to a proposed change that is requested by an organization of its customers or users.

resiliency In Windows Storage Spaces, the degree to which the configuration can resist or recover from drive failure.

Resilient File System (ReFS) A file system that offers excellent fault tolerance and compatibility with virtualization and data redundancy in a RAID system; ReFS is included in Windows 10 Pro for Workstations.

resolution The number of pixels on a monitor screen that are addressable by software (for example, 1024 × 768 pixels).

Resource Monitor A Windows tool that monitors the performance of the processor, memory, hard drive, and network.

resource pooling Cloud computing services to multiple customers that are hosted on shared physical resources and dynamically allocated to meet customer demand.

restore point A snapshot of the Windows system, usually made before installation of new hardware or applications. Restore points are created by the System Protection utility.

Resultant Set of Policy (RSoP) A Windows command and console (rsop.msc) that displays the policies set for a computer or user.

REt (Resolution Enhancement technology) The term used by Hewlett-Packard to describe the way a laser printer varies the size of the dots used to create an image. This technology partly accounts for the sharp, clear image created by a laser printer.

G

retinal scanning As part of the authentication process, some systems acquire biometric data by scanning the blood vessels on the back of the eye; this method is considered the most reliable of all biometric data scanning.

reverse lookup A way to find the host name when you know a computer's IP address. The nslookup command can perform a reverse lookup.

revoked signature database (dbx) A Secure boot database that is a blacklist of signatures for software that has been revoked and is no longer trusted.

RFID (radio-frequency identification) A wireless technology used on small tags that contain a microchip and antenna; RFID is often used to track and identify car keys, clothing, animals, and inventory.

RFID badge A badge worn by an employee and used to gain entrance into a locked area of a building. An RFID token transmits authentication to the system when the token gets within range of a query device.

RG-59 coaxial cable An older and thinner coaxial cable once used for cable TV.

RG-6 coaxial cable A coaxial cable used for cable TV that replaced the older and thinner RG-59 coaxial cable.

RIMM An older type of memory module developed by Rambus, Inc.

riser card A card that plugs into a motherboard and allows for expansion cards to be mounted parallel to the motherboard. Expansion cards are plugged into slots on the riser card.

risk analysis The process of identifying potential problems that might arise as a change plan is implemented; this process is done before the change begins.

RJ-11 *See* RJ-11 jack.

RJ-11 jack A phone line connection or port found on modems, telephones, and house phone outlets. *Also called* RJ-11 port.

RJ-11 port *See* RJ-11 jack.

RJ-45 A port that looks like a large phone jack and is used with twisted-pair cable to connect to a wired network adapter or other hardware device. RJ stands for registered jack. *Also called* RJ-45 port *or* Ethernet port.

RJ-45 port *See* RJ-45.

robocopy (robust file copy) A Windows command that is similar to and more powerful than the xcopy command; it is used to copy files and folders.

root account In Linux and macOS, the account that gives the user access to all the functions of the OS; the principal user account.

root certificate The original digital certificate issued by a Certificate Authority.

root directory The main directory, at the top of the top-down hierarchical structure of subdirectories, created when a hard drive or disk is first formatted. In Linux, it's indicated by a forward slash. In Windows, it's indicated by a backward slash.

rooting The process of obtaining root or administrator privileges to an Android device, which then gives you complete access to the entire file system and all commands and features.

rootkit A type of malicious software that loads itself before the OS boot is complete and can hijack internal OS components so that it masks information the OS provides to user-mode utilities such as Windows File Explorer or Task Manager.

router A device that manages traffic between two or more networks and can help find the best path for traffic to get from one network to another.

RS-232 A 9-pin serial connector used with rack server consoles and older mice, keyboards, dial-up modems, and other peripherals.

run-time environment The environment provided by the operating system in which commands contained in a script file are interpreted and executed.

S1 state On the BIOS/UEFI power screen, one of the five S states used by ACPI power-saving mode to indicate different levels of power-saving functions. In the S1 state, the hard drive and monitor are turned off and everything else runs normally.

S2 state On the BIOS/UEFI power screen, one of the five S states used by ACPI power-saving mode to indicate different levels of power-saving functions. In S2 state, the hard drive and monitor are turned off and everything else runs normally. In addition, the processor is also turned off.

S3 state On the BIOS/UEFI power screen, one of the five S states used by ACPI power-saving mode to indicate different levels of power-saving functions. In S3 state, everything is shut down except RAM and enough of the system to respond to a wake-up. S3 is sleep mode.

S4 state On the BIOS/UEFI power screen, one of the five S states used by ACPI power-saving mode to indicate different levels of power-saving functions. In S4 state, everything in RAM is copied to a file on the hard drive and the system is shut down. When the system is turned on, the file is used to restore the system to its state before shutdown. S4 is hibernation mode.

S5 state On the BIOS/UEFI power screen, one of the five S states used by ACPI power-saving mode to indicate different levels of power-saving functions. S5 is the power-off state after a normal shutdown.

SaaS (Software as a Service) A cloud computing service that is responsible for hardware, the operating systems, and the applications installed.

Safe Mode The technique of launching Windows with a minimum configuration, eliminating third-party software, and reducing Windows startup to only essential processes. The technique can sometimes launch Windows when a normal Windows startup is corrupted.

safety goggles Eye goggles worn while working in an unsafe environment such as a factory, where fragments, chips, or other particles might cause eye injuries.

sag *See* brownout.

SATA (Serial Advanced Technology Attachment or Serial ATA) An interface standard used mostly by hard drives, optical drives, and other storage devices. Current SATA standards include SATA3, SATA2, and eSATA.

SATA Express An interface standard that uses a unique SATA connector and combines PCIe and SATA to improve on the performance of SATA3. SATA Express is three times faster than SATA3 but not as fast as NVMe.

SATA power connector A 15-pin flat power connector that provides power to SATA drives.

SC (subscriber connector or standard connector) A type of snap-in connector that can be used with either single-mode or multimode fiber-optic cables. It is not used with the fastest fiber-optic networking.

scanstate A command used by the User State Migration Tool (USMT) to copy user settings and data from an old computer to a safe location such as a server or removable media. *Also see* loadstate.

scope of change Part of a change plan that defines the key components of change and how they will be addressed, the people, skills, tasks, and activities required to carry out the change, how the results of the change will be measured, and when the change is complete.

screen orientation The layout or orientation of the screen, which is either portrait or landscape.

screen resolution The number of dots or pixels on the monitor screen, expressed as two numbers such as 1680 × 1050.

Screen Sharing In macOS, a utility to remotely view and control a Mac; it is similar to Remote Desktop in Windows.

script A text file that contains a list of commands that can be interpreted and executed by the OS.

SCSI (Small Computer System Interface) An interface between a host adapter and the CPU that can daisy-chain as many as 7 or 15 devices on a single bus.

SD (Secure Digital) card A group of standards and flash memory storage cards that come in a variety of physical sizes, capacities, and speeds.

SDK (Software Development Kit) A group of tools that developers use to write apps. For example, Android Studio is a free SDK that is released as open source.

secondary logon Using administrator privileges to perform an operation when you are not logged on with an account that has these privileges.

secondary-click An action in macOS applied to an item on the macOS screen, such as displaying a shortcut menu for a file; it is similar to a right-click in Windows. By default, the action is a tap with two fingers on the Mac trackpad.

sector On a hard disk drive or SSD, the smallest unit of bytes addressable by the operating system and BIOS/UEFI. On hard disk drives, one sector usually equals 512 bytes; SSDs might use larger sectors.

Secure boot A UEFI and OS feature that prevents a system from booting up with drivers or an OS that is not digitally signed and trusted by the motherboard or computer manufacturer.

Secure Digital (SD) card A type of memory card used in digital cameras, tablets, cell phones, MP3

G

players, digital camcorders, and other portable devices. The three standards used by SD cards are 1.x (regular SD), 2.x (SD High Capacity or SDHC), and 3.x (SD eXtended Capacity or SDXC).

Secure DNS A security service offered by providers such as Comodo to interrupt a phishing attack by monitoring a browser's requests for websites and redirecting the browser when it attempts to visit a known malicious site. To implement Secure DNS, use the provider's DNS server addresses for your DNS service.

Secure FTP (SFTP) A TCP/IP protocol used to transfer files from an FTP server to an FTP client using encryption.

Secure Shell (SSH) A protocol used to pass login information to a remote computer and control that computer over a network using encryption.

security profile A set of policies and procedures that restrict how a student or employee can access, create, and edit the organization's resources.

security token A smart card or other device that is one factor in multifactor authentication or can serve as a replacement for a password.

self-grounding A method to safeguard against ESD that involves touching the computer case or power supply before touching a component in the computer case.

separate pad *See* separation pad.

separation pad A printer part that keeps more than one sheet of paper from moving forward.

serial ATA (SATA) *See* SATA (Serial Advanced Technology Attachment or Serial ATA).

serial port A male 9-pin or 25-pin port on a computer system used by slower I/O devices such as a mouse or modem. Data travels serially, one bit at a time, through the port. Serial ports are sometimes configured as COM1, COM2, COM3, or COM4. *Also called* DB-9 *or* DB9 port.

server lock A physical lock that prevents someone from opening the computer case of a server.

Server Manager A Windows Server console, also available in Windows 10, that contains the tools used to manage Active Directory.

Server Message Block (SMB) A protocol used by Windows to share files and printers on a network.

server-side virtualization Using this virtualization, a server provides a virtual desktop or application for users on multiple client machines.

service A program that runs in the background to support or serve Windows or an application.

service pack A collection of several patches or updates that is installed as a single update to an OS or application.

Service Set Identifier (SSID) The name of a wireless access point and wireless network.

Services console A console used by Windows to stop, start, and manage background services used by Windows and applications.

Settings app In Windows 10, an app to view and change many Windows settings.

setup BIOS/UEFI Firmware used to change motherboard settings. For example, you can use it to enable or disable a device on the motherboard, change the date and time that is later passed to the OS, and select the order of boot devices for startup BIOS/UEFI to search when looking for an operating system to load.

shadow copy A copy of open files made so that they are included in a backup.

share permissions A method to share a folder (not individual files) to remote users on the network, including assigning varying degrees of access to specific user accounts and user groups. These permissions do not apply to local users of a computer; they can be used on an NTFS or FAT volume. *Compare with* NTFS permissions.

sheet battery A secondary battery that fits on the bottom of a laptop to provide additional battery charge.

shell The portion of an OS that relates to the user and applications.

shell prompt In Linux and macOS, the command prompt in the terminal.

shell script A text file of Linux commands that can be executed as a batch.

shielded twisted-pair (STP) cable A cable that is made of one or more twisted pairs of wires and is surrounded by a metal shield.

Short Message Service (SMS) A technology that allows users to send a test message using a cell phone.

shoulder surfing As you work, other people secretly peeking at your monitor screen to gain valuable information.

shredder A device, such as a paper shredder or multimedia shredder, that destroys sensitive data by destroying the paper or storage device that holds the data.

shutdown The Windows command to shut down the local computer or a remote computer.

Side button The physical button on the upper-right side of an iPhone or iPad.

signature database (db) A Secure boot database that holds a list of digital signatures of approved operating systems, applications, and drivers that can be loaded by UEFI.

signature pad A device with a touch screen used to capture a handwritten signature made with a stylus or finger.

SIM (Subscriber Identity Module) card A small flash memory card that contains all the information a device needs to connect to a GSM or LTE cellular network, including a password and other authentication information needed to access the network, encryption standards used, and the services that a subscription includes.

SIMM (single inline memory module) An outdated miniature circuit board used to hold RAM. SIMMs held 8, 16, 32, or 64 MB on a single module. SIMMs have been replaced by DIMMs.

Simple Network Management Protocol (SNMP) *See* SNMP (Simple Network Management Protocol).

simple volume A type of volume used on a single hard drive. *Compare with* dynamic volume.

single channel The memory controller on a motherboard that can access only one DIMM at a time. *Compare with* dual channel, triple channel, *and* quad channel.

single sign-on (SSO) An account that accesses multiple independent resources, systems, or applications after signing in one time to one account. An example is a Microsoft account.

single-core processing An older processor technology whereby the processor housing contains a single processor or core that can process two threads at the same time. *Compare with* multicore processing.

single-sided A DIMM that has memory chips installed on one side of the module.

site license A license that allows a company to install multiple copies of software or allows multiple employees to execute the software from a file server.

slack Wasted space on a hard drive caused by not using all available space at the end of a cluster.

sleep mode A power-saving state for a computer when it is not in use. *Also called* standby mode *or* suspend mode. *Also see* S3 state.

sleep timer The number of minutes of inactivity before a computer goes into a power-saving state such as sleep mode.

SLP (Service Location Protocol) A TCP/IP protocol used by AFP to find printers and file sharing devices on a local network.

small form factor (SFF) A motherboard used in low-end computers and home theater systems. An SFF is often used with an Intel Atom processor and sometimes purchased as a motherboard-processor combo unit.

S.M.A.R.T. (Self-Monitoring Analysis and Reporting Technology) A BIOS/UEFI and hard drive feature that monitors hard drive performance, disk spin-up time, temperature, distance between the head and the disk, and other mechanical activities of the drive in order to predict when it is likely to fail.

smart camera A digital camera that has embedded computing power to make decisions about the content of the photos or videos it records, including transmitting alerts over a wired or wireless network when it records certain content. *Also called* a vision sensor.

smart card Any small device that contains authentication information that can be keyed into a sign-in window or read by a reader to authenticate a user on a network.

smart card reader A device that can read a smart card to authenticate a person onto a network.

smart speaker A speaker that includes voice-activated digital assistant software and connects by Wi-Fi or other wireless technology to the Internet.

smart TV A television that has the ability to run apps, store data, and connect to the Internet.

smartphone A cell phone that can send text messages with photos, videos, and other multimedia content, surf the web, manage email, play games, take photos and videos, and download and use small apps.

SMB (Server Message Block) A file access protocol originally developed by IBM and used

G

by Windows to share files and printers on a network. The current SMB protocol is SMB3.

SMB2 *See* CIFS (Common Internet File System).

S/MIME (Secure/Multipurpose Internet Mail Extensions) A protocol that encrypts an outgoing email message and includes a digital signature; S/MIME is more secure than SMTP, which does not use encryption.

SMTP (Simple Mail Transfer Protocol) A TCP/IP protocol used by email clients to send email messages to an email server and on to the recipient's email server. *Also see* POP *and* IMAP.

SMTP AUTH (SMTP Authentication) An improved version of SMTP used to authenticate a user to an email server when the email client first tries to connect to the email server to send email. The protocol is based on the Simple Authentication and Security Layer (SASL) protocol.

snap-in A Windows utility that can be installed in a console window by Microsoft Management Console.

snapshot In macOS, a backup created by Time Machine that is stored on the hard drive when the computer is not connected to backup media and copied to backup media when connectivity is restored.

SNMP (Simple Network Management Protocol) A versatile TCP/IP protocol used to monitor network traffic and manage network devices. The SNMP server works with SNMP agents installed on devices being monitored.

social engineering The practice of tricking people into giving out private information or allowing unsafe programs into the network or computer.

socket (1) In computer hardware, a rectangular connector with pins or pads and a mechanism to hold the CPU in place; it is used to connect a CPU to the motherboard. (2) In networking, an established connection between a client and a server, such as the connection between a browser and web server.

SO-DIMM (small outline DIMM) A type of memory module for laptop computers that uses DIMM technology. A DDR4 SO-DIMM has 260 pins, and a DDR3 SO-DIMM has 204 pins. A DDR2 or DDR SO-DIMM has 200 pins.

soft boot To restart a computer without turning off the power; for example, in Windows 10/8,

press Win+X, point to Shut down or sign out, and click Restart. *Also called* warm boot.

soft reset (1) For Android, to forcefully reboot the device (full shut down and cold boot) by pressing and holding the power button. (2) For iOS, to put the device in hibernation and not clear memory by pressing the Wake/sleep button.

software piracy The act of making unauthorized copies of original software, which violates the Federal Copyright Act of 1976.

software RAID Using Windows to implement RAID. The setup is done using the Disk Management utility.

software token An app or digital certificate that serves as authentication to a computer or network.

solid-state device (SSD) An electronic device with no moving parts. An SSD is a storage device that uses memory chips to store data instead of spinning disks (such as those used by magnetic hard drives and CD drives). Examples of solid-state devices are jump drives (also known as key drives or thumb drives), flash memory cards, and solid-state disks used as hard drives in notebook computers designed for the most rugged uses. *Also called* solid-state disk (SSD) *or* solid-state drive (SSD). *Compare with* magnetic hard drive.

solid-state drive (SSD) *See* solid-state device (SSD).

solid-state hybrid drive (SSHD) *See* hybrid hard drive (H-HDD).

Sound applet An applet accessed through Control Panel to select a default speaker and microphone and adjust how Windows handles sounds.

sound card An expansion card with sound ports.

South Bridge The portion of the chipset hub that connects slower I/O buses (for example, a PCI bus) to the system bus. *Compare with* North Bridge.

Space In macOS, one desktop screen. Multiple desktops or Spaces can be open and available to users.

spacer *See* standoff.

spanning A configuration of two hard drives that hold a single Windows volume to increase the size of the volume. Sometimes called JBOD (just a bunch of disks).

SPDIF (Sony-Phillips Digital InterFace) sound port A port that connects to an external home theater audio system, providing digital audio output and the best signal quality.

spear phishing A form of phishing where an email message appears to come from a company you already do business with.

spoofing Tricking someone into thinking an imitation of a website or email message is legitimate. For example, a phishing technique tricks you into clicking a link in an email message, which takes you to an official-looking website where you are asked to enter your user ID and password to access the site.

spooling Placing print jobs in a queue so that an application can be released from the printing process before printing is completed. Spool is an acronym for simultaneous peripheral operations online.

Spotlight In macOS, the search app that can be configured to search the local computer, Wikipedia, iTunes, the Maps app, the web, and more.

spudger A metal or plastic flat-head wedge used to pry open casings without damaging plastic connectors and cases when disassembling a notebook, tablet, or mobile device.

spyware Malicious software that installs itself on your computer or mobile device to spy on you. It collects personal information about you and transmits it over the Internet to web-hosting sites that intend to use the information for harm.

SSD (solid-state drive or solid-state device) See solid-state device (SSD).

SSH (Secure Shell) A protocol and application that encrypts communication between a client and server and is used to remotely control a Linux computer.

SSID (Service Set Identifier) See Service Set Identifier (SSID).

SSO (single sign-on) See single sign-on (SSO).

ST (straight tip) connector A type of connector that can be used with either single-mode or multimode fiber-optic cables. The connector does not support full-duplex transmissions and is not used on the fastest fiber-optic systems.

standard account The Windows 10/8/7 user account type that can use software and hardware and make some system changes, but cannot make changes that affect the security of the system or other users. *Compare with* administrator account.

standard image An image that includes Windows, drivers, applications, and data, which are standard to all the computers that might use the image.

standby mode See sleep mode.

standoff Round plastic or metal pegs that separate the motherboard from the case so that components on the back of the motherboard do not touch the case.

Start screen In Windows 8, a screen with tiles that represent lean apps, which use few system resources and are designed for social media, social networking, and the novice end user.

startup BIOS/UEFI Part of UEFI or BIOS firmware on the motherboard that is responsible for controlling the computer when it is first turned on. Startup BIOS/UEFI gives control to the OS once the OS is loaded.

startup disk In macOS, the entire volume on which macOS is installed.

startup items In macOS, programs that automatically launch at startup. Apple discourages the use of startup items, which are stored in two directories: /Library/StartupItems and /System/Library/StartupItems. Normally, both directories are empty.

startup repair A Windows 10/8/7 utility that restores many of the Windows files needed for a successful boot.

static electricity See electrostatic discharge (ESD).

static IP address A permanent IP address that is manually assigned to a computer or other device.

static RAM (SRAM) RAM chips that retain information without the need for refreshing, as long as the computer's power is on. They are more expensive than traditional DRAM.

storage card An adapter card used to manage hardware RAID rather than using the firmware on the motherboard.

Storage Spaces A Windows utility that can create a storage pool using any number of internal or external backup drives. The utility is expected to replace Windows software RAID.

STP (shielded twisted-pair) cable Twisted-pair networking cable that shields or covers each pair of wire in the cable to prevent electromagnetic interference.

G

straight-through cable An Ethernet cable used to connect a computer to a switch or other network device. *Also called* a patch cable.

string In scripting and programming, a type of data that can contain any character but cannot be used for calculations.

striped volume The term used by Windows for RAID 0. A striped volume is a type of dynamic volume used for two or more hard drives; it writes to the disks evenly rather than filling up allotted space on one and then moving on to the next. *Compare with* spanned volume. *Also see* RAID 0.

striping *See* RAID 0.

strong password A password that is not easy to guess.

stylus A device that is included with a graphics tablet and works like a pencil on the tablet.

su A Linux and macOS command to open a new terminal shell for a different user account; su stands for "substitute user."

subdirectory A directory or folder contained in another directory or folder. *Also called* a child directory *or* folder.

subnet A group of local networks tied together in a subsystem of the larger intranet. In TCP/IP version 6, a subnet is one or more links that have the same 16 bits in the subnet ID of the IP address. *See* subnet ID.

subnet ID In TCP/IP version 6, the last block (16 bits) in the 64-bit prefix of an IP address. The subnet is identified using some or all of these 16 bits.

subnet mask In TCP/IP version 4, 32 bits that include a series of ones followed by zeroes—for example, 11111111.11111111.11110000.0000 0000, which can be written as 255.255.240.0. The 1s identify the network portion of an IP address, and the 0s identify the host portion of an IP address. The subnet mask tells Windows if a remote computer is on the same or different network.

subscription model A method of licensing software with a paid annual subscription and the software is installed on your local computer. For example, Office 365 uses a subscription model.

sudo A Linux and macOS command to execute another command as a superuser when logged in as a normal user with an account that has the right to use root commands. Sudo stands for "substitute user to do the command."

superuser A user who is logged in to the root account.

surge protector A device that protects against voltage spikes by blocking or grounding excessive voltage. *Also called* surge suppressor.

surge suppressor *See* surge protector.

suspend mode *See* sleep mode.

S-Video port A 4-pin or 7-pin round video port that sends two signals over the cable, one for color and the other for brightness, and is used by some high-end TVs and video equipment.

swap partition A partition on a Linux hard drive used to hold virtual memory.

swapfile In macOS, the file used to hold virtual memory, similar to pagefile.sys in Windows.

switch A device used to connect nodes on a network in a star network topology. When it receives a packet, it uses its table of MAC addresses to decide where to send the packet.

Sync Center A Control Panel applet that allows two computers to sync the contents of a shared folder or volume.

synchronization app An app on a mobile device or other computer to sync data and settings to cloud storage accounts such as Google Cloud and iCloud and between devices.

synchronous DRAM (SDRAM) The first DIMM to run synchronized with the system clock; it has two notches and uses 168 pins.

Syslog A protocol that collects event information about network devices, such as errors, failures, and users logging in or out, and sends the information to a Syslog server.

Syslog server A server that receives and analyzes syslog data to monitor network devices and create alerts when problems arise that need attention.

system BIOS/UEFI UEFI (Unified Extensible Firmware Interface) or BIOS (basic input/output system) firmware on the motherboard that is used to control essential devices before the OS is loaded.

system board *See* motherboard.

system bus The bus between the CPU and memory on the motherboard. The bus frequency in documentation is called the system speed, such as 400 MHz. *Also called* the memory bus, FrontSide Bus, local bus, *or* host bus.

system clock A line on a bus that is dedicated to timing the activities of components connected to it. The system clock provides a continuous pulse that other devices use to time themselves.

System Configuration A Windows utility (Msconfig.exe) that can identify what processes are launched at startup and can temporarily disable a process from loading.

System File Checker (SFC) A Windows utility that verifies and, if necessary, refreshes a Windows system file, replacing it with one kept in a cache of current system files or downloaded from the Internet with the help of Windows Updates.

system image The backup of the entire Windows volume; it can also include backups of other volumes. The system image works only on the computer that created it, and is created using Windows 10/8 File History or the Windows Backup and Restore utility.

System Information A Windows tool (Msinfo32.exe) that provides details about a system, including installed hardware and software, the current system configuration, and currently running programs.

system partition The active partition of the hard drive, which contains the boot loader or boot manager program and the specific files required to start the Windows launch.

System Preferences In macOS, a utility to customize the macOS interface; it is available on the Apple menu.

System Protection A utility that automatically backs up system files and stores them in restore points on the hard drive at regular intervals and just before you install software or hardware.

system repair disc A disc you can create in Windows 10/7 to launch Windows RE. The disc is not available in Windows 8.

System Restore A Windows utility used to restore the system to a restore point.

system state data In Windows, files that are necessary for a successful load of the operating system.

system tray *See* notification area.

System window A window that displays brief but important information about installed hardware and software and gives access to important Windows tools needed to support the system.

systray *See* notification area.

T568A Standards for wiring twisted-pair network cabling and RJ-45 connectors; in T568A, the green pair of wires is connected to pins 1 and 2 and the orange pair is connected to pins 3 and 6.

T568B Standards for wiring twisted-pair network cabling and RJ-45 connectors; in T568B, the orange pair of wires uses pins 1 and 2 and the green pair is connected to pins 3 and 6.

tablet A computing device with a touch screen that is larger than a smartphone and with functions similar to a smartphone.

TACACS+ (Terminal Access Controller Access Control System Plus) A Cisco AAA service specifically designed for network administrators to remotely connect to a network and configure and manage Cisco routers, switches, firewalls, and other network devices. The service authenticates, authorizes, and tracks activity on the network and can work with Active Directory.

tailgating When an unauthorized person follows an employee through a secured entrance to a room or building.

tap pay device A device in a point-of-sale system that uses an encrypted wireless NFC connection to read and send payment information from a customer's smartphone to a vendor's account.

Task Manager A Windows utility (Taskmgr.exe) that lets you view the applications and processes running on your computer as well as information about process and memory performance, network activity, and user activity.

Task Scheduler A Windows tool that can set a task or program to launch at a future time, including at startup.

Task View A Windows 10 feature used to create and manage multiple desktops.

taskbar A bar normally located at the bottom of the Windows desktop that displays information about open programs and provides quick access to others.

taskkill A Windows command that uses the process PID to kill a process.

G

tasklist A Windows command that returns the process identifier (PID), which is a number that identifies each running process.

TCP (Transmission Control Protocol) The protocol in the TCP/IP suite of protocols that works at the OSI Transport layer, establishes a session or connection between parties, and guarantees packet delivery.

TCP/IP (Transmission Control Protocol/Internet Protocol) The group or suite of protocols used for almost all networks, including the Internet. Fundamentally, TCP is responsible for error-checking transmissions and IP is responsible for routing.

TCP/IP model In networking theory, a simple model used to divide network communication into four layers. This model is simpler than the OSI model, which uses seven layers.

technical documentation Digital or printed technical reference manuals that are included with software packages and hardware to provide directions for installation, usage, and troubleshooting. The information extends beyond that given in user manuals.

Telnet A TCP/IP protocol and application used to allow an administrator or other user to control a computer remotely.

Teredo In TCP/IP version 6, a tunneling protocol to transmit TCP/IPv6 packets over a TCP/IPv4 network; it is named after the Teredo worm that bores holes in wood. Teredo IP addresses begin with 2001, and the prefix is written as 2001::/32.

terminal In Linux and macOS, the command-line interface. In macOS, the terminal is accessed through the Terminal utility in the Applications group of the Finder window.

tether To connect a computer to a mobile device that has an Internet cellular connection so that the computer can access the Internet by way of the mobile device.

thermal compound A creamlike substance that is placed between the bottom of the cooler heat sink and the top of the processor to eliminate air pockets and help draw heat off the processor.

thermal paper Special coated paper used by thermal printers.

thermal printer A type of line printer that uses wax-based ink, which is heated by heat pins that melt the ink onto paper.

thermal transfer printer A type of thermal printer that uses a ribbon containing wax-based ink. The heating element melts the ribbon onto special thermal paper so that it stays glued to the paper as the feeder assembly moves the paper through the printer.

thick client A regular desktop computer or laptop that is sometimes used as a client by a virtualization server. *Also called* fat client.

thin client A computer that has an operating system but little computing power and might only need to support a browser used to communicate with a virtualization server.

thin provisioning A technique used by Storage Spaces whereby virtual storage space can be made available to users who do not have physical storage allotted to them. When the virtual storage space is close to depletion, the administrator is prompted to install more physical storage.

third-party drivers Drivers that are not included in BIOS/UEFI or Windows and must come from the manufacturer.

thread Each process that the processor is aware of; a thread is a single task that is part of a larger task or request from a program.

Thunderbolt *See* Thunderbolt 3 port.

Thunderbolt 3 port A multipurpose standard and connector used for communication and power. Early versions were limited to Apple products and used a modified DisplayPort. The current version 3 uses modified USB-C ports on Apple and non-Apple devices.

ticket An entry in a call-tracking system made by the person who receives a call for help. A ticket is used to track and document actions taken, and it stays open until the issue is resolved.

Time Machine In macOS, a built-in backup utility that can be configured to automatically back up user-created data, applications, and system files to an external hard drive attached either directly to the computer or the local network.

TKIP (Temporal Key Integrity Protocol) A type of encryption protocol used by WPA to secure a wireless Wi-Fi network. *Also see* WPA (Wi-Fi Protected Access).

tone generator and probe A two-part kit used to find cables in the walls of a building. The toner connects to one end of the cable and puts out a pulsating tone that the probe can sense. *Also called* a toner probe *or* tone probe.

tone probe   *See* tone generator and probe.

toner probe   *See* tone generator and probe.

toner vacuum   A vacuum cleaner designed to pick up toner used in laser printers; the toner is not allowed to touch any conductive surface.

topology   In networking, the physical or logical pattern or design used to connect devices on a network.

touch pad   A common pointing device on a notebook computer.

touch screen   An input device that uses a monitor or LCD panel as a backdrop for user options. Touch screens can be embedded in a monitor or LCD panel or installed as an add-on device over the monitor screen.

tower case   The largest type of personal computer case. Tower cases stand vertically and can be up to two feet tall. They have more drive bays and are a good choice for computer users who anticipate making significant upgrades.

TPM (Trusted Platform Module)   A chip on a motherboard that holds an encryption key required at startup to access encrypted data on the hard drive. Windows 10/8/7 BitLocker Encryption can use the TPM chip.

TR4 (Threadripper 4)   A land grid array socket for AMD Ryzen processors and X399 chipsets. The socket is used with high-end AMD processors.

trace   A wire on a circuit board that connects two components or devices.

tracert (trace route)   A TCP/IP command that enables you to resolve a connectivity problem when attempting to reach a destination host such as a website.

track   One of many concentric circles on the surface of a hard disk drive.

tractor feed   A continuous feed within an impact printer that feeds fanfold paper through the printer rather than individual sheets; this format is useful for logging ongoing events or data.

transfer belt   A laser printer component that completes the transferring step in the printer.

transfer roller   A soft, black roller in a laser printer that puts a positive charge on the paper. The charge pulls the toner from the drum onto the paper.

transformer   An electrical device that changes the ratio of current to voltage. A computer power supply is basically a transformer and a rectifier.

trim   To erase entire blocks of unused data on an SSD so that write operations do not have to manage the data.

trip hazards   Loose cables or cords in a traffic area where people can trip over them.

triple A   *See* AAA (authenticating, authorizing, and accounting).

triple channels   When the memory controller accesses three DIMMs at the same time. DDR3 DIMMs support triple channeling.

Trojan   A type of malware that tricks you into downloading and/or opening it by substituting itself for a legitimate program.

Troubleshooting applet   A Control Panel applet used to automatically troubleshoot and fix many common Windows problems involving applications, hardware, sound, networking, Windows updates, and maintenance tasks.

trusted source   A source for downloading software that is considered reliable, such as app stores provided by a mobile device manufacturer and websites of well-known software manufacturers.

TV tuner card   An adapter card that receives a TV signal and displays it on the computer screen.

Twisted Nematic (TN)   A class of LCD monitor that has fast response times to keep fast-moving images crisper. TN monitors are brighter, consume more power, and have limited viewing angles.

twisted-pair cabling   Cabling, such as a network cable, that uses pairs of wires twisted together to reduce crosstalk.

two-factor authentication (2FA)   When two tokens or actions are required to authenticate to a computer or network. Factors can include what a person knows (password), what she possesses (a token such as a key fob or smart card), what she does (such as typing a certain way), or who she is (biometric data).

Type 1 hypervisor   Software to manage virtual machines that is installed before any operating system is installed.

Type 2 hypervisor   Software to manage virtual machines that is installed as an application in an operating system.

G

UDF (Universal Disk Format) A file system for optical media used by all DVD discs and some CD-R and CD-RW discs.

UDP (User Datagram Protocol) A connectionless TCP/IP protocol that works at the OSI Transport layer and does not require a connection to send a packet or guarantee that the packet arrives at its destination. The protocol is commonly used for broadcasting to multiple nodes on a network or the Internet. *Compare with* TCP (Transmission Control Protocol).

UEFI (Unified Extensible Firmware Interface) *See* Unified Extensible Firmware Interface (UEFI).

UEFI CSM (Compatibility Support Module) mode Legacy BIOS in UEFI firmware.

ultra-thin client *See* zero client.

unattended installation A Windows installation in which answers to installation questions are stored in a file that Windows calls so that they do not have to be typed in during the installation.

unicast address Using TCP/IP version 6, an IP address assigned to a single node on a network.

Unified Extensible Firmware Interface (UEFI) An interface between firmware on the motherboard and the operating system. UEFI improves on legacy BIOS processes for managing motherboard settings, booting, handing over the boot to the OS, loading device drivers and applications before the OS loads, and securing the boot to ensure that no rogue operating system hijacks the system.

Unified Threat Management (UTM) A computer, security appliance, network appliance, or Internet appliance that stands between the Internet and a private network. A UTM device runs a firewall, anti-malware software, and other software to protect the network, and is considered a next-generation firewall.

uninterruptible power supply (UPS) A device that raises the voltage when it drops during brownouts.

unique local address (ULA) In TCP/IP version 6, an address used to identify a specific site within a large organization. It can work on multiple links within the same organization. The address is a hybrid between a global unicast address that works on the Internet and a link local unicast address that works on only one link.

Universal Plug and Play (UPnP) *See* UPnP (Universal Plug and Play).

unmanaged switch A switch that requires no setup or configuration. *Compare with* managed switch.

unshielded twisted-pair (UTP) cable *See* UTP (unshielded twisted-pair) cable.

upgrade path A qualifying OS required by Microsoft in order to perform an in-place upgrade.

UPnP (Universal Plug and Play) A feature of a SOHO router that enables computers on the local network to have unfiltered communication so they can automatically discover services provided by other computers on the network. UPnP is considered a security risk because hackers might exploit the vulnerability created when computers advertise their services on the network.

USB (Universal Serial Bus) Multipurpose bus and connector standards used for internal and external ports for a variety of devices. Current USB standards are USB 3.2, 3.1, 3.0, and 2.0.

USB port A type of port designed to make installation and configuration of I/O devices easy. It provides room for as many as 127 devices daisy-chained together.

USB 2.0 A version of USB that runs at 480 Mbps and uses cables up to 5 meters long. *Also called* Hi-Speed USB.

USB 3.0 A version of USB that runs at 5 Gbps and uses cables up to 3 meters long. *Also called* SuperSpeed USB.

USB 3.0 B-Male connector A USB connector used by SuperSpeed USB 3.0 devices such as printers or scanners.

USB 3.0 Micro-B connector A small USB connector used by SuperSpeed USB 3.0 devices. The connectors are not compatible with regular Micro-B connectors.

USB lock A type of port lock used to control access to a USB port on a computer.

USB optical drive An external optical drive that connects to a computer via a USB port.

USB to Bluetooth adapter A device that plugs into a USB port on a computer to connect to Bluetooth devices.

USB to RJ-45 dongle An adapter that plugs into a USB port and provides an RJ-45 port for a network cable to connect to a wired network.

USB to Wi-Fi dongle An adapter that plugs into a USB port and provides wireless connectivity to a Wi-Fi network.

USB-C A USB connector that is flat with rounded sides and used by smartphones and tablets. The connector is required for USB 3.2 devices to attain maximum speeds.

User Account Control (UAC) dialog box A Windows security feature that displays a dialog box when an event requiring administrative privileges is about to happen.

User Accounts A Windows utility (netplwiz.exe) that can be used to change the way Windows sign-in works and to manage user accounts, including changing passwords and changing the group membership of an account. *Also called* Network Places Wizard.

user mode In Windows, a mode that provides an interface between an application and the OS, and only has access to hardware resources through the code running in kernel mode.

user profile A collection of files and settings about a user account that enables the user's personal data, desktop settings, and other operating parameters to be retained from one session to another.

user profile namespace The group of folders and subfolders in the C:\Users folder that belong to a specific user account and contain the user profile.

User State Migration Tool (USMT) A Windows utility that helps you migrate user files and preferences between computers to help a user make a smooth transition from one computer to another.

Users group A type of Windows user account group. An account in this group is a standard user account, which does not have as many rights as an administrator account.

usmtutils A command used by the User State Migration Tool (USMT) that provides encryption options and hard-link management.

UTM (Unified Threat Management) *See* Unified Threat Management (UTM).

UTP (unshielded twisted-pair) cable Twisted-pair networking cable commonly used on LANs that is less expensive than STP cable and does not contain shielding to prevent electromagnetic interference.

variable The name of one item of data used in a script or program.

VBScript A scripting language that creates scripts modeled after the more complex Visual Basic programming language. VBScripts have a .vbs file extension.

VDI (Virtual Desktop Infrastructure) *See* Virtual Desktop Infrastructure (VDI).

VGA (Video Graphics Adapter) port A 15-pin analog video port popular for many years. *Also called* DB-15, DB15 port, DE15 port, *or* HD15 port.

VGA mode Standard VGA settings, which include a resolution of 640 × 480.

vi editor In Linux and macOS, a text editor that works in command mode (to enter commands) or in insert mode (to edit text).

video capture card An adapter card that captures video input and saves it to a file on the hard drive.

video memory Memory used by the video controller. The memory might be contained on a video card or be part of system memory. When it is part of system memory, the memory is dedicated by Windows to video.

virtual assistant A mobile device app that responds to a user's voice commands with a personable, conversational interaction to perform tasks and retrieve information. *Also called* a personal assistant *or* digital assistant.

virtual desktop When a hypervisor manages a virtual machine and presents the VM's desktop to a user. A remote user normally views and manages the virtual desktop via a browser on the local computer.

Virtual Desktop Infrastructure (VDI) A presentation of a virtual desktop made to a client computer by a hypervisor on a server in the cloud.

virtual LAN (VLAN) A subnet of a larger network created to reduce network traffic. Managed switches are commonly used to set up VLANs.

virtual machine (VM) Software managed by a hypervisor that simulates the hardware of a physical computer, creating one or more logical machines within one physical machine.

virtual machine manager (VMM) *See* hypervisor.

G

virtual memory   A method whereby the OS uses the hard drive as though it were RAM. *Also see* pagefile.sys.

virtual NIC   A network adapter created by a hypervisor that is used by a virtual machine and emulates a physical NIC.

virtual printing   Printing to a file rather than directly to a printer.

virtual private network (VPN)   A security technique that uses encrypted data packets between a private network and a computer somewhere on the Internet.

virtualization   When one physical machine hosts multiple activities that are normally done on multiple machines.

virtualization server   A computer that serves up virtual machines to multiple client computers and provides a virtual desktop for users on these client machines.

virus   A program that often has an incubation period, is infectious, and is intended to cause damage. A virus program might destroy data and programs.

vision sensor   *See* smart camera.

VM (virtual machine)   *See* virtual machine (VM).

Voice over LTE (VoLTE)   A technology used on cellular networks for LTE to support voice communication.

VoIP (Voice over Internet Protocol)   A TCP/IP protocol and an application that provides voice communication over a TCP/IP network. *Also called* Internet telephone.

volt (V)   A measure of potential difference or electrical force in an electrical circuit. A computer ATX power supply usually provides five separate voltages: +12 V, -12 V, +5 V, -5 V, and +3.3 V.

volume   A primary partition that has been assigned a drive letter and can be formatted with a file system such as NTFS. *Compare with* logical drive.

VPN (virtual private network)   *See* virtual private network (VPN).

VR (virtual reality) headset   A device worn on the head that creates a visual and audible virtual experience.

wait state   A clock tick in which nothing happens; it is used to ensure that the microprocessor isn't getting ahead of slower components. A 0-wait state is preferable to a 1-wait state. Too many wait states can slow down a system.

Wake-on-LAN   Configuring a computer so that it will respond to network activity when the computer is in a sleep state. *Also called* WoL.

WAN (wide area network)   A network or group of networks that span a large geographical area.

WAP (wireless access point)   *See* wireless access point (WAP).

warm boot   *See* soft boot.

watt   The unit of electricity used to measure power. A typical computer may use a power supply that provides 500W.

wear leveling   A technique used on a solid-state drive that ensures the logical block addressing does not always address the same physical blocks; this technique distributes write operations more evenly across the device.

wearable technology device   A device, such as a smart watch, wristband, arm band, eyeglasses, headset, or clothing, that can perform computing tasks, including making phone calls, sending text messages, transmitting data, and checking email.

WEP (Wired Equivalent Privacy)   An encryption protocol used to secure transmissions on a Wi-Fi wireless network; however, it is no longer considered secure because the key used for encryption is static (it doesn't change).

whitelist   In filtering, a list of items that is allowed through the filter—for example, a list of websites that computers on a local network are allowed to access. *Compare with* blacklist.

Wi-Fi (Wireless Fidelity)   The common name for standards for a local wireless network, as defined by IEEE 802.11. *Also see* 802.11 a/b/g/n/ac.

Wi-Fi analyzer   Hardware and/or software that monitors a Wi-Fi network to detect devices not authorized to use the network, identify attempts to hack transmissions, or detect performance and security vulnerabilities.

Wi-Fi calling   On mobile devices, voice calls that use VoIP over a Wi-Fi connection to the Internet.

Wi-Fi Protected Setup (WPS)   A method to make it easier for users to connect their computers to a secured wireless network when a hard-to-remember SSID and security key are used. WPS is considered a security risk that should be used with caution.

wildcard   An * or ? character used in a command line that represents a character or group of characters in a file name or extension.

Windows 10   The latest Microsoft operating system for personal computers and tablets and an upgrade to Windows 8.

Windows 10 Mobile   A Microsoft OS for smartphones.

Windows 7   A Microsoft OS whose editions include Windows 7 Starter, Windows 7 Home Basic, Windows 7 Home Premium, Windows 7 Professional, Windows 7 Enterprise, and Windows 7 Ultimate. Each edition comes at a different price with different features and capabilities.

Windows 8 reset   A clean installation of Windows 8 that first formats the Windows volume. If an OEM recovery partition is present, the system is reset to its factory state. If no recovery partition is present, the installation is performed from a Windows 8 setup DVD.

Windows 8.1   A free update or release of the Windows 8 operating system.

Windows 8.1 Enterprise   A Windows 8 edition that allows for volume licensing in a large, corporate environment.

Windows 8.1 Pro for Students   A version of Windows 8 that includes all the same features as Windows 8 Pro, but at a lower price. This version is available only to students, faculty, and staff at eligible institutions.

Windows 8.1 Professional (Windows 8.1 Pro)   A version of Windows 8 that includes additional features at a higher price. Windows 8.1 Pro supports homegroups, joining a domain, BitLocker, Client Hyper-V, Remote Desktop, and Group Policy.

Windows as a service   Beginning with Windows 10, the Microsoft strategy to deploy Windows and then provide ongoing, incremental updates to service the OS with no end-of-life limitation. In comparison, earlier versions of Windows had more discrete and significant updates, and end-of-life limitations required you to eventually upgrade to a new version of Windows.

Windows Assessment and Deployment Kit (ADK)   In Windows 8, a group of tools used to deploy Windows 8 in a large organization; the ADK contains the User State Migration Tool (USMT).

Windows Boot Loader   One of two programs that manage the loading of Windows 10/8/7. The program file (winload.exe or winload.efi) is stored in C:\Windows\System32, and it loads and starts essential Windows processes.

Windows Boot Manager (BootMgr)   The Windows program that manages the initial startup of Windows. For a BIOS system, the program is bootmgr; for a UEFI system, the program is bootmgfw.efi. The program file is stored in the root of the system partition.

Windows Defender Anti-malware   Software embedded in Windows 8/7. In Windows 8, the software can detect and remove many types of malware. In Windows 7, the software can detect and remove only spyware.

Windows Defender Antivirus   Anti-malware software embedded in Windows 10 that can detect viruses, prevent them, and clean up a system infected with viruses and other malware. In Windows 8/7, a similar tool is called Windows Defender.

Windows Defender Offline (WDO)   Scanning software available in Windows 10 or downloaded from the Microsoft website that launches before Windows to scan a system for malware. WDO works in the WinPE environment.

Windows Easy Transfer   A Windows tool used to transfer Windows user data and preferences to a Windows installation on another computer.

Windows Explorer   The Windows 7 utility used to view and manage files and folders. *Compare with* File Explorer.

Windows Firewall   A personal firewall in Windows that protects a computer from intrusion and is automatically configured when you set your network location in the Network and Sharing Center.

Windows pinwheel   A Windows graphic that indicates the system is waiting for a response from a program or device.

Windows Preinstallation Environment (Windows PE)   A minimum operating system used to start a Windows installation. *Also called* WinPE.

G

Windows Recovery Environment (Windows RE) A lean operating system installed on the Windows 10/8/7 setup DVD and on the Windows volume that can be used to troubleshoot problems when Windows refuses to start.

Windows RT A Windows 8 edition that is a lighter version designed for tablets, netbooks, and other mobile devices.

Windows Subsystem for Linux (WSL) A Windows component that supports the Bash on Ubuntu on Windows shell.

Windows.old folder When using an unformatted hard drive for a clean installation, this folder is created to store the previous operating system settings and user profiles.

wire stripper A tool used when terminating a cable. The tool cuts away the plastic jacket or coating around the wires in a cable so that a connector can be installed on the end of the cable.

wireless access point (WAP) A wireless device that is used to create and manage a wireless network.

wireless LAN (WLAN) A type of LAN that does not use wires or cables to create connections, but instead transmits data over radio or infrared waves.

wireless locator A tool that can locate a Wi-Fi hotspot and tell you the strength of the RF signal.

wireless wide area network (WWAN) A wireless broadband network for computers and mobile devices that uses cellular towers for communication. *Also called* a cellular network.

WLAN (wireless LAN) *See* wireless LAN (WLAN).

WMN (wireless mesh network) Many wireless devices communicating directly rather than through a single central device. This technology is commonly used in IoT wireless networks.

workgroup In Windows, a logical group of computers and users in which administration, resources, and security are distributed throughout the network without centralized management or security.

worm An infestation designed to copy itself repeatedly to memory, drive space, or a network until little memory, disk space, or network bandwidth remains.

WPA (Wi-Fi Protected Access) A data encryption method for wireless networks that use the TKIP (Temporal Key Integrity Protocol) encryption method. The encryption keys are changed at set intervals while the wireless LAN is in use. WPA is stronger than WEP.

WPA2 (Wi-Fi Protected Access 2) A data encryption standard compliant with the IEEE802.11i standard that uses the AES (Advanced Encryption Standard) protocol. WPA2 is currently the strongest wireless encryption standard.

WPA3 (Wi-Fi Protected Access 3) A standard that offers improved data encryption over WPA2 and allows for Individual Data Encryption, whereby a laptop or other wireless device can create a secure connection over a public, unsecured Wi-Fi network.

wpeinit The Windows command that initializes Windows PE and enables networking. *Also see* Windows Preinstallation Environment (Windows PE).

WPS (Wi-Fi Protected Setup) *See* Wi-Fi Protected Setup (WPS).

WWAN (wireless wide area network) *See* cellular network.

x86 processor An older processor that first used the number 86 in the model number; it processes 32 bits at a time.

x86-64 bit processor A hybrid processor that can process 32 bits or 64 bits.

XaaS (Anything as a Service or Everything as a Service) An open-ended cloud computing service that can provide any combination of functions depending on a customer's exact needs.

xcopy A Windows command more powerful than the copy command that is used to copy files and folders.

xD-Picture Card A type of flash memory device that has a compact design and currently holds up to 8 GB of data.

XPS Document Writer A Windows feature that creates a file with an .xps file extension. The file is similar to a .pdf file and can be viewed, edited, printed, faxed, emailed, or posted on websites.

Yahoo! An email provider owned by Verizon.

zero client A client computer that does not have an operating system and merely provides an interface between the user and the server.

zero insertion force (ZIF) socket A processor socket with one or two levers on the sides that are used to move the processor out of or into the socket so that equal force is applied over the entire socket housing.

zero-day attack An attack in which a hacker discovers and exploits a security hole in software before its developer can provide a protective patch to close the hole.

zero-fill utility A hard drive utility that fills every sector on the drive with zeroes.

zero-touch, high volume deployment An installation strategy that does not require the user to start the process. Instead, a server pushes the installation to a computer when a user is not likely to be manning it.

ZIF connector A connector that uses a lever or latch to prevent force from being used on a sensitive connection. ZIF stands for zero insertion force.

Zigbee A wireless standard used by smart devices that works in the 900-MHz band, has a range up to 100 m, and is considered more robust than Z-Wave, a competing standard.

zombie A computer that has been hacked to run repetitive software in the background without the knowledge of its user. *Also see* botnet.

Z-Wave A wireless standard used by smart devices that works in the 900-MHz or 2.4-GHz band and has a range up to 20 m. Z-Wave competes with Zigbee but is not considered as robust as Zigbee.

G

INDEX

I

I

I

I

I

I